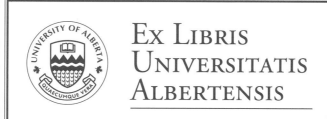

The Cambridge Encyclopedia of Child Development

The Cambridge Encyclopedia of Child Development is an authoritative, accessible and up-to-date account of all aspects of child development. Written by an international team of leading experts, it adopts an multidisciplinary approach and covers everything from prenatal development to education, pediatrics, neuroscience, theories, and research methods to physical development, social development, cognitive development, psychopathology, and parenting. It also looks at cultural issues, sex differences, and the history of child development. The combination of comprehensive coverage, clear, jargon-free style, and user-friendly format will ensure this book is essential reading for students, researchers, health-care professionals, social workers, education professionals, parents, and anyone interested in the welfare of children.

Features include:

- Foreword by Jerome Bruner
- Comprehensive coverage
- Cross-references between entries
- Extensive glossary
- Biographies of key figures
- Companion web site
- Clear, user-friendly format

BRIAN HOPKINS is Professor of Psychology at Lancaster University and has published extensively in the field of developmental psychology. He is co-editor of *Neurobiology of Infant Vision* (2003) and *Motor Development in Early and Later Childhood* (1993), as well as editor of the journal *Infant and Child Development*.

RONALD G. BARR is the Canada Research Chair in Community Child Health Research at the University of British Columbia and Professor of Pediatrics in the Faculty of Medicine there.

GEORGE F. MICHEL is Professor of Psychology at the University of Carolina at Greensboro, co-author of two books on developmental psychobiology, and editor-in-chief of *Developmental Psychobiology* (the official journal of the International Society for Developmental Psychobiology).

PHILIPPE ROCHAT is Professor of Psychology at Emory University. In addition to numerous research articles, he is the editor of *The Self in Infancy* (1995), *Early Social Cognition* (1999), and the author of *The Infant's World* (2001).

The companion website for this title can be found at www.cambridge.org/hopkins. It includes an extended glossary, biographical sketches, relevant organizations and links.

The Cambridge Encyclopedia
of CHILD
DEVELOPMENT

Edited by BRIAN HOPKINS

Associate Editors: Ronald G. Barr, George F. Michel, Philippe Rochat

CAMBRIDGE UNIVERSITY PRESS
Cambridge, New York, Melbourne, Madrid, Cape Town, Singapore, São Paulo

Cambridge University Press
The Edinburgh Building, Cambridge CB2 2RU, UK

Published in the United States of America by Cambridge University Press, New York

www.cambridge.org
Information on this title: www.cambridge.org/9780521651172

First published 2005

Printed in the United Kingdom at the University Press, Cambridge

A catalogue record for this book is available from the British Library

Library of Congress Cataloguing in Publication data
The Cambridge Encyclopedia of child development / edited by Brian Hopkins; associate editors Ronald G. Barr . . . [*et al.*].
    p.   cm.
Includes bibliographical references and index.
ISBN 0 521 65117 4
1. Child development – Encyclopedias.   I. Hopkins, B.   II. Barr, Ronald G.
HQ767.9+   305.231′03 – dc22   2004047291

ISBN-13 978-0-521-65117-2 hardback
ISBN-10 0-521-65117-4 hardback

CONTENTS

Part III Prenatal development and the newborn

Part IV Domains of development: from infancy to childhood

Part V Selected topics

Part VI Developmental pathology

CONTRIBUTORS

RYAN ADAMS, Department of Psychology, Concordia University

DIMA AMSO, Department of Psychology, New York University

ROGER BAKEMAN, Department of Psychology, Georgia State University

SIMON BARON-COHEN, Autism Research Centre, University of Cambridge

MARTIN C. O. BAX, Department of Paediatrics, Imperial College of Science, Technology & Medicine, London

JOYCE F. BENENSON, Department of Psychology, University of Plymouth

MARK BENNETT, Department of Psychology, University of Dundee

ANN BIGELOW, Department of Psychology, St. Francis Xavier University, Nova Scotia

JOHAN J. BOLHUIS, Behavioural Biology, Utrecht University

MELISSA BOWERMAN, Max-Planck-Institut für Psycholinguistik, Nijmegen, The Netherlands

GAVIN BREMNER, Department of Psychology, Lancaster University

JEROME S. BRUNER, School of Law, New York University

PETER BRYANT, Department of Psychology, Oxford Brookes University, Oxford

WILLIAM M. BUKOWSKI, Department of Psychology, Concordia University

TARA C. CALLAGHAN, Department of Psychology, St. Francis Xavier University, Nova Scotia

JANE E. CLARK, Department of Kinesiology, University of Maryland

PATRICIA R. COHEN, New York State Psychiatric Institute & School of Public Health, Columbia University

JENNIFER COLE, Committee on Human Development, University of Chicago

MICHAEL COLE, Laboratory of Comparative Human Cognition, University of California

MARGARET COUSINS, Department of Psychology, Lancaster University

MORAG L. DONALDSON, Department of Psychology, University of Edinburgh

JUDY DUNN, Social, Genetic and Developmental Psychiatry Research Centre, Institute of Psychiatry, London

THALIA C. ELEY, Social, Genetic, and Developmental Psychiatry Research Centre Institute of Psychiatry, London

DIGBY ELLIOTT, Department of Kinesiology, McMaster University

JOHN C. FENTRESS, Department of Biology, Dalhousie University, Nova Scotia

WILLIAM P. FIFER, Developmental Psychobiology, New York State Psychiatric Institute, Columbia University

BARBARA L. FINLAY, Departments of Psychology and Neurobiology and Behavior, Cornell University

KURT W. FISCHER, Department of Human Development, Harvard University

PETER FONAGY, Department of Psychology, University College London

NATHAN A. FOX, Institute for Child Study, University of Maryland

NORMAN H. FREEMAN, Department of Experimental Psychology, University of Bristol

ROGER D. FREEMAN, Neuropsychiatry Clinic, British Columbia Children's Hospital, University of British Columbia

CHRISTOPHER GILLBERG, Department of Child and Adolescent Psychiatry, University Hospital, Göteborg

IAN M. GOODYER, Developmental Psychiatry Section, Department of Psychiatry, University of Cambridge

GILBERT GOTTLIEB, Center for Developmental Science, University of North Carolina, Chapel Hill

ALBERT GRAMSBERGEN, Department of Medical Physiology, University of Groningen

MARYKE GROENVELD, Department of Psychiatry, British Columbia Children's Hospital, University of British Columbia

MICHELLE DE HAAN, Institute of Child Health, University College London

MIJNA HADDERS-ALGRA, Developmental Neurology, University Hospital Groningen

ERIN R. HANNON, Department of Psychology, Cornell University

LAUREN J. HARRIS, Department of Psychology, Michigan State University

WILLIAM A. HARRIS, Department of Anatomy, University of Cambridge

JANE S. HERBERT, Department of Psychology, University of Sheffield

JAN B. HOEKSMA, Department of Child and Adolescent Psychology, Vrije Universiteit, Amsterdam

JERRY A. HOGAN, Department of Psychology, University of Toronto

BRIAN HOPKINS, Department of Psychology, Lancaster University

CLAIRE HUGHES, Department of Experimental Psychology, University of Cambridge

JULIE HWANG, Department of Psychology, University of Oregon

MARK H. JOHNSON, Centre for Brain and Cognitive Development, Birkbeck College, London

SCOTT P. JOHNSON, Department of Psychology, New York University

RAY D. KENT, Waisman Center, University of Wisconsin

FREDERICK K. KOZAK, British Columbia Children's Hospital, University of British Columbia

KURT KREPPNER, Max-Planck-Institut für Bildungsforschung, Berlin

ADINA R. LEW, Department of Psychology, Lancaster University

CHARLIE LEWIS, Department of Psychology, Lancaster University

MICHAEL LEWIS, Institute of Child Development, Rutgers University, New Jersey

BRIAN MacWHINNEY, Department of Psychology, Carnegie Mellon University, Pittsburgh

ROBERT M. MALINA, Department of Kinesiology, Tarleton State University, Stephenville, Texas

DENIS MARESCHAL, Centre for Brain and Cognitive Development, Birkbeck College, London

MICHAEL F. MASCOLO, Department of Psychology, Merrimack College, Massachusetts

JOHN J. McARDLE, Department of Psychology, University of Virginia

JAMES J. McKENNA, Department of Anthropology, Notre Dame University

EDWARD C. MELHUISH, Institute for the Study of Children, Families and Social Issues, Birkbeck College, London

ANDREW N. MELTZOFF, Department of Psychology, University of Washington

ELIZABETH G. MENAGHAN, Department of Sociology, The Ohio State University

CELIA MOORE, Department of Psychology, University of Massachusetts, Boston

PIERRE MOUNOUD, Faculté de Psychologie et des Sciences, Université de Génève

ULRICH MÜLLER, Department of Psychology, University of Victoria

CHARLES A. NELSON, Institute of Child Development, University of Minnesota

DAVID OLSON, Ontario Institute for Studies in Education, University of Toronto

RONALD W. OPPENHEIM, Wake Forest Medical School, Wake Forest University, North Carolina

WILLIS F. OVERTON, Department of Psychology, Temple University, Philadelphia

SIMON H. PARSON, School of Biomedical Sciences, University of Leeds

SERGIO M. PELLIS, Department of Psychology and Neuroscience, University of Lethbridge

YPE H. POORTINGA, Department of Psychology, Tilburg University, The Netherlands

HELLGARD RAUH, Institute for Psychology, University of Potsdam

RICHARD R. RIBCHERTER, Division of Neuroscience, University of Edinburgh

JOHN E. RICHARDS, Department of Psychology, University of South Carolina

MICHAEL J.L. RIVKIN, Departments of Neurology and Radiology, Children's Hospital, Boston, Massachusetts

SCOTT R. ROBINSON, Laboratory of Comparative Ethogenesis, Department of Psychology, University of Iowa

HILDY S. ROSS, Department of Psychology, University of Waterloo

MARY K. ROTHBART, Department of Psychology, University of Oregon

GREGOR SCHÖNER, Institut für Neuroinformatik, Ruhr-Universität Bochum

CARLA SHARP, Developmental Psychiatry Section, Department of Psychiatry, University of Cambridge

LESLIE SMITH, Department of Educational Research, Lancaster University

PETER K. SMITH, Unit for School and Family Studies, Goldsmiths College, London

MARY M. SMYTH, Department of Psychology, Lancaster University

MARGARET J. SNOWLING, Department of Psychology, University of York

YVETTE SOLOMON, Department of Educational Research, Lancaster University

CATHERINE E. SPIELMACHER, Department of Psychology, University of Waterloo

IAN ST. JAMES-ROBERTS, Thomas Coram Research
Unit, Institute of Education, University of London

FIONA STANLEY, Department of Paediatrics,
School of Medicine, University of Western
Australia

ROBERT J. STERNBERG, Department of Psychology,
Yale University

JAMES E. STEVENSON, Centre for Research into
Psychological Development, University of
Southampton

CYNTHIA STIFTER, Department of Human
Development and Family Studies, Pennsylvania State
University

EUGENE SUBBOTSKY, Department of Psychology,
Lancaster University

ERIC TAYLOR, Department of Child and Adolescent
Psychiatry, Institute of Psychiatry, London

RICHARD E. TREMBLAY, Department of Psychology,
Université de Montréal

WENDA R. TREVATHAN, Department of Anthropology,
New Mexico State University

ELLIOT TURIEL, Department of Education, University
of California, Berkeley

BEATRIX VEREIJKEN, Human Movement Sciences
Section, Norwegian University of Science and
Technology

ALEXANDER VON EYE, Department of Psychology,
Michigan State University

CLAES VON HOFSTEN, Department of Psychology,
Uppsala University, Sweden

JOHN S. WATSON, Department of Psychology,
University of California, Berkeley

HELEN L. WESTCOTT, Psychology Discipline, Faculty
of Social Sciences, The Open University

GERT WESTERMANN, Department of Psychology,
Oxford Brookes University, Oxford

PETER H. WOLFF, Department of Psychiatry,
Children's Hospital, Boston

JOHN WOROBEY, Department of Nutritional Sciences,
Rutgers University

ROBERT H. WOZNIAK, Department of Psychology,
Bryn Mawr College, Philadelphia

EDITORIAL PREFACE

The subject matter of child development has grown exponentially over the last fifty years such that its study has become a vast multidisciplinary enterprise. The roots of this enterprise can be traced back to the 1930s, when the likes of Arnold Gesell, Myrtle McGraw, and Jean Piaget embarked on systematic programs of research, each one encompassing a variety of disciplines in different ways.

Common to these pioneering attempts at forging a multidisciplinary approach to the study of child development was an appreciation that ontogenetic development and biological evolution were somehow inextricably linked, and as such it shaped the questions being asked and the answers provided. Subsequently, and perhaps for justifiable reasons at the time, child development was studied bereft of evolutionary considerations and all things 'biological.' With the rise of molecular developmental genetics during the last decade or so, together with renewed insights into the relationships between ontogeny and phylogeny, the landscape of research on ontogenetic development has been changed irrevocably, and as a consequence that on child development will have to take into account newly emerging fields of study such as evolutionary developmental biology.

Another theme that stands out in the book concerns the impact of neuroscience on how child development, both 'normal' and 'deviant,' is presently studied. Ranging from specific animal models through non-invasive neural imaging techniques to computational modeling, the wealth of information generated about the changing nature of brain–behavior relationships during development is truly staggering. The challenge now, and one to which this book is geared, is how to integrate this plethora of new knowledge and that contained in the first theme so that progress can be made toward the provision of more unified theories of ontogenetic development that cross disciplinary boundaries.

A further theme includes the historical roots and controversies that have motivated the study of child development and which form essential reading for understanding the two main issues that continue today: the origin problem and the change problem. The first calls for a better understanding of the ways in which prenatal development relates to that after birth, and the second for the use of longitudinal designs and associated statistical techniques for teasing out the salient features of intra-individual change in whatever domain of development. As an additional theme, this book strives wherever possible to encourage the study of child development across domains (e.g. cognitive, motor, social) rather than within domains as one means of achieving greater theoretical integration.

There is no pretense made of having covered every possible topic that might fall under the heading of 'child development.' Given the limitations of space and those imposed by our own experiences in studying child development, we have endeavored nevertheless to provide a coverage that is as comprehensive as possible. Having said this, there are no separate entries, for example, that deal with 'attachment theory' or 'qualitative research.' Despite not having dedicated slots, such topics are given consideration across a number of entries. Furthermore, the book will have a companion web site by means of which readers will be able to communicate with the editor about the structure of the book and its contents as well as make suggestions for revisions or for correcting any inaccuracies. It will also contain an extended glossary, a large number of web site addresses for relevant scientific organizations, as well as further information relevant to specific entries, and short biographical sketches of additional individuals who have, directly or indirectly, had an influence on the study of child development.

Finally, we wish to thank a number of individuals who enabled this book to come to fruition. To begin, there are the numerous referees whose reviews of the initial proposal helped us to refine both structure and content. In approaching authors for particular topics, the recommendations of Jonathan W. Hill (University of

Liverpool), William P. Fifer (Columbia University), Albert Gramsbergen (University of Groningen), and Claudio Stern (University College London) were particularly helpful. Throughout the whole process of editing the book, Ronald W. Oppenheim (Wake Forest University) was a consistent source of valuable advice, and in the run-in to completion Thomas C. Dalton (California Polytechnic State University, San Luis Obispo) provided a much-needed and coherent description of the term 'consciousness' for the glossary. A number of people kindly accepted the job of reviewing a selection of first drafts, which resulted in some very helpful comments that improved the quality of subsequent versions. These particular individuals have been acknowledged on a separate page. A special debt of gratitude goes to the in-house editorial team at Cambridge University Press: Sarah Caro, Gillian Dadd, Alison Powell, and especially Juliet Davis-Berry. Their advice, patience, and support throughout the arduous task of completing such a large book were unfailing and of the highest professional quality. Another special debt of gratitude goes to Leigh Mueller, copy-editor *par excellence*. To everyone who has helped us in one way or another, we are most grateful.

Brian Hopkins
Lancaster, January 2005

FOREWORD

The course of human development used to be a topic for the specialist – the pediatrician, the development psychologist, the child welfare worker, and even the anthropologist in search of the origins of cultural difference. There was also, to be sure, a wider audience of parents, in search of advice about how best to 'raise' their children, and the better educated among them often browsed in the technical developmental handbooks for clues about how to deal with their children's 'difficulties,' like dyslexia or persistent bedwetting or failure to meet the 'norms' popularized in such widely read manuals as Arnold Gessell's endlessly revised and reissued *Manual of Child Development*.

That degree of specialization is no more. 'Child development' and its course has, in the last quarter-century, become an issue of general, even political concern, a passionate issue. To a degree never before seen, the cultivation of childhood has become central not only in debates about schooling and parenting, but also in discussions of broader policy: anti-poverty programs in our inner cities, budgetary policy nationally, even international policy where aid for the care and education of the young has become a central issue. Indeed, there are few issues that are as publicly scrutinized as, for example, *when* and *how* 'education' should start, even before a child ever gets to school. *What* should schools take as their objective, and *in what ways* might the larger social environment harm or help a child's readiness for later school learning?

Indeed, the introduction of Head Start in America in the 1960s (and comparable programs elsewhere) provoked a blizzard of debate on how and whether poverty disables a young pre-school child for later schooling. In a like vein, intense debates rage about the possibly irreversible effects of childhood 'deprivations' in the Third World. As never before, the adage "The child is father to the man" has emerged into open debate about policy.

All of these concerns make it all the more urgent that there be available not only to the expert, but also to the engaged citizen, some informed and intelligent guidance regarding human growth and development. It is our hope that *The Cambridge Encyclopedia* will fill that function. It is written by distinguished specialists in child development, but written with a view to being accessible to the intelligent reader concerned with the growth and welfare of the young.

One special point needs emphasis. Over the last quarter-century, there has been a remarkable burgeoning of research on early childhood. Inevitably, this research on early growth and the factors affecting it has come to concentrate more than before on neural as well as psychological processes that might be affected by early encounters with the world. Such research is well represented in this volume, and to good effect. For many current debates swirl futilely around the issue, for example, of whether certain early experiences produce 'irreversible' effects on the 'brain.' The reader will find a well-balanced approach to this feverish issue in this *Encyclopedia*.

The contributors to this volume, as well as its editors, are to be congratulated, finally, for maintaining a happy balance between the general and the particular. For, indeed, the details of development cannot be understood without appreciating the broader contexts in which they occur, nor can general trends be grasped without reference to the specific mechanisms that make them possible. The relation between early experience and the state of the brain is, indeed, a two-way street.

Jerome S. Bruner
New York University

ACKNOWLEDGMENTS: EXTERNAL REVIEWERS

The following colleagues provided reviews of one or more first drafts for just over thirty entries:

MAGGIE BRUCK (Department of Psychiatry and Behavioral Science, Division of Child and Adolescent Psychiatry, Johns Hopkins Medical Institutions)

ADELE DIAMOND (Department of Psychiatry, University of British Columbia)

KIERAN EGAN (Faculty of Education, Simon Fraser University)

REBECCA EILERS (Department of Psychology, University of Maine)

GLEN H. ELDER (Carolina Population Center, University of North Carolina, Chapel Hill)

DALE HAY (School of Psychology, Cardiff University)

DENNIS HAY (Department of Psychology, Lancaster University)

ROB HENDERSON (Medical Stats Unit, Department of Mathematics and Statistics, Lancaster University)

CHRISTOPHER HENRICH (Department of Psychology, Georgia State University)

MARTIN L. HOFFMAN (Department of Psychology, New York University)

ALAN LEVITON (Neurodevelopmental Unit, Children's Hospital, Harvard Medical School)

SHU-CHEN LI (Max Planck Institute for Human Development, Center for Lifespan Psychology, Berlin)

PHILIP LIEBERMAN (Department of Cognitive and Linguistic Sciences, Brown University)

ELENA LIEVEN (Max Planck Institute for Evolutionary Anthropology, Leipzig)

CAROLYN B. MERVIS (Department of Psychological and Brain Sciences, University of Louisville)

DEBRA L. MILLS (Department of Psychology, Emory University)

TOMAS PAUS (Department of Neurology & Neurosurgery, McGill University)

DANIEL PÉRUSSE (Hôpital Sainte Justine et Université de Montréal)

CHING-FAN SHEU (Psychology Department, DePaul University)

STEPHANIE A. SHIELDS (Department of Psychology, Penn State University)

JAMES H. STEIGER (Department of Psychology, University of British Columbia)

FRED R. VOLKMAR (Yale University Child Study Center)

KATE WATKINS (Cognitive Neuroscience Unit, Montreal Neurological Institute)

INTRODUCTION

What is development and interdisciplinarity?

The aim of this section is to provide a setting for the rest of the book. This is achieved in two ways. Firstly, by historical overviews and evaluations of the debates about the nature of development, which culminate in contemporary interpretations of ontogenetic development. Secondly, by providing the rudiments of an interdisciplinary framework for studying child development and pinpointing the challenges arising from such a framework.

The concept of development: historical perspectives

CELIA MOORE

Introduction

The concept of development is rooted in the biology of the individual life cycle. It encompasses the subsidiary ideas of growth, differentiation from homogeneous to heterogeneous matter, and morphogenesis (the assumption of ordered form, an idea included as part of differentiation for most of history). Development also comprises the concept of reproduction, in which the origin of an individual from parents is related both to the resemblance of offspring and parents (heredity) and to the observation that species breed true to type. The history of developmental psychology has been fed by many streams, but developmental biology was the wellspring for its origin during the closing decades of the 19th century.

The ancient legacy

Aristotle (384-322 BP) presented the first detailed conception of development, along with a vivid natural history of embryology in diverse life forms, in *On the Generation of Animals*. He replaced the atomistic preformationism of earlier thinkers with an epigenetic conception in which the embryo differentiates progressively from a homogeneous origin, with parts such as heart, lungs, and limbs and their spatial arrangement only gradually taking shape. Both epigenesis (Fig. 1) and preformationism were destined to endure as the two grand synthesizing images that have competed in the minds of developmentalists throughout history.

The three central features of Aristotelian epigenesis derived from his material, efficient, and final causes. These included a distinction between the material cause from which the embryo is produced and nutrients to support the growth and maintenance of the embryo; an explanation of differentiation as the action of a non-material generative principle in the semen of males (the efficient cause) on the formative material from females (menstrual blood of humans, the white of a bird egg, etc.); and an explanation of the particular form taken by an organism and its parts in terms of final causes (purpose or plan). The central epigenetic idea was that there was a male principle that acts on generative material secreted by females, setting developmental processes in motion that progressively actualize potentials inherent in the material. Although his theory of generation mixed metaphysics with science, including as it did both vitalistic and teleological elements, Aristotle nevertheless defined the major developmental questions and led the way for empirically minded successors to continue the inquiry some two millennia later.

Concepts from 17th- and 18th-century embryology

The modern history of developmental science can be started with the 17th-century scientists who resumed the work of the ancients (Needham, 1959). Of these, William Harvey (1578–1657), most celebrated for his discovery of the circulation of blood, stands as an important transitional figure in the history of developmental thought. His work on generation, as it was then still called, took Aristotle's epigenesis as a starting point. Harvey believed that all life begins from an egg. One of the major developmental issues of Harvey's time centered on the nature of embryonic nutrition and the distinction between nutrients and formative matter in the egg. Harvey demonstrated that the distinction was meaningless: nutrients were assimilated by the embryo as it took form. He reconceived epigenesis as the entwined, synchronous processes of growth (increase in mass) and differentiation. This contrasts with Aristotle's equation of epigenesis simply with differentiation of a finite mass of formative material. It also contrasts with the preformationism of Harvey's contemporaries.

Preformation was developed in part out of dissatisfaction with the vitalistic leanings of epigenesis and in part out of the enthusiasm that attends a major technological advance. The newly invented microscope was revealing a previously invisible world and opening the possibility of even smaller worlds awaiting technical improvements in lenses. It prepared a way around the problem of differentiation by making it plausible to deny its necessity. Turning the microscope on eggs revealed a high degree of organization in the tiniest of embryos, giving rise to the ovists; turning it on semen revealed a swarm of active animalcules (spermatozoa), giving rise to the spermists. If such organization was present so early, why not from the very beginning? Although most preformationists were ovists who thought that life was preformed in eggs, the enduring icon of preformation is Nicholas Hartsoecker's 18th-century drawing of what such a human animalcule would look like if only it could be seen clearly. This was not, however, the clearer vision that was to come with improved microscopy. Anatomists such as Caspar Friedrich Wolff (1733–94) saw such things as tubular structures growing out of the folding of two-dimensional sheets, and not from the swelling of miniature tubular structures. The 18th-century debates ended with embryos that were epigenetic in Harvey's sense: simultaneously growing and taking shape. These debates, however, left the problem of heredity unsolved.

As use of the term 'generation' suggests, the concept of development through the 18th century included reproduction along with growth and differentiation. The most salient feature of reproduction in this context is what we would now call heredity. Offspring are of the same type as parents: chickens invariably come from chicken eggs, and ducks from duck eggs. These and similar regularities in nature were taken to reflect the over-arching plan behind the whole of existence. The preformationist concept of embôitement (encasement), which was promoted by Wolff's adversary Albrecht von Haller (1708–1777), was an attempt to eliminate the problem of heredity. In this conception, progressively smaller embryos were stacked inside one another such that all generations were present from one original creation. This was a plausible idea at the time because of the generally shared presumption of a short history of life on earth.

Qualitative change was established as a central fact of development by the end of the 18th century. However, it is possible to read too much into that victory for epigenesis. Firstly, developmental thought during this formative period was focused on the embryo, which is an early stage of life. By pushing back the time of differentiation far enough, the difference between a preformed and an emergent embryo becomes negligible (Needham, 1959). This is particularly true for developmental psychology, which is concerned with post-embryonic life. Secondly, the conceptions of heredity that came to dominate in the 19th and 20th centuries

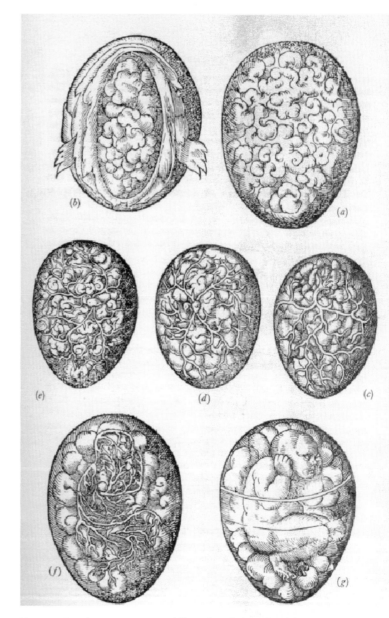

Figure 1. A 16th-century conceptual illustration of what Aristotle's epigenesis might look like if observed. Drawing from Jacob Rueff, as reproduced in J. Needham, 1959. *A History of Embryology*. New York: Abelard-Schuman.

have more in common with the preformationist concept of preexistence than with the epigenetic concept of emergence. Of all the concepts comprised by the ancient idea of generation, heredity was the one that has dominated biology during most of the history of child development.

Development beyond the embryo

Embryology thrived during the early 19th century as a comparative, descriptive science of anatomical development. Its dominance in biology fitted well with the general intellectual climate of the time. The concept of cycle. This connected embryology with comparative anatomy and taxonomy, allowing von Baer also to extend the concept of development to include diversity of life forms. From this broad array of data, von Baer observed that shared traits in a group of embryos appear earlier than special traits; that more general structural relations in traits appear before the more specific; that embryos of different forms in the same group gradually separate from one another without passing through states of other differentiated forms; and that embryos of higher forms never resemble adults of lower forms, only their embryos. These observations and ideas left a deep mark on Charles Darwin's mid-century theory of evolution. They were seen to support the idea of evolution as descent with modification from ancestral forms.

In the first textbook of the field, Herbert Spencer (1820–1903) presented psychology as a division of biology, new in its subject matter of the conscious mind, but otherwise using methods and concepts general to the life sciences. Spencer had an abstract concept of development as progress, which he applied across many disciplines. He saw progress as related to the epigenetic tradition of Aristotle, Harvey, Wolff, and von Baer in embryology. This viewpoint was adopted by the influential James Mark Baldwin (1861–1934), who brought the organic tradition of the embryologists into 20th-century developmental psychology. Concepts of assimilation, growth, and differentiation that were first articulated for nutrients and anatomy were re-worked to accommodate experience and the mind. These ideas, in concert with the powerful influence of Darwinian evolutionary theory and the subsequent rise of functionalism, shaped the emergence of developmental psychology and its history well into the 20th century (Kessen, 1983).

It would have been a logical next step for a developmental theory to grow out of von Baer's embryology to explain how evolution works, but efforts in this direction did not flourish (Gould, 1977). Instead, first evolution and then genetics took on the task of explaining development while embryology declined to a marginal field. Ernst Haeckel (1834–1919) popularized the parallel between embryology and evolution (Fig. 2), giving these concepts new names and proposing their relationship in the Biogenetic Law: ontogeny recapitulates phylogeny. Haeckel's recapitulation concept reverted to the old idea of the linear progression of life from monad to man, ignoring von Baer's evidence of the ramified nature of biological diversity and the emergence of diversity in embryonic stages. However retrograde, the idea was very influential for a time. Development came to be seen as pushed by evolution, with adult forms of 'lower' animals as stages in the ontogenetic progression of 'higher' species. This stage conception retained epigenesis of form during ontogeny,

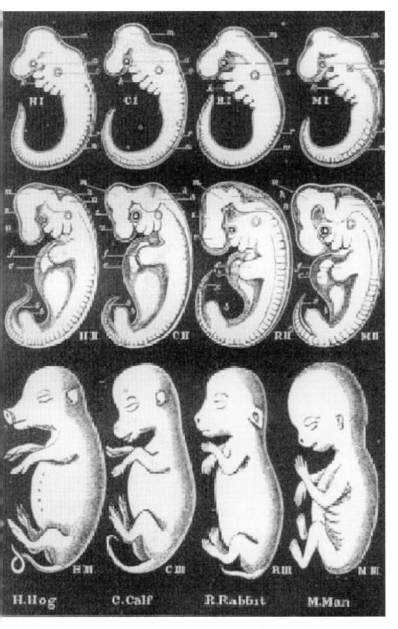

Figure 2. A 19th-century illustration of the relation between ontogeny and phylogeny. From E. Haeckel, 1897. *The Evolution of Man*. New York: D. Appleton and Co. Haeckel's illustrations are presented as empirical, but exaggerate the similarity across species. From S. J. Gould, 1977. *Ontogeny and Phylogeny*. Cambridge, MA: Harvard University Press.

progress was in the air, shaping new ideas in cultural anthropology, sociology, and philosophy as well as those in the natural sciences. This led in natural science to a reconception of the grand plan of nature, that great chain of being, from a static structure to a work in progress and, eventually, to the theory of evolution as the foundation of the life sciences.

Karl Ernst von Baer (1792–1876) synthesized the growing field of anatomical embryology in a set of generalizations that extended the concept of epigenesis beyond the embryo, through the adult stage of a life

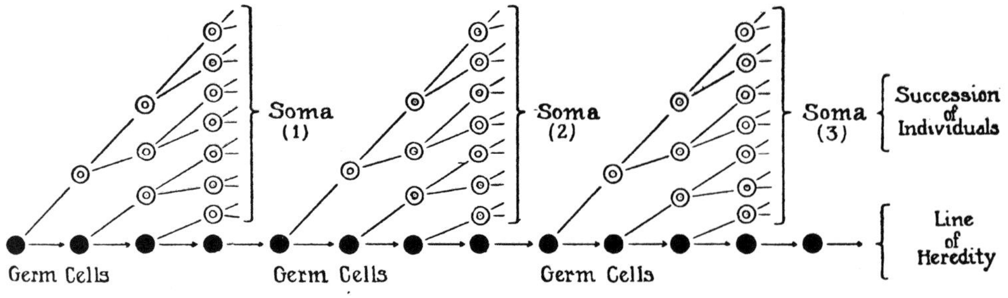

Figure 3. In Weismann's theory, heredity is sequestered in a separate line of germ cells (filled dots) that cross generations. Somatic cells (open dots) originate from inherited germ cells but cannot cross generations. From E. B. Wilson, 1925. *The Cell in Development and Heredity*, 3rd. edn. New York: MacMillan, p. 13.

but placed the cause of change in a preexistent phylogeny.

The schools of developmental psychology that arose early in the 20th century derived core conceptions from 19th-century embryology and evolutionary biology, but each took something different from these sources. The stage conceptions of development elaborated by G. Stanley Hall and Sigmund Freud built on Haeckel's flawed concept. These theorists proposed that human development recapitulated the history of human evolution and that healthy development required support of this predetermined sequence through childhood. Heinz Werner's orthogenetic principle of development as progress from a global, undifferentiated state to an articulated, hierarchically integrated state was an abstract statement meant to distinguish development from other temporal change. It was Spencerian in the breadth of its application and Aristotelian in its view of epigenesis.

William Preyer (1841–1897) was a physiological embryologist in the epigenetic tradition of von Baer who brought both concepts and methods from this field to the study of behavioral development. His 1882 book (*The Mind of the Child*), often used to date the birth of developmental psychology, demonstrated a way to transform empirical approaches from embryology for use in postnatal mental development. Preyer's concept of development, shaped by his physiological work, included an active organism contributing to its own development and the idea that achievements from early stages provide substrates for later stages. This concept had a major influence on James Mark Baldwin, who integrated Preyer's ideas with von Baer's principles and Darwin's natural selection into a developmental theory that served as a foundation for many schools of 20th-century developmental psychology, including those associated with Lev Vygotsky, Jean Piaget, Heinz Werner, Leonard Carmichael, and T. C. Schneirla.

Baldwin's concept of development focused on the relationship between the active organism and its social milieu as the source of developmental transformation. Applied to the mind of the child, this led him to notions of circular reaction and genetic epistemology that were later to be extensively elaborated by Piaget. Vygotsky and Werner applied the ideas broadly, including cultural and phyletic evolution in their conceptions, along with ontogenetic development that served as their primary focus. Comparative developmentalists, such as Carmichael and Schneirla who used experimental methods to study behavioral development in diverse animals, remained closest to their roots in physiological embryology. They mirrored early 20th-century experimental embryology with experimental approaches to behavioral development.

Heredity and development

The fact of organic evolution and Darwin's theory of natural selection to explain how it works were widely accepted by the end of the 19th century. This made a mechanism of heredity the most important missing link in biology. Evidence for Lamarckian inheritance had been found wanting, which was disappointing in the light of the adaptability of organisms through use and disuse. The search for a genetic mechanism took a decisive turn away from the organism with the introduction by August Weismann (1834–1914) of the germ plasm concept at the close of the century (Fig. 3). The cell had been established as the basic unit of life by 1838. Egg and sperm were subsequently identified as cells, and the first step in ontogeny was reconceived as their fusion. Weismann demonstrated that the cell divisions giving rise to egg and sperm occurred in a specialized population of cells sequestered from the rest of the body. This had the effect of separating the concepts of reproduction and heredity from that of development, and making the hereditary material preexistent to development.

If the 19th century was the age of progress, the 20th century was the age of information. The metaphors used to discuss development were drawn from the cultural well of cybernetics and computers (Keller, 1995). In keeping with this new orientation, the concept of plan was reintroduced to guide the progressive emergence of form during epigenesis. However, the 20th-century plan was written in a digital code inherited from a line of ancestors, not an idea carried on the informing breath of an agent in semen as it was for Aristotle.

The search for a hereditary mechanism led to the rediscovery of Gregor Mendel's non-blending hereditary particles, the location of these particles on chromosomes in the cell nucleus, the discovery of the DNA molecule, and the definition of a gene as a code that specifies phenotype. In 1957, Francis Crick (1916–2004) stated the central dogma of biology as the one-way flow of information from gene to product. The central dogma had taken its place alongside Darwinian evolution as one of the twin pillars of biology. The study of development thus became incidental to the major biological agenda. Indeed, molecular geneticists adopted single-celled bacteria as their organism of choice, in part because they do not undergo the irrelevant complications of metazoan development. The term 'developmental biology' came into wide use as a replacement for embryology by the middle of the 20th century to describe a field that was now largely focused on cytoplasm in cells rather than on either organisms or the hereditary molecules found in cell nuclei.

Conclusions

The success of genetics fostered a new generation of predeterminists who conceived development as differentiation under the control of plans inherited in genes. They took a biologically differentiated organism as their starting point, using mainstream genetic ideas to explain biological development. Predeterminists and environmentalists debated developmental theory in terms of the nature–nurture dichotomy. The predeterminists claimed a major informative role for nature, which they equated with inherited plans; the environmentalists claimed a major informative role for nurture acting on a *tabula rasa* organism. The ascendancy of the central dogma had the effect of putting constructivists in the Baldwinian tradition outside mainstream biological thought for most of the 20th century. Constructivists have an organic conception of epigenesis as emergent differentiation entwined with growth, achieved through organism–environment transactions. This conception is not compatible with either preexistent plans or the nature–nurture dichotomy.

There are signs that the long reign of the central dogma is coming to an end in biology. Developmental genetics has focused attention on the activation of genes and made cytoplasmic elements at least equal in importance to an increasingly passive DNA molecule. The embryo has re-emerged as a central figure in both development and evolution. With some irony, the age of information that gave us simplifying genetic codes has now given us the science of complexity, making it not only possible but fashionable to study complex, developing organisms with new tools. It remains to be seen what lasting changes in the concept of development will follow these current trends.

Acknowledgments

Supported by a grant from the National Science Foundation (IBN-9514769).

See also:
Understanding ontogenetic development: debates about the nature of the epigenetic process; Constructivist theories; Dynamical systems approaches; Conceptions and misconceptions about embryonic development; Behavioral embryology; Behavior genetics; Developmental genetics; James Mark Baldwin; Jean Piaget; Wilhelm T. Preyer; Lev S. Vygotsky; Heinz Werner

Further reading

Oyama, S. (2000). *The Ontogeny of Information: Developmental Systems and Evolution*, 2nd edn. Durham, NC: Duke University Press.

Peters, R. S. (1965). *Brett's History of Psychology*. Cambridge, MA: MIT Press.

Pinto-Correia, C. (1997). *The Ovary of Eve: Egg and Sperm and Preformation*. Chicago: University of Chicago Press.

Understanding ontogenetic development: debates about the nature of the epigenetic process

GILBERT GOTTLIEB

Introduction

The debates concerning individual development go back 2,500 years to the time of Aristotle in the fourth century before the present era. During his investigations of the embryo and fetus in a wide variety of species, Aristotle opened up fertilized eggs at different stages of incubation and noted that new structures appeared during the course of incubation. He was the first to perceive the antithesis between *epigenesis* (novel structures emerge during the course of development) and *preformation* (development is the simple unfolding or growth of preexisting structures). All subsequent debates about the nature of the developmental process are founded to some extent on this dichotomy. I say 'to some extent' because when one surveys the history of embryological thought, as, for example, embodied in Joseph Needham's (1959) marvelous work, *A History of Embryology*, there is a second debate of utmost importance that is really at the heart of all debates about the nature of the developmental process: what causes development? What causes development to happen?

By the late 1700s and early 1800s, the debate over preformation and epigenesis was resolved in favor of epigenesis. Before proceeding to a review of the debates about the causes of epigenetic development, it is informative to go a bit deeper into the notions of preformation and epigenesis.

Preformation: ovists and animalculists

There were two main versions of preformation. Since, according to this view, the organism was preformed in miniature from the outset, it was believed by some to lie dormant in the ovary of the female until development was started by fertilization. This view was held by the ovists. To other thinkers, the preformed organism resided in the semen of the male and development was unleashed through sexual union with the female. These were the animalculists.

Many of the preformationists, whether ovists or animalculists, tended to be of a religious persuasion. In that case they saw the whole of humankind having been originally stored in the ovaries of Eve if they were ovists or in the semen of Adam if they were animalculists. Based upon what was known about the population of the world in the 1700s, at the time of the height of the argument between the ovists and animalculists, Albrecht von Haller (1708–1777), the learned physiologist at the University of Göttingen, calculated that God, in the sixth day of his work, created and encased in the ovary of Eve 200,000 million fully formed human miniatures. Von Haller was a very committed ovist.

The sad fact about this controversy was that the very best evidence to date for epigenesis was at hand when von Haller made his pronouncement for preformation: "There is no coming into being! [*Nulla est epigenesis.*] No part of the animal body was made previous to another, and all were created simultaneously . . . All the parts were already present in a complete state, but hidden for a while from the human eye." Given von Haller's enormous scientific stature in the 1700s, we can only assume that he had an overriding mental set about the question of ontogenesis (development of the individual), and that set caused him to misinterpret evidence in a selective way. For example, the strongest evidence for the theory of encasement, as the theory of preformation was sometimes called, derived from Charles Bonnet's observations, in 1745, of virgin plant lice, who, without the benefit of a male consort, reproduce parthenogenetically (i.e., by means of self-fertilization). Thus, one can imagine the ovist Bonnet's excitement upon observing a virgin female plant louse give birth to ninety-five females in a 21-day period and, even more strikingly, observing these offspring themselves reproduce without male contact. Here was Eve incarnate among the plant lice!

Epigenesis: emergent nature of individual development

The empirical solution of the preformation–epigenesis controversy necessitated direct observation of the course of individual development, and not the outcome of parthenogenetic reproduction, as striking as that fact itself might be. Thus it was that one Caspar Friedrich Wolff (1733–1794), having examined the developmental anatomy and physiology of chick embryos at various times after incubation, provided the necessary direct evidence for the epigenetic or emergent aspect of individual development. According to Wolff's observations, the different organic systems of the embryo are formed and completed successively: first, the nervous system; then the skin covering of the embryo; third, the vascular system; and finally, the intestinal canal. These observations not only eventually toppled the doctrine of preformation but also provided the basis for the foundation of the science of embryology, which took off in a very important way in the next 150 years.

Fortunately, the microscopes of the late 1800s were a significant improvement over those of the late 1600s, whose low power allowed considerable reign for the imagination. Figure 1 shows the drawing of a human sperm cell by Nicholas Hartsoeker in 1694. Needless to say, Hartsoeker was a convinced animalculist prior to looking into the microscope.

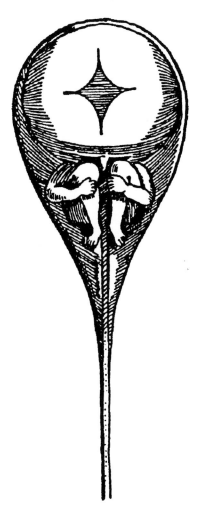

Figure 1. Drawing of the contents of a human sperm cell by the preformationist Nicholas Hartsoeker in 1694. From J. Needham (1959). *A History of Embryology*. New York: Abelard-Schuman.

Nature versus nurture: the separation of heredity and environment as independent causal agents

The triumph of epigenesis over preformation eventually ushered in the era of experimental embryology, defined as the causal-analytic study of early structural development, which unhappily coincided with the explicit separation of the effects of heredity and environment in Francis Galton's formulation of the nature-nurture dichotomy in the late 1800s.

Francis Galton's influential legacy

Francis Galton (1822–1911) was a second cousin of Charles Darwin and a great admirer of Darwin's concept of natural selection as a major force in evolution. Galton studied humans and advocated selective breeding or non-breeding among certain groups as a way of, respectively, hastening intellectual and moral evolution and saving humankind from degeneracy. Galton coined the term *eugenics*, and its practice in human populations eventually resulted from his theories, among others. He advocated positive eugenics, which encouraged people of presumed higher moral and intellectual standing to have larger families. (Negative eugenics, which he did not explicitly advocate, resulted in sterilization laws in some countries, including the United States, so that people judged unfit would have fewer children.)

Galton failed completely to realize that valued human traits are a result of various complicated kinds of interactions between the developing human organism and its social, nutritional, educational, and other rearing circumstances. If, as Galton found, men of distinction typically came from the upper or upper-middle social classes of 19th-century England, this condition was not only a result of selective breeding among 'higher' types of intelligent and moral people, but was also due in part to the rearing circumstances into which their progeny were born. This point of view is not always appreciated even today; that is, the inevitable correlation of social class with educational, nutritional, and other advantages (or disadvantages) in producing the mature organism. Negative eugenics was practiced in some European countries (e.g., Sweden, Switzerland) and in some states in the USA for much of the twentieth century.

Galton's dubious intellectual legacy was the sharp distinction between nature and nurture as separate, independent causes of development, although he said in very contemporary terms, "The interaction of nature and circumstance is very close, and it is impossible to separate them with precision" (Galton, 1907, p. 131). While it sounds as if Galton opts for the interpenetration of nature and nurture in the life of every person, in fact he means that the discrimination of the separate causal effects of nature and nurture is difficult only at the borders or frontiers of their interaction. Thus, he wrote:

> Nurture acts before birth, during every stage of embryonic and pre-embryonic existence, causing the potential faculties at the time of birth to be in some degree the effect of nurture. We need not, however, be hypercritical about distinction; we know that the bulk of the respective provinces of nature and nurture are totally different, although the frontier between them may be uncertain, and we are perfectly justified in attempting to appraise their relative importance.
>
> (Galton, 1907, p. 131)

Since we still retain, albeit unknowingly, many of Galton's beliefs about nature and nurture, it is useful to examine his assumptions more closely. He believed that nature, at birth, offered a potential for development, but that this potential (or reaction range, as it is sometimes called) was rather circumscribed and very persistent. In 1875, he wrote: "When nature and nurture compete for supremacy on equal terms . . . the former proves the stronger. It is needless to insist that neither is self-sufficient; the highest natural endowments may be starved by defective nurture, while no carefulness of nurture can overcome the evil tendencies of an intrinsically bad physique, weak brain, or brutal disposition." One of the implications of this view was, as Galton wrote in 1892: "The Negro now born in the United States has much the same natural faculties as his distant cousin who is born in Africa; the effect of his transplantation being ineffective in changing his nature." The conceptual error here is not merely that Galton is using his upper-middle class English or European values to view the potential accomplishments of another race, but it is rather that he has no factual knowledge of the width of the reaction range of African blacks – he assumes it not only to be inferior, but to be narrow and thus without the potential to change its phenotypic expression.

This kind of assumption is open to factual inquiry and measurement. It requires just the kind of natural

experiment that Galton would have marveled at, and perhaps even enjoyed, given its simple elegance, namely, the careful monitoring and measurement of presumptively in-built traits *within generations* in races that have migrated to such different habitats, sub-cultures, or cultures that their epigenetic potential would be allowed to express itself in previously untapped ways. Thus, we can draw a line of increasing adult stature as Oriental groups migrate to the United States and substantially change their diet. More importantly we can measure the increase in IQ of blacks (within as well as between generations) as they move from the rural southern United States to the urban northeast, and its further increase the longer they remain in the urban northeast (Otto Klineberg's book, *Negro Intelligence and Selective Migration*, published in 1935). The same is true for lower-class whites coming from the rural south to the urban northeast. Galton's concept of 'like begets like,' whether applied to upper-class Englishmen or poor blacks and whites, requires that their rearing circumstances and opportunities remain the same.

Galton's dubious intellectual legacy is notoriously long-lived, no matter how many times the nature-nurture controversy has been claimed to be dead and buried. An analysis of psychology textbooks reveals the heartiness of Galton's dichotomous ideas up to the late 20th century (Johnston, 1987).

Dichotomous thinking about individual development in early experimental embryology

In the late 1800s and early 1900s, the main procedure of experimental embryology, as a means of implementing a causal analysis of individual development, was to perturb normal development by deleting cells or moving cells to different places in the embryo. Almost without exception, when normal cellular arrangements were changed developmental outcomes were altered, giving very strong empirical support to the notion that cell–cell or cell–environment *interactions* are at the heart of individual development: interactions of one sort or another make development happen (i.e., make development take one path rather than another path).

This major conceptual advance was only incompletely realized because of the erroneous interpretation of one of the earliest experiments in the new experimental embryology. In 1888, Wilhelm Roux (1850–1924), one of the founders of experimental embryology, used a hot needle to kill one of the two existing cells after the first cleavage stage in a frog's egg and observed the development of the surviving cell. The prevalent theory of heredity at the time held that one-half of the heredity determinants would be in each cell after the first cleavage, and, indeed, as called for by the theory, a roughly half embryo resulted from Roux's experiment.

However, when Hans Driesch (1867–1941), another of the founders of experimental embryology, performed a variation of Roux's experiment by separating the two cells after cleavage by shaking them completely loose from one another, he observed an *entire* embryo develop from the single cells. Eventually, Roux accepted that the second, dying cell in his experiment interfered with the development of the healthy cell, thus giving rise to the half-embryo under his conditions.

Before he accepted that, however, Roux had begun theorizing on the basis of his half-embryo results and came up with a causal dichotomy that continues to haunt embryology to the present day: *self-differentiation* versus *dependent differentiation*. These two terms were coined by Roux as a consequence of his half-embryo experiment, which he believed erroneously to be an outcome of self-differentiation, implying an independent or non-interactive outcome, in contrast to dependent differentiation where the interactive component between cells or groups of cells was necessary to, and brought about, the specific outcome. The concept of self-differentiation is akin to the concept of the *innate* when the term is applied to an outcome of development, as in the innate (hereditary) – acquired (learned) dichotomy that is prevalent in much of psychological theorizing.

Roux, himself, gave up the self- and dependent-differentiation dichotomy as he came to accept Driesch's procedure as being a more appropriate way to study the two post-cleavage cells. Unfortunately, Roux's concepts lived on in experimental embryology in disguised form as *mosaic development* versus *regulative development*. In the latter, the embryo or its cells are seen as developing in relation to the *milieu* (environment), whereas the former is understood as a rigid and narrow outcome fostered by self-differentiation or self-determination, as if development were non-interactive. Here is the way the American embryologist W. K. Brooks (1902, pp. 490–491) expressed concern about the notion of self-differentiation:

> A thoughtful and distinguished naturalist tells us that while the differentiation of the cells which arise from the egg is sometimes inherent in the egg, and sometimes induced by the conditions of development, it is more commonly mixed; but may it not be the mind of the embryologist, and not the material world, that is mixed? Science does not deal in compromises, but in discoveries. When we say the development of the egg is inherent, must we not also say what are the relations with reference to which it is inherent?

This insight that developmental causality is relational (interactive or coactive) has eluded us to the present time, as evidenced in the various causal dichotomies extant in the developmental-psychological literature of today: nature-nurture, innate-acquired, maturation-experience, development-evolution, and so forth. We need to move beyond these dichotomies to understand individual development correctly.

Predetermined and probabilistic epigenesis

At the root of the problem of understanding individual development is the failure to truly integrate biology into developmental psychology in a way that does empirical justice to both fields. The evolutionary psychologists, for example, are still operating in terms of Galton's legacy, as witnessed by the following quotations. They start off seemingly on the right foot, as we saw in Galton's introductory remarks about nature and nurture: "The cognitive architecture, like all aspects of the phenotype from molars to memory circuits, is the joint product of genes and environment . . . EPs [evolutionary psychologists] do not assume that genes play a more important role in development than the environment does, or that 'innate factors' are more important than 'learning.' Instead, EPs reject these dichotomies as ill-conceived" (Cosmides & Tooby, 1997, p. 17). However, several pages later, when they get down to specifics, the nature-nurture dichotomy nonetheless emerges: "To learn, there must be some mechanism that causes this to occur. Since learning cannot occur in the *absence* of a mechanism that causes it, the mechanism that causes it must *itself* be unlearned – must be innate" (Cosmides & Tooby, 1997, p. 19). Since one must certainly credit these authors (as well as others who write in the same vein) with the knowledge that development is not preformative but epigenetic, in 1970, extending Needham's (1959, p. 213, note 1) earlier usage, I employed the term 'predetermined epigenesis' to capture the developmental conception of the innate that is embodied in the above quotation. (Cosmides and Tooby do not stand alone; other evolutionary theorists such as the ethologist Konrad Lorenz (1903–1986) posited an 'innate schoolmarm' to explain the development of species-specific learning abilities.) The predetermined epigenesis of development takes this form:

Predetermined Epigenesis
Unidirectional Structure – Function Development
Genetic activity (DNA → RNA → Protein) →
structural maturation → function, activity, or
experience (e.g. species-specific learning abilities)

In contrast to predetermined epigenesis, I put forward the concept of probabilistic epigenesis:

Probabilistic Epigenesis
Bidirectional Structure – Function Development
Genetic activity (DNA ↔ RNA ↔ Protein) ↔ structural
maturation ↔ function, activity, or experience

In this view, prior experience, function, or activity would be necessary for the development of species-specific learning abilities. Epigenesis is probabilistic because there is some inevitable slippage in the very large number of reciprocal coactions that participate in the developmental process, thereby rendering outcomes probable rather than certain.

By way of defining the terms and their relationships, as it applies to the nervous system, *structural maturation* refers to neurophysiological and neuroanatomical development, principally the structure and function of nerve cells and their synaptic interconnections. The unidirectional structure-function view assumes that genetic activity gives rise to structural maturation that then leads to function in a non-reciprocal fashion, whereas the bidirectional view holds that there are reciprocal influences among genetic activity, structural maturation, and function. In the unidirectional view, the activity of genes and the maturational process are pictured as relatively encapsulated or insulated, so that they are uninfluenced by feedback from the maturation process or function, whereas the bidirectional view assumes that genetic activity and maturation are affected by function, activity, or experience. The bidirectional or probabilistic view applied to the usual unidirectional formula calls for arrows going back to genetic activity to indicate feedback serving as signals for the turning on and turning off of genetic activity.

The usual view in the central dogma of molecular biology calls for genetic activity to be regulated by the genetic system itself in a strictly feed-forward manner, as in the unidirectional formula of DNA $\rightarrow$ RNA $\rightarrow$ Protein above. Thus, the central dogma is a version of predetermined epigenesis. Note that genetic activity is involved in both predetermined and probabilistic epigenesis. Thus, what distinguishes the two conceptions is not genes versus environment, as in the age-old nature-nurture dichotomy, but rather the unidirectional (strictly feed-forward or -upward influences) versus the bidirectional nature of the coactions across all levels of analysis. There is now evidence for all of the coactions depicted in the probabilistic conception, including those at the genetic level of analysis (Gottlieb, 1998). Given that genes, however remotely, are necessarily involved in all outcomes of development, it is dismaying to see that that fact is not universally recognized, but rather is seen as some outdated relict of hereditarianism: ". . . although genetic effects of various kinds have been conclusively demonstrated, hereditarian research has not produced conclusive demonstrations of genetic inheritance of complex behaviors . . . The behaviorists' approach . . . should be – and generally is – to accept a genetic basis only if research designed to identify effects of social or other environmental variables does not reveal any effects" (Reese, 2001, p. 18). This is a particularly blatant example of either/or dichotomous causality: develop-

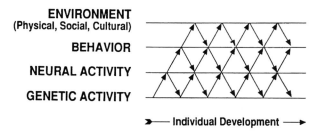

BIDIRECTIONAL INFLUENCES

Figure 2. Probabilistic-epigenetic framework: depiction of the completely bidirectional and coactional nature of genetic, neural, behavioral, and environmental influences over the course of individual development. From G. Gottlieb, 1992. *Individual Development and Evolution*. Oxford: Oxford University Press, with permission.

mental outcomes are caused either by genes or by environment. Given the recent date of the quotation, this is evidence that the nature-nurture dichotomy is not dead and, if it is buried, it has been buried alive.

From central dogma of molecular biology to probabilistic epigenesis

In addition to describing the various ramifications of the nature-nurture dichotomy, the other purpose of this entry is to place genes and genetic activity firmly within a developmental-physiological framework, one in which genes not only affect each other and mRNA (messenger RNA that mediates between DNA and protein), but are affected by activities at other levels of the system, up to and including the external environment. This developmental system of bidirectional, coactional influences is captured schematically in Figure 2. In contrast to the unidirectional and encapsulated genetic predeterminism of the central dogma, a probabilistic view of epigenesis holds that the sequence and outcomes of development are probabilistically determined by the critical operation of various endogenous and exogenous stimulative events (Gottlieb, 1997).

The probabilistic-epigenetic framework presented in Figure 2 not only is based on what we now know about mechanisms of individual development at all levels of analysis, but also derives from our understanding of evolution and natural selection. As everyone knows, natural selection serves as a filter and preserves reproductively successful phenotypes. These successful phenotypes are a product of individual development, and thus are a consequence of the adaptability of the organism to its developmental conditions. Therefore, natural selection has preserved (favored) organisms that are adaptably responsive to their developmental conditions, both behaviorally and physiologically. As noted above, genes assist in the making of protein; they

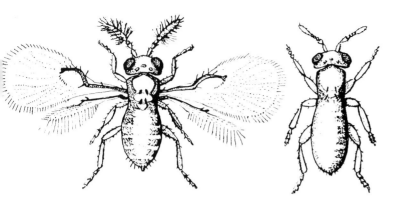

Butterfly Host   **Alder Host**

Figure 3. Two very different morphological outcomes of development in the minute parasitic wasp. The outcomes depend on the host (butterfly or alder fly) in which the eggs were laid. The insects are of the same species of parasitic wasp (*Trichogramma semblidis*). Adapted on the basis of V. B. Wigglesworth, 1964. *The Life of Insects*. Cleveland, OH: World Publishing Co.

do not predetermine or make finished traits. Thus, organisms with the same genes can develop very different phenotypes under different ontogenetic conditions, as witness the two extreme variants of a single parasitic wasp species shown in Figure 3 and identical twins reared apart in the human species (Fig. 4).

Since the probabilistic-epigenetic view presented in Figure 2 does not portray enough detail at the level of genetic activity, it is useful to flesh that out in compa-

rison to the previously mentioned central dogma of molecular biology.

As shown in Figure 5, the original central dogma explicitly posited one-way traffic from DNA → RNA → Protein, and was silent about any other flows of 'information' (as Francis Crick wrote in 1958). Later, after the discovery of retroviruses (RNA → DNA information transfer), Crick (1970) did not claim to have predicted that phenomenon, but, rather, that the original formulation did not expressly forbid it. At the bottom of Figure 5, probabilistic epigenesis, being inherently bidirectional in the horizontal and vertical levels (Fig. 2), has information flowing not only from RNA → DNA but between Protein ↔ Protein and DNA ↔ DNA. The only relationship that is not yet supported is Protein → RNA, in the sense of reverse translation (protein altering the structure of RNA), but there are other influences of protein on RNA *activity* (not its structure) that would support such a directional flow. For example, a process known as *phosphorylation* can modify proteins such that they activate (or inactivate) other proteins (Protein → Protein) which, when activated, trigger rapid association of mRNA (Protein → RNA activity). When mRNAs are transcribed by DNA, they do not necessarily become immediately active but require a further signal to do so.

The consequences of phosphorylation could provide that signal (Protein → Protein → mRNA activity → Protein). A process like this appears to be involved in the expression of 'fragile X mental retardation protein' under normal conditions and proves disastrous to neural

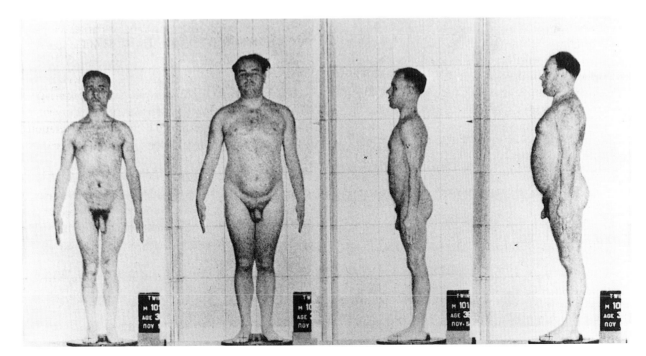

Figure 4. Remarkable illustration of the enormous phenotypic variation that can result when monozygotic (single egg) identical twins are reared apart in very different family environments from birth. From J. M. Tanner, 1978. *Foetus Into Man*. Cambridge, MA: Harvard University Press.

and psychological development when it does not occur. The label of 'fragile-X mental retardation protein' makes it sound as if there is a gene (or genes) that produces a protein that predisposes to mental retardation whereas, in actual fact, it is this protein that is *missing* (absent) in the brain of fragile X mental retardates, and thus represents a failure of gene (or mRNA) expression rather than a positive genetic contribution to mental retardation. The same is likely true for other 'genetic' disorders, whether mental or physical: these most often represent biochemical *deficiencies* of one sort or another due to the lack of expression of the requisite genes and mRNAs to produce the appropriate proteins necessary for normal development. Thus, the search for 'candidate genes' in psychiatric or other disorders is most often a search for genes that are not being expressed, not for genes that are being expressed and causing the disorder.

So-called cystic fibrosis genes and manic-depression genes, among others, are in this category. The instances that I know of in which the presence of genes causes a problem are Edward's syndrome and trisomy 21 (Down's syndrome), wherein the presence of an extra, otherwise normal, chromosome 18 and 21, respectively, causes problems because the genetic system is adapted for two, not three, chromosomes at each location. In some cases, it is of course possible that the expression of mutated genes can be involved in a disorder, but, in my opinion, it is most often the lack of expression of normal genes that is the culprit. Most mutations impair fitness. In one of the very rare cases of benefit, in sickle-cell anemia (a defect in red blood cells), the bearer is made resistant to the malaria parasite. Amplifying the left side of the bottom of Figure 5, it is known that gene expression is affected by events in the cytoplasm of the cell, which is the immediate environment of the nucleus and mitochondria of the cell wherein DNA resides, and by hormones that enter the cell and its nucleus. This feed-downward effect can be visualized thusly:

Gene expression influenced by

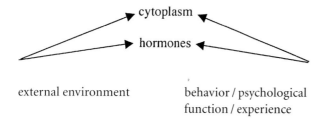

According to this view, different proteins are formed depending on the particular factors influencing gene expression. Concerning the effect of psychological functioning on gene expression, we have the evidence of decreased interleukin 2 receptor mRNA, an immune system response, in medical students taking academic

Genetic Activity According To Central Dogma

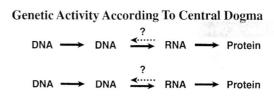

Genetic Activity According To Probabilistic Epigenesis

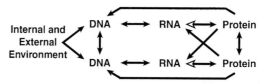

Figure 5. Different views of influences on genetic activity in the central dogma and probabilistic epigenesis. The filled arrows indicate documented sources of influence, while the open arrow from Protein back to RNA remains a theoretical possibility in probabilistic epigenesis and is prohibited in the central dogma (as are Protein ↔ Protein influences). Protein → Protein influences occur (1) when prions transfer their abnormal conformation to other proteins and (2) when, during normal development, proteins activate or inactivate other proteins as in the phosphorylation example described in the text. The filled arrows from Protein to RNA represent the activation of mRNA by protein as a consequence of, for example, phosphorylation, and the reshuffling of the RNA transcript by a specialized group of proteins called spliceosomes ('alternative splicing'). DNA ↔ DNA influences are termed 'epistatic,' referring to the modification of gene expression depending on the genetic background in which they are located. In the central dogma, genetic activity is dictated solely by genes (DNA → DNA), whereas in probabilistic epigenesis internal and external environmental events activate genetic expression through proteins (Protein → DNA), hormones, and other influences. To keep the diagram manageable, the fact that behavior and the external environment exert their effects on DNA through internal mediators (proteins, hormones, etc.) is not shown; nor is it shown that the protein products of some genes regulate the expression of other genes. (Further discussion in text.) Reprinted in modified form from G. Gottlieb, 1998. Normally occurring environmental and behavioral influences on gene activity: from central dogma to probabilistic epigenesis. *Psychological Review*, 105, 792–802; with permission of the American Psychological Association.

examinations (Glaser *et al.*, 1990). More recently, in an elegant study that traverses all levels from psychological functioning to neural activity to neural structure to gene expression, Cirelli, Pompeiano, & Tononi (1996) showed that genetic activity in certain areas of the brain is higher during waking than in sleeping in rats. In this case, the stimulation of gene expression was influenced by the hormone norepinephrine flowing from locus coeruleus neurons that fire at very low levels during sleep, and at high levels during waking and when triggered by salient environmental events. Norepinephrine modifies neural activity and excitability, as well as the expression of certain genes. So, in this case, we have evidence for the interconnectedness of events relating the external environment and psychological functioning to genetic

Table 1. Developmental–behavioral evolutionary pathway.		
I: Change in behavior	*II: Change in morphology*	*III: Change in gene frequencies*
First stage in evolutionary pathway: change in ontogenetic development results in novel behavioral shift, which encourages new environmental relationships.	Second stage in evolutionary change: new environmental relationships bring out latent (already existing epigenetic) possibilities for morphological–physiological change.	Third stage of evolutionary change resulting from long-term geographic or behavioral isolation (separate breeding populations). It is important to observe that evolution has already occurred phenotypically before stage III is reached.

expression by a specifiable hormone emanating from the activity of a specific neural structure whose functioning waxes and wanes in relation to the psychological state of the organism.

Role of ontogenetic development in evolution

Though not a debate about the nature of ontogenetic development or the epigenetic process as such, the role of development in evolution takes two very different forms. In its most conventional form, a change in genes (via mutation, sexual recombination, or genetic drift) brings about an enduring change in development that results in the appearance of different somatic, behavioral, and psychological features. That is the standard sequence of events in bringing about evolution in what is called the 'Modern synthesis' in biology. A change in genes results in a change in development in this scenario. Since evolution need not occur in only one mode, in another, more recent, scenario, the first stage in the evolutionary pathway is a change in ontogenetic development that results in a novel behavioral outcome. This novel behavior encourages new organism–environment relationships. In the second stage, the new environmental relationships bring out latent possibilities for somatic-physiological change without a change in existing genes. The new environmental relationships activate previously quiescent genes that are correlated with a novel epigenetic process, which results in new anatomical and/or physiological arrangements. This evolutionary scenario is based on two facts: firstly, the empirical fact that specific kinds of changes in species-typical development result in the appearance of behavioral novelties (e.g., increased exploratory behavior, changes in learning ability or preferences, enhanced coping with stress), and, secondly, there is a relatively great store of typically unexpressed genetic (and, therefore, epigenetic) potential that can be accessed by changing developmental conditions.

As long as the changed developmental circumstances prevail, in generation after generation, the novel behavior will persist without any necessary change in genes. Now, eventually, long-term geographic or behavioral isolation (separate breeding populations) may result in a change in gene frequencies in the new population, but the changes in behavior and morphology will already have occurred before the change in genes. No one is denying that genetic mutations, recombination, or drift can bring about evolution; the point is that those are not the only routes to evolutionary change. The three-stage developmental-behavioral evolutionary scenario is shown in Table 1.

That a developmental change in behavior can result in incipient speciation and in genetic change has recently been demonstrated in the apple maggot fly, *Rhagoletis pomonella*. The original native (USA) host for the female apple maggot fly's egg laying was the hawthorn, a spring-flowering tree or shrub. Domestic apples were introduced into the USA in the 17th century. Haws and apples occur in the same locale. The first reported infestation of apple trees by apple maggot flies was in the 1860s. There are now two variants of *R. pomonella*, one of which mates and lays its eggs on apples and the other of which mates and lays its eggs on haws (Table 2). The life cycles of the two variants are now desynchronized because apples mature earlier than haws. Incipient speciation has been maintained by a transgenerational behavior induced by early exposure learning: an olfactory acceptance of apples for courting, mating, and ovipositing based on the host in which the fly developed (Bush & Smith, 1998).

The cause of the original shift from hawthorns to apples as the host species for egg laying can only be speculated upon. Perhaps the hawthorn hosts became overburdened with infestations or, for other reasons, died out in a part of their range, bringing about a shift to apples in a small segment of the ancestral hawthorn population that did not have such well-developed olfactory sensitivity or an olfactory aversion to apples. This latter supposition is supported by behavioral tests, in which the apple variant accepts both apples and haws as hosts, whereas in the haw variant only a small percentage will accept apples and most show a strong preference for haws. As indicated by single host acceptance tests, the apple-reared flies show a greater percentage of egg-laying behavior on the apple host than do the hawthorn-reared flies. Thus, the familiarity-inducing rearing experience (exposure learning) makes the apple-reared flies more accepting of the apple host, although they still have a preference for the hawthorn host.

Given the ecological circumstances, the increased likelihood of acceptance of the apple host, even in the face of a preference for hawthorn, would perpetuate the transgenerational courting, mating, and laying of eggs in apple orchards. Apple maggot flies hatch out at the base of the tree in which their mother had laid their egg the previous summer. While becoming sexually mature, even though they have wandered tens or hundreds of yards, they are still in the vicinity of the apple orchard, if not still in the orchard. The scent of the apples attracts them, and the early rearing experience having rendered the apple scent acceptable, the cycle renews itself, because of the high probability that the early maturing apple maggot fly will encounter the odor of apples rather than hawthorns (see Table 2). In support of incipient speciation, the two variants are now genetically somewhat distinct and do not interbreed freely in nature, although they are morphologically the same and remain interfertile.

In contrast to the transgenerational behavioral scenario being put forward here, conventional evolutionary biological thinking would hold that "most likely some mutations in genes coding for larval/pupal development and adult emergence" brought about the original divergence and maintain the difference in the two populations (Ronald Prokopy, personal communication, August 2000). Although we cannot know with certainty, present evidence (below) would suggest a genetic mutation was not necessary. This is not a behavior versus genes argument; the transgenerational behavioral initiation requires genetic compatibility, otherwise it would not work. The question is whether the original interaction (switch to the apple host) required a genetic mutation or not. The developmental timing change in the life histories of the two forms (Table 2) has resulted in correlated genetic changes in the two populations. That finding is consonant with the evolutionary model presented here (i.e., gene frequencies change some time after the behavioral switch).

From the present point of view, another significant feature of the findings is that, when immature hawthorn flies (pupae) are subjected to the pre-wintering environment of the apple flies (pupae), those that survive have a genetic make-up that is similar to the apple flies, signifying that environmental selection is acting on already-existing developmental-genetic variation. Most importantly, this result shows that there is still sufficient individual developmental-genetic

Table 2. An example of the developmental behavioral basis of evolution: incipient speciation in two variants of apple maggot fly (Rhagoletis pomonella).

Time	Apple host	Hawthorn host
Year 1	Eggs laid	Eggs laid
	Fruit matures earlier than haw	Fruit matures later than apple
Year 2	Hatch late summer	Hatch early fall
	5–12 days	5–12 days
Year 3	OFFSPRING court and mate on or near host, and female lays eggs on same host	OFFSPRING court and mate on or near host, and female lays eggs on same host
	Cycle repeats	Cycle repeats

Adapted from G. L. Bush and J. J. Smith, 1998. The genetics and ecology of sympatric speciation: a case study. *Research in Population Ecology*, 40, 174–187; and R. Prokopy and G. L. Bush, 1993. Evolution in an orchard. *Natural History*, 102, 4–10.

variation in the hawthorn population, even at this late date, to support a transgenerational behavioral initiation of the switch from hawthorns to apples without the necessity of a genetic mutation.

To summarize, a developmental-behavioral change involving the apple maggot fly's choice of oviposition site puts it in a situation where it must be able to withstand certain pre-wintering low temperatures for given periods of time, and that differ between the apple and hawthorn forms (Table 2). This situation sets up the natural selection scenario that brings about changes in gene frequencies that are correlated with the pre-wintering temperature regimen. The change in egg-laying behavior leads the way to genetic change in the population, the genetic change thus being a consequence of the change in behavior.

Conclusions

After hundreds of years of debate, epigenesis triumphed over preformation. Thus, the nature of the process of individual development was finally understood to be of an emergent character, wherein new structures and functions appear during the maturation of the organism. The next debates concerned the sources of these new structures and functions, and these were partitioned into nature (heredity or genes) and nurture (environment or learning). Recently, as probabilistic epigenesis has more or less triumphed over predetermined epigenesis, the cause of development is now understood to be relational (coactive), in which genetics, neurology, behavior, and environmental influences are all seen as essential and as acting in concert to bring about developmental outcomes, whether physical or psychological. Finally, ontogenetic development, particularly changes in behavioral development, can have a role in initiating evolution prior to genetic changes in the population.

See also:
The concept of development: historical perspectives; Neuromaturational theories; Ethological theories; Cross-species comparisons; Twin and adoption studies; Conceptions and misconceptions about embryonic development; Normal and abnormal prenatal development; Sleep and wakefulness; Behavioral and learning disorders; Down's syndrome; Behavior genetics; Developmental genetics

Further reading

Johnston, T. D. and Edwards, L. (2002). Genes, interactions, and the development of behavior. *Psychological Review*, 109, 26–34.
Lerner, R. M. (2002). *Concepts and Theories of Human Development*, 3rd edn. Mahwah, NJ: Erlbaum.
Moore, D. S. (2001). *The Dependent Gene: The Fallacy of "Nature vs. Nurture."* New York: Henry Holt.
Wahlsten, D. and Gottlieb, G. (1997). The invalid separation of nature and nurture: lessons from animal experimentation. In R. J. Sternberg and E. Grigorenko (eds.), *Intelligence, Heredity, and Environment*. New York: Cambridge University Press, pp. 163–192.

Acknowledgments

The author's research and scholarly activities are funded, in part, by grants from the National Institute of Mental Health (P50-MH-52429) and the National Science Foundation (BCS-0126475).

One section of this entry, "From central dogma of molecular biology to probabilistic epigenesis," was taken from Gottlieb (1998), with permission of the American Psychological Association.

What is ontogenetic development?

BRIAN HOPKINS

Introduction

Take any textbook on human development and then look for whether it provides a definition of 'development.' You will probably find that such a definition is absent or that it is provided in a couple of unenlightening sentences. In fact, most of these textbooks provide only a cursory definition of the term. The reason is not hard to find: development is one of those terms that we freely use in everyday language and yet when we try to pin it down with a precise definition it assumes an almost evanescent-like quality. As the satirist and evolutionist Samuel Butler (1835–1902) wrote in his Note-Books (1912), published posthumously, "Definitions are a kind of scratching and generally leave a sore place more sore than it was before." Scratching the surface of the term development exposes a host of seemingly related terms such as differentiation, evolution, growth, and phylogeny. Scratch a bit more and up pops 'ontogenetic development.'

In what follows, there is no pretense made to distinguish between all these terms, as space limitations do not permit that. The main focus is on comparing ontogenetic development with ontogeny. This brings with it the need to distinguish development from evolution and evolution from phylogeny. Finally, mention will be made of the long-standing pursuit to bring ontogenetic development and biological evolution into a scientifically credible relationship, which is currently leading to the emergence of a new discipline called evolutionary developmental biology.

Ontogeny and development

Ontogeny

Like phylogeny, this is a term created by Ernst Haeckel (1839–1919) from combining the Greek word for 'being' with that for 'birth' or 'born of.' Typically, ontogeny is defined as the life history of an individual from the zygote to the mature adult. Thus, it concerns the description of a historical path (i.e., the life cycle) of the 'common' individual of a particular species from fertilization to sexual maturity. In the past, it was restricted to the time between conception and birth, with the term ontogenesis being reserved for the history of a particular individual as in, for example, case studies. In either case, ontogeny or ontogenesis, such a history is conveniently broken down into periods, phases, or stages according to some metric of chronological age in order to indicate major age-specific changes and to describe the products of these temporal delineations.

Development

A more general and abstract concept than ontogeny, development has assumed a number of different meanings such that it was treated as being synonymous with the terms differentiation, growth, and evolution. As a concept, particularly prior to the 20th century, it was intended to indicate organized change toward some certain end condition or hypothetical ideal. Thus, like evolution, it was represented as a progressive process of 'improvement' applicable to all levels of organization.

The distinction between growth and differentiation, with both serving as synonyms for development, continued to separate the preformationists (development is growth) from the epigeneticists (development is differentiation) throughout the 19th century. However, during the same century, growth started to become something different from development, with the advent of cell theory as formulated by Theodor H. A. Schwann (1810–1887) following Matthias Schleiden (1804–1881). While much of Schwann's theory proved to be untenable, it led to growth being restricted to quantitative change (viz., increase in cell number by cell division and increase in cell size), and thus continuing compatibility with preformationism. Subsequently termed

Table 1. Examples of quantitative and qualitative regressions during ontogenetic development at different levels of organization.

Level	Quantitative	Qualitative
Behavioral	Decrease in associated movements	Fetal GMs, rooting, suckling, and some reflexes, imitation, swimming in human newborn
Morphological		Egg-tooth
Physiological		Yolk-sac, placenta
Neuromuscular	Poly- to monoinnervation	
Neural	Apoptosis, synapse elimination	Cajal-Retzius cells, axon and dendrite retraction, radial glia, neurons in the dorsal horn of spinal cord

Quantitative regressions involve a decrease in the number of elements (e.g. neurons; synapses). Qualitative regressions consist of replacements of existing structures and behaviors, or their disappearance, once their adaptive functions have been fulfilled. The quantitative change from poly- to monoinnervation occurs with a change from many to just one axon innervating a muscle fiber, which seems to occur both prenatally and during early postnatal life in humans. The egg-tooth is found in birds and crocodiles at the end of their beaks or snouts, respectively. Together with spontaneous and rather stereotyped head movements, it enables the hatchling to be born by breaking open the eggshell. Once it has served this function, it drops off. GMs: general movements of the whole body that are expressed in the healthy fetus and infant with variations in amplitude, speed, and force, and give the impression of being fluent and elegant in performance. Evident at about 10 weeks after conception, they remain in the behavioral repertoire until about 2–3 months after birth. After this age, they are replaced by more discrete movements that have a voluntary-like appearance (e.g., reaching). All told, convincing evidence for qualitative regressions in behavioral development is less easy to come by than at the other levels.

appositional or isocentric growth, it was contrasted with allometric growth (i.e., change in shape) in order to account for qualitative change, largely through the work of Julian Huxley (1887–1975). Treating growth as manifesting both types of change led to a blurring of distinctions between it and development that continues today.

With the rise of systems thinking during the 20th century, further attempts were made to discriminate development from other sorts of change such as growth and metabolism. One such attempt was made by Nagel (1957) who defined the concept of development as involving: ". . . two essential components. The notion of a system possessing a definite structure and a definite set of pre-capacities; and the notion of a sequential set of changes in the system yielding relatively permanent but novel increments not only to structure, but to its modes of operation as well" (p. 17). The core of Nagel's definition is that development consists of changing structure-function ('modes of operation') relationships at all levels of organization, an issue that goes to the heart of attempts to explain ontogenetic development at the individual level.

Ontogenetic development

When, in 1870, Herbert Spencer (1820–1903) suggested that the development of the individual was analogous to embryonic growth, the way was open to combine ontogeny with development to give ontogenetic

development. Once done, it was not long before individual development was divided up into successive, time-demarcated periods, phases, or stages. The result was an even more difficult term to pin down unambiguously. What then do we mean by 'ontogenetic development'? One definition, capturing those given in some textbooks on developmental (psycho-) biology, is the following: "Species-characteristic changes in an individual organism from a relatively simple, but age-adequate, level of organization through a succession of stable states of increasing complexity and organization."

Defined as such, we are confronted with what is meant by 'relatively simple,' 'organization,' and 'stable,' as well as the previously mentioned term 'differentiation.' Moreover, the definition alludes to ontogenetic development being progressive, while at the same time ignoring the possibility of transitional periods between the stable states. Evidence from avian and non-human mammalian species, and to a lesser extent for humans, indicates both quantitative regressions (e.g., cell death) and qualitative regressions (e.g., the replacement of one set of cells by another) as being a normal part of 'normal' development (Table 1). Such evidence forces us to consider ontogenetic development as being both progressive and regressive, and in which there are both quantitative (continuous) and qualitative (discontinuous) changes (Fig. 1). If there is qualitative change (i.e., the emergence of new properties), then there must be transitional periods during which the

• **Linear change**

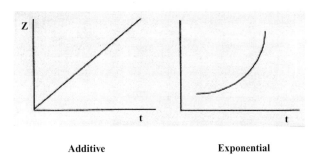

Additive   Exponential

• **Continuous change to a steady state**

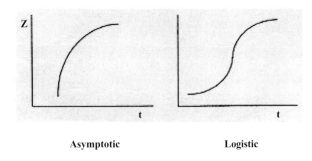

Asymptotic   Logistic

• **Discontinuous change**

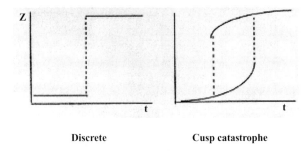

Discrete   Cusp catastrophe

Figure 1. A classification of a variety of developmental functions. Quantitative and continuous changes can reveal linear or exponential functions as well as ones that are asymptotic or comply with a logistic growth function (i.e., there is an initial exponential trajectory that gives way to deceleration and the achievement of a final steady state). Qualitative and discontinuous changes may be manifested in one of two ways. The first consists of a discrete step or sudden jump from one stable state to another, but more complex, state with no intermediary ones. The second, termed a cusp catastrophe, has the same properties but additionally includes a hysteresis cycle, which can be interpreted as a regressive phenomenon. Hysteresis is a strong indication that a developing system is undergoing a transition between two qualitatively different states. With special thanks to Raymond Wimmers for permission to use the plots of the developmental functions.

developing organism undergoes transformation (Fig. 2). Thus, ontogenetic development is typified by progressions and regressions, quantitative and qualitative changes, and instabilities (i.e., transitions) between stable states that become increasingly complex

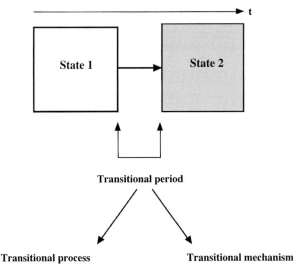

Figure 2. A transition in the behavior of a linear system (e.g., a thermostat) is gradual and continuous. For non-linear systems such as living organisms, change can be abrupt and lead to a qualitatively different and more complex state. As illustrated for such systems, that part of the time (t) taken to complete a transition (the transitional period) should be shorter than that spent in the preceding and subsequent states. In the first instance, what one wants to know is how behavior is organized during the period of transition (the transitional process) relative to the preceding and subsequent states. In dynamical systems terminology, this is captured by an order parameter, an example of which might be movement units in studying the development of reaching. The next step would be to identify the event that triggered the transition (the transitional mechanism). Using the same terminology, this is referred to as control parameter, which in the case of reaching could be the degree of postural stability when performing this action.

by some criteria. Furthermore, it takes on two forms, one direct and the other indirect or metamorphic (Fig. 3).

In suggesting metamorphosis as a metaphor for non-metamorphic development, Oppenheim (1982a) makes his point as follows:

> Destruction followed by a dramatic reorganization or even the appearance of entirely new features are familiar themes of development in such forms, and the nervous system and behavior are no exceptions. Although I do not wish to offend my colleagues in developmental psychology by claiming that the ontogeny of the nervous system and behavior in 'higher' vertebrates is metamorphic in nature, I would argue that even some of the regressions and losses, and other changes that occur during human development are only slightly less dramatic than the changes that amphibians undergo in their transformation from tadpoles into frogs.
>
> (p. 296)

Comparing ontogenetic development across phyletic levels in this way brings us to the distinction between phylogeny and evolution.

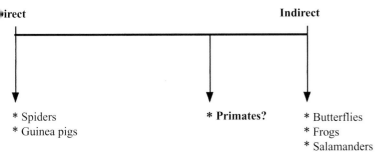

Direct development: newborn or hatchling resembles adult form and mainly undergoes growth to achieve adult-end state.

Indirect (or metamorphic) development: newborn or hatchling differs markedly from adult in terms of behavioral, morphological, physiological and other traits.

Figure 3. The differences between direct and indirect forms of ontogenetic development, taken to be two extremes of a continuum of possibilities. Direct development is more or less synonymous with growth. Indirect development, which is the defining feature of metamorphosis, involves radical transformations at different levels of organization, including the behavioral level. It has been suggested that the ontogenetic development of non-metamorphic species such as primates may in fact be better characterized as lying closer to the indirect end of the continuum. In developmental psychology, there is an ongoing debate about whether infants are born with innate cognitive structures for acquiring physical knowledge and thus that subsequent development is analogous to the growth of these structures. Those who oppose this view argue that such structures are emergent properties of the developing cognitive system. Thus, the first view is consonant with the direct form of development and the latter with its indirect counterpart.

Phylogeny and evolution

Phylogeny

Phylogeny (or phylogenesis) refers to the historical paths taken by evolving groups of animals or plants. More precisely, it is a history made up of the histories of a class of organisms in which every member is the ancestor of some identifiable class of organisms. The key to understanding this more precise definition is identifying what is meant by 'histories of a class of organisms.'

One interpretation derives from Haeckel's theory of recapitulation, later amended to the Biogenetic Law: phylogeny is a successive build up of adult stages of ontogeny, with descendants adding on a stage to those 'bequeathed' them by their ancestors. Accordingly, organisms repeat the adult stages of their ancestors during their own ontogeny. They do so, however, such that previous adult stages appear increasingly earlier during the ontogeny of descendants thereby allowing for the terminal addition of a new stage. Over the years, Haeckel's brainchild was summarized and handed down with the felicitous phrase 'ontogeny recapitulates phylogeny.'

Recapitulation theory became discredited when Thomas H. Morgan (1866–1945) showed it to be

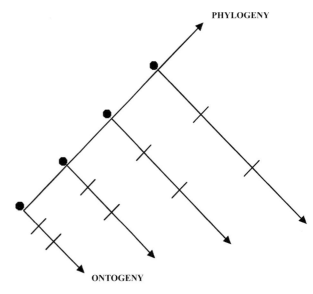

Figure 4. Phylogeny refers to the histories of a class of organisms in which every member is the ancestor of some identifiable class of organisms. These histories can be considered as a successive series of ontogenies that begin with fertilization (●). In this idealized reconstruction, each succeeding ontogeny becomes longer. Furthermore, identifiable stages (–) become proportionally extended with each ensuing ontogeny. Thus, heterochronic alterations in the mechanisms that regulate the process of ontogeny can precipitate phylogenetic change in the form of, for example, speciation.

incompatible with Mendelian genetics. In its place came a diametrically opposed interpretation articulated by Walter Garstang (1868–1949) and Gavin de Beer (1899–1972). Now, 'histories of a class of organisms' was interpreted as phylogeny consisting of a succession of *complete* ontogenies across many generations (Fig. 4). The crucial point about this interpretation is that phylogenetic change occurs through heterochronic alterations in the timing of ontogeny (i.e., by retardation as well as through the acceleration of ontogeny). More specifically, it involves alterations in the timing of somatic growth relative to reproductive maturation (Gould, 1977).

Evolution

When the controversy between supporters of epigenesis and preformationism was in full flow during the 18th century and into the second half of the 19th century, evolution (from the Latin word 'evolutio' meaning the unfolding of existing parts) was treated as being synonymous with development. Seemingly introduced by Charles Bonnet (1720–1793) or Albrecht von Haller (1708–1777), both radical preformationists, it was taken to denote any process of change or growth. Once again, it was Spencer who changed things. In his essay the 'Developmental hypothesis,' published seven years before Darwin's *Origin of Species* (1859), he offered it as a metaphor for organic change, while still retaining the notion of improvement. Although Darwin avoided the term 'evolution' in his theory of descent with modification (except as the very last word in the first edition of the *Origin*), he was, together with the geologist Charles Lyell (1797–1875), instrumental in restricting its scientific usage to biological evolution as distinguished from cultural evolution.

Biological evolution

It is sometimes not fully appreciated that Darwin had two theories of biological evolution: descent with modification and natural selection. In the 20th century, these two master theories spawned a number of associated theories (Fig. 5). His theory of descent with modification, which concerned phylogenetic change or macroevolution (i.e., speciation), led to disputes between proponents of phyletic gradualism and punctuated equilibrium. In contrast, the theory of natural selection, which addresses evolutionary change or microevolution (i.e., continuous small changes in gene frequencies within a population), was united with the theory of population genetics to give rise to the Modern synthesis. In formulating the theory of descent with modification, Darwin accorded ontogenetic development (embryology in his terms) a role in creating phylogenetic change and a chapter in the *Origin*, although he never spelt out in detail how this might occur. The Modern synthesis, for its part, dispensed with ontogenetic development as being irrelevant to an understanding of evolutionary change, in part because its supporters regarded embryology as still harboring remnants of vitalistic thinking and anti-materialistic doctrines (Mayr, 1982). As a consequence, Darwin's two master theories have proved to be difficult to integrate. The emergence of evolutionary developmental biology in the last decade is yet another attempt to provide such an integration. Before considering this discipline-in-the-making, a few final comments on the distinction between biological evolution and phylogeny are needed.

To begin with, evolution in the biological sense is a theory proposing a number of mechanisms (e.g., natural selection, mutations, genetic drift) that can be made to account for micro- and macroevolutionary changes. Unlike the study of phylogeny as pursued by paleontologists, evolutionary theory is ahistorical and concentrates on the determinants that bring about these changes. Thus, there is a distinction to be made between the reconstruction of a phylogenetic history and the mechanisms of events that can explain the processes implicated in that history. Put another way, the study of phylogeny involves the description of a succession of products while evolutionary theory addresses the processes and mechanisms underlying such successive products. In this sense, the distinction between phylogeny and evolution parallels that between ontogeny

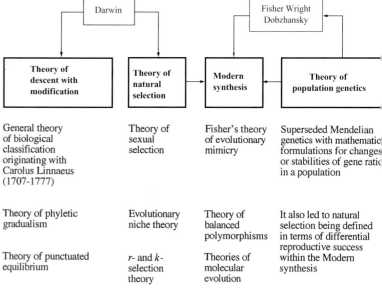

Figure 5. A summary of some of the many adjunct theories derived from Darwin's master theories of descent with modification and natural selection. The Modern synthesis arose from an integration of the theories of natural selection and population genetics during the first half of the 20th century, chiefly, but not only, through the work of Ronald A. Fisher (1890–1962), Sewall Wright (1889–1988), and Theodosious Dobzhansky (1900–1975). In turn, the synthesis gave rise to a number of adjunct theories. The theories of punctuated equilibrium and molecular evolution are difficult to classify exclusively: the former because it incorporates *r*- and *k*-selection theory and the latter in that they attempt to address phylogenetic descent. Punctuated equilibrium, more than the other theories, tries to take account of the nexus between ontogeny and phylogeny. More specifically, it rests on the assumption that alterations in the timing of ontogenetic development can lead to phylogenetic changes.

and development (i.e., ontogenetic development is not a function of time, but rather a system of processes and related mechanisms that take place over time).

To round off the comparisons, it was claimed in the past that the basic difference between ontogenetic development and biological evolution was that the former relies on deterministic processes and the latter on stochastic processes. Now, however, both are regarded as being based on determinism (i.e., 'necessity') and on (constrained) stochasticity (i.e., 'chance'). With this distinction in mind, we can turn to evolutionary developmental biology.

Evolutionary developmental biology

Haeckel's recapitulation theory had the effect of driving a wedge between developmental and evolutionary biology for many years thereafter. Nevertheless, individuals such as Richard Goldschmidt (1878–1958), with his 'hopeful'

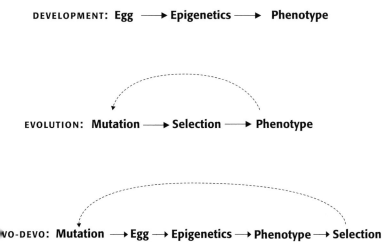

DEVELOPMENT: Egg ⟶ Epigenetics ⟶ Phenotype

EVOLUTION: Mutation ⟶ Selection ⟶ Phenotype

EVO-DEVO: Mutation ⟶ Egg ⟶ Epigenetics ⟶ Phenotype ⟶ Selection

Figure 6. In ontogenetic development, epigenetics serves to mediate the connections between genotype and phenotype (top). Such an intermediary agent is replaced by selection in the Modern synthesis, which acts on the variation created by mutations (middle). Until recently, and most notably with Edelman's theory of neuronal group selection, the concept of Darwinian selection has not been ascribed a prominent role in the study of ontogenetic development. Evolutionary developmental biology attempts to go beyond the Modern synthesis in accounting for the role of epigenetics in biological evolution as well as for selection processes acting on ontogenetic development at any stage (bottom). The solid arrows indicate events within a generation and the dashed ones those that take place between generations. Adapted from B. K. Hall, 2003. Unlocking the black box between genotype and phenotype: cell condensations as morphogenetic (modular) units. *Biology and Philosophy*, 18, 219–247.

monsters arising as a consequence of small changes in the timing of embryonic development, and Conrad H. Waddington (1905–1975), with his diachronic biology and its associated concept of epigenetics, made valiant efforts to overcome the neglect of ontogenetic development in the Modern synthesis. What they lacked was the present day array of techniques in molecular biology that would have allowed them to test their ideas more fully. In recent years, there has been a renewal of interest in forging closer links between developmental and evolutionary biology with the arrival of what promises to be a new synthesis, namely, evolutionary developmental biology (or evo-devo for short).

The starting point for evo-devo is credited to the Dahlem Workshop (1981) on evolution and development (Bonner, 1982). At that time, there were major advances in molecular biology such as recombinant DNA technologies that enabled cross-species comparisons of developmental mechanisms at the molecular level. In addition, a distinction had been made between developmental regulator genes and structural genes, starting with the François Jacob - Jacques Monod (1910–1976) operon model (1961). Whereas the Modern synthesis, or more correctly population genetics, assumed that ontogenetic development was

stable and resistant to change, and therefore irrelevant for understanding evolutionary change, evo-devo treats it as a major agent of such change.

What are the defining features of evo-devo? They can be summarized as follows:

1. Genes alone can explain neither development nor evolution.
2. Developmental processes (i.e., epigenetics) link genotype to phenotype (Hall in Sarkar & Robert, 2003). Due to the stochastic nature of such processes, there is no one-to-one relationship between genotype and phenotype.
3. Developmental mechanisms evolve.
4. Developmental constraints act on particular kinds of phenotypic variation and thus restrict the availability of evolutionary pathways. According to Gilbert (2003), these consist of physical constraints (e.g., elasticity and strength of tissues), morphogenetic constraints (e.g., there are only a limited number of ways a vertebrate limb can be formed), and phyletic constraints (e.g., due to the genetics of a species' development). In these respects, ontogenetic development exerts deterministic influences on biological evolution.
5. Evolutionary biology should not persist in trying to explain adaptation, but instead should try to account for evolvability (i.e., the potential for evolution). Stated otherwise, this means accounting for the possibility of complex adaptations via transformations in ontogenetic development. And finally, the key feature of evo-devo:
6. Most evolutionary changes are initiated during ontogenetic development. The implication here seems to be that alterations in the actions of regulator genes rather than structural genes give rise to macroevolutionary changes.

If all of the above signal a new synthesis, how then does it differ from the Modern synthesis? Figure 6 attempts to encapsulate the main differences.

Evo-devo is one of at least three current initiatives to integrate ontogenetic development with biological evolution in a testable and unifying theory. Another is developmental evolutionary biology (abbreviated to devo-evo) and a third is dynamical systems theory (DST). At the present time, there is a lack of clarity as to the essential differences between them. Both devo-evo and DST have been criticized for underplaying the roles of genes in evolution, while at the same time emphasizing those for developmental constraints (Gilbert in Sarkar & Robert, 2003). For example, DST, as represented in Brian Goodwin's book *How the Leopard Changed its Spots* (1994), accords explanatory equality to all levels of organization, and thus does not assign instructive or at least permissive roles to genes. Such differences in emphasis between scientists engaged in a common cause are perhaps a hallmark of the first stages in forming a new discipline. If this is achieved, then we will have a foundation for promoting new insights into ontogenetic development that Waddington and his contemporaries could only have dreamed about.

Conclusions

The main thrust of this entry has been to capture the phenomenological features of ontogenetic development that distinguish it from other terms such as evolution, ontogeny, and phylogeny. Furthermore, evolution was contrasted with phylogeny in order to prepare the ground for an introduction to evolutionary developmental biology with its promise of unifying the developmental and evolutionary sciences. To quote Samuel Butler again, it is to be hoped that we have not left ". . . a sore place more sore than it was before."

With regard to ontogenetic development, two related points can be emphasized. Firstly, we still need a theory of developmental transitions that is sufficiently detailed to guide us toward teasing out the processes and mechanisms involved in specific instances. Secondly, if the primary aim of studying ontogenetic development is to describe and explain change *within* individuals over time, then we also require a better understanding of the functional significance of the considerable variability that typifies intra-individual change. If such variability both increases and decreases over time, what does this mean? Does, for example, increasing variability herald the onset of a developmental transition and a decrease its offset? Most grand theories of development have either ignored or paid insufficient attention to such issues.

Finally, a comment on the new arrival evolutionary developmental biology. It has resulted in reuniting ontogenetic development with biological evolution through the aegis of molecular biology. While appearing to hold great promise for understanding the causal relationships between genotype and phenotype both within and between generations, it remains to be seen what impact it will have on the practice of studying child development. As the saying goes, "In theory, there is no difference between theory and practice, but in practice there is a great deal of difference." Hopefully, this will not be the case if the theoretical implications of evolutionary developmental biology become more widely appreciated amongst those of us who study child development.

See also:
The concept of development: historical perspectives; Understanding ontogenetic development: debates about the nature of the epigenetic process; Dynamical systems approaches; Conceptions and misconceptions about embryonic development; Brain and behavior development (II): cortical; Anthropology; Developmental genetics

Further reading

Ford, D. H. and Lerner, R. M. (1992). *Developmental Systems Theory*. Newbury Park, CA: Sage.

Hall, B. K., Pearson, R. D. and Müller, G. B. (eds.) (2003). *Environment, Development and Evolution: Toward a Synthesis*. Cambridge, MA: MIT Press.

Hopkins, B. (2004). Causality and development: past, present and future. In A. Peruzzi (ed.), *Causality and Mind*. Amsterdam: John Benjamins, pp. 1–17.

McNamara, K. J. (1997). *Shapes of Time: The Evolution of Growth and Development*. Baltimore: Johns Hopkins University Press.

van der Weele, C. (1999). *Images of Development: Environmental Causes in Ontogeny*. Albany, NY: State University of New York Press.

The challenge of interdisciplinarity: metaphors, reductionism, and the practice of interdisciplinary research

BRIAN HOPKINS

Introduction

Go to Google and type in 'interdisciplinary' as a search word. What do you get? In the first instance, the answer is almost 1.8 million entries or 'hits.' Not quite as many as for George W. Bush at almost more than 3.4 million hits or Manchester United at just 2 million, but nevertheless an impressive number. Combining 'interdisciplinary' with 'psychology' delivers over 360,000 entries, 20.2 percent of the total number for 'interdisciplinary' alone, and noticeably more (in descending order) than for 'sociology,' 'anthropology,' 'developmental biology,' and 'behavior genetics.' Within psychology, 'social psychology' results in many more hits than, for example, 'cognitive psychology' and 'developmental psychology' when combinations with 'interdisciplinary' are made. Nevertheless, each one provides an imposing numerical outcome. Repeating the whole exercise with 'interdisciplinary research' and 'interdisciplinarity' does little to alter by very much any of these relative comparisons (Table 1).

At first flush, this trawl through the Internet would seem to suggest that interdisciplinarity is well established in some areas of study represented in this volume. Unfortunately, the quantitative findings do not tally with qualitative considerations. Why not? First of all, because there is a lack of clarity about the meaning of interdisciplinarity or what constitutes interdisciplinary research. Further confusion is engendered when attempting to distinguish among interdisciplinarity, cross-disciplinarity, multidisciplinarity, and transdisciplinarity. Yet we now appear to be in the age of the inter-discipline prefixes and suffixes, with proliferations of bio-, etho-, psycho-, and socio-, together with the recent arrival of scientific endeavors dubbed 'social neuroscience' and 'neuroeconomics.' As for 'child development,' the number of Google entries is relatively large (Table 1). Once again, however, the numbers game masks a range of different designations as to the meanings of interdisciplinarity and interdisciplinary research. Certainly, interdisciplinarity has had something of a bad press in the past.

The up and downs of interdisciplinarity

If it appears that something of an interdisciplinary Zeitgeist is upon us, it has been achieved in the face of some strong pockets of resistance in the past. One example is epitomized by the remark of Leslie A. Smith (1900–1975) in his book *The Science of Culture* (1949) to the effect that cultural anthropologists ". . . have sold their culturological birthright for a mess of psychiatric pottage" (p. xix). During the 1960s, some leading biologists opposed what they saw as the threat of their discipline being reduced to the laws and principles of physics, or more specifically to classical mechanics. The same mistrust is still evident in attempting to preserve disciplinary boundaries (e.g., that between psychology and neuroscience).

Why then has interdisciplinarity (ID) become the mantra of current scientific policy? Before getting anywhere near answering that question, we need to address a number of converging issues: the meaning of ID relative to cross- and multidisciplinary as well as to transdisciplinarity, levels of (biological) organization and the associated problem of reductionism, and the use of metaphors and other tropes (e.g., analogy) in science more generally. What follows is essentially a personal view derived from the experience of being a member of so-called interdisciplinary programs of research in child development. Undoubtedly, this view will have its dissenters, particularly with regard to the restricted meaning accorded to ID. Such an imposition should be seen as a debating point, rather than a firmly held belief as to how interdisciplinary research (IDR) should be construed. The hope is that it will highlight some of the structures and processes needed for IDR in child development that go beyond mere cross-disciplinarity and multidisciplinarity.

The discipline of interdisciplinarity

In 1996, the final report of the US Gulbenkian Commission on the Reconstruction of the Social Sciences was published. While favorably disposed to IDR, it did little more than recommend it could be achieved by granting academics tenure in two departments. Nowhere in the report was there a systematic attempt to distinguish ID from the other three similar terms. In short, among other things, it is a shared language (or what might be termed a scientific Esperanto) between the participating disciplines that embraces both theory and method (Table 2).

With the establishment of such a linguistic 'trading zone' at the frontiers of disciplines, the task of dissipating barriers to ID has begun. If this first step is seen as a 'mission impossible,' there are examples in science to suggest otherwise. For instance, the interdiscipline of biophysics was established through the combined efforts of physicists, biochemists, and computer scientists to learn each other's theoretical vocabulary in order to gain fresh insights into biomolecular mechanisms involving, for example, protein synthesis in membranes. Nearer to home, cognitive neuroscience arose from a lack of models in clinical neuropsychology that could be used to address the effects of focal brain injuries. During the 1960s, such models were sought in cognitive psychology, with the result that the neuropsychologists began to share the language and methods of cognitive psychologists.

Even more germane were the efforts of Arnold Gesell and Myrtle McGraw in the 1930s and 1940s to found the study of child development on principles drawn from embryology and particular branches of physics such as thermodynamics. Other pertinent examples are: the birth of biochemistry through François Magendie (1783–1855) bringing together organic chemists and physiologists to study collectively the relevance of nitrogen for animal nutrition, and the way in which Walter Nernst (1864–1941) and collaborators integrated what was then known about electrochemistry with thermodynamics during the early 20th century to give birth to what is now inorganic chemistry.

To label a scientific activity as an ostensive example of IDR is a common occurrence and a source of some obfuscation. IDR can take on at least three types, with, for example, one discipline coming to subordinate the

Table 1. Approximate number of Google entries for interdisciplinary, interdisciplinary research, and interdisciplinarity. These terms are then combined with psychology, followed by doing the same for developmental, cognitive, and social psychology. The procedure is repeated for what might be regarded as 'sister' disciplines (sociology; anthropology), for two others that have a bearing on theorizing and research in developmental psychology (developmental biology; behavior genetics), and for child development.

Search word	Interdisciplinary	Interdisciplinary research	Interdisciplinarity
On its own	1,790,000	1,590,000	46,000
Psychology	362,000	414,000	9,150
Developmental psychology	954,000	189,000	1,940
Cognitive psychology	108,000	117,000	6,170
Social psychology	284,000	267,000	5,330
Sociology	284,000	224,000	6,170
Anthropology	237,000	224,000	4,520
Developmental biology	76,800	120,000	1,160
Behavior genetics	30,600	51,600	341
Child development	189,000	243,000	2,610

others brought together to address a common problem beyond the bounds of a single discipline. Once more, what makes a distinction is a commonly shared language that 'cracks' the linguistic codes of the participating disciplines (Table 3).

If only it were that simple. For example, disciplines can share identical words, but they can have contrasting meanings in each one. Examples include different interpretations of growth and individuation across the developmental sciences and even that pertaining to causality. When one gets down to this level of discussion, proposed IDR projects can eventuate in disarray and the loss of a common cause. The interdisciplinary gap widens instead of closing.

Bridging the gap: levels of organization and reductionism

Levelism

One way in which disciplinarity is portrayed is to arrange disciplines along a hierarchy of levels of organization and then at each level to pigeon-hole them under 'structure,' 'function,' and 'evolution.' Table 4 depicts such a hierarchy for the life sciences, broadly defined.

It should be evident that the number of levels and how they are labelled is, together with the disciplines included, an arbitrary exercise (e.g., ecology could have been allocated to the top and particle physics to the bottom of the hierarchy). Nevertheless, one person's hierarchy looks very much like another's demarcation of

Table 2. Starting from a consideration of what constitutes disciplinarity, interdisciplinarity (ID) is compared to three other forms of scientific collaboration. There is still confusion and a general lack of agreement about the meaning of ID and how it should be practiced. The defining features of ID are deliberately presented in conservative terms so as to draw distinctions with the other forms of scientific collaboration that are often taken as being synonyms. Transdisciplinarity is the most vague term used to denote cooperation between disciplines. It appears to be an attempt to get science galvanized into focusing on the provision of solutions to a variety of social and economic concerns that may be national or, more commonly, worldwide in scope (e.g., environmental pollution, and its effects on child development).

	Defining features	*Comments*
Disciplinarity	During the early part of the 20th century, there was a 'drive for disciplinarity': establishment of 'bounded' disciplines, with their own theories, methods, and standards of scientific rigor. Gave rise to modern-day discipline structures having their own scientific societies and accreditation committees	Until the late 19th century, disciplines as they existed were more loosely 'bounded' in that science was pursued as an enterprise based on a broad-ranging critical reflectivity across many areas of knowledge. Such was the case, for example, in descriptive embryology. With the 'push for specialization,' new disciplines were founded (e.g., pediatrics, which became a 'bounded' discipline in the 1930s). Largely as a result of the Cold War, area studies and systems approaches to science began to emerge in the late 1950s which ultimately gave rise to what have been termed 'interdisciplines' (e.g., cybernetics)
Interdisciplinarity (ID)	Well-established disciplines working together on a common problem, but with the express aim of adjusting their theories and methods so that they can be integrated into a new discipline or interdiscipline. It involves generalizing from multidisciplinary settings so that a common language covering theory and method can be established	In the past, there have been a number of unsuccessful attempts to establish a common scientific language (e.g., behaviorism; logical positivism; General system theory) and the quest continues (e.g., on a more restricted scale with the theory of embodiment). Apart from that, most individuals participating in this 'strong' form of scientific collaboration do so not only to contribute to another field, but also to take back new ideas to their own disciplines (thus preserving discipline independence)
Multidisciplinarity	Disciplines working together on a common problem, but not changing their approaches or adjusting to the knowledge base or techniques of other disciplines. Participating disciplines then tend to present their findings in discipline-dedicated conferences and journals	Most so-called ID research takes on this 'weak' form of scientific collaboration
Cross-disciplinarity	Takes on two forms: 1. researchers in one discipline (e.g., physics) choose to work in another discipline (e.g., biology)[1] 2. researchers trained in two disciplines (e.g., psychology and neuroscience or psychology and anthropology)	Two noticeable and increasing features of modern-day science are: 1. cross-appointments between departments (e.g., between computer science and psychology) 2. cross-disciplinary training programs (e.g., within the context of the neurosciences)
Transdisciplinarity	A sort of half-way house between disciplinarity and ID in which the aim is to provide a forum or platform for the generation of new ideas that can then be applied across a number of disciplines	If properly understood, it seems to be a medium created so that non-scientists, can have a say in the decision-making process as to which scientific problems need to be addressed. Consequently, it tends to lead to calls for science to tackle issues such as diseases and discrimination, and to providing a better standard of living for all

[1] Outstanding examples of this type of cross-disciplinarity are Max Delbrück (1906–1981) and Leo Szilard (1898–1964), both trained in quantum mechanics, who applied their knowledge acquired in physics to the study of cell reproduction. Their work made a significant contribution to the discovery of the DNA double helix attributed to John D. Watson and Francis H. C. Crick.

Table 3. Three types of interdisciplinary research, which ultimately depend on whether or not the participating disciplines share a common language, and for which possible examples involving psychology and possible common problems are given.

Type	Interpretation	Possible example	Possible common problem
Communality in vocabulary	Two or more disciplines focusing on a common problem, with a common scientific language and set of concepts and techniques as well as shared standards of rigor and proof. While a common shared language may be assumed, it could turn out that some terms have different meanings between the participating disciplines	Psychology and Behavioral biology	Development of attachment
Disparity in vocabulary	Two or more disciplines with different languages and concepts as well as techniques, and standards of proof. The problem to be tackled is divided up so that each part can be dealt with by relevant disciplines. Findings from the parts then have to be integrated in some way	Psychology and Anthropology	Cross-cultural comparisons of parent-child communication
Disparate in vocabulary and subordination of one discipline to another	Two or more disciplines with very different languages, research methods techniques, and standards of proof. There is a search for a common language, which requires major adjustments in concepts, methods, and techniques. The outcome can be a hierarchically arranged research strategy in which one discipline is subordinated to another in tackling a common problem.	Psychology and Pediatrics	Development of very preterm infants

Table 4. Levels of organization in relation to structure (being), function (acting), and evolution (becoming) and the (sub-)disciplines that address each one. Evolution is meant to denote the study of change over different time scales (viz., real, developmental, and geological time).

Level	Structure	Function	Evolution
Macro-societal	Cultural anthropology	Sociology	History
Institutional	Management science	Political science	Cultural anthropology
Micro-societal	Social psychology	Social psychology	Developmental psychology[1]
Individual	Linguistics	Psychology	Developmental psychology
Organic	Anatomy	(Neuro-)physiology[2]	Embryology
Cellular	Histology	Biochemistry	Embryology
Sub-cellular	Molecular biology	Molecular biophysics	Developmental genetics

[1] Developmental psychologists carry out research at this level when, for example, it involves the analysis of family dynamics

[2] Neurophysiology can be interpreted as covering neuroscience and developmental neuroscience and thus can feature, for example, at both the organic and cellular levels under 'Evolution'

levels and assignment of disciplines. What is this stratified hierarchy meant to convey? There are two responses. One is that as you move up the hierarchy, disciplines have to address increasingly complex phenomena, together with the emergence of properties not manifested at the lower levels. The other is that as you move down it, increasing explanatory power can be gained, which has led to the claim that science should be unified from the bottom up rather than top down. Whichever way you move, you are confronted with a task of almost Sisyphean dimensions, namely, climbing the slippery slopes of reductionism.

Reductionism

Here is not the place to embark on a detailed diatribe about the provenance of reductionism in science in general and for IDR in particular, and which assumes not one, but a number of slippery slopes. Instead, we focus just on theoretical reductionism. To begin with, what is meant by theoretical reductionism?

Termed intertheoretic reductionism by Churchland (1986), it concerns the explanation of the reduced theory (e.g., the theory of gases) by the reducing theory (e.g., statistical mechanics). On a grander scale, it encompasses the pursuit of a Theory of Everything as strived for by General system theory in the past and by such as string theory, superstring theory, and M-theory at present. In the context of the deductive-nomological model of scientific explanation originating with Carl Gustav Hempel (1905–1997) and Paul Oppenheim in 1948, theoretical reductionism is supposed to work through the implementation of bridge laws or principles. These devices act as transformation rules for linking two distinct linguistic expressions with two theories at different levels. Self-organization is sometimes treated as possessing the potential to become a bridge law as are Piaget's functional universals (viz., assimilation, accommodation, and equilibration). The problem with bridge laws is that they can become too cumbersome to put into practice such that they defeat the purpose of ever attempting theoretical reductionism in the first place (a case in point being the way in which Piaget attempted to operationalize equilibration). If this is so, and which appears to be borne out by the fact that the most successful reductions in the history of science (e.g., of Mendelian to molecular genetics) did not have recourse to bridge laws, then an alternative strategy is needed.

If not bridge laws, then what? Let's put this question to one side for a minute and consider two classic problems of theoretical reductionism. These are genetic determinism and the relationship between psychology and neuroscience.

1. Genetic determinism: with the success of the Human Genome Project, there is an increasing tendency to regard genes as the ultimate determinants of development and of developmental disorders. Knowing the sequence of many human genes, however, is not going to be particularly revealing about development, given the protein-folding problem and continuing ignorance of the pathways between genotype and phenotypes during development. Genetic determinism brings with it the danger of reification: reducing something that is a dynamical process to a static trait and then searching for its single (genetic) determinant. Examples include aggression, intelligence, and syndromes such as ADHD. Without doubt, genes influence virtually all behavior, but virtually no behavior is determined by them. Structural genes manufacture proteins and enzymes whose translation and regulation are critical to phenotypical changes in ontogenetic development (and biological evolution). However, the environment can inject some degree of developmental specificity as well (e.g., the sex of a turtle depends on the temperature of incubation and not on the dictates of chromosomes). In this example, the environment is instructive and the genotype permissive.

2. Psychology and neuroscience: without doubt, one of the most enduring themes in the history of science is how to conflate psychology and neuroscience into a unified theory of behavior or cognition. Can psychology be reduced to neuroscience as some contend (Churchland, 1986)? Or is neuroscience irrelevant to psychology as maintained by others who see their task as defending the autonomy of psychology from intrusions by other sciences (Fodor, 1975)? The nub of the issue is whether mental states (e.g., emotions, feeling, and consciousness more generally) can be reduced to corresponding neural states. Recent attempts that have been made to resolve this issue include Gerald Edelman's theory of neuronal group selection. Churchland's (1986) response, in a pro-reductionist mode, has been to argue that a psycho-neuro symphysis can be achieved by what she calls theoretical co-evolution: theories at different levels may co-evolve such that they inform and correct each other, thus bringing them ever closer to assuming a common theory. As Churchland herself realizes, while concordant development has worked for the marriage of thermodynamics and statistical mechanics as well as for physics and chemistry more generally, there are still formidable problems to be overcome in fusing psychology with neuroscience. Why? Because it is still unclear how knowledge of the brain exerts constraints on theorizing about psychological functions. Ultimately, clarity can only be achieved through further insights into structure-function relationships. For developmental psychology, understanding such constraints seems at best remote given the ever-changing relationships between structure and function during development. Thus, psycho-neuro IDR concerned with child development faces considerable hurdles, not just because of linguistic disparities between the two fields of study (Table 3), but rather due to the lack of a common theory that goes beyond correlating changes in structure and function.

So, if not bridge laws, then what? An alternative to such laws is the use of analogies to connect two or more different levels of organization. Perhaps the most frequently cited example of the value of analogies in promoting scientific advancement is how Darwin arrived at his theory of natural selection. To begin with, he drew an analogy between artificial selection as used by animal and plant breeders and the process of natural selection. He then addressed another analogy, namely, that between the theory of population pressure developed by Thomas R. Malthus (1766–1834) and the process of speciation. In combining these two analogies, Darwin created the very foundation of modern biology.

If analogical reasoning worked as a first step for Darwin, then we can ask if it serves the same function in getting IDR off the ground (i.e., whether it provides a starting point for the development of a common language). Asking this question raises the more general issue of the role of tropes in science. To begin with, let's take a trip to Milton Keynes.

Headline news: "Milton Keynes is to double in size over the next 20 years" (*Guardian* newspaper, January 6, 2004)

Metaphor, analogy, and homology

Milton Keynes (MK), like Basildon, is one of the so-called new towns built in the UK during the late 1940s. Apart from having the longest shopping mall in the world according to the *Guinness Book of Records*, it was built on a grid network system of roads and is now home to a range of light industries. Doubling its size will make it comparable to Pittsburgh in terms of the number of inhabitants. One of these inhabitants might say:

1. MK is paradise on earth
2. Although designed differently, MK has the same functions as Basildon, which also has a number of light industries
3. Although both have a grid system, MK has different functions than Pittsburgh, with its traditional base of heavy industries

Admittedly, these comparisons stretch credulity a bit, but they do raise some relevant points. What are these points? They are that:

1. is a metaphor (note it is not a simile as our inhabitant would have said: "MK is *like* paradise on earth")
2. is an analogy (viz., two different structures have similar functions)
3. is a homology, which is not a trope (viz., two corresponding structures have different functions). Relatedly:
4. Asking whether MK will have the same structures or functions in 2024 as now is a question about serial homology (viz., with development or evolution, whether or not organisms retain the same structures or functions).

A metaphor is a figure of speech in which an expression about an object or action is used to refer to something it does not literally denote in order to suggest a similarity. It is one of two master tropes, with analogy being a sub-class of metaphors. To complete the picture, the second master trope is metonymy, with synecdoche as a sub-class.

Like a metaphor, an analogy is a linguistic device or form of reasoning that logically assumes that if two things agree in some respects (mainly their relations), then they probably agree in others. To this extent, an analogy is regarded as an extended metaphor or simile. And like a 'metaphor,' it gives insights into the unfamiliar and unknown by comparison with something familiar and known. Furthermore, analogies are made explicit by similes and are implicit in metaphors. In practice, it is hardly feasible to delimit the use of metaphors, analogies, and similes in science. Thus, for the time being, these tropes will not be distinguished further, with the term 'metaphor' being used for all three.

Aristotle (384–322 BP) in his *Poetics* stated that the greatest thing by far was to be master of the metaphor and that to have achieved mastery is a sign of genius. A bit of an overstatement perhaps, but it is widely accepted that the functions of metaphor are indispensable to science, with a minority who think otherwise. Its acknowledged functions are: aids to communication, resources for the discovery of novel insights and the generation of new theories, and in applying a theory to data by means of metaphorical redescription (i.e., in mediating its application to real-life phenomena). Examples abound, across many branches of science, about the theory-invigorating properties of metaphors (Table 5).

Having championed metaphors as a first-staging post in implementing IDR, it is well to consider what has been said about their limitations. In short, according to some, there is a price to pay for using metaphorical identifications (Table 6). Despite such pitfalls, it is questionable whether there can be a metaphor-free knowledge of whatever phenomenon we are striving to explain.

What about homologies? What role, if any, can they be accorded in IDR? Posing this question brings in its wake the more general concept of isomorphisms between levels of organization.

Homologies and isomorphisms

While homology is one of the most important concepts in biology, it is used for quite different purposes (e.g., some morphologists define homology with reference to

Table 5. Examples of theories and concepts that emerged from particular metaphors (or analogies) in terms of who used them ('Source'), where they came from originally, and to what field of study they were applied. Freud and Piaget are renowned for their use of metaphors in generating their respective theories. James Clerk Maxwell was openly honest about the sources of his metaphors and another one who used them widely in his work. ? = Could it have been Aristotle?

Example	Source	From	To
Theory of natural selection	Darwin	Animal breeding	Evolutionary biology
Theory of electricity and magnetism	Maxwell	Fluid mechanics	Electromagnetic fields
Epigenetic landscape	Waddington	Geology	Embryology
Emotion	Freud/Lorenz	Hydraulics	Psychology/Ethology
Assimilation and accommodation	Piaget	Digestive system functioning	Genetic epistemology/Developmental psychology
Differentiation	?	Psychology	Embryology

Table 6. Three problems put forward as being associated with the use of metaphors (and analogies) in science. Lewontin's metaphorical distortion is by far the most problematic.

Pitfall	Description	Comment
Misplaced metaphor or Lavoisier's problem	Proposing a metaphor that turns out to have no value in understanding the target phenomenon	Antoine L. Lavoisier (1743–1794) proposed that a living organism is like a combustion engine. While subsequently shown to be completely incorrect, it brought together chemistry and biology, thereby encouraging physiologists of the time to take account of chemistry in their work. This eventually gave rise to modern insights and formed the basis for the initial establishment of biochemistry. Thus, misplaced metaphors can lead to advances in science, even when they are shown to be wrong, by means of testing them out
Metaphorical distortion[1]	A theory provides explanations and a model the related analytical techniques. In applying the model to a real-world phenomenon, the latter needs to be associated with some metaphor. Such metaphorical identification can give rise to metaphorical distortion (or what others have termed 'sort-crossing')	An example of a metaphorical distortion is treating evolution as though it were a process of trial and error. Doing so runs the risk of imposing concepts such as 'intention' and 'will' on what is seen as generally being a random process
Overreliance on metaphors	"Major reasons for psychology's lack of progress in accounting for brain-behavior relationships stem from a reliance on metaphorical explanations as a substitute for a real understanding of neural mechanisms"[2]	Such a statement is not supported by the vast literature on metaphors in general and their use in science in particular. For example, if Charles S. Sherrington (1857–1952) had not put forward his notion of a (then unseen) synapse as metaphor for neural connectivity, then S. Ramón y Cajal (1832–1934) would probably never have fully developed the neuron doctrine

[1] R. C. Lewontin, 1963. Models, mathematics and metaphors. *Synthese*, 15, 222–244.
[2] V. S. Ramachandran and J. J. Smythies, 1997. Shrinking minds and swollen heads. *Nature*, 386, 667–668.

a common developmental origin and although a different concept it is sometimes the case that the two homologies can be congruent). In evolutionary biology, it stands for correspondences between species in parts of morphological structure, a segment of DNA, or an individual gene. It becomes controversial when applied to behavior and development. Why? Because, in principle, homology is a qualitative concept (viz., something is homologous or not) and thus it can only be applied with considerable difficulty to phenomena that show a great deal of variability such as behavior and development. Despite this problem, there are ongoing attempts to convert homologies into mathematical isomorphisms and to account for development in terms of serial homologies.

The distinction between homology and analogy is embedded within the more general concept of isomorphisms. There are three sorts of isomorphisms to be drawn between different levels of organization:

1. Analogical isomorphisms: also known as the 'soft' systems approach, the concern is to demonstrate similarities in functioning between different levels. However, they say nothing about the causal agents or governing laws involved.
2. Homological isomorphisms: also known as the 'hard' systems approach, the phenomena under study may differ with regard to causal factors, but they are governed by the same laws or principles based on mathematical isomorphisms. The latter can be derived, for example, from allometry, game theory, and linear or non-linear dynamics, as well as a broad range of frequency distributions (e.g., Poisson distribution).
3. Explanatory isomorphisms: the same causal agents, laws, or principles are applicable to each phenomenon being compared.

The interdisciplinary exercise of approaching ontogenetic development as a process of interacting dynamical systems in developmental psychology has been mainly confined to (1), but it strives to attain (2), and for which there are some recent examples (e.g., in applying chaos theory to the study of how fetal and infant spontaneous movements are organized).

A serial homology addresses the issue of whether repetitive structures within the same organism are the same or different. When brought to bear on development, it results in questions such as: in what ways is behavior pattern A at time T_1 the same as or different from that at T_2? Are they served by homologous or analogous structures at the two ages or by those that are partially homologous and partially analogous? Such questions confront what in essence calls for IDR, namely, the evergreen topic concerning the development of structure-function relationships.

We now turn from the abstract to things more pragmatic: the practicalities of doing IDR (with the remark that the *OED* defines 'pragmatic' as dealing with things sensibly and realistically in a way that is based on practical rather than theoretical considerations).

News flash: "Pushing the frontiers of interdisciplinary research: an idea whose time has come" (*Naturejobs*, March 16, 2000)

This five-year-old news flash was a blurb for a number of US research initiatives that were accorded the adjective "interdisciplinary." In particular, coverage was given to the Bio-X project housed in the Clark Center at Stanford University, which gathers together researchers from engineering, the chemical and physical sciences, medicine, and the humanities. What is the project meant to achieve? One senior academic associated with the project answered as follows: "What's really interesting is the possibility that we have no clue what will go on in the Clark Center. That's the point. Much of what we think works is this random collision that has a physics person talking to somebody interested in Alzheimer's" (p. 313).

The Bio-X project, as with others of the same ilk, is an example of 'big science,' largely concerned with the development of new (biomedical) technologies. In its present instantiation, it is best labeled as a cross-disciplinary program of research that, perhaps with more of the random collisions, could evolve into a series of IDR projects. Certainly, it is a more expensive way of achieving truly IDR than 'small science.' The latter, as an ID enterprise, begins with a focus on a commonly defined problem emanating from negotiated theoretical settlement arrived at through the medium of metaphorical reasoning and the like. How small should 'small' be though? If forming an across-discipline group to establish guidelines for achieving desired outcomes in patient care is of any relevance, then the recommendation is not to exceed twelve to fifteen members, with a minimum of six (Shekelle *et al.*, 1999). Too few members restrict adequate discussion and too many disrupt effective functioning of the group.

Assuming that a common problem has been identified, what are the further practical considerations to be borne in mind when attempting to carry out IDR? Some, but by no means all, can be captured under three headings: preliminary questions, having clarity about general guidelines and goals, and overcoming threats to IDR.

○ Preliminary questions
 1. What does IDR achieve that would not be attained by a single discipline?
 2. In what ways would IDR give rise to improved and more powerful explanations?
 3. What disciplines should be included and excluded (or at least held in abeyance)?
 4. Does a new vocabulary interpretable by all participating disciplines need to be developed?
 5. Do new methods and techniques need to be developed?
○ General guidelines and goals
 1. The main aim of IDR should be to predict and explain phenomena that have not been studied previously or are only partially understood and resolved.
 2. Establish criteria for judging what counts as good quality IDR. As yet, there are no well-defined

(i.e., operationalized) criteria for making such a judgment. On a personal note, at least one good indication that an IDR project is proceeding well is if a member of the team (e.g., psychologist) is able to report findings relevant to another from a different discipline (e.g., pediatrician) coherently at a conference mainly for colleagues of the latter.

3. The publications stemming from IDR should report not just the methods of data collection and analysis, but also how ID collaboration was achieved. Incorporating how this was done can be of benefit to others attempting to initiate IDR, as well as providing a source of reference for developing and improving the practice of such research.

4. At all costs, avoid the 'Humpty-Dumpty' problem: allowing participants to pursue their own discipline-related research agendas without regard to what has been defined as the common problem, such that at a later stage the pieces have to be put together to form a coherent whole. In order to prevent this:

5. Constantly ask what the common problem and related questions are in the first instance. Are we still 'on track' or are we losing sight of the original plan for achieving the desired outcomes? What were the desired outcomes and do we need to alter them in some way, given how things have gone?

○ Threats to IDR: apart from one discipline riding atop a hierarchy of subordinated disciplines as mentioned previously, others are –

1. Continuation of research funding that endorses existing disciplinary boundaries

2. Career paths in academia continue to be dependent on discipline-best performance criteria

3. Not encouraging technical staff (the lifeblood of most research activities) to publish in their own right. However:

4. Ensuring that the research is not primarily driven by the availability of technological innovations. While the development of new techniques is a laudable goal in IDR, they can assume a life of their own in that they permit questions to be pursued across disciplines that would not otherwise be answered. The opposite of this and another threat is:

5. Technical inertia: as pointed out by Paul Galison in his book *Image and Logic* (1998) for the case of particle physics, techniques, instruments, and experimental expertise can possess an inertia that determines the course of the research. And last, but not least:

6. *The First Law of Scientific Motivation*: "what's in it for me?"

As a final comment on the practicalities of IDR, its defining character is to have a shared common problem that can only be addressed by two or more disciplines working closely together. In tackling it, Hodges' Law of Large Problems has a very practical implication: inside every large problem is a small (and more manageable) problem struggling to get out.

Conclusions

Research in child development has long been distinguished by multidisciplinarity, if not interdisciplinarity. In the 1930s and 1940s, both Gesell and McGraw had embarked on research programs addressing core issues about the nature of infant development that were both theoretically and in practice steadfastly committed to the ethos of interdisciplinarity. McGraw, for example, brought together an interdisciplinary team consisting of researchers from biochemistry, neurophysiology, nursing, pediatrics, physiology, and psychology as well as requisite technicians during her time at the Babies' Hospital of Columbia University (Dalton & Bergenn, 1995b, p. 10). Her studies were sponsored by the Rockefeller Foundation, which had a special commitment to the promotion of IDR.

Times have changed and nowadays it is less common to find such an array of disciplines collectively focused on resolving a common set of problems concerning child development using a judicious interplay of cross-sectional and longitudinal methods. This is not to imply that IDR is a good thing and specialization a bad thing for research on child development. Many breakthroughs have been achieved (e.g., in studying cognitive development) from within a more or less monodisciplinary framework. IDR is mandated by the start point for any sort of research: "What's the question?" What is at issue is whether the question, when pared down so as to render more specific ones that are methodologically tractable, unequivocally carries with it the necessity of crossing disciplinary borders.

The success of IDR depends initially on the thoroughness of attempts to develop a common language of communication framed around a common problem. Achievement of a common language should suggest isomorphisms between levels of organization representative of the disciplines involved and which emerge from the skillful use of metaphors and analogies, and perhaps ultimately homologies. The power of metaphorical reasoning to achieve communication between individuals from different backgrounds has been demonstrated, for example, in research on consultations between pulmonary physicians and their patients (Arroliga *et al.*, 2002). If it works so successfully in this sort of setting in which such a marked disparity in language use has to be overcome, then this is surely an indication of its potential for fostering IDR.

Inevitably, reductionism in one form or another looms large in the context of IDR. Despite the rise of radical reductionism in the guise of genetic determinism during recent years, there is little evidence to suggest it has any real significance for the way in which most developmental scientists conduct their research. What one finds is that reductive analysis (i.e., induction) is combined with holistic synthesis (i.e., deduction), which have commonly (and mistakenly) been represented as mutually exclusive types of scientific explanation. Embryologists such as Paul A. Weiss (1898–1989), a staunch defender of holism, long ago argued for the necessity of maintaining both approaches in research on living systems. Put another way, it is an argument that both upward and downward causation should be accounted for in IDR.

Organizational structures need to be in place in order for IDR to flourish and in this regard the USA is still ahead of the game. On the one hand, there are agencies that continue to promote and support IDR networks, such as the MacArthur Foundation, some of which are committed to the study of child development (e.g., Network on Early Experience and Brain Development). On the other hand, there is considerable encouragement for the establishment of interdisciplinary teaching, at least with respect to the undergraduate level, through the activities of the Association for Integrative Studies. In order to overcome the confusion about the meaning of interdisciplinarity, this organization commissioned a task force whose work culminated in a report entitled "Accreditation Criteria for Interdisciplinary Studies in General Education" (2000). While a first step in identifying good practice in interdisciplinary teaching, this document also helps in removing some of the ambiguities surrounding the use of the term inter-disciplinarity more generally.

Why has interdisciplinarity become the mantra of scientific policy? The optimist might answer that it is because it provides the sort of intellectual challenge that leads to scientific breakthroughs. Apart from mentioning the potential financial savings to be gained from replacing a diverse multidisciplinarity with a more unified interdisciplinarity (or in other words, amalgamating departments when there are cash-flow problems), the pessimist would point out that the policy makers have overlooked Barr's Inertial Principle: asking scientists to revise their theory is like asking a group of police officers to revise the law. Now there's a challenge.

See also:
Understanding ontogenetic development: debates about the nature of the epigenetic process; Neuromaturational theories; Constructivist theories; Dynamical systems approaches; Conceptions and misconceptions about embryonic development; Behavioral embryology and all other entries in Part VII; Jean Piaget

Further reading

Bickle, J. (1998). *Psychoneural Reduction: The New Wave.* Cambridge, MA: MIT Press.

Brown, T. L. (2003). *Making Truth: Metaphor in Science.* Champaign-Urbana: University of Illinois Press.

Klein, J. T. (1996). *Crossing Boundaries: Knowledge, Disciplinarities and Interdisciplinarities.* Charlottesville, VA: University of Virginia Press.

Sarkar, S. (1998). *Genetics and Reductionism.* Cambridge: Cambridge University Press.

Weingardt, P. and Stehr, N. (eds.) (2000). *Practising Interdisciplinarity.* Toronto: Toronto University Press.

PART I

Theories of development

The aim of this part is to explain the main features of theoretical approaches to development that have shaped contemporary developmental sciences in general and developmental psychology in particular. The strengths and weaknesses of each approach will be indicated. The final section on the application of dynamical systems approaches to development enables further details to be added to the interdisciplinary framework outlined in the Introduction.

Neuromaturational theories **Brian Hopkins**
Constructivist theories **Michael F. Mascolo &**
   Kurt W. Fischer
Ethological theories **Johan J. Bolhuis &**
   Jerry A. Hogan
Learning theories **John S. Watson**
Psychoanalytical theories **Peter Fonagy**
Theories of the child's mind **Noman H. Freeman**
Dynamical systems approaches **Gregor Schöner**

Neuromaturational theories

BRIAN HOPKINS

Introduction

Ontogenetic development occurs as a consequence of genetically determined structural changes in the central nervous system that can in turn give rise to orderly modifications in function. Thus, whatever the function, development conforms to an inevitable and invariable linear sequence of achievements (or milestones), with little or no assistance from the prevailing environment.

Redolent of the theory of the immortal germ plasm designed by August Weismann (1834–1914) to account for the genetic mechanisms of inheritance, this depiction of development continues to persist in textbooks on human development that devote a section (rarely a chapter) to what has become known as neuromaturational theories. Typically, two names have been associated with such theories: Arnold L. Gesell (Fig. 1) and Myrtle B. McGraw (Fig. 2). Consequently, the history of so-called neuromaturational accounts of development is restricted to brief, and as a result distorted, descriptions of the research endeavors of these two eminent developmental scientists. Such descriptions inevitably go on to report the demise of neuromaturational theories of development, with the epitaph "of historical interest, but no longer relevant." Nothing could be further from the truth, and it leaves one pondering whether some writers of developmental textbooks have ever read the original (as in 'source' and 'originality') writings of Gesell and McGraw.

Previewing the conclusions

Scientists, unlike hermits, do not work in a vacuum divorced from contemporary and historical influences on their research interests. As Isaac Newton (1642–1727) wrote to fellow physicist Robert Hooke (1635–1703) in a letter dated February 5, 1675: "If I have seen further it is by standing on the shoulders of giants." Who were the influential 'giants' with regard to the research and writings of Gesell and McGraw? Answers to this

question lead to the conclusion that neuromaturational theories as depicted above are a caricature when applied to influences that motivated the wide-ranging works of Gesell and McGraw.

It becomes further evident that neither was a 'neuromaturationist' in the strictest sense when one considers what they actually wrote. Even though both frequently used the term maturation, they did so as a means of combating the excesses of behaviorism and its doctrinal insistence that the human newborn was nothing more than a tabula rasa. Thus, perhaps we should conclude that 'neuromaturational' is an inappropriate adjective with which to qualify their respective theoretical stances – a conclusion they reinforced by the fact that they not only converged, but also most noticeably diverged, in their speculations about the determinants of development.

Historical and contemporary influences

From Comenius to Dewey

The intellectual heritage implicit in the writings of both Gesell and McGraw can be traced back to Jean-Jacques Rousseau (1712–1778) and before him John Amos Comenius (1592–1670). Rousseau offered the first psychological theory of child development in his book *Emile* (1762). While he portrayed development as an internally regulated process, he was by no means a strict maturationist as he emphasized that the spontaneously active child is ultimately a product of his own exploratory behavior and the environmental challenges it creates.

The intermediary link between Rousseau's ideas on the nature of the child and those of Gesell and McGraw was John Dewey (1859–1952). Fascinated by the latter's theory of enquiry and related research on infant and child development, the teenaged McGraw corresponded with Dewey from 1914 to 1918, and subsequently followed his courses at Columbia University. Dewey had

Figure 1. Arnold Lucius Gesell (1880–1961).

Figure 2. Myrtle Byram McGraw (1899–1988), photograph by Victor Bergenn.

Figure 3. Granville Stanley Hall (1844–1924).

a crucially important influence on McGraw's research agenda and in turn his theorizing substantially benefited from her findings (Dalton & Bergenn, 1995b, pp. 1–36). As for Gesell, he was influenced by Dewey's theory from two sources. Firstly, through the writings of G. Stanley Hall (Fig. 3) on child education, and secondly by his wife and some time co-author Beatrice Chandler who was a devotee of Dewey's pragmatic philosophy.

Dewey's rich and complex theory as expressed in his ideas on the development of judgment was an attempt to resolve the mind-body problem such that a static 'being' could be reconciled with a dynamical 'becoming.' Important in this respect were the related theories of Michael Faraday (1791–1867) and James Clerk Maxwell (1831–1879) on electrical and magnetic forces. Dewey believed that the laws of energy derived from these theories could be applied to the study of infant development. This step was taken by McGraw in one of her most detailed investigations on the development of bipedal locomotion, which for its time was technically sophisticated (Fig. 4).

For Dewey, and for McGraw, infants devote a considerable expenditure of kinetic energy in their first attempts at counteracting the gravitational field and subsequently in sitting, prehension, and the various forms of locomotion. For bipedal locomotion, at least, the dissipation of kinetic energy is expressed in a non-linear fashion, with the transition from unsupported to supported walking as shown by McGraw (Fig. 4). In general, however, development involves a gradual reduction in this expenditure through improvements in the transformation and redistribution of energy by the brain (and presumably by the musculoskeletal system in interaction with the central

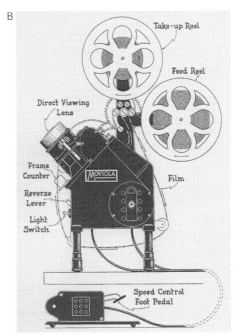

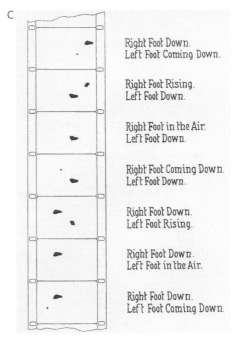

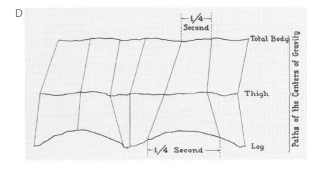

Figure 4. Methodological aspects of the study by McGraw and Breeze (1941) on the energetics of unsupported and supported walking in fifty-two infants. (A) Infants walked across a glass-topped table covered in evaporated milk and on top of which was placed a rubber mat. Positioning a mirror below the table at an angle of 45° enabled images of footprints to be recorded. Black markers were attached to the lower legs and thighs and another to that ". . . corresponding to the level of the center of gravity as a whole" (p. 276). Successive footprints and displacements of the markers on both sides of the body were registered by means of a 16mm camera at a sampling rate of 32 frames per second. (B) An editing camera was used to to project recordings onto a screen so that single and double stance times as well as changes in marker displacements could be plotted frame-by-frame. (C) A frame-by-frame plot of footprints indicating single and double stance phases. (D) A frame-by-frame plot of paths followed by the centers of gravity of the whole body, thigh, and lower leg. A number of measures to capture the 'energetic efficiency of locomotion' were derived. One was based on translational kinetic energy: average kinetic energy of a projectile / average kinetic energy of the leg moving over the same horizontal distance. This ratio revealed little change throughout supported walking and a sudden increase with the onset of unsupported walking. Subsequently, there was evident variability, both between and within infants, in the amount of kinetic energy expended. From M. B. McGraw and R. W. Breeze, 1941. Quantitative studies in the development of erect locomotion. *Child Development*, 12, 267–303.

nervous system). The outcome is a series of overlapping phases during which there is a selective elimination of unnecessary movements in such actions. During these phases, movements become increasingly integrated and coordinated, thereby allowing more stable energy-efficient states of 'being' to be achieved.

The notions of integration and coordination, according to Dewey, were evident in the continuing bidirectional relationships between motor and cognitive functions. Consequently, it was for him an artificial exercise, and thus biologically inappropriate, to compartmentalize development into separate functions. Doing so would undermine our understanding of how consciousness developed as it involves not just the mind, but also the mind in interaction with the body. To use Dewey's terminology, the development of consciousness was the "awareness of difference in the making."

Dewey, like Baldwin and Piaget, took account of Darwin's impact on psychology in his theory building, as did Gesell through his exposure to the arch-Darwinist and avid supporter of recapitulation theory, Stanley Hall. While Dewey never fully ascribed to Darwin's claim that development abided by a universal sequence, Gesell adopted it as a cornerstone of his theory. Apparently, McGraw displayed some hesitancy in applying Darwinian thinking to her work, feeling that it diverted attention away from a proper understanding of proximate mechanisms in development (Dalton & Bergenn, 1995a, pp. 207–214). Nevertheless, both she and Dewey can be read as subscribing to Darwin's theory of natural selection, at least in terms of a metaphor applicable to development. Dewey's selectionist account of development is echoed in McGraw's (1935) conclusion that developing infants are engaged in a process of selecting and refining combinations of movements and postures best suited to gaining ascendancy over a new task or challenge. In this sense, they foreshadowed a key feature of Gerald Edelman's theory of neuronal group selection.

Embryology

An important contemporary influence on Gesell and McGraw was the rise of experimental embryology, which reached a peak during their most research-intensive period (viz., the 1930s and 1940s). Figures in this field such as Ross G. Harrison (1873–1959) had already expressed the view that embryogenesis was not predetermined, but instead relied on interactions between cells and between them and the extracellular environment, a view in keeping with Gottlieb's concept of probabilistic epigenesis. By the time Gesell and McGraw embarked on their respective programs of research, such a view had become a commonly held

principle among embryologists. For certain, they were keenly aware of such embryological principles and readily incorporated them into their work. Thus, we find Gesell writing: "The organismic pattern of one moment, responsive to both internal and external environments, influences the pattern of succeeding moments. In a measure, previous environmental effects are perpetuated by incorporation with constitution" (Gesell & Thompson, 1934, p. 294). For her part, McGraw expressed her indebtedness to embryology in the following way: "... it is the experimental embryologists and not psychologists who deserve credit for formulating the most adequate theory of behavior development. It is they who are revealing the process of morphogenesis, and it is they who are bringing the most convincing experimental evidence to bear upon an evaluation of the intrinsic and extrinsic factors in the process of growth" (McGraw, 1935, p. 10). She then goes on to state in a manner equally applicable to Gesell: "In many ways development as manifest in the early metamorphosis of the germ cells is extraordinarily similar in principle to that shown in the development of behavior in the infant and young child" (p. 10). Undoubtedly, the embryologist with the greatest impact on Gesell and McGraw was George E. Coghill (Oppenheim in Dalton & Bergenn, 1995a, pp. ix–xiv). Coghill had embarked on an intensive study of changes in the swimming movements of salamander larvae and embryos in 1906, with the aim of identifying the neural mechanisms underlying their behavioral development. His theoretical approach and findings influenced Gesell and especially McGraw in a variety of ways (Fig. 5). Three of these relevant to both of them can be mentioned. Firstly, behavioral development stemmed from an orderly sequence of changes in the nervous system (a standpoint perhaps shared more by Gesell than McGraw). Secondly, from the beginning, behavior is expressed as a total integrated pattern and from which individual functions emerge during development (Coghill's principle of the integration and individuation of behavior, according to which experience and learning make significant contributions to development). Thirdly, behavioral development does not originate in a bundle of reflexes triggered into a chain-like response to external stimulation. Instead, it commences as a coordinated pattern generated by a spontaneously active nervous system (another standpoint perhaps shared more by Gesell than McGraw). This last point reveals something about Coghill's strong opposition to behaviorism and its close cousin in neurophysiology, reflexology (Fig. 6).

Behaviorism

If embryology, with its emphasis on reciprocal structure-function relationships during development,

Figure 5. A specific instance of Coghill's influence on McGraw's research. (A) The S-stage in the development of swimming movements in the salamander larva, one of three stages identified by Coghill, with the prior two being termed the Early Flexure and Coil stages. (From Coghill, 1929, as cited in George E. Coghill, this volume.) These observations provided McGraw with the motivation for studying developmental changes in the swimming movements of human infants. (B) Phases in the swimming movements of the human newborn (A), at about 2–3 months (B) during which they become more variable, and approximately coinciding with the achievement of unsupported bipedal locomotion (C). The newborn movements, no longer present when the infant is placed in water after phase B, suggest that they are ontogenetic adaptations to the intrauterine environment, with their 'reappearance' at phase C having to do with practice effects as in her co-twin study. They also demonstrate the effects of decreasing gravitational constraints on the behavior of the newborn and McGraw considered them to be better organized than either neonatal crawling or stepping movements. From M. B. McGraw, 1943. *The Neural Maturation of the Human Infant*. New York: Columbia University Press.

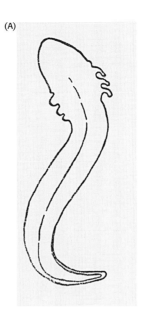

(A)

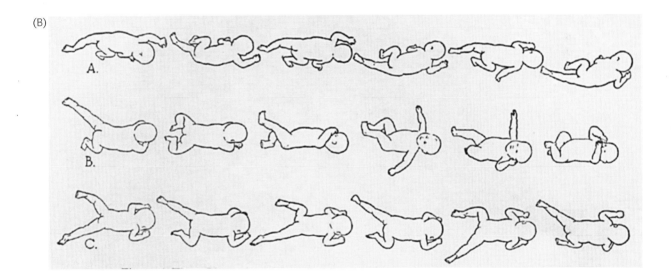

(B)

was a source of inspiration for Gesell and McGraw, then behaviorism posed a definite threat to the future of their research. Of course, we are not talking about just any sort of behaviorism, but rather the radical formulation promulgated by John B. Watson (1878–1958). Attaining the apex of its dominance during the 1930s and 1940s, Watson's radical environmentalism banned not only the use of the introspective method, but also concepts having to do with the internal regulation behavior that were so essential to the visions of development held by Gesell and McGraw. Why he espoused such an extreme view is not entirely clear. His Ph.D. thesis (1903) concerned the issue of how behavior and cortical myelination co-developed in the rat, and subsequently he carried out ethological research together with his student Karl S. Lashley (1890–1958) on the behavioral

development of terns. Perhaps the turning point was his justifiable dissatisfaction with the concept of instinct as could be found in the writings of William McDougall (1871–1938) at the time. Whatever the case, Watson never studied child development, except for an abortive attempt to classically condition the human newborn. He did manage, however, to divorce mainstream (American) developmental psychology from its roots in biology that had been established by the likes of Baldwin and Stanley Hall before him.

Given their affinity with Coghill and Dewey, it is not surprising that Gesell and McGraw also opposed radical behaviorism as a means of understanding development. Certainly, Gesell was more outspoken in this respect and both he and McGraw were forced by Watson's polemics to defend and refine their own theoretical stances on

Table 1. Gesell's seven morphogenetic principles, with their interpretations, examples taken from his own writings and analogous terms used by others. Most of them were derived from embryology and some of them have interdependent meanings. The overriding principle is that of self-organization.

Principle	Interpretation	Gesellian example	Similar terms
1. Individuating fore-reference	Two aspects: 1. organism develops as a unitary whole from which differentiated functions arise (i.e., 'being' is sustained in the face of 'becoming'); 2. neural mechanisms present before they are functionally expressed	Neural 'machinery' for locomotion is developed before the child can walk	Systemogenesis and environmentally or experience-expectant development of structures and functions
2. Developmental direction	Development proceeds in invariant cephalo (proximal) – caudal (distal) direction as well as following a proximo-distal trend	Infant gains control over muscles of the eyes, neck, upper trunk, and arms before those of the lower trunk and legs	Gradients in morphogenetic fields
3. Spiral reincorporation	Loss and (partial) recurrence of behavioral patterns (regressions as well as progressions) that lead to emergence of new ones, with development appearing to repeat itself at higher levels of organization	As the infant changes from being able to move in prone, elevated, and finally the upright position, there is a partial repetition of previous forms of leg activity.	Repetition (of abilities at increasingly higher levels of organization)[1]
4. Reciprocal interweaving	Periodic fluctuations in dominance between functions, and between excitation and inhibition. Applied not only to the changing dominance between flexor and extensor muscles, but also to perceptual and emotional development. Similarity with Piaget's concept of *décalage* and thus to the process of equilibration	Alternations in hand preference during infant development that include a period of no preference.	Heterochrony and systemogenesis
5. Functional asymmetry	Development begins in a symmetrical state that has to be 'broken' in order to achieve lateralized behavior	Symmetry is 'broken' initially with the appearance of the asymmetrical tonic neck posture in neonatal life, which forms the origin of a subsequent hand preference	Symmetry breaking (in physics)
6. Self-regulatory fluctuation	Developing system in state of formative instability in which periods of equilibrium alternate with periods of disequilibrium. Accordingly, development is a non-linear process	Evident in changes in the developing relationships between sleep and wakefulness	Self-organization
7. Optimal tendency	Achievement of end-states in development through the action of endogenous compensatory mechanisms, which serve to 'buffer' the developing organism from undue external perturbations	Most infants achieve independent bipedal locomotion without any specific training at about the same age, despite temporary setbacks such as illnesses	Canalization and the mechanism of homeorhesis, both of which stem from the concept of equifinality

[1] Derived from T. G. R. Bower and J. G. Wishart, 1979. Towards a unitary theory of development. In E. B. Thoman, ed., *Origins of the Infant's Social Responsiveness*. Hillsdale, NJ: Erlbaum, and a feature of Bower's model of descending differentiation applied to both perceptual and motor development.

child development. What were the defining features of their respective theories?

Arnold Gesell the theoretician and tester

On the possibility of a behavioral morphogenesis

The anchor point of Gesell's theory of development was morphogenesis, the study of change in the physical shape or form of the whole organism by means of growth and differentiation across ontogenetic (or phylogenetic) time. In this respect, he was greatly influenced by the Scottish zoologist D'Arcy Wentworth Thompson (1860–1948) and his book *Growth and Form* (1917). Today the mechanisms of growth and differentiation are couched in terms of symmetry breaking following the seminal work of Alan Turing (1912–1954) on modeling the effects of chemical gradients in morphogenetic fields, something that Gesell was aware of toward the end of his working life.

According to Gesell, behavior had a changing morphology, and development, like physical growth, was a morphogenetic process that was revealed in transformations of the ". . . architectonics of the action system" (Gesell & Amatruda, 1945, p. 165). Morphogenesis was more than just a metaphor for Gesell: behavioral development conformed to the same processes of pattern formation as for the growth of anatomical structures, and its study required a topographical approach (partly via cinematography) in order to capture age-related alterations in the patterns of movement (e.g., prehension) and posture (e.g., the asymmetrical tonic neck configuration of head, arms, and legs). He endeavored to encapsulate these processes in his seven morphological principles or laws of growth (Table 1) and to depict their most salient features with the aid of spatial-temporal illustrations (Fig. 7).

What is clear from reading the later publications of Gesell (e.g., Gesell & Amatruda, 1945) is that his theory of behavioral morphogenesis complied with one overarching principle: self-regulation or what is now referred to as self-organization in open systems. He, like McGraw, was acquainted with General system theory as propounded by Ludwig von Bertalanffy (1901–1972) in his attempt to provide a theoretical framework for the unification of biology and physics through the agency of irreversible thermodynamics. Gesell was also becoming familiar with the approach of Ilya Prigogine (1917–2003) to this branch of physics and thus to how living systems evade the maximum entropy created by the Second law of thermodynamics. One can only speculate how Gesell would have incorporated the non-linear dynamics of irreversible thermodynamics and related theories into his own morphogenetic theory, but it is indisputable that for him development was a self-organizing process.

On the meaning of maturation

If development was a process imbued with self-organizing capacities, what then was the mechanism of ontogenetic change in Gesell's theory? It is in this regard that we confront the most persistent representation of his theory, namely, that the 'motor' driving such change was maturation. Originating in embryology, the meaning of maturation was restricted there to the formation of gametes (ova and spermatozoa) from the oogonia and spermatogonia of the female and male gonads, respectively. As such, it refers to the first of the major stages in metazoan embryological development that is followed by fertilization, cleavage, and the stages of the blastula and neurula. In Gesell's theory, maturation was not only a formative agent in development, but also even more so a stabilizing mechanism that ensured the ontogenetic achievement of species-characteristic end states. Thus, it has considerable kinship with the notion of canalization as advanced by the geneticist-cum-embryologist Conrad H. Waddington (1905–1975).

The obdurate misrepresentation of Gesell's theory stems not only from a neglect of how he conceptualized development, which he used to replace the by-then-outmoded instinct concept. What tends to be overlooked is that he accorded both learning and experience equality with maturation as is evident in the previous citation from Gesell & Thompson (1934). What united learning, experience, and maturation in Gesell's theoretical edifice was his concept of growth (Oppenheim, 1992). Growth for him was the functional enhancement of behavioral adaptations that included responses to internal and external environments, with the rider that the distinction between 'internal' and 'external' was ultimately an inexpedient exercise. Over the years, and perhaps as a debating point to counteract the excesses of radical behaviorism, he subtly altered his stance on the maturation versus learning debate that came to replace the hereditary-environment controversy. So, by the middle of the 1940s, he expressed the following, much-quoted, statement: "The so-called environment, whether internal or external, does not generate the progressions of development. Environmental factors support, inflect, and specify; but they do not engender the basic forms and sequences of development" (Gesell, 1946, p. 313). Such a statement is strikingly reminiscent of the roles of experience in development delineated by Gottlieb: maintenance (cf., support), facilitation (cf., inflect), and induction (cf., specify).

(A)

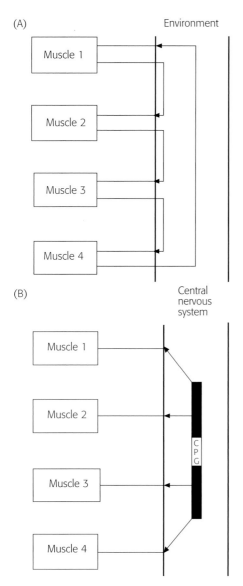

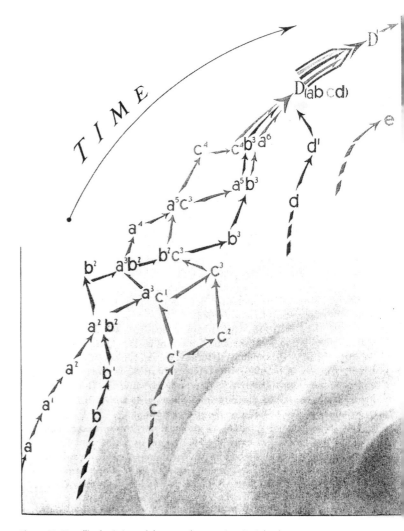

Figure 7. Gesell's depiction of the morphogenetic principles he proposed as giving rise to the formation of behavioral patterns and which he termed a 'time-space diagram' or 'dynamic map.' The shaded area refers to the 'corpus of behavior', which consists of potential and achieved expressions of the developing action system. The lower-case letters a, b, c, and d stand for traits or their parts, which over time merge into a developed complex of traits (D). The numbers associated with these letters represent the enhancement or elaboration of a trait, either of itself or through its integration with a related one. The broken lines denote latent traits that still have to be expressed in behavior, while the solid lines indicate dominant ones, with the former serving as replacements for the latter should that be required (e.g., as a consequence of focal brain damage). The behaviors at the edge of the shaded area (b^2, a^4, etc.) are those that are overtly manifest. In particular, this map illustrates the principle of reciprocal interweaving. From A. Gesell and C. S. Amatruda, 1945. *The Embryology of Behavior: The Beginnings of the Human Mind.* New York: Harper.

Figure 6. (A) Reflexology: a schematic representation of the chain-reflex model. When the first reflex associated with a muscle is elicited by external stimulation, its output triggers the next reflex and so on. With elicitation of the last reflex in the chain, its output serves to re-elicit the first one and thus the movement is repeated as in locomotion. Opposed by Coghill, this model was also severely criticized by Lashley in 1930 as an unrealistic model of motor control. (B) Coghill's approach to behavioral development was akin to the Preyer-Tracy hypothesis of autogeneous motility, which today is reflected in the central pattern generator (CPG) theory. A CPG is taken to be a network of of spontaneously active interneurons situated, for example, in the spinal cord and which emits modulated rhythmical electrical discharges that activate muscles in coordinated fashion, such as those involved in locomotion. With thanks to Hans Forssberg for both illustrations.

On developmental testing

Gesell was not only a psychologist, but also a pediatrician by training. The fusion of these two professions in his academic career led him inexorably to what has become his defining contribution to

developmental psychology: the derivation of normative, age-based, criteria for use in developmental diagnosis, which culminated in his battery of tests referred to as the Gesell Developmental Schedules.

As pointed out by others, there is curious tension between Gesell the theoretician and Gesell the tester. On the one hand, he had articulated a complex and subtle theory designed to capture the development of the *whole* child. On the other hand, his schedules appear to bear little relationship to his theory, with the 'typical' child's development being disassembled into one of several functional domains that have been incorporated into subsequent scales of infant development. His test battery, which covered ten ages, was intended to serve two main purposes. Firstly, to identify signs of deviant development as early as possible, despite the fact that the norms for each item were appropriated from testing children from middle-class families of North European ancestry. Secondly, and resting on the embryological concept of competence, to provide an indication of 'readiness for schooling.' In pursuit of that purpose, it was never really made clear by Gesell whether it also implied a 'readiness for learning.'

A maturationist?

The truncated overview of Gesell's prodigious and diverse publications does not entirely justify his continuing categorization as a 'maturationist' who simply rendered an account of ontogenetic development within the restrictive confines of neural determinism. A careful reading of his more theoretically oriented publications (e.g., Gesell & Amatruda, 1945) should dispel the commonplace supposition that he held such a 'one-cause' theory of development. Gesell was a pioneering student of child development who had many 'firsts' to his name: the first to employ the co-twin method, the first to use one-way observation mirrors together with cinematography in recording infant and child behavior, and the first to employ these and other techniques to study systematically the development of sleep and wakefulness (and the transitions between them) in both preterm and fullterm infants. He was, however, not an experimenter (except perhaps within the context of his co-twin study) and thus left an incomplete theory of how brain and behavior co-develop. McGraw, in contrast, can be said to have gone further than Gesell in these respects.

McGraw the theoretician and experimenter

Reflexology and the cortical inhibition hypothesis

In a paper published in 1985, McGraw contends that she had never worked out her own theory of development (McGraw in Dalton & Bergenn, 1995a, pp. 57–64). If she did not have her own theory, then she certainly took guidance from those of Dewey and Coghill, and at least one of the tenets of reflexology, in formulating the theoretical underpinnings of her broadly based program of research.

While the doctrine of reflexology was evident in how she interpreted her findings, McGraw was selective in her use of it. She never accepted that newborn behavior amounted to just a bundle of reflexes (or a 'mid-brain preparation') that were somehow activated and chained together by the grace of external stimulation. Rather, it was predicated in the first instance on a spontaneously active brain.

What she did extract from reflexology was the cortical inhibition hypothesis. In the Introduction to the 1962 edition of McGraw (1943), she expressed regret at having given prominence to this hypothesis as providing an explanation for what she saw as a change from sub-cortical to cortical mediation of behavior occurring around 2–3 months after birth. It is recognized, also in her time, that cortical activity is both inhibitory and excitatory. Moreover, the hypothesis has been refuted by both animal and human developmental studies and in particular by the fact that movements in near-term anencephalic fetuses are qualitatively different from those of their healthy counterparts. Nevertheless, it still lingers on as an explanatory construct in some quarters of developmental psychology.

A reductionist?

Some recent evaluations of McGraw's published work have led to the assertion that it bears the badge of a reductionist in the sense that she claimed that behavioral development was prescribed by changes in the brain. In the same breath, she is portrayed as being more of a 'maturationist' than Gesell. Her writings speak firmly against such an adumbration. Take, for example, the following conclusion about the nature of development in McGraw (1946): ". . . it probably is the interrelationship of a multitude of factors which determines the course of behavior development at any one time" (p. 369). As another example, consider this comment from her *Psychological Review* paper published in 1940:

> In studying the development of reaching-prehensile behavior of the infant, for example, the object in the field of vision is just as much an integral part in the organization of the behavior as are the arms, fingers and eyes of the baby . . . One manipulates arms and fingers quite differently when picking up a bowl a water from the way one does when trying to catch a fly. In that the object determines the configuration of neuromuscular movements, and as such might be considered an "organizer" of behavior.
>
> (McGraw in Dalton & Bergenn, 1995a, p. 218)

Does this sound familiar? It should do as it conveys the essence of organism-environment mutualism that is the foundation of J. J. Gibson's affordance concept.

Structure and function

On the issue of structure-function relationships during development, McGraw was more explicit than Gesell. For example, in McGraw (1946), she writes:

> It seems fairly evident that certain structural changes take place prior to the onset of overt function; it seems equally evident that cessation of neurostructural development does not coincide with the onset of function. There is every reason to believe that when conditions are favorable function makes some contribution to further advancement in the structural development of the nervous system . . . Obviously, rigid demarcation between structure and function as two distinct processes of development is not possible. The two are interrelated, and at one time one aspect may have greater weight than the other.
>
> (p. 369)

Similar commitments to a bidirectional model of development are dispersed throughout both her books (McGraw, 1935; 1943).

Based on her studies concerned with the development of locomotion, McGraw (1943) went beyond Gesell in acknowledging that structure-function relationships emerged from ongoing interactions between the central nervous system (CNS) and the energy-converting musculoskeletal system (MSS). In McGraw's case, the MSS was the interface between the CNS and the infant's external environment (Fig. 8), an insight commonly accredited to Nikolai A. Bernstein (1896–1966).

Just motor development?

Beyond Bernstein, connections to Piaget's theory of development are also to be found in her publications. McGraw (1935), in her co-twin study, regarded the attainment of dynamical balance not only as a necessary condition for persistent bipedal locomotion to be achieved, but also as contributing to the development of problem-solving abilities and thereby to the promotion of consciousness. This was another example of McGraw putting Dewey's theory of development to the test. To do so, her famous twins Johnny (with practice) and Jimmy (without practice) Woods had to resolve balance problems in, for example, roller skating before they could walk habitually, climbing up inclines at various angles, and demounting from pedestals of different heights. Her ingenuity in devising such age-appropriate manipulations matches that of Piaget. Both still stand as exemplars in their attempts to link theory with apposite methods in studying development through presenting infants with challenges on the cusp of their current abilities. Allowing them to discover their own solutions when challenged in this way complies with Piaget's assertion that the resolution of conflict is a motivating force in generating development.

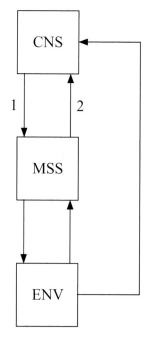

Figure 8. The central nervous system (CNS) interacts with the musculoskeletal system (MSS) throughout development. Moreover, the latter functions as the interface with the external environment (ENV), with which it also interacts. In a very simplified way, this figure illustrates some of the features of Bernstein's (1967) approach to resolving issues about motor control and coordination which he applied to the development of upright walking in infants. McGraw (1943) also treated motor development, and specifically locomotion, as consisting of bidirectional influences between the CNS and the MSS, and between the MSS and the ENV. The arrow labeled (1) signifies the common interpretation imposed on neuromaturational theories (structure → function), which therefore can be seen as omitting the many interactions between intrinsic and extrinsic factors considered by McGraw. The one labeled (2) refers to an interesting proposal by Bernstein (1967) that has implications for understanding (motor) development, which he communicates as follows: ". . . the reorganization of the movement begins with its biomechanics . . . ; this biomechanical reorganization sets up new problems for the central nervous system, to which it gradually adapts" (pp. 87–89). Thus, according to this rather radical viewpoint, developmental transformations occur not just because the brain changes, but rather the opposite, namely, there are changes in the biomechanical properties of the body segments (i.e., the MSS) to which the developing brain adjusts.

Gesell and McGraw: similarities and differences

There are similarities, but even more so differences, between Gesell and McGraw in terms of the theoretical assumptions and associated methods they assimilated into their research programs. Some similarities have been mentioned previously. Others that stand out are:

1. Reciprocal interweaving: McGraw, like Gesell, envisaged development to consist of alternating and overlapping phases, which resulted in both progression and regression. It seems to be the case

that McGraw (1935) used weaving as a metaphor to capture the non-linearity of development some four years before Gesell introduced into the literature his related principles of reciprocal interweaving and spiral reincorporation (Dalton in Dalton & Bergenn, 1995a, pp. 134–135).

2. The role of movement: for both Gesell and McGraw, movement was a 'final common pathway' for the enhancement of all aspects of development (e.g., cognitive, social, emotional, etc.). While Gesell (& Thompson, 1934) alluded to movement as an essential ingredient in the development of exploration (or what he considered to be movement-generated 'sensory experience'), he also included posture in this context. He went so far as to say that "Posture is behavior," by which he meant ". . . the position of the body as a whole or by its members, in order to execute a movement or to maintain an attitude" (Gesell & Amatruda, 1945, p. 46). In Gesell's view, the asymmetrical tonic neck (ATN) posture, or what he termed "This new visual postural visual-manual-prehensory pattern" (Gesell & Amatruda, 1945, p. 458), exerted a formative influence on the development of handedness. This conjecture brings us to the first of the differences between Gesell and McGraw.

1. Antecedent-consequence relationships: a consistent theme in Gesell's writings is that mature expressions of behavior can be observed in incomplete forms earlier in development, with both being part of the same developmental sequence. His Developmental Schedules reflect this point of view. McGraw did not share such an ontogenetic scenario. This is exemplified in her interpretation of the ATN posture: it was not an antecedent condition for the acquisition of a hand preference, but instead forms part of an age-appropriate righting response that later becomes incorporated into prone locomotion (Dalton in Dalton & Bergenn, 1995a, p. 144). While neither of them referred to ontogenetic adaptations as such, it is clear McGraw envisaged development as being more of a discontinuous process than Gesell.

2. Heterochrony: during development, there are differential rates in the timing with which new structures and functions appear (i.e., the accelerated development of particular brain areas and behaviors relative to others). While Gesell and McGraw depicted development as essentially heterochronic in nature, they differed in this regard on one important aspect based on the findings of their respective co-twin studies. According to McGraw, but not Gesell, early experiences could affect heterochronicity between functions in the sense of accelerating slower developing components (or what she labelled as 'ontogenetic skills' as opposed to 'phylogenetic skills').

3. Intra-individual differences: inter-individual differences in intra-individual change, to use a somewhat clumsy formulation, should be the overriding concern in studying ontogenetic development. Only possible to address with a longitudinal design, it tends to be neglected in research on child development. Such was not the case with McGraw and her attention to tracking change within individual infants is considered to have been a key feature of her research (Touwen in Dalton & Bergenn, 1995a, pp. 271–283). Together with her co-workers, she devised a number of analytical techniques for detecting differences in developmental trajectories between infants (McGraw, 1943). Gesell, on the other hand, gave little regard to intra-individual change and at most considered it to be an indication of deviant development (i.e., 'deviant' in not complying with the sequential age-related norms in his Development Schedules). Drawing on the distinction between population and typological thinking, McGraw was representative of the former and Gesell of the latter.

4. Chronological age: in keeping with Baldwin and Piaget, McGraw was not particularly concerned with mapping the development of various abilities as a function of chronological age (McGraw in Dalton & Bergenn, 1995a, p. 60). Instead, she was more interested in the 'how' and 'why' rather than the 'when' of developmental achievements. To say that Gesell did not address all three questions would be to do him a disservice. As Gesell the theoretician, he did so, but as his program of research progressed the questions of 'how' and 'why' tended to become subordinated by Gesell the tester to a focus on the modal chronological ages at which particular abilities were attained. Unfortunately, that is what he is chiefly remembered for in the developmental literature despite the fact he distinguished astronomical (i.e., chronological) time from biological (i.e., developmental) time in the following way: "Astronomical time is rigid, neutral, two-way, reversible. Biological time is elastic, cyclical, one-way, irreversible" (Gesell & Amatruda, 1945, p. 16). His observations on preterm infants, never studied by McGraw, reveal an attempt to reconcile these two time scales, and he was one of the first to assert the importance of using corrected age when evaluating their postterm development. In his more popular writings aimed chiefly at parents, Gesell the tester really comes to the fore. Here, parents are confronted with age-encapsulated caricatures of children (e.g., the assentive and conforming three-year-old as

against the assertive, lively four-year-old). Such an example of typological thinking was completely absent from McGraw's publications.

There are many other points of departure that can be discerned when comparing the published work of Gesell and McGraw (e.g., McGraw's attempts to apply mathematical modeling to her data as outlined in Fig. 4 for one of her studies). However, it should be clear that their approaches to the study of ontogenetic development were so divergent as to leave us wondering why they are still lumped together under the rubric 'neuromaturational theories.'

Conclusions

If unbridled genetic determinism defines the essence of neuromaturational theories of development and Gesell and McGraw are taken to be their standard-bearers, then we continue to labor under false pretenses. Neither of them held to such a reductionistic and monocausal view of development. Their theoretical formulations were much more subtle than this and still bear insights that resonate with current dynamical systems approaches to development. Recognition that development is a self-organizing phenomenon, and intimations that there is a circular causality between perception and action, are readily apparent in both their writings. If the label 'neuromaturationist' does in any way seem to be appropriate, then perhaps it is more applicable to Gesell when defending his theory against attacks from the radical behaviorists. Outside this context, both he and McGraw strove to find the middle ground in the maturation versus learning debate of the time.

With the foundation of experimental embryology in the late 19th century by Wilhelm Roux (1850–1924), the bidirectionality of the relationship between structure and function during development became an undisputed maxim (at least among the embryologists). In drawing theoretical inspiration from such a source, both Gesell and McGraw transported this dictum into the realm of postnatal behavioral development. All of this suggests that at least by the end of the 19th century, there was no such thing any more that complied with a radical neuromaturational theory. The irony is that now in fact we have such theoretical radicalism as contained, for example, in theories of innate knowledge and language acquisition as well as those addressing the role of the prefrontal cortex in the development of executive functions. At the same time, Gesell and McGraw continue to be castigated as representatives of an overly simplistic maturational stance on the mechanism of development.

In conclusion, it is long overdue that Gesell and McGraw should no longer be classified as 'neuromaturationists.' More germane would be something like 'developmental psychobiologists,' while at the same time acknowledging important differences between them in how they endeavored to describe and explain ontogenetic development. The last word is perhaps best given to Myrtle McGraw, the consummate developmentalist:

> In the present state of knowledge a more profitable approach lies in the systematic determination of the changing interrelationships between the various aspects of a growing phenomenon. It has been suggested that relative rates of growth may afford a common symbolic means by which the underlying principles of development may be formulated. Once the laws of development have been determined the maturation concept may fade into insignificance.
>
> (McGraw, 1946, p. 369)

If only . . .

See also:
The concept of development: historical perspectives; Understanding ontogenetic development: debates about the nature of the epigenetic process; Learning theories; Dynamical systems approaches; Developmental testing; Cross-sectional and longitudinal designs; Twin and adoption studies; Conceptions and misconceptions about embryonic development; Motor development; Brain and behavioral development (I): sub-cortical; Brain and behavioral development (II): cortical; Executive functions; Handedness; Locomotion; Prehension; Sleep and wakefulness; Prematurity and low birthweight; Behavioral embryology; Cognitive neuroscience; Developmental genetics; Pediatrics; James Mark Baldwin; George E. Coghill; Viktor Hamburger; Jean Piaget; Milestones of motor development and indicators of biological maturity

Further reading

Ames, L. B. (1989). *Arnold Gesell: Themes of his Work*. New York: Human Sciences Library.

Dalton, T. C. and Bergenn, V. W. (eds.) (1995). *Reconsidering Myrtle McGraw's Contribution to Developmental Psychology*. Special Issue *Developmental Review*, 18, 472–503.

Thelen, E. and Adolph, K. E. (1992). Arnold L. Gesell: The paradox of nature and nurture. *Developmental Psychology*, 28, 368–380.

Constructivist theories

MICHAEL F. MASCOLO AND KURT W. FISCHER

Introduction

Constructivism is the philosophical and scientific position that knowledge arises through a process of active construction. From this view, knowledge structures are neither innate properties of the mind nor are they passively transmitted to individuals by experience. In this entry, we outline recent advances in constructivist models of cognitive development, beginning by analyzing the origins of constructivist developmental theory in the seminal writings of Piaget. We then examine the ways in which theoretical and empirical challenges to his theory have resulted in the elaboration of a more powerful constructivism in the form of neo-Piagetian and systems models of human development.

Piagetian foundations of constructivist theory

Piaget's theory of cognitive development is simultaneously a structuralist and constructivist theory. For Piaget, psychological structures are constructed in development. The basic unit of cognitive analysis is the psychological structure, which is an organized system of action or thought. All psychological activities are organized, whether they consist of a 6-month-old's reach for a rattle, an 8-year-old's logical solution to a conservation problem, or a 15-year-old's systematic manipulation of variables in a science experiment.

Psychological structures, or schemes, operate through the dual processes of assimilation and accommodation. Piaget appropriated these notions from the prior work of James Mark Baldwin. Drawn from the biological metaphor of digestion, assimilation refers to the process by which objects are broken down and incorporated into existing structures, while accommodation reflects complementary processes of modifying or adapting an existing structure to accept or incorporate an object.

Any psychological act requires the assimilation of an object into an existing structure and the simultaneous accommodation of that structure to the incorporated object. For example, to perform the sensorimotor act of grasping a rattle, an infant incorporates (assimilates) the rattle into her grasping scheme. However, to grasp the rattle, the infant must modify her scheme to the particular contours of the incorporated object.

Piaget maintained that psychological structures undergo successive transformations over time in a series of four stages. Within his theory, stages exhibit several important properties. Firstly, each stage corresponds to a particular type or quality of thinking or psychological organization. From this view, infants are not simply small adults – they think in fundamentally different ways from older children and adults. Secondly, the stages form a hierarchical progression with later stages building upon earlier ones. Thirdly, the stages form a single, universal, and unidirectional sequence. Regardless of the culture in which a child resides, thinking develops in stages toward the common endpoint of formal operations. Fourthly, Piagetian stages form *structures d'ensemble* (i.e., 'structures of the whole'). Piaget's position on the organization of thinking within stages was complex. On the one hand, the concept of stage implies homogeneity of organization. Within a given stage, Piaget held that schemes are general and have wide application to broad ranges of cognitive tasks. On the other hand, he also invoked the concept of *décalage* – the idea that cognitive abilities within a stage develop at different times. Despite such *décalage*, Piaget held that as children resolve the conflicts that exist between cognitive sub-systems, psychological structures develop into increasingly broad and integrated wholes.

According to Piaget, for the first two years of life, infant schemes function within the sensorimotor stage of development. Sensorimotor schemes consist of organized systems of action on objects. Piaget held that infants cannot form representations (images) of events in the absence of direct sensory input. As such, sensorimotor schemes reflect integrations of the sensory and motor aspects of action. Thinking emerges between 18 and 24 months of age with the onset of the semiotic function during the pre-operational stage of development. During this stage, children are capable of forming representations of events (e.g., words, images), but are incapable of manipulating these images in logical or systematic ways. Pre-operational intelligence is marked by the emergence of symbolic play, deferred imitation, and the use of words to refer to present and absent objects. During the concrete operational stage, thinking becomes systematic and logical. Children are able to operate logically on concrete representations of events. The capacity for concrete operations underlies a child's ability to perform various logical tasks, including conservation, class inclusion, seriation, transitivity judgments, etc. It is not until the formal operational stage (adolescence onward) that individuals are able to free their logical thinking from concrete content. In formal operations, adolescents become capable of operating using abstract forms. In so doing, thinking becomes abstract, and adolescents and adults can conceptualize hypothetical and systematic solutions to logical, mathematical, and scientific problems.

The concept of equilibration provides the backbone of Piaget's constructivist theory of development. Equilibration refers to an inherent, self-regulating, compensatory process that balances assimilation and accommodation and prompts stage transition. Piaget elaborated upon several forms of equilibration. The first involves the detection of a conflict or discrepancy between an existing scheme and a novel object. He held that a state of equilibrium results when an object is successfully incorporated into a given scheme, and thus when assimilation and accommodation are in a state of balance. A state of disequilibrium results when there is a failure to incorporate an object into a given scheme. A child who only has schemes for cats and dogs will have little difficulty identifying common instances of these two classes, but his schemes would be in disequilibrium when first encountering a rabbit. Disequilibrium, in turn, motivates successive acts of accommodation that result in a significant modification of the existing schemes. A new scheme thus emerges from the failure of existing schemes. Where there were initially only schemes for cats and dogs, there are now schemes for cats, dogs, and bunnies.

Piaget discussed additional forms of equilibration, which involve the resolution of conflict between two competing cognitive schemes (e.g., when conservation of length and conservation of number come into conflict), and between individual schemes and the larger systems of which they are a part (e.g., integrating conservation of length, number, and mass into an abstract understanding of conservation). Piaget also acknowledged other processes that contribute to development. For example, in order for a stage transition to occur, there must be a requisite level of neurological maturation; a child must actively experience the world by acting on objects and people; a child must receive cultural knowledge in the form of socially transmitted and linguistically mediated rule systems (e.g., mathematics, science). Nonetheless, disequilibrium engendered by cognitive conflict provides the driving force of development.

Questions about Piaget's structuralism

Table 1 describes five basic problems and criticisms that emerged with regard to central principles in Piaget's theory of development. The first four critiques concern the Piagetian notion of cognitive structure or stage. Each critique is a variant on the idea that there exists more variability in children's cognitive functioning than would be predicted by a strong notion of stage. Research has indicated that the developmental level of even a single child's cognitive actions can change with variations in the level of contextual support provided to the child, the specific nature of the task, the conceptual domain in which the task occurs, and the child's emotional disposition. For example, Western European and North American children generally conserve number by 6–7 years of age, mass by 8 years, and weight by 10 years, but generally do not solve tasks about inclusion of sub-classes within classes until 9 or 10 years of age.

Research also suggests that providing training and contextual support for concrete operational tasks lowers the age at which children succeed in performing such tasks. For example, Peter Bryant and Thomas Trabasso demonstrated that providing young children with memory training (e.g., having them memorize which of each pair of adjacent sticks was larger or smaller) lowered the age at which they were able to perform a transitivity task, determining which stick in a pair is larger by inferring from comparisons of other pairs of sticks. Studies like these challenge the idea that children's thinking develops in broadly integrated and homogeneous structures (i.e., stages). Instead, they suggest that thinking is organized in terms of partially independent cognitive skills that develop along different pathways. Researchers have also criticized Piagetian concepts such as equilibration, assimilation, and accommodation as difficult to translate into clear and testable hypotheses. Finally, others have noted that Piaget did not pay enough attention to the ways in which social processes contribute to development. This last issue requires additional elaboration.

Table 1. Moving toward the new constructivism.		
Piagetian construct	*Source of problem*	*Analysis of developing skills*
Structural principles **I. Inner *competence* as property of individual child**. Individual *cognitive structures* function as basic units of cognitive activity. Cognitive structures are seen as properties of individual children.	Social context and affective state play a direct role in modulating level of functioning. Evidence suggests that performance on similar tasks in the same children vary dramatically with changes in contextual support and affective state.	**Skill as property of individual in social context**. Skills reflect actions performed on physical and social objects in particular social contexts. Child and social context collaborate in the joint construction of skills.
II. Limited number of broad stages. Piaget postulated four broad stages of cognitive development with a series of sub-stages.	**Variability in performances as a result of task complexity**. Differences in the complexity of tasks used to test children's stage acquisition produce different assessments of operative ability.	**Precise developmental yardsticks**. Skill analyses allow both broad and fine-grained analysis of development across a total of thirteen *levels* with a large number of smaller *steps* between levels.
III. Stage as *structure d'ensemble*. Piaget held that cognitive structures entail broad abilities having wide application to multiple tasks.	***Décalage***. Unevenness in the development of skills is the rule rather than the exception in ontogenesis, even for abilities presumed to be at the same developmental level.	**Skills develop within particular tasks, domains, and social contexts**. Rejecting the notion of globally consistent stages, skill analyses assess skill development within particular conceptual domains, tasks, and social contexts.
IV. Development as unidirectional ladder. Piaget proposed a unidirectional model of stage progression in which cognitive capacities in all cultures follow the same abstract progression of stages.	**Varied sequences of development**. Evidence suggests variation in developmental sequence in different children, tasks, and cultures, as well as failures to observe predicted Piagetian sequences.	**Development as multidirectional web**. Different skills develop along different trajectories for different *tasks*, *domains*, *persons*, *contexts*, and *cultures*. As such, development proceeds as a web of trajectories rather than as a ladder of fixed or universal steps.
Process principles **V. Individual action as primary source of developmental change**. Piaget viewed cognitive *disequilibria* as the primary mover of development, suggesting a central role for the individual child as the main mover of development.	**Limited focus on social, cultural, biological, and emotional organizers of developmental change**. Evidence suggests that social interaction, language, culture, genetics, and emotion play important roles in the constitution of psychological structures.	**Developmental change occurs as a product of *relations between* biological, psychological, and sociocultural processes**. Biological, psychological, social, and cultural processes necessarily coact in the formation of novel psychological structures.

Sociocultural challenges to the primacy of individual action

Piagetian constructivism relies heavily, but not exclusively, on the notion that children's own actions are primary movers of development (equilibration). According to Piaget, thinking emerges in the pre-operational stage as children abbreviate and internalize sensorimotor actions to form mental images (inner abbreviated action). Constructing an image of one's mother involves the abbreviated and internal reconstruction of actions that one performs when one actually looks at one's mother. Thus, thinking becomes a matter of internally manipulating images that have their origins in the actions of individual children.

Sociocultural psychologists, especially those inspired by Vygotsky, noted that Piaget's constructivism neglected the role of social interaction, language, and culture in development. From a Vygotskian perspective, children are not solitary actors. They work with adults and peers in the creation of any higher-order developmental process. In social interaction, partners direct each other's actions and thoughts using language and signs. Signs function as important vehicles of enculturation. Unlike symbol systems, such as mental images or pictures, signs are used to represent relatively arbitrary meanings that are shared within a linguistic community. For example, understanding the meaning of words such as 'good' or 'democracy' involves learning a relatively arbitrary cultural meaning that is shared and understood among individuals who comprehend a certain language, such as English. Vygotsky maintained that all higher-order psychological processes are mediated by signs. Development of higher-order mental functions occurs as children internalize the results of sign-mediated interactions that they have with others. As children come to use signs to mediate their thinking, they think in culturally not merely personally organized ways.

In his explanation of the social origins of higher-order functions, Vygotsky (1978) invoked his general genetic law of cultural development: "Any function in children's cultural development occurs twice, or on two planes. First, it appears on the social plane and then on the psychological plane. First it appears between people as an interpsychological category and then within the individual child as an intrapsychological category" (p. 57). The concept of internalization explains how sign-mediated activity that initially occurs between people comes to be produced within individuals in development. For example, to help his 6-year-old remember where she put her soccer ball, a father may ask, "Where did you last play with it?" In so doing, the father and daughter use signs to regulate the mental retracing of the girl's actions. As the girl internalizes these sign-mediated interactions, she acquires a higher-order memory strategy – 'retracing one's steps.'

This vignette illustrates the Vygotskian principle of the zone of proximal development (ZPD). The ZPD refers to the distance between a child's level of functioning when working alone and her developmental level working with a more accomplished individual. In the above example, the father's questions raise his child's remembering to a level beyond that which she can sustain alone. The child's remembering strategy is formed as she internalizes the verbal strategy that originated in joint action. In this way, the research spawned by sociocultural theory challenges the primacy of children's individual actions as main movers of development.

Reinventing constructivist theory: trajectories of skill development

In what follows, we will elaborate the major tenets of dynamic skill theory, a neo-Piagetian constructivist theory of psychological development. We describe how skill development can explain cognitive development and address key challenges to Piaget's theory elaborated in Table 1. Rather than speaking of broad logico-mathematical competences, according to dynamic skill

theory the main unit of acting and thinking is the developing skill.

The concept of skill

The concept of skill provides a useful way to think about psychological structures. A skill refers to an individual's capacity to control her behavior, thinking, and feeling within specified contexts and within particular task domains. As such, a skill is a type of control structure. It refers to the organization of action that an individual can bring under her own control within a given context. The concept of skill differs from the Piagetian notion of scheme or cognitive structure in several important ways. To begin with, a skill is not simply an attribute of an individual; instead, it is a property of an individual-in-a-context. The production of any instance of skilled action is a joint product of person and context (physical and social). As such, a change in the context in which a given act is performed can result in changes in the form and developmental level of the skill in question. In this way, context plays a direct role in the construction of skilled activity.

Contexts differ in the extent to which they support an individual's attempt to produce skilled activity. Contexts involving high support provide assistance that supports an individual's actions (e.g., modeling desired behavior; providing cues, prompts, or questions that prompt key components to help structure children's actions). Contexts involving low support provide no such assistance. Level of contextual support contributes directly to the level of performance a person is able to sustain in deploying a given skill. A person's optimal level refers to the highest level of performance one is capable of achieving, usually in contexts offering high support. A person's functional level consists of his or her everyday level of functioning in low support contexts. In general, a person's optimal level of performance under conditions of high support is several steps higher than his functional level in low support contexts.

Figure 1 depicts developmental variation in a child's story telling in a variety of high and low support conditions. In the context of elicited imitation, a child is asked to imitate a complex story modeled by an adult. In elicited imitation, the child's story functions at a level that is several steps higher than when he or she tells stories in free play, or is asked to tell his or her best story – both conditions of low support. Minutes later, when an adult prompts the child by stating the key components of the story, the child again functions at optimal level. Then after a few more minutes low support conditions result in reduction of the child's performance to functional level again. These fluctuations in skill level occur in the same child on the

Step	Performance Level	Social Support
1		
2		
3	Functional level	None
4		
5		
6	Optimal level	Priming through modeling, etc.
7		
8	Scaffolded level	Direct participation by adult
9		

Figure 1. Variation in skill level for stories as a function of social-contextual support. In the high-support assessments, the interviewer either modeled a story to a child (elicited imitation) or described the gist of a story and provided cues (prompt); the child then acted out the story. In low support assessments, the interviewer provided no such support but either asked for the child's best story or simply observed story telling in free play.

same task across varying conditions of contextual support separated by mere minutes.

Contexts involving high and low support differ from contexts involving scaffolded support. In contexts involving high or low support, the child alone is responsible for coordinating the elements of a given skill. For example, an adult may model a complex story for a child who then produces the story without further assistance. In scaffolded contexts, an adult assists the child by performing part of the task or otherwise structures the child's actions during the course of skill deployment. Scaffolding allows adult-child dyads to function at levels that surpass a child's optimal level. When a mother helps her 6-year-old tell a story by intermittently providing story parts and asking the child leading questions, the dyad can produce a more complex story than the child could tell alone, even with high support. As a result of contextual support and scaffolding, children do not function at a single developmental level in any given skilled activity. Instead, they function within a developmental range of possible skill levels.

A second way in which the concept of skill departs from Piagetian theory is that skills are not general structures. There are no general, de-contextualized, or all-purpose skills. Skills are tied to specific tasks and task domains. Skills in different conceptual domains (e.g., conservation, classification, reading words, social interaction, etc.) develop relatively independently of each other at different rates and toward different developmental endpoints. Assessments of the developmental level of one skill in one conceptual domain (e.g., conservation) will not necessarily predict the developmental level of skills in a different domain (e.g., classification), or even in conceptually similar tasks

(conservation of number versus conservation of volume). One can chart developmental sequences only for skills within a given domain and within particular social contexts and assessment conditions.

Levels of skill development

Skills develop through the hierarchical coordination of lower level action systems into higher-order structures. Table 2 presents the levels of hierarchical organization of a developing skill based on Fischer's dynamic skill theory (Fischer, 1980; Fischer & Bidell, 1998). In this model, skills develop through four broad tiers: reflexes refer to innate action elements (e.g., sucking; closing fingers around an object placed in the hand); sensorimotor actions refer to smoothly controlled actions on objects (e.g., reaching for an object); representations consist of symbolic meanings about concrete aspects of objects, events, and persons (e.g., "Mommy eat candy"); abstractions consist of higher-order representations about intangible and generalized aspects of objects and events (e.g., "Conservation refers to no change in the quantity of something despite a change in its appearance"). Within each broad tier, skills develop through four levels. A single set refers to a single organized reflex, action, representation or abstraction. Mappings refer to coordinations between two or more single sets, whereas systems consist of coordinations of two or more mappings. A system of systems reflects the intercoordination of at least two systems and constitutes the first level of the next broad tier of skills. For example, a *system* of sensorimotor systems constitutes a single representational set.

In this way, dynamic skill theory specifies four broad qualitatively distinct tiers of development comprising a total of thirteen specific levels. It also provides a set of tools for identifying a variable number of steps between any two developmental levels. These levels have been documented in scores of studies in a variety of different developmental domains. In the following sub-sections, we illustrate dynamics of skill development through an analysis of how sample skills move through the levels and tiers specified in Table 2.

Development in infancy

Here, we examine the development of visually guided reaching as an example of skill development. Like all skills, reaching does not emerge at any single point in time. Instead, like all skills, it develops gradually over the course of infancy and takes a series of different forms over time. In addition, at any given point in development, an infant's capacity to reach for seen objects varies dramatically depending upon the task at hand, the

Table 2. Tiers and levels of skill development.

Level	Reflex	Sensorimotor	Representational	Abstract	Age[1]
Rf1: Single reflexes	$[A]$ or $[B]$				3–4 wk
Rf2: Reflex mappings	$[A\text{———}B]$				7–8
Rf3: Reflex systems	$\left[A_F^E \longleftrightarrow B_F^E\right]$				10–11
Rf4/Sm1: Single sensorimotor actions	$\left[\begin{array}{c}A_F^E \longleftrightarrow B_F^E \\ \updownarrow \\ C_F^E \longleftrightarrow B_D^E\end{array}\right] \equiv [\mathbf{I}]$				15–17
Sm2: Sensorimotor mappings		$[\mathbf{I}\text{———}\mathbf{J}]$			7–8 mo
Sm3: Sensorimotor systems		$\left[\mathbf{I}_N^M \longleftrightarrow \mathbf{J}_N^M\right]$			11–13
Sm4/Rp1: Single representations		$\left[\begin{array}{c}\mathbf{I}_N^M \longleftrightarrow \mathbf{J}_N^M \\ \updownarrow \\ \mathbf{K}_P^O \longleftrightarrow \mathbf{L}_P^O\end{array}\right] \equiv [Q]$			18–24
Rp2: Representational mappings			$[Q\text{———}R]$		3.5–4.5 yr
Rp3: Representational systems			$\left[Q_V^U \longleftrightarrow R_V^U\right]$		6–7
Rp4/Ab1: Single abstractions			$\left[\begin{array}{c}Q_V^U \longleftrightarrow R_V^U \\ \updownarrow \\ S_X^W \longleftrightarrow T_X^W\end{array}\right] \equiv [\mathcal{Y}]$		10–12
Ab2: Abstract mappings				$[\mathcal{Y}\text{———}\mathcal{Z}]$	14–16
Ab3: Abstract systems				$\left[\mathcal{Y}_P^Q \longleftrightarrow \mathcal{Z}_Q^P\right]$	18–20
Ab4: Principles				$\left[\begin{array}{c}\mathcal{Y}_Q^{\mathcal{L}} \longleftrightarrow \mathcal{Z}_Q^{\mathcal{L}} \\ \updownarrow \\ \mathcal{A}_P^{\mathcal{L}} \longleftrightarrow \mathcal{B}_Q^{\mathcal{L}}\end{array}\right]$	23–25

[1] Ages are modal times that a level first emerges according to research with middle-class American and European children. They may differ across social groups.

Note: In skill diagrams, each letter denotes a component of a skill. A large letter = a main component (set), and a subscript or superscript = a subset of the main component. Plain letter = component that is a reflex, in the sense of innate action-component. Bold letter = sensorimotor action; italic letter = representation; and script letter = abstraction. Line connecting sets = relation that forms a mapping, single-line arrow = relation that forms a system, and double-line arrow = relation that forms a system of systems.

trajectory of an object's movement, degree of postural support, and other variables.

The first tier of skill development consists of reflexes. In skill theory, reflexes refer to simple elements of controlled action, present at birth, that are activated by environmental events. Reflexes do not simply consist of encapsulated reactions such as eye blinks or knee jerks. Instead, they consist of more molar elements of action over which infants exert limited control in contexts that activate them. These include action elements such as simple acts of looking at an object held in front of the face, sucking objects placed in the mouth, as well as emotional acts such as cooing or smiling. At the level of single reflexes (Rf1), infants in the first month of life are capable of exerting limited control over several action elements that function as precursors to visually guided reaching. Soon after birth, infants engage in pre-reaching, which involves making arm movements in the direction of objects. In addition, at this level, infants actively look at an object placed in front of the face. An infant is capable of making wobbly adjustments of the head to track an object that moves slowly within his line of vision. In addition, a baby is also capable of various reflex actions, such as the palmar reflex, in which pressure on the hand prompts the infant to close her fingers together. In each of these reflex actions, a situation or object must be made available to the child (e.g., an object in front of the eyes; a situation placing the body in a particular position).

Beginning at about 7 weeks of age, infants gain the capacity to construct reflex mappings (Rf2), which consist of active coordinations of two or more single reflexes. At this level, for example, an infant coordinates two or more simple movements into short swiping movements toward a seen object. Such swipes at this age tend to be rigid and ballistic motions that are poorly coordinated for grasping or touching objects. Over the next month, infants gain the capacity to coordinate multiple reflex mappings into reflex systems (Rf3). As a result, arm movements are smoother but still poorly coordinated. In highly supportive contexts, depending upon the precise placement of the target and the child's posture, infants sometimes hit their targets.

At around 15–17 weeks of age, infants gain the capacity to coordinate two reflex systems into a system of reflex systems (Rf4/Sm1). Systems of reflex systems are also the first level of the next broad tier of development, because they engender sensorimotor actions (Sm1). Sensorimotor actions consist of single more highly controlled actions on objects in the environment. Unlike reflex acts, sensorimotor actions are more modulated by the child, with less need for activation by environmental events. Using sensorimotor actions, in high support contexts, an infant can produce the first successful reaches. When an infant's posture is supported, she is capable of directing arm movements toward a seen object such as an object moving toward her. Initial movements are generally jerky, consisting of multiple action segments that do not follow a straight line. At this level, although an infant can reach for an object while looking at it, looking and reaching are not yet fully differentiated. The child must already be in the process of looking at the object to reach for it. In so doing, she looks mainly at the object and not at her arm. As such, looking operates primarily to trigger movement. The infant does not yet map variations in arm extension to variations in looking in a controlled and coordinated way.

Over the next several months, within the level of single sensorimotor acts, looking and reaching become increasingly differentiated and coordinated. In one study, after watching an object moving back and forth in a slow and constant motion, 5-month-old infants were able to reach for and intercept the moving object. In so doing, the infant exhibits a degree of coordination of looking and reaching in order to predict the trajectory of the object. In another study, 6-month-old infants were

presented with an object that moved toward them from one of two corners of a stimulus display. As the object moved within reach, it either continued to move along its linear trajectory, or else it turned in a 90-degree angle and continued movement. On trials when the object switched directions, infants moved their heads and reaches in the direction of the anticipated path of the object. This study indicates further visual-motor planning in the reaching of 6-month-olds.

Although reaching in 6-month-olds involves the simultaneous use of looking and reaching within the same object-directed action, it is not until the onset of sensorimotor mappings (Sm2), beginning around 7–8 months of age, that infants are fully able to coordinate distinct acts of looking and reaching in relation to each other. At this level, infants can begin to map variations in looking with variations in reaching. For example, an infant can reach for an object in order to bring it in front of the face and look at some aspect of the object. Similarly, a child can look at a moving object and map changes in the movement of his or her hand to changes in the movement of the object. In addition, infants can detour their reaches around barriers placed between themselves and target objects. For example, if an adult attempts to block a child's reach toward an object, the infant can redirect his action around the obstacle. From this point onward, visually guided reaching becomes increasingly smooth and deployed for more complex purposes. Beginning around 11–12 months, infants become capable of coordinating two or more sensorimotor mappings into a sensorimotor system (Sm3). At this point, infants are capable of using multiple coordinated acts of looking and reaching in order to explore an object from a variety of angles, as in Piaget's descriptions of a 1-year-old's systematic variation of the position and orientation of a toy in order to see how to get it through the bars of a crib or how to make it fall in different ways.

Nativism and the question of innate abilities in infancy

Challenges to a constructivist model of infant development have also come in the form of neo-nativist claims that infants are born with innate rules or abilities for particular conceptual domains. For example, with regard to language development, Noam Chomsky has claimed that deep structured rules of syntax are innate. More recently, such claims have also been made for concepts such as gravity and inertia, space, numerical addition. From this view, certain foundational abilities are not constructed gradually in development, but are instead present at birth.

An illustrative case in point concerns recent work on the development of object permanence. Piaget maintained that infants gradually construct an understanding that objects continue to exist even while absent from sight, sound, and touch. He argued that this ability undergoes transformation as infants coordinate early grasping and looking schemes into more complex schemes for understanding how objects can behave, as described above. For example, at about 6 months, infants are able to retrieve a partially hidden object, but fail to retrieve a fully hidden object, even when they have seen the object being hidden. A key transition occurs a few months later, when infants begin to coordinate two schemes to enable search for fully hidden objects. At this point, an infant removes a cover in order to retrieve a rattle that she has seen hidden under it, making a major advance in object permanence. Children's understanding of object permanence continues to develop throughout the sensorimotor stage and beyond.

A well-known challenge to this constructivist view comes from work by Baillargeon (1987). Infants from 3 to 5 months of age were habituated to the sight of a small door that swung upward from a flat position (the top of the door facing the child) in a 180-degree arc to lie flat again on a solid surface (the top now facing away from the child). They were then shown two scenes involving objects placed behind the rotating door. In one scene, called the possible event, the door swung up but stopped at the object. In the impossible event, the object was removed surreptitiously and the door appeared to swing right through the space occupied by the object. Infants as young as 3 to 4 months dishabituated to the impossible event to a greater degree than they did to the possible event. Baillargeon interpreted this behavior as evidence for object permanence and concluded that infants achieve it four to five months earlier than Piaget had reported.

Based on such studies, neo-nativists often offer interpretations that proceed from what might be called an argument from precocity. They argue that if one can demonstrate behaviors that are an index of a given concept (such as object permanence) at an age much earlier than reported in previous work, then the concept in question is likely to be innate. Such arguments are seriously flawed by the failure of researchers to assess the full range of variability involved in the developmental phenomenon. Evidence that infants look longer at the impossible versus possible display is interesting – even fascinating! An interpretation that such evidence indicates object permanence, however, suffers major flaws. Firstly, it implies that object permanence consists of a singular, monolithic, or abstracted ability, rather than a capacity that, like all developing skills, takes different forms over time. Secondly, the action taken to indicate object permanence – looking time – is very simple and requires very little responding by the infant. What the infant actually can do with the stimulus

display is at best unclear. Thirdly, differences in looking are assessed in a complex task that richly supports the baby's action (viz., a visuospatial field involving moving objects exhibiting Gestalt properties of good or bad form). Such rich perceptual information raises the question of whether such tasks measure perceptual processing rather than cognitive concepts.

Researchers are beginning to conduct studies that address these issues. A series of studies has examined the question of whether dishabituation to the impossible display in Baillargeon's paradigm occurs because infants understand the possibility or impossibility of the events observed, or because of the relative novelty or familiarity of the stimulus display (Bogartz, 2000). In a series of studies with infants ranging from 4 to 8 months of age, researchers varied the extent to which infants were familiarized with the various possible and impossible displays used in their study. They reported evidence that infant looking time reflected preferences for novelty and familiarity, and did not indicate understanding of the possibility or impossibility of a given display. Regardless of whose findings are ultimately supported by future research, the main point is that skills emerge over time, not at a single point in development: for a reliable sense of the developmental course of any given skill, children's actions must be assessed across a broad range of ages, behaviors, tasks, and assessment conditions.

Extending the paths: webs of representational development

As Table 1 (points III and IV) indicates, research conducted over the past three decades underscores the idea that unevenness in the emergence of skills is the rule rather than the exception in development. Skills from different conceptual domains develop relatively independent of each other, moving through their own developmental trajectories. Development takes place in a multidirectional web of pathways rather than a unidirectional ladder – a metaphor depicted in Figure 2. Developing skills do not move in a fixed order of steps in a single direction, but they develop in multiple directions along multiple strands that weave in and out of each other in ontogenesis. The developmental web portrays variability in developing skills within individuals, not only between them. For development in an individual child, different strands represent divergent pathways in the development of skills for different tasks or conceptual domains. For example, the development of addition and subtraction skills might occupy one strand, skills for producing stories another, and skills for reading words still another. As such, the developmental web provides a metaphor for understanding how different skills develop through diverging and converging pathways toward or away from different endpoints.

Source: adapted from K. W. Fischer and T. R. Bidell (1998). Dynamic development of psychological structures in action and thought. In R. M. Lerner, ed., *Handbook of Child Psychology*, Vol. I: *Theoretical Models of Human Development*, 5th edn. New York: Wiley, pp. 467–56.

Figure 2. The developmental web, which provides a metaphor for understanding development in terms of multiple divergent and converging paths. Strands of development represent different skills in individual children, or different trajectories of the same skills in different children.

According to dynamic skill theory, there are no generalized or 'all-purpose' skills. As a result, a precise analysis of developmental changes in a skill can be performed only within particular conceptual domains, tasks, and social contexts. Figure 3 depicts pathways through which many American and Western European children pass as they construct representational skills for telling stories about nice and mean social interactions. The pathways depicted are meant to illustrate the types of trajectories through which skills at the representational level develop within a given task domain. While the pathways depicted may generalize to the development of related skills in similar children (e.g., stories involving similar content), no assumption is made that the sequences necessarily generalize beyond the specified task domain, social group, and assessment contexts. Typically, skills do not spontaneously generalize to different domains and contexts. Generalization of skills can and does occur, but it requires actions linking existing skills to new content, domains, and/or contexts.

Figure 3 was derived from a series of studies conducted by Fischer and his colleagues (Fischer & Bidell, 1998; Lamborn, Fischer, & Pipp, 1994) who assessed children's story-telling skills in highly supportive contexts. To support children's capacity to function at their optimal levels, using dolls and props, adults modeled stories of different levels of complexity about characters who acted nice or mean toward one another. Children then told or acted out the stories modeled by the adult. In Figure 3, each diagram of *YOU* or *ME* acting *NICE* or *MEAN* represents a story exhibiting a certain structure. In skill theory, beginning around 18–24 months of age, children gain the capacity to coordinate two sensorimotor systems into a system of sensorimotor systems, which is equivalent to a single representation (Sm4/Rp1). In a single representation, a child uses one sensorimotor system (e.g., moving a doll or uttering a word) to stand for or represent a single concrete meaning (e.g., the movement of a doll represents the act of walking). At the level of single representations, two-year-old children tell a story about a character who exhibits a single *NICE* or *MEAN* action. For example, a child makes a doll representing *YOU* or *ME* act nice (e.g., by offering candy to another doll) or mean (e.g., by knocking another doll down).

Stories about nice and mean interactions function as starting points for two trajectories in different (albeit related) interpersonal domains (nice and mean, respectively). At the second row, these two strands of development begin to come together as children gain the capacity to shift the focus of their attention between a single *NICE* representation and a single *MEAN* representation. At this step, a 2- to 3-year-old tells part of a story about a nice interaction and another separate part of a story about a mean interaction. Note that separate *NICE* and *MEAN* representations are juxtaposed and not yet fully coordinated. A child, for example, makes one doll give candy to a second doll, and then, later in the story, makes one of the dolls act in a mean way, without connecting the two events.

With the stories in the third row, children can move in three different directions along the developmental web. All three directions involve skills at the level of representational mappings (Rp2), beginning around 3.5 to 4.5 years of age, in which children fully coordinate two representations in terms of a relationship such as reciprocity, causality, temporality, etc. Moving along the *NICE* strand, a child tells a story involving reciprocal nice actions (e.g., one character gives candy to another, who returns the favor with a hug). Similarly, moving along the *MEAN* strand, a child tells a story involving reciprocal mean actions. In the central strand, bringing *NICE* and *MEAN* together, a child tells a story in which a *MEAN* act is opposed by a *NICE* act, or vice versa. Within the level of representational mappings, children tell increasingly complex stories by stringing together multiple *NICE* or *MEAN* representations in different ways. This is represented by the story structures depicted at Steps 4, 5, and 6.

At Step 7, which arises around 6–7 years of age, children coordinate two representational mappings into a higher order representational system (Rp3). A child is able to construct a fully coordinated understanding of

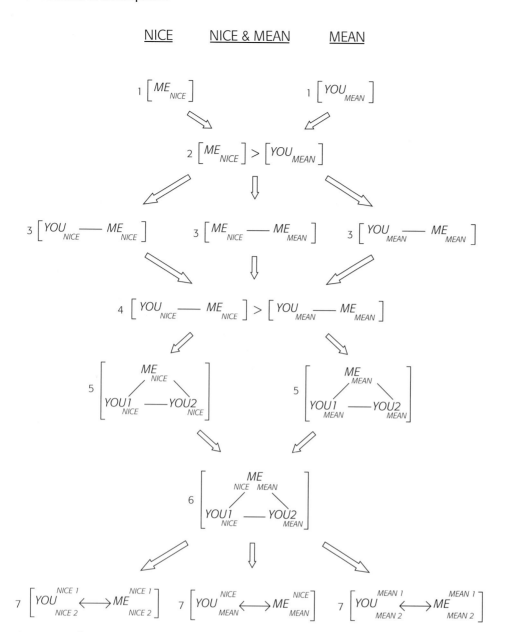

Figure 3. Developmental web for nice and mean social interactions. The numbers to the left of each set of brackets indicate the complexity ordering of the skill structures. The words inside each set of brackets indicate a skill structure.

how one concrete relationship between *NICE* and *MEAN* maps onto another such concrete relationship. For example, a child acts out a story in which one doll invites another doll to play (*NICE*), while playfully slapping the other doll on the arm (*MEAN*); the other doll responds by accepting the invitation to play (*NICE*), but by sternly saying that the hitting must stop (*MEAN*). In this example, a child understands how one concrete relation (e.g., asking me to play while you teasingly hit me) is related to another (i.e., I'll play but only if you stop hitting). The ability to construct representational systems underlies children's capacities to perform various Piagetian tasks at the level of concrete operations (e.g., conservation, seriation, transitivity,

etc.). Figure 3 specifies the structure of three types of stories involving *NICE* and *MEAN* interactions at the level of representational systems.

As indicated in Table 2, around 10–11 years of age, pre-adolescents enter a new tier of development marked by the emergence of abstractions. Abstractions refer to generalized and intangible aspects of events, people, or things. Beginning around 10–11 years, in high support contexts, children gain the capacity to intercoordinate two concrete representational systems into a system of representational systems, which entails a single abstraction (Ab1). A child 'abstracts' across or generalizes what is common about at least two concrete descriptions of an event. For example, given two concrete stories depicting separate acts of kindness from one person to another (e.g., one child gives his lunch to another who forgot his; a student helps another study for a test when she wanted to go out and play), an 11-year-old can 'abstract' across these two stories and identify what is common to them: "Kindness is helping somebody in need, even if they can't help in return." Prior to this age, children have difficulty separating intangible from concrete aspects of events.

Beginning around 14–15 years of age, adolescents gain the capacity to coordinate two abstractions into an abstract mapping (Ab2). At this level, an individual can represent the relation between two abstract concepts. For example, an adolescent can understand the complex concept of a 'social lie' in terms of the contrast between 'honesty' and 'kindness,' or he might offer an explanation like "Honesty is telling the truth about something even when it is easier to lie. Kindness is helping someone in need. In a social lie, a person gives up honesty in order to be kind." With further development, beginning around 18–20 years of age, young adults become capable of coordinating two abstract mappings into a single abstract system (Ab3). At this level, an individual can form an abstract conception of 'constructive criticism' in terms of the intercoordination of two abstract aspects of 'honesty' and two abstract elements of 'kindness': "Constructive criticism combines two types of honesty and two types of kindness. It involves being honest about praising another person's accomplishments while criticizing his shortfalls. This expresses kindness as one helps to improve another person's skills while being compassionate in not hurting his feelings." At the final level, beginning at about 25 years of age, a person interprets multiple systems of abstractions in terms of general principles, such as a broad moral principle of treating others justly.

The epigenesis of psychological structures

As indicated in Table 1 (point V), theorists and researchers have criticized several aspects of Piaget's constructivist view of developmental change. In this section, we describe an epigenetic model of cognitive change that builds upon Piaget's model and addresses these issues. Traditionally, many have assumed that development proceeds as a result of two independent processes: heredity and learning. Recent theory and research has called into question the separability of genes and environments as causes of development. Researchers have examined development as an epigenetic process in which cognitive skills emerge

over time rather than being predetermined by genes or transmitted from social experience. From an epigenetic view, organisms function together with their environments as multi-leveled systems, the elements of which necessarily coact (affect each other) in the production of any set of actions, thoughts, or feelings.

One can differentiate among three broad levels of individual-environment processes. 'Biogenetic systems' refers to all biological systems below the level of the experiencing person. Biogenetic systems are multi-leveled with lower-order systems embedded in higher-order systems. For example, DNA is located in chromosomes, which themselves are hierarchically nested within cell nuclei, the cell matrix, cells, tissues, organs, organ systems, and the organism as a whole. 'Individual-agentic systems' refers to processes at the psychological level of action and experience – individual agents controlling actions. Such processes correspond to psychological systems of acting, thinking, and feeling and the control structures (skills) that regulate them. Although individual-agentic processes are themselves biological, they have emergent properties (e.g., meaning, control) that are absent in their lower-level constituents. Such systems function within larger sociocultural systems (the third level), which consist of patterns of interaction between persons and the shared symbolic meanings distributed among members of a given community. Symbol systems, particularly words, represent conventionalized meanings common to a linguistic community.

The main proposition of an epigenetic view holds that anatomical and psychological structures emerge as a result of coactions that occur over time both within and between these broad sets of systems. Coaction refers to the ways in which component systems act together mutually to regulate and influence each other's functioning. Component systems coact both horizontally (e.g., gene with gene; cell-cell; organ-organ; organism-organism) and vertically (e.g., biogenetic with individual-agentic). For example, while gene action affects the functioning of the components of the cell, changes in the cell matrix also influence gene action. The direction of influence of component systems is dynamical and bidirectional rather than linear or unidirectional. The following contains a brief outline of how biogenetic, individual-agentic, and sociocultural systems necessarily coact in the development of cognitive skills.

Biogenetic processes

Developmental changes in biogenetic systems are necessary for the emergence of new levels of cognitive skill. Recent research suggests that brain development exhibits discontinuities that are related to the emergence of new psychological skills. Research on the development of cortical (electroencephalogram or EEG) activity, synaptic density, and head growth provides evidence for discontinuities in brain development for at least twelve of the thirteen levels of skill development listed in Table 2. Little research exists to test hypothesized brain-behavior relations for the thirteenth level. For example, in a series of studies, American, Swedish, and Japanese infants demonstrated spurts in brain growth (EEG and head circumference) at approximately 3–4, 7–8, 10–11, and 15–18 weeks of development and at 2–4, 6–8, 11–13, and 24 months. As indicated in Figure 4, studies measuring EEG activity in various cortical regions show discontinuities at approximately 2, 4, 8, 12, 15, and 19 years of age. There are many different brain systems and different classes of behavior that develop relatively independently of each other, but research suggests patterns of concurrent growth over time in related systems, especially during rapid growth of new skills. For example, Ann-Marie Bell and Nathan Fox assessed the relations between growth functions for EEG activity and the development of object search, vocal imitation, and crawling skills in infancy. They found that for many individual infants between 8 and 12 months of age, connections between specific cortical regions involving planning, vision, and control of movement exhibited a surge while the infants were mastering crawling. The surge disappeared after they had become skilled crawlers.

Within the representational and abstract tiers of development, transformation from one level of skill to another (e.g., from single sets to mappings, etc.) seems to be supported by the production of new systems of neural networks that link different brain regions. Matousek & Petersen (1973) examined changes in EEG activity for each of four cortical brain regions (viz., frontal, occipital/parietal, temporal, and central) in children and adolescents. Their results suggested that for the representational (2–10 years of age) and abstract tiers (10–20 years), transitions to different levels within a developmental tier are marked by cyclic changes in brain activity in different cortical regions. Within this cycle, a new tier emerges with a maximal spurt in the frontal cortex: the first level is marked by a maximal spurt in the occipital-parietal region, one in the temporal region marks the second level, and one in the central region marks the third. Another maximal surge in the frontal region marks the onset of the next broad tier of development. These changes illustrate the systematic relations between movement through skill levels and cyclic changes in brain activity.

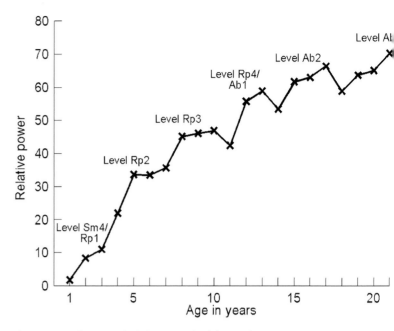

Figure 4. Development of relative power in alpha EEG in occipital-parietal area in Swedish children and adolescents. Relative power is the amplitude in microvolts of absolute energy in the alpha band divided by the sum of amplitudes in all bands. From Matousek & Petersen (1973).

Individual-agentic processes

Biogenetic changes are necessary but not sufficient for the emergence of new skill levels. While any given level of skill requires a requisite level of brain development, skill development also requires action at the level of individual children. For novel skills to develop, individual children must perform controlled acts that coordinate lower-level skill components into higher-order structures. Fischer and his colleagues have identified a series of transformation rules that describe the active processes by which children coordinate skill elements into higher-order structures. Substitution occurs as children perform a previously constructed skill on a novel object. For example, an infant who has acquired the skill of grasping a rattle might use this new skill to grasp a small teddy bear. Shift-of-focus occurs when children redirect their attention from one component of skilled activity to another. Children often use shift-of-focus to reduce task demands. In such contexts, children break down complex tasks into simpler sub-tasks and then shift the focus of their attention from one task element to another. For example, 3-year-olds, who are generally unable to imitate a story modeled for them at the level of representational mappings (e.g., Bobby acts mean to Sally because Sally was mean to him), can simplify the story by breaking it into two separate parts and directing attention first to one part (Sally is mean to Bobby), and then the other (Bobby is mean to Sally). Such shifts function as initial attempts to integrate skill components beyond a child's immediate grasp.

Children can use compounding to construct more complex skills within a given developmental level. A child links a series of skill elements at the same developmental level. For example, 5-year-olds often tell stories by combining in a single story characters that act out distinct roles, such as doctor, patient, and nurse. Compounding involves integration among skill elements without re-organizing them to form a higher-level skill. The only change mechanism that produces movement to a new level or developmental tier is intercoordination. Using intercoordination, children go beyond merely compounding together skill elements. Instead, skill elements become reciprocally coordinated to form a single higher-level skill. For example, as indicated in Figure 3, when telling stories about nice and mean interactions, children move from row 2 (shift-of-focus between representations) to row 3 (representational mappings) by connecting two representations in terms of some type of relation (e.g., "Bobby gave Sally a kiss because Sally gave him her lunch"). In this way, higher-order skills emerge from the intercoordination of lower-order components.

Another important process by which individuals create new knowledge involves a process called bridging (Granott, Fischer, & Parziale, 2002). Bridging arises from the capacity to function simultaneously at two developmental levels in a one-skill domain. It occurs when individuals establish a target level of skill and then direct their knowledge construction toward that target. In so doing, the to-be-constructed level of understanding functions as a shell for constructing a new level of knowledge. The shell helps to bridge one level to a higher level of understanding. For example, in a study in which a pair of adults observed the operation of self-moving robots in order to figure out how they worked, one person experimented with a robot by putting his hand around it in different positions. His partner noted: "Looks like we got a reaction there." In using the word reaction, the partner made a vague reference to cause and effect, but did not provide specifics about the cause or effect. By speaking of a reaction, he created a bridging shell postulating a link between two unknown variables, **X** and **Y**, related to each other:

$$\left[(\mathbf{X}) \; \frac{\text{reaction}}{\text{SHELL}} \; (\mathbf{Y}) \right]$$

Further observations allowed the observers to establish a causal connection that filled in the shell to create a

mapping (i.e., when the robot moves under a shadow, its behavior changes):

$$\begin{bmatrix} \textbf{UNDER} & \dfrac{\text{reaction}}{} & \textbf{CHANGES} \\ \textbf{SHADOW} & & \textbf{BEHAVIOR} \end{bmatrix}$$

As such, shells function as a kind of self-scaffold that helps to explain how individuals bootstrap their knowledge to new developmental levels based upon existing lower-level knowledge.

Sociocultural processes

While individual children must actively coordinate lower-level components to produce new skills, they act in a rich sociocultural environment, not in a vacuum. Interactions with others play a direct role in the formation of psychological structures in at least two ways. Firstly, in face-to-face social interaction, partners engage in continuous reciprocal communication. In so doing, both partners are simultaneously active as senders and receivers of meanings. As a result, they continuously adjust their ongoing actions, thoughts, and feelings to each other. In so doing, neither partner exerts complete control over his behavior, but instead they co-regulate each other's actions. In this way, social partners function as actual parts of each other's behavior.

Secondly, in constructing new knowledge, children work with others using cultural meanings, tools, and artifacts. As children's thinking becomes mediated by cultural tools – particularly language and other symbolic vehicles that represent shared cultural meanings – their thinking develops in directions defined by cultural meanings and practices. In this way, sociocultural systems play an active role in the constitution of cognitive skills.

Co-regulated interaction with children, especially when it involves sign-mediated guidance by adults or more accomplished peers, raises children's thinking to levels that they would be incapable of sustaining alone. It is from this social matrix that children construct novel skills. Rogoff (1998) has offered the concept of participatory appropriation to refer to the ways in which individuals seize novel meanings from their participation in social interaction. Appropriation occurs as children coordinate lower-level meanings into higher-order skills in ways that are structured by their interactions with social and cultural agents. As such, appropriation involves more than simply incorporating other people's meanings. When a child appropriates meanings from her interactions with others, she transforms those meanings in ways that are biased by her existing skills and meanings.

This process can be illustrated by a study on the development of a child's causal understanding in the context of parent to child story telling. The study traced the production and resolution of question–answer sequences as a parent read a 4-year-old boy the same children's book over the course of six evenings. In four of the six sessions, the boy asked questions about a part of the story in which a character (Pig Won't) caused soap suds to splash in his eye and sting it. In the second session, the following dialogue occurred:

CHILD: Why does it sting?
PARENT: Well *because when soap gets on your, in your eyes, it stings.*

In this reading, the parent responds to the child's question by drawing a causal relationship (a representational mapping) between the action of the soap ("When soap gets in your eyes") and a consequential result ("it stings"). The question of stings was next raised in the third reading session:

CHILD: Why does it sting?
PARENT: Why DOES it sting?
CHILD: *'Cause it hurts.*
PARENT: Soap hurts your eyes.

In this sequence, we again see the child trying to represent the cause of the stinging. When the parent prompted the child to elaborate his own thinking, the child responded at the level of single representations ("'Cause it hurts"). The child has not yet differentiated the cause from the effect in this concrete incident. By the sixth session, the following interchange occurred:

CHILD: That's sad.
PARENT: Why is that sad?
CHILD: It's sad that Pig Will has stings.
PARENT: Yeah? Why? Why is it sad that it stings?
CHILD: *Because when soap gets in your eyes it stings.*
PARENT: Right.
CHILD: When bumble bee stings, me. Does that stings?
PARENT: When bumble bees sting do they sting? You betcha' it does.
CHILD: Why?
PARENT: Well when bumble bees put their little stinger inside of you, it pierces the skin, and it stings.

Here, the child responds to the adult's question with virtually the same representational mapping that was produced by the adult in earlier sessions. These exchanges illustrate a series of points about the role of sociocultural systems in development. Firstly, the exchanges involve co-regulated interactions that function to raise the child's understanding to levels that he could not sustain alone. Secondly, the interaction is mediated by cultural tools, practices, and artifacts (e.g., words, causal story content, bedtime reading rituals, use of books). Thirdly, through the verbal exchanges, the child is able to appropriate a novel meaning. He does so by coordinating lower-level skill elements (single representations) into a higher-order meaning (representational mapping). Thereafter, the child initiates an act of substitution involving the application of his new causal knowledge about 'stinging' to new content (i.e., bee stings). These exchanges illustrate how a child's novel meanings are jointly created but individually appropriated though individual acts of hierarchic integration.

Conclusions

The new constructivism in cognitive development builds upon central tenets of Piaget's thinking. Cognitive development involves qualitative and quantitative changes in psychological structures. However, the new constructivism maintains that transformations in psychological structures are tied to specific tasks, domains, and social contexts. While retaining the principle that individual action functions as a central organizer of cognitive change, the new constructivism more fully embraces the joining of biological, psychological, and sociocultural processes as coacting causes of cognitive change.

Future research is needed to address several questions. Firstly, to the extent that skills are defined in terms of tasks and domains, what are the boundaries of developing skills? Is it possible to specify a relatively distinct set of psychological skills that cluster together in development for a particular domain? Secondly, given that change processes involve bidirectional coactions among vertical and horizontal dimensions of organism-environment systems, how do these coactions move development? How do different component systems affect each other? Thirdly, although not discussed at length in this entry, the new constructivism is built around the premise that cognitive development is inextricably linked to socioemotional development. Emotion is a central organizer of all behavior, intentional or otherwise. Thus, a major contemporary question is, "How do emotional and cognitive processes coact in the creation of developmental pathways?"

See also:
Understanding ontogenetic development: debates about the nature of the epigenetic process; Theories of the child's mind; Dynamical systems approaches; Cognitive development in infancy; Cognitive development beyond infancy; Motor development; Social development; Emotional development; Moral development; Brain and behavioral development (II): cortical; Imitation; Prehension; Socialization; Cognitive neuroscience; Education; James Mark Baldwin; Jean Piaget; Lev S. Vygotsky

Further reading

Case, R. and Okamoto, Y. (1996). The role of central conceptual structures in the development of children's thought. *Monographs of the Society for Research in Child Development*, Serial 246, Volume 61, Number 1–2.

Dawson, G. and Fischer, K. W. (eds.) (1994). *Human Behavior and the Developing Brain*. New York: Guildford Press.

Fischer, K. W., Yan, Z. and Stewart, J. (2003). Adult cognitive development: dynamics in the development web. In J. Valsiner and K. J. Connolly (eds.), *Handbook of Developmental Psychology*. London: Sage, pp. 491–516.

Ethological theories

JOHAN J. BOLHUIS & JERRY A. HOGAN

Introduction

Ethology was originally defined as the study of animal behavior within the framework put forward by Lorenz (1937) and Tinbergen (1951). Later, 'ethology' was used more generally to describe any scientific study of the behavior of animals in relation to their natural environment. A modern inclusive term for the discipline is behavioral biology.

Classical ethological theory had surprisingly little to say about the development of behavior, in spite of the fact that Lorenz (1903–1989) himself had earlier (1935) published a landmark paper on the concept of imprinting. Tinbergen's (1951) book, for example, has only one short chapter on development, and only one paragraph on imprinting. Lehrman (1953), in his influential critique of ethological theory, pointed out this neglect of developmental questions, which subsequently led many ethological workers to consider problems of development (Kruijt, 1964). It also led Tinbergen (1963), ten years later, to reformulate his views on the aims of ethology. In this seminal paper, he stated that ethologists should aim to answer four major questions about behavior: its causation, function, evolution, and development. Although Tinbergen (1907–1988) emphasized that understanding behavior required addressing all four of these questions, we shall only discuss some of the major contributions ethologists and other behavioral biologists have made to the study of development. We shall see that many concepts and findings concerning behavioral development in animals have had important consequences for the study of human development.

Lorenz and the nature-nurture debate

In his early papers, Lorenz postulated that behavior could be considered a mixture of innate and acquired

Full references for works cited in this entry which do not appear in the Bibliography can be found in one of the reference links in either Bolhuis & Hogan (1999), Hogan (2001), or Johnson & Bolhuis (2000).

elements (*Instinkt-Dressur-Verschrankung*: intercalation of fixed action patterns and learning), and that analysis of the development of the innate elements (fixed action patterns) was a matter for embryologists. In reaction to Lehrman's (1953) critique of ethological theory, Lorenz (1965) changed his formulation somewhat, and argued that the information necessary for a behavior element to be adapted to its species' environment can only come from two sources: from information stored in the genes or from an interaction between the individual and its environment. This formulation also met with considerable criticism from many who insisted that development consisted of a more complex dynamic. Gottlieb (1997) discusses many aspects of this debate, and we have recently republished some of the original papers (Bolhuis & Hogan, 1999). Here, we will mention only two important aspects of the debate.

To begin with, Lehrman (1970) pointed out that he and Lorenz were really interested in two different problems: Lehrman was interested in studying the effects of all types of experience on all types of behavior at all stages of development, very much from a causal perspective, whereas Lorenz was interested only in studying the effects of functional experience on behavior mechanisms at the stage of development at which they begin to function as modes of adaptation to the environment. Hogan (1988, 2001) has argued that both these viewpoints are equally legitimate, but that Lorenz's functional criterion corresponds to the way most people think about development. Nonetheless, it is essential not to confuse causal and functional viewpoints (cf. Hogan, 1994a; Bolhuis & Macphail, 2001). In this entry, we consider development from a causal perspective.

A second aspect of the debate is that even behavior patterns that owe their adaptedness to genetic information require interaction with the environment in order to develop in the individual. As Lehrman (1953) states: "The interaction out of which the organism develops is *not* one, as is so often said, between heredity and environment. It is between *organism* and environment! And the organism is different at each different stage of its development" (p. 345). We give examples later that illustrate this interactionist interpretation of development.

Imprinting: sensitive periods and irreversibility

Filial imprinting is the process through which early social preferences become restricted to a particular stimulus, or class of stimuli, as a result of exposure to that stimulus. This early learning phenomenon is often regarded as a classic example of a developmental process involving sensitive periods. The idea of a sensitive period has been extremely important (and controversial) in the study of behavioral development. Here we adopt the definition given by Bateson & Hinde (1987): "The sensitive period concept implies a phase of great susceptibility [to certain types of experience] preceded and followed by lower sensitivity, with relatively gradual transitions" (p. 20). Lorenz and other authors use the term 'critical period', borrowed from embryology, for this concept. However, Bateson & Hinde argue that the periods of increased sensitivity are not sharply defined, and consequently they suggested the use of the term 'sensitive period,' which is now widely (but by no means universally) used. We shall discuss recent evidence concerning sensitive periods in the context of filial imprinting.

Early imprinting researchers concluded that there was a narrow sensitive period within which imprinting could occur. This sensitive period was thought to occur within the first twenty-four hours after hatching in ducklings and chicks, and to last for not more than a few hours. Subsequent research has demonstrated that the sensitive period for filial imprinting is not so restricted in these species (Bateson, 1979; Bolhuis, 1991).

In the analysis of sensitive periods, it is important to distinguish between the onset and the decline of increased sensitivity, as there are often different causal factors for these two events. In filial imprinting, it is likely that the onset of the sensitive period can be explained in terms of immediate physiological factors, such as increases in visual efficiency and in motor ability in precocial birds some time after hatching. Different causal factors are thought to be involved at the end of the sensitive period for imprinting. Sluckin & Salzen (1961) suggested that the ability to imprint comes to an end after the animal has developed a social preference for a certain stimulus as a result of exposure to that stimulus. The animal will stay close to the familiar object and avoid novel ones; it will thus receive very little exposure to a novel stimulus and there will be little opportunity for further imprinting. This interpretation implies that imprinting will remain possible if an appropriate stimulus is not presented. Indeed, chicks that are reared in isolation retain the ability to imprint for longer than socially reared chicks. An apparent decline in sensitivity in isolated chicks can be explained as resulting from the animals' imprinting to stationary visual aspects of the rearing environment (Bateson, 1964). Thus, it is the imprinting process itself that brings the sensitive period to an end.

The conventional view of the causes of sensitive periods in a number of disciplines is that they are due to some sort of physiological clock mechanism (Bornstein, 1987; Rauschecker & Marler, 1987). The evidence from filial imprinting studies, however, is not consistent with an internal clock model, but requires instead that experience with the imprinting stimulus is the causal factor for the end of the sensitive period. Bateson (1987) proposed just such a model: the competitive exclusion model. He pointed out that neural growth is associated with particular sensory input from the environment. His model assumes that there is a limited capacity for such growth to impinge upon the systems that are responsible for the execution of the behavior involved (e.g., approach, in the case of imprinting). Input from different stimuli 'competes' for access to these executive systems. Once neural growth associated with a certain stimulus develops control of the executive systems, subsequent stimuli will be less able to gain access to these systems. Furthermore, insofar as these early neural connections are permanent (Shatz, 1992; Hogan, 2001, pp. 263–269), this interpretation also explains the general irreversibility of many aspects of early learning. Evidence from recent studies of sexual imprinting (Bischof, 1994) and bird song learning (Marler, 1991; Nelson, 1997) is also consistent with an experience-dependent end to the sensitive period. These results all show that it is necessary to investigate the causes for both the beginning and end of any sensitive period before reaching conclusions about the mechanisms responsible.

Perceptual development as a continuous interactive process

In his classic paper on imprinting, Lorenz (1935) proposed the concept of 'schema,' which is a kind of perceptual mechanism that 'recognizes' certain objects (Hogan, 1988). In the development of a social bond between parents and young, Lorenz noted that in certain bird species (such as the curlew, *Numenius arquata*) the newly hatched chicks came equipped with a schema of the parent that he considered to be 'innate,' while in others (such as the greylag goose, *Anser anser*) the schema of the parent developed as a result of specific experience (imprinting). It is now known that the development of almost all perceptual mechanisms that have been studied requires some kind of experience. In some cases the experience that is necessary is tightly constrained, and the animal is predisposed to be affected by very specific classes of stimuli, while in other cases the experience can be quite general. We shall discuss examples of both kinds.

Most songbird species need to learn their song from a tutor male (Thorpe, 1961; Marler, 1976; Nelson, 1997). Under certain circumstances, young males of some species can learn their songs, or at least part of their songs, from tape recordings of tutor songs. When fledgling male song sparrows (*Melospiza melodia*) and swamp sparrows (*Melospiza georgiana*) were exposed to taped songs that consisted of equal numbers of songs of both species, they preferentially learned the songs of their own species. Males of both species are able to sing the songs of the other species. Thus, it appears that they are predisposed to perceive songs of their own species; Marler (1991) called this 'the sensitization of young sparrows to conspecific song' (p. 200). It is noteworthy that many aspects of birdsong learning have been found to be relevant to the development of human language (Marler, 1976; Doupe & Kuhl, 1999). For example, Kuhl and her colleagues have shown that infants less than 6 months of age learn to perceive phonemes unique to their linguistic environment, but that they do not learn to utter these sounds until several months later.

In an extensive series of experiments published between 1975 and 1987, Gottlieb (1997) investigated the mechanisms underlying the preferences that young ducklings of a number of species show for the maternal call of their own species over that of other species. He found that differential behavior toward the species-specific call could already be observed at an early embryonic stage, before the animal itself started to vocalize. However, a post-hatching preference for the conspecific maternal call was only found when the animals received exposure to embryonic contact-contentment calls, played back at the right speed and with a natural variation, within a certain period in development. Thus, the expression of the species-specific preference in ducklings is dependent on particular experience early in development.

The development of filial behavior in the chick involves two perceptual systems that are neurally and behaviorally dissociable (Bolhuis, 1996; Bolhuis & Honey, 1998; Horn, 1985, 1998). On the one hand, there is an effect of experience with particular stimuli (i.e., filial imprinting). On the other hand, there is an emerging predisposition to approach stimuli resembling conspecifics (see Fig. 1). Training with a particular stimulus is not necessary for the predisposition to emerge: the predisposition can emerge in dark-reared chicks, provided that they receive a certain amount of

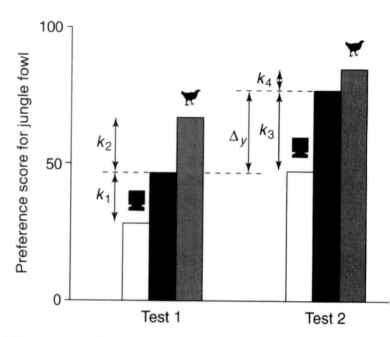

Figure 1. Mean preference scores, expressed as a preference for the stuffed fowl, of chicks previously trained by exposure to a rotating stuffed junglefowl (gray), a rotating red box (white), or exposure to white light (black). Preference scores are defined as: activity when attempting to approach the stuffed jungle fowl divided by total approach activity during the test. Preferences were measured in a simultaneous test either 2 h (Test 1) or 24 h (Test 2) after the end of training. $k1–k4$ represent the differences between the preferences of the trained chicks and the controls; Δy represents the difference in preference between the control chicks at Test 2 and at Test 1. Adapted from Horn (1985), by permission of the Oxford University Press, after Johnson *et al.* (1985).

non-specific stimulation within a certain period in development (Johnson *et al.*, 1989).

The stimulus characteristics of visual stimuli that allow the filial predisposition to be expressed were investigated in tests involving an intact stuffed junglefowl versus a series of increasingly degraded versions of a stuffed junglefowl (Johnson & Horn, 1988). The degraded versions ranged from one where different parts of the model (wings, head, torso, legs) were re-assembled in an unnatural way, to one in which the pelt of a junglefowl had been cut into small pieces that were stuck onto a rotating box. The intact model was preferred only when the degraded object possessed no distinguishable junglefowl features. Further studies showed that the necessary stimuli are not species- or even class-specific: eye-like stimuli are normally important, but other aspects of the stimulus are also sufficient for the expression of the predisposition (Bolhuis, 1996).

There are interesting similarities between the development of face recognition in human infants, and the development of filial preferences in chicks. Newborn infants have been shown to track a moving face-like stimulus more than a stimulus that lacks these features,

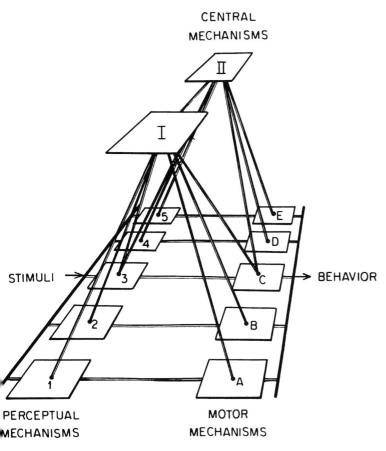

CENTRAL
MECHANISMS

STIMULI → → BEHAVIOR

PERCEPTUAL
MECHANISMS

MOTOR
MECHANISMS

Figure 2. Conception of behavior systems. Stimuli from the external world are analyzed by perceptual mechanisms. Output from the perceptual mechanisms can be integrated by central mechanisms and/or channeled directly to motor mechanisms. The output of the motor mechanisms results in behavior. In this diagram, central mechanism I, perceptual mechanisms 1, 2, and 3, and motor mechanisms A, B, and C form one behavior system; central mechanism II, perceptual mechanisms 3, 4, and 5, and motor mechanisms C, D, and E form a second behavior system. Systems 1-A, 2-B, and so on can also be considered less complex behavior systems. From Hogan, 1988.

or in which these features have been jumbled up. Similarly, in both human infants and young precocial birds, the features of individual objects need to be learned. Once learned, both infants and birds react to unfamiliar objects with species-specific behavior patterns that tend to bring them back to the familiar object or caregiver (Blass, 1999; Johnson & Bolhuis, 2000).

Development of behavior systems

Kruijt (1964), in his classic monograph on the development of social behavior in the junglefowl (*Gallus gallus spadiceus*), suggested that in young chicks – and obviously, in the young of other species as well – many of the motor components of behavior appear as

independent units prior to any opportunity for practice. Only later, often after specific experience, do these motor components become integrated into more complex systems such as hunger, aggression, or sex. Hogan (1988) has generalized this proposal by Kruijt and suggested a framework for the analysis of behavioral development using the concept of behavior system (see Fig. 2). A behavior system consists of different elements: a central mechanism, perceptual mechanisms, and motor mechanisms. These mechanisms are considered to be structures in the central nervous system, and one could also call them cognitive structures. The definition of a behavior system is ". . . any organization of perceptual, central, and motor mechanisms that acts as a unit in some situations" (Hogan 1988, p. 66). According to Hogan, behavioral development is essentially the development of these mechanisms and the changes in the connections among them. Often, these mechanisms and their connections only develop after functional experiences (i.e., experience with the particular stimuli involved, or with the consequences of performing specific motor patterns).

An example of a developing behavior system is the hunger system in the junglefowl chick (Hogan 1971, 1988). This system includes perceptual mechanisms for the recognition of features (e.g., color, shape, size), objects (e.g., grains, mealworms), and functions (food versus non-food). There are also motor mechanisms underlying behavior patterns such as ground scratching and pecking, and there is a central hunger mechanism. Importantly, several of the connections between the mechanisms (shown by dashed lines in Fig. 3) only develop as a result of specific functional experience. For instance, only after a substantial meal will the chick differentiate between food items and non-food items (Hogan-Warburg & Hogan, 1981). On the motor side of the system, a young chick's pecking behavior is not dependent on the level of food deprivation before 3 days of age. Only after the experience of pecking and swallowing some solid object do the two mechanisms become connected, and only then is the level of pecking dependent on the level of food deprivation (Hogan 1984).

A similar phenomenon occurs with respect to suckling in rat pups, kittens, puppies, and human infants (Hinde, 1970, p. 551). For instance, human newborns sucked more when satiated and experimentally aroused than when food-deprived. In the case of rat pups, suckling does not become deprivation-dependent until about two weeks after birth (Hall & Williams, 1983). Unlike with chicks, we do not yet know what experience is needed to connect the suckling motor mechanism with the central hunger mechanism in the rat pup or human newborn.

The development of behavioral structure is not uniform, but may proceed along different pathways for

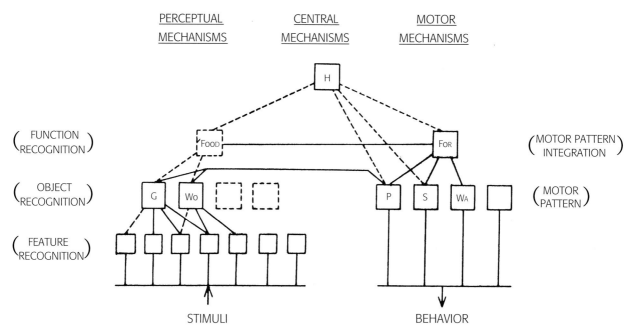

Figure 3. The hunger system of a young chick. Perceptual mechanisms include various feature-recognition mechanisms (such as of color, shape, size, and movement), object-recognition mechanisms (such as grain-like objects and worm-like objects), and a function-recognition mechanism (food). Motor mechanisms include those underlying specific behavior patterns (such as pecking, ground scratching, and walking) and an integrative motor mechanism that could be called foraging. There is also a central hunger mechanism (H). Solid lines indicate mechanisms and connections that develop prefunctionally; dashed lines indicate mechanisms and connections that develop as the result of specific functional experience. From Hogan, 1988.

different behavior systems. For example, dustbathing is a behavior that adult birds of many species frequently engage in. It consists of a sequence of coordinated movements of the wings, feet, head, and body that serve to spread dust through the feathers. The function of this behavior in adult fowl is to remove excess lipids from the feathers and to maintain good feather condition (van Liere & Bokma, 1987). Unlike the development of feeding behavior in rats or chicks, dustbathing is deprivation-dependent as soon as it appears in the animal's behavioral repertoire (Hogan *et al.*, 1991). Thus, in this case, chicks do not require functional experience to connect the motor mechanisms with the central dustbathing mechanism. On the perceptual side, other experiments have shown that initially the chick will perform dustbathing on virtually any kind of surface, including wire mesh, suggesting that the perceptual mechanism and the central mechanism are not yet connected (Vestergaard, Hogan and Krisijt, 1990; Petherick *et al.*, 1995).

The perceptual mechanism itself develops more quickly with some substrates (peat or sand) than with others (wood shavings or wire mesh), which is similar to the development of perceptual mechanisms in song learning (Marler, 1991) and filial predispositions (Bolhuis, 1991). Furthermore, preferences for function-ally unlikely surfaces (in this case a skin of junglefowl

feathers) can be acquired as a result of experience with them (Vestergaard & Hogan, 1992). This is another example of the development of a perceptual mechanism, and one that is not dissimilar to filial imprinting.

Finally, Hogan (2001, pp. 254–257) has discussed how it is possible to consider human language to be a behavior system that is similar in many respects to those we have just discussed. Learning to perceive and produce phonemes has been mentioned above. It is also possible to identify two major central components of the language system: the semantic system (Shelton & Caramazza, 1999) and the syntax system (Chomsky, 1965; Pinker, 1994). The basic lower-order units of the language system are morphemes (words). Numerous studies have shown that the same morphemes can be expressed equally well with auditory-vocal units (normal spoken language) or visual-manual units (sign language). Development of the organization of both the semantic system and the syntax system proceeds in the same way regardless of how the morphemes are expressed.

Attachment theory

Ethological theories and methods have played an important role in the formulation and development of

John Bowlby's (1969, 1991) theory of attachment in humans. This theory was originally developed to explain the behavior of children who had been separated from their mother and raised in a nursery during the Second World War, and was greatly influenced by Lorenz's ideas about imprinting. This is not the place to discuss attachment theory in detail, but we can point out that, in many ways, the attachment system postulated by Bowlby is analogous to the filial behavior system in young birds. In both cases, the newborn infant or chick possesses a number of behavior patterns that keep it in contact with the parent (or other caregiver) and that attract the attention of the parent in the parent's absence. Furthermore, both infant and chick must learn the characteristics of the parent, which is considered to be the formation of a bond between the two. Factors influencing the formation of the bond are also similar, including all the factors we have discussed above such as length of exposure, sensitive periods, irreversibility, and predispositions. Studying the importance of these factors in the human situation has resulted in a large body of literature, some of which has supported the theory, and some not (Rutter, 1991, 2002). The theory itself has been modified to take these results into account, and has also been expanded to include development of attachments throughout life.

Gathering data to test hypotheses about human behavior always presents special challenges because of the ethical issues involved. To study the effects of maternal separation on infant behavior, Harlow (1958), for example, raised infant rhesus monkeys in complete social isolation, which led to horrific effects on the infant's subsequent behavior. Less intrusive methods such as raising infants with other infants (Harlow & Harlow, 1962), or separating infants from their mothers for brief periods of time (Hinde & Spencer-Booth, 1971; Hinde, 1977) led to less dramatic results, but these methods are still unacceptable for human research. Bowlby felt that the best method for studying human development was to observe infants in real-life situations, in much the same way as many ethologists study the behavior of other animals in natural or semi-natural settings.

Much of his theorizing about human attachment was based upon such research carried out by Mary Ainsworth (1913–1999). She and her colleagues (1978) developed a standardized 'Strange Situation' test in which a stranger approaches an infant with and without the parent being present, and various aspects of the infant's behavior are measured. This method is now widely used, and has allowed researchers to characterize specific patterns of attachment and their determinants. Use of basically similar methods has allowed results from both human and other animal studies to be more easily compared, and has led to mutual benefits with respect to both theory (Kraemer, 1992) and methods (Weaver & de Waal, 2002).

Conclusions

Ethology, as a set of theories distinct from those in other disciplines, no longer exists. Nonetheless, many workers trained in the framework of ethology have made important contributions to the study of behavioral development. The debate over the conceptualization of the roles of nature and nurture, ubiquitous in the older literature, has led to a modern synthesis that is generally accepted by all developmental biologists. This can be seen in the studies of filial imprinting and behavior system development that we have reviewed, as well as in studies of sexual imprinting and birdsong development. These studies, in turn, have had an important influence on such topics in child development as early attachment, face recognition, and language development. Students of behavioral biology interested in development are now devoting much of their energy toward investigating aspects of cognition in humans and other animal species using techniques from neuroscience and psychology, as well as the observational and experimental techniques used by the early ethologists. The search for grand theories is likely to continue, but in a much wider context.

See also:
Understanding ontogenetic development: debates about the nature of the epigenetic process; Learning theories; Cross-species comparisons; Observational methods; Ethical considerations in studies with children; The status of the human newborn; Perceptual development; Language development; Development of learning and memory; Face recognition; Cognitive neuroscience; Ethology; John Bowlby

Further reading

Bolhuis, J. J. and Giraldeau, L.-A. (eds.) (2005). *The Behavior of Animals. Mechanisms, Function, and Evolution.* Oxford: Blackwell Publishing.

Doupe, A. J. and Kuhl, P. K. (1999). Birdsong and human speech: common themes and mechanisms. *Annual Review of Neuroscience*, 22, 567–631.

Goldberg S. (2000). *Attachment and Development.* New York: Oxford University Press.

Learning theories

JOHN S. WATSON

Introduction

The normal human transition in cognitive ability from birth to maturity is vast and, as yet, without adequate explanation. During the last century, scientific consensus changed from a view that newborns possess virtually no knowledge of the world or of themselves to a view that they actually possess considerable innate bias that guides their interaction with their physical and social environment. The conception of learning mechanisms that might help explain the dramatic development of competence has undergone considerable change as well.

The idea that learning might play a strong role in development from birth to maturity has existed since the earliest of written history. Herodotus (485–425 BP) recorded in 440 BP concern for the role of learning in children's development of language. The primary alternative to learning is usually stated in terms of the maturation of innate ability. While these opposing notions are of ancient origin, they continue their competition in developmental psychology at the present time.

In the past centuries, academic theories of learning were the outgrowth of scientists trying to replace folklore about the experiential role of repetition, effort, and temporal association in the production of such things as abilities, habits, and resilience of memories. The effort was to find objective laws like those being uncovered in physics and chemistry. For psychology, this would mean finding the laws that controlled the way experience changed an individual's capacity and/or propensity to behave.

S-S learning

In 1927, when Ivan Petrovich Pavlov (1849–1936) published his classic work on the 'conditioned reflex,' it was seen to be exactly what had been hoped for. The loose notion of experience was replaced with defined categories of stimulus (S) and response (R), and further sub-categorical distinctions relating to the learning process, termed 'conditioning.' Thus, a law of learning was provided whereby systematic manipulation of stimuli would lead to a predictable change in an individual's propensity to produce a particular response under specified conditions. Adding to the majesty of Pavlov's laws of learning was the fact that timing of the manipulation of stimuli was very important, just as is so in the laws of physics and chemistry.

In the simplest terms, Pavlov uncovered a law for giving power to a stimulus that previously had little or none. The change in power was evidenced by the change in the conditioned individual's response to the conditioned stimulus (CS). For example, as illustrated in Table 1, prior to applying the law of conditioning to a naive dog, the stimulus sound of a bell has no power to elicit salivation. However, after a number of pairings of this stimulus (the CS) just shortly prior to the presentation of meat (an unconditioned stimulus, UCS, that already possessed the power to cause salivation), the bell acquires the power to elicit salivation.

Pavlov's experiment demonstrates how animals are sensitive to the temporal contingency between events. The dog experienced a series of trials in which presentation of meat was contingent on the bell having just sounded. The conditioning is dramatically weakened if the temporal contingency is reversed so that the meat precedes the bell. Pavlov investigated the lawful effects of varying the trial conditions and varying the timing between stimuli. Experiments of this kind are commonly referred to as 'S-S learning' and they continue to be investigated in many labs to this day. Renewed interest in this type of learning in humans has recently occurred in conjunction with techniques of brain imaging in studies of brain structure and function. For example, monitoring brain activity with event-related functional magnetic resonance imaging (efMRI) during classical conditioning of an angry face (CS) with an aversive sound (UCS) supports speculation of the special involvement of the amygdala in this form of learning (Morris, Buchel, & Dolan, 2001).

Table 1. S-S contingency learning: passing pre-existing power by classical conditioning.

Time	Learning progression
t1	Sound of bell has no power to cause dog's salivation. Meat has power to cause dog's salivation.
t2	Dog exposed to meat contingent on prior sound of bell for some number of conditioning trials.
t3	Sound of bell now has power to cause salivation.

Table 2. S-(R-S) contingency learning: making new power by discriminative operant conditioning.

Time	Learning progression
t1	Sound of bell has no power to cause dog to sit. Food has no power to cause dog to sit.
t2	Dog receives food contingent on sitting within five seconds of sound of bell for some number of learning trials.
t3	Sound of bell now has power to cause dog to sit.

John Broadus Watson (1878–1958) was probably the most eloquent promulgator of Pavlov's laws as these might apply to development, particularly human development. He appeared to believe that S-S learning could account for virtually all of the variation in human ability and self-control. It was in relation to the latter, and his conditioning and extinguishing of fear in infants, that he gained a broad non-academic following for practical advice on child rearing during the 1920s and 1930s. Watson viewed his successful conditioning of fear as a blueprint for properly understanding the origins of the many irrational fears and emotional maladjustments that were often being treated by psychoanalysis at that time. An experiment by one of his students, Mary Cover Jones (1896–1987), extinguishing fear in an infant by presenting the fearful CS in association with naturally pleasant stimulation (UCS), has been acknowledged as the first experiment in therapeutic behavior modification, a clinical field begun in the 1950s with extensions of Pavlov's findings by Joseph Wolpe (1915–1997).

Watson's influence on the academic field of psychology and its effort to account for human development is arguably as great as and longer lived than his popular writings on child rearing. Pavlov's laws of conditioning were perfect examples of the power of objectifying variables in the laws of psychology. Philosophically, Watson had been championing the virtue of behaviorism as a replacement for the subjective introspective methodology that psychology had relied on in its first steps as a science in the 19th century. One could, he argued, remove any reference to an individual's subjective mental state when constructing laws that would adequately explain human behavior and development. Stimuli associated in specifiable patterns of temporal contingency would provide a sufficient causal reference in a philosophically sound science of psychology.

R-S and S-(R-S) learning

In the mid-thirties, Burrhus Fredric Skinner (1904–1990) introduced a behavioristic formalization of what was commonly viewed as goal-oriented or instrumental learning. It was a refinement and further objectification of what Edward Lee Thorndike (1874–1949) had termed the 'law of effect.' In contrast to Pavlov's focus on the contingency between experiencing CS and UCS, Skinner's focus was on the contingency between an unconditioned behavior, termed an operant response (R), and a subsequent unconditioned stimulus termed a reinforcer (Sre). He reframed the everyday notions of working for incentives and goals from their reference to anticipated future events which he found unacceptable. Skinner proposed instead a reliance solely on past contingency between behaviors and reinforcers that had followed them and stimuli that had marked these occasions of contingency. He believed that these basic categories of experience are sufficient to explain the development of even that most complex of human behaviors, language.

We noted that S-S learning might be viewed as a method of passing power from one stimulus to another in terms of the power to elicit some specific behavior. In Pavlovian learning, however, the power that can be given to an initially powerless stimulus is limited to the set of available powers existing in unconditioned stimuli. In R-S learning theory, by contrast, power can be constructed in the absence of an available UCS for the target behavior. How this is done is termed discriminative learning (S-[R-S]). As summarized in Table 2, when the target behavior occurs, it is reinforced. This R-S contingency is itself made contingent on the presence of another stimulus. This new stimulus is called a discriminative stimulus (Sd) because it provides a basis to discriminate occasions in which the target behavior has been reinforced. After some number of trials in which the Sd is present and others in which it is absent, the individual will begin to emit the target behavior in response to the occurrence of the Sd. Thus, the trials have constructed an eliciting power for the Sd without a need for a UCS that possessed such eliciting power beforehand.

This expansion of learning theory to provide a behavioristic account of what is commonly called purposive or goal-oriented behavior was joined by a number of other notable theorists. Clark Hull (1884–1952) developed a set of inter-related lawful formulations that, like the laws of mechanics in physics, were intended to account for not only the occurrence but also the strength of learned behavior. Unlike Skinner, Hull and his student Kenneth Wartinbee Spence (1907–1967) tried to account for the power of some stimuli to function as rewards (or reinforcers in Skinner's terminology) by appealing to a notion of biological needs that set up motivating 'drives' in the individual. Edward Chace Tolman (1886–1959) offered another significant variant of learning theory that explicitly tried to account for the philosophical notion that purposive behavior involves an individual possessing some cognitive representation of the goal being pursued. This shift from radical behaviorism to what was called purposive behaviorism opened the door for more recent theorizing about how maturation of memory and information processing capacities might alter learning and its effect on subsequent development.

Although Skinner did not receive the degree of attention that Watson did in the area of popular guidance for child rearing, Skinner's theoretical perspective has had deep and lasting influence in the USA in the areas of special education and classroom management of children in primary school grades. This may be due to the relative clarity and simplicity of his prescriptions for modifying behavior. It may also be due in part to Skinner's novel *Walden Two* (1948), which was, in effect, a treatise on his view of ideal rearing conditions. That book was widely read in undergraduate courses of humanities and social philosophy during the second half of the twentieth century.

The radical behaviorism that Watson and Skinner espoused greatly influenced academic psychology in the United States until the mid 1950s. This was less true in Europe and within the sub-field of developmental psychology where Freudian psychoanalytic theory, the cognitive developmental theory of Jean Piaget (1896–1980), and various bio-maturational theories maintained many adherents regarding how maturation and early experience affect human development. In the USA, there was a productive tension in the lingering theoretical struggle between learning theory and psychoanalytic theory that resulted in the collaborative collection and analysis of cross-cultural data in an archive known as the Human Relations Area Files (HRAF) at Yale University (now accessible on the Internet). Initially, cultural anthropologists and developmental psychologists compiled observations of the variation in child rearing as this could be discerned across a variety of reasonably independent cultures (now more than ninety) accounted for by the HRAF. The ethnographic observations made were in part guided by

the goal of testing differences in the developmental predictions that would follow from the theoretical frameworks of learning theory and Freudian theory. Overall, learning theory has tended to fair better in this contest.

Social learning theory

Albert Bandura (1925–) and others loosened the grip of behaviorism on learning theory. This occurred in three important respects. Initially, it was on the basis of a specific concern for the process of imitation or observational learning. Bandura and his colleagues pointed out that when a child changed a propensity to behave in a certain way simply by observing another person perform that behavior, the learning (i.e., the change in propensity) should be viewed as occurring in the absence of a learning trial. That is, imitation appeared to be unlike the simple laws of Pavlovian S-S learning or Skinnerian R-S learning, wherein the conditioning of the individual involved some number of trials in which the focal behavior occurred – as elicited by the UCS in the case of Pavlovian learning or as emitted and reinforced in the case of Skinnerian learning. By contrast, imitation involved only the observation of another individual enacting the target behavior. Bandura highlighted the uniqueness of this by labeling it 'no-trial learning.' In addition, the fact that the ease and strength of imitation was found to vary in relation to social characteristics of the model was a serious barrier to any concerted effort to classify stimuli in strictly physical terms as was the preference of radical behaviorism.

The third issue raised by Bandura's work, and that of others, was the effect of the individual's attribution of control to the model. Imitation is more likely if the observer evaluates the model's behavior as truly causing the apparent consequences. However, the research of Andrew Meltzoff with newborns indicates that imitation can proceed without such contextual evaluation in the beginning. On the other hand, a recent study suggests that imitation by 14-month-olds depends in part on whether the model's behavior is perceived as rational under the circumstances in which the behavior is modeled (Gergely, Bekkering, & Kiraly, 2002). The preceding findings and related work with animals (e.g., Michael Tomasello's work with chimpanzees) has lead to debate regarding the possibility that imitation develops from a response with no inference, to a response based on a rational and eventually an intentional stance. Some extension of this debate may come from brain imaging research such as that of Jean Decety and his colleagues who have recently used positron emission tomography (PET) to distinguish the neural mechanisms

Table 3. Four ways to perceive contingency of event E2 on event E1.

Basis of perception	Mechanism involved
Contiguity	Detection of short time span between instances of E1 and E2
Correlation	Computation of co-variation in time of instances of E1 and E2
Conditional probability	Computation of probability of E2 in time following instances of E1 and probability of E1 in time preceding instances of E2
Logical implication	Deduction of contingency by combining evidence of truth for each of the following relations: E1 implies E2, E1 implies not-E2, not-E1 implies E2, and not-E1 implies not-E2

underlying acts of imitation and the perception of being imitated.

New forms of learning theory

The learning process, as conceived by the radical behaviorists, was meant to stand objectively independent of the learner. We have noted above that later theorizing has seriously eroded the independence of learning from the subjective/cognitive processes of the learner. The effectiveness of a contingency in S-S learning, R-S learning, or even in learning by imitation, now appears to become soon dependent on the cognitive-perceptual activity of the individual. Learning depends on contingency, but on contingency as perceived by the learner. When put in this perspective, it becomes important to consider just how a contingency (be it between stimuli or between behavior and stimuli) might be perceived.

Contingency perception

As outlined in Table 3, there have been at least four theoretical proposals for how contingency might be perceived: contiguity, correlation, conditional probability, and logic. Contiguity was favored by the radical behaviorists. It had the appeal of simple dependence on temporal separation. The greater the time between events, the less likely the learning. The generality of this 'law of contiguity' was seriously undermined in the 1960s by John Garcia who found food aversion learning in which strong S-S learning occurred despite extensive delay between a novel food CS and a subsequent noxious UCS. It was further undermined by

findings of 'learned helplessness' wherein R-S learning fails to occur despite short delay between behavior and normally reinforcing stimuli that previously were experienced as being non-contingent or independent of behavior (Peterson, Maier, & Seligman, 1993).

The proposals of contingency being perceived in terms of correlation, conditional probability, or logic each carry a computational assumption regarding the learner's capacity to evaluate the experience of a contingency. These three potential indices of contingency respectively make reference to progressively more details in the representation of the contingency. Correlation centers on a single index of co-variation between, say, events E1 and E2. Conditional probability introduces two indices, the prospective probability of E2 occurring given E1 has occurred, and the retrospective probability of E1 having occurred given E2 occurs. Logical inference, as proposed by Thomas G. R. Bower, involves evidence in relation to four possible connections: E1 implies E2, E1 implies not-E2, not-E1 implies E2, and not-E1 implies not-E2. Most work to date has been framed in terms of either contiguity or conditional probability.

Constraints on learning

In recent decades, as learning theory has become more cognitive, it has also become increasingly integrated with evolutionary theory. The earlier hopes of finding universal laws of learning that would account for development similarly across species were strained by the reports of species-specific imprinting uncovered by ethologists as well as by the species variation of food aversion learning reported by Garcia and others. Likewise, the attempt to encompass the complexity of language acquisition in laws of R-S contingencies by Skinner and others lost favor to the seemingly more adequate account provided by Noam Chomsky and his students that incorporated an assumption that humans are innately equipped with an abstract learning mechanism containing the primitive categories of language structure. Language learning was thus a very constrained matter of discriminating sound patterns that fit the preset linguistic categories. Of note was the apparent fact that language learning progressed without the need for reward and in a manner that seemed self-guided, as evidenced in such phenomena as the English-speaking child's errors of over-regularization of the past tense suffix '-ed' for previously mastered cases of irregular verbs (e.g., "mommy goed out"). Such special constraints on general learning laws suggest that learning mechanisms are part of the evolved equipment each species has obtained in its adaptation to environmental pressure.

John Bowlby (1907–1990) was influenced by the findings of ethology and the growth of cognitive learning theory in his construction of a new theory of early socio-emotional development called attachment theory. Bowlby replaced Freud's speculations (basically Pavlovian in form) about the role of stimulus associations in children's development of emotional attachment to their parents. He emphasized instead the interplay of proximity control signals that have evolved in humans. In this view, children clearly must learn who to love and how to manage their emotional states. However, rather than building this learning through associations of people and stimulus events that reduce somatic tension as claimed by Freud, Bowlby proposed a central role for a restricted sub-set of stimulus events that were part of an evolved system of infant and parental behaviors that would help them maintain spatial proximity. The system served to protect immature members of our species from predation, especially in the prehistoric environments of our ancestors or what Bowlby called the "environment of evolutionary adaptedness."

Contingency as a stimulus

The idea that the contingencies of learning need to be perceived in order to be effective undermines the prospect of finding laws of learning that can be formulated without concern for the mental processes of the learner. It also introduces a new option for the potential effects of contingency experience. As an object of perception, contingency experience can be viewed as a stimulus in its own right. From this perspective, the infant controlling the mobile in Figure 1 by movement on pressure-sensitive pillows is not only perceiving the mobile turn, but the contingency of its turning as well. A responsive mother can display her attention to her baby by any number of auditory, tactile, or visual reactions to any number of actions on the part of her infant. The baby's perception that her reactions are contingent on his behavior may have a psychological impact that is separate from and far more important than the stimulus impact of her behavior itself. In this manner, contingency experience has been proposed to have unconditioned eliciting power in human infants in their early phases of social development. In this view, part of what initially defines the mother is her characteristic level of contingency as perceived by the infant. Moreover, this view allows that contingency may be misperceived and certain forms of misperception may have predictable developmental consequences (Watson, 2001).

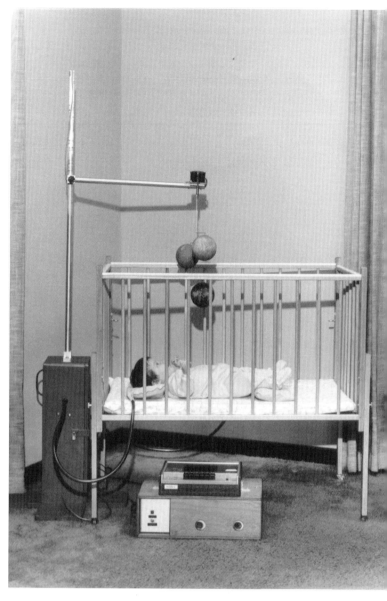

Figure 1. Infant learning to control mobile movement using pressure-sensitive pillows.

Probability learning

Studies examining the sensitivity of infants and young children to the contingency structure of their environment have increased in recent years. These range from testing how contingent responsiveness of a mobile affects subsequent reactions to it to how inter-stimulus contingency level may be used to segregate words in speech. The latter work is an interesting challenge to one aspect of Chomsky's proposed abstract linguistic categories.

Chomsky and his students have argued that linguistic structure had such variable distribution in the continuous stream of natural speech that it was not decipherable without some prior knowledge. This argument for an inborn guidance to language development (or so-called 'language acquisition device') has been weakened by the discovery that the transitional probability structure of the phonemic sequences in natural speech can reveal at least some of its underlying linguistic structure. Moreover, researchers have shown that 8-month-old infants are sensitive to conditional probability structure in continuous streams of an artificial language (Aslin, Saffran, & Newport, 1998). Thus, it would seem that some of the presumably innate grounding of language development may really be provided by the human infant's capacity for probability learning.

Neural-net models and new views of learning and maturation

Since the early 1990s, the elaboration of cognitive learning models has been spurred on by techniques of computer simulation of neural-net learning. Despite the seminal work of Donald O. Hebb (1904–1985), the most influential learning theories of the past century did not speculate as to how their learning laws were supported by an animal's neurophysiological structure. The picture is quite the opposite today. Neural-net modeling, for example, is an explicit attempt to approximate the mechanics of neurological adaptation to experience. These models have just primitive features, such as neuronal nodes, their activation, their synaptic-like inter-connection, their inter-node conductivity (termed 'weights'), and their form of inter-connection across layers of nodes. The neural-net simulations have been applied to a wide variety of classic developmental issues. Although neural nets embody no use of symbolic representation, they have managed to learn to perform tasks that had previously been assumed to require symbolic thought. For example, James L. McClelland and his colleagues have shown that neural nets can do quite well in simulating the developmental progression in solving various conservation tasks that were highlighted in the classic work on human cognitive development by Piaget.

Neural-net modeling of learning has spawned ideas about how maturation and learning may be viewed as cooperative in the explanation of development. Jeffrey L. Elman found that a neural net was incapable of mastering an artificial language even though the net had a theoretically sufficient amount of memory capacity as provided by feedback connections between layers. The net could master the language if the linguistic examples were initially simple and then later of full complexity. However, real world learning does not occur with sequential exposure to partial then full language

structure. So Elman arranged to have the net begin with a limited memory followed by a maturational shift to full memory. In this case, the net succeeded (Elman, 1993). It seems reasonable to expect that evolution may have worked out a cooperation between maturation and learning for many recurrent environmental challenges.

Conclusions

The past century has seen a dramatic shift in theorizing about the role of learning in development. Dominance has shifted from a preference for formulating laws of contiguity between external stimuli and behavior to a preference for formulating models with various degrees of biologically based computational activity and novel assumptions of evolved bias in guiding adaptation to the contingency structure of the physical and social environment (Table 4). In addition, recent advances in brain imaging and neural-net simulation techniques hold some promise for further insights into the

Table 4. Potential developmental consequences of contingency experience.

S-S contingencies	R-S and S-(R-S) contingencies
Extend range of stimuli that cause behavioral reactions (e.g., learn to fear fire).	Increase strength and likelihood of behavioral reactions and create new causal classes of stimuli for discriminative control of those behaviors (e.g., learn to squeeze toy to hear squeak).
Learn categories of S-S contingency structure in sequential stimuli (e.g., learn the word segmentation of linguistic utterances).	Learn categories of responsive objects (e.g., learn mom is person who is especially responsive to cry).
Learn causal powers of environmental objects (e.g., learn that only certain objects will float).	Learn extent of personal efficacy (e.g., learn where, when, and what things can be caused by one's own behavior).
Learn association of feelings and sights of own action (e.g., learn hand motion sequence to assist imitation of mom's clapping of hands).	Learn social signals that mark change in responsiveness of others (e.g., learn the face and body confirmations that display the mood, emotional states, and intentions of another person)

biological substrate of learning mechanisms and their evolved constraints.

See also:
Neuromaturational theories; Constructivist theories; Ethological theories; Psychoanalytical theories; Magnetic Resonance Imaging; Experimental methods; Perceptual development; Language development; Connectionist modeling; Imitation; Cognitive neuroscience; Ethology; Linguistics; John Bowlby; Jean Piaget

Further reading

Elman, J. L., Bates, E. A., Johnson, M. H., Karmiloff-Smith, A. *et al.* (1996). *Rethinking Innateness: A Connectionist Perspective on Development.* Cambridge, MA: MIT Press.

Mower, R. R. and Klein, S. B. (eds.) (2001). *Handbook of Contemporary Learning Theories.* Mahwah, NJ: Erlbaum.

Whiting, J. W. M. and Child, I. L. (1953). *Child Training and Personality.* New Haven: Yale University Press.

Psychoanalytical theories

PETER FONAGY

Introduction

Psychoanalytical theory is not a static body of knowledge; it is in a state of constant evolution. This was as true during Sigmund Freud's life (1856–1939) as it has been since. Nevertheless, a core assumption of psychoanalytical theory throughout has been the so-called genetic or developmental point of view, seeing current functioning as a consequence of developmentally prior phases, which all psychoanalytical texts acknowledge as central. This places theories of individual development at the very heart of most psychoanalytical formulations.

An essential idea running through all phases of Freud's thinking was the notion that pathology recapitulated ontogeny; that disorders of the mind could be best understood as residues of childhood experiences and primitive modes of mental functioning (S. Freud, 1905). A developmental approach to psychopathology has continued to be the traditional framework of psychoanalysis. It aims to uncover the developmental stages and sequelae of different disorders of childhood and adulthood, and the factors that influence them. Psychoanalytical theories have evolved through diverse attempts to explain why and how individuals in psychoanalytical treatment deviated from the normal path of development and came to experience major intrapsychic and interpersonal difficulties. Bringing together psychoanalysis and developmental psychopathology makes explicit what has been at the core of psychoanalytical theorizing and treatment, from Freud's day onward. Each theory reviewed here focuses on particular aspects of development or specific developmental phases, and outlines a model of normal personality development derived from clinical experience.

Freud's psychoanalytical theory

Freud (Fig. 1) was the first to give meaning to mental disorder by linking it to childhood experiences, and to the vicissitudes of the developmental process. For example, Freud's theory of narcissism or self-development during infancy was invoked to explain adult psychosis, and, conversely, his view of psychic life during infancy was constructed largely on the basis of observations of adult psychopathology. His notion of infantile grandiosity is derived from that observed in many instances of psychosis (e.g., the delusional belief of an individual suffering from paranoia that he is being targeted by the combined intelligence agencies of the Western world or that he has superhuman powers).

One of Freud's greatest contributions was undoubtedly the recognition of infantile sexuality. His discoveries radically altered our perception of the child from one of idealized innocence to that of a person struggling to achieve control over his biological needs, and make them acceptable to society through the microcosm of his family. Pathology was correspondingly seen as failures in this process. Childhood conflict was thought to create a persistence of the problem aggravated by current life pressures, generating significant anxieties that could only be resolved by 'neurotic compromise': giving in partially to infantile sexual demands, in the context of a self-punitive struggle against these.

Freud's final model went beyond sexual concerns and posited aggressive or destructive motives independent of the sexual, which faced the child with a further developmental task of accommodation (Fig. 2). This involves gradually having to tame natural destructiveness or otherwise suffer from a life-time of psychic pain as destructiveness is dealt with by being turned against the self or projected outward and becoming a focus of anxiety. Freud, and many of his followers, considered genetic predisposition to be a key factor in abnormal reactions to socialization experience.

Beyond Freud: some general comments

Post-Freudian models of development, which dominated the second half of the last century of

Figure 1. Sigmund Freud, 1920.

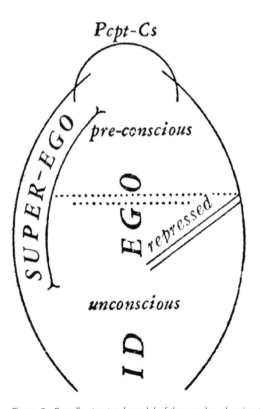

Figure 2. Freud's structural model of the psyche, showing the relations of id, ego, and super-ego to the older terminology of unconscious and pre-conscious, and the interface of these systems with the system of perception-consciousness (Pcpt-Cs) at the top of the figure.

psychoanalytical thinking, broadly fall into three geographical-conceptual categories: (1) in the USA, Freud's most complex model of the mind, the structural theory of id, ego, and super-ego, was expanded to include a concern with adaptation to the external or social world in addition to the intrapsychic. This approach is known as ego psychology; (2) in Europe, particularly in the UK, concern with internal representations of the parental figures dominated psychoanalytical thinking. This class of theories came to be known as object-relations theories because of the emphasis they give to the fantasies that individuals can have about their relationship with the internally represented object; (3) more recently, both approaches have given way in the USA to an interpersonalist tradition that is primarily concerned with the actual observable nature of the infant-caregiver relationship as well as the vicissitudes of the social construction of subjective experience. These approaches are generally considered under the heading of relational theories.

Ego psychology

Heinz Hartmann (1844–1970)

Ego psychologists balanced the Freudian picture by focusing on the evolution of the child's adaptive capacities, which he brings to bear on his struggle with his biological needs. Hartmann's model (Hartmann,

Kris, & Loewenstein, 1949) attempted to take a wider view of the developmental process, to link drives and ego functions, and show how very negative interpersonal experiences could jeopardize the evolution of the psychic structures essential to adaptation. He also showed that the reactivation of earlier structures (regression) was the most important component of psychopathology. Hartmann was also amongst the first to indicate the complexity of the developmental process, stating that the reasons for the persistence of particular behavior are likely to differ from the reasons for its original appearance.

While conflicts over oral dependency and gratification may account for an infant's eating problems, this is unlikely to explain eating disturbance in adolescence or problems of obesity in adulthood. Amongst the great contributions of ego psychologists are the identification of the ubiquity of intrapsychic conflict throughout development, and the recognition that genetic endowment, as well as interpersonal experiences, may be critical in determining the child's developmental path. This latter idea has echoes in the developmental psychopathological concept of resilience.

Anna Freud (1892–1982)

Psychoanalysts with ego psychological orientations were among the first to study development through the direct observation of children, both in the context of child psychoanalysis and the observation of children in the nursery. Child analysts discovered that symptomatology is not fixed, but rather is a dynamical state superimposed upon, and intertwined with, an underlying developmental process. Continuity of personality traits and symptoms across childhood was the exception rather than the norm.

Anna Freud's study of disturbed and healthy children under great social stress led her to formulate a relatively comprehensive developmental theory, where the child's emotional maturity could be mapped independently of diagnosable pathology. Particularly in her early work in the war nurseries, she identified many of the characteristics that later research linked to resilience. For example, her observations spoke eloquently of the social support that children could give one another in concentration camps, which could ensure their physical and psychological survival. Similarly, she found that children during the London Blitz were less frightened of objective danger than they were of the threat that separation from their parents represented, and that their caregivers' anxieties predicted their own level of distress. More recent research on children experiencing severe trauma has confirmed her assumption of the protective power of sound social support and the risk of parental pathology in coping with threat or danger. Anna Freud's

work stayed so close to the external reality of the child that it lent itself to a number of important applications (e.g., child custody in case of divorce, treatment of children with serious physical illness).

Anna Freud was also a pioneer in identifying the importance of an equilibrium between developmental processes (A. Freud, 1965). Her work is particularly relevant in explaining why children deprived of certain capacities (e.g., sensory capacities or general physical health), by environment or constitution, are at greater risk of psychological disturbance. Epidemiological studies have supported her clinical observation. She was the first psychoanalyst to place the process and mechanisms of development at the center-stage of psychoanalytical thinking. Her approach is truly one of developmental psychopathology, insofar as she defines abnormal functioning in terms of its deviation from normal development, while at the same time using the understanding gained from clinical cases to illuminate the progress of the normal child. It is a logical development of her work to explore the nature of the therapeutic process also in developmental terms. It is important to remind ourselves that often psychoanalysts apply developmental notions to the therapeutic process metaphorically, but essential components of treatment, particularly with children, and with personality disordered adults, inevitably involve the engagement of dormant developmental processes.

Margaret Mahler (1897–1986)

A pioneer of developmental observation in the USA, Mahler drew attention to the paradox of self-development: that a separate identity involves giving up a highly gratifying closeness with the caregiver (Mahler, 1968). Her observations of the ambitendency of children in their second year of life threw light on chronic problems of consolidating individuality. Mahler's framework highlights the importance of the caregiver in facilitating separation, and helps explain the difficulties experienced by children whose parents fail to perform a social referencing function for the child, which would help them to assess the realistic dangers of unfamiliar environments. A traumatized, troubled parent may hinder rather than help a child's adaptation, while an abusive parent may provide no social referencing. The pathogenic potential of withdrawal of the mother, when confronted with the child's wish for separateness, helps to account for the transgenerational aspects of psychological disturbance.

Joseph Sandler (1927–1998)

In the UK, Sandler's development of Anna Freud's work and that of Edith Jacobson (1897–1978) represents the best integration of the developmental perspective with psychoanalytical theory. His comprehensive psychoanalytical model has enabled developmental researchers to integrate their findings with a psychoanalytical formulation, which clinicians were also able to use. At the core of Sandler's formulation lies the representational structure that contains both reality and distortion, and is the driving force of psychic life. He moved away from an emphasis on drives and proposed derivative affects as organizers of human motivation. An important component of his model is the notion of the background of safety (Sandler, 1987), which suggests that individuals seek above all to experience a feeling of security in relation to their internal and external world. Often what is familiar, even if objectively aversive such as situations of abuse, can feel paradoxically 'safer' than the alternative that is expected.

Object-relations theories

Melanie Klein (1882–1960)

The focus of these theories on early development and infantile fantasy represented a shift in world view for psychoanalysis from a tragic to a somewhat more romantic one. Melanie Klein and her followers, working in London, constructed a developmental model that at the time met great opposition because of the extravagant assumptions these clinicians were ready to make about the cognitive capacities of infants. Surprisingly, developmental research appears to be consistent with some of Klein's claims concerning perception of causality and causal reasoning. Kleinian developmental concepts have become popular because they provide powerful descriptions of the clinical interaction between both child and adult patient and analyst. For example, projective identification depicts the close control that primitive mental function can exert over the analyst's mind. Post-Kleinian psychoanalysts were particularly helpful in underscoring the impact of emotional conflict on the development of cognitive capacities.

W. R. D. Fairbairn (1889–1964) and D. W. Winnicott (1896–1971)

The early relationship with the caregiver emerged as a critical aspect of personality development from studies of severe character disorders by the object-relations school of psychoanalysts in Britain. Fairbairn's (1952) focus on the individual's need for the other helped shift psychoanalytical attention from structure to content, and profoundly influenced both British and North American psychoanalytical thinking. As a result, the self as a central part of the psychoanalytical model emerged in, for example, the work of Winnicott (1971). The concept of the caretaker or false self, a defensive structure created to master trauma in a context of total dependency, has become an essential developmental construct. Winnicott's notions of primary maternal preoccupation, transitional phenomena, the holding environment, and the mirroring function of the caregiver, provided a clear research focus for developmentalists interested in individual differences in the development of self-structure (Fonagy *et al.*, 2002). The significance of the parent-child relationship is consistently borne out by developmental studies of psychopathology. These studies in many respects support Winnicott's assertions concerning the traumatic effects of early maternal failure, particularly maternal depression and the importance of maternal sensitivity for the establishment of a secure relationship.

Heinz Kohut (1913–1981)

There have been many attempts by North American theorists to incorporate object-relations ideas into models that retain facets of structural theories. Kohut's self-psychology was based primarily on his experience of narcissistic individuals. His central developmental idea was the need for an understanding caretaker to counteract the infant's sense of helplessness in the face of his biological striving for mastery. Kohut emphasizes the need for such understanding obtains throughout life and these notions are consistent with accumulating evidence for the powerful protective influence of social support across a wide range of epidemiological studies. He also borrowed freely from Winnicott and British object-relations theorists, although his indebtedness was rarely acknowledged. The mirroring object becomes a self-object, and the need for empathy drives development, which culminates in the attainment of a cohesive self. Drive theory becomes secondary to self theory in that the failure to attain an integrated self-structure both leaves room for, and in itself generates, aggression and isolated sexual fixation. However, the self remains problematic as a construct in Kohut's model as it assumes both the person (the patient) and the agent control the person. Nevertheless, Kohut's descriptions of the narcissistic personality have been powerful and influential examples of the use of developmental theory in psychoanalytical understanding.

Kohut's hypotheses concerning the profound and long-term consequences of a self 'enfeebled' by the failure of emotional attunement of the self-object find a powerful echo in the risk literature. Recent evidence has shown a clear link between early trauma and disorganization and delay in self-development. The effectiveness of actions undertaken by the child is at the center of Kohut's concept of self-esteem. Kohut's formulations were probably helpful in the operationalization of the concept of self-confidence, although in some studies

Personality disorders: their mutual relationships

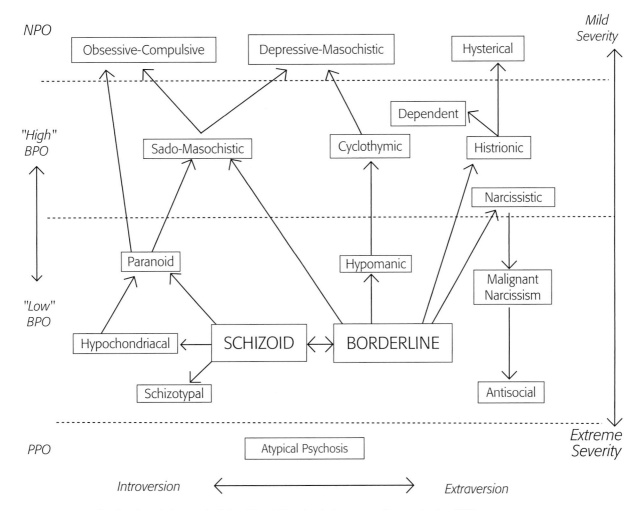

Figure 3. Personality disorders: their mutual relationships. BPO = borderline personality organization; NPO = neurotic personality organization; PPO = psychotic personality organization.

problem-solving skills and self-esteem appear to be independent indicators of resilience.

Otto Kernberg

An alternative integration of object-relations ideas with North American ego psychology was offered by Kernberg. His contribution to the development of psychoanalytical thought is unparalleled in the recent history of the discipline. His systematic integration of structural theory and object-relations theory (Kernberg, 1987) is probably the most frequently used psychoanalytical developmental model, particularly in relation to personality disorders (Fig. 3). His understanding of psychopathology is developmental, in the sense that personality disturbance is seen to reflect the limited ability of the young child to address intrapsychic conflict. Neurotic object-relations show much less defensive disintegration of the representation of self and objects into libidinally invested part-object relations. In personality disorder, part-object relations

are formed under the impact of diffuse, overwhelming emotional states, which signal the activation of persecutory relations between self and object.

Kernberg's models are particularly useful because of their level of detail and his determination to operationalize his ideas far more than has been traditionally the case in psychoanalytical writing. It is not surprising, therefore, that a considerable amount of empirical work has been done to test his proposals directly, and the clinical approach that he takes toward serious personality disturbance.

Beyond object-relations

Relational theories

With the gradual demise of ego psychology in the USA and the opening of psychoanalysis to psychologists and other non-medically qualified professionals, a fresh intellectual approach to theory and technique gained ground in theoretical and technical discussions. The relational approach is arguably rooted in the work of Harry Stack-Sullivan (1892–1949) and Clara Thompson (1893–1958) in the USA and the work of John Bowlby in the UK. An outgrowth of the former tradition is the interpersonalist approach (Mitchell, 1988), which has revolutionized the role of the analyst in the therapeutic situation. Influenced by post-modernist ideas, this group of clinicians generally conceive the analytic relationship as far more of two equals rather than of patient and doctor. They recognize the fundamentally interpersonal character of the sense of self and thus the irreducibly dyadic quality of mental function. They consistently acknowledge the influence of the inter-personal nature of the mind on the process of therapy, and the active role that the analyst as a person plays in the treatment process. Particularly controversial is the insistence of many interpersonalists that enactments by the analyst within the therapy are almost as inevitable as those by the patient in the transference. Until recently, there has not been a strong developmental approach as part of this tradition.

John Bowlby (1907–1990)

In the meantime, in the UK, Bowlby's work on separation and loss also focused developmentalists' attention on the importance of the security (safety, sensitivity, and predictability) of the earliest relationships. His cognitive-systems model of the internalization of interpersonal relationships (internal working models), consistent with object-relations theory and elaborated by other attachment theorists, has been increasingly influential. According to Bowlby, the child develops expectations regarding a caregiver's behavior and his or her own behavior. These expectations are based on the child's understanding of experiences of previous interaction, and organize the child's behavior with the attachment figure and (by extension) with others. The concept has had very broad application. Bowlby's developmental model highlights the transgenerational nature of internal working models: our view of ourselves depends upon the working model of relationships that characterized our caregivers. Empirical research on this intergenerational model is encouraging as an accumulating body of data confirms that there is intergenerational transmission of attachment, security and insecurity.

A number of theories have drawn deeply from the developmental research tradition, combining attachment theory ideas with psychoanalytical conceptions within a general system theory frame of reference favored explicitly by Bowlby. There have been a number of major contributors such as Stern (1985) whose book represented a milestone in psychoanalytical theorization concerning development. His work is distinguished by being normative rather than patho-morphic, and prospective rather than retrospective. His focus is the reorganization of subjective perspectives on self and other as these occur with the emergence of new maturational capacities. Stern is the most sophisticated amongst psychoanalytical writers in dealing with several qualitatively different senses of self, each developmentally anchored. Many of his suggestions have proved to be highly applicable clinically, including his notion of an early core self and the role of the *schema of being with* the other. Other general system theory interpretations of psychoanalysis originated in the work of practitioners of brief psychotherapy.

Mentalization-based theories

Most recently, the work of psychoanalysts as part of the long-term collaboration of the Anna Freud Centre and University College London has advanced a develop-mental model in the relational tradition (Fonagy *et al.*, 2002). Their ideas originate within attachment theory, but also draw strongly on the object-relations tradition. They focus on the emergence of the self, not as a representation but as an experiential agent of change. They suggest that prior to the self experienced as a thinking and feeling entity is an intersubjective self that acquires understanding of its own functioning through the reaction of the caregiver. Thinking of the actions of self and other is teleological, cause–effect thinking based merely upon what is observable.

The development of a psychological self that is able to experience itself and others it interacts with as thinking, feeling, and desiring arises from the integration of two primitive modes of experiencing the mental world: psychic equivalence and pretend or non-serious modes. In the former, all that is felt to be happening inside the mind is also thought to be occurring in physical reality. In the pretend mode, physical reality and the mental world are totally decoupled and one is assumed to have no possible consequence for the other. The two modes of functioning are prototypically integrated through playful interactions with the caregiver. As a conse-quence, when such interactions are undermined by maltreatment or constitutional problems on the part of the child, mentalization (thinking of the other and the self as motivated by mental states) will not be acquired fully and severe attachment-related personality problems will arise.

Conclusions

We have seen that the assumption of a correspondence between development and psychopathology is present in all psychoanalytical formulations. There are divergences in terms of the exact period of development involved in particular disorders, or the aspect of the developmental process underlying a particular pathology, but there is a shared assumption that the study of development and the study of pathology concern the same psychic processes. Psychoanalytical theories have come under considerable criticism over recent years for excessive reliance on single case studies and lack of reliable observation to back up generalizations. Interestingly, information pertinent to psychoanalytical ideas has been accumulating from both cognitive science and neuropsychological studies at very rapid rates. In fact, we are at a historical point when as more is learnt about the brain the clearer the appropriateness of a number of basic psychoanalytical propositions might appear (e.g., the predominantly non-conscious nature of human cognition).

If psychoanalytical developmental theory is to become part of the intellectual future of the mind sciences, changes in the way psychoanalytical knowledge is accumulated must take place. In particular, psycho-analysis needs to restrict the number of assumptions concerning normal development it makes, and an increase in the effectiveness of its interface with other disciplines studying the mind in development will be necessary. At the moment, too many incompatible theoretical formulations are vying for acceptance. The choice is made on the basis of usefulness in completing personal narratives in the context of psychotherapeutic consultations rather than observations of actual development. If psychoanalysis is able to meet the challenge that integration with modern cognitive psychology and neurosience represents, then taking psychoanalytical ideas more seriously could have a very beneficial effect on the future of developmental psychopathology. This particularly applies to the central psychoanalytical developmental notion that complex and, at times, conflicting representations of unconscious beliefs and affects created early in life, influence behavior and experience throughout the lifetime.

A widening perspective could, for example, lead to a shift in emphasis from self-report to narrative data. It could also lead to a closer examination of patterns of narration, as opposed to observations of narrative content, and to a greater concern with discordance and conflict among response systems rather than a single-minded search for congruence and consistency. Psychoanalytic theory is alive, and its potential for enriching our understanding of development and psychopathology was not fully exploited in the century that has just closed.

See also:
Constructivist theories; Theories of the child's mind; Clinical and non-clinical interview methods; Self and peer assessment of competence and well being; Epidemiological designs; Cognitive development in infancy; Play; Selfhood; Socialization; 'At-risk' concept; Behavioral and learning disorders; Child depression; Behavior genetics; Cognitive neuroscience; John Bowlby; Donald Winnicott

Further reading

Bronstein, C. (ed.). (2001). *Kleinian Theory: A Contemporary Perspective*. London: Whurr.

Fonagy, P. and Target, M. (2003). *Psychoanalytic Theories: Perspectives from Developmental Psychopathology*. London: Whurr.

Mollon, P. (2001). *Releasing the Self: The Healing Legacy of Heinz Kohut*. London: Whurr.

Theories of the child's mind

NORMAN H. FREEMAN

Introduction

A good way of approaching any theory is to try and diagnose what serious purpose might be animating the author. Researchers into child development are conscious of having to carry three responsibilities.

One responsibility is to explain why the child's mentality is as it is during the tortuous route to adulthood. Any theory of the child's mind is in part a theory of the striking peculiarities of change during phases of childhood. Much research is driven by curiosity about the fact that some early changes irreversibly mark us for life, whilst other changes that may affect us deeply during childhood do not seem to last into adulthood.

A second responsibility is to reconstruct something of what it is like to be a young child. That reconstruction is a necessary task because we adults have long forgotten what the events in our early autobiography felt like to us at the time. There is continuing interest in decoding the significance of the experiences that we feel we have lost.

A third responsibility is to explain what it is about childhood that explains why adults are as we are. There are vast differences between adults in individual patterns of abilities, skills, tastes, and sensibilities. If our adult patterns of thinking are often very specialized, one wonders to what extent that is because we become increasingly uneven during the course of childhood itself.

There is no agreed-upon unified grand theory that is adequate to discharge all three responsibilities. From one point of view, the lack of such a theory vexes the undeniably dedicated researchers. Yet from another point of view, it is entirely realistic for researchers to hold back from the ambition to generate a single definitive theory that would live up to the different responsibilities in equal measure. Unequal measure has perforce given shape to current theories of the child's mind.

What is a theory?

The *Concise Oxford Dictionary* (1999) defines a theory as "a supposition or system of ideas intended to explain something, especially one based on general principles independent of the thing to be explained." A theory thus comes out as a supposition – something abstract that has an explanatory function, and a domain of application. A theory is made up of a mix of principles that may be right or wrong, and propositions that may be true or false. The principles and propositions allow the development of models that may or may not fit the domain the theory is supposed to address. In turn, the models themselves allow one to adduce which hypotheses do or do not hold in the real world.

The above standard ordering of conceptual complexity, from theory to model to hypothesis, does not mean that advances always occur by theoretical development having a trickle-down effect. Development of models can impel a re-evaluation of what principles should go into a theory. In practice, a lively interplay between models and theories can come into operation when an ambitious theory comes under attack and begins to look less coherent than before. Such a situation arose with the assimilation of lessons learned during controversies that had raged during the 1960s and 1970s over Piagetian constructivist theory. It became evident that ambitious theory had repeatedly failed to facilitate the devising of explanatory models that would capture the complexity of development. By the beginning of the 1980s, developmental psychology had become marked out by several explanatory theories that had been partly impelled by an interest in building models.

Different models serve to make salient different things to test for projection onto the real world. Consider model ships. For one model ship, it might be essential that it float, regardless of the precise shape of the prow. For another model ship, it might be essential that its prow be shaped to measure water-flow past it; and if the model does not float, it can be held up in a clamp. Anything that can be modeled in one way can be modeled differently. Researchers interested in modeling the child's mind ceased to assess positions with reference to a single dominant approach. The theoretical pluralism has continued into this new millennium. Accordingly, it is necessary here to review the situation that currently sustains theoretical pluralism.

From broad stages to narrow phases

The background to the current theoretical pluralism is that analysis of models of adult smooth-running competencies repeatedly revealed that the competencies can be decomposed into separate components. Developmental research revealed how the components came together. The theoretical task then was to characterize the operation of the separate components of the child's mind, and to explain how it functions.

In this pluralist era, there is usually not a great deal of weight given to trying to explain development by synchronic across-the-board changes in the child's mind. It is now rather uncommon for theorists to hold to a conception of stages of development such as that of Piaget. Stage theory relied on an implicit metaphor whereby the major part of development was seen as rather along the lines of a child climbing a ladder, with each rung of the ladder representing a new level of attainment. The metaphor involved all children stepping on the same ascending order of rungs so that a great deal of uniformity was envisaged; nevertheless there was scope for envisaging individual differences arising whenever individual children pause for variable lengths of time on any rung, according to temperament and experience.

It is more common nowadays to theorize developing minds as containing ideas that are acquired in independent phases. This newer metaphor is rather along the lines of development consisting of a gradually lengthening sort of rope that is woven, in which the separate narrow strands are woven together in a somewhat individual pattern for each child. Dynamical systems theory is one approach that is informed by such a conception. It is good to see a respect for individual differences being built into the theories. The danger in all such theorizing is that it is possible to lose sight of the wood for the trees: in theorizing the separate strands of development, the child as a whole is in danger of becoming invisible to the theorist.

A great deal of debate has arisen about how to characterize the separate strands of development. The informal term 'strand' has become the formal 'domain' in the 1990s. The term 'domain' has become firmly embedded in developmental psychology as a label for a ". . . set of representations sustaining a specific area of knowledge; language, number, physics, and so forth"

(Karmiloff-Smith, 1992, p. 6). The representations sustaining knowledge in any domain do not grow haphazardly, but are organized according to a set of underlying principles specific to that domain. The idea common to a large family of theories is that the child is born with a set of constraints that channel the child's mind toward a limited number of domains of knowledge and encourage the growth of knowledge in a different way in each domain (Hirschfeld & Gelman, 1994). Some constraints may operate from birth whilst others only find expression later in development.

Constraints force the learner's attention to key inputs that are relevant to knowledge acquisition within the domain. Key inputs differ between domains: inputs that have to be processed for a mastery of language differ from those required to master basic arithmetic. The principle of building into one's theory a firm respect for domain-specificity is perfectly in accordance with the proposition that developmental theory has to be compatible with basic evolutionary thinking. The proposal that comes out time and time again from evolutionary research is that biological organisms evolve in piecemeal fashion, solving distinct local problems of survival, like the task of developing signals to attract a mate, or of developing sensitivity to the color of ripening fruit. A biological approach is applicable to any why-question whatsoever that is asked about any behavioral or mental activity. That does not mean that sociocultural facts of development should become chased out of developmental theory by reductionist argument. It means that theorists of social development have to make their models at least moderately compatible with the operation of biological constraints.

Phases of development in different domains

A sense of number might be mediated by entirely different neural and mental mechanisms from those that mediate a sense of balance. The crucial point for modeling children's learning is that emerging concepts of counting might not impinge on finding a solution to a problem involved in the intuitive physics of how things balance. There is no reason why there has to be a single pacemaker governing the rate of development of all the domains to which an individual mind becomes addressed. It makes sense to envisage somewhat separate domain-specific developments, with one child racing ahead with, say, language while being not as advanced in number skills as her less articulate friend. Modern theories of the child's mind take it for granted that individual children are very uneven in the sophistication and coherence of their thinking. In short, the child's mind is heterogeneous. Furthermore, ". . . there is a great deal of variability of thinking within each domain" (Siegler, 1996, p. 12). At any moment, the child might stick to one strategy of working something out (e.g., by counting on her fingers), or be in the process of switching to another strategy (e.g., be busy recalling number facts). Siegler (1996) added that ". . . variability is a basic property of human thought" (p. 12).

Precisely how many domains are there for the child to master? Answers vary widely. However, the situation is not entirely chaotic. For a start, everyone accepts that children's mental change is a product of their interaction with the world of things and people. Out of the interactions, children come to construct explanatory networks of beliefs along with rules of application to domains. In addition to theories of language and number, children are innately prepared to construct theories of physics (e.g., categorizing objects and the forces that operate on them), biology (e.g., objects that move by themselves and initiate activities), and psychology (e.g., the significance of attention, intentions, and mental representations of reasons for acting). There is a long road for the child to travel in order to attain an explicit theory in any domain.

An appealingly simple example of the emergence of children's ideas comes from Karmiloff-Smith (1992). The general model is that there is inside the child a battery of internally powered motors of representational development. Thus, in the domain of intuitive physics, the early representations of, say, heaviness, embedded within the child's experience of actions, are reworked until eventually the heavily revised representations will become available to the child's reflective awareness, and be at the service of flexible thinking. Eventually, the child may come to decompose the intuitive concept of 'heaviness' into 'weight' and 'density.' It may, however, require a physics teacher to guide the child at that rarefied level of complexity.

In a study of children trying to balance weights on a board resting on a fulcrum, some of the weights had small pieces of lead hidden toward one end, so that their density was unbalanced such that the weights did not balance around their geometric midpoints. The 4-year-olds did well: they solved the balance problems by feel. That is, they were data-driven, basing their actions and reactions on the evidence of their senses. The 6-year-olds did very poorly: they had extracted a representation of balancing and fallen into the grip of an idea, the idea that things ought to balance around their geometric midpoints. The children were admirably persistent, trying the same unproductive strategy again and again. The 8-year-olds did well. Having broken out of the simple theory 'there is one way to balance,' they had become flexible, and reasoned out what to do when the simple strategy failed. Note that 'being in the grip of a simple theory' has been documented for many

domains of judgment, for many age groups. A child may be in the grip of a simple theory in one domain while being advanced and flexible for a similar-seeming problem in another domain.

Karmiloff-Smith (1992) sought out, predicted, and tested for, a variety of symptoms of representational development from being data-driven to theory-led in the five domains of physics, depiction, number, language, and psychology. A decade later, there had been theoretical development in predicting and then identifying some cross-talk between domains. The obvious place to look for cross-talk is between domains that involve some concepts of representation: theory of mind, language, number, and pictures. Bloom (2001) surveyed a range of experiments from a cross-talk perspective, and in particular a direct linkage of the child's developing theory of mind and language development. It had been known that normal infants do not simply learn words by registering how often a word is paired with an object (unlike children with autism). As young as 18 months of age, infants learn to associate a noun with the object that the speaker is looking at. In contrast, if it is unclear what salient object the speaker is looking at, then no evident learning may occur. By 4 years, a speaker whom the child can presume to be knowledgeable ("I made this object myself") induces better word-learning than if the speaker seemingly might be rather ignorant ("This was made by a friend").

There are also early links between preschoolers' theory of mind and their launching of a theory of pictures. It has often been proposed that children learn to identify pictures by virtue of a resemblance between the picture and what it depicts. That realist model has been as much under threat as the simple associationistic view of language acquisition. In one study reviewed by Bloom (2001), preschool children were asked to draw things like a lollipop and a balloon on a string. Such drawings often come out identical in the work of such young children (mostly a sort of circle on top of a sort of straight line). So, resemblance was equal between each drawing and each topic, but the children did not view matters that way. To them, the meaning of the picture went by their recalled intention when they were producing it. Some of the children even became testy when the experimenter labeled the child's drawings contrary to the child's prior intention in making each drawing. Being able to recall a prior intention is one of the key components of having a theory of mind around which children structure their intuitive understanding of psychology.

To summarize, a new metaphor of development appears to be emerging as the 21st century gets under way. Development seems to be construed as a slowly growing model of strands as in a model of DNA, but with very many intertwining strands to stand for the growth of each domain of knowledge, and only a few reciprocal links standing for cross-talk between those strands.

The rise of clusters of categories

Despite the cross-links, there is little doubt of the fact of separateness in strands of development. The child has to come to grips with a complex world in which things get called by different terms on different occasions; and what may be a pet dog at one time may become a reserve meal for the tribe if winter closes in. That is, order is imposed from nature (the existence of natural objects such as dogs) and from culture (the generation of cultural categories such as 'pet'). Entities fall into categories that have various relationships between them, and there are many fuzzy and marginal instances. Categories fall into clusters, with as many clusters as there are regular practices such as cookery or woodwork. The same applies to more intellectual activities such as understanding kinships and ethics. Each cluster of categories can be labeled a 'conceptual domain' within which the child has to do mental work. These clusters burst the early bounds of the core domains of number, physics, biology, and psychology.

The domain of language itself becomes a key source that powers the differentiation of concepts in the construction of new domains. Keil (1989) offered an account of compartmentalized change in the development of concepts and beliefs within a language community. Key notions are that the child has to make essentially the same revolutionary discovery within each domain, and that same decisive step will be taken early for some domains and later for others. Briefly, for domain after domain, the child starts off by relying on recognizing regularities in their experience or in the information they have been given. This early data-driven phase will eventually give way to obeying conventional definitions that can hold true despite appearances.

To illustrate the process, Keil made up pairs of short stories. In one type of story, an entity was presented as having the usual characteristics, but it was explicitly presented as lacking the defining attribute. In the other type of story, the entity fitted the definition but contained atypical characteristics. For example, in one story a mean smelly old man with a gun in his pocket came and took away the television set at the request of your parents because they did not want it any longer. Despite appearances, the man was not a robber. In the contrasting story, a cheery and affectionate woman took away your toilet-bowl without permission and never brought it back. Despite appearances, the woman was indeed a robber. At the end of each story, the child was asked whether the protagonist was a robber. Pairs of stories were written for many concepts. The question was at what age children shift from reliance on appearances to reliance on the socially defined reality. The results were rather beautiful.

First, even 5-year-olds understood rather well the 'moral' domain with terms 'lie,' 'tease,' steal,' 'cheat.' That is a useful finding, because such concepts are what the child acquires knowledge about as her theory of mind develops. Second, a lot of the data pointed to a regularity whereby if one term in a domain was grasped (e.g., the cooking term 'bake'), then other common terms in that domain tended to be grasped (e.g., 'boil' and 'fry'). That is, concepts do indeed seem to differentiate out in little clusters. Thirdly, the mastery of basic terms in different domains was a long process, spread out over years. Finally, there was just enough material to suggest that the process should be investigated as a human universal across different socio-cultural formations. The work shows how it is possible to put children's thinking under a microscope and expose something of what it is like to be a child. Imagine that you are a child with your parents having a picnic on a small island when the tide starts rising. Unless you firmly understood that the defining characteristic of an island is to be entirely surrounded by water, you would not share your parents' concern to abandon the picnic and to secure a precipitate retreat. There are ample opportunities for adult and child minds to be at cross-purposes through no-one's fault. Cross-purpose can always arise where two people understand concepts differently yet use the same words.

In summary, research into cognitive development since the early 1980s, has largely swept away the old concept of children progressing by great across-the-board intellectual changes, in favor of vastly complicated models in which progress is made in mini-domain after mini-domain as the child comes to acquire a working idea that explains the reality behind the appearance. The outcome of that mental work is that the child will come to do more than to know about what is in a domain. She will come to know what it is to know about the domain. In that sense, the child can develop a theory of any domain. She can develop into an amateur linguist, mathematician, biologist, or physicist. No matter how bright the child may be, though, nothing guarantees that her theoretical grasp of one domain will energize her advance in another domain. It may or may not. Many a brilliant mathematician flounders inarticulately in language class, and many a brilliant linguist retreats from working out the area of a triangle.

Mental work and mental play

Are the theories of domain-specific learning at all adequate to deal with one of the most puzzling of all aspects of human beings? One would think that evolutionary pressure would put the highest premium on an organism being kept in firm contact with reality. It comes naturally in all cultures, however, to spend a lot of our time during early childhood with our heads in clouds of pretense. In pretense, as has been discussed at inordinate length in the theory-of-mind literature, truth conditions are suspended. It does not contradict pretense to point out to a child that her pretend game is not true to the brute facts of reality. That would not deter the child from continuing to play.

It is in pretend play that one sees impressively long series of joined-up thinking being done by very young children long before they can puzzle through problems with a similar structure that demand reality-testing at each step along the way. There is a role for children in feeding their nascent theories into the imagination. It is a way of overcoming our minds' fragmentation into domain-specific forms of knowledge, especially if refreshed by the ample use of analogy and metaphor that comes naturally to our species. The end result is the emergence of whole ideologies that are mixes of reality and magical thinking. In the process of laying down the basis for reality-oriented theories of the world, the child builds up creative and imaginative ways of putting her ideas to work. Children's addiction to playfulness is a vital part of their mental growth. Variability is often best expressed and easiest explored once the trammels of reality become a bit loosened.

Conclusions

Although it is never possible to foresee how theory will develop, it is straightforward to identify current preoccupations of many researchers as reflected in the strength of research trends that fill the journals. One ambition is to refine theory so as to get a unified account that propounds cognitive change along with behavioral change. Thus, with age, children generally learn to avoid blurting out something before they have given themselves time to think things through. That sort of phenomenon is often found under the general heading of 'executive functions.' It is a challenge to model executive-control processes so that they become integral to an account of domain-specific conceptual change. Such research needs a secure grounding in developmental neuropsychology. Neuromodeling has an important component that rests on making comparisons with populations who develop differently. Important advances are currently being made in respect of people with autism and Williams syndrome. Such broadening of theoretical scope is one of the most encouraging aspects of research over the past generation.

See also:
Constructivist theories; Dynamical systems approaches; Clinical and non-clinical interview methods; Cognitive development beyond infancy; Moral development; Executive functions; Play; Autism; Williams syndrome; Cognitive neuroscience; Jean Piaget

Further reading

Barrett, L., Dunbar, R. and Lycet, J. (2002). *Human Evolutionary Biology*. Basingstoke: Palgrave.

Bornstein, M. H. and Lamb, M. E. (eds.) (1999). *Developmental Psychology: An Advanced Handbook*, 4th edn. Hove: Erlbaum.

Kuhn, D. and Siegler, R. S. (eds.) (1999). *Handbook of Child Psychology*. New York: Wiley.

Dynamical systems approaches

GREGOR SCHÖNER

Introduction

When a liquid is heated from below, convection patterns may form in which warm currents rise to the surface in the centers of tightly packed hexagons, while the cooler parts of the liquid sink to the bottom at the boundaries of the hexagons. Such patterns are 'self-organized' in the sense that they arise from the laws of fluid flow and of heat transport through an instability, in which a small initial fluctuation grows into the full, regular convection pattern. The theory of such pattern-forming systems is based on the mathematics of non-linear dynamical systems.

One origin of dynamical systems approaches to development was an analogy between such forms of self-organization and the emergence of ordered patterns of nervous and behavioral activity in organisms. Although the analogy turned out to hold only superficially, the language of dynamical systems has proven fertile for a new perspective on developmental processes. An entry point was the study of patterns of coordinated movement, from which a dynamical systems approach to the development of motor behavior was initiated (Thelen & Smith, 1994). More recently, these ideas were extended to a dynamic field theory that addresses cognitive aspects of motor behavior and spatial representations (Thelen, Schöner, Scheier, & Smith, 2001). At a more abstract level, analogies between behavioral transitions and mathematical phenomena in catastrophe theory and non-linear dynamics were used to describe processes of change during development (van Geert, 1998). Also, neural network models are formally dynamical systems, a fact that has been made explicit in a number of connectionist models.

This entry first provides a brief tutorial of the relevant mathematical background of dynamical systems theory. The coordination of movement is used to illustrate the dynamical systems approach to the development of motor behavior. Dynamic field theory is illustrated in the context of the Piagetian A-not-B task. Links to other variants of dynamical systems approaches and to connectionism are discussed last.

What are dynamical systems?

The notion of dynamical systems comes from the branch of mathematics that has formed the foundations of most applications of mathematical formalization to the sciences. Through the theory of differential equations, this notion is central to physics and engineering, but is also used in a wide range of other fields.

A system is called 'dynamical' if its future evolution can be predicted from its present state. This lawfulness of temporal evolution comes to light only if appropriate state variables (lumped into a vector $\mathbf{x}$) are identified. Given any possible initial state, the future evolution of the state variables is coded into the instantaneous direction and rate of change, $d\mathbf{x}/dt$. This vector points from the initial state to the state in which the system will be found an infinitesimal moment in time later. The dynamical system thus ascribes to every possible value, $\mathbf{x}$, of the state variables, a vector, $\mathbf{f}(\mathbf{x})$, that indicates the direction and rate of change from this particular value. This vector field is the dynamical function appearing on the right-hand side of the differential equation that formally defines the dynamical system:

$$d\mathbf{x}/dt = \mathbf{f}(\mathbf{x})$$

In physics and other disciplines, the principal task consists of finding appropriate state variables, $\mathbf{x}$, and identifying the associated dynamical function $\mathbf{f}(\mathbf{x})$, which together capture the determinism and predictability of a system.

How might a specific scientific approach arise from a setting as general as this? Dynamical systems approaches to development are based on a much more specific class of dynamical systems, those having attractor solutions. Figure 1 illustrates the idea for the simplest case, in which the state of the system can be captured by a single state variable, $\mathbf{x}$. For any possible initial state, $\mathbf{x}$, the rate

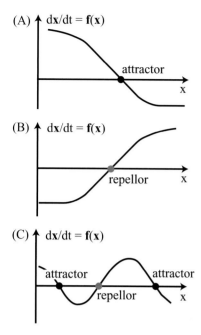

(A) dx/dt = **f(x)**

attractor
x

(B) dx/dt = **f(x)**

repellor x

(C) dx/dt = **f(x)**

attractor   attractor
repellor   x

Figure 1. The dynamical function, **f(x)**, determines the rate of change, d**x**/dt, of state variable, **x**, for every initial value of **x**. Intersections with the x-axis (marked with filled circles) are fixed points. (A) Fixed points are attractors when the slope of the dynamical function is negative. (B) A positive slope makes the fixed point unstable. (C) A bistable dynamical system has two attractors, separated by an unstable fixed point.

of change, d**x**/dt, determines whether **x** will increase (positive rate of change) or decrease (negative rate of change). The cross-overs between these two regimes are points at which the rate of change is zero, the so-called fixed points. When the initial state of the system is in a fixed point, the state does not change further, and the system remains fixed at the initial state.

In part (A) of the illustration, the region with positive growth rate lies at smaller values of the state variable than the region with a negative growth rate, so that the dynamical function has a negative slope around the fixed point. Therefore, from a small initial value, the state variable increases as long as the growth rate remains positive, that is, up to the fixed point. From a large initial value, the state variable decreases as long as the growth rate remains negative, that is, up to the fixed point. Thus, the fixed point attracts nearby initial states. Such a fixed point is an attractor state. An attractor is a stable state in the sense that when any perturbation pushes the state away from the attractor, the system is attracted back to this state. Conversely, if through some change in the system, the attractor state is displaced, the system follows that change, tracking the attractor.

When the arrangement of regions of positive and negative rate of change is reversed (part [B] of the figure), an unstable fixed point emerges at their boundary. Now, the dynamical function, d**x**/dt = **f(x)** intersects with a positive slope at the fixed point, so that

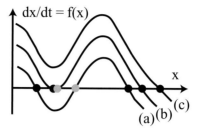

dx/dt = f(x)

x

(a)(b)(c)

Figure 2. Three dynamical functions representing three points in a smooth change of the dynamical function, which consists of shifting the function upwards. (a) Initially, the dynamical function has three fixed points, two attractors (black filled circles) and one unstable fixed point (circle filled in gray). (b) As the function is shifted upward, one attractor and the unstable fixed point move toward each other until they collide and annihilate at the instability. (c) When the function is shifted up more, only one attractor remains.

small deviations from the fixed point are amplified. When a perturbation pushes the system away from the fixed point to larger levels, the positive rate of change drives the system further up. Analogously, a perturbation to lower values is enhanced by the negative rate of change.

Unstable solutions separate different attractor states. Part (C) of Figure 1 shows a case in which there are two attractors, one at small values, the other at larger values of the state variable. At each attractor, the slope of the dynamical function is negative. Between the two attractors is an unstable fixed point marking the boundary between the two attractors. Any initial state to the right of the unstable fixed point is attracted to the right-most fixed point and any initial state to the left of the unstable fixed point is attracted to the left-most attractor.

Clearly, a linear dynamical function, **f(x)**, cannot generate multiple fixed points, because a straight line intersects the **x**-axis only once. Thus, multistability, that is, the co-existence of multiple attractors and associated unstable fixed points, is possible only in non-linear dynamical systems.

When a system changes, the dynamical function may be altered. Mathematically, such change can be described through families of dynamical functions that smoothly depend on one or multiple parameters. Most smooth changes of the dynamical function transform the solutions of the dynamical system continuously. There are, however, points at which a smooth change of the dynamical function may lead to qualitative change of the dynamics, that is, to the destruction or creation of attractors and unstable fixed points. Such qualitative changes of a dynamical system are called instabilities. Figure 2 provides an example in which an initially bistable system is changed by increasing the overall rate of change. This pushes the left-most attractor and the unstable fixed point toward each other until they collide and annihilate. Beyond this point, only the right-most attractor remains. Thus, a particular attractor disappears as the dynamical function is changed in a global, unspecific manner. As the instability is approached, the slope of the dynamical function near the doomed attractor becomes flat, so that attraction to this fixed point is weakened. Thus, even before the instability is actually reached, its approach is felt through lessened resistance to perturbations (hence the term 'instability'). If the system was initially in the left-most attractor, the instability leads to a switch to the right-most attractor.

Coordination dynamics

How are such abstract mathematical concepts relevant for understanding behavior and development? That stability is a fundamental concept for understanding nervous function has been recognized since the early days of cybernetics. For any given nervous function or behavior, the large number of components of the nervous system and the complex and ever changing patterns of sensory stimulation are potential sources of perturbation. Only nervous functions that resist such perturbations, at least to an extent, may persist and actually be observable.

What is it though, that needs to be stabilized against potential perturbations? To visualize the ideas think first of the generation of voluntary movement. Most fundamentally, the physical movement of an effector (e.g., a limb, a joint angle, a muscle) must be stabilized against all kinds of forces such as the passive, inertial torques felt at one joint as a result of accelerations at other joints. Stability at that level of motor control may be helped by the physics of the system (such as the viscous properties of muscles that dampen movement), although the nervous system clearly contributes.

In a slightly more abstract analysis, the time courses of the effectors must be stabilized. Dancing to music, for instance, not only requires stable movement, but also the maintenance of a particular timing relationship with the music. When the dancer has fallen behind the beat of the music, she or he must catch up with the rhythm. When the dancer has drifted ahead of the rhythm, he or she must fall back to the correct timing. Similarly, a bimanual reach requires the two hands to arrive at the same time at the object. This is the problem of coordination, either between a movement and an event in the world (e.g., to catch a ball or to keep up with a rhythm), or between different movement effectors (e.g., to coordinate different limbs or to keep an effector on a trajectory through space). The stability of timing is thus the maintenance of temporal alignment between different movement events or between movement events and events in the world.

At an even more abstract level, the overall form of a movement is described by such parameters as direction or amplitude. These parameters must be assigned values to initiate a movement and those values must be stabilized. When, during the initiation of a goal-directed hand movement, for instance, the movement target is displaced, then an automatic adjustment of the movement trajectory brings the hand to the correct target.

Stability is thus a concept that cuts across different levels of neural control of motor behavior. To illustrate the ideas, the rest of this section focuses on a single level and behavior: interlimb coordination during rhythmical movement, perhaps the behavior best studied to date using the concepts of dynamical systems approaches (Schöner, Zanone, & Kelso, 1992). The relative time order of the movement of two limbs can be experimentally isolated from other levels of control by minimizing mechanical demands and mechanical coupling (e.g., in finger movements at moderate frequencies) and by keeping spatial constraints constant. The relative phase between the trajectories of the two limbs can then serve as a state variable (Fig. 3A). It characterizes the relative time order of the two limbs independently of the trajectory shapes and movement amplitudes.

The two fundamental and ubiquitous patterns of relative time order in coordinated rhythmical movement are synchronous movement and alternating movement. Variations of these patterns underlie locomotory gaits, but are also observed in speech articulatory movements, in musical skills, and many other motor behaviors. However, both patterns are not available under all conditions. Scott Kelso discovered that when the frequency of the alternating rhythmical movement pattern is increased, the variability of relative phase increases, leading to a degradation of the alternating pattern until it can no longer be consistently performed (Schöner & Kelso, 1988). As illustrated in Figure 3, this leads, under some conditions, to an involuntary shift to the synchronous pattern of coordination. The intention to perform the alternating pattern (as manipulated by instruction) helps stabilize the pattern, but does not make it immune to degradation at higher frequencies.

From a dynamical systems perspective, the two basic patterns of coordination must be attractor states of an effective dynamical system controlling relative timing. Nervous activity of various structures putatively contributes to this effective dynamical system including sensory processes reflecting the position of each effector in its cycle, central processes reflecting movement plans, intentions, attention, and other possible cognitive factors, and finally motor processes reflecting the activation of muscles and effectors. The resulting

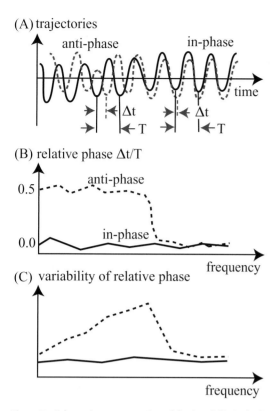

(A) trajectories

(B) relative phase Δt/T

(C) variability of relative phase

Figure 3. Schematic representation of the instability in rhythmic bimanual coordination. (A) The trajectories of the right (solid) and left (dashed) finger are shown as functions of time. The movement is initially coordinated in phase alternation, but switches to in-phase in the middle of the trial. This transition is induced by an increase in movement frequency. The relative timing of the two fingers can be represented by the relative phase, the latency between matching events in the two fingers' trajectories (here: minima of position) expressed in percent of cycle time. (B) The relative phase as a function of frequency (dashed line) reflects this shift from anti-phase (relative phase near 0.5) to in-phase (relative phase near 0.0). When movement starts out in the in-phase coordination pattern then it remains in that pattern (solid line). (C) That the loss of anti-phase coordination at higher frequencies is due to an instability is demonstrated by the observation that the variability of relative phase increases with increasing frequency in the anti-phase pattern (dashed line), but not in the in-phase pattern (solid line).

network has attractors whose stability is a matter of degree. Multiple processes contribute to that stability. When the stability of a pattern is ultimately lost, the performed coordination pattern changes.

Two additional observations are informative. Firstly, when at a fixed movement frequency a switch from synchronous to alternating coordination or back is performed purely intentionally, this process is not immune to the stability of the two patterns. Switching into the less stable pattern takes longer than switching into the more stable pattern. The process of achieving a desired pattern of coordination is helped by the mechanisms of stabilization of that pattern. In fact, from a theoretical perspective the conclusion is even more radical: to achieve a particular pattern, nothing but

stabilization is needed. With the appropriate stabilization mechanisms in place, the pattern emerges through the convergence of the dynamical state toward the attractor.

Secondly, when a new coordination skill is being learned, what evolves is not just the performance at the practiced pattern, but also performance at nearby, non-practiced patterns. For instance, after extensive practice at producing an asymmetrical, 90° out-of-phase pattern of rhythmical finger movement, participants are systematically affected when they try to perform similar, unpracticed patterns (e.g., 60° or 120° out-of-phase). They are biased toward the practiced pattern, performing patterns intermediate between the instructed relative phase and 90°. In some individuals, this effect is strong enough to reduce the stability of the basic coordination patterns of synchrony and alternation, leading to instabilities induced by the learning process itself. Thus, what evolves during learning is the entire dynamical function governing the stability of the attractor states such as to stabilize the practiced pattern. Learning consists of the shaping of the dynamical function from which performance emerges as attractor states.

The conditions under which stable performance of a particular pattern emerges may therefore include both unspecific factors (movement frequency, mechanical load) and specific factors (intention, practice). The landscape of stable states is changed through instabilities. How do these insights impact on our understanding of the development of motor abilities? Three main insights to be gained from a range of studies are the following (Thelen & Smith, 1994). Firstly, at any point in the development of motor behavior, any particular movement pattern cannot be said to be either present or absent from the behavioral repertoire. The effective dynamical function underlying the relevant motor ability may be such that the pattern may emerge under appropriate environmental conditions or with appropriate motivation. Developmental change is thus characterized more adequately in terms of the range of conditions under which the pattern emerges as a stable state. This is clearly an insight linking gradualist thinking (at the level of mechanism, here of effective dynamical functions) and theories of the discontinuous change of abilities (at the level of the absence or presence of an attractor generating a particular action in a particular situation).

Esther Thelen (1941–2004) has shown, for example, that rhythmical stepping movements can be elicited at a much earlier age than the onset of walking, simply by providing mechanical support of the body and by transporting the feet on a treadmill (Thelen & Smith, 1994). More dramatically, when a split treadmill imposes different speeds on either leg, the coordination tendency toward alternation can still be detected. Thus, coordination mechanisms supporting stepping are already in place, waiting to emerge until other behavioral dimensions such as balance and strength change.

Secondly, learning a new motor ability means changing a dynamical function to stabilize the practiced pattern. Developmental processes that lead to the emergence of new motor abilities can therefore be understood as inducing change in the underlying dynamical functions that increase the stability of the new pattern. The theoretical insight is that such gradual stabilization is sufficient for the new pattern to emerge, either continuously or abruptly through an instability. The development of reaching movements in infants is a well-studied exemplary case. A number of studies have established that, during the months over which this ability is developed, the kinematic and kinetic patterns generated by the infant reduce in variance, although the specific patterns onto which this process converges at this stage are highly specific to the individual.

Thirdly, instabilities drive differentiation. If the dynamical function characterizing motor behavior in an early stage of development permits only a small number of attractor states, new states may emerge from instabilities through which these attractors split and multiply, in each case in relation to environmental and internal conditions. The empirical support for this rather broad theoretical conclusion is less direct. One indication is the transition from an early tendency to display stereotypical movements to a capacity later in motor development to generate task-specific movements. Convergent evidence comes from the general tendency for younger infants to have greater difficulty in disengaging from a specific motor activity, gaze direction, or from a particular stimulus, than older infants.

The dynamic field approach

The dynamical systems ideas reviewed up to this point lend themselves naturally to the analysis of overt motor behaviors, for which state variables at different levels of observation can be identified. The evolution of these state variables can be observed continuously in time, and, on that basis, the stability of attractor states can be assessed through the variability in time or from trial to trial.

Even within the motor domain, limitations of this approach can be recognized. When a goal-directed movement is prepared, for example, movement parameters such as direction, amplitude, amount of force to apply, duration, and others are assigned values, which may be updated when the relevant sensory information changes. More generally, however, the assumption that each movement parameter has a unique value at all times that evolves continuously is a strong one, but for which there is only limited support. There is, for instance, not always a trace of previous values when a new motor act is prepared. When moving to more abstract forms of cognition, the need for additional concepts becomes clearer still. While spatial memory, for example, can still be conceived of as being about an underlying continuous variable, the quality of having memorized no, one or multiple spatial locations must also be expressed. In perception, sets of stimuli might be thought to span continuous spaces of potential percepts, but the presence or absence of a particular stimulus and a particular percept must be represented as well.

An important extension of the dynamical systems approach is, therefore, the integration of the concept of activation into its framework. Activation has been used in theoretical psychology and the neurosciences many times to represent information. In connectionism, for instance, computational nodes (i.e., neurons) are activated to the degree to which the information they represent is present in the current input. This is the space code principle of neurophysiology, according to which the location of a neuron in a neural network determines what it is that the neuron represents (i.e., under which conditions the neuron is activated). Activation thus represents the absence (low levels of activation) or presence (high levels of activation) of information about a particular state of affairs, coded for by the neuron.

The link between the notion of activation and the dynamical systems approach is made through the concept of a dynamic field of activation that preserves the continuity of that which is represented, such as the continuity of the space of possible movements or the continuity of memorized spatial locations. At the same time, information about those spaces is likewise represented through continuous values of state variables by introducing continuously valued activation variables for each possible point in the underlying space. The result is activation fields, in which an activation level is defined for every possible state of the represented quantity.

Figure 4 illustrates the different states of affairs such an activation field may represent. To make things concrete, think of the field as representing the direction of a hand movement. A well-established movement plan consists of a peak of activation localized at the appropriate position in the field. In the absence of any kind of information about an upcoming movement, the activation field is flat. More typically, however, there is prior information about possible upcoming movements. Such information may come from the perceptual layout of work space, from the recent history of reaching, from cues, etc., and is represented by graded patterns of activation.

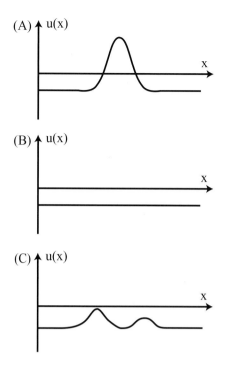

Figure 4. Patterns of activation in an activation field u(x) may represent (A) particular values of the underlying dimension, x, through the location of a peak of activation; (B) the absence of any specific information about that dimension; or (C) graded amounts of information about multiple values of the underlying dimension.

The preparation of a movement then consists of the generation of a peak of activation localized at the appropriate value of the underlying dimension, starting out from a more or less pre-structured pattern of prior activation. This generation is conceived of as the continuous evolution in time of the activation field, as described by a dynamical function that links the rate of change of the activation field to its current state.

In the simplest case, the activation field evolves toward attractors set by input. When, for example, a unique movement goal is specified by the perceptual layout (e.g., a single object is visible in work space), perceptual processes may be assumed to provide input to the movement parameter field that drives activation up at field locations representing movement parameter values appropriate to achieve reaching to that object. This input-output mode of operation requires perceptual analysis, extraction of metric information from the scene, and coordination transformations to translate spatial information into information about corresponding movement parameter values.

It is easy, however, to encounter situations that inherently go beyond this input-output scheme. Natural environments have rich visual structure in work space so that a form of selection or decision making must occur to prepare a particular movement. The classical Piagetian A-not-B task, for instance, involves a form of such decision making (Thelen *et al.*, 2001). Infants between 7 and 9 months of age are presented with a box

into which two wells have been set, each covered by a lid. With the infant watching, a toy is hidden in one well, a delay imposed, and then the whole box is pushed toward the infant, so the lids can be reached for. At the time a reach is initiated, there are two graspable objects in the visual layout, the two lids of the two wells. Almost always, the infant reaches for one of the two lids, and thus makes a decision.

Most commonly, infants reach for the lid to which their attention was attracted when the toy was hidden. Subsequently, they will often recover the toy (although sometimes they enjoy just playing with the lids as well). Occasionally, however, infants may reach to the other lid, under which no toy was hidden. This error becomes quite frequent when the lid under which the toy is hidden is switched, so that after a number of trials in which the infant retrieved the toy under the A lid, the toy is now hidden under the other, B lid. The rate at which the toy is successfully retrieved in such switch trials is much smaller than the rate observed during the preceding A trials.

Older infants do not make such A-not-B errors. Are their motor plans more input-driven? A detailed analysis reveals the contrary. At least three sources of input contribute to the specification of the reaching movement in the A-not-B paradigm. The act of hiding the toy under one lid, together with attention-attracting signaling, provides input that is specific to the location of the hidden toy. This input is present only temporarily before the delay period, after which the infant initiates a reach. In contrast, the lids themselves provide constant input that is informative about the two graspable objects. Finally, the effect of prior reaches can be accounted for by assuming that a memory trace of previous patterns of activation is accumulated over time, biasing the motor representation to maintain the motor habit, that is, to reproduce the previous movement.

In a dynamic field model built on these three types of input (Fig. 5), the A-not-B error arises because input from the memory trace at A dominates over activation at B. Although specific input first induced activation at B on a B trial, this activation decays during the delay. This explains why there is less A-not-B error at short delays than at longer delays. In order to avoid the A-not-B error at longer delays, activation at the cued location must be stabilized against decay and be enabled to win the competition with the activation induced by the memory trace of previous reaches. This requires interaction, that is, the interdependence of the evolution of the field at different field sites. Activation at neighboring field sites belonging to a single peak of activation may be mutually facilitatory, which helps sustain activation even when input is reduced. Activation at field sites that are sufficiently distant to contribute potentially to separate peaks of activation may be mutually inhibitory, so that the field sites in effect compete for activation. When the

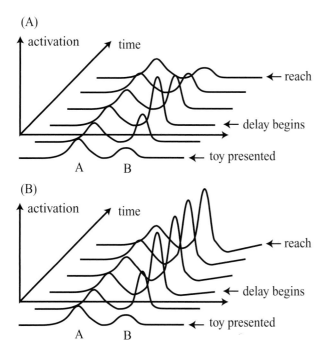

Figure 5. The temporal evolution of an activation field representing reaching targets in the A-not-B task during a B trial. Perceptual input at the two locations A and B pre-activates the field initially. At the A location, there is additional pre-activation due to the memory trace of prior reaches to A. When the toy is presented at B, activation near that location increases. (A) In the input-driven system modeling younger infants, this activation peak decays during the delay period, so that when the reach is initiated, activation at A is higher. (B) The interaction-driven system modeling older infants self-sustains the peak even as specific input at B is removed. When the reach is initiated, activation at B is higher.

relative weight of interaction compared to the weight of input increases, an instability occurs.

At low levels of interaction, the field is input-dominated, so that for every input pattern, there is a unique matching activation pattern. At sufficiently large levels of interaction, the field may become interaction-dominated. Now there is no longer a unique mapping from input to activation patterns. New, self-stabilized patterns of activation may arise. One such pattern is self-sustained activation, in which a peak first induced by input remains stable even when the input is removed. Another related pattern is decision making, in which two sites receive input, but only one site develops a peak of activation.

The hypothesis underlying the dynamic field account of the A-not-B effect stipulates that the field goes through such an instability, transforming itself from an input-driven system at younger ages to an interaction-driven system at older ages. According to this hypothesis, older infants do not make the A-not-B error, because the dynamic field representing planned reaching movements is capable of sustaining activation at the initially cued site and stabilizing this sustained activation in B trials against input from the memory trace of previous A trials.

The hypothesis is supported by a wealth of detailed effects that can successfully be predicted or explained. For instance, the rate of spontaneous reaches to B during trials in which the toy was hidden at A is linked by the theory to the rate of A-not-B errors. Before the instability, both spontaneous and A-not-B errors are frequent while beyond the instability both are infrequent.

A number of different factors may put any given dynamic field on either side of the instability. Thus, whether an infant perseverates or not depends on the behavioral and stimulus context. The A-not-B error may be enhanced by providing more opportunity to reach to A first (building up a stronger memory trace there). It is reduced by spontaneous errors when infants reach to the B location on A trials. This happens because a memory trace is built up at the B location as well. Experiments in which the A and B locations are switched several times (maybe even dependent on the infants' responses) potentially lead to memory traces at both locations reflecting each particular history of reaching, so that conclusions about the underlying representation become tenuous. The rate of A-not-B errors also depends on the perceptual layout (how visually distinct and symmetrical the two lids are), and on the reinforcement received from successful retrieval (e.g., lids that flash and make sounds when lifted up lead to a stronger memory trace than plain lids).

In these kinds of experiments, the locations to which reaches may be directed are always perceptually marked by the visible lids. In the theory, this is reflected by the fact that the perceptual layout pre-activates the field at these two locations. The underlying continuum of possible movements is thus not directly accessible to experimental observation. This is different in the sandbox version of the experiment, which reproduces the A-not-B experiment, except that the toy is hidden by burying it in the sand in one of two locations and then smoothing the sand over, so that no perceptual marker of the hiding location remains (Spencer, Smith, & Thelen, 2001). Toddlers retrieve the toy by digging for it after the imposed delay period. The location at which they begin to search is used to assess the movement plan. After a series of A trials, 2-year-olds show a clear pattern of attraction toward the A location when the toy is first hidden at the B location. Figure 6 illustrates how this attraction effect comes about in the dynamic field model. The peak induced when the toy is hidden at the B location drifts in the direction of the A location attracted by activation there due to the memory trace. This drift is suppressed in the traditional A-not-B experiment by input at both locations from the perceptual layout. The dynamic field account for this continuous version of an A-not-B error leads to the prediction that the attraction should be the larger, the more time is left between induction of the peak and execution of the movement.

(A)

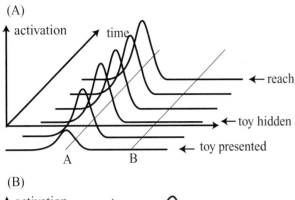

(B)

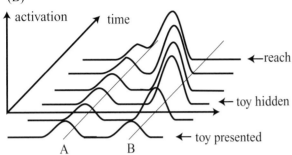

Figure 6. The temporal evolution of an activation field representing reaching targets in the sandbox task, in which there is no permanent input from the perceptual layout. (A) Thus, on an A trial there is no perceptual pre-activation at location B, so that the peak induced at A is unperturbed. (B) On a B trial, a peak is induced at the B location when the toy is presented. Activation at location A induced by the memory trace of prior reaches begins to attract that peak once the toy is hidden, as there is no input at B that stabilizes the peak's position.

Such enhanced attraction at longer delays was indeed found.

The dynamic field account of the A-not-B error operated with the underlying continuum of movement plans, graded patterns of activation, and their continuous evolution in time. The toy as an object did not actually play any particular role, other than perhaps modulating the effective strength of the specific input. In fact, Linda Smith and Esther Thelen have demonstrated that the A-not-B error can be observed when the toy is completely removed from the paradigm (Smith, Thelen, Titzer, & McLin, 1999). The hiding of the toy is replaced by a waving of a lid, to which attention is attracted until it is put down over the well. Thus, less embodied forms of cognition, such as representing the hidden toy as an object independently of the associated action plan, are not necessary to understand the error. We may be learning nothing about such forms of cognition from the A-not-B paradigm. Instead, the paradigm informs us about a simple form of embodied cognition, the maintenance of an intention to act that is stabilized against the tendency to repeat a habit. This cognitive ability emerges whenever activation is sufficient to launch neuronal interaction.

In terms of the dynamic field framework, what is it then that develops? Just as in the earlier approach to movement coordination, the answer is that it is the dynamical function, now of the field, that develops. Specifically, the regime of self-sustained activation is enlarged so that the induced activation can be stabilized against the memory trace of previous movements over a wider set of perceptual layouts, specific cues to the hiding location, distractor information, and delays. How this change of the dynamical function is propelled by the ongoing sensory and motor experience of the infant is not yet understood.

Relationships to similar theoretical perspectives

At a conceptual level, connectionist approaches to development overlap broadly with dynamical systems approaches. The notion of distributed representation shares the emphasis on the graded, sub-symbolic nature of representation. Both the notion of activation-carrying network nodes of connectionism and the notion of activation fields are compatible with basic concepts of neurophysiology. Many connectionist networks are, technically speaking, dynamical systems, so that activation patterns in the networks evolve gradually in time under the influence of input and interaction. While there are technical differences in how instabilities are used and analyzed, these are not fundamental and may vanish as both approaches develop.

Dynamical systems approaches have hardly addressed the actual mechanisms of learning, focusing as a first step on an assessment of what it is that evolves during learning. In contrast, the explicit modeling of learning mechanisms has been central to connectionist approaches. One important observation of those is that characteristic signatures of such learning mechanisms may emerge from simple learning rules. For example, a fixed neuronal learning rule may lead to a time-varying rate at which new vocabulary is acquired (low rates initially, a maximal rate at intermediate levels of competence, with a return to low rates at relatively high levels of competence).

This form of emergence is analogous to the emergence of a particular attractor under appropriate conditions from the dynamical function characterizing a particular function in dynamical systems approaches. In such approaches, the states that emerge when perceptual or task conditions are changed are particular states of behavior or performance, and emergence comes from the dynamical function characterizing behavior. In contrast, in connectionism, the signatures that emerge are properties of the processes of learning, occurring on a longer time scale, while at any fixed time during the learning process, the system is typically characterized by its input-output function.

Linking these two complementary aspects of the two approaches is an obvious next step of scientific inquiry. Thus, dynamical systems approaches must be expanded to include dynamical accounts of the actual processes of learning. Connectionist models must be expanded to address dynamical properties of behavior at any given point during learning processes, including non-unique input-output relationships and the continuous evolution of activation on the fast time scale at which behavior is generated. First steps toward such a fusion of the approaches are now being made.

Perhaps because they were originally developed most strongly in the motor domain, dynamical systems approaches have provided accounts that link behavior quite closely to underlying sensorimotor processes, and thus to their neural and physical substrates. The dynamic field concept is an attempt to extend this thinking to the level of representations, again providing strong links to continuous sensory and motor surfaces. In contrast, connectionist approaches have been particularly strong in the domain of language, and thus were often constructed on the basis of relatively abstract levels of descriptions. Network nodes that represent letters, phonemes, keys to press, or even perceived objects are commonly used as input or output levels. This lack of a close link to actual sensory or motor surfaces weakens the strength of the gradualist, sub-symbolic stance of connectionism and gives some of the connectionist models the character of simplified, if exemplary, toy-like models. A second potential line of convergence could arise if connectionist models were scaled up to provide closer links to sensory and motor processes.

There are variants of dynamical systems approaches, represented by authors like Han van der Maas (catastrophe theory) and Paul van Geert (logistic growth models), that do not emphasize this link to sensory and motor processes as much (van Geert, 1998). These approaches are based on a theoretical stance somewhat similar to connectionist thinking. They depart from the discovery of analogies between characteristic signatures of developmental processes such as stages, dependence on individual history, or dependence on context on the one hand, and properties of non-linear dynamical systems such as bifurcations, sensitive dependence on initial conditions, or the existence of structure on multiple scales on the other hand. These analogies are exploited at a relatively abstract level. There is less emphasis on a systematic approach toward identifying the state variables that support such processes, as well as the specific dynamical functions that characterize these processes. These forms of dynamical systems approaches are thus less directed toward maintaining a close link between behavior and motor and sensory processes.

Conclusions

Stabilization is necessary for any behavior to emerge, not only at the level of motor behavior, but also at the level of representation. Conversely, once stabilization mechanisms are in place, behavioral or representational states may emerge under appropriate conditions. Instabilities lead to change of state and are thus landmarks of qualitative shifts in behavior and cognitive capacity. Dynamical systems provide the theoretical language in which these properties of behavior can be understood.

Dynamical systems ideas are impacting on our scientific understanding of development in a variety of ways. The most important implication is, perhaps, that what develops is the dynamical function, from which the various observable behavioral states may emerge as attractors. Thus, appropriate landmarks of development are not these states as such, but rather the range of sensory, behavioral, or environmental contexts in which the states become stable. Development may lead to the stabilization of a particular behavioral or representational state. It may also, however, facilitate the suppression of particular states and the associated inputs through instabilities, leading to flexibility and the differentiation of the dynamical landscape of behavior.

See also:
Neuromaturational theories; Constructivist theories; Learning theories; Cognitive development in infancy; Perceptual development; Motor development; Development of learning and memory; Connectionist modeling; Locomotion; Prehension; Sleep and wakefulness; Cognitive neuroscience; Jean Piaget

Further reading

Fischer, K. W. and Bidell, T. R. (1998). Dynamic development of psychological structures in action and thought. In R. M. Lerner (ed.), *Handbook of Child Psychology (fifth edition)*, Vol. 1: *Theoretical Models of Human Development*. New York: Wiley, pp. 467–561.

Schutte, A. R. and Spencer, J. P. (2002). Generalizing the dynamic field theory of the A-not-B error beyond infancy: three-year-olds' delay- and experience dependent location memory biases. *Child Development*, 73, 377–404.

Thelen, E. and Smith, L. B. (1998). Dynamic systems theories. In R. M. Lerner (ed.), *Handbook of Child Psychology (fifth edition)* Vol. 1: *Theoretical Models of Human Development*. New York: Wiley, pp. 563–634.

PART II

Methods in child development research

This part reviews a number of the key aspects of methodology used in the study of child development. It is emphasized that each of them has appropriate applications, which stem from questions about development arising from the theories in Part I. The final section considers the sometimes neglected ethical issues that can arise from such questions, particularly with regard to research involving children.

Data collection techniques

Magnetic Resonance Imaging **Michael J. L. Rivkin**
Clinical and non-clinical interview methods
   Morag L. Donaldson
Cross-cultural comparisons **Ype H. Poortinga**
Cross-species comparisons **Sergio M. Pellis**
Developmental testing **John Worobey**
Observational methods **Roger Bakeman**
Experimental methods **Adina R. Lew**

Data collection techniques

Magnetic Resonance Imaging

MICHAEL J. L. RIVKIN

Introduction

During infancy through early childhood and on into adolescence, there occur fascinating changes in cognitive, social, and motor development that can be inferred to reflect changes in brain development. Certain postnatal biological correlates of these developmental changes such as myelination and synaptogenesis have been studied in detail in animal models and in human tissue. However, investigation of the complex process of human postnatal brain development has been hindered by the dearth of tools for non-invasive, high-resolution in vivo study of brain structure and function.

Attempts to understand the reasons for delay in cognitive development have prompted interest equal to that in normal development. These delays may range from global mental retardation to autism to more discrete learning disabilities. For example, despite the discovery of anatomical and some functional differences in comparisons of autistic patients and controls, little is known about the functional organization of the brain of the child suffering from autism. Similarly, about 53,000 very low birthweight (VLBW) infants are born each year in the USA. More than 50 percent of these children will require some form of special needs or educational support in school because of learning difficulties. At least half of these children possess normal-appearing brains when evaluated with conventional structural magnetic resonance imaging (sMRI). Improved understanding of the brain's functional organization in these children is essential if more effective treatment strategies are to be developed. Clinical populations such as these are likely to benefit from the application of new imaging tools for non-invasive, high-resolution in vivo study of brain structure and function.

There are several neuroimaging or neurophysiological methods available for the non-invasive study of brain development. Each offers relative advantages and disadvantages (Table 1). The current entry focuses upon the structural and functional information afforded by Magnetic Resonance Imaging (MRI) techniques about brain development in children. MRI techniques provide the powerful capability for the non-invasive investigation of human neurodevelopment. Recent efforts to use MR neuroimaging to plumb the depths of brain and cognitive development during childhood will be addressed. Firstly, the application of structural and quantitative volumetric MRI to study postnatal brain development will be reviewed. Secondly, the technique of diffusion tensor imaging will be presented. Finally, use of functional MRI (fMRI) to investigate cerebral function in children will be explored.

Structural and volumetric Magnetic Resonance Imaging techniques

Non-invasive MRI methods have permitted close scrutiny of postnatal myelination in the brain. Myelination data derived from these studies have compared favorably to data derived from neuropathological investigations. Several aspects of early brain development have been studied with MRI techniques, such as changes in cerebral gyration and sulcation in preterm and term neonates. MR images were obtained from preterm infants between the gestational ages (GA) of 30 and 42 weeks. Five stages of advancing sulcal-gyral development were identified beginning at 30 weeks and extending to 41 weeks. Sulcal and gyral development was most advanced in regions of the central sulcus and medial occipital lobes at birth while anterior frontal and temporal regions were most immature at birth. Similarly, inferior and anterior frontal and temporal regions demonstrated the slowest rate of sulcal and gyral development. Using T1 signal-weighted (T1-W) and T2 signal-weighted (T2-W)

Table 1. Comparison of selected non-invasive techniques for measurement of brain function.

Technique	Description	Technique advantage	Technique disadvantage
Electroencephalography (EEG)	scalp electrodes detect electrical potentials generated by underlying neurons	good temporal resolution	poor spatial resolution
Evoked response potentials (ERP)	scalp electrodes detect responses of underlying neurons to sensory stimulation	good temporal resolution	poor spatial resolution
Magnetoencephalopgraphy (MEG)	scalp measurement of local magnetic field generated by underlying neuronal activity	no volume- or tissue-dependent signal attenuation	limited availability
Positron emission tomography (PET)	measures positron emission from intravenously administered radioactive isotope	provides information about blood flow or receptor density in brain	radioactivity exposure
Functional Magnetic Resonance Imaging (fMRI)	measures BOLD signal from neural activity-related changes in regional blood flow	good spatial and temporal resolution	requires focused subject compliance
Optical imaging	measures neural activity-related changes in cortical light reflectance	good spatial and temporal resolution	non-invasive use possible only in infants

techniques, one study found a very simple brain at 25 weeks GA almost devoid of cortical folding. Only elementary sylvian and parieto-occipital fissures, central and calcarine sulci, and cingulate sulci were observed. Thus, the sulcal and gyral configuration of the developing brain matures at a region-dependent rate. Furthermore, as GA advances so do sulcal and gyral formation (van der Knapp *et al.*, 1996).

MRI has been used to quantify total brain volume and that of its tissue constituents in infants and older children. Three-dimensional MRI has been combined with post-imaging data processing that assigns each image voxel to one of the tissue sub-classes of background, skin, cerebrospinal fluid (CSF), cortical gray matter, sub-cortical gray matter, unmyelinated white matter, or myelinated white matter. Total brain tissue volume was found to increase linearly from 28 weeks GA to term. Cortical gray matter increased fourfold in the same time period. Similarly, sub-cortical gray matter volumes increased during this period. Finally, a rapid and widespread increase in the volume of myelinated white matter was found late in the third trimester (Huppi *et al.*, 1998). An example of such a tissue segmentation of an infant's brain is found in Figure 1.

Although MRI has proven effective in demonstrating the structural changes in the brain during the immediate postnatal period, conventional MRI techniques have not been equally successful in discerning structural changes in the brain that accompany developmental advances of

children from 1 year of age until the attainment of adulthood. Recently, however, advances in development of quantitative algorithms have permitted determination of global and regional brain volumes during this longer epoch of child development.

Morphometry, an imaging technique that can determine the volume occupied by a specific structure(s) that constitutes an organ of interest, has been performed on the brain. Using this technique cerebrum, cerebellum, and basal ganglia, as well as specific sub-regions of these central nervous system (CNS) structures have been determined in children. In a group of males and females ranging in age from 3 months to 30 years, cortical gray matter volume increased throughout early childhood, reached its apogee by 4 years of age, and gradually declined thereafter. Predictably, white matter volume increased until the twentieth year. Similarly, a longitudinal MRI study of brain development demonstrated that gray matter volume increased throughout childhood only to decrease late in adolescence before adulthood (Giedd, Blumenthal, Jefferies, *et al.*, 1999).

A study of typically developing children revealed effects of both age and sex upon brain development. Basal ganglia volume decreases while temporal lobe structures such as the hippocampus and amygdala increase in volume with age (P. M. Thompson *et al.*, 2000). Males demonstrate larger cerebral, cerebellar, putaminal, and pallidal volumes than females. Caudate nuclei in females are larger than in males. While boys

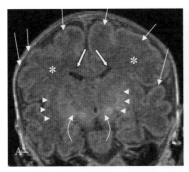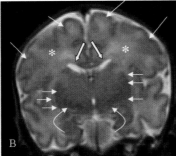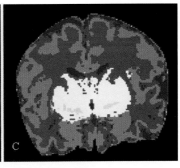

Figure 1. Example of quantitative MRI imaging for the purpose of tissue segmentation in the developing brain. **(A)**: T1-W spoiled gradient recalled (SPGR) coronal brain image from a healthy 35 weeks gestation premature infant. High signal is found in the cortical gray matter (arrows), and scant myelinated white matter (curved arrows). Low signal is found in unmyelinated white matter (asterisks) and ventricles (bold arrows). The sub-cortical gray matter (arrowheads) provides a signal intermediate between cortical gray matter and unmyelinated white matter. **(B)**: T2-W image of same slice as in A. Low signal is found in the cortical gray matter (large arrows), and scant myelinated white matter (curved arrows). High signal is found in the water-rich unmyelinated white matter (asterisks) and ventricles (bold arrows). The sub-cortical gray matter (small arrows) provides a signal intermediate between cortical gray matter and unmyelinated white matter. **(C)**: resultant segmentation of same coronal slice shown in (A) and (B). Cortical gray matter is denoted by gray color, unmyelinated white matter by red color, sub-cortical gray matter by white, cerebrospinal fluid by blue color, and myelinated white matter by yellow.

possess a total cerebral volume that is 10 percent larger than that found in girls, neither cerebral nor cerebellar volumes change appreciably after 5 years of age. Quantitative MRI study of the temporal lobe has revealed a similar pattern of sex-specific characteristics. The volume of the amygdala increases with age in males as compared to females. Conversely, hippocampal volume increases with age more in females than in males, and was found to be greater in young adult females than in males.

Recently, maturational changes in the brain have been detected during adolescence using three-dimensional (3D) quantitative MRI. Several investigators have observed that gray matter volume reduction has been counterweighed by enlargement of white matter to produce a stable total brain volume well into adolescence. Statistical mapping techniques applied to high-resolution MRI data sets reveal that reduction in gray matter was most evident in dorsal regions of both frontal and parietal lobes. These regions of gray matter reduction segmented as gray matter in younger children only to become classified as white matter in older adolescents. Taken together, these data indicate that volumetric changes can be observed beginning in the newborn period, and continue to be evident on a regional basis in the brain throughout early childhood and adolescence.

Myelination and diffusion tensor imaging

While the sequence of myelination has been studied extensively in neuropathological series, several investigators have used MRI techniques to study its progress in the term and preterm newborn infant. Myelination is predominantly a postnatal process. Its progress is best detected using T1-W images during the first six months of life and with T2-W images, thereafter. Using these techniques, myelination has been detected in cerebellar peduncles at 25 weeks GA followed by the crura cerebri, inferior colliculi, globus pallidus, dorsolateral putamen, and ventrolateral thalamus. Myelination can also be discerned in the posterior limb of the internal capsule by 37–38 weeks gestation using T2-W pulse sequences.

Despite the important information about myelination of the preterm and term newborn brain provided by conventional MRI techniques, information has been lacking about the architecture of white matter in the newborn. Recently, diffusion tensor magnetic resonance imaging (DTI) has been applied to study of the newborn brain. This method measures the ability of water to move in the medium studied. In the case of the two studies mentioned previously, the relevant medium was white matter. Diffusion of water in the cerebral white matter is dependent on the extent to which fiber tracts limit its movement. This property derives from water's ability to move more easily in parallel rather than perpendicular to white matter fibers. Diffusion anisotropy refers to the ability of water to move more in certain directions than in others dependent on the orientation of white matter fiber tracts surrounding it.

Using DTI, the diffusion tensor can be calculated on a voxel-by-voxel basis. The diffusion tensor describes the principal direction of water movement in a given voxel. As a result, it provides indirect but accurate information

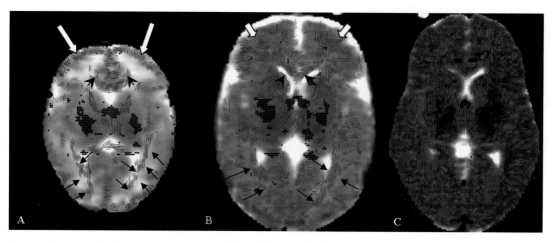

Figure 2. Examples of diffusion tensor images in children. **(A)**: brain diffusion tensor map for an axial brain slice from a premature infant at the age of 34 weeks gestation. Red lines denote anisotropic water diffusion in the image plane while black stippling indicates water diffusion perpendicular to the image plane. The anterior aspect of the corpus callosum (black arrowheads) and the optic radiations (black arrows) are visible. Areas of black stippling indicate the internal capsules, bilaterally. No evidence of anisotropic diffusion is found in the frontal lobes (bold white arrows). **(B)**: similar axial slice obtained from the same child as in (A), but at the age of 42 weeks gestation. Post-image processing and threshold determination were identical to those used in (A). Once again the anterior corpus callosum (black arrowheads) and optic radiations (black arrows) are visible. Note that anisotropic diffusion is much more evident in the frontal lobes bilaterally than was evident in (A) (bold white arrows), indicating more advanced white matter development than is found at the earlier age. **(C)**: diffusion tensor map from a 10-year-old male for an axial slice similar to those seen in (A) and (B). Note the greater anisotropic water diffusion throughout both hemispheres than is found in either (A) or (B).

about the orientation of the white matter fibers that determine the magnitude and direction of water movement. This method has been used on a regional and global basis to study white matter microstructure in human infants.

Interestingly, the ability of water to diffuse in the human brain is highest during infancy and progressively declines thereafter. This characteristic is attributable to the scarcity of white matter myelination found at birth. However, the progressive reduction of water mobility at such an early age is a subject of considerable interest. When the diffusion properties of white matter in the brains of preterm infants were examined longitudinally between the ages of 32 and 42 weeks GA at loci in the posterior limb of the internal capsule, anterior corpus callosum, and frontal white matter, an increasing tendency for water to move more in certain directions than in others was observed.

Careful histochemical study of the developing newborn brain has established that evidence of myelination is not found in the posterior limb of the internal capsule, the anterior corpus callosum, and the frontal lobe until 40 weeks, 52 weeks, and 52 weeks GA, respectively. Therefore, these data provide important evidence of change in white matter diffusion properties in the brain of the preterm infant prior to the onset of myelination (Vajapeyam *et al.*, 2002). Changes in diffusion tensor measurements are not limited to the

neonatal and early infant period as they extend well beyond early childhood and have been detected during adolescence (Fig. 2).

Functional magnetic resonance imaging

Functional magnetic resonance imaging (fMRI) has recently provided identification of regional cerebral activity during tests of human cognition performed by adults. This approach has produced compelling maps of human cognitive activity that are superimposed on detailed neuroanatomical images of the brain. This technique takes advantage of the different magnetic properties of deoxyhemoglobin as compared to those of oxyhemoglobin.

Activated areas of human brain show localized increases in blood flow. While blood flow increases to a region of brain actively engaged in function, the amount of oxygen extracted from the increased volume of blood is unchanged from that extracted when cerebral tissue is at rest. This results in a net increase in the amount of oxygenated hemoglobin flowing through an activated region of brain. This regional increase in oxyhemoglobin concentration produces an increase in the derived MR signal. An MR signal difference may be calculated for a given region of brain from the higher signal obtained during activation as compared to that found during rest.

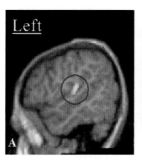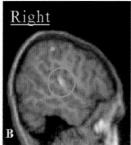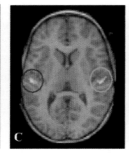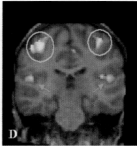

Figure 3. Composite fMRI map for fifteen children 9–11 years of age who performed paced alternating bimanual finger tapping to a 3 Hz metronome. These difference maps compare activation for tapping to metronome versus rest. **(A)** and **(B)**: sagittal slices of brain show activation found in posterior superior temporal gyrus on the left and right, respectively. **(C)**: axial view at the level of sub-cortical gray matter reveals activation found in posterior superior temporal gyri, bilaterally. **(D)**: coronal view reveals bilateral activation in primary motor cortices (circles) to correspond with the subjects' alternating bimanual finger tapping movements. Activation of posterior superior temporal gyri is indicated by green arrows.

The patient is asked to perform 'activation' tasks such as reading words or watching visual patterns to activate a cerebral region of interest. Thus, the fMRI signal difference derived from comparison of two or more cognitive states is blood oxygen level dependent and forms the basis for the Blood Oxygen Level Dependent (BOLD) signal that serves as the comparative basis for fMRI. Recently, it has been demonstrated that the BOLD signal corresponds more closely to the local field potentials associated with the afferent neural signal to a given region rather than to the action potentials that emanate from it (Logothetis *et al.*, 2001).

Despite exciting brain mapping work performed already in adults, this approach has not been applied as frequently to the study of cognitive development. Nonetheless, important data from children have begun to emerge. One study employed fMRI in conjunction with the activation paradigms of antonym and verb generation to localize language in a 9-year-old child. In addition, comparisons of children and adults performing a single-word processing task have revealed a developmentally dependent pattern of activation to a language activation paradigm. Finally, in a developmental fMRI study of performance on a go/no-go task, children demonstrated different patterns of activation than adults.

Clinically, fMRI language paradigms have been used to map language centers prior to the performance of epilepsy surgery or brain tumor extirpation. Furthermore, fMRI has been applied to the study of patients with attention deficit disorder (ADD) and attention deficit-hyperactivity disorder (ADHD). Differences in fronto-striatal activation have been identified between children with ADD and normal controls using fMRI and the go/no-go task as an activation paradigm.

Functional MRI has been applied to the study of motor control in children (Rivkin *et al.*, 2003). Children 9 to 10 years of age recruited as normal volunteers were studied while listening to a metronome cadence and matching its rhythm with alternating bimanual index finger tapping (Fig. 3). The images revealed a picture of a distributed neural network necessary for tapping to match a rhythm provided by auditory means. In short, there was regional activation of auditory, primary motor, supplementary motor, and pre-supplementary motor cortices and cerebellum.

Conclusions

The development of human cognitive function constitutes a fertile and fascinating field of research. MRI techniques now afford a high-resolution, non-invasive in vivo view of the human CNS. A panoply of MRI techniques may be used together with neuropsychological and neurological evaluations to study neurodevelopment in children. Importantly, current MRI techniques will be complemented by other techniques, such as evoked potentials, electro- and magnetoencephalography, and transcranial magnetic stimulation, to provide greater spatial and temporal resolution than is currently available.

It is likely that further refinement of imaging techniques will permit direct measurement of the induced small magnetic fields produced by neuronal activation. Further, new molecular contrast agents are likely to permit cellular and molecular MR imaging, and thus the study of location and function of discrete neuronal populations in the brain. Much like the field of human molecular biology in the early 1990s, an assortment of tools for the quantitative and rigorous exploration of human cognitive development are now available. The results of their use in the decade ahead will yield insight into the development of the human mind and brain that will indeed be fascinating.

See also:
Cross-sectional and longitudinal designs; Normal and abnormal prenatal development; Cognitive development in infancy; Cognitive development beyond infancy; Motor development; Language development; Attention; Brain and behavioral development (I): sub-cortical; Brain and behavioral development (II): cortical; Executive functions; Face recognition; Imitation; Sex differences; Autism; Behavioral and learning disorders; Cerebral palsies; Dyslexia; Prematurity and low birthweight; Williams syndrome; Cognitive neuroscience; Pediatrics

Further reading

Davidson, M. C., Thomas, K. M. and Casey, B. J. (2003). Imaging the developing brain with fMRI. *Mental Retardation and Developmental Disabilities Research Reviews*, 9, 161–167.

Rivkin, M. J. (2000). Developmental neuroimaging of children using magnetic resonance techniques. *Mental Retardation and Developmental Disabilities Research Reviews*, 6, 68–80.

Peterson, B. S., Anderson, A. W., Ehrenkranz, R., Staib, L. H., Tageldin, M., Colson, E., *et al.* (2003). Regional brain volumes and their later neurodevelopmental correlates in term and preterm infants. *Pediatrics*, 111, 1432–1433.

Clinical and non-clinical interview methods

MORAG L. DONALDSON

Introduction

Interview methods typically involve face-to-face interaction between a researcher and a participant, with the researcher asking questions and the participant giving verbal answers. In child development studies, interview methods have been used with various types of participants, most notably children, parents, and teachers, to investigate many aspects of development, and to address a wide range of theoretical and applied issues. Here, we will focus mainly on the use of interviews with child participants to investigate their knowledge, reasoning, and understanding (i.e., their cognitive development).

Interviews versus other methods for developmental research

The use of interview methods to investigate children's cognitive development can be contrasted with a variety of other research methods, including observations of children in natural settings, reports from teachers and parents, psychometric tests of intelligence, and experimental techniques. However, the distinction between interviews and experimental tasks is not entirely clearcut. Once children are old enough to use and understand language reasonably proficiently, experimental studies on their cognitive development will often incorporate aspects of the interview method, in that the researcher will ask questions in the context of a structured, specially designed task that will typically involve both verbal and non-verbal activities. Similarly, while interview methods tend to be more constrained, focused, and artificial than observational methods, the data obtained from observations of children interacting with adults (especially in classroom settings) will often include question-and-answer sequences that have much in common with those that occur in interviews.

Piaget and his interview method

Historically, interview methods for studying cognitive development have their origins in the work of Jean Piaget (1896–1980). Piaget's central aim in interviewing children was to uncover and describe their cognitive structures (i.e., the general principles underpinning their knowledge, reasoning, and understanding). He therefore adopted an approach that had much in common with that used by psychiatrists in diagnostic interviews, and that has therefore become known as the 'clinical (interview) method'. He wanted to encourage children to talk freely about particular topics, so rather than asking a standard set of questions to all children, he based his questions on the individual child's responses to previous questions.

Subsequent research on cognitive development has been heavily influenced by Piaget's pioneering work, so interview methods have continued to figure prominently. There has been an increasing tendency, though, to follow a pre-determined script in which the questions are the same (or at least similar) for all children. This type of interview method is generally referred to as 'non-clinical', but the distinction between clinical and non-clinical methods is probably best regarded as being a matter of degree.

The key features of clinical and non-clinical interview methods will now be described before turning to a consideration of their strengths, weaknesses, and applications.

Table 1. An example of the clinical interview method.

Adult:	*When you are out for a walk what does the sun do?*
Child:	*It comes with me.*
Adult:	*And when you go home?*
Child:	*It goes with someone else.*
Adult:	*In the same direction as before?*
Child:	*Or in the opposite direction.*
Adult:	*Can it go in any direction?*
Child:	*Yes.*
Adult:	*Can it go wherever it likes?*
Child:	*Yes.*
Adult:	*And when two people go in opposite directions?*
Child:	*There are lots of suns.*
Adult:	*Have you seen the suns?*
Child:	*Yes, the more I walk and the more I see, the more there are.*

J. Piaget (1929). *The Child's Conception of the World.* London: Kegan Paul, Trench, Trubner.

Table 2. Types of responses in Piaget's clinical interviews.

Type of response	What the child does . . .
Answer at random	Provides an answer without thinking about it, because not interested in the question or does not understand it.
Suggested conviction	Is led to a particular response by the nature of the researcher's question and/or by a desire to satisfy the researcher.
Romancing	Engages in playful fantasy and invents an answer that is not really believed.
Liberated conviction	Bases answer on original reasoning, but without having previously considered the issue addressed.
Spontaneous conviction	Bases answer on original reasoning carried out previously.

Clinical interview method

A flavor of the clinical interview method can be gained from the extract in Table 1 in which a 6-year-old child is being interviewed to investigate whether young children regard the sun as being animate and capable of engaging in purposeful activities.

Piaget (1929) emphasized that in conducting such interviews, the researcher needs to steer a middle course to avoid the two dangers of ". . . systematisation due to preconceived ideas and incoherence due to the absence of any directing hypothesis" (p. 9). In other words, the researcher has to try to avoid leading the child in a particular direction through suggestion, while at the same time making the most of opportunities to formulate and test hypotheses about the nature of the child's understanding. Similarly, in interpreting children's answers, it is important to avoid the two extremes of assuming either that all answers are 'pure gold' (i.e., can be taken entirely at face value), or that they are all 'dross' (i.e., are of no value whatsoever). Instead, Piaget advises researchers to consider carefully the status of individual responses, by being alert to the distinctions amongst five main types of response (see Table 2).

In Piaget's view, the first two types of response (answers at random and suggested convictions) should be discounted since they are uninformative regarding the nature of children's thinking. He regarded spontaneous convictions as the most informative type of response, although liberated convictions can also be revealing and romancing responses may be interesting so long as they are interpreted cautiously. The status of responses cannot be determined by considering individual responses in isolation. Rather, it is necessary to consider an individual child's pattern of responses throughout an interview, and to compare these responses to those of other children of the same and different ages, as well as to observations of spontaneous speech. For example, Piaget argues that random answers and suggested convictions are typically unstable, and so they can be identified if a child changes answers when questions are repeated in different guises or when counter-suggestions are introduced.

A counter-suggestion is a comment or question that challenges the child's answer by highlighting a potential contradiction, and that is designed to counteract the possible suggestive influence of an earlier question. For instance, in the extract in Table 1, the interviewer challenges the child's claim that the sun follows people by asking what happens when two people go in opposite directions. Piaget argues that if it were simply the nature of the interviewer's initial question ("When you are out for a walk what does the sun do?") that had led the child to reply in animistic terms, then the child would be likely to change his answers when faced with a potential contradiction. In this case, though, the child persists with a similar line of argument, so Piaget concludes that the answers reflect spontaneous convictions (i.e., thinking that is systematic and relatively stable, albeit erroneous).

Non-clinical interview methods

Non-clinical interview methods are more structured than the clinical interview method in that the researcher follows a more standard protocol. The degree of structure and standardization varies from study to study, depending on such factors as the topic under investigation, the children's age, and the researcher's aims. In most cases, the researcher will try to present the same basic set of questions to all the participants, and in reporting the study will specify the nature of and rationale for any variations.

As in clinical interviews, the questions in non-clinical interviews are usually designed to test the researcher's hypotheses about the nature of children's thought processes. However, the way in which particular questions will be used to test hypotheses is worked out in advance and is used to guide the design of the interview protocol, rather than being worked out 'on line' as the interview progresses. For example, in order to investigate children's theory of mind, Perner, Leekam, & Wimmer (1987) asked 3- and 4-year-olds a series of questions about a scenario in which John puts some chocolate in one location (e.g., a drawer in the living room), but his mother transfers it to another location (e.g., the kitchen cupboard) while he is away at the playground. On the basis of previous research, Perner *et al.* hypothesized that 3-year-olds have a fundamental conceptual inability to attribute false beliefs to another person, and therefore that they will give incorrect answers to the test question:

> When John comes home where will he look for his chocolate?

That is, they will say that John will look in the kitchen cupboard, where the chocolate really is, rather than in the living-room drawer, where he falsely believes it to be. Since incorrect answers might reflect difficulties in remembering or understanding key aspects of the story rather than in reasoning about false beliefs, some additional control questions were included to test this alternative hypothesis:

> Where did John put the chocolate in the beginning?
> Where did John's mother put John's part of the chocolate?
> Where was John when mother put it there?
> So did John see her put it there?

Thus, as in clinical interviews, children's answers to a single question are not taken at face value. Instead, alternative interpretations are evaluated by asking a series of carefully constructed questions. However, in non-clinical interviews, the questions are typically planned in advance as part of the design of the study and are the same for all participants, rather than being formulated in the course of the interview for each individual child.

Strengths and weaknesses of interview methods

In discussing the strengths and weaknesses of clinical interviews, Piaget (1929) compared them on the one hand to observational methods and on the other hand to psychometric tests of intelligence. He regarded his clinical method as combining some of the advantages of these two alternative methods, while avoiding many of their disadvantages. At an early stage in his career, Piaget worked in the laboratory of Alfred Binet (1857–1911), one of the pioneers of intelligence testing in children. While appreciating the value of standardized intelligence tests for making quantitative assessments of the extent to which individual children's intellectual abilities are consistent with the norm, Piaget's goal was to characterize the qualitative aspects of children's thinking. He was therefore interested not so much in how many correct answers the children gave as in the types of errors they made and what these might reveal about their underlying cognitive processes. He argued, nevertheless, that standard tests were not well suited to his aim of exploring children's thinking in depth. For example, since the questions always had to be asked in the same way, it was hard to tell whether the particular way a question was worded had influenced the child's answer.

Piaget's clinical method was designed to create a less artificial and broader context in which the researcher could probe the basis of the child's answers. By considering children's answers in context, the clinical method preserves one of the key advantages of observational methods. Indeed, Piaget argued that, before conducting clinical interviews, the researcher should engage in 'pure observation' of children's spontaneous questions, and use this as a basis for deciding on the types of questions to ask in the interviews. At the same time, the clinical method enables researchers to exercise a greater degree of control than observational methods do, in that they can ask questions in order to test their hypotheses about the nature of the child's reasoning, and in order to encourage the child to consider issues that might not arise spontaneously.

On the other hand, as Piaget himself acknowledged, the clinical method does have some drawbacks. Conducting clinical interviews and interpreting children's responses requires high levels of skill, sensitivity, and experience on the part of the researcher. Piaget recommended at least a year of daily practice! Also, the heavy reliance on the individual researcher's skill and intuitions, as well as the inevitable variations in the form of the interview from child to child, raises concerns about the generalizability and replicability of findings. These are some of the reasons why more recent research has tended to employ non-clinical interview methods, which involve a greater degree of structure and uniformity in the questions asked.

Non-clinical interview methods, like clinical interview methods, occupy an intermediate position relative to observational methods and psychometric tests, and hence enable researchers to exercise more control over the direction and focus of their investigation than observational methods would allow, but within a more natural and flexible context than is typical of psychometric tests. Non-clinical interviews lie somewhat closer to psychometric tests than clinical interviews do because they use a more structured and predetermined schedule of questions.

The higher degree of structure in non-clinical interviews, compared to clinical interviews, brings both advantages and disadvantages. Non-clinical interviews are more readily compatible with the research paradigms, methods of statistical analysis, and scientific reporting styles that are dominant in contemporary experimental psychology. It is easier to compare findings, both across studies and within a study (e.g., between different age groups of children). On the other hand, there is usually less opportunity to pursue lines of questioning that an individual child's answers suggest might be interesting. Also, if the interview script is very rigid, it can be difficult to resolve the confusions that may arise if a child misunderstands a particular question, and it can be difficult to make the sequence of questions flow naturally if a child gives an unexpected answer. In practice, though, most interviewers aim to achieve an appropriate balance between consistency and flexibility, rather than adhering to an absolutely rigid script.

One of the potential advantages of interviews (both clinical and non-clinical) as a method for studying children's understanding is that they are based on the intrinsically meaningful activity of answering questions, an activity with which children are familiar from their everyday conversations. However, while the similarity between interview methods and everyday conversations may help children to feel at ease and to grasp the basic nature of what they are expected to do, it may also mislead them into carrying over strategies that are appropriate in a conversational context but inappropriate in the more constrained, artificial context of a research study.

Donaldson (1978) argues that young children's understanding of everyday conversations is inextricably linked to their understanding of human purposes, and involves making sense of the overall verbal and non-verbal context. In contrast, researchers' interview questions typically require children to focus specifically on the exact wording of the questions themselves, in isolation from the interactional context in which they are embedded. For example, in a typical Piagetian conservation task, children are asked the same question (e.g., "Are there more red counters or more blue counters or are they both the same number?") both immediately before and immediately after the researcher carries out an action (e.g., moving the red counters closer together). Donaldson reports that young children are more likely to answer the second question correctly when the action

is made to appear accidental than when it is carried out in a deliberate manner. She interprets this as evidence that the researcher's deliberate action misleads the child into inferring that the action is relevant to the ensuing question, and hence into interpreting the question as referring to some property other than number (e.g. the length or density of the row of counters).

The developmental psychology literature contains many further examples of children's responses to interview questions being influenced by the way the questions are worded or by the context in which they are presented. When conducting interview-based studies, it is therefore important to take account of the ways in which the interaction may differ from a typical conversation. Before drawing firm conclusions, it is advisable to investigate how children respond to different wordings and different contexts, although this will often require a series of studies, to avoid confusing or overloading individual children with too many different questions within a single study.

A number of studies have shown that children aged between about 5 and 8 years are remarkably willing to answer questions that are bizarre or nonsensical, such as "Is red heavier than yellow?" (Waterman, Blades, & Spencer, 2001). However, this holds primarily for 'closed' questions (i.e., questions that can be answered "yes" or "no"). When children are asked nonsensical 'open' questions, such as "What do feet have for breakfast?" they usually say that they do not understand or that they do not know the answer. Similarly, when children are asked questions that are intrinsically sensible but unanswerable because the relevant information has not been supplied, they typically answer closed questions, but acknowledge that they do not know the answer to open questions. These findings suggest that presenting interview questions in an open rather than a closed format is likely to be advantageous, but the situation is complicated in that children sometimes find it difficult to respond to open questions even when they do have relevant knowledge.

Conclusions

Interview methods play a key role not only in research studies, but also in a variety of applied contexts. For instance, in forensic settings where children are interviewed as witnesses or victims of an alleged crime, it is crucial to develop interview techniques that will maximize the reliability of children's testimony and thus reduce the risk both of non-disclosure and of false allegations. Although further research is required, the currently available evidence suggests that beneficial factors include the interviewer being unbiased, asking neutral questions, minimizing the number of interviews and of repeated questions, and avoiding the use of threats, bribes, or peer pressure (Bruck, Ceci, & Hembrooke, 1998).

See also:
Constructivist theories; Theories of the child's mind; Developmental testing; Observational methods; Experimental methods; Parental and teacher rating scales; Self and peer assessment of competence and well-being; Ethical considerations in studies with children; Language development; Intelligence; Alfred Binet; Jean Piaget

Further reading

Flavell, J. H. (1963). *The Developmental Psychology of Jean Piaget*. Princeton, NJ: D. Van Nostrand.
Lewis, C. and Mitchell, P. (eds.) (1994). *Children's Early Understanding of Mind: Origins and Development*. Hove: Erlbaum.
Siegal, M. (1991). *Knowing Children: Experiments in Conversation and Cognition*. Hove: Erlbaum.

Cross-cultural comparisons

YPE H. POORTINGA

Introduction

The study of individual development across cultures ideally requires longitudinal research conducted in a range of societies, with data on individuals as well as cultural contexts. Such a combination implies a large investment of time and effort. Most cross-cultural research is cross-sectional, and the relatively few longitudinal studies tend to be limited both in time span and in the number or diversity of cultural groups examined (Berry, Dasen, & Saraswathi, 1997). Apart from less than optimal designs, cross-cultural research also has problems of method related to data interpretation.

In what follows, we first consider the issue of equivalence (i.e., the question of whether scores have the same meaning cross-culturally). Next, we address the two major theoretical perspectives of relativism and universalism that by and large correspond to the methodological distinction between 'qualitative' and 'quantitative' research. Thereafter, attention is paid to an issue that recently has been gaining more attention, namely, the distinction between cultural-level and individual-level data. The entry concludes with a brief reflection on the state of the art in cross-cultural methods and expected future developments.

Equivalence of data

Specific problems of cross-cultural comparison of data center on the notion of equivalence (van de Vijver & Leung, 1997). In a narrow sense, equivalence or inequivalence (i.e., cultural bias) refers to the question of whether scores obtained in different cultural groups can be interpreted in the same way. A broader and more basic question is whether the concepts of interest in a study have the same meaning and can be operationalized identically in procedures and instruments across cultures. For example, do similar reactions to the Strange Situation, often used to assess attachment in young children, reflect mother-child relationships similarly in all cultural contexts? Is adolescence found everywhere as a distinguishable developmental phase? And is 'filial piety' (respect for elderly parents) in China a characteristic that differs from concern for ageing parents in the West?

For the analysis of equivalence of cross-cultural data, researchers make use of multivariate techniques, such as exploratory and confirmatory factor analysis. A set of psychological variables, like items in a questionnaire or sub-tests in a cognitive battery, is considered equivalent in a qualitative (or structural) sense when a similar factorial structure is found in the cultures compared. Where such analyses are common (e.g., in cross-cultural research on personality traits), positive evidence for structural equivalence is often found. However, there is an important caveat: such studies tend to be limited to literate samples.

Even if cross-cultural data meet conditions for structural equivalence, there remain reasons why quantitative differences in scores should not be interpreted at face value. Firstly, score levels can be affected by biased items or stimuli in an instrument (item bias). Such incidental bias can be identified by analyzing whether differences in the statistics of a separate item deviate from expectations based on the entire set. Secondly, there are sources of bias that can affect all items of an instrument in a similar way (irrespective of whether the instrument is a questionnaire, interview, or observation schedule). Such method bias is difficult to identify, unless there is a common standard or criterion, and that is usually absent for data collected in geographically separated societies. Of the many kinds of method bias, cross-cultural differences in response styles (e.g., in social desirability, acquiescence) are perhaps the most likely to distort the meaning of results. For example, when asked about their children's behavior, parents' answers tend to be influenced by cultural norms. As a result, cross-cultural differences in the actual behavioral repertoire of children will be misrepresented in the data set.

Cultural relativism and universalism

The notion of equivalence is challenged by researchers from relativistic traditions who emphasize the specificity of culture-behavior relationships. In relativism, psychological functioning is seen as inherently embedded in culture. Also, the crystallization of such functioning in words and concepts is cultural. Thus, psychological concepts are formulated, and should be understood, within a given sociohistorical tradition. According to relativism, each culture is a unique developmental system (also called a developmental niche) that has to be analyzed and understood in its own terms. Research in different cultures employing standard experiments and instruments is frowned upon because it implies an imposition of one's own (usually Western) cultural understandings on others.

In this tradition, phenomenological and hermeneutic analysis, often referred to as 'qualitative methodology,' is advocated, which can bring out culturally unique and complex interactions of individuals within a developmental niche (e.g., Valsiner, 2000). A problem with much qualitative research is the question of the validity of results. One rarely finds attempts at confirmation (or falsification) of ideas and findings with procedures that are independent of rather subjective interpretations by the researcher. However, there are exceptions. A record of data in the form of videotapes can help to alleviate problems of subjective interpretation, as such data provide a permanent record that can be re-analyzed by other researchers.

Culture-comparative research, which largely follows the perspective of universalism, continues to form the main tradition in cross-cultural psychology. In terms of formal logic, any comparison requires concepts that apply equally to all the individuals or populations that are being compared. Such concepts acquire the status of universal psychological characteristics when they are shared across all cultures. However, in good comparative research, universals are not merely assumed to be present. The extent to which variables across cultures refer to shared and invariant characteristics is an issue to be answered empirically. Such characteristics can be defined in various ways, corresponding to various levels of psychometric equivalence, as mentioned before (van de Vijver & Leung, 1997).

Although cultural specificity and universality are often presented as a dichotomy, it is more fruitful to think of these two notions as the endpoints of a dimension. This implies the use of research designs in which both the culturally unique and the culturally common can emerge, and in which cross-cultural differences are expressed on a continuous scale (e.g., proportion of variance explained by culture). While applied cross-cultural research is mostly undertaken to emphasize the importance of cultural variation, basic research is also conducted with a view to identifying communalities underlying observed cultural diversity.

Individual level and culture level

Further methodological issues arise from the fact that data may not be equivalent across the two levels inherent in cross-cultural research, namely, the cultural level and the individual level. In psychological research, data are typically obtained from individuals. A relatively high frequency or mean score in a sample is then easily interpreted as a characteristic of the culture. Subsequently, any person from that culture tends to have that characteristic attributed to them. The inappropriateness of such attributions to individuals is readily apparent. For example, even in a society with a high rate of pregnancy, only a fraction of the women are pregnant at any moment in time. Similarly, it is a fallacy to attribute a collectivistic orientation indiscriminately to all members of a society with a high mean score on a scale of collectivism (van de Vijver & Poortinga, 2002).

Cross-cultural differences in mean scores on a wide variety of individual psychological variables, such as socialization practices, personality dimensions, and cognitive abilities, are correlated with country-level variables like national wealth (GNP) and quality of school education. Differences at country level on psychological variables may not reflect the same traits as individual-level scores. For example, cognitive ability at individual level and quality of school education at country level may be confounded, or there can be differential effects of non-target traits like response styles. Research design and analysis (so far) often do not allow one to distinguish such artifacts from valid psychological differences in the target traits.

Conclusions

Culture-comparative research is often limited to a few variables. A quasi-experimental design tends to be followed in which ecocultural or sociocultural conditions are antecedents and individual outcomes the consequent or dependent variables. This sort of design is confronted with two challenges. On the one hand, the restricted number of variables leads to poor representation of dynamical and complex interactions between the developing individual and the socializing context. On the other hand, there is a need for strict controls since culture is an extremely diffuse and encompassing concept, making ad hoc explanations of observed differences almost trivial. Hence, there is a continuous tension between the scope and relevance of studies for understanding development in cultural context, more emphasized in relativistic approaches, and validity issues, more emphasized in universalistic approaches. A variety of approaches may be needed rather than a single perspective. However, it remains a challenge to find a balance between ill-founded speculative accounts and stifling methodological requirements.

Methodological difficulties of culture-informed developmental research reflect to an important extent the absence of more precise and testable theories. Probably the most promising perspectives are those that will combine biological and cultural-contextual underpinnings of behavior (Keller, Poortinga, & Schölmerich, 2002). Cross-cultural studies can make an important contribution to the testing of such theories, providing data to help differentiate between species-wide processes and contextually bound variations in developmental patterns.

See also:
Experimental methods; Cross-sectional and longitudinal designs; Group differences in developmental functions; Cognitive development beyond infancy; Anthropology

Further reading

Berry, J. W., Poortinga, Y. H., Segall, M. H. and Dasen, P. R. (2002). *Cross-cultural Psychology: Research and Applications*, 2nd. edn. Cambridge: Cambridge University Press.
Cole, M. and Cole, S. R. (1999). *The Development of Children*. New York: Freeman.

Cross-species comparisons

SERGIO M. PELLIS

Introduction

Two children don 'Ninja Turtle' dress and proceed to engage in rough-and-tumble play (i.e., mock combat). Among mammals, such play fighting, as it is better known in the animal literature, varies from being completely absent in some species to being very common in others. The question of why such play exists and why it should vary in prevalence has defied

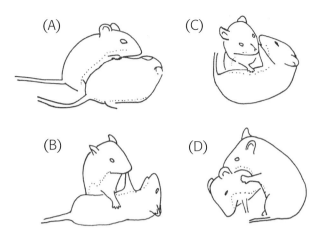

Figure 1. A sequence of play fighting is shown in a pair of deer mice. An attack to the nape of the neck by the animal on the left (A), leads to a defensive rotation to supine by the recipient (B), which then counter-attacks by lunging at the attacker's nape (C). This results in a role reversal (D). Adapted from S. M. Pellis, V. C. Pellis, and D. A. Dewsbury (1989). Different levels of complexity in the play fighting by muroid rodents appear to result from different levels of intensity of attack and defense. *Aggressive Behavior*, 15, 297–310.

satisfactory explanation. A comparative perspective reveals that even among those species that exhibit play fighting, the content can vary markedly. This information can then be used to ask a simpler set of questions. What are the sub-components of play fighting? Have these sub-components co-evolved? And what are the neurobehavioral mechanisms that regulate these sub-components, and how do these mechanisms emerge during development?

Analytical steps in comparative research

Cross-species comparisons can thus supplement the traditional tool kit of developmental studies. Differences between species can be used to fractionate a behavior that appears to be very complex into its constituent components, and then help identify the processes by which those components are integrated. Some of the analytical steps taken in using cross-species comparisons will be further illustrated using play fighting.

Step one: description

The first step of a comparative analysis is to describe the behavior in question. Play fighting involves attack, whereby one animal attempts to gain some advantage, such as contacting a particular body part of its partner, and defense, whereby the attacked animal takes actions to prevent its partner from attaining that advantage. A third component is counter-attack: after successfully defending against an attack, the defender attacks its partner (Fig. 1).

During serious fighting, an attack is often accompanied by a defensive maneuver by the attacker so as to

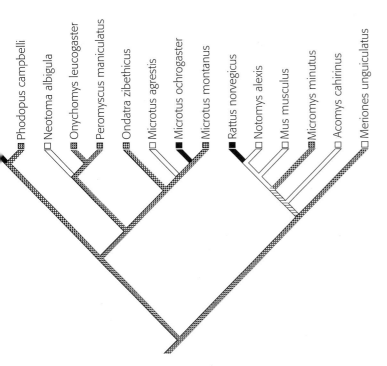

Figure 2. The complexity of play fighting in fifteen species of rodents was scored on a three-point rating system, with 0 being the least complex and 2 the most (see A. N. Iwaniuk, J. E. Nelson, and S. M. Pellis, 2001. Do big-brained animals play more? Comparative analyses of play and relative brain size in mammals. *Journal of Comparative Psychology*, 115, 29–41). Based on molecular and morphological data, the species were mapped onto a cladogram, showing differing degrees of relatedness. Finally, the 'character state' (i.e., 0, 1, or 2) for each species is mapped onto the cladogram, using a computer program (i.e., MacClade) that is capable of identifying the tree with the least or most parsimonious number of changes from ancestral to extant species (W. P. Maddison and D. R. Maddison, 1992. *MacClade: Analysis of Phylogeny and Character Evolution*, Version 3.05. Sunderland, MA: Sinauer). Thus, the transitions in character states from ancestral to extant species can be inferred. Note that in this case, the most likely ancestral state is for a moderate level of complexity in play fighting (gray for 1), with different lineages then either increasing (black for 2) or decreasing (white for 0) the complexity of their play fighting. One further point to note is that some transitions cannot be resolved as to the state of an ancestral node (shown as cross-hatched lines). Such unresolved portions of a cladogram help researchers identify potentially useful species for further analysis. Common names of species from left to right: Syrian golden hamster, Djungarian hamster, cotton rat, grasshopper mouse, deer mouse, muskrat, field vole, prairie vole, montane vole, Norway rat, hopping mouse, house mouse, harvest mouse, spiny mouse, Mongolian gerbil.

limit the ability of the opponent to counter-attack. Similarly, defensive actions are very vigorous, so as to block attacks. In play fighting, however, the attack is not accompanied with a defensive action, and defensive actions are not as vigorous as they are in serious fighting. Thus, in play fighting, attack and defense are organized in such a way as to promote the ability of the partner to counter-attack successfully. In this way, both animals have the opportunity to gain the advantage and

so maintain the reciprocal relationships typical of social play (Pellis & Pellis, 1998a).

When the species-typical proportions of attack, defense, and counter-attack are combined, many species differences in play fighting can be explained. Most of the remaining species differences appear to involve differences in the organization of the motor patterns used for attack, defense, and counter-attack. The juveniles of some species use the same tactics of attack and defense as do the adults in non-playful contexts (e.g., voles), whereas other species (e.g., rats) modify either the form or the frequency of use of those tactics (Pellis, Pellis, & Dewsbury, 1989).

Step two: accounting for phylogenetic relationships

The next step is to evaluate the distribution of these components across a range of related species. However, to do this requires that the comparisons take the phylogenetic relationships among the species into account. The reason for this is that similarity between two species could result from two different mechanisms. Species may be similar because their common ancestor was similar (homology), or because they converged on the same solution to a similar problem (analogy). For example, the wings of sparrows and hawks are homologous, whereas the wings of sparrows and butterflies are analogous. Therefore, to make cross-species comparisons, the phylogenetic relationship among the species has to be known. Figure 2 illustrates the mapping of the complexity of play fighting onto a cladogram for several species of rodents. Note that the most complex instances of play fighting appear on separate branches of the tree, suggesting that changes in complexity arise from convergence and not because of shared ancestry.

Domesticated Norway rats have the most complex play fighting among the group of related species of rodents represented in Figure 2. In part, domestication may have exaggerated the complexity of play present in rats, but the few data available suggest that wild rats have a similar pattern. Compared to the more simplified play fighting of mice and voles, the greater complexity of play in rats has required the evolution of novel behavioral, hormonal, and neural mechanisms. The analytical steps of fractionation and phylogenetic mapping have permitted the research to focus on those key features unique to a specific branch of the tree. The next step involves re-synthesis. That is, what processes bring together the combination of shared and unique features typical of play fighting in rats?

Step three: re-synthesis

Rats and mice not only differ in the complexity of play fighting, but also in a wide range of behavioral and cognitive capacities. Rats learn to solve a spatial navigation puzzle more quickly, manipulate food items more effectively, and have a greater range of behavioral options in dealing with other conspecifics. This shifts the comparative question from why play fighting is simpler in mice than in rats, to why behavioral and cognitive capacities generally are simpler, or less flexible, in mice than rats. A possible answer is that mice mature faster than rats and more of their brain growth occurs prior to birth, suggesting that delayed maturation of the nervous system may be related to increased behavioral flexibility (Whishaw, Getz, Kolb, & Pellis, 2001). Indeed, the amount of brain growth occurring after birth is a better predictor of species differences in the complexity of play fighting than is overall brain size (Iwaniuk, Nelson, & Pellis, 2001).

It is also possible that at least some of the mechanisms regulating play fighting in rats evolved in response to specific problems confronted by rats. For example, both rats and golden hamsters have complex play fighting (Fig. 2). However, in rats, but not hamsters, play fighting is retained in adulthood, and can be used for social assessment and manipulation, such as in dominance relationships (Pellis & Pellis, 1998a). Thus, some of the regulatory mechanisms in rats may not be just by-products of an overall difference in the rate of maturation, as signified by how quickly sexual maturity is achieved. When comparing rats with mice and hamsters, the issue becomes an empirical one: how many of the unique changes in the regulation of play present in rats can be accounted for by species differences in rates of development? The residual mechanisms not explicable by differences in the rates of maturation are the ones that need answering in terms of what novel conditions have led to their evolution.

Conclusions

What about the children in Ninja Turtle outfits? Play fighting in children includes all the elements present in rats, but can also include highly sophisticated levels of pretense, thus requiring additional levels of control not present in rats. Comparative studies of development in a wide range of primates can, as is illustrated for rodents, be used to determine what those levels of control may be and why the lineage leading to our species has developed them the way it has.

The example of play fighting shows that a comparative approach can change the question from a seemingly intractable one – "why do animals play fight?" – to one that is more manageable – "why do particular species have particular features in their play fighting?" Similarly, there are several complex human behavioral and cognitive capacities that have resisted decomposition into their fundamental constituents. A comparative

approach is beginning to yield novel insights into these phenomena (Parker & McKinney, 1999).

See also:
Ethological theories; Aggressive and prosocial behavior; Play; Ethology; Viktor Hamburger

Further reading

Brooks, D. R. and McLennan, D. H. (eds.) (2002). *The Nature of Diversity. An Evolutionary Voyage of Discovery.* Chicago, IL: University of Chicago Press.

Burghardt, G. M. (2004). *The Genesis of Play: Testing the Limits.* Cambridge, MA: MIT Press.

Pellis, S. M. (2002). Keeping in touch: play fighting and social knowledge. In M. Bekoff, C. Allen, and G. M. Burghardt (eds.), *The Cognitive Animal: Empirical and Theoretical Perspectives on Animal Cognition.* Cambridge, MA: MIT Press, pp. 421–427.

Pellis, S. M. and Pellis, V. C. (1998b). The play fighting of rats in comparative perspective: a schema for neurobehavioral analyses. *Neuroscience and Biobehavioral Reviews,* 23, 87–101.

Developmental testing

JOHN WOROBEY

Introduction

Developmental testing refers to the assessment of infants' or children's abilities across a number of domains in relation to their age, through the use of standardized tasks and procedures. Although certain aspects of traditional intelligence are usually measured, developmental testing entails a more comprehensive approach, with multiple areas of child functioning, such as motor and social development, also being assessed. As its name implies, such testing endeavors to capture the child's behavioral status at a particular point in time, recognizing that development is a dynamical process by which the normal child's abilities become increasingly more complex. To understand the rationale for developmental assessment in early childhood, it is useful to consider first the history of the testing of mental abilities.

A historical overview

European pioneers

As the 'Father of mental testing', Francis Galton (1822–1911) first constructed simple tests of memory, motor, and sensory functions in England in the late 19th century in order to differentiate between high and low achievers. At around the same time, Charles Darwin (1809–1882) suggested that studying early behavior might shed light on understanding the pattern of human development. His work inspired baby biographers, such as Wilhelm Preyer (and Millicent Shinn, 1858–1940, in the USA), who demonstrated that a regular sequence of behavior characterized the human infant, but that individual differences in rates of development were also important. In France, the challenge of identifying and treating the mentally deficient led people like Jean-Marc Itard (1775–1838), Etienne Esquirol (1772–1840), Edouard Sequin (1812–1880), and especially Alfred Binet, to construct a means for diagnosing and identifying the mentally retarded who might benefit from special education (Kelley & Surbeck, 1991).

By the beginning of the 20th century then, the science of mental testing was established. However, the early tests were predicated on the belief that intelligence was solely determined and fixed by genetics, and displayed via sensory functioning. Binet and Theodore Simon (1873–1961) are credited with developing the first test of mental ability in 1905 that attempted to measure judgment, reasoning, and comprehension in school-age children. While formulated around a century ago, their work convinced others that such tests should follow standard procedures for administration, should be simple in their scoring, and should provide results that distinguish the normal from the delayed (Kelley & Surbeck, 1991).

North American pioneers

In the early 1900s, a child study movement began in the United States, led by G. Stanley Hall (1844–1924). Two of his students, Henry Goddard (1866–1957) and Fred Kuhlmann (1876–1941), translated Binet's scales for American use, advocated early diagnosis, and extended the test items downward into infancy. Institutes of child welfare for the study of child development sprang up at land-grant universities across the States, with another of Hall's students, Arnold Gesell, becoming the first to explore systematically the developmental change and growth of normal children from birth to age 5. Like many of his predecessors, Gesell believed that biology predetermined growth and development, and took a maturational approach to the 'whole child.' That is, instead of a focus on intelligence, he presented a developmental schedule for the normal child that covered motor, language, adaptive, and personal-social behavior. Along with tests designed by his contemporaries at other institutes throughout the country, these normative scales generated a great deal of research, though initially with respect to their adequacy as measurement devices.

From intelligence to developmental testing: a US perspective

While new tests continued to be developed throughout the mid-part of the 20th century, the theory that guided the testing of children was fundamentally altered when psychologists began to reformulate their views of the nature of intelligence. Intelligence was now seen as multi-faceted, but, even more important, as environmentally influenced and therefore as modifiable. The recognition that the child's environment could exert a substantial effect on the child's test score, along with a confluence of other political factors, led the US government to create Head Start, a compensatory early childhood education program that was implemented nationally in 1965. It was soon realized, however, that the infant and child assessment instruments available up to that time had weak validity, were culturally unfair, and appeared to be inadequate for describing children's functioning. In 1975, Public Law 94-142 (Education for the Handicapped Act) was passed and mandated the provision of free and public education in the least restrictive environment. As required by the law, every handicapped preschool-age child must have an Individualized Education Plan (IEP) developed for him or her, which necessitates the evaluation and diagnosis of the individual child's level of functioning.

In response to these federal mandates, a veritable explosion in test construction took place, with estimates of more than 200 assessment instruments being constructed and published during the years from 1960 to 1980 (Kelley & Surbeck, 1991). Moreover, a shift from intelligence testing to the evaluation of overall development had clearly occurred. In fact, Public Law 99-457, which extended the provisions of PL 94-142 in 1986 and mandates an Individualized Family Services Plan (IFSP) for infants and toddlers, requires a statement of the infant or toddler's present levels of development in five domains. These areas are cognitive, psychosocial, language and speech, physical, and self-help skills (Gilliam & Mayes, 2000).

As it applies to early assessment and testing, cognitive development refers to the child's mental abilities and includes the sensorimotor abilities of infancy, such as object permanence, and the pre-academic skills of childhood, such as concept development. Psychosocial development includes attachment behavior, peer interaction, temperament, and adjustment. Language and speech development is comprised of communication abilities, both receptive and expressive. Physical development includes reflexes and muscle tone along with fine motor abilities, such as grasping and stacking, and gross motor abilities, such as walking and climbing. Self-help skills include those that allow for independent functioning, such as feeding, toileting, and dressing without assistance.

Testing for developmental delays and beyond

In contrast to intelligence testing, which may be done routinely by some school districts, or to help document giftedness, or solely for research purposes, developmental testing is largely undertaken in order to determine if an infant or young child is delayed in certain abilities and may benefit from some type of specialized early intervention. To this end, there are a number of applications that are served by developmental testing (Gilliam & Mayes, 2000). In screening, a brief device such as the Denver Developmental Screening Test is used to identify infants or children who may be at risk for a developmental delay, with a formal assessment to follow if the results warrant. Indeed, some screening tests, such as the Ages and Stages Questionnaire, which can be completed by parents as an initial step in early identification, are now also available.

The ideal screening instrument is inexpensive in terms of training and brief in its administration, and should err in the direction of false positives. That is, a good screening test will over-refer, so that children who may not have a delay are re-examined, rather than passed because the test could not detect a delay that they truly have. In diagnosis, a more comprehensive test is given in order to confirm or dismiss the possibility of a delay.

Normative-based tests such as the Bayley Scales of Infant Development devised over many years by Nancy Bayley (1899–1994) and the McCarthy Scales of Children's Abilities may be used to identify a general delay that derives from a mental, motor, or perceptual problem. It may, however, appear obvious from screening that a delay in a particular area is suspected, in which case a test that specifically assesses speech, language, cognition, or motor abilities may be employed. For example, the Kaufman Assessment Battery for Children might be used to obtain cognition scores for mental processing and achievement, while the motor domain of the Battelle Developmental Inventory can provide a breakdown of coordination, locomotion, and motor abilities.

For placement, the results of developmental or other domain-specific tests are used to determine whether or not a child is eligible for an early intervention program. A delay in one or more of the five areas described above is a sufficient criterion in qualifying for early intervention services. For intervention planning purposes, the child's IEP or IFSP requires a statement of the child's present levels of development in the five areas. Hence, the test results provide an entry-point for developing an instructional plan to meet individualized goals. Subsequently, the results of repeated developmental tests may be used for evaluation purposes, both to determine progress for an individual child, and across children to

determine the effectiveness of an intervention program. Finally, developmental testing is frequently employed in outcomes-based research, where the impact of ecological factors such as poverty or nutrition may be assessed (Klebanov, Brooks-Gunn, McCarton, & McCormick 1998; Lozoff *et al.*, 2000).

Challenges in developmental testing

While inherently rewarding, the testing of infants and children is nevertheless beset by a number of challenges. The absence of or limitations in language mean that verbal instruction cannot be given, and a substantial number of test items must be performance-based, with an objective way of measuring success. Although they are linguistically incompetent, infants are nevertheless quite skilled in their ability to communicate. That is, an uninhibited versus wary approach to the examiner means that the tester must be on guard not to reward ambiguous responses based on the infant's cuteness, or downgrade performance because the toddler appears to be shy. In addition to direct assessment, the examiner must often supplement testing with observations and caregiver reports (Gilliam & Mayes, 2000).

Because young children, and certainly infants, are not motivated to do their best, test items must also be attractive and interesting in order to arrest and sustain the child's attention. At the same time, because of an attention span that is relatively shorter the younger the child, the examiner must be sufficiently proficient in the particular test so that flexibility in administration can be assured. The testing of preterm infants may present additional problems. However, allowances by correcting for age are routinely made.

Conclusions

Despite their common purpose in identifying the strengths and weaknesses of the child's repertoire, the tests used for infants and children may vary considerably. Many tests take what is referred to as a developmental milestones approach, where items are included if they meet a 50th percentile criterion for a particular age (e.g., picking up a cube at 6 months). Others may take a stage approach, where the toddler's understanding of a Piagetian concept like means-end relations is assessed (e.g., using a small stick to obtain a small toy that is just out of reach). Finally, some tests may reflect a functional approach, where the child's ability to tie a shoelace, for example, is the behavior of interest. Although some tests are markedly superior to others, with their validity generally improving with increasing age of the child, extensive research in their use has resulted in the current availability of a number of devices, both new and revised, that meet appropriate standards for reliability and validity. Nevertheless, new approaches to testing will inevitably continue to evolve, and will serve more effectively to meet the challenge of measuring development. As the first step in identifying a child's strengths and weaknesses, developmental assessments will maintain a primary role in helping educators to optimize early development.

See also:
Neuromaturational theories; Clinical and non-clinical interview methods; Parental and teacher rating scales; Indices of efficacy; Cognitive development in infancy; Cognitive development beyond infancy; Motor development; Social development; Language development; Speech development; Intelligence; Temperament; Prematurity and low birthweight; Alfred Binet; Jean Piaget; Wilhelm T. Preyer; Milestones of motor development and indicators of biological maturity

Further reading

Culbertson, J. L. and Willis, D. J. (eds.) (1993). *Testing Young Children: A Reference Guide for Developmental, Psychoeducational, and Psychosocial Assessments.* Austin, TX: PRO-ED Inc.

Guralnick, M. J. (ed.) (2000). *Interdisciplinary Clinical Assessment of Young Children with Developmental Disabilities.* Baltimore, MD: Paul H. Brookes.

McLean, M. E., Wolery, M. and Bailey, D. B. (2004). *Assessing Infants and Preschoolers with Special Needs.* Columbus, OH: Merrill.

Observational methods

ROGER BAKEMAN

Introduction

Observational methods admit to a variety of meanings, but two stand out. According to the broader of the two meanings, they might include procedures by which informed observers produce narrative reports, such as those by Jean Piaget or Charles Darwin and other baby biographers when describing the development of their infants. Such reports have greatly enriched our understanding of child development, but require talent and wisdom on the part of the observer that is not easily reduced to a list of techniques and tools. In contrast, according to the narrower meaning, observational

methods are often understood by students of child development to refer to procedures that result in quantification of the behavior observed. The requisite techniques and tools are relatively easy to describe and are the subject of this entry.

If data are understood as generally quantitative, then data collection means measurement, which is defined by procedures that, when applied to things or events, produce scores. This entry describes measurement procedures that permit investigators of child development to extract scores from observed behavior that can then be analyzed with conventional statistical techniques. Other entries in this first section of Part II focus on different data collection techniques such as parental and teacher rating scales, whereas the other two sections consider issues of research design and data analysis. The first three sections of Part II work together. Matters of design (second section) define the circumstances of data collection, and measurement produces the scores that then become grist for the data analytic mill (third section).

What makes observational methods different from other measurement approaches? In an attempt to address this question, I consider five topics in turn and explain their relevance for observational methods. These topics are coding schemes, coding and recording, representing, reliability, and reducing. Then, at the end of this entry, I will address two further questions: for what circumstances are these methods recommended? And what kinds of researchers have found them useful?

Coding schemes

Coding schemes, which are measuring instruments just like rulers and thermometers, are central to observational methods. They consist of sets of pre-defined behavioral categories representing the distinctions that an investigator finds conceptually meaningful and wishes to study further. One classic example is Parten's (1932) coding scheme for preschool children's play. She defined six categories (viz., unoccupied, onlooking, solitary, parallel, associative, and cooperative) and then asked coders to observe children for one minute each on many different days and to assign the most appropriate code to each minute.

Examples of other coding schemes can be found in Bakeman & Gottman (1997) and throughout the literature generally, but most share one thing in common: like Parten's scheme, they consist of a single set of mutually exclusive and exhaustive codes (i.e., there is a code for each event, but in each instance only one applies) or of several such sets, with each set coding a different dimension of interest. In the simplest case, a set could consist of just two codes, presence or absence of the event. Thus, if observers were asked to note occurrences of five different behaviors, any of which could co-occur, this could be regarded as five sets with each set containing two codes, "yes" or "no."

It is sometimes objected that coding schemes are too restrictive and that pre-defined codes may allow potentially interesting behavior to escape unremarked. Earlier, I referred to observing without the structure of a coding scheme as observation in a broad sense, and I assume that such qualitative, unfettered observation occurs while coding schemes are being developed and will influence the final coding schemes. Once defined, however, coding schemes have the merits of replicability and greater objectivity that they share with other quantitative methods. Even so, coders should remain open to the unexpected and make qualitative notes as circumstances suggest. Further refinement of the measuring instruments is always possible.

Coding and recording

Armed with coding schemes, and presented with samples of behavior, observers are expected to categorize (i.e., code) quickly and efficiently various aspects of the behavior passing before their eyes. One basic question concerns the coding unit: to what entity is a code assigned? Is it a neatly bounded time interval such as the single minute used by Parten? Or is it successive n-second intervals as is often encountered in the literature? Or is it an event of some sort? For example, observers might be asked to identify episodes of struggles over objects between preschoolers and then code various dimensions of those struggles. Alternatively, as often happens, they might be asked to segment the stream of behavior into sequences of events or states, coding the type of the event and its onset and offset times.

A second basic question concerns the scale of measurement. Most coding schemes require observers to make categorical (or nominal) judgments, yet some coding schemes ask them to carry out ordinal judgments (e.g., rating the emotional tone of each n-second interval on a 1 to 7 scale). Categorical judgments are also called qualitative and should not be confused with qualitative reports: the counts and sequences that result from categorical measurement can be subjected to quantitative analysis in a way that qualitative narrative reports cannot, unless the qualitative reports are themselves coded.

Some observations can be automated (e.g., the position of an animal in an enclosure or a person's physiological responses). In contrast, coding schemes used in child development, especially when social behavior is studied, often require human judgment and would be difficult if not impossible to automate. Human

observers are required and need to record their judgments in some way. It is possible to observe behavior live in real time, recording the judgments made simply with pencil and paper, some sort of hand-held electronic device, or a specially programmed lap-top computer. More likely, the behavior of interest will be video recorded for later coding, which permits multiple viewings, in both real time and slow motion, and reflection (literally, re-view) in a way live observation does not. With today's video systems, usually time will be recorded as a matter of course, but it has not always been so.

Especially in older literature, observers used interval recording, which is often called zero-one or partial-interval or simply time sampling (Altmann, 1974). Typically, rows on a paper recording form often represented quite short successive intervals (e.g., 15 seconds) and columns represented particular behaviors; observers then noted with a tick mark the behaviors that occurred within each interval. The intent of the method was to provide approximate estimates of both frequency and duration of behaviors in an era before readily available recording devices automatically preserved time. It was a compromise, reflecting the technology of the time, and no longer seems recommended.

Representing

Occasionally, investigators may refer to video recordings as data, but making a video recording is not the same as recording data. Thus, the question arises: how should coding of video recordings be recorded? More generally, how should any data be represented (literally, re-presented) for subsequent computer processing? Since a low-tech approach to coding relies only on pencil and paper and the naked eye, and alternatively a high-tech approach connects computers and video recordings, then a relatively mid-tech approach to coding video material might use video recording but rely on a visual time code displayed on the monitor (instead of an internal, electronically recoded one). This would allow observers to record not just behavioral codes, but also the time they occurred. Almost always, data will ultimately be processed by computer so observers viewing video could use pencil and paper for their initial records, and then enter the data in computer files later. Alternatively, they could key their observations directly into a computer as they worked, whichever they find easier. Such a system retains all the advantages that accrue to coding previously video-recorded material, and is attractive when budgets are constrained.

When feasible, a more high-tech approach has advantages and a number of systems are available. Such

Table 1. An agreement matrix.							
					Observer B		
Codes		*Unoccupied*	*Onlooking*	*Solitary*	*Parallel*	*Associative*	*Cooperative*
Observer A	Unoccupied	7	2	0	0	0	0
	Onlooking	1	13	1	3	0	0
	Solitary	3	0	24	4	1	0
	Parallel	0	0	1	27	3	0
	Associative	0	0	0	2	9	3
	Cooperative	0	0	0	0	0	6

Rows represent Observer A and columns Observer B. In this case, 110 samples were coded. Percentage agreement was 78 percent (i.e., 86 of the 110 tallies were on the upper-left to lower-right diagonal, representing exact agreement). The pattern of disagreements (i.e., off-diagonal tallies) suggests that Observer B sees more organized behavior than Observer A (e.g., 4 samples that Observer A coded Solitary, Observer B coded Parallel; 3 samples that Observer A coded Parallel, Observer B coded Associative; and another 3 samples that Observer A coded Associative, Observer B coded Cooperative; the corresponding Observer B to A errors occur only 1, 2, and 0 times). Thus, even though the kappa is a respectable .72, recalibration of the observers is suggested.

systems combine video recordings and computers in ways that serve to automate coding. Perhaps the best known is The Observer (Noldus, Trienes, Henriksen, Jansen, & Jansen, 2000). In general, computer-based coding systems permit researchers to define the codes they use and their attributes. Coders can then view previously video-recorded information in real time or slow motion as they decide how the material should be coded. Subsequently, computer programs organize codes and their associated times into computer files. Such systems tend to the clerical tasks, freeing coders to focus on their primary task, which is making decisions as to how behavior should be coded.

No matter how coding judgments are captured initially, they can be reformatted using Sequential Data Interchange Standard (SDIS) conventions for sequential data; such data files can then be analyzed with the Generalized Sequential Querier (GSEQ), a program for sequential observational data that has considerable flexibility (for both SDIS and GSEQ, see Bakeman & Quera, 1995).

Reliability

The accuracy of any measuring device needs to be established before weight can be given to the data collected with it. For the sort of observational systems described here, the instrument consists of trained human observers applying a coding scheme or schemes to streams of behavior, often video-recorded. Thus, the careful training of observers and establishing their reliability is an important part of the enterprise. As previously noted, usually observers are asked to make categorical distinctions. For this reason, the most

common statistic used to establish inter-observer reliability is Cohen's kappa, a coefficient of agreement for categorical scales (Bakeman & Gottman, 1997). Cohen's kappa corrects for chance agreement and thus is much preferred to the percentage agreement statistics sometimes used, especially in older literature. Moreover, the agreement matrix required for its computation is useful when training observers due to the graphic way it portrays specific sources of disagreement (see Table 1).

Reducing and analyzing

Observational methods often result in voluminous data, thus data reduction is often a necessary prelude to analysis. A useful strategy is to collect slightly more detailed data than one intends to examine. In such cases, initial data reduction will consist of lumping some codes. Other data reduction may involve computation of conceptually targeted indices (e.g., an index of the extent to which mothers are responsive to the gaze of their infants), which then serve as scores for multiple regression or other kinds of statistical analyses. Several examples of this useful and productive strategy for observational data are given in Bakeman & Gottman (1997).

Conclusions

Historically, observational methods have proven useful when process aspects of behavior are emphasized more than behavioral outcomes, or for studying any behavior that unfolds over time. They have been widely used for studying non-verbal organisms (e.g., infants), non-verbal behavior generally, and all kinds of social interaction. Mother-infant interaction and emotion regulation are two areas in which observational methods have been widely used, but others include school and classroom behavior. Observational methods seem to have a kind of naturalness not always shared with other measurement strategies. Observers are not always passive or hidden and situations are often contrived, and yet the behavior captured by these methods seems freer to unfold, reflecting a target's volition more than seems the case with, for example, self-report questionnaires. Self-reflection is not captured, but aspects of behavior outside immediate articulated awareness often are.

With recent advances in technology, observational methods have become dramatically easier. Handheld devices can capture digital images and sound, computers permit playback and coding while automating clerical functions, and computer programs permit flexible data reduction and analysis. In the past, potential users of observational methods may have been dissuaded by technical obstacles. Whether or not future investigators select observational methods will come to depend primarily on whether these methods are appropriate for the behavior under investigation.

See also:
Clinical and non-clinical interview methods; Parent and teacher rating scales; Ethological theories; Social development; Emotional development; Play; Ethology; Jean Piaget

Further reading

Bakeman, R., Deckner, D. F. and Quera, V. (2005). Analysis of behavioral streams. In D. M. Teti (ed.), *Handbook of Research Methods in Developmental Science*. Oxford: Blackwell.

Bakeman, R. and Quera, V. (1995). Log-linear approaches to lag-sequential analysis when consecutive codes may and cannot repeat. *Psychological Bulletin*, 118, 272–284.

Long, J. (1996). *Video Coding System Reference Guide*. Caroga Lake, NY: James Long.

Experimental methods

ADINA R. LEW

Introduction

The basic assumption underlying scientific endeavor is that nature behaves in lawful ways. The scientist's task is to uncover these lawful relations between entities. In the physical sciences, theories concerning particular

domains are usually expressed in terms of mathematical equations, stating the relation between different variables such as heat and pressure. These theories are tested in experiments, which seek to measure quantities predicted by the equations. In psychological experiments, it is much more common for theories to state relations between variables in informal and less precise ways (e.g., there will be a relation between the amount of violence that individuals view on television and the amount of violence they show in real life). In order to test such theories, a group of people are exposed to some form of the hypothesized causal variable (e.g., viewing violent programs), and their subsequent performance on the outcome variable is measured (e.g., violent behavior). This performance is compared to that of another group of people (known as the control group) who are not exposed to the treatment of interest.

Ideally, any differences observed between experimental and control groups should be attributable to exposure to the variable that was manipulated in the experiment (e.g., viewing violent programs). A combination of attention to how people are assigned to the different groups (ideally this should be random), care in minimizing differences in the treatment received by both groups other than the experimental treatment, and the use of appropriate statistical analysis, makes it more likely that differences between groups can be attributable to the treatment of interest rather than to extraneous factors or natural variation between individuals.

Are informal theories just a reflection of the relative youth of scientific psychology, eventually to give way to precisely stated theories? This is unlikely, as the large majority of psychological processes involve many factors interacting in ways that are hard to predict, in much the same way that other complex self-organizing systems such as weather produce unpredictable outcomes. Such systems are best understood using modeling techniques. These models are developed together with experimental studies, being both constrained by experimental findings and suggestive of new experiments.

Construct validity

The first problem encountered when trying to test a theory experimentally is that there has to be a good match between a theoretical construct (e.g., aggression) and behavior measured in the experiment, an issue termed construct validity. A well-known example of an experiment that has attracted much criticism in terms of construct validity is that of Bandura, Ross, & Ross (1963), who addressed the issue of whether viewing a model perform violent acts leads to aggression in children. Children observed either a live or televized adult model being aggressive to a Bobo doll (i.e., kicking

Figure 1. Does this smiling face suggest aggression or rough-and-tumble play? See text for details.

and punching it), and they then had the opportunity to play with the doll themselves. The question was whether the children who had observed the aggression would be more likely to display these behaviors themselves, relative to a group of children who had seen non-aggressive play with the doll.

While there was indeed a greater degree of kicking and punching in the children who had seen these acts modeled, critics have argued that these children were engaging in rough-and-tumble play rather than aggression, as evidenced by their smiling faces (see Fig. 1). Another difficulty with the study is that taking part in the experiment does not match real TV viewing. This is because children, like adults, try to make sense of their experience, and in the case of the experiment will be attempting to figure out what is wanted of them by the experimenter (so-called demand characteristics). A reasonable assumption after viewing the model is that the experimenter *wants* me to kick the Bobo doll.

Demand characteristics

One could ask whether the issue of demand characteristics invalidates most psychological experiments, given that it is present whenever a person is aware of being a participant. The answer is "yes" and "no." In the case of the effects of TV on violent behavior, such criticisms have led to a withdrawal of research effort from experimental approaches. In the case of Piagetian tasks concerning the development of logical thinking, such critiques have arguably led to a reconceptualization of the origins of logical thinking that emphasizes sociocultural factors. One such task is Piaget's conservation of number task, where children younger than about 7 years claim that a row of counters that is longer than another has more counters. They do this having just seen both rows in one-to-one

correspondence, agreeing with the experimenter that there are the same number of counters in each row. They have also witnessed the experimenter move one row such that the counters are more spread out, prior to being asked again whether both rows contain the same number of counters. At this point, most children prior to about 7 years give a non-conserving answer. Piaget argued that these children had not discovered which actions on objects lead to reversible transformations (e.g., moving counters about), a discovery made through protracted experience of playing with objects. Hence they could not understand that the property of numerosity of a set of objects remains invariant over rearrangements.

It has been found that the form in which the task was done is a strong determinant of children's responses. For example, if a naughty teddy messed up the counters prior to the second question concerning numerocity, younger children were far more likely to say that the number of counters had remained unchanged. A potential stalemate could have emerged, with some researchers arguing that Piaget's procedure has the demand characteristic of signaling to the child that an important transformation has taken place, with the counter-argument being that game-like formats give the child the signal that the transformation should be ignored, so that we can all get on with playing the game. However, researchers began a productive analysis of task differences. As a consequence, they came to the conclusion that most Piagetian tasks demand precise attention to the words used in questions and instructions, which are sometimes at variance with what might be reasonably assumed by the child about the nature of the task (i.e., the difference between what is meant and what is said). Schooling appears to have precisely the effect of socializing the child into treating language in this disembodied way. A key property of language is that there can be internal consistency irrespective of the real-world truth value of statements, a property that underpins logical reasoning of the 'if A then B' kind. Thus, the development of such reasoning may be closely linked to the development of the mean/say distinction.

Construct validity over developmental time

An issue of validity that is particularly salient for developmental researchers concerns the measurement of a construct at different periods of development. For example, the construct of attachment developed by John Bowlby refers to a biologically based propensity on the part of an infant to form a deep emotional bond with a principal caregiver. According to Bowlby, such a propensity evolved to maintain proximity between infant and parent, clearly necessary for survival in altricial species. Bowlby also believed that the attachment relationship in infancy formed a basis for a working model of intimate love relationships that the individual maintained throughout the lifespan. Mary Ainsworth and her colleagues developed a method for assessing individual differences in attachment behavior in infants, based on reactions to brief separation and reunion episodes with parents. They found reliable differences in reactions, potentially signaling differences in security of attachment.

Subsequent research has attempted to chart the development of attachment representations beyond infancy. Mary Main and co-workers developed an interview technique termed the Adult Attachment Interview (AAI) for assessing attachment in adults. This complex instrument asks adults about their attachment experiences as children and how they think these have affected their current personality. The material is analyzed not just in terms of the content of memories, but also in terms of the emotional openness of the respondent and how they have come to terms with their experiences. Part of the validation of this instrument lies in theoretical argument and empirical analysis excluding competing models of what construct is being measured by the AAI (e.g., verbal fluency or introspectiveness of the respondent).

Another part of the validation of the AAI lies in a correlation found between the AAI scores of young adults and scores they obtained as infants using the Ainsworth procedure, in a twenty-year follow-up study (Waters *et al.*, 2000). Interestingly, another such follow-up study failed to obtain correlations between infant and adult scores (Lewis, Feiring, & Rosenthal, 2000). However, these latter authors did not conclude that their results challenge the construct validity of the AAI. Rather, they argue that attachment is far more fluid and evolving than the classic formulation of Bowlby would allow. Ultimately, there is no experimental way of determining whether two measures do indeed relate to the same construct at different ages. The researcher has to present plausible theoretical arguments to support his or her case.

Internal validity

Once the issue of construct validity has been addressed, it is necessary to make sure that any differences between experimental groups are attributable to the treatment of interest rather than extraneous factors (termed internal validity). Campbell & Stanley (1966) emphasize that random allocation of participants to treatment and control conditions is crucial for balancing out extraneous sources of variation, going so far as to use the term 'quasi-experiments' for studies in which this does not occur. This means that any study using different groups of individuals in which age is one of the

treatment variables can be considered to be a quasi-experiment. This is because a group of children of a particular age will differ from a group of an older age on dimensions other than age (e.g., they belong to a different birth cohort).

While care has to be taken to consider such cohort factors, in practice it is only of major concern to researchers studying development across large age-spans. For example, there is a general belief that IQ declines with age. Such effects were greatly exaggerated, however, due to the fact that education has improved over the last century, so that a comparison between young and old adults in the 1960s would have encompassed both any declines in IQ with age *as well as* any cohort differences between young and old adults. Methods have been developed involving a combination of cross-sectional and longitudinal measurement at two or more historical time-points in order to try to separate age from historical and cohort effects.

External validity

A final design issue, termed 'external validity,' concerns the generalizability of findings from a study to the behavior of people in general. This is often an important issue for applied researchers who want to know whether a treatment that has been found to be efficacious experimentally will also be efficacious in the population at large. Obtaining a representative sample of participants becomes a critical issue. As Mook (1983) argues, however, this is often not a concern in basic research, and the question of sample representativeness has perhaps been overemphasized. As he asks, who wants to be 'invalid'? Sometimes, deliberately extreme situations or unusual populations are sought because they provide a means of testing a theory.

The case for the basis of attachment being a primary emotional bond rather than a result of rewards such as feeding came from Harry Harlow's study of maternally deprived captive monkeys in the 1950s (from today's vantage point, we would question the ethics of such studies). When stressed, such infants ran to a terry towel mother substitute rather than to a wire mesh substitute where food was regularly provided. Mook makes the point that the representativeness of either the sample of monkeys or the situation was not relevant to the theoretical point being made, in that when warmth and food provision are artificially separated, warmth wins out. In summary, it is easy to criticize most research on the grounds of lack of sample representativeness, as it is known that people from more disadvantaged groups tend to be less willing research participants. Whether such criticisms invalidate results, however, depends on the question being studied.

Conclusions

This brief overview of the principles underlying good experimental design in developmental research has focused on the link between theoretical concepts and what is measured in experiments (construct validity), and the need to ensure that the treatment being applied to experimental groups is responsible for any differences observed relative to control groups (internal validity). In terms of the fundamental focus of developmental research, however, that is processes of change in development, experimental methods form only one tool out of the many that are required.

See also:
Theories of the child's mind; Dynamical systems approaches; Parent and teacher rating scales; Cross-sectional and longitudinal designs; Ethical considerations in studies with children; Cognitive development beyond infancy; Aggressive and prosocial behavior; Connectionist modeling; Play; Schooling and literacy; John Bowlby; Jean Piaget

Further reading

Light, P. (1986). Context, conservation and conversation. In M. Richards and P. Light (eds.), *Children of Social Worlds.* Cambridge: Polity Press, pp. 170–190.
Schaie, K. W. and Willis, S. L. (1991). *Adult Development and Aging*, 3rd edn. New York: Harper Collins.
Teti, D. (ed.) (2005). *Handbook of Research Methods in Developmental Science.* Oxford: Blackwell.

Parent and teacher rating scales

ERIC TAYLOR

Introduction

Rating scales are important research tools; they have not only advantages, but also some disadvantages. To ensure their advantages, certain challenges have to be confronted. In what follows, consideration is given to the pros and cons of rating scales and to such challenges as the application of these research tools to the study of developmental psychopathology.

Advantages

The description of children's behavior and emotions by raters who know them well has unique advantages.

Behavior can be sampled in a comprehensive way, based on the whole of a child's life rather than a brief observation period. The behavior that is assessed is natural, in that it is not influenced by the artificial context of an observation or the presence of an unfamiliar observer. Cognitive as well as behavioral and emotional development can be assessed. Parents can report, for example, on the early language development of their young children, with the results reflecting its known course by a particular age (Feldman *et al.*, 2000). Assessments can be quite brief, with a rating scale taking typically ten to twenty minutes to complete, and thus allowing large amounts of data to be generated economically. Standardization is feasible, and therefore children's scores can be related to existing population norms. This has been a particular strength in studies focusing on individual differences rather than the normative course of development.

Disadvantages

A questionnaire is a device for communication, and many barriers can arise. The wording of items needs to mean the same things to raters and investigators. This in turn often requires that the child qualities to be rated must be described in clear and concrete terms. The rating of depression, for example, risks being interpreted by one rater as referring only to misery, by another as including irritable outbursts, and by an investigator as present only if there is a whole complex of associated changes. 'Frequent tearfulness' conveys a more precise significance, but a more restricted one. Minor variations in wording can have major effects upon the prevalence of items (Woodward *et al.*, 1989).

Fine and subtle distinctions can often not be made reliably; and the timing of transitions in, or influences on, development is prone to serious falsification by recall. Terms denoting frequency and intensity of behaviors are also prone to misunderstanding between investigator and rater. How often should tantrums occur to be described as 'frequent'? Expectations vary greatly between raters, and so do the ratings. Teachers' ratings are often said to be less vulnerable to such effects as they have a better professional understanding of the range of variation. However, the experience of the teacher is not ordinarily reckoned into the results of questionnaire surveys.

The relationship of the rater with the child colors the report that is made. For example, the impact of a behavior problem upon the parent, rather than the actual severity of the problem, may generate the rating. More generally, rating scales contain variance that is attributable to the rater, the setting in which the rating is made (e.g., home or school), and the instrument used, as well as to the individual child. When this is structurally modeled, it is evident that scores are far more complex than simply a record of a child (Fergusson, 1997).

For all these reasons, questionnaire ratings lend themselves best to large group studies, and to longitudinal studies where the raters and settings are constant for an individual child. For practical purposes (e.g., the selection of children for special educational interventions), they are valuable as screening measures, but seldom sufficient for the accurate identification of individuals.

Particular issues arise when parental or teacher ratings are used to capture both the qualities of the child and those of the child's social environment. Contamination can result in misleading interpretations of associations. For example, if a mother's account of her child's depression is exaggerated by her own depression, but taken as evidence for an intergenerational transmission.

The challenge of the age factor

The same behavior may carry different psychological significance at different ages, so intelligent interpretation is required and the age boundaries of a scale should be known and respected. The extent to which age influences ratings will depend upon the wording of items and instructions. The more exact and molecular the behavior to be noted, the more it is likely to show age trends, but also the more likely it is to be valuable only for a very restricted age range. When a general rating of behavior is made, raters are likely to adapt their rating to their underlying expectation of what should be present at that age. For example, ratings of impulsiveness and inattention show rather small age trends in community surveys in contrast to test and observation measures of the same constructs that reveal large changes. The method makes allowance for age changes, which may be very convenient to the investigator, but it throws the responsibility of determining what is age-appropriate back to the rater rather than making it a subject of enquiry.

The challenge of rater and situational effects

The agreement between different raters is at best moderate and frequently low. Achenbach, McConaughy, & Howell (1987) reported a meta-analysis of 119 studies of ratings of behavior. Agreement was moderate (around 0.6) when the raters were reporting on the same situation (e.g., mother and father), but lower (around 0.3) when different settings were involved (e.g., mother

and teacher). It is often idle to ask which rating is best as they capture different aspects of the child. Teachers are likely to be less sensitive than parents to alterations of mood in the child, and both to be less sensitive than the child's self-report. In contrast, teachers may be the best informants about a child's attention. Multiple informants are usually necessary. Their ratings may be combined into a composite scale, used as raw material for investigator judgment, put together following an algorithm, or entered into structural equations to model a latent trait.

People using rating scales need to make decisions about whether to use absolute scores or scores that are corrected for sub-cultural or gender norms. No general answer is available, but the most useful rating scales include standardization so that the decision can be made rationally.

The challenge of cultural expectancies

Investigators in non-Western cultures often find Western questionnaires very attractive. There may be a high degree of sophistication that has gone into their construction, and the perceived prestige of the instruments may favor their use. This risks, however, imposing a framework of expected development that is not valid for the culture. Cruelty to animals, to take just one example, may have very different significance in a liberal and urbanized culture than in a traditionally organized rural society.

The challenge of psychopathology

Most problem behaviors in young people are continuously distributed, with progressively fewer cases at higher levels of severity. Many adolescent girls diet, but less than 1 percent develop anorexia nervosa. Both dimensional and categorical approaches are used to describe altered function. Psychopathology (e.g., in depression and attention deficit) is often defined as a cut-off on a scale. Issues of where to place the cut-off therefore become substantial scientific questions. Statistical methods, such as the application of signal detection theory and latent class analysis, are increasingly used, and cut-offs validated by their ability to predict developmental risk (Fombonne, 1991).

The challenge of the choice of scales

A wide range of rating scales is available. The choice, obviously, depends upon the purpose. Selection of a measure should focus on the psychometric properties (interrater reliability, stability over time), the adequacy of standardization when this is important for the purpose in hand, the feasibility (e.g., the time required for completion), and, above all, the relevance to the construct that is to be measured. Relevance is estimated either by the face value of the questions asked, the instrument's prediction of a good measure of the construct, or by a network of predictions to relevant associations (i.e., construct validity).

Conclusions

Rating scales are an indispensable tool in population studies. They also have real limitations that potential users need to understand. Future development will emphasize more sophisticated analytical methods mentioned above, and validation against more objective measures. For example, a rating scale, in which child behaviors are expressed in general phrases, can be judged against its ability to predict detailed measures of the same behavior drawn from direct observation or a standardized interview with the same rater. A validation study such as this uses much more expensive instruments and may only be feasible for small numbers, but the resulting questionnaire can then be applied to large groups with knowledge of how it can be interpreted.

Potential users of existing scales should think carefully about the questions they need to ask and the ability of the scale to answer them. This will mean attention to the psychometric properties of the scale and, if cross-cultural use is intended, to rigor in translation and back-translation. Crucially, users need to know what factors can affect parental and teacher reports besides the constructs that are the targets of measurement. Confounding factors can often be allowed for in design and analysis, but only when they are recognized.

See also:
Cross-cultural comparisons; Experimental methods; Observational methods; Cross-sectional and longitudinal designs; Structural equation modeling; Language development; 'At-risk' concept; Behavior and learning disorders; Child depression

Further reading

Myers, K. and Winters. N. C. (2002). Ten-year review of rating scales. I: overview of scale functioning, psychometric properties, and selection. *Journal of the American Academy of Child and Adolescent Psychiatry*, 41, 114–122.

O'Brien, G., Pearson, J., Berney, T., and Barnard, L. (2001). Measuring behaviour in developmental disability: a review of existing schedules. *Developmental Medicine and Child Neurology* (Supplement, July), 87, 1–72.
Verhulst, F. C. and van der Ende, J. (2002). Rating scales. In M. Rutter and E. Taylor (eds.), *Child and Adolescent Psychiatry*, 4th edn. Oxford: Blackwell.

Self and peer assessment of competence and well-being

WILLIAM M. BUKOWSKI & RYAN ADAMS

Introduction

Peer and self-assessments are commonly used research techniques for indexing aspects of social functioning, competence, and well-being in samples of school-age early adolescent boys and girls. In so far as children have multiple opportunities to observe their peers in a broad range of contexts, peer assessments of social functioning and competence can be a highly valid and efficient source of information. Self-ratings provide unique measures of children's evaluations of skills, affective states, and experiences, as well as their impressions and representations of events and of other people. Several peer-based procedures are available to measure children's social behavior according to broad and narrow band constructs (Zeller *et al.*, 2003). Moreover, direct assessment of children's liking and disliking of peers can be used to index the positive and negative bonds that exist among the children in the group (Bukowski *et al.*, 2000).

Sociometry

Peers can be used to provide two forms of critical information about children's functioning. The first form of assessment, known as sociometry, refers to the procedures used to measure the attractions and repulsions that occur between children. Attractions are the positive forces that bring persons together, and repulsions are the negative forces that keep persons apart. According to sociometric theory, these forces are neither antithetical nor unrelated to each other. Attractions and repulsions are seen as two sides of a triangular model whose third side is the derivative dimension known as indifference.

According to this model, a person could have feelings of attraction, repulsion, or indifference toward another individual. Using measurements of the attractions and repulsions that exist between children, one can produce independent indices of the extent to which a child is liked (i.e., accepted) by peers and disliked (i.e., rejected) by peers. These dimensional scores (i.e., acceptance and rejection) can be used to assign children to sociometric or popularity groups known as popular (high acceptance, very low rejection), rejected (very low acceptance, high rejection), neglected (low acceptance, low rejection), controversial (high acceptance, high rejection), and average (at or near the mean on both dimensions). Although sociometric procedures have typically relied on nomination techniques in which children individually identify the peers whom they like and dislike the most, efforts have been made to develop sociometric procedures that use rating scale techniques (Bukowski & Cillessen, 1998).

Peer assessment procedures

Peers can be used also as a source of information about what a child is like. In these procedures, children are asked to indicate, via nomination or rating procedures, the extent to which a child has a particular characteristic or generally behaves in a particular way, such as being helpful, shy, or aggressive. These questions frequently involve asking children to nominate the peers in their school class or grade who best fit a particular character or behavior (e.g., "Who in your class is a good leader?"; "Who gets into fights?"; or "Who likes to play alone?"). The number of times a child is chosen for each role is used as a score on that item. These scores are then aggregated to form either broad or narrow band scale scores. Those created often reflect the three basic behavioral dimensions of moving toward others (e.g., sociability and helpfulness), moving away from others (e.g., withdrawal and isolation), and moving against others (e.g., aggression and disruptiveness). Perhaps the best-known peer assessment technique is the Revised Class Play (Masten, Morrison, & Pelligrini, 1985; Zeller et al., 2003). Peer assessment techniques can also produce measures of other constructs such as status and prominence within the peer group. Although most peer assessment techniques have employed nomination procedures, rating scales have also been used.

Self-ratings

Whereas peer assessments involve the collection of information from individual children in an effort to obtain measures of other children's behavior, self-ratings are used to capture measures of how individual children see themselves. Although the most widely used form of self-assessment is concerned with the construct known as self-esteem (i.e., one's overall evaluation of one's

worth and competence), self-ratings can be used whenever one wants to understand how individuals think about themselves and their experiences. That is, ratings of the self can either assess content (i.e., the characteristics or traits that one ascribes to oneself) and evaluation (e.g., whether one sees the self as 'good' or 'bad' or as competent or incompetent). Although researchers cannot use self-ratings as objective measures of a person's performance, they do provide unique information about how a person sees his or her functioning and well-being and how one experiences life. In this way, such measures complement other sources of information about individuals' functioning. The concept of the self has been discussed by Susan Harter who also developed a widely used measure of self-perceptions of competence (Harter, 1998).

Conclusions

Peer and self-assessments provide researchers with unique and reliable information about children's social behavior and experience, and of how children see themselves. While peer assessment techniques have been used in a large number of studies, research on the factors that influence how children perceive others has been rare. Even rarer have been efforts to understand the process of peer and self-ratings from a theoretical and developmental perspective.

See also:
Clinical and non-clinical interview methods; Parental and teacher rating scales; Aggressive and prosocial behavior; Peers and siblings; Play; Selfhood; Sex differences

Further reading

Newcomb, A. F., Bukowski, W. M. and Pattee, L. (1993). Children's peer relations: a meta-analytic review of popular, rejected, neglected, controversial, and average sociometric status. *Psychological Bulletin*, 113, 99–128.

Pekarik, E. G., Prinz, R. J., Liebert, D. E., Weintraub, S. and Neale, J. M. (1976). The Pupil Evaluation Inventory: a sociometric technique for assessing children's social behavior. *Journal of Abnormal Child Psychology*, 4, 83–97.

Rubin, K. H., Bukowski, W. M. and Parker, J. G. (1998). Peer interactions, relationships and groups. In W. Damon (series ed.) and N. Eisenberg (vol. ed.), *The Handbook of Child Psychology*. New York: Wiley, pp. 619–700.

Younger, A. J., Schwartzman, A. E. and Ledingham, J. E. (1986). Age-related differences in children's perceptions of social deviance: changes in behavior or perspective? *Developmental Psychology*, 22, 531–542.

Research design

Epidemiological designs

PATRICIA R. COHEN

Introduction

Observational epidemiological designs have been shaped by two classic concerns. The first concern is the onset and course of disease, conceived as a dichotomous variable (you have it or you do not). The second is a focus on risk for the disease, which may also be dichotomized as present or absent. Although more recent epidemiological work often investigates outcomes that vary in a continuous fashion (e.g., blood pressure, depression), this focus on risk for disease or disorder has shaped much of epidemiological thinking about study design. The developmental aspects of disease are captured in epidemiologists' attention to the distinction between incidence (when a condition began) and prevalence (current status with regard to the condition), and by attention to the course of the condition over time. Such attention has led to research designs that foster the distinction between risks related to onset of the disease or condition and risks related to its course over time.

Case-comparison design

Within observational epidemiological studies, the fact that some disorders are relatively rare has made the case-comparison design (previously, but not as accurately, called case-control design) a particularly efficient method of investigation (Kelsey *et al.*, 1996). In this design, participants who have the disorder or condition of interest are identified, often through service providers. Another group that is as comparable as possible in other respects that may be relevant to the onset or detection of the disease is examined with regard to the presence or absence of the risk or risks being investigated in the study. Classically, such a study proceeds by determining, by report or record, differential exposure to putative risks of the case and comparison groups. For developmental studies, a group may be selected on a developmental outcome (e.g., reading disorder) and a comparison group selected who do not have this outcome.

A key aspect of the epidemiological perspective is attention to the population; the sample studied should be representative of the population to which generalization of findings is to be made. This population, then, defines both the case and the comparison groups, thus effectively controlling for a number of shared risks, whether measured in the study or not. Such a strategy permits less ambiguous interpretation of findings with regard to the risks that are the study's focus.

Attention to unintended or biasing differences between groups is a universal focus of epidemiological concern. For example, in some groups the likelihood of detection of early forms of the problem or condition being studied may be increased by a putative risk factor. Even agreement to participate in research on a given topic may select atypical subjects with regard to relevant variables.

An aspect of epidemiological research that is relevant to its application in developmental research is attention to the rate of development of a given problem or disease over the time period following the initial exposure to a risk. Thus, in addition to information on average proportionate increase in a negative outcome, epidemiologists are traditionally concerned about the effect of exposure duration or, if the exposure has ceased, the time period over which the negative outcome typically develops.

Longitudinal designs

Observational epidemiological studies of development employ one of several alternative longitudinal designs. One widely used design is the prospective cohort design, in which a random or representative sample is drawn at an age at which the earliest risks of interest are likely to be manifest and followed over a period of time for emergence of, or change in, the developmental factor of interest. Such a design may include those exposed to a given risk and a comparison group that is otherwise as similar as possible. This design is not really different from that used commonly in other behavioral sciences, but with one exception. The epidemiological concern about the population to which study findings may be generalized leads to considerable attention to both the original sampling scheme and the extent of, and potential bias introduced by, attrition from the study.

An alternative panel design selects subjects without regard to the risk or outcome process being studied, often on the basis of some common institutional or residential frame, such as a school, hospital, or community. These persons may already have experienced the risks being studied, and may already have begun to manifest the outcomes. One particularly useful panel is a birth cohort, in which selection into the study is based on date of birth and residence. Such a study may include births over a period of days, or weeks, or even years.

Epidemiologists have long appreciated the fact that for a given study three variables, age, cohort, and period, are generally confounded. Cohort refers to the date of birth, and period refers to the historical date at which the investigation took place. Developmentalists are primarily interested in age effects. However, it is not possible to separate developmental effects from period or cohort effects unambiguously. If a finding from a 1990 study of children seen originally in 1988 is reported as a developmental change from age 8 to age 10 (an age effect), can we be sure that this change wasn't different for 10-year-olds born in 1970 (a cohort difference)? Or might it have been affected by the historical climate for 10-year-olds in 1990 (a period effect)?

The problem is made more complicated by the fact that once you know age and cohort the period is fixed, once you know age and period the cohort is fixed, and once you know cohort and period the age is fixed. Therefore, longitudinal studies of multiple cohorts are required to disentangle these effect sources completely. When cohort selection includes birth dates over a relatively longer period such as multiple years, or even decades, the subsequent analyses of longitudinal data over a comparatively long time will include the opportunity to separate age or true developmental effects from cohort and period effects.

Historically, a large number of longitudinal studies beginning in childhood have been based on samples of convenience, and thus of unknown generalizability to the overall population. However, there is an increasing tendency to sample very large birth cohorts for both the long-term study of developmental processes and determination of the long-term effects of early risk

exposure. These studies were mostly initiated after the mid 20th century and predominantly in Europe, especially in Great Britain (e.g., Richards, Hardy, Kuh, & Wadsworth, 2001), as well as Finland and Sweden (e.g., Pulkkinen, Virtanen, Klinteberg, & Magnusson, 2000). The magnitude of some of these studies provides strong statistical power for producing reliable findings, even on outcomes that are quite infrequent. It is widely recognized that the amount of expense and effort involved in maintaining and following these cohorts makes it highly desirable that information on as wide a range of health and developmental issues as possible be gathered. Increasingly, such data are available to researchers in the field, and in some cases qualified professionals may arrange to have new measures or procedures added to the longitudinal protocol.

Another longitudinal design is a follow-back design, in which subjects are sampled from some past frame (e.g., a clinical service or special program) and traced forward to assess some current status. An example of such a design is Robins' (1966) classic study of boys with identified antisocial behavior/conduct disorder, traced when they became adults for the presence of criminal records. A comparison group of boys matched for residential block, but without a childhood record of antisocial behavior, was employed to show that, although most antisocial boys did not have adult criminal records, almost no men with criminal records did not also have a childhood history of antisocial behavior. When such a design can be based entirely on officially recorded information such as birth, school, child welfare, or criminal justice records, actual contact with the subjects may not be necessary. Current concerns about informed consent may rule out some such designs.

Sampling strategies

Epidemiological designs examining developmental issues may include alternative sampling ratios for subjects with different potential risk levels. Thus, rather than confining one's study to some children at high risk of a particular developmental outcome, a preferable epidemiological strategy is to include children with different levels of early risk at different sampling ratios. Some screen for risk, or for the early manifestation of the developmental aspect of interest, is administered, and children at high levels are sampled with a higher probability of inclusion in the study than children with lower levels. Such a design permits both a higher statistical power to identify risks for unusual patterns of development and also generalization to a known, larger population. More complex sampling strategies involving combinations of risks may also be employed to increase the statistical power and precision for issues of particular interest (e.g., oversampling high-risk neonates for developmental follow-up).

Conclusions

Epidemiological longitudinal designs are likely to be employed for more and more developmental research because of increased awareness of (a) possibly atypical local study participants, (b) sample size requirements for producing study findings with the necessary precision, and (c) the problematic substitution of data on age differences for data on age changes in making developmental inferences. To the extent that large longitudinal data bases can be generated with sophisticated developmental input, it is likely that more and more developmental research will be based on analyses of these data.

See also:
Cross-sectional and longitudinal designs; Indices of efficacy; Ethical considerations in studies with children; 'At-risk' concept; Behavioral and learning disorders; Cerebral palsies

Further reading

Johnson, J. G., Cohen, P., Kasen, S., Skodol, A. and Brook, J. S. (2000). Age-related change in personality disorder trait levels between early adolescence and adulthood: a community-based longitudinal investigation. *Acta Psychiatrica Scandinavica*, 102, 265–275.
Kuh, D., Hardy, R., Rodgers, B. and Wadsworth, M. E. J. (2002). Lifetime risk factors for women's psychological distress in midlife. *Social Science & Medicine*, 55, 1957–1973.
Werner, E. E. and Smith, R. S. (2001). *Journeys from Childhood to Midlife: Risk, Resilience and Recovery*. Ithaca, NY: Cornell University Press.

Cross-sectional and longitudinal designs

CHARLIE LEWIS

Introduction

If developmental psychology is quintessentially the study of 'change within organisms over time,' then which methods should it employ? This is an old question, but is one that remains in want of a complete answer. Measuring change is very difficult for both conceptual

and statistical reasons. This entry divides into four sections. The first compares cross-sectional and longitudinal designs. The second section focuses upon the latter to highlight their centrality in studying change. The third part examines the controversies that have prevented longitudinal methods from becoming more evident within developmental psychology. Finally, the fourth section briefly reviews attempts to overcome some of the interpretative problems in longitudinal research.

Cross-sectional and longitudinal studies: different beginnings, different ends

The term 'cross-section' is used in the biological sciences to refer to the process of cutting through one or more dimensions of an organism, usually by identifying layers of tissue types within such a section. The analogy transfers into psychology to apply to different groups within the same sample. These groupings might include divisions by gender or social class, but usually involve comparisons between different age periods. In such designs, individuals within different age groups are studied just once, and any difference on a dependent measure is attributed to the hypothesized process of change between them.

It is not difficult to criticize the cross-sectional approach. Differences between age groups reveal just that – differences – and not the process of developmental change within the child. However, there is also much to commend in the cross-sectional approach. For example, it allows us to identify the developmental issues confronting individuals within a particular age range. There is no point in undertaking a longitudinal study unless we know something about the timing of changes. Cross-sectional studies help us to identify the age-demarcated transitions during which one or more changes take place, and individual differences in the ages at which an ability is acquired. For example, several hundred cross-sectional studies over the past twenty years have identified the period around the child's fourth birthday as the age when the false belief test is passed for the first time, suggesting that the understanding of the mind undergoes an important shift at 4 years of age. However, these age differences have led to many contrasting accounts of the nature of change.

As a number of commentators have long pointed out, the tensions between cross-sectional and longitudinal approaches have centered on deeper philosophical divisions. For example, Overton (1998) contrasts the essentialism associated with cross-sectional designs – the attempt to identify crucial causal variables – with the attempts to explore weaker causal links in the longitudinal approach.

Longitudinal research: one paradigm or many?

Two broad traditions of longitudinal research are subsumed within one methodology. Firstly, longitudinal investigations chart the dynamics of change. There are a number of possible patterns. The most simple is a linear function in which change in an individual is constant (i.e., the individual maintains her/his rank relative to others over age). More complex are functions in which there are dramatic or step-like progressions, as typified in stage models, or exponential patterns in which there is an accelerated period of change that continually slows toward an asymptote. Even more complex are U-shaped developmental trajectories in which the development of a particular function seems to disappear and then to reappear. Researchers who explore the dynamics of change in this way tend to examine the developmental function (Wohlwill, 1973), defined as the average change of a group of individuals over time. Secondly, the longitudinal approach has been used to examine individual differences and their stability over time (McCall, 1977). Such research designs are used mainly to examine issues related to personality or intelligence, but which have developmental implications in terms of whether individuals with different abilities (e.g., children with autism versus typically developing children, or preterm versus fullterm infants) develop in the same way and at equivalent rates.

Baltes & Nesselroade (1979) suggested five fundamental goals of longitudinal research. The first three are to identify and describe the key developmental trends: (1) change within individuals; (2) differences between individuals in their patterns of change; (3) interrelationships between the factors that change in development. The final two are about the determinants of change and analyze (4) the causes of change within individuals; (5) the causes of changes in individual differences. Goals 4 and 5 are the gold standard of longitudinal research, but they are hard to realize. An additional goal is whether individual differences in one domain of functioning predict those in another domain (Schneider, 1993).

Issues in longitudinal research

That longitudinal data require repeated measures imposes practical constraints. To begin with, it is necessarily costly, in that it involves research time and efforts to collect data. This could be solved by reducing the sample or the number of test visits required. However, most statistical techniques for longitudinal data analysis require large samples for sufficient statistical power (and this is only one of a legion of problems in conducting such research). Longitudinal studies, particularly those which cover greater periods of time, are renowned for participant attrition through mobility and morbidity. This causes massive headaches in terms of the generalizability of the research, its cost in efforts to maintain contact with the sample, and the statistical headache of coping with missing data. However, general mixed linear models provide some compensation for lost data.

Psychologists have been relatively unsophisticated about a related issue – the influence of repeated contact upon the participants and the resulting data. This has been shown in some studies to lead to Hawthorne effects (positive change), but in other projects to 'screw you' effects (decrements in performance), simply as a result of the researcher's interest. Another problem concerns the equivalence of measures over time. For example, crying may not serve the same function in a 3-month-old and a 12-month-old, let alone a 4-year-old. Partly as a result, we must be cautious about the nature of correlations over time as they do not necessarily indicate causal relationships. Research I conducted with John and Elizabeth Newson (C. Lewis, Newson, & Newson, 1982) found that one of two predictors of success at national school exams at 16 and avoiding a criminal record by age 21 was reported father involvement at ages 7 and 11. However, we were at pains to point out possible explanations other than a naïve belief in paternal influences (e.g., an involved father might be a marker of a closer family).

Such theoretical issues concerning correlation-causation confounds are echoed in the problems in designing statistical procedures for analyzing longitudinal data. In the 1970s, it was fashionable to analyze possible mutual forms of influence using cross-lagged correlations in which the relative strengths of variables a and b at times 1 and 2 were assessed. If, for example, the correlation of $a1$ and $b2$ was significantly stronger than that between $b1$ and $a2$, then it was thought that causal inferences could be made (Fig. 1). However, authors like Rogosa (1988) have been very critical of the assumptions behind such inferences. He points out that false statistical assumptions have to be made, and that such analyses often single out pairs of variables from a range of possible influences, thus inflating the likelihood of Type 1 errors. More importantly, they hypothesize simple causal effects, when such reciprocal influences are notoriously complex and difficult.

Recent advances have been made by means of structural equation models in which covariance matrices are explored, particularly those involving the latent factors underlying manifest variables. Rogosa (1988)

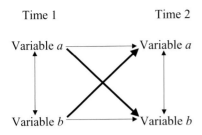

Figure 1. An example of a cross-lagged correlation showing the relative influence of the two key variables upon each other over time.

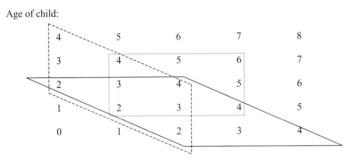

Figure 2. Cross-sequential (............), time-sequential (- - - -) and cohort-sequential (—) designs. After W. K. Schaie, 1965. A general model for the study of developmental problems. *Psychological Bulletin*, 64, 92–107.

was equally critical of these because they do not provide us with an analysis of the mechanisms of development. He favored more simple models that are built up by examining the growth curves for each individual followed by a broader comparison of collections of the developmental patterns across a sample.

A third issue concerns theoretical confounds that inspired so much writing on longitudinal methods in the 1960s. This is between developmental processes that are the focus of the study and three other factors: age, time of assessment, and cohort. The problem here is that these are not clearly independent of one another, and getting to the heart of developmental processes is impeded by them. Any well-designed study that charts a developmental trajectory cannot rule out the possibility of this pattern of change being a feature of this particular cohort, which itself is susceptible to unique genetic and environmental influences. The lessons to learn are that: (1) the three other factors are not part of the causal story that the developmentalist wants to tell about changes in psychological functioning, they are just possible confounds that have to be taken into consideration; (2) they have to be treated as non-experimental features

of a research design since they cannot be manipulated. The end result is that only replication of a change in more than one population will identify a generalizable developmental effect.

Conclusions

Hoppe-Graff (1989) argues that whether and how we can observe change relies upon both one's concept of change, and thus on the theoretical stance one takes. He claims first that only a complete theoretical account of the dynamics of change has a hope of being tested, and that the differences between cross-sectional and longitudinal designs are trivial by comparison. Others, like Rogosa (1988), contend that if longitudinal studies are to gain the advantage they must first develop closer ways of analyzing within-participant growth and development curves and subsequent comparisons of different individuals. However, such modeling processes remain relatively uncommon.

There are three shortcuts that can be used to redress the imbalance between cross-sectional and longitudinal studies. Firstly, researchers can combine cross-sectional and longitudinal designs, using techniques originally proposed to overcome the confounds between age, time, and cohort (Wohlwill, 1973). These condense the research period and allow for replication so that cohorts can be compared. Figure 2 shows these techniques in a hypothetical design in which children are studied once a year within the age period 2–6. In the cross-sequential design, represented in the dotted rectangle, the researcher starts with three cohorts and studies them at three time points, covering the age-span of 2–6 years involving 4-year-olds in each group and one comparison between two samples at ages 4–5. The problem here is that cross-age comparisons cannot fully be made. The time-sequential design, in the dashed parallelogram, is essentially three cross-sectional studies of 2- to 4-year-olds with extra longitudinal data so that 2–3 and 3–4 transitions can be explored, each in two cohorts. However, this design does not allow cohort effects to be completely explored. In the black parallelogram, the cohort-sequential design is the successive comparison of three cohorts over three years. The problem with this design is that it takes two years longer to complete, but it does allow for cohort and age effects to be untangled, at least partially. None of the designs in Figure 2 is *the* solution to the problems of confounds and the time limitations on research, but they can be used to good effect.

Secondly, there are ways of examining the dynamics of change. While there are various techniques, including intensive case studies, the most used is the microgenetic method (Granott & Parziale, 2002) in which a known transition phase is studied in depth and the individual is subjected to intensive trial-by-trial analysis over that period. Such research allows for the examination of an individual's developmental trajectory, and for the possibility that different individuals reach the same end at different rates or via different routes. Indeed, some authors using this method search for the possibility that we may use a diversity of old and new skills to varying degrees when making a developmental transition (Siegler in Granott & Parziale, 2002).

The third means of condensing the longitudinal study is to carry out an intervention to effect change through training or by experimental manipulation. Where there are competing explanations for a developmental change, training studies can manipulate both sets of precursors to see whether one is more effective. As with microgenetic studies, there is always the danger of teaching skills that do not develop spontaneously. Indeed, the term 'microgenetic' was coined to describe such studies, in part because the training aspect might effect change that does not spontaneously occur in development. However, the training study is an important research tool as it condenses the period in which change might occur. Studying the relationship between different types of intervention and different outcomes allows us to make theoretical claims about the nature of change in general. The bottom line is that no research technique provides all the answers, but a healthy combination of the techniques described here is the solution in most developmental studies.

See also:
Theories of the child's mind; Developmental testing; Epidemiological designs; Indices of efficacy; Group differences in developmental functions; Multilevel modeling; Structural equation modeling; Sociology; Heinz Werner; Milestones of motor development and indicators of biological maturity

Further reading

Appelbaum, M. I. and McCall, R. B. (1983). Design and analysis in developmental psychology. In P. H. Mussen (ed.), *Handbook of Child Psychology: History, Theory and Methods*, 3rd. edn. New York: Wiley, vol. 1, pp. 415–476.

Magnusson, D. (1981). Some methodology and strategy problems in longitudinal research. In F. Schulsinger, S. A. Mednik, and J. Knop (eds.), *Longitudinal Research: Methods and Uses in Behavioural Science*. Boston: Martinus Nijhoff, pp. 192–215.

Strauss, S. and Stavy, R. (eds.) (1982). *U-shaped Behavioral Growth*. New York: Academic Press.

Twin and adoption studies

JIM STEVENSON

Introduction

The resemblance between family members has long been of interest. Francis Galton (1822–1911) suggested that the differential resemblance between monozygotic (MZ) and dizygotic (DZ) twins could be used to determine the extent to which individual differences in measured characteristics (phenotype) were influenced by inherited factors (heritability). Thereafter, the study of twins has been one of the main tools to address the nature-nurture issue. This issue dominated the study of individual differences in child development during the 20th century. It centered on whether children's behavior and psychological make-up were determined primarily by the genes they inherited (nature) or by the environment they experienced (nurture). These two influences were seen to be mutually exclusive (i.e., either nurture or nature, but not both, was paramount). The behaviorists (e.g., John Watson) believed that behavior was shaped by experience and that genetic predisposition was of less relevance. By contrast, others (e.g., Cyril L. Burt, 1883–1971) adopted a position that emphasized the genetic contribution to intelligence and other aspects of behavior. Burt's conviction of the significance of genetic factors would appear to have led him to falsify data (Hearnshaw, 1979). This added to a crisis of uncertainty about the value of twin studies.

Contemporary studies of twins

More recent twin studies have consistently replicated the findings from earlier ones about the role of genes and the environment in influencing individual differences in intelligence. It is no longer necessary to rely on older twin studies with suspect methodology. More recent studies have been both more systematic in the identification of samples and, with increases in sample size, have greater power to detect both genetic and environmental influences. There are now a number of longitudinal twin studies that can address important questions concerning development and change in children's abilities. The Louisville Twin Study provided important and original findings indicating an increase in heritability of intelligence with age – a finding that ran counter to expectations that with age the cumulative effects of experience would lead to a reduction in the impact of genetic differences between individuals (Wilson, 1983).

The field has also matured so that the stark contrast between nature and nurture has been recast into an appraisal of a range of influences on individual difference in development. In addition to genetic effects, the environment is now seen as being decomposed into the effects of those producing resemblance between family members (shared environment) and those producing differences (non-shared environment). For most aspects of cognition and personality, it is the non-shared aspect of the environment that is most salient. A broad generalization is that similarity in psychological characteristics within families arises from genes and differences from genes and experience.

The impact of adoption studies

Adoption studies were first systemically applied to IQ, but it was the study of the mental health of the adopted-away offspring of schizophrenic mothers by Leonard Heston in 1966 that had an important impact. This changed the view of schizophrenia as being engendered by dysfunctional parenting. While twin studies are a powerful tool for detecting the presence of genetic effects, adoption studies have most power to detect the effects of shared environments. In this sense, twin and adoption studies are complementary although, of course, they can be combined. The reared-apart studies of MZ twin pairs have been the cause of much public and media interest. If MZ twins have been adopted away from each other and reared in independent families, any resemblance represents an index of genetic influences plus any differences in the prenatal and postnatal environment up to the time of adoption. The largest systematically studied sample of such reared-apart twins has been assembled by Tom Bouchard in Minnesota.

One of the most extensive exercises in gathering information on adopted children and their families repeatedly during development is the Colorado Adoption Project (DeFries, Plomin, & Fulker, 1994). This study has shown how there is a pattern of changing genetic influences with age. During cognitive development, genetic influences become more important and shared environmental influences less so. Indeed, genes are seen as effecting change in cognitive development, with the environment acting to maintain stability of individual differences.

The rationale and methodological assumptions of the twin studies

The logic of the twin study is that the different contributions of genes and environment to resemblance between MZ and DZ twins can be used to estimate additive genetic (A), shared environment (C), and non-shared environmental (E) influences on individual differences. The mathematics behind this approach was first formulated by Ronald A. Fisher (1890–1962) in a classic paper in the *Transactions of the Royal Society of Edinburgh* dated 1918. (The current approach to the analysis of such data is described in Appendix 3 by Thalia Eley.)

There are a number of assumptions that underlie the use of twins to estimate genetic and environmental influences. The first is that zygosity is known reliably (i.e., whether the pairs are MZ or DZ). This designation can be based on biological markers such as blood typing or DNA, but for many purposes physical resemblance data has sufficient validity. The second is that the two zygosity groups are treated equally similarly within their families – the equal shared environment assumption. It might be thought that the more similar MZ pairs would evoke more similar treatment by parents than that given to DZ pairs. Where this has been examined, there is little difference in the similarity of experience in those aspects of the environment relevant to psychological development. Where differences are found, it is thought that these arise from the greater genetic difference between the DZ pairs (i.e., the differences in the environment experienced are consequences not a cause of behavioral differences between the children). The final assumption is that the development of twins is representative of the general population where singleton births are the overwhelming majority. In terms of their early development, twins are lighter at birth than singletons, tend to be born prematurely, and may experience a less optimal intrauterine environment.

These differences indicate that some caution may be needed when generalizing from findings with twins to the general population. However, with the exception of language development, which tends to be somewhat delayed in twins, it is thought that twins are not more vulnerable to difficulties in development or adjustment, and that with caution the estimates of genetic and environmental effects based on twins' psychological development can be generalized to the rest of the population. It is particularly valuable when the findings from twin and adoption studies agree with one another since the assumptions underlying the methods are different.

The rationale and methodological assumptions of adoption studies

Adoption studies are of different types, but the most usual design is where there are data on children and their adoptive parents and siblings (but not their biological parents). It is argued that any resemblance between biological siblings adopted into different families is a reflection of genetic factors. Similarly, any resemblance between a child and their adoptive siblings or adoptive parents is a pure measure of shared environmental effects. The analysis of such data is based on the methods of model fitting described by Thalia Eley in Appendix 3.

There are two main assumptions behind the adoption study. The first is that children are placed at random into adoptive homes. This is often not the case because adoption agencies may try to 'match' the adoptive parents to known characteristics of the biological parents (e.g., in respect of ethnicity). The second assumption is that the adopted children and their adoptive families are representative of the general population. In both cases, this is unlikely to be true. Children coming to adoption are often from parents with multiple difficulties that might be related to psychological factors, and families making themselves available for adoption, and then selected by placement agencies are likely to be 'super-normal' (i.e., have been screened for the absence of social and psychological difficulties). Possible concerns about the assumptions of twin and adoption studies mean that particular attention should be given to convergent findings from these two types of studies.

One relatively recent advance in the analysis of twin data has been the method developed by John DeFries and David Fulker. This is particularly valuable when one of the twins in a pair has been selected as being extreme on a continuum such as being highly anxious or showing very poor reading attainment. The analysis is based on the notion that if genes are responsible for the twin being in this extreme group, then if the pair are DZ the other twin (co-twin) will have a score on this continuum that is closer to the population mean than if the co-twin is in an MZ pair. When based upon samples of MZ and DZ pairs, the means for the DZ co-twins will be less extreme than the mean of the MZ co-twins. This is represented in Figure 1. If the scores are appropriately transformed, DeFries and Fulker showed that double the difference between the means for MZ and DZ co-twins was a direct estimate of the extent to which genes are responsible for extreme group membership (i.e., group heritability). This approach to the analysis of twin data has been used to identify the extent to which poor reading attainment is due to genetic differences between children.

When data are available on a total population of twin pairs, it is possible to use this analysis to address the question of whether more extreme cases of under-achievement or of behavioral difficulties are due to a different mix of genetic and environmental factors than are operating to produce individual differences within the normal range. This question is important when arguing for the presence of disordered development in children. Parsimony dictates that if the mix of gene and environmental influences is the same at the extreme as

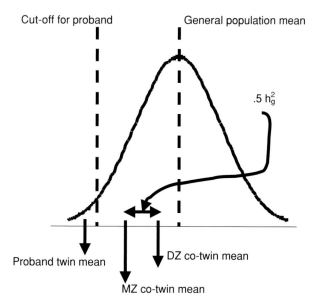

Figure 1. DeFries and Fulker analysis of twin data identifies group heritability (h_g^2) from the mean scores of twins with extreme scores (probands) and their co-twins. Probands have extreme scores at one end of the range and by definition have a mean far from the population mean. The co-twins have less extreme scores (i.e. their means regress toward the population mean). The greater genetic similarity between an MZ proband and their co-twin results in less regression to the mean for the MZ co-twins than the DZ co-twins. The difference in the means of the co-twins of MZ probands and the co-twins of DZ probands is an estimate of half the value of h^2 g.

for the range of normal individual differences, then there is no evidence of disordered development. Underachievement or maladjustment is best explained as an extreme of normal variation, and additional causal factors producing disorders are absent.

This pattern has been found for both reading and spelling ability and for hyperactivity. However, for language delay, there is evidence that more extreme forms of delayed language development at 2 years of age are primarily due to genetic differences between children. By contrast, individual differences in language development in the normal range and less severe degrees of delay are accounted for primarily by shared environmental factors. It is interesting to note that this also reflects higher heritability estimates seen in clinically defined cases with language disorders as compared to studies of individual differences in the normal range.

Findings from twin and adoption studies on cognitive development

By far the most extensive set of studies concerns the measurement of IQ in twins and adopted children. The overall pattern of results is clear. Just under 50 percent of the variance in IQ in the population is due to genetic differences between people. The remaining variance is roughly equally divided between the shared and the non-shared environment. The contribution of genetics gradually increases with age, and this continues into old age.

Not all the effects of genes on cognition are via an impact on general intelligence. There is evidence that more specific cognitive abilities such as memory, reading, and language ability have specific genetic influences, although it should also be noted that there is considerable overlap between the genetic influences on many aspects of cognition, indicating a genetic 'g.' These findings have now led to the start of the identification of specific genes involved in reading, using both linkage and association methods in molecular genetics.

Findings from twin and adoption studies on personality

The evidence from both twin and adoption studies suggests that the shared environment has little if any role to play in personality development. This contrasts with cognition where some 25 percent of the variance is attributed to shared experiences. Across all personality dimensions, whether measured using the two-factor model of Hans Eysenck (1916–1997) or the Big Five of Robert McCrae and Paul Costa, approximately 40 percent of the variance is attributable to genetic differences and the remainder to non-shared environmental effects.

Adoption studies have provided the best evidence for the operation of gene-environment interactions on behavior. For example, children with no history of criminality in their biological parents were themselves only marginally above the population level of criminality, even if they were raised by criminal adoptive parents (Mednick, Gabrielli, & Hutchings, 1984). Those children with a criminal biological parent were at increased risk, but especially so if they were adopted into a criminal home. The combination of biological and social risk was a particularly potent influence, and demonstrates a gene-environment interaction.

The place of twin and adoption studies in the era of molecular genetics

The first few years in the third millennium are witnessing the initial results from the Human Genome Project. Genes are being identified that contribute to individual differences in cognition (FOXP2 and language) and to personality (e.g., dopamine receptor 4 gene and novelty seeking). It may therefore be thought that the era of usefulness for twin and adoption studies is over. Molecular genetic studies are able to identify the specific genes, and this must make the crude aggregate assessments of genetic and environmental influences from twin and adoption studies redundant. In fact, the value of such quantitative genetic approaches is greater than ever (Martin, Boomsma, & Machin, 1997). The identification of which aspects of child development are genetically influenced is an essential prior step before molecular genetic studies can be undertaken.

Any evidence of shared genetic influences between different aspects of development, such as can be obtained from multivariate twin studies, can be used to guide the search for candidate genes likely to influence a specific characteristic. Adoption studies will also increase in importance. As genes are identified that influence children's development, it will be of paramount importance to identify how these genes interact with environmental factors. It will therefore be possible to use adopted siblings to establish the differential impact of genes in contrasting settings.

Conclusions

Twin and adoption studies have an established place in the study of child development. Both will continue to play a central role in the investigation of the joint influences of genes and experience on development.

See also:
Understanding ontogenetic development: debates about the nature of the epigenetic process; Neuromaturational theories; Cross-sectional and longitudinal designs; Group differences in developmental functions; Language development; Development of learning and memory; Attention; Intelligence; Parenting and the family; Reading and writing; Temperament; 'At-risk' concept; Behavioral and learning disorders; Prematurity and low birthweight; Behavior genetics; Developmental genetics; The statistics of quantitative genetic theory

Further reading

Bouchard, T. and Propping, P. (1993). *Twins as a Tool of Behavioural Genetics*. Chichester: Wiley.
Loehlin, J. C. (1992). *Genes and Environment in Personality Development*. Newbury Park, CA: Sage.
Plomin, R. and Crabbe, J. (2000). DNA. *Psychological Bulletin*, 126, 806–828.

Data analysis

Indices of efficacy

PATRICIA R. COHEN

Introduction

There are two overall kinds of indices of efficacy, those related to the efficacy of measurement and those reflecting the magnitude of influences on developmental outcome. These indices (measurement efficacy, influence efficacy) form the focus of this entry, which at the same time considers percent agreement (together with kappa). It also introduces a third index of efficacy (attributable fraction) in the concluding comments that may be less well known to some readers.

Measurement efficacy

Measurement efficacy is often indexed by a function of the frequencies in a 2 by 2 table reflecting agreement between a dichotomous measure and a dichotomous variable that represents the criterion or true status. These functions can be seen by reference to Table 1. Measurement efficacy expressed as a fraction of the true status includes sensitivity, the proportion of positive cases correctly identified or $D/(B + D)$. Similarly, specificity is the proportion of non-cases correctly identified or $A/(A + C)$. Indices that are expressed as a fraction of the measured status would include the positive predictive value reflecting $D/(C + D)$ or the proportion of identified cases that are true cases, and the negative predictive value $A/(A + B)$ or the proportion of those identified as non-cases that are true non-cases.

Percent agreement

Simple percent agreement has often been used as an index of overall agreement between categorical variables,

especially as an indicator of inter-rater reliability. Percent agreement is, however, strongly influenced by the relative frequencies of the different categories, and is thus not recommended. For example, if each of two raters put 90 percent of the cases in Table 1 in the negative category, we would expect 81 percent of the cases to be in the A cell even if one or both were, in effect, randomly assigning cases, so there was no validity to the distinction between the − and + assignment at all. Coefficient kappa is the most widely used indicator for inter-rater reliability. With this index, observed percent agreement is corrected by the percent agreement expected on the simple basis of marginal frequencies. This coefficient has been generalized to the situation in which some disagreements are judged to be less important than others, as, for example, when there is an ordinal (ordered) aspect to the different categories (Cohen, 1968). It may also be adapted to more than two categories and to more than two raters (Shrout & Fleiss, 1979).

Influence efficacy

Influence efficacy indices reflect magnitudes of effects on development processes or outcomes. For influences measured as scaled variables, these indices include effect size measures such as correlations, regression coefficients, standardized regression coefficients, standardized mean differences, and proportions of shared variance or variance accounted for. For influences measured as dichotomous or ordinal variables, these same measures of effect size may be used when the outcome of interest is a scaled measure. If, however, the developmental outcome is dichotomous (e.g., presence or absence of teenaged pregnancy or college graduation), the efficacy of an influence may be indexed by the odds ratio (OR). The OR is the ratio of the odds of attaining the status for those positive on the predictor (D/C in Table 1) to the odds of attaining the status for those negative on the predictor (B/A in Table 1). This measure is widely used,

Table 1. Frequencies in a 2 by 2 table.			
		Criterion or outcome	
		−	+
Test outcome or risk	−	A	B
	+	C	D

despite its somewhat lesser familiarity than a simple rate ratio, $D/(D + C)$ over $B/(A + B)$, because of its greater mathematical tractability. Because the rate ratio and the odds ratio are often reasonably close in magnitude (although the odds ratio is larger), odds ratios are often interpreted as if they were rate ratios (e.g., if the value is 2.0 it is interpreted to mean that the negative outcome is twice as likely for those with the risk than for those without it).

In developmental studies, the goal may be identifying influences on the time taken or age required to reach some developmental outcome. In such a case, given appropriate longitudinal data, the analytical method of choice may be a survival analysis. With a dichotomous predictor, the hazard ratio indexes the ratio of the odds of attaining the outcome between the two classes of the predictor variable. A beauty of the hazard ratio (HR) is that it is a unit-free index of efficacy in producing or predicting change (i.e., it may be generalized to any time period of interest). The provision for checking the assumption that it is constant over time is available in any major statistical package that includes survival analysis. Like the OR, if the predictor is an ordinal variable with more than two levels, the HR is a kind of weighted value of the hazard ratio for adjacent unit increases in the predictor (Willet & Singer, 1995).

Conclusions

Another index of efficacy that is less familiar to developmentalists than would be desirable is the attributable fraction. Conceptually, this index reflects the expected reduction in rate of a dichotomous outcome if certain conditions did not exist in the population. For example, it could be used to index the reduction in the prevalence of cases of some level of developmental delay that would be expected in the absence of toxic lead exposure. Since it refers to a particular population, it is necessary to know the rates of both risk and outcome in the population, as well as the relationship between risk and outcome. Its value estimated from a random or representative sample from a known population is (population rate − low risk rate) divided by the population rate. Thus, for example, if the

rate of developmental delay in a population were .12, and the rate in a no-lead-exposure sample were .08, the attributable fraction would be $(.12 − .08)/.12 = .33$. Thus, a third of the cases of developmental delay in this (hypothetical) population may be attributable to toxic lead exposure. This method assumes that the developmental delay in those exposed to lead is actually due to the lead exposure, and not to some other correlate such as low socioeconomic status or neighborhood characteristics. Methods to correct for these potential confounders are also available (Greenland & Drescher, 1993).

See also:

Epidemiological designs; Cross-sectional and longitudinal designs; Group differences in developmental functions; 'At-risk' concept

Further reading

Cohen, J., Cohen, P., West. S. G. and Aiken, L. S. (2002). *Applied Multiple Correlation/Regression Analysis for the Behavioral Sciences*, 3rd. edn. Mahwah, NJ: Erlbaum, pp. 151–192.

Kraemer, H. C. (1993). Reporting the size of effects in research studies to facilitate assessment of practical or clinical significance. *Psychoneuroendocrinology*, 17, 527–536.

Kraemer, H. C., Kazdin, A. E., Offord, D. R., Kessler, R. C., Jensen, P. S. and Kupfer, D. J. (1999). Measuring the potency of a risk factor for clinical or policy significance. *Psychological Methods*, 4, 257–271.

Group differences in developmental functions

ALEXANDER VON EYE

Introduction

Constancy and change of behavior are the main topics of developmental research, and when individual differences in development are of interest, research designs usually include longitudinal components of data collection. Elementary designs used in developmental research include cross-sectional, longitudinal, and time-lag designs, while more complex designs combine these three basic approaches.

Data from repeated observations can be analyzed from a number of perspectives. For example, one can ask whether, in the population being studied, means change over time. If there are significant mean changes, one can attempt to describe the developmental trajectory in functional form. Resulting developmental functions describe the ups and downs of mean changes.

Examples of such functions have been used to describe the development of intelligence over the human life span, the emergence of cognitive abilities in adolescence, the pathways of delinquent behavior over the lifespan, the quantity of drug use in adolescence and adulthood, and the acuity of vision in old age. Each of these examples describes development in the form of changes in mean performance levels.

There exist many statistical methods for the analysis of changes in means. Among the most popular and useful is Analysis of Variance (ANOVA). This entry discusses ANOVA in two parts. We begin with a description of the statistical model of ANOVA. We also discuss the conditions that must be fulfilled for proper use of ANOVA. Furthermore, we discuss the use of ANOVA when samples are heterogeneous, that is, when there may be more than one population from which a sample was drawn. The second part of this entry presents examples of the many uses of repeated measures ANOVA in developmental research, with an emphasis on group differences.

The statistical model of Analysis of Variance

The method of ANOVA is a member of the family of Generalized Linear Models (GLM). The general form of the GLM is

$$f(\mu) = X\beta$$

where μ is expectancy of the dependent variable, X is the matrix of independent variables and their interactions, and β is a parameter vector. The function f is called the link function. In the context of ANOVA, the link function is typically the identity function, that is, $f(\mu) = Y$. In log-linear models, where variables are categorical, the link function is the logarithmic function $\log(\mu)$ (Agresti, 2002).

The matrix X is called the design matrix. X contains the effects under study in the form of column vectors. These vectors express the contrasts of interests. In ANOVA, contrasts are specifications of hypotheses about means. In other words, the design matrix X contains vectors that indicate which means are compared to each other. In addition, the design matrix X can contain vectors that indicate interactions. Planned comparisons can also be part of X, and so can covariates.

The vectors in X are created such that they fulfill the conditions of orthogonality. This implies that all vectors are orthogonal to each other. More specifically, let x_{ij} be the ith element of vector j. Then, two vectors j and j' are

orthogonal to each other if the inner product

$$\sum_i x_{ij} x_{ij}j^i = 0$$

for $j \neq j'$. In addition, each vector is typically specified such that $\sum_i x_{ij} = 0$. When an ANOVA design is balanced, that is, when the cells contain the same number of cases, both conditions can easily be met and, as a result, parameters will be uncorrelated, and effects can be tested independently. If, however, a design is not balanced, parameter estimates can be biased and correlated.

For proper application of ANOVA, a number of conditions must be fulfilled. The following list contains the most important of these conditions.

(1) The dependent variable, Y, must be scaled at the interval or ratio scale level.
(2) The dependent variable must be normally distributed for the significance tests to be valid.
(3) The sample must be representative of the population about which statements are intended.
(4) The design matrix X of factors, their interactions, and covariates must be of full rank, and the inverse of the matrix product $X'X$ must exist.
(5) There must be homoscedasticity of the residuals.
(6) In repeated measures analysis, it is assumed, in addition, that the covariance matrix of the observations displays a specific structure. Two of these structures have been discussed in particular, compound symmetry and sphericity. Compound symmetry is the more restrictive of the two assumptions. It posits that the variance-covariance matrix of the observations be of the form

$$\sigma^2\{Y\} = \begin{bmatrix} \sigma_Y^2 & \omega\sigma_Y^2 & \omega\sigma_Y^2 \\ \omega\sigma_Y^2 & \sigma_Y^2 & \omega\sigma_Y^2 \\ \omega\sigma_Y^2 & \omega\sigma_Y^2 & \sigma_Y^2 \end{bmatrix},$$

that is, the diagonal contains the constant variance of the observed scores, and the off-diagonal elements contain the constant covariances.

Less restrictive is the requirement of sphericity, which is that the variance of the difference between any two treatment means be constant. This requirement can be met without simultaneously meeting the requirement of compound symmetry. A test for sphericity relates the arithmetic and geometric means of the covariance matrix to each other. A χ^2-distributed statistic can then be calculated to determine whether deviations from sphericity are larger than random. If the null hypothesis of random deviations must be rejected, either the degrees of freedom for the ANOVA tests are reduced, or correction factors ε are calculated with which F is multiplied. These factors are equal to 1 if the null hypothesis of sphericity prevails. They are less than 1 if deviations from sphericity exist. Typically, two variants of ε are calculated. The Greenhouse-Geisser variant is more conservative (results in smaller F-values). The Hyunh-Feldt variant is less conservative.

No assumptions are made concerning the nature of the factors and covariates. Factors and residuals can be at any scale level, and they do not have to be normally distributed. However, the values of the factors and covariates are assumed to be error-free.

In the study of developmental functions and differences in such functions, repeated measures ANOVA plays a most important role. The next section presents specifics of repeated measures ANOVA.

Repeated measures Analysis of Variance

ANOVA of repeated observations decomposes the total variance into two parts. The first part is known from cross-sectional ANOVA. It is the variance between individuals. The second part is the variance within individuals. Each of the variance components can be further decomposed into main effects, interactions, covariate effects, and the effects of planned comparisons.

Consider a simple case of a repeated measures design, one with one factor and one dependent variable that is observed repeatedly. In the present context, we assume that the factor distinguishes among groups of individuals. The ANOVA design typically employed for such cases is the additive model

$$Y_{ij} = \mu_{..} \rho_i + \tau_j + \varepsilon_{ij},$$

where $\mu_{..}$ is a constant, specifically the grand mean, the ρ_i are independent, normally distributed person-specific parameters, the τ_i are constants that specify the effects of the factor (mean comparisons), and the ε_{ij} are the independent and normally distributed residuals, often called errors (Neter, Kutner, Nachtsheim, & Wasserman, 1996). The τ_i are subject to $\sum \tau_i = 0$, and the ρ_i and the ε_{ij} are independent of each other. In words, a repeated measures ANOVA decomposes the variability of the observed scores into components that are person-specific, time-specific, and other components that remain unexplained (the residuals). More complex models typically include (1) more factors and (2) interaction terms. Interactions with the person factor suggest that means or developmental trajectories vary across groups. The following four assumptions are made about the observed scores Y_{ij}:

$$E\{Y_{ij}\} = \mu_{..} + \tau_j.$$

In words, this assumption states that the expected score of Person i at Time j is determined by the time-point-specific deviation from the grand mean only.

$$\sigma^2\{Y_{ij}\} = \sigma_Y^2 = \sigma_\rho^2 + \sigma^2.$$

This assumption states that the expected variance of the observed scores is invariant over time and does not vary across individuals.

$$\sigma\{Y_{ij}, Y_{ij'}\} = \sigma_\rho^2 = \omega \sigma_Y^2$$

for $j \neq j'$. This assumption also states that the covariance between observations from different points in time is the same across individuals and depends on the variance of the observed scores and the magnitude of the autocorrelations, ω. The latter two parameters are assumed to be constant. The correlation between two observations for the same individual is $\omega = \sigma_\rho^2 / \sigma_Y^2$. The fourth assumption is that

$$\sigma\{Y_{ij}, Y_{i'j'}\} = 0$$

for $i \neq i'$ and $j \neq j'$. This assumption states that the covariance between scores from different individuals, observed at different points in time, is equal to zero, that is, these scores are independent.

The covariance structure obtained under this model is somewhat unrealistic for repeated measures data, in which typically covariances decrease as time separation increases. Adjustments can be made to accommodate this characteristic. These adjustments come in the form of the ε-factors mentioned above.

It is well known that the repeated measures model of ANOVA is identical to the randomized block model or MANOVA with random block effects (Neter *et al.*, 1996; Schuster & von Eye, 2001). There is also a close relation with multilevel models. Therefore, the same methods can be applied in both models to test whether the selected ANOVA model is appropriate. One aspect of the appropriateness is that the variance of the residuals be constant. Residuals e_{ij} are defined as the difference between the estimated and the observed scores, or $e = Y - Xb$. Plots of the independent variable scores against the residuals can be used to determine whether the variance of residuals is constant. The responses Y_{ij} can be plotted and checked for lack of parallelism. If the responses are not parallel, the additive model given at the beginning of this section may not be the proper one. Furthermore, a normal probability plot (= Q-Q plot) of the estimated subject main effects can be used to determine whether the subject main effects, ρ_i, are normally distributed.

Most important for repeated measures ANOVA is the inspection of the within-subjects variance-covariance matrix. This matrix should show constant variances and covariances. As always, the term *constant* means that random deviations are deemed of low impact.

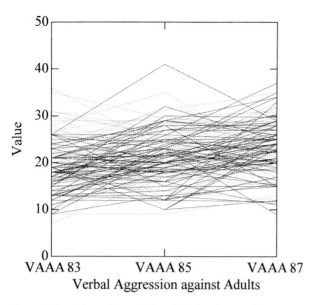

Figure 1. Parallel coordinate display of the developmental trajectories of VAAA scores in 67 girls (dotted lines) and 47 boys (solid lines).

Table 1. Gender-specific average verbal aggression scores in 1983, 1985, and 1987.

	Gender	Mean	Std. Deviation	N
VAAA 83	Girls	17.9406	4.4226	67
	Boys	21.0137	6.7064	47
	Total	19.2076	5.6605	114
VAAA 85	Girls	20.5986	5.8951	67
	Boys	22.6967	6.1717	47
	Total	21.4636	6.0729	114
VAAA 87	Girls	22.7791	6.0699	67
	Boys	23.5743	5.6737	47
	Total	23.1069	5.8973	114

Table 2. ANOVA table of Time × Gender repeated measures analysis.

Between subjects

Source	SS	df	MS	F	p
Gender	327.785	1	327.785	5.355	0.022
Error	6855.425	112	61.209		

Within subjects

Source	SS	df	MS	F	p
Time	763.693	2	381.846	19.167	0.000
Time*Gender	72.156	2	36.078	1.811	0.166
Error	4462.624	224	19.922		

Greenhouse-Geisser epsilon: 0.9886
Huynh-Feldt epsilon: 1.0000

The expected pattern of variances and covariances is described by the concept of sphericity.

Variance-covariance matrices in randomized block designs and in repeated measures designs are also expected to display sphericity. If a variance-covariance matrix violates the sphericity condition, the F-test used in ANOVA can be adjusted to take into account the degree of violation. Most of the modern statistical software packages perform sphericity tests by default and adjust the F-test accordingly.

Sample applications of repeated measures ANOVA

In this section, we present a re-analysis of a data set that was published by Finkelstein, von Eye, and Preece (1994). They studied physical pubertal development and the development of various aspects of aggression in 114 adolescents over a span of four years. The sample included 67 girls. Data were collected in 1983, 1985, and in 1987. In the following analyses, we look at the scale Verbal Aggression against Adults (VAAA). The parallel coordinate display of the raw data appears in Figure 1, and suggests that, on average, verbal aggression against adults increases over the four years of observation. The means for 1983, 1985, and 1987 appear in Table 1, by gender.

In the following three sections, we ask whether (1) a repeated measures ANOVA supports the conclusion drawn from visual inspection, and whether there are gender differences. We also ask, whether (2) the developmental trajectories are linear in nature, (3) the trajectories are gender-specific, and (4) whether there

are particularly significant mean increases from 1983 to 1985 or from 1985 to 1987.

Standard repeated measures ANOVA

We first check whether the sphericity assumption is violated, using the the Mauchly test statistic, W. This statistic is small and non-significant. We thus retain the null hypothesis according to which there is no violation. The standard ANOVA table appears in Table 2. The table reports only the standard F-tests that tend to be overly liberal if sphericity exists. The adjusted F-values and their tail probabilities were the same because the correction terms ε (indicated below the table) are equal to or close to 1.0.

The results in Table 2 indicate that verbal aggression against adults increases during puberty (significant Time effect), that verbal aggression against adults is stronger in boys than in girls (significant Gender effect), and that the increase in boys and girls is parallel (non-significant Time × Gender effect). The effect size, η^2, for the Time effect is solid ($\eta^2 = 0.146$), the effect

Table 3. Within-subjects tests of polynomial contrasts and their interactions.

Source	Polynomial trend	Type III sum of squares	df	Mean square	F	P	Eta squared
Polynomial	Linear	756.115	1	756.115	34.879	.000	.237
trend	Quadratic	7.577	1	7.577	.417	.520	.004
Trend*Gender	Linear	71.661	1	71.661	3.306	.072	.029
	Quadratic	.495	1	.495	.027	.869	.000
Error (Factor 1)	Linear	2427.981	112	21.678			
	Quadratic	2034.642	112	18.166			

Table 4. Profile analysis of verbal aggression against adults over three observation points.

Source	Time	Type III sum of squares	df	Mean square	F	P	Eta squared
Time	Level 2 vs. Level 1	520.528	1	520.528	12.945	.000	.104
	Level 3 vs. Previous	755.143	1	755.143	25.503	.000	.185
Time*Gender	Level 2 vs. Level 1	26.259	1	26.259	.653	.421	.006
	Level 3 vs. Previous	88.540	1	88.540	2.990	.087	.026
Error (Time)	Level 2 vs. Level 1	4503.471	112	40.210			
	Level 3 vs. Previous	3316.332	112	29.610			

size for the Gender effect is very small ($\eta^2 = 0.046$), and the effect size for the non-significant interaction is close to zero ($\eta^2 = 0.016$).

The next step in an ANOVA involves testing pairs of means for significant differences. We skip this step here because the third part of our analyses (below) covers all of the interesting post-hoc tests.

The shape of the growth curve

As an alternative to standard repeated measures ANOVA, polynomial ANOVA is often recommended. Polynomial ANOVA fits orthogonal polynomials to the observed series and tests the trends for statistical significance. For a series with k observation points, a polynomial of order $k - 1$ will be fit. This approach to repeated measures ANOVA allows one to test hypotheses concerning the statistical significance of the linear, quadratic, cubic, or higher-order trends. It can also be tested whether these trends differ over the categories of the between-subjects factors.

In the present data example, we have three observation points. Thus, the linear and quadratic trends can be tested, and the interactions of these two trends with the Gender factor can be examined. The main effect Gender will be as before. Therefore, we focus here on the polynomials, as they were not included in the standard repeated measures ANOVA. Table 3 displays the results for this part of the ANOVA, which suggest that the linear trend is significant, whereas the quadratic trend fails to be statistically significant. The increase over time in the overall scores in verbal aggression against adults can

thus be described most parsimoniously with a straight-line function. None of the interactions of the linear or quadratic trends with Gender is significant. It should be noted, however, that the observed power of all tests except the one for the overall linear trend is low. Thus, a replication of this study with a larger sample may be needed to confirm the results in Table 3.

Bock's profile analysis

In many contexts, for instance in intervention studies, it is of interest to identify the time span within which change is most rapid. Bock (1975) proposed what is known as multivariate profile analysis. This method is a repeated measures ANOVA that compares scores from time-adjacent observations with each other. If changes are significant in one of these comparisons but not in others, the researchers will know the period in time during which change was most pronounced.

In the present data example, we ask whether the change from 1983 to 1985, that is the change in the early adolescent years, is as significant as the change from 1985 to 1987. In addition, we ask whether there is an interaction with Gender. Table 4 displays the results, which suggest that the increases in verbal aggression are significant both from 1983 to 1985, and from 1985 to 1987. The effect strength for the second transition is higher. So, one might assume that this increase is stronger (statistical tests would have to be performed to confirm; note that we would expect that these tests would suggest that the differences in increase are non-significant, given that only the linear, and not the quadratic, component of the curve, was significant). Again, there is no interaction with Gender. However, the interaction of Gender with the second transition might have been significant, given more power. Thus, again, a larger-sample replication study is needed.

Conclusions

The discussion and the examples presented in this entry suggest that ANOVA is a flexible and powerful method for the analysis of development or change over time. Questions can be asked concerning change, trends in change, the location of change, and whether any of these aspects of change interacts with between-subject factors. In addition to the conditions that must also be met in cross-sectional ANOVA, the data subjected to repeated measures ANOVA must satisfy sphericity assumptions (this requirement does not apply when polynomials are fitted). ANOVA is known to be robust, however, for deviations from normality. When data are non-orthogonal and nested, some researchers may find the recently developed methods of hierarchical linear modeling useful. These methods allow one to accommodate more realistic correlation structures, and they can also be used when individuals differ in the length of the series of data they provide.

See also:
Cross-sectional and longitudinal designs; Multilevel modeling; Aggressive and prosocial behavior; Sex differences

Further reading

Dobson, A. J. (1990). *An Introduction to Generalized Linear Models*. London: Chapman and Hall.
Kirk, R. E. (1996). *Experimental Design. Procedures for the Behavioral Sciences*, 3rd. edn. Pacific Grove: Brooks/Cole.
von Eye, A. (2002). *Configural Frequency Analysis – Methods, Models, Applications*. Mahwah, NJ: Erlbaum.
von Eye, A. and Schuster, C. (1998). *Regression Analysis for Social Sciences – Models and Applications*. San Diego: Academic Press.

Multilevel modeling

JAN B. HOEKSMA

Introduction

Developmentalists study change within individuals. They study how changes vary from individual to individual and how different changes are related to each other. Most importantly, they try to offer explanations. In pursuit of this goal, developmentalists generally try to relate their theoretical accounts to empirical data. Statistical models and techniques play an important role in this endeavor. They are used as an intermediate stage between gathered data and the propositions derived from developmental theory.

Models are used to translate theoretical hypotheses into testable predictions or to reveal structure in empirical data to be interpreted in the light of some theory or body of knowledge. Advances in statistical modeling (Collins & Sayer, 2001) have greatly eased the task of researchers studying change and development. In particular, multilevel modeling and structural equation modeling have had major impacts in this respect. The former is the topic of this entry.

Sampling

No sample, no empirical research. Samples are drawn in many ways. Researchers will often try to minimize their efforts, without compromising their research. For that reason, they often resort to so-called multi-stage samples. Such samples are drawn in steps. Relatively large units are sampled first, followed by sampling within units. Researchers interested in educational performance may start sampling schools, followed by classes within schools, and next by students within classes. Such samples have multiple levels, together forming a hierarchy. The students are the first level, classes make up the second level, whereas the schools form the third level.

Developmental research requires measurements in time. Longitudinal samples are a *sine qua non* for studying change and development. Longitudinal samples can be seen as two-stage samples with a hierarchical or multilevel structure. In the first step, individuals, children, or adults are sampled, followed by a sample of measurement occasions. In actual research, developmentalists often use sampling schemes with measurements at fixed ages, but end up with samples that are less systematic or neat. In either case, longitudinal samples have a hierarchical or multilevel structure. The measurement occasions are nested within individuals. From a multilevel perspective, the sampled measurement occasions comprise the first level while the individuals form the second.

Modeling attachment behavior

Multilevel models (Goldstein, 2003) or hierarchical linear models (Raudenbush & Bryk, 2002) are meant to analyze multilevel or hierarchical data. In developmental

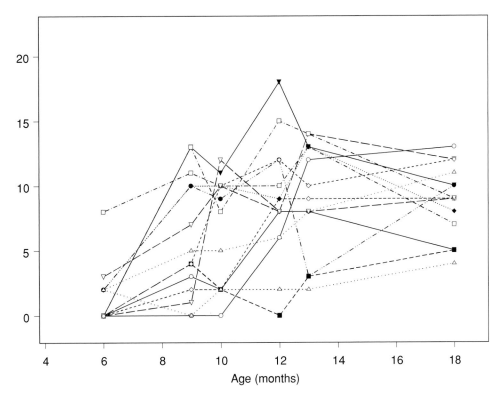

Figure 1. Perceived Attachment Behavior (PABS) against age (fourteen cases): raw data.

research, the model is used to analyze *change* on the basis of longitudinal data.

We will explain the longitudinal multilevel model by means of an example taken from attachment research. It is hypothesized that the development of the child's attachment behavior is related to early sensitivity of his or her mother. We start, however, by asking how attachment behaviors *change* during early childhood.

The Perceived Attachment Behavior Scale (PABS) was used to measure the child's attachment behavior six times between 6 and 18 months of age. The mother filled it out. The sample consisted of thirty-four children with cleft lip and palate and thirty-three normal children and their mothers. Figure 1 displays the raw data of fourteen cases. The measurement occasions are unequally spaced. The raw observations will be designated by y_{ti}, where the index t refers to the measurement occasion (in our data t runs from 1 to 6) and i refers to number of the child (in our data i runs from 1 to 34 for children with cleft lip and palate, and from 35 to 67 for children without cleft lip and palate). At approximately 10, 13, and 18 months, about one third of the sample was not measured. The total number of observations is 347. The sample average PABS score is 5.7 and the sample standard deviation is 4.8.

The sample has a clear hierarchical or multilevel structure. The children and their mothers were sampled first, followed by a sample of measurement occasions. The children, sampled first, comprise the *second*

(highest) level. The measurement occasions, sampled last, comprise the *first* (lowest) level. During actual analyses, the terms *level 2* and *level 1* are often used as adjectives. It is important to remember that in longitudinal research *level 2* often refers to adults or children, whereas *level 1* refers to repeated measurements.

Absence of change

The first question we want to answer is how does the level of attachment behavior change as a child becomes older? To answer this question, we start our analyses with a simple model, the random intercept model. It embodies the hypothesis of 'no change'. The model is

$$y_{ti} = \beta_0 + u_{0i} + e_{ti}.$$

In words, this model refers to the attachment behavior y (the score on the PABS) of child i at occasion t and equals the *intercept* β_0, plus the *level 2* residual u_i, plus the *level 1* residual e_{ti}. The intercept β_0 is designated the fixed part of the model. It corresponds to the population mean PABS across age and is estimated from the data to be 5.7 with a standard error of 0.4. The *level 2* residual u_i is specific to child i. It indicates to what extent the child i's repeated PABS scores deviate from the general mean β_0. The u_i's vary randomly from child to child. Their variance is designated by σ_{u0}^2. It is called *level 2* variance because it refers to variation between units at *level 2* (i.e., children). In our sample, $\sigma_{u0}^2 = 7.5$. The *level 1* residual e_{ti} is considered error and consists of random chance fluctuations including measurement error. Their variance is designated by σ_e^2. It is the *level 1* variance and its estimated value is 15.2 from our sample.

The random intercept model embodies the hypothesis of no change. The age variable is not involved. The child's constant level of attachment behavior β_{0i} is given by $\beta_0 + u_i$. It can be visualised as a horizontal developmental curve (see Fig. 2A). The curve is a member of a population of developmental curves with mean curve β_0.

Introducing change

The next hypothesis is: 'attachment behaviors increase linearly with age' (Fig. 2B). The model corresponding to this hypothesis is obtained by adding Age as an explanatory variable. The regression coefficient β_1 is called the linear coefficient and corresponds to the developmental velocity. The resulting model is:

$$y_{ti} = \beta_0 + \beta_1.\text{Age}_{ti} + u_{0i} + e_{ti}.$$

According to the model, the observed attachment behavior (PABS score) of child i at occasion t consists of a general constant β_0 (the intercept) plus a quantity β_1 times the age of the child at occasion t. In our sample, age runs from 6 to 18 months. For ease of interpretation, the age variable is re-scaled by subtracting 6 months from the original age. As a result, the numerical values run from 0 to 12 (note that 0 now corresponds to age 6 months in the original time scale, whereas 12 corresponds to the age 18 months). The first two terms $(\beta_0 + \beta_1.\text{Age}_{ti})$ comprise the fixed part and describe how attachment behavior changes linearly with age. The *level 2* residuals u_{0i} and the *level 1* residuals e_{ti} and their corresponding variances σ_u^2 and σ_e^2, have the same meaning as in the previous model.

Applying the model to our attachment data gave the following result. The fixed parameters were $\beta_0 = 3.4$ ($se = 0.5$) and $\beta_1 = 0.4$ ($se = 0.05$). The random parameters were $\sigma_u^2 = 8.2$ and $\sigma_e^2 = 11.8$. Fixed parameters that exceed more than twice their associated standard error are considered significantly different from 0 at $p < 0.05$. Our interest is in β_1. It appears to exceed its standard error approximately 8 times. It is highly significant. For that reason, it is concluded for the time being that attachment behaviors change linearly with age. Given the estimate of the linear coefficient, attachment behaviors increase by $\beta_1 = 0.4$ score point on the PABS per month.

The preceding model implies that attachment behavior increases by the same amount each month. When the developmental velocity changes in time, curvilinear developmental patterns will result. By adding Age-square as an explanatory variable, curvilinear patterns can be accounted for (Fig. 2C). The regression

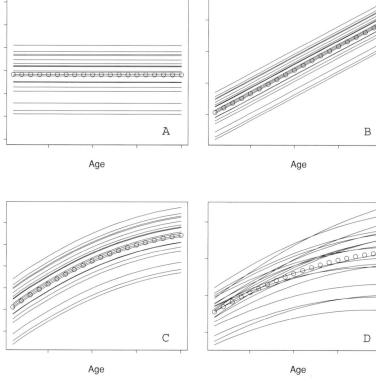

Figure 2. Four patterns of developmental curves.

coefficient β_2 is called the quadratic coefficient and is proportional to developmental acceleration. The resulting model is:

$$y_{ti} = \beta_0 + \beta_1.\text{Age}_{ti} + \beta_2.\text{Age}_{ti}^2 + u_{0i} + e_{ti}.$$

In our sample, the following estimates were obtained: $\beta_0 = 2.2$ ($se = 0.5$), $\beta_1 = 1.2$ ($se = 0.1$) and $\beta_2 = -0.06$ ($se = 0.01$), and $\sigma_u^2 = 8.2$ and $\sigma_e^2 = 11.8$. All fixed parameters making up the average developmental curve exceed twice their standard error. The fixed part corresponds to the average developmental curve. At $\text{Age}_{ti} = 0$, corresponding to 6 months of age, the level of attachment behavior is $y_0 = 2.2$. During the next month ($\text{Age}_{ti} = 1$), it vastly increases to $y_2 = 2.2 + 1.2 * 1 - 0.06 * 1 = 3.34$. Then, the next month the level becomes $y_3 = 2.2 + 1.2 * 2 - 0.06 * 2^2 = 4.84$, etc.

Introducing individual development differences

The models so far assume that the development of attachment behavior follows the same developmental course for each child. As any parent knows, however, this assumption is generally mistaken. Developmental patterns differ markedly from child to child.

The major strength of the longitudinal multilevel model is that it accounts for individual developmental differences easily. Figure 2D shows a so-called fan spread pattern. When attachment behaviors of different children develop at different velocities, the pattern displayed in Figure 2D may result. This and similar

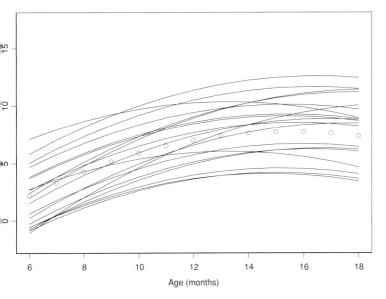

Figure 3. Estimated individual developmental curves of Perceived Attachment Behavior (nineteen cases).

patterns are obtained by replacing the fixed linear coefficient β_1 with $\beta_1 + u_{1i}$, where u_{1i} is a random quantity specific to child i. The resulting model after rearranging terms is:

$$y_{ti} = \beta_0 + \beta_1.\text{Age}_{ti} + \beta_2.\text{Age}_{ti}^2 + u_{0i} + u_{1i}.\text{Age}_{ti} + e_{ti}.$$

The attachment score of child i at occasion t consists of three parts. The first three terms ($\beta_0 + \beta_1.\text{Age}_{ti} + \beta_2.\text{Age}_{ti}^2$) make up the fixed part and describe the average developmental curve. Both u_{0i} and u_{1i} are random *level 2* residuals. The terms $u_{0i} + u_{1i}.\text{Age}_{ti}$ describe how the individual developmental curve of child i deviates from the average developmental curve. If u_0 is positive, the initial level of child i's attachment is above average, if negative it is below average. The *level 2* residual u_{1i} pertains to child i's developmental velocity. Positive values point to an initial developmental velocity higher than average. Negative values point to an initial developmental velocity lower then average. The respective variances of u_{0i} and u_{1i} are σ_{u0}^2 and σ_{u1}^2. The covariance of the level 2 residuals u_{0i} and u_{1i} is σ_{u1}^2. The covariance captures the linear association between the initial level of a child's attachment and the rate of change of his/her attachment over time.

The intercept of the individual developmental curve of child i is given by $\beta_{0i} = \beta_0 + u_{0i}$ and the linear coefficient is given by $\beta_{1i} = \beta_1 + u_{1i}$. Both are considered random quantities drawn from a population with means β_0 and β_1.

The model contains three fixed and four random parameters. The following estimates were obtained in our sample of attachment data. The fixed parameters (describing the average developmental curve) were $\beta_0 = 2.3$ ($se = 0.52$), $\beta_1 = 1.1$ ($se = 0.15$), $\beta_2 = -0.6$

($se = 0.1$), all highly significant. The *level 2* variances were $\sigma_{u0}^2 = 11.6$, $\sigma_{u1}^2 = 0.10$, and $\sigma_{u01} = -0.7$. Using the so-called deviance statistic, the addition of individual differences by means of the parameters σ_{u1}^2 and σ_{u01} proved to be significant, $\chi^2 = 15.6$, $df = 2$, $p < .01$. (Use of this statistic will be discussed shortly.)

What do these results mean? The best way to interpret the model is to use its parameters to plot average and individual developmental curves. Given the parameter estimates of the fixed part, the average developmental curve is described by $y_t = 2.3 + 1.1 * \text{Age} - 0.6 * \text{Age}^2$. Substitution of the values 0 (corresponding to 6 months) to 12 (corresponding to 18 months) gives the average developmental curve (o) displayed in Figure 3.

The individual developmental curves consist of the average developmental curve plus the individual deviation. That is, $y_{ti} = 2.3 + 1.1 * \text{Age} - 0.6 * \text{Age}^2 + u_{0i} + u_{1i}.\text{Age}_{ti}$. To plot the developmental curve of child i, we have to know his or her *level 2* residuals u_{0i} and u_{1i}. They are implicit in the *level 2* variances σ_{u0}^2, σ_{u1}^2, and covariance σ_{u01}. For each child, both u_{0i} and u_{1i} were computed and added to the average developmental curve. The resulting curves are displayed in Figure 3. It shows how the developmental curves converge. That is, the initial individual differences decrease when the children grow older.

The pattern shown is only valid if the model does not need extension with additional parameters to account for yet unknown variation in the data. It may come as a relief to some readers that the model does need to be extended.

Evaluating parameters

So far, we have estimated a number of longitudinal models to answer the question: how do attachment behaviors change from 6 to 18 months onward? At each step, a fixed or random parameter was added. Fixed parameters describe the average developmental curve. They are evaluated by comparing them to their standard error on the assumption that the estimates are normally distributed. If they exceed twice (or more precisely 1.96) their standard error, they are significantly different from 0 at $p < .05$ (two-sided).

Testing for significance of *level 2* variances is a bit more complicated because the assumption of normality is not warranted. Instead, the so-called deviance statistic is used. It is produced by the computer program used to estimate the significance of the model parameters. Each time one or more parameters are added to the model, the deviance statistic decreases. This change may be evaluated using a chi-square distribution, with df (degrees of freedom) equal to the number of parameters added to arrive at the more complex model. When the deviance decreases significantly the parameters are retained, otherwise they are deleted. To illustrate, by adding σ_{u1}^2 and σ_{u01}, the deviance decreased from Dev = 1915.9 to Dev = 1900.3, and the difference Dev_{change} = 15.6 is highly significant when looked up in a chi-square table with $df = 2$.

The next step in our analyses would be to add additional parameters to describe more complex patterns of development. One option is to take into account the differences between children with and without cleft lip and palate. For that purpose, an explanatory variable Z_i is created and added to the fixed part of the model. It contains 1's if an observation y_{ti} belongs to a child with cleft lip and palate and 0's otherwise. When added, the coefficient $\beta_z = -0.3$ $(se = 0.7)$ did not appear significantly different from zero. So we did not pursue this line any further.

Sensitivity and attachment

The main goal of the analysis was to test the relationship between early sensitivity of the mother and the development of the child's attachment behavior. The analyses so far revealed individual differences with respect to both initial *level* and developmental *velocity*. The final step is to extend the last model in order to test the hypothesized relationship between early sensitivity and the development of attachment behavior. A detailed description of the model involved is beyond the scope of this entry. A hunch is nevertheless easily given.

The mother's level of sensitivity was rated twice from four video recordings of mother-child interactions made around 6 months of age. The observations are nested within mothers. Mothers form *level 2* and the observations are *level 1*. There is no meaningful time structure. The random intercept model, discussed earlier, is used to describe the sensitivity data.

The crux is to combine the random intercept model describing the variability of sensitivity with the longitudinal model describing the development of attachment behavior. Using the superscripts *S* and *A* to refer respectively to mother's sensitivity and the child's attachment behavior, the combined model is:

$$\left.\begin{array}{l} y_{ti}^S = \beta_0^S + u_{0i}^S + e_{ti}^S \\ y_{ti}^A = \beta_0^A + \cdots + u_{0i}^A + u_{1i}^A.\text{Age}_{ti} + e_{ti}^A \end{array}\right\}$$

Note that the terms $\beta_1.\text{Age}_{ti} + \beta_2.\text{Age}_{ti}^2$ are replaced by two dots. The answer to our question is contained in the *level 2* residuals. u_{0i}^S pertains to the mother's mean level of sensitivity, whereas u_{0i}^A and u_{1i}^A refer to the initial *level* and the developmental velocity of the child's attachment behavior. As noted before, *level 2* residuals are random variables that co-vary and thus can be correlated. In our data, the correlation between u_{0i}^S (the mother's level of

sensitivity) and u_{0i}^A (the child's initial level of attachment behavior) was negligibly small, $r = .04$. In contrast, the correlation between u_{0i}^S (the mother's level of sensitivity) and u_{1i}^A (the developmental velocity of the child's attachment behavior) was substantial (viz., $r = -.37$). The latter indicates that the attachment behavior of children of initially low-sensitive mothers increases relatively fast.

Conclusions

The analysis of longitudinal data by means of multilevel models was introduced by Harvey Goldstein in 1986. Laird & Wair (1982) introduced an equivalent class of models under the label 'random-effects models,' while Raudenbush & Bryk (2002) prefer the name 'hierarchical linear models.'

Since their introduction, multilevel models have been extended and applied in many ways. They can be used for all sorts of hierarchical data, including categorical and dichotomous outcome variables. They have been applied in many fields of research, ranging from psychology and econometrics to geography and health research. The interested reader may refer to Goldstein (2003) as a starting point for other applications.

With respect to the field of growth and development, the longitudinal multilevel models offer flexible ways to describe developmental data. Of course, there are more models and options than presented here (Plewis, 2001; Hoeksma & Knol, 2001).

Longitudinal multilevel models allow researchers to describe changes within individuals, how changes vary from individual to individual, and how these changes are related to other variables. Certainly, their main benefit is that they force theorists and researchers to think about change, that is to think developmentally.

See also:
Parental and teacher rating scales; Cross-sectional and longitudinal designs; Group differences in developmental functions; Structural equation modeling; Social development

Further reading

Hoeksma, J. B. and Koomen, H. M. Y. (1992). Multilevel models in developmental psychological research: rationales and applications. *Early Development and Parenting*, 1, 227–248.

Kreft, I. G. and de Leeuw, J. (1998). *Introducing Multilevel Modeling*. Thousand Oaks, CA: Sage.

Snijders, T. A. B. and Bosker, R. J. (1999). *Multilevel Analysis: An Introduction to Basic and Applied Multilevel Modeling*. London: Sage.

Structural equation modeling

JOHN J. MCARDLE

Introduction

There are many effective techniques for analyzing developmental data. Many of these techniques offer good ways to examine substantive questions about processes and change over time and age (Collins & Sayer, 2001; Gottman, 1995). In this entry, we discuss a few contemporary techniques from the recent literature on structural equation modeling (SEM) for longitudinal data.

Most good longitudinal analyses start with a clear description of the raw data. Figure 1 is a plot of longitudinal data for individuals measured at several points in their lifespan – each line representing one person, and each picture a different measure of intellectual ability (N = 111 from McArdle *et al.*, 2001). The individual lines in these plots highlight questions about the shapes or trajectories over time. We may ask "Do the scores rise in a straight line?" or "Do they change shape at some time point and rise again at a later time?" or "Are the shapes of the variables different?" for multiple individuals, or multiple groups, or as multiple variables. We are interested in data analysis models that allow us to examine these questions as hypotheses about the patterns of change over time. Additional questions also arise about the time-based relationships among these multivariate trajectories such as "Which scores are precursors, or leaders, of the others?"

In many cases, developmental questions about processes and change require a mixture of different types of analyses. For example, we can use a MANOVA or a mixed-effects model to examine the size and shape of the change over time in the group averages (i.e., the means). We might also calculate sets of test-retest correlations to describe the pattern of the stability and change of the individual differences over time. Finally, we can run a set of factor analyses to better understand systematic changes in the structure of the measurements over different occasions. These analyses may lead us back to a revision of the plots of individual and group trajectories with possibly new results. These popular procedures are easy to calculate and permit a developmental researcher to answer common questions about processes and change.

Structural equation modeling (SEM) techniques

It is also common for developmental researchers to ask questions about change over time not completely covered by these standard techniques. The SEM approach is useful here because in any SEM analysis the researcher is required to specify a theoretical model for the observed scores for groups and individuals. The SEM approach is most often used as a clear and flexible 'confirmatory' specification of developmental hypotheses, but SEMs also permit 'exploratory' analyses.

The technical aspects of SEM are highly developed, and are not presented in detail here (but see Further reading). In SEM, we represent any model hypothesis by placing a set of *a priori* restrictions on the specific model parameters. This is accomplished by the placement of fixed, free, and equal parameters in a model. The score model is used to form a set of expectations about the summary statistics (means, standard deviations, correlations) that can be compared to the observed statistics for goodness-of-fit (e.g., using a χ^2 test). In addition, simple graphical displays termed path analysis diagrams have made these SEM techniques more effective in communication, available to a broad audience, and useful in theory-based interpretations of change. A variety of recent computer programs, including AMOS, CALIS, LISREL, Mplus, Mx, RAMONA, and SEpath, among many others, have made it easier to use these concepts.

The purpose of this entry is to give a brief overview of some unique features of SEM techniques for longitudinal and developmental research. This discussion focuses on the aspects of the SEM approach that can be useful beyond the traditional uses of ANOVA, regression, path and factor analysis. Five different types of basic SEMs are highlighted to consider measurement concepts, alternative models for

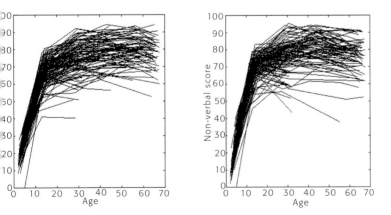

Figure 1. Multivariate lifespan intellectual ability data (from J. J. McArdle, F. Hamagami, W. Meredith, K. P. Bradway (2001). Modeling the dynamic hypotheses of Gf-Ge theory using longitudinal lifespan data. *Learning and Individual Differences*, 12, 53–79).

describing process and change, opportunities to deal with group differences, and the introduction of dynamical concepts. These five types of models are presented in more detail in the cited references.

SEM Type I: developmental measurement models

A primary use of SEM is to organize the information among multiple measures made within an occasion. One common model in SEM assumes that a large number of observed behaviors, labeled W, X, Y, and Z, are a direct result of a smaller number of unobserved or 'latent' factors, labeled f. These classical models of common factor analysis can be expressed by linear equations written as

[1a]　$Y_n = \Lambda_y f_n + u_{yn}$　and　$X_n = \Lambda_x f_n + u_{xn}$,

so the f score is the common predictor of both variables Y and X (and presumably W and Z as well) with a set of factor loading coefficients Λ and unique residuals u.

This common factor model is presented as a SEM path diagram on both the left- and right-hand sides of Figure 2. In this kind of a diagram, squares are used to represent the observed or manifest variables (e.g., Y) and circles to represent the unobserved or latent variables (e.g., f). The factor loadings (Λ_y) are drawn as one-headed arrows (from f to y), and these represent the strength of the relationship of the factor score to the observed score. The two-headed arrows attached to each variable represent variance or covariance terms. On each side of this diagram, we have drawn a single latent factor among all observed variables.

In cases where we have four measures of one common factor, the concept of an underlying latent factor may be rejected from information about the correlations among the multiple variables. The chi-square test (χ^2) and other goodness-of-fit indices are available for this purpose. In general, the overall hypothesis of a factor structure may be in the form of a classical simple structure, or it may reflect a pattern of factor loadings determined by known features of the experimental design. SEM analyses with categorical outcomes (e.g., items, rating scales) may also include a classical true-score measurement model through the estimation of a set of thresholds (τ_m, drawn as dark triangles).

The repeated observation of multiple variables leads to a latent variable model for two-occasion longitudinal data where the same variables (W, X, Y, Z) are repeatedly measured at a second occasion over time and/or age. A SEM model with more than one time point ($t = 1$ to T)

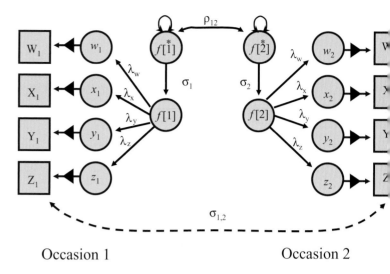

Occasion 1　　　　　　Occasion 2

Figure 2. A common factor model with invariance over time model applied to item-level data.

can be expressed as

[1b]　$Y[t]_n = \Lambda_y[t] f[t]_n + u_y[t]_n$　and
　　　$X[t]_n = \Lambda_x[t] f[t]_n + u_x[t]_n$.

These models are important to developmental research because they can be used to evaluate quantitative changes in the scores of a factor over time as well as qualitative changes in the meaning of a measured construct over time. That is, although the same variables are measured at repeated occasions, we are still not assured that the same constructs are being measured at each occasion. For example, there may have been an experimental intervention between occasions that altered the persons' views of the measurements. Alternatively, the persons may have developed in ways that have altered their response to different aspects of the measures. In order to examine the hypothesis of construct equivalence over time, we can require the exact equality of the factor loadings at one time and another (i.e., $\Lambda_x[1] = \Lambda_x[2]$, and $\Lambda_y[1] = \Lambda_y[2]$) and examine the comparative goodness-of-fit (e.g., using χ^2 test).

If this equality hypothesis provides a reasonable fit to multiple occasion data, we can further examine changes in the common factor scores. Stability of individual differences can be examined using the correlation over time among the factor scores. If this factor intercorrelation is high, then the individuals exhibit few or no shifts in the relative position of their factor scores from time 1 to time 2. If this correlation is low, we assume there are notable shifts in the factor scores from time 1 to time 2. Either result can occur and this kind of factor score stability is apparent in studies of intellectual ability, but is not found in those on mood states. Most usefully, this two-occasion multiple variable model

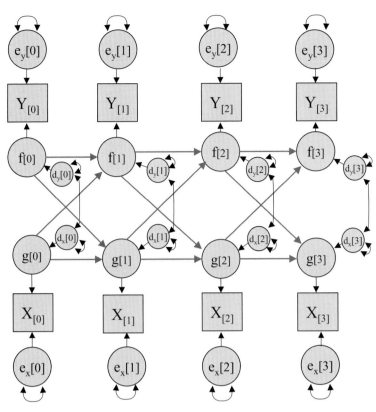

Figure 3. A latent variable cross-lagged regression model.

allows us to separate the stability due to (a) the internal consistency reliability of the factors and (b) the test-retest correlation of the factor scores.

SEM Type II: autoregressive models of change

Another distinguishing feature of SEM is that latent variables can be used either as dependent outcomes or as independent predictors in any analysis. This is most useful when the original measures have substantial measurement error, or they are considered complex mixtures of constructs. In one extension of the previous model (Type I, Fig. 2), we can examine how much the 'independent' time 1 factor score $f[1]$ affects the deviations on the 'dependent' time 2 factor score $f[2]$. This impact can be indexed by adding a regression coefficient (α_{21}) from time 1 to time 2. This simple principle has been extended to consider multiple scores over several occasions, and we write

$$[2a] \quad Y[t] = y[t] + e[t]_n \quad \text{and}$$
$$y[t]_n = \alpha[t]\, y[t-1]_n + d[t]_n$$

where the observed score at any occasion is made up of a true score (labeled lower-case $y[t]$), plus a random

error ($e[t]$). Here, we only have one indicator for each true score so we can only separate out the random components and not the unique factors ($u[t]$ as in [1a]). We do have a time-series, however, so we can postulate that the latent score at any occasion ($y[t]$) is partially due to the state of the latent score at some previous time point ($y[t-1]$), and partially due to a latent disturbance ($d[t]$). This is generally termed an autoregressive model and means are not usually considered here. This kind of model will represent a good fit in data where the pattern of correlations is progressively lower for scores further apart in time. Since we only consider that change in score deviations is around some equilibrium or steady state point, this model can be useful for studying developmental processes thought to be represented as fluctuations around their average values.

An autoregressive model for two variables ($X[t]$ and $Y[t]$) measured at four occasions is drawn as the path diagram of Figure 3. In this popular SEM model, we assume there are latent variables at several occasions $y[t]$ and these latent scores at a previous time, $y[t-1]$, are responsible for the scores of the latent variables at the next occasion. We also assume there is a second set of observed variables $X[t]$ and corresponding latent variables $x[t]$, and

$$[2b] \quad y[t]_n = \alpha[t]\, y[t-1]_n + \beta[t]\, x[t-1]_n + d[t]_n$$

and this is termed a latent variable cross-lagged regression model. In this model, the changes in one variable ($\Delta y[t]$) come from the prior changes in another variable ($\Delta x[t]$), and vice versa. Variations of this popular SEM include additional static variables (e.g., W, Z, etc.) or time-varying variables (e.g., $W[t]$, $Z[t]$, etc.) that can be added to account for other aspects of this covariation over time. Of course, all of these concepts about sequences of change over time are hypotheses that can be examined for both accuracy and meaningful interpretation.

This cross-lagged model has recently been used to examine the sequential development of many different behavioral processes, including the relationships among knowledge and reasoning, and self-esteem and academic achievement. Such a model is widely used in the analysis of time-sequence data, including studies of long-term changes in panel studies of persons, and in time-series research where only a few individuals are studied over a relatively large number of occasions.

SEM Type III: latent growth models

Alternative models for longitudinal data are useful when we are trying to describe developmental processes that grow in a systematic fashion. One popular SEM for this purpose is termed a latent growth curve and a bivariate form of this model is displayed in the path diagram of Figure 4. This model is used to characterize both the group average changes over time and the individual differences around these averages. The observed scores $Y[t]$ on the right-hand side of the diagram are written as

[3a] $Y[t] = y_0 + A[t]\,y_s + e[t]$

so there are three sources used to describe the trajectory over time. The first latent factor score is an intercept or level score labeled y_0, the second factor score is a latent slope or latent change score labeled y_s, and the third score is the random error labeled $e[t]$. The relationships between the latent slopes y_s and all observed scores $Y[t]$ are assigned a value based on a set of basis coefficients termed $A[t]$. The triangle in the diagram is a constant, and it is included to capture the group mean changes over time.

Any latent growth model will only be a good fit to longitudinal data when both the covariances and means follow a pattern in the form of the $A[t]$ basis. In latent growth models, the shape of the group curve depends on the application, and these may be fixed or estimated from the data. If we fix the basis at a straight line (i.e., $A[t] = [1, 2, 3, 4]$), we can estimate the parameters of a linear growth model. If we force a non-linear shape on these coefficients (i.e., $A[t] = [1, 2, 2, 1]$), we can examine non-linear shapes as an alternative hypothesis. If we estimate some parameters of the basis (i.e., $A[t] = [1, \alpha_2, \alpha_3, \alpha_4]$), we can obtain an optimal non-linear group curve. The flexible features of this model make it ideal for a number of applications, so that it has been used in studies that range from physical growth to the decline of intellectual abilities.

The latent growth model in Figure 4 includes such a model for two different measured variables ($Y[t]$ and $X[t]$). For each variable in this model, we postulate levels (x_0, y_0) and slopes (x_s, y_s) with separate latent basis ($A_x[t]$ and $A_y[t]$) and allow all components to covary. We write

[3b] $Y[t] = y_0 + A_y[t]\,y_s + e_y[t]$ and
$\qquad X[t] = x_0 + A_x[t]\,x_s + e_x[t].$

We can first consider concepts of factorial invariance if we happen to have comparable measurements. For example, if $X[t]$ represents the score of the child and $Y[t]$ represents the score of the parent on the same measures, we might be interested in testing a direct equality of the shapes of the two curves (i.e., does $A_y[t] = A_x[t]$?). More often, the primary interest here is the covariance or correlation of the slopes ($\rho_{sx,sy}$), as these parameters summarize the way individual differences in change over time in one variable are related to individual differences in change in another variable. This is a model of

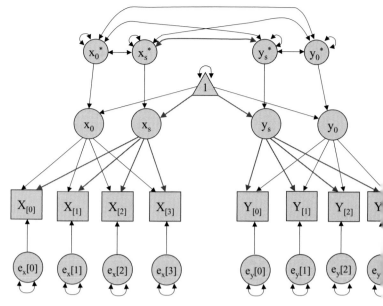

Figure 4. A bivariate latent growth model.

correlated changes where, unlike the cross-lagged model, we do not use the time-sequence to try to determine the flow of one variable from the other.

SEM Type IV: multiple group models

Another type of SEM is used for describing change over multiple groups. Once again, these are not easy problems for any statistical technique, but SEM again offers some clarity and some alternative choices. Some alternative SEMs for multiple group problems are described in Figure 4 using the latent growth model, but the results apply to any SEM.

Figure 5 is a latent growth model with the regression of the time-related factor scores from an external grouping variable. In this model, we assume the entire group can be described by a single shape ($A[t]$), but the variations around the level and slope are partly accounted for by the regression on the external group variable, labeled G. This model is written as the previous equation [3a] with the addition of

[4a] $y_0 = \omega_{0g} + \omega_{1g}\,G + e_0$ and
$\qquad y_s = \omega_{0s} + \omega_{1s}\,G + e_s.$

This SEM can be a simple way to account for the individual differences in the latent level and slope scores. This is a popular model because it is easy to use and interpret, and it is the SEM equivalent of a mixed-effects or multilevel model. The model in Figure 5 also includes some additional circles (hence, unobserved or latent) mixed in with the squares (observed) to represent that an equal-interval time spacing of the occasions was not

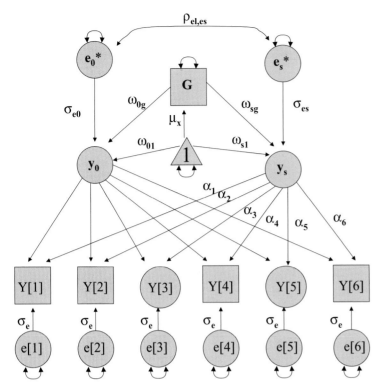

Figure 5. A latent growth model with group differences and incomplete data.

represents the SEM version of the commonly used assumption of data missing at random (MAR).

The multiple group approach also leads to another kind of useful analysis. In almost any data set, we can consider the possibility that there is heterogeneity with respect to the change pattern (i.e., there are some groups in the data with different growth curves, but we do not know how to form these groups). In cases where the groupings of persons are unobserved, we can apply techniques based on a growth-mixture model. This kind of model assumes that there are some basic group trajectories in the data, and that each individual has some probability of being a member of each group. Different kinds of models can be fitted and compared to other models with different numbers of latent groups. As in all other SEMs, the concept of a latent group can be treated as a hypothesis to be examined.

SEM Type V: latent difference score models

There is a large family of longitudinal curves that can be generated using the previous models. One way to summarize and extend this approach is to describe the changes in terms of a set of latent difference scores. Figure 6 is a path diagram of a seemingly complicated model, but this SEM can be described for each variable by a few simple equations as

[5a] $y[t] = y[t-1] + \Delta y[t]$ and
$$\Delta y[t] = \alpha + \beta y[t-1].$$

For variable $Y[t]$, we introduce a latent difference score by entering fixed value of unity (1). By fixing the 1 from factor $y[1]$ to factor $y[2]$, we can define a new variable as the difference in the latent scores ($\Delta y[t]$). In SEM, we do not calculate the differences among any variables, but we repeat this structural system of equations so we have an implied factor score at each time point and an implied difference between these scores. In this model, we add successive latent variables and successive latent difference scores followed by some theoretical model of the differences in terms of other variables. These difference score models can include some kind of constant change (i.e., the α), some kind of auto-regression (i.e., the $\beta y[t-1]$), or a more complex combination of both (i.e., $\alpha + \beta y[t-1]$). Since all previous SEMs can be written as specific models of change, this latent difference approach can encompass aspects of all other change and permit a variety of interesting hypotheses about change over time.

A bivariate latent difference score model is presented in Figure 6. This overall model uses the basic concept of the latent difference score as the key outcome, but now the change in one variable ($\Delta y[t]$) can be affected by the previous level of the other (i.e., $\gamma x[t-1]$).

actually measured. This kind of unbalanced data collection now poses no barrier to growth analysis.

One classical assumption in the mixed-effects model is that the basis of change ($A[t]$) is the same for all persons under study. Of course, this assumption of homogeneity may not be realistic for a number of substantive or methodological reasons. To examine these issues, we can (a) split up the data into separate groups, (b) consider model [3a] for each group, and (c) examine the invariance of the curve shape across groups by fitting

[4b] $A[t]^{(1)} = A[t]^{(2)} = A[t]^{(G)}$.

This type of SEM permits hypotheses about the mean differences across groups (as in the multilevel model [4a]), but it also uses factorial invariance principles on the trajectories over time. It offers a direct way to examine whether or not differences between the groups are in the shape of the growth curve itself.

This multiple group model is important in a number of other contexts. In real applications, we will have dropouts, deaths, returnees, etc. (Fig. 1), and this implies different persons have been measured on different numbers of variables. If we can assume the invariance of the model parameters across these different-sized groups, we can use a multiple group model to accumulate information about the entire data set. This assumption of factorial invariance over multiple independent groups with different variables

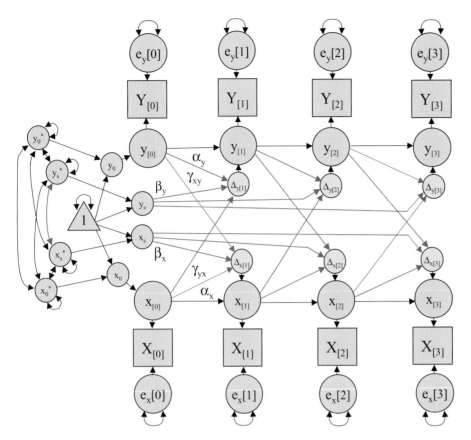

Figure 6. A latent difference score (LDS) model.

In theory, this may result in a complex system of inter-determination or dynamical coupling written as

[5b] $\Delta y[t] = \alpha + \beta y[t-1] + \gamma x[t-1]$

and the parameters are not exactly equivalent to the cross-lagged model (2b). In theory, this SEM representation of latent difference scores for both variables includes both the time-sequence determination and the latent growth interpretations of the previous models.

Many substantive questions in developmental data analysis deal with an improved understanding of the sequence of events that lead to outcomes, and there are several ways to make such predictions from these equations. Figure 7 is a vector field plot of the expectations for two variables measured over many occasions. In this plot, each line represents the expectation of change for a person with a pair of scores at some specific time ($x[t]$, $y[t]$) and the small arrows show the bivariate direction ($\Delta x[t]$, $\Delta y[t]$) that is expected over the next interval of time ($x[t+1]$, $y[t+1]$). The general direction and flow seen here is the result of a SEM (fitted to Fig. 1) based on latent variables and dynamical parameters. This specific result shows that the patterning of changes may not be the same for all initial score points, and the overall dynamical flow is a key

interpretive feature of this kind of SEM. These kinds of dynamical models have been used to study the time-sequence of multiple abilities in aging, the leading impacts of neurological declines on subsequent memory losses, and the relationships between early reading achievement and delinquency.

Conclusions

SEM offers a variety of unique and useful options for developmental data analysis. The overview presented here was intended to illustrate the range of current SEM applications. The key benefit of SEM is that seemingly different types of models of change can all be represented using contemporary SEM techniques for latent variables, and can all be fitted to the same data using the same SEM computer programs. In this way, SEM can be an informative tool for expressing a developmental theory, and in some cases it is possible to reject one change concept in favor of another. In this general sense, SEM can be a useful way to organize both the concepts and the practices of developmental data analysis.

SEM research has also provided a lead on some difficult problems for other statistical techniques, including the ability to deal with different models of change, multiple variables, and incomplete data. In these cases, SEM offers some clarity and some interesting

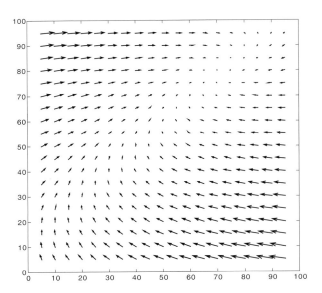

Figure 7. The resulting vector field as an expression of developmental changes over two variables.

alternative choices. Of course, there remain active debates on the meaning and interpretation of SEM parameter estimates and goodness-of-fit indices, and so on. These controversies are partly classical problems in statistics dealing with hypothesis testing and causal inference, but they also reflect classical problems in psychometric theory about the certainty of our measurement procedures. In many good longitudinal studies, the SEM approaches described here are not directly used for data collection or data analysis. Nevertheless, the SEM concepts have clarified the way researchers think about developmental issues, and hopefully this useful trend will continue.

See also:
Cross-sectional and longitudinal designs; Group differences in developmental functions; Multilevel modeling; The statistics of quantitative genetic theory

Further reading

Marcoulides, G. A. and Schumacker, R. E. (eds.) (2001). *New Developments and Techniques in Structural Equation Modeling*. Mahwah, NJ: Erlbaum.

McArdle, J. J. and Bell, R. Q. (2000). Recent trends in modeling longitudinal data by latent growth curve methods. In T. D. Little, K. U. Schnabel, and J. Baumert (eds.), *Modeling Longitudinal and Multiple-group Data: Practical Issues, Applied Approaches, and Scientific Examples*. Mahwah, NJ: Erlbaum, pp. 69–108.

McArdle, J. J., Ferrer-Caja, E., Hamagami, F. and Woodcock, R. W. (2002). Comparative longitudinal multilevel structural analyses of the growth and decline of multiple intellectual abilities over the life-span. *Developmental Psychology*, 38, 115–142.

Research and ethics

Ethical considerations in studies with children

HELEN L. WESTCOTT

Introduction

Diverse methods and approaches to research on child development are found in this book and ethical considerations are fundamental to all of them. Professionals carrying out research on, or with, children must be aware of the national and international legal regulations and conventions which apply, such as the United Nations Convention on the Rights of the Child (UNCRC) 1989, US federal regulations, data protection acts, and so on. Furthermore, researchers may be bound by the ethical guidelines of their profession, such as those issued by the British Psychological Society, or the Society for Research in Child Development. Such guidelines and regulations are not included here, but principles are introduced that should form the basis for ethical considerations in research with children.

Researchers in the UK working with children should, however, be aware of the recent (and not unproblematic) requirement to register with the 'Disclosure' service provided by the government's Criminal Records Bureau. The ethical considerations discussed here apply to all stages of the research process, irrespective of whether that research takes place in a laboratory, in a field observation, or in a health treatment program. They may also arise from aspects of a study that are not routinely apparent (e.g., implications for the siblings of a child participant).

Three fundamental and linked principles relevant to research involving human participants were laid down in 1979 by the National Commission for the Protection of Human Subjects of Biomedical and Behavioral Research (NCPHS) in the United States: 'beneficence,' 'justice,' and 'respect for persons.' Respect in the context of research with children goes beyond treating child participants in the manner in which we ourselves would like to be treated (Christensen & James, 2000). As Alderson (2000) has commented, ". . . respect links closely to rights, and rights conventions offer a principled, yet flexible, means of justifying and extending respectful practices" (p. 241). Nor do notions of respect and acting ethically equate with researcher comfort (Graue & Walsh, 1998). In planning and conducting research with children that is ethical, we can expect conflicts of interests, as well as challenges to our theoretical perspective and methodological interventions.

Developmental considerations

Children may be particularly vulnerable in research (Stanley & Sieber, 1992) as a result of:

- power imbalances between children and adults generally, and researchers specifically;
- children's distinctive cognitive and social developmental characteristics;
- children's greater difficulty in understanding the research process as a result of these characteristics, and of children's lesser life experience;
- the institutional context of much research with children (e.g., school, clinic) that may make it difficult for children to avoid cooperating with research projects or programs that make them feel uncomfortable.

Such considerations may be more or less relevant to any individual child, but should not devalue the potential of children's contributions to research. Rather, they should make our responsibilities as researchers even more apparent. They may also lead us to re-evaluate the role children can have in research projects, such as giving them and researchers the opportunity to design and implement projects together (Alderson, 1995; 2000).

Three fundamental principles

Beneficence

Beneficence is the obligation to maximize possible benefits, and minimize possible harms, for child participants. In calculating risk-benefit ratios, a number of interrelated issues are apparent: are benefits *direct* for the child involved, or are they *indirect*, and likely to apply to other children? Risks are less likely to be justified if the benefits to participants are indirect rather than direct. A second consideration is whether potential risks (and benefits) are psychological or physical in nature. Psychological risks may be less apparent, but for younger children may include the more limited success of debriefing and dehoaxing procedures, and for older children may include threats to self-esteem, embarrassment, or coping with violations of privacy (R. Thompson, 1992). Estimations of risk and benefits must also vary with the age of the child and should be re-visited at different stages of longitudinal projects. Benefits for younger children may include more concrete and direct aspects of the research process such as researcher praise, fun in participating, or receiving a sticker for participation. Older children may find benefits in less direct aspects of research such as satisfaction with participating, and thus helping the researcher and other children (Thompson, 1992). Different groups of children (e.g., abused versus non-abused, disabled versus non-disabled, sick versus healthy) also require vulnerabilities, risks, and benefits to be assessed differently.

Justice

Justice essentially demands that "equals ought to be treated equally" (NCPHS, 1979, p. 5), although this interpretation is not unproblematic (Stanley & Sieber, 1992). The principle of justice can be viewed as urging fair and impartial treatment of child participants at all stages of the research process (e.g., in sampling or in allocating to experimental conditions, in debriefing, in recompense for participation).

Respect for persons

Respect for persons is often linked to discussions of autonomy, a particularly pertinent issue for child participants and the concept of informed consent. This principle also relates to researchers' guarantees of confidentiality; protection of participants' privacy (both during research and in dissemination); minimizing deceptive practices; and providing full debriefings and dehoaxings (Thompson, 1992).

Traditionally, much research *on* children has relied on consent being obtained only from parents or carers, or instead on reports 'by proxy' from adults. In more recent research *with* children, researchers have sought to obtain children's own consent, as well as that of the adults responsible for them. With research into sensitive topics involving child participants increasing (e.g., children with HIV, children who are drug users, children who are abused) comes the issue of whether and under what conditions children are able to give consent independently, when parents or carers may be inappropriate gatekeepers (Stanley & Sieber, 1992).

In order for children (or adults) to give informed consent, they must understand:

- the purpose of the research;
- the anticipated nature of the research findings, their likely value and dissemination;
- that participation is voluntary;
- that they can withdraw at any time, without consequences;
- what their role in the research is, and what participation involves.

Box 1. Ten topics in ethical research

1. *The purpose of the research*

   If the research findings are meant to benefit certain children, who are they, and how might they benefit? How will the success of the research be evaluated in practice?

2. *Researching with children – costs and hoped-for benefits*

   How can researchers promote possible benefits, and prevent or reduce any risks? How may a research observation, or diagnosis (e.g., of a developmental disorder), affect how the child is subsequently treated by their parents or other professionals?

3. *Privacy and confidentiality*

   How much choice can children exercise over the nature of their involvement in a study (e.g., when and where they participate)? What will the researcher do in the event that a child is identified as being at risk of harm from self or others? How will the child be made aware of this eventuality and what is the likely impact on the research outcome?

4. *Selection, inclusion, and exclusion*

   Can the exclusion (of any children) be justified? For example, may non-participating peers become distressed? What obligations does this impose on the researcher?

5. *Funding*

   Should children be paid or given some reward after helping with research? How and when should children be made aware of such reward? Could it be seen as coercion to consent, or as unfair to children whose carers refuse consent? How might non-participating children be otherwise recompensed?

6. *Review and revision of the research aims and methods*

   Has a committee, a small group, or an individual (or children and carers) reviewed the protocol specifically for its ethical aspects and approach to children? What should a researcher do if easy access is promised by a gatekeeper (e.g., institutional principal or school headteacher) who disregards the need for parental or child consent?

7. *Information for children, parents, and other carers*

   How does a researcher describe a study's design, when it is likely that the full description may be off-putting to parents or children, even if no deception is involved? Are 'half-truths' on a consent form acceptable? How can children contact a researcher if they wish to comment, question, or complain?

8. *Consent*

   Do children know they can ask questions, perhaps talk to other people, and ask for time before they decide whether to consent? If a child requests a toilet break, or a school bell rings for break just before completion of a test or interview, is it ethical to ask the child to stay for 'just one more question'?

9. *Dissemination*

   Will the children and adults involved be sent short reports of the main findings? How might such feedback be made age-appropriate? Should a researcher give individual details (e.g., to carer) if they think this might help a child, despite initial promises only to feed back group data?

10. *Impact on children*

    Do researchers try to balance impartial research with respect for children's worth and dignity? When researchers have initially indicated their research will have no negative consequences for children, do they subsequently follow-up child participants to check that this is true?

In studies with children, obtaining consent requires more than formalities (e.g., completion of the consent form), and researchers must be aware of child participants' likely needs and fears. In this respect, a steering group, perhaps involving children or carers or both, may be helpful. Researchers must be sensitive to non-verbal as well as verbal signals of distress, or of the child wishing to withdraw. It is debatable – even in studies not involving deception – whether young children are ever truly able to express the wish to participate (or not). Children who have communication and/or learning impairments require special attention in this respect.

Practicalities and dilemmas

Translating responsibilities imposed by these principles into practical considerations of ethics is not easy. Alderson (1995, pp. 2–6) lists ten topics to be addressed in ethical research, which are summarized in Box 1.

The topics in Box 1 apply to the various stages of the research process, but the degree to which children are actively involved alongside researchers in addressing each will vary from study to study (i.e., from no involvement to consultation to initiation of research projects). Nonetheless, researchers can improve a study's ethics by exploring each topic in turn. Pilot studies can also be used to evaluate the success of ethical considerations alongside experimental manipulations (e.g., are leaflets designed to enable children to give informed consent successful?). If deception is deemed necessary, it may be helpful to get an impartial colleague or steering group (again, perhaps involving children and/or carers) to evaluate the research design and possible implications for child participants' welfare. These implications too can be evaluated in the post-pilot stage of a study.

Conclusions

Three fundamental principles that researchers should promote in working with participants have been considered, and particular issues arising when those participants are children have been summarized. An awareness of the potential of the research process to exploit children highlights the responsibility of the researcher toward the children involved. Different ways of working with children in planning and carrying out future studies have been hinted at, ways which may permit a more participatory role for children. Greater participation leads to greater control of the research process by children, and, as a result, to better insights into the research questions and design. Effective methodology and effective ethics are parallel considerations in research. As Thompson (1992) observed: "The limitations accepted by researchers because of their ethical responsibilities to research participants can at times have profound implications for the generalizability, validity and quality of the data they gather . . . Yet their acceptance of these limitations reveals the underlying humanistic values guiding their scientific enterprise" (p. 61).

See also:
Clinical and non-clinical interview methods; Developmental testing; Observational methods; Experimental methods; Cross-sectional and longitudinal designs; 'At-risk' concept; Autism; Sociology

Author's note

I would like to thank Dr. Clare Wilson for her helpful comments on an earlier draft of this entry.

Further reading

Greig, A. and Taylor, J. (1999). *Doing Research with Children.* Thousand Oaks, CA: Sage.
Pezdek, K. (ed.) (1998). *Applied Cognitive Psychology Special Issue*, 12, 3 (discussion of ethical issues in the experimental study of children's 'false memories').
Ward, L. (1997). *Seen and Heard: Involving Disabled Children and Young People in Research and Development Projects.* York, UK: Joseph Rowntree Foundation.

PART III

Prenatal development and the newborn

This part of the book aims to provide up-to-date information on normal and abnormal development during the prenatal period – a period that has been largely neglected by mainstream developmental psychology. This information has far-reaching consequences for the theories discussed in Part I, as well as for our understanding of the birth process in humans relative to other species and subsequent postnatal development.

Conceptions and misconceptions about embryonic* development

RONALD W. OPPENHEIM

Introduction

As a Developmental Biologist who has spent more than forty years studying the embryonic development of the nervous system and behavior, it is both informative and disheartening to read the following statement made recently by two eminent molecular biologists: ". . . the encapsulated instructions in the gametes are passed on to a fertilized egg and then they unfold spontaneously to give rise to offspring" (Lander & Weinberg, 2000, p. 1777). This statement is disheartening in that such a view seems to lead inexorably to the mistaken argument that all one needs to know about an organism in order to understand its development is the DNA sequence of its genome, which is a modern form of preformationism. At the same time, from a historical perspective this view is informative in that, despite the triumph in embryology of epigenesis over preformationism more than a century ago, preformationism (which is a prototypical example of an embryological misconception) appears to linger on today in the intellectual framework of at least a few highly influential biologists.

The developmental issues embodied in the debate over epigenesis versus preformation have a long history stretching back to antiquity, and some of these issues have persisted into more modern times in the form of questions about nature versus nurture, genetic versus environmental factors, and instinct versus learning (Oppenheim, 1982b; 1992). Although these concepts are dealt with in detail in other entries, I mention them here only because they also represent opposing views or concepts of embryonic development. However, except for their historical interest (and despite the statement quoted above), such views represent anachronisms and misconceptions, that no contemporary developmental

scientist would subscribe to. Rather, it is now an accepted principle of developmental biology that genetic information requires both permissive and instructional signals involving cell-cell interactions within the developing organism, as well as environmental signals from outside to generate the normal features characteristic of each stage of development. Although this general framework is applicable to the development of all tissues and organs, it is especially relevant for neurobehavioral development in which developmental plasticity driven by the environment and individual experience is a common *Leitmotiv*.

Some major questions

Because I would argue that neurobehavioral development, especially during embryonic stages, is best understood within the more general framework of developmental biology, it is informative to consider briefly some of the major questions addressed by developmental biologists (Gilbert, 2003). These include:

- **The question of differentiation.** Since all cells beginning with the zygote contain the same genetic material, how are the hundreds of diverse cell types generated?
- **The question of morphogenesis.** Diverse cell types arise by differentiation, but then become organized into tissues and organs. What regulates the creation of these supra-cellular patterns during morphogenesis?
- **The question of growth.** How do precursor cells know when to stop dividing and how do individual post-mitotic cells know when to stop growing?
- **The question of evolution.** Evolution occurs by inherited changes in the development of organisms. Advances in developmental genetics and molecular biology have now made it possible to isolate phylogenetic changes in specific genes, and in their means of regulation and expression during

---

* The term 'embryonic' is used here to refer to the entire period between fertilization and birth or hatching. This is a more all-encompassing term than prenatal, fetal, in utero or in ovo in that it is applicable to virtually all invertebrate and vertebrate species.

development in different species. This new field of developmental evolution provides a framework in which, for the first time, it is possible to determine how development has been altered to produce structures and functions that permit both developing and adult animals to adapt to specific conditions.

○ **The question of environmental integration.** Most organisms require cues or signals from the external environment for normal development. This is especially true for neural and behavioral development. When and how this occurs is a key issue in developmental neurobiology.

Since behavioral development is predicated on a properly constructed nervous system, all of the above questions are relevant for understanding both pre- and postnatal stages of development. However, because behavioral development also involves issues related to neuronal function, a major focus of interest has been on questions related to the formation of synaptic connections between neurons and the extent to which endogenous neuronal activity and environmental (sensory) inputs regulate connectivity and functional/behavioral development. Because neurons begin to function at early stages of embryogenesis, such an analysis forces one to begin the study of neurobehavioral development during the period prior to birth or hatching.

Embryonic neurobehavioral development

Neuronal function during embryonic stages has been shown to be important for the development of the lungs, the vascular system, skeletal muscle, and the skeleton (joint formation). The normal development and maintenance of skeletal muscle, for example, requires that the muscle fibers contract, an effect that is maintained by spontaneous movements of the embryo that are generated by spinal cord activity. These same embryonic movements are also important for regulating neuronal survival. Most populations of developing neurons undergo an adaptive process of programmed cell death whereby some proportion of the population (usually about one half) degenerate prior to birth or hatching. For developing motoneurons, the number of cells that survive depends upon functional nerve-muscle interactions. Paralysis of developing embryos rescues most of the motoneurons that would otherwise die (Fig. 1).

Later in development, the formation and maintenance of synaptic connections is also modulated by neuronal activity (Fig. 2), a form of plasticity that is related to and is a precursor of the kinds of changes required postnatally for learning, memory, and other forms of

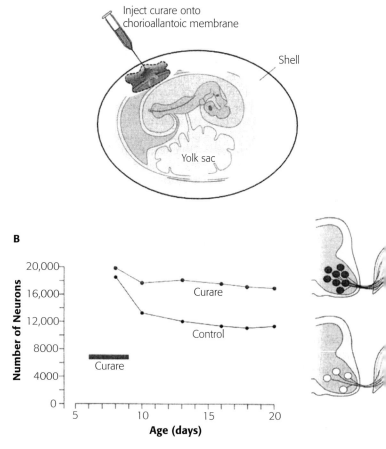

Figure 1. Blocking synaptic transmission prevents normal motoneuron cell death. (A) Neuromuscular transmission can be blocked by applying curare onto the chorioallantoic membrane of chick embryos. (B) In control animals, over 30 percent of motoneurons die after embryonic day 5 (E5). When animals are treated with curare from E6 to E9, the magnitude of normal cell death is greatly diminished. Adapted from Sanes, Reh, & Harris (2000).

experience-dependent changes in the nervous system. Therefore, an important principle of nervous system development, first manifest during embryonic life, is the fundamental role of neuronal function. By the induction of new gene transcription and post-transcriptional events, neuronal activity leaves a lasting imprint on the developing brain. Although many aspects of embryonic and postnatal neuronal development also involve diverse kinds of cell-cell interactions that occur normally without the benefit of function, it is now clear that neuronal activity must be added to these other developmental events if the nervous system is to develop its normal structure and the capacity to generate adaptive behaviors. When viewed from this perspective, it becomes impossible to accept the common misconception of embryonic development, which is the notion that behavioral ontogeny first begins at birth or hatching and that the period prior to birth is mainly important

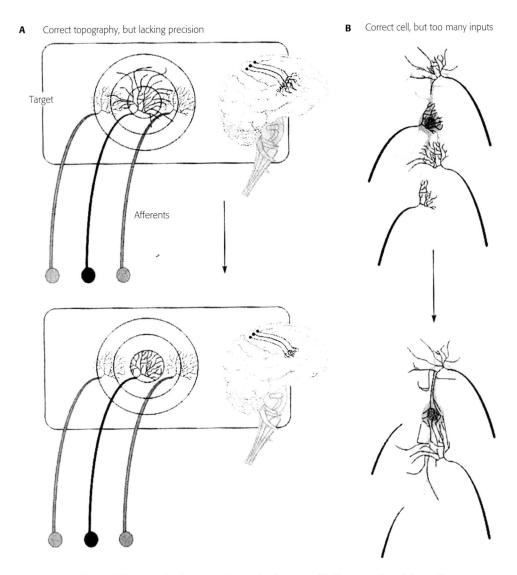

A Correct topography, but lacking precision

Target

Afferents

B Correct cell, but too many inputs

Figure 2. Two kinds of afferent projection errors during development. (A) The projection of three afferents to the cortex is shown, and each one centers its arborization at the topographically correct position in the target. However, one of the arbors initially extends too far (top) and these local branches are eliminated (bottom) during development. (B) A single neuron is shown to receive input from four afferents initially (top), and two of these inputs are eliminated (bottom) during development. Note that the remaining afferent arbors may spread out on the postsynaptic neuron. Adapted from Sanes, Reh, & Harris (2000).

for anatomical-morphological development. Other entries document the occurrence and significance of embryonic behavioral development.

Ontogenetic adaptations

A major conception of development is that the events occurring during embryonic, prenatal, and postnatal stages represent a preparation for adult life. From this perspective, development is viewed as a gradual progression in which each step or stage represents a closer approximation to the adult situation. In its most extreme form, this view assumes that the only possible

way to understand ontogeny is with reference to what is to come, and thus that developmental events are only an anticipation, an imperfect form of adult features. Because much of the research in the developmental sciences is predicated on this concept, there is obviously a great deal of truth in such a view. A problem arises, however, if one takes this to be the whole truth and nothing but the truth. By excluding a whole class of ontogenetic events that can be viewed as important in their own right and not just as stepping stones to adulthood, such a view ignores a major feature of development.

Life histories are often complex and embryos, fetuses, larvae, neonates, and juveniles frequently inhabit

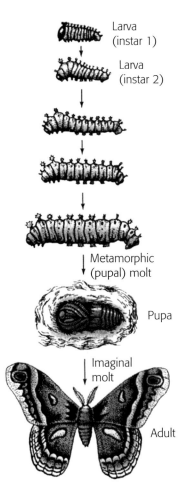

Larva (instar 1)

Larva (instar 2)

Metamorphic (pupal) molt

Pupa

Imaginal molt

Adult

Figure 3. Mode of metamorphosis in the moth. Adapted from Gilbert (2003).

environments that differ amongst themselves as well as from the adult environment. Each of these stages may be adaptive in its own right and require unique anatomical, physiological, biochemical, and behavioral mechanisms. I have previously referred to these as ontogenetic adaptations and have provided numerous examples (Oppenheim, 1981; 1984), some of the most obvious of which are hatching in egg-laying species, suckling in mammals, swimming and many other transient features in amphibian tadpoles, larval stages in insects, and imprinting in many precocial species of birds. Because by their very nature these are transient characteristics, their major role in development cannot merely be as precursors of adult features. Furthermore, being short-lived, their loss often requires regression or reorganization of the cellular, physiological, and anatomical mechanisms that mediate them.

I have often used the process of metamorphosis in amphibians and insects as a metaphor for the transient nature of ontogenetic adaptations in non-metamorphic species such as birds and mammals (Fig. 3). In fact, although the underlying mechanisms may differ, ontogenetic adaptations in these species may only represent less striking instances of the same needs of

metamorphic species to adjust to changing environments. The period of childhood in mammalian development, for example, has often been viewed as a new stage in the vertebrate life cycle that is required for optimal brain development, and puberty in humans can also be thought of as a kind of metamorphic transition even down to its regulation by hormones. Admittedly, the life histories of most vertebrates do not include the radical, hormonally driven transformations and regressions that characterize metamorphosis in amphibians and insects, but this is a difference in degree not kind.

Genes, development and evolution

As implied in the term 'ontogenetic adaptation' it is assumed that, regardless of whether one refers to behaviors or other transient features of developing organisms, the characteristics in question have evolved by natural selection and therefore represent genetically controlled shifts (re-programing) in developmental pathways (Wilkins, 2002). As noted above, one of the major questions of development is how inherited alterations in development produce evolutionary changes. One notable area in which significant progress has been made in this field is in our understanding of the regulation of anterior-posterior (head-to-tail) axis specification (the body plan) in the animal kingdom. A family of nuclear transcription factors, the homeobox or *Hox* genes, have been evolutionarily conserved from invertebrate species to mammals and serve to specify the basic body plan in all of these forms (Fig. 4). The protein products of *Hox* genes function by binding to specific DNA sequences (genes) in the cell nucleus that through a cascade of complex developmental (epigenetic) events control the specification of specific body parts along the anterior-posterior axis. Variations in *Hox* gene expression and the downstream genes they regulate are the basis for many of the major evolutionary changes in body plan. For example, the loss of limbs during the evolution of snakes from lizards has been shown to result from alterations in *Hox* gene expression during the development of snake embryos (Fig. 5). The enormous variety in appendages of arthropods (e.g., insects) is perhaps the most completely understood example of how genetic re-programing in develop-mental pathways involving *Hox* genes can mediate micro- and macroevolutionary changes.

Another example more relevant to the topic of this entry is the developmental events responsible for the evolution of the central nervous system (CNS). The same set of genes that control the induction of the nervous system have been conserved in animals as diverse as insects and mammals. These genes control specific cell-cell interactions in the ectoderm (the tissue

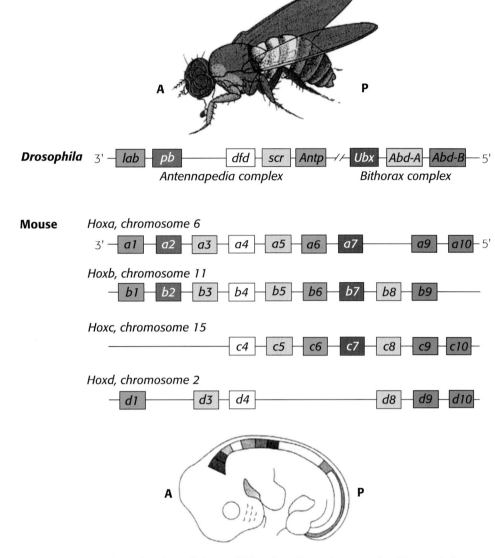

Figure 4. *Hox* gene clusters in arthropods (*Drosophila*) and vertebrates (mouse embryo) have a similar spatial organization and similar order along the chromosomes. Their position on the chromosome is related to their role in anterior-posterior (A-P, head to tail) specification of the body in both flies and mammals. Adapted from Sanes, Reh, & Harris (2000).

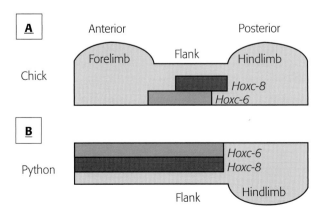

Figure 5. Loss of limbs in snakes. *Hox* expression patterns in chick (A) and python (B). The expression of *Hoxc-8* and *Hoxc-6* specifies rib versus forelimb development in the python. Adapted from Gilbert (2003).

layer that can generate either skin or neural tissue) by converting the fate of the ectoderm from skin to the nervous system (Fig. 6). Although the means for inducing the CNS has been conserved, later in evolution developmental changes occurred that resulted in the striking differences one observes between the complexity of the CNS of a fly and the human brain.

Changes in developmental timing: a source of evolutionary change

The relevance of these observations from developmental evolutionary studies for understanding embryonic development and ontogenetic adaptations is that evolutionary differences between animal groups involve

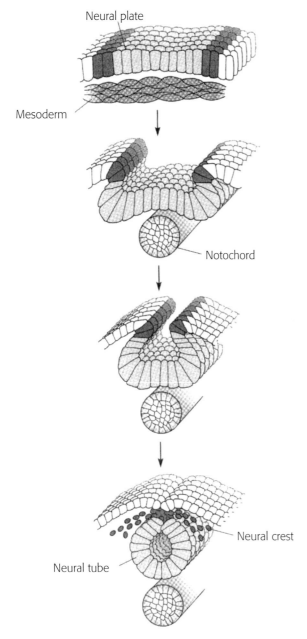

Neural plate

Mesoderm

Notochord

Neural crest

Neural tube

Figure 6. The neural plate (top) rolls up into a tube separating from the rest of the ectoderm. The mesoderm cells condense to form a rod-shaped structure – the notochord – just underneath the neural plate. The neural plate begins to roll up and fuse at the dorsal margin. A group of cells known as the neural crest arises at the point of fusion of the neural tube. Adapted from Sanes, Reh, & Harris (2000).

changes in developmental as well as in adult features. For example, although most amphibian species have a transient larval (tadpole) stage during development that is adapted for an aquatic environment, some frog species living in environments where standing pools of water are scarce have abandoned the larval stage such that the newly hatched animal is a miniature adult rather than a larval tadpole. This is one example of a common occurrence in developmental strategies (viz., heterochrony), by which changes in the relative timing of ontogenetic events drive evolution. By the early activation of adult genes and the suppression of larval

genes, the tadpole stage is eliminated and replaced by adult structures.

Such changes in timing represent only one of several kinds of developmental re-programming events by which changes in ontogeny affect phenotypes. Others include, spatial re-programming (e.g., changing the location of a structure from dorsal to ventral), quantitative re-programming (e.g., changing limb size) and qualitative (type) re-programming (e.g., forming a wing in a formerly wingless body segment). It is important to point out, however, that all re-programing events, though mutation- and thus gene-based, are also influenced by epigenetic and environmental factors.

The appearance and disappearance of larval stages in the evolution of different species underscores another important point, namely, that both early and late stages of development can be the substrate for evolutionary change. Regardless of the time during development when genetic alterations occur, however, the resulting phenotype must be adaptive. Accordingly, the conceptual framework provided by developmental evolution studies is a valuable tool for understanding pathways of individual development (i.e., ontogeny). It provides a means for integrating genetic, epigenetic, embryological, and evolutionary evidence in an attempt to understand the direct development of the adult phenotype, as well as the transient phenotypes (i.e., ontogenetic adaptations) that characterize intervening stages between the egg and the adult.

Conclusions

As a leading developmental biologist has noted:

> Between fertilization and birth, the developing organism is known as an embryo. The concept of an embryo is a staggering one, and forming an embryo is the hardest thing you will ever do . . . One of the critical differences between you and a machine is that a machine is never required to function until after it is built. Every animal has to function as it builds itself.
>
> (Gilbert, 2003, p. 3)

This statement is as valid for the development of the nervous system and behavior as it is for the development of the heart, lungs, and muscles of embryos.

See also:
The concept of development: historical perspectives; Understanding ontogenetic development: debates about the nature of the epigenetic process; What is ontogenetic development?; Neuromaturational theories; Cross-species comparisons; Prenatal development of the musculoskeletal system in the human; Normal and abnormal prenatal development; The status of the human newborn; Development of learning and memory; Brain and behavioral

development (I): sub-cortical; Brain and behavioral development (II): cortical; Cognitive neuroscience; Developmental genetics; Behavioral embryology; George E. Coghill; Viktor Hamburger

Further reading

Gottlieb, G. (ed.) (1973, 1974). *Studies on the Development of Behavior and the Nervous System*, Vols. I and II. New York: Academic Press.

Hall, W. G. and Oppenheim, R. W. (1987). Developmental psychobiology: prenatal, perinatal and early postnatal aspects of behavioral development. *Annual Review of Psychology*, 38, 91–128.

Oppenheim, R. W. (2001). Early development of behavior and the nervous system: a postscript from the end of the millennium. In E. Blass (ed.), *Handbook of Behavioral Neurobiology*, Vol. XII: *Developmental Psychobiology*. New York: Plenum Press, pp. 15–52.

Prenatal development of the musculoskeletal system in the human

SIMON H. PARSON AND RICHARD R. RIBCHESTER

Introduction

Behavior is ultimately constrained by the limits of articulation in bones and joints, mediated by muscle contraction. Skeletal muscles of the trunk and limbs ensure the maintenance of posture as well as underpinning a diverse repertoire of voluntary movement. Furthermore, the musculature of the head, neck, and face mediate many forms of verbal and non-verbal communication. An understanding of musculoskeletal anatomy, physiology, and development is important for those interested in child development. In this entry, we overview principles of musculoskeletal anatomy, physiology, and development, and discuss briefly recent advances in understanding of molecular and physiological mechanisms.

Overview of musculoskeletal morphology and physiology in adults

There are three main classes of muscle: skeletal, smooth, and cardiac. Skeletal muscles are composed of hundreds or thousands of multinucleate fibers, up to 100 μm in diameter and 50 cm in length, each of which generates force by virtue of calcium-dependent, molecular cross-bridge cycling between cytoskeletal proteins organized into myofilaments. The contractile proteins involved include myosin (making up anisotropic 'A' bands) and actin (isotropic 'I' bands), the latter being tethered to transverse slabs of protein ('Z' bands) that demarcate the sarcomeres. The organization of these proteins confers their characteristic striated appearance when viewed under phase or polarized light microscopes. The energetic cost of cross-bridge recycling is met by hydrolysis of adenosine triphosphate (ATP).

Muscle contraction generates force against a load. If the force generated is greater than the load, then the muscle will shorten and move the load, something that is termed isotonic contraction. If the force generated is insufficient to move the load, then the muscle will not shorten, this being an isometric contraction. As muscle contraction begins, isometric contractions that normally precede isotonic ones equal the load and then shorten unless, of course, the load is too great, and the muscle fails to shorten. To generate force, sarcomeres shorten by relative sliding of the thick myosin and thin actin filaments. Contractions are triggered by membrane depolarization, coupled to release of Ca ions from intracellular stores, mainly in the sarcoplasmic reticulum (SR). Relaxation of muscle is mediated by Ca-pumps in the SR membranes that re-sequester cytoplasmic Ca. Depletion of energy stores such as glycogen, creatine, and ATP, and/or build-up of metabolites including lactic acid, lead to irregular control of muscle force, including fatigue, cramp, and – ultimately – rigor (mortis).

Most voluntary muscles are attached to bones via tendons (in contrast to ligaments that sustain the orientation of bones at joints), which allow joints to be moved. The organization of muscles in antagonistic, opposing groups – flexors and extensors – provides a mechanism for moving the joints they span in opposing directions. For example, the biceps and triceps brachii muscles span the elbow joint on anterior and posterior surfaces, and respectively flex and extend the elbow joint.

Denervation, a consequence of nerve injury and degeneration, and paralysis or prolonged disuse also trigger changes in gene expression and emergence of a host of curious physiological properties (e.g., 'fibrillation' or 'fasciculation,' characteristic forms of spontaneous, involuntary twitching, and changes in pharmacological sensitivity to toxins and neurotransmitter agonists/antagonists). Thus, ultimately, muscle activity is an important regulator of muscle development, metabolism, and function.

From somites to segmentation of muscle

One of the most basic levels of organization during development is the generation of primitive layers (gastrulation). The middle layer of this sandwich is the mesoderm, the others being ectoderm (outer) and endoderm (inner). This mesoderm ultimately gives rise to the majority of the axial skeleton and skeletal muscle of the trunk and limbs. Mesoderm rapidly segments into somites, which first appear on about embryonic day 20 (i.e., 20 days after fertilization), and arise from paraxial mesoderm via an intermediate whorl-like somitomere. Here, an important division begins to arise as the first (cranial) 6–7 somites develop within structures known as the pharyngeal arches, and go on to form much of the musculature of the face and neck. More caudally, by day 30, 37 pairs of somites have formed, which become all of the vertebrae from cervical to coccygeal and some of the base of the skull. At the same point, the paraxial mesoderm induces the overlying ectoderm to develop into the neural plate from which the central nervous system forms. Spinal and cranial motoneurons that go on to innervate skeletal muscle develop from this structure.

Pattern formation: genes and environment

In chick embryos, somites are generated regularly every ninety minutes, which has led to the suggestion that a developmental clock determines somite formation and identity. Many mechanisms have been proposed to account for this, and several candidate genes and proteins have been identified. One interesting contender for a clock gene is *c-hairy1*. This putative transcription repressor molecule shows a cyclical pattern of expression in developing somites that co-ordinates well with the timing of their generation, and ultimately becomes confined to the caudal portion of the somite when it forms. It is thought that *c-hairy1* is not THE clock gene, but rather a downstream manifestation of it (Dale & Pourquie, 2000; Stern & Vasiliauskas, 1998). Downstream, *notch* is known to be important in pre-somitic tissues segmentation, and very recent work suggests a role for a glycosyltransferase (*Lfng*) that oscillates in pre-somitic tissue. In doing so, it periodically inhibits *notch*, and in synchrony with somitogenesis, may have the primary clock function (Dale *et al.*, 2003).

Development of the skeleton

Newly formed somites now become segregated into dorsolateral dermomyotome and ventromedial sclerotome, which together form trunk muscle, dermis, and skeleton. Interestingly, sclerotome, which migrates medially and develops most rapidly, comes to enclose completely the notochord (and future neural tube), blocking the emergence of spinal nerves. However, sclerotomes split longitudinally and recombine to form intersegmental structures, between which spinal nerves emerge (see Box 1). A large family of *Hox* genes are of key importance to this process of segmentation, and, in mice at least, their boundaries of expression closely match segmental boundaries. Furthermore, experiments in which *Hox* genes are mutated clearly demonstrate that they have the ability to re-specify the identity of vertebrae. An important signaling molecule possibly acting up-stream of *Hox* genes is retinoic acid. This has been suggested to operate as a gradient switch for *Hox* genes, and is a known teratogen. It is rather more difficult to match expression patterns of *Hox* genes exactly to either somatic or intersegmental sclerotome boundaries.

Intervertebral discs arise from sclerotomal cells remaining after division, and invading cells from the notochord. At about day 35, the newly formed thoracic vertebrae alone begin to form the costal process, which will develop into the true (direct sternal articulating), and false (indirect sternal articulating) ribs. Ribs will ossify (become bone) from cartilaginous precursors.

Sonic hedgehog (a small peptide homologue of *drosophila* Hedgehog) is important in the induction of sclerotome by the notochord and neural tube. *Sonic hedgehog* is a diffusible factor, and can operate over considerable distances in the embryo. It appears able to induce *Pax-1* expression, which is an important transcription factor in sclerotome differentiation.

Segmentation of muscles (including segmental and non-segmental muscles)

Returning to the dermomyotome (that portion of the somite not developing into sclerotome), this splits to give dermotome and myotome. The latter further divides to form two rudiments, which in the trunk independently form the erector spinae (the epimere)

Box 1. Eight cervical spinal nerve roots, but only seven cervical vertebrae?

This occurrence also explains why there are eight cervical nerve roots, but only seven cervical vertebrae. Here, the cranial-most part of the first cervical vertebra combines with those forming the occipital part of the skull while the caudal-most half of the eighth cervical vertebra fuses with the anterior portion of the first thoracic vertebra. Spinal nerve C1 emerges above the first cervical vertebra, and spinal nerve C8 below the seventh cervical vertebra.

and tri-laminar anterior-lateral abdominal wall / thoracic wall musculature (the hypomere). These latter muscles include the external and internal oblique and transversus abdominis muscles of the abdomen, and external, internal, and innermost muscles of the intercostal spaces (Fig. 1).

At about the same time, musculature of the pharyngeal arches develops from paraxial mesoderm and occipital somites in the future head and neck. Muscles from each arch become innervated by a single cranial nerve (CN), even though they may migrate to different ultimate locations. The first arch gives rise to the muscles of mastication (CN V), the second to those of facial expression (CN VII), the third to stylopharyngeus only (CN IX), and the fourth to pharyngeal muscles (CN X).

Formation of the limbs, appendicular skeleton, and musculature

The upper and lower limb buds appear between the middle and end of the 4th week. Hand rudiments are apparent by the middle of the 5th week, and development proceeds until about the 8th week. Each limb bud has a mesoderm-derived mesenchymal core, surrounded by ectoderm, and specifically an apical ectodermal ridge, which stimulates limb elongation. Experimental removal of this structure halts limb bud extension. Mesenchyme begins to condense (Hall & Miyake, 2000) along the central long-axis of the limb buds around the 5th week, and these will develop into the skeletal elements, via a process of chondrification (cartilage formation) and ossification (bone formation) (Karsenty & Wagner, 2002). Furthermore, peripheral nerves begin to invade the newly formed limb bud during the 4th week. The limb thus rapidly elongates at its tip, simultaneously differentiating into muscular and skeletal elements behind this growth front. These structures are then rapidly invaded by neural growth cones.

Segregation of muscle masses

At limb levels, somitic mesoderm also begins to invade the newly formed limb buds at this time, and goes on to form the skeletal muscles of the limbs. Those on the ventral surfaces become flexors and pronators/adductors of the upper and lower limbs, while those on the dorsal surface form extensors and supinators/abductors of the upper and lower limbs, respectively.

For the developmental events so far considered, the key milestones in the human are indicated in Table 1.

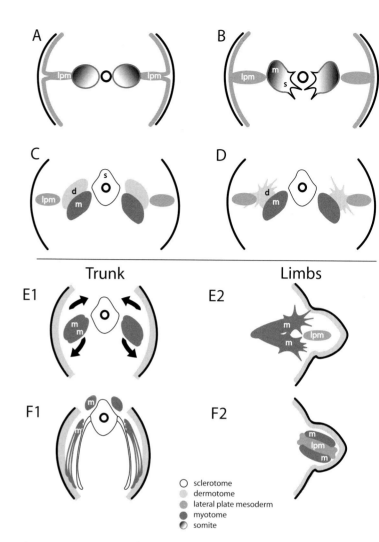

Figure 1. Formation of axial (trunk) and appendicular (limb) skeleton and musculature. (A) Invagination of mesoderm forms a shelf in the midline of the embryo. The most medial parts form the somite, and the more lateral parts the lateral plate mesoderm. (B) The somite differentiates into dorsolateral dermomyotome and ventromedial sclerotome. The sclerotome erupts and migrates medially. (C) The sclerotome comes to surround the notochord, while the dermomyotome differentiates into dermotome and myotome. (D) Dermotome migrates laterally. (E1) In the trunk, myotome splits into epimere and hypomere, which migrate dorsally and ventrally respectively. (E2) In the limbs, myotome divides into presumptive dorsal and ventral muscle masses. (F1) In the trunk, epimere forms the erector spinae muscles, and hypomere the trilaminar thoracic and abdominal walls, while limb bones begin to condense from mesenchyme. (F2) In the limbs, the dorsal muscle mass forms extensors, supinators, and abductors and the ventral mass flexors, pronators, and adductors, while the ribs form by vertebral outgrowth.

The rudiments of the axial (trunk) musculoskeletal system are now formed. These are bones of the vertebrae and ribs, formed from the early-differentiating sclerotome portion of the somites, and trunk musculature from the later differentiating myotomal portion of the somite.

Box 2. Development of structures necessary for vocalization

Meaningful sounds are produced by movements of the laryngeal cartilages brought about by the intrinsic muscles of the larynx. That sound is modulated by the tongue and lips, and to some extent the fixed shape of the oral and nasal cavities. Considering the development of these structures individually:

Larynx – The cartilaginous portions of the larynx are derived from the cartilages of the fourth to the sixth arches. These are thought to be derived from lateral plate mesoderm rather than neural crest. Arytenoid swellings first develop in the 5th week, but do not begin to chondrify until the 7th week. The epiglottis, which is formed of elastic, rather than the hyaline cartilage of the other laryngeal cartilages, does not develop until the 5th month, and is thought to arise from migrating mesenchyme, which invades the region of the fourth arch. Paraxial mesoderm from the first and second occipital somites enters the sixth arch and forms the intrinsic musculature of the larynx.

Hyoid bone – The cartilage of the second arch (Reichert's), arises from neural crest derived from the mesencephalon/ rhombencephalon boundary, and together with the cartilage of the third arch goes on to form the hyoid bone, which supports the larynx and gives attachment to the muscles of the tongue.

Tongue – Some occipital somites also migrate into endoderm-covered swellings on the floor of the pharynx to form the tongue. The anterior two thirds and posterior one third of the tongue arise from the first and second pharyngeal arches, respectively, which explains their dual sensory nerve supply. Equally, motor supply comes from another cranial nerve, the hypoglossal (CN XII).

Lips – These are moved by the muscles of facial expression, such as orbicularis oris and risorius. As stated above, these muscles arise from the second arch and are innervated by the facial nerve (CN VII).

Table 1. Milestones of muscle development in humans.

Week	Day	Event
3	16	Mesoderm begins to form and differentiate into dermomyotome and sclerotome
	17	Intermediate and lateral plate mesoderm begins to form
	20	Somites begin to form (cranial)
4	22	Neural tube begins to form from neural plate
	24	Upper limb bud forms
	26	Sclerotome begins to migrate to surround notochord and neural tube formation is complete
	28	First dorsal root ganglia form (from migrating neural crest), and ventral motor columns begin to form, lower limb bud forms
5	30	Last somites formed, (caudal) ventral roots begin to form
	31	Spinal nerves begin to invade the myotomes
	33	Costal processes that begin to form on vertebrate growth cones enter the upper limb bud, and mesenchyme begins to condense in the limbs. Hand plate is visible in the upper limb
	35	Ribs begin to form in the thoracic region, dorsal and ventral muscle masses begin to form in the limbs, chondrification of mesenchyme begins
6	37	Myotomes begin to split into epimere and hypomere
	38	Finger rays appear
	40	Ossification of upper limb bones begins
7	48	Spinal and trilaminar thoracic wall musculature established
8		Neuromuscular junctions begin to form

Modified from W. J. Larsen, 2001. *Human Embryology* 3rd. edn. New York: Churchill Livingstone.

Cytogenesis of muscle fibers

Differentiation of muscle involves activation of specific transcription factors, myoblast proliferation, arrest of cell cycle (becoming post-mitotic), fusion of myoblasts to form myotubes, and expression of structural muscle proteins. Initially, myoblasts (embryonic muscle cells) fuse to form primary myotubes at about the same time as motor axons invade muscle blocks. Notably, this development is independent of innervation, as is the initial specification of fiber type. Secondary myotubes have some degree of autonomous development, but their survival is tightly linked to innervation, and denervation leads to loss of many developing fibers. Experiments suggest that the sequence of transcription factor activation in skeletal muscle is as follows: *Wnt* and *sonic hedgehog* induce *Pax 3*, *7*, and *Myf-5*, which trigger *MyoD*, *myogenin*, and *MRF4*, which in turn induce structural proteins in the muscle cells.

Multinucleate myotubes lose the capacity to divide further. However, a reserve of undifferentiated myoblasts remain. These are satellite cells, which retain the capacity to divide following exercise or injury.

Muscle fiber type

Skeletal muscle fibers come in several flavors. These are broadly slow-twitch, oxidative, Type 1 (red) and fast-twitch, glycolytic, Type 2 (white). As most muscles are made up of varying amounts of the two, most appear pink upon dissection. Fast fibers are specialized for rapid, short-lived powerful contractions, such as occur during running. However, these fibers fatigue rapidly. Slow fibers are tonically active, provide lower levels of contraction, but do not readily fatigue, which makes them excellent postural muscles. Fiber types can be further sub-divided biochemically by the type of myosin polypeptide chains present within a particular muscle fiber. Currently Types 1, 2A, and 2B are recognized by one of three possible variant myosin heavy chains that make up the head of the myosin molecule. Type 2A fibers are relatively rare in humans and other primates.

Determinants of muscle fiber type

At birth, the vast majority of muscle fibers are Type 1. Type 2 fibers only emerge during early postnatal life. It has been demonstrated that the most important factor determining muscle fiber type is the pattern of innervation of the motor nerve. Thus, experimentally altering the pattern of nerve discharge can cause muscle fibers to switch between slow and fast metabolic pathways. However, as touched on above, at least to some extent, cytoskeletal proteins are formed even in the absence of muscle innervation.

Formation of bone

All the bones of the limbs and associated girdles (pectoral and pelvic) are derived by a process of endochondral ossification. This means that cartilaginous structures form first, and these slowly ossify. Only the clavicle is different as it undergoes membranous ossification (i.e., direct ossification from mesenchyme, with no intermediate cartilaginous stage). For the majority of bones, a cartilaginous precursor (*anlage*) of each bone is formed, which undergoes ossification from a primary center (diaphyses), toward the ends of the bone. At birth, bone shafts are ossified, but the portions adjacent to joints remain cartilaginous. After birth, these regions develop secondary ossification centers (epiphyses), which only finally fuse with the diaphyses when growth is completed at about 20 years of age. This pattern of development at least partially explains why the limbs of an infant appear so much more flexible than those of an adult, because of the increased cartilaginous nature of the ends of joints. This is particularly true of the wrist.

Hox genes are again important in the proximo-distal organization of skeletal elements in the developing limb bud, with a stepwise increase in number of genes expressed in different limb regions from one *Hoxd* gene proximally (scapula), to 5 *Hoxd* genes distally

(hand). Interestingly, this patterning appears to be generated by the amount of time a migrating mesenchymal cell spends in the progress zone. Critically, absence of individual genes results in absence of particular skeletal elements.

The regions of mesenchyme between distinct ossification centers (adjacent bones) give rise to joints. Diarthrodial (synovial) joints first produce fibroblastic tissue from the undifferentiated, interzone mesenchyme. Portions adjacent to limb bones form cartilage, the central core forms menisci and interjoint ligaments, while vacuoles form and coalesce to produce the joint cavity. Finally, the joint capsule is formed from surrounding mesenchymal cells.

Innervation pattern

Axons begin to invade the newly formed limb bud around 33 days. In fact, the first axonal growth cones to leave the developing spinal cord are those of ventral horn motoneurons. These migrate exclusively through the cranial portion of each segmental sclerotome, probably because of inhibitory cues present in caudal sclerotome. In the upper limb, branches from the primary ventral rami of spinal nerves C5 to T1, which constitute the brachial plexus, supply almost all appendicular muscles. In the lower limb, spinal levels L4 to S3 form the lumboscaral plexus. As nerve axons enter the base of the limb buds, they undergo a complex period of re-organization and directional specification. In general terms, the dorsal division of this ventral rami supplies dorsal mesoderm-derived muscles (epimere), while ventral branches of the ventral rami supply ventral mesoderm-derived muscles (hypomere). Sensory fibers

Box 3. Formation of the digits

The hand of the developing limb bud begins as a simple paddle shape by day 33 in which condensations or digital rays gradually emerge by day 38. Interestingly, what then takes place is a carefully orchestrated period of programmed cell death, directed at the areas between the digital rays. Bone morphogenetic protein (BMP) appears important here as increasing the amounts available leads to excessive cell death in the interdigital necrotic zone (INZ), while removal results in webbed digits (syndactyly).

Box 4. Ossification of the wrist

At birth, a radiograph of the wrist will show no bony elements. From this point onward, the spirally directed ossification of the eight carpal (wrist) bones provides an excellent way of aging human skeletons, much in the same way that the eruption of teeth does for a horse. As a rule of thumb, ossification proceeds approximately annually in the following fashion (years in brackets): capitate and hammate (1), triquetrum (3), lunate (4), scaphoid (5), trapezoid and trapezium (6), and pissiform (12). It should be noted that, as with all bone development, the female skeleton is precocious, with major landmarks being reached on average two years earlier.

growing out from the dorsal root ganglion are bipolar in nature, sending one axon into the developing spinal cord, and one into the periphery. These fibers emerge later, and grow more slowly, than the motor axons and generally follow established pathways, only diverging at the last to innervate sensory organs in the skin, muscle spindles, and tendon organs, etc.

Axons are generally prevented from entering dense mesenchyme such as the *anlage* of the limbs, and diverge around these into ventral and dorsal groups along permissive pathways, largely demarcated by surrounding inhibitory cues, which channel the axons into a pathway. The first axons to penetrate these pathways are known as pioneers, and following axons tend to fasciculate (grow along) these in preference to finding their own way.

Axons come to innervate muscle and sensory organs in a roughly segmental pattern, with motoneurons arising from the upper levels of the brachial and lumbosacral plexuses supplying muscle and skin in proximal portions of the upper and lower limb, respectively. These progress along the limbs resulting in the most distal portions being supplied by the lower levels of the respective plexuses. The major disturbance to this uniform pattern are two periods of limb rotation. The first is when the limb rotates from a coronal to a parasagital location, and the next when they rotate on their long axis in the 5th to 6th week, the upper limb doing so laterally and the lower limb medially. These rotations explain at least to some extent why the flexors of the upper limb lie anteriorly, and the flexors of the lower limb posteriorly, and also why the original ventral surface of the lower limb bud has become the caudal surface of the lower limb (Fig. 2).

Development of motor innervation

In terms of specificity, somatic motoneurons are located in spatially demarcated columns in the spinal cord. The medial motor column (MMC) supplies the axial muscles and the lateral motor column (LMC) the appendicular muscles. As a result of this, the MMC extends throughout all vertebral levels, while LMCs are only present at the levels of the brachial and lumbosacral plexuses. Further sub-divisions are possible: medial MMC neurons project to epimere-derived erector spinae muscles, while more lateral neurons projecting to the hypomere-derived musculature of the trunk wall are found only at thoracic levels. In the same way, the most lateral LMC neurons project to the ventral muscle mass, while the more lateral LMC neurons project to the dorsal muscle mass of the limbs. These sub-sets are very accurately demarcated by homeodomain proteins of the *Lim* family, which are expressed by all motoneurons.

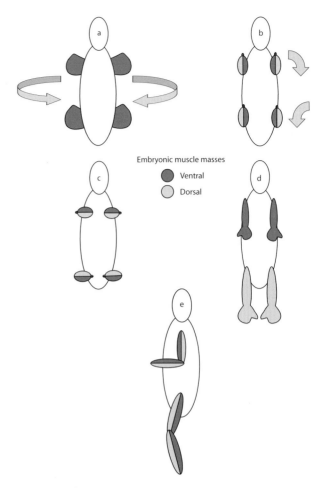

Figure 2. Limb rotations
(a) Original embryonic body plan, with limb buds directed laterally. (b) Upper and lower limb buds rotate from coronal to parasagittal (essentially medially). (c) Limbs rotate around their long axis: upper limb laterally (externally); lower limb medially (internally). (d) Placing the limbs in their adult orientation shows that tissue which was originally ventral is now anterior in the upper limb, but posterior in the lower limb. The thumb is now in a lateral position, while the big toe lies medially. (e) A lateral view clearly indicates that ventral musculature, although now displaced posteriorly in the lower limb, is still concerned with flexion.

These groupings are further sub-divided into motor pools, where closely defined groups of motoneurons project to single muscles. The identities of these motoneurons appear to be determined at an early stage of development (stage 13 of 46 in the chick), and govern the pathfinding behavior of their axonal growth cones. Even more interestingly, it appears that pools of motoneurons, which will innervate fast or slow muscle as well as flexors and extensors, are apparent at early stages of development. In fact, antagonistic patterns of bursting electrical activity can be recorded in flexor and extensor motor pools, possibly driven by early-forming interneuron circuits in the developing spinal cord (Landmesser, 2001).

Sensory feedback from muscle: development of muscle spindles and tendon organs

There are two chief proprioceptive sensory organs in muscle. These are muscle spindles and (Golgi) tendon organs. Both detect stretch, which is fed back to motoneurons by a monosynaptic reflex arc, thus constantly providing information as to the disposition of antagonistic muscle pairs. Most is known about muscle spindles. The spindle is composed of modified (intrafusal) muscle fibers that have both motor and sensory innervation. The largest diameter axon present is the primary (1a) afferent, which supplies all intrafusal fibers. Other innervation comes from smaller diameter sensory afferents and branches of motoneurons that either exclusively or partially innervate intrafusal fibers. The motor supply serves to modulate the receptivity of the muscle spindle so as to tune it to differential stretch.

Sensory neurons are not clustered within dorsal root ganglia (DRG) in the way that motoneurons are, and it has been difficult to adopt the same kinds of anatomical tracing methods utilized for motoneurons. Therefore, much less is understood about the development of sensory compared to motor innervation of muscle. However, experiments have demonstrated that the presence of sensory but not motor innervation to a muscle spindle is essential for its development, and that the loss of proprioceptive neurons results in a failure of muscle spindle development. It appears that in a similar manner to motoneurons, sensory neurons are specified relatively early in development, and both the neurotrophin NT3 and its receptor TrkC appear to play important roles. In addition, a basic helix-loop-helix protein neurogenin 2 (*Ngn2*) appears to specify proprioceptive neuronal sub-types. Once peripheral contacts have been formed, afferents must form highly stereotypical contacts with specific motoneurons in the LMC. These contacts are modeled by activity, but once again it seems that even the first contacts made are accurate (Chen *et al.*, 2003). In summary, it appears that

sensory neurons, much like motoneurons, are specified at relatively early stages of development, in terms of both their peripheral and central contacts.

Conclusions

The development of the musculoskeletal system is complex, involving differentiation of the skeleton and musculature of the trunk and limbs, and concurrent innervation by invading peripheral nerves. Once initial functional nerve-muscle contacts are established, patterned movements begin to occur in the embryo/fetus. These patterns of activity help to refine the system in terms of culling supernumerary neurons and connections, and to determine muscle fiber type. Once this basic pattern is established, growth, maturation, and further fine-tuning occur prior to and for a period after birth, until the stable adult pattern is established. Perhaps surprisingly, our musculoskeletal system is not fully mature until the end of puberty.

See also:
Understanding ontogenetic development: debates about the nature of the epigenetic process; Conceptions and misconceptions about embryonic development; Normal and abnormal prenatal development; Motor development; Speech development; Brain and behavioral development (I): sub-cortical; Sex differences; Behavioral embryology; Developmental genetics; George E. Coghill; Viktor Hamburger; Milestones of motor development and indicators of biological maturity

Further reading

Matthews, G. G. (2003). *Cellular Physiology of Nerve and Muscle*, 4th. edn. Oxford: Blackwell.

Moore, K. L., Persaud, T. V. N. and Chabner, D.-E. B. (eds.) (2003). *The Developing Human: Clinically Oriented Embryology*, 7th. edn. Philadelphia: W. B. Saunders.

Normal and abnormal prenatal development

WILLIAM P. FIFER

Introduction

Until recently, the richness and complexity of fetal-environment interactions were inaccessible, with the consequence that the dynamical nature of normal fetal development is only just beginning to be appreciated. Investigation and characterization of the evolving brain-behavior relationships are the first steps toward understanding the fetal origins of child and adult behavior. In this entry, the earliest stages of human development are described first, followed by an overview of the emergence of fetal phenotypes during each trimester. Risks for abnormal outcomes are addressed next, and how understanding the timing and nature of aberrant gene-environment interactions can uncover the roots of both normal and abnormal developmental trajectories.

Normal development

First trimester

Prior to conception, gene-environment interactions come into play in the developmental process. A host of factors have helped shape the first environment of the fetus. These range from the health, age, and diet of the mother, to the reproductive history of the grandmother, to paternal factors tied to sperm production and viability, such as age and alcohol use. Maternal diet, stress, or infection can affect even the several days' journey of the fertilized egg down the fallopian tube and into the uterus. When fertilization occurs, 23 chromosomes from the egg and 23 from the sperm line up in pairs and replicate themselves exactly. This process occurs again and again, each cell dividing and producing two new cells each the same as the first. Sometimes when a cell divides the genetic material is not copied exactly and a mutant gene occurs. This type of mutation can occur when exposed to radiation or carcinogens.

For conception to be successful, a ball of cells, the blastocyst, must implant in the wall of the uterus. Once the implantation has been successful, several changes take place rapidly within the womb that constrain the influence of external factors, including the fact that the cervix becomes sealed off with a mucous plug to prevent any infection from disrupting the pregnancy. Conception is only considered to have occurred if the fertilized egg successfully implants in the uterine wall. The wall then provides shelter and nourishment for the developing fetus.

The second month is a period of very rapid development for the fetus. The tiny bundle of cells begins to differentiate. One set of cells becomes the amniotic sac and another group forms the placenta, which enables the exchange of vital nutrients and oxygen from the mother's blood with carbon dioxide and waste products from the fetal blood. It also acts as a barrier against some potentially disruptive environmental influences (e.g., infections and many, but not all, toxins). In between these two structures, the embryo is formed, a tiny disk of elongated cells with a head and tail. At the earlier part of this month, there is little difference between the appearance of an embryonic human or fish.

By the end of the second month, however, the fetus does look more distinctly human as can be seen with the aid of 3-D ultrasound recordings (Fig. 1). A primordial brain and spinal cord have begun to form. The embryo's head is very large in relation to the rest of the body, and a small tail is still present. The face is beginning to form, eyes and ears are growing, the mouth and jaw are formed, and there are dental buds within the mouth. The heart is beating and the other major organs have formed, but are not yet fully developed. Small arms and legs have formed from limb buds and small indentations at the end show where the fingers and toes will develop.

The brain and spinal cord become important control centers for all fetal behaviors. By the end of the second month, the fetus will be making small flexing movements. These are simply spontaneous movements

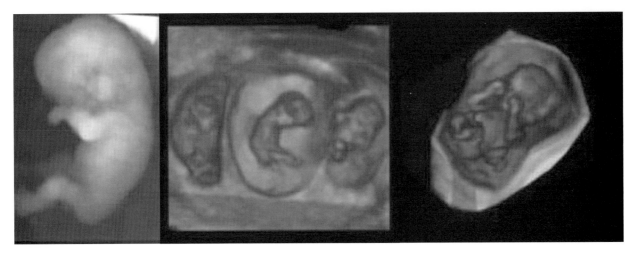

Figure 1. Non-invasive 3-D ultrasound technology essentially captures several ultrasound images and compiles them into a 3-D 'volume,' thereby providing the images above. A 10-week-old fetus is shown on the left, an image of 11-week-old triplet fetuses in the middle, and on the right is a 12-week-old singleton fetus.

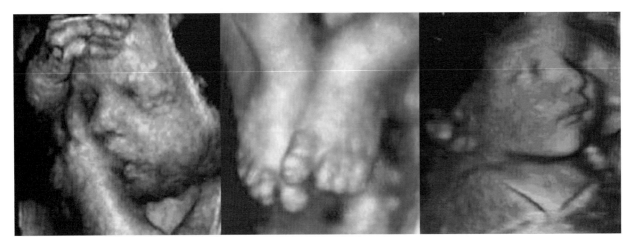

Figure 2. 3-D ultrasound images illustrating the extent of detail available to image fetal behaviors such as thumb sucking seen on the left, morphology such as digits in the middle, and facial expressions as might be inferred from the image on the right. Emerging improvements in technology aimed at near real-time data visualization offer potential access to more dynamical patterns of fetal behavior.

that are controlled by very simple circuits. These circuits probably only consist of a few sensory cells directly connected to some motoneurons, and may exist independently of the brain within the spinal cord itself. As the brain develops, more sophisticated control centers will emerge gradually, and these will act directly on the basic systems currently in effect. The major source of environmental input during this period is via the placenta. It forms a barrier against infection, but viruses and many teratogens can pass through it. The growth of the placenta is influenced both by hormonal control and by metabolism, and recent evidence suggests that even some fetal growth hormones may be under the influence of nutrients. The role the placenta plays in 'programming' of adult disease will be covered later. However, it is important to note there are other factors

that may affect early placental growth, and consequently fetal growth including maternal smoking and maternal anemia. Recreational exercise on the other hand is thought to have a beneficial effect and may even promote placental growth.

By the end of the third month, the fetus is well formed and has similar proportions to a fullterm newborn. Although all the organs are present by this time, the fetus cannot survive outside the protective environment of the uterus. While the fetus is only about 2.5 inches long head to toe and weighs 0.5 oz, it displays an incredible range of body movements such as stretches, hiccups, and movements of the head, jaw, tongue, and fingers. Others include hand-to-face contacts in which fingers may be inserted in the mouth (Fig. 2). Yawns and eye movements will intermittently occur and fluids

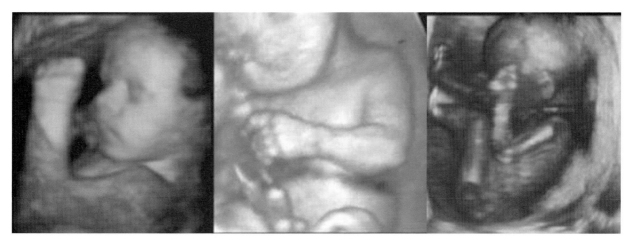

Figure 3. 3-D ultrasound images illustrating the range of body positions typical of the second trimester.

are exchanged by swallowing, 'breathing' movements, and urination. The brain is beginning to differentiate and to exert control over a variety of functions. Observation of non-viable exteriorized fetuses confirms that the sense of touch also begins to develop about this time. By the end of this month, there is almost constant movement, with only brief periods when the fetus is physically inactive. It is thought that movement serves to promote not only the development of the nervous system, but also the growth of muscles, tendons, and ligaments, as well as the formation of joints. Additionally, frequent changes in position, head rotations followed by rump rotations, alternating extensions of the legs, and bending the head backward may help to prevent skin adhesions and promote better circulation. At this stage, neural control is primarily reflexive with very little refinement in the control of motor behavior until higher centers form in the brain and develop circuits that can modulate behavior. At the same time as the fetus initiates a wide range of body movements, a number of other specialized behaviors also develop late in this trimester. These behaviors result in the movement of amniotic fluid through the fetal body: it is swallowed through the mouth and expelled from the fetal bladder, and continues to be taken into the lungs during hiccupping and breathing movements.

During this month, hiccupping is seen much more frequently than breathing movements. When breathing movements do occur, respiratory patterns are atypical in that the diaphragm moves downward, the thorax inward and the abdomen outward. Despite their atypicality, these behaviors are thought to serve as 'practice' for the environment outside the womb when the fetus is born. However, they also serve other developmental functions. Swallowing is thought to play a role in regulating the amount of amniotic fluid, and breathing movements must bring fluid into the lungs to physically stimulate further lung development.

Second trimester

The fetus is now 5 in. in length and weighs about 3 oz. The fetal face has a baby-like quality, with a large rounded forehead, small snub nose, and a well-defined chin. Although the eyelids are closed, frequent eye movements continue. The fetus may start to have longer periods without movement and adopt a range of different body positions (Fig. 3). The fourth month is an important time in the development of the visual system. The gross structures of the eyes are almost completely formed. The eyelids have developed and are now fused together, and will not open until the end of the second trimester of pregnancy. The inner surface of the eye, the retina, is just beginning to develop into different types of cells. Specifically, ganglion, amacrine, bipolar, and horizontal cells are now present.

Very soon, the light-sensitive cells, the rods and cones, will develop. The nerve fibers from each retina have grown into the brain, and there is some crossing over of the fibers so that each side of the brain will receive information from both eyes. This is necessary for the development of binocular vision and depth perception after birth.

The senses of taste and smell are often linked together under the heading of chemosensation. The nostrils are formed at about 8 weeks, and are plugged with tissue until about the fourth month of pregnancy. When these plugs reabsorb, amniotic fluid then circulates through the nose stimulating the olfactory receptors within it. The fetus actually inhales twice as much fluid as it swallows so these receptors are continuously being bathed in amniotic fluid. Aromatic substances within the amniotic fluid will be sensed. They may also stimulate the chemoreceptors by diffusion into the fetal bloodstream. If sugar-containing substances are present in the amniotic fluid, then the fetus will actually swallow more amniotic fluid, which indicates a neurobehavioral sensitivity to the chemical composition of the fluid.

Maternal diet will influence the composition of the amniotic fluid. In particular, lactic and citric acids, uric acids, and amnio acids are most likely to stimulate fetal chemoreceptors. Highly aromatic foods, such as garlic, cumin, curry, and coffee, also are likely to affect the odor or taste of the amniotic fluid, or both. Consequently, in addition to the important nutritional component of the diet, the fetus is now beginning to have sensory experiences paired with the diet. This may set the conditions for the beginning of an early learning process in utero in that these experiences may facilitate later chemosensory preferences.

Within the inner ear, the vestibular apparatus is now active, consisting of three semicircular canals set at right angles to each other. Each canal is filled with fluid and so any movement will cause the fluid within the canals to move, thereby stimulating the receptors within. Depending on direction and plane of movement, one semicircular canal may be stimulated more than another. This information is then sent to the brain and information about the fetal position and head movement is processed. Animal model research confirms vestibular function in utero, but human fetal vestibular reactivity has been difficult to demonstrate. However, according to Jean-Pierre Lecanuet, it seems likely that the vestibular system will be influenced by maternal movement and position, providing a level of stimulation to this system that will probably not be matched until the infant starts to walk as an infant. This vestibular stimulation may underlie future maturation of motor behavior as well as head and body position prior to birth.

Support for the contention that environmental experience once again plays an integral developmental role is the observation that preterm infants, deprived of this naturally occurring stimulation, appear to benefit from supplemental gentle rocking and other movement stimulation. Throughout the pregnancy, maternal diet will have an impact on the growth and development of the fetus. The fourth month is just as important as any other in maintaining adequate nutrition for the fetus. As an example, adequate amounts of vitamin A in the diet are required for the development of the retina.

By the end of the fifth month, the fetus weighs about 8 oz and is 8 to 10 in. in length. The brain is developing rapidly and the cerebral hemispheres expand in size considerably. This development is accompanied by a change in the control of fetal behavior. During this month, there are distinct periods of activity and rest. The fetus is able to exhibit quite a range of facial movements, including arching the eyebrows. Hiccups occur less frequently, but breathing movements are now becoming more common. Instead of isolated breaths, the fetus will breathe intermittently at a rate of less than one breath per second. There are fewer startles and stretches, the periods between movements are getting longer, and overall there are fewer body movements. However, during every movement, nerve impulses are sent back and forth from the brain to the limbs strengthening the connections between them, and ensuring that these movements continue to develop. For example, it is known that, early in development, one nerve cell may activate many muscle cells in a limb. However, as more nerve cells form connections, something closer to a 1:1 relationship develops between nerve cells and muscle cells, and the earlier connections from just one nerve cell become eliminated. This in turn allows for more sophisticated types of movement to develop. In summary, the fetus is no longer in a state of nearly constant motion because of the change in the neural (inhibitory) control of movement.

The cerebral hemispheres of the brain are developing rapidly at this time (Fig. 4). They develop from two balloon-like structures at the front of the brain, that increase tremendously in size, and so by this point in time they now cover the rest of the brain. The outer crust of these structures is called the cerebral cortex, and the cells within it are rapidly dividing and migrating to specific locations where they become specialized. These higher control centers will ultimately be responsible for memory, language, thought, and the further integration of movement and the senses.

By 6 months, the fetus is about 13 in. long, weighs about 1.75 pounds, and is covered by a creamy colored, waxy substance called vernix caseosa, which protects the skin from the amniotic fluid, but also hinders external monitoring of fetal electrophysiological activity. The fetal brain is still developing, folding inward forming grooves and convolutions, and the number of nerve cells in the cerebral cortex has now reached its maximum. Myelination of the nerve fibers is just beginning, leading to an increase in speed of travel for the nerve impulses, which then results in a more fluent and rapidly responding system. Bones are beginning to harden. The genitals are now fully formed, so the sex can often be determined during ultrasound examination. The fetus is often moving and responding to sounds outside the uterus.

The fetus appears to have a very rich auditory environment. In addition to the background maternal vascular noises, which change in tempo and intensity as the mother or fetus moves, the mother's digestion sounds can be heard by the fetus. External sounds are generally heard at a lower intensity, with more bass than treble sounds filtering through. At this age, the fetus can respond to loud sounds with changes in heart rate and by either initiating or stopping movement. Normal development continues to depend on adequate nutrition (e.g., myelin requires the intake of fatty acids).

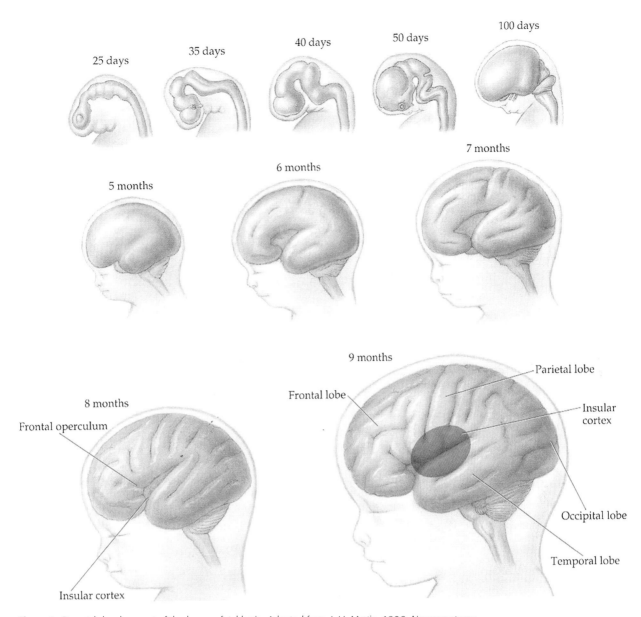

Figure 4. Prenatal development of the human fetal brain. Adapted from J. H. Martin, 1996. *Neuroanatomy Text and Atlas*, 2nd. edn. Stamford, CT: Appleton & Lange, p. 51.

Third trimester

The fetus weighs approximately 3 pounds by the end of the seventh month. The eyelids are no longer fused. The eyes can open and close and though the uterine environment provides minimal visual stimulation, the fetus has the capacity to see. However, visual acuity, contrast sensitivity, and color vision are relatively poor as shown by preterm infants of the same gestational age. The protective blink reflex is observed in the preterm infant, which can be elicited by a bright light or an approaching object. Spontaneous irregular eye movements occur very frequently at this time. The visual cortex has begun to organize its nerve cells in layers, similar to those seen in the adult brain. Vision is not very good at this point, although the lens of the eye has

formed, enabling the fetus to change focus and look at objects at different distances. The lungs are still immature such that survival outside the womb would not be possible without intensive care. This is an important time for neural development. In many areas of the brain, the number of nerve cells present has reached adult maturity, but the complex patterns of connectivity between cells that are required for cognitive and motor abilities are still to develop. As the brain gets larger, it convolutes further in order to fit into the skull.

The lungs are undergoing important maturational changes. Inside them, air sacs (alveoli) are formed in ever increasing numbers. Blood vessels around the alveoli begin to multiply. The lungs begin to

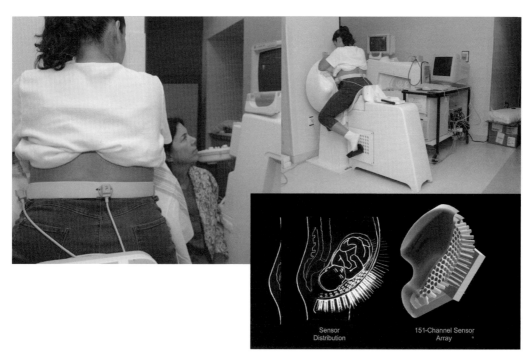

Figure 5. Device used to collect magnetic fields generated during electrical activation of any organ. In this instance, magnetoencephalography is used to monitor fetal brain activity non-invasively. From Curtis L. Lowry Jr., University of Arkansas Medical Center.

manufacture surfactant. An important part of lung development occurs when the fetus breathes in the amniotic fluid, which is merely a mechanical action at this stage since oxygen is obtained from the mother via the placenta until birth. When the fetus is born, in order to exchange oxygen for carbon dioxide and prevent the lungs from collapsing, there have to be adequate levels of surfactant present.

By the end of the eighth month, the fetus is about 18 in. long and weighs about 5 pounds. Brain development is occurring rapidly during this time, with myelinization of the nerve fibers progressing, and an overabundance of synaptic connections forming between neurons. Most sensory systems, such as those subserving smell, taste, hearing, touch, and vision, are functioning, and it is likely that naturally occurring, early sensory experiences continue to play an important role in stimulating and shaping the development of the neural system. Lung surfactant and fat are still developing.

At this age, two dominant patterns of behavior have emerged: active sleep and quiet sleep. At about 32 weeks of pregnancy, the fetus will spend 70 to 80% of the time in active sleep. During this REM-like sleep, many vital systems are being stimulated. Bursts of electrical activity occur in the brain, and eye muscles, heart, blood pressure, and respiration systems are all being activated and exercised. These intermittent periods of 'high activity' may be necessary for the growth of brain cells, and for the connections between them to be formed. By

exercising these vital systems in a state of active sleep rather than wakefulness, the fetus is able to conserve energy.

During this period before birth, further deposits of brown fat are laid down. These serve as important means of internal temperature regulation by the fetus who will soon no longer be in the warm uterine environment. The lungs mature and the surfactant is adequate for the ability to breathe air without risk of the lungs collapsing. At this time, organized patterns of sleep/wake cycles have emerged. Many of the fetal movements in place during this time will ensure survival outside the womb (e.g., breathing movements, rooting for subsequent nipple attachment, and stepping, which may aid departure from the womb during labor).

Though the auditory environment of the fetus is largely limited to lower-frequency sounds, it is quite varied near term. Mother's voice is by far the most frequently heard, and loudest auditory stimulus, and those pathways that sense pressure, touch, and movement are also stimulated during respiratory activity coupled with maternal speech (Lecanuet & Schaal, 1996). Although much of the evidence for brain reactivity at this stage comes from pre- and fullterm infants, differential heart rate and movement responses to sounds have been demonstrated at this age. Magneto-encephalographic techniques (i.e., monitoring magnetic fields generated by neural activity) are now being used to measure fetal responses to both sound and light stimulation (Fig. 5). This methodology offers great promise for the systematic study of fetal neuro-behavioral development.

The near-term fetus likely exhibits not only the behavioral repertoire of the newborn, but comparable sensory and perceptual abilities as well. The strongest evidence for in utero stimulation effects is the newborn's preference for olfactory and auditory cues emanating from the mother, including the odor of her amniotic fluid and her voice. Though claims of the benefits of fetal extra-stimulation programs are scientifically unsound, there is credible evidence in support of the benefits of supplemental stimulation for the preterm newborn. Deprived of normal uterine experience, recent studies suggest that efforts to reduce over-stimulation in the Neonatal Intensive Care Unit and to judiciously provide compensatory vestibular, auditory, and tactile stimulation may improve the developmental course of fetuses born before their time.

Abnormal development

Fetal risk

As is the case throughout infancy, normal fetal development demands constant and complex interactions between genes, environment, and the emerging organism. Although certain developmental pathways are more highly canalized than others (i.e., resistant to perturbations), the opportunities for altering trajectories are abundant. Abnormal developmental trajectories can have their origins in parental preconception conditions, as well as emerge from gene-environment interactions throughout embryogenesis and gestation. In addition to fetal and newborn demise, atypical outcomes range from serious congenital malformations such as microcephaly (see below) to subtle variations with putative minor clinical significance.

Though genetic defects alone account for somewhere between 10 and 15 percent of abnormalities, and toxic exposures in the absence of genetic influences may account for a similar percentage, the vast majority of anomalies are likely to be the result of gene-environment interactions. Abnormal developmental trajectories, ranging from subtle to significant, also can be associated with intrapartum risks such as labor complications (e.g., hypoxia during delivery or those resulting from multiple births). These complications can result in an increased incidence of low birthweight and preterm deliveries, both strong risk factors for abnormal outcomes.

Chromosomal disorders

Chromosomal abnormalities are seen in 1/200 live births and in 50–70 percent of first trimester miscarriages.

Abnormal numbers of chromosomes are usually caused by an error in their separation into appropriate daughter cells during meiotic division. The most common chromosomal defects are monosomies in which there is only one copy of a chromosome pair, or trisomies in which there are three representatives of a chromosome pair. Most monosomies are not viable, except for Turner's syndrome in which the individual is phenotypically female but sterile. The most common trisomy, Down's syndrome, is characterized by varying degrees of mental retardation, anomalous facial features, and heart defects.

Disorders can result from a single gene abnormality. The risk of an affected individual having a child with the disorder depends on their partner's status with respect to the genetic mutation, and therefore on how rare the disease is. Examples of autosomal genetic disorders are sickle cell disease, cystic fibrosis, Tay-Sachs disease, Huntington's disease, and Marfan syndrome. Certain ethnic groups are at greater risk for specific genetic disorders than others. For example, in Ashkenazi Jews of Eastern European descent, 1 in 30 is a carrier of Tay-Sachs disease, while approximately 8 in 100 African Americans are carriers of the sickle cell gene. New techniques utilizing molecular (DNA) testing are currently evolving, and becoming universally utilized to increase the accuracy of testing for a rapidly expanding list of putative genetic disorders.

Environmental influences

A teratogen is any drug, chemical, infectious or physical agent that causes structural damage or functional disability in the fetus, and they are estimated to be responsible for approximately 10 percent of all human birth defects. Drugs of abuse such as cocaine and heroin have long been implicated as teratogens. Alcohol is probably the most researched teratogenic agent. Heavy maternal alcohol consumption profoundly influences fetal and child development. For the children who survive, the effects include mild to severe physical anomalies and cognitive and behavioral impairments. However, other adverse fetal outcomes include increased risk for spontaneous abortion, stillbirth, premature placental separation (i.e., abruptio placentae), intrauterine growth restriction, and, as some studies suggest, preterm birth – itself a risk factor for future health problems, poor development, and newborn mortality. Follow-up studies of behavior and cognitive development indicate that significant in utero exposure to alcohol is associated with attentional deficits, mental retardation, and poor academic performance. Research into the mechanisms underlying the toxic effects of fetal alcohol exposure and improvements in exposure assessment are the *sine qua non* for development of

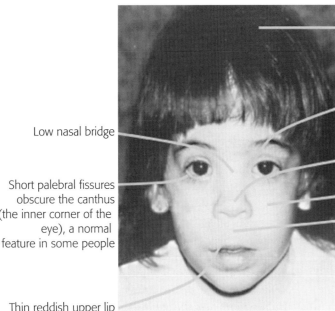

Small head circumference

Epicanthic folds

Low nasal bridge

Short nose

Short palpebral fissures obscure the canthus (the inner corner of the eye), a normal feature in some people

Short midface

Indistinct philtrum (an underdeveloped groove in the center of the upper lip between the nose and lip edge)

Thin reddish upper lip

Figure 6. Facial features associated with the Fetal Alcohol Syndrome. From Larry Burd, Fetal Alcohol Syndrome Center, University of North Dakota, www.online-clinic.com.

intervention strategies. One prenatal prevention candidate, based on animal studies, involves the use of growth peptide agonists to ameliorate the alcohol-induced fetal death, growth restriction, and microcephaly associated with the Fetal Alcohol Syndrome (Fig. 6). Another promising postnatal treatment may emerge from animal work demonstrating that a regimen of complex motor training in adult rats rehabilitated motor performance deficits induced by binge alcohol exposure when they were neonates.

The adverse consequences of prenatal exposure to maternal smoking are well known and it remains one of the most preventable risk factors for an unsuccessful pregnancy outcome. Although negative effects may even begin at conception, it is during the third trimester when the fetus gains weight at the fastest rate that maternal smoking has the greatest impact on fetal growth. On average, babies born to smokers weigh 100–200 g less than those of non-smokers and have twice the risk for fetal growth restriction. Furthermore, independent of the risks for lower birthweight, smoking is associated with risk for prematurity and perinatal complications, such as placenta previa or premature detachment of the placenta (i.e. abruptio placentae). Cigarette smoking is also associated with a two- to three-fold increase in cot death and may induce abnormalities in the cardiorespiratory and vascular control centers in the fetal brain. Nicotine directly alters vasoconstriction in the placental and fetal vascular beds, reducing oxygen and nutrient input to the fetus. Carbon monoxide, which binds to hemoglobin to form carboxyhemoglobin, reduces the oxygen-carrying capacity of the blood. It also increases the affinity of hemoglobin for oxygen so that oxygen release to tissues is inhibited. More subtle effects of fetal exposure to maternal smoking have been found during childhood.

Behavioral problems and cognitive weaknesses, including problems with attention and visuoperceptual processing, have been associated with smoking during pregnancy. Some of the newest research focuses on the effects of passive smoking or environmental tobacco smoke (ETS) during pregnancy on birth outcome. Studies suggest that exposure to passive smoking during pregnancy is associated with reductions in fetal weight ranging from 25 g to 40 g, as well as greater likelihood of a low-birthweight baby. In recent epidemiological studies, ETS has emerged as a major risk factor in cot death. In a very recent study of inner-city, minority populations at high risk for adverse birth outcomes, environmental contaminants including ETS, polycyclic aromatic hydrocarbons, and pesticides were all independently associated with such outcomes.

Nutrition

As described previously, throughout pregnancy specific nutritional requirements must be met in order to support the developing fetus. For example, women must increase their caloric intake to reach between 2,700 and 3,000 calories per day, monitor calcium intake for fetal bone and muscle, iron for red blood cells and transmitter production, and folic acid for protein synthesis required for neural tube development. A recent series of studies have demonstrated deficits in recognition memory in the first year of life linked to fetal iron deficiency. Research from epidemiological and animal studies has shaped a recent large-scale research effort investigating the link between low birthweight and increased risk for future cardiovascular disease (CVD). To account for this association, it has been hypothesized that aspects of fetal cardiovascular functioning are 'programmed' in utero by maternal nutritional or hormonal factors or both (Godfrey & Barker, 2001). Although the emerging data with human pregnancy are not entirely consistent with this hypothesis, animal studies support this line of thinking. Other possible mechanisms that might account for the association between maternal protein intake, low fetal weight, and increased risk for CVD include the possibility that low protein intake reduces the size of the pancreas and glucose tolerance, leading to low birthweight and alterations in metabolism.

Both birthweight and maternal nutrition during pregnancy have been implicated in risk for future disease. Maternal consumption of less than 1,000 calories a day during the first two trimesters is thought to have an impact on fetal brain organization that is occurring rapidly at this time, and leads to increased risk for schizophrenia or antisocial personality disorders. This evidence was based on epidemiological research involving children born to undernourished Dutch women during the Nazi food embargo in the Second World War. In contrast, high birthweight appears to be correlated with increased risk for breast cancer. Continued epidemiological and animal research is needed to define the underlying mechanisms linking birthweight to later disorders.

Psychosocial stress

Psychosocial stress during pregnancy has long been linked to negative birth outcomes such as low birthweight and prematurity (Hobel & Culhane, 2003; Mulder *et al.*, 2002). In animal models, offspring whose mothers are exposed to acute stress during pregnancy versus controls exhibit long-term changes in behavior and the regulation of stress hormones. Prenatally stressed animals show inhibited, anxious, fearful behavior throughout the lifespan, hypothesized to result from their excessive level of endogenous arousal. In tests with non-human primates, prenatal stress is associated with poorer neuromotor maturity and distractibility. The offspring of rats exposed to an acute stressor compared to controls also have elevated stress hormone responses as preweanlings, and increased stress-induced

corticosterone secretion as adults. It is likely that over the course of pregnancy, the frequency and magnitude of maternal stress may have a cumulative effect, shaping fetal and child central and peripheral nervous system development.

Psychosocial stress during pregnancy has also been associated with alterations in markers of fetal neuro-behavioral development. Fetuses of pregnant women who reported greater life stress had reduced parasympathetic or increased sympathetic activation or both as measured by reduced fetal heart rate variability. Moreover, fetuses of mothers who reported greater stress and had faster baseline heart rate showed a delay in the maturation of the coupling of fetal heart rate and movement, hypothesized to be an index of impeded central nervous system development. Low socio-economic status, often with increased social stress, is associated with higher and less variable fetal heart rate throughout the second and third trimesters. The pregnant woman's anxiety is associated with differences in fetal heart rate reactivity.

During a cognitively challenging laboratory task (e.g., mental arithmetic), fetuses of women describing themselves as more anxious showed significant heart rate increases while the fetuses of less anxious women exhibited non-significant decreases during the mental stressor. Antenatal maternal anxiety is reported to predict child behavioral/emotional problems independently of postnatal depression. The data indicate that over the course of gestation, maternal psychological variables such as stress, anxiety, and mood, acting via alterations in maternal physiology, may influence fetal neurobehavioral development and ultimately child and adult phenotypes.

Conclusions

Future fetal research will be led by improvements in technology employing 3-D ultrasound and cerebral blood flow measurement to image fetal structures and function more clearly. An emerging technique, magnetoencephalography, which has been used non-invasively to study brain function in adults, offers a promising tool for studying brain activity in the fetus. New advances in genomic research will fuel the need to go beyond identification of the genes involved in early brain-behavior development. The next task will be to unravel the 'epigenetic code,' that is, to investigate how the intrauterine and extrauterine environments effect the expression of those genes in both normal and abnormal development. Such advancements will ultimately lead to a better understanding of the sources of individual differences and timely assessment of fetal well-being and future risk.

See also:
Understanding ontogenetic development: debates about the nature of the epigenetic process; Neuromaturational theories; Learning theories; Magnetic Resonance Imaging; Cross-species comparisons; Epidemiological designs; Conceptions and misconceptions about embryonic development; The birth process; The status of the human newborn; Cognitive development in infancy; Perceptual development; Motor development; Emotional development; Language development; Development of learning and memory; Attention; Brain and behavioral development (I): sub-cortical; Brain and behavioral development (II): cortical; Sex differences; Sleep and wakefulness; 'At-risk' concept; Behavioral and learning disorders; Down's syndrome; Prematurity and low birthweight; Sudden Infant Death Syndrome; Behavioral embryology; Behavior genetics; Developmental genetics; Pediatrics; Viktor Hamburger

Further reading

Hopkins, B. and Johnson, S. P. (eds.) (2005). *Prenatal Development of Postnatal Functions*. Westport, CT: Praeger.

Lecanuet, J. P., Fifer, W. P., Krasnegor, N. A. and Smotherman, W. P. (eds.) (1995). *Fetal Development: A Psychobiological Perspective*. Mahwah, NJ: Erlbaum.

Nathanielsz, P. W. (1996). *Life Before Birth: The Challenges of Fetal Development*. New York: Freeman.

Nilsson, L. and Hamberger, L. (2003). *A Child is Born*, 4th. edn. Aliso Viejo, CA: Delacorte Press.

The birth process

WENDA R. TREVATHAN

Introduction

Birth is a critical moment in the lives of two individuals, the child being born and the mother giving birth. What happens at this time may have a profound impact on subsequent development of the infant, and on the quality of the relationship between the mother and infant. Certainly, this includes mortality and morbidity related to the risks associated with childbirth. Mortality associated with birth has been high throughout human history and remains so in many parts of the world today. Thus, it is not surprising that there is a great deal of ritual surrounding childbirth designed to ensure the health of mother and infant in this perilous period. In modern countries, for those who can afford it, the danger associated with birth has led to the common practice of giving birth in hospitals surrounded by highly trained medical personnel and elaborate obstetrical technology.

Unfortunately, too much intervention in normal birth may interfere with the developing relationship between the mother and infant and, in some cases, may increase morbidity. In other words, while the decrease in mortality associated with the movement of birth from home to hospital is certainly welcomed, the impersonal and mechanical way in which births can occur in hospitals is less than satisfying to most, and may have a negative impact on the developing relationships between parents and infant.

Impact of bipedalism on birth

A common misconception is that labor and delivery are a great deal more stressful and longer in humans than in other mammals, including other primates. Because monkeys and apes, like humans, have large heads relative to their body sizes, the process of passing a neonatal head through the birth canal is not much easier for these primates than it is for humans (see Fig. 1). Exceptions to this generalization are the Great Apes (chimpanzees, gorillas, and orangutans) whose neonates are somewhat smaller relative to maternal pelvic size, leading to relatively fewer restrictions in the passage through the birth canal (Fig. 2). Additionally, the human newborn is larger overall relative to maternal bodyweight in comparison with other primates. If humans were like other primates, a mother weighing 65 kg would give birth to a baby of 2.2 kg when in fact the mean birthweight for humans is about 3.3 kg. The relatively larger size of the human fetus contributes to complexities in human deliveries.

Based on behaviors observed during labor, contractions during the birth process are painful for most monkeys and apes, and there is no evidence that the infants are born quickly or easily. But for humans, the pelvic changes resulting from the evolutionary transition from four-legged to two-legged walking have meant greater difficulty giving birth and upper limits on the size of the birth canal. These limits, associated with increase in adult brain size in the last two million years of human evolution, have meant that the human infant is much less developed at birth than our closest primate relatives. Certainly, an immature infant places further demands on the mother, in part because maintaining proximity between them is entirely the mother's responsibility.

Bipedalism has had a number of impacts on the birth process beyond the narrowing of the birth canal and increasing immaturity of the infant. Most non-human primate infants enter and exit the birth canal in a single plane and are born facing their mothers, which facilitates reaching down and guiding the infant out of the birth canal (Fig. 3).

The human bipedal pelvis, unlike the monkey pelvis, is twisted in the middle so that the entrance and the exit of the birth canal are perpendicular to each other. This means that, for most pelvic shapes, the human fetus must negotiate a series of rotations as it works its way through the birth canal so that all maternal and fetal dimensions, including the shoulders of the fetus, line up with each other during this tight passage. Thus, the

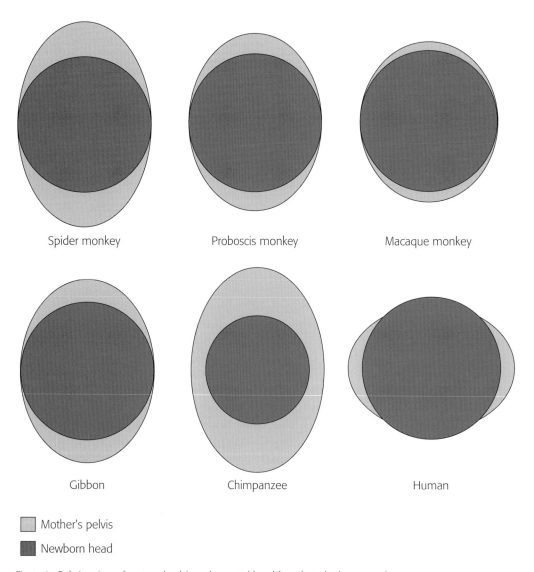

Spider monkey   Proboscis monkey   Macaque monkey

Gibbon   Chimpanzee   Human

Mother's pelvis

Newborn head

Figure 1. Relative sizes of maternal pelvis and neonatal head for selected primate species.

human fetus most commonly enters the birth canal facing side to side and exits facing front to back (Fig. 4). This is because the human pelvis, designed for bipedalism, has a shape that best accommodates the fetal head in a manner that results in the baby emerging from the birth canal facing toward the mother's back. This means that the mother must reach behind her in order to guide the fetus out or she must find someone to assist her (Fig. 4).

Such added difficulty might explain why humans routinely seek assistance at the time of birth rather than isolation as do most other mammals, including most other primate species. Simply having someone else there to guide the baby out, to wipe the face so breathing can begin, and to keep the umbilical cord from choking the baby can significantly reduce mortality associated with birth. In fact, a survey of world cultures reveals that it is extremely unusual for a woman to give birth alone (Trevathan, 1987). Even in cultures where the ideal may be to give birth alone, such as among the !Kung of

southern Africa, it rarely happens that way, especially with a first birth (Konner & Shostak, 1987).

Emotional support and the birth process

In addition to the reduced mortality and morbidity associated with having another person assist the laboring woman at the time of birth, there are clear emotional advantages to receiving support from another person rather than delivering alone. In fact, the mechanism that has been proposed to lead a woman to seek assistance at the time of birth is emotional as it is based on fear and anxiety (Rosenberg & Trevathan, 1996). In support of this are studies that consistently demonstrate the positive effects of social and emotional support at the time of birth. Furthermore, the positive effects of assistance at birth seem to persist in the first few weeks after birth, suggesting that such emotional support may have an impact on the developing mother-infant relationship. In

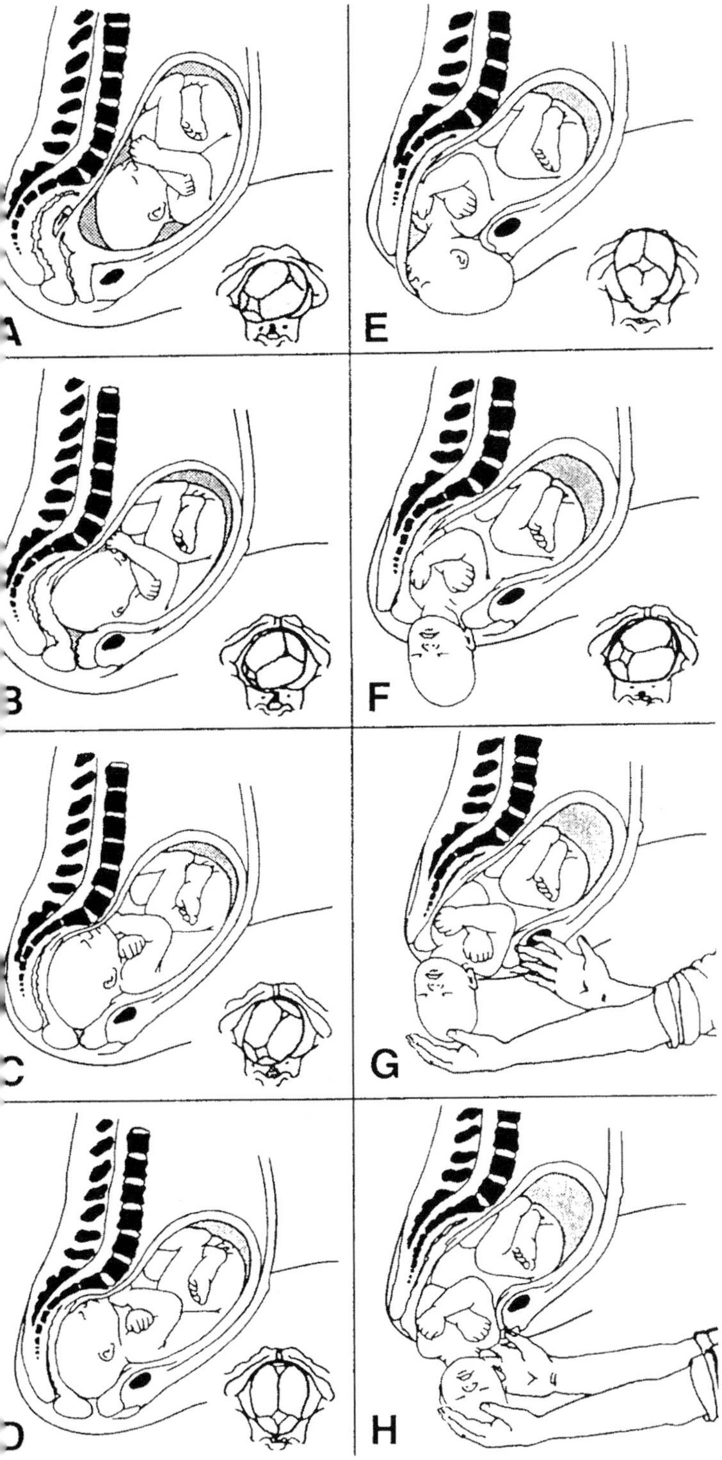

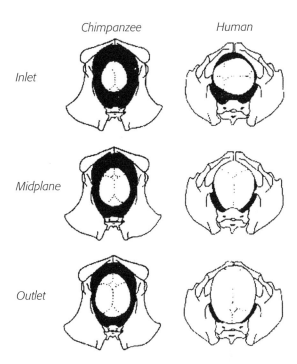

Figure 2. Midwife's view of chimpanzee and human deliveries. Note position of the anterior fontanelle.

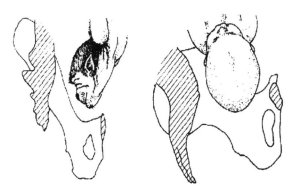

Figure 3. Lateral view of monkey and human passage through birth canal.

The concept of bonding

The idea that the mother-infant relationship is affected by events surrounding birth is not without controversy (Eyer, 1992). More than two decades ago, American pediatricians Marshall Klaus and John Kennell published *Maternal-Infant Bonding*, in which they argued, among other things, that attachment between mother and infant most optimally forms soon after birth. They referred to the process of attachment as bonding, a concept that was embraced by activists working to reform childbirth practices in US, Canadian, British, and Australian hospitals. Within a few years of publication of their book, birth routines in some hospitals had changed to include allowing fathers and other family members to attend deliveries, minimal separation of mothers and

Figure 4. Lateral view of the human birth process showing benefits of assistance at delivery.

one study, mothers who received extra emotional support at birth showed significant differences in comparison with a control group (Klaus *et al.*, 1992). These differences included increased breastfeeding, more time spent with the infant, less anxiety, lower scores on a depression scale, higher self-esteem, and more positive feelings about partners and infants.

newborn, use of birthing rooms, early breastfeeding, and minimal use of medications during labor and delivery.

'Bonding' became a household word, a rallying point, and, unfortunately, a source of guilt and worry for those who feared that if they were not with their infants immediately after birth (the optimal bonding period), they would not be able to bond with their children. Criticism came from feminists who argued that the concept of bonding served to reinforce stereotypes of what a 'good mother' is, and served to keep women out of the workplace during their childbearing years. These and other criticisms of the bonding research led most researchers and practitioners to abandon the idea that immediate postpartum bonding was part of the human behavioral repertoire, or that it was in any way necessary for the development of attachment.

Part of the central argument about bonding in the postpartum period was the suggestion by Klaus and Kennell that there is a maternal sensitive period in the first few hours after birth during which mothers are able to bond more readily and easily with their newborns. Additionally, they proposed that human mothers exhibit species-specific behaviors at birth that facilitate bonding. These behaviors include: (1) a progression of tactile contact with the infant, beginning with fingertip exploration of extremities and face and moving on to fully embracing the infant; (2) the tendency to hold the infant on the left side of the body regardless of maternal handedness; (3) the tendency to elevate the pitch of the voice when orienting toward the infant; and (4) attempting to look into the infant's eyes with heads in the same plane, a position known as *en face*.

Maternal behavior after birth

Observations of mammalian mothers interacting with their newborns reveal a number of complex and often predictable behaviors, many of which appear to fulfill fairly specific functions. These include licking or stroking the infants to establish respiration, digestion, and elimination, and to dry them so that they can maintain optimal body heat. Characteristic vocalizations are often noted that function to initiate interaction or nursing and that facilitate recognition. Most mammalian mothers position their bodies in such a way that the young can find the mammary glands. These behaviors may be regarded as bonding mechanisms, or simply as behaviors that enhance neonatal survival. The two functions are not mutually exclusive, of course. For example, licking may serve the immediate need of stimulating respiration, but it also serves to enhance maternal recognition, and thus contributes to attachment.

The behaviors described above for human mothers have been examined almost exclusively for their effects on bonding. An enlarged perspective forces the broader question: how might they have contributed to survival in the past? For example, holding and tactile exploration of the infant may be to humans what licking is to many mammals, and thus may stimulate breathing, digestion, and thermoregulation. Accounts of left-side holding have ranged from the soothing effect of the heartbeat on the infant (not one supported by subsequent studies), the tendency for infants to turn their heads to the right, and facilitation of communication between mother and infant.

Vision is the most important sensory mechanism most primates use to get information about their environments. It is, therefore, not surprising that human mothers expend great effort looking into the eyes of their infants when they first have the opportunity to do so. Furthermore, there is evidence that human neonates can focus on objects 10–20 inches from their faces. Eye contact is one of the few behaviors under direct control of the relatively helpless human neonate. Some authors have suggested that the amount of time spent looking into an infant's eyes (the *en face* position) is an indication of maternal-infant attachment. Eye contact appears to calm infants, suggesting aspects of the behavior that may have been beneficial in the past. Although olfaction may not be as important in human interaction as vision, there is evidence that the human infant can recognize the mother's scent within several hours after birth (Porter & Winberg, 1999; see Trevathan, this volume).

Vocalizations between mothers and infants of various species serve a number of functions, including maintaining proximity, facilitating individual recognition, and initiating nursing. It has been reported that human mothers unconsciously elevate the pitch of their voices when directing their speech to or toward their infants. Additionally, the human infant seems to respond more rapidly and more intently to the higher-pitched female voice. As with *en face* behavior, talking to the infant in a high-pitched voice appears to have a calming effect, and was likely a common part of early mother-infant interaction among hominids in the past, as well as in the present.

Conclusions

There is scant evidence that contact between mothers and infants during the immediate postpartum period is necessary for survival or for adequate bond formation today. But thousands of years ago, the only infants who survived were those whose bond with their mothers began at birth and continued to an age at which food, protection, and nurturance could be derived from other sources. As with other species, we thus have a heritage of mechanisms, hormonal or otherwise, that ensures that each mother-infant dyad has optimal opportunity to initiate that bonding process, even while the infant is in utero.

Further research focusing on the relationships among mother-infant interaction, the hormones of labor and delivery, and immediate postpartum behaviors may help to elucidate the significance of contemporary environments and experiences of normal childbirth for subsequent infant development and maternal and child health. For example, there is evidence that skin-to-skin contact between mother and infant in the immediate postpartum period may have positive effects on breastfeeding success, digestion and metabolism, and in lower blood pressure and cortisol levels for the mother. These may be related to the hormones oxytocin and prolactin.

Oxytocin is involved in mother-infant attachment in many animal species, so it is likely that it plays a role in human behavior in the postpartum period and more studies of its role would be welcome. Because it is a peptide hormone, however, it is not measurable in saliva or urine and is much more difficult to assess. For this reason, many studies of its effect on maternal behavior have been correlational. Uvnäs-Moberg (1999) suggests that oxytocin released at the time of birth (enhanced by estrogen, which is high at delivery) may help calm both mother and infant, reduce stress, and promote growth. If true, clinicians need to be aware of the impact of various obstetrical drugs and routines on oxytocin release. This may be particularly true for the more vulnerable preterm infant.

Far from being an isolated event, birth is just one phase in the on-going life cycle of two individuals. A broad evolutionary perspective on birth and bonding suggests that allowing women and infants to spend time together as soon as possible after birth may have a positive effect on long-term mother-infant relationships, although it is clearly not necessary for strong attachments to form. Although the idea of a sensitive period for bonding has not been supported, when we consider the intense physical and emotional experience of giving birth and the hormonal actions that accompany this process, it is hard to maintain that the first hour after birth is no different from any other hour the mother shares with the infant. If obstetrical care can complement evolved human behaviors with emotional as well as biomedical support, then mothers, fathers, infants, and society will gain.

See also:
Ethological theories; Cross-cultural comparisons; Normal and abnormal prenatal development; The status of the human newborn; Perceptual development; Social development; Handedness; Locomotion; Prematurity and low birthweight; Pediatrics

Further reading

Blaffer Hardy, S. (1999). *Mother Nature: A History of Mothers, Infants, and Natural Selection*. New York: Pantheon Books.

Klaus, M. H., Kennell, J. H. and Klaus, P. H. (1995). *Bonding*. Reading, MA: Addison-Wesley.

Rosenberg, K. and Trevathan, W. (2001). The evolution of human birth. *Scientific American*, 285, 72–77.

The status of the human newborn

WENDA R. TREVATHAN

Introduction

Several decades of research coupled with what parents have always known have laid to rest the nineteenth-century notion that humans were born with a blank slate, a *tabula rasa*, on which parents and cultures wrote their versions of what it is to be human. Furthermore, the previous view, offered by William James, that the newborn human infant perceives the world as "one great blooming, buzzing confusion" has given way to one in which they come into the world equipped with a number of abilities that enable them to respond and adapt to their new environments.

At birth, newborns face dramatic changes in every aspect of their internal and external environments. Most of the stresses encountered would be sufficient to elicit symptoms of shock in an adult, but infants are apparently equipped to withstand the challenges they face in adapting to the extrauterine environment. Placental support of oxygen is replaced with respiration, the oxygen delivery system switches to the lungs, heart rate increases, and systems for the control of body temperature, digestion, and elimination begin to function. Significantly, the neonate is also equipped with behavioral mechanisms, shaped over eons of evolutionary history, that serve to attract the mother and induce her to care for her infant. Of course, the mother is also equipped with behavioral mechanisms shaped over human evolution that serve to induce her to provide warmth, food, and care.

In some ways, the human infant in the first several months of life shows growth patterns similar to those of other primates during fetal development, leading to the suggestion that the human newborn is more like an 'exterogestate fetus' than a non-human primate infant (Montagu, 1989). This is true in ossification rates, enzyme development, central nervous system development, and brain growth (Fig. 1). Because brain size is directly related to head size, and head size affects passage through the birth canal, it has been argued that increased brain size in adult humans over

the course of evolution has come at the expense of relatively less maturity of almost all systems critical for infant survival. Advantages gained from being born in such an immature state include greater plasticity and earlier exposure to environmental stimuli important for learning a variety of abilities, not the least of which is language.

Altricial and precocial infants

Reproductive ecologists use the terms 'altricial' to describe infants born in a relatively immature state and 'precocial' for those who are somewhat mature at birth. In general, altricial infants have their eyes closed and are unable to regulate their body temperature. They tend to be highly dependent and are often left in nests or burrows. Precocial infants, on the other hand, are usually able to move about very soon after birth, can regulate their body temperature, and follow their mothers. Related to the state of development is the composition of milk produced by each species (Fig. 2). Although there are exceptions, milk of altricial mammals tends to be somewhat higher in nutrients than the milk of precocial mammals. Milk composition is, in turn, related to nursing behavior and frequency. Mothers with nutrient-dense milk can leave their altricial infants in nests or burrows while they forage for their own food, whereas mothers with nutrient-poor milk have precocial infants that follow them and are able to nurse 'on demand.'

Although there is great variation in the order, most primate species, such as monkeys and apes, give birth to precocial infants who are able to cling to their mothers soon after birth and nurse at will. Predictably, the milk of monkeys and apes (including humans) is relatively nutrient-poor with approximately 88% water, 4% fat, less than 2% protein, and 6–7% carbohydrate.

Looking only at milk composition would lead one to expect that human infants would be precocial like their monkey and ape counterparts, but, clearly, human

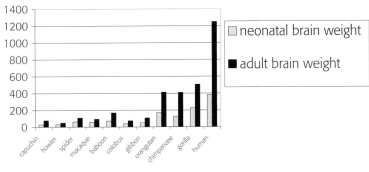

primate species

Figure 1. Neonatal brain weight in selected primate species. From P. H. Harvey, and T. H. Clutton-Brock, 1985. Life history variation in primates. *Evolution*, 39, 559–581.

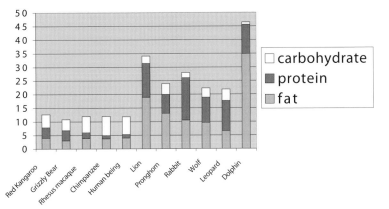

Figure 2. Composition of milk in selected mammals. From D. M. Ben Shaul, 1962. The composition of the milk of wild animals. *International Zoo Yearbook*, 4, 333–342.

infants do not have the motor abilities that would enable them to cling to their mothers even if they had prehensile feet and their mothers had fur. This phenomenon led to the concept of 'secondary altriciality' to describe the status of the human newborn whose eyes are open, but who is completely dependent on the mother for maintaining contact between the two. It is likely that humans are descended from primate ancestors that gave birth to precocial infants but, for reasons described above, now give birth to more dependent, less mature neonates. They have retained the 'precocial milk' of their ancestors, however, so they are 'on-demand' feeders and nurse frequently. This secondary altriciality places huge demands on the human mother who, in contrast with the infant, is entirely responsible for maintaining contact and nursing.

Newborn assessment

Concern about distinguishing between abnormal and normal infant neurological and behavioral status at birth has resulted in the development of several assessment tools. In the United States and many other countries, birth attendants use the Apgar scoring technique to quickly assess infant well-being at 1 and 5 minutes following birth. Five vital signs (color, heart rate, reflex, muscle tone, and respiration) are evaluated and scored 0–2 points. A score of 7–10 indicates a vigorous infant, 4–6 indicates a depressed infant, and a score below 4 is clear cause for concern. Typically, the score increases from 1 to 5 minutes. Although the test is useful in helping obstetrical attendants recognize emergency situations, the Apgar score has limited ability to predict future neurological status of the infant.

Early attempts to assess neurological and behavioral maturity of infants at birth resulted in the development of a number of assessment tools including the Prechtl Neurological Examination of the Fullterm Newborn, the Brazelton Neonatal Behavioral Assessment Scale (NBAS), and the NICU Network Neurobehavioral Scale (NNNS). These instruments have varying goals, including distinguishing between healthy and compromised fullterm newborns, assessing individual differences in the behavior of fullterm, healthy newborns, and assessing the status of an at-risk infant, respectively. They are used to evaluate the relationships between obstetrical complications and later neurological development, and in designing interventions when abnormalities are detected. Most of them assess the infant's capacity to respond and adjust to stimulation in a self-organized manner.

The newborn infant brain

At birth, the neonatal human brain weighs between 300 and 400 g, approximately one quarter the size it will be in adulthood. The birth event itself is associated with rapid formation of synapses in the neonatal brain, perhaps in preparation for the environmental changes the infant faces in the transition from the uterine to the external environment. Much of fetal and early neonatal behavior seems to be governed by sub-cortical parts of the brain (midbrain and hindbrain) that are relatively mature at birth, in contrast to the somewhat immature neocortex. Brain growth in the first few months following birth is due to the development of synaptic connections, with their associated increased metabolic demands and blood vessels that support the neurons. Certainly, a rapidly growing brain is dependent on energy resources to fuel its growth. During gestation, the placenta provided the carbohydrates needed to meet the metabolic demands of the growing brain, and carbohydrate reserves are stored in the liver of the fullterm infant to meet initial postnatal demands until nursing is established, 2–3 days after birth.

Following birth, the infant's experiences will alter neocortical structures in ways that enhance or inhibit cognitive development and affect behavioral responses in adulthood. Furthermore, the effects of experience vary by age, sex, and culture of the infant. In some instances, experiences can lead to modifications in the brain and perhaps laying down of new neurons following injury or illness. The evidence for the influence of experience on brain development is the basis for arguing that a 'rich' environment is better for learning than an 'impoverished' one, although an actual definition of a 'rich' environment is far from certain, given great variation in environments of infancy across cultures.

Sensory development at birth

Although the terms 'altricial' and 'precocial' may be useful in comparing very general developmental states of infants across species, they do not suffice to describe the specifics of neurological, behavioral, or physical development in the human neonate. In fact, there are differences in the maturity of the sensory systems at birth, with, for example, touch, olfaction, and taste being more advanced than vision.

Touch

When we consider that licking is the most common initial reaction to a newborn infant by mammalian mothers, it is not surprising that touch is an important mediator of maternal-infant interaction at birth in humans. The tactile system matures early in fetal development, and the licking that most mammalian infants receive at birth appears to facilitate development of the respiratory and gastrointestinal systems. Additionally, licking may enhance maternal recognition of the infant and play a role in attachment in many mammals. Licking of the newborn is extremely rare in humans, but its function seems to be filled by the mother rubbing and stroking the infant with her hands, behaviors that are commonly reported by observers of human births. Rubbing and stroking stimulate and maintain breathing and may serve to warm the infant.

The human newborn is covered with a fatty substance, vernix caseosa, that protects the skin from drying, and from viral and bacterial agents when it is rubbed into the skin. Mothers typically cradle their infants (most often on the left, over the heart), and explore fingers, face, hands, and extremities with their hands in a pattern that likely facilitates recognition and bonding. Furthermore, Tiffany Field's research has

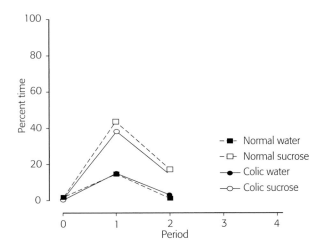

Figure 3. Percent time mouthing after water (black symbols) and sucrose (white symbols) in infants with (circles) and without (squares) colic before taste administration (period 0) and in each minute after stimulus administration (periods 1 and 2) when tastes are administered to crying infants before a feeding. From R. G. Barr, S. N. Young, J. H. Wright, R. Gravel, & R. Alkawaf, 1999. Differential calming responses to sucrose taste in crying infants with and without colic. *Pediatrics*, 103, 1–9.

demonstrated positive benefits from infant massage, especially for preterm and drug-exposed infants.

Taste

Human infants and those of most other primates seem to be born with a 'sweet tooth.' Tongue protrusions, lip smacking, and lip sucking are common positive reactions to sweet substances in human infants before they ingest any food substance postnatally. Neonates presented with sour or bitter tastes commonly exhibit averse facial expressions and movements. Furthermore, sucrose serves to calm newborn infants and to reduce heart rate. Apparently, it is the actual sweetness of sucrose rather than its nutritive value that induces calming (Fig. 3). In addition to their calming effects, sweet tastes also induce mouthing movements and hand-to-mouth contacts in newborn infants (R. G. Barr & Young, 1999), including those with colic (R. G. Barr *et al.*, 1999). All of these behaviors can be seen as predisposing an infant to nurse, enhancing survival at a critical point in development.

Vision

Although the infant's visual system at birth is not fully developed, a newborn infant is able to focus on objects approximately 8–12 inches away. This is roughly the distance to the mother's face when the infant is nursing. Even at less than an hour old, infants show preference for features characteristic of a human face over any other object presented to them. The patterns and movements of the human face appear to be optimal for maximal neural firing rate. In an evolutionary sense, it is not surprising that the neonatal visual system and the most predicted object in the neonatal environment (viz., the mother's face) combine to enhance visual development. Furthermore, by the time they are a few hours old, infants apparently distinguish between a familiar and an unfamiliar face, typically preferring the mother's face to all others, perhaps even discriminating facial expressions. Learning of individual faces appears to be very rapid, and neonates seem to prefer faces that adults judge to be attractive to those judged to be unattractive. There is debate over whether this early learning results from a face-specific learning mechanism or is due to general ability to process complex visual stimuli.

Neural activation is necessary for the maintenance of the visual abilities present at birth and for the further development of the visual system. In fact, the structuring of the visual system begins in utero, where it has been demonstrated that there is rhythmical firing of retinal cells involved in vision. Infants just a few minutes old show the ability to turn their heads and smoothly follow an object suggesting, on the one hand, that gaze stabilization is facilitated prenatally. On the other hand, there is no evidence that visual acuity, color perception, or contrast sensitivity are as developed in the neonate as they are in the older infant (3–6 months of age) and adult. Visual acuity, for example, is estimated to be only about 5 percent of that in an adult (Slater, 1998). There is some evidence that human newborns can compare color information from long and medium-length cones. Finally, there is evidence for some contrast sensitivity in human newborns, but in the subsequent two to three months it steadily improves, with a sudden appearance of being able to perceive lower spatial frequencies.

Neonatal imitation has been the subject of inquiry for several decades, and remains somewhat controversial. In some experiments, newborns have shown the ability to imitate a variety of facial gestures, leading some researchers to suggest that they enter the world equipped to communicate, albeit in a simple fashion. Despite the fact that neonates may not perceive depth, color, or contrast as well as they will several months later, they are quite capable, as many have noted, of seeing what they need to see and responding in ways that are appropriate for eliciting caretaking.

Olfaction

Olfactory centers appear to be fairly well developed at birth, fitting with the prediction that evolutionarily older sections of the brain will mature more rapidly than more recently evolved parts. As it is with most

mammals, olfaction is likely a primary route of recognition between mother and infant, and may play a role in attachment or bonding between the two. Particularly salient for newborn infants is the smell of the mother's breast (Porter & Winberg, 1999). Infants under a week old have been shown to turn their heads longer and more frequently toward their mother's smell when given a choice between a gauze pad from their mother's breast and one from another woman. Within an hour of birth, neonates placed on their mothers' abdomens have been observed crawling unassisted toward the mothers' breasts, apparently using olfactory cues to guide them. One basis for the attraction may be fetal learning of the odor of amniotic fluid, which has been shown to have chemical similarities to breast milk. In general, newborns seem to be attracted to odors from breasts of lactating women, although they consistently prefer the odors of their own mothers, especially if they are breastfed. In fact, one study shows that bottle-fed infants prefer the scent of lactating females, but are not able to discriminate their mothers from strangers by olfactory means (Cernoch & Porter, 1985). It should be noted that there is also extensive evidence that mothers can recognize the odors of their infants soon after birth.

Hearing, communication, and language

One of the characteristics that set humans apart from other animals is the capacity for and dependency on language. The auditory system begins functioning in utero and several studies have demonstrated that infants recognize sounds after birth to which they were exposed in utero. These include mother's voice, her heartbeat, and the father's voice. Neonates can apparently discriminate between male and female voices, preferring higher-pitched sounds. Mothers frequently slow down the speed of speech and raise the pitch of their voice when they talk to or toward their infants in an apparently unconscious manner (referred to as 'motherese'). Newborns also show preferences for listening to poems that they were exposed to in utero.

Newborns appear to be able to discriminate phonemes (units of sound such as syllables and tones) and seem to recognize paralinguistic differences among languages. For example, 3-day-old infants are able to discriminate phonological phrase boundaries in several languages although their ability to discriminate is greater between two languages that are quite different from each other (Mehler *et al.*, 1988). This ability probably enhances language development in the first year of life. Apparently, human infants are born able to process language in general. However, as they develop in the context of a specific linguistic environment, their receptive abilities narrow and become language-specific.

Evolutionary significance of neonatal behaviors

In 1958, John Bowlby identified five behaviors, referring to them as fixed action patterns, which he claimed were present at birth in the human infant: clinging, crying, smiling, following with the eyes, and sucking. He described them as behaviors that promote attachment between mother and infant, and argued that they must be understood in the context in which they evolved (i.e., the environment of evolutionary adaptedness). The psychological literature stresses that the way in which the mother responds to these behavioral signals from the infant has an impact on their continuing relationship, and on the feelings of security that develop in the infant. In general, mothers who respond sensitively to infant signals (vocalizations, smiles, crying) have babies that are more securely attached when they are older. Furthermore, mothers who are informed of their babies' abilities to communicate through these behaviors during the newborn period usually develop sensitive responses to the signals. This has led to proposals that early intervention to increase responsiveness of caregivers in the newborn period, particularly for mother-infant dyads at risk, may enhance the long-term quality of the mother-infant relationship.

Considering neonatal behaviors as evolved behaviors requires examination of their adaptive significance beyond their role in promoting attachment. For example, when the newborn makes initial attempts to nurse by licking and suckling the mother's breast in the immediate postpartum period, these nipple contacts stimulate the release of oxytocin in the mother, which facilitates uterine contractions, expulsion of the placenta, and inhibition of postpartum bleeding. Sucking on the nipple also releases prolactin, which stimulates milk production. It is not likely that the infant receives nutritional sustenance from these initial attempts to nurse (although the colostrum has been proposed as being beneficial to the newborn's immune system), but the actions serve to enhance postpartum adaptation for the mother and may even save her life if uterine bleeding is excessive.

Conclusions

For years, there has been debate about the importance for bonding of mother-infant contact in the first hour after birth. Some early studies suggested that the first hour was a 'sensitive period' for bonding and that when the infant was removed from the mother, as was common in hospital births, the quality of the mother-infant bond would be compromised. Certainly, the immediate postpartum period is a time of heightened awareness in both mother and infant, and the physical and hormonal sensations surrounding birth converge to create a unique moment in the developing relationship between the two. Whether or not this unique moment is essential or even contributes in a significant way to the security of the mother-infant bond is unclear, but it is unlikely that rapid bond formation at birth is part of the evolutionary legacy of humans, as perhaps it is for some other mammals. Future research may help to clarify the impact of birth and the immediate postpartum period on early maternal and infant development.

See also:
Normal and abnormal prenatal development; The birth process Perceptual development; Motor development; Social development; Language development; Brain and behavioral development (I): sub-cortical; Brain and behavioral development (II): cortical; Face recognition; Imitation; Prematurity and low birthweight; Prolonged infant crying and colic; Pediatrics; John Bowlby

Further reading

Lewis, M. and Ramsay, D. (eds.) (1999). *Soothing and Stress.* Mahwah, NJ: Erlbaum.
Simion, F. and Butterworth, G. (eds.) (1998). *The Development of Sensory, Motor, and Cognitive Capacities in Early Infancy: From Perception to Cognition.* Hove, UK: Psychology Press.
Singer, L. T. and Zeskind, P. S. (eds.) (2001). *Biobehavioral Assessment of the Infant.* New York: Guilford Press.

PART IV

Domains of development: from infancy to childhood

The aim here is to present concise overviews of the main lines of research and associated questions that currently typify the study of postnatal development in different domains. Theoretical frameworks, both within and across domains, are identified and examples given of studies linking domains (e.g., between perceptual and motor development).

Cognitive development in infancy

GAVIN BREMNER

Introduction

Cognitive development is such a vast topic that it would be impossible to do it justice in one short entry. Fortunately, however, research on the topic splits rather naturally into two developmental periods, infancy and childhood. This is largely a historical division, and toward the end I shall comment on the fact that there are few clear links between the two literatures, fewer than there should be. My task is to write about cognitive development in infancy. Even limiting attention to the first two years of life still leaves a vast topic, including issues regarding infants' understanding of causality, space, and time, their problem-solving abilities, and so on. My aim here is thus to focus attention on what has become the hallmark of infant cognitive development, namely, the development of object knowledge.

Object knowledge has its roots in object perception. The ability to identify objects in the surroundings is a fundamental of human and animal perception. Consequently, it is no surprise that researchers have put great effort into investigating the origins of object perception and knowledge in infancy. This effort has been pursued at several different levels. Firstly, there are basic questions regarding the ability of infants to resolve contour detail and to scan their visual environment. There are also questions about infants' depth perception, which is needed not just to identify the distance of objects but also to identify their three-dimensionality. Johnson, Hannon, & Amso deal with all these basic issues in their entry on Perceptual development. Here, the aim is to supplement the material in that entry by focusing on infants' object perception, providing research evidence on questions regarding their ability to detect organization in visual information, to identify objects as 3-D solids with constant size and shape, and to segregate them from other objects and the visual background. This will be followed by consideration of higher-level object properties, in particular object identity and permanence, and infants' knowledge of the rules governing object movements relative to other objects and surfaces.

Form perception

It is clear that even at birth infants' visual perception is sufficient to discriminate between two-dimensional forms such as triangles and squares. What is much less clear is the level at which they are making these discriminations. Most of the work on form perception involves measures of infant looking time. If a form is presented repeatedly, the time infants spend looking at it declines, a phenomenon known as habituation. Following habituation, we can test infants' discrimination by presenting a new stimulus. If they discriminate it from the old stimulus, looking should show recovery, whereas if they do not discriminate, looking should remain at the previous habituated level and indeed should continue to decline. While this technique frequently yields positive results, we cannot immediately tell what the basis for discrimination is. It could be that infants are showing recovery because some low-level variable such as overall stimulus brightness or amount of contour has changed. Even when this is equated between stimuli, it is still possible that infants discriminate on the basis of presence or absence of a single feature.

These difficulties have led investigators to take a different approach, investigating infants' ability to discriminate elements of form at progressively higher levels. Key features of rectilinear forms are the orientation of linear elements and the angles at which they intersect. There is clear evidence that newborns discriminate different line orientations. Furthermore, there is evidence that they discriminate different angular relations between intersecting lines. It has to be noted, however, that the result with newborns is contentious. But certainly this ability appears to be well established by 4 months (Slater, 2001).

Size and shape constancy

Size constancy is the principle that the true size of an object remains unchanged despite changes in its distance from the observer and hence changes in the size of the retinal image. Shape constancy is the principle that the true shape of an object remains unchanged despite changes in its slant in the depth plane, and hence changes in the form of the retinal image. From the classical standpoint, perception on the basis of both of these principles relies on depth perception: size constancy because distance information is necessary in order to compute the true size from retinal image size, and shape constancy because perception of slant in the depth plane is necessary to compute the true shape of a surface from retinal form. It should be noted, however, that direct realist accounts of perception deny the need to construct true shape and size from retinal image information, the objective structure of the world being directly available in the dynamic information yielded as the individual moves through space.

   Early accounts such as Piaget's viewed both of these constancies as developing toward the latter part of the first year. However, recent applications of more sensitive techniques have yielded evidence that both shape and size constancy are present at birth. This appears to be important indirect evidence for form perception at birth, since it is hard to see how these constancies could govern newborn perception in the absence of form perception (Slater, 2001).

Object unity and object segregation

An object is a bounded single entity and perception of it as such involves being able to treat it as a unit even if parts of it are hidden (object unity), and to segregate it from other objects and the background. As indicated in the entry 'Perceptual development', 4-month-old infants perceive object unity, and even 2-month-olds do under certain circumstances. The typical test of object unity is illustrated in Figure 1. Infants are habituated to a rod moving back and forth behind a box, and are then tested for novelty preference (recovery of looking) on displays in which the box is removed and they see (a) the complete rod, or (b) just the parts that were visible during habituation. The rationale is that if they perceive unity, they should treat the broken rod as novel, because they perceived a whole rod during habituation. Infants aged 4 months show object unity, looking longer at the broken rod, and 2-month-olds do so provided the box is made quite narrow so that the part of the rod that has to be interpolated is small. In contrast, newborns show a preference for the complete rod, a finding that has

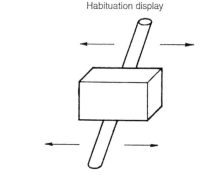

Habituation display

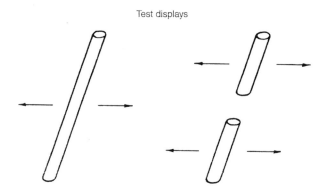

Test displays

Figure 1. Displays used to measure object unity in infancy.

persisted despite all attempts to make the task simpler. Thus, it appears that object unity develops some time after birth, only appearing in robust form at 4 months.

   It is important to note that common motion of the visible parts of the rod is a necessary condition for perception of unity. However, common motion is not in itself a sufficient condition, since other factors also contribute. For instance, if the rod parts are displaced from one another so that they are not directly relatable, 4-month-olds do not perceive unity despite common motion. In addition, at 4 months, object unity is only perceived when rod motion leads to deletion and accretion of background texture. Indeed, it may be this rather than common motion in itself that supports object unity. One view is that deletion and accretion segregates the rod from its background and from the box in the foreground, leading it to be perceived as an object, with perception of unity following from that. This is not the whole story, however, because, as noted above, the relatability of the parts of the rod is also an important factor, and further work has indicated that Gestalt 'good form' in the partially occluded object leads to perception of unity (S. P. Johnson, 2000).

   Direct tests of object segregation generally involve investigating whether infants perceive objects as separate despite there being physical contact between them. Typically, infants view two objects in contact and see a hand appear, grasp the nearer object, and pull it across a surface. In one case, only the grasped object moves (consistent with segregation), and in the other case, both objects move (consistent with lack of segregation). If objects are featurally similar and are in contact along a linear boundary, 8-month-olds treat them as a single unit and expect them to move together. However, if, prior to the movement event, infants see a blade move between the objects, they then treat them as separate. Featural differences between objects in contact help to support segregation. Additionally, prior experience of seeing the objects spatially separate led 4-month-olds to segregate them when they were subsequently placed in contact.

A potential problem with this means of testing object segregation is that the test confounds segregation with understanding of basic physical relationships between objects. Specifically, if the hand pushed rather than pulled the near object, we would expect both to move together even if they are not connected. This raises the issue of whether young infants have difficulties with object segregation or in understanding pushing versus pulling relationships (principles that tie in with causality). The fact that featural differentiation leads to segregation at 4 months would appear to make such an alternative unlikely. However, it has been shown that infants do not segregate featurally different objects when one is on top of the other. Could this be more to do with infants' incomplete understanding of the distinction between supporting and supported objects?

Perception of support relationships

There are frequent examples of support relationships in the everyday world: books on bookshelves, a vase of flowers on a table, and so on. As adults, we know what sorts of support relationships will work and which will not. For instance, we know that placing the vase partly over the edge of the table is risky, and placing it more than half off the table will inevitably result in catastrophe. The same does not seem to be true of young infants. Apparently, they expect any form of contact between the object and the supporting surface to result in support, even when much more than half of the object extends over the edge of the surface. In contrast, older infants have much more precise notions about the conditions for adequate support. Infants of 6.5 months look longer at an object that does not fall when the contact relationship with a surface would not provide support than they do at cases in which there is adequate support. Here longer looking is taken as evidence that they have detected the anomaly of continued stability, expecting the object to fall. One suggestion is that the infant's own experience of stacking objects is a causal factor in the progression from rudimentary notions

about support in which contact equals support, to more precise appreciation of the conditions for support.

The reader may be asking whether the young infant's incomplete understanding of support is not to do with support but with failure to segregate the object from the surface; if object and surface are perceived as a single unit, then support of one by the other is just not an issue. However, two points make this interpretation unlikely. Firstly, the object and surface are featurally distinct, circumstances under which quite young infants segregate objects. Secondly, as part of the experimental procedure, infants see the object moved along the surface, an event that is likely to support object-surface segregation.

Object permanence and perception of physical reality

Object permanence involves awareness that an object continues to exist over time, despite the fact that it may be completely out of sight for periods of time. Traditionally, object permanence is treated as a form of knowledge that infants construct laboriously over the first two years of life. However, more recently, evidence has accumulated suggesting that infants as young as 4 to 6 months perceive or understand object permanence. Some investigators treat object unity as a perceptual basis for the beginnings of object permanence, because infants who exhibit object unity are effectively filling in an absent part of the object, a step toward filling in an absent whole.

Not all would agree with this analysis, however, and recent studies of object permanence have tended to use a rather different technique known as the violation of expectation technique. This involves habituating infants to an event sequence of some sort, after which they are presented with two test trials, one of which is normal with regard to the way objects move relative to each other, and one of which violates some principle of physical reality. For instance, in one study, often referred to as the 'drawbridge study,' 5-month-old infants were habituated to a flap that repeatedly rotated from flat on the table through 180 degrees and then back again (Fig. 2). After this, test trials were presented in which a block was placed in the path of the flap. In the possible test trial, the flap rotated until it came to rest against the block. In the impossible test trial, the flap made its usual 180° rotation, apparently passing through and annihilating the block. The elegance of this design lies in the fact that in basic perceptual terms, the impossible event is more familiar relative to the habituation event than the possible event: it involves the same 180° rotation. However, infants looked longer at the impossible event, a finding that the investigators interpret as evidence that infants perceive or know that the block still exists once occluded by the flap, and that they realize one object cannot pass through another. This finding has been replicated with 3.5-month-olds.

There is, however, some controversy over the basis of this result. It has been suggested that even though infants were habituated to the 180° rotation, this event remained more stimulating than the smaller rotation as it involved more stimulus change. Thus, others argue, infants look longer at the impossible event simply because it provides more low-level perceptual stimulation. However, when the original investigators tested this by presenting post-habituation trials involving the full rotation versus the partial rotation, but no obstructing block, they no longer obtained longer looking at the 180° rotation. Controversy continues, however, because under these circumstances one would really have expected longer looking at the perceptually novel partial rotation (Cashon & Cohen, 2000).

Another study tackles similar questions in a way that has been harder to find fault with. The events presented to infants are shown in Figure 3. Infants are first habituated to an event in which (a) a screen is raised and lowered to reveal nothing behind it, and (b) a truck runs down a track, goes behind the screen, and emerges again. Following habituation, two test trials are presented. In the possible test trial, when the screen is lifted, a block is revealed resting behind the track, whereas in the impossible event, the block is revealed resting on the track and hence impeding the truck's progress. What made this event impossible was that the truck emerged from behind the screen as usual. Children aged 6 and 8 months looked longer at the impossible event, evidence that they both detected the continued existence of the block on the track and realized that the truck could not move through it. Again, this is an elegant design because, once the screen is lowered, both test events are identical to the habituation event. Yet infants look longer at the event that follows screen lowering in the impossible condition.

Again, an alternative interpretation is possible. Maybe the on-track placement of the block is more perceptually stimulating simply because the block is closer, and the effects of this greater stimulation lead to longer looking that persists over time. However, it seems we can rule out this interpretation because the effect was replicated when the possible event involved placement of the block in front of the track. Again, infants looked longer at the impossible event, despite the fact that the block was further away than in the possible test event. It is thus hard to find an interpretation of this result that does not imply object permanence and knowledge of the rules governing object movements. Furthermore, in a simplified task, this effect has been obtained with 2.5-month-olds.

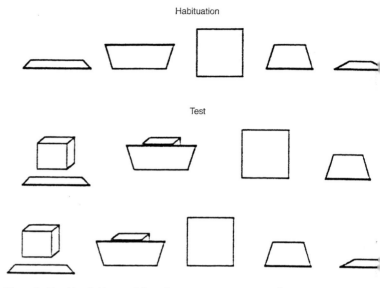

Figure 2. The 'drawbridge study' used to measure awareness of object permanence and rules governing object movement.

It should be noted, however, that young infants do not have a full understanding of the conditions governing object movements. Although they appear to understand that one object cannot move through another, whether it is travelling horizontally or vertically, they do not appear to understand that an object will continue to move under gravity until it reaches a solid surface, being unperturbed when a falling object is subsequently revealed hanging in midair. At first sight, this is a surprising finding. But possibly young infants apply basic rules for object movement that they incorrectly generalize to movements under gravity. Due to friction forces, balls moving across the floor do come to rest without hitting obstructions. Possibly infants apply the same principle to falling objects.

Other work reveals findings that apparently point not just to object permanence in young infants, but to quite precise expectations regarding how the size of an object determines its history of invisibility and visibility on passing behind a screen. Infants are habituated to an event in which either a tall or a short object moves behind a screen and re-emerges. On test trials, the solid screen is replaced by one with a window cut in its top half. This is so placed that part of the tall object but not the short object should appear during its passage behind the screen. Infants of 3.5 months looked longer at the tall object test event, apparently evidence that, given its size, they expected it to reappear.

Although replicated, this result is open to criticism. The objects were either carrots or rabbits, and both contained facial features near their top. It has been argued that in the case of the tall object, infants fixate the facial features and track along that line. Thus, tracking is higher for the tall object, and it is only in this case that they note the window in the screen.

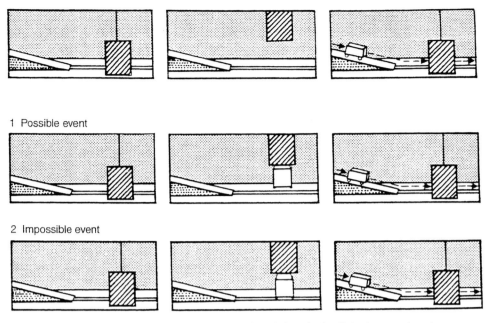

1 Possible event

2 Impossible event

Figure 3. A procedure used to test young infants' object knowledge. The familiarization event is at the top and the two test events are below.

Consequently, longer looking in the tall object event arises not because an event did not occur that infants expected, but because they note that the screen is different. However, one must question the plausibility of this interpretation. After all, infants do not have tunnel vision: one would expect them to notice the window even if it was not directly on their scan path.

Numerical identity

Similar techniques have been extended to investigate infants' awareness of the number of objects that must be involved in an event to make it possible. For instance, consider the case in which an object disappears behind a screen, reappears, moves behind a second screen, and reappears again. Particularly if the movement is of constant velocity, an event such as this is liable to be treated by adults as a case of a single object in motion. However, if the center part of the trajectory is omitted, we would tend to interpret this as one object moving behind the first screen and a different one emerging from the second screen (Fig. 4). Event sequences of this sort have been presented to infants, after which the screens are lowered or removed to let infants 'behind the scenes'. In the case of the discontinuous trajectory, 10-month-old infants look longer when only a single object is revealed, whereas they look longer when two objects are revealed after the continuous trajectory event. Other workers have used similar techniques to gain similar findings from infants of only 3 to 4 months.

Surprisingly, infants of up to 10 months do not seem to use featural differences to detect that more than one object is involved. Evidence for this comes from work in which only a single screen is used, but distinctly different objects appear at each side of the screen (with timing of emergence in keeping with a single object on a constant trajectory). Children aged 10 months showed no signs of expecting there to be two objects in this case, whereas by 12 months infants did appear to expect there to be two objects involved. Nor do 3- to 4-month-old infants use constant trajectory as an indicator that a single object is involved, or departure from constant trajectory as an indicator that more than one object is involved. The conclusion that these investigators draw is that, before 12 months, infants only use continuity versus discontinuity of motion as a basis for detecting how many objects are present. Neither object features nor smoothness of motion appear to be used.

One study, however, suggests that at least featural information is used as an indicator that more than one object is involved. The task just involved events in which one object moved behind a screen and another appeared from the other side. This sequence was presented either with a wide screen, capable of hiding both objects, or with a narrow screen capable of hiding only one of the objects. Infants of 7 months looked longer at the narrow screen event, and it was concluded that they do this because they note that two objects are involved and realize that both cannot be hidden behind the narrow screen simultaneously. However, an alternative possibility is that infants only note the object change when the gap with no object visible is very small, as in the case of the narrow screen, and that registration of the object change is the sole reason for longer looking. This was controlled for by repeating the study with smaller objects, both of which could fit behind the screen. Infants treated this event in the same way as they had the wide screen event with the larger objects, a finding that has been used to argue that screen width or time out of sight is not at the root of the result.

There is, however, growing evidence that young infants have difficulty linking events either side of a screen. For instance, 4-month-olds only treat an object trajectory as continuous if the time or distance over which it is out of sight is very short. This must lead to questions regarding the numerical identity work, in which various screen widths and object speeds have been used. In particular, comparison of double screen and single screen conditions is made problematic by the fact that the single screen has typically been much wider than even the combined width of the two screens. It is clear that further work is needed to assess these rather lower-order perceptual variables before clear conclusions can be drawn regarding numerical identity (Bremner, 2001).

Perception of addition and subtraction operations

Probably one of the most controversial claims made in recent years about young infants' capabilities is that they can detect violations of simple acts of addition and subtraction. The technique used is simple, and is illustrated in Figure 5. In the case of addition, infants see a single object, which is then hidden by a screen. Following this, a second object is placed behind the screen. Finally, the screen is lowered to reveal either one object (the inappropriate outcome) or two objects (the appropriate outcome). In the subtraction case, the initial array contains two objects and after screening one is removed. In both cases, 4- to 5-month-olds looked longer at the inappropriate outcome, suggesting that they appropriately perceived addition and subtraction operations and noted violations of the outcome of these. It appears that this is more than a simple ability to note that there should be more or fewer objects after addition or subtraction because, following a 1 + 1 addition operation, infants looked longer at a three object outcome than a two object outcome.

This area is controversial, and a number of investigators do not believe that any true perception of number is involved. However, the alternative interpretations of these data, though based at a lower level, are generally rather low in plausibility. In consequence, there remains a strong possibility that infants detect the principles of

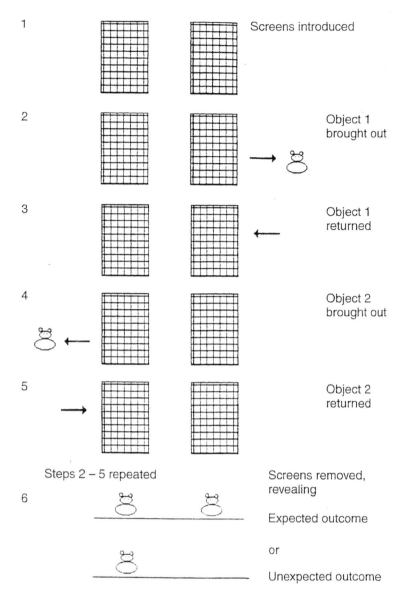

1 Screens introduced

2 Object 1 brought out

3 Object 1 returned

4 Object 2 brought out

5 Object 2 returned

Steps 2 – 5 repeated

6 Screens removed, revealing

Expected outcome

or

Unexpected outcome

Figure 4. A discontinuous movement event that adults interpret as involving two objects. After familiarization with the event sequence, the screens are removed to reveal either one or two objects.

addition and subtraction, at least in very simple cases such as 1 + 1 and 2 − 1.

Nativism, direct realism, or lower-level interpretation?

The evidence for object permanence and awareness of the rules governing object movement is generally interpreted from a nativist stance. Infants are credited with innate core knowledge of physical principles and the ability to reason about the events they see on the basis of this knowledge. This is very clearly a cognitive account with a large innate component. However, it should be noted that these accounts recognize that core knowledge is severely limited. For instance, although

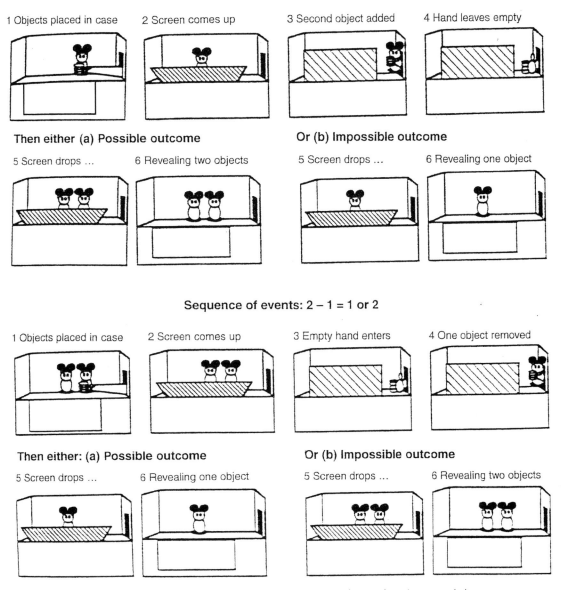

Sequence of events: 1 + 1 = 1 or 2

1 Objects placed in case 2 Screen comes up 3 Second object added 4 Hand leaves empty

Then either (a) Possible outcome

5 Screen drops ... 6 Revealing two objects

Or (b) Impossible outcome

5 Screen drops ... 6 Revealing one object

Sequence of events: 2 − 1 = 1 or 2

1 Objects placed in case 2 Screen comes up 3 Empty hand enters 4 One object removed

Then either: (a) Possible outcome

5 Screen drops ... 6 Revealing one object

Or (b) Impossible outcome

5 Screen drops ... 6 Revealing two objects

Figure 5. Displays used to measure addition and subtraction: addition events above, subtraction events below.

infants understand continuity (that objects move along continuous paths) and solidity (that objects occupy space and no two objects can occupy the same space simultaneously), they do not understand gravity or inertia. They also have very limited understanding of support relationships. Understanding of these principles follows from experience, possibly in large part self-structured experience as infants begin to build towers of bricks and cast objects to the ground.

Not all investigators accept the strongly cognitive account presented by the nativists, doubting whether it is appropriate to describe young infants as reasoning about reality. An extreme contrast is seen in the direct realism approach, according to which perception of the world is objective from birth, not because the infant has innate cognitive structures to interpret retinal images, but because objective reality is there to be picked up directly. The objective nature of the world extends to cases in which parts of objects and whole objects are temporarily out of sight. The way in which they disappeared, through either their own movement or the movement of the organism, specifies their continued existence. Referring back to the evidence presented above, such perceptually based accounts would not credit the young infant with the ability to reason about events, particularly since the only evidence for this is the fact that infants look longer at one event than another. Instead, longer looking may simply indicate that the infant has detected a departure from normal perceptual experience. Even though the key events in test trials are subsequently hidden, perception is seen as a continuous process over time in which objects that are subsequently screened retain their integration with ongoing events.

Another anti-nativist account with certain similarities, but with different theoretical underpinnings, is based on the premise that infants benefit from a short-term sensory store, which maintains a memory trace for events that are screened from view. It is pointed out that the startling positive findings presented above tend only to be obtained when periods of occlusion are very short. According to proponents of this account, these periods are sufficiently short for the sensory store to fill in the hidden information, and so it is as if the screens did not exist. Since many of the interpretations summarized above rely crucially on certain information being hidden from the infant, this presents a definite challenge. However, the account is limited due to lack of evidence for such processes (at least at conscious level) in adults. Other critics claim that the data on which nativists base their arguments can be explained on the basis of infants' responses to perceptual novelty rather than their detection of violation of rules of physical reality. There is not space to expand on the evidence and arguments here, but the interested reader is referred to Cashon & Cohen (2000) as a good example. This paper is part of a thematic collection in which the arguments for and against the nativist account are fully aired. As such, the whole collection is well worth reading.

Later infancy: linking perception and action

Despite evidence for objective perception of the world in early infancy, such awareness is not generally revealed in the infant's actions. For instance, despite evidence for perception or knowledge of permanence in the early months, it is not until about 8 months that infants begin to search manually for a hidden object, and it has been shown that lack of search cannot be put down to inability to organize the appropriate action. And even once infants begin to search, they make systematic errors, tending to search only at the first place that the object has been hidden. One of the important questions since the early 1990s has concerned how to reconcile the apparent contradiction here.

The predominant view now is that infants are not initially capable of using perception or rudimentary knowledge to guide action. Thus, early information about the world is implicit in the sense that it does not guide action, and a major developmental process in later infancy concerns building links between perception and action (Bremner, 2000). Object search errors can be seen as problems of executive function in which the infant has not recognized what information is needed in guidance of action. Neuroscience approaches identify

these limitations of executive function as arising from immaturity of frontal cortex. One should be wary, however, of concluding that development follows simply from the maturation of the frontal cortex. It has been clearly demonstrated that brain development depends upon experience, and so it is most likely that development of the frontal cortex supporting executive functions arises from the infant's experiences while acting on the world.

Links with cognitive development after infancy

As mentioned at the beginning, research on infant cognitive development is somewhat compartmentalized. This is largely due to the influence of Piaget's stage theory, in which infancy is the first major period. Although developments in this first period are crucial precursors for later development according to Piaget's theory, these later ones are qualitatively different from those taking place in infancy. While the influence of Piaget's theory has waned, we are left with a historical division of literatures that is probably not fully warranted. True enough, the emergence of language and symbolic thought sets later cognitive development apart from developments in infancy. However, there are more continuities than was once thought. Also, there is much to be done to explore how developments taking place in infancy set the scene for abilities that emerge in childhood.

Conclusions

As the reader will have noted, most of the evidence regarding infant perception, at all levels, involves simple measures of looking time. While measures of visual scanning are used to elucidate the basic processes of perception, almost all evidence regarding *what* is perceived is based on looking time. Although habituation-recovery and violation of expectation techniques have proved enormously productive, they begin to creak under the strain when used to support high-level accounts based in infants' ability to reason about events. It appears that there is an urgent need to supplement these measures with others.

Eye-tracking technology is now sufficiently good to allow accurate measurement of *where* infants are looking, in the case of both static patterns and dynamical events. Such information is very much more rich than simple looking time, and is likely to yield important supplementary information regarding the bases of perception in early infancy. Methods of measuring brain activity have also moved forward, making it possible to carry out non-invasive measurements of cortical activity while infants are exposed to perceptual events. This kind of information is beginning to supplement behavioral measures, and helps to distinguish between alternative interpretations of infants' overt responses to events, leading in the process to a more secure account of infant perception and knowledge.

See also:
Constructivist theories; Dynamical systems approaches; Experimental methods; Cognitive development beyond infancy; Perceptual development; Motor development; Development of learning and memory; Attention; Executive functions; Cognitive neuroscience; Jean Piaget

Further reading

Slater, A. (ed.) (1998). *Perceptual Development: Visual, Auditory, and Speech Perception in Infancy*. Hove, UK: Psychology Press.

Cognitive development beyond infancy

TARA C. CALLAGHAN

Introduction

Since 1970s, research on the origins of human knowledge about the physical and social world has fueled a revolution in ideas of when and how humans begin to represent, reason, and accumulate a base of knowledge about objects, people, and the self. Current views construe cognitive development as a complex process that is grounded both in biological preparedness, and in the highly evolved cultural context that surrounds and nurtures the child from infancy and beyond. Along with revolutionary findings have come major shifts in theories of cognitive development, notions of continuity and discontinuity in that development, and the topics that engage researchers. To provide an overview of this vast research area, we focus on the theoretical filters that have dominated research, the major findings in key research areas, and research directions for the future.

Theories and filters: past and present

For many years, the theoretical foundations of cognitive development came mainly from Jean Piaget's unparalleled works. Almost as soon as the works of Piaget were translated into English, his biologically influenced, organismic view of the construction of intelligence across successive, qualitatively distinct chronological stages became the target of harsh criticisms from behaviorists, who viewed the child as essentially a passive, blank slate upon which experience etched the individual. In contrast to this view, Piaget believed the developing child was a biologically prepared organism engaged in the active construction of physical knowledge through a precise succession of necessary stages, culminating in the emergence of formal logical thought by early adulthood. Although Piaget's ideas revolutionized the study of cognitive development, some justly argue that his model neglected the important role of socialization. Nevertheless, the theory continues to evolve in the writings of neo-Piagetians and others using a dynamical systems approach to account for qualitative change over development.

Another perspective comes from the writings of Lev Vygotsky. He offered the novel view that thought develops first and foremost in social interaction, only later becoming internalized via language and inner speech. For Vygotsky, the child's cognition develops in a social context with a strong supporting cast. The parents, siblings, peers, and educators of the child play a critical role in shaping the context in ways that support development. Thus, it is during the social engagement of children in their social settings that cognition develops.

Both Piaget and Vygotsky left a legacy of ideas that define the way many contemporary researchers view cognitive development. These include the view that infants and children are actively involved in constructing their knowledge, that the foundations for cognitive development lie in both biological preparedness and social supports, and that development is a lengthy process of refinement. From these historical theoretical foundations, a number of contemporary theories of cognitive development have emerged that help to frame current research findings.

Innate, modularity theories

Mental modules are specialized to process domain-specific input (e.g., language) with encapsulated processing mechanisms, and are considered to be hard wired in the organism's biological makeup with outputs that are resistant to modification from experience. A number of developmental researchers with nativist leanings have softened the original modular claim in order to account for changes over development. For example, rather than a single encapsulated module for theory of mind reasoning, it has been suggested that a sequence of mental modules come on line over development. In another model, a process called representational re-description is proposed as a mechanism that allows the organism to change implicit, modularized information into explicit knowledge that can then be modified through theory building, thought experiments, and the like.

Still other researchers supporting the modular account distinguish between core concepts (e.g., solidity and contact), which develop early and are resistant to change, and non-core concepts (e.g., gravity) that develop later and are influenced by real world experience with physical objects and gravity. However, this view is challenged by researchers who propose that the development of physical knowledge of objects is influenced by the maturation of motor abilities such that infants come to interact with the world and derive very different information as a function of whether they can reach, grasp, and manipulate those objects. In spite of these modifications, the 'softer' modular theorists retain a distinctly nativist flavor, and aim to identify initial states and constraints on cognitive development.

Domain-specific expertise models

In contrast to the strongly nativist claims of modular theorists, other researchers propose that islands of competence are carved out by high levels of practice in specific domains. It is clear that gaining specific information about a domain through the effects of practice can improve knowledge acquisition in those domains. However, what is difficult to reconcile with a purely practice account of knowledge development is the fact that children are not always explicitly exposed to the information that forms the basis of their knowledge and beliefs. Thus, while expertise does influence the nature of the knowledge base in particular domains, it is clear from research in this field that biological preparedness also plays a role in predicting developmental outcome.

Hybrid theories

Many contemporary theorists see a role for both biology and social support in cognitive development. The relative influence of biology and culture on development is perhaps most strongly debated in accounting for language acquisition, wherein some researchers take a distinctly nativist, modular view of the process (Pinker, 1994), while others argue that social influences play a critical role along with the speech perception and learning mechanisms present at birth (Tomasello, 2003). Similar arguments are found in theories of children's developing theories of mind. Some researchers claim that infants begin life with an initial theory of the world that is based on action (much as Piaget claimed), and an initial understanding of self that is founded on an imitation mechanism present at birth. Then, during infancy and through childhood, social cognitive understanding (e.g., of intentionality and the self/other distinction) is developed through imitating others

(i.e., their bodily actions, actions on objects, and intentions), and then revised and reconstituted much like the process of theory building.

Theoretical accounts of cognitive development have been heavily influenced by infancy research, and most attempt to account for the clear foundational role that early years of development play in later cognitive refinement. The origins of humans' abilities to represent, reason, and build knowledge about physical and social worlds clearly lie in infancy (Rochat, 2001). The refinement of these representations, reasoning abilities, and knowledge bases is the work of childhood.

Continuity/discontinuity and the special case of symbols

While many researchers have criticized Piaget's view that cognitive development encompasses a sequential unfolding of multiple, qualitatively distinct ways of knowing and forms of knowledge, it is clear that qualitative distinctions do exist. One such discontinuity in cognitive development is the onset of an ability to use representations as the currency of communicative exchange – the onset of the symbolic mind. Symbols are representations intended to refer to entities outside of themselves, and their use is specific to the human species and universal across cultures. They are also cultural artifacts, or ways that cultures have evolved to ensure a meeting of minds in communicative exchanges. The questions of when symbolic understanding emerges, what precursors are necessary for its development, and whether it is driven by a domain-general or domain-specific process are hotly debated.

We know that infants are patently pre-symbolic organisms. We also know that symbolic proficiency in language emerges toward the end of infancy, first in gestures and then in verbal language, but that profound refinements of this ability continue throughout life as children increase their fluency and come to understand the more subtle uses of language such as metaphor and irony. The trend of increasing refinement in symbolic functioning also occurs for other symbols, such as play, maps, and pictures. Some research suggests that language develops first, followed closely by symbolic play, and visual symbolism. Additionally, language appears to help children break into other symbolic systems, and children's symbolic development appears to be supported by social facilitation from other people who are more advanced symbol users. Although research in this field has been dominated by language, it is likely that the priority cultures give to particular symbol systems will influence the trajectory of their development. In American-European culture, the priority is clearly verbal language as parents engage

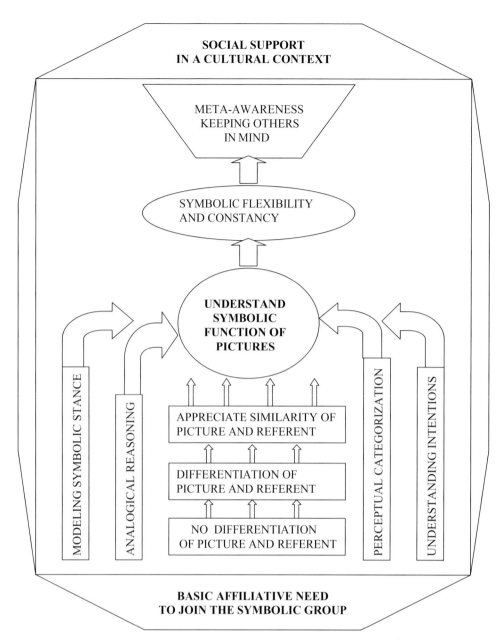

Figure 1. A six-level model of symbolic development – adapted from P. Rochat and T. C. Callaghan, (in press). What drives symbolic development? The case of pictorial comprehension and production. In L. Narry, ed., *The Development of Symbolic Comprehension and Use*. Mahwah, NJ: Erlbaum, suggesting that perceptual, learning, cognitive, and social mechanisms support development. It is claimed that the onset and refinement of symbolic functioning is influenced by the combination of many social cognitive foundations laid down during infancy (e.g., intentional understanding, learning through modeling, forming analogies and categories), the social support of expert symbol users, and the child's own drive to affiliate with the symbolic cultural group.

infants in proto-conversations from birth, and this priority may account for the relatively early development of linguistic as compared to other symbols.

The ability to use symbols is a paradigm shift for the human organism, and affects cognition of all types once it is achieved. Studies of symbolic development provide a fertile ground for discussion of the domain-specificity issue. Some researchers suggest that the onset of symbolic systems has a distinctly modular flavor,

supporting the domain-specific view. In contrast, others (Rochat & Callaghan, in press) argue that the domain-general mechanisms found in infancy – notably the appreciation of similarity and analogical reasoning, understanding of intentions, propensity to reproduce the actions of others, and basic social affiliative needs – pave the way for the development of the insight that symbols serve as representations of entities outside of themselves (see Fig. 1 for more details on this model of symbolic development). To understand better whether symbolic development is domain-general or specific, more research needs to be devoted to the study of this development both across symbolic systems and across cultures.

Selected contemporary topics

Foundational knowledge

Foundational knowledge refers to fundamental insights that change the way we view the world, such as the concept that objects continue to exist even when we no longer see them. In the domain of physical knowledge, children between the ages of 3 and 10 years appear to judge objects on the basis of what kind of thing it is and generalize their knowledge to similar kinds of things. Children at this age also appear to have a naïve theory of matter as they judge that irrelevant changes of size and weight do not have an impact on enduring physical properties like material. In the domain of psychological understanding, commonly called theory of mind, it is clear that by 3 to 4 years children turn to desires, emotions, and perceptions as the explanatory cons-tructs for people's actions. By 5 years, children come to understand the role of beliefs in predicting and explaining action. Specifically, at this age children have the critical insight that another person could hold a belief that is false, that is different from their own, and that will result in a particular action.

Further refinement of psychological understanding is found in 6- to 10-year-olds who begin to make correct judgments of actions based on the more subtle distinc-tions of mixed, hidden, and social (pride, shame, and guilt) emotions. In the domain of biological knowledge, there is evidence that preschool children have core knowledge of a very basic distinction between animate/inanimate entities and know, for example, that animals breathe, eat, have similar body parts, and so on. However, there is equally compelling evidence to suggest they have persistent misconceptions surrounding animacy that undergo radical re-organization during childhood.

Memory

The study of memory in childhood has recently focused on a variety of themes including strategies, domain knowledge, and eyewitness testimony to name a few. Children do not appear to utilize memory strategies spontaneously for improving recall prior to early elementary school age, but can be easily trained to use them even in the preschool years. A number of studies have shown that increasing amounts of knowledge within a domain improves accuracy and influences how information is organized in memory. For example,

Figure 2. Mother and toddler in market in Thailand.

children who were chess experts sometimes reached the same level of performance as adult experts, and were better than adult novices at recalling meaningful chess arrangements. In eyewitness testimony research, preschoolers are usually found to be accurate, especially for personally meaningful information, but they recall less information than older children. Preschoolers are also more suggestible than older children, and a number of researchers have identified specific characteristics of questions that lead these youngsters astray, helping forensic psychologists to improve interview techniques for child witnesses.

Reasoning

Reasoning can be based on a variety of relationships between kinds, including perceptual and conceptual similarities, analogies, and rules. Children are clearly influenced in their reasoning by perceptual similarity, but so too are adults. As they get older and gain knowledge about the concepts and categories in their world, their reasoning will focus more on features that define category membership (e.g., has wings made of feathers) than on simple perceptual features (e.g., is yellow). Children of 3 to 6 years can reason analogically about causal relations as long as they are familiar with the relationship (e.g., cutting results in more pieces), and even adults have difficulty reasoning about more complex causal relations such as the dynamics of objects.

Figure 3. Preschoolers in Peru.

Young preschoolers are fairly rigid rule followers, and once they learn a rule they have difficulty changing it. They can also induce relatively abstract rules, such as 'pick the one that's different' across diverse problems. What is clear from research in this field is that while the content of knowledge may become more complex over development, even very young children are remarkably adept at using the same learning, memory, and reasoning tools that serve adults well.

Future directions for research: situating a biological organism in a cultural context

In contemporary cognitive development research, a marriage of perspectives is emerging that focuses on the initial states of knowledge and processes, as well as on the contexts in which these subsequently develop.

Social and cultural influences on cognitive development

Recently, a number of researchers have shown that a variety of social factors, those that are core to the learning occurring in close social interactions, are fundamental to cognitive development. For example, symbolic functioning has been found to improve as a result of certain parenting practices, the verbal and pre-verbal communication styles of parents, and adult modeling. A few researchers have gone outside of the dominant American-European context to examine the role of cultural factors, and found both universal trends as well as diversity in cognitive developmental outcome. More studies of social influences are needed, especially those that compare across diverse cultures, to help us understand what is universal in early development and how open subsequent development is to influence from cultural forces. Researchers need to clarify the extent to which diversity in early experience, such as in the Thai preschooler who spends her days with her mother in her market stall, or the Peruvian preschoolers who learn to march with their teacher (see Figs. 2 and 3), leads to diversity in developmental outcome.

Cultural and sociocultural conceptualizations of development.

A rather new paradigm shift is taking hold whereby cognitive development is construed as a process of co-construction between children and their cultural context (Rogoff, 2003). For example, in a growing body of research, evidence is found that even early in life a concept of self is developed through participation in a given cultural system of meanings and practices that can be distinctive, and hence may effect diverse developmental outcomes. Many researchers in this area have focused on distinctive notions of self that emerge in cultures that encourage collaboration and interdependence between people as compared to those that foster individual achievement and independence. However, there is no simple principle of developmental outcome given cultural context; diversity can develop within as well as between broadly defined cultural groups.

Conclusions

A general theme that emerges from this review is that cognitive development beyond infancy appears to be based on both biological pre-dispositions and sociocultural experiences. Fundamental questions have been raised that need to be addressed in future research. What are the initial states of knowledge in humans? To what degree are these initial states modifiable by experience? Is there continuity in the processes underlying cognitive development? Are domains of knowledge and the symbol systems used to manipulate that knowledge sharply bounded in encapsulated modules? Or are the boundaries between domains and symbol systems more permeable? Specifically, can expertise in one domain influence development in another?

Infancy research will continue to address these fundamental questions by identifying the importance of prenatal development and the initial state of the human organism before postnatal experience in the physical and social world. Child research that looks for universal milestones of cognitive development across diverse cultures, especially in the early years, can also help to answer these questions. When a study of universality is coupled with a search for the diversity of outcomes that are afforded by cultural influences, it can potentially lead to a deeper understanding of human cognitive development.

See also:
Constructivist theories; Theories of the child's mind; Dynamical systems approaches; Cross-cultural comparisons; Cognitive development in infancy; Motor development; Social development; Language development; Development of learning and memory; Executive functions; Imitation; Play; Selfhood; Socialization; Anthropology; Jean Piaget; Lev S. Vygotsky

Further reading

W. Damon (series ed.), and D. Kuhn and R. S. Siegler (vol. eds.) (1999). *Handbook of Child Psychology*, 5th edn. Vol. II: *Cognition, Perception and Language*. New York: Wiley.

Goswami, U. (ed.) (2003). *Blackwell Handbook of Childhood Cognitive Development*. Malden, MA: Blackwell.

Tomasello, M. (1999). *The Cultural Origins of Human Cognition*. Cambridge, MA: Harvard University Press.

Perceptual development

SCOTT P. JOHNSON, ERIN E. HANNON, & DIMA AMSO

Introduction

Casual observations of infants reveal little evidence that they have knowledge of relationships among objects or people, that they understand cause and effect, or that they have any kind of commonsense notions of objects, space, or time. Indeed, it can be hard to tell if an infant has functioning senses at all. But how accurate is this characterization? How much do infants know about their environment? How well are infants able to discover visual, auditory, and other kinds of important information that surrounds them in determining the fundamental facts of the world? And how might we find out, given that infants have few or no linguistic abilities to tell us what they know?

Remarkable advances in methods in the second half of the 20th century, coupled with the ingenuity and curiosity of dedicated researchers, have begun to sketch some answers to these important questions. The central focus of much of this research has been the nature and limits of infant perception and its development, because perception is the principal means through which we acquire information about the environment. As we shall see, infants are initially well equipped to make sense of their world. Vision is partly organized from birth, as is coordination of perception and action systems (such as hearing and head turning), and there are important developments in these abilities during and after infancy. Compared to vision, audition, olfaction, and touch are more mature at birth, relatively speaking. Intermodal perception (detection and integration of information about a single event from multiple sources, such as vision and audition) begins early, but there are fundamental improvements across infancy. Within weeks and months following birth, infants develop the capacity to comprehend complex associations among objects and events. However, perception of higher-order relations does not seem to be available as early as are basic perceptual abilities.

Visual perception

Basic visual functions

In order to see the objects and events in the environment, infants must be able to discern detail, to see motion, and to distinguish between various levels of brightness, colors, and patterns, as well as detect depth differences among object surfaces. In addition, they must be able to direct their visual attention appropriately to selected targets. Studies of newborn infants have revealed that they are born with the rudiments of these abilities, and there is rapid improvement across the first several months after birth (Atkinson, 2000).

Acuity is rather poor at birth, estimated to be between 20/200 and 20/400 for most newborns, but improves quickly over the next few months, along with contrast sensitivity and wavelength sensitivity. Development of motion perception is somewhat more complex, due in part to the diverse nature of motion information itself (Fig. 1). Sensitivity to different types of motion develops at different rates, suggesting differences in maturation of separate processing mechanisms, but these differences are not large, and full motion sensitivity is probably nearly complete by 6 months (Banton & Bertenthal, 1997). Taken together, research on these fundamental visual functions indicates that vision is near adult levels by 6–8 months after birth, though other visual capacities continue to develop over months, even years, beyond this time.

Depth perception, likewise, appears to develop in a piecemeal fashion. True depth perception is the ability to detect absolute distance, but most experiments exploring depth perception in infancy have tested responses to the relative distance of objects, without necessarily any perception of absolute distance. The first depth cue to which infants are sensitive is kinetic depth information. There are two of these motion-based cues, kinetic occlusion and motion parallax. Infants have been found to be sensitive to kinetic depth information

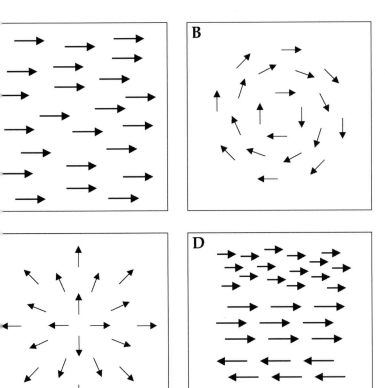

Figure 1. Four kinds of motion processed by the visual system. All visible motion is produced by movement of points in the visual image, relative to the observer. A. Translation: image points move together across the scene. B. Rotation: image points rotate around a single locus. C. Expansion/contraction: image points move out from, or toward, a single locus. D. Shear: image points in distinct areas of the scene move relative to one another, either at different rates, in different directions, or both. One or more of these patterns can be produced either by motion of objects in the environment, or by movement of the observer. Figure adapted from T. O. Banton & B. I. Bertenthal, 1997. Multiple developmental pathways for motion processing. *Optometry and Vision Science*, 9, 751–760.

as early as two months after birth, and perhaps earlier.

The second depth cue to which infants become sensitive is binocular disparity (also known as stereopsis). This provides information about relative distances of objects as a function of their relative horizontal positions in the visual field. Binocular disparity is especially useful at providing information about distances of objects and surfaces within reach, and adults are able to make extremely fine-grained discriminations of depth in near space (e.g., in threading a needle). Sensitivity to binocular disparity emerges between 3 and 5 months in most infants. Finally, there is a class of information composed of pictorial depth cues (Fig. 2). Despite the fact that there are so many pictorial depth cues, the ability to extract information about depth from such cues commonly appears between 5 and 7 months.

By 7 months, therefore, infants have nearly fully developed depth perception abilities (Yonas & Granrud, 1984). Their emergence is fortuitous, linked probably to progress in the development of basic abilities such as reaching for objects and independent locomotion.

Visual attention

Research on attention in infancy reveals a complex pattern of development that is best described with reference to two kinds of attentional mechanism: overt and covert attention. There are four kinds of overt eye movements: optokinetic and vestibulo-ocular responses, saccades, and smooth pursuit (Fig. 3). Optokinetic eye movements occur in response to large-field motion, or whole-scale movement of the visual field, such as when looking out the window of a moving train. Vestibulo-ocular eye movements occur to compensate for head and body motion when the observer's goal is to fixate a stationary (or moving) target. Both these eye movement patterns can be observed at birth. Saccades, too, can be elicited at birth, and these consist of a series of scans from one object to another. However, saccades and scanning undergo improvements across the first four months after birth such that they seem to become more purposive and less random, changes that are thought to reflect underlying maturation of the ability to direct overt attention volitionally (as opposed to reflexively). Finally, there is smooth pursuit, the ability to track small moving targets with a smooth eye movement pattern. This ability emerges within three to four months after birth, with the timing similar to that of motion discrimination, suggesting some direct or indirect relation between the two. In contrast to overt orienting, emergence of covert attention requires much longer to reach adult-like competence, and may take several years to develop fully, perhaps due to increasing demands imposed by its inherently cognitive nature.

Higher-level visual functions

If many basic visual functions appear to be in place at or around birth, followed by rapid improvements across infancy, what about more complex, higher-level visual functions? The best evidence to date reveals a general trend: infants at first do not perceive higher-order relations among visible object parts and motion. With experience and maturation of the visual system, they become able to integrate information across time and space. Some kinds of integration emerge rapidly, but others take many months or years of experience.

Examples of higher-level visual perception that emerge within the first year after birth are perception of illusory contours, perception of causality, perception of object unity, and perception of biological motion (Fig. 4). Initially, infants perceive the individual elements in these stimuli as disconnected and, perhaps, unrelated. Adults, in contrast, tend to see the relations among elements easily. For example, when viewing a partly occluded object moving behind a horizontal screen, newborns perceive the top and bottom object parts. However, they do not seem to perceive yet that the two visible parts of the object moving behind the screen are actually connected. By 2 months, and only under certain circumstances, infants begin to perceive the visible parts of the object as connected (i.e., if the parts of a regular, smooth shape move together). It is not until 8 months that infants seem to begin perceiving object unity regardless of shape. An analogous developmental trend is evident in research on perception of causality, although the age at which full causal perception is in place is probably after 12 months.

Examples of visual stimuli that are not perceived accurately until later in childhood include displays in which an object moves behind a screen with an aperture, such that only small portions are visible at any one moment through the opening. The observer's task in this case is to perceive the entire shape or extent of the object despite the challenge imposed by aperture viewing, and it appears that children have difficulty with such tasks even into the school-age years. A second example is a display in which small elements are arranged to form a global pattern, as when most are scattered randomly but a small sub-set form a shape that is camouflaged by the other members of the stimulus. Such patterns are often not at all visible to young children.

In summary, many basic visual functions are in place at birth or within several months after birth, such as the ability to see detail, color, and motion, and the ability to direct attention with the eyes to scan large static stimuli or to track small moving objects. Depth perception takes the better part of the first postnatal year to develop, and some aspects of covert attention take longer still. The ability to integrate information (e.g., object parts) across space and time, likewise, takes several months or years to develop fully.

Auditory perception

Basic auditory perception

The task of hearing is different in several respects than vision. Firstly, the auditory system is more highly developed at birth than is the visual system in terms of basic function, as determined by such metrics as sensitivity thresholds, by assessing discrimination of frequency, loudness, and timbre, and by examining temporal resolution. Secondly, a listener does not

Figure 2. Pictorial cues to depth and distance. A. Texture gradients: the individual squares of concrete that compose the sidewalk become progressively smaller as they are higher in the picture plane. B. Linear perspective: the boundary lines of the sidewalk become closer together as they are higher in the picture plane. C. Occlusion: the walking man occludes part of the tree and fence, and is perceived as relatively closer to the vantage point. D & E. Familiar and relative size: the observer has knowledge of the general height of people, and their comparative size provides information for their distances relative to the observer. F. Height in the picture plane: the position of the base of each tree provides information for its distance relative to the observer.

have to face in direction of an object or an event in order to receive and attend to auditory information. Nevertheless, we often turn toward the direction of a sound, a process known as localization. As with vision, however, there are important developments in these functions, though the pace of improvement is not as steep as it is in many visual tasks. Not surprisingly, we see earlier emergence of competence in the context of simple perceptual discrimination tasks and later-developing proficiency in relation to more complex tasks, also in parallel with vision.

Humans start hearing about two-thirds of the way through gestation. The cochlea is structurally mature by the end of pregnancy (although it may still undergo important developments in the first few weeks after birth), and fetuses are sensitive to auditory information in the womb that is retained after birth. For example, newborns prefer recordings of their own mother's speech to another woman uttering the same words, a preference likely based on prenatal exposure. Auditory sensitivity thresholds in infants, however, are higher than those of adults, meaning simply that infants have reduced auditory sensitivity. Newborn thresholds are

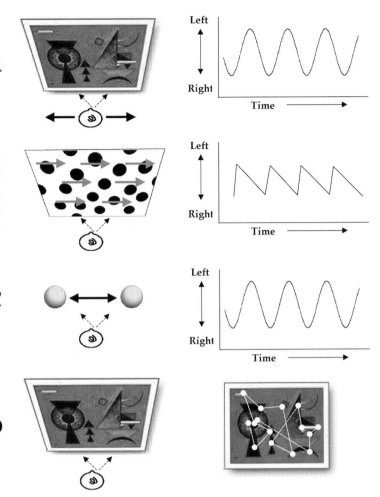

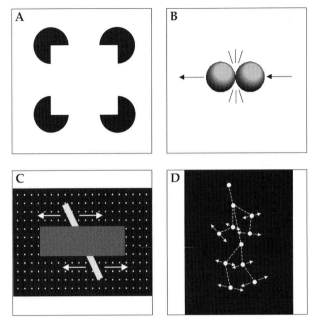

Figure 4. Examples of stimuli that require integration of visual information across space and/or time. Very young infants do not perceive the displays in the same way as do adults, implying that general improvements in spatiotemporal integration are required to achieve higher-level visual processing. A. Illusory contours. The square is readily seen by adults, but is not defined by visible boundaries. B. A causality display. Adults perceive the first ball as launching the second. C. Object unity. In this example, the rod parts are aligned and move together. D. Biological motion, produced in this example by attaching luminous patches to the joints of a walking human figure. The dotted lines and arrows are provided for illustrative purposes, and serve to highlight the relative motions and positions of the luminous points in producing the percept.

Figure 3. Four kinds of eye movement. These schematic illustrations depict an overhead view of an infant observing a stationary or moving stimulus in panels A–D at left; in panels A–C at right are idealized graphs showing horizontal eye movements (i.e., left and right), and a series of fixations and saccades in panel D. A. Vestibulo-ocular response. The infant is moved back and forth while viewing a stationary pattern. The eyes move back and forth in the opposite direction to the motion of the infant to maintain stable gaze on the target. The vestibulo-ocular response can be elicited at birth. B. Optokinetic response. The infant is stationary while viewing a large display of smoothly moving elements that are replaced at one side (here, at left) as they move off the screen on the other side (here, at right). The eyes fixate a single target element as it moves, then 'snap' back to find another element, track it, snap back to find another element, and so forth, producing an alternating slow-fast sawtooth pattern. This response can be elicited at birth. C. Smooth pursuit. The infant is stationary while viewing a small target that moves across the visual field. As the object translates back and forth, the infant tracks it with smooth eye movements that keep the object fixated. Very young infants exhibit little smooth pursuit as their eye movements tend to be jerky and lag behind that of the object. D. Saccades. The infant is stationary and views a stationary stimulus with a series of stable fixations interspersed with quick eye movements (saccades), the most common eye movement pattern when observers inspect a scene. Improvements in scanning efficiency can be observed over the first six months after birth.

closer to adults in the lower frequencies, but different in the higher frequency range. In adults, audibility is more sensitive as frequency gets higher. The shape of infant audibility curves becomes more adult-like (less flat) by 6 months, but thresholds are still elevated across the frequency range.

The greater improvement of higher over lower frequency thresholds continues through childhood until about 10 years of age, when children's thresholds resemble those of adults across all frequency ranges and even surpass adult thresholds at very high frequencies, such as 20 kHz. There is still some debate as to whether behavioral changes in thresholds result from the development of the ear and cochlea, changes in the auditory nervous system, or from non-sensory processes such as attention and motivation. However, the variability of the audibility curves is fairly similar for infants and adults, suggesting that age differences reflect true changes in sensory capacities (Werner & Gray, 1998). Infants and children also have elevated masked thresholds. Some of the apparent developmental differences may be due to improvements in attention, or 'selective listening.'

How well can infants and children detect differences in frequency, loudness, and timbre? Even newborns can detect large differences in pitch, and improvements in discrimination occur more rapidly for high than for low relative pitch. At 3 months, infants' frequency discrimination is generally poor, and low frequency discrimination is better than high frequency discrimination. At 5–8 months, however, infants can discriminate higher frequency changes (1–3 kHz) with an accuracy close to adult discrimination. In contrast, for lower frequencies such as 440 Hz, more improvement in discrimination occurs between the ages of 4 and 6 years (Werner & Gray, 1998).

Current findings are mostly based on a presentation of pure tones to the infants despite the fact that sounds heard in nature are complex, being composed of a fundamental frequency and many component frequencies above it (which often are harmonically related to the fundamental). When the relative amplitudes of these frequency components change, so does the timbre of the sound, and such changes allow us to discriminate between, say, different vowels or musical instruments. Infants can discriminate vowels soon after birth, and by 7 months they can categorize complex tones on the basis of timbre. However, when older children (4–9 years) are tested in a more naturalistic task involving masking noise, even the oldest children do not yet demonstrate an adult level of discriminability.

Good temporal resolution early in infancy may be essential for language acquisition. There is evidence that newborns can detect gaps and tempo changes in an auditory stream, and that their sensitivity to such sound features continues to develop into childhood. Sensitivity to rapid auditory changes is important for representing phonemes in speech. Normal children have significantly smaller gap detection thresholds than the thresholds of children from families with a known history of language impairment.

A final aspect of basic auditory function to be discussed is proficiency at localization, which is one of the earliest complex coordinated actions reliably expressed at birth. Newborns are able to discriminate between the general direction of a sound (left or right, far or near), but they are rather inaccurate at orienting toward more subtle variations in location. It is likely that the representation of auditory space is somewhat unstable until the head reaches a fixed size (and the interaural timing and intensity differences between inputs to the two ears become fixed). A second possible explanation is that binaural hearing involves basic auditory processes requiring some degree of brain maturation. Because the brain undergoes much more postnatal development than the peripheral auditory system, changes in localization accuracy may depend on auditory cortex maturation (Werner & Gray, 1998).

Higher-level auditory function

In everyday life, sounds need to be sorted out in order to be perceived as meaningful information, not mere noises or auditory cacophony. How do listeners determine which sounds are important, which components of a complex sound belong together, and which sounds are separate despite their temporal simultaneity? Adults group incoming sound according to spectral, pitch, intensity, and spatial information. Discrepancies in these parameters predict the perception of separate versus unified sound sources. Infants' perceptual grouping abilities parallel those of adults in many ways. For example, streaming that results from pitch, timbre, and spatial proximity interferes with adults' as well as with the newborn's abilities to discriminate a cycling melody from its opposite, suggesting that at least some basic organizational mechanisms are present at birth.

The abilities of 6- and 8-month-old infants to detect duration changes placed between pitch-based perceptual groups (such as AAA EEE) are greatly diminished in comparison to their detection of duration changes placed within perceptual groups (such as AA AEEE). Likewise, young infants group musical phrases according to melody, and discriminate among different melodies according to contour. In fact, infants are better than adults at perceiving certain 'mistunings' in the musical contexts of other cultures, such as when a Western listener hears a Javanese scale, suggesting that musical perception abilities are tuned with experience.

Language acquisition has long been an important topic of study, but the development of speech perception has received less attention, perhaps because of very young infants' striking and precocious capacities for many aspects of speech perception. This may have led many past researchers to assume that speech perception abilities are already in place at birth, and that language learning occurs independent of the sound patterns characteristic of speech. More recently, researchers have found that many aspects of infant speech processing are indeed adult-like at an early age, but there are several important developmental changes that take place over the first year after birth. For example, 2- to 3-month-old infants, like adults, can discriminate the fine acoustical differences between phonemes such as /da/, /ba/, and /pa/ (Werker & Tees, 1999). Infants shift their perception of phonemes in a manner similar to adults, in the sense that they detect some equal-sized acoustical changes along a continuum more readily than others. Some researchers have called this the 'perceptual magnet effect' because non-prototypical members of a phonemic category are drawn toward, or perceived as more similar to, a phonetic prototype rather than to each other.

Several findings actually suggest that for some types of phonetic contrast, young infants' performance is superior to that of adults. Adults can discriminate phonetic contrasts that are used to differentiate meaning in their own language, but are poor perceivers of contrasts unique to other languages. A classic example of these adult limitations comes from Japanese adults, who often cannot perceive the difference between /r/ and /l/, let alone pronounce it. Adults may also have difficulty discriminating contrasts that occur in their own lan–guage but are not used to distinguish meaning, such as /da/ versus /sta/ without the [s]: native English-speaking adults hear the two as identical (Werker & Tees, 1999). In contrast, before 6 months of age, infants can discriminate all contrasts in native and non-native languages, but not some of those that do not occur in any language. By 10–12 months, however, infant auditory perception becomes much more adult-like, with attenuated perception of non-native (but not native) contrasts. This re-organization in sensitivity may mark a general trend from universal discrimination abilities to an expertise that is more language-specific.

In summary, infants begin hearing even before birth, and many basic auditory functions are in place within several months, such as the ability to distinguish different frequencies, timbres, tempos, and levels of loudness. Even newborns are able to localize sounds by head turning. Finding the units of the auditory stream is a more protracted process, and there is ample evidence for perceptual 'tuning' upon exposure to music and speech, another phenomenon that is extended across development.

Intermodal perception

We do not merely watch events unfold, as more often than not we also hear them. Objects are not just seen, but also heard, touched, and sometimes (especially by infants) tasted and smelled. How do individuals come to understand the relation between different types of simultaneous sensory experience?

Many studies have suggested that infants are capable of perceiving and understanding intermodal relations. Newborns can perceive some arbitrary auditory-visual relations presented during a period of familiarization (e.g., a particular shape paired with a particular sound). However, most intermodal relations in the world are not arbitrary, but rather specific. Some of these real-world intermodal relations are described as amodal. For example, speech can be simultaneously heard and seen in a talking face. By 6 months, infants are able to detect some changes in auditory-visual synchrony and microstructure. Infants were familiarized with auditory-visual events with the same synchrony, such that visual impact corresponds with a sound, and microstructure, so that the number of objects involved

in the impact is reflected in the complexity of the sound. They subsequently noticed a change in both the synchrony and the microstructure. In contrast, same-age infants tested following familiarization with events that were not matched for synchrony or microstructure did not appear to notice changes in those relations. Other studies point to synchronization of onset and offset of intermodal information as an important cue for binding across modalities (Lewkowicz, 2000).

Infants' abilities to coordinate auditory-visual events may depend also on the intermodal temporal contiguity window (Lewkowicz, 2000). In order to accurately detect changes in synchrony, 2- to 8-month-old infants need a difference of 350 ms with a sound that preceded a bounce, and a 450 ms gap when the bounce preceded the sound. In contrast, adults require an asynchrony of 65 ms for detecting that the sound preceded the bounce, and 112 ms for detecting that the bounce preceded the sound. The differences in detection as a function of which modality stimulus came first may be due to the longer neural transduction speed of the visual as opposed to the auditory signals as auditory temporal resolution is superior to visual temporal resolution.

Another example of how intermodal perception develops involves matching a shape that is perceived both visually and haptically (i.e., by touch). This ability does not appear to be functional in very young infants, but, by 4–5 months, infants can recognize the unity or independence of two objects, either joined rigidly or with a string. However, findings on tactile-visual matching are rather inconsistent and much remains to be learned in this area.

All told, many studies suggest that, at a very early age, infants are sensitive to some intermodal relations. Other findings suggest that intermodal perception for amodal pairings emerges only after 6 months or older, suggesting that at least some intermodal relations are learned through experience, or at least come on-line only after particular modalities reach certain developmental levels (Lewkowicz, 2000).

Other senses

In contrast to the many empirical studies on develop-ment of vision, audition, and intermodal perception in infancy, other perceptual systems such as gustation (taste), olfaction (smell), and touch have received relatively little attention. Though this research literature is smaller, evidence exists demonstrating a remarkable organization at birth in the ability to seek olfactory and tactile information that is meaningful to the infant. The best example of this organization is sensitivity to different odors in newborn infants. Newborns are particularly proficient at olfactory discrimination, being capable of discriminating between the scent of their own mother's breast milk or amniotic fluid, and those of a female stranger. Other kinds of early olfactory discrimination are evident as well (e.g., between common spices). These well-developed abilities, particularly in the sensitivity to maternal odor, suggest that the uterine environment may be akin to a 'liquid atmosphere' rich in chemicals that stimulate developing chemoreceptors in the nasal membranes of the fetus. The particular mix of substances, unique to each mother, may initiate a special receptivity to her smell upon birth (Schaal, Orgeur, & Rognon, 1995).

Studies of infant touch, likewise, have revealed the prenatal origins of coordinated movements, and there is evidence for the rudiments of a cooperative interplay between vision, hand-mouth coordination, and taste that is functional at birth: newborns given a weak sucrose solution showed an increase over baseline in hand-mouth contacts. They also exhibit differentiation of objects placed in the mouth (e.g., pacifiers varying in shape and substance). Improvements in movement coordination are observed over the next several months, the most obvious example being reaching (Rochat & Senders, 1991).

Conclusions

Careful, controlled studies, employing highly specialized methods, suggest that human infants are born with perceptual mechanisms that are highly tuned to information specifying objects and events in the world. Sensory systems undergo much development over the first months after birth and become able to make increasingly subtle discriminations, but, from the start of postnatal experience, infants can discover many of the individual sensory units that surround them and make up the perceptual environment. With ontogeny comes the ability to put smaller units of information together into coherent, enduring wholes that have substance and meaning. This development accompanies and contributes to later abstract reasoning and other higher levels of cognitive operations.

See also:
Ethological theories; Experimental methods; Normal and abnormal prenatal development; The status of the human newborn; Cognitive development in infancy; Cognitive development beyond infancy; Motor development; Speech development; Language development; Development of learning and memory; Attention; Brain and behavioral development (I): sub-cortical; Brain and behavioral development (II): cortical; Connectionist modeling; Locomotion; Prehension; Hearing disorders; Behavioral embryology; Cognitive neuroscience

Further reading

Hopkins, B. and Johnson, S. P. (eds.) (2003). *Neurobiology of Infant Vision*. Westport, CT: Praeger.

Jusczyk, P. W. (1997). *The Discovery of Spoken Language*. Cambridge, MA: MIT Press.

Kellman, P. J. and Arterberry, M. E. (1998). *The Cradle of Knowledge: Development of Perception in Infancy*. Cambridge, MA: MIT Press.

Motor development

BEATRIX VEREIJKEN

Introduction

When a newborn infant makes an entry into our life, every movement and motor achievement become the focus of attention for an extended audience. For years to come, parents will proudly report to friends and family what new ability their infant has demonstrated for the first time today, and change their house and behavior in accordance with the changing capacities of the new addition to the family. Professionals in baby-care clinics closely follow the child's progression from one stage of motor competence to the next, so that they can estimate the functional integrity of the infant's nervous system. For their part, psychologists carefully study changes in motor behaviors to advance their understanding of motor development in particular and the process of development in general, and to predict possible problems of development like delays, abnormalities, or neural disorders.

Throughout history, scientific interest in motor development has waxed and waned. After centuries of sporadic interest from philosophers and biologists, motor development became a focal point of attention in psychology during the first half of the 20th century. Pioneering developmental scientists like Arnold Gesell, Myrtle McGraw, and Mary Shirley provided fine-grained descriptions of countless motor stages children pass through in their seemingly orderly march to adulthood. The resulting elaborate catalogues of motor milestones, combined with the prevailing view that development was genetically programmed, left subsequent developmental psychologists with little to do. Motor development seemed to be both described and understood. When interest shifted to cognitive psychology and information processing in the 1960s, research on motor development as good as vanished from the scientific literature. By way of example, there has not been an independent chapter on motor development in the *Handbook of Child Psychology* since the mid-1940s.

The rise of dynamical systems theory since the early 1980s and the realization that even the more 'psychological' domains of perceptual, cognitive, and social development are heavily mediated by the development of movement and posture, gave a renewed impulse to the interest in motor behavior and its development. This change in emphasis in the study of motor development is reflected in the most recent *Handbook of Child Psychology* (1998), in which a chapter is included by Bennett Bertenthal and Rachel Clifton on perception and action. Nowadays, motor development is studied both in its own right, and as an early testing ground for general principles of development.

Descriptions of motor development and learning

The humble beginnings

Initially, the newborn infant seems anything but a deft movement artist. On the contrary, movements seem erratic, accidental, and reflective of a poor level of motor control. Yet, at a second more thorough look, we see hints and signs of admirable control, even in the newborn. One example is the exquisite coordination of sucking-swallowing-breathing cycles during feeding, and another the use of crying as an effective captor of attention. And even the earliest attempts of newborns to use their flailing arms are more goal-directed and less random than we once presumed.

Of course, the newborn does not arrive in our life as a clean sheet. Development, including motor development, started many months before birth, giving the fetus ample opportunity to start exercising body parts while still in the womb. Ground-breaking research on prenatal activity, started in the 1980s by Heinz Prechtl and co-workers, showed in fact that fetal behavior was largely unaltered by birth. Using real-time ultrasound recordings to monitor the movements of the fetus, they highlighted a remarkable continuity between newborn and prenatal behaviors. In that respect, birth does not mark as dramatic a transition for the fetus as was once widely held.

The organized newborn

Compared to many other mammals, the nervous system of the human newborn is relatively underdeveloped at birth. Brain development after birth includes dramatic changes in the number of neurons and their connectivity, cell migration, cell differentiation, myelination of axons, and glia tissue. The newborn state of affairs leaves the infant with limited possibilities for skilled actions, and has led several authors to characterize the newborn as an 'extrauterine fetus.' Despite the immaturity of the nervous system and ensuing precarious control of voluntary body movements, newborn behavior is surprisingly well organized and displays a wide range of behaviors, even at such a young age. Newborns can habituate to vision, sounds, and touch, orient eye and head movements, and modulate their sucking rate on a pacifier to effectuate events in the environment such as focusing a film projection on a screen, choosing between alternate soundtracks, or selecting their mother's voice on a loudspeaker.

In addition to these voluntary-like and goal-directed movements, there is a wide range of so-called infantile responses, organized behaviors that can be elicited from the newborn under specific environmental conditions. Well-known examples are the grasp response, the rooting response, the Moro response, the asymmetrical tonic neck reaction, the Babinski response, and the stepping response.

Another common feature of behavior during infancy are the so-called rhythmical stereotypies, which consist of rapid, repetitive movements of the head, torso, and limbs. As described by Esther Thelen (1941–2004), healthy infants spend an average of approximately 5 percent of their waking time engaged in this behavior, which takes the form of, for example, scratching the skin, swaying the body back and forth, waving the arms, banging objects, kicking the legs, or bouncing up and down in so-called baby bouncers. She suggests that these repetitive movements serve to promote the development of neuromuscular coordination and timing which, in turn, benefit the development of temporal and spatial characteristics of gross motor abilities. In children with Down's syndrome and blind children, frequencies of rhythmical movements are much higher, reaching levels up to as much as 40 percent of waking time. High frequencies of rhythmical stereotypies can thus signal underlying neurological damage.

New abilities and subsequent improvements

At about 3 months of age, dramatic changes take place in the development of infants. They achieve unsupported head control allowing the eyes and head to move together, visual abilities improve (e.g., visual acuity), and they display longer periods of wakefulness without crying. Whereas newborn behavior was largely state-dependent, the infants now start to exert increasing state control. In the words of Nathaniel Kleitman, they move on from 'wakefulness of necessity' to 'wakefulness of choice.' On the performance front, the above changes are mirrored by marked improvements in motor control. Whereas newborn and fetal behaviors were continuous, movements now become qualitatively different. Control of arm and hand movements becomes more functional, several infantile responses start to diminish and disappear, and the remaining responses and spontaneous movements come increasingly under afferent control. The state of alert activity increases and, to the delight of their parents, infants start flashing their first social smile.

From this age on, infants steadily acquire one motor milestone after the other, each new accomplishment reflecting increasing postural control and advancing mastery over internal and external forces. They start to reach and grasp, demonstrate increasing control of first the sitting then the standing posture, learn to crawl (Adolph, Vereijken, & Denny, 1998) and, around the end of the first year, they begin to walk, first with support, later independently (Adolph, Vereijken, & Shrout, 2003). The early developmental psychologists in particular described each identifiable milestone in such meticulous detail that their publications still represent valuable resources about motor development to date. Figure 1 depicts Shirley's famous illustration of motor milestones. It portrays the major milestones in the first fifteen months of life, spanning the period from the curled-up posture of a newborn to the erect, bipedal toddler.

This sequence of motor milestones reflects increasing control over posture and movement in a gravitational field, with each new postural achievement marking a small victory over gravity. By the time infants have mastered the erect posture for standing and walking without support, they basically master the fundamental components underlying further development of both fine and gross motor abilities. Development then takes the shape of improving existing abilities and enlarging the movement repertoire with additional ones. Grasping for small items, for example, develops from a rather clumsy palmar grasp to a refined pincer grip. The early walking pattern becomes extended to include running, jumping, hopping, and skipping. Throwing movements develop from a simple underarm throw to a complex

Figure 1. Depiction of motor milestones from fetal posture (top left) to walk alone (bottom right). From M. M. Shirley, 1933. *The First Two Years: A Study of Twenty-five Babies*. Minneapolis: University of Minnesota Press.

overarm throw accompanied by a contralateral step. And several abilities are combined to form complex activities such as climbing and swimming, and bouncing, hitting, or kicking a ball.

Processes of motor development and learning

Characteristics of motor development and learning

When looking at motor development 'from the outside' (i.e., describing its appearance), one fundamental characteristic about its nature readily stands out. Motor development is strongly interactive, and as such reverberates at many different levels. At the most common everyday level, movements typically reflect an interaction with the environment through the musculoskeletal system. Children act upon the environment, extract information from it, and effect changes in it. This continuous interaction between the organism and its environment formed one of the cornerstones of James J. Gibson's (1904–1979) ecological theory of perception, and became known as the perception-action cycle. Organisms have to act in order to perceive, and

perceive in order to act. Which one has primacy in development becomes a moot debate, a chicken and egg problem. This interactive cycle is mirrored within the nervous system in that the gradual growth of new structures enables new functions, the repeated execution of which allows further development of structures. Neither one has primacy over the other. Development in both is necessary for continued increase in and improvement of the behavioral repertoire. The same stand is echoed extensively in the writings of Piaget.

The significance of repeated perception-action cycles stretches far beyond the domains of perceptual and motor development. In 1988, Eleanor J. Gibson (1910–2003) argued that perception-action cycles in infancy often take the form of exploratory behavior and form the building blocks for the acquisition of knowledge, and thus for the development of cognition. It is only by exploring the world that we learn about its objects, events, and regularities. By manipulating objects, infants gain knowledge about their form, texture, taste, and rigidity. In that respect, the status of early motor development paces development in other domains. With the ability to control arm and hand movements, comes the possibility for infants to grasp objects and explore them. With the development of self-induced mobility, an infant can follow an object rolling out of sight and discover that it has not disappeared. Likewise, by interacting with other children and adults, infants learn about the social structure of their culture, its rules, and its language. This pervasive interplay between new motor achievements and other arenas of development has been exquisitely described by Campos and his colleagues (2000). Taking the onset of self-produced locomotion as an exemplary case, they illustrate the intricate interplay between motor experience and subsequent transitions in perception, spatial cognition, and social and emotional development.

There is another striking characteristic of early motor development and learning that is linked to the previous discussion. Young infants are critically dependent upon information from the environment to aid their memory. That is, early motor development and learning are highly context-specific. This point is illustrated by the research program of Carolyn Rovee-Collier on infant memory. By using the ability of young infants to learn the contingency between their own body movements and subsequent jiggling of attractive overhead mobiles, she and her colleagues have shown that early memory depends on detailed replication of the context. Small changes in the crib, mobile, or ambient environment disrupt the memory of the mobile task even after one day. With increasing age and skill level, performance becomes more and more independent of the context and transfers more readily to other contexts, and sometimes even to other tasks. The issue of specificity and transfer will be considered in more detail later in this entry.

Explaining motor development and learning

The processes of motor development and learning have been explained in a variety of different theories, as attested to by entries in Part I. As progression through the series of motor milestones seemed universal rather than unique to each infant, the pioneering developmental scientists sought explanation of development in terms of cortical maturation, a process driven by our common genetic heritage. Those focusing on motor learning, on the other hand, tended to emphasize stages of information processing and the conditions under which optimal learning could take place. Although these theories may differ widely in their assumptions and explanations, they share a common feature in that they are all hierarchical. They stipulate a structure at the top of the hierarchy, usually the central nervous system, that gives instructions to the rest of the body about what to do, when to do it, and how to do it (Fig. 2A). Unfortunately for hierarchical theories, Nicholai Bernstein (1896–1966) showed that there is no one-to-one relationship between the neural codes, the

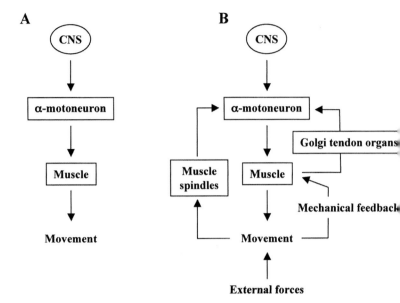

Figure 2. A simplified hierarchical model of a straightforward relation between neural codes and resulting movement (A), and a more complex model (B). Mechanical feedback refers to characteristics like the force-velocity and the force-length relationships.

activation of muscle fibers, and the resulting movement (Bernstein, 1996). The neural code, traveling from the cortex to the periphery, is integrated and changed at the synaptic nodes. The relationship between activation of muscle fibers and the force they generate is dependent on the state of the muscle. And the resulting movement depends not only on the muscle force generated, but also on additional intrinsic and extrinsic forces acting on the body (Fig. 2B). As this so-called non-univocality between the central signal and the resulting movement cannot be modeled in sufficient detail ahead of time, any hierarchical model of movement control necessarily falls short. The inevitable conclusion, Bernstein realized, is that goal-directed actions can only be planned at an abstract level, and that many sub-systems, including the environment, can and will contribute to the eventual movements.

At first sight, the inclusion of 'many sub-systems' into a theory of motor development and learning seems to complicate matters beyond comprehension. How does an infant acquire control of the body under such conditions? Contemporary views propose that the movement patterns that emerge during development are due to changing constraints imposed on action, rather than to evolving blueprints or descending commands. Constraints on action exclude or limit certain movement possibilities by reducing the available degrees of freedom from which a specific task solution can be assembled. The lack of motor control acts as a constraint early in development, as do gravity, motivation, and the physical growth of body parts. Karl Newell proposed a general classification scheme of constraints based on

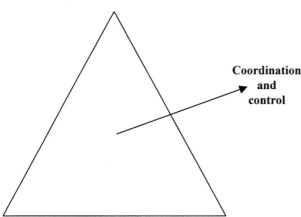

Organismic constraints

Coordination and control

Environmental constraints   **Task constraints**

Figure 3. Classification of constraints based on their sources of origin. Redrawn from K. M. Newell, 1986. Constraints on the development of coordination. In M. G. Wade & H. T. A. Whiting (eds.), *Motor Development in Children: Aspects of Coordination and Control*. Dordrecht: Nijhoff, pp. 341–360.

whether they originate in the organism, in the task, or in the ambient environment. The confluence of these interacting constraints subsequently shapes movement coordination and control (Fig. 3).

From an engineering perspective, such a multitude of interacting variables governing the task solution is a curse to any modeling attempt. There is, however, a theory available that explicitly deals with organization arising in systems with many interacting components, dynamical systems theory. Applying this theory to motor development and learning, the infant becomes a problem-solving system who uses available constraints and possibilities to discover solutions to a problem. The problem of coordination is not hampered by the many interacting variables but simplified by them, as they allow exploitation of the natural properties of the system and the complementary support of the environment (Thelen, 1995). They give the system flexibility to meet the demands of a task within a continually varying environment.

This dynamical view also provides a unifying perspective on the co-existence of global similarities in motor development across infants and cultures on the one hand, yet pervasive individual differences even between monozygotic twins on the other. As infants tend to have a similar organismic make-up, grow up in similar physical environments facing similar challenges, their individual pathways of motor development will reflect a high degree of similarity as well. This model is in accordance with the contemporary perspective on development in general as a probabilistic epigenetic process.

Lingering issues and future directions

In this final section, some of the hard 'motor nuts' to crack for developmental psychologists are considered. These include the origins of new motor abilities, the driving force behind motor development, the issue of specificity of learning versus learning transfer, and the roles of growth and experience for development and learning. In addition, some reflections are offered as to where the study of motor development should go in the future for the field to advance.

The origins of new motor abilities

Arguably the most fundamental question within motor development has been haunting the field since its inception. Where do new abilities come from? From one theoretical perspective to another, different answers have been suggested throughout history. Could new abilities result from a simple unfolding of pre-existing structures and functions? The answer is "no," according to a wide range of biological and other scientific evidence. Can they result from a central structure in the brain? Not unless one is willing to embrace the idea of infinite regress to an intelligent homunculus. The contemporary view on the origin of new motor abilities is that they are properties that emerge gradually by a process of sequential changes in structure and function. This process is not instructed or predetermined, but probabilistic and heavily influenced by both internal and external factors, and functional activity itself.

One way to visualize such a process is offered by the epigenetic landscape, introduced by the embryologist Conrad Waddington (Fig. 4). This landscape depicts the process of canalization and the constraints the latter imposes on increasing differentiation of tissues and organs during embryogenesis. In particular, it illustrates why stable, species-typical phenotypes arise despite variations in genetic inheritance and environmental condition. The valleys in this landscape are formed by the organism's genotype and represent end states such as wings, antenna, or the mouth. Different initial conditions can be represented by the bias of the balls as they travel down the surface. Deeper valleys give the traveling balls more resistance to perturbations than shallow valleys, so that within the pathways themselves, disturbances tend to be compensated.

Thelen adapted Waddington's epigenetic landscape into an ontogenetic landscape that illustrates the emergence of new abilities in an individual as a series of changes of relative stability and instability. One of her examples, concerning the development of locomotion, is represented in Fig. 5. Developmental time runs from the top to the bottom of the figure. The horizontal lines are slices of time representing the probability that the infant displays a particular movement organization. The hills and valleys represent behavioral options and their stability. The relative width of a valley represents the variability of that behavior. A steep and narrow valley represents few, highly stable behavioral choices. Several small hillocks in a valley indicate that behavior can take on a number of different, less stable options. Small changes in anatomy, motivation, or environmental support can change the shape of the landscape, with preferred states continuously emerging and disappearing. The landscape provides a powerful metaphor for the intricate nature of the developmental process. As structures mature, the infant can face both old and new challenges with an increased set of possibilities. Through a process of exploration and selection of different movement organizations, infants discover new actions that, with repeated practice, can become more skilled and stable.

Mechanisms for spurring change

The next hard nut to crack is closely related to the previous one: what causes development to happen? What drives the process forward from a less-advanced stage or milestone to one that is more advanced? Here, as well, different suggestions have been made. The process of repeated perception-action cycles is one of them, and these take the shape of exploratory behavior in the writings of Eleanor Gibson (1988). Infants continuously push their own boundaries forward by exploring current abilities, the characteristics of new tasks, and the properties of the environment, and by linking experiences back to the system. This is similar to the process of equilibration in Piaget's work. Closely linked to this perspective is that of Thelen (1995) who emphasizes variation in movement behavior and subsequent selection of alternatives as pushing development forward. The starting points for her as well are the capacities and structures already available to the infant. By modulating current abilities and exploring a variety of movement configurations, infants converge on a 'ball park' solution to a new challenge that works. Through further cycles of acting and perceiving the consequences, infants can fine-tune the solution to make it smooth, reliable, and efficient. In this view, the challenge a task poses to the infant can become the driving force, the motivation, for change. Why challenges seem to be so motivating for healthy infants, whereas many infants with disorders and adults can often be seen to give up or settle for inadequate performance, remains an issue to be addressed by future research.

A question related to the mechanism for change is why change so often appears continuous at the local level of developing components, but discontinuous and stage-like at the global level of developing behavior. Each

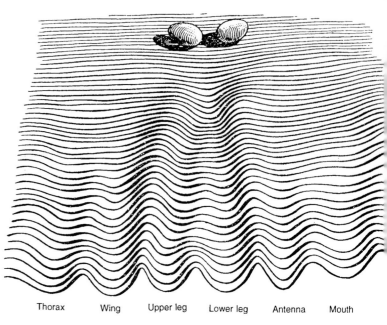

Figure 4. Waddington's epigenetic landscape. The balls at the top represent developing phenotypes, the curvatures in the landscape depict different pathways of change. From C. H. Waddington, 1956. Genetic assimilation of the *Bithorax* phenotype. *Evolution*, 10, 1–13.

Thorax   Wing   Upper leg   Lower leg   Antenna   Mouth

of the motor milestones seems to kick in one day as a discrete transition, but measurements of underlying sub-components suggest that these are developing continuously. The best answer to date comes from a dynamical systems perspective on development. According to this perspective, the emergence of each new ability or milestone requires the functional readiness of many underlying variables. Each of these variables may follow its own developmental trajectory and change continuously at its own rate. The last component ability to develop acts as a control parameter that pushes the system into a new configuration. Again, this is not a predetermined process, but a self-organizing process heavily influenced by individual differences, the social and cultural context, the history of the infant, and her intentions and motivations. Thus, different variables can serve as control parameters at different times in development, and the last component to develop for a new ability may differ from individual to individual.

Specificity of learning versus learning transfer

Another enduring puzzle of motor development and learning concerns the nature of the changes over time. Do these changes transfer to other abilities or skills and other contexts, or are they specific? Above, it was described how early developmental and learning changes are often context-specific, but that, with increasing skill, infants' performance becomes more and

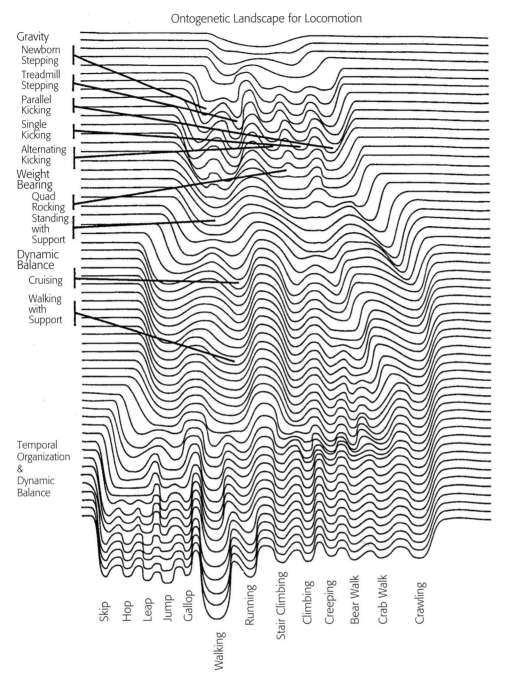

Figure 5. Thelen's adaptation of the epigenetic landscape into an ontogenetic landscape for locomotion. The valleys represent preferred states of movement organization, the depth of each valley its stability, and their width the number of available choices. From Thelen & Smith, 1994.

more resistant to contextual changes. With respect to learning transfer between different abilities or skills, the picture is more mixed. On the one hand, several studies have shown that practice and experience with one skill has limited beneficial effects for the development and learning of other skills. One of the most dramatic examples of this is McGraw's famous study on Johnny and Jimmy. The infant Johnny was given physical training through unusual motor experiences, like

climbing and roller-skating, that were unavailable to his twin brother Jimmy. Johnny outperformed his untrained twin on tests of physical strength and agility, but on the basic abilities of reaching, sitting, and walking, Johnny did not develop better or more quickly than Jimmy. A later study by Philip Zelazo and colleagues confirmed that young infants receiving enhanced practice of the stepping response stepped more and infants receiving enhanced practice of the sitting posture tended to sit in longer boots, but that these benefits did not transfer to the non-practiced skill. These studies thus indicate specificity of learning effects.

These examples, though, tested for learning transfer across different postures, for example sitting and stepping. In other words, the practiced task and the tested transfer task built on different underlying postural abilities. Especially in early development, postural control acts as a critical constraint on performance (Hopkins & Rönnqvist, 2002). For example, infants can reach for objects at younger ages when their trunk is stabilized in a slightly reclining chair compared to a situation in which they have to control sitting posture themselves. When gravity prevents infants held upright from continuing stepping movements after rapid fat gain, they will continue kinematically similar kicking movements in a supine position (Thelen, 1995). Could learning effects of practicing one ability transfer to a different one if both had similar postural characteristics? A recent study on learning to crawl (Adolph, Vereijken, & Denny, 1998) showed that indeed they can.

Infants with extended experience of crawling on their belly were more proficient at crawling on hands and knees than those who had skipped the belly-crawling period (Fig. 6). Robust, positive transfer occurred from belly to hands and knees despite structural differences in interlimb coordination and timing in the two forms of crawling. These differences between former belly crawlers and non-belly crawlers were not due to infants' age or body dimensions. Such results suggest that specific experience with particular interlimb movement patterns, particular coordinative timing patterns, or even particular muscle actions is not critical for transfer. Rather, positive transfer may result from shoring up constituents underlying both forms of locomotion, like strengthening the arms, gaining experience coping with the consequences of disequilibrium, and drawing attention to visual and mechanical information for balance control.

In summary, learning effects can be context-specific and task-specific, or generalize to other contexts and other tasks, depending on the developmental status of the infant and similarities in underlying components of the different abilities. By carefully examining situations where experience does and does not show evidence of transfer in future studies, we may arrive at a better understanding of the factors underlying developmental change.

The roles of growth and experience

A final hard nut to crack is the role of growth and experience in motor development. Although there is no debate that important changes take place in both factors during infancy, the literature has sustained fierce battles

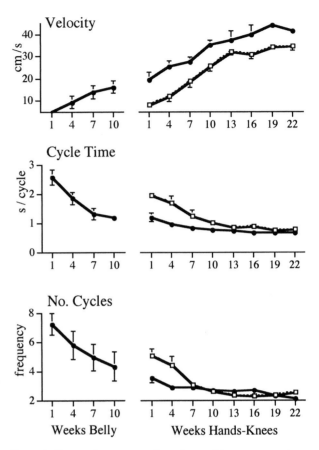

Figure 6. Changes in measures of crawling proficiency over weeks on belly and weeks on hands and knees. Solid circles indicate former belly crawlers. Open squares indicate non-belly crawlers. Bars reflect standard errors.

concerning the relative importance of experience, body growth in general, and neural maturation in particular. Whereas the maturational view emphasized the importance of changes in neural structures and downplayed the role of experience, behaviorists focused on experience-related changes to the detriment of maturational factors. Movement scientists have pointed out that changing body dimensions and body proportions affect, for example, the biomechanical constraints on movement, thereby altering movement possibilities available to the infant. And as indicated above, a large part of brain development takes place after birth, especially with regard to interneuron connectivity. The resulting growth in structure enables an increase in functions, the execution of which feeds back to further the development of brain structures. How does each of these factors contribute to motor development? As simultaneous experimental manipulation of these factors is not viable, teasing apart their independent contributions to development depends on statistical procedures performed on a large data sample.

A recent study by Adolph, Vereijken, and Shrout (2003) took up this challenge. We measured improvement in walking in over 200 infants, obtained measures of their body dimensions, and used their chronological age and duration of walking experience as crude estimates for capturing the effects of neural maturation and practice. Our findings indicated that body dimensions, testing age, and walking experience were interrelated in that older infants tended to have larger bodies and more walking experience. More importantly, the developmental factors that these measures represent are likely to have bidirectional and interactive effects. We statistically controlled for the effects of pairs of factors in a series of hierarchical regression analyses. These showed, first of all, that changing body dimensions did not explain improvements in walking independent of infants' testing age and duration of walking experience. The independent contribution of age was significant, but only accounted for an additional 1% of the variance. In contrast, walking experience played the single most important role in the development of walking proficiency. It explained an additional 19%–26% of the variance after controlling for body dimensions and age.

How does experience facilitate development? A tentative answer can in fact be found in any textbook on motor learning or physical education. The advice to aspiring coaches has been that practice should be massed, variable, and distributed. Looking at infants struggling to walk, we see a dramatic case in point. They try, fall, get up, and try again, seemingly tirelessly. They endlessly vary smaller and bigger aspects of their feeble attempts in order to arrive eventually at a solution that works. And they keep repeating this process in long bouts until they suddenly shift gear for an hour or the rest of the day, and happily busy themselves with a different task. Practice in young infants is truly massive, in that they can take hundreds of steps per hour and thousands of steps per day. It is also variable, as each step is slightly different from the last due to variations in the terrain and the continuously varying constraints on the body. And it is wonderfully distributed in bouts of activity, providing rest periods and enhancing motivation. What they do is in essence what Bernstein told us to do half a century ago: repeat without repetition. From this perspective, motor development is not learning to remember solutions to problems, but learning to solve the problem by generating solutions. Over and over again.

Conclusions

Since the 1980s, the study of motor development has re-emerged as a progressive and innovative field of inquiry. Through meticulous analysis of the development of fundamental motor abilities in infancy, leading scientists within the field have shown not only how such abilities develop, but also how tightly interwoven motor development is with development in other domains like perception, cognition, motivation, and communication. In that respect, motor development transcends traditional topics and provides us with a unique and captivating window into the fundamental questions of developmental psychology in general.

To further our insight into the intricate nature of development, detailed analyses of changes in motor abilities are needed in two directions in particular. Firstly, detailed longitudinal studies are needed to scrutinize how the fundamental motor abilities continue to develop after the infancy period and throughout childhood. For example, how do patterns of locomotion develop into obstacle avoidance and way-finding? How do early manual activities develop into drawing and writing? Secondly, detailed analyses are needed of less conventional motor systems such as tool use, emotional expression, and movements in the context of communication, such as gestures, facial expressions, and vocalizations. By carefully analyzing the motor aspects of these abilities and skills, new insights will be gained into how perceptual, cognitive, social, and motor systems interact in the performance of everyday activities.

See also:

Understanding ontogenetic development: debates about the nature of the epigenetic process; Neuromaturational theories; Constructivist theories; Learning theories; Dynamical systems approaches; Developmental testing; Normal and abnormal prenatal development; The status of the human newborn; Cognitive development in infancy; Perceptual development; Social development; Emotional development; Development of learning and memory; Brain and behavioral development (I): sub-cortical; Brain and behavioral development (II): cortical; Locomotion; Prehension; Sleep and wakefulness; Blindness; Developmental coordination disorder; Down's syndrome; Prematurity and low birthweight; Behavioral embryology; Cognitive neuroscience; James Mark Baldwin; George E. Coghill; Viktor Hamburger; Jean Piaget; Milestones of motor development and indicators of biological maturity

Further reading

Bertenthal, B. I. and Clifton, R. K. (1998). Perception and action. In W. Damen, D. Kuhn, and R. S. Siegler (eds.), *Handbook of Child Psychology*, Vol. II: *Cognition, Perception, and Language*. New York: John Wiley, pp. 51–102.

Elman, J. L., Bates, E. A., Johnson, M. H., Karmiloff-Smith, A., Parisi, D. and Plunkett, K. (1996). *Rethinking*

Innateness: A Connectionist Perspective on Development. Cambridge, MA: MIT Press.

Hopkins, B. (2001). Understanding motor development: insights from dynamical systems perspectives. In A. F. Kalverboer and A. Gramsbergen (eds.), *Handbook on Brain and Behavior in Human Development.* Dordrecht: Kluwer, pp. 591–620.

Acknowledgments

Parts of the research reported here were funded by the Norwegian Research Council (grant no. 129273/330) and the Royal Netherlands Academy of Arts and Sciences.

Social development

HILDY S. ROSS & CATHERINE E. SPIELMACHER

Introduction

From the outset, infants are social beings who are welcomed into the worlds of their families, communities, and cultural groups. With development, children's social interactions change radically and their relationships increase in number and variety. In this entry, we highlight some of the transformations that mark this social journey. The literature on children's social development is multifaceted and extensive; to help us understand the changes that are taking place, we highlight three themes. First, we treat social development within the context of children's close relationships with others, emphasizing those with parents, siblings, and peers. Second, we treat social development as bi-directional, which entails both partners, be they adults or children, contributing to the development of relationships. Third, we highlight communication as the basic medium of children's relationships with others.

Why focus on relationships?

Because children are never 'social' in a vacuum, it will always be necessary to consider what others are contributing to children's social development. Specific forms of interaction and processes of social influence will differ from one relationship to another. This variety, in itself, holds its own fascination. Furthermore, relationships do not remain static. As children develop, so do their relationship partners and, in a fundamental way, so do the characteristics of their relationships. The mother with whom a 2-year-old plays is quite different from the partner she will be six or twelve years later as she interacts with her 8-year-old or adolescent child. The meaning of friendship will be quite different when we consider 2-year-olds, 8-year-olds, or 16-year-olds.

Each relationship is shaped by the contributions of two individuals. This proposition is easy to accept when we examine children's interactions with peers because equality and reciprocity have always been recognized as the hallmarks of such relationships. Reciprocity also plays a central role in relationships between siblings. In the study of parent-child relationships, however, many developmental psychologists have asked how the parent shapes or socializes the child, without asking how the child, in turn, influences her interaction with parents. A hostile parent can be either creating or reacting to an aggressive child, while a sensitive, caring parent can create or react to an empathic child. Once we realize that parental behavior can be influenced by the characteristics of their children, and consider bi-directional influences with respect to the formation of social relationships, we are faced with far more uncertainty about basic developmental processes. Developmental psychologists, however, have accepted the challenge of this complexity: the easy assumptions of the past have given way to a more critical attitude toward the study of social development. With the view that the child also has an influence on the parent comes an emphasis on social relationships as the joint product of individuals interacting with one another.

In addition, we focus on the ways in which relationship partners communicate with one another. Communication develops as a fundamental aspect of social development. What is the message of an infant's cry, a young child's laugh, a parent's admonition or praise, a personal story, a bully's taunt, or an adolescent's argument? Communication occurs within all social interactions – it carries both informational and emotional content, and it gives meaning to all relationships in which the developing child participates. Communication forms the basis of mutual influence and understanding, and gives substance to the factors that distinguish among relationships and mark changes within relationships.

Our emphasis is on three forms of close personal relationships: the parent-child relationships, the sibling relationships, and peer relationships. Each of these is considered as foreground, but the backdrop of the extended family, the broader peer group, and the

Figure 1. Children develop within the contexts of their families, embedded within the structure of the larger social and cultural groups.

prevailing culture form the context for our examination of developing relationships (Fig. 1). To realize the complexity of the social network, we consider the interdependence among relationships in the family, and examine the formation of friendships within the broader peer group.

Parent-child relationships

From birth, parents and their offspring communicate. Perhaps the first form of communication occurs when infants cry and parents respond. Both the quality of the infants' acoustic signals and the interpretative stance of the adult influence how parents will react. For example, high-pitched and raspy a-tonal cries convey more urgency and distress in young infants' crying, and prompt adults to intervene more quickly. As infants develop, they are more easily soothed, and some may even begin to quiet when they hear their mother's approach. Adults' own feelings of efficacy, their physiological response to the crying, their psychological well-being, and their understanding of why an infant is crying also influence their reactions.

Of course, parent-child communication, even in the early months, takes more positive forms as well. From about the age of 2 months, parents and infants collaborate in well-structured, engaging, and mutually responsive bouts of interaction. These begin with direct face-to-face encounters where parents and children watch one another, vocalize, smile, and touch. The degree to which interpersonal communication is involved in these episodes is most dramatically illustrated when adults become unresponsive to their

infants. When adults stop responding to infants' cues by adopting a still face, most babies become disinterested or distressed, although some try to signal to their parents that the play should continue. In one study, babies saw either a video of their mothers who were able to watch and respond to them, or the same picture being played later in time, when the mother's behavior was no longer related to what the baby was doing (Murray & Trevarthen, 1986). The infants were animated and engaged when mothers were acting in synchrony with their own signals, and distressed or uninterested when mothers were out of sync.

By the time babies are 4 months of age, vocal responsiveness predominates. Infants appear to set the tone for most sequences of contingent interaction and mothers appear to be more highly responsive, but when it comes to object play, the reverse seems to be the case. When mothers introduce objects, infants quickly become engaged in object play, but when infants are playing with things, maternal responsiveness to what the baby is doing diminishes. Toys may also become the medium through which adult-infant games are developed. Games of peek-a-boo, ball, stack and topple, drop and retrieve are common forms of fun in the infants' second six months. Roles are invented and enacted repeatedly and in turn. When adults stop playing, infants reliably signal with gaze and gestures that they should take a turn.

Another factor that seems to change the pattern of parent-child communication is the infants' growing ability to move around in the world. With mobility comes increased independence and a greater need for parents to exert control at a distance. Prohibitions are one means of doing so, and parents of infants who can crawl about are more likely than parents of non-crawling infants to discipline their offspring. Also counteracting this greater level of independence is the development of parent-infant attachment. One prominent feature of attachment is the security that infants feel in the presence of their parents and the corresponding distress they show in the parents' absence. According to Bowlby's (1969) original formulation, mothers serve their children as a 'base of exploration.' Infants move away from their mothers to the interesting world beyond, but it is mothers' continued availability that makes these forays possible. Infants return to 'base' often to share their discoveries.

A second way in which families adjust to the child's growing independence is through the emergence of social referencing. When infants from 7 or 8 months of age find themselves in ambiguous situations, perhaps being confronted by a barking mechanical dog or a looming adult stranger, they will frequently look to their parents for information on how to interpret their experiences. Mothers' and fathers' positive or negative emotional reactions will often guide the infants' own responses. It is not just the baby's immediate response that is influenced by how the parent seems to feel about the situation, but later encounters are also guided by past parent reactions.

What do infants need to understand to use parents as sources of such information? They have to know what the emotional messages mean and to what event the adult is reacting. A recent experiment (Moses *et al.*, 2001) has shown that children get information about what makes an adult either pleased or apprehensive by knowing what objects comprise the focus of the adult's attention. Picture a 12-month-old baby about to approach a very interesting, jiggling, plush octopus. A woman, either in sight of the infant or out of sight, utters either an enthusiastic "Nice . . . Wow!" or an equally animated "Iiuu . . . Yecch!" The woman's emotional reaction will guide the infant to approach either more rapidly or more slowly only if she is in the room, and the baby can see that she is looking at and evaluating the octopus.

When she is outside the room, the target of these same emotional reactions is ambiguous, and the adult's outburst does not influence the baby's reactions to the toy. It does not matter that the information concerns the current object of the infant's own attention; the baby wants to know what the adult is referring to and this information makes her communication meaningful. These same researchers have shown that a similar process facilitates children's learning new words from parents. If parents indicate through the direction of their gaze what they are referring to when they name something new for their baby, the baby will be likely to learn the word. By 18 months, toddlers will actively check the speaker to see which of several objects is being labeled, and they will then associate the new label with the appropriate object. Thus, emotional and linguistic information is both sought and communicated in the context of early parent-infant relationships.

Just a little later, around 2 years of age, children will begin to share memories of past events with their parents. Together, they engage in joint story telling (Fivush, 1993). Consider the following example of an exchange between mother (M) and child (C):

M: What were you doing?
C: Playing.
M: Where? In the what? By the what?
C: By the park, on the hill.
M: No, remember, weren't you by the pond?
C: Yeah.
M: Was mommy mad?
C: Yes.
M: Why was I mad?
C: Guess that we were in the pond.

Notice how the mother prompts and corrects the child's recollection, and prompts both emotional and evaluative information from her daughter. The mother helps her daughter to shape the narrative, but also elicits causal and explanatory information that justifies her own past emotional reactions. Such stories about the past allow parents and children to share assumptions about social life, to construct links between causes and effects, to reinforce socializing standards, and to construct personal views of self and others. Accordingly, children's memories of their own pasts are not entirely private matters, but are part of the social discourse that takes place within the family.

Not all parent-child communication proceeds with this same level of harmony. Parents and children also have conflicts with one another. Until recently, parent-child discord was conceptualized almost exclusively as related to situations of discipline: the parent issued an order or made a request, and the child either complied or disobeyed. Current observations, however, paint a more varied picture. Children also make requests of their parents, and parents are actually somewhat less compliant than their preschool-aged offspring (Eisenberg, 1992). Children, in turn, resist their parents' demands in a variety of ways; even young children bargain, propose alternatives to parents' requests, offer and seek explanations for their own or their parents' positions, and successfully resist their parents' wishes. Children's negotiation increases with age and is associated with parents' explanations, bargaining, and affection. When parents and young children negotiate together, parents tend often to change their positions with respect to their children's sibling conflicts, and resolutions often come about that are antithetical to parents' original suggestions (Perlman & Ross, 1997).

Parent-child conflict also provides an opportunity to convey the moral principles that might guide social life. Parents' discipline often involves instructing children in morally and socially acceptable behavior. When parents intervene in disputes between their children, they tend to address the child who has violated the siblings' rights or welfare, they support moral principles, and children tend to adhere to those principles. Children also play a role in developing the principles that will help them get along with others. The resolution of young children's property disputes reflects the priority of owners to control their belongings. Children endorse this principle in their justifications, and in the disputes that they settle without parent involvement. When they intervene, however, parents are more ambiguous, endorsing the rights of those who currently hold the toy equally with those of owners, and urging their children to share. Nonetheless, disputes are still resolved in favor of owners when parents intervene.

Sibling relationships

Sibling rivalry is such a commonplace phrase that we can barely say one of these two words without immediately calling up connections with the other. Yet rivalry is not a fair characterization of these lifelong relationships that have so many other facets and dimensions. Siblings are genetically related, and thus alike in many ways. They are playmates and teachers. They provide support in circumstances where parents cannot. Siblings are intimate companions who share the everyday adventures of family life. They hold memories in common that provide links to the past. And yes, they do fight with one another, but conflict and rivalry are not exactly the same thing.

The birth of a younger brother or sister is often an eagerly anticipated family event. Caring for a newborn, however, can often divert parents' attention from an older sibling. Some mothers share the care of the newborn with older brothers or sisters. When mothers and their first-borns talk frequently about the newborn as a distinct person, with feelings and needs, and when mothers actively encourage their preschooler to help care for the new baby, the two siblings develop friendlier, more positive relationships over the next year (Fig. 2). The preschoolers' own references to their infant siblings' internal states are also found more often among children with positive sibling relationships. Such conversations may help children imagine what their siblings' perspectives might be on the events they experience together. Indeed, it has been found that having a sibling helps children recognize that others have internal thoughts, knowledge, desires, or beliefs that may differ from their own.

The preschool period is when siblings spend a lot of time together, and there are a number of ways in which their interactions change during that time. To begin with, children of about 3 years of age spend time in conversational interactions with both their mothers and their siblings, but over the next year there is a notable increase in conversations with siblings as talk with mothers goes down in frequency. At the same time, children are also likely to talk to their parents about their siblings and such talk becomes increasingly positive, functioning more and more to connect family members rather than to create barriers among them. There are also some forms of talk that are especially important for the sibling relationship: siblings appraise one another frequently, and, over the preschool years, those appraisals become increasingly positive. Positive emotional expressions are also more frequent in conversations with siblings than with mothers, as are play, humor, and fantasy. Thus, relationships with siblings are quite exciting, engaging, and emotional.

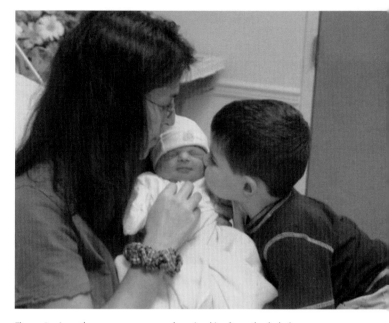

Figure 2. A mother encourages a welcoming kiss from the baby's big brother.

Interestingly, children are less likely to express their own self-interests to their siblings than to their mothers, and expressions of self-interest, conflict, and accompanying expressions of anger and distress decrease over the preschool years.

Despite these decreases, conflict remains a significant aspect of sibling relationships. According to some accounts, disputes decrease from about six each hour when children are between 2 and 4 years of age, to approximately four fights when they are two years older – a substantial decline, but still a substantial number of fights. Although conflict sometimes involves physical aggression, damage to valued property, and angry exclusion or derogation, it is also an occasion in which children express, defend, and justify their own positions, and one in which the perspectives of the sibling are made clear. When they are asked to remember their own past conflicts with sisters and brothers, children report more violations, especially serious violations, by their siblings than by themselves, and are more likely to justify their own wrongdoings; however, they are also able to understand and convey a coherent account of what their siblings wanted, and what they did to achieve their goals.

Parents are also likely to become involved when young children fight. Mothers or fathers intervene in slightly more than half of their children's disputes, and that does not decrease over the preschool period. In fact, children actually seek their parents' interventions by tattling on their siblings (Ross & den Bak-Lammers, 1998). Although we are often told that it is the younger sibling who runs to report on older brothers and sisters, it is actually the other way around – older siblings are more

Figure 3. A newly formed peer group of 3-month-old babies.

likely to tattle. They do so both when they need parents' help to resolve their differences ("She won't share. Mommy, she won't share"), and when they only want to inform the parent that the sibling misbehaved ("He peed on the rug"). Tattling also increases rather than decreases over the preschool years. It expresses children's awareness of their parents' roles in enforcing social and moral rules. Children seem to place great value in the idea that they should be treated fairly in their relationships with their siblings. In fact, if parents favor one of their children over the other, or if children perceive that they do so, then the sibling relationship suffers.

Parents' roles as mediators in their children's disputes as well as the impact of parents' differential treatment of their offspring remind us that sibling conflicts, indeed, sibling relations in general, are not isolated from but embedded within other family relationships. The family is a system of intersecting relationships, and we have to recognize its functioning if we are to understand children's social development. Indeed, the impact of the various relationships within the family is also illustrated by children's reactions to interparental conflicts. Children are highly distressed by conflict between their parents, especially if it is hostile and aggressive. They cry, cover their ears, try to leave, and feel angry, sad, guilty, or worried. Also, children do not seem to get used to witnessing their parents' fights, but react more strongly when they have been exposed to parental conflict in the past. When parents fight often or violently, there are also often problems within parent-child relationships. Additionally, sibling relationships show less warmth and more hostility when parents engage in more conflict.

Although it is difficult to tell whether conflict in the parental relationship is the source of other negativity in the family, the evidence suggests that the relationship between spousal conflict and sibling conflict depends on there also being negativity in the parent-child relationship. By the same token, less conflictual spousal relationships, well-functioning and warm parent-child relationships, and close, positive sibling relationships reinforce the general harmony of the family. Thus, even a small nuclear family creates a complex context in which social development takes place.

Children's peer relationships

As children develop, they spend an increasing amount of time with peers (Fig. 3). Many children enter daycare settings during the preschool years and remain segregated with same-aged peers during the school years. Children also form relationships with peers from their neighborhoods, after-school organizations, and sport teams.

Children associate with peers in different ways. Children interact with peers when they reciprocate another child's behavior. Each child's contribution to an interaction functions as both a response to the other and a stimulus for the other's response. An example of an interaction is a conversation, in which each child reciprocates by taking turns in the shared talk. The content of the talk could include gossip, encouragement, self-disclosure, banter, or disputes. Children prefer interacting with particular peers, and may choose to form long-lasting friendships with them. Groups are more than mere aggregates of relationships, as they have norms or distinctive patterns of behavior and attitudes that characterize group members and differentiate them from members of other groups. Groups are highly cohesive and are often organized in a hierarchical fashion, with leaders who guide the interactions of a group's members. Interactions with peers, friends, and groups become increasingly complex as children develop.

Infants as young as 2 months of age interact with their peers. They will reciprocate eye-gazing with peers, and, by 12 months, infants will imitate peers' vocalizations, smiles, finger points, and other playful activities (Eckerman, Whatley, & Kutz, 1975). By 2 years, peer interactions become increasingly complex. Lengthier interactions become organized around games. During these games, toddlers direct social actions to one another, respond appropriately to these social actions, invent specific rule-governed routines, take their own turns, and encourage peers to do so as well.

One of the chief challenges of the preschool years is to join in when others are at play. Competent entry into ongoing peer activity involves the ability to observe what the play partners are doing, approach and play beside potential play partners, and engage the players in conversation about the ongoing activity. Preschool-aged children direct more speech to their peers than do younger children. Children whose communications are skillful (e.g., by making sure they have obtained the listener's attention and by positioning themselves within an arm's length of the listener) are more likely to meet their social goals than those whose verbal directives are less skillful. Preschool children adroitly modify the context and grammar of their speech.

The topic of children's conversations differentiates mutual friends from mutual non-friends. Children are more likely to talk about their own and their peers' activities in the context of interactions with friends than with non-friends. Moreover, preschool children alter their speech to suit the needs of their listeners. For example, speech directed to 2-year-old listeners is shorter and less grammatically complex than speech that is directed to agemates or adults. Preschool children's communication skills are flexible, and young children who recognize their limited verbal repertoires will resort to the use of gestures to communicate their intended meaning to listeners.

The proportion of peer interaction increases from approximately 10 percent of all social interaction for 2-year-olds to more than 30 percent for children in middle childhood. Furthermore, the form of play changes over this time period. During middle child-hood, there is a decline of pretend and rough-and-tumble play. Replacing these forms of interaction are games, and unstructured activities such as 'hanging out' or watching television.

From quite a young age, children demonstrate a preference for interacting with specific children. Reciprocity, stability, and a voluntary relationship mark these friendships. Toddlers develop reciprocal relationships with peers in terms of mutual exchanges of positive and conflict behavior. For example, they share toys with children who had shared with them earlier, and they grab toys from children who had previously taken their toys. Toddler friends generally prefer one another and play together more than either child does with other agemates. Such relationships emerge gradually as children interact with one another, but toddler friendships can remain stable over periods of a year or more.

By preschool age, children demonstrate a preference for play partners who are the same age and sex, and these preferences are stable over time. As with toddlers, once preschoolers form friendships, their behavior with these individuals is distinct from that with other children who are familiar but not friends. For example, friends spend more time actually interacting with one another than do non-friends, and positive social exchanges and mutuality occur more among friends than non-friends. However, preschool children also demonstrate more quarreling and more hostility with friends than with non-friends.

The number of children's reported 'close friends' increases with age up to about 11 years after which it begins to decline. Moreover, children's friendships with opposite-sex peers drop off sharply after 7 years of age. Observational data reveal that children at this age interact differently with same- and opposite-sex children. When interacting with opposite-sex peers, children make more negative facial expressions and remarks, and they exhibit more negative gestures than when interacting with same-sex peers. Children report that they like opposite-sex peers less than same-sex peers, and they are not interested in becoming friends with opposite-sex peers. The gap between friends and non-friends continues to exist in middle childhood, as friends are more emotional and more likely to display emotional understanding than non-friends. However, in middle childhood, pairs of friends engage in about the same amount of conflict as pairs of non-friends. There is, however, a major difference in the conflict resolution strategies that friends and non-friends adopt, as friends are more concerned about achieving an equitable resolution to conflicts, and attempt to resolve conflicts in a way that will preserve the continuity of their relationships.

During middle childhood, the size of peer groups becomes considerably larger than it had been during the preschool period. Children's concerns about acceptance in the peer group rise sharply, and these concerns appear to be related to an increase in the salience and frequency of gossip. At this age, gossip reaffirms children's membership in important same-sex groups, and reveals the core attitudes, beliefs, and behaviors comprising the basis for inclusion in or exclusion from these groups (Gottman & Mettetal, 1986). Much gossip among children at this age is negative, involving the defamation of third parties. Nevertheless, a great deal of children's gossip involves discussion of the important interpersonal connections among children and other children's admirable traits. The gossip of boys and girls is more similar than different. However, there is some evidence that boys who are not close friends use gossip to find common ground between them, whereas girls who are not close friends avoid gossip more than close friends. A new form of social involvement that emerges in middle childhood is the participation in stable cliques. Cliques are voluntary, friendship-based groups that almost always comprise same-sex, same-race members. By 11 years of age, children report that most of their peer interaction takes place in the context of the clique, and nearly all children report being a member of one.

Parents' socializing influence begins to diminish as the power of peer influence increases. Children's peer groups reinforce attitudes and behaviors that may be quite different from those of adults, but because children spend more of their time with peers than with parents, they identify more closely with the norms of their peer groups. It is important to situate children's peer friendships in a larger relationship context, however, as children's conceptualizations and feelings about their primary relationships are internalized and lead to expectations about what other relationships should be like. Children bring to peer interaction more or less stable temperaments that dispose them to be more or less aroused physiologically to social stimuli, and a repertoire of social skills for social perception and problem solving. It can be misleading, however, to attribute these characteristics of interaction solely to individual differences in temperament or social competence. One must also consider the relational interdependencies, that is, the unique adjustments made by individuals to one another that define their particular relationship.

A useful tool for untangling the various influences on relationships is the Social Relations Model (Kenny & La Voie, 1984). Individuals impact peer interactions by carrying their characteristic behavior into the relationships (actor effect), and by eliciting behavior from others that is common across several relationships (partner effects). For example, a particularly shy child may be generally reluctant to initiate interactions with other children (actor effect), and others may generally ignore this child when it comes to finding playmates (partner effect). However, specific relationships can influence interaction in a way that goes beyond the characteristic influences of the individuals, by prompting special adjustment of an actor to a particular partner (relationship effect). For example, our shy child may take a leadership role when interacting with a particular friend and her friend may choose her at playtime. The actor, partner, and relationship effects are intertwined in a web of mutually influencing relationships in both families and peer networks.

Conclusions

We have touched on the increasing body of research that illuminates processes of children's social development. Forms of communication, from early crying to peer gossip, play their roles in providing the substance of social interaction and in marking developing social relationships. Mutual understanding emerges time after time as the central component of communication:

infants refer to their parents for signals of how to react to ambiguities; toddlers develop rule-governed games that they play with one another; preschoolers imagine what their siblings desire and think, and support their younger siblings' understanding that others have beliefs and desires that are independent of their own; parents and their offspring, brothers and sisters, and friends and acquaintances, learn to negotiate with one another and to resolve differences; school children gossip as they form and cement relationships; adolescents fight with their parents when they do not share assumptions about responsibility and choice in certain domains of social conduct.

Children participate as active partners in quite different relationships, yet each relationship intersects, in some way, with the others. This is most apparent in the family, and in the way that friendships emerge within broader peer social groups. Children act in different ways within different relationships and evoke different reactions from their various social partners. The relationship itself, and not just the individual characteristics of participants, is a determining component of social development. Although each relationship is unique, together the web of relationships teaches children about social behavior, attitudes, and beliefs, and this knowledge is brought into children's relationships and shared.

See also:
Theories of the child's mind; Parental and teacher rating scales; Self and peer assessment of competence and well-being; Emotional development; Moral development; Aggressive and prosocial behavior; Daycare; Parenting and the family; Peers and siblings; Play; Socialization; Temperament; Sociology; John Bowlby

Further reading

Brody, G. H (ed.) (1996). *Sibling Relationships: Their Causes and Consequences*. Norwood, NJ: Ablex.
Bukowski, W. M., Newcomb, A. F. and Hartup, W. W. (eds.) (1996). *The Company they Keep: Friendship in Childhood and Adolescence*. Cambridge: Cambridge University Press.
Shantz, C. U. and Hartup, W. W. (eds.) (1992). *Conflict in Child and Adolescent Development*. Cambridge: Cambridge University Press.

Emotional development

NATHAN A. FOX & CYNTHIA A. STIFTER

Introduction

The study of emotional development has made great strides since the 1970s. Prior to this period, emotions in infancy were viewed as diffuse responses of physiological arousal to changes in stimulation. Emotions were not necessarily linked to specific psychological states in the infant, but rather viewed for the effects they had on caregiver behavior. Theories regarding the development of emotions were linked to traditional psychoanalytical approaches. For example, infant wary responses to unfamiliar adults around 9 months of age were called "stranger anxiety," and these 'anxious' responses were viewed as a function of potential object loss (e.g., loss of a love object such as the mother). Alternative models of the development of emotion behavior approached the subject from an operant learning perspective suggesting that crying and smiling responses were a function of conditioning and reinforcement. There were exceptions to these two views, of course. Bronson (1972) wrote on the origins of fear in the young infant, carefully describing the stimulus conditions that could elicit fear, the behaviors that reflected this emotion, and its developmental course. However, it was not until the seminal writings of Ekman (Ekman, Friesen, & Ellsworth, 1972) on the role of emotion in human psychological behavior and Izard (1977), who presented a model of the development of emotions and their role in behavior, that the study of emotional development found its renaissance.

The contributions of Paul Ekman and Carroll Izard

Both Ekman and Izard revived the study of emotions as psychological states with important social and evolutionarily adaptive functions. In addition, they focused on the study of facial expressions as important signals of emotion. This renaissance in the study of emotion was based upon the classical work of Charles Darwin (1872, 1965) who was the first to call attention to the importance of emotions as behavioral states that signal critical information to conspecifics and to others. Darwin specifically focused on the role of facial expressions as important means for conveying emotion information (Fig. 1).

One of the most important aspects of this revival was the notion that emotion, particularly in the face, could be accurately measured. Ekman developed a coding system based upon the movement of each of the various facial muscles. He called these facial movements action units (AUs), and noted that certain combinations of facial movements represented what he determined were primary or discrete affects. A number of researchers have utilized Ekman's Facial Action Coding System (FACS) for use with infants and young children.

Izard, as well, created a coding system for examining facial movements and their role in combining to form emotional expressions specifically in infants and young children. Termed the Maximally Discriminative Facial Coding System (MAX), it divides the face into three regions (eyes, mouth, brows), and identifies movements or changes in each region that together form an emotion expression.

Both Ekman (Ekman *et al.*, 1972) and Izard (1977) have argued that specific patterns of facial movement that create certain emotional expressions are universally recognized as communicating emotional states, and provide shared meaning across cultures. While there is some debate about the universality of these discrete emotions, one important position in the field is that there are a limited number of discrete emotions (perhaps five) portrayed by different facial expressions that are highly recognizable across cultures. These emotions include joy, disgust, fear, anger, and sadness.

On the co-development of cognition and emotion

This revival in the study of emotion brought with it debate about the identity of facial expression and the

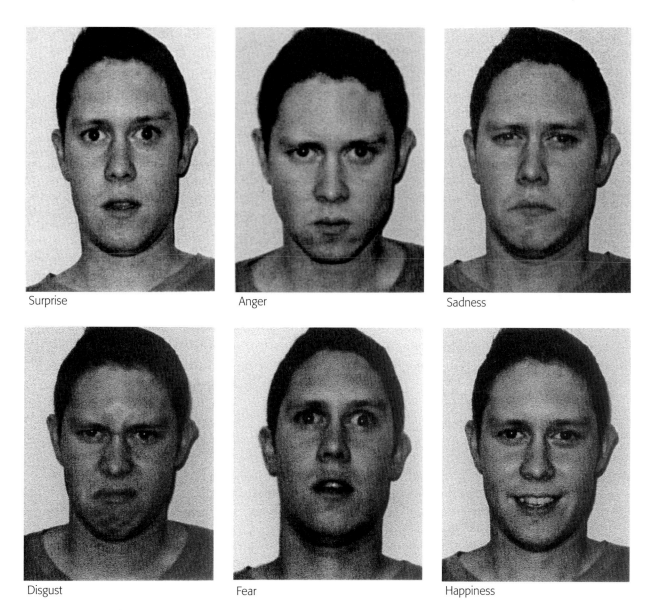

Surprise   Anger   Sadness

Disgust   Fear   Happiness

Figure 1. Darwin's six basic emotions linked to particular facial expressions, which he suggested could be distinguished from each other in terms of the muscle groups involved. Darwin believed expressions of emotion were not learnt, and that they were universal across cultures and species-specific. For him, facial expressions were vestiges of once-useful physiological reactions, for which he proposed three principles (viz., [1] serviceable associated habits: when the same brain state is induced, there is a tendency for the same movement patterns out of habit, even when they have no use whatsoever; [2] antithesis: when an opposite brain state is induced, there is an involuntary tendency to perform movement patterns of a directly opposite nature to those produced previously; [3] direct action of the nervous system: every movement pattern is determined by the brain, but in this respect Darwin excluded those performed in obedience to the will or through habit). Photographs by Juliet Davis-Berry based on Darwin (1872).

psychological state of emotion, the link between emotion and cognition, and, among developmentalists, the functional significance of emotions in development. A number of emotion researchers have staked out differing positions on the importance of facial expression for identifying emotion in individuals. For example, a position derived from attachment theory argues that emotional expressions serve the purpose of either attracting the caregiver to the infant (through positive expressions such as smiling) or signaling danger to the caregiver (through expressions of distress or fear). Others view the emergence of facial expressions of emotion in the first years of life as serving a more general functional purpose involved in the development of social communication with caregivers.

There has also been discussion regarding the interpretation of these facial expressions. Do they reflect internal states, communicate important social information, or both? Given the inability to ask the infant what he or she is feeling, developmental researchers must rely upon behavioral changes to infer the presence of an emotional state. The manner in which facial, vocal, and bodily changes affect social interaction has been a means for interpreting the functional communicative role of early emotional behaviors.

The role of cognition in the experience of emotion continues to be debated. There are those who argue that all emotion involves some level of cognitive appraisal, while others believe that emotional states may exist independently. During the first years of life, such debates revolve around thinking about the cognitive abilities of the young child. There is substantial evidence that infants are capable of complex perceptual discriminations early in the first year, and these abilities may underlie appraisal leading to an emotional response.

These debates have important consequences for a developmental theory of emotion. On the one hand, if facial expression alone signifies the presence of an emotion, then the data suggest that infants at birth are capable of expressing (and hence experiencing) a number of discrete emotions (e.g., disgust or joy). If, on the other hand, some form of appraisal is necessary for infants to experience emotion, then questions may be raised about whether they have the cognitive sophistication to do so. Most developmentalists would agree that infants are capable of experiencing certain emotions at birth and during the first weeks of life. If so, how do these psychological states change with development? Finally, given that both Ekman and Izard have argued for the universality of a number of discrete emotions, what is the developmental timing of these expressions? Below we review, briefly, the emergence of these emotions.

The emergence of affective neuroscience

Recent advances in the study of emotion include linking behaviors associated with emotion to neuroscientific methods. Two different streams of research are responsible for this linkage. The first consists of the research of Davidson (1993) and colleagues who examined changes in physiology coincident with the appearance of specific facial expressions. Davidson argued that, to investigate the neural correlates of emotion, specific methods must be used to identify the presence or absence of such a psychological state. In a series of studies, he and his co-workers demonstrated changes in physiology that were associated with the facial expressions of discrete emotions. Arguing for

specificity and precision in the methods used in emotion research, Davidson was able to define a field currently called affective neuroscience – the study of the neural correlates of affective experience.

A second stream of research linking emotion and neural systems was the approach of Davis (1992) and LeDoux (1996). Both Davis and LeDoux examined the neural systems involved in conditioned fear. Using a classical fear conditioning paradigm, both identified structures within the limbic system that appeared to be responsible for eliciting and potentiating fear responses in animals. They specifically identified the amygdala and its nuclei as playing central roles in the detection of threatening stimuli and in the elicitation of fear-related behaviors. By providing the first evidence of a specific neural system for a discrete emotional state, this work encouraged human emotion researchers to examine the physiological correlates of fear and anxiety.

Both streams of research have influenced developmental work. Fox & Davidson (1986) examined patterns of EEG power recorded over prefrontal and posterior scalp locations. They found that infants as young as 1 week of age exhibited patterns of asymmetry in the activation of the EEG that were correlated with their emotional reactions to different liquid tastants (sweet and sour). Fox & Davidson (1988) also examined patterns of EEG power that were recorded synchronously with 10-month-old infants' facial expression of emotion. They reported different patterns of frontal EEG asymmetry depending upon the type of facial expression exhibited by the infant. Infants exhibiting expressions of joy displayed patterns of left frontal EEG activation, while those exhibiting facial expressions of distress or sadness exhibited patterns of right frontal EEG activation.

Unfortunately, this developmental work has been hampered by the difficulties in recording physiological responses in awake, alert, and responsive infants and young children. Furthermore, it is not possible to utilize some of the more invasive imaging technologies, such as functional magnetic resonance imaging (fMRI) used in the study of neural processes and emotion in adults. For these reasons, we still know little about the development of specific regions of the brain that may underlie the development of discrete emotions and the emergence of more complex emotional behaviors.

Emergence of specific emotions

Disgust and interest

The presence of emotions in young infants has been inferred via the coding of patterns of facial movement in response to stimuli thought to elicit a particular emotion. Several studies have demonstrated that newborn infants respond differently to different liquid tastes. Infants displayed facial expressions of disgust to citric acid and quinine, and an open-eyed brightened expression to the sugar water (coded in Izard's MAX system as the emotion of interest). More recently, newborns' EEG patterns were found to change as a function of whether the liquids were hedonically pleasant or aversive.

Joy

At about 3 months of age, infants begin to smile to human faces. This smiling does not appear to be specific to an individual, and specificity in response develops only later in the first year of life. However, it is clear that this emotional state is specific to social interaction rather than a response to novelty. Thus, the psychological state exhibited in infant smiling may reflect an underlying approach motivation for social interaction and the positive reward state that is engendered by social contact.

Distress

Emotional communication occurs early on by vocal as well as facial expression. Infants cry to signal their distress. A number of studies have examined adult abilities to identify discrete emotional states via infant cries. These studies have found that infant cries could be differentiated into those conveying hunger, pain, and distress by 3 months of age. There has also been work aimed at identifying the specific parameters of the acoustic signal that appear to reflect these different motivational states. There may be a difference, however, between the motivational state of hunger or pain (and its accompanying cry) and the discrete emotional states that are signaled in the face. Specific types of cries and facial expression may accompany states such as hunger or pain. These cries and facial expressions may reflect a range of emotional states from anger to distress. Hunger is not an emotion. The experience of hunger may create an emotional state, which is then reflected in the cry and face.

Anger

By 5 to 6 months of age, it is possible to elicit states of anger that are accompanied by discrete facial expressions. At least two conditions under which anger may be reliably elicited have been identified: one in which the infant's hands were briefly restrained, and the other in which an attractive object or piece of food is systematically given and then taken away. As infants become frustrated, they are observed to show expressions of anger. Darwin (1872) theorized that anger expressions were a result of being blocked in obtaining a desired goal. More recently, anger responses have been elicited as early as 2 months of age in response to the violation of expectancy. When a previously contingent action that the infant produced by pulling on a string tied to an audiovisual stimulus was stopped, infants expressed more anger and arm pulling than prior to the violation and when the contingency was restored.

Fear

The emergence of fear during the first year has been a much-investigated phenomenon. Two situations have been examined in some detail. The first involves the infant's developing wariness of unfamiliar adults during the second half of the first year of life. The second involves examining the infant's response to placement on or near the deep end of a visual cliff. Around 7–9 months, infants will display wariness and distress when confronted with unfamiliar adults, which is hypothesized to indicate stranger anxiety or fear. For example, when infants were confronted with unfamiliar adults, adult midgets, and young children, they reacted with wariness to the combination of both height and age of the model, but did not show wariness to unfamiliar children. Others have demonstrated that wary responses are heightened when unfamiliar adults approach in the absence of the mother as opposed to when the mother is present. Attachment theorists identified this behavior as signaling the infant's developing discriminative relationship with an attachment figure as compared to earlier non-discriminative affiliation with adults. Although some research has revealed changes in both central and peripheral physiology (e.g., changes in heart rate) during the approach of unfamiliar adults at this age, few studies have found or identified facial expressions of fear. Rather, it is the complex of facial, motor, and vocal changes that have been related to the expression of stranger fear.

A similar story emerges with regard to infants' responses to a visual cliff. Prior to 6 months, infants do not show signs of wariness or distress in response to placement on the deep side of the visual cliff. However, during the second six months, wariness and distress emerge when infants are placed on the deep side or on the edge and encouraged to cross from the shallow to the deep side of the cliff. A number of studies have examined the correlates of this wariness. Specifically, the onset of crawling has been associated with the emergence of fear of the visual cliff. Infant wariness appears to increase as a function of onset of crawling, suggesting that perceptual changes associated with crawling may underlie that response to depth cues. Experience with crawling (and perhaps falling off heights) may also contribute to wariness. In line with this, significant changes in hemispheric EEG coherence that accompanied the onset of crawling have been shown. These changes may facilitate organization of the brain centers responsible for these fear responses.

Sadness

Another negative emotion emerging during the second half of the first year of life is sadness. Darwin's (1872) notion of sadness was that it reflected a response on the part of the individual to the loss of an important person, and the physiological attempt to regulate expression of distress at that loss. Bowlby (1972) invoked Darwin's description to illustrate the exhibition of sadness in response to the loss of an attachment figure. Although the full facial configuration of sadness appears only in the second half of the first year, a partial facial configuration becomes apparent earlier in the first year. The 'horse shoe pout' (the turning down of the corners of the mouth) is believed to be an attempt to suppress crying and distress. This configuration figures prominently in the expression of sadness, and is present by around 6 months of age. By the end of the first year, infants exhibit full-blown facial sadness, particularly in response to maternal separation.

By the end of the first year, infant emotional development produces a wide range of emotions that may be identified by distinct facial configurations, and that are appropriate for particular conditions. These emotions appear to function as important signals of social communication as well as internal psychological states. Infant emotional life is linked to the caregiving environment and to responses that the infant elicits from his or her world. During the following year, these emotions are further differentiated as new emotions tied to the development of the self-system emerge.

Self-conscious emotions

During the second and third years, there are profound changes in children's ability to monitor their own behavior and control their responses. Developments in response inhibition and in the control of attention are accompanied by an emerging sense of the self. A marker of the emergent self is seen in the mirror task, in which the child can identify a perturbation in his or her appearance as seen in the mirror (e.g., a red spot on his or her nose). This self-recognition in the mirror is accompanied by changes in emotional expression that have been called 'self-conscious emotions.' These emotions are psychological states generated by some threat or challenge to the self. They are affects that result from calling attention to the self, from comparison of the self to external standards, or from negative evaluations of the self. The affects in question include embarrassment, shame, guilt, and pride. Michael Lewis has done a good

deal of empirical work in which he has described the stimulus conditions that elicit these different emotions (M. Lewis, 1993). He has argued that they each have a unique facial expression and body posture, and that each is the result of a specific challenge to the self.

These self-conscious emotions mainly involve the experience of negative affect, or distress, when the self is challenged or threatened, and have been discussed frequently with regard to the socialization of conscience, prosocial behavior, compliance, and moral values. Parents have elicited embarrassment or shame in the service of socializing compliance in their offspring. Two other emotions that emerge during this time are empathy and sympathy. Empathy is defined as an emotional state that is congruent with the emotion (usually distress) of another. The elicitation of empathy may lead to avoidance (withdrawal from the situation to reduce distress), freezing, or active helping behavior on the part of the young child. Sympathy is the feeling state elicited by someone in distress accompanied by an active attempt to comfort or help that individual. Neither of these emotions has a unique facial expression though both may involve prolonged psychological states. Both most probably are the outcome of appraisal of the external environment and context, with accompanying physiological changes consonant with distress.

Emotional processes

The evidence reviewed above indicates that infants are capable of expressing an array of emotions within the first two years. Additional research has shown that adults respond contingently and appropriately to these different emotional displays, thus demonstrating that infants are clearly communicating their internal states. What is not as yet obvious is whether this understanding of emotional communication is reciprocated. In other words, do infants read and respond appropriately to emotion in others? The current research findings suggest that, indeed, they do.

Emotional awareness

Infants are capable of discriminating emotion in the face and voice in the second six months. Whether infants assign meaning to these emotional displays is debatable. Many of the studies used static faces expressing an emotion. Dynamic presentations using both facial and vocal cues improved the infant's ability to discriminate different emotions, but whether this represents an understanding of the meaning of these displays remains questionable. The infants' responses may have been due to the differences in acoustical or facial cues. Nevertheless, the ability to discriminate these features in emotional expressions is an important first step toward developing emotional awareness.

Studies on the recognition and discrimination of emotional expressions are typically conducted under controlled laboratory conditions. Other research using more naturalistic methods confirms that infants as young as 3 months are aware of changes in adult facial expressions. The still-face procedure in which an adult, usually the mother, interacts with the child and then becomes unresponsive, consistently elicits changes in infant affect and behavior. During such staged mother-infant interactions, infants exhibit more positive affect when mothers are smiling, and more negative affect when mothers are either neutral or posing a negative emotional expression. Together, the evidence clearly indicates that infants are sensitive to different facial and vocal expressions of emotion presented statically, dynamically, and within a social context.

That infants are aware that certain social signals such as those conveyed by the face and voice have emotional meaning can be found in studies on social referencing. Social referencing refers to the process of looking toward another person for information about how to react and feel about a typically ambiguous event in the environment. The assumption is that, if an infant can 'read' and understand the meaning behind an emotional display, then responding will occur with appropriate affect and behavior. Social referencing research indicates that this ability emerges by 12 months. Studies in which a novel toy, for example, was presented to an infant with an adult directing either positive or negative facial expressions toward the toy have shown emotional and behavioral responses in accordance with the affect presented. More recently, the voice alone when expressing fear has been shown to elicit less toy proximity and more negative affect.

Emotional regulation

Another avenue through which we might infer that infants have awareness of their own emotions and feeling states is their need and capacity to regulate their emotions. Emotional regulation is defined as the ability to modulate, maintain, and enhance emotion (R. A. Thompson, 1994) and, depending on the theoretical perspective, is proposed to be dependent upon physiological, cognitive, and social developmental processes. From birth, infants have the capacity to regulate input that creates discomfort. Turning away from a bright light and putting a hand to the mouth when distressed are adaptive behaviors that occur automatically without thought or planning. However, within the first few months, the visual and motor systems mature and the infant begins to perform voluntary actions. Self-soothing behaviors such as

thumb sucking and the ability to disengage attention allow infants to actively control their internal states. These same abilities can be used to maintain or enhance emotion through self-initiated attention to social partners and objects. With development, a more varied and complex repertoire of regulatory strategies emerge.

Infants graduate from simpler behaviors such as self-comforting to information-seeking behaviors like social referencing. Increasing attentional control gives the infant more regulatory flexibility, not only in disengaging from negatively arousing stimuli but also in shifting attention to more pleasurable activities or stimuli. Importantly, several studies have demonstrated that the behaviors infants use when negatively aroused are effective in reducing distress. Equally importantly, the finding that regulatory behaviors such as distraction and withdrawal are specific to the emotion being expressed (e.g., anger, fear) suggests that infants are aware of the different emotions they are experiencing.

The emergence of these and other developmental processes allows for regulatory input from the environment. While the young infants possess an array of putative regulatory behaviors, these strategies are only effective at low levels of emotional arousal. Caregivers, therefore, are critical to the modulation of infant emotion, particularly when the intensity of the emotion is high. Moreover, caregivers, through their ministrations, convey to infants what are acceptable levels of emotional expression. As the infant develops self-regulatory abilities, the role of the caregiver shifts from directly soothing distress to supporting and scaffolding the infant's existing abilities. The family increasingly becomes an important agent for transmitting expectations for emotional expression.

Early childhood and beyond

Toddlers and preschoolers continue to learn which emotions to express and where and when to do so, and to develop emotional understanding that involves the ability to label emotions, to use emotion language, and to know the causes and consequences of emotions.

Expanded social interactions and environments require the young child to learn ways of communicating non-verbal emotional signals in socially appropriate ways. The complexity of the emotions expressed, the knowledge of the appropriate emotion for a given situation, and the cultural rules for displaying a given emotion are the result of within-person differences, as well as interpersonal interactions that contribute to the child's abilities. By 3 years of age, children are able to decode and label other's emotions correctly. Interestingly, they are able to label and generate appropriate situations for positive emotions before negative emotions. In preschoolers, understanding the causes and consequences of emotion is quite sophisticated. However, they are more adept at describing the causes of their own emotions than those of peers and parents. Emotional understanding is also enhanced through the use of emotion language. Children as young as 2 years of age use emotion words to describe their internal states and influence the behavior of others. Talking about emotion, particularly within the family, is an important vehicle for teaching young children about emotions in themselves and others, and for dealing with emotionally charged events.

For preschoolers, adhering to the cultural or display rules that suggest when to mask or substitute a felt emotion for prosocial reasons appears to be a difficult task. This is most likely because it involves a complex understanding of rules, contexts, and gender expectations. However, these abilities develop rapidly in school-age children, and girls assimilate these rules into their repertoire sooner than boys.

The abilities described above are not traits that young children develop at specified time points. Rather, their development is the result of interactions that socialize the child over time. These interactions are embedded within the larger cultural context, which also exerts a socializing influence. The complexities of the process of emotion socialization are many. The individual characteristics of the parent and the child, the child's age, sex, and siblings, are just some of the many factors that may influence this essential but complicated developmental process.

Conclusions

During the first three years, there is rapid development of complex emotional states. These states may involve the expression of discrete facial expressions, or they may involve more prolonged mood states (e.g., empathy or sympathy). Development of emotional life in the first years appears to involve three motivating forces. Firstly, discrete emotions emerge along basic motivational continua of approach and withdrawal to novelty and uncertainty. Disgust, fear, interest, and joy all appear early in life, and are the result of the infant's fundamental hedonic responses to stimulus intensity and novelty. Fear or wariness is a response to novelty or perceived threat. That is, with development, infants may appraise certain situations as threatening and hence respond with wariness or fear.

Secondly, emotions emerge as a function of social interaction. Social smiling and anger are two discrete and distinct emotions surfacing early in the first year of life that are a result of social interaction. Sadness, as well, is a result of the loss of positive social interaction.

The third force is the emerging ability to monitor behavior and particularly to self-monitor responses. The development of self-control is paralleled by an increasing appreciation of the self. Self-conscious emotions that involve threats to the self emerge with that increasing self-appreciation.

Emotional development involves not only the emergence of specific emotions, but also the development of abilities to understand and appropriately communicate emotions. By the end of the first two years, infants display a rich array of emotions that guide their own behavior, as well as that of those in their social sphere. As this social context expands, the toddler participates fully in emotional communication, and through these interactions obtains a rudimentary understanding of emotion labels and the situations that generate these emotions. During the preschool years, their knowledge of the causes and consequences of emotion expands along with their understanding of the rules that govern their expression. Each of these interrelated emotion abilities is a component of emotional competence, a developmental goal that is vital in understanding one's own experiences and negotiating successful interactions with others.

The study of the development of emotion will benefit from future research in three areas of work. Firstly, developmental psychologists recognize the need for specificity in describing both the stimulus and the context in which the stimulus is presented when eliciting emotion in the infant or young child. Enhanced specificity will provide a level of precision regarding the elicitors of emotion that is necessary for behavioral description and study of the development of emotional responses.

Secondly, multiple levels of measurement will enhance the study of emotion. In particular, use of psychophysiological responses provides a means for examining reactions to stimulus events in the absence of self or verbal report. Physiological changes coupled with overt behavioral signs of emotion are solid indicators, which together may be used to study emotional development in preverbal infants and young children.

Thirdly, research in affective neuroscience with adults will lead the way in identifying brain areas underlying different emotions and mood states. Such data may serve as clues for examining the underlying developing brain structures responsible for normative emotional behavior. Developmental work will provide important information on the effects of early experience on the development of these brain regions and the emotional behaviors they support. Finally, a hallmark in the development of emotions is the emergence of control or regulation of emotions over the course of childhood.

The study of emotional regulation will benefit from all of the areas mentioned above: greater specificity of definition and context, use of multiple measures including psychophysiological assessment, and evidence from adult research on emotion control and the underlying brain structures supporting such control. Together, they will provide the means for the scientific study of emotion and the development of its regulation.

See also:
Constructivist theories; Psychoanalytical theories; Magnetic Resonance Imaging; The status of the human newborn; Cognitive development in infancy; Perceptual development; Motor development; Social development; Moral development; Aggression and prosocial behavior; Attention; Peers and siblings; Selfhood; Sex differences; Sleep and wakefulness; Socialization; Temperament; Prolonged infant crying and colic; Cognitive neuroscience; John Bowlby

Further reading

Barrett, K. and Campos, J. (1987). Perspectives on emotional development II: A functionalist approach to emotions. In J. Osofsky (ed.), *Handbook of Infant Development*, Vol. II. New York: Wiley, pp. 555–578.

Davidson, R. J. and Sutton, S. (1995). Affective neuroscience: the emergence of a discipline. *Current Opinion in Neurobiology*, 5, 217–224.

Denham, S. A. (1998). *Emotional Development in Young Children*. New York: Guilford.

Ekman, P. (1984). Expressions and the nature of emotion. In K. Scherer and P. Ekman (eds.), *Approaches to Emotion*. Hillsdale, NJ: Erlbaum, pp. 319–344.

Saarni, C. (1999). *The Development of Emotional Competence*. New York: Guilford.

Moral development

ELLIOT TURIEL

Introduction

The topic of morality has received serious, sustained attention in several disciplines, including philosophy, sociology, anthropology, branches of biology, and psychology. Especially in the early part of the 20th century, sociologists and anthropologists emphasized the societal and cultural sources of morality. Most notable in this respect were the French sociologist, Emile Durkheim (1858–1917), and the American cultural anthropologist, Ruth Benedict (1887–1948). Durkheim proposed that morality is defined by a shared respect individuals feel for their society. Children's morality develops through the formation of a strong emotional attachment to the group, by which they incorporate its rules and values as their own. Similarly, Benedict held that children learn to accommodate to the standards and customs of their culture, which form an integrated pattern that may well differ from the standards and customs of another culture.

The idea that morality is defined by the standards and values of society, and that its acquisition by children entails the incorporation of those values and standards, constitutes one of the common approaches to morality and its development. Through one means of learning or another, children come to accept as their own the moral precepts of their society, culture, or religion. Since morality is viewed as the acquisition of such standards, within these perspectives it is often presumed that it is particular to the group. Accepting these propositions regarding the sources of morality, some psychologists have focused in their research on the mechanisms that would explain how children learn to behave in accord with group values or standards. Various explanations have been offered, including learning through punishments and rewards, imitations of others, and a global identification with parents (as in the theory of Sigmund Freud).

In psychological explanations of mechanisms for the acquisition of group values or standards, emotions of anxiety and guilt play a central role. For example, Freud proposed that anxiety is part of the process of acquisition, and that guilt is necessary for the maintenance of the moral standards of individuals. During the latter part of the 20th century, there was a shift to a greater focus on emotions referred to as positive (e.g., love, sympathy, and empathy). Within these perspectives, it is proposed that young children's positive emotions are the primary basis for such moral behaviors as altruism and caring. Positive emotions are also seen as contributing to the process of acquisition of group values.

The main focus: development of moral judgments

The focus of this entry, however, is on another perspective that emphasizes moral judgments. In this perspective, children, through their social experiences, develop moral judgments that entail understandings about human welfare, justice, and rights. Rather than accommodating to standards and values defined by society, individuals construct several types of social understandings that include concepts of social relationships, social institutions, systems of authority, and legal systems. Moral judgments are not based on understandings of societal or legal systems, but are distinct from them. This perspective on moral development was articulated by Piaget (1932) in his book on *The Moral Judgment of the Child*, which is closely linked to philosophical analyses. In philosophy, the topic of morality has received the most and longest-standing attention.

Moral philosophy has been a central topic in the discipline since the time of Plato and Aristotle. Several philosophers are well known for their treatments of morality (e.g., David Hume, John Stuart Mill, and Immanuel Kant). In philosophy, there are disagreements and debates about the sources and nature of morality, including debates as to whether it is culturally derived and relative, or based on (universal?) processes of reasoning. There is, however, a very strong tradition of philosophers stressing the role of reasoning that includes J. S. Mill, Kant, and several contemporary philosophers, who have influenced research on children's moral development by providing definitional bases for psychological investigations. Perhaps the most influential contemporary philosopher is John Rawls (1971), who is well known for his landmark work, *A Theory of Justice*. Other contemporaries who have had an impact on psychological explanations are Ronald Dworkin, Alan Gewirth, and Martha Nussbaum. As articulated by Nussbaum (1999), the general approach is based on the idea ". . . that human beings are above all reasoning beings, and that the dignity of reason is the primary source of human equality" [p. 71].

Social experiences and the development of moral judgments

Nussbaum (1999) also stated that philosophical perspectives on reason as a source of morality have their roots in a long tradition: "They owe much to their forebears in the Western philosophical tradition, in particular the Greek and Roman Stoics, whose conception of the dignity of reason as a source of equal human worth profoundly influenced Kant, Adam Smith, and others" (p. 71). Piaget was influenced by Kant and others in a variety of ways. The major thrust of his work was on children's development in non-social realms (e.g., their understandings of causality, space, number, and logic). As noted, however, in one set of early studies he examined children's moral judgments. In turn, Piaget's research influenced Lawrence Kohlberg (1927–1987), whose theorizing and research in the 1960s and 1970s forwarded understandings of the development of moral judgments.

There are several features of note in the contributions of Piaget and Kohlberg – some of which have been carried into subsequent research and some of which have not. One of Piaget's major contributions is that he demonstrated how children's moral development is due to their multiple social interactions, and not solely to the consequences of how adults (parents, teachers) influence them. Correspondingly, he showed that children do not solely accommodate to the social environment, but instead progressively construct their own understandings of morality, social relationships, and social institutions. As he put it (Piaget 1951/1995): ". . . socialization in no way constitutes the result of a unidirectional cause such as the pressure of the adult community upon the child through such means as education in the family and subsequently the school . . . it involves the intervention of a multiplicity of interactions of different types and sometimes with opposed effects" (p. 276).

Piaget's focus on the multiplicity of interactions centered on the variety of children's experiences and the related proposition that they systematically interpret those experiences. That is, moral development is influenced by relationships with adults, with other children, and the emotional reactions of self and other, especially those of sympathy and empathy. Nearly forty years after Piaget published his treatise on the development of moral judgments, the topic was again researched extensively by Kohlberg. An added dimension in Kohlberg's work was an emphasis on sound analyses of the nature (definitions, meanings, substance) of the realm of morality in the psychological study of development, judgment, and action. Guided by philosophical formulations, such as those of Kant and Rawls, Kohlberg explicitly specified what was implicit in Piaget's writings – that morality entailed non-relativistic, generally applicable concepts of welfare, justice, rights, and equality.

The idea that the psychological study of morality should be coordinated with philosophical analyses is linked closely to the proposition that laypersons, starting in childhood, think systematically about moral issues. Kohlberg coined the phrase "the child as a moral philosopher" to convey the idea that through their social experiences children construct ways of thinking about right and wrong (not that they functioned like professional moral philosophers). Following Piaget, he maintained that morality is not based on adult impositions on children or on avoidance of negative emotions like anxiety and guilt. It is, instead, based on the formation of judgments built on emotions like sympathy, empathy, and respect.

Piaget and Kohlberg formulated somewhat different age-related sequences to depict the development of moral judgments, but with one key feature in common (viz., that children about 4 to 8 years of age base their moral judgments on authority, rules, obedience, or punishment). Developmentally, there is a process of differentiating the moral (e.g., welfare, justice) from the dictates of authority and the conventional rules of the social system. Piaget proposed that there are two types of morality connected to two general types of social relationships in childhood. In early childhood, it is relationships with adults that are predominant. Such relationships, which usually entail inequalities, provide the means by which children first develop a sense of obligation. The sense of obligation comes about from young children's one-way or unilateral respect for adults in authority (especially parents). Unilateral respect for adults structures young children's moral judgments,

---

Table 1. Kohlberg's stages of moral judgment.

Level I.   Moral value resides in external, quasiphysical happenings, in bad acts, or in quasiphysical needs rather than in persons and standards.

   Stage 1. Obedience and punishment orientation. Egocentric deference to superior power or prestige, or a trouble-avoiding set.

   Stage 2. Naïvely egocentric orientation. Right action is that instrumentally satisfying the self's needs and occasionally others'. Awareness of relativism of value to each actor's needs and perspectives. Naïve egalitarianism and orientation to exchange and reciprocity.

Level II. Moral value resides in performing good or right roles, in maintaining the conventional order and the expectations of others.

   Stage 3. Good-boy (girl) orientation. Orientation to approval and to helping and pleasing others. Conformity to stereotypical images of majority or natural role behavior, and judgment by intentions.

   Stage 4. Authority and social order maintaining orientation. Orientation to 'doing duty' and to showing respect for authority and maintaining the given social order for its own sake. Regard for earned expectations of others.

Level III. Moral value resides in conformity by the self to shared or shareable standards, rights, or duties.

   Stage 5. Contractual legalistic orientation. Recognition of an arbitrary element or starting point in rules or expectations for the sake of agreement. Duty defined in terms of contract, general avoidance of violation of the will or rights of others, and majority will and welfare.

   Stage 6. Conscience or principle orientation. Orientation is not only to actually ordained rules but to principles of choice involving appeal to logical universality and consistency. Orientation to conscience as a directing agent and to mutual respect and trust.

From L. Kohlberg, 1969. Stage and sequence: the cognitive-developmental approach to socialization. In D. A. Goslin, ed., *Handbook of Socialization Theory and Research*. Chicago: Rand McNally, pp. 347–480 (p. 376).

---

which are 'heteronomous.' At the heteronomous level, morality is based on obedience to authorities and the maintenance of social rules: authority is regarded as always right and rules are seen as fixed and unchangeable. It is important to note that, according to Piaget, even at the level of heteronomy children interpret their social experiences. Unilateral respect stems from children's perceptions and interpretations of the size, power, and status of adults.

With increasing age, children form ideas about fairness and justice that are not based on authority or fixed rules, but in part stem from shifts in their relationships. To a greater extent than at earlier ages, there is a focus on relationships with peers in middle childhood. Because relationships with other children are more equal than with adults, they can more readily engage in reciprocal relations and, in that way, construct judgments of equality, fairness, and cooperation. Consequently, in Piaget's formulation, the development of morality requires an element of liberation from the constraints of authority and rules in favor of conceptions of fairness and justice in the service of mutual respect and cooperation. The morality of heteronomy shifts to a morality of autonomy, in which maintaining the moral purposes of rules or laws replaces the idea that they are fixed and unalterable, and in which justice is judged over authority when the two are in conflict. A central aspect of this formulation is that at the level of autonomy children are not simply judging by tradition or existing standards, but form understandings that are not

limited to adherence to authority or social rules as they exist.

Kohlberg presented children, adolescents, and young adults with complex dilemmas depicting moral conflicts (the most well-known is of a man who has to decide whether to steal a drug in an attempt to save the life of his wife who has cancer). On the basis of these interviews, Kohlberg proposed a sequence of six stages that differed from the levels proposed by Piaget (Table 1). In this sequence, children up to about 10 years of age make moral judgments that are not based on feelings of respect for adults, but are structured by considerations of rewards and punishments, and a perceived need to obey authority due to a concern with sanctions. In a second stage, children's judgments take into account the needs of others, and endorse facilitating the attainment of desires and interests of self and others. There is an understanding of a system of exchange so that each person's needs are met (the first two stages being grouped into a 'pre-conventional' level).

It is not until adolescence (the next two stages, grouped into a 'conventional' level) that individuals develop a sense of obligation based on respect for rules and authority, along with conceptions of social systems and perceived needs for social order. At these stages, judgments are based on role obligations, stereotypical conceptions of good persons, and respect for uniformities, rules, law, and the authority legitimated in the social system. It is not until the next stages that there may be perceived discrepancies and conflicts between conceptions of morality and societal arrangements. At the last two stages (grouped into a 'post-conventional' level), judgments are based on contractual agreements, mutual respect, and differentiated principles of welfare, justice, and rights. It is through the application of these principles that individuals might critique and protest societal practices and arrangements.

The multiplicity of social experiences and moral judgments

The idea that children's development is a function of a multiplicity of interactions of different types, sometimes with opposed effects, was not fully implemented in Piaget's (or Kohlberg's) analyses of young children's moral judgments since it is mainly interactions with adults that he emphasized. If we take seriously the multiplicity of social interactions, then it is more plausible to think that children attend to a variety of features of the social environment. In addition to relationships with adults and peers, children attend to people's physical and emotional reactions to events and the consequences of actions. In a series of observational studies of social interactions in preschools and elementary schools, it has been found that the ways children relate to each other and with adults vary with the types of issues involved. Two basic categories of social issues were represented in these studies.

One involved moral issues pertaining to welfare, fairness, and justice. Events that could be classified as moral included those relating to welfare (e.g., hitting, teasing that results in emotional distress), fairness (e.g., favoritism, failure to share equitably, not taking turns), and property jurisdiction (e.g., taking what belongs to another, taking what has been for a time allocated to another). The second category involved what have been referred to as conventional issues. Social conventions are uniformities in behaviors that serve to coordinate interactions within social systems. Conventional uniformities pertaining to matters like dress, greetings, and forms of address are linked to a social system and may well vary from one to another. Conventional events in the observational studies with preschoolers and school children included failure to sit in assigned places, speaking out of turn, and several types of violations of classroom rules.

Two types of consistent findings from this series of studies are informative with regard to children's moral development. One is that the type of social interactions that occurred among participants (children and adults) differed for moral and conventional events. For the most part, moral events entailed communications about hurt, injury, and pain experienced, as well as exhortations to see matters from the other's point of view. Often, the children (especially the victims) reacted emotionally (sadness, anger) to transgressions of a moral kind. By contrast, communications about conventional events pertained to the need to follow rules, to adhere to commands of those in authority, and to matters of social order. It appears that children have a variety of different types of social experiences and that these experiences vary systematically by type of event.

A second finding indicated that young children judge moral transgressions differently from the ways they judge conventional transgressions. In the context of the naturally occurring events, preschoolers were asked if it would be wrong when there were no rule governing it. Most of them thought that acts of the moral type would be wrong even in the absence of a rule, whereas they thought that the conventional acts would not be wrong if no rule existed.

Judging the two types of acts differently with regard to rules is part of broader sets of conceptions in the 'domains' of morality and social convention. Thinking about morality is based on concepts of welfare, justice, and rights. In addition to judging that moral issues are not contingent on rules, children judge that such issues are not dependent on authority dictates or expectations, and that they are not determined by existing or commonly accepted practices, norms, or agreements. Thinking about social conventions is based on concepts of the coordination of interactions in social systems and, thereby, conventional issues are judged to be contingent on rules, authority, and agreed-upon or accepted norms and practices.

Research showing that children distinguish, on the above-listed dimensions, between the domains of morality and convention is important to an understanding of morality and its development. That such a distinction is made demonstrates that children's moral thinking is not heteronomous or preconventional. That is, children's moral judgments are not based on a unilateral respect for adult authority, a conception of rules as fixed and unalterable, or on avoidance of punishment. Children, by the age of 5 or 6 years, have nuanced understandings of the roles and jurisdiction of both adults and peers who are in positions of authority with regard to moral and non-moral matters. Children do not regard adults as all-knowing or their dictates and rules as synonymous with the good or right, and they do not believe that where fairness conflicts with the wishes of authority that authority is right.

In evaluating commands from persons in authority, children take seriously the type of act commanded, and consider an authority's command wrong if they judge the act to be wrong. A consistent finding is that, with acts like stealing or inflicting physical harm, children as young as 5 or 6 years of age judged by the nature of the actions rather than by what is commanded by persons in authority. For instance, whether or not they hold positions of authority in a school, commands from peers or adults that children stop fighting were judged legitimate. In addition, commands from peers (with or without positions of authority in a school) that children stop fighting were judged more legitimate than conflicting commands from adult authority, such as a teacher, that children be allowed to continue fighting.

A large number of studies conducted in several cultures have documented that children make moral judgments based on their developing understandings of welfare, justice, and rights (Turiel, 2002). One set of studies is particularly informative since judgments about morality and religious precepts were examined. Although it is sometimes thought that religious doctrines determine what is moral, this research shows that more involved processes are at work, and that religiously committed people do not simply judge moral issues by religious dictates. The judgments of children and adolescents from Amish-Mennonite, Dutch Reform Calvinist, and two Jewish groups (conservative and orthodox) were studied with regard to moral rules pertaining to stealing, hitting, slander, and property damage, and to rules connected to the authority and rituals of the religion, such as day of worship, women's or men's head-covering, circumcision, and keeping kosher.

Although non-moral religious practices are strictly maintained by these groups, most judged these rules to be dependent on the religious context. The non-moral religious rules were not seen as applicable to people of other religions, and it was thought that members of their own religion would not be obligated to follow the rules if there were nothing in the Bible about them. Judgments about the moral rules entailed a different kind of connection to religion. It was thought that members outside one's religion were also obligated to follow those rules, and evaluations of the moral acts were not judged to be dependent on God's word. Acts like hitting others or stealing would be wrong even if there were nothing in the Bible or if God had not said anything about these acts, because of harm, or injustice. The findings indicate that the relationship between religion and morality entails an interweaving between moral judgments and what is given and should exist in religious precepts. Moral criteria of welfare, justice, and rights are applied to religion to at least the same extent as religious doctrine is seen to establish the good. Practices of importance to the religion, but of conventional types, are judged differently in that they are seen as binding only to members of the religion and contingent on rules and authority within the religious system.

Studies bearing on the role of religious affiliation and commitment, along with many of the other studies on morality and convention, looked at judgments about situations stated in hypothetical terms. These studies tell us about thinking outside of contexts in which people engage in social interactions. However, on the basis of the type of philosophical idea maintained by Nussbaum (1999) that ". . . human beings are above all reasoning beings" (p. 71), we would expect that moral and social judgments are connected closely to actions. Some of the studies already mentioned indicated that this is the case. More detailed and direct evidence of connections between social thought and action comes from research on social interactions around moral and conventional events, and the judgments that children made about those events.

Observations of social interactions in elementary and junior high school settings, across the ages of about 6 to 12 years, revealed that many events were of a moral or conventional kind (as well as those that included a mixture of components of each domain). The moral events often involved transgressions on the part of children, including inflicting physical or psychological harm, taking things from others, and failure to share. The conventional events involved transgressions of classroom rules, disobedience of authorities, and violations of school procedures. As in the observational studies discussed, participants' reactions and communications in moral events differed from those in conventional events (communications about injury, hurt feelings, and matters of fairness as opposed to discussions about rules, authority, and social order). The participants' judgments were examined in two ways. Firstly, many of the children who had participated in the observed events were interviewed on the same day they had occurred. Secondly, the same children were again interviewed approximately one month later about comparable events described in hypothetical terms.

The majority of children in each of the grades evaluated the actual moral and conventional transgressions as wrong. However, judgments about the two domains of events differed. Most thought that moral transgressions would be wrong if no rule existed in the school about them and even if acceptable to the teacher. The reasons given for these judgments involved the need to prevent harm to persons, act in fair ways, and respect rights. By contrast, it was judged that the conventional transgressions would be acceptable if no rules were in place, or if the teacher found them acceptable. The reasons for these judgments involved the role of traditions, customs, and authority in the social organization of the classroom and school.

It appears, therefore, that children's judgments are interconnected with their social interactions. Their judgments about experienced events were in keeping with the types of reactions and communications that occurred during the events, and entailed the types of conceptual discriminations between morality and social convention typically made in non-behavioral contexts. These same children's judgments about hypothetical situations, assessed at a later time, corresponded closely with judgments about the actual events. We know, consequently, that there are close connections between moral thought and action. However, a great deal is still unknown about how it is that in some situations people act on their moral judgments and in other situations they may not. A key element in answering this question will be how people make priorities among the different types of domains or judgment they apply to complex and multifaceted situations.

Morality and social resistance

There is abundant evidence demonstrating that children make moral judgments at a relatively early age. They judge that it is wrong to inflict harm on others and that fairness should be maintained. Changes in moral thinking do occur with age. Adolescents, in addition to holding concepts about welfare, form better under-standings of reciprocity in social relationships, equity, and the need to maintain justice and rights.

Since children, adolescents, and adults make moral judgments that are not confused with authority, rules, or needs and desires, it might be expected that social relationships are generally harmonious and absent of much conflict. This would seem counter-intuitive to many, who perceive social relationships, especially in childhood and adolescence, to entail a fair amount of conflict. Indeed, it is correct that conflicts occur and all is not harmonious – even among adults. However, the sources of conflict are not simply or solely due to adults' efforts to socialize children into a moral point of view.

Research with children has shown that there are several moral strands in social development. Children do develop moral judgments and actions that result in caring for others, efforts to help, and, more generally, socially positive actions. Yet, studies also show that children act in opposition to others and become involved in conflicts, including those with parents. There are at least two sources of opposition and conflicts. One is that, along with development in the moral and conventional domains, there is development in a domain that can be termed 'personal.' The personal domain reflects concerns with areas of activity legitimately deemed within the purview of personal jurisdiction. An interplay of moral judgments and conceptions of personal jurisdiction make for a combination of sociability and opposition among children. Moral judgments, too, can be sources of conflicts insofar as children judge the acts or demands of others as unfair.

Adolescents and parents, too, get into conflicts, but most of the time not about moral issues. Research shows that parents and adolescents are often in agreement about issues in the moral domain. Disagreements and conflicts are more likely to occur over social conventions and areas of personal choice. Often adolescents are unwilling to accept the conventional regulations that are expected by their parents. Furthermore, parents often believe that their adolescents are too young to make certain choices of a personal kind (e.g., regarding sex, drugs, alcohol, education) that the parents think would be acceptable at older ages. Conflicts emerge insofar as adolescents believe that they are already capable of making those choices.

Differences in moral perspectives do produce disagreements and conflicts among adults when societal arrangements and cultural practices around social hierarchies are perceived by some to be unjust or detrimental to the welfare of a group. Tensions and conflicts are evident between people of different social classes, and when minority groups are treated unequally or denied their basic rights. The most frequently studied tensions and conflicts stemming from social hierarchies have been those between females and males. It is sometimes thought that arrangements of dominance and subordination between males and females, especially within families, are accepted because people in dominant or subordinate positions believe they should fulfill their respective roles. However, psychological and anthropological research that has examined the perspec-tives of women has shown that they often express strong discontent with their roles. They judge societal arrange-ments to be unfair and as violating their rights. In their everyday lives, women in cultures with traditional social arrangements simultaneously identify with their culture and are critical of it. The criticisms entail the judgment that certain cultural practices are unfair and actions are taken in efforts to subvert and change the system. For instance, women in traditional cultures typically use a variety of strategies to get around the control imposed upon them by men in their daily lives, and to subvert practices like arranged marriages and polygamy.

Conclusions

Psychological research on opposition to societal arrangements from the perspective of people's moral judgments provides another important connection between moral psychology and moral philosophy (Nussbaum, 1999; Turiel, 2002). Future research is likely to give more attention to how moral, social, and personal judgments are applied by people in different positions in the social hierarchy to the ways societies are organized. It is also likely to focus more on pinpointing the age-related changes that occur in moral thinking. The question of how moral judgments are related to actions is another topic requiring much more research.

See also:
Constructivist theories; Psychoanalytical theories; Theories of the child's mind; Social development; Parenting and the family; Peers and siblings; Socialization; Anthropology; Education; Jean Piaget

Further reading

Kohlberg, L. (1984). *Essays on Moral Development: The Psychology of Moral Development*. San Francisco: Harper & Row.

Nucci, L. (2001). *Education in the Moral Domain*. Cambridge: Cambridge University Press.

Turiel, E. (1998). The development of morality. In W. Damon (gen. ed.), N. Eisenberg (vol. ed.), *Handbook of Child Psychology*, 5th edn. Vol. III: *Social, Emotional, and Personality Development*, New York: Wiley, pp. 863–932.

Speech development

RAYMOND D. KENT

Introduction

Speech development in children is a complex process that occurs over several years, beginning in some of its aspects in the neonate and extending in its finer details to at least the ages of puberty and adolescence. A substantial research effort has been made to specify the age at which particular speech milestones are achieved, and much of the contemporary understanding rests on this kind of knowledge. Most commonly, speech development is described in terms of the mastery of phonemes (the distinctive sound elements used to form words and morphemes in a particular language). Mastery of this kind typically is determined as the correct production of sounds according to a percentage criterion (e.g., 50%, 75%, or 100% correct production). With a 75% criterion, most children will have completed speech development by the age of 7 or 8 years, meaning that all of the phonemes are produced correctly at least 75% of the time. Phonemic mastery is particularly important to clinical assessment of articulatory or phonological disorders in children. To be sure, phonemes are not the only unit of speech behavior, and the full description of speech ability recognizes the interplay of units of different kinds and sizes, including phonetic features, phonemes, syllables, and words. But a child's progress toward speech competence is generally described in respect to the ability to produce the phonemes of the language.

It can be misleading to indicate an exact age at which any speech sound, let alone all the sounds in a language, should be acquired. Children exhibit considerable variability in the age at which sounds are mastered, so that averages based on group studies should be used with caution. Differences among languages and dialects also must be taken into account, although developmental data are simply not available for many of the world's languages. It is also misleading to say that the process of speech development stops at any particular point in childhood. Careful observation reveals that speech undergoes gradual adjustments even after phonemic mastery is judged to have occurred. Furthermore, phonemic mastery is a manifestation of several underlying processes, including perception of the acoustic cues for phonemic recognition, control over the muscles of the speech production system, and application of the phonological regularities of the ambient language. All of these depend on the maturation of the nervous system and the systems of speech production, including the respiratory system, larynx, and the vocal tract (consisting of the pharynx, jaw, tongue, velum, and lips). These processes are typically interactive and disruption of any one of them places the child at risk for delayed or disordered spoken language.

On the complexity of speech

It is well to note that speech is actually a quite demanding behavior. This assertion may be difficult to reconcile with the apparent ease with which many individuals utter speech for long periods without evidence of fatigue or exertion. But speech is arguably our fastest discrete mechanical performance. The mature speaker can readily produce speech at the rate of 7 to 8 syllables per second, with each syllable typically containing 2 or more phonemes (yielding a rate in the range of 14 to 20 phonemes per second). Each of the phonemes has its own spatiotemporal characteristics, and these add further complexity to the task. No other mechanical performance rivals that serial pace, which can be maintained for several seconds until the need for inspiration intervenes. Speaking also involves more motor fibers than any other routine motor activity, giving it a remarkable complexity.

Speech is exquisitely controlled in its temporal patterns, perhaps requiring more temporal precision than any other motor act. And, beyond this, the motor actions must be linked to be the complexity of language, to ensure that a linguistic message is executed in a timely and accurate fashion. Therefore, speech development is a remarkable, yet commonplace, accomplishment that

Table 1. Summary of major advances in speech development that are typical of different ages.

Age period	Developmental advance
Prenatal	Functional maturation of hearing at about 5 months gestational age: fetus hears, especially maternal sounds including speech.
Birth	Ability to discriminate virtually all sounds in the world's languages. Transition to breathing to support life; vocalization begins.
Birth to 1 month	Vegetative or reflexive stage of phonetic development: vocalizations include especially cries, fusses, belches, hiccups, and some simple moans and coos.
2 to 3 months	Cooing stage: simple vocalizations containing mostly vowels, but sometimes accompanied by a limited number of consonants.
4 to 5 months	Expansion stage: vocal tract is remodeled to look more like that of the adult human, and the phonetic repertoire increases.
6 to 10 months	Babbling stage: sequences of syllables such as "ba ba ba ba." Syllables are more reliably structured, and prosodic patterns may resemble those in adult speech. Vocalizations begin to reflect the ambient language.
11 to 18 months	Auditory discrimination of speech is tuned to the ambient language and children may begin to lose the discrimination of some contrasts from non-native languages. The phonetic inventory begins to grow but is quite limited.
19 to 24 months	By the age of 2 years, children possess 10 to 20 consonants and have sufficient phonetic ability to learn many new words, and therefore to establish phonological principles that will guide further lexical acquisition.
25 to 36 months	Continued growth in phonetic inventory, along with vocabulary and syntax. Stuttering is often first noticed at about this age.
3 to 4 years	Almost all vowels are mastered by this age, along with a number of consonants.
4 to 6 years	Closing in on phonemic mastery, with the exception of fricative (noise) sounds.
6 to 9 years	Phonemic mastery typically completed, but refinements in speech production continue.
9+ years	For practical purposes, speech development is complete, but developmental changes can be observed (e.g., voice change in adolescence).

opens the door to the power of language, which some believe to be the most distinctive feature of humans. The eminent speech scientist Dennis Fry referred to our species as *homo loquens* (talking animal). One can debate at length, although probably unprofitably, whether we talk because we are wise (*homo sapiens*) or if we are wise because we talk (*homo loquens*).

Major achievements in speech development

Accounts of speech development frequently describe the process with respect to age-related stages, as though the child progresses from one plateau of speaking ability to the next. Although the stages will not fit each individual child perfectly, they have a general value in portraying developmental advances, and are one of the few ways of economically describing a complex phenomenon. A stage description will be used here, but with the caveat that stages force a somewhat artificial categorical mold on a process that is continuously unfolding. It should be recognized that stage descriptions can be an artifact of observation techniques and analytical conventions. Yet they capture some fundamental advances that have theoretical and empirical significance. For additional

information, see Fletcher and MacWhinney (1995), Locke (1993), Oller (2000), and Vihman (1996).

Major developments are summarized in Table 1, and the following discussion is keyed to the developmental periods listed in the table. Before continuing, it should be noted that it is difficult to describe the development of speech, or any aspect of speech, without using the symbols of the International Phonetic Alphabet to identify speech sounds unambiguously. Because not all readers will be familiar with these phonetic symbols, a keyword in italics is given each time a phonetic symbol is introduced. For example, the phonetic symbol [i] designates the sound of the vowel in the word *he*. It is also helpful to use a few articulatory descriptions that refer to where speech sounds are made.

Figure 1 is a simplified drawing of the vocal tract, showing the major articulators for speech as seen in a midsagittal section that divides the head into left and right halves. The descriptors for place of consonant articulation are illustrated in Figure 2. These are: (1) bilabial (both lips), (2) labio-dental (lower lip and upper incisors), (3) lingua-dental (tongue tip and upper incisors), (4) lingua-alveolar (tongue tip and alveolar ridge), (5) lingua-palatal (tongue blade and palate), (6) lingua-velar (tongue dorsum and velum), and

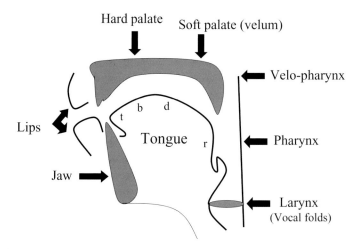

Figure 1. Drawing of a midsagittal section of the vocal tract, showing the major articulators of speech. The tongue is divided into the functional regions of tip (t), blade (b), dorsum (d), and root (r).

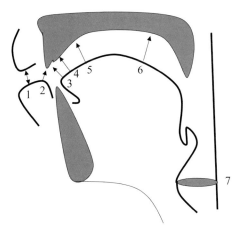

Figure 2. Places of articulation for the consonants of English: (1) bilabial, (2) labio-dental, (3) lingua-dental, (4) lingua-alveolar, (5) lingua-palatal, (6) lingua-velar, and (7) glottal.

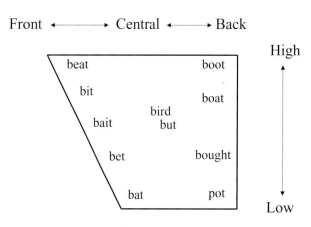

Figure 3. The vowel quadrilateral formed by the articulatory dimensions of tongue height (low to high) and tongue advancement (front to back). Keywords for selected vowels of American English are positioned in the quadrilateral to show the lingual articulation of the vowels.

(7) glottal (the glottis is the space between the vocal folds). Vowels of American English are shown in Figure 3 as a quadrilateral diagram formed by two dimensions of tongue position: front-back and high-low. Keywords for selected vowels are positioned in the diagram to show their lingual articulation (e.g., the vowel in the word *beat* is a high-front vowel).

Prenatal period

Although we may say in a general way that all human behaviors are rooted in events that occur during the embryonic and fetal stages, there is good reason to mark the beginning of speech during fetal development with respect to specific processes that shape early behavioral preferences. The human ear, an important sensory organ in speech acquisition, is well developed by about 5 months gestational age, which allows a fetus to hear maternal and some other environmental sounds. Although these acoustic stimuli are attenuated by their passage through the maternal tissues of flesh and fluid, they have sufficient energy that a fetus is exposed to important acoustic cues pertaining to the mother's voice and to the language used by those in close proximity. As a consequence of this exposure, the newborn shows a preference for the mother's voice over those of other women and for certain aspects of the parental language over other languages (Jusczyk, 1997). Fetal hearing prepares the newborn for a world in which sound has immense social value. In this sense, speech development, at least in its perceptual aspects, begins before birth, and a baby enters the world with an auditory bias to the mother's voice and the dominant language used in the home.

Birth to 1 month

At birth, the lungs fill with air for the first time, and the success of this vital physiological transformation is signaled by vocalization, often, but not necessarily, a cry. The author's daughter announced her arrival with a series of coos (crying came later). Strength of cry is one of the rated variables used to calculate the Apgar score, which, among other things, indicates the need for resuscitation. Whatever these natal sounds may be, they open the way to a lifetime of vocalization, proceeding from the gurgles, coos, and babbles of infancy (from the Latin for 'incapable of speech') to the articulate pronouncements of the adult speaker, and finally to the moans that announce the end of life. Sounds produced within the first month of life include cries, grunts, hiccups, and other sounds that are collectively labeled 'reflexive or vegetative vocalizations.' The newborn's speech production system differs considerably from that of the adult, not only in size but also in the relative shape of individual structures and their relationship to one another. The neonate's larynx is relatively high in the neck, the tongue nearly fills the oral cavity, the teeth have not erupted to form a dental boundary for the tongue, and the vocal tract has a gentle angle along its course from larynx to lips. These features can be seen in Figure 4, which is a magnetic resonance image of a 2-week-old. Taken together, these anatomical features give the neonate's vocal tract a shape that contrasts with that of an adult male (Fig. 5). Note in particular the short length of the pharynx (double-headed arrow) in the neonate, compared to the adult.

2 to 3 months

Many observers note a qualitative change by the age of 2 months, with the appearance of coos, goos, and other simple vocalizations. In recognition of these sounds, some writers identify a cooing stage that extends from about 1 to 2 months of life up to about 3 or 4 months. Although laypersons may apply the term 'babbling' to any infant vocalization, most specialists use the term more restrictively, as will be explained in the following discussion of the period of 6 to 10 months (Fletcher & MacWhinney, 1995; Oller, 2000). Historically, it was assumed that speech movements are derived from earlier-appearing movements for chewing and swallowing, but recent evidence indicates that speech movements may develop separately from these nutritive behaviors, and have distinctive patterns of interstructural coupling (e.g., the muscular interaction between lips and jaw). Speech in its earliest forms may diverge from vegetative behaviors that use essentially the same musculature, but this issue is not entirely resolved and awaits further study.

It is generally accepted that newborns have the auditory ability to discriminate phonetic contrasts in the parent language (Jusczyk, 1997; Vihman, 1996). That is, babies enter the world equipped with an auditory analyzer that is suited to detect the sounds of any ambient language. Newborns have been credited with possessing a 'universal phonetic analyzer,' which certainly would be advantageous as the baby orients to the complex world of acoustic signals, an important subset of which pertain to spoken language. As we shall see, this analyzer changes significantly in the first year of life.

An account of speech development cannot be given accurately without attention to the auditory capabilities that introduce the child to the parent language, and that enable the learning and monitoring of the intricate patterns of speech. Although speech can be learned

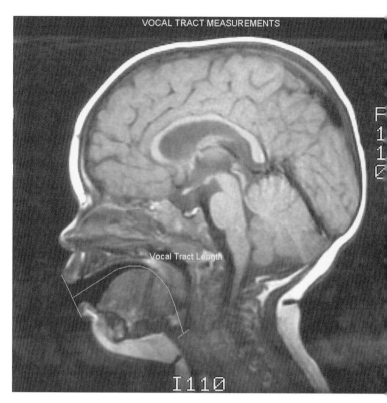

Figure 4. Magnetic resonance image of a neonate's head, showing the vocal tract length. This image shows the midsaggital appearance of the articulators identified in Figure 1. Image courtesy of Dr. Houri K. Vorperian.

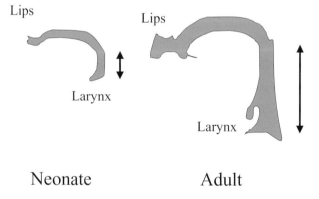

Figure 5. Comparison of the vocal tracts of a neonate and an adult male. The double-headed arrows illustrate the relative lengths of the pharynx.

without auditory cues, other routes of learning are effortful and often not fully successful. Individuals who are born deaf or lose their hearing in infancy typically encounter substantial difficulties in learning speech, even when visual and tactile cues are emphasized as alternatives to auditory information. This is not to say that it is impossible for deaf children to acquire spoken language, but rather that relatively few reach the goal of speech that is highly intelligible and of normal quality. However, the picture is changing with the introduction of cochlear implants, which may bring about substantial improvements in spoken language.

4 to 5 months

At about 4 months, new capabilities emerge. Vocalizations are increasingly accompanied by adjustments of the articulatory system (jaw, tongue, lips) to produce more complex sound patterns. These supralaryngeal actions (i.e., actions above the level of the larynx or voice box) combine with voice energy from the larynx to generate an enlarging repertoire of sounds that resemble adult speech (Vihman, 1996). It is at this time that adults ascribe 'speechiness' to infantile sounds, apparently because syllable structure is increasingly evident.

An increase in the number of sounds that the infant produces at this stage has prompted some observers to describe this period as an expansion stage in phonetic development (Fletcher & MacWhinney, 1995; Oller, 2000; Vihman, 1996). Certainly, many factors contribute to these changes, but one is a remodeling of vocal tract anatomy from a pattern typical of non-human primates such as the chimpanzee to a configuration resembling that of adult humans. The remodeling of vocal tract anatomy during this early period may set the stage for important phonetic advances (Lieberman, Crelin, & Klatt, 1972). Vowel sounds that are most frequently heard during this period resemble those in the words *bid*, *bed*, *bud* (see Fig. 3 for the location of these vowels in the articulatory quadrilateral). The consonants that occur most frequently in the early part of the period are the glottals (e.g., the initial sound [h] in *hat*) and the lingua-velar stops (the initial sounds [k] in *cap* and [g] in *gap*).

6 to 10 months

This period is a bridge between the relatively simple vocalizations of early infancy and the more complex sound patterns that may prefigure early words. During this period, the vowel-to-consonant ratio (V/C) declines so that vocalizations are enriched by an increasing number of consonants. However, only a small number of sounds account for the majority that are heard in babbling, and, at least in the early part of this period, there is a compelling similarity in the sounds produced by infants who are raised in different language environments (Locke, 1993; Oller, 2000; Vihman, 1996). Cross-language research shows that infants tend to produce bilabial [p b m] (as in *pat*, *bat*, *mat*, respectively) and lingua-alveolar [t d n] (as in *tip*, *dip*, *nip*, respectively) consonants in preference to consonants produced at other places of articulation and these sounds dominate in babbling. Bilabials, in particular, have a nearly universal appearance in infantile vocalizations.

It appears that phonemic differences among languages do not strongly influence vocalizations until after about 6 to 7 months of age, which some writers take to mean that universal factors, such as biology, account for sound patterns in the first half-year of life. The effects of experience with a particular language become more evident after about 6 months of age. And so begins a lifelong process in which ease of articulation (minimal energy) is at odds with efforts needed to ensure conformity with language-specific sound patterns (intelligibility).

Evidence that auditory experience begins to shape a child's sound patterns comes from studies of infants with hearing impairment and from those of hearing infants from different language communities. It might be noted in passing that babies born deaf do babble, but their vocalizations differ from those of hearing babies and often decline with age. It is particularly notable that deaf infants lag behind hearing infants in the onset of babbling, to which we now turn.

One of the most striking developmental advances at this stage is the appearance of true babbling, characterized by the production of multisyllabic strings, such as "da da da da" or "ba ba ba ba." This vocal pattern, known by names such as canonical babbling, multisyllabic babbling, or repetitive babbling, is reliably identified by parents and others, and is therefore a conspicuous landmark in vocal development (Locke, 1993; Oller, 2000). One of the most common syllable shapes in canonical babbling is the CV (consonant + vowel), which is also a dominant syllable shape in the languages of the world. Babbling appears to be a major stride toward speech. Firstly, it marks a linkage noted earlier between audition and motor control insofar as babbling is influenced both by the child's hearing status and by the phonetic patterns in the ambient language. Secondly, it seems to be a signal motor accomplishment in that the infant produces regular and fairly reliable syllable patterns that may be a foundation for speech. Indeed, some syllables from babbling may be incorporated in first words. Some accounts of speech development give special emphasis to syllables as formative units that help to explain developmental changes in speech sound patterns. But it should be emphasized that syllables are generally identified by their phonetic constituents (vowels and consonants).

The vowels most likely to occur in babbling during the second half-year of life are central, mid-front, and low-front. This is not to say that high vowels such as [i] (as in *beat*) and [u] (as in *boot*) are avoided entirely by all infants, but rather to say that these sounds are relatively rare in group data. The most likely consonants are the voiced stops [b d g] (as in *bill, dill, gill,* respectively), the nasals [m n] (as in *met, net,* respectively), the fricative [h] (as in *hat*), and the glide [w] (as in *way*). One of the major differences between consonants produced in the first half-year and those produced in the second half-year is that glottals like [h] and lingua-velars like [g k] (as in *gill, kill,* respectively) predominate in the former, whereas lingua-alveolars [d t n] (as in *doe, toe, no,* respectively) and bilabials [b p m] (as in *bay, pay, may,* respectively) predominate in the latter. This shift in articulatory position from back to front is a general index of speech development.

11 to 18 months

During the early part of this period, infants have adjusted their speech perception systems to align with the phonetic contrasts of the ambient language. Evidence for this is seen in data showing that infants at about 1 year of age no longer discriminate many non-native-language phonetic contrasts that were discriminated earlier in life. In short, a child's auditory analysis of speech has been tuned to the native language, and this may facilitate the rapid analysis of speech signals (Jusczyk, 1997; Vihman, 1996).

At least for American English, the phonetic inventory is relatively stable from about 8 months to 18 months, with the average inventory of consonants being about six in number, typically from the set [b d g t m n h w l] (respective keywords: *bay, day, gay, tape, may, nay, hay, way, lay*). About two to three times as many consonants are used in syllable-initial position as in syllable-final position. Consonants in syllable-initial position tend to be the voiced stops [b d g], the nasals [m] or [n], and the fricative [h]. Consonants likely to appear in syllable-final position are [t m h s] (s as in *say*). Therefore, the word *bus* is more likely at this stage than the word *sub*, even though they contain the same phonemes and have the same syllable structure (consonant + vowel + consonant). One implication is that speech sounds are not always initially learned in the same syllable position.

19 to 24 months

Inventory size increases at about 18 to 22 months. A typical 2-year-old has an inventory of about ten to twenty consonants, enough to begin learning the phonology of the parental language. But some major limitations are at work. The inventory of syllable-initial

consonants, which are mostly voiced (e.g., *dog, bear, door*) grows more rapidly than that for syllable-final consonants, which are more likely to be voiceless (e.g., *cat, nap, juice*). These patterns exert a powerful influence on the phonetic form of early words. Putting sounds into word patterns is the subject of phonology, a branch of linguistics. Some writers assert that phonological learning begins in earnest in this period because a child has now acquired a sufficient number of sounds so that some economy of scale is needed. That is, rather than learn and store the sound patterns for each new word (a quickly formidable task as vocabulary grows), a child begins to recognize recurring patterns that can be described by phonological rules or processes.

Observers of early language learning in children have been struck by the apparently systematic nature of the ways in which children simplify and restructure adult words. For example, very young children tend to produce *juice* as "doos," *soup* as "toop," *lamb* as "yam," *green* as "deen," and *balloon* as "bawoon." Analysis of these simplifications and restructurings gave rise to various theories of phonological development that frequently involve the derivation of rules or processes (Vihman, 1996). A phonological rule expresses the systematic relationship between a child's production and the adult target. It is often expressed in the form $X => Y/Z$, which can be verbalized as: X is replaced by (or realized as) Y in the environment Z. A phonological process is similar to a rule in that it accounts for systematic adjustments in phonological realization. It has been suggested that a relatively small number of phonological processes is sufficient to account for patterns at particular points in development, and also for changes in these patterns with increasing phonological ability. Examples of phonological processes are Final Consonant Devoicing (consonants in word-final position are produced as voiceless rather than voiced: *pick* for *pig*); Cluster Reduction (consonant clusters are reduced to simpler forms such as single consonants; *tick* for *stick*) and Stopping (fricative consonants are replaced by stops; *tip* for *sip*). Processes are sometimes classified as whole-word processes and segment change processes. The former simplify word or syllable structure, or segmental contrast within a word. The latter specify changes in segments or types of segments, no matter what the location of the segment may be in a word or syllable.

25 to 36 months

A child in this age range typically acquires additional phonemes and ventures into longer sound sequences. But most children have conspicuously limited or poor production of fricative sounds like [s] (as in *say*) and [z] (as in *zoo*), or liquids like [r] (as in *ray*) or [l] (as in *lay*). This is the age at which parents are most likely to note stuttering, and some experts believe that the difficulty of pairing an immature motor system with a rapidly growing but possibly inefficient language system creates the opportunities for disfluencies (sound or word repetitions, prolongations, and pauses).

3 to 4 years

By the age of about 4 years, children usually have acquired all of the vowels, except for the rhotic (r-colored) vowel in the word *bird*. Mastery of the vowels reflects maturing control of mandibular, lingual, and labial articulation, and is an important accomplishment in phonology. Consonant acquisition proceeds rapidly during this time, and most children achieve mastery of a large number of consonants, with the likely exception of the initial sounds in the words *jay, van, zoo, this, thin*.

4 to 6 years

During this period, most children converge on adult phonology and are capable of producing accurately nearly all of the vowels and consonants, with the possible exception of some fricatives (like [z s] in *zip, sip, this, thin*, respectively), the lateral [l] as in *lay*, and the rhotic [r] as in *ray*. With the loss of the temporary dentition beginning at about 6 years, many children will experience a temporary period of fricative misarticulation owing to the loss of the central incisors. Although children may appear to produce speech quite easily at this age, speaking is harder work for children than for adults, as gauged by the aerodynamic work expended. Children need to develop higher pressures of air (subglottal air pressure, or the air pressure below the vocal folds) than adults to achieve comparable levels of loudness. In addition, children generally have slower speaking rates than adults, and they tend to be less precise in the spatiotemporal patterns of articulation.

6 to 9 years

This period marks a transition between the variable and error-prone patterns of early childhood and the more assured and competent articulatory skills of the pre-pubescent. To be sure, some developmental articulation errors may be noted in the speech of some children, especially for the fricatives that begin the

words *sip, zip, ship, this, then*, but most children produce highly intelligible speech at this age, and acoustic and physiological studies of speech production evince strong similarities to the remarkable precision of adult speech.

9 years and later

By this age, the great majority of children demonstrate phonemic mastery even by rather strict criteria such as 100 percent correct production of all speech sounds, but refinements continue in the motor aspects of speech production, as judged by children's ability to produce a phonetic pattern repeatedly with a stable acoustic or articulatory pattern. The age of puberty (approximately 12 years) is an interesting divide between the capability to learn a second language with native-like pronunciation versus production of that language with an accent that reflects the sound patterns of the first language. Although some individuals can learn other languages with native-like proficiency even in adulthood, the majority do not fare so well. This is one form of evidence used to argue for critical or sensitive periods in speech development, the idea being that certain developmental epochs favor rapid and sure progress in speech acquisition. Although the explanation is not entirely clear, many authorities favor the view that the neural mechanisms of language lose flexibility or plasticity by the age of puberty. If the child is not able to use these epochs to full advantage, because of sensory deprivation, social isolation, or illness, long-term deficiencies may result.

Some of these later-appearing developmental changes are easily heard, as in the case of the adolescent voice change, also known as the mutation. The beginning of mutation is typically between 10 and 12 years of age, and the mean change in fundamental frequency is much more pronounced in males than females. No significant changes are observed after the age of 15 years, which indicates that the voice change is effectively complete by that age. Other less noticeable adjustments are also underway, especially in boys, who experience considerable growth of the vocal tract structures, often continuing up to the age of 18 years.

Conclusions

Speech development is a complex process with an indefinite beginning and ending. Although some of the most noticeable events occur in early childhood, there is reason to place the beginning of speech even in the womb and the final phase of maturation in late adolescence. Phonemic mastery is a commonly used gauge of development, but it masks the complexity of the process. Fortunately, most children acquire speech with apparent readiness and then apply this unique sensory and motor skill to the manifold aspects of social communication.

See also:
Developmental testing; Normal and abnormal prenatal development; The status of the human newborn; Perceptual development; Language development; Sex differences; Hearing disorders; Prolonged infant crying and colic; Linguistics

Further reading

Boysson-Bardies, B. de (1999). *How Language comes to Children*. Cambridge, MA: MIT Press.

Kent, R. D. (1999). Motor control: neurophysiology and functional development. In A. J. Caruso and E. A. Strand (eds.), *Clinical Management of Motor Speech Disorders in Children*. New York: Thieme, pp. 29–71.

Locke, J. L. (1983). *Phonological Acquisition and Change*. New York: Academic Press.

Smith A. and Zelazink, H. N. (2004). Development of functional synergies for speech motor coordination in childhood and adolescence. *Developmental Psychobiology*, 45, 22–33.

Language development

BRIAN MACWHINNEY

Introduction

Almost every human child succeeds in learning language. As a result, people often tend to take the process of language learning for granted. To many, language seems like a basic instinct, as simple as breathing or blinking. But, in fact, language is the most complex ability that a human being will ever master. The fact that all people succeed in learning to use language, whereas not all people learn to swim or do calculus, demonstrates how fully language conforms to our human nature. In a very real sense, language is the complete expression of what it means to be human.

Linguists in the Chomskyan tradition (Pinker, 1994) tend to think of language as having a universal core from which individual languages select out a particular configuration of optional features known technically as 'parameters' (Chomsky, 1982). As a result, they see language as an instinct driven by specifically human evolutionary adaptations. In their view, language resides in a unique mental organ that has been given as a Special Gift to the human species. This mental organ contains rules, constraints, and other structures that can be specified by linguistic analysis. Without guidance from this universal core, the child would be unable to piece together the intricate details of language structure.

Many psychologists (Fletcher & MacWhinney, 1995) and linguists who reject the Chomskyan approach view language learning from a very different perspective. To the psychologist, language development is a window on the operation of the human mind. The patterns of language emerge not from a unique instinct, but from the operation of general processes of evolution, cognition, social processes, and facts about the human body. For researchers who accept this emergentist approach, the goal of language acquisition studies is to understand how regularities in linguistic form emerge from the operation of low-level physical, neural, and social processes. Before considering the current state of the dialogue between the view of language as a

hard-wired instinct and the view of language as an emergent process, let us review a few basic facts about the developmental course of language acquisition and some of the methods used to study it.

Early auditory development

William James (1890) described the world of the newborn as a "blooming, buzzing confusion." However, we now know that, at the auditory level at least, the newborn's world is remarkably well structured. The cochlea and auditory nerve provide extensive pre-processing of signals for frequency and intensity. In the 1970s and 1980s, researchers discovered that human infants were specifically adapted at birth to perceive contrasts such as that between /p/ and /b/, as in *pit* and *bit*. Subsequent research showed that even chinchillas are capable of making this distinction. This suggests that much of the basic structure of the infant's auditory world can be attributed to fundamental processes in the mammalian ear and cochlear nucleus. Beyond this basic level of auditory processing, it appears that infants have a remarkable capacity to record and store sequences of auditory events. It is as if the infant has something akin to a tape recorder in the auditory cortex that records input sounds, replays them, and accustoms the ear to their patterns, well before learning the actual meanings of these words (Fig. 1).

One clever method for studying early audition relies on the fact that babies tend to habituate to repeated stimuli from the same perceptual class. If the perceptual class of the stimulus suddenly changes, the baby will brighten up and turn to look at the new stimulus. If the experimenter constructs a set of words which share a certain property and then shifts to words that have a different property, the infant may demonstrate awareness of the distinction through preferential looking (Fig. 2). For example, a baby may slowly habituate to a long string of syllables that have the form ABA, such as *badaba-nopano-rinori-punapu*. If the string then shifts

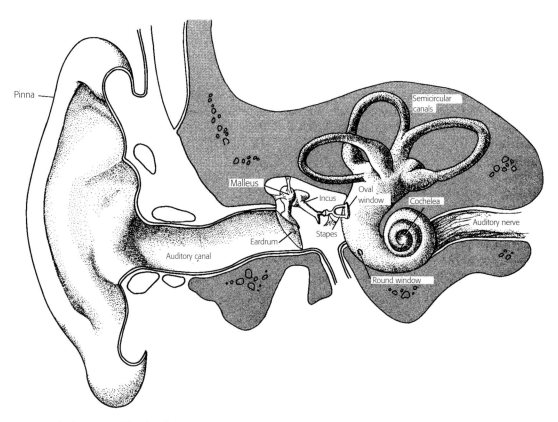

Figure 1. The human peripheral auditory apparatus.

to an ABB structure, as in *badada-rinono-satoto-punana*, the infant will perk up and show increased attention to the new string.

Infants also demonstrate preferences for the language that resembles the speech of their mothers. Thus, a French infant will prefer to listen to French, whereas a Polish infant will prefer to listen to Polish. In addition, they demonstrate a preference for their own mother's voice, as opposed to that of other women. Together, these abilities and preferences suggest that, during the first eight months, the child is remarkably attentive to language. Although babies are not yet learning words, they are acquiring the basic auditory and intonational patterns of their native language. As they sharpen their ability to hear the contrasts of their native language, they begin to lose the ability to hear contrasts not represented in that language. If the child is growing up in a bilingual world, full perceptual flexibility is maintained. However, when growing up as a monolingual, flexibility in processing is gradually traded off for quickness and automaticity.

Early articulation

During the first three months, babies produce cries that express hunger, distress, and sometimes pain. By 3 months, at the time of the first social smile, they begin to make the delightful little sounds that we call 'cooing'

(Fig. 3). By 6 months, the infant is producing structured vocalizations, including a larger diversity of individual vowels and consonants, mostly structured into the shape of the consonant-vowel (CV) syllables like *ta* or *pe*. The basic framework of early babbling is built on top of patterns of noisy lip-smacking that are present in many primates. These CV vocal gestures include some form of vocal closure followed by a release with vocalic resonance.

Until the sixth month, deaf infants babble much like hearing children. However, well before 9 months, deaf infants lose their interest in babbling. This suggests that their earlier babbling is sustained largely through proprioceptive and somaesthetic feedback, as the baby explores the various ways in which she can play with her mouth. After 6 months, babbling relies increasingly on auditory feedback. During this period, the infant tries to produce specific sounds to match up with specific auditory impressions. It is at this point that the deaf child no longer finds babbling entertaining, since it is not linked to auditory feedback. These facts suggest that, from the infant's point of view, babbling is essentially a process of exploring the coordinated use of the mouth, lungs, and larynx.

In the heyday of behaviorism, researchers viewed the development of babbling in terms of reinforcement theory. They thought that the reinforcing qualities of language would lead a Chinese baby to babble the sounds of Chinese, whereas a Quechua baby would babble the sounds of Quechua. This was the theory of 'babbling drift.' However, closer observation has indicated that no drift toward the native language occurs until well after 9 months. By 12 months, there is some slight drift in the direction of the native language, as the infant begins to acquire the first words. Proponents of universal phonology have sometimes suggested that all children engage in babbling all the sounds of all the world's language. Here, again, the claim seems to be overstated. Although it is certainly true that some English-learning infants will produce Bantu clicks and Quechua implosives, not all children produce all of these sounds.

The first words

The emergence of the first word is based on three earlier developments. The first is the infant's growing ability to record the sounds of words. The second is the development of an ability to control vocal productions that occurs in the late stages of babbling. The third is the general growth of the symbolic function, as represented in play, imitation, and object manipulation.

Piaget (1954) characterized the infant's cognitive development in terms of the growth of representation or the 'object concept.' In the first six months of life, the child is unable to think about objects that are not physically present. However, a 12-month-old will see a dog's tail sticking out from behind a chair and realize that the rest of the dog is hiding behind the chair. This understanding of how parts relate to wholes supports the child's first major use of the symbolic function. When playing with toys, the 12-month-old will begin to produce sounds such as *vroom* or *bam-bam* that represent properties of these toys and actions. Often these phonologically consistent forms appear before the first real words. Because they have no clear conventional status, parents may tend to ignore these first symbolic attempts as nothing more than spurious productions or babbling.

Even before producing the first conventional word, the 12-month-old has already acquired an ability to comprehend as many as ten conventional forms. The infant learns these forms through frequent associations between actions, objects, and words. Parents often realize that the pre-linguistic infant is beginning to understand what they say. However, they are hard-pressed to demonstrate this ability convincingly.

Researchers deal with this problem by bringing infants into the laboratory, placing them into comfortable highchairs, and asking them to look at pictures, using the technique of visually reinforced preferential looking. A word such as *dog* is broadcast across loudspeakers. Pictures of two objects are then displayed. In this case, a dog may be on the screen to the right of the baby and a car may be on the screen to the left. If the child looks at

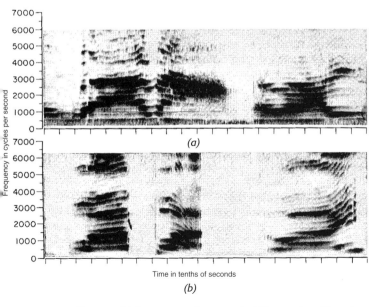

Figure 2. The preferential looking task in which changes in infant gaze signal discrimination of differences in words. From J. Berko and N. Bernstein Ratner, 1993. *Psycholinguistics*. Fort Worth: Harcourt Brace Jovanovich.

Figure 3. (a) Spectogram of a 3-month-old boy cooing. (b) Mother imitating her child after listening many times to a tape-loop on which the baby noises are recorded. From E. Lenneberg, 1967. *Biological Foundations of Language*. New York: John Wiley.

the picture that matches the word, a toy bunny pops up and does an amusing drum roll. This convinces the baby that they have chosen correctly, and they then do the best they can to look at the correct picture on each trial. Some infants get fussy after only a few trials, but others last for ten trials or more at one sitting and provide reliable evidence that they have begun to understand a few basic words. Many children show this level of understanding by the tenth month – two or three months before the child has produced a recognizable first word.

Producing the first word is a bit like stepping out on stage. In babbling, the only constraints infants faced were ones arising from their own playfulness and interest. However, when faced with the task of producing standardized word forms, the child's articulation must be accurate enough to fit within conventional limits. In practice, the forms of early words often deviate radically from the adult standard. Children tend to drop unstressed syllables, producing *hippopotamus* as *poma*. They repeat consonants, producing *water* as *wawa*. And they simplify and reduce consonant clusters, producing *tree* as *pee*. These phonological processes echo similar processes found in the historical development and dialectal variation of adult language. What is different in child language is the fact that so many simplifications occur at once, making so many words difficult to recognize.

Word meanings

As the child's stock of words grows, it becomes harder to keep words apart from each other. To solve this problem, children must strike a delicate balance between two opposing strategies. On the one hand, children may try to be conservative in their first uses of words. For example, a child may use the word *dog* to refer only to the family dog and not to any other dog. Or a child may use the word *car* to refer only to cars parked outside a certain balcony in the house and not cars in any other context. This tendency toward undergeneralization can only be detected if one takes careful note of the contexts in which a child avoids using a word. The flip side of this coin is the strategy of overgeneralization. It is extremely easy to detect overgeneralizations. If the child calls a tiger a *kitty*, this is clear evidence for overgeneralization.

At first, both undergeneralization and overgeneralization are applied in a relatively uncontrolled fashion. Early undergeneralizations are quickly corrected. For example, parents will soon teach the child that the word *dog* refers not to just the family dog, but to all the dogs that live on the block, as well as dogs in pictures. The child's first attempts at generalization are also often wildly overproductive. For example, a child may use the

word *duck* first to refer to the duck, then to the picture of an eagle on the back of a coin, then to a lake where she once saw ducks, and finally to other bodies of water. These 'pleonastic' extensions of forms across situations are fairly rare, but they provide interesting commentary regarding the thinking of the toddler when they do occur.

Scholars from Plato to Quine have considered the task of figuring out word meaning to be a core intellectual challenge. Quine (1960) illustrated the problem by imagining a scenario in which a hunter is out on safari with a native guide. Suddenly, the guide shouts "Gavagai!" and the hunter, who does not know the native language, quickly has to infer the meaning of the word. Does it mean "Shoot now!" or "There's a rhino" or perhaps even "It got away"? Without some additional cues regarding the likely meaning of the word, how can the hunter figure this out? Fortunately, the toddler has more cues to rely on than the hunter. Foremost among these cues is the parent's use of joint attention and shared eye gaze to establish common reference for objects and actions. If the father says "hippo" while holding a hippopotamus in his hand, the child can use the manual, visual, verbal, and proxemic cues to infer that the word *hippo* refers to the hippopotamus. A similar strategy works for the learning of the names of easily produced actions such as falling, running, or eating. It also works for social activities such as *bath*, or *bye-bye*. The normal child understands the important role of contact through the eyes well before learning the first words. At 3 months, children maintain constant shared eye gaze with their parents. In normal children, this contact persists and deepens over time.

Blind children use touch and other methods to establish a similar domain of shared attention. For many autistic children, contact is less stable and automatic. As a result, autistic children may be delayed in word learning and the general development of communication.

Shared reference is not the only cue toddlers use to pick out the reference of words. They also use the grammatical form of utterances to derive the meanings of new words. For example, if the toddler hears the sentence *Here is a zav*, it is clear that *zav* is a common noun. However, in the sentence *Here is Zav*, then *Zav* must be either a proper noun or perhaps the name of a mass quantity, like sand. If a toddler hears *I want some zav*, then it is clear that *zav* is a quantity and not a proper or common noun. Cues of this type can give a child a rough idea of the meaning of a new word (L. B. Smith, 1999). Other sentential frames can give an even more precise meaning. If the child hears *This is not green, it is chartreuse*, then it is clear that *chartreuse* is a color. If the child hears *Please don't cover it, just sprinkle it lightly*, then the child knows that *sprinkle* is a verb of the same general class as *cover*. The use of cues of this type leads to a fast, but shallow, mapping of new words to new meanings.

Word combinations

Throughout the second year, the child struggles with perfecting the sounds and meanings of the first words. For several months, the child produces only isolated single words. However, the real power of language lies in the process of word combination and the child soon realizes the importance of combining predicates such as *want*, *more*, or *go* with arguments such as *cookie* or *Mommy*. The association of predicates to arguments is the first step in syntactic development. As in the other areas of language development, these first steps are taken in a very gradual fashion. Before producing a smooth combination of two words such as *my horsie*, children will often string together a series of single-word utterances that appear to be searching out some syntactic form. For example, a child might say *my, that, that, horsie* with pauses between each word. Later, the pauses will be gone and the child will say *that horsie, my horsie*. This tentative combination of words involves groping on both intonational and semantic levels. On the one hand, the child has to figure out how to join words together smoothly in production. On the other hand, the child also has to figure out which words can meaningfully be combined with which others.

As was the case in the learning of single words, the production of the first word combinations is guided by earlier developments in comprehension. Here, again, researchers have used the preferential looking paradigm to measure early sentence comprehension. In a typical form of this experiment, there is a TV monitor to the child's right with a movie of Big Bird tickling Cookie Monster. To the child's left, there is a TV monitor with a movie of Cookie Monster tickling Big Bird. The experimenter produces the sentence *Big Bird is tickling Cookie Monster*. If the child looks at the matching TV monitor, a correct look is scored. Using this technique, researchers have found that 17-month-olds already have a good idea about the correct word order for English sentences. This is about five or six months before they begin to use word order systematically in production.

The grammar of the child's first combinations is extremely basic. The child learns that each predicate should appear in a constant position *vis à vis* the arguments it requires. For example, in English, the word *more* appears before the noun it modifies, and the verb *run* appears after the subject with which it combines. Slot-filler relations can control this basic type of grammatical combination. Each predicate specifies a slot for the argument. For example, *more* has a slot for a following noun. When a noun, such as *milk*, is selected to appear with *more*, that noun becomes a filler for the slot opened up by the word *more*. The result is the combination *more milk*. Later, the child can treat this whole unit as an argument to the verb *want* and the result is *want more milk*. Finally, the child can express the second argument of the verb *want* and the result is *I want more milk*. Thus, the child gradually builds up longer sentences and a more complex grammar. This level of simple combinatorial grammar is based on individual words as the controlling structures. Such word-based control of grammar is important even in adults. In languages with strong morphological marking systems, word-based patterns specify the attachment of affixes, rather than just the linear position of words. In fact, most languages of the world make far more use of morphological marking than does English. In this regard, English is a rather exotic language.

Filling in the missing glue

The child's first sentences are almost all incomplete and ungrammatical. Instead of saying, *This is Mommy's chair*, the child says only *Mommy chair* with the possessive suffix, pronoun, and copula all deleted. Just as the first words are full of phonological deletions and simplifications, the first sentences include only the most important words, without any of the relational glue. In some cases, children have simply not yet learned the missing words and devices. In other cases, they may know the 'glue words' but find it difficult to coordinate the production of so many words in the correct order. Because so much relational structure is missing, early utterances may be highly ambiguous. For example, it is not clear whether the phrase *Mommy chair* means *This is Mommy's chair* or *Mommy is sitting in the chair*, although the choice between these interpretations may be clear in context.

Children's learning of grammatical markings is driven by several factors. To begin with, children learn that certain markings are never omitted. For example, the progressive verb suffix *-ing* is one of the first suffixes learned by the child. This suffix is never omissible and children come to realize this. In addition, children tend to pick up markings that are highly regular and analytic. For example, the suffix *-s* is a reliable, consistent marker of plurality in English. However, if a form is highly frequent, children will learn it even if it is irregular and non-analytic. For example, children learn past tense forms such as *went*, *came*, or *fell* early on because of their high frequency. At the same time, they are also learning somewhat less frequent regular forms such as *wanted* and *dropped*. As the child learns more and more regular forms, the productivity of the regular past tense *–ed*

This is a WUG

Now there is another one.
There are two of them.
There are two _____.

Figure 4. Stimuli designed to test children's ability to inflect novel words productively in the 'wug' study (by J. Berko, 1958. The child's learning of English morphology. *Word*, 14, 150–177).

increases and we find errors such as *goed* and *falled*. Productivity for grammatical markings can be demonstrated in the laboratory by teaching children names for new objects. For example, we can show a child a picture of a funny-looking creature and call it a 'wug' (Fig. 4). If we then show the child another one of these creatures and ask "what are these?" the child will produce the productive form *wugs* (MacWhinney, 1978).

Children aged 3 also demonstrate some limited productive use of syntactic patterns for new verbs. However, children tend to be conservative and unsure about how to use verbs productively until about age 5. Laboratory experiments with strange new toys and new words tend to encourage a conservative approach. As they get older and braver, children start to show productive use of constructions such as the double object, the passive, or the causative. For example, an experimenter can introduce a new verb like *griff* in the frame "Tim griffed the ball to Frank" and the 5-year-old will productively generalize to "Tim griffed Frank the ball."

The control of productivity is based on two complementary sets of cues: semantics and co-occurrence.

When hearing *a wug*, the child correctly infers that *wug* is a count noun. Given a picture of a cute little animal, the child also infers that *wug* is a common, count, name for an animate creature. These semantic features allow the child to generalize the use of the plural suffix to produce the form *wugs*. At the same time, this extension illustrates the application of co-occurrence learning. The child learns that words that take the indefinite article (*a dog, a wug*) also form plurals (*dogs, wugs*). On the other hand, words that take the quantifier *some* (*some bread*) do not form plurals. In this way, children use both semantic and co-occurrence information to build up knowledge about the parts of speech. This knowledge can then be fed into existing syntactic generalizations to produce new combinations and new forms of newly learned words. The bulk of grammatical acquisition relies on this process.

Special Gift or emergence?

This overview has tended to view language acquisition as a developmental process, rich with opportunities for learning. The control of vocalization is seen as emerging from practice with the vocal apparatus. The process of trimming the meanings of the first words is viewed as emerging from interactions between parents and children. The learning of the patterns governing word combinations is viewed as emerging from operations on individual lexical items that slowly build up syntactic groups. How can we reconcile an emergentist view of this type with the Special Gift vision favored by Chomskyan linguists? Part of the solution lies in understanding the scope of the two accounts. The emergentist account tends to focus on the moment-to-moment processes of learning, whereas the Special Gift account focuses more on the general issue of whether language learning could occur without at least some genetic guidance.

Evidence for the Special Gift comes from the study of children who have been cut off from communication by cruel parents, ancient Pharoahs, or accidents of nature. The Special Gift position holds that, if the special gift for language is not exercised by some early age, perhaps 6 or 7, it will be lost forever. However, none of the isolation experiments that have been conducted can be viewed as good evidence for this claim. In many cases, the children are isolated because they are brain-injured. In other cases, the isolation itself produces brain injury. In a few cases, children as old as 6–8 years of age have successfully acquired language even after isolation. Thus, the most we can say from these experiments is that it is unlikely that the Special Gift expires before age 8. A better form of evidence of the importance of the Special Gift comes from the manual language produced by hearing children of deaf parents. These children piece

Figure 5. A transcript in CHAT format linked to a quicktime movie playable over the web from the CHILDES site (http://childes.psy.cmu.edu).

together a crude form of communication with certain language-like properties, without guidance from exposure to any standard language.

A second form of evidence in favor of the notion of a Special Gift comes from the fact that children are able to learn some grammatical structures without apparent guidance from the input. The argumentation involved here is sometimes rather subtle. For example, Chomsky notes that children would never produce "Is the boy who next in line is tall?" as a question deriving from the sentence "The boy who is next in line is tall." Instead, they will inevitably produce the question as, "Is the boy who is next in line tall?" The fact that children always know which of the forms of the verb "is" to move to the front of the sentence, even without ever having heard such a sentence from their parents, indicates to Chomsky that language must be a Special Gift. Although the details of Chomsky's argument are controversial, the basic insight here seems solid. There are some aspects of language that seem so fundamental that we hardly need to learn them. One of these is the fact that word combinations join together items that are meaningfully related. It is likely that evolution has provided genetic support for a few core linguistic abilities, including the linkage of sound to meaning and the ordering of words into relational structures.

Language emergence and time scales

A more comprehensive view treats this genetic determination of language structure as a type of emergent process operating on a particular time scale. In general, we can view developmental processes as emerging on five separate time scales:

1. *Evolutionary emergence.* The slowest-moving emergent structures are those that are encoded in the genes. Emergentist accounts of evolutionary processes emphasize continuity, and the ways in which evolution has reused older forms for new functions. The study of the last three million years of hominid evolution provides good evidence for the emergent and gradual nature of this process.

2. *Epigenetic emergence.* Translation of the DNA in the embryo triggers a further set of processes from which the initial shape of the organism emerges. The shape of neural development and the structuring of the infant brain emerges from these dynamical interations.

3. *Developmental emergence.* Piaget's genetic psychology (Piaget, 1954) was the first fully articulated emergentist view of development. Current emergentist accounts of human development use mechanisms derived from connectionism, embodiment, and dynamical systems theory to explain the complexities of developmental emergence.

4. *On-line emergence.* The briefest time frame for the study of emergent processes is that of online language processing. Emergentist accounts are now showing how language structure emerges from the pressures and loads imposed by real-time on-line processing. These pressures involve social processes, memory mechanisms, attentional focusing, and motor control of the vocal tract.

5. *Diachronic emergence*. We can also use emergentist thinking to understand the changes that languages have undergone across the centuries. These changes emerge from a further complex interaction of the previous three levels of emergence (epigenetic, developmental, and online).

Conclusions

The major challenge now facing the theory of language development is to work out how language structure emerges across each of these diverse time frames. In the search for emergentist explanations, developmentalists are making use of new models and new technological tools. Advances in computing and robotics will soon allow us to build a cybernetic 'baby' that can use visual and auditory input to build up a human-like lexicon. By moving through its environment, this robot will develop a spatial and body map much like that of a human infant. Another major advance will rely on the linkage of videotape data to transcripts of interactions of real children with their parents and peers. Using web-based systems like CHILDES (Fig. 5) and TalkBank,

researchers will be able share data that will help us understand how social mechanisms support the development of language and communication.

See also:
The concept of development: historical perspectives; Understanding ontogenetic development: debates about the nature of the epigenetic process; Constructivist theories; Dynamical systems approaches; Normal and abnormal prenatal development; The status of the human newborn; Cognitive development in infancy; Perceptual development; Social development; Speech development; Connectionist modeling; Autism; Blindness; Hearing disorders; Linguistics; Jean Piaget

Further reading

Berko Gleason, J. and Bernstein Ratner, N. (1998). *Psycholinguistics*, 2nd edn. Austin: HBJ.

MacWhinney, B. (ed.) (1999). *The Emergence of Language*. Mahwah, NJ: Erlbaum.

O'Grady, W. (1997). *Syntactic Development*. Chicago: University of Chicago Press.

Development of learning and memory

JANE S. HERBERT

Introduction

Researchers have long been intrigued by the development of learning and memory during infancy. For example, young ducklings at hatching have been shown to imprint and become attached to any moving object they observe. That is, the infant duckling is born ready to learn. Early experiences have an immediate impact on the duckling's behavior, and are retained over the long term. The study of learning reflects how we respond and adapt to events that occur in our environment. The most general definition of learning refers to behavioral change as the result of training or practice, while excluding changes in behavior due to biological maturation or physical growth, and temporary states such as sensory adaptation or changes in arousal. The permanence and pervasiveness of changes resulting from learning experiences provide the basis for the study of memory. The most general definition of memory refers to the recall or more rapid relearning of previously experienced behaviors. This entry provides a brief review of four of the main procedures used in the assessment of learning and memory in human infants, and a synthesis of their findings that provide insight into the way these abilities emerge and develop from before birth and throughout the period of infancy.

Prenatal learning

By the thirty-third week of gestation, the human fetus is able to discriminate between familiar and unfamiliar auditory stimuli. In one study, Anthony DeCasper and colleagues (1994) had pregnant mothers read aloud a children's short rhyme three times a day every day between 33 and 37 weeks gestation. In the thirty-eighth week of gestation, fetal heart rate was measured during the presentation of the familiar rhyme compared with an unfamiliar rhyme. Heart rate fell in response to the familiar rhyme, indicating that the fetuses had learned the sound patterns of the story they were exposed to in the womb.

Further research conducted by DeCasper and Spence (1986) suggests that infants may actually retain some information from their prenatal experiences after they are born. In this study, a group of pregnant mothers were asked to read aloud a passage from a *Dr. Suess* book twice a day for a month and a half prior to their due date. In the test procedure, two or three days after delivery, the newborns were able to control the presentation of the recording of either the familiar or a novel passage being read by their mother by modifying their suck rate on a non-nutritional pacifier. Because infants modified their sucking patterns in order to maintain the presentation of the familiar story, the authors concluded that the infants' prenatal experiences influenced their neonatal preferences.

The long-term influence of intrauterine experiences is not limited to auditory preferences, extending also to the acquisition of olfactory and gustatory preferences. For example, infants whose mothers ingested carrot juice on a regular basis near the end of pregnancy showed preferences for these flavors months after birth. Experiences that occur within the womb, and as the result of stimulation from the external environment, can obviously have a long-lasting impact on behavior.

Postnatal learning

At birth, the opportunities for learning and memory are enormous. Researchers no longer share William James' view that the infant's world is a "blooming, buzzing confusion." All the infant's sensory systems are functioning at some level at birth and continue to develop rapidly afterwards, providing researchers with a range of opportunities to assess developmental changes in learning. Reviewed here are four of the main techniques used to examine learning during the infancy period: habituation, classical conditioning, operant conditioning, and imitation. These procedures have been used to address a range of questions about the age at which different types of learning emerge, and whether early learning opportunities have a long-lasting impact on behavior.

Habituation

Much of the early research on infant learning capitalized on the finding that infants are more interested in objects and events that are novel than those that have previously been observed. Habituation – a decrease in responding to the repeated presentation of a particular stimulus – provides evidence that learning has occurred. For example, newborn infants tested by Rachel Clifton and her colleagues (Swain, Zelazo, & Clifton, 1993) spontaneously turned their heads toward the initial occurrence of speech sounds, but ceased to exhibit this response if the sounds were repeatedly presented in a consistent manner. This represents a stimulus-specific decrease in responding rather than a more general sensitization to all speech sounds because, if the word was altered, infants once again orientated in the direction of the new word. The habituated pattern of responding is, however, relatively short-lived, typically enduring for only a few minutes to a few days. As such, this type of learning appears to have only a limited impact on behavior over the long term.

The rate at which habituation occurs can, however, provide important information about the speed and quality of information processing during infancy. Shorter habituation times during training have been thought to reflect more effective information processing abilities. For example, in 1964, Robert Fantz observed that older infants habituated more rapidly to visual stimuli than younger infants. In his study, 3.5- and 5-month-olds habituated following repeated exposure to a single visual stimulus. That is, at these ages infants showed a decrease in the amount of time they spent looking at a stimulus across multiple presentations. Children aged 2 months, on the other hand, did not exhibit habituation under the same conditions. These findings indicate that there may be age-related changes in the rate of this simple form of learning, at least between 2 and 6 months of age. It is important to note, however, that age is frequently confounded with experience in these types of studies. At younger ages, the experience of the infant is such that many more things are novel, and hence habituation at later ages may be confounded by generalization from previous stimuli to the 'novel stimulus.'

Classical conditioning

Early research with classical conditioning procedures demonstrated that neonates could learn to associate sounds or sensations with the presentation of food.

Using these procedures, even very young infants are able to show awareness that environmental events are relevant to them. Conditioning procedures have therefore allowed the assessment of a fundamental building block of learning – the formation of simple associations. One procedure in particular, classical eyeblink conditioning, has been used extensively with adult humans and animals to examine the neural structures underlying learning and memory.

In the typical eyeblink conditioning procedure, a neutral stimulus, such as a tone, is presented together with a response-eliciting stimulus, such as a gentle puff of air directed toward the subject's eye. The airpuff causes the subject to blink their eye, while initially the tone does not. Over time, as the two events are presented together, the tone becomes associated with the airpuff and begins to elicit a blink (the conditional response), even when it is presented in the absence of an airpuff.

Simple variations in this procedure have provided a wealth of information on the neural circuitry underlying learning and memory, and have begun to reveal the limits and parameters that support learning at different ages. In the delay conditioning version of this task, the tone precedes and overlaps with the airpuff, and both stimuli terminate at the same time. Damage to the cerebellum, and the cerebellar cortex in particular, yields deficits in the ability of humans and animals to form associations on this task. In the trace conditioning version of this task, a brief temporal gap is inserted between the end of the tone and the onset of the airpuff. This temporal separation between the stimuli requires the maintenance of a memory representation of the tone to form an association with the airpuff. Learning in trace conditioning involves the cerebellum as well as higher cortical structures such as the hippocampus and prefrontal cortex.

Developmental studies with infant rats by Mark Stanton and colleagues have demonstrated that delay eyeblink conditioning emerges postnatally in association with the development of the cerebellum (Stanton & Freeman, 2000). Comparisons between 5-month-old human infants and adults tested in virtually identical procedures reveal learning emerges at a slower rate in infants (Fig. 1). The slower learning rate does not, however, preclude 5-month-olds from reaching and maintaining the same level of learning as adults across two acquisition sessions of delay conditioning. In contrast, human infants and infant rats have difficulty learning a trace conditioning procedure. Control conditions have revealed, however, that the slower learning rate actually appears to be due to increased cerebellar demands resulting from the much longer interstimulus interval between the tone onset and the airpuff onset inherent in the trace procedure, and not necessarily due to deficits in short-term memory. When given additional training in the trace procedure,

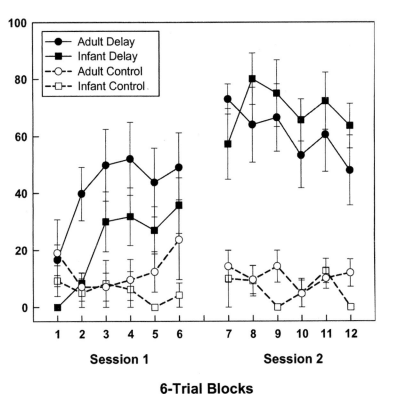

6-Trial Blocks

Figure 1. The mean percent conditional responses produced by 5-month-old infants and adults in paired and unpaired control conditions. Learning is observed emerging in the first session of paired conditioning and reaches an asymptote in the second session one week later. Figure adapted from J. S. Herbert, C. O. Eckerman, & M. E. Stanton, 2003. The ontogeny of human learning in delay, long-delay, and trace eyeblink conditioning. *Behavioral Neuroscience*, 117, 6, 1196–1210.

5-month-olds exhibit learning in this task at the same rate as those trained in delay procedures with similarly long interstimulus intervals.

Although human developmental research with the eyeblink conditioning procedure is still in its infancy, the findings to date reveal that infant learning is more constrained than adult learning by parametric variables such as the interval between stimuli. Changes in these variables undoubtedly change the demands made on the infant's immature neural circuitry and the inter-connections between brain regions. It is these variables that need to be accounted for before claims can be made about the brain development and cognitive functioning of infants. Although the hippocampus is clearly not functioning at mature levels during infancy, it appears that 5-month-olds have at least limited access to these learning circuits.

Operant conditioning

Recognizing that there is a relationship between actions and consequences is one of the key forms of learning in infancy, as it is later in development. Learning about these types of contingencies is referred to as instru-

mental or operant conditioning. Most operant conditioning procedures use positive reinforcement so that producing a particular behavior results in a positive outcome, or reward, and leads to an increase in the likelihood of the behavior being produced again.

A revolution in understanding infant learning occurred in the 1960s when Hanuš Papoušek (1922–2000) used a combination of classical and operant procedures to demonstrate that from 3 to 4 months of age onward, infants could learn relatively complex reinforcement schedules, perform discrimination tasks, and appeared to actively seek solutions for problems. In Papoušek's basic head turning paradigm, the infant was reinforced with milk when he or she turned the head to the left by 30° following the sound of an electric bell presented at the midline. Thus, conditioning signals (the bell as a conditional stimulus and the milk as the unconditional stimulus) were combined with operant reinforcement (the head turn must occur before the milk reinforcement is given). Using this procedure, Papoušek observed that learning rate increased rapidly across the first six months of life and that individual differences in conditioning were observed from birth.

The strength of the association formed by the infant is perhaps best illustrated in discrimination versions of this procedure. In 1961, Papoušek trained eleven infants, aged 4–6 months, that an electric bell signifying sweet milk reinforcement was available to the left, while a buzzer indicated that a bitter solution (quinine) was available to the right. The stimulus-reinforcement relationship developed so strongly that when the discrimination stimuli were reversed infants responded quite inappropriately to the solution they received. Apparently, an infant would spit out the milk solution if it was signaled by the buzzer previously associated with quinine. Similarly, an infant would drink the quinine solution for the whole ten-second trial period if it was signaled by the bell previously associated with the milk solution. Gradually, as they learned the new stimulus-reinforcement rule, infant responding developed appropriately for the solution they received.

Operant conditioning procedures have continued to play a pivotal role in research on learning and memory in infancy since the 1960s. The most comprehensive picture of developmental changes in learning during the first eighteen months of human development has emerged from two operant conditioning paradigms designed by Carolyn Rovee-Collier and her colleagues (Rovee-Collier, Hayne, & Colombo, 2000). The mobile conjugate reinforcement paradigm is used with infants between the ages of 2 and 6 months. In this paradigm, the infant is placed in a crib and a ribbon is tied from the infant's ankle to an overhead mobile (Fig. 2). Infants quickly discover that kicking causes the mobile to move, and form an association between their own behavior (kicking) and reinforcement (movement of the mobile).

This is observed when the infant produces a higher rate of kicking during the non-reinforced response period at the end of the session than during the non-reinforced baseline response period at the start of the session. At all ages, infants learn the response contingency rapidly within the first training session. There is, however, some age-related variability in the time required to learn the contingency during the acquisition phase. While 2-month-olds demonstrate learning by increasing the number of foot kicks they produce within the first 4–6 minutes of training, 3-month-olds require only 1 minute and 6-month-olds learn the contingency within the first minute of training.

The second operant conditioning procedure, the operant train task, was designed by Rovee-Collier and her colleagues to cater for infants aged 6 to 18 months as they become increasingly active. Using a virtually identical training procedure to the mobile conjugate reinforcement paradigm, infants in this task are taught to press a lever that causes a miniature train to move around a track. The response contingency is learnt rapidly within the first few minutes of the acquisition phase, and rate of responding does not vary with age. Familiarity with this type of action (pressing a lever) is undoubtedly a factor in making the rate of learning so rapid that if age-related differences in learning are present, they can no longer be observed.

Imitation

Imitation, or observational learning, has long been recognized as an important means by which children learn new behaviors. By 6 months of age, infants are able to reproduce a wide range of behaviors by simply observing the actions of others around them. In a typical imitation experiment, the infant watches an experimenter demonstrate an action or series of actions, and the infant's ability to replicate these actions is then assessed either immediately or after a delay. The final level of learning is assessed by comparing the immediate performance of infants in the demonstration condition to that of infants who have not seen the target actions or the objects prior to the test.

Harlene Hayne and her colleagues have used imitation procedures to assess changes in learning by infants between 6 and 24 months of age (Barr & Hayne, 2000). By using exactly the same task with infants across this broad age range, imitation studies provide convincing evidence of the age-related change in the rate of learning. Even when provided with double the exposure of older infants to a three-step sequence of target actions, the performance of 6-month-olds lags behind that of their older counterparts. When tested immediately after the demonstration, 6-month-olds perform only a single action, while 18-month-olds

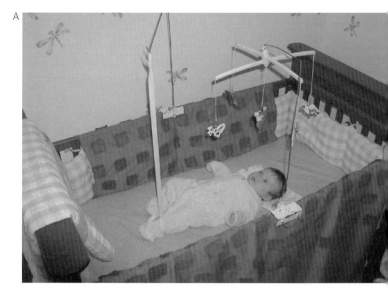

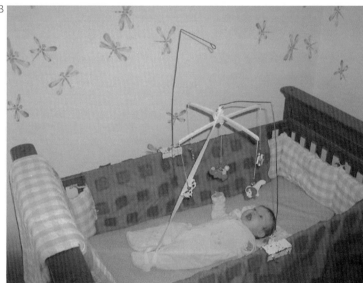

Figure 2. The mobile conjugate reinforcement paradigm used with a 3-month-old infant. (A) A non-reinforcement phase: the ribbon is attached from the infant's foot to an empty mobile stand, so that kicks cannot produce movement in the mobile. This phase provides a baseline measure of kicking, and is also used to measure learning (and retention) following reinforcement. (B) A reinforcement (acquisition) phase: the ribbon is attached to the same stand as the mobile so that kicks produce movement in the mobile. Photographs courtesy of Carolyn Rovee-Collier.

perform two out of three of the possible target actions. In other words, older infants appear to encode the information at a faster rate than younger infants.

In addition to faster learning, older infants imitate new behaviors from a wider range of sources than younger ones. By at least 14 months of age, infants can learn some simple actions demonstrated by peers or modeled on television, though this ability continues to develop with age. In one study, Rachel Barr and Hayne demonstrated that there are age-related changes in the ability of infants to imitate actions they have seen on television. Following a live demonstration, 12-, 15-, and 18-month-olds exhibit learning as evidenced by the ability to reproduce the target actions after a 24-hour delay. Immediately following a video demonstration of the same actions, 12- and 15-month-olds failed to reproduce the actions they had observed, while 18-month-olds were able to reproduce the target actions even after a 24-hour delay. These findings suggest that at younger ages, infants have not acquired sufficient information from the video demonstration to perform the task.

Summary of infant learning

Taken together, these procedures have revealed two important points about infant learning. Firstly, the age at which learning is observed is related to the complexity of the response required from the infant. When the experimental task requires the modification of a naturally occurring behavior such as sucking, looking, or blinking, then learning is observed within the first weeks of life. When the task requires production of novel actions, thereby increasing the motoric demands, then evidence of learning may not occur until much later in infancy. Secondly, across all the tasks reviewed, there are changes in the rate of learning as a function of age. Older infants learn faster than younger infants. Faster, more efficient learning may also contribute to the ability of older infants to learn from a wider range of sources than younger infants. Controlling for these factors will be essential prior to assessing the development of higher cognitive abilities such as memory.

Memory

The earliest emergence of memory in young organisms is largely determined by how memory is defined, and by the procedures used to probe for it. If we apply a strict definition of memory that refers to the conscious recollection of a specific past experience, then the pre-verbal nature of the infant makes it extremely difficult to determine memory ability. However, if we consider the ability of past experiences to influence present behavior as evidence of memory, then even the neonate may be capable of demonstrating retentive abilities (e.g., DeCasper and Spence, 1986).

Many memory researchers continue to debate whether procedures that allow the infant to produce the target behavior during learning (e.g., operant and classical conditioning) are measuring vastly different memory processes than those in which the infant is merely an observer during learning (e.g., habituation and imitation). In contrast, presented here is a synthesis of findings from across the memory development literature irrespective of the procedure used to assess memory performance. This approach is well suited to work with developing children who demonstrate rapid changes in interests and motor abilities across retention intervals. Furthermore, it allows the identification of overarching findings that are not unique to the assessment procedure *per se.*

Short-term memory

Short-term memory is a term used to define the system that holds information for rehearsal, usually for periods of less than twenty seconds. The recency effect, enhanced recall for items at the end of the list, has been thought to reflect short-term memory processing, while the primacy effect, enhanced recall for items at the beginning of a list, has been used to demonstrate that events are rehearsed and stored in long-term memory.

In general, there is no evidence to suggest that there are major differences in the short-term memory abilities of children compared to adults. Within the first year of life, human infants exhibit evidence of both the primacy and the recency effect when presented with serial lists in procedures such as operant conditioning. These findings reveal that retention at all ages is influenced by the order in which events are experienced. There is also no evidence to suggest that at some time point in development, humans might be limited to only short-term memory. There are, however, developmental differences in the duration over which memories can be retrieved as the short-term delay between encoding and retrieval increases.

Long-term memory

An early focus on visual recognition procedures such as habituation initially led memory researchers to assume that infants' retentive abilities were limited to seconds or minutes. As other procedures were developed to capture the abilities and interests of infants, evidence of retention over days, weeks, and months emerged. By this time, age-related changes in the duration of retention had been well documented in the animal literature across tasks and species including avoidance learning by rats, conditioned responses by rhesus monkeys, and simple escape learning by mice. Age-related changes in long-term memory by the human infant have been, and continue to be, most systematically addressed by Rovee-Collier with the operant conditioning paradigms. In the mobile conjugate reinforcement paradigm, 2-month-olds exhibit retention for 1 day, 3-month-olds for 7 days, and 6-month-olds for at least 14 days. By 18 months of age, infants show retention 12 weeks after participating in the operant train task (Fig. 3).

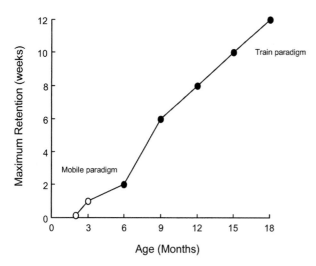

Figure 3. The absolute duration of retention obtained by independent groups of infants in the operant conditioning tasks. Infants aged 1 to 6 months are tested in the mobile conjugate reinforcement paradigm. Infants aged 6 to 18 months are tested in the operant train task. (From K. Hartshorn, C. Rovee-Collier, P. C. Gerhardstein, R. S. Bhatt, T. L. Wendoloski, P. Klein, G. Gilch, N. Wurtzel, & M. Campos-de-Carralho, 1998. The ontogeny of long-term memory over the first year-and-a-half of life. *Developmental Psychobiology*, 32, 69–89; reprinted by permission of John Wiley & Sons)

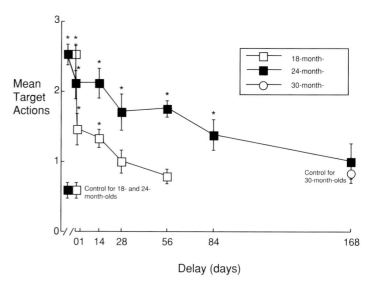

Figure 4. The mean number of target actions (out of 3) produced by independent groups of 18- and 24-month-old infants either immediately after demonstration (a delay of 0 days) or following a delay of 1 to 168 days. The mean scores of age-matched infants in control conditions who did not observe the target actions or objects prior to the test are indicated in the figure by three single points (control for 18-, 24-, and 30-month-olds). An asterisk indicates that the mean number of target actions imitated is significantly above the mean number of target actions produced by the age-matched control group. Data are re-plotted from J. S. Herbert and H. Hayne, 2000. The ontogeny of long-term retention during the second year of life. *Developmental Science*, 3, 50–56.

Age-related differences in retention persist in both animals and humans, even in the absence of differences in the levels of original learning or in the spontaneous production of the target behaviors. For example, in a deferred imitation task where there are identical levels of baseline responding and no age-related differences in immediate imitation, 18-month-olds exhibit retention for actions demonstrated with novel objects for 14 days, while 24-month-olds do so for at least 56 days (Fig. 4). The duration of retention exhibited at any given age is, however, not absolute and can be modified by changing the behavioral requirements of the task, the parameters of the training session, or events occurring during the retention interval.

Forgetting and retrieval failure

Differences in the duration of retention across ontogeny could be the result of changes in one of three main processes: the encoding, storage, or retrieval of information. To some degree, differences in retention early in development may reflect changes in the way in which memories are encoded into the sensory store and transferred to more permanent memory stores through rehearsal. However, the most thorough examination of developmental changes in the retention interval has focused on features of the retrieval process. Reviewed below is the effect of reminders and reactivation treatments, and the principle of encoding specificity.

These concepts are not unique to the infancy period, but may create stronger constraints on memory retrieval during early infancy than at any other point in development.

Reinstatement and reactivation

Although the forgetting function during infancy is quite steep, periodic re-exposure to a brief portion of an experience (reinstatement) can sustain retention over substantial periods. For example, a conditioned fear response in 25-day-old rat pups can be maintained for at least a month by providing weekly reminders of the original experience. Furthermore, a single brief reminder experienced just prior to the retention test can be just as effective as several reminders distributed throughout the retention interval. In comparison to reinstatement, which is thought to maintain the memory throughout the retention interval, a single reactivation session alleviates forgetting, allowing a previously inaccessible memory to be recovered and expressed at a subsequent session.

Reminders and reactivation treatments are important factors in the long-term maintenance of early experiences by human infants. When appropriate reminders are given, even very young infants can maintain their memories over quite remarkable delays.

Recently, Kristen Hartshorn (2003) used reinstatement with 6-month-olds to maintain memory of participation in the operant train task substantially beyond the typical 2-week retention period. Following original training, infants were provided with a 2-minute reinforced exposure to the train task at 7, 8, 9, 12, and 18 months of age. As a result of these multiple brief exposures, infants trained at 6 months of age were still exhibiting retention for this task at 2 years of age. In contrast, infants who participated in the reinstatement sessions, but did not receive the original training, showed no evidence of retention at any of the time points. Thus, it appears that very early memories can be retained over the long term if appropriate reminders are experienced on a regular basis.

Encoding specificity

Studies of verbal learning with adults suggest that the retrieval of information from memory is disrupted by changes in context or stimulus material at the time of the test. The greater the discrepancy between the conditions present at the time of original encoding and at the time of retrieval, the greater the disruption in memory performance. These findings suggest that a specific event can only be recalled if there is a good match between the attributes stored during original encoding and those present during retrieval. This phenomenon has been referred to as the principle of encoding specificity. Although this principle was originally developed to account for findings obtained in studies of verbal learning with adults, some of the best empirical support has come from studies with pre-verbal infants. In the mobile conjugate reinforcement paradigm, for example, even minor changes in the mobile at the time of testing disrupt memory performance in the first six months of life. In one study conducted with 2- and 3-month-olds, memory retrieval was precluded when infants were tested with a five-object mobile that contained more than one novel component.

Studies conducted with operant conditioning and deferred imitation procedures reveal that even very young infants encode contextual information in their memory representations. A match between the conditions present during encoding and at the time of retrieval facilitates memory performance during infancy, as at older ages. The effect of a mismatch between the conditions present during encoding and at retrieval, however, varies as a function of age within the infancy period. Irrespective of the paradigm used to assess memory performance, memory retrieval by younger infants appears to be more bound by the contextual details of the original experience than memory retrieval at later ages. For example, 6-month-olds tested by Hayne and her colleagues (2000) exhibited

no retention in a deferred imitation task if the demonstration occurred in the laboratory and the test occurred in the home. The same environmental change had no impact on the retention exhibited by 12-month-olds.

As infants develop, they become more resilient to the disruptive effects of changes in the cues present at retrieval and progressively more capable of retrieving their memories in a wide range of situations, such as generalizing knowledge between physically different but functionally similar objects (Fig. 5), or from 2- or 3-dimensional representations to real objects. Changes in the constraints imposed by these mechanisms are likely to account for retrieval failures and the observed rapid forgetting of early memories. The gradual loosening of these contextual constraints enhances the opportunity for retrieval in novel situations, and is therefore likely to increase the duration over which a memory can be retrieved. Similarly, as novel objects and events become capable of functioning as retrieval cues, the opportunity for being reminded of old objects and events improves, and may increase the duration over which a memory can be maintained.

Childhood amnesia

Memory development research to date reveals there is continuity in basic memory processes across development. With age and experience, there are changes in the duration over which a memory can be maintained and increases in the range of effective cues that can retrieve the original memory. These findings suggest that there may be no magic age when infants suddenly gain access to more advanced memory systems. Rather, these abilities appear present in a basic form from very early on in development. The perspective that there may be a qualitative shift from infancy to later childhood in memory processes has developed to account for the phenomenon of childhood amnesia, the inability of adults to recall memories for events that occurred prior to 3 years of age. Explanations for this phenomenon have included the repression of unacceptable impulses, the immaturity of the declarative memory system, the development of a sense of self, and the development of the ability to use language as a retrieval cue.

Although the precise mechanism responsible for childhood amnesia differs across these theories, the underlying assumption is the same: at some point during infancy or early childhood, there is a qualitative shift in the way in which memories are processed that allows them to be maintained over the long term. Contrary to these theoretical views, the empirical research reviewed above demonstrates that changes in learning and memory processing early in development are predominantly quantitative in nature: the duration

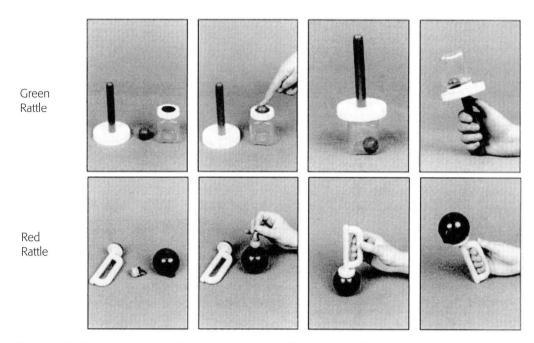

Green
Rattle

Red
Rattle

Figure 5. Stimuli used in a generalization version of the deferred imitation procedure. The two sets of stimuli differ in color and form, but can be used to produce the same three target actions (pictured left to right). The infant observes the actions with one set of stimuli and is then tested with either the identical stimuli or the similar set. These stimulus sets were used in J. S. Herbert and H. Hayne, 2000. Memory retrieval by 18- to 30-month-olds: age-related changes in representational flexibility. *Developmental Psychology*, 36, 473–484. Copyright © 2000 by the American Psychological Association. Reprinted with permission.

of retention and the flexibility of memory retrieval increase systematically across infancy. Unlike the emergence of a self-concept, and the ability to participate in past-event conversations that may be unique to humans, the changes in learning and memory that have been observed in infancy are not uniquely human. Infantile amnesia – the more rapid forgetting by infants – is commonly seen in the animal literature (e.g., Campbell & Campbell, 1962). The presence of this related phenomenon in other species suggests that the answer to childhood amnesia may lie at least partially in understanding quantitative changes in basic learning and memory processes.

Conclusions

There is a fundamental similarity between learning and memory systems observed in infants and adults: learning occurs rapidly, memories are forgotten gradually, and the information acquired and retrieved contains highly detailed information. Across development, however, there are changes in the limits and parameters that support learning and memory at different ages. At younger ages, additional learning opportunities may be required, some events may simply be harder to learn, and constraints on memory retrieval may be so specific that there is a retrieval failure.

Systematic infant research has highlighted the need to examine the factors that control the expression of different types of learning and memory at different ages. This approach has the potential to prove much more productive than simply pursuing the age when different systems or abilities come on line. At least two classic themes of developmental research will undoubtedly continue to guide researchers in the 21st century. Firstly, in what ways are learning and memory development continuous processes and in what ways are they discontinuous across infancy and childhood? And secondly, what accounts for the behavioral changes that are observed? As the range of tasks available for addressing these questions continues to grow and our understanding of current tasks develops further, we are in good stead for understanding the complexities of brain development and experience in accounting for changes in cognitive abilities during infancy and early childhood.

See also:
Understanding ontogenetic development: debates about the nature of the epigenetic process; Ethological theories; Learning theories; Experimental methods; Normal and abnormal prenatal development; The status of the human newborn; Cognitive development in infancy; Perceptual development; Connectionist modeling; Imitation; Cognitive neuroscience

Further reading

Campbell, B. A. and Spear, N. E. (1972). Ontogeny of memory. *Psychological Review*, 79, 215–236.

Diamond, A. (ed.) (1990). The development and neural basis of higher cognitive functions. *Annals of the New York Academy of Sciences*, 608.

Steinmetz, J. E., Gluck, M. A. and Solomon, P. R. (eds.) (2001). *Model Systems and the Neurobiology of Associative Learning: A Festschrift in Honor of Richard F. Thompson*. New Jersey: Erlbaum.

Stone, L. J., Smith, H. T. and Murphey, L. B. (eds.) (1974). *The Competent Infant: Research and Commentary*. London: Tavistock.

Tulving, E. and Craik, F. I. M. (eds.)(2000). *The Oxford Handbook of Memory*. New York: Oxford University Press.

PART V
Selected topics

This part focuses on key topics in child development, some of which will have been referred to in Part IV. The aim is to identify the main issues associated with each topic based on recent publications. Where appropriate, any studies adopting an interdisciplinary perspective are highlighted. Each topic ends with three to five 'burning questions' that need to be addressed in the future.

Play **Peter K. Smith**
Prehension **Claes von Hofsten**
Reading and writing **Peter Bryant**
Schooling and literacy **Yvette Solomon**
Selfhood **Michael Lewis**
Sex differences **Joyce F. Benenson**
Siblings and peers **Judy Dunn**
Sleep and wakefulness **Peter H. Wolff**
Socialization **Mark Bennett**
Temperament **Mary K. Rothbart & Julie Hwang**

Aggressive and prosocial behavior

RICHARD E. TREMBLAY

Introduction

Behavioral scientists borrowed the word 'aggressive' from common language, and invented the word 'prosocial.' The *American Heritage Dictionary* (1985) included the following comment under the verb "aggress": "Though the verb *aggress* has a long and honorable history, it has lately come to be associated primarily with the jargon of psychology and is often objected to."

Socialization theories suggest that 'adequate' environments will help children learn behaviors that benefit others (prosocial), while behaviors which hurt others (aggression) are learned in 'inadequate' environments. Unfortunately, most studies on the development of aggression did not include prosocial behavior, and vice versa. This surprising disconnection between the 'prosocial' and 'aggressive' behavior investigators is highlighted by the fact that the *Handbook of Child Psychology* has traditionally devoted two separate chapters to aggression and prosocial behavior (Damon & Eisenberg, 1998). The studies, which did include assessments of both behavioral dimensions, generally reported a small negative correlation between these two 'social' behaviors, while some studies of young children indicated small positive correlations. Thus, individuals who tend to be helpful can also hurt, while those who tend to aggress can be helpful. Does this mean that environments in which one learns to aggress can also foster prosocial behavior? And does it mean that environments that foster prosocial behavior can also train children to aggress?

Developmental origins of aggression and prosocial behavior

The lack of studies targeting both aggression and prosocial behavior is partly due to the fact that those who study the development of prosocial behavior have tended to focus their attention on early childhood, while studies of aggression tend to use school-age children. These different choices of populations highlight an important implicit theoretical assumption: prosocial behavior is learned during early childhood, while aggression is learned during middle childhood and adolescence. Recent longitudinal studies of aggression with large samples and frequent assessments over many years have challenged not only the idea that physical aggression is learned during the school years, but, more fundamentally, the idea that physical aggression is learned.

Because physical aggression by adolescents and young adults is a major concern in all modern societies, criminologists, psychiatrists, and psychologists have tried to understand how playful and innocent young children become hard-core violent juveniles. The risk of being arrested and found guilty of delinquent behavior is higher during late adolescence and early adulthood than at any other point in one's lifetime. This fact was first highlighted in the early 19th century by the Belgian astronomer-mathematician-developmentalist-social reformer Adolphe Quetelet (Fig. 1). The rapid increase in arrests during adolescence, and its relatively rapid decline during adulthood, has been labeled the 'age-crime curve.' The theories which attempt to explain this developmental curve ranged from biological explanations, such as the rapid increase in testosterone during adolescence, to the traditional sociological explanation (poverty), and to learning explanations, such as imitation of aggressive parents, aggressive friends, and violence in the media.

In 1993, the USA National Academy of Sciences Panel on the Understanding and Control of Violent Behavior highlighted the fact that 89 percent of those arrested for violent crimes in the USA were males. The Panel's analysis of research on the causes of violent behavior led them to conclude that:

> Modern psychological perspectives emphasize that aggressive and violent behaviors are *learned* responses to frustration, that they can also be learned as instruments

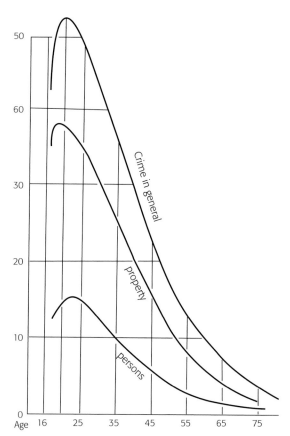

Crimes during the 19 years from 1826 to 1844 (France)

Figure 1. The age-crime curve according to Adolphe Quetelet. From A. Quetelet, 1869. *Physique sociale ou Essai sur le développement des facultés de l'homme.* Bruxelles: C. Muquardt.

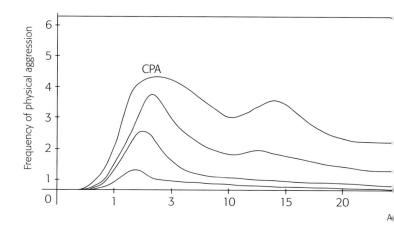

Figure 2. Hypothetical trajectories of physical aggression. From R. E. Tremblay, 2003. Why socialization fails? The case of chronic physical aggression. In B. B. Lahey, T. E. Moffitt, & A. Caspi, eds., *The Causes of Conduct Disorder and Juvenile Delinquency.* New York: Guilford Press, pp. 182–224.

physical aggression than males. The decline of the frequency of physical aggression with age is not expected from the traditional social learning approach to aggression, since exposure to models of physical aggression increases with age. The longitudinal studies also showed that it was extremely unlikely that a child who had not been highly physically aggressive in the past would start to show important problems with physical aggression later (Broidy, Nagin, Tremblay *et al.*, 2003; Tremblay & Nagin, 2004).

From physical to indirect aggression

If most children are at their peak in frequency of physical aggression at school entry, when do children learn to physically aggress? In 1931, Florence Goodenough published data collected from mothers on the frequency of angry outbursts in a small cross-sectional sample of preschoolers. Her results suggested that physical aggression was present during the second year after birth, and that its frequency decreased with age. Verbal aggression appeared to replace physical aggression as age increased. Recent longitudinal studies with large population samples confirmed these early observations. These studies show that if children learn to physically aggress by observing models, most of the learning must be done during the first 18 to 24 months after birth. Indeed, by that age, most mothers report that their child has used some form of physical aggression. However, there are important differences in the frequency of physical aggression among infants as well as among toddlers. Some infants appear to make very infrequent use of physical aggression while others meet the American Psychiatric Association criteria for

for achieving goals, and that the learning occurs by observing models of such behavior. Such models may be observed in the family, among peers, elsewhere in the neighborhood, through the mass media, or in violent pornography, for example.

Reiss & Roth, 1993, p. 7.

So why are males more likely to learn to physically aggress? And why during adolescence?

Recent findings

The interpretation of aggression's developmental course by the National Academy of Sciences Panel has recently been challenged. Studies that followed large random samples of children from school entry to adolescence, in Canada, New Zealand, and the USA, clearly indicate not only that the frequency of physical aggression does not increase with age, but that it tends to decrease. Most children were at their peak level in frequency of physical aggression during their kindergarten years. The same phenomenon applies to females and males, although females systematically show lower frequencies of

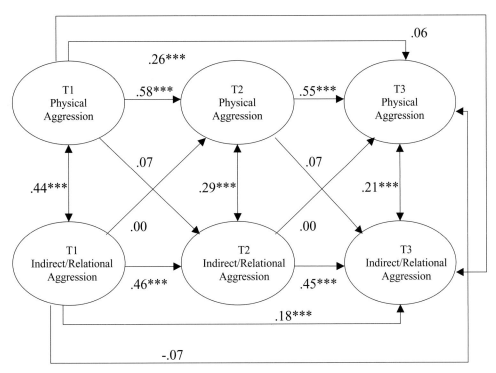

Figure 3. Lisrel analysis of physical and indirect aggression development of Canadian children from 4 to 11 years of age (N = 3089). T1, etc. = Time 1, etc. From T. Vaillancourt, M. Brendgen, M. Boivin & R. E. Tremblay 2003. A longitudinal confirmatory factor analysis of indirect and physical aggression: evidence of two factors over time? *Child Development*, 74, 1628–1638.

conduct disorder, mainly because of physically aggressive behaviors.

Thus, the available data on the development of physical aggression indicate that, for most children, frequency of such aggression increases during the first thirty months after birth, and then decreases steadily (Fig. 2). Compared to boys, fewer girls tend to reach the highest frequency levels, and girls tend to reduce their frequency more rapidly. The available data suggest that the preschool years are a sensitive period for learning to regulate physical aggression. The small group of children (5–10%) who continue to show high levels of physical aggression during the elementary school years (chronic physical aggression, CPA in Fig. 2) are those most at risk of physically violent behavior during adolescence.

Interestingly, while the frequency of physical aggression starts decreasing after the third or fourth year after birth, the frequency of indirect aggression (getting at others behind their back) increases substantially from 4 to 7 years of age. However, there is no evidence that indirect aggression replaces physical aggression (Fig. 3). Once children have the cognitive abilities to use indirect aggression, they use both physical and indirect aggression, or use either one or the other. A large survey of 8-, 11-, and 15-year-old boys and girls from Finland, Italy, Israel, and Poland (Fig. 4) indicates that girls use indirect aggression more often than verbal aggression or physical aggression, while boys use it less. A

longitudinal study of a large population sample of Canadian children has confirmed the female-male difference for indirect aggression (see reference for Fig. 3). Indirect aggression is probably the most frequent form of aggression during adulthood. It has been shown to be of frequent use in different workplace environments, including universities!

Prosocial behavior

Until recently very few studies had monitored changes in prosocial behavior for long periods of time during childhood and adolescence. A 1998 review of age differences in frequency of prosocial behaviors, based largely on cross-sectional data, concluded that results differed depending on the type of behavior that was observed, but that overall the frequency of prosocial behavior appeared to increase with age (Damon & Eisenberg, 1998). Recent analyses of helping behavior trajectories with large samples of children, in Canada and Italy, indicate that the frequency of these behaviors generally increases from 2 to 10–11 years of age, but appears to level off during the elementary school years, and then decrease during adolescence. These analyses also confirmed results from smaller studies suggesting that girls tend to use prosocial behavior more often than boys from infancy to adolescence (e.g. Côté, Tremblay,

Nagin *et al.*, 2002). The period with the most important increases in helping behaviors appears to be the preschool years. It is not clear if the decrease in helping behavior during the early part of adolescence is followed by an increase during later adolescence and adulthood.

Determinants of aggressive and prosocial behavior

Many studies have tried to identify determinants of aggressive and prosocial behavior. Unfortunately, the majority of these studies simply look for correlates, often at one point in time, or, at best, at two points in time. Experimental evidence of causal factors could be obtained from preventive and corrective interventions, which randomly allocate families or children to treatment and control groups. However, most of these experiments do not specifically measure prosocial behavior and different forms of aggression for long periods after the intervention. There is some evidence that parent training and social skills training do have a positive impact on disruptive behaviors if the intervention is intensive and lasts over many years. There is also some indication that an intervention during early childhood can have a more lasting impact than an intervention during later childhood and adolescence.

The most frequently found correlates of aggressive and prosocial behavior can be separated into two categories, individual and environmental characteristics. Individuals with high levels of aggression and low levels of prosocial behavior tend to be males who are fearless, sensation-seeking, inattentive, hyperactive, insensitive to social rewards, and who have cognitive deficits. From a physiological perspective, they tend to have low heart rates, high levels of testosterone, and low levels of serotonin, all of which may have a genetic basis. From a physical environment perspective, they are more likely to have been affected during pregnancy by nicotine and alcohol. They are also more likely to have suffered from birth complications. High concentrations of lead in their environment and poor nutrition have also been linked to disruptive behavior. From a social environmental perspective, their parents have a history of problem behavior, low education, low income, and poor parenting skills. Most of the preceding physical and social environmental factors are linked to parental characteristics, and are obviously highly correlated. They are also correlated with genetic factors and neighborhood factors such as poverty, violence, poorly performing schools, and deviant peers. Most studies have not been designed to take all these factors into account.

In summary, aggressive and prosocial behaviors are mutually exclusive only when an individual is observed at a given point in time. Interactions between two

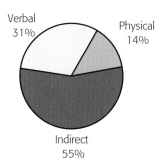

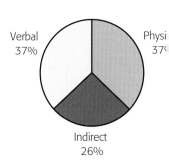

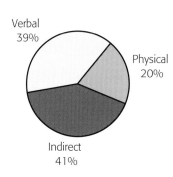

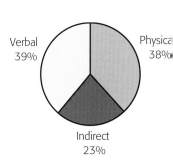

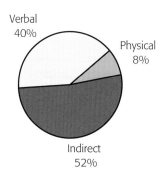

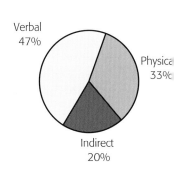

Figure 4. Proportions of physical, verbal, and indirect aggression in percentage of total aggression scores. Peer-estimated data for girls (n = 1025) and boys (n = 1069) for three age groups from Finland, Israel, Italy, and Poland. From K. Österman, K. Björkqvist, and K. M. J. Lagerspetz *et al.*, 1998. Cross-cultural evidence of female indirect aggression. *Aggressive Behavior*, 24, 1–8.

individuals can show a sequence of aggressive and prosocial behaviors by the same person. From a developmental perspective, children appear with age to learn to help others and not to physically aggress. Those who do not learn to inhibit physical aggression are at high risk of being excluded. Although most children learn to fit in their social environment, socialization is a thin veneer that can always crack under stress. Thus, despite the fact that individual differences in frequency of aggressive and prosocial behaviors are relatively stable over time, highly prosocial individuals will resort to aggression when needed, and individuals with a history of frequent physical aggression can make frequent use of prosocial behaviors. Many risk factors have been identified, but none have been clearly shown to have causal effects, mostly because of a lack of experimental studies.

Conclusions

From a descriptive perspective, we need to understand better how different forms of aggressive and prosocial behaviors develop from early childhood to adolescence, and to what extent these two types of behaviors are associated over time. Do most individuals start life with relatively high levels of physical aggression, and low levels of prosocial behavior and become adults with relatively high levels of prosocial behavior and low levels of physical aggression? How many individuals maintain high levels of aggressive and prosocial behaviors throughout their lives? To answer such questions, we need to follow large samples of individuals from birth to adulthood, and frequently measure different forms of aggressive and prosocial behaviors.

From an experimental perspective, we need to identify which factors influence the developmental trajectories of aggressive and prosocial behaviors. The best opportunities for experimental work in this area are preventive interventions. Well-designed preventive experiments are still needed to verify such influences (Tremblay, 2003).

Sex differences in aggressive and prosocial behaviors offer an exceptional opportunity to investigate genetic and environmental effects. By including females and males in longitudinal-experimental studies to address the questions described above, we should be able to obtain more adequate answers to long-standing questions about sex differences in the development of these behaviors.

Preventive experiments will help answer these questions if they are planned accordingly. Investigators in this area of research need to increase the level of interdisciplinary and international collaborations. Future studies should be large scale longitudinal-experimental multisite international studies that assess genetic and environmental factors, including both physical and social environments.

Questions

1. What are the intra-individual joint trajectories of aggressive and prosocial behavior from birth to adulthood?
2. To what extent can the manipulation of putative causal factors change the developmental trajectories of aggressive and prosocial behaviors?
3. To what extent do aggressive and prosocial behaviors have the same determinants at different developmental periods?
4. To what extent are there sensitive periods:
   a) to learn not to use physical aggression?
   b) to learn to help individuals that are hard to get along with?
   c) to learn not to use indirect aggression?
   d) to learn to be assertive?
   e) to learn to help others?
5. What factors lead females to use prosocial behavior more often than males, and males to use physical aggression more often than females?

See also:

Neuromaturational theories; Learning theories; Experimental methods; Cross-sectional and longitudinal designs; Normal and abnormal prenatal development; Social development; Attention; Parenting and the family; Peers and siblings; Sex differences; Socialization; 'At-risk' concept; Behavioral and learning disorders; Behavior genetics; Sociology

Further reading

Leavitt, L. A. and Hall, M. B. (eds.) (2004). *Social and Moral Development: Emerging Evidence on the Toddler Years*. New Brunswick, NJ: Johnson & Johnson Pediatric Institute.

Lacourse, E., Côté, S., Nagin, D. S., Vitaro, F., Brendgen, M. and Tremblay, R. E. (2002). A longitudinal-experimental approach to testing theories of anti-social behavior development. *Development and Psychopathology*, 14, 909–924.

Tremblay, R. E., Hartup, W. W. and Archer, J. (eds.) (in press). *Developmental Origins of Aggression*. New York: Guilford.

Attention

JOHN E. RICHARDS

Introduction

Attention may be defined as the selective enhancement of some behavior at the expense of other behavior. Writings on attention often cite William James, *Principles of Psychology* (1890), ". . . everyone knows what attention is." This is because we all have a commonsense notion of what attention is, and that it is ubiquitous across all types of behavior (e.g., attention to objects, joint attention with others, social attention, motor abilities). It is defined both as a specific psychological mechanism and as a characteristic of individual psychological behavior. Thus, in a developmental perspective, there may be a separate cognitive process called 'attention' that develops independently of other psychological mechanisms, as well as attention development specific to behavior. Attention development is often linked to the development of brain areas that are involved in attention.

Newborn attention: stimulus orienting

Attentive behavior may be observed in newborns. Newborns show a form of attention called 'stimulus orienting,' which involves the movement of sensors to enhance the quality of external information. For example, a rattle shaken to the side of a newborn will result in a head turn that enhances hearing and vision as both eyes and ears can be aligned with a sound by means of turning the head. Attention is limited, however, by the infant's perceptual apparatus (poor vision, poor hearing), and by brain areas that are yet to develop. Many changes in visual and auditory behavior over the first six months involve development of the receptors themselves (e.g., eyeball size, density of retinal connections), or development in the primary sensory areas in the cortex that support perceptual activity (e.g., connections within the primary visual cortex). Thus, changes in the range of stimuli to which stimulus orienting may occur, or the number of situations in which it does or does not occur, are not likely to be due to a change in the ability to show stimulus orienting, but to development other than stimulus orienting *per se*.

Young infant attention development: from stimulus orienting to sustained attention

The greatest change in attention during the first eighteen months is in sustained attention (also called focused attention). Sustained attention is an extended selective engagement of a behavior system that primarily enhances information processing in that system. It is similar to a state of arousal during which cognitive processing is enhanced. Many interesting cognitive and social activities of the infant occur mainly during episodes of sustained attention. For example, infants prefer to look at relatively novel objects, faces, and sounds. Novel stimuli elicit an initial stimulus orienting and then sustained attention. During sustained attention the infant 'memorizes' and becomes familiar with the aspects of the stimulus (Richards, 1997). The infant then will be less likely to show either stimulus orienting or sustained attention in response to the stimulus.

Infants as young as 3 months of age will engage in five- to ten-second periods of sustained attention (Richards, 2001). From 3 months of age to the middle of the second year, the duration of sustained attention increases. For example, heart rate changes that are known to accompany sustained attention will occur for longer durations in older infants than in younger infants, and the infants will show longer looks toward interesting stimuli. Stimulus orienting (present at birth) and sustained attention (developing from 3 to 18 months) are two processes that are basic in the human cognitive and behavior system. By the middle of the second year (18 months), these two basic attention processes are fully developed.

The development of sustained attention during the period of infancy is closely related to that of brain systems controlling arousal and state. Sustained

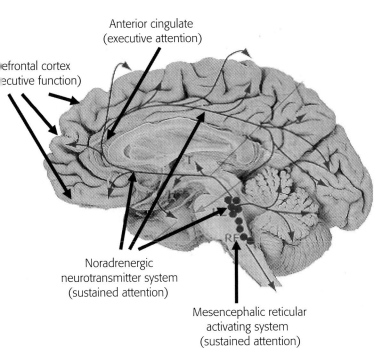

Anterior cingulate (executive attention)

efrontal cortex ecutive function)

Noradrenergic neurotransmitter system (sustained attention)

Mesencephalic reticular activating system (sustained attention)

Figure 1. The areas of the brain involved in attention development. The noradrenergic neurotransmitter system and the mesencephalic reticular activating system control sustained attention and show developmental changes in infants. The prefrontal cortex and anterior cingulate gyrus control executive attention and show developmental changes from early childhood through adolescence.

attention is a manifestation of a 'global arousal' system, not unlike sleep and other behavioral states. This arousal system controls responsiveness to events in the environment and affects sensory systems. It is closely associated with the mesencephalic reticular activating system, and is mediated by the noradrenergic and cholinergic neurotransmitter systems (Robbins & Everitt, 1995). Figure 1 shows several areas of the brain that are involved in attention development, including the noradrenergic neurotransmitter system and the reticular activating system. These neurotransmitter systems have a widespread influence over cortical sensitivity and excitability. Thus, sustained attention represents the activation of this arousal system in situations calling for attention. The behavioral (decreased peripheral activity and movements, increased processing) and physiological (heart rate, scalp-recorded brain activity) indices of sustained attention are also signs that these brain systems are active. Thus, developmental changes in the neurochemical systems controlling arousal are manifested and correspond to developmental changes in sustained attention in infants.

Infant attention and visual fixation

There is a counter-intuitive relation between attention and duration of visual fixation in infants. Many

researchers define visual attention as coincident with visual fixation. That is, a dependent variable in psychological research on infant attention will often be the duration that the infant keeps the eyes directed toward a visual stimulus. However, infants can look at visual patterns and actually be in an inattentive state. This is particularly true in the first three months of life. An infant's look toward a visual pattern may be captured by the pattern even though other signs indicate the infant is inattentive (heart rate change, brain activity, psychological manipulations, no later recognition memory). For example, heart rate changes can be used to indicate that a child is in an attentive state, during which heart rate decelerates, or that an attentive state has ended with heart rate returning to baseline (Richards, 2001). Young infants will often continue to look at a visual pattern even when their heart rate shows that they are no longer aroused (i.e., sustained attention is not occurring).

Between 3 and 12 months, with the increase in sustained attention, there is concomitant decline in looking duration to simple visual patterns. Figure 2 (top panel) shows the changes in visual fixation duration to relatively simple stimuli that have been found in a number of studies of infants. There is an initial increase in look duration from birth to 2 months followed by a decline through 6 months of age. This change has been interpreted as indicating an increase in processing speed over this age range. The decline in looking duration to simple patterns may indicate increases in sustained attention, leading to more efficient cognitive processing, and a decline in the amount of time necessary to process simple visual patterns. Alternatively, across this same period there is an increase in looking duration to complex and varied visual patterns, or complex auditory-visual patterns.

Figure 2 (bottom panel) shows the average look duration to the television program *Sesame Street* or to simple computer-generated black-and-white geometric forms. There is an increase in look duration from 6 months to 2 years for the *Sesame Street* program, but no change in the amount of time spent looking at the simple forms. The increase in looking time to complex visual patterns indicates that infants will engage in selective enhanced processing if sufficient complexity exists in the stimulus.

Individual differences in the development of attention

There are individual differences in attentive behavior in infants that may be stable through early childhood. At a specific age, say 6 months, one can find that some infants engage in more attentive behavior than other infants.

For example, changes in behavior (fast processing time, body movements, recognition memory) or physiological indices (heart rate change, brain activity) indicate that the degree of attentiveness differs among infants, and that this difference exists across several types of stimulus situations. One can measure similar behaviors at two different ages (e.g., 6 and 12 months), and find that individuals showing high levels of attentiveness at the first age are also those showing attentiveness at the second age. This relationship between multiple behaviors at a single age (intra-age stability) and that between behaviors across age (inter-age stability) are typically measured with a correlation coefficient. Correlations between early and later behavior in months 6 to 12 typically range from .2 to as high as .8.

A remarkable finding is that some aspects of early infant behavior are correlated with measures of intellectual outcome in early childhood (e.g., 5 years), and perhaps through the adolescent years. For example, it has been shown repeatedly that the amount of attention to a novel visual stimulus in 6-month-old infants is negatively correlated with measures of intelligence (e.g., Stanford-Binet IQ) in 11-year-old children (Rose, Feldman, Futterweit, & Jankowski, 1997). The interpretation of this finding is that infants with faster processing speed, and presumably higher levels of attention, look at a simple stimulus for a shorter period of time, and have higher intellectual abilities in early childhood. Thus, individual differences in infant attention occur that are very stable across short periods of time, and that remain relatively stable through the childhood years.

Development of executive attention

The period from 18 months through mid-adolescence is accompanied by an extended development of executive attention and executive functioning. Executive function is a description of psychological activities that control behavior, allocate cognitive resources, evaluate behavior progress, and direct activity with goals and plans. One aspect of executive function is the ability to allocate attention in a way that is consistent with self-established goals and plans. For example, if young children decide to play with a set of toys and construct a small setting from the toys, they must attend to the relevant characteristics of the toys (e.g., building connections, framework for a scene, characters in the setting). At the same time, characteristics of the toys that are irrelevant to the planned setting must be ignored, such as toys that do not belong in the setting, particular attributes of the toys, or how many toys or people are available. Similarly, other activities in the environment that might be of interest to the child must be ignored, or it will disrupt the planful behavior. The executive functioning that

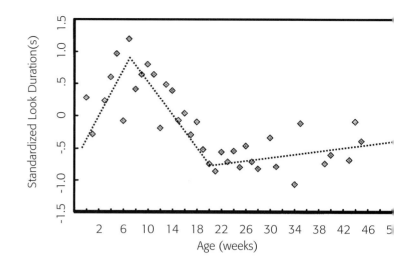

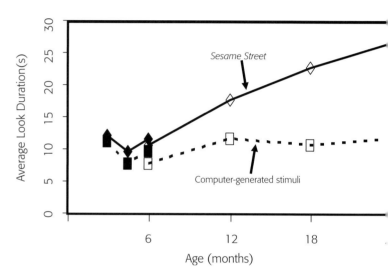

Figure 2. Changes in fixation duration reflecting attention development in infants. The top panel shows a systematic decline in fixation to simple stimuli reflecting an increase in processing speed and decline in the amount of time necessary to process simple visual patterns (compiled by John Colombo). The bottom panel shows an increase in fixation duration to *Sesame Street* and no change to simple geometric patterns, reflecting increases in sustained attention for stimuli of sufficient complexity (solid symbols for a study from 3 to 6 months; empty symbols for a study from 6 to 24 months).

guides such planful behavior selectively enhances attention to the particular aspects of the environment that are consistent with this behavior, and inhibits attention to things that are inconsistent with it.

As with sustained attention, executive attention and executive functioning are closely related to brain activity, in particular to the prefrontal cortex. Figure 1 shows several areas of the brain that are involved in the development of attention, including the prefrontal cortex. This area of the brain controls the ability to engage in goal-directed behavior, to inhibit intrusive behavior, and coordinate multiple actions to be consistent with goals and plans. Specific areas in the prefrontal cortex may be related to executive attention. Some studies have shown that the anterior cingulate region of the prefrontal cortex (Fig. 1) is involved in shifting attention from one object to another in situations demanding internal control of attention. Presumably, development in the areas of the brain controlling executive functions is partially responsible for the extended period of development of executive function and executive attention measured in behavior (i.e., 18 months through adolescence).

Mental effort and development of attention

There are apparent changes during childhood in the amount of attention used on a task due to the close link between attention and mental effort. When mental effort is necessary to solve a task or is required for a psychological process, one observes attention being used in the task. Both basic processes (e.g., stimulus orienting, sustained attention) and more complex processes (viz., executive attention) will be engaged in proportion to how effortful a task may be. There are dramatic developmental changes in several cognitive functions that employ mental effort. For example, the amount of working memory increases throughout childhood as does speed of information processing, which lead to a decrease in the effort and time to complete a mental task. Along with the decrease in mental effort during childhood, there is a decrease in the amount and duration of attention to the task. Similarly, with increased working memory and increased skills, some tasks may be engaged in for increased periods of time as the child grows older. This would be accompanied by an increase in the amount and duration of attention devoted to the task. These apparent increases or decreases in attention are not developmental changes in attention itself. Rather, they reflect the close association of attention with other behaviors and changes intrinsic to other behavioral or cognitive processes.

ADHD and childhood attention

One type of attention difficulty seen in young children, particularly as they enter school, is Attention Deficit Hyperactivity Disorder (ADHD). ADHD affects from 5 to 10 percent of school-aged children. It is characterized by inattentiveness, hyperactivity, poor impulse control, and behavior management problems. These children often come to the attention of health-care professionals when entering school because they do poorly in situations demanding sustained behavior control. ADHD is usually separated into three sub-types: ADHD-

Inattentive (ADHD-I), ADHD-Hyperactive (ADHD-H), and ADHD-Combined (ADHD-C). The children who are diagnosed as ADHD-I have problems in attention control, sustained attention, and show a great deal of inattentiveness. The children diagnosed as ADHD-H show poor impulse control and exhibit high levels of activity. The ADHD-C children show signs of both inattentiveness and hyperactivity. The treatment for ADHD is generally pharmacological (e.g., the methylphenidate Ritalin).

The types of ADHD may be related to the distinction between sustained attention and executive attention. A popular hypothesis about the cause of ADHD-H subtype is a poorly functioning executive function system. Supporting this, ADHD-H children have been shown to do poorly on tasks requiring plans, the inhibition of reflexive or automatic behavior, and impulse control. Several studies link deficits in the prefrontal cortex to ADHD-H children. Alternatively, children with the diagnosis of ADHD-I perform nearly as normal children on executive function tasks. However, they show deficits on tasks requiring sustained attention, such as in the continuous performance task, covert shifting of attention, and selective attention (Aman, Roberts, & Pennington, 1998). The ADHD sub-types may be due to differences in the brain regions controlling sustained attention and executive attention.

Individual differences in sustained attention in the early part of infancy may be related to ADHD-I outcomes, particularly in infants showing extremely low amounts of sustained attention. Deficits in parts of the brain that allow the sustaining of attention over extended time periods may be damaged or impaired leading to consistently poor performance for these infants and children. Alternatively, ADHD-H is not predicted by individual differences in attention observed prior to 2 or 3 years of age. This is likely due to the fact that the areas of the frontal cortex controlling executive attention are not yet sufficiently developed. Individual differences in impulse control depend on prefrontal brain development.

Conclusions

Attention is the selective enhancement of some behavior at the expense of other behavior. Developmental changes occur in infants in stimulus orienting and sustained attention. Stimulus orienting involves the general orientation of sensory systems and receptors to important environmental events, and sustained attention involves the enhanced and selective processing of information for specific psychological behaviors. Thus, by the end of infancy these two basic functions of attention are fully developed. Development of attention in early and middle childhood involves the development of executive attention, which is the ability to carry out tasks with planfulness, allocate attention to self-established goals and plans, and monitor one's progress in complex tasks. Changes in sustained attention and executive attention are closely linked to brain development. One of the most recognized childhood disorders, ADHD, is closely related to problems in the executive attention system, and may be caused by a deficit in the brain areas involved in the development of executive function and executive attention.

Questions

1. The development of sustained attention is hypothesized to be closely related to changes in brain systems mediating arousal (e.g., noradrenergic and cholinergic neurotransmitter systems). Are there direct measures of these neurotransmitter systems, such as MRI or fMRI, that could be tested in human infants and young children? Would these changes show the same developmental time course as sustained attention?

2. Executive attention and executive function are controlled by the prefrontal cortex. Children with Attention Deficit Hyperactivity Disorder (ADHD) have been hypothesized to have a disorder in the prefrontal cortex and thus show deficits in tasks of executive functioning. Would it be possible to get direct measures of the deficits in the prefrontal cortex in individuals with ADHD? Since pharmacological treatment (e.g., Ritalin) is an effective treatment for the behavioral disorders seen in ADHD, could it be shown that such drug treatment improves brain functioning in those children who show improvement in the behavior deficits?

3. There is a paradoxical relationship between improvement in sustained attention and look duration (i.e., with increases in the development of sustained attention, information processing becomes more efficient and look duration decreases). Can stimuli be found for which an increase in sustained attention leads to an increase in look duration? What aspects might characterize such stimuli?

See also:

Magnetic Resonance Imaging; Experimental methods; The status of the human newborn; Cognitive development in infancy; Perceptual development; Development of learning and memory; Brain and behavioral development (II): cortical; Executive functions; Intelligence; Sleep and wakefulness; Behavioral and learning disorders; Cognitive neuroscience

Further reading

Colombo, J. (2000). The development of visual attention in infancy. *Annual Review of Psychology*, 52, 337–367.

Richards, J. E. (2001). Attention in young infants: a developmental psychophysiological perspective. In C. A. Nelson and M. Luciana (eds.), *Developmental Cognitive Neuroscience*. Cambridge, MA: MIT Press, pp. 321–338.

Ruff, H. A. and Rothbart, M. K. (1996). *Attention in Early Development: Themes and Variations*. New York: Oxford University Press.

Brain and behavioral development (I): sub-cortical

ALBERT GRAMSBERGEN

Introduction

Systematic research into neuro-ontogeny started only in the last quarter of the 19th century. Since then, the processes underlying development as well as the relationships between behavioral changes and neurobiological transitions have been the subjects of intense research to identify causal factors in development.

A considerable amount of the around 30,000 genes estimated to constitute the human genome come to expression in the central nervous system (CNS). During early development, sets of proneural genes and the processes they control induce neurogenic genes to come to expression in intricate cascades and in complex time schedules. It seems that during earlier stages in which neural circuitries are globally established, genetic factors predominate, while at later stages epigenetic processes, such as the functioning of the nervous system in interaction with the environment, become increasingly important in shaping circuitries and modulating connectivities. Growing insights into the nature of these interactions, however, have stressed the complexities involved, and warn against any simple categorizations.

Some further caveats

One point of consideration is the timing of developmental processes. Environmental needs in the fetal period differ from those in postnatal phases, and this requires adaptations in behavioral patterns and their neuronal circuitries. Brain functions that are vital at a certain stage may develop ahead of others, some are actively inhibited for a certain period, and still others are only active during a short time span. This warns us against proposing any simple morphogenetic gradient in development. Another point is that some aspects of development are genetically determined, while others are triggered by physiological changes (e.g., those occurring at birth) or new behavioral abilities (e.g., standing). As such, they stand as evidence against the formulation of simple relationships between neurobiological and behavioral changes in neuro-ontogeny.

Sub-cortical regions in the CNS are involved in numerous tasks ranging from regulating homeostatic processes, autonomic responses, the sleep-wakefulness cycle, attentional processes, and motor behavior. In mature individuals, many of these processes involve the entire CNS, including the cortex and spinal cord. However, as cortical development during early stages lags behind that of the brain stem, functional relations at early stages differ from those at a later age. In the visual system, for example, perceptual and cognitive processing in the cortex still develops in the first years postnatally, but directing gaze and shifting attention occur already shortly after birth when these processes mainly involve sub-cortical circuits. In the motor system, the laterally descending corticospinal tract (CST) in the first year probably overrules projections such as the rubrospinal tract that develops earlier, while cerebellar processing, even later, starts complementing motor commands from the motor cortex. Such knowledge contradicts any simple trends in behavioral development.

A further point to be considered is to what extent data from animal research can be extrapolated to human development. Modern brain imaging techniques such as PET scans provide insights into brain development and metabolic processes in the human. However, details on the development of circuitry, the transmitters involved, and aspects of molecular biology depend on animal experimentation. Homologues of proneural and neurogenic genes in insects have also been identified in vertebrates, and it seems that the functions of these genes were globally retained during the evolution from insects to primates. On the other hand, behavioral competences in humans and in other animals often differ drastically, reflecting alternative neural circuitries. Differences in behavioral strategies and neuroanatomical structures should therefore be taken into account. Other problems

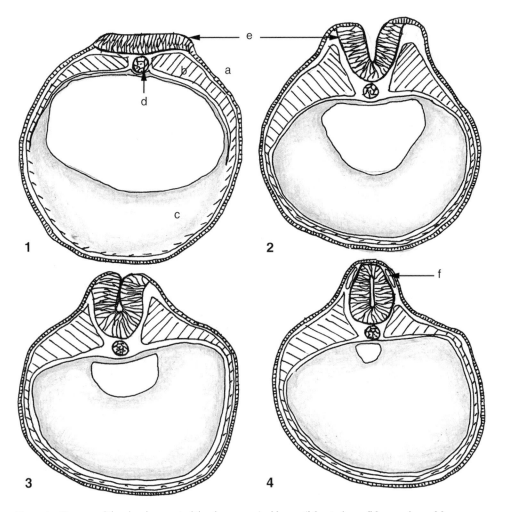

Figure 1. Diagram of the development of the three germinal layers ([a] ectoderm; [b] mesoderm; [c] entoderm), the notochord (d), neural tube (e), and the neural crest (f), in a vertebrate embryo. Trend in development follows 1, 2, 3, 4. Adapted from J. W. Saunders, 1970. *Patterns and Principles of Animal Development*. Macmillan, New York.

in extrapolating from animal studies are the varying speeds of development and the timing of birth. The human brain at term is analogous to that of a rat of about 13 days after birth, or to that of a monkey around 40 days before birth. When studying neuro-ontogeny, therefore, developmental stages, not ages, should be compared.

This entry will be concerned with motor behavior and some related topics in relation to sub-cortical development. For aspects of development concerned with the regulation of respiration, cardiac function, and metabolism, the reader is referred to the specific literature on these topics (e.g., Teitel, 1998). The development of behavioral state regulation and sexual differentiation is discussed elsewhere in this volume. In the next section, a few aspects will be highlighted about early brain development, specifically relevant to the development of sub-cortical brain areas and the spinal cord. In the sections thereafter, a brief review will be given of the development of motor behaviors in the light of relevant neurobiological knowledge.

On early brain development

At an early stage of development, the few hundred cells in the so-called blastula stage are arranged into three germinal layers (Jacobson, 1991). The inner, entodermal layer gives rise to the intestinal canal and connected organs, the mesodermal layer to muscles and skeleton as well as the cardiovascular and urogenital systems, and the outermost ectoderm to the skin and the nervous system (Fig. 1). The differentiation of the ectoderm into the nervous system, neurulation, starts in the blastopore region (the 'organizer zone') through induction agents both in the underlying mesoderm and in the ectoderm itself. Bone morphogenetic proteins (BMPs) induce ectodermal cells to transform into cells for the skin (epidermal cells). This BMP-signaling is under the influence of transforming growth factor-b (TGF-b), and preventing the binding of such factors to receptors on the ectodermal cells induces them to develop into neural cells. Other factors such as noggin, a protein which is expressed in the organizer zone, directly blocks BMP

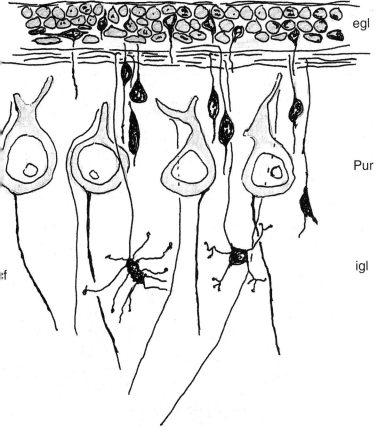

Figure 2. Diagram of the development of the cerebellar cortex. Adapted from Ramon y Cajal, 1890. *Monatschrift für Anatomie und Physiologie* (Leipzig) 7, 12–31.
Abbreviations – egl: extragranular matrix; Pur: Purkinje cell layer; igl: internal granular layer; cf: climbing fibers; pf: parallel fibers.

and fibroblast growth factor (FGF) leading to neurulation, but the actual factors that are effective in induction are as yet unknown.

A groove invaginates over the length of the embryo, deepens, and the neural tube then separates from the ectoderm that closes over this primordial nervous tissue. The neural and glial cells proliferate from the progenitor cells lining the neural tube, while the ganglia and the sensory nerves derive from the neural crest on both sides of the neural tube. Interactions between the notochord, a mesodermal structure, and the overlying neural tube lead to the expression of cascades of regionally specific genes (so-called homeobox genes), thereby specifying the axes in the CNS and the differential development of nuclei and their connections. The large variety of neural and glial cell types in the CNS is induced by intrinsic factors, cellular interactions, and the timing of their generation.

Once generated, the neuroblasts leave the proliferative matrix and migrate along radially oriented glial cells toward their destination. The intricacies of this process are illustrated best in the cerebellum (Fig. 2). At an early stage, the neuroblasts for vestibular and other brain stem

nuclei, for cerebellar nuclei, and finally for Purkinje cells, migrate toward their location. Much later (in the human around term birth), groups of proliferative cells from the central matrix migrate and spread over the Purkinje cell layer. After arrival, cells in this so-called extragranular matrix start proliferating, and the neuroblasts (generating granular cells and interneurons) migrate in an inward direction. In the spinal cord, the neuroblasts forming the large motoneurons are the first to generate. These cells migrate toward the ventral horn, to be followed by the smaller interneurons, as has been shown in frogs. Migratory processes in the cerebral cortex are considered elsewhere in this volume.

The outgrowth of axons and dendrites is regulated by attracting or repulsive factors, acting over shorter or longer ranges (e.g., netrins and semaphorins), and also by mechanical factors. Specific factors promote growth toward and across midline regions along common trajectories, and others induce axons to divert from this path. Near their target, the axonal growth cones in the CNS are attracted by cell adhesion molecules of the immunoglobulin and cadherin superfamilies that are located on the cellular membrane or in the extracellular medium. They also may be repelled (e.g., by protein tyrosine kinases on the membrane), and together with subtle balances in a large array of signaling factors, this guides the axon toward its target neuron, leading to global projections in some cases but highly specific somatotopic relations in others (Goodman & Tessier-Lavigne in Cowan, Jessell, & Zipursky, 1997).

Considerable proportions of neurons and glial cells die during development, a process that is termed programmed cell death or apoptosis. A first stage of apoptosis occurs shortly after neurulation in the proliferative matrix, probably in order to adjust proliferation and to sculpt neural tissue. A second stage occurs much later after neural circuits have been established. Evidence indicates that in this stage neurons are doomed to die unless they are saved by target-derived neurotrophic factors, such as Nerve Growth Factor (NGF), Brain Derived Neurotrophic Factor (BDNF), and others. These factors bind to receptors on the membrane, leading to the upregulation in the production of proteins that protects the cells from apoptosis, processes in which caspases play a key role. This apoptosis, dependent upon the activity of cells in the target area and affecting about half of the neuronal population, plays a role in matching the sizes of neuronal and glial cell populations (Oppenheim in Kalverboer & Gramsbergen, 2001).

Still later, pruning takes place in neural connections through the withdrawal of axons and synaptic connections. One example is the regression in the poly-innervation of muscle fibers. Muscle fibers initially are innervated by multiple axons, but subsequently the supernumerary axons are retracted. In the human psoas muscle, which is active during sitting, this final situation is reached around 3 months after birth (Fig. 3). In rats, this regression in the intercostal muscles has finished before birth, when respiration starts, but only at 2 weeks after birth in the hindpaw muscles, indicating that the regression of polyneural innervation is related to functioning. Indeed, blocking neuromuscular transmission by α-bungarotoxin brings regression to a halt, and a retrograde influence from the active muscle fiber probably leads to this regression (Ribchester in Kalverboer & Gramsbergen, 2001).

A similar regression of supernumerary connections occurs in the cerebellum. Neurons in the inferior olivary nucleus initially innervate several Purkinje cells, but then supernumerary axons withdraw such that a one-to-one relationship is established between neurons and Purkinje cells. In rats, this point is reached a few days before the cerebellum starts functioning in motor control. Also in the cerebral cortex, an impressive decline in the number of synapses has been observed.

On behavioral development in the prenatal period

Human fetuses start moving at an amazingly early stage of development. Davenport Hooker, as reviewed in his book *The Prenatal Origin of Behavior* (1952), studied fetuses after abortion and found that the first movements emerge by the seventh week of postmenstrual age (PMA). By stimulating the fetus in the neck region at this same age (with Von Frey hairs), he elicited a contraction of neck and trunk muscles, and this led to the claim that the initial movements are reflex-like in character. The introduction of real-time ultrasound scanning in human fetal research has fundamentally changed insights into prenatal motor development.

Prechtl and his co-workers (Prechtl, 1984) demonstrated that the first movements occur spontaneously at 6–7 weeks PMA. These movements are small and performed slowly, but shortly thereafter they become more extensive and vigorous. By 12 weeks PMA, a repertoire has developed consisting of, for example, movements in the arms, legs, trunk and of the head, as well as generalized or general movements (GMs), sucking and breathing movements. Movements initially occur only sparsely and they are randomly scattered over time, but their incidence increases, and from about halfway in pregnancy most of the movements occur in periods with increased activity. Sleep and wakefulness states, as defined by the presence or absence of GMs, eye movements, and regular or irregular respiration, only emerge from 34 weeks PMA in fetuses and also in preterm infants of the same PMA (Prechtl, 1984).

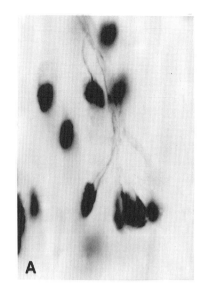
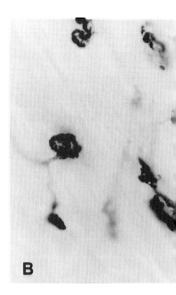
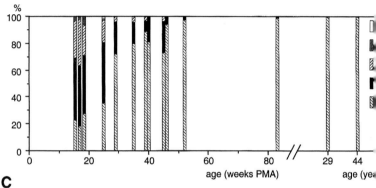

Figure 3. Micrographs of motor end plates with nerve terminals in the psoas muscle of the human. (A) fetus, age 28 weeks PMA (note the polyneurally innervated and immature motor end plates); (B) fetus, age 35 weeks PMA (note the increased size of the end plates and the polyneurally innervated end plate in the center); (C) percentages of end plates with 1–5 endings in fetuses and infants at ages ranging from 15.5 to 85 weeks PMA as well as in two adults.

Investigations in fetal and neonatal rats allow one to relate these trends to neurobiological developments. The first movements in rats emerge at the fifteenth embryonic day (E15), which is about a day after motoneuronal axons of cervical segments have reached their muscles. These movements are restricted to the head and neck region, and by the end of that day tactile stimulation of the head region induces movements. In the following days, the repertoire expands and the movements become more vigorous. Mouth movements, eye blinking, and foreleg-mouth contacts occur in the last days before parturition, at E21. At birth, the rat's developmental stage is comparable to that of a human fetus of 6 to 7 months.

Experiments in chick embryos have shown that the axons of the motoneurons in the ventral portions of the ventral horn are the first to grow out toward the myoblasts in the ventral plate, giving rise to the extensor muscles at a later stage. Somewhat later, the axons of the dorsally located motoneurons are heading for the future flexor muscles in the dorsal plate. The myoblasts induce the release of acetylcholine (Ach) from the approaching axon as shown in tissue cultures of *Xenopus laevis*, and the Ach receptor concentrates at the connection site (viz., the future motor end plate) on the myoblasts. Initially, the transmitter release is low and only enables short contractions and small movements, but this release increases, particularly after the multiple innervation of muscle fibers has been eliminated.

Reflexes can be elicited from embryonic day 15 (E15) by stimulating the neck region. To begin with, the neurites from the dorsal ganglia neurons contact their skin area, and only thereafter does the central branch grow via the dorsal horn toward the interneurons surrounding the motoneurons. Electrical stimulation of the dorsal roots from around E15 elicits discharges in the motoneurons indicating a polysynaptic coupling, which is typical for exteroceptive reflexes. Proprioceptive reflexes, elicited by stretching muscle spindles, only develop from E19 and these involve monosynaptic connections with motoneurons. The maturation of muscle spindles still continues in the first postnatal weeks.

Investigations in the rat indicate a close correspondence between the establishment of neuromuscular connections and the occurrence of the first movements. Even these first trunk and extremity movements require a programmed activation of several groups of motoneurons. Such patterning seemingly develops without experience, suggesting that the circuitries involved largely develop autonomously.

Rest-activity cycles in rats can be observed in the last fetal days, but sleep-wakefulness cycles only occur from several days after birth (Gramsbergen in Kalverboer & Gramsbergen, 2001). Adrenergic and serotonergic descending projections from the locus coeruleus and the raphe nuclei in the brain stem are instrumental in the modulation of motor activity in the different behavioral states (absence or presence of activity, normal or decreased muscle tone, etc.). These monoaminergic projections are among the first to descend, but their initial synaptic patterns in the spinal cord differ remarkably from those at later age, suggesting that these projections fulfill alternative functions at early stages.

Significance of early movements

The question arises why movement patterns such as breathing and extremity movements occur long before becoming functional. Some patterns are adaptations to the fetal environment. It has been suggested that movements might prevent adhesion of the fetus to the uterine wall. Another example is the leg movements in the last half of pregnancy that enable the fetus to assume a position with the head downward, a position which is achieved in about 95 percent of human pregnancies. Other patterns anticipate their postnatal function, such as breathing movements. Swallowing and thumb sucking have been observed, and these might be anticipations of drinking after birth. Physiologically, it makes sense that practicing movements increases muscle strength and adjusts the patterning of contractions. However, it remains puzzling how future needs could initiate this development. Piortr Kur'mich Anokhin (1898–1974) proposed that an evolutionary pressure on the development of patterns subserving vital functions might explain their precocial occurrence, an outcome he termed systemogenesis (Touwen, 1976).

Early movements have an important role in histogenesis. The prevention of movements (by blocking neuromuscular transmission or mechanical restriction) has demonstrated that this leads to a decreased number of sarcomeres in the muscle fibers, to a decreased growth rate in shaft bones, and to abnormally shaped joints. In the CNS, it has been shown that as soon as neurons are integrated in circuits, action potentials emerge, and this activity shapes and refines neural circuits. Apoptosis, and the regression of supernumerary synapses, depend on neural activity and transmission.

Postnatal development

Feeding behavior

Nutritive sucking is of vital importance after birth. This pattern is an intricate interplay between sucking movements of the lips and facial muscles, negative pressure in the mouth, peristaltic tongue movements, and swallowing, all of which are coupled to grasping movements of the hands. Within days after birth, sucking becomes very efficient and can be elicited by stimulating the perioral region around the mouth. After having been functional in the months after birth, this complex behavior disappears altogether in the human, possibly along with its neural substrate.

General movements

GMs are the most frequently occurring pattern in the fetal and early postnatal period. They are defined as a series of gross movements of variable speed and amplitude involving all parts of the body, and lasting from a few seconds to several minutes (Hopkins & Prechtl in Prechtl, 1984). The evaluation of GMs in terms of their quality has been demonstrated to be a powerful tool in the early detection of neurological deficits (Prechtl, 1990). Extremity and trunk movements in the early fetal period are generated autonomously in the spinal cord, as has been shown in human and rat fetuses. As severe brain lesions already at early stages lead to GMs of abnormal quality, this indicates that the spinal cord activity is modulated by descending projections from the brain stem, such as the reticulospinal tract and monoaminergic projections.

Postural control

Already in their first week infants, when supported in a sitting position, can lift their head and keep it upright for a few seconds. With the further development of muscle strength and coordination, infants at 2 months are able to control the position of the head unaided. Touwen (1976) studied the neurological development of normal infants and reported that the ability to sit unsupported was achieved between 7 and 10 months. Standing with support developed between 9 and 13 months, and shortly preceded the age at which they could walk with support. The median age for standing freely (around 15 months) preceded by a few months that at which they were able to walk without support.

Static postures are controlled by feedback mechanisms on the basis of proprioceptive information from muscles and tendons, and the vestibular and visual systems. Movements, on the other hand, require anticipatory adjustments (based on feedforward mechanisms) and the cerebellum plays a decisive role in this type of control, and the question is how this sensory information and processing develops. Proprioceptive afferents are functional from a few months before birth in the human, suggesting that the feedback control of postures starts prenatally. However, the vestibular and visual systems giving information on the orientation of the body in space are not yet functioning. The vestibular apparatus already at 10 weeks PMA has an adult-like morphology, and further morphological development is finished by mid-gestation. Its function, however, remains inhibited as indicated by the absence of reactions to tilting experiments during pregnancies. This inhibition might in part be due to a low oxygen saturation in the fetal blood as experiments in guinea pigs at a late fetal stage have revealed.

Within days after birth, the vestibulum starts functioning as indicated by the presence of vestibular reflexes. Nystagmic eye movements can be elicited by vestibular stimulation in preterm infants as early as 31 weeks PMA, suggesting that the vestibular system is ready for functioning before term age. Studies in the rat have shown that the projections of the vestibular nuclei reach the lower levels of the spinal cord already from E18. Electrical stimulation of the vestibulospinal projections indicated that these projections are functional on the first postnatal day, but further maturation including

re-arrangement of the synaptic terminals still requires one or two weeks.

Although visual information plays a role in the control of head position in the newborn, its function in postural control becomes more prominent in older infants. Infants who recently acquired the ability to stand unsupported were tested when standing in a so-called moving room. The walls and ceiling of the room were shifted in a horizontal direction, and infants at that stage experienced great difficulties in keeping their standing position when the room moved. This indicates the great influence of visual input ('visual proprioception') on postural control, particularly when new motor patterns arise by virtue of more advanced postural control strategies. In this perspective, it is surprising that the development of walking in congenitally blind infants is only retarded by a few months. Similarly, rats visually deprived from the tenth day start walking fluently at the normal age (see below). This indicates that effective compensation is possible between the visual and vestibular systems in such situations.

On the roles of the cerebellum and basal ganglia in motor control

The cerebellum at adult age plays an important role in adjusting the recruitment of motoneurons, in coupling movements to postural control, and in learning motor abilities. Both inputs to the Purkinje cells, via the parallel fibers that stem from the granular cells as well as via the climbing fibers from the inferior nuclei, develop late. In contrast, the axons of the Purkinje cells, the sole output of the cerebellum, have established their projections already long before birth in rats. The development of the cortical circuitry occurs in the human around birth, and this parallels the protracted development of motor behavior in the human, relative to other primates. Another consequence of this late development is that cerebellar development is particularly vulnerable to a decreased supply of nutrients or teratological influences in the postnatal period.

The basal ganglia, a complex of four closely interconnected nuclei, play an important role in motor control and cognitive functions. The cortical and thalamic nuclei project onto the striatum that is connected to the globus pallidus and the substantia nigra, and further to the sub-thalamic nucleus. The two output nuclei, the pars reticulata of the substantia nigra and the internal segment of the pallidum, tonically inhibit thalamic nuclei and by that cortical control of movements. These nuclei are influenced by a direct pathway that via the output nuclei disinhibits thalamocortical activity, and by an indirect pathway via the external segment of the pallidum that through the output nuclei further inhibits thalamocortical activity. More recent research has pointed to differential inputs to the striatum, with a diffuse input from the cortex, hippocampus, and amygdala to patches of cells (striosomes) within a matrix of cells receiving a topographically organized input from the cortex. The striosomes are rich in opiate receptors, and it has been suggested that they might mediate a reinforcement of certain memories.

The generation and migration of the neurons of the basal ganglia in rats occurs early (from E12), and in the human fetus the differentiation of the nuclear complexes starts from the sixteenth week. However, virtually no knowledge exists with regard to the functional development of the basal ganglia.

Reaching, grasping, and manipulating

The first arm extensions (referred to as pre-reaching movements) occur already in the first week of life, and initially they might play a role in directing attention. Such movements often coincide with the newborn looking at an object. Visual acuity is low at birth, but it improves rapidly during the first year through foveal development and improved cortical processing. As also the CST is not yet functional at birth, it seems that such behavior, if goal directed, is largely controlled by sub-cortical visual processing and motor projections from sub-cortical centers. Developmental changes in both these systems will contribute to the transition from pre-reaching movements to controlled reaching, starting around the age of 2 to 3 months. From about 4 months, such movements in sitting infants are accompanied by specific EMG patterns in the neck and trunk muscles, reflecting improvements in postural control.

Stimulation of the palm of the hand elicits a grasp reflex in newborns, and it gradually disappears in the course of the first year to be replaced by voluntary control over individual finger movements, which is achieved around 12 months (Touwen, 1976). Such movements in primates and humans are made possible by virtue of monosynaptic connections between neurons in the primary motor cortex and the motoneurons of the distal arm and hand muscles in the spinal cord. In developing monkeys, a relationship has been found between the entrance of the CST fibers into the ventral horn and the emergence of isolated finger movements around the middle of the first year (Armand in Kalverboer & Gramsbergen, 2001). In humans, individual finger movements occur toward the end of the first year, and extrapolation of data obtained in monkeys suggests the establishment of synaptic contacts between CST fibers and motoneurons of the wrist and hand muscles around that age.

In rats, the number of CST fibers amounts to about 400,000 at postnatal day P4, but thereafter it decreases to 150,000 fibers by adult age. This decrease is largely dependent on the withdrawal of collaterals, for example, from the visual cortex. The significance of this development and whether a similar initial overproduction of the CST also occurs in the human are not known.

Development of locomotion

In the first one or two months after birth, stepping movements can be elicited in human infants when they are supported in an upright position. Alternating leg movements also occur in the fetal period and this stepping seems to be the remnant of the prenatal pattern. The response normally disappears after one or two months although alternating leg movements still occur in crawling and kicking movements. Infants are able to stand around 11–12 months, and from this same age supported walking develops (Touwen, 1976). These walking movements initially resemble the neonatal pattern in terms of foot placing and EMG patterns. A few months thereafter, infants walk without support as a consequence of increased strength in leg and trunk muscles and further improvements in postural control.

The alternating leg movements in the fetal period, the neonatal stepping response and walking are probably all generated by so-called central pattern generators (CPGs) in the lumbar spinal cord. These neural circuits are controlled by supraspinal brain regions with regard to initiation, halting, and speed modulation. Developmentally, the onset of walking is related to neuro-biological changes in the motor cortex and the CST, and the cerebellum, as well as to increases in muscle strength. Other researchers, adherents of the dynamical systems approach to development, particularly emphasize the immensely complex interactions between changes in muscular properties, increasing mass and dimensions of extremities, and other developmental processes, with the environment counteracting the increasing mass and forces. Accordingly, the 'silent period' after the waning of the stepping response is considered to be induced by an increase in the mass of the legs, without an appropiate increase in the muscle force.

Research on walking development in young rats has pointed to the close relationship between postural development and leg movements during locomotion. At the age of 1 week, rats can stand and make a few staggering steps, but at P15, in the course of one day, this immature pattern is replaced by a smooth and adult-like walking pattern. Until this age, EMG recordings show irregular activity and co-contractions in antagonistic muscles (as in human newborns), but after this transition clearly delineated bursts occur without co-contractions (Fig. 4). Several lines of evidence indicate that this sudden transition is linked to the development of anticipatory postural control mechanisms. Simultaneously with the transition in walking at P15, postural muscles in the trunk start to be specifically activated, in phase with walking activity. An even stronger argument in favor of postural control being the limiting factor for the development of fluent walking is that vestibular deprivation in rats from P5 leads to a retarded postural development, and as a consequence to a delay of the shift to fluent walking.

Conclusions

The development of the brain passes through a series of stages, some of which are specific solutions to problems posed at a particular time. Comparative ethological analyses have also suggested that evolutionarily older patterns of behavior at certain early phases of development have been conserved. Some of these behaviors and the underlying circuitry probably disappear during development. The intriguing question is to what extent parts of the earlier circuitries and behaviors are incorporated into later patterns.

Early neural development is to a certain extent genetically determined while at later stages sets of neurons and circuitries are selected, or selectively stabilized, on the basis of their role in functioning. The question remains whether these selection processes are limited in time, and whether abilities attained later in life remain dependent upon the shaping of dormant circuitries. Related to these sorts of questions is the conclusion that the human genome differs only marginally from that of the mouse in terms of the number of genes. How then have the increases in cognitive and motor abilities during evolution been accomplished by this limited increase in genomic capacity?

In early development about twice as many neurons are produced as the final number, and several hypotheses have been formulated to explain this seeming waste. Examples include efficiency in using a limited genetic informational capacity, or this overproduction being a safeguard for future evolutionary possibilities. Neuronal proliferation almost comes to a halt in the second year of life, although limited proliferation continues lifelong in the olfactory bulb, hippocampus, and cortex. For those involved in research into the effects of brain lesions imposed during early life, the question is if and how the overproduction of neurons and connections during development can be exploited beneficially for treatment purposes. These and many other intriguing problems make the investigation of brain and behavior

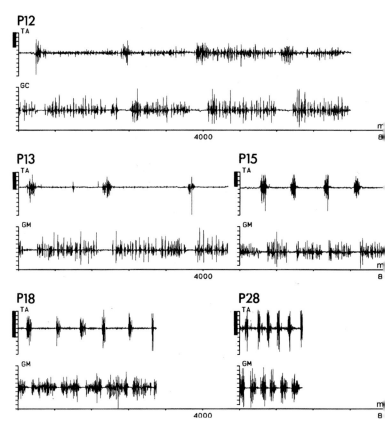

Figure 4. EMG recordings of two hind leg muscles during locomotion in the developing rat: tibialis anterior muscle (TA) is active during the swing phase and gastrocnemius muscle (GM) during the stance phase. Recordings at P12 and at P13 show irregular electrical activity in both muscles and simultaneous activity, (i.e., 'coactivation') whereas from P15 onward EMG bursts are more regular. The time scale is identical in all recordings. Note the increase in walking speed.

mechanisms during development a passionate enterprise for numerous generations of scientists to come.

Questions

1. The young brain is vulnerable to damage by trauma or physiological de-regulations around birth. In this same period, the brain is highly plastic as circuitries are still being formed and connections are not yet stabilized. Thus, what are the optimal therapeutical strategies to exploit this plasticity beneficially for the compensation of perinatal brain lesions?
2. The circuitries of the brain and their functions are the result of a long evolutionary history. Some traces of older patterns are still obvious shortly after birth, but then disappear. If so, how are elements of the earlier circuitries and behaviors incorporated into later patterns?
3. The human genome only marginally differs from, for example, that of the mouse or the rat in terms of the

number of genes. How then have the increases in cognitive and motor abilities during evolution been accomplished by this limited increase in genomic capacity?

See also:
Neuromaturational theories; Dynamical systems approaches; Magnetic Resonance Imaging; Cross-species comparisons; Conceptions and misconceptions about embryonic development; Prenatal development of the musculoskeletal system in the human; Normal and abnormal prenatal development; The status of the human newborn; Perceptual development; Motor development; Brain and behavioral development (II): cortical; Locomotion; Prehension; Sleep and wakefulness; Blindness; Prematurity and low birthweight; Behavioral embryology; Developmental genetics; Ethology; George E. Coghill; Viktor Hamburger

Further reading

Blass, E. M. (ed.) (2001). *Handbook of Behavioral Neurobiology*, Vol. XIII: *Developmental Psychobiology, Developmental Neurobiology and Behavioral Ecology: Mechanisms and Early Principles.* New York: Plenum Press.

Connolly, K. J. and Forssberg, H. (eds.) (1997). *Neurophysiology and Neuropsychology of Motor Development.* London: MacKeith Press.

Squire, L. R, Bloom, F. E., McConnell, S. J., Roberts, J. L., Spitzer, N. and Zigmond, M. (eds.) (2003). *Fundamental Neuroscience.* San Diego: Academic Press, Section 3, Nervous system development.

Brain and behavioral development (II): cortical

BARBARA FINLAY

Introduction

The changing structure of the cerebral cortex can be put to many uses in understanding behavioral and cognitive development. Developmental psychologists often look to biology for structural confirmation of the theories about the developing organization of behavior, for physical realization of stages, connections, and modules. Alternatively, structure is often invoked to imply constraints on behavior (e.g., perhaps the absence of some essential physical building block, such as a certain transmittter or myelination of a pathway, prevents the emergence of some particular behavior until a certain age). The role of cause and constraint can also be reversed: the onset of a particular sensory experience or maternal interaction often induces structural alterations in the brain greater than the simple registration of the event, changing the character of future information handling. Overall, structure and physiology give an added dimension to the description of behavioral change, and often can supply direct insights into the causes of behavioral and cognitive determinants.

Since cortical cells are electrophysiologically active from the moment they are generated, even in transit from their natal site to their terminal position, it is wrong to say the cortex 'turns on' at any particular developmental point. Rather, the cortex is in a continually changing state of activity, and uses its own activity to construct itself in combination with the instructions of intracellular and extracellular molecules specified by the genome. Later, information from the external environment is added to the mix, as represented by the activity of inputs to the cortex.

Our main goal will be to describe this complex system in the appropriate dynamical terms. We will begin with a description of fundamental cortical structure: how and when the cortex develops in early embryogenesis. The embryology will be considered in light of evidence for and against early cortical specialization and modularity. Then we will consider maturational gradients of various kinds as they have been described in the cortex

and how they might be related to behavioral maturation. These events are primarily prenatal and concern the structure with which the cortex first addresses the world. Finally, we will consider the postnatal development of the brain and how it links to behavioral development.

Structure of the cerebral cortex

Adult organization: cortical layers, columns, and their specializations

The six-layered scheme to describe the cortex laid out by Korbinian Brodmann (1868–1918) in his publications on cortical architecture in the period 1903–1918 is the one still in use today (Figs. 1 and 2). First, a note on nomenclature. The word 'cortex' when used technically refers to any layered, external structure. In this entry, we are discussing the neocortex or isocortex, the six-layered structure that dominates the surface of the human brain. As commonly, but not technically used, the words 'cortex' and 'cerebral cortex' will refer to the isocortex or neocortex.

The key to understanding cortical structure, in both development and adulthood, is to understand that the cortical column (the fundamental, repeating unit of the cortex, see below) does a stereotyped intake, transformation, and distribution of information within a matrix of local and distant influences from the rest of the cortex, though the functional contents of a column are wildly diverse (Rakic, 1990). The principal input to the cortex comes from the thalamus, a collection of nuclei in the diencephalon that gets its input from: (1) the senses including sight, sound, touch, and kinesthesis, (2) other parts of the brain that give information about the body's state of motion, homeostasis, and arousal state, and (3) other cortical areas (Fig. 1). The input from the thalamus goes to the middle layer, Layer IV, and, to a lesser extent, to the upper part of Layer VI (Fig. 2).

This thalamic information in Layer IV is then relayed up and down, to Layers II and III, and to Layers V and

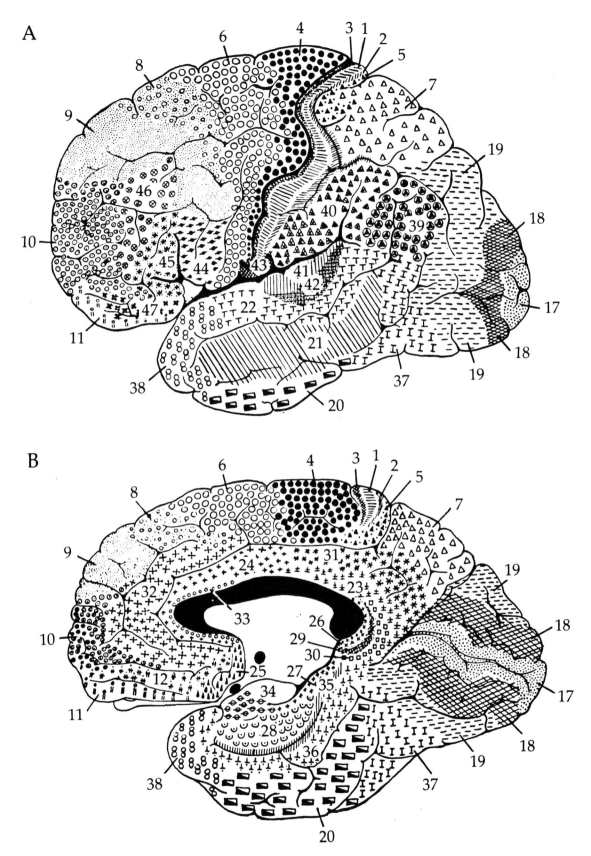

Figure 1. Areas of the cortex as described by Brodmann. Lateral (A) and medial (B) views of the cortex are shown. The numbered divisions are based on the thickness, density, and cell size of the cortical layers.

VI (Fig. 2). The majority of synaptic connections most input cells of the cortex will make are restricted to the column several cells wide that extends perpendicularly from Layer IV to the cortical surface, and down to Layer VI. All the cells in a particular column participate in similar contexts. For a few examples, taken from widely separated parts of the cortex, one column might fire to stimulation of a particular location and type of sensation on the body surface, another before a particular trajectory of arm movement, and another might fire when the individual is anxious in a social context.

The activity in these columns is continually modified by the local and distant context supplied from other cortical areas. Output from Layers II and III is long-range and connects the cortex to itself. Axons from these areas distribute to neighboring cortical areas (e.g., from primary to secondary visual cortex), to distant cortical areas (e.g., from secondary visual cortex to visuomotor fields in frontal cortex), and across the corpus callosum to the cortex on the other side of the brain. The cells of Layer V distribute their axons sub-cortically to every sort of effector center throughout the brain, including the motoneurons of the spinal cord. The principal output connection of Layer VI is a reciprocal connection back to the thalamus, which can be massive.

This same organization of layers and repeating columns is found throughout the cortex. At the next layer of organization, the cortical area has inputs, descending connections, and specializations of layers that reflect their relative position in the intake or distribution of information (Fig. 2). The primary visual cortex, which receives a massive thalamic input relayed from the retina, has an unusually large number of cells in Layer IV. In the motor cortex, Layer IV is almost absent, and the cells of Layer V, the output layer connecting to downstream motor centers and the spinal cord, are unusually large and prominent. Each cortical area typically contains a topographic representation of a sensory, motor, or other computed dimension (any derived ordered array, such as location in 3-D auditory space, which has no sensory surface like the retina). Each area has unique input and output and a limited repertoire of physiological transformations of its thalamic input, such as the elongated, orientation-selective visual receptive fields of the primary visual cortex that are constructed from the symmetrical center-surround visual fields of their visual input.

It is critical to understand what is meant by a cortical area because many of the questions that have been raised about the relationship of behavioral development to cortical development assume that particular perceptual and cognitive mechanisms can be mapped directly onto particular cortical areas, using the concept of a cortical module to subsume both structure and function. Such functions can vary from basic perceptual operations to

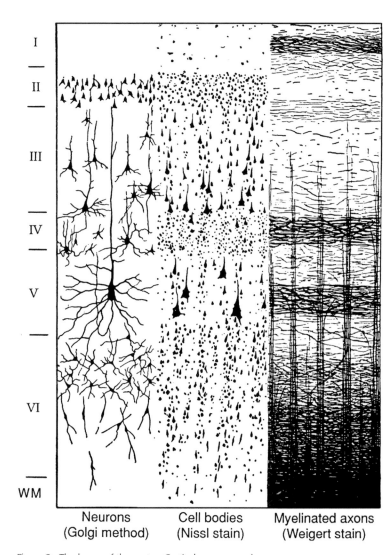

Figure 2. The layers of the cortex. Cortical neurons and axons are arranged in six principal layers designated by Roman numerals; WM refers to 'white matter,' the myelinated axons passing underneath the cortex. Three types of stains are represented: the Golgi method, which stains whole cells and all their processes, the Nissl stain, which shows only cell processes, and the Weigert stain, which stains axons.

complex aspects of cognition, like mapping spatial trans-locations over time ('A-not-B') or syntax in language. For example, if there is a 'face recognition area' located in the mature cortex necessary and sufficient for all face recognition, then to understand the maturation of that area is to understand the maturation of face perception. Many investigators, however, emphatically disagree with the idea of modular structure-function relationships realized in the cortical area, arguing for a more distributed representation, which sets a very different agenda for developmental research. The pieces of developmental information that will bear on this question relate to when each cortical area is specified for its function, how that function is realized, and how plastic the functions of each area are.

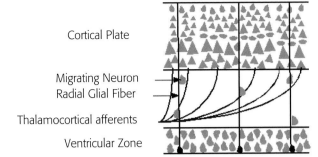

Figure 3. A schematic diagram illustrating the general development of the cortex. Cortical neurons are generated in the ventricular zone and migrate into the cortex along radial glial fibers (black vertical lines) or tangential pathways (not shown). Neurons settle within the developing cortical plate according to an inside-out gradient. Afferents from thalamic nuclei begin to colonize the intermediate zone as cortical neurons migrate through them.

Cortex development

Making layers and columns

The area where cells that will make up the cerebral cortex divide and propagate is called the ventricular zone (Fig. 3). Early in development, before the proliferation of many cells and their connections, the ventricular zone and cortical plate (the primordial cortex) are directly apposed. Later, however, as the region between them fills up with cells from other regions and connecting processes, the cells migrate along progressively stretching glial cells that hang on to their connection to the ventricular zone on the inside and the cortical wall on the outside, letting go only when all cortical cells have been generated. Due to these glial highways, each location in the ventricular zone makes a column (or more properly, a column-shaped zone) extending the depth of the mature cortex (Rakic, 1990). The second dimension of developmental time corresponds directly to the cortical layers, from inside (VI) to outside (II). Recently, a second population of interneurons of the cortex have been discovered that arise from a special generative region in the ventricular zone, separate from the source of radially migrating neurons described here, and migrate tangentially through the cortex to populate it.

Several structural aspects of this pattern of development are significant for behavioral development, particularly the debate about the modular nature of the cortex. Firstly, most of the cellular constituents of a cortical area come from a particular region of the ventricular zone, and thus could capably transmit genetic instructions that are locally specified in the ventricular zone, such as instructions for particular wiring patterns or neurotransmitter expression. Secondly, most of the events just described happen very early in development, before three months

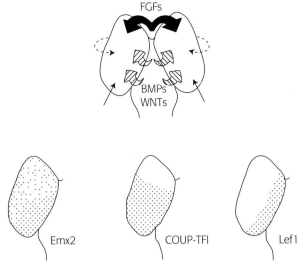

Figure 4. Schematic diagrams of cortical area patterning in the embryonic mouse cerebral cortex showing signaling centers that set up patterns of transcription factors controlling regional differentiation and differential growth, and the patterns of transcription factor expression. (Top) Signaling centers, sources of proposed polarizing molecules (FGFs, BMPs, WNTs). (Bottom, left to right) Spatial distribution of the transcription factors Emx2, COUP-TFI, Lef1 expressed in the cortex consequent to the action of the polarizing molecules. Transcription factors can control the expression of particular cell properties such as neurotransmitters or thalamus-to-cortex recognition signals. Redrawn from C. W. Ragsdale & E. A. Grove, 2001. Patterning the mammalian cerebral cortex. *Current Opinion in Neurobiology,* II, 50–58.

post-conception. Finally, the principal input to the cortex, the thalamus, can influence cortical organization from the very earliest stages, as the axons from the thalamus are in fact a large part of developing processes interposed between the ventricular zone where cortical neurons are generated, and the cortex, where they eventually mature. The cortical neurons migrate directly through their eventual input. The thalamus could potentially transmit information on the fetus's own movement, the body surface, or any structured or unstructured activity arising in any part of the brain.

Making areas

What is the source of the information that gives cortical areas their distinct input and output connections and other specialized local features? Only recently, the cortex has come to be understood in the same genomic terms that structures like the entire vertebrate body plan, or spinal cord segmentation, are understood (Grove & Fukuchi-Shimogori, 2003) (Fig. 4). These schemes are rather counter-intuitive to the adult human architect's first guess about how to build something, where expression of Gene A corresponds to Segment A or Cortical Area A, and Gene B to Segment B, and so on. Rather, adult 'parts,' like a spinal cord segment or cortical area, correspond to regions in overlapping and nested patterns of regulatory genes. These genes will in time control the expression of other regulatory genes and, eventually, particular molecules like structural proteins, cell-cell recognition molecules, and transmitter production and uptake systems that are the physical components of the cortex. Very rarely would the domain of expression of an early regulatory gene be identical with a recognizable chunk of adult morphology. With the exception of a few genes and other markers that are partially localized to the primary sensory cortices, particularly visual and somatosensory, there is no mosaic organization of gene expression that in any way mirrors the adult mosaic of cortical areas.

A 'polarizer' has been discovered at the front of the growing cortical plate that appears to control the orientation of the cortex. Thus, if this region is transplanted to the back, the topographic organization of cortical areas turns around from the normal arrangement, such that the somatosensory cortex is at the back and the visual cortex in the front (Fig. 4). This polarizer could control the expression of genes in the proliferative zone for the cortical plate, the cortical plate itself, and secondarily the recognition molecules that direct particular regions of the thalamus to particular parts of the cortex. So far, predominating types of gene expression found to be under control of these polarizers are different kinds of cell recognition molecules that control axon pathway selection.

One clear outcome of this specification is that thalamic input to the cortex is very topographically precise in early development. For example, in the adult, the lateral geniculate nucleus in the thalamus gets a point-to-point projection from the retina and confers this representation directly on the visual cortex. Even on first contact, the topology of the projection from the retina to the cortex is nearly as specific as it is in adulthood. The timing and precise placement of thalamic input is well suited to specify further many of the local features of cortical areas. Thalamus-controlled differentiation steps include differences in numbers of cells in the various layers, expression of particular transmitters, and, perhaps most important, the effects of the nature and pattern of activity relayed through the thalamus on how cortical neurons wire up.

In great contrast to the thalamic connections, the early connections of the cortex with itself are made wholesale (Bates *et al.*, 2002). In rodents, the first connections from a very small area of the cortex are in potential reach of a third to half of the entire cortical surface. Intracortical connections are the principal substrate of cortical plasticity of all types that involve reallocation of the cortex to new functions, from gross to fine functional readjustments. Demonstrations of this range from local plasticity that might be caused by producing a gap in the sensory information coming in

from the periphery within a particular sensory modality, to experimental 're-wiring' of the cortex done by inducing retinal axons to innervate auditory centers, which causes the auditory cortex to take on visual properties (Pallas, 2001). A recent demonstration of multimodal activation of the visual cortex in the early blind, including activation during Braille reading, almost certainly uses intracortical pathways to produce the observed re-organization (Sadato *et al.*, 1996).

The significance of embryology for modularity and plasticity

Understanding the cortex in terms of general vertebrate (and invertebrate!) mechanisms that produce the basic body plan opens a wealth of analogies and models. Segmentation of a uniform field into a number of repeating units, and then subsequent differentiation of each unit is the central strategy for creation of the body in embryos, from the segments of an insect body or a worm, to the segments of the vertebrate spinal cord. This 'theme-and-variation' strategy maps in a fairly direct way onto an 'easy' evolutionary alteration of the genome that preserves function while allowing adaptation: duplications of individual genes or groups of genes, followed by modification of the duplicate gene while conserving the original. A typical modification would allow different genes to come under the control of the regulatory genes in separate segments of a segmented structure. Consider the spinal cord of a fish, which has a repeating segmental structure that maps onto the relatively uniform (front to back) musculature of the fish trunk for the rhythmical motion of swimming. In animals with limbs, those segments that innervate the limbs must have evolved to acquire new instructions, including some very specific new wiring for complicated limb musculature. Yet, if these same segments are transplanted into the body trunk region, they are capable of expressing the old trunk pattern and wire up successfully. By analogy, the question of whether particular cortical areas, like the 'face area' or the 'motion area,' are wired for particular functions or are generic has a very likely answer in this developmental context: both.

Maturational gradients: what is the sequence of maturation of cortical areas, and how does it correspond to behavior?

Neurogenesis and innervation

Anyone hoping for fundamental simplicity in the patterning of the early maturation of the cortex will be disappointed. There is no single dimension of

GRADIENTS OF NEUROGENESIS

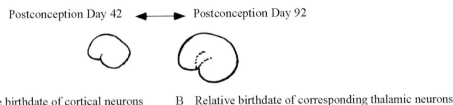

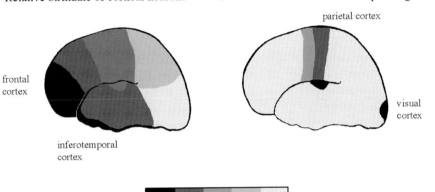

A   Relative birthdate of cortical neurons   B   Relative birthdate of corresponding thalamic neurons

First generated   Last generated

Figure 5. Maturational gradients in the early postnatal development of the human cortex on the day of birth (Postconception day 270). (A) Neurogenesis of cortical neurons begins at the rostrolateral margin of the cortex and proceeds posteriorly through the parietal cortex to the primary visual cortex, framing a period of genesis of about fifty days (Postconception days 42 to 92). (B) Neurogenesis of corresponding thalamic neurons begins with the medial geniculate body (auditory cortex, in black), the lateral geniculate body (on the pathway from the retina to the visual cortex, in black), and the ventrobasal complex (somatosensory cortex, next to the motor cortex) followed by neurons that innervate the motor cortex (in gray). The last thalamic neurons to be produced are located in the nuclei that innervate the frontal, parietal, and inferotemporal cortex.

'maturational state' that any area of the isocortex can be retarded or advanced on (which makes it even less likely there could be a moment when a region 'turns on'). Rather, each isocortical area is best viewed as an assembly of different features, including neurogenesis, the maturation of its input, and the maturation of its output, all of those in the context of the maturation of the entire organism (Bates *et al.*, 2002). Because different areas of the brain follow maturational gradients that do not match in order, interesting mismatches occur. Thus, in some areas, intracortical connections will be relatively more mature than thalamic connections (the frontal cortex), and in others, the reverse will hold (primary visual cortex). Figure 5 compares the gradients of original generation for two central aspects of cortical development: the timing of the original generation of the cortex itself compared to the order of innervation of each cortical region by the thalamus.

The cortex has an intrinsic gradient of maturation. Neurogenesis begins at the front edge of the cortex and proceeds back to the primary visual cortex; the limbic cortices on the midline also get an early start. As depicted in the maturational gradients in Figure 5, paradoxically, the frontal cortex, viewed in hierarchical models as the last maturing cortical area, is in fact one of the first to be produced and thus quite 'mature' in some

features. The order of thalamic development is quite different. In general, the primary sensory nuclei in the thalamus are generated first and establish their axonal connections to the cortex first. Various other nuclei, motor and cingulate, are intermediate in their timing, and the last to be produced are the thalamic nuclei that innervate the frontal, parietal, and part of the inferotemporal cortex. The thalamic order of neurogenesis suggested a hierarchical notion of cortical development (primary sensory areas mature early, 'association' areas late), but it is not the whole story.

So what might the dual gradients mean for the frontal cortex, the area so often described as "maturing late?" The fact that the frontal cortex matures early, but receives its input from the thalamus relatively late, could predispose it for intracortical processing. In other words, this difference in developmental gradients might mean that the frontal cortex is primed for higher-order associative function from the start, not by virtue of being 'out of the circuit' early on.

A uniform perinatal burst of synaptogenesis

Synapses begin to be formed in the cortex from the time that the first neurons move into place, and a fair number are in evidence at 6 months post-conception. The first synapses must account for the many demonstrations of early activity-dependent organization in the cortex, and perhaps for several types of in utero learning (e.g., preferences for the language rhythms of the mother). Just before birth, all over the cortex, the density and number of excitatory synapses surge ten- to a hundredfold. What causes the dramatic acceleration of synaptogenesis? Using the visual cortex as a test case, the possibility that this marked increase is actually caused by the barrage of experience that occurs around birth was investigated. When monkeys were deprived of visual input, the initial acceleration and peak of synaptogenesis were unchanged. A second complementary experiment showed that when monkeys were delivered three weeks prematurely, so that experience began much sooner than it would normally occur, the peak of synaptogenesis still occurred on the monkey's anticipated birthday, not its premature one. In both experiments, secondary effects on types and distributions of synapses were also seen in this study, so experience does matter, but not to the timing of the synaptic surge (Bates *et al.*, 2002).

Why are the connections between neurons made just around birth, before most experience, rather than as experience occurs? In fact, the number of synapses produced is in excess of the eventual adult number. The immediate postnatal phase of development is distinguished by axon retraction and synapse elimination, regressive events, as well as growth and addition. In the mature nervous systems, synapses are both added and subtracted during learning. Perhaps the developing nervous system is both allowing activity (though initially disorganized) to be easily propagated through itself, and also allowing itself the possibility of both addition and subtraction of synapses, rather than simply additive ones, by the installation of large numbers of synapses just prior to experience. This initial overproduction of synapses may be a way of producing continuity in mechanisms of synaptic stabilization from initial development to adulthood. The impressive statistical learning capabilities of infants soon after birth may require this highly elaborated substrate.

Experience-induced maturation

One of the best-studied features of perinatal development from both behavioral and neural perspectives is the development of binocular vision, and its relationship to binocular interactions in the visual cortex, both anatomically and physiologically defined (Dannemiller, in Nelson & Luciana, 1999). Several observations of interest about structure-function links arise from this work. Firstly, in normally developing individuals with normal experience and reasonable optics, there is a critical period for the establishment of a balance of influence from the two eyes on perceptual decisions, for sorting information by eye-of-origin, and for the

development of stereoscopic depth perception that happens in the first several years of life. Absence of activity in either eye or incoordination of the eyes can permanently derail the development of normal visual function during this period. If all experience is denied, however, and both eyes are closed (in experimental animals), what occurs is delay of the critical period – the representation of the two eyes does not begin its segregation into ocular dominance columns, and the special neurotransmitters and receptors that are responsible for this structural change are held at their initial state. When experience is re-instated, anatomical, pharmacological, and physiological events then progress, as they would have, independently of the animal's age (to a point).

Presumably this allocation of cortical tissue to particular functions on the basis of activity occurs everywhere in the cortex. Initial function to structure allocation is often called maturation and the property of maturity is ascribed to the tissue, but the example above shows this need not be so. For example, the immaturity of the frontal cortex on which many executive and self-monitoring functions depend could reflect an absence of events likely to activate frontal cortex in early childhood, not a maturational deficit of the tissue itself.

Continuous brain, discontinuous behavior

One instructive structure-function relationship that appeared in the binocular interaction research was a mismatch between the gradual spatial segregation of the neurons responsive to either the right or left eye in the cortex, and a stepwise change in an aspect of visual behavior likely to be dependent on it, the development of binocular rivalry. In early infancy, as demonstrated in the laboratory of Richard Held, infants presented with horizontal stripes to one eye and vertical stripes to the other indicate by their behavior that their experience is a checkerboard, and not the alternating rivalry between the horizontal and vertical stripes that an adult experiences. In longitudinal studies, the infants switched in a matter of days from the immature to mature perception at about 3 months of age, while no such instant of sharp segregation has ever been described in the presumably corresponding anatomy. A different discontinuity with a similar lesson was described in the development of infant walking by Esther Thelen. At birth, all infants will show an alternating stepping movement when supported over a surface, which disappears around 2–3 months, with real walking appearing at about 1 year of age. This progression was first described as a spinal reflex becoming supplanted by cortical control as the cortex matured. In fact, the spinal reflex never disappears, is the basis of adult walking, and can be elicited at any time if the infant is appropriately weighted and balanced. In this case, spinal circuitry can produce many different rhythmical patterns at any age, dependent on the particular pattern of peripheral load, and 'maturation' lies in the changing periphery.

Mapping complex changing functions onto complex changing tissue

The point of the prior section on maturation is to discount as much as possible the notion of cortical areas maturing as single functional modules blossoming one at a time, and rather to emphasize the continuous activity of the cortex from the time of its generation, with a single point of punctuation in the surge of synapse production at the time of birth. What then is known about the postnatal maturation of the cortex and its relationship to behavior? Until quite recently, very little. Attempts had been made to locate discontinuities or inflections in graphs of changes in the volume or structure of brain tissue, synapses, and process and correlate them with discontinuities in behavior (e.g., the period of very rapid vocabulary addition in learning), although, as we have discussed, the assumption that anatomical and physiological discontinuities should correspond is questionable (Bates *et al.*, 2002). Myelination, the growth of the insulating glial sheaths that increase the speed of axon conduction of impulses, is something that occurs postnatally, and could be correlated with behavior, but not with any great insight. Measurements of spontaneous electrical activity in the cortex (electroencephalograms, EEGs) and evoked activity (ERPs) could be compared from infant to adolescent to adult, with the typical result revealing that the frontal cortex, and sometimes the parietal cortex, showed the mature pattern later than sensory cortices.

Better imaging techniques of all kinds now allow closer structure-function mappings (M. H. Johnson, 2002). While behavioral information about children with brain damage was always available, now various Magnetic Resonance Imaging techniques give a much better idea about what part of the brain is damaged, which is particularly useful for longitudinal studies. Techniques for employing functional magnetic resonance imaging (fMRI) to image the brain's activity while the individual is employed in some task are being adapted to use with children. Exotic techniques, like diffusion tensor imaging, can look at the development of tracts with different physical properties in fully alive subjects; high-density ERPs can be registered with appropriate computer data-gathering that add much more spatial resolution to the already high temporal resolution of the technique. This list is not comprehensive, and it is growing.

Some striking results have already emerged, consistent across both brain damage and imaging studies (Bates *et al.*, 2002; Nelson & Luciana, 1999). Although the cortical areas involved in early and adult performance of the same tasks are rarely disjunct, they are never identical. The structures important for learning language are quite different to those required for mature language performance, both in laterality and in anterior-posterior position, as determined in longitudinal studies of children with early brain damage. A different constellation of areas is activated for facial and spatial judgments in children, though general adult divisions are employed. Overall, there is an interesting tendency for the right hemisphere to be preferentially involved in early learning (in both children and adults). The frontal cortex was found to be *more* active in children engaged in response inhibition tasks than adults, though its activity was not related to success in the task. Identification and understanding of neural structures that are specialized for the acquisition of new knowledge, rather than the performance of practiced abilities, will probably be one of the first outcomes of this research enterprise.

Conclusions

The field of developmental cognitive neuroscience is itself in early development, such that it is not possible to survey the conclusions reached, and suggest new directions. Rather, it is a time to scrutinize fundamental assumptions that guide research, while gathering basic descriptive information. The grammar, the fundamental classificatory scheme for cortex-behavior relationships, is the cortical area. These areas, however, might be not much more than the visible correlate of a mechanism to precisely fan out thalamic information over the cortical surface, to be integrated wholesale later by more general intracortical connections, and may be an unnatural unit for behaviorally defined functions. Are there any intrinsically determined wiring differences between cortical areas, or induced differences? What is the nature of regions of the cortex that are brought into performance early in learning versus those that are employed for mature abilities? Outside of primary sensory areas, we know virtually nothing about how response properties in cortical regions start out and organize, even in experimental animals. The most important fact to remember in all future investigations, however, is that, no matter how privileged the cortex might seem for the unique aspects of human cognition, it is part of the vertebrate body, evolving in the same context, developing with the same genome, with the same rules.

Questions

1. Do any regions of the cortex contain circuitry specific for their mature task (such as face recognition, or syntactic processing), or is cortical circuitry initially task-independent?

2. How do 'cortical areas,' other than primary sensory areas, develop in the primate cortex? Are they specified from the start, or do they arise epigenetically using mechanisms like activity-dependent segregation?

3. What is the best way to organize and understand the vast amount of data about cortical activity varying in space and time collected with all of the new functional and morphological imaging techniques?

See also:
Understanding ontogenetic development: debates about the nature of the epigenetic process; Magnetic Resonance Imaging; Conceptions and misconceptions about embryonic development; Normal and abnormal prenatal development; The status of the human newborn; Cognitive development in infancy; Perceptual development; Motor development; Speech development; Language development; Development of learning and memory; Attention; Brain and behavioral development (I): sub-cortical; Executive functions; Face recognition; Locomotion; Blindness; Cognitive neuroscience; Developmental genetics; Behavioral embryology; George E. Coghill

Further reading

Kingsbury, M. A. and Finlay, B. L. (2001). The cortex in multidimensional space: where do cortical areas come from? Commentary article. *Developmental Science*, 4, 125–156.

Quartz, S. R. and Sejnowski, T. J. (1997). The neural basis of cognitive development: a constructivist manifesto. *Behavioral and Brain Sciences*, 20, 537–596.

Wilkinson, A. S. (2002). *The Evolution of Developmental Pathways*. Sunderland, MA: Sinauer Associates.

Connectionist modeling

GERT WESTERMANN & DENIS MARESCHAL

Introduction

Computational models provide a useful tool for developing and testing theories of cognitive and behavioral development. Building a model involves making precise and specific assumptions about the mechanisms underlying cognitive development. By implementing and testing the model as a running computer simulation, one can verify if these assumptions do indeed generate a behavior that is comparable to that of developing infants and children.

In recent years, connectionist models (artificial neural networks) have emerged as a paradigm that is especially attractive for modeling developmental change. This is because neural networks learn from data, and they develop their own internal representations as a result of interactions with an environment. After learning, they can generalize their knowledge to new instances. A model's performance during learning and its generalization ability can then be compared to that of children to explain their behavior in terms of the model's mechanisms. The model can also be used to generate novel predictions about development that can be tested empirically.

Principles of connectionist models

Connectionist models consist of a number of simple processing units with weighted connections between them. Activation flows from unit to unit via the connections. A unit becomes active when the activation flowing into it is either larger than a threshold value, or when it falls within a certain range. The models learn by adjusting the weights of the connections between the units. Items such as objects or words are represented in the models by patterns of activity over the units.

Connectionist models are loosely inspired by the functioning of neurons in the brain in that a large number of simple, non-linear associators with complex interconnections give rise to higher-level behavior.

However, the similarity between such networks and the brain should not be overstated as biological and artificial neurons differ in important aspects. It may be more useful to see connectionist models simply as complex associative learning systems with similar computational properties to the brain rather than as implementations of specific neurobiological ideas. For example, many connectionist models are very simple and only contain some 100 units, but this does not imply that the part of the brain solving the corresponding task only uses 100 neurons. Instead, individual units are sometimes taken to represent pools of neurons or cell assemblies. According to this interpretation, the activation level of the units corresponds to the proportion of neurons firing in the pool. Nevertheless, some models have aimed for a higher degree of biological plausibility, taking into account known connection pathways in the cortex, response properties of biological neurons, realistic methods for weight adjustment (Hebbian learning), and aspects of neural development.

There are four basic methods of training a neural network. In *supervised* learning, an external teaching signal is provided. The network gradually learns to associate a given input with this teaching signal by computing the discrepancy between its output and the teaching signal (i.e., the output error), and adjusting the connection weights so as to reduce this discrepancy. The most popular method for training a model in this way is the backpropagation algorithm (Rumelhart, Hinton, & Williams, 1986). A common architecture for supervised connectionist models is a three-layer feed-forward network (Fig. 1). It consists of an input layer that receives data from the environment, a hidden layer in which the model develops internal representations necessary to solve the learning task, and an output layer where an output is generated.

In *unsupervised* learning, there is no teaching signal, and the task of the network is often to detect similarities between different inputs or to cluster the input data. In *reinforcement* learning, there is no direct teaching signal, but only feedback (reward) about the success of a task

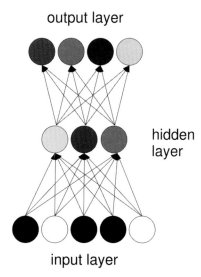

output layer

hidden layer

input layer

Figure 1. A three-layered neural network. Different unit activations are indicated by gray scale.

performed by the network. Finally, *self-supervised* learning is similar to supervised learning, but here the teaching signal is generated by the network itself rather than being external. All of these training methods have been used in the modeling of development, and when building a model it is important to consider which method is appropriate for the task at hand.

Although they are associationist, connectionist models are not *tabula rasa* empirical learning systems. Each model involves a number of choices that form constraints on the learning task. These constraints concern, for example, the number of processing units and the structure of their interconnections, or the learning algorithm used to train the model. The selection of initial constraints is important because it will influence if and how the model learns a certain task. Any model involves abstraction, but the abstraction of an aspect of processing that is important for learning the task, or the introduction of constraints that do not exist in the real world task and that might make learning easier, can compromise the validity of a model. With this in mind, the chosen constraints can inform theories of cognitive development in children.

Representational constraints, such as the features used to represent objects in category learning, or the amount of overlap between the representations of different verbs in learning inflections, can shed light on which representations are necessary for the child to solve a certain task. *Architectural* constraints such as integration between orthographic and semantic components in learning to read, or the number of units in the model that constrain its overall capacity to learn, can show which resources are necessary for learning a task. Further constraints are *processing* constraints such as the specific unit activation function and the weight update rule, and *environmental*

constraints that can give insights into the effect of the structure of the environment on learning (e.g., what can be learned based on a set of experimental stimuli in a within-task learning model, or what is learned from the experience in a structured environment such as the linguistic input to a child).

Varying the initial constraints of models has been used to explain abnormal development. For example, aspects of different types of developmental dyslexia have been successfully modeled in a connectionist model of normal reading by reducing the number of processing units (Harm & Seidenberg, 1999). Such models can therefore give new explanations for the causes of developmental disorders as well.

Specific connectionist models of development

Connectionist models have been used to model both behavioral and cognitive development. Examples of modeled behaviors are habituation (the decrease of response to a stimulus after repeated exposure) and perseveration (repetition of a behavior even after circumstances change and the behavior is no longer appropriate, such as in the A-not-B task) (Munakata, 1998).

Connectionist models of cognitive development have addressed the trajectory of development across a number of tasks. Examples include the balance scale task (Shultz, Mareschal, & Schmidt, 1994), the acquisition of the English past tense, learning the meaning of words, phonological development (Westermann & Miranda, 2004), the emergence of object-directed behaviors in infants (Mareschal, 2001), and concept and category acquisition. Models of within-task learning at a certain stage in development have also been devised, such as category learning and speech sound discriminations in 4- and 10-month-olds (Mareschal, 2001). In this way, connectionist models can explain both the mechanisms underlying cognitive change and those that are responsible for infant learning on a shorter time scale.

One recent example of within-task learning is a model of novelty preference. Infants direct more attention to unfamiliar and unexpected stimuli, and the standard interpretation of this behavior is that they are comparing an input stimulus to an internal representation of the same stimulus (Fig. 2B). A bigger discrepancy between the stimulus and the internal representation results in a longer looking time because the infant updates the latter to reduce the discrepancy. This behavior has been translated into connectionist models with so-called auto-encoder networks (Fig. 2A). These are simple three-layer feed-forward networks where the input signal and the target signal are the same (i.e., the

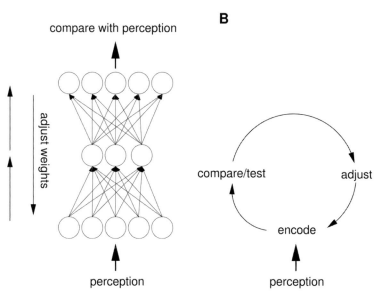

Figure 2. An auto-encoder neural network model (A) that implements the analogy of the infant looking time model (B).

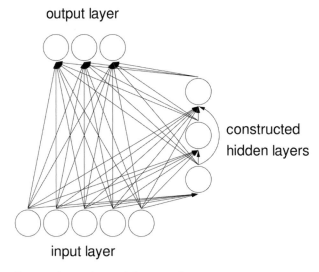

Figure 3. A cascade-correlation network.

These 'constructivist' models have been especially successful in accounting for stage-like development in Piagetian tasks, and for regressive behavior (the unlearning of previously learned behavior typical of U-shaped learning). Furthermore, constructivist models have been useful in formalizing Piaget's notions of assimilation, accommodation, and equilibration.

An example for a constructivist connectionist network is the cascade-correlation algorithm (Fig. 3). This model starts out with a minimal architecture comprising only the input and output layers. It is trained in a supervised way, and when the task cannot be learned in the present architecture, a new, hidden, unit is inserted, and training continues with the new architecture. This process is repeated until the task has been learned. Each new unit is connected to all previously inserted units as well as the input units, and can thus develop into a higher-level feature detector that helps in learning the task. While the precise mechanisms of structural change in the cortex are not well understood, they are certainly different from those in constructivist neural network models. Nevertheless, the models highlight the importance of structural change and adaptation to the environment in cognitive development.

Conclusions

Since the early 1980s, connectionist models of development have become an indispensable tool for furthering our understanding of the mechanisms that underlie behavioral change. They draw inspiration from the functioning of biological neurons in the brain, but they also abstract from many aspects of real neurons and introduce some new constraints. An important step in modeling, which is sometimes omitted, is to re-translate a successful model into a developmental theory. This step specifies the relevant aspects of the model that have led to the observed behavior, and whether they find their counterpart in the real world. It also makes sure that the model does not succeed only because hidden assumptions have been made that have nothing to do with the modeled phenomenon.

All connectionist models of development are located in the large gap that looms in our understanding of the connections between brain and cognitive development. They can serve to narrow this gap, and a promising direction of future models might be to incorporate more biological plausibility while still addressing relatively high-level cognitive behavior. Existing models are biologically plausible to different degrees, but more plausible models often address low-level phenomena like visual or auditory processing. The challenge for connectionist models is to address high-level tasks that involve behavior normally explained with symbolic

model learns to reproduce the input at the output layer). To learn this task, the model develops internal representations in the form of activation patterns of the hidden units for all stimuli. When a novel stimulus is presented to the network, its output will be more different from the target signal, resulting in a higher output error. Here, the error in the model is equated with the looking time of the infant. With this paradigm, several aspects of categorization behavior in early infancy have been successfully modeled.

Another class of connectionist models has been based on recent evidence that the structural experience-dependent adaptation of the cortex in the first years of life plays a major role in cognitive change during development. These models change their structure while they learn a task, by adding or deleting units and connections.

processing, such as reasoning, inference, analogy, and decision making.

Connectionist models have been successful in addressing many developmental phenomena, but they are mainly adapted to specific isolated tasks. A challenge is therefore to build models that account for multiple interacting tasks. Such models would have to address the question of how knowledge that has developed in separate domains is subsequently integrated, and how the models can capitalize on previously acquired knowledge. Another important question concerns the role of embodiment in learning. Connectionist models take their inspiration from learning and processing in the brain, but as such they are divorced from a body. However, proactive behavior of a learner, that is, manipulating the environment to generate new information and new learning situations, probably plays an important role in cognitive development. Therefore, a future direction of connectionist research should be to incorporate these models into embodied systems that have the ability to manipulate their environment.

Questions

1. How can connectionist models account for the development of higher-level skills such as reasoning?
2. How can connectionist networks capitalize on previously acquired knowledge from different domains?
3. How can connectionist models further narrow the gap between brain and cognitive development?
4. How can connectionist models address multiple tasks?
5. What is the role of embodiment in learning?

See also:
Learning theories; Dynamical systems approaches; Cognitive development in infancy; Cognitive development beyond infancy; Perceptual development; Speech development; Language development; Development of learning and memory; Brain and behavioral development (II): cortical; Dyslexia; Cognitive neuroscience; Jean Piaget

Further reading

Elman, J. L., Bates, E. A., Johnson, M. H., Karmiloff-Smith, A., Parisi, D. and Plunkett, K. (1996). *Rethinking Innateness: A Connectionist Perspective on Development*. Cambridge, MA: MIT Press.

Marcus, G. (2001). *The Algebraic Mind*. Cambridge, MA: MIT Press.

Munakata, Y. and McClelland, J. L (2003). Connectionist models of development. *Developmental Science*, 6, 413–429.

Quinlan, P. T. (ed.) (2003). *Connectionist Models of Development: Developmental Processes in Real and Artificial Neural Networks*. Hove, UK: Psychology Press.

Shultz, T. R. (2003). *Computational Developmental Psychology*. Cambridge, MA: MIT Press.

Acknowledgments

The writing of this chapter was supported by grants from the Economic and Social Research Council (R00239112) and the European Commission (HPRN-CT-1999-00065).

Daycare

EDWARD C. MELHUISH

Introduction

Daycare refers to childcare by someone other than the parent and most research is concerned with the years 0–5. As research has revealed the complexity of daycare, theoretical models for it have become more sophisticated, and produced three waves of research. The first wave was influenced by concerns, deriving from attachment theory, that repeated separations from the mother may weaken attachment to her, and addressed the question of whether daycare is bad for children. The second wave recognized the diversity of daycare environments and considered how the quality of daycare affects development. The third wave considered the inter-relationship between home and daycare environments and how the interaction may affect child development. However, the social context beyond the family should also be considered, and this should be a fourth wave of research.

Social context and cross-national comparisons

The impact of daycare upon children is dependent upon context, or social ecology. Most industrialized societies have seen marked increases in maternal employment since the early 1970s. For example, in the USA in 1975, 39% of mothers with a preschool child were in employment. By 2000, this had increased to 67%. However, much of this was part-time employment and over 60% of preschool children had at least one parent who did not work full-time. Countries have responded differently to the increased demand for daycare. In some countries, daycare provision is seen as a state responsibility (e.g., Sweden had 85% of mothers of a preschool child in employment in the early 1990s, and provided high levels of publicly funded daycare). In English-speaking countries in the twentieth century, daycare was a private concern with little public funding.

In these circumstances, the quality and type of daycare becomes more diverse. For example, in the USA, in 1995, where mothers were employed, 22% of preschool daycare was center-based; 24% was family daycare (nanny, or babysitter); 27% was provided by a relative; and 27% was provided by the father. Most daycare in the USA is funded by parents and the quality varies considerably, partly because states have markedly different regulations concerning daycare. Where daycare costs fall to parents, parents are likely to choose on the basis of cost, particularly as information on quality is not readily available.

Social ecology and daycare

Where daycare is publicly funded, cost constraints are reduced, and quality of daycare is usually regulated to acceptable minimum standards, and there is investment in training for daycare workers. Other factors such as parental leave will also influence daycare practices. Consequently, the range of quality, quantity, and age of use for daycare vary markedly between societies. These aspects mediate relationships between daycare and child development, and hence such variation between societies would be expected to produce different patterns of these relationships. Social ecology also influences the kinds of research undertaken. The social ecology of relationships is represented in Table 1.

Daycare and child development

Some preschool provision has explicit educational aims, and is usually targeted on children from 3 years upward (e.g., nursery school, kindergarten). Other provision is care-orientated and, while operating for under-3s, also caters for older children (e.g., daycare centers). These distinctions are becoming increasingly blurred with changes in provision. Quality of daycare or differences in children's experiences may have developmental consequences, and be part of the explanation of whether daycare or preschool experiences are beneficial or not. There are alternative perspectives on the quality of care, but most research adopts the perspective that quality reflects what is beneficial for children's development, based upon expert judgment or upon empirical research of the relationship between indicators of quality and developmental outcomes.

Daycare of high quality has been associated with short-term and long-term cognitive, social, and emotional benefits for children's development (e.g., Peisner-Feinberg *et al.*, 2001). The strongest effects appear to occur for children from disadvantaged backgrounds. Longitudinal studies indicate long-term gains from high-quality preschool experience, related to crime, welfare dependence, unemployment, teenage pregnancy, school dropout, and family instability (e.g., Behrman, 1995). Apparently, these long-term benefits can easily justify the costs of preschool provision. Common features of high-quality preschool programs are:

1. adult-child interaction that is responsive, affectionate, and readily available;
2. well-trained staff who are committed to their work with children;
3. facilities that are safe and sanitary and accessible to parents;
4. ratios and group sizes that allow staff to interact appropriately with children;
5. staff development that ensures continuity, stability, and improving quality;
6. a developmentally appropriate curriculum with educational content.

Long-term benefits may stem from effects on parents' and children's attitudes and consequently home experience, resulting in better motivation and long-term gains in social development and adjustment.

While the results from research on preschool education for 3-year-olds and older have been fairly consistent, the research evidence on the effects of earlier daycare upon development has been equivocal, with some studies finding negative effects, some no effects, and others positive effects. Discrepant results may relate to age of starting as well as with the quality and quantity of daycare. Also, daycare effects are mediated by family background, or aspects of parenting. One model of the interrelationship of quality of care at home and in daycare predicts that negative, neutral, and positive effects may occur depending on the relative balance of quality of care at home and in daycare. With quality of care in both settings equivalent, there is likely to be little effect from attending daycare. Where quality of care in daycare is superior to the home, then children receiving daycare are likely to show beneficial effects, as seen in several studies of children from disadvantaged families

Table 1. Ecological perspective on daycare and effects upon children	
Level	*Unit of study*
SOCIETY	Culture and social context (e.g., labor markets and ideology) ↓
INSTITUTIONS	Daycare provision ↓
SETTINGS	Daycare center, individual daycare, etc. ↓
SOCIAL EXPERIENCE	Patterns of interaction ↓
INDIVIDUAL	Children's development

receiving good-quality daycare. However, where the quality of daycare is inferior to that at home, then negative or detrimental effects may occur, as reported in studies where children attend poor-quality daycare. This model would predict that the strongest effects of quality would occur for disadvantaged families, which is increasingly receiving empirical support.

The National Institutes for Child Health and Development (NICHD) study

This study is following over 1,100 children from nine states of the USA from birth onward (NICHD, 2002). The issue of whether daycare was bad for children re-emerged in the 1980s with the proposition that infant daycare may be a risk factor for insecure attachment to the mother, and increased aggressiveness and disobedience (e.g., Belsky, 2001), and this controversy led to the funding of the NICHD study. This study could find no direct or main effect of amount, quality, or type of daycare on attachment security. At 15 months of age, children with more than twenty hours per week of non-parental care in the first year of life were not significantly more likely to have an insecure attachment to their mother. However, where children had a less responsive home environment and poor-quality daycare, or unstable daycare, or higher levels of daycare, there were increased levels of insecure attachment. Thus, greater non-parental care in the first year is a risk factor, but it only results in increased insecurity of attachment at 15 and 36 months of age when combined with another risk factor (e.g., poor responsiveness at home). Conversely, responsive home environments, responsive daycare, and stable daycare can be regarded as protective factors.

The NICHD results for the children aged $4^1/_2$ years reveal effects for quality and quantity of daycare. These effects were independent and influenced different aspects of development. The quality effect occurred primarily for cognitive and language development, whereby those children whose caregivers provided more language stimulation and were more responsive to children's utterances had better cognitive and language scores. The quantity effect (time in daycare) occurred for socio-emotional aspects of development, such that children in non-parental care for long hours across their first $4^1/_2$ years were rated as having more behavior problems. For example, 17% of children in non-parental care for more than 30 hours per week were rated as aggressive to other children, whereas only 6% of children in non-parental care for less than 10 hours per week were rated similarly. This quantity effect is consistent with concerns that high levels of daycare may be a risk factor. Further evidence consistent with these results is emerging. For example, data analyzed from the National Longitudinal Study of Youth (NLSY) found that high levels of maternal employment in the first year of life (and consequent daycare) was predictive of poorer cognitive and behavioral outcomes, after allowing for demographic factors (Han, Waldfogel & Brooks-Gunn, 2001).

Besides the effects of quality and quantity within the NICHD study, there was a separate effect for type of care, whereby children in group care tended to have better language and memory skills, but also more behavior problems than children in individual child care. The effects of home-related variables such as socio-economic status and responsiveness in the home were consistently related to cognitive, language and social development. The effect sizes of quality and quantity of daycare were about half that of home background factors, indicating the greater importance of home-related experience.

Sensitive mothering has been a consistent predictor of child competencies. Similar points have been made with regard to responsiveness and sensitivity affecting social relationships and social development. The NICHD findings indicate that increased quantity of daycare is associated with less maternal engagement with children, and higher-quality daycare with greater maternal sensitivity. Thus, there is an inevitable problem in dissociating the effects of daycare from those of the family when there are subtle and complex interactions between these two domains.

The NICHD study has reinforced the evidence that quality of daycare is important despite indications that the sampling procedures may under-represent both poor-quality daycare and unresponsive home environments, and hence lead to an underestimation of the effects of quality of home and daycare. The results also replicate earlier findings on the impact of quality of care and specifically responsiveness within the linguistic environment on language development (Melhuish, 2002). While the daycare effect sizes were about half that for family factors, such factors incorporate unmeasured genetic influences, in addition to environmental ones such as responsiveness. Hence, family and daycare effects may be much more equivalent in terms of environmental influence than the NICHD results imply. Family factors and daycare quality co-vary, with low-income families tending to have lowest quality of daycare. The analytical strategy of the NICHD study, in common with many others, attributes variance to daycare factors only after that attributed to the family has been extracted. Where the two co-vary, this will produce underestimates or conservative estimates of daycare effects.

Measures of the quality of daycare

Most measures of quality focus on the setting (i.e., a center or a daycare home), and indicate what is typical for children in that setting. A widely used method is the Early Childhood Environment Rating Scale (ECERS), which consists of observational ratings of aspects of care judged by 'expert opinion' to be important for development. Such observations have the disadvantage that the experiences of individual children within one setting may vary substantially. Methods focusing on individual children overcome this disadvantage, and give more accurate information for the specific child, but the results may not generalize to other children.

Another perspective on quality derives from answering the question: does a particular institution attended by a child make a difference? This approach identifies the effectiveness of specific centers. Effectiveness here means the extent to which the child's development deviates either positively or negatively from the expected developmental trajectory for a child with given characteristics. This effectiveness measure can be taken as a measure of the quality, where quality is defined in terms of beneficial effects upon child development. While measures of daycare quality consist of characteristics presumed by 'experts' to be representative of quality, a definition of quality rooted in demonstrable beneficial effects on child development is an advance. Once a specific effective (high-quality) or ineffective (low-quality) institution is identified, the processes producing effectiveness can be investigated.

A study using such an approach is the Effective Provision of Preschool Education (EPPE) project that identifies the effectiveness of specific preschool centers (e.g., Sammons *et al.*, 2002). This study considers the quality of a setting in terms of both observational ratings of child experience (e.g., ECERS) and effects on developmental outcomes, and different settings vary in quality according to different criteria. A center rated highly from observations may not be associated with improved developmental progress, whereas one rated as mediocre may be associated with significant developmental progress to that expected from intake characteristics. In terms of effectiveness, such a setting would be of high quality, yet it may not score well on observational ratings, and, in terms of 'expert opinion,' appears to be low quality. Research incorporating quality measures based on observations and developmental outcomes will increasingly reveal this dilemma. This raises the issue of values (i.e., what values are placed on different development outcomes and what is the relative value of children's experience and their developmental progress?). Such findings will require a re-conceptualization of the issue of quality in children's environments.

Conclusions

In summary, research confirms the importance of the characteristics of daycare and the relationship with home care. Type, timing, quantity, and quality of daycare are all important. Future research needs to integrate alternative approaches to quality, which incorporate validation through links with developmental outcomes. This will have to consider the proximal processes underlying quality to produce a new synthesis of the relationships between environmental characteristics (community, family, and daycare), child experience, and developmental outcomes. The interaction of quality, quantity, and timing of daycare will need further differentiation, particularly in the first two years. Also, it is now the norm for children in most industrialized societies to experience some form of child care/education in the early years. Hence, all longitudinal studies should incorporate measurement of this experience as part of the full range of experiential factors affecting development. If longitudinal studies also include genetic factors in the analysis of developmental patterns, the analysis of child-care experience may contribute to the perennial issue of gene/environment interaction. Overall, the improvement in measures of children's experience or quality in child

care facilitate the incorporation of such measures into mainstream developmental studies, integrating the study of daycare more firmly within developmental psychology.

Questions

1. Are the effects of daycare uniform across types of daycare, types of family and children, or between societies?
2. How do quality, quantity, type, and timing of daycare interact in affecting child development?
3. How should quality of daycare be defined and measured? Has this concept become too simplistic?
4. What are the processes underlying good-quality daycare?
5. How are daycare effects mediated or modulated by other aspects of the child's world?

See also:
Cross-sectional and longitudinal designs; Social development; Emotional development; Aggression and prosocial behaviors; Parenting and the family; Socialization; 'At-risk' concept; Behavioral and learning disorders; Pediatrics; John Bowlby

Further reading

Fox, N. and Fein, G. G. (eds.) (1990). *Infant Day Care: The Current Debate.* Norwood, NJ: Ablex.

Melhuish, E. C. and Moss, P. (eds.) (1991). *Day Care for Young Children: International Perspectives.* London: Routledge.

Lamb, M. E. (1998). Nonparental child care: context, quality, correlates and consequences. In W. Damon, I. E. Sigel and K. A. Renninger (eds.), *Handbook of Child Psychology*, Vol. IV: *Child Psychology in Practice.* New York: John Wiley, pp. 73–133.

Executive functions

CLAIRE HUGHES

Introduction

Following William James' famous example of going upstairs to change and discovering himself in bed, cognitive psychologists have recognized that some actions require conscious effortful control, but others are executed automatically (and so can lead to 'capture errors' of the kind described by James). This distinction is not simply a contrast between simple and complex actions, as well-learned complex actions can be automatic (e.g., driving a car); nor between externally and internally driven actions as the latter can be based on internally driven automatic processes (e.g., memory recall). Instead, the distinction between controlled and automatic actions hinges upon three key features: the execution of novel versus familiar action sequences, making a choice between alternative responses versus executing a single action sequence, and the execution of acts that do / do not require access to consciousness.

The term 'executive function' (EF), therefore, refers to a complex cognitive construct encompassing the whole set of processes underlying these controlled goal-directed responses to novel or difficult situations, processes which are generally associated with the prefrontal cortex (PFC), the regions of which are shown in Figure 1. The cognitive importance of the PFC first became apparent through studies of First World War veterans, which demonstrated that soldiers with frontal lobe injuries were unimpaired on routine tasks, but had difficulty mastering new tasks or grasping the whole of a complicated task. This led to the view that EF was important for abstract or high-level thought, abilities only manifested in adulthood, and to the subsequent neglect of EF in childhood for much of the last century.

Luria's influence

Research into the development of EF can be traced back to the theoretical and empirical work of the Soviet psychologist Alexander R. Luria (1902–1977), who proposed a less ambitious but more practical role for the frontal lobes, namely, the responsibility for programming, monitoring, and regulating behavior. This view continues to be influential, and has been expressed computationally by the characterization of the PFC as a 'Supervisory Attentional System' (SAS). A recent version of this model is shown in Figure 2.

Luria's empirical work was equally seminal. In particular, his account of developmental improvements showing a peak between the ages of 4 and 7 in children's ability to plan, monitor, and regulate their behavior has been well replicated. In addition, several tasks developed by Luria (1966) in his work with adult clinical groups and with young children continue to be widely used. These include tasks such as the 'Go / No Go test' (in which the child must execute a response to stimulus A, but withhold this response when presented with stimulus B) and non-verbal Stroop tasks. Examples of non-verbal Stroop tasks include the picture-based 'Day/Night' task (in which the child must say 'Day' for a picture of the moon, and 'Night' for a picture of the sun), the Tapping game (in which the child must tap once in reply to two taps, and twice in response to a single tap), and the Hand game depicted in Figure 3.

Executive function tasks

Other EF tasks that are simple enough even for infants have since been developed. These include tests such as (i) the A-not-B test in which the infant is invited to retrieve an object that is hidden in location A for a few trials, and then hidden in a new location B (younger infants will continue to search at A, even when the object is visible at B); (ii) the object reversal test in which an established reward contingency is reversed (performance is rated by the number of trials needed to learn this reversal); and (iii) object retrieval tasks that tap the ability to perform a means-end action, such as making a detour around a barrier to retrieve a desired object. Both animal lesion studies and human imaging studies indicate that particular clusters of tasks differentially activate distinct sub-regions of the PFC. For example, 'hot' (affectively laden) EF tasks that involve changing reward values (e.g., the object reversal task described above, and gambling tasks that involve high- and low-risk card decks) appear to activate the orbitofrontal PFC, whilst 'cool' EF tasks (e.g., working memory tasks that require processing as well as storage) activate the dorsolateral PFC (Fig. 1).

These simple tasks have also led to dramatic improvements in our understanding of the development of EF. For instance, it is now known that EF: (i) begins to emerge in the first few years of life; (ii) becomes fully mature in late adolescence and declines with normal ageing; (iii) sub-divides in children and adults in similar ways (in each case the three most widely reported factors are inhibitory control, attentional flexibility, and working memory / planning); (iv) shows stage-like age-related changes; and (v) has important consequences for other cognitive functions (e.g., early vocabulary development is strongly predicted by individual differences in the functioning of one component of working memory termed the phonological loop).

Current research topics

This rapid progress in our understanding of the basic development of EF has exciting consequences, and there are now several hot topics for research. Firstly, impairments in the control of action contribute to the behavioral problems that set children on a trajectory toward deviance, delinquency, and anti-social conduct. For instance, in a study of 'hard to manage' 3- and 4-year-olds, individual differences in EF were significantly associated with antisocial behavior (Hughes et al., 2000). Studies that deepen our knowledge of normative age-related improvements in EF may therefore help to identify children with poor regulatory control who could benefit from intervention programs, and so has clear societal importance. Thus, interest in early EF is closely tied to the growth of the new discipline of developmental neuropsychology. In particular, impairments in EF are thought to play a key role in several childhood disorders, including Attention-Deficit Hyperactivity Disorder (ADHD) and autism, though the latter is more controversial.

Secondly, studies with children offer the promise of differentiating the components of EF. In particular, the technique of manipulating task parameters may be especially fruitful in studies of children, since their relatively limited processing capacity makes them more sensitive to effects of increased demands for particular functions. This provides a direct solution to the low discriminant validity shown by traditional EF tasks.

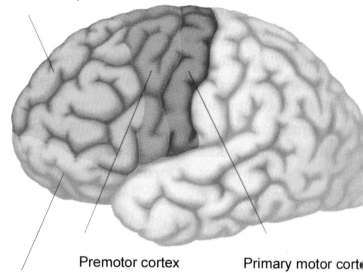

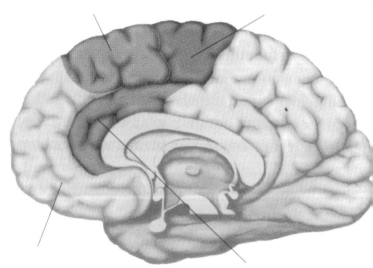

Figure 1. Surface and medial views of the brain, showing key regions of the prefrontal cortex.

Because such tasks are typically complex and multi-componential, different clinical groups may perform equally poorly for different reasons. For example, ADHD and autism have quite different clinical presentations, and yet both groups show substantial EF deficits (scoring $\approx$ 1 standard deviation below control groups). At first glance, one might therefore expect EF impairments to be rather non-specific. However, studies that adopt an information-processing approach (involving simplified tasks that allow comparisons based on specific rather than global performance measures) have revealed both quantitative and qualitative

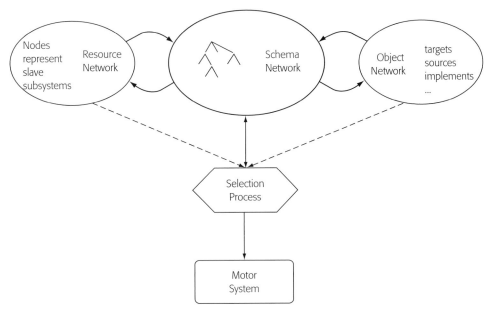

Figure 2. The Cooper and Shallice implementation of the 'Supervisory Attentional System' model. At the center of the model is a hierarchically structured network of interactive action schemas that compete for activation. Schemas receive excitation and inhibition from various sources, including higher-level schemas, the representation of the environment, and competing schemas. The model has been applied to a range of tasks, including preparing coffee and packing a lunchbox. From R. Cooper & T. Shallice, 2000. Contention scheduling and the control of routine activities. *Cognitive Neuropsychology*, 17, 297–338.

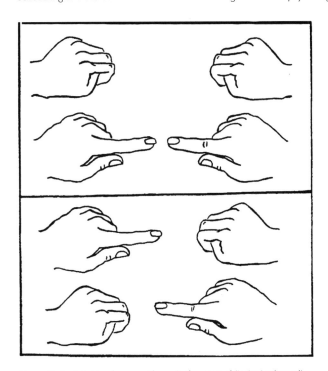

Figure 3. Luria's Hand game. Above is the control 'imitation' condition. Below is the test 'conflict condition' in which the child has to show a fist if presented with a finger, but point a finger if shown a fist. Performance is scored by the number of correct conflict trials/12.

distinctions between EF impairments in these two disorders.

Thirdly, there is converging evidence for a functional link between EF and 'theory of mind' (ToM) defined as the ability to attribute mental states to oneself and others: (i) pronounced impairments in both EF and ToM among children with autism; (ii) the developmental synchrony of improvements in both EF and ToM among typically developing pre-schoolers; and (iii) robust correlations between individual differences in EF and ToM, even with effects of age and IQ controlled. Since the topic of ToM continues to attract intense research interest, the nature and significance of its association with EF is a matter of considerable debate.

Empirically, there is longitudinal evidence for a predictive association between individual differences in EF at age 4 and in ToM one year later (even controlling for initial ToM), but no association between early ToM and later EF (Hughes, 1998). This asymmetry suggests a direction of influence (EF → ToM), but findings from intervention studies are needed to establish a causal path. In addition, it may be that associations between EF and ToM are specific rather than global. For example, Carlson & Moses (2001) have reported particularly strong associations between inhibitory control and ToM. Further support for this view comes from the findings in several imaging studies, demonstrating that ToM tasks activate the orbitofrontal PFC (the subregion previously identified as important in inhibitory control). Since individuals with autism are known to show profound impairments of ToM, this finding suggests that research into EF impairments in autism should focus on 'hot' EF tasks that are associated with the orbitofrontal PFC (previous research in this field has generally employed traditional 'cool' EF tasks that are typically associated with the dorsolateral PFC). Thus, one positive consequence of the debate surrounding the relation between ToM and EF is the integration of brain-based research with studies of both normative and atypical development.

Methodological challenges

Despite the various advances outlined above, it should be emphasized that EF research remains besieged by methodological problems. In particular, much more work is needed to achieve a fine-grained analysis of the distinct components of EF. This fractionated approach is also important as a solution to the homunculus problem raised by terms such as 'effortful control,' since it allows EF to be compared with a set of automatic tools, rather than an engineer. In addition, it is very difficult to design 'pure' tests of EF, or even tasks that show good test-retest reliability (an inherent problem with EF research is that any task is only novel once). Progress in our conceptual understanding of EF depends critically upon innovative and rigorous solutions to these methodological challenges.

Conclusions

The challenges for future research in the above areas are vast and varied. However, one that deserves a special mention is the need to investigate whether contrasts in EF help explain differences in the form and severity of behavioral symptoms. Research on this topic may enable us to elucidate *specific* links between EF and behavior. Such links may be best described in terms of distinct behaviors, such as reactive versus proactive forms of aggression (for disruptive behavior disorders), or catastrophic responses to change versus ritualistic routines (for autism). Alternatively, links between EF and behavior may be clearest for specific contexts (e.g., peer interactions that are not scaffolded by familiar routines). Addressing the relationship between variability in EF and in behavior also provides a promising alternative to simply comparing diagnostic groups, in that disorders with overlapping symptoms (e.g., ADHD and Conduct Disorder) may show relative rather than absolute differences in EF. For many reasons then, research that combines innovative task

manipulations with valid and reliable observational methods is vital.

Questions

1. To what extent do executive function deficits explain differences in the form and severity of behavioral symptoms?
2. Can distinct types of executive function deficit be identified with different disorders?
3. How do individual differences in executive function relate to individual differences in other cognitive skills, such as theory of mind or verbal ability?

See also:
Theories of the child's mind; Magnetic Resonance Imaging; Cross-sectional and longitudinal designs; Cognitive development in infancy; Cognitive development beyond infancy; Aggressive and prosocial behaviors; Brain and behavioral development (II); cortical; Attention; Autism; Behavioral and learning disorders; Cognitive neuroscience; Ethology; Jean Piaget

Further reading

Diamond, A. (1991). Developmental time course in human infants and infant monkeys, and the neural bases of inhibitory control in reaching. *Annals of the New York Academy of Sciences: Part VII. Inhibition and Executive Control*, 637–704.

Hughes, C. and Graham, A. (2002). Measuring executive functions in childhood: problems and solutions? *Child and Adolescent Mental Health*, 7, 131–142.

Pennington, B. F. and Ozonoff, S. (1996). Executive function and developmental psychopathology. *Journal of Child Psychology & Psychiatry*, 37, 51–87.

Perner, J. and Lang, B. (2000). Theory of mind and executive function: is there a developmental relationship? In S. Baron-Cohen, H. Tager-Flusberg, and D. J. Cohen (eds.), *Understanding Other Minds: Perspectives from Autism and Developmental Cognitive Neuroscience*, 2nd edn. Oxford: Oxford University Press, pp. 150–181.

Zelazo, P. R. and Jacques, S. (1997). Children's rule use: representation, reflection and cognitive control. In R. Vasta (ed.), *Annals of Child Development: A Research Annual*, Vol. XII. Bristol, PA: Jessica Kingsley, pp. 119–176.

Face recognition

CHARLES A. NELSON

Introduction

Scientific interest in face recognition dates back at least to Darwin (1872), who compiled detailed observations of his infant son's facial expressions. Since Darwin, of course, interest in this topic has grown among researchers representing a number of disciplines. For example, cognitive psychologists are interested in face recognition because of evidence that faces are somehow perceived differently than other patterned objects. In turn, this has led to speculation that faces represent a 'special' class of stimuli. Neuroscientists are interested in face recognition for a similar reason: that the neural circuits subserving face recognition may be distinct from those for object recognition. Finally, developmental psychologists have long been interested in face recognition because, prior to the onset of language, faces provide an early channel of communication between infant and caregiver.

Is face recognition a special case of object perception?

There is evidence from many quarters to suggest that there is something special about face recognition. This includes the study of adults with brain damage, neuro-imaging, and perceptual studies with human adults, as well as single unit recording studies with monkeys. With regard to lesion studies, a well-known manifestation of a visual agnosia is prosopagnosia, the inability to recognize familiar faces (generally due to lesions in the occipital-temporal pathway). For example, Farah, Levinson, & Klein (1995) reported on patient L. H., who at age 18 (tested at age 37) suffered a closed head injury, leading to bilateral damage with the occipital-temporal region and right inferior frontal lobe and anterior temporal lobe. L. H. cannot recognize his wife, children, or even himself. Like other prosopagnosic patients, he

performs in the normal range of visual perception tasks that do not involve faces. An even more specific facial agnosia can be found in patients with damage restricted to the amygdala, who may have difficulty recognizing specific facial expressions like fear, as with patient S. M. (Adolphs et al.,1995).

Support for the specificity of face processing can also be found in neurologically intact individuals. For example, neuropsychologically normal adults typically perform worse on face identification tasks when faces are presented in an inverted versus upright orientation (Valentine, 1988). In contrast, stimulus inversion typically does not interfere with object recognition. Thus, at the perceptual level, faces and objects appear to be processed by separate neural systems, or alternatively the same system that employs different strategies or algorithms.

In terms of more direct evidence of face recognition specificity, there are now many reports that the fusiform gyrus is selectively activated when viewing faces. For example, there are reports of increased activation in the fusiform gyrus to faces in general, although less activation is observed if the faces are presented upside down. There are also reports of increased activation in the amygdala to fearful faces, but decreased activation to happy faces (Morris, Frith, Perrett, & Rowland, 1996).

Animal studies employing single unit recordings have also supported the cytoarchitectonic independence of face versus object perception. For example, a number of investigators have reported the existence of neurons in the adult monkey brain (most commonly in the superior temporal polysensory area and adjacent areas in TE cortex of the inferior temporal lobe) that respond selectively to faces. And, consistent with the human functional imaging work, neurons responsive to faces have also been observed in the amygdala, with some nuclei found to be responsive to individual faces, whereas others are to individual expressions (Nelson, 2001).

Caveats

Thus far, I have presented evidence that, in the adult, faces are perceived as a separate class of stimuli, distinct from objects. The mechanism responsible for this segregation is hotly debated, with some arguing for innate specificity, and others that expertise lies behind such segregation. I shall return to this debate in a subsequent section.

Developmental studies

There are now numerous demonstrations of face recognition abilities being present at or near the time of birth. For example, when confronted with two moving stimuli, one face-like and another not, infants 'prefer' (e.g., track longer) the face-like stimulus. Curiously, this preference for face-like stimuli gradually wanes toward the second month, and then returns shortly thereafter (Morton & Johnson, 1991).

There is considerable development in this ability beyond the newborn period (Nelson, 2001), with the first marked change in face processing occurring around 2 months of age. For example, at this age infants' gaze falls on the inner features of the face, rather than the outer edges, and infants are less captured by faces moving in the periphery (Maurer & Salapatek, 1976).

By approximately 4 months of age, infants begin to show evidence of perceiving faces as distinct from other patterned objects. Here, for example, they will exhibit difficulty in discriminating two upside down faces (as occurs in adults), whereas earlier than this inverted and upside down faces are treated comparably (Fagan, 1972). Despite this shift, infants' processing of faces still differs markedly from that of adults. For example, studies using event-related potentials (ERPs) in 6-month-old infants have shown that face-responsive ERP components are more specific to human faces in adults than in infants. Furthermore, in adults the effect of stimulus inversion on the so-called 'face' component of the ERP – the N170 – is specific to human faces and does not occur to monkey faces or sheep faces.

In 6-month-old infants, the P400 (believed to be the infant analogue to the adult N170), is, like the N170, affected by stimulus inversion. However, as reviewed in detail by de Haan (2001), the infant P400 and the adult N170 differ on a number of dimensions (Fig. 1). Firstly, the effect of stimulus inversion is evident in the ERPs at a much longer latency in infants than in adults. Secondly, although infants and adults show an inversion effect bilaterally for human faces, only infants also show an inversion effect over left hemisphere electrodes for monkey faces. This observation suggests that the infant's

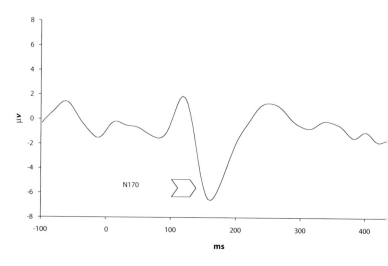

ADULT

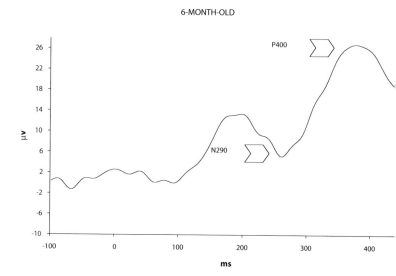

6-MONTH-OLD

Figure 1. A face-specific component of the event-related potential (ERP) has been observed in adults and two such components in infants. The former (top figure) is negative in polarity and occurs with a latency of approximately 170 ms (and is termed the N170). In infants (bottom figure), components include the P400, which, as the name implies, is positive in polarity with a latency of approximately 400 ms and the N290, which is negative in polarity with a latency of about 290 ms. μ_v = microvolts; ms = milliseconds. Adapted and reprinted with permission from Fig. 5 in M. de Haan, O. Pascalis, M. H. Johnson, 2002. Specialization of neural mechanisms underlying face recognition in human infants. *Journal of Cognitive Neuroscience, 14*, 1992–2009.

face processing system is more broadly tuned to faces than is the adult's.

Face processing continues to develop well into the second year of life. One example of this change can be found in the 'other race' effect. For example, whereas Caucasian 6-year-olds are equally good at recognizing Caucasian and Asian faces, older Caucasian children and adults are better at recognizing Caucasian than Asian faces. These results might indicate that as 'late' as 6 years of age, the representation of 'facedness' is still broader and less specific in children than in adults (Chance, Turner, & Goldstein, 1982).

What is developing?

There are currently two primary contrasting viewpoints on how face recognition develops. Morton & Johnson (1991), for example, have proposed that infants less than 2 months old are drawn to face-like objects because of a sub-cortical mechanism referred to as CONSPEC. CONSPEC is purported to be an innate mechanism that primes infants to attend to and prefer face-like stimuli. As infants traverse 2 months of age, a more cortically driven mechanism is employed (CONLERN), in which experience with faces largely engenders development. A strength of this approach is that it does a satisfactory job in accounting for newborn face preferences; a concern, however, is that in most newborn studies, only face-*like* stimuli are used, and, thus, it remains to be determined if the preferences observed by a number of investigators are truly to faces *qua* faces as much as to stimuli that simply resemble faces.

An alternative perspective can be found in a recent model I have put forth (Nelson, 2001), in which an analogy is drawn between the development of face recognition and speech perception. In this model, the face recognition system is tuned very broadly to include all or most faces, regardless of species. With experience, this system is tuned to the faces to which the infant is most exposed. Support for this model can be found in a recent study by Pascalis, de Haan, & Nelson (2002), in which 6-month-old infants were reported to be able to recognize and discriminate equally well faces of both humans and monkeys. In contrast, 9-month-olds' and adults' recognition was limited to human faces. Unknown, of course, is how much experience is necessary to tune the perceptual system, and whether this experience needs to take place during a sensitive period of development.

Conclusions

Within the first half-year of life, infants demonstrate a remarkable ability in recognizing faces, although this ability improves well beyond the first year of life. Indeed, some have claimed that this ability is still not adult-like until early adolescence (de Haan, 2001). Although there are no studies that have directly examined the neural systems involved in face recognition in preverbal children, there is suggestive evidence using ERPs that as infants approach 1 year of age, neural circuits similar to those employed in face recognition in the adult are utilized. What drives the development of these circuits remains unknown, although both Morton & Johnson (1991) and Nelson (2001) have argued that experience with faces plays an important role. Whether such experience leads infants to become experts at face recognition is unknown, although this hypothesis is likely more parsimonious than arguing for an innate or genetic mechanism.

Questions

1. Since the 1970s, the pendulum has swung back and forth on the question of whether face recognition represents an innate ability, or one that depends on experience for its emergence and subsequent elaboration. What data can be cited to support both sides of this argument, and how can the study of the development of this ability shed light on mature function?
2. Since the initial observation that newborns prefer faces over non-faces, debate has ensued over the functional significance of this finding. Some have cited these and similar data to suggest that infants prefer faces *qua* faces, whereas others suggest that such preferences may simply reflect biases toward certain perceptual aspects of the face, such as the orientation or position of specific facial features. In surveying all the newborn data collected to date, what is the most parsimonious conclusion that can be drawn?
3. The disorder prosopagnosia has received considerable attention from psychologists and neuroscientists alike, mostly because of the theoretical implications such findings have for the 'specialness' of face perception. What areas of the brain have been implicated in this disability, and do these data correspond to the functional neuroimaging data on neurologically intact individuals' processing of faces?
4. What do human and non-human primates have in common with regard to the development of the ability to perceive and recognize faces?

See also:
Ethological theories; Magnetic Resonance Imaging; Cross-species comparisons; The status of the human newborn; Perceptual development; Brain and behavioral development (II): cortical; Autism; Williams syndrome; Cognitive neuroscience

Further reading

Farah, M. J. (1996). Is face recognition "special"? Evidence from neuropsychology. *Behavioural Brain Research*, 76, 181–189.

Farah, M. J., Rabinowitz, C., Quinn, G. E. and Liu, G. T. (2000). Early commitment of neural substrates for face recognition. *Cognitive Neuropsychology*, 17, 117–123.

Gauthier, I. and Nelson, C. A. (2001). The development of face expertise. *Current Opinions in Neurobiology*, 11, 219–224.

Acknowledgments

The writing of this paper was made possible by grants from the National Institutes of Health (NS329976), and the John D. and Catherine T. MacArthur Foundation, through their support of a research network on *Early Experience and Brain Development*.

Handedness

LAUREN JULIUS HARRIS

Introduction

The topic of this entry is the development of handedness. For adults, handedness is a universal characteristic, meaning that virtually all adults use one hand preferentially and usually more proficiently on tasks requiring speed, precision, force, skill, and especially coordinated sequences of movements. The difference is seen in such familiar activities as writing letters, drawing pictures, throwing balls, peeling fruit, using utensils and other tools, and opening and closing jars and boxes. The 'dominant' hand often can work alone, but, depending on the task, the other hand usually plays a supporting role such as by adjusting the position of the paper while writing, or by holding and turning the fruit while peeling.

Evidence from self-report questionnaires and direct observation of hand use, along with performance on such tasks as peg-moving and finger-tapping, shows that handedness is distributed continuously in the population. Both directions, right and left, are represented as are all degrees of bias as indexed by the number of different tasks for which the same hand is used. The overall distribution, however, is skewed sharply to the right, like the letter J. Lacking a universal classification rule, many investigators therefore divide adults into two groups, 'right-handers' and 'left-handers,' counted as 85–90 percent and 10–15 percent, respectively. Others include one or more groups in between, variously called 'mixed-handed' or 'weak-' or 'inconsistently' right- or left-handed, with true 'ambidexterity' being extremely rare. The evidence also shows that preference and proficiency differences are often smaller in left-handers, and that left-handers as a group are more varied, with proportionately more being inconsistently handed. Direction of handedness is also familial: the chances of being left-handed rise from about 10 percent when neither parent is left-handed to about 25 percent when both are left-handed. Left-handedness is also slightly more common in men than women.

Many questions can be asked about the development of handedness. When and in what form does a bias first appear? Once it does, is it stable, or does it change over time in degree or even direction? If the initial bias is unstable, when is stability normally achieved? Does development follow the same course in all individuals, including right- and left-handers and males and females? And what causes handedness and guides its development? Only main points and a small sampling of evidence can be covered here; the recommended readings give further information.

Overview of the evidence

Developmental studies of handedness begin as early as the first fetal trimester and extend through adolescence. Cross-sectional studies provide age norms and can reveal bias direction and degree at the group level, but only longitudinal studies can show the path of development, along with details of individual differences. For every age, data for both kinds of studies come from direct observation of hand use and, as early as 5 months, from assessments of its proficiency or quality. Self-report questionnaires, though feasible for older children and adolescents, are rarely used.

Developmental studies also must meet certain measurement needs. Choice of tasks should take into account age changes in physical size, strength, and general motor ability. For example, where ability is limited so that hand preference can be assessed only on simple tasks, such as reaching for and grasping objects, the object's distance should be adjusted to the child's arm length. That puts the object proportionately close or far for all age groups. Likewise, object size and weight should be scaled to the size and strength of the child's hands and fingers. The relationship between object size and grip type required also should be considered. A piece of cereal, by requiring a pincer grip that makes greater demands on fine-motor ability, might elicit a more lateralized response than a larger object such as a ball, requiring a palmar grasp. The child's understanding of task demands should be considered as well. For example, to assess hand preference for opening a box of candy, the child must know not only how to lift the lid, but that it must be lifted to get the candy.

Representative findings for different age periods

The following review describes representative behaviors and tasks for which lateral biases have been documented over the fetal through childhood period.

By the 7th gestational week, fetuses begin making whole body movements. By 9–10 weeks, when they can move their limbs independently, biases appear. In an ultrasound study of 72 10-week-old fetuses, 54 made more right-arm movements, 9 more left-arm movements, and only 9 showed no bias (Hepper, McCartney, & Shannon, 1998). By 15 to 18 weeks, many fetuses also suck their thumbs, more often the right (Fig. 1).

If fetuses show lateral biases, so should neonates. The change from uterine to terrestrial environment, however, can affect motility. The limbs, no longer supported by amniotic fluid, are heavier, making movements more effortful, especially for lifting and extension. Nevertheless, neonates move their arms often and even take uncoordinated 'swipes' or 'swings' at objects (referred to as 'pre-reaching'). The majority swipe more often with the right arm. For most neonates, objects placed in the hands also usually elicit a stronger grasp reflex on the right (Tan *et al.*, 1992). When supine, most neonates usually lie in a head-to-right position (Fig. 2).

By 2–3 months, when the infant is stronger and has more voluntary motor control, other biases appear. One is length of time holding a rattle, right-hand times usually being longer for most infants. By 4 months, infants show 'directed reaching' for objects and can take hold of the target by 6 months. This period also marks the gradual replacement of bimanual with unimanual reaching, and, by 9–10 months, one hand either leads and makes contact first or is used predominantly. Again, most infants favor the right hand, like the 1-year-old, shown in Figure 3, reaching for a piece of birthday cake.

For reaching and grasping, early differences also appear in quality of performance. In a longitudinal study from 5 to 8 months, most infants, while often still reaching bimanually, had shorter movement times for the right hand, at least in part because it was continuously more directly oriented toward the target, thus requiring fewer direction changes, or corrections (Morange-Majoux, Peze, & Bloch, 2000).

From 13 to 24 months, physical strength and motor control continue to increase so that, among other accomplishments, infants can eat with a spoon, draw with crayons, put pegs in a pegboard, bang with a

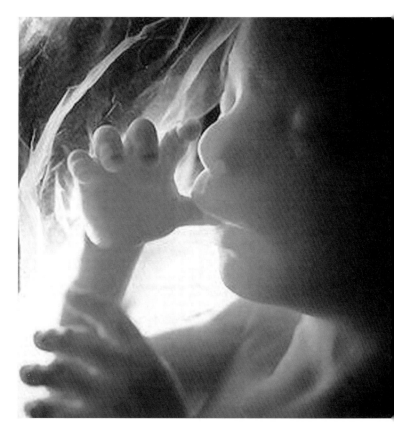

Figure 1. Fetus aged 18 weeks sucking the right thumb.

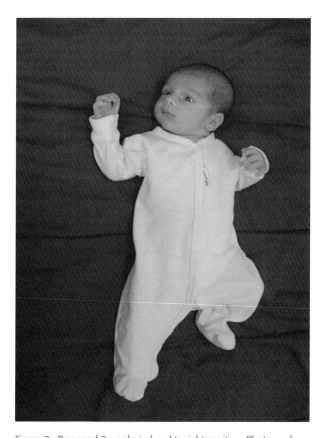

Figure 2. Boy aged 2 weeks in head-to-right position. Photograph courtesy of Zach Kron.

Figure 3. Boy aged 1 year reaching for a piece of his birthday cake. Photograph courtesy of Christopher Strehlo and Robin Leichenko.

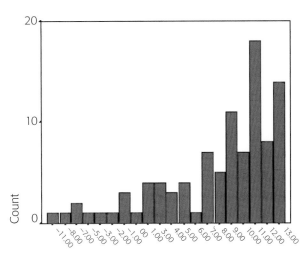

Figure 4. Distribution of hand-use scores for 97 4-year-old children on 13 separate tasks. Figure courtesy of Jason B. Almerigi.

hammer, and use their fingers like pincers to pick up small objects. Again, most favor the right hand (Cornwell, Harris, & Fitzgerald, 1991). Coincident with their increasing skill and growing understanding of task demands, they also show increasing differentiation of hand use for tasks requiring two hands. For example, whereas 9-month-olds usually just mouth a nut-and-bolt toy, 13- and 20-month-olds increasingly manipulate it, turning the bolt with one hand, holding the nut with the left, with the manipulation hand for most children being the right (Cornwell *et al.*, 1991).

From 2 to 6 years, with still further advances in strength and motor control, children increasingly can be assessed on complex skilled tasks, including printing and drawing, using scissors and other tools, throwing a ball, and stringing beads. Scores for ninety-seven 4-year-olds on 13 such tasks are shown in Figure 4, where positive scores = right bias, negative scores = left bias. As in adults, the distribution is skewed sharply to the right. The pattern continues in tests with older children and adolescents. At least by age 4, most children are also more proficient with their preferred hand.

Stability or change?

The evidence shows group-level and predominantly right-sided biases from the ninth or tenth gestational week through early childhood and beyond. Less clear is whether, over this period, individual biases are stable or

change. For bias direction, one sign of stability is that at most ages the percentages of right- and left-biased individuals at least roughly match those found for adults. In Figure 4, they are about 85 percent and 15 percent for positive (right-hand) and negative (left-hand) scores, respectively. Does this mean that right-biased fetuses, neonates, infants, or preschoolers become right-handed adults, while their left-biased counterparts become left-handers? Direct evidence will require long-range longitudinal studies.

So far, only short-range studies are available, and they give a mixed picture. For example, in terms of stability, a study of seventeen fetuses observed at three-week intervals from 12 to 27 weeks revealed stable biases in twelve fetuses, ten for the right arm, two for the left (McCartney & Hepper, 1999). Similarly, most children who as neonates were right head-turners favored the right hand for reaching at 19, 60, and 74 weeks, whereas left-turners favored the left (Michel & Harkins, 1986). Other studies, however, find changes over these same early periods. One study of thirty-two infants, tested repeatedly from 18 to 52 weeks on a 27-trial reaching task, found emerging right-hand preference for the group, but also one or more reversals in direction in nearly half the sample (Harris & Carlson, 1993). From reports that the more common shift is left to right, some investigators have even hypothesized early transient left handedness as part of normal development.

Stability looks more impressive during childhood as indicated by longitudinal studies that find stable directional biases for individual tasks. Stability, now of proficiency as well as direction, likewise is implied in cross-sectional studies showing that about 80 percent of all 4- to 12-year-olds perform pegboard or finger-tapping tasks faster with the right hand, and by a similar margin at every age (e.g., Annett, 1985). Together, this evidence suggests that handedness direction is relatively stable, even fixed, as early as 3 years. For degree of handedness, however, many studies find increases until age 7 or even later. Assuming that, by early childhood, the underlying directional bias is stable, it may be that improvements in skill and motor control allow for clearer expression of that bias and that it takes time for children to discover and consolidate their preferences across tasks, especially for new, complex tasks.

Finally, whenever 'mixed handedness' appears, as in the children in Figure 4 whose scores cluster around the zero point, *inter-task* stability must be distinguished from *intra-task* stability. As Bishop (1983) noted, "A child who always uses the left hand to throw a ball but the right hand to write with is . . . showing a more mature pattern than one who is equally likely to use either hand for both tasks. Both children are mixed-handers, but one has a stable pattern of hand use for skilled tasks, whereas the other does not" (p. 168).

Individual differences

Individual differences no doubt contribute to the mixed picture of stability and change. Just as infants and children vary in their general motor development, they vary in the development of handedness, with the process occurring sooner, faster, and more stably in some individuals than others. In a longitudinal study of 154 infants classified as right-, left-, or non-preferrers at each of three ages (7, 9, and 11 months) based on hand use for reaching, only 47% showed a 'stable' or 'fairly stable' preference, while the rest showed a 'shifting distribution' of preferences (Michel, Sheu, & Brumley, 2002). Evidence also suggests that instability is more common among left-preferrers. In the same study, of infants with a 'stable' preference, 32% were for the right, none for the left. Likewise, in another longitudinal study, now from 7 to 24 months, performance on unimanual and bimanual tasks was less stable for left-preferrers (Fagard & Jacquet, 1989). It is the same in school-age children. In a cross-sectional study of 5-, 7-, and 10-year-olds, left handers (based on writing hand) in every age group were less stable than right-handers on a variety of preference and proficiency measures (Bruml, 1972). Similarly, in a longitudinal study at 5, 8, and 11 years, hand preference at 5 predicted preference at 11 for only 74% of left-handers versus 97% of right-handers (Fennell, Satz, & Morris, 1983).

As in adults, left handedness is more common in boys than girls. The difference appears as early as 4 or 5 years. Girls also often show larger hand differences on finger-tapping and certain other speeded tasks, and their lateral biases appear sooner. For example, in some studies of the neonatal grasp reflex, only girls showed significant hand differences. In infancy, girls also show earlier hand preference for reaching (Harris & Carlson,

1993) and more stable preference for executing a pincer grip by 24 months (Humphrey & Humphrey, 1988).

Explanations

As we have seen, most individuals at every age have a lateral bias, whether right or left. The path to established handedness, however, is often unstable, especially in individuals with left-sided patterns. A variety of explanations have been proposed for these and other features of the development of handedness. Five are summarized below. Each posits an asymmetrical state, or condition, that, in the modal case, leads to right handedness, in the amodal case to left handedness.

According to the *brain explanation*, handedness reflects structural and/or physiological asymmetries in brain regions relevant for motor control. Regions at several levels, from spinal cord to cerebellum to basal ganglia to cerebral cortex, are assumed to contribute, with different regions more relevant for certain features and at certain developmental periods. Thus, early fetal asymmetries in arm movement are assumed to reflect asymmetries in lower (sub-cortical) centers, since functional connections between cortical motoneurons and spinal cord regions serving the fingers, hands, and arms are not yet established. Even after connections are complete, however, lower-level control can predominate. For example, neonatal head-turn biases probably are mostly sub-cortically based, since cortical motor regions are still functioning only rudimentarily. Only by 2 or 3 months, when the infant is cortically more mature and behavior, including head turning, is more voluntary, are cortical asymmetries likely to play key roles.

At the cortical level, the brain explanation posits a relationship between side of control for handedness and side of control for speech on the view that dominant hand abilities reflect the cerebral specialization for programming movement sequences of the kind required for speech. The relationship is compelling for right handers, 95% or more of whom are left-dominant for speech. For left handers, the figure is closer to 66%, with the rest being either right-dominant or bilateral, implying a sharing, or overlapping, of function. Consistent with the group scores on handedness preference and proficiency, asymmetries in cortical as well as sub-cortical regions relevant for motor control are usually larger and/or more consistent in right- than left-handers.

Like the brain explanation, the *gene explanation* seeks to account for the lower prevalence of left handedness, but also for its familiality. The most prominent explanation posits that handedness is determined by a single gene with two alleles, one from each parent (Annett, 1985). Like the brain explanation, it assumes, at least in right handers, a relationship between side of control for handedness and speech, the dominant allele thus predisposes left-hemisphere control of speech and right handedness, whereas in individuals receiving the recessive allele, this predisposition is absent, and chance determines side of control for both functions. Because these chance factors are assumed to work independently, these individuals are equally likely to become left- or right-dominant for speech, and equally likely to become right or left handed.

Neural and genetic explanations emphasize the biological foundations of handedness. Other explanations emphasize environmental foundations, both prenatally and postnatally. The *uterus explanation* posits that handedness originates in the infant's position in utero. Of infants born in a left-vertex position (the most common), about two-thirds lie with their backs toward the mother's left side in the last weeks before delivery. In this position, the mother's pelvis and backbone are assumed to constrain the infant's left side, facilitating rightsided movement and control as well as the right head turn bias at birth. The *head explanation* posits that, in consequence of the postnatal head-to-right position, the right hand is more often in the infant's field of view (Fig. 2). It therefore receives more practice in eye-hand coordination, setting a course for right handedness.

Finally, the *social-cultural explanation* emphasizes the role of education, socialization, and culture. It draws support from evidence that handedness is strongest for acts requiring special training and practice, such as writing and use of utensils; that left handedness is less prevalent in societies that prohibit, or discourage, left-hand use for such acts; and that, even in 'left-hand tolerant' societies, left-handedness is less prevalent among the elderly, suggesting that prohibitions once were strong but have weakened over time. Even in these societies, however, the predominance of 'right-handed' objects of every sort, from scissors and school desks to camera buttons and guitars, can make left-hand use difficult or even preclude it altogether, with possible consequences for handedness development.

Conclusions

In summary, handedness is the product of a multifaceted biosocial process, beginning prenatally and continuing well into postnatal life. So far, no single explanation has managed to account for all its features. Instead, a variety of mechanisms probably operate, and with varying degrees of influence depending on the features and time periods. Furthermore, none of the explanations, whether 'biological' or 'environmental,' are mutually exclusive; even at the level of gene expression, handedness, like all human characteristics, should be seen as

'nature via nurture,' not 'nature versus nurture.' This view is in keeping with the principle that plasticity is a fundamental feature of the nervous system, and that neural systems underlying handedness are malleable however much they may appear to be 'hard-wired' and under genetic control. Further research, therefore, should focus not only, for example, on identifying environmental biases that affect hand use but on whether, in doing so, they 'tune,' or shape, the developing neural substrates.

More information is needed on when, how, and for what acts education and culture affect handedness degree and even direction. For example, although formal training for writing begins at least by first grade, informal training could start as soon as a parent places a crayon in one of the child's hands, or models hand use for the child to imitate. Instruction in utensil use might begin when a parent places a spoon closer to one hand, or into that hand directly. But is the parent's behavior necessarily planned, or is it in response to cues sent out by the child? And how effective are such actions? To date, we have mostly anecdotes and single-case reports to go on. What is needed are longitudinal studies of everyday social-environmental transactions.

The complete story of the development of handedness remains to be told. It is a story well worth pursuing. By elucidating the roles of the brain, genes, and environment, it can enrich our understanding not only of the development of handedness, but of the development of brain-behavior relationships in general.

Questions

1. Perhaps the most fundamental question is, how are the earliest lateral biases in arm movements and grasp strength and duration related to later, more 'mature' forms of handedness? Can they be linked to one another via a definable and measurable set of processes? If so, what might those processes be?

2. Even in societies that do not prohibit left-hand use for certain acts, do parents, overtly or covertly, still influence the development of handedness in their children? If so, what do they do, and what are the effects? Is left handedness more common in boys at least in part because any such practices are imposed less on boys or, alternatively, because boys are less compliant or less able to accommodate?

3. In development, which comes first, hand preference or hand skill, or proficiency? If it is preference, then it may be that, over time, the preferred hand becomes more proficient by being used more often. Alternatively, if skill comes first, it may lead to preference as the child becomes increasingly aware of greater success with that hand. Still another possibility is that

preference and skill emerge together in co-influence and co-dependency.

4. Are there either 'sensitive' or 'critical' periods for the development of handedness comparable to those identified for other functions, such as speech or ocular dominance? If so, are these periods limited to development in the purely biological sense, or is there a 'cultural sensitive period' comparable to what has been proposed for social-emotional adjustment?

5. How does the development of handedness correspond in time to the development of other cognitive and higher cortical functions such as speech, memory, and problem-solving?

See also:
Cross-sectional and longitudinal designs; Group differences in developmental functions; Normal and abnormal prenatal development; The status of the human newborn; Motor development; Brain and behavioral development (I): sub-cortical; Brain and behavioral development (II): cortical; Prehension; Sex differences; Socialization; Behavior genetics

Further reading

Bishop, D. V. M. (1990). *Handedness and Developmental Disorder*. Oxford: Blackwell.

Harris, L. J. (1990). Cultural influences on handedness: historical and contemporary evidence. In S. Coren (ed.), *Left-Handedness: Behavioral Implications and Anomalies*. Advances in Psychology volume 67. Amsterdam: Elsevier, pp. 195–258.

(1992). Left-handedness. In F. Boller and J. Grafman (series eds.), *Handbook of Neuropsychology*, Vol. VI: Section 10: (Part 1) *Child Neuropsychology* (vol. ed. I. Rapin and S. J. Segalowitz). Amsterdam: Elsevier, pp. 145–208.

Hopkins, B. and Rönnqvist, L. (1998). Human handedness: developmental and evolutionary perspectives. In F. Simion and G. Butterworth (eds.), *The Development of Sensory, Motor, and Cognitive Capacities in Early Infancy*. Hove, UK: Psychology Press, pp. 189–223.

Mandal, M. K., Bulman-Fleming, M. and Tiwari, G. (2000). *Side Bias: A Neuropsychological Perspective*. Dordrecht: Kluwer.

Molfese, D. L. and Segalowitz, S. J. (eds.) (1988). *Brain Lateralization in Children: Developmental Implications*. New York: Guilford.

Imitation

ANDREW N. MELTZOFF

Introduction

Imitation is a key component of classic theories of child development such as those of Baldwin and Piaget. Recently, it has emerged as a focus of interdisciplinary work cutting across cognitive, social, evolutionary, and brain sciences (Meltzoff, 2002).

Imitation has adaptive value because it is a powerful learning mechanism. Imitative learning provides flexibility that goes beyond the innately fixed motor patterns. It is less dangerous for the child than trial-and-error learning, and it is faster than independent invention. Just as DNA transmits inherited information, imitation is the vehicle for the transmission of acquired characteristics across generations. Imitation is crucial in the formation and evolution of human culture.

What is imitation?

Imitation involves cognitive and social components. In order to imitate, the child must see the adult's act, 'translate' perception into an action plan and execute the motor output. Imitation raises classic issues in attention, cross-modal coordination, and motor control. If imitation occurs after a delay, memory is implicated. Such imitation goes beyond visual recognition memory, and provides a way of investigating recall memory in infants. Imitation also draws on fundamental social processes. It involves children's recognition that they can do what another person does, that they are in some sense like the model. This perception of 'like me' equivalence at the level of action provides a foundation for more advanced forms of interpersonal connectedness and social cognition, including empathy and theory of mind.

Newborn imitation

Traditional theories such as Piaget's assumed that facial imitation was a cognitive milestone first passed at about 1 year of age. When reports emerged in the 1970s–1980s demonstrating facial gestures in newborns, this sparked great interest and much discussion. These reports forced a revision in traditional theories that had held that newborns were 'solipsistic' creatures – isolated from others and without the sensorimotor or cognitive skills to connect self and other (see Meltzoff, 2002 for a historical review of the debate and what was at stake). It has now been established in many independent laboratories that newborns imitate facial movements such as tongue protrusion, mouth opening, and lip protrusion (Fig. 1). This is intriguing because although newborns attend to the faces of others, a newborn has not seen his own face.

How can they match a gesture they see another perform with one that is invisible on the self? Detailed studies of imitation provide a clue. They correct their behavior over successive attempts. This indicates that they are using a cross-modal matching process. The adult facial expression is the target, and infants use the proprioceptive feedback from their own facial movements to correct their efforts so that their actions more accurately match the visual target. Imitation has an innate basis; however, it is not an isolated reaction, but rather a springboard for further developments in understanding people.

Imitation beyond the newborn period

Imitation is an important mechanism for acquiring new behaviors and skills. Albert Bandura showed that 3- to 5-year-old children learn novel acts through imitation. Human infants also imitate novel acts. In one study, 14-month-old infants were shown a novel act of touching a panel with one's forehead. Fully 67 percent of them imitated when given the object, compared to 0 percent of the controls who did not see the adult's demonstration (Fig. 2). Infants imitate not only single actions, but also novel event sequences (e.g., how to use simple tools, a telephone, etc.).

Imitation would have restricted value if children were limited to direct mimicry. Scientists have investigated the length of delay that can be inserted between the observation of a model and the imitative response. In the second half-year of life it is about twenty-four hrs, and by 14 months it rises to at least four months. Children learn not only from live models, but also from television. In one study, 2-year-old children were shown how to play with a toy on television. They readily copied what they saw on television (Fig. 3), and even imitated when presented with the object after a one-day delay. The latter illustrates the long-term effect of television viewing on pre-verbal infants. In older children, complex information about gender-stereotyped behavior and violence is conveyed via television and leads to imitation, often with deleterious effects.

Imitation and brain science

Scientists are beginning to explore the brain basis of imitation. The essential problem posed by imitation is the 'correspondence problem': how does the subject convert action perception into motor commands that produce matching behavior? One possible solution is that perception and production are associated during development. If a child sees his own hand opening and closing, he associates the sight of this event and the

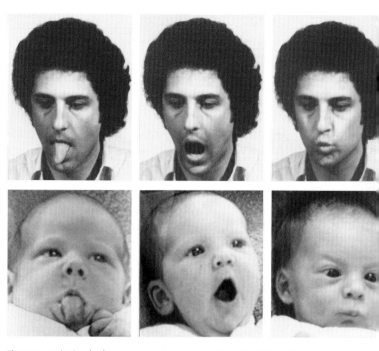

Figure 1. Imitation by human neonates. From A. N. Meltzoff & M. K. Moore, 1977. Imitation of facial and manual gestures by human neonates. *Science*, 198, 75–78.

motor commands to perform it. When the adult shows hand-opening-and-closing, the child can produce the associated behavior. Such association may occur, but it is not an adequate account of newborn facial imitation,

Figure 2. A 14-month-old imitates a novel act. From A. N. Meltzoff, 1999. Origins of theory of mind, cognition, and communication. *Journal of Communication Disorders*, 32, 251–269.

Figure 3. An infant imitates an act seen demonstrated on television. © A. N. Meltzoff.

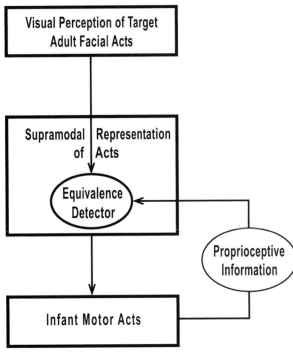

Figure 4. The AIM mechanism for solving the 'correspondence problem' in imitation. From A. N. Meltzoff & M. K. Moore, 1997. Explaining facial imitation: a theoretical model. *Early Development and Parenting*, 6, 179–192.

because infants cannot see their own faces. Meltzoff & Moore (1997) proposed that imitation is based on active intermodal mapping (AIM) in which the viewer forms a supramodal representation of the model's act (Fig. 4). This representation is not modality specific, but rather provides the *lingua franca* connecting vision and action. More recently, experimental psychologists studying adult imitation and related phenomena (e.g., stimulus-response compatibility) independently articulated a 'common coding' thesis by which the adult codes perception and action in the same form (e.g., Prinz & Hommel, 2002). Both the AIM model and the common coding thesis are psychological models, and make predictions about the brain mechanisms involved in imitation.

In 1996, 'mirror neurons' were discovered in the premotor cortex of monkeys (Rizzolatti *et al.*, 2002). These neurons fire both when the monkey observes an act performed by others (e.g., grasping an object), and

also when the monkey produces the act itself. It is tempting to think that mirror neurons explain human imitation. They are, however, most compatible with immediate mimicry. Young children imitate from memory and also correct their responses, neither of which is explained by mirror neurons alone. This has led scientists to the concept of 'shared neural representations' – human brain networks that are broader than single mirror neurons and serve to govern both action perception and action planning through common neural circuits.

Adult imitation has been studied using brain imaging techniques (fMRI, PET). The inferior parietal lobe and medial prefrontal cortex are consistently activated in adult motor imitation (Meltzoff & Decety, 2003). The involvement of the inferior parietal lobe fits with clinical neuropsychological findings that this region is important for body awareness, as well as the sense of self-agency; abnormalities in the region are found in schizophrenia and apraxia. The involvement of the medial prefrontal cortex in imitation is noteworthy because it is also activated in high-level theory of mind tasks (Blakemore & Decety, 2001). Children with autism consistently show deficits on both motor imitation and theory of mind tasks, although the same children may perform normally on memory and spatial reasoning tasks. Extreme deficits in imitation, gaze following, and pretend play in early infancy are strongly associated with a subsequent diagnosis of autism in the 4- to 5-year-old age range.

Imitation: unique to humans?

The human capacity for imitation is unrivaled in the animal kingdom. "Monkey see, monkey do" is misleading. Monkeys show little or no imitative capacity. Their behavioral matches can be explained by mechanisms simpler than imitation. One example is 'stimulus enhancement' wherein the animal becomes interested in an object because someone else is manipulating it, and reproduces the desired effect by chance. Another example is outcome-duplication, sometimes called 'emulation,' where the animal achieves the same end but does so using different actions (e.g., the model uses a stick to open a box to obtain food and the observer tears apart the box, thus 'copying' the end, but not imitating the body movements). The classification of such simpler mechanisms is hotly debated among comparative psychologists, but one widely accepted synthesis is that monkeys and other mammals, save for the great apes, have little or no capacity for the type of spontaneous and generalized imitative learning of novel acts manifested by the human young.

The artificial intelligence (AI) community is turning to imitative learning in the hope that robots can be programmed by observing an expert's action. Instead of laboriously writing code to get a robot to pour a cup of tea, the robot's performance would be mapped onto the visual input of a tutor. Robotic imitation is one aspect of a larger trend of using realistic biological models as a basis for creating AI systems that learn. To date, flexible open-ended routines, such as learning by watching, are beyond the reach of machines.

Is imitation a solution to an old problem?

In humans, imitation not only serves for learning new motor abilities and skills, but also for learning about other people. A longstanding puzzle in philosophy is the problem of Other Minds. The problem arises because we seem to know self and other in incommensurate ways. We know our own inner feelings and thoughts, but not how others see us. We see how others look, but we do not know their inner states.

Imitation, and the brain system subserving it, may be Nature's way of solving the Other Mind problem. Infants are not born with the knowledge that others have mental states such as beliefs and desires, but they are born being able to imitate simple behavioral actions. This shows a fundamental connectedness between self and other rather than an incommensurability. Infants then use this self-other mapping to develop a richer understanding of people. In particular, when they see others acting like they do, they make the attribution that these people feel the same way. Others who behave 'like me' have invisible beliefs, desires, and intentions just like me. The child is using his or her own case as an interpretive framework for understanding others. This is an example of developmental bootstrapping, rather than strict nativism or blank-slate empiricism.

Conclusions

Future empirical work will be directed at investigating the vital role that imitation plays in cognitive and social development. Two promising areas are: (a) elaborating the neural and psychological mechanisms underlying imitation, and (b) tracing developmental changes in imitation throughout the lifespan. Studies indicate a progression from imitating facial gestures (newborns), to imitating actions on objects (about 9 months of age), to imitation of another's intentions (what they 'meant' to do even if they failed to do so, occurring at about 15–18 months of age); to imitative role-play and imaginatively 'standing in another's shoes' for empathy and perspective-taking (2 years to adulthood). The progression is from recognizing the similarity between self and other at the level of *behavior* to recognizing higher-order similarities between self and other at the level of *mental attitudes* that underlie and generate the behaviors. One hypothesis is that simple motor imitation of early infancy provides the platform for developing these higher abilities (Meltzoff, 2002). Or, more poetically: through imitating and understanding the motor actions of others, we come to understand their souls.

Questions

1. What neural and psychological mechanisms solve the 'correspondence problem' in imitation?
2. Is imitation linked to feeling empathy for others and developing a theory of mind? If so, why?
3. Why do children with autism fail to imitate?
4. When in evolution did the capacity for modern-day human imitation emerge?
5. Can we build robots that learn by watching human tutors?

See also:

Ethological theories; Learning theories; Theories of the child's mind; Magnetic Resonance Imaging; Experimental methods; The status of the human newborn; Perceptual development; Motor development; Development of learning and memory; Attention; Face recognition; Autism; Cognitive neuroscience; James Mark Baldwin; Jean Piaget

Further reading

Dautenhahn, K. and Nehaniv, C. L. (2002). *Imitation in Animals and Artifacts.* Cambridge, MA: MIT Press.

Meltzoff, A. N. and Prinz, W. (eds.) (2002). *The Imitative Mind: Development, Evolution and Brain Bases.* Cambridge: Cambridge University Press.

Tomasello, M. (1999). *The Cultural Origins of Human Cognition.* Cambridge, MA: Harvard University Press.

Intelligence

ROBERT J. STERNBERG

Introduction

Intelligence may be defined as the ability to learn and think and to adapt to the environment. There are many different theories of intelligence. How one conceives of the development of intelligence depends, in part, on the theory one accepts.

It used to be thought that infant intelligence represents some kind of sensorimotor program that is relatively distinct from the program that unfolds later on during childhood. The reason for this view was that infant intelligence (measured as sensorimotor abilities) does not much correlate with childhood and adult intelligence (measured as learning and thinking abilities). More recent work has shown, however, that there are ways of conceiving of infant intelligence that are more useful than the conventional one.

Although age of acquisition of sensorimotor abilities generally does not predict later intelligence, one thing that does so is an infant's preference for novelty. This apparent preference for novelty is associated with the moderate-discrepancy hypothesis, according to which infants prefer stimuli that are moderately discrepant, or different, from what they already know.

The preference for novelty explains why infants learn about things only when they are ready to learn about them. They do not waste their time attending to completely familiar things, or to things so new that they are overwhelming. Indeed, it may be that infants who prefer some degree of novelty are more intelligent than are those who do not. Joseph Fagan and Marc Bornstein have found that infants who show stronger preferences for novelty at ages 2 to 6 months are more likely to have high scores on intelligence tests at ages 2 to 7 years. Thus, new methods of measuring intelligence in infants show that infant intelligence may predict later intelligence.

What, exactly, is 'later intelligence'? Several different views have been presented about what it is, and how it develops.

The psychometric view

A traditional view of intelligence is a psychometric one, according to which intelligence can be understood in terms of a set of underlying mental abilities that, in combination, work together to produce intellectual performance. Charles Spearman (1863–1945), a British psychologist, proposed at the turn of the 20th century that intelligence can be understood largely as comprising a single, general ability (g), which he believed to be mental energy. Another theorist, the American Louis Thurstone (1887–1955), believed that the essence of intelligence is not in a single factor, but rather in multiple primary mental abilities, such as verbal comprehension ability (e.g., vocabulary), inductive reasoning ability, and spatial ability. Most recently, Carroll (1993) has suggested that a hierarchical model can well explain intelligence, with general ability at the top, multiple primary abilities hierarchically below this general ability, and specific abilities under those.

According to the psychometric view, intelligence can develop in several different ways. The number of abilities (measured as factors) can increase, or abilities that already exist can split off into more refined and differentiated abilities (the so-called differentiation hypothesis), or children's efficacy in applying the abilities can increase.

Most existing tests of intelligence are loosely based on the psychometric view of intelligence. There are two major tests. One test, the Stanford-Binet (now in its fourth edition), dates back to the work early in the 20th century of Alfred Binet (1857–1941) and Theodore Simon (1873–1961). The other, more widely used test is actually a set of tests, the Wechsler Intelligence Scales. There are separate scales for preschool and primary-school children, and for children who are older. Both tests yield IQs, or intelligence quotients, which have a mean of 100 and a standard deviation of 16 (in the case of the Stanford-Binet) or 15 (in the case of the Wechsler). These tests measure higher-order knowledge and judgment skills, such as vocabulary, arithmetical reasoning, and spatial skills.

The genetic-epistemological view

During the 1960s and 1970s, views of the development of intelligence were dominated by the Piagetian approach. Although the approach is no longer as influential as it once was, no theory has been as important in thinking about the development of intelligence as that devised by Piaget.

Piaget, who had worked with Binet and Simon, revolutionized the study of children's intelligence by proposing that researchers could learn as much about children's intellectual development from examining their incorrect answers to test items as from examining their correct answers. Through his repeated observations of children, including his own children, and especially through investigation of their errors in reasoning, Piaget concluded that coherent logical systems underlie children's thought. These systems, he believed, differ in kind from the logical systems that adults use. If we are to understand development, we must identify these systems and their distinctive characteristics.

Piaget believed that the function of intelligence is to aid in adaptation to the environment. In his view (Piaget, 1972), the means of adaptation form a continuum ranging from relatively unintelligent means, such as habits and reflexes, to relatively intelligent means, such as those requiring insight, complex mental representation, and the mental manipulation of symbols. In accord with his focus on adaptation, he believed that cognitive development is accompanied by increasingly complex responses to the environment. Piaget further proposed that with increasing learning and maturation, both intelligence and its manifestations become differentiated (i.e., more highly specialized in various domains).

Piaget believed that development occurs in stages that evolve via equilibration, in which children seek a balance (equilibrium) between both what they encounter in their environments and what cognitive processes and structures they bring to the encounter, as well as among the cognitive capabilities themselves. Equilibration involves three processes. In some situations, the child's existing mode of thought and existing schemas (mental frameworks) are adequate for confronting and adapting to the challenges of the environment; the child is thus in a state of equilibrium.

At other times, however, the child is presented with information that does not fit with the child's existing schemas, so cognitive disequilibrium arises. That is, imbalance occurs when the child's existing schemas are inadequate for new challenges the child encounters. The child consequently attempts to restore equilibrium through assimilation (i.e., incorporating the new information into existing schemas).

Under some circumstances, the child must somehow modify his schemas to allow for the new information, perhaps creating an overarching schema for animals into which he fits his existing schema for dogs. Piaget suggested that sometimes children modify existing schemas through accommodation (i.e., changing the existing schemas to fit the relevant new information about the environment). Together, the processes of assimilation and accommodation result in a more sophisticated level of thought than was possible previously. In addition, these processes result in the re-establishment of equilibrium, thus offering the individual higher levels of adaptability.

According to Piaget, the equilibrative processes of assimilation and accommodation account for all of the changes associated with intellectual development. In Piaget's view, disequilibrium is more likely to occur during periods of stage transition. That is, although Piaget posited that equilibrative processes go on throughout childhood as children continually adapt to their environment, he also considered development to involve discrete, discontinuous stages. In particular, he divided cognitive development into three main stages summarized here: the sensorimotor, concrete-operational, and formal-operational stages. Others have added a preoperational stage, which may be better treated as a period of transition between the sensorimotor and concrete-operational stages. Because these stages are discussed elsewhere in this volume, they are not considered further here.

Neo-Piagetian views

Neo-Piagetian theorists build upon a broad understanding of Piaget's theory of cognitive development. Although each neo-Piagetian is different, most of them (a) accept Piaget's broad notion of developmental stages of cognitive development; (b) concentrate on the scientific or logical aspects of cognitive development (often observing children engaging in many of the same tasks as those used by Piaget); and (c) retain some ties with the notion that cognitive development occurs through equilibration. Only a few neo-Piagetian theories are considered here.

Firstly, fifth-stage theorists do not posit an entirely different theory of cognitive development; instead, they build on the Piagetian four stages by suggesting a fifth stage beyond formal operations. Patricia Arlin proposed that a fifth stage of cognitive development is problem finding. In this stage, individuals come to master the tasks of figuring out exactly what problems they face, and deciding which problems are most important and deserving of their efforts toward solution.

Secondly, several theorists have suggested that logical reasoning beyond Piagetian formal operations might proceed to a fifth stage of dialectical thinking. Dialectical thinking recognizes that in much of life, there is no one final, correct answer, but rather a progression of beliefs whereby we first propose some kind of thesis, then later see its antithesis, and finally effect some kind of synthesis between the two, which then serves as the new thesis for the continuing evolution of thought. For example, adults use dialectical thinking when considering one extreme and then the other, subsequently incorporating only the best elements of each extreme.

The sociocultural view

In Piaget's theory, cognitive development proceeds largely 'from the inside out' through maturation. Environments can foster or impede development, but Piaget emphasized the biological and hence the maturational aspect of development. Vygotsky's (1978) theory takes an entirely different approach in emphasizing the role of the environment in children's intellectual development. He suggested that cognitive development proceeds largely 'from the outside in' through internalization (i.e., the absorption of knowledge from context). Thus, social, rather than biological, influences are key in Vygotsky's theory of cognitive development. According to Vygotsky then, much of children's learning occurs through interactions within the environment, which largely determine what the child internalizes.

This interactive form of learning relates to Vygotsky's second major contribution to educational and developmental psychology: the construct of the zone of proximal development (ZPD), sometimes termed the zone of potential development. The ZPD is the range of potential between a child's observable level of realized ability (performance) and the child's underlying latent capacity (competence), which is not directly obvious. When we observe children, what we typically observe is the ability that they have developed through the interaction of heredity and environment. To a large extent, however, we are truly interested in what children are capable of doing – what their potential would be if they were freed from the confines of an environment that is never truly optimal. Before Vygotsky proposed his theory, people were unsure how to measure this latent capacity.

Vygotsky argued that we need to reconsider not only how we think about children's cognitive abilities, but also how we measure them. Typically, we test children in a static assessment environment, in which an examiner asks questions and expects the child to answer them. Whether the child responds correctly or incorrectly, the examiner moves to the next question or task on the list of items in the test. Like Piaget, Vygotsky was interested

The triarchic theory of successful intelligence

Conventional (Analytical) Intelligence

Creative Intelligence

Practical Intelligence

Figure 1. The components of the triarchic theory of successful intelligence.

not only in children's correct responses, but also in their incorrect responses to questions.

Thus, Vygotsky recommended that we move from a static assessment environment to a dynamical assessment environment, in which the interaction between child and examiner does not end when the child responds, especially not if the child responds incorrectly. In static testing, when a child gives a wrong answer, the examiner moves on to the next problem. In dynamical assessment, when the child gives a wrong answer, the examiner gives the child a graded sequence of guided hints in order to facilitate problem solving. In other words, the examiner serves as both teacher and tester. The examiner provides the scaffolding children need in order to go from wherever they are in problem solving to the next step beyond. In general, learning proceeds most efficiently when scaffolding is provided to ensure that children have the necessary prerequisites for advancing beyond their current understandings.

The ability to use hints is the basis for measuring the ZPD, because this ability indicates the extent to which the child can expand beyond her or his observable abilities at the time of testing. Two children may answer a given problem incorrectly. However, a child who can profit from instruction can potentially go far, whereas a child who cannot is unlikely to acquire the abilities needed to solve not only the problem being tested, but also related ones. Several tests have been created to measure the ZPD.

Systems approaches

Two modern theorists have proposed theories of intelligence and its development that view intelligence as a system.

Gardner (1999) has proposed a theory of multiple intelligences, according to which there are eight intelligences: linguistic, logical-mathematical, spatial, musical, bodily-kinesthetic, naturalist, interpersonal, and intrapersonal. Gardner believes that each intelligence is modular and largely independent of the others. Thus, development of one intelligence proceeds relatively independently of development of the others. Complex behavior requires an integration of the intelligences. The mechanism for this integration is not clearly specified by the theory.

Sternberg (1997) has proposed a triarchic theory of intelligence, according to which there are three different aspects of intelligence: analytical intelligence, creative intelligence, and practical intelligence. The analytical aspect of intelligence is the kind measured by traditional tests of intelligence (Fig. 1). The creative and practical aspects of intelligence are not measured by such tests. Sternberg has offered a theory of intellectual development that emphasizes the role of information processing in development. In particular, children develop in terms of acquiring new processes, strategies, and ways of mentally representing information.

Conclusions

What constitutes intelligence and how it develops continue to be sources of much debate and disagreement among psychologists. We are now confronted with a range of theories about intellectual development, each with its own appeal, and each focusing on different aspects of what may constitute intelligence. Nevertheless, current theories do manifest some common ground (e.g., a concern with changes in information processing abilities in Sternberg's theory and in the approach adopted by neo-Piagetians). It remains to be seen whether anything approaching a unified theory about the development of intelligence can ever be achieved. Future research needs to seek more measures of what might constitute precursors to childhood intelligence during infancy that arise from a well-articulated theory. In this respect, a concern for cortical brain development as is evident in the emerging field of developmental cognitive neuroscience has potentially much to offer. In addition, we need to know more about the mechanisms of developmental transitions in intelligence, in which this emerging field may play a vital role.

Questions

1. One might say that intelligence both increases and decreases with age. Why does such a statement make sense?
2. Describe two conceptions of intelligence, and how they are similar and different.
3. Can someone be intelligent but foolish? Intelligent but not very wise?
4. Why do so many societies seem to value intelligence so much more than they value wisdom?

See also:
Constructivist theories; Theories of the child's mind; Developmental testing; Twin and adoption studies; Cognitive development during infancy; Cognitive development beyond infancy; Attention; Cognitive neuroscience; Alfred Binet; Jean Piaget; Lev S. Vygotsky

Further reading

Ceci, S. J. (1996). *On Intelligence*. Cambridge, MA: Harvard University Press.

Gardner, H. (1983). *Frames of Mind: The Theory of Multiple Intelligences*. New York: Basic Books.

Jensen, A. R. (1998). *The g Factor*. Westport, CT: Praeger.

Lubinski, D. (ed.) (2004). Cognitive abilities: 100 years after Spearman's (1904) '"General intelligence," objectively defined and measured.' *Journal of Personality and Social Psychology*, Special section, 86, 96–199.

Sternberg, R. J. (1990). *Metaphors of Mind*. New York: Cambridge University Press.

Sternburg, R. J. (ed.) (2000). *Handbook of Intelligence*. New York: Cambridge University Press.

Locomotion

JANE E. CLARK

Introduction

Locomotion is a fundamental characteristic of living things. To move, to change location, ensures an animal's survival. Humans, while not the fastest animals, have a rich repertoire of locomotor capabilities. Crawling, walking, running, galloping, hopping, and skipping are all human phylogenetic patterns of coordination. In addition, cultures have created variations on these patterns, with their dances and sport forms. But unlike most other animals, humans take years to develop their locomotor abilities. Indeed, the human infant takes nearly a year to master bipedal walking, and several years more before the later emerging locomotor abilities appear (Table 1).

The origins of locomotion are observed in the movements of the human fetus as she changes positions and moves about in the womb, starting around the second month after conception. At birth, the newborn is challenged with a new environment where gravitational forces are nearly three times larger than they were in the womb. With weak muscles and a large mass (averaging about 7–8 pounds), the neonate's movements are limited primarily to the arms and legs. Moving the torso and head is much more difficult. It is not until about five months after birth that the infant can roll over from lying on the back to the front and sit upright with support. It takes about eight months from birth before crawling and independently pulling the body up to a standing position are achieved. Independent walking is a first birthday milestone, although the age range for the appearance of the first walking steps spans from 9 to 18 months of age.

Functions of locomotion

Locomotion not only affords survival by fleeing from predators, but it also opens up the world. Objects and people are now in reach for touching, holding, or acting upon. Locomotion offers autonomy and willful action,

separation from caregivers, and a new view on the world that many scientists believe changes the way infants think about the world. Indeed, psychologists have long asked what role these early perceptual-motor experiences created by locomotion play in the development of cognition. Similarly, those in kinesiology and rehabilitation have studied the development of action, and locomotion in particular, to understand how adult motor control or the lack of it occurs. Indeed, the study of locomotion development involves understanding the neuromotor control and coordination not just of the human's multisegmented body in ever changing contexts, but of an embodied mind in which action, perception, and cognition are inextricably intertwined (Thelen, 2000).

Changing views on the development of walking

In Western countries, walking seems to appear without much attention given to specifically teaching an infant how to achieve it. Nevertheless, the development of walking was at the heart of the nature-nurture debate in the early 1930s. Theoretical explanations of behavioral development were grounded in maturational and neurophysiological changes in the brain. To support the maturational explanations, researchers at that time trained one twin in various motor behaviors while the second twin acted as a control. These studies revealed that the twins demonstrated motor abilities including walking at about the same time, despite differences in experience. Interestingly, these results are not confirmed by studies of cultures where the development of walking is 'taught' or, at least, culturally promoted, and where infants walk much earlier than in cultures where no specific physical exercises or practices are promoted. Surely, all human infants learn to walk, with movement patterns that are much the same. These walking patterns are phylogenetic or fundamental abilities of the species. Their similarities in form emerge in large measure

Table 1. Mean first ages of appearance and age range for locomotor milestones.

Locomotor ability	Average age of appearance	Age range for appearance
Crawling	8 months	7–14 months
Walking	11.5 months	9–18 months
Running	17.5 months	15–24 months
Galloping	22 months	**
Hopping	3 years	**
Skipping	5 years	**

** No data available.

because of similar constraints within and around the infant.

These constraints include the infant's body, the physical and social environment, and the task of locomotion. The human body itself constrains the infant to certain movement patterns and not others. For example, the hip, knee, and ankle joints shape the configuration of the leg such that walking forward is easier than doing so backward. The earth's gravitational field creates another constraint as the force of gravity pulls the upright infant downward, toppling those first attempts at independent bipedal locomotion, while later being exploited to pull one forward into walking. Upright locomotion is also favored as it is a ubiquitous and efficient movement behavior for our physical environments, irrespective of culture.

For decades, the stage-like progression of motor milestones (rolling over, sitting, crawling, standing, cruising, and walking) reinforced the notion that maturation of the central nervous system (CNS) drove motor development (McGraw, 1940). From a maturational perspective, the maturing CNS first produces reflexes such as newborn stepping, and then inhibits them so that voluntary walking can occur. Since the early 1980s, new theoretical perspectives, referred to as the dynamical systems approach and ecological psychology, that consider behavioral development to emerge from changes in many systems not just the CNS, have replaced the maturational view. One of the first challenges to the maturational view came from findings that practicing the stepping reflex prolonged its existence and accelerated the onset of independent walking (Zelazo, Zelazo, & Kolb, 1972). A second challenge came from a compelling experiment in which stepping 'disappeared' after the legs of infants were weighted (Thelen, Fisher, & Ridley-Johnson, 1984). Conversely, for those infants who no longer demonstrated stepping, it 're-appeared' when the unweighted legs were submerged in water. This led to the conclusion that the disappearance of the stepping reflex was not the result of neuromaturation, but rather due to infants' legs becoming too heavy to step.

Today, most developmental scientists would agree that the developing nervous system plays an important role in attaining the ability to walk, but they would also recognize that many other systems develop and offer constraining influences on the growing infant. Current theorizing about the development of walking recognizes the richness of these multicausal influences. To walk upright over two small feet with a top-heavy tottering trunk and head is a difficult task. The infant has spent months learning to sit, roll over, crawl, stand, cruise, and finally walk. With the attainment of each motor milestone, the infant has developed improved postural control that maintains the head and trunk positions in the desired orientation and coordinated with the legs. Sensory information from the vestibular system, vision, and proprioception is integrated and coupled to the evolving action system.

Control of a multisegmented body

Like other behaviors that infants exhibit during the first year or so of life, walking engages a physical entity – the multisegmented body. This structure has unique physical properties that influence the infant's locomotor behavior. At birth and for a few more months, the infant is too weak to lift up the trunk and head in order to crawl. Later, balancing the many segments atop each other is a challenging task, made all the more daunting when attempting to step forward whilst keeping the segments upright. Add to that task, repeatedly stepping, turning, and negotiating obstacles and the difficulty of learning to walk becomes apparent. In fact, to walk requires the control and coordination of hundreds of muscles, with each leg alone having fifty and not counting the muscles of the neck, trunk, and arms that are also involved in walking.

To solve the problem, the new walker 'freezes' the so-called degrees of freedom (i.e., the many choices that the nervous system would have to make to walk). This 'freezing' results in a biomechanically rigid system, with the head-neck-torso moving as a block and arms that are held up and unmoving (the so called 'high guard' position). As the infant walks, shifting the body's weight from one leg to the other, twisting forces are created. Freezing the degrees of freedom simplifies the task and reduces the forces. With practice, the infant frees some degrees of freedom, thus enabling the resulting forces to be exploited to their biomechanical advantage. But it takes time for the infant's brain to know the body it lives in. So, while infants take their first steps around their first birthday, it is many years later before they can exploit the body's dynamics to walk like an adult. In addition, the infant's body dimensions change dramatically, particularly in the first two years of life. This poses a developmental challenge to infants who must adjust their locomotor behavior to these physical changes.

Later-emerging locomotor abilities

In addition to crawling and walking, humans have four other common patterns of locomotion (Clark & Whitall, 1989). Walking is thought to emerge first owing primarily to its symmetrical properties that give it inherent stability. Running emerges next, and again is a symmetrical pattern with the same interlimb coordination (i.e., an alternating bilateral leg action in which one leg's footfall occurs at 50 percent of the other leg's cycle). The two gaits differ in that running has a flight phase where both feet are off the ground at the same time, while walking always has at least one foot and sometimes two on the ground. The emergence of running occurs about six months after walking when the infant has achieved the force and postural control required for the lift off and landing of a run.

The third gait to emerge is the gallop that appears just after running. This is the first asymmetrical gait form to emerge, and appears to be selected voluntarily by the child, probably as a 'playful' action. Because it is asymmetrical, it requires more balance control than walking or running. The gallop is defined as a walking step in which one limb is followed by a running step (or leap), with the leading limb beginning its cycle approximately 35 percent of the way through the cycle of the rear limb. The appearance of hopping and then skipping follow around one to two years later depending on the child's experience. A hop is a one-legged gait in which take-off and landing are on the same foot. It is more difficult than a gallop as it requires the ability to balance on one foot repeatedly, and also the strength to propel the body up with only one leg. Skipping follows hopping as it requires more complex symmetrical coordination involving a step and hop on each foot alternately. As with walking, all the later emerging gaits take months, if not years, to become well controlled.

Conclusions

As is the case with all abilities, cognitive or motor, children are better able to adjust their locomotion to a wide variety of contexts with increasing experience. Through childhood, locomotor abilities are combined with other movement patterns such as throwing and striking. Culturally specific forms of locomotion also develop in early to late childhood. For example, children learn locomotor dance skills, such as the polka and those found in ballet, through specific instructions provided by adults. There are several challenges for future research on the development of locomotion. The complex relationships between perception, cognition, and action present an important puzzle to be solved. How these relationships unfold, interplay, and change from birth to later childhood has yet to be studied in depth. Few have examined the role of experience in the development of locomotor abilities, perhaps, in part, because they are presumed either tacitly or explicitly to be predetermined. And yet, the level of a child's competence in these essential abilities may well interact with other developing systems (e.g., cognitive, perceptual, emotional, social).

Questions

1. Walking is considered a phylogenetic or species-typical behavior, suggesting that it requires very little environmental influence for its emergence and development. However, the range for the first age of appearance of walking is almost nine months (viz., between the ages of 9 and 18 months). In addition, there is considerable individual and cultural variation in the onset of walking. What might be the basis for (i.e., the influences on) these examples of variability in the development of upright locomotion?

2. The alternating leg pattern of walking is evident in the fetus and later in the stepping response of the newborn. What systems and/or abilities must develop in the neuromotor system to enable the infant to walk without falling in a cluttered environment? In other words, what develops when locomotion develops?

3. Many changes occur in the infant's cognitive abilities about the time that self-produced locomotion (i.e., crawling) emerges. What might be the relationship between 'acting' and 'thinking'?

4. Is there a sensitive period for the development of locomotion? Are there any conditions or constraints (e.g., physical, environmental, social) under which infants would not develop walking?

5. Some people can dance, some seem to have two left feet. Can we find the roots of these differences in locomotion in individual developmental trajectories?

See also:
Neuromaturational theories; Dynamical systems approaches; Cross-cultural comparisons; Normal and abnormal prenatal development; The status of the human newborn; Motor development; Brain and behavioral development (I): sub-cortical; Prehension; Behavioral embryology; Behavior genetics; Milestones of motor development and indicators of biological maturity

Further reading

Adolph, K. E., Vereijken, B. and Shrout, P. E. (2003). What changes in infant walking and why. *Child Development*, 74, 475–497.

Campos, J. J., Anderson, D. I., Barbu-Roth, M. A., Hubbard, E. M., Hertenstein, M. J. and Witherington, D. (2000). Travel broadens the mind. *Infancy*, 2, 149–219.

Dickinson, M. H., Farley, C. T., Full, R. J., Koehl, M. A., Kram, R. and Lehman, S. (2000). How animals move: an integrative view. *Science*, 288, 100–106.

Parenting and the family

CHARLIE LEWIS

Introduction

Sigmund Freud was not the first theoretician to suggest that individual consciousness is most influenced by family relationships, but he has been the greatest influence upon developmental theories of parenting and the family. He stressed the importance of early parent-child relationships, and their possible pathological patterns in the development of the child's current and later identity. The 20th century witnessed the rise of two grand theories in the area, psychoanalysis and learning theory, followed by their decline. Today, a massive amount of literature is produced on family relationships, but this has become increasingly focused on the many smaller-scale issues that comprise parenting. Marc Bornstein presents the most detailed review of the area that exemplifies its diversity. This entry attempts to identify the major themes in contemporary parenting research, the current trends, and some issues that will undoubtedly be developed in the future.

Mapping the history of contemporary parenting research

Authors like Tom O'Connor often pointed out that there is no 'unifying theory' of parenting, as if such a theory were possible. There are two ways of regarding theoretical divisions in the field: either it is still in its infancy and will develop into a fully fledged and comprehensive theory, or a diversity of perspectives reflects the complex nature of the parental experience and its influences on child development. What are the legacies of the major perspectives? At first glance, it might appear that complexity of, and a lack of defeasibility within, psychodynamic theory has prevented it from influencing contemporary research on the family. However, this would overlook the presence of psychoanalytic strands explicitly within current research, theory, and clinical practice, particularly in the field's multidisciplinarity (e.g., psychiatry, social policy, social work, nursing,

psychology), and in a heavy emphasis on the problems experienced by families who come into contact with the many professions who work with them. These professions share what appear to be naïve accounts of parenting that simply attempt to chart the transmission of parenting practices, mainly psychopathological, from one generation to the next.

Social learning theory has had clear and lasting influences upon family studies in its emphases on the observation of patterns of interaction, and the importance of parents as role models in the child's identification with adult norms. Like psychoanalysis, it stresses the importance of parenting regimes in the development of normative patterns of behavior in the child. Yet, it has long been exposed to criticism, notably by Richard Q. Bell who pointed out that its theoretical focus was upon the 'effects' of parents on their children. He brought together evidence showing that children influence their parents just as much (e.g., Bell & Harper, 1974). From outside, the critique of social learning accounts has centered upon the narrow focus on parent-child influences. Among the plethora of criticisms are that the many cross-cultural comparisons of childhood made in the 1950s and any theory of human development have to be understood within an ecological niche in which immediate family relationships are nested within the complexity of sub-cultural and cultural processes (Bronfenbrenner, 1979). However, psychoanalysis and social learning theory had profound effects on contemporary parenting research, and we all too often neglect their influences on our assumptions.

Contemporary strands

While it is hard to tease apart contemporary strands of research, let alone summarize them in a nutshell, it is possible to discern five themes. Firstly, there is a line of research that has attempted to identify styles of parenting and their effects on children. This tradition, inspired by Diana Baumrind, began in the 1960s and continues. She

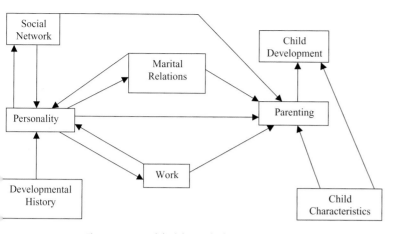

Figure 1. A model of the multiple influences on parenting skills. Adapted from J. Belsky, 1984. The determinants of parenting: a process model. *Child Development*, 55, 83–96.

distinguished four patterns of parenting: authoritarian, authoritative, permissive, and non-conformist. Accordingly, authoritarian parents value obedience and the forceful imposition of their will, permissive parents think that they should be non-intrusive but 'available,' while non-conformist parents oppose authority, but are more controlling than permissive parents. Between the extremes of authoritarian and permissive parenting lie authoritative parents, who encourage independence and attempt to shape their preschoolers' behavior using rational explanation.

Much contemporary research replicates the original finding that firm and responsive parenting is related to greater cooperation, less delinquency, and higher social and cognitive competence in children. However, it also complicates the picture. In African-American families, authoritarian parenting, particularly if associated with physical punishment regimes, may not be linked to childhood problems. This suggests that the pattern of findings might be culture-specific. As argued by others, Baumrind has yet to document the developmental processes by which authoritative parents facilitate their children's socialization.

The second strand of research also derives from social learning theory, and Bell's re-analysis. It emphasizes the importance of the parent-child system, contending that parent-child relationships should be regarded in terms of the system as a whole, rather than simple bi-directional patterns of influence. Some parents, for example, unwittingly train their children to be manipulative, or fail to extinguish their children's undesirable behaviors. At the same time, conduct-disordered teenagers have been shown to elicit coercive behavior from adults (Anderson, Lytton, & Romney, 1986). Such insights have been the basis of intervention programs designed to help parents exercise more effective control over their children's conduct. However, this approach does not fully account for the complexities

of the experience of parenting and family relationships. As with the first strand of research, it does not explore, for example, why parents might adopt the strategies that they do.

The third perspective, attachment theory, derives from an integration of ethology, psychoanalysis, systems theory, and social learning theory. It explores the behavioral systems within the adult-infant dyad that develop to promote the latter's survival, but which also instill working models about trust within relationships. Within this framework, the quality of parenting is essential for the child's current and future psychosocial functioning. Recent research has shown that there are continuities in individuals' attachments from infancy to early adulthood, and between adults' own attachment constructions in pregnancy and their subsequent attachment relationships with their children. However, it must be borne in mind that attachments are theorized to be relationship-specific, and that it is too easy to slip into thinking about them as personality attributes.

The legacy of Uri Bronfenbrenner's analysis is that many theoretical accounts now, fourthly, acknowledge that parenting is embedded within a complexity of factors forming the child's social environment. They contend that parental styles and the parent-child system must be understood within a network of other systems of relationships, including extended kin and each family member's non-familial contacts. Current models of the determinants of parenting clearly nest the parent and child within an interacting social network (Fig. 1). Subsequent perspectives have been very useful in framing research agendas, taking into consideration major life experiences, such as extrafamilial care or parental divorce.

The fifth strand of research on parenting, behavior genetics, can be traced back to the 1930s, but has become increasingly visible since the 1980s. This tradition uses comparisons between mono- and dizygotic twins, and between adopted and non-adopted children, to tease apart genetic influences from both shared and non-shared environmental factors. The main focuses of attention in childhood have been on behavior problems, especially aggression, and personality development, although the effects of parenting have been considered. Such studies have suggested that parental responsiveness and affective engagement between parent and child have a genetic component (Deater-Deckard, 2000). The evidence for a need to take into account the complexities of the gene-environment interaction seems compelling. Within a longitudinal adoption study, O'Connor *et al.* (1998) compared adoptees at genetic risk for anti-social behavior (their biological mother had such a history) with those not obviously at risk. They found that children with such a risk for antisocial behavior received more negative treatment from their adoptive parents and parental negativity correlated with children's behavior problems, even when their children's genetic predispositions had already been taken into account. While this is a growth area, the relative contributions of genes and environment are still under debate.

The present and the future

Given the diversity of approaches to parenting, research in the field is lively. In one respect, the area has been called into question with the publication of a series of books downplaying the importance of parental influences because of the importance of the peer group or genetic influences (e.g., Rowe, 1994). One reason for this critique stems from the very diversity of the field and the healthy debate between the camps, which seems from the outside to indicate a failure to reach a consensus. However, recent large-scale reviews of the area are a celebration of the diversity of family life, and the possible methods used for researching such diversity. The future holds many good prospects for two reasons. Firstly, given the diversity of contemporary work, improvements in the multivariate analyses of longitudinal data, and an agreement that a developmental approach is needed, research on the family has shifted to the study of complex relationships over time.

Secondly, there has been a move in research over the past few years to accommodate to this shift in methods, and to external criticisms of the area such as that by Rowe (1994). It has been noted that some areas of parenting (e.g., the transition to parenthood and adolescence) are heavily over-represented in the literature, while others (e.g., parenting young adults or children in middle childhood) are relatively neglected. Much current activity aims to link together previously unrelated areas. For example, there is the recent attempt to unravel the patterns of influence between the family and peer systems, showing that they are highly interrelated (Parke *et al.*, 2002). At the same time, researchers within behavior genetics and the other traditions have recently combined forces to examine the complexity of genetic and social factors in relation to one another (Hetherington *et al.*, 1999). Only through combining different approaches will we free ourselves of paradigm-bound analyses and inter-group feuding.

Conclusions

While great strides have been made to understand the complexities of parenting, there are three key issues that will need to be more closely addressed in the literature in the coming years. Firstly, there are many gaps in our understanding of research methods. As O'Connor (2002) suggests, a mixture of methods is virtuous, but brings with it particular problems, notably what to do when they produce results that do not square with each other. Secondly, we persist in treating 'parenting' as 'mothering,' as mothers continue to take the major role in caretaking and are more available to study. However, recent research suggests that we should distinguish paternal and maternal relationships and their influences. Finally, as Hay and Nash (2002) point out, we continue to hold in mind the assumption that the nuclear family is the blueprint against which all other types should be compared – and usually unfavorably. The challenge for future research is to acknowledge that psychologists tend to stick rather conservatively within their white, predominantly Anglo-Saxon hegemony, even though the nuclear family continues to be a minority that does not reflect the diversity and complexity in contemporary family life.

Questions

1. Is a 'unifying theory of parenting' possible, given all the possible influences upon parenting by men and women? If so, how can we reconcile the contributions of genetic and social factors with the fact that parenting is a dynamical process (i.e., children influence their parents as much as parents influence their children)?
2. How can we identify patterns of parenting like the categories 'authoritarian' and 'authoritative' within Baumrind's theory?
3. At a practical level, can we use the evidence on parenting to help parents be more skillful in the ways in which they rear children?

See also:
Learning theories; Psychoanalytical theories; Parental and teacher rating scales; Cross-sectional and longitudinal designs; Twin and adoption studies; Social development; Aggressive and prosocial behavior; Daycare; Peers and siblings; Socialization; 'At-risk' concept; Behavioral and learning disorders; Behavior genetics; John Bowlby; Donald Winnicott

Further reading

Amato, P. R. (1998). More than money? Men's contributions to their children's lives. In A. Booth and A. C. Crouter (eds.), *Men in Families. When do they Get Involved? What Difference does it Make?* Mahwah, NJ: Erlbaum, pp. 241–278.

Baumrind, D. (1989). Rearing competent children. In W. Damon (ed.), *Child Development Today and Tomorrow*. San Francisco: Jossey-Bass, pp. 349–378.

Bornstein, M. (ed.) (2002). *Handbook of Parenting*, 2nd edn. Vols. I–V. Mahwah, NJ: Erlbaum.

Collins, W. A., Maccoby, E. E., Steinberg, L., Hetherington, E. M., and Bornstein, M. H. (2000). Contemporary research on parenting: the case for nature and nurture. *American Psychologist*, 55, 218–232.

Play

PETER K. SMITH

Introduction

This entry reviews the main different types of play, and the kinds of developmental benefits they may bring to children. The ubiquity of play in childhood (and in most species of mammals when young) strongly suggests its benefits for development, but what these benefits are, and how important or essential they are, are still debated. Classic perspectives on the development and function of play can be found in the writings of Piaget and Vygotsky. Let us begin by tackling the issue of what constitutes play, and then turn to how it undergoes age-related changes.

Defining play

Play is often defined as activity that is both done for its own sake, and characterized by 'means rather than ends' (i.e., the process of the play is more important than any end point or goal). These criteria contrast play with, for example, exploration (which may lead into play as a child gets more familiar with a new toy or environment), with work (which has a definite goal), and fighting (different from play fighting as discussed later). Additional characteristics of play are flexibility (objects being put in new combinations, roles acted out in new ways), positive affect (children often smile and laugh in play, and say they enjoy it), and pretence (use of objects and actions in non-literal ways).

Main types of play

Although classifications differ, the following main types of play are well recognized: object play, pretend play and sociodramatic play, and physical activity play (exercise play; rough-and-tumble play). Of these, object play and physical activity play are seen widely in other species of mammals. Pretend and sociodramatic play are only seen in humans, apart from some possibly very elementary forms of pretence in great apes. Besides play, there is the related concept of games. Games with rules are more organized forms of play in which there is some goal (e.g., winning the game) and are not reviewed further.

Object play

This starts in infancy and may help children develop creative problem-solving skills. Researchers such as Jerome Bruner and Kathy Sylva have reported experiments with children in which they are given a chance to play with objects, then solve a task. Those with the play experience solved the task better. However, subsequent research has suggested that instruction can often be equally effective (Johnson, Christie, & Yawkey, 1999). The benefits of play need to be balanced against those of instruction, bearing in mind the ages of the children, the nature of the task, and the specificity of the learning expected – whether for specific skills or a more generally inquisitive and creative attitude.

Pretend play

This develops from about 15 months, with simple actions such as 'pretending to sleep' or 'putting dolly to bed,' developing into longer story sequences and role play (Fig. 1). Much early pretend play can be with parents, and older siblings. In Western societies especially, it is common for parents to model or 'scaffold' early pretend play actions. By 3 to 4 years, pretend play becomes common with same-age peers.

Pretend play among children is seen very widely in different societies. It is often imitative of adult roles (e.g., in rural societies, children may play at 'herding cattle' with stones and at 'pounding maize' with sticks and pebbles). Such play might be considered as 'practice' for the adult activities concerned. However, rather more ambitious developmental benefits for pretend play have been put forward.

Leslie (1987) argued that pretend play is an early indicator of theory of mind abilities. In simple object

Figure 1. Pretend play. Photograph by John Walmsley.

substitution pretence, the knowledge or representation that 'this is a banana' becomes 'this banana is a telephone.' Correspondingly, in theory of mind, the representation that 'this is a banana' is related to the representation that 'X believes that the banana is a telephone.' Leslie argued that this similarity suggested that pretence might be very important in theory of mind acquisition. However, this early pretend play before 3 years is often very imitative, and it is not clear whether a young child who talks into a banana is actually having the cognitive representations that Leslie describes, or is simply imitating what older children or adults do. The nature of any relationship between pretend play and theory of mind is still disputed.

Sociodramatic play

Defined in terms of social play with others, sustained role taking, and a narrative line, this is something that children from about 3 years of age engage in a lot. Such play can be quite complex, involving an understanding of others' intent and role, sophisticated language constructions, and the development of sometimes novel (sometimes less novel!) story lines. Smilansky (1968) suggested that sociodramatic play assists language development, cognitive development, creativity, and role taking. She also claimed that pretend and

sociodramatic play were less frequent and less complex in disadvantaged children. This led her and others to develop play tutoring (intervention by an adult) to raise levels of these kinds of play; adults would provide suitable props, visits, etc. and encourage the sociodramatic play of children in nurseries and kindergartens, such that subsequently they became more able to sustain this play themselves.

Smilansky's ideas about the value of sociodramatic play were tested by a number of experimental studies, including play-tutoring studies. In these, a group or class of children that received play tutoring were compared with those who did not. Generally, the play-tutored children improved more on measures of cognition, language, and creativity, apparently supporting Smilansky's views.

A number of critiques were made of these studies. Many of them pointed to flaws due to selective interpretation of results, effects of experimental bias, and the use of inappropriate control groups. For example, in the traditional play-tutoring study, the play-tutored children received more stimulation and adult contact generally, so one cannot really conclude that it is the extra play that brought about the developmental benefits. Further studies took account of these criticisms. This step included balancing play-tutoring with skills tutoring (e.g., coloring, picture dominoes) and assessing

Table 1. Some criteria distinguishing play fighting and real fighting.

Criterion	Play fighting	Real fighting
Facial expression	Smiling, laughing	Frowning, tearful
Restraint	Kicks and blows are not hard or do not make contact	Kicks and blows are hard or make contact
Role-reversal	Voluntarily take it in turns to be 'on top' or be 'chased'	Aims to be 'on top' or to chase the other
How encounter starts and finishes	Starting by invitation and ending with continued play or activity together	Starting with challenge and ending in separation

outcomes blind to the child's treatment condition. Doing so failed to reveal many differences (P. K. Smith, 1988), which suggests that benefits of sociodramatic play need not be essential for development. Nevertheless, play-tutoring does work out as equal to skills tutoring in many domains, and it is generally enjoyable and sociable for children in the preschool years, so there are sound reasons to encourage it in the nursery curriculum.

One kind of pretend play, often not encouraged in nurseries, is war play, which is pretend play with toy guns or weapons, or military action figures. Many educators believe that this play encourages real aggression, though others emphasize its pretend nature and feel that no real harm results from it.

Physical activity play

This refers to playful activity involving large body activity, particularly exercise play that includes running, climbing, and other large body or large muscle activity, as well as rough-and-tumble play, that covers play fighting and play chasing. These forms of play have been reviewed by Pellegrini & Smith (1998).

Exercise play

This increases in frequency from toddlers to preschool children, peaks at early primary school ages, and then declines. Young children seem to need opportunities for physical exercise more than older children, and are more likely to get restless after long sedentary periods and to run around when released from them. Boys do more of this kind of play than girls. It is often hypothesized to support physical training of muscles, for strength and endurance, and skill and economy of movement. Another hypothesis is that exercise play encourages younger children to take breaks from being overloaded on cognitive tasks (the cognitive immaturity hypothesis). The argument here is that younger children have less mature cognitive capacities, so benefits of concentrating on a cognitively demanding task decrease after a shorter time than for older children. The 'need' to exercise thus helps children 'space out' these cognitive demands.

Figure 2. Rough-and-tumble play. Photograph by John Walmsley.

Rough-and-tumble play

This seems to increase from toddlers through preschool and primary school children, to peak at late primary age, and then decline in frequency. It takes up some 10 percent of playground time, though varying by the nature of the surface, physical conditions, etc. Boys do more than girls, especially play fighting. Rough-and-tumble play looks like real fighting, but can be distinguished from it by several criteria (Table 1; Fig. 2).

Most children can distinguish playful from real fighting, and from 8 years give similar cues to those described in Table 1. In one study, English and Italian children were found to be accurate in judging videotapes of play fighting and real fighting, irrespective of which nationality they were watching.

During the primary school years, only about 1% of rough-and-tumble episodes usually turn into real fighting, although many teachers and lunchtime supervisors think it is as much as about 30%. However, 'rejected' children (those disliked by many peers and seldom liked much) more often respond to rough-and-tumble aggressively (around 25% of episodes). So, it is possible that teachers or lunchtime supervisors are making general judgments about children, based on these 'rejected' children who may be taking up a lot of their supervisory time.

Rough-and-tumble is often between friends. By early adolescence, however, there appears to be some change, with dominance/status becoming important in choosing play partners, as well as friendship, with a greater risk of play fights turning into real fights. It is hypothesized that rough-and-tumble play in younger children may (in addition to benefits of exercise play) provide practice in fighting/hunting skills, at least in earlier human societies. By adolescence, however, it may involve dominance relationships (e.g., using rough-and-tumble play to establish or maintain dominance in the peer group).

What do children learn from play?

Evolutionary arguments suggest that the propensity to play has been selected for, so we can expect there to be benefits to playing, and that these may vary by species, and by types of play. There can be a lot of incidental benefits to play such that it keeps children active and provides them with opportunities to encounter new situations. With human children, and with object, pretend, and sociodramatic play, there may be a balance to draw between benefits of playing and of instruction. Instruction can be more focused on a precise goal, but play is often more enjoyable for young children and, even if less efficient for a precise goal, may foster a more generally inquisitive and creative approach to problem-solving.

Conclusions

Among the theoretical issues in play research remaining unresolved, two are currently especially noteworthy. The first relates to rough-and-tumble play. We know that this is primarily friendly and non-exploitative in pre-adolescents, but how does this change as children move into adolescence? Does the function of this form of play then change and, in particular, is it used for purposes related to dominance, especially for boys? The second issue relates to pretend play. An earlier phase of research queried the findings from play tutoring studies, but, more recently, pretend play has been proposed as an important component of developing a theory of mind. Greater conceptual clarity and empirical evidence are called for here, together with a willingness to learn from the problems encountered in the earlier studies (e.g., experimenter bias).

Amongst practical issues, the issue of war play continues to be debated in early education. There have been moves to ban war play in many nursery schools; however, there is also a recognition that such play may be generally harmless in itself and a rather natural play format, especially for boys (Holland, 2003). Regarding educational practice through the school years, there has been a general movement toward shortening or eliminating playground breaks. However, leaving aside social benefits of playtime, the benefits for physical activity and for providing breaks between instruction (cf., the cognitive immaturity hypothesis), argue for retaining playground breaks. More systematic study is still needed in these areas.

Questions

1. What value does physical activity play have in providing spacing for concentration on school-based tasks?
2. How does rough-and-tumble play change in form and function from the primary to secondary school ages?
3. Does young children's war play have any connection with later aggressiveness?
4. Does pretend play have any important role in helping young children develop a theory of mind?

See also:
Cross-cultural comparisons; Cross-species comparisons; Theories of the child's mind; Social development; Aggressive and prosocial behavior; Peers and siblings; Sex differences; Anthropology; Jerome S. Bruner; Jean Piaget; Lev S. Vygotsky; Donald Winnicott.

Further reading

Lancy, D. F. (1996). *Playing on the Mother-Ground: Cultural Routines for Children's Development*. New York: Guilford Press.
Pellegrini, A. D. (2002). Rough-and-tumble play. In P. K. Smith and C. Hart (eds.), *Handbook of Social Development*. Oxford: Blackwell, pp. 438–453.
Power, T. (2000). *Play and Exploration in Children and Animals*. Mahwah, NJ: Erlbaum.

Prehension

CLAES VON HOFSTEN

Introduction

Although prehension is one of the most prominent behaviors to develop in infancy, it has been little studied. Piaget made one of the first thorough descriptions of its development and related it to other aspects of infant cognition. H. M. Halverson (1931–), in the tradition of Arnold Gesell, made one of the first attempts to describe and measure various qualities of its development in detail. Halverson's studies were made by tediously filming infants and then analyzing the films frame by frame. With the availability of video and other quantitative means of recording movements in the 1970s, studies of the development of prehension became more feasible, and a firmer body of knowledge about its development started to form.

Although children do not successfully reach for and grasp objects until they are about 4 months old, the development of prehension starts much earlier. Von Hofsten (1982, 2003) found that newborn infants make goal-directed arm movements toward an object presented in front of them. They do not grasp the object reached for, however. One reason for this is that their arm and hand movements are coupled to each other in extension and flexion synergies. They will open the hand as they reach out (Fig. 1), but the opening of the hand is not a preparation for grasping the object because the same thing happens when the child extends the arm without looking. Lawrence & Hopkins (1976) also observed this synergistic pattern in newborn rhesus monkeys, and found that they had difficulties in closing their fingers around an object they had reached out for. If they eventually managed to do so, they had problems in releasing the object after they had pulled it toward themselves.

Pre-reaching and other newborn movements

Newborn reaching is controlled by multiple perceptual systems. When the reach is initiated, vision defines the position of the object in space and proprioception the location of the arm. When the arm extends, the hand enters the visual field. Closing the visual-manual loop in this way is of crucial importance for the development of manual control. It makes it possible for the infant to explore the relationship between seen and felt hand position, between motor commands and movements within visual space, and to discover the possibilities and constraints of exploring visual space with manual movements.

Another kind of goal-directed arm and hand movement that newborns engage in is putting finger(s) or thumb into their mouth (Butterworth & Hopkins, 1988). These movements are guided by proprioception and they are coordinated with mouth movements in a prospective way in that the mouth opens in anticipation of the arrival of the hand rather than as a response to it. This pattern is especially distinct just before feeding.

Viewing their hands is attractive to neonates, and they will make an effort to continue to view them. Placed on their back, they extend the arm toward which their head is turned and flex the other. This posture has traditionally been described as the Asymmetric Tonic Neck Reflex, and is assumed to be elicited by neck proprioception. Evidence against this interpretation is provided by van der Meer, van der Weel, & Lee (1995) who showed that it is rather an effort to keep the seen arm in the visual field. When the newborns' arms were pulled gently downward, the extended arm they were viewing resisted this pull, but not the other one, just as predicted by the reflex notion. However, when they viewed the other arm on a TV monitor placed between the face and the extended arm, they resisted the pull on the seen arm. In another experiment, van der Meer (1997) placed newborns in a dark room with a spotlight in front of them in such a way that the hand was illuminated when it was positioned in the light beam. When this happened, they spent significantly more time with their hand in that region of space than in other regions. If the spotlight was re-directed, their preferred region of space moved to the new bright region. This

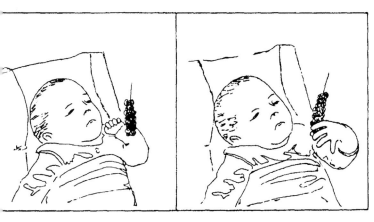

Figure 1. A newborn reach. Although the object is inside the hand of the infant the fingers do not flex around it.

shows that newborns can use visual feedback to re-direct the arms into a region of space where they can view them.

From pre-reaching to functional reaching

During the first two months of life, the pre-reaching activity diminishes, and the quality of the movements changes dramatically. Instead of the hand opening during the extension of the arms, it tends to become fisted when the arms are extended, and the movements show signs of being more vigorous. This suggests that the global extension-flexion pattern is broken up, and arm-hand control is in transition toward a more differentiated mode. After this age, the amount of pre-reaching activity goes up again and the hand will start opening during the forward extension, but only when the infant is engaged in goal-directed reaching. The infant will then also start closing the hand on the object, demonstrating more independent and functional hand control.

The transition from pre-reaching to functional reaching usually occurs around 4 months of age. Thelen and colleagues (1993) found large individual differences in the way the arms were moved during early reaching attempts; some infants moved them in a slow and damped way and others more vigorously. Overall, these attempts were characterized by much variability rather than being stereotyped. During the transition from pre-reaching to successful reaching and grasping, the movements became less variable as the infants came to control the intrinsic dynamics of their arms.

Early reaches are made up of several segments or movement units (3–5 per second), each consisting of an acceleration and a deceleration phase in contrast to adult reaches that mainly consist of one bell-shaped velocity function (von Hofsten, 1993; 2003). With development, the number of segments decrease and their functions become differentiated. One segment becomes much larger than the rest and responsible for the transport of the hand to the object. The remaining ones take care of the adjustments in the grasp component. This development reflects improvements in the prospective control of reaching.

From reaching to catching

A remarkable ability of infants to time their manual actions relative to an external event is demonstrated in early catching behavior, such that they successfully intercept moving objects at the very age they began mastering reaching for stationary ones. It was found that reaches were aimed toward the meeting point with the object and not to the position where the object was seen at the beginning of the reach (von Hofsten, 1993; 2003). Moreover, 8-month-old infants successfully caught an object moving at 120 cm/sec. The initial aiming of these reaches was within a few degrees of the meeting point with the target, and the variable timing error was around 50 ms. This shows that infants predict the future positions of a moving object, and move there in anticipation of the arrival of the object.

Such abilities rely on assumptions of how objects move. One such basic assumption that guides infant catching is that objects will continue to move in the same way as before (i.e., that they adhere to the principle of inertia). Accordingly, when 6-month-olds reached for an object that abruptly changed its direction of motion, they continued to reach for it along the extension of its previous trajectory. This tendency persists even after repeated observations of objects whose trajectories suddenly turned in the same way at the same position.

Problems to be overcome

Several problems need to be dealt with in advance when reaching for an object (von Hofsten, 1993; 2003). Firstly, the reach will push the body out of its postural equilibrium if nothing is done about it. Therefore, the effects of reaching movements must be foreseen and prepared for in order to maintain ongoing activity. Infants aged 9 months sitting astride on their parent's knee make such pre-adjustments of their trunk muscles before reaching out (Fig. 2), and 15-month-olds pre-adjust their leg muscles to counteract the forces that arise when pulling a drawer. Secondly, the reaching hand needs to adjust to the orientation, form, and size of the object (Fig. 3). The encounter must be timed in such a way that the hand starts to close around the object before it

Figure 2.   An infant reaching for an object while sitting astride the parent's knee.

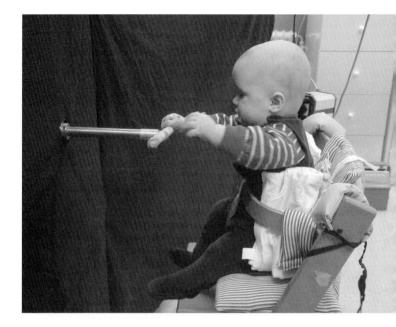

Figure 3.   Infants aged 6 months reaching for a horizontal and a vertical rod.

arrives there. Such spatial and temporal adjustments are only possible under visual control.

Almost from the onset of successful reaching, infants pre-adjust the orientation of the hand to that of the object. Pre-adjusting the opening of the hand to the size of an object develops somewhat later. Thus, 9- and 13-month-old infants, but not 5-month-olds, adjusted the opening of the hand to the size of the object reached for. Infants time the grasping movement from the onset of reaching. Children of 9 months and younger first move the hand to the vicinity of the object, and then close the hand around it. Those aged 13 months, however, typically start to close the hand during approach and well before touch. This is an indication that reaching and grasping become coordinated into one continuous action.

In mature grasping, the whole hand is used to grasp large objects, while only the thumb and the index finger are used to grasp small ones. This differentiation of grasping is not present in early reaching. The medial part of the hand then plays a more prominent role, and the whole hand is used to grasp any object. During the second part of the first year, the focus of the grasp moves toward the radial part of the hand, and the infant starts to use a pincer grasp in picking up small objects. Younger infants tend to avoid picking up such objects, but when they start to control the thumb and the index finger independently between 9 and 12 months of age,

they demonstrate obvious pleasure in doing so. The independent control of finger movements is made possible by the establishment of direct corticomoto-neuronal connections. It marks the beginning of the development of fine manipulation that continues throughout childhood.

Conclusions

An important next step in the study of prehension in infancy is to investigate the perceptual and cognitive basis for this development. Smooth and skillful actions require sophisticated planning, and this in turn pre-disposes the child to be able to perceive and represent what is going to happen next. Understanding how an object moves is crucial for preparing to grasp it in the right way. After the object has been grasped, it is equally important to understand how to move it in order to accomplish the intended actions associated with the object. This requires a firm prospective and retrospective base of information.

Another important next step is to investigate how the development of prehension is affected by various developmental pathologies. There are good possibilities that the study of prehension in deviant infant populations can help us to identify the nature of the abnormalities as well as their causes and effects.

A third important next step is to investigate how manual actions are learnt. What is the role of imitation in this process? Recent research by Rizzolatti, Fadiga, and co-workers (2002) has shown that part of the prefrontal cortex, containing 'mirror neurons,' is specialized in mirroring the manual actions of others. This opens up an important shortcut to learning about prehension and other manual actions.

Questions

1. Clarify the meaning of prospective control, and then show how it can be applied to development of actions such as reaching and grasping.
2. What are the main changes in the development of prehension during the first year, and what do they tell us about the development of action more generally?
3. What are pre-reaching movements and how might they be related to later functional prehensile actions?
4. Why should 'mirror neurons' identified by Rizolatti and others open up an important shortcut to learning about prehension and other manual actions?
5. If postural control and prehensile actions co-develop, how might this perspective serve as an aid in the early detection of infants at-risk for subsequent perceptual-motor disorders, and in some form of therapeutic intervention for such children?

See also:
Neuromaturational theories; Dynamical systems approaches; The status of the human newborn; Perceptual development; Motor development; Brain and behavioral development (I): sub-cortical; Brain and behavioral development (II): cortical; Handedness; Imitation; Prematurity and low birthweight; Cognitive neuroscience

Further reading

Bertenthal, B. I. and Clifton, R. K. (1998). Perception and action. In W. Damon (editor-in-chief), *Handbook of Child Psychology*, Vol. II. *Cognition, Perception, and Language*, ed. D. Kuhn and R. Siegler 5th. edn. New York: Wiley, pp. 51–102.

Halverson, H. M. (1931). Study of prehension in infants. *Genetic Psychology Monographs*, 10, 107–285.

Piaget, J. (1953). *The Origins of Intelligence in the Child*. New York: Routledge.

Reading and writing

PETER BRYANT

Introduction

Since writing translates spoken language into visual symbols, the starting point for most psychological research on children's reading has been the strong relationships that exist between their knowledge of spoken language and their progress in learning to read. Psychologists have established that children's progress in learning about written language is linked to three aspects of spoken language: phonology, morphology, and comprehension. In each case, the evidence suggests that children's awareness of the rules of spoken language affects how well they learn to read, and also that the experience of learning to be literate transforms children's explicit understanding of phonological, morphological, and semantic relationships. These two-way links, as Ravid & Tolchinsky (2002) have shown, become increasingly sophisticated as children grow older, and are important in adulthood as well.

Phonology and literacy

All scripts represent speech sounds in some way, and therefore children's sensitivity to the sounds in words should be at the heart of their learning how such scripts work. In alphabetic scripts, the individual letters, for the most part, represent individual phonemes. In syllabaries, such as the kana scripts in Japanese, each character signifies a syllable. In the Chinese script, each character represents a morpheme (a basic unit of meaning) rather than a unit of sound, but most Chinese characters also contain a 'phonological component', which tells readers something about the sound of the morpheme that it represents. Not surprisingly, therefore, much research has demonstrated that children's awareness of phonological structure plays a crucial role in reading.

Even before children are taught to read, they develop hypotheses about what the letters or characters in their written language represent. Early on, according to research by Ferreiro & Teberosky (1983) in Argentina,

children think that each letter represents a syllable. Preschool children are also alive to certain formal characteristics of alphabetic scripts: the children in this study were able to judge that a written word consisting entirely of a repeated letter was not a proper (Spanish) word. More recently, Marie Cassar and Rebecca Treiman in the United States as well as Pacton, Perruchet, Fayol & Cleermans (2001) in France, confirmed that children are soon aware that, in the English and French scripts respectively, words often contain a doublet (i.e. a repeated letter as in 'kiss'), but never at the beginning of a word. Ferreiro and Teberosky argued that these early discriminations are a matter of the children being aware of the 'form', but not yet of the 'function', of spelling sequences. This hypothesis recently received strong support from an experiment by Annukka Lehtonen with Finnish children. In Finnish, doublets have a form and a function: consonant doublets do not appear at the beginning of words (form), but when they do in other parts of the word they signal long phonemes (function): 'kk' and 'aa', for example, represent speech sounds that last longer than those represented by 'k' and 'a' on their own. Lehtonen showed that Finnish children are aware of the formal constraints on consonant doublets (not at the beginning of the word) before they are aware of the function of doublets when they are used (longer speech sounds).

Once children begin to write an alphabetic script, they quickly become aware of many of the phonological functions of the letters that they are using. However, they have a long way to go before they conquer conventional spelling patterns, particularly with scripts that have complex sets of spelling rules such as English and French. Charles Read, an American linguist, showed that young children often produce phonetic representations in their spellings, even though their spellings are not the conventional ones (e.g. 'kwyit' for 'quiet' and 'wodr' for 'water'). Figure 1 gives an extract from a charming story written by an English 7-year-old girl, which shows that even at this age children often persist in plausible, but non-conventional, phonetic spellings.

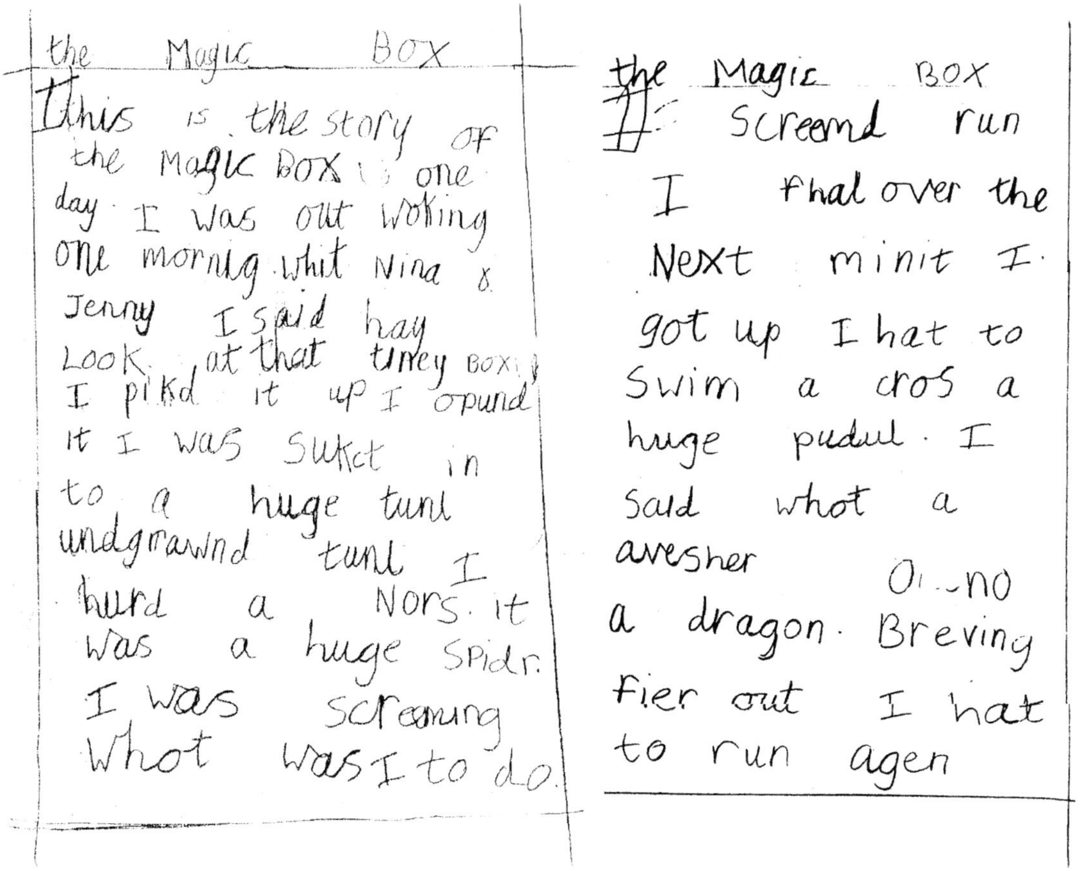

Figure 1. Extract from a story by an English 7-year-old girl, which shows how she adopts largely phonetic transcriptions (e.g.'minit,' 'pudul,' 'agen'), and ignores conventional spellings for morphemes (e.g. 'sukct,' 'opund').

Treiman's (1993) work supports this view in research on American children's spellings. In spoken American English, for instance, there is no separate vowel sound in syllables with a syllabic *r*, such as 'girl.' American children often misplace the letter for the vowel sound in such words (e.g. 'gril'). Treiman also showed a difference between American- and British-speaking children in the way that they deal with such syllables. British children tend to leave out the *r* altogether, because in the standard British dialect the *r* in words like 'girl' and 'better' is not pronounced.

Children's initial ingenious, but rather too literal, attempts to associate single letters with single sounds or, in other words, to use simple grapheme-phoneme correspondence rules in their writing, indicate the importance of phonological skills in early attempts to conquer reading. The significance of these skills has been amply confirmed in tasks that measure children's sensitivity to the phonological structure of words. Some phonological awareness tasks test children's awareness that words consists of phonemes (c-a-t: s-t-i-ck), and others their sensitivity to the intrasyllabic phonological units, onset, and rime (c-at: st-ick). Onset-rime tasks (e.g., which is the odd one out: [onset] cat, bed, cup?

[rime] bed, red, fan?) are easier for children than phoneme tasks, but longitudinal studies have shown that children's performance in both kinds of task are excellent predictors over several years of children's success in reading. The reason for the influence of sensitivity to rime is probably that it alerts children to the fact that words with common rimes often share spelling sequences too (light-night, lent-sent).

Most research on phonological rules in reading has concentrated on associations between single letters and single sounds (grapheme-phoneme correspondences), but there are rules that go beyond these basic links. These are 'conditional' rules: they apply when the same letter represents one sound in one context and a different sound in another context, or when the same sound is indicated by different letters or letter sequences depending on the context. The best-known conditional rule in English is the 'split-digraph': vowel sounds are lengthened if the syllable that they are in is followed by an 'e' ('hop'-'hope', 'hat'-'hate'). There are many conditional spelling rules in English, and Richard Venezky has demonstrated that, when these rules are taken into account, this orthography is much more predictable than it is usually believed to be.

Conditional rules exist in other orthographies too. For example, in Portuguese many words end in the sound /u/: this ending is spelled as 'o' in words whose stress is on the penultimate syllable (the most common stress pattern in Portuguese words), but it is spelled as 'u' in words in which the last syllable is stressed (e.g., 'bambu' [bamboo], 'caju' [cashew]). Terezinha Nunes found that beginning spellers in Brazil usually spell the ending phonetically – as 'u' – all the time. With more experience, they begin to adopt the non-phonetic, but more common, 'o' ending, but use this new spelling altogether too often, generalizing it to words that should have the 'u' ending (e.g., 'bambo'). It takes most Portuguese-speaking children many years to learn this conditional rule and to apply it effectively, and English-speaking children seem to have similar difficulties with their own conditional rules.

Morphology and literacy

Morphological rules also play an important part in many scripts. Morphemes are units of meaning and many words contain more than one morpheme. 'Kissed' is a two-morpheme word: its first morpheme is the verb 'kiss' and the second morpheme is the /t/ sound ending that tells us that the word refers to a past action. We spell this final sound as 'ed' in 'kissed,' but not in 'list,' because '-ed' is the non-phonetic spelling for the past tense ending in regular verbs. The correct spelling for the /z/ sound ending in 'trees' is 's,' but not in 'freeze,' and the /s/ ending in 'socks,' and not in 'box,' because this is the way to spell plural endings in regular English nouns.

In French too, morphology is at the center of written language: plural endings in nouns, adjectives, and verbs, for example, are represented in writing, but usually not pronounced in speech. Thus, French children must learn to write silent morphemes. In Greek, there are few vowel sounds and many ways to spell them, and when these vowel sounds occur in inflectional endings, there are firm rules about how they should be spelled. For example, the /i/ sound is written as η with feminine singular endings, as οι with masculine plural endings, as ι with neuter endings, and as ει with third person singular verb endings.

Three salient facts have emerged from research on children's learning of such spelling rules. One is that it takes years. In learning Greek, French, and English, children master phonological spelling rules first and morphological ones later (Fig. 1). By around 6 years, they spell phonetically represented endings in words like 'list' and 'lord' nearly perfectly, but still have great difficulty with morphological spellings, such as the endings of 'kissed' and 'bored' (Nunes, Bryant, &

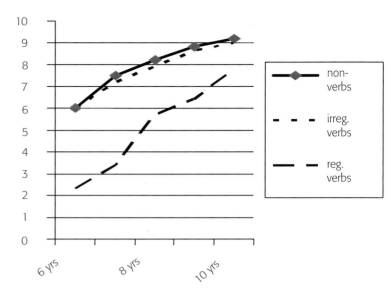

Figure 2.   Mean number of times (out of 10) that children spelled correctly the endings of non-verbs ending in /d/ and /t/ (e.g., ground, soft), irregular past verbs (e.g., found, slept), and regular past verbs (e.g., called, dressed). Note that the scores for the regular past verb endings, in which the 'ed' spelling is morphologically based, are much worse than the other two spellings. Data from T. Nunes, P. Bryant, and M. Bindman, 1997. Morphological spelling strategies: developmental stages and processes. *Developmental Psychology*, 33, 637–649.

Bindman, 1997). Children aged 10 years often make mistakes with these particular endings (Fig. 2). Even adults have problems with such rules as many of them do not know the rule that the /z/ ending in plural words ('cars,' 'trees') is always spelled as 's' (Kemp & Bryant, 2003). It is a similar story with the French plural endings and with the Greek inflections. French and Greek children also learn morphological rules after the phonological ones.

A second point is that there is a connection between awareness of morphological structure and learning morphological spelling rules. The more children know about morphemes, the more likely they are to learn morphologically determined spellings. Research in English by Terezinha Nunes and in Hebrew by Iris Levin, Dorit Ravid, and Sharon Rapaport shows that children's knowledge of morphological structure affects how they learn morphologically based spelling patterns, but also that their experience with these spelling rules promotes their awareness of morphemes.

The third point is that Terezinha Nunes, Peter Bryant, and Jenny Olsson have shown that explicit instruction about spelling and morphemes enhances children's learning of these spelling rules. This is significant because in English-speaking schools, and probably elsewhere, teachers give children little instruction about morphemes and spelling, and often such instruction emphasizes the relationship between sounds and spelling sequences, rather than between meanings and spelling. Thus, teaching practices sometimes wrongly treat morphological spelling rules as phonological ones.

Comprehension and literacy

So far, we have dealt only with children's learning about reading and spelling single words, but of course the main aim of learning to read and to write is to understand and to produce meaningful passages of written prose (and occasionally verse). Until recently, this distinction between reading single words and reading meaningful prose was the center of heated debate. Several researchers, including Kenneth Goodman and Frank Smith, argued that children learn to read by using the context provided by prose – a process which Goodman called the 'psycholinguistic guessing game.' He claimed that, when children cannot read a word in a meaningful sentence, they use the context of the rest of the sentence to guess the meaning of this difficult word. As a result of doing so, they are more likely to be able to read that word properly when they meet it again. The empirical evidence that Goodman produced was entirely about the first part of the hypothesis, that children use context whenever it can help them to decipher difficult words.

The importance of children's use of context has been disputed by Charles Perfetti and Keith Stanovich on the grounds that good readers do not depend on it as much as less advanced readers do. This research, however, misses the main point, which is the need for a direct test of the second part of Goodman's hypothesis, namely, that children learn to read new words as a result of guessing their meaning. This claim has now been tested by Nicola Archer and Peter Bryant who confirmed that children do use context to decipher difficult words, and showed that this experience helps them decipher such words when they see them next. This study also revealed that simply telling children what a difficult word means is just as effective a way of helping them to learn the word well enough for them to read it correctly on the next occasion. Thus, the use of context is an effective way of learning to read new words, but not the only way.

A great deal of research suggests that children's understanding of what they read depends partly on their ability to decipher single words, and partly on their general level of understanding of connected prose (listening comprehension). Philip Gough showed that measures of these two variables together accounted for a large amount of the variance in children's reading comprehension. There is evidence too from longitudinal research in England by Lucia Rego, and subsequently by Margaret Snowling, of a considerable independence between (a) the contribution of children's phonological awareness, which mainly predicts single word reading,

and (b) the impact of their ability to use context to guess the meaning of a difficult word (Goodman's psycholinguistic guessing), which mainly predicts reading comprehension. Thus, everyone turns out to have been right in the protracted battle between those who concentrated on deciphering single words and those who insisted on the importance of reading for meaning.

The studies of comprehension mentioned so far treated it either as a predictive or a predicted variable, without examining what psychological steps children must take in order to comprehend a passage of prose. There is also some research on the psychological processes that underlie children's comprehension. Jane Oakhill claims that the crucial factor in children's comprehension is their ability to make inferences. Inferences, she argues, are necessary because even the most explicit prose passages leave certain facts and conclusions for the readers to make themselves. Mention that some people start off on a trip carrying towels and buckets, and that, when they get to their destination, they listen to seagulls and build sand castles, and it is a fair bet that these people are spending a day at the beach, even though nothing is said about the beach or the sea in the story. These have to be inferred. Oakhill collected cross-sectional and longitudinal data that showed a strong relationship between children's ability to make such inferences and their success in standardized tests of reading comprehension. She also demonstrated that children's reading comprehension improves when they are taught how to make inferences about stories that they hear and read.

Conclusions

Research since the early 1980s has established strong and widespread links between children's awareness of the structure of spoken language and the progress that they make in learning to be literate. This connection works on at least three levels: phonology, morphology, and comprehension and verbal inferences. The direction of cause and effect in this connection is a two-way one. Children's sensitivity to the structure of spoken language influences their reading and spelling, but their success in reading and spelling also increases their explicit understanding, and appreciation, of their own language. Attempts to teach children explicitly about the relationships between spoken and written language (at the levels of phonology, morphology, and verbal inferences) have had excellent effects on children's reading and spelling. Children benefit from being shown the richness of the connections between the language that they speak and the language that they read and write.

Psychologists have two main problems still to solve in future work on children's reading. We know a lot about what children learn, but not nearly enough about how they learn. We still need to know, for example, how much of learning to read and to spell is implicit (i.e., to what extent children are unaware of the rules that they learn and use), and we also need to know much more about the experiences that help children learn to read and to spell. The second problem is how to translate the considerable advances made in our understanding of how children read and spell into educational programs that work. If psychologists can solve these problems as well, their study of children's reading will be a truly successful enterprise.

Questions

1. Which aspects of learning to read and to spell are explicit and which implicit?
2. To what extent will children benefit from explicit instruction about conditional phonological and morphological spelling rules, many of which they now have to learn without help from their teachers?
3. How can we best enhance the inferences that Oakhill has shown to be so important in understanding text?

See also:
Constructivist theories; Cross-sectional and longitudinal designs; Connectionist modeling; Schooling and literacy; Behavioral and learning disorders; Dyslexia

Further reading

Harris, M. and Hatano, G. (eds.) (1999). *Learning to Read and Write: a Cross-linguistic Perspective.* Cambridge: Cambridge University Press.
Rayner, K., Foorman, B., Perfetti, C. A., Pesetsky, D. and Seidenberg, M. S. (2001). How psychological science informs the teaching of reading. *Supplement to Psychological Science*, 2, 31–74.

Schooling and literacy

YVETTE SOLOMON

Introduction

Research in the field of literacy and its place in schooling has developed rapidly since the 1980s. It now encompasses a range of interconnected issues concerned with the development of text-based skills within a social framework, hence spanning the disciplines of linguistics, education, sociology, anthropology, and psychology. An emphasis on literacy as a social phenomenon and a corresponding recognition of the connection between literacy and politics, policy, power, and disadvantage finds a particular focus in the arena of schooling. The role of language in reproducing social inequality via the institution of the school has been recognized and developed since the 1960s by major theorists such as Basil Bernstein (1924–2000) and Pierre Bourdieu (1930–2002). This focus, combined with the revival of the work of Lev Vygotsky and of the linguist Mikhail Bakhtin (1895–1975), provided the theoretical impetus for a conceptualization of literacy within a sociocultural framework.

While literacy has been perceived in the popular view as an unproblematic and school-based means of empowerment, this interdisciplinary research focus has identified the presence of multiple literacies embedded within different cultural contexts, as opposed to a single literacy. Schooling, as the site of transmission of a narrow but high-status range of literacy practices, is thus the major medium of social reproduction and the means by which thought and action can be constricted via the power of 'dominant literacies.' However, it also has the potential to liberate through (i) enabling access to powerful forms of literacy; and (ii) making explicit the inner workings of text and its use as a social instrument.

The recognition of multiple literacy practices

The work of Scribner & Cole (1981) is a classic early indication of the need to recognize the variety of literacy practices associated with different social and cultural contexts. Their influential study of the Vai in Liberia demonstrated the capacity of communities to develop literacy independently of schooling: the Vai writing system was informally transmitted while Arabic and English were taught formally. These different literacy practices corresponded with specific cognitive skills, which depended on the sociocultural contexts of their occurrence and usage. Importantly, Vai literacy did not equip learners with the same skills as those acquired by formally schooled learners. Similarly, Heath (1983) observed that African-American and working-class children in South Carolina interacted with text in ways which were different from those of children from white and middle-class families, and were in addition less compatible with the use of text in school settings. This disjunction between home or community and school gives rise to a pervasive perception of deficit rather than difference, with the result that 'vernacular' or community literacies have frequently been misinterpreted and excluded from definitions of legitimate literacy practices.

Consequences for pedagogy

Responses to this recognition of the importance of socially situated literacies have taken a number of courses. Many theorists and practitioners have argued that literacy teaching can and should be adapted to include and build on the differences that children bring to school, capitalizing, for instance, on multicultural backgrounds and gendered experiences. Such a response entails a challenge to the 'school standard' and a recognition of 'multiple literacies,' which acknowledges other, potentially more important, sources of literary competence drawn from community or vernacular literacies and personal literacies – ways of knowing and communicating that are based in individual experience and a sense of self. This approach, labeled as critical literacy, aims to make explicit to learners the ways in which texts support and transmit ideology, thus diffusing their power.

A contrasting, but not necessarily opposed, approach is that of the largely Australian tradition of systemic functional linguistics or genre theory (Christie & Misson, 1998). This group focuses on the functional use of language to construct meaning through the making of particular choices in particular contexts. Thus, school subjects and academic disciplines represent specific ways of reasoning and constructing knowledge. Gaining access to such knowledge and its reasoning processes is a question of learning its related language patterns, and taking command of the genres or text types in which knowledge is conveyed.

The development of school literacies

While popular views of literacy often portray it as a task of the primary school years, the development of genre command in fact extends throughout the compulsory years, and indeed into tertiary education where academic literacy is a major task in all disciplines. Early writing has characteristic speech-like dependence on personal narrative and material processes ("we went on the bus"), and is sequenced in the past tense as a string of clauses joined by frequent additive connections ("and then"). However, later writing exploits the ability of written text to pack information more densely within a single clause through the use of complex nominal groups ("the super-heated chromospheric gases") and grammatical metaphor ("cosmology involves the formation of theories about the universe which make specific predictions for phenomena that can be tested with observations").

Control of written language in this way accompanies the development of genre from narrative forms through recount and report to scientific, factual, and argument genres. Examples of the development of genre control can be found in Figures 1, 2, and 3. Literacy educators working in the genre-based tradition argue that, because genre is central to the construction of meaning, schooling should focus on making explicit the ways in which texts make meaning. Enabling pupils to manipulate consciously and even critique those genres that are controlled by dominant groups is seen as a means of re-distributing power, with particular benefits for those from disadvantaged backgrounds.

The impact of literacy

These insights from the fields of linguistics and anthropology underline the complexities of assessing both the cognitive impact and the skills base of literacy

in the development of a model of teaching and learning. Learning to write is a question of learning to control different socially embedded genres, as well as the more obvious skills of handwriting, spelling, punctuation, and sentence construction. Reading involves the making of strategic choices against the backdrop of a range of socially situated relationships with print: whether to read alone or with others; whether to read sequentially or to jump around within a text; whether to pay attention to detail or overall form; whether to decode individual words or memorize whole passages; how to interpret analogies and illustrations; how to treat texts according to their situation within scientific, humanities, and arts disciplines; and so on.

Some theorists have argued that literacy has direct and universal effects on the development of higher modes of thought, while others have suggested that it impacts on language development beyond the preschool years as a consequence of its development of conscious access to linguistic knowledge (Ravid & Tolchinsky, 2002). However, the development of literacy cannot easily be disengaged from its occurrence within a range of institutional and cultural settings and their related forms of education and socialization.

A major contribution of Vygotskian approaches has been the development of a theoretical bridge between individual psychological processes and the wider social context of literacy (Lee & Smagorinsky, 2000). Emphasizing the collaborative activity of teachers and students in the construction of knowledge, this perspective aims to describe the formation, operation, and maintenance of communities of practice within the school setting, and the role of individual learners and teachers within them. For example, Anne Haas Dyson studied child writers' co-construction of stories in a classroom community characterized by differences in ethnicity, class, and gender and their concomitant social tensions. These social structures and relationships were visible in both the stories and the group writing process itself. The teacher's role was to foster dialogue about these issues through the production and discussion of text, encouraging the children to consider their own roles and responsibilities as authors in the community, and the need to make genre and other textual choices with awareness of the consequences for others. Gordon Wells argues similarly for a transformation of schooling that recognizes the value of collaborative dialogical enquiry about text in building collective and individual understanding for both teachers and pupils.

Education policy and literacy

Wells' and Dyson's recognition that classroom communities are affected by the values and expectations

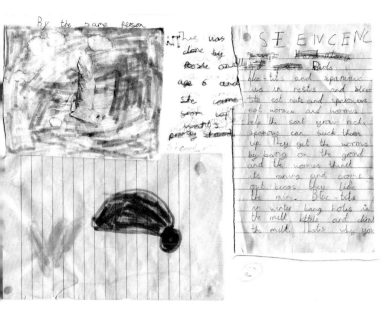

Figure 1. 'Science': spontaneous writing produced by a 6-year-old. The audience was her mother, known to the child to be interested in writing. Note that this is not writing produced in or for school. It shows an awareness of the science genre as information presentation and explanation. The drawings are integral to the piece, but the author feels bound to point out that they are "By the same person." She also adds a legend to stress her authorship, thus personalizing the work.

Insulations 6.1.97
What keeps tins warmest?

What we used:
tins, materials, thermometer, hot wat.
tymer
What we did:
We put the same amount of hot water in each tin. We tested the temperature every 10 minutes.

Material	2.25	2.35	2.45	2.55	3.05
newspaper	89°	69°	60°	49°	45°
tin foil	80°	64°	52°	46°	40°
fur fabric	85°	70°	54°	50°	45°
Yellow paper	85°	64°	54°	49°	41°
black paper	81°	64°	54°	50°	40°
polystyrene	82°	70°	57°	50°	45°
nothing	75°	59	58°	41°	37°

I predict newspaper will work best
I predict nothing will work worst
I was right.

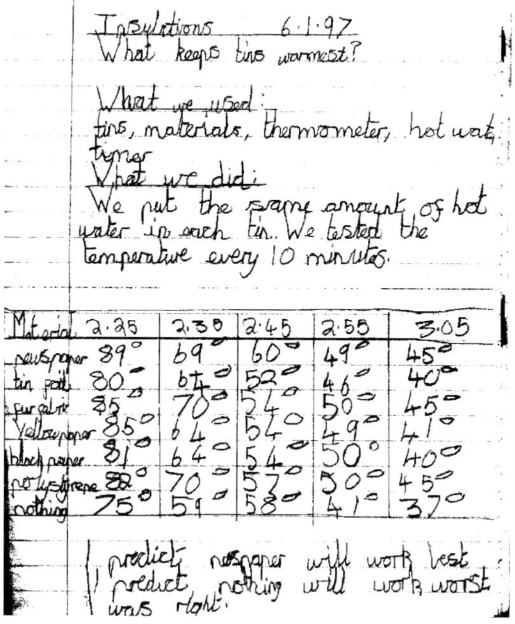

Figure 2. 'Insulations': science writing produced at school by an 8-year-old. Note that the science genre is more developed here in terms of the opening question, 'recipe-like' list of materials, past-tense report of "what we did," tabular presentation of results, and appropriate lexical choice of "predict" and "material." However, the author loses control of the genre in the concluding remarks, slipping into a personal account in the future tense and the final 'I was right' abandonment of the science lexicon and genre.

An Inspector Calls

The play is a platform for the debate; what role we should play in society? . . . Towards the end of the play the Inspector and therefore Priestley rounds up his views in a speech. ... This speech summarises everything that Priestley tries to tell us about society and its ills, and uses dramatic irony of the First World War to demonstrate the relevance of the Inspector's speech. . . . For the entirety of the story we, as characters and as the audience have assumed that the Inspector is in fact an Inspector, then it is worked out that he isn't in fact an Inspector. After the relief felt by some of the characters that the whole thing was just a hoax, the phone rings and the play ends with, '*That was the police. A girl just died ... And a police Inspector is on his way here- to ask some- questions-.*' The point of ending the play on a twist like this is to send the audience out of the play thinking 'who was the first Inspector?' and hence from this question, to question themselves on the way they act towards others and how small things can lead to horrific events.

Figure 3. Analysis of *An Inspector Calls*. English literature writing produced at school by a 14-year-old. These extracts from a more extended piece, word-processed in the original, show not only a developing command of the English literature analysis genre – note the lexical choice of "dramatic irony," "characters," and "audience," the impersonal tone (this is not the personal response that a younger writer might make), the use of italicized quotations, and the confident authorial voice – but also the ability to make observations on the genre and social context of *An Inspector Calls*. The author is aware of the power of writing to make social comment and of the importance of the reader's response.

of the institutions and society of which they are part, underlines the crucial role of education policy in literacy and schooling. As current theorizing about the social context of literacy suggests, the relationship between literacy and economic and cultural capital has significant and often controversial policy implications for pedagogy and the organization of schooling. An emphasis on the part played by literacy in national economic success and social inclusion has led to the widespread institution of literacy programs in both the developing and developed worlds. State intervention is particularly evident in the UK, South Africa, and Australia, where primary education programs based on testing and benchmarking have had considerable impact on the nature of schooling. Such initiatives may run counter to the recognition of literacy as socially situated practice, however.

The National Literacy Strategy in the UK has the potential for a more inclusive pedagogy with explicit aims and methods that involve and empower both learners and their parents. However, its implementation within a market-driven system that promotes the use of setting (banding) results in different educational experiences for different children, despite the strategy's emphasis on reducing underachievement. Thus, while the strategy draws pupils' attention to different genres, for instance, children in higher-ability sets are more likely to be introduced to ways of controlling and even critiquing genres, while those in lower sets are more likely, as Bernstein's theory suggests, to be controlled *by* genres, and subjected to a 'teaching to the test' curriculum of employability-related facts and skills.

Conclusions

The impact of information technology illustrates well the fact that literacy is socially and historically situated, and that literacy practices develop and change. In the case of computer literacy, the new practice is one that for many has been acquired through informal learning, although its absorption into the realm of dominant literacies means that it is now the subject of formal education and training and is highlighted in educational policy in many countries. Moreover, in these countries it is perceived as a major element of economic power.

A major focus for literacy researchers concerns the impact of information technologies on the geography of literacy, as practices shift in terms of focus and place. Thus, a new emphasis on knowing where to look for information as opposed to the possession of factual knowledge gained from books has to some extent shifted the power balance between home and school as private Internet access challenges the dominance of schooling, and in an increasing number of cases enables its total rejection. The influence of information technology on writing itself is less clear. Computer literacy and computer-supported informal learning in areas of special interest have introduced a number of new and powerful genres frequently used outside of school. However, a major question for literacy researchers is how and to what extent these new genres will be appropriated or assimilated by schooling in order to support its already existing aims, and, conversely, how far schooling will accommodate itself to the new 'techno-literacy,' for good or ill.

A related question concerns the extent to which schooling will change as a result of the recognition of and requirement for a wide range of literacy practices in the world of work. Policy and labor market contexts have a visible influence on the nature of schooling and an emphasis on 'life-long learning' is prevalent in developed economies, where new learning demands as a consequence of transfer within and between job spheres are common. Thus, a major contribution of schooling may be to develop skills of transfer in the form of the ability to ascertain the implicit rules, structures, value systems, and assumptions of new genres or practices. A question for both literacy researchers and educationalists is what this ability involves and how its development can be supported.

Perhaps the most important question for a society that concerns itself with life-long learning is that of the role of literacy education in achieving social inclusion. As both the genre and critical literacy theorists have shown, the resolution of power imbalance is a central concern. Literacy is not a single neutral skill located solely in the school. A final question concerns whether school practices can be changed in such a way as to accommodate pupils from whatever background, and, if they can, how this is to be done.

Questions

1. How has the advent of computer word-processing technology changed the process of writing? How has it influenced thinking and planning in the writing process? Has it created new literacy forms, new genres? Has it enhanced access to literacy?
2. How can we reconcile the tension between the need to build on personal literacies and the need to empower learners with access to more powerful genres? What bridges can we build between literacy practices in the home and community, and those of schooling?

3. What can we learn from the study of the development of writing and literacy that can be transferred to other spheres, such as mathematics and science – that is, what exactly are mathematical and scientific literacy, and how can we support their development?

See also:
Reading and writing; Socialization; Behavioral and learning disorders; Dyslexia; Anthropology; Education; Linguistics; Sociology: Lev S. Vygotsky

Further reading

Barton, D., Hamilton, M. and Ivanic, R. (eds.) (2000). *Situated Literacies: Reading and Writing.* London: Routledge.

Gallego, M. and Hollingsworth, S. (eds.) (2000). *What Counts as Literacy.* New York: Teachers College Press.

Snyder, I. and Lankshear, C. (2000). *Teachers and Technoliteracy: Managing Literacy, Technology and Learning in Schools.* St Leonard's, New South Wales: Allen & Unwin.

Selfhood

MICHAEL LEWIS

Introduction

The easiest way to describe what we mean by self is to give two examples, the first being cognitive, the second, emotional. When I say, "I know that you know I know it is Friday," the idea of a self is explicitly held to exist. That I know something about what you know, and that what you know is something I know, means that there is a self (in this case, *me*) that knows about another's knowledge, implying another and self-differentiation. It also implies that the other has knowledge about something I know. Only a creature with consciousness or self-awareness can have such a mental construct.

When I say "I am happy that I got an A in physics," I mean by such a statement that I am in an emotional state. There may or may not be physiological concomitants to that state, but I am aware of experiencing it. Moreover, that state and experience of mine – an internal process not necessarily visible to anyone else – is caused by my getting an A grade in an academic course. While animals and human newborns may have such emotional states as happiness or fear, it is most unlikely that they have an awareness of those states, since to experience them also requires a self awareness of itself.

What is a self?

Since the 1970s, we have come to learn about the development of a self. Nevertheless, considerable confusion exists around the term 'self-development,' since, for some, the term 'self' and its development speak to aspects of a self-system that does not require a mental construct. For others, it represents mostly the development of a mental construct. It is the difference between 'knowing' and 'knowing I know.' Thus, in order to understand the concept of self, we need to disentangle the common term, self, into at least two aspects. I have suggested we call these 'the machinery of the self' and 'the idea of me.' They have been referred to as objective self-awareness, which reflects the idea of me, and

subjective self-awareness, which reflects the machinery of self (M. Lewis, 1992). The same objective–subjective distinctions have been considered by Duval & Wicklund (1972). In any consideration of the concept of self, especially in regard to adult humans, it is important to keep in mind that both biological aspects exist. There is, unbeknownst to us most of the time, an elaborately complex machine that controls much of our behavior, learns from experience, has states, and affects our bodies, most likely including what and how we think. The processes are, for the most part, unavailable to us. What is available is the idea of me, a mental state.

Brain function and self

What is particularly impressive is recent research on brain function pointing to the possibility that different brain areas may be associated with these different functions. Thus, both the machinery of the self and the mental state involving the idea of me appear to be the consequences of different biological processes and locations. For example, LeDoux (1990) points to specific brain regions that may be responsible for different kinds of self-processes. Working with rats, he found that even after the removal of the auditory cortex, the animals were able to learn to associate an auditory signal and shock. After a few trials, they showed a negative emotional response to the sound, even though there was no auditory cortex. These findings indicate that the production of a fear state is likely to be mediated by sub-cortical structures, probably the thalamic-amygdala pathways.

Similar findings have been reported in humans, suggesting that states can exist without one part of the self experiencing them. Weiskrantz (1986) reported on a phenomenon called 'blindsight' in patients who lack the visual cortex, at least in one hemisphere. When asked if they could see an object placed in their blind spot, they reported not being able to (i.e., they did not have experience of the visual event). The self, reflecting on

Figure 1. Self-recognition.

itself, my recognition of what I know, the 'me' – the mental state – in fact, does not see. When, however, the patients were asked to reach for it, they showed the ability to do so, at least some of the time. Thus, they can 'see' the event, but cannot experience their sight. These findings, as well as work on split-brain patients, suggest that separate brain regions are responsible for the production and maintenance of both the machinery of self-processes and the mental state of me. A similar analysis involving memory has been suggested by Tulving (1985).

The self, then, is greater than the 'me,' the me being only a small portion of myself. Many features of the self exist early and exist as part of the system from birth or soon after. The idea of me – the knower who knows – is not developed until somewhere in the middle of the second year of life (M. Lewis, 1992).

Early features of the machinery of self

Two early features of the self are self-other differentiation and self-regulation. Both features are likely to be part of the machinery of the self, and not related to the idea of me. Certainly, by 3 months, and most likely from birth, an infant can differentiate self from other. Self-other differentiation also has associated with it a type of self-awareness. It is the self-awareness of elements of a system in communication with one another. This type of recognition and the self-other differentiation are part of the hardware of any complex system. T-cells recognize and differentiate themselves from foreign protein. A rat does not run into the wall, but runs around it. A newborn recognizes and responds appropriately to intersensory information. Therefore, we should not expect that these aspects of self are the differentiating

features when we compare widely different organisms. All organisms, as systems, should have these capacities.

What may distinguish organisms in regard to their system organization is the complexity of the machinery of these systems. What may differentiate humans from most other living organisms are not the functions of the system, but the ability to have mental states and, more specifically, the mental states related to the idea of me.

On the development of the mental state of me

There is clear evidence for the onset of this mental construct or self-representation by the middle of the second year of life. Self-recognition has been assessed by surreptitiously applying a spot of rouge to children's faces, and then observing whether they touch the mark when in front of the mirror. Figure 1 presents a picture of a 20-month-old child touching her nose. In normally developing children, this mark-directed behavior has been found to emerge reliably between 15 and 24 months of age and not before. Moreover, self-recognition appears to be a prerequisite for children's expression of various self-conscious emotions, such as embarrassment, empathic behavior, and altruism.

Based on these findings, it has been argued that self-recognition onset marks more broadly the emergence of self-awareness, reflecting children's understanding that they are objects in their own mental representations of the world (M. Lewis, 1997). Children also begin to use personal pronouns including 'me' and 'mine' by the latter part of the second year of life, which also provides a demonstration of the emergence of the idea of me (Hobson, 1990). In fact, one can observe two children playing together and see that one child will take a toy from the other, bring it toward herself, away from the other child, and say "mine." This action of bringing the toy toward the space occupied by the self and away from the space of the other child, and at the same time saying 'mine,' strongly suggests that language usage reflects a linguistic marker of self-awareness.

There is good reason to suppose that this meta-representation is necessary for pretense. A self-representation is necessary for there to be the dissociable relationship between the literal and pretend situation. Piaget (1962) understood that pretense requires an awareness of self in order for children to distinguish between what is reality and what is fantasy. The child feeding a doll imaginary food, or drinking an imaginary cup of liquid, must know that the act is not real. If children did not know that their actions on objects were not real, their play would not be pretense, but a hallucination. Pretense involves, in effect, a negation by the self that "this is what I pretend to be" rather than what it actually is. Similarly, Leslie (1987) included a self-representation in this model of pretend play and theory of mind (cf., the "I pretend –" function of the 'manipulator' in the model). Thus, the origins of a theory of mind involve a self pretending (i.e., the appearance of the self that knows that it knows and knows that its play is not real).

From a variety of theoretical perspectives, therefore, pretense is an early manifestation of the ability to understand mental states including one's own and those of others. The dissociative relationship (the dual representation of the literal and pretend situation) allows the child to distinguish between appearance and reality, and provides the cognitive basis for a theory of mind. Research by Piaget (1962) and subsequent investigators indicates that pretense emerges in children by the middle to latter part of the second year of life, thus suggesting that it too emerges at the same time as self-recognition and personal pronoun use.

In summary, there is evidence of the idea of me by the middle of the second year of life. This emergence is further supported by studies indicating that children who are mentally challenged with a mental age of less than 18 months are not able to recognize themselves in the mirror task. The emergence of self-recognition as a function of maturation can be found in the data on myelinization of the frontal lobes, which suggests that while it is not complete by the middle of the second year, it is well on its way (Staudt *et al.*, 1994).

Self-recognition, personal pronoun use, and pretend play all indicate the capacity for self-representation. Consistent with these findings is work that indicates children's emerging understanding of a theory of mind by the middle of the second year of life.

The self and cognitive development

Piaget's (1962) theory of sensorimotor intelligence did not emphasize the development of the self although it would appear that self-awareness is a necessary aspect of various representational abilities including pretense. In this regard, Bertenthal & Fischer (1978) found a high degree of correspondence between the development of object permanence and the development of various mirror-directed behaviors, including the mark-directed behavior indicative of self-recognition. Moreover, any theory of mind requires that the child have the ability to understand that their mind (me) is different from another's mind, and therefore a mental state or the idea of me. Such relationships are consistent with a central, perhaps organizing, role for self-knowledge in cognitive development (Lewis & Brooks-Gunn, 1979).

Figure 2a. Embarrassment.

Figure 2b. Shame.

Figure 2c. Pride.

The self and emotional development

Even more important is the finding that with the emergence of self-awareness, children become capable of intentions as well as allowing for the development of emotions such as embarrassment, shame, and pride, which in turn help the child in making plans and in choosing actions they wish to engage in. Figures 2a, b, and c present the emotions of embarrassment, shame, and pride, which emerge only after the development of self-awareness.

Conclusions

Self-awareness provides the scaffolding necessary for the beginning of a theory of mind as well as the source for the development of complex self-conscious emotions, which include empathy, embarrassment, shame, guilt, and pride. These abilities lead in turn to complex social relationships, built upon knowledge of others and their knowledge of you, as well as on the ability to put oneself in the place of the other.

New research on the development of the self suggests that, beside the role of the interaction between child and mother, the child's temperament plays an important role. Children with difficult temperaments, and who have problems in regulating their responses to stress, are those who are more likely to show early self-recognition, and are more likely to show more subsequent shame and guilt to failure. Such early individual differences may provide answers to questions of how school-age children cope with stress and failure.

Questions

1. What role does the social environment play in the emergence of the mental state of the idea of me?
2. What is the relationship between the early emergence of this mental state and the types of ideas about the self (good, bad, strong, weak, loved, not loved, etc.)?
3. What brain re-organization is necessary for the emergence of this mental state?
4. What is the role of infant characteristics such as differences in emotional reactivity and regulation in the emergence of this mental state?

See also:
Theories of the child's mind; Self and peer assessment of competence and well-being; The status of the human newborn; Cognitive development in infancy; Cognitive development beyond infancy; Emotional development; Moral development; Imitation; Play; Socialization; Temperament; James Mark Baldwin; Erik Erikson; Jean Piaget; Donald Winnicott

Further reading

Gazzaniga, M. S. (1988). Brain modularity: towards a philosophy of consciousness experience. In A. J. Marcel and E. Besearch (eds.), *Consciousness in Contemporary Science*. Oxford: Clarendon, pp. 218–256.

Meltzoff, A. N. (1995). Understanding the intentions of others: re-enactment of intended acts by 18-month-old children. *Developmental Psychology*, 31, 838–850.

Sex differences

JOYCE F. BENENSON

Introduction

Differences between males and females have been reported for virtually every human characteristic. Most of these sex differences are small, indicating large individual variability within each sex and much overlap between the sexes. Furthermore, for cognitive and social characteristics, the direction and magnitude of sex differences frequently are highly dependent on the context. Developing a meaningful model of the effect of sex differences on human development, therefore, requires first identifying those sex-differentiated characteristics that exert the greatest impact on human lives. Explanatory models then can be constructed and tested to account for the divergent developmental trajectories of these characteristics for each sex.

In the field of child development, little agreement currently exists regarding which sex-differentiated characteristics are most important for influencing the development of children of each sex. To complicate matters further, within the broader social sciences, some researchers argue that the category of sex itself is problematic. These researchers base their conclusions on individuals whose reproductive structures are not clearly male or female, whose gender identity (feeling that one is either male or female) or sex role (behavior considered typical for each sex) is discordant with their reproductive structures, and whose sexual relations do not occur solely with individuals of the other sex. The plasticity of chromosomal, hormonal, and internal and external reproductive structures and of gender identity, sex role, and sexual orientation have been acknowledged since John Money and Anke Ehrhardt's classic work on prenatal development. Cross-cultural reports of individuals with atypical gender identities, sex roles, or sexual orientations confirm the widespread variability that occurs within each sex category.

Nevertheless, the majority of individuals have reproductive structures typical for their sex as well as gender identities, sex roles, and sexual orientations that correspond with their reproductive structures. Because the continuation of the species requires that individuals with typical reproductive organs of each sex mate, the emphasis here is on differences between boys and girls who have typical reproductive structures, and corresponding gender identities and who are expected to reproduce in adulthood. Furthermore, the current emphasis is on identifying those cognitive and social characteristics that differentiate the sexes in their quests to survive, reproduce, and raise their own children.

Sex differences in growth rates and vulnerability

In most cultures, parents prefer to have sons over daughters. Accordingly, sons are more likely than daughters to receive resources, obtain an education, and hold positions of status within the family and larger society. Paradoxically, morbidity and mortality rates from deformities, disease, and injuries are higher for boys than girls, beginning even before birth and peaking in adolescence. The sex difference in survival rates is so robust that female infanticide is suspected when more male than female infants and children survive. Figure 1 displays infant mortality rates for diverse countries.

Part of the reason for males' greater vulnerability is believed to arise from females having two of the same sex chromosomes so that anomalies on one may be overridden by the other, and from males' slower rate of maturation. Although boys are slightly heavier and taller than girls from infancy onwards, girls are more advanced than boys in their rate of maturation. The sex difference in rate of maturation becomes most marked at adolescence when girls reach puberty on average two years before boys (Fig. 2).

Another major factor in boys' higher rates of morbidity and mortality stems from their universally greater risk-taking behavior that peaks in adolescence and young adulthood. Beginning in early childhood,

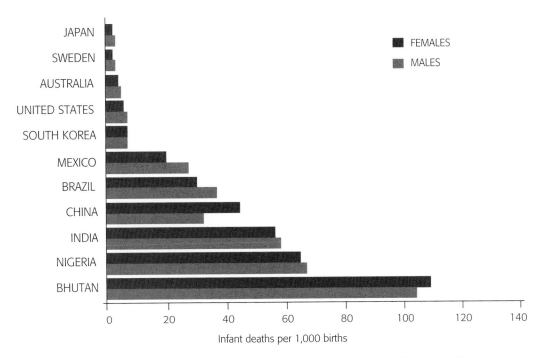

Figure 1. Cross-national data on infant mortality rates. From UNESCO, 2002. Infant mortality rates. *Teaching and Learning for a Sustainable Future*, version 2.0. Web document.

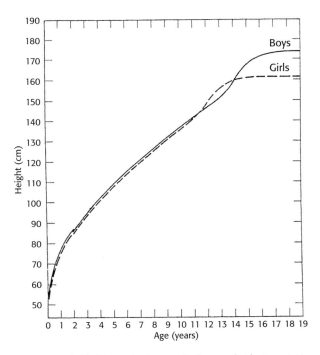

Figure 2. Typical height-attained curves for boys and girls. From J. M. Tanner, 1970. Physical growth. In P. H. Mussen, ed., *Carmichael's Manual of Child Psychology*, 3rd. edn. New York: Wiley, pp. 77–155.

boys take more risks than girls do. These risks include such behaviors as ignoring adult prohibitions, climbing in dangerous places or bicycling recklessly, physically aggressing against or directly verbally denigrating others, taking intellectual risks that could increase payoffs but reduce odds of success, and, when older, gambling, driving at high speeds, and engaging in sexual behaviors that facilitate contraction of diseases. Girls are more careful and remain closer to adults who can provide protection. When girls aggress against one another, they are much less likely than boys to employ physical or overt methods that could invite physically injurious retaliation from their opponents.

Robert Trivers' theory of parental investment suggests that sex differences in risk-taking behavior reflect the higher reproductive payoffs to males than females for outperforming one another and attracting females. Campbell's (2002) interpretation focuses on the greater role that females play compared to males in ensuring the survival of their children. Relative to males, risk-taking behavior in females not only does not enhance reproductive success, but also can be detrimental to the survival of children.

Sex differences in psychiatric disorders and symptoms

In childhood, serious psychiatric disorders are also more common in boys than girls (Table 1). In particular, boys are diagnosed with more language problems and externalizing disorders. Many of these difficulties relate to abilities important for formal schooling, generating stress in those boys from modern cultures who cannot cope with educational demands. It is not until adolescence that significant numbers of girls begin to exhibit serious psychiatric difficulties. At that time, girls compete to find a potentially reliable heterosexual partner. A young woman who can mate with a stable partner strongly enhances her children's academic and social outcomes. The stress of searching for a partner, then assuming primary responsibility for raising children, likely contributes to the cross-culturally consistent finding that, beginning in adolescence, females outnumber males in rates of internalizing disorders by more than 2 to 1.

Even at sub-clinical levels of symptoms under less stressful conditions, boys exhibit more externalizing symptoms including attention deficit hyperactivity disorder, conduct disorder, and oppositional defiant disorder, and girls more internalizing symptoms, such as major depressive disorder, separation anxiety disorder, and overanxious disorder. These consistencies suggest that each sex is predisposed to confront problems in differing ways. Aggressive behaviors may enhance reproductive success in males by contributing to elevation of internal status and defeat of external enemies, whereas depressive or anxious behaviors may enhance reproductive success in females by preventing harm from befalling dependent offspring.

For example, across cultures that differ enormously in absolute levels of homicide, males nevertheless commit over 90 percent of the homicides, with a peak in the rate of homicides in late adolescence and early adulthood. Martin Daly and Margo Wilson attribute this sex and developmental difference to male competition for sexual partners. Males also experience higher levels of self-esteem than females, though again absolute levels vary by culture and ethnicity. Wrangham (1999) believes that high levels of aggression and self-esteem may enhance successful engagement in intergroup warfare that traditionally has been the exclusive domain of males. In contrast, for females who are more responsible than males for the care of offspring, anxious behaviors are likely to enhance protection of offspring, whereas depressive behaviors may elicit help from others in caring for offspring.

One of the more uncommon but serious disorders to begin in childhood is gender identity disorder (GID), which is diagnosed when an individual is uncomfortable with his or her designated sex. Kenneth Zucker reports that signs of GID begin in early childhood, with prevalence rates six times higher for boys than girls. Children with GID compared to controls wish to be the other sex, dress up like the other sex, engage in cross-sex fantasy play, and prefer to play with other-sex peers, and concomitantly experience difficulties in peer interaction and general behavioral problems. GID in early childhood is predictive of homosexuality in adulthood.

Table 1. Sex ratios for psychiatric disorders in childhood and adolescence reported in the *DSM-IV*. (From C. M. Hartung and T. A. Widiger, 1998. Gender differences in the diagnosis of mental disorders: conclusions and controversies of the *DSM-IV*. *Psychological Bulletin*, 123, 260–278.)

Disorder	Sex ratio
Mental retardation	1.5M:1F
Reading disorder	1.5–4M:1F
Mathematics disorder	–
Written expression disorder	–
Developmental coordination disorder	–
Expressive language disorder	M > F
Mixed language disorder	M > F
Phonological disorder	M > F
Stuttering	3M:1F
Autistic disorder	4–5M:1F
Rett's disorder	F only
Childhood disintegrative disorder	M > F
Asperger's disorder	M > F
ADHD	4–9M:1F
Conduct disorder	M > F
Oppositional defiant disorder	M > F
Pica	–
Rumination	M > F
Feeding disorder	M = F
Tourette's disorder	1.5–3M:1F
Chronic motor or vocal tic	–
Transient tic disorder	–
Encopresis	M > F
Enuresis	M > F
Separation anxiety disorder	F > M
Selective mutism	F > M
Reactive attachment disorder	–
Stereotypic movement disorder	M > F

'–' indicates no data available.

Sex differences in schooling and on cognitive tests

Schooling

As previously reviewed, the structure of formal education is more conducive to learning for girls than boys. From early childhood onward, compared to boys, girls maintain closer proximity to teachers, comply more with adult-generated rules, work and study harder, and exhibit more concern about their school performance. They also receive higher grades in elementary through high school, and, in cultures where they are permitted to do so, attain higher levels of education. In contrast, compared to girls, boys experience higher rates of both serious language and externalizing disorders. More generally, boys have greater difficulties sustaining attention, as well as remaining sedentary and inhibiting their actions, all of which interfere with learning and create discipline problems for teachers.

Cognitive tests

There are more boys than girls who receive extreme scores on cognitive tests. Although boys are at least four times more likely than girls to suffer from serious mental handicaps, a sub-set also obtains slightly higher scores than girls on general intelligence tests (e.g., Wechsler Intelligence Scales for Children or Adults) and achievement tests (e.g., Scholastic Aptitude Test). Although the cognitive abilities that underlie scores on these tests are not well understood, current cross-cultural research confirms what Eleanor Maccoby and Carol Nagy Jacklin reported in the 1970s: girls excel at some verbal tasks, whereas boys are superior at some mathematical and visual-spatial tasks.

Not only do girls suffer from fewer serious language disorders than boys, but Kimura (1999) reports that girls also learn language more quickly, are superior at grammar and spelling, read and write more proficiently through high school, and excel at verbal memory tasks, such as word or digit recall or memory for the content of material. In mathematics, girls are superior at computational skills, whereas boys excel at understanding and applying concepts or problem-solving. At the very highest level of math performance, boys outnumber girls by as much as 10 to 1. On visual-spatial tasks, whereas girls have a better memory for where specific objects are located, boys outperform girls on mental rotation tasks as when, for example, the same two-dimensional object must be identified from differing angles. Boys also are somewhat superior to girls on spatial perception tasks, such as estimating the position of water in a tilted glass.

Some research suggests that boys and girls may solve the same task using differing approaches. Sex differences in navigational skills provide an interesting example. Research suggests that girls and women are more likely than males to refer to landmarks to find their way. In contrast, boys and men use distances and directions, and learn to navigate more quickly. Sex differences in verbal, mathematical, spatial, and navigational skills likely reflect adaptations by males and females that differentially enhanced survival and reproductive success in the environment in which humans evolved.

Sex differences in activities and social organization

Across cultures, the largest sex differences are found in preferences for interests and occupations. By early childhood, boys are more interested than girls in mechanical objects and how they work. At the same time, when asked what they would like to be when they grow up, boys select a wider variety of occupations, such as construction worker, doctor, pilot, soldier, or fireman, whereas girls mention teacher, nurse, or mother. From early adolescence onward, males are more likely than females to demonstrate interest in subjects and vocations that involve interaction with inanimate objects and which require the use of mathematics, spatial skills, and computer programming. In contrast, females are more interested than males in subjects and vocations that focus on directly helping other people. Despite women entering many previously all-male professions in Western societies, large sex differences remain in the choices of subjects and professions made by children, adolescents, and adults.

Similarly, consistent sex differences in social behaviors are found in developmental preferences for activities. Girls are more likely than boys to respond to vulnerability in others, beginning as early as the newborn period when girls cry more than boys to another newborn's distress. Between 2 and 3 years of age, girls exhibit greater interest than boys in doll play, dressing up, and preparing food. By 3–5 years, in traditional cultures, girls care for younger siblings. Likewise, in Western societies, girls' social play contains caregivers (mothers, teachers) who respond to vulnerable individuals (babies, younger siblings, or other helpless animals or people). At the same time, girls enact the roles of vulnerable and attractive women (princesses, Barbie dolls) who search for a powerful person to marry and protect them.

By middle childhood and continuing into adolescence, girls are more likely than boys to take turns talking about mutual vulnerabilities and supporting one another. Girls also learn to soften conflicting perspectives with one another by employing mitigated speech forms (e.g., "do you want to play with this?", "let's both go there"), and indirect aggression (e.g., telling a third person what a friend has done wrong, using non-verbal gestures to express disagreement). Girls become interested in media (television, movies, computer games) that portray familial and romantic interactions, as well as in adventure stories and some sports. By adolescence, girls discuss in great depth their own and others' romantic and sexual relationships.

In contrast to girls, from the newborn period onward, boys engage in more gross motor activity, and quickly become more interested in physical domination of others and protection against vulnerability. By 2–3 years of age, boys are more likely to play with vehicles (cars, airplanes, bulldozers), weapons (guns, swords), and tools (hammers, saws). By 3–5 years, Robert Malina reports that boys hold a small advantage over girls in a number of gross motor abilities such as running and kicking, but particularly throwing. Boys' social play

Boys

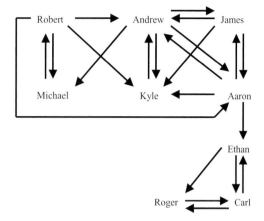

Girls

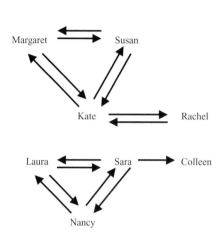

Figure 3. Typical sex differences in social organization (arrows indicate friendship choices) as found in a class of 10-year-old children. Adapted from J. F. Benenson, 1990. Gender differences in social networks. *Journal of Early Adolescence*, 10, 472–495.

revolves around physically powerful 'supermen' (good soldiers, cowboys, policemen) who vanquish enemies (enemy soldiers, ferocious animals, aliens). Simultaneously, they engage in rough-and-tumble play, which requires physical dominance and submission.

By middle childhood and continuing thereafter, boys enjoy adventure games and stories replete with physical feats in which 'good' guys destroy 'bad' guys using vehicles, weapons, and tools. Unlike girls, competition is often overt. For example, boys denigrate each other using direct speech forms ("you're stupid," "do it my way"), and play directly competitive physical sports. After puberty, boys far surpass girls in the development of motor abilities and skills that require strength, speed, and physical power, facilitating even greater domination of others. They also begin to develop romantic and sexual relationships.

Cross-cultural evidence demonstrates that the social organization of the two sexes also differs with both parents and peers. From early childhood through adolescence, girls spend more time than boys in proximity to mothers and, when needed, serve as maternal substitutes. In contrast, boys spend more time than girls with fathers, when fathers are present. The same-sex peer relationships of boys are more segregated from families, adult authority figures, and peers of the other sex than those of girls. Fathers also are more likely to behave punitively toward sons as opposed to daughters who deviate from standard same-sex peer group behavior. In general, fathers are more concerned than mothers with appropriate sex-typed behavior in their children.

With same-sex peers, beginning in middle childhood, girls are more likely than boys to interact with one friend at a time. Dyadic relationships are exclusive and egalitarian. In adolescence, girls also often join cliques. Clique membership is related to status, both of which are associated with degree of attractiveness to boys. Unlike girls, after age 5, boys interact in dense peer groups in which boys' friendships are interconnected (Fig. 3). Boys' groups are hierarchically organized with status usually based on relative physical prowess and alliances.

Sex differences in interests, activities, and relationships likely reflect the unfolding of differential strategies that males and females adopted in the environment in which they evolved for enhancing personal survival, reproductive success, and the well-being of offspring. Nonetheless, variations in the ecological constraints in the environments in which humans evolved would have required that each sex retain flexible strategies. Availability of food resources and of kin, as well as number of same- and other-sex peers who were competitors or allies, are likely candidates for factors that strongly influenced variability in strategies utilized by each sex.

Proximate determinants of sex differences

The major thrust of explanatory models of sex-differentiated characteristics focuses on disentangling proximate biological from environmental influences. This enterprise is riddled with complexities, however.

Table 2. Outline of stages of prenatal sexual differentiation.

Typical female	Typical male	Atypical examples
Sex Chromosomes		
XX	XY	XO, XXX, XXXX (female) XYY, YYYY, XXY, XXXY (male)
Bi-potential Gonad		
2 Ovaries	2 Testes	1 ovary + 1 testis; 2 of each; 1 ovitestis; 2 ovitestes
Hormones		
Estrogens > androgens + De-masculinizing hormones	Androgens > estrogens + De-feminizing hormones	Absence of estrogens or androgens results in female development; absence of de-masculinizing or de-feminizing hormones results in reproductive structural anomalies
Internal Reproductive Structures and Brain Morphology		
Female internal reproductive structures (e.g., fallopian tubes, uterus, upper vagina), + female brain structures (e.g., smaller pre-optic area of hypothalamus)	Male internal reproductive structures (e.g., Wolffian ducts, seminal vesicles, vas deferens) + male brain structures (e.g., larger pre-optic area of hypothalamus)	Combination of male and female internal reproductive structures or neither male nor female reproductive structures; changes in brain structures
Undifferentiated Genital Tubercle		
Female external genitalia (e.g., lower vagina, clitoris)	Male external genitalia (e.g., penis, scrotum)	Examples of viable mismatches: XX + excess androgens produces female internal reproductive structures (can bear children), male brain structures, penis; XY + insensitivity to androgens + de-feminizing hormones produces no clear internal reproductive structures (sterile), female brain morphology, clitoris

For example, as Maccoby (1998) emphasizes, it is difficult to assess the influence of parents on the development of children's sex-typed behavior. Parent-child interactions are based on continually evolving adjustments between the parent, other environmental factors, and a child's biological transformations. Ethical considerations prohibit experimental manipulation of these factors. Reviewing data from rhesus monkeys, however, Wallen (1996) provides clear experimental evidence that sex-differentiated characteristics result from a combination of hormones and rearing environments. Even in rhesus monkeys whose behaviors are highly sexually dimorphic, most sex differences vanish without a specific combination of hormones and rearing environment.

Researchers who have studied human prenatal development are able to document the effects of chromosomes, hormones, and brain morphology on a number of significant sex differences (Table 2). Even after birth, postnatal and pubertal hormonal surges further influence sex-differentiated characteristics. The whole system is highly malleable, however, and mismatches can occur so that one stage results in female development and another in male development in the same individual. Marcia Collaer and Melissa Hines reviewed the influence of hormones on human sex differences based on natural mismatches that occurred during development or through hormonal treatments. Evidence is presented that hormones (masculinizing, de-masculinizing, feminizing, and de-feminizing) influence rate of maturation, gender identity, sexual orientation, language difficulties, and performance on tasks involving attention, verbal memory, spatial rotation and perception, and mathematics. In addition, hormones also affect behaviors that once were considered to be determined solely by the social environment, including activity level, rough-and-tumble play, physical aggression, risk-taking behavior, assertiveness, preference for play with guns and transportation vehicles versus with dolls and dressing-up, level of interest in families or athletics, play with same-sex versus other-sex peers, and self-esteem.

At present, it is unknown how much normal variations in hormonal levels in typical males and females influence sex differences in these characteristics, or to what extent hormones as opposed to other biological or environmental factors influence these characteristics. For example, the number of older same-sex siblings influences sexual orientation in typical boys, but the mechanism remains unclear.

Research on non-human mammals indicates that the timing of hormonal influxes influences sex-differentiated characteristics, suggesting that one individual can be more like typical males on some characteristics and more like typical females on others. In addition to hormones, other biological factors such as extra chromosomes have been associated with physical growth, motor skills, learning difficulties, and psychiatric disorders. The hypothalamus also appears to regulate sex-differentiated characteristics though its function is less understood.

Contextual factors clearly are also necessary for sex differences to appear, though no compilation yet exists of those that influence specific characteristics. Developmental psychologists traditionally focused on the reinforcement that parents provide for sex-appropriate behaviors, as well as on self-labeling that motivates children to identify with adults of the same sex. Cross-cultural studies by Beatrice Whiting and Carolyn Pope Edwards demonstrate that boys and girls learn sex-typed activities from their same-sex parents, indicating that relationships with same- versus other-sex parents influence sex-typed characteristics. Maccoby (1998) emphasizes the importance of same-sex peers for sex-typed behavior. For example, studies show that frequency of interaction with same-sex peers enhances activity level and rough-and-tumble play, and reduces compliance with adult directives for boys, whereas the reverse pattern occurs for girls. For both sexes, interaction with several same-sex peers at a time, as opposed to with only one other peer, augments direct competition and diminishes responsiveness to others' needs. Because boys are more likely than girls to interact in groups, whereas girls spend more time with one other individual, direct competition is enhanced in boys and responsiveness in girls.

Sociologists and anthropologists focus on broader contextual factors. Polygynous households, cultures that discriminate against women, and socioeconomic status influence many critical sex differences such as mortality rates and levels of education for girls, number and spacing of children, as well as rates of male physical aggression. Sex differences have also been reported to be higher for Whites than for African-Americans and Asians on some social variables, such as degree of assertiveness in speech. Until instruments are developed that can measure biological factors and studies include precise information on contextual factors, however, understanding how these interactions operate remains a goal of future research.

Evolutionary biologists believe that males and females evolved brains that differed to the extent that each sex confronted unique problems in the environment in which humans evolved. Trivers has shown that non-human males and females differ in the energy they expend on parenting versus mating effort in order to maximize their reproductive success. For humans, females are more limited than males in the number of children they can produce, and hence invest more heavily in each of their offspring. Competition between females occurs over access to mates who can provide resources for themselves and their children. Human males can produce more offspring than females, and therefore invest more heavily in mating effort by competing with other males for resources and status and concomitant access to females. The most successful males can inseminate many females, and often also provide many resources as well as protection for their reproductive partners and offspring. Besides competition, however, cooperation amongst males is also crucial for success in intragroup and intergroup conflicts. Cooperation amongst females with kin and mates is important for the survival and success of offspring.

Aletha Huston summarizes evidence from human children and adolescents indicating that the largest sex differences occur in preferences for differing academic, cognitive, and social activities, as well as in the expression of psychopathology. These childhood sex differences can be viewed as precursors of differing roles for mothers and fathers. Cross-culturally, human mothers invest more than fathers in vulnerable offspring, and fathers engage in greater intragroup and intergroup dominance and aggression, as well as invest more heavily in extra-familial activities.

Nevertheless, the idea that the female and male brains have evolved to pursue differing strategies is not without its critics. Anne Fausto-Sterling is a strong advocate of the position that sex is a social construction that develops with age, changes with the context, and is not necessarily internally consistent. For example, having male or female reproductive structures may not correspond with gender identity, sex role, marital status, sexual orientation, or typical sex-typed personality beliefs and displays. These positions are not mutually exclusive, however. Most researchers believe that the brain exerts a significant influence on the degree and kind of many sex-differentiated characteristics, and that the environment is crucial for these characteristics to develop and remain stable.

Conclusions

Researchers continue to attempt to characterize in more depth how the two sexes differ in their cognitive structures and social behaviors, and to provide explanatory mechanisms that include both biological and environmental factors. Developmental psychologists are beginning to examine longitudinally the development of sex-typed cognition and social behaviors, taking into account both variations in prenatal and postnatal hormonal levels and their interactions with specific contexts, such as degree of parental sex-typing or frequency of interaction with same-sex peers. Anthropologists compare the structure of societies, including marital forms and stability, residence patterns, and the availability of defensible resources, to determine how the roles of men and women develop.

Researchers who study non-human primates are able to examine both experimentally and under naturalistic conditions the influence of hormonal factors and different rearing environments on sex differences in various species who vary in their ecological niches. Interest in differences within each sex as well as between the sexes is steadily growing as researchers develop richer characterizations of sex differences in cognition and social behaviors along with more complex biological and environmental proximate and evolutionary explanations.

Questions

1. How do specific environments, such as being raised by same-sex or other-sex parents or having same-sex or other-sex siblings or friends, interact with prenatal levels of hormones to produce individuals who differ in their degree of sex-typing or in specific sex-typed behaviors?
2. How does investment in offspring versus in mating vary with availability of resources and the marital and occupational structure of a society for each sex?
3. How much do the outcomes of cooperation and competition with kin and peers influence the reproductive success of males versus females?
4. What was the social and physical environment to which early female and male humans adapted that produced current sex-typed neurological structures?
5. Which aspects of sex-differentiated behaviors are the most biologically 'hard-wired' and least amenable to environmental input?

See also:
Cross-cultural comparisons; Normal and abnormal prenatal development; The status of the human newborn; Motor development; Social development; Language development; Aggressive and prosocial behavior; Intelligence; Peers and siblings; Play; Schooling and literacy; Socialization; Temperament; 'At-risk' concept; Behavioral and learning disorders; Child depression; Sociology; Milestones of motor development and indicators of biological maturity

Further reading

Geary, D. C. (1998). *Male, Female: The Evolution of Human Sex Differences*. Washington, DC: American Psychological Association.

Halpern, D. (2000). *Sex Differences in Cognitive Abilities*, 3rd. edn. Hillsdale, NJ: Erlbaum.

Moffitt, T. E., Caspi, A., Rutter, M. and Silva, P. A. (2001). *Sex Differences in Antisocial Behavior*. New York: Cambridge University Press.

Siblings and peers

JUDY DUNN

Introduction

Children's relationships with their siblings and peers have been the focus of a great increase in research in recent years. Among the several sources of this interest, three stand out. The first is that interaction between children has special importance in children's social understanding, relationships, and moral development – an idea that has a key place in Piagetian theory. Children's relations with their peers and siblings have been studied as a context in which children make intellectual advances (e.g., mindreading and understanding emotions as a window on their understanding of others, their perceptions of themselves, and on the nature of their relationships).

The second source of interest is the growing evidence that there are associations between troubled peer and sibling relationships, and concurrent and later adjustment problems; this has led to a large literature on peer rejection, aggression and bullying, and social isolation, and on the protective nature of friendships. The third source of interest is more controversial: it concerns an argument that it is children's relationships with their peers, rather than their parents, that form the key influence on the development of individual differences (Harris, 1998).

Siblings

Most people grow up with siblings (around 80 percent in the UK and USA). And our sibling relationships are probably the longest-lasting we will have in our lives. Scientific research on siblings is relatively recent, but it has raised some general challenges to developmental psychologists. There are four key issues. Firstly, do brothers and sisters influence each other's development, and if so how? We will take the case of links with adjustment, as an example. Secondly, continuing with the theme of adjustment, we ask in what ways siblings and parents influence each other in this respect. Thirdly, why do brothers and sisters differ so strikingly from one another, even though their genetic resemblance is 50 percent, and they grow up in the same family? Fourthly, can the study of siblings change our picture of children's social understanding?

Sibling influence: the example of adjustment

Sibling relationships differ very strikingly in their qualities: some siblings are hostile and irritable, others are affectionate, concerned, and constant companions. Emotion is freely expressed between siblings, and this can be aggression or affection. Moreover, not only do siblings share their parents – a source of potential problems – but they know each other very well. Thus, the nature of the sibling relationship suggests it may well be important in fostering aggression, in feelings of inadequacy and low self-esteem. And research now confirms that siblings are likely to exert influence on both 'externalizing' problems such as aggression and conduct disorder, and on 'internalizing' problems such as worrying, anxiety, and low self-esteem (Brody, 1998). The influence is both from older to younger and vice versa. Children who have 'deviant' peers also begin to draw their siblings into these groups during middle childhood.

Siblings and parents

How far are these associations with adjustment linked to parent-child relationships, rather than solely sibling effects? Children are extremely sensitive to differences in the ways they and their siblings are treated. Thus, in families in which more attention, affection, and less discipline is shown by a parent to one sibling than to another ('differential parenting'), there is a higher probability of children's adjustment difficulties. This effect is particularly clear in families under stress, such as those which have recently suffered parental separation, those with children who are sick or have disabilities. Of course, in all these studies, the links

374

between adjustment and children's relationships are correlational, and we cannot come to firm conclusions about the direction of causal effects.

Psychologists disagree about how far and in what ways parent-child relationships influence those between siblings. Is the security of children's attachments to their parents linked to the quality of their sibling relationships? Yes, according to some studies, which show warm positive relationships between parent and child are linked to friendly ones between siblings. But plenty of questions remain: is it that parents influence sibs, or that sibs influence parents? What are the processes linking the relationships? These are likely to operate at varied, different levels. One new direction of research has shown that how parents talk to their very young children about others – including new siblings – influences the relationship between them. Another research direction has shown how parents' own relationships with each other influence their children.

Why do siblings differ? Challenges to ideas on family influence

A second theme in recent sibling research with general implications for psychology has grown from the evidence that siblings differ from one another, notably in personality, adjustment, and psychopathology (Dunn & Plomin, 1990). This evidence challenges the conventional view of family influence, as the features of family life thought to be important (parents' well-being, educational background, neighborhood, family social class) are apparently shared by the siblings, who in spite of this grow up to be very different from one another. How can this be?

One answer seems to be that the sources of influence on individual differences appear to operate within families. The message is not that families are unimportant, but that experiences *within the same family* are very different for the children growing up in that family. It is a major challenge for those studying families to work out how and why these experiences differ among brothers and sisters. One response has been to emphasize peers – rather than families – as the key influence on individual differences (Harris, 1998).

Can the study of siblings change our view of children's social understanding?

Observations of young siblings teasing, cooperating, showing concern for each other, and sharing an imaginary world in make-believe play, have transformed our picture of the development of social understanding in young children. In the emotional drama and the familiarity of their interactions with each other, they show powers of reading each other's minds and feelings much earlier than the understanding shown in more formal assessments. So the study of siblings has contributed to our understanding of children's discovery of the mind, by offering a new perspective on their abilities. One general lesson from the sibling research is that social processes are likely to play a significant role in shaping the remarkable individual differences in what children understand about each other.

Peers

Children's relationships with peers range from intimate friendships to passing acquaintanceship. From the early years, they are members of both close relationships and of larger groups, and these relationships are of central importance to their well-being, and their self-esteem. Moreover, within peer groups, children's relationships differ markedly in closeness, conflict, and companionship (Rubin, Bukowski, & Parker, 1998). One major theme in research on peers has been the evidence that problems with peers in middle childhood are associated with later adjustment difficulties; this has added urgency to the need to clarify what the processes might be that link different kinds of peer relations to problematic outcomes.

Relationships with the peer group: popularity and rejection

Children's relationships with the others in their class or peer group have been extensively studied through getting children to nominate those whom they like and dislike. We now know that there is much heterogeneity in classifications such as 'rejected.' For instance, children who are aggressive-and-rejected have different worries and social concerns than those who are rejected but not aggressive. How stable are such 'status' classifications? With younger children, they are not very stable. However, by 10 years old, one study reports that 50 percent of children classed as rejected remained so for a further five years. Popular children at all developmental stages are reported to be helpful, friendly, and considerate. There are, however, developmental changes in the behavior linked to rejection: aggressive actions by preschoolers are not necessarily linked to rejection as they are in middle childhood. Social withdrawal becomes more clearly related to rejection as children grow up. There is disagreement still about the causal links between peer relationships and adjustment problems. Some argue that rejection leads to withdrawal, others that withdrawal itself results in not being liked by peers.

Peer relationships and social understanding

Are children unpopular and rejected because they have problems in social understanding – in reading the emotions and intentions of their peers? There is some evidence for this. Aggressive children tend to misperceive the intentions of others and to interpret ambiguous acts by other children as aggressive, and to react aggressively themselves. Research into bullying, which is distressingly common among school-age children, has shown that disruptive behavior can be used in socially manipulative ways, and may reflect the goals of bullies, rather than deficits in social competence.

At a more general level, psychologists have asked whether children's experience with their peers has special significance for the development of their understanding of other people. It has been suggested that in conflict with peers and siblings, cognitive and moral development may be particularly fostered. It is clear that how children act when they are in conflict can be an illuminating window on what they understand about social rules, and about other people's feelings and intentions, but whether such arguments play a causal role in developing understanding is less firmly established.

Peers in educational contexts

The idea that interaction between peers can be intellectually important has led to a focus on learning from peers in educational contexts – by peer tutoring, peer cooperative learning, and peer collaboration (consisting of two novices working together on a problem in which neither takes the lead). These three types of interaction, which differ in the degree of symmetry and mutuality between the peers, have all been shown to be linked to intellectual gains, but little is known about how far the effects generalize beyond the particular setting.

Friendships

Children's friendships can begin early (e.g., in the second year of life). They are not invariably fleeting, but can last for several years even in the pre-school period (Howes, 1996). They can differ notably in quality, from very intimate relationships in which secrets and problems are shared, to close companions who chiefly do things together. Sex differences have been noted, with girls in particular valuing shared intimacy. Children can show their most mature and sophisticated behavior in the context of their close friendships, in terms of their emotional understanding and moral sensibility.

Friendship and adjustment

Friendships can play a key supportive role in children's lives. This has been shown, for example, in studies of children's adjustment to school (which goes more smoothly if they make the transition with a friend), and their response to the birth of a sibling (friendship buffers children as young as 3 from the stress of family changes involved). Separation from friends can induce stress and anxiety, even among preschoolers. And studies of children's perspectives on their experience of parental separation and family change show that friends provide the major sources of communicating and sharing confidences about problems.

Links between friendship and adjustment are particularly clear in middle childhood. Children without friends report loneliness and unhappiness regardless of their 'peer status,' their popularity and rejection within the class. Troubled children have difficulty forming and maintaining friendships. The question of what is the causal direction here remains unanswered, as it does with regard to difficult parent-child relationships.

Peers, friends, and parents

The question of whether and how family relationships are linked to children's relationships with peers is of much current interest. There has been a particular focus on attachment. Children who are insecurely attached to their parents as toddlers are at higher risk for difficulties with aggressive and antisocial behavior, and with their peers later on. However, again the causal connection between these relationships is not clear. And where children have been followed from infancy through to middle childhood, some intriguing patterns of developmental change are reported. Links between other aspects of children's family lives, such as discipline, parental mental health, difficult marital relations and family disruption, and negative life events, have all been linked to children's difficulties in peer relationships. There is much less research into links between parent-child relationships and close friendships. What evidence we have indicates that securely attached children are likely to form close and rewarding friendships.

Conclusions

We have learned a great deal in the last decades about how much children's relationships with other children matter to them, and to their development. What issues remain of particular importance? Answers can be found when addressing the questions for discussion. All are important and practical questions that deserve our attention.

Questions

1. How significant are early individual differences in friendship and in peer relationships for later development, and do they play the major role Harris (1998) has suggested? If so, where does genetics fit in the story?

2. How does the role of the family *differ* in its significance for children's peer relationships in other cultures and class communities? Our sources of information are, to date, very narrow. What family processes, besides attachment quality, are important?

3. At a practical level, how can interventions to help children with peer problems be made both effective and realistic?

See also:
Theories of the child's mind; Self and peer assessment of competence and well-being; Social development; Moral development; Aggressive and prosocial behavior; Parenting and the family; Play; Sex differences; Socialization

Further reading

Bukowski, W. M., Newcomb, A. F. and Hartup, W. W. (eds.) (1996). *The Company they Keep: Friendship in Childhood and Adolescence.* Cambridge: Cambridge University Press.

Dunn, J. (1993). *Young Children's Close Relationships.* Newbury Park: Sage Publications.

Sleep and wakefulness

PETER H. WOLFF

Introduction

Biologists have long recognized that complex organisms do not operate like steady-state systems. Rather, they will frequently switch from one marginally stable pattern of organization to another. The relative stability of states and the phenomenon of state transitions reflect the influence of many factors with interactive effects. Living things, unlike clocks or automobiles, often will switch from one state to another over relatively short intervals, either spontaneously or in response to environmental perturbations. In the course of such state transitions, the individual's sensitivity to stimuli and behavioral repertoire, and indeed the relations between stimuli and the individual's behaviors, change quantitatively or qualitatively (Kauffman, 1993; Wolff, 1993). Thus, organisms exhibit all the attributes of complex self-organizing systems whose states, state transitions, and variable, non-linear input-output characteristics are sensitive to the organism's initial conditions.

In humans, this non-linearity is clearly illustrated by the dramatic changes of spontaneous behavior and responsiveness as subjects alternate between sleep and waking states. This state-dependence of behavior is probably expressed most clearly during the early months after birth, such that the concept of behavioral state affords a useful framework for investigating the development of the sleep-waking cycle in human infants.

Historical background

Kleitman's pioneering investigations (Kleitman, 1963) have over the past fifty years inspired a spate of physiological and behavioral studies on the development of sleep and waking in human infants. The majority of these studies have concluded that a minimum taxonomy of four 'basic' behavioral states of quiet sleep, active sleep, waking, and crying, is essential if one is to make sense of the infant's apparently random fluctuations in physiological parameters and observable behavior. Moreover, they agree that four behavioral criteria, comprising the pattern of respiration (regular or irregular), status of eyes (open or closed), quantity of movements, and vocalization, are sufficient to discriminate between the behavioral states of infants (Prechtl & O'Brien, 1982).

Sleep

During the first week after birth, healthy fullterm newborns sleep on average for 16–17 hours of every 24-hour day, and are awake – or at least, not asleep – for at most 7–8 hours. The total duration of sleep per day remains relatively constant over the first six months (about 15 hours per day), but the organization and distribution of epochs of sleep and waking are extensively transformed. During the first week, infants sleep on average for 4 hours at a time, and they are awake (or at least not asleep) for at most 2 hours. By the end of the fourth month, they sleep without interruption for up to 8–9 hours and stay awake without crying for up to 4 hours (Fig. 1). At the same time, they have adjusted more or less successfully to the diurnal sleep-waking patterns of their parents, although they still take extended naps during the day.

Such studies have also demonstrated that the sleep of infants, adults, and for that matter most mammals, consists of at least two qualitatively different behavioral states. They are variously referred to as quiet, non-REM, slow-wave, or state 1 sleep on one hand, and active, Rapid Eye Movement (REM), or dream-sleep on the other hand (for behavioral state criteria of sleep, see Kleitman 1963; Prechtl & O'Brien, 1982; Wolff, 1987). This demonstration has motivated many systematic investigations on the functions and neurophysiological substrates of the different sleep states, and it has stimulated renewed interest in the age-old question of why we must sleep at all in order to survive. The demonstration that infants behave in qualitatively

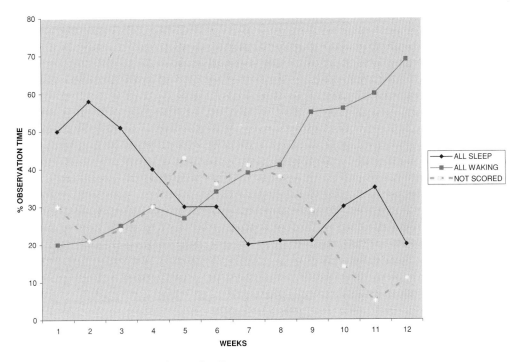

Figure 1. Day-time distribution of sleep and waking.

different ways during active and quiet sleep has also focused attention on the fundamental importance of the behavioral state concept for all empirical studies of early psychological development.

Electromyographic (EMG) recordings indicate that tonic muscle activity is at a relatively high level during quiet sleep, but disappears almost entirely as soon as the infant switches to active sleep. Monosynaptic reflexes like the knee jerk are very active during quiet sleep and non-cry waking, but weak or absent during active sleep or when the infant is crying. Polysynaptic reflexes like the grasp reflex, on the other hand, are absent in quiet sleep, prominent during active sleep, but weak when the infant is awake and not crying. Exteroceptive pain reflexes, in contrast, are active across all four behavioral states (Prechtl & O'Brien, 1982).

On the state dependency of behavior

Even the simple 'reflexes' of clinical neurology demonstrate the exquisite sensitivity of the infant's behavioral repertoire to its initial behavioral state. The same holds for the extensive array of other, and often more complex, physiological and behavioral attributes that characterize states of sleep and wakefulness. Under some initial conditions, a quantitative change in one component state variable (e.g., body temperature) will precipitate a discontinuous shift from one behavioral state to another, and a corresponding switch in the infant's overall sensorimotor characteristics. Under

other initial conditions, the ensemble of component variables as a whole may effectively absorb the same quantitative change, so that the perturbing stimulus has no detectable effect on the infant's behavioral state or sensorimotor characteristics.

For example, as long as the infant is in quiet sleep, innocuous environmental stimuli or minor visceral discomforts usually have no perceptible impact on the overall state organization. When the perturbing stimulus does elicit a transient motor response, the infant quickly returns to quiet sleep once left in peace. During active sleep, by contrast, the same perturbation will often waken the infant, and sometimes it will provoke a bout of fussing or crying (Wolff, 1987). As one consequence of such differences in the relative stability of the two sleep states and their sensitivity to perturbation, the mean duration of quiet sleep epochs falls within a fairly narrow time window of 21–25 minutes, whereas the durations of those during active sleep are much more widely distributed (Fig. 2).

Wakefulness

The finding that behavioral states of sleep differ qualitatively in their resistance to perturbation, and in their capacity to maintain stability and return to their initial condition, should in principle also hold for behavioral states of wakefulness. A taxonomy of wakefulness is obviously of greater theoretical and methodological interest for any theory of psychological development

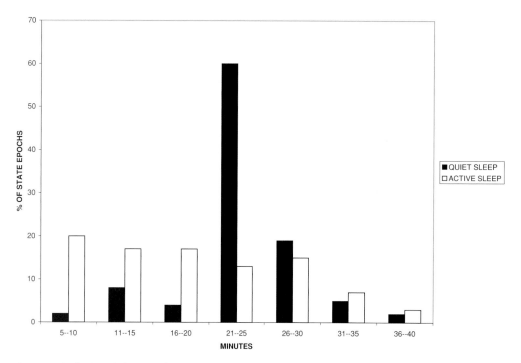

Figure 2. Distribution of sleep epochs as a function of behavioral state.

than a taxonomy of sleep states. However, we know much less about the organizational principles of wakefulness. For example, it remains a largely unanswered question whether the alert wakefulness of the young infant merely consolidates and stabilizes over time, or differentiates into a number of qualitatively distinct behavioral states with their own unique input-output relations.

The total duration of wakefulness increases progressively from 24 percent of total observation time during the first two weeks at home, to 64 percent of observation time at 12 weeks. During the first week, infants stay awake and alert for up to seven minutes before fussing or falling asleep. However, even these short periods of alert waking are easily aborted by a wide range of perturbations, including intrusive environmental events, visceral discomforts such as hunger or wet diapers, and by minor increases above a low threshold in the infant's self-initiated motor activity (Wolff, 1987).

By 12 weeks, on the other hand, infants can stay awake and alert for up to three hours. Moreover, sustained periods of non-cry wakefulness are much less vulnerable to disruption by visceral discomforts, environmental perturbations, or by vigorous limb movements (Fig. 3). Mildly noxious stimuli that might have provoked a bout of crying in the first month may now provoke a brief period of consternation or fussing, but more often than not the infant quickly returns to an alert state. By 12 weeks, wakefulness therefore also exhibits a capacity for self-correction (Wolff, 1987; 1993).

Nearly all of the studies on early psychological development summarized in other entries are based on the a priori assumption that alert wakefulness is the fundamental pre-condition for any meaningful research on perception, attention, cognition, learning, language acquisition, and contingent interactions with the social partner. Studies are, therefore, scheduled accordingly, especially those involving young infants. The perhaps obvious exception is crying that has a number of the functional attributes of a behavioral state of wakefulness, and that is sometimes used as a framework for investigating the development of emotions and parent-child interactions.

Even within the global frame of non-cry wakefulness, the infant's spontaneous behavior and coordinated responses to environmental contingencies may change discontinuously and unpredictably. This fact raises the tactical, and perhaps even the strategic, question of whether such variations can be treated as random noise smoothed over by statistical manipulations, or whether they are the outward expressions of shifts among discrete behavioral waking states. Decisions on this point may have important implications for the interpretation of findings in many of the studies summarized in other entries.

The unobtrusive observation of infants suggests that not only the coordinated behavior itself, but also the infant's sensitivity to changes in behavioral states of wakefulness, change dramatically over the first 4–6 months. For example, 1-month-old infants will intermittently pursue 'interesting' moving targets, smile

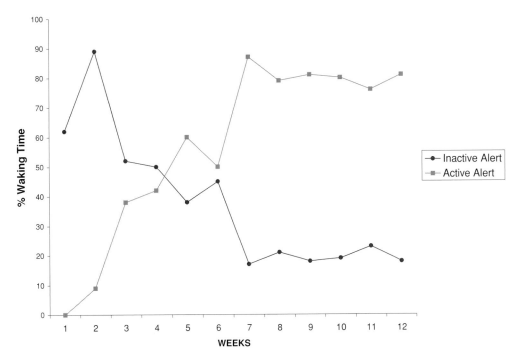

Figure 3. Development of waking states.

contingently to a nodding familiar face, and engage in a limited repertoire of other goal-directed actions as long as they are awake, quiet, and 'alert.' However, as soon as the infant begins to move the limbs actively or responds with discomfort to visceral stimuli, such actions immediately stop. By 4 months, infants have no difficulty carrying out two coordinated actions concurrently, tracking a moving target with their eyes while shaking a rattle, and looking back and forth between two objects rather than being stimulus-bound to one visual object (Wolff, 1987).

These, and many similar observations, suggest that it should be possible in principle to construct a developmental taxonomy of behavioral states of wakefulness on the basis of behavioral criteria. However, a number of conceptual and methodological problems stand in the way of such a strategy. Polygraphic recordings are undoubtedly helpful as independent criteria for classifying sleep states. Since they are essentially useless for classifying waking states, a taxonomy of wakefulness has to rely almost exclusively on behavioral criteria as these emerge and are extensively differentiated during the first three to six months. Not only is the logic of a strategy for tracking the development of behavioral states circular, it would also require the identification of an entirely new set of age-specific criteria for each major advance in development.

Most discrete studies of behavioral development therefore proceed implicitly on the assumption that non-cry wakefulness is a homogeneous disposition that remains relatively unchanged from infancy through childhood and beyond, except in its quantitative duration and distribution over the 24-hour day. Yet, systematic investigations have demonstrated that the physiological, cognitive, and linguistic behavior patterns of psychotic patients with rapidly cycling manic-depressive psychoses or multiple personalities change qualitatively and discontinuously as patients switch from one psychotic waking state to another. Also, psychological constructs of mood and levels of consciousness suggest that normal adults exhibit discontinuous fluctuations of behavior, albeit in a less dramatic form.

Conclusions

In summary, a theoretical formulation is needed to capture what is important about behavioral states as organizing principles of coordinated behavior across the life cycle. As a point of departure, I will assume that behavioral states are not autonomous brain mechanisms controlling behavioral output, but the collective term for different ensembles of the same or different physiological and behavioral variables. Among all logically possible combinations of variables, only a small number of ensembles will be realized. Those that are realized exhibit attributes of coherence among component variables, resistance to perturbations, the capacity for self-correction, and state-specific input-output (sensorimotor) characteristics.

The rules of spontaneous pattern formation governing the induction of behavioral state ensembles are probably too complex to submit to an empirical analysis by currently available tools. However, in principle, they should be susceptible to experimental investigation. Perhaps at this time, they may be best understood by using modeling techniques that are constrained by current experimental findings and tested by the new experiments they suggest. As a minimum, the concept of behavioral state reminds us that perception, action, memory, emotion, and attention are not discrete and autonomous psychological faculties. Instead, they are the emergent properties of very large numbers of interactive component variables, even if it may be necessary to compartmentalize them in order to study their development.

Questions

1. Name some of the theoretical and methodological advantages and disadvantages of applying either of the two very different definitions of behavioral state, discussed in the text, as a framework for investigating the behavior of young infants.
2. What is the evidence for the claim that qualitatively distinct behavioral states of waking are also present in the older child or adult?

3. Give some concrete examples that would support the claims that: (a) that the input-output characteristics of all living things are distinctly non-linear; and (b) that the non-linearity of input-output relations is sensitive to the organism's initial conditions (in this case, to the organism's behavioral state).

See also:
Dynamical systems approaches; Observational methods; The status of the human newborn; Perceptual development; Emotional development; Attention; Brain and behavioral development (I): sub-cortical; Connectionist modeling; Prolonged infant crying and colic; Ethology

Further reading

Churchland, P. S. (1998). What should we expect from a theory of consciousness? *Advances in Neurology*, 77, 19–32.

Kelso, J. A. S. (1995). *Dynamic Patterns*. Cambridge, MA: MIT Press.

Sejnowski, T. J. and Destexhe, A. (2000). Why do we sleep? *Brain Research*, 886, 208–223.

Socialization

MARK BENNETT

Introduction

Socialization is the process by which children acquire the values, standards, practices, and knowledge of the society into which they are born. It is through this process that children typically come to share many aspects of the behavior, cognition, and emotion of members of their society. Until fairly recently, and at least since John Locke in the 17th century, socialization has been conceived as something imposed by adults upon children. However, since the 1970s, psychological research has demonstrated that this unidirectional view fundamentally misconceives the means by which children become enculturated.

Early psychological work on socialization came from two quite distinct theoretical traditions: learning theory and Freudianism. For learning theorists, socialization was merely the individual's reinforcement history. That is, children's acquisition of the norms of their society was seen as the result of the particular rewards and punishments to which they were subject. This position was elaborated in social learning theory, which, though continuing to assert the centrality of reinforcement, introduced the concept of vicarious reinforcement to account for observational learning. Freudian theory, on the other hand, viewed socialization as a process through which children's powerful instinctual impulses to self-gratification were regulated by parents. That is, socialization was seen to involve the transformation of an entirely hedonistic being into one capable of *self*-regulation in accordance with the norms of the wider society. Despite profound differences between these two theoretical traditions, their conception of socialization was identical in one important respect: for both, it was a unidirectional process in which children are essentially passive recipients of parents' rearing practices.

Today, there are no monolithic accounts of the process of socialization. Moreover, contemporary researchers typically address the topic not in a comprehensive and general manner, but in a domain-specific way (e.g., independently examining moral socialization, gender socialization, cognitive socialization, emotional socialization, etc.). Notwithstanding the absence of an overarching theoretical account embracing the many biological, cognitive, and cultural factors that are implicated in children's socialization, a unifying theme in current work is the view that, from the outset, children play an *active* role in their own socialization.

The active infant

First of all, infants are active participants in their relationships with caregivers. They manifest a degree of 'social fittedness' that suggests a biological preparedness for socialization. For example, soon after birth, infants show strong preferences for faces rather than other high-contrast patterns. They also evince preferences for human voices (especially the mother's voice) over other sounds. Furthermore, newborns have a rudimentary capacity for imitation of others' facial expressions. Interestingly, within months this latter capacity is lost, suggesting that it is essentially innate. However, increasingly, from the second month of life, infants smile at those around them. Despite such changes in the early forms of sociality, it is clear that infants produce many behaviors that make them compelling social partners to caregivers. They thus have an active part in establishing early relationships.

A second sense in which children are seen as active in their own socialization is that they play a fundamental role in shaping the environments they occupy. Thus, research inspired by Bell's (1968) ground-breaking paper on 'child effects' has demonstrated that innately given individual differences between children can have an important bearing upon parents' behavior toward them, and hence influence their environment. For example, children's gender, physical attractiveness, and most importantly temperament, have all been found to have marked influences on parental behavior. Thus, from birth, parents treat girls and boys in systematically different ways, both wittingly and unwittingly. Physical attractiveness, too, is characteristically associated with a range of more positive responses from parents and other adults. For example, fathers of physically attractive daughters have been found to be subject to significantly fewer displays of child-directed anger than have those of less attractive daughters, suggesting that attractiveness may serve a buffering function.

Most significantly, however, children's temperament has been found to strongly influence parental behavior. Thus, an infant with a 'difficult' temperament (i.e., one who is irritable in response to many stimuli, irregular in terms of basic functions like eating and sleeping, and given to negative mood states) is likely to be treated differently from 'easy' siblings within the same family. In particular, by comparison with their 'easy' brothers and sisters, 'difficult' children typically experience lower levels of parental attention, have less stimulating contact, and are liable to greater levels of restriction and punishment. It is clear, then, that innately given differences between children have significant conse-quences for how others react to them, and, hence, for children's environments. Socialization practices thus are influenced by children themselves.

A further sense in which children are actively involved in their own socialization is reflected in research on identity development (Martin, 2000). Such research has revealed that children actively seek out information relevant to their social identities. For example, having categorized themselves as a boy or girl (something that typically happens by the age of 2 years), children increasingly attend to information relevant to their own sex. Boys may learn that skipping games are 'for girls,' and, as a result, cease further information- search. Girls on the other hand, recognizing that "this is relevant to me," are likely to attempt to supplement their existing knowledge about such games. Consequently, children develop an own-sex schema that guides the acquisition and processing of potentially self-relevant information. To summarize, it is clear that children demonstrate a greater interest in information that is relevant to their ascribed identities than to other identities. In this respect, children actively engage in their own socialization. Action theorists, moreover, go further by contending that with increasing age children come to play a *directive* role in their socialization in that they set goals for their own development and pursue means to achieve those goals. Thus, from this relatively new perspective, socialization is to some extent a self-conscious process; by late childhood, the child is seen as a driving force in his or her own development.

development in this field has been the shift toward understanding socialization in terms of a systems approach (Sameroff, 1983). Key to this approach is that the child is conceived as embedded in a variety of mutually influencing relationships and social structures. Within the apparently simple triadic structure of the nuclear family (i.e., mother, father, and child), complex networks of reciprocal influence can be observed, with each party influencing the behavior of each other party, and each dyadic relationship influencing each other such relationship. For example, that between child and mother, itself the interactive outcome of characteristics of each, has a bearing upon the relationship between the mother and father, with temperamentally difficult children posing greater challenges to the parents' relationship with one another than are posed by easy children. Similarly, the parents' relationship influences that of the mother's with her child. For example, mothers who enjoy close, supportive relationships with their partners typically interact with greater patience and sensitivity toward their child than do mothers whose relationships with their partners are marked by discord. From a systems perspective, the complexity of the basic family triad is thus substantial. Such complexity is significantly increased when we consider the arrival of further children, and when we take into account the nuclear family's relationship within the wider, extended family. Families, then, are complex, multifaceted systems. Moreover, they are dynamical systems inasmuch as each person and relationship within the system is subject to change and development.

As a context for socialization, the 'microsystem' of the family must be understood as embedded in broader social networks, including the school, peer groups, and parental employment: all exert direct and indirect effects, on both the child and the family as a whole. Additionally, consideration must be given to the 'macrosystem' of the wider society. The macrosystem represents a broad range of factors that have a variety of largely indirect influences upon other systems relevant to the child. For example, both family and school are influenced by societal beliefs about how children develop, how they should be treated, and what can reasonably be required of them at different points in childhood. The systems approach, then, contends that a full account of human socialization must recognize complex reciprocal relationships at many levels of analysis, from the individual to the societal (Bronfenbrenner, 1989).

Socialization and systems approaches

Beyond the move toward conceptualizing socialization as an active process, a related and fundamental

Folk wisdom and parenting

Despite an increasing recognition of complexity in socialization processes, some findings have emerged that attest to widely held aspects of folk wisdom. Foremost amongst them is that some styles of parenting have more positive socialization outcomes than others. Thus, regardless of child temperament, parenting styles characterized by authority and warmth have been found to be more likely to encourage social, moral, and self-regulatory competence than those characterized by, for example, authoritarianism and aloofness. Similarly, parental acceptance and responsiveness, along with the absence of coercive control, are associated with relatively low levels of aggressive and defiant behavior in children. However, the point should be reiterated that parenting styles are themselves influenced by child characteristics (e.g., temperamentally difficult children are more likely than easy children to promote coercive forms of parenting, though this is by no means inevitable).

Although some aspects of folk wisdom have thus been confirmed (albeit with significant caveats), recent work has also challenged pervasive lay views that the socialization of children is most effectively accomplished within the conventional nuclear family unit. Thus, single-parent families, though more often associated with adverse outcomes for children, are not inevitably inferior agents of socialization: such adverse outcomes reflect the difficulties frequently associated with single-parent families, such as stress and financial problems, rather than single-parent status *per se*. Where such problems are absent, outcomes are typically no different from those associated with two-parent families. Similarly, recent work dispels the myths that adoptive parents are less nurturing than biological parents, and that gay and lesbian parents are less effective in promoting positive developmental outcomes than are heterosexual parents. That is, it is type of parenting rather than type of family that makes the more important contribution to development.

As within Western culture generally, parenting has long been conceived by psychologists as the domain primarily of mothers. However, since the 1970s, social changes have increasingly focused attention on the role of fathers. Psychological research confirms that fathers have an important role in socialization. For example, recent studies show that father-child play in the preschool years is related to children's feelings of self-worth up to age 16 and to the quality of peer interaction in the primary years. Also, closeness between fathers and their children at 16 years has been found to predict feelings of self-confidence in relationships at 33 years.

Conclusions

Given the vast scope of the term, recent advances in our understanding and conceptualization of socialization have been considerable, with developments in statistical technology making it feasible for researchers to examine the many nested systems of socialization agents. Importantly, too, researchers are increasingly sensitive to the insights of disciplines beyond psychology, such as anthropology, economics, demography, paediatrics, psychiatry, and sociology (Parke, Ornstein, Reiser, & Zahn-Waxler, 1994). Nonetheless, despite advances, important challenges remain. For example, more needs to be understood about the process of internalization, by which 'outer' control of behavior by parents becomes transformed into 'inner,' self-directed control by children themselves. Moreover, notwithstanding the acknowledgment of bidirectional influences between parents and children, understanding at the level of the detail is relatively limited (which in part may reflect the lack of an adequate theoretical language for the description of emergent properties of relationships).

More work, too, is needed to address the *changing* nature of socialization processes during the course of development. Furthermore, although the systems approach has emphasized partnership and synergy between families and other agents of socialization, much remains to be discovered about their relative influence at different points in childhood, and the extent of their influence upon one another. For example, throughout the 1990s, much research examined 'neighborhood effects' (Leventhal & Brooks-Gunn, 2000), demonstrating the adverse effects on child development of growing up in neighborhoods characterized by poverty. Such effects have been shown to be independent of 'family effects,' but more needs to be understood about the pathways through which the macrosystem impacts upon children's development.

Finally, technologies have introduced important changes to the process of socialization: through media such as television and the Internet, children now have greater access to the adult and adolescent spheres than was previously the case. The impact of such media on children's socialization, especially when promulgating norms and values at odds with those of parents, represents an important domain of future inquiry.

Questions

1. Should child-rearing be taught? Should it be more closely monitored by government agencies?
2. Is smacking an acceptable or effective tool in the socialization process?
3. How might siblings influence the socialization process? Similarly, how might the transition to school impact upon the socialization process?
4. How exactly does the process of 'outer control' by socialization agents become transformed into the process of inner self-control?

5. What are the pathways through which aspects of the macrosystem (e.g., poverty, neighborhood) impact upon the microsystem of the family?

See also:
Learning theories; Psychoanalytical theories; Parental and teacher rating scales; Self and peer assessment of competence and well-being; Multilevel modeling; Social development; Moral development; Aggressive and prosocial behavior; Imitation; Parenting and the family; Sex differences; Siblings and peers; Temperament; Anthropology; Sociology; Pediatrics; John Bowlby

Further reading

Bugental, D. B. and Goodnow, J. J. (1998). Socialization processes. In N. Eisenberg (ed.), *Handbook of Child Psychology*, 5th edn. New York: Wiley, Vol. III, pp. 389–462.

Parke, R. D. and Buriel, R. (1998). Socialization in the family: ethnic and ecological perspectives. In N. Eisenberg (ed.), *Handbook of Child Psychology*, 5th edn. New York: Wiley, Vol. III, pp. 463–552.

Schaffer, H. R. (1999). Understanding socialization: from unidirectional to bi-directional conceptions. In M. Bennett (ed.), *Developmental Psychology: Achievements and Prospects*. Philadelphia, PA: Psychology Press, pp. 272–288.

Temperament

MARY K. ROTHBART AND JULIE HWANG

Introduction

Since the early 1970s, research on temperament in infancy and childhood has burgeoned. Temperament has been defined as constitutionally based individual differences in emotional, motor, and attentional reactivity, and self-regulation (Rothbart & Bates, 1998). Reactivity refers to the excitability, responsiveness, and arousability of behavioral and physiological systems. It can be measured in the latency, intensity, and duration of children's emotional, motor, and attentional reactions to arousing events. Self-regulation refers to processes that modulate reactivity, such as attentional control and motor inhibition. Temperamental characteristics demonstrate consistency across situations and relative stability over time. They undergo developmental change, and their measurement is basic to identifying trajectories of social-emotional and personality development.

Constructs of temperament

Research on temperament in childhood has been greatly influenced by the New York Longitudinal Study (NYLS; Thomas & Chess, 1977). Thomas and colleagues interviewed parents about the behaviors of their 2- to 6-month-old infants. Through content analysis of the parents' descriptions, they identified nine dimensions of temperament: activity level, rhythmicity, approach-withdrawal, adaptability, threshold, intensity, mood, distractibility, and attention span-persistence. Many subsequent parent-report questionnaires have been based on these dimensions.

Since the NYLS list of dimensions was developed, however, major revisions to it have been proposed, based on factor analyses of children's temperament that revealed statistical relationships among temperament items (Rothbart & Bates, 1998). The revised list of dimensions in infancy and early childhood refers to individual differences in positive affectivity, activity level, fearfulness, anger/frustration, attentional orienting, and, in early childhood, effortful control. The latter refers to the capacity to inhibit a dominant response (e.g., running about in the classroom) in order to perform a sub-dominant response (e.g., focusing on a reading text). During childhood, three broad factors have consistently been found in parent reports of temperament: Surgency or Extraversion, related to positive affect and activity; Negative Affectivity, related to all of the negative affects; and Effortful Control, defined above, and these factors have been linked to emotional and attentional systems in humans and in non-humans (Rothbart & Bates, 1998, in press).

Because temperamental individual differences in early infancy and childhood are likely based on neural structure and physiology, they can also provide insight into the biological bases for personality development. In Table 1, we list some of the broad dimensions of temperament along with neural structures and neuro-chemicals that are likely to underlie those dimensions (see also Rothbart & Bates, 1998).

Methods for evaluating temperament

Research on temperament in childhood has been based on multiple methods. These include parent-report questionnaires, laboratory assays of children's behavioral and physiological responses to standardized stimuli, and independent observations of children's behavior in school or home. Each of these methods has advantages as well as disadvantages for the measurement of temperament (Rothbart & Bates, 1998, in press). Parent-report questionnaires are inexpensive to administer and based on the wide range of behaviors parents observe on multiple occasions. Laboratory observations allow researchers to control and manipulate the environment, allowing more precise measures of reactivity and regulation, and home or school observation allow both coder objectivity and ecological validity.

The disadvantages of each of these methods lie in their potential sources of error. Caregiver reports may be biased by parents' desires to portray their children in a desirable way. Laboratory observations are often limited in the range and frequency of behaviors elicited, and suffer from the carryover of one elicited emotion to the elicitation of others. Natural observations in home or school can be expensive and time consuming, requiring multiple visits to adequately sample children's behavior. While no one method is completely error-free, each of these methods has provided tools to better our understanding of the development of temperament in childhood, and of relations between temperament and developmental outcomes.

Research in behavior genetics has established genetic links with temperament (Rothbart & Bates, 1998). More recent research has used behavior genetics methods, combined with careful assays of the environment, to study both genetic influences on children's choices of environment (e.g., the kinds of friends children select, influenced by the child's preference for quiet or excitement), and the interaction between genetic inheritance and specific environments in influencing developmental outcomes (Dick & Rose, 2002). These improved methods will prove increasingly helpful as knowledge of the human genome allows us to study more specific gene-environment influences developmentally.

Development of temperament

Central to our understanding of temperament is the observation that it undergoes development, with initial reactive tendencies becoming increasingly influenced by later-developing regulatory systems (Rothbart & Bates, in press). During the first few months of life, individual differences in orienting, distress proneness, positive affect, and approach can be observed. By 6 months of age, when presented with novel objects, some infants will rapidly approach in order to reach and contact them, while others do so more slowly. These tendencies, along with infant smiling and laughter elicited in the laboratory, have been associated with later parent-reported extraversion at 7 years (Rothbart, Ahadi, & Evans, 2000). Children who are more extraverted in infancy also demonstrate greater tendencies toward anger/frustration and aggression later.

By 9 months, individual differences in fearfulness or inhibition toward novel or intense stimuli can be observed. The development of fear modulates approach tendencies, so that some infants who previously responded rapidly to new objects may now become

Table 1. Neuropsychology of temperament.

Temperament dimension	Related neural structures / neurochemicals
Surgency / Extraversion	Basolateral amygdala VTA, nucleus accumbens / dopamine
Fear	Lateral and central amygdala, hippocampus / norepinephrine, serotonin
Irritability / Anger	Approach circuits, ventromedial hypothalamus, periacqueductal gray / dopamine
Effortful control	Mid-prefrontal structures including anterior cingulate, motor cortex / dopamine

Adapted from D. Derryberry and M. K. Rothbart, 1997. Reactive and effortful processes in the organization of temperament. *Development and Psychopathology, 9,* 633–652.

more inhibited, or not approach at all. Early fearfulness is related to the later development of empathy, guilt, and shame in childhood, and plays an important role in moderating effects of parental influences on the development of conscience (Rothbart & Bates, in press). Fearful children tend to develop greater early signs of conscience, and Grazyna Kochanska's research suggests that fearful children also benefit from gentle parental discipline in promoting internalized conscience. More fearless children appear to benefit more from maternal responsiveness and their own security of attachment in conscience development (Rothbart & Bates, 1998).

Toward the end of the first year, another system begins to develop, providing additional means for regulating reactive tendencies. Effortful control, allowing inhibition of a dominant response in order to perform a sub-dominant one, develops over the preschool years and beyond, and appears to be critical to socialization. As this system develops in young children, so does the ability to maintain focused attention for longer periods of time. Developing capacities in the deployment of attention allow children to regulate their own emotional reactivity and behavior. Kochanska and her colleagues found that infant behaviors, including sustained attention and the ability to refrain from touching a prohibited toy at 9 months, significantly predicted effortful control at 22 months (Kochanska, Murray, & Harlan, 2000). It appears that there is also long-term stability in children's ability to delay gratification and their control of attention and emotion. Preschoolers' ability to delay gratification predicted adolescent parent-reported attentiveness, ability to concentrate, and control over negative affect (Rothbart & Bates, 1998). In addition, effortful control is strongly related to the development of empathy and guilt or shame in children.

Temperament and environment

The concept of 'goodness-of-fit' put forward by Thomas & Chess (1977) describes how well or poorly children's temperamental characteristics meet the demands and expectations of their environments. A temperament characteristic may be appropriate in one context (e.g., the home, school, or play yard), but fail to fit expectations and demands of another context. Within a single context, a child's temperament may meet some demands, but fail in others, or show success within one developmental period, but not in another. Temperament research has made considerable contributions to our understanding of children's adaptation to the classroom. Awareness that there are biological bases of individual differences and a recognizable structure of temperament can allow educators to better accept and work with children's differences, rather than only making negative attributions about children's motivation and attitude.

Correlations have been found between child temperament and parenting, such as those between temperamental fearfulness, mother's gentle discipline, and the development of conscience described above. In addition to temperament, personality in children is related to variables including the child's age, gender, parental characteristics (e.g., maternal depression), and social/cultural factors (e.g., socioeconomic status and culture). In the future, the study of interactions between temperament and these variables will give us an increasingly fine-grained understanding of child development (Rothbart & Bates, in press).

Significant links have been found between adult temperament and the Big Five or Five Factor Model of personality traits (Rothbart *et al.*, 2000). This model was derived from lists of self-descriptive adjectives that were subsequently factor analyzed, yielding the broad personality factors of extraversion, agreeableness, conscientiousness, neuroticism, and openness to experience. Temperamental surgency was related to extraversion, temperamental negative affectivity to neuroticism, and effortful control to conscientiousness (Rothbart *et al.*, 2000). In addition, an adult temperament measure of orienting sensitivity was positively related to the Five Factor openness to experience. However, the developmental course of temperament in relation to the development of personality has not yet been extensively studied.

Temperament and psychopathology

Several theoretical links between temperament and the development of psychopathology have been considered (Rothbart & Bates, in press). Extreme temperamental characteristics may in themselves be closely related to pathology (e.g., when extreme shyness is related to the development of anxiety disorder). Temperament can also influence the child's choice of environments, providing specific social experiences that can lead to pathology or positive adjustment. For example, children with high attentional control may be able to complete tasks and schoolwork, and thereby receive rewards that contribute to their positive school adjustment. Other children with problems in school may be rejected by other students, then tend to seek out deviant friendships, contributing to subsequent delinquency and substance use. Temperament may also heighten responses to stressful events or buffer against risk. Correlations have been found between temperament and psychopathology, both concurrently and over time (Rothbart & Bates, in press). Examples of these linkages include relationships between temperamental negative affectivity and depression, and between parent ratings of temperament and later child psychiatric diagnoses.

Conclusions

How can we improve our measures of temperament? Development of better measures of temperament and its underlying processes continues to be a major need in the area. In addition to improvements in questionnaires and observational procedures, improving laboratory methods based on our knowledge of brain networks will be important for future directions. Examples include conflict tasks marking the executive attention network that underlies effortful control, or startle paradigms related to the functioning of fear circuits.

What are the dynamics of temperament in relation to the developing personality? It is important to study links among temperamental dimensions, leading to identification of common mechanisms, and how one or more reactive characteristics may be affected by self-regulative temperament systems. This research will be best accomplished at multiple levels, studying behavior and underlying neural systems, as well as associations between temperament, social behavior, and experience.

By using differentiated concepts of temperament and social outcomes, how can we identify multiple pathways in development? Developmental studies, like those of Kochanska on conscience (Kochanska *et al.*, 2000), Dymph van den Boom on attachment, and Nancy Eisenberg on prosocial behavior and behavior problems, have used measures of individual differences in temperament to study personality development and differential influences of caregiver behavior (Rothbart & Bates, in press). This research serves as a model for the identification of different developmental trajectories and outcomes that depend on temperament, as well as demonstrating how similar outcomes result from different temperaments, depending on the nature of the intervening experiences.

How shall we apply temperament ideas to social settings? Temperament provides an important rubric for applied work in schools and clinical settings. The effectiveness of different interventions may depend upon temperamental characteristics, as well as the child's level of cognitive development. Additional research investigating culture and the value placed on temperamental characteristics will also be of great interest. Different cultures appear to have different valuations of temperament characteristics. The Chinese culture, for example, stresses reserve, whereas more outgoing and extraverted characteristics are prized in the United States. A given child may 'fit' one culture better than another, and a poor fit between cultural valuation and the child's temperament may lead to negative outcomes. Different cultures may also exert different pressures toward changing temperament-linked behaviors.

Finally, can we link genetic mechanisms to temperament and its development? Studying temperament from the point of view of molecular genetics will be a new frontier in the understanding of temperament and how it develops (Dick & Rose, 2002). Early research established clear genetic contributions to temperament, but we do not yet know how gene expression unfolds in a social context so as to lead to particular developmental outcomes. Identifying genes associated with temperamental characteristics will allow the study of their detailed relationships with behavior throughout development.

Questions

1. Do our current assessment methods adequately measure all aspects of temperament? How might current methods be improved or new ones added?

2. What are the mechanisms of self-regulation? Consider regulation of behavior, emotion, and thought.

3. What genetic polymorphisms can be linked to dimensions of temperament (e.g., effortful control)?

4. How does temperament in interaction with culture influence the development of self?

5. In what ways is it helpful to distinguish between temperament and personality? Can cognitive aspects of personality influence temperament?

See also:

Observational methods; Parental and teacher rating scales; Experimental methods; Cross-sectional and longitudinal designs; Twin and adoption studies; Social development; Emotional development; Aggressive and prosocial behaviors; Attention; Executive functions; Selfhood; Sex differences; Socialization; Behavioral and learning disorders; Behavior genetics; Cognitive neuroscience; Developmental genetics; Ethology

Further reading

Eisenberg, N., Fabes, R. A., Guthrie, I. K. *et al.* (1996). The relations of regulation and emotionality to problem behavior in elementary school children. *Development and Psychopathology*, 8, 141–162.

Halverson, C. F., Jr., Kohnstamm, G. A. and Martin, R. P. (eds.) (1994). *The Developing Structure of Temperament and Personality from Infancy to Adulthood*. Hillsdale, NJ: Erlbaum.

Posner, M. I. and Rothbart, M. K. (2000). Developing mechanisms of self-regulation. *Development and Psychopathology*, 12, 427–441.

PART VI
Developmental pathology

This part presents a number of topics that illustrate the nature and scope of studies on abnormal and deviant development during childhood. The strength of this part is that it provides ready examples of multidisciplinary research involving developmental psychologists among others. Most topics consider the theoretical and therapeutic implications of recent findings.

'At-risk' concept **Hellgard Rauh**
Autism **Simon Baron-Cohen**
Behavioral and learning disorders
    Christopher Gillberg
Blindness **Ann Bigelow**
Cerebral palsies **Fiona Stanley**
Child depression **Ian M. Goodyer & Carla Sharp**
Developmental coordination disorder
    Mary M. Smyth & Margaret Cousins
Down's syndrome **Digby Elliott**
Dyslexia **Margaret J. Snowling**
Hearing disorders **Roger D. Freeman,
    Maryke Groenveld & Frederick K. Kozak**
Prematurity and low birthweight
    Mijna Hadders-Algra
Prolonged infant crying and colic
    Ian St. James-Roberts
Sudden Infant Death Syndrome **James J. McKenna**
Williams syndrome **Michelle de Haan**

'At-risk' concept

HELLGARD RAUH

Introduction

The at-risk concept lies at the heart of developmental and clinical psychology and is a fundamental concept in understanding developmental pathology. Children are called developmentally 'at-risk' when biopsychological characteristics, or social factors, or both, suggest that they will, with high probability, develop into maladapted unsuccessful adolescents or adults. Examples of such outcomes include school failure, persistent unemployment, delinquency, aggression, risky behaviors, alcoholism, drug abuse, eating disorders, psychosomatic disorders, and psychopathology.

Early research endeavors aimed at detecting signs of deviant development, or of deviant conditions for development, as early as possible in order to be able to suggest preventive, or compensatory interventions. More recent research and theorizing has elaborated the at-risk concept and extended risk models to include related concepts, such as 'vulnerability', and complementary concepts, such as 'protective factors' and 'resilience.'

Empirical approaches

Risk evidence is based on retrospective analyses and, ideally, on prospective follow-up or longitudinal research. Retrospectively, most children with school problems, and most maladapted adolescents or adults, have indeed disproportionately unfortunate childhoods, often correlated with early health problems. Longitudinal and follow-up studies have also confirmed that early health risks (preterm birth, prenatal teratogenic influences, perinatal problems), as well as early social or family problems (e.g., poverty, low educational level of the parents, family discord), significantly and substantially predicted later personality and behavioral problems. However, under equivalently adverse circumstances, some children developed into well-adapted, healthy, and successful adults. They appeared to be 'resilient,' or 'invulnerable,' or 'resourceful.'

Results from most empirical studies apply only at a group level. In other words, they are useful for identifying variables in early childhood that are significantly associated with later poor outcomes, but not every individual with them has such outcomes. The term 'at-risk' simply implies an increased probability of poor outcome, not a certain outcome for each individual. More recent research endeavors, therefore, include the analyses of individual pathways, and the search for those factors that enable a person to withstand the odds, or to recover from deviation.

The at-risk concept, vulnerability, and resources

In psychological research, the term 'at-risk' has mainly been used to characterize persons with limited personal, health, social, or cultural resources. Under optimal and supportive conditions, they would have a fair chance of developing inconspicuously, but they would fail to cope with additional stress associated, for instance, with developmental transitions (e.g., puberty), or with highly probable critical events (e.g., school change, change of peer network), or with hazards of life (e.g., parental divorce, loss of family member, major school failure, major sociopolitical changes). In this regard, children who are born preterm, or those with chronic illnesses, are considered as developmentally at-risk, or at least as 'vulnerable.' Similarly, physically healthy children who come from poor and from unfavorable homes may lack the necessary social and emotional support to cope with additional stressful situations. Some early personality characteristics (e.g., difficult temperament, shyness) and sub-optimal emotional relationships (e.g., insecure attachments) may also function as limited resources in challenging situations.

Finally, periods of developmental transition, such as that from sensorimotor intelligence to representational

Table 1. Delineation of what is involved in the 'at-risk' concept.

Level	Risk	Protection
Factors	Biological risks, social risks Established risks versus at-risk	Biological, social, and cultural resources
Personal level	Vulnerability	Resilience
Mechanisms	Inadequate coping Inadequate parenting Lack of curiosity and exploration	Coping Positive parenting Stress training Curiosity and exploration
	Risky behavior Negative transactions	Consideration Positive transactions
Outcome	Maladaptation Psychopathology	Psychologically healthy person

thought, or puberty, may disclose latent vulnerabilities and emotional instabilities. Children at developmental risk may lack the necessary variability and flexibility of responses (or resiliency), or they have insufficient access to social resources, to cope successfully with these new challenges (O'Connor & Rutter, 1996).

Developmental risk and sensitive periods

The notion of 'critical' or 'sensitive' periods implies a very specific susceptibility to external influences. With regard to noxious (i.e., teratogenic) influences on the developing organism, the early embryonic period is considered to be particularly perilous for organ malformations, whereas during the fetal period and early infancy, in times of rapid brain growth, the formation of neural connections can be disrupted or distorted by teratogenic influences (e.g., maternal drug exposure).

The notion of sensitive periods has also been used with regard to experiences during developmentally specific 'time-windows'. In the case of 'experience-expectant processes,' specific kinds of experiences are necessary in order to fine-tune and complete a particular function (e.g., stereoscopic vision), or to orient the child's attention to certain aspects of the world (e.g., the visual or the acoustical world, specific aspects of the mother tongue). In a broader sense, infancy and toddlerhood constitute a sensitive period for the development of language, communication, and socioemotional attachment. If developmentally appropriate experiences are missed, or distorted, or extremely delayed, as might occur with blind or deaf infants or in cases of massive neglect, later acquisition of these competencies will at best be more arduous, but the result may also be deviant. Also, the kinds of experiences that the infant encounters lay the grounds for usually long-lasting individual

differences, as shown, for instance, in the cases of language development and attachment formation.

The term 'sensitive period' has also been used for a child's cognitive and motivational 'readiness' to learn cultural standards and techniques with age-appropriate ease. There has been a never-ending debate over whether there are general or specific optimal time-windows for specific cultural learning experiences (e.g., toilet training, learning to read and to write, mathematics, school entry generally), and whether 'precocious' or 'delayed' learning constitute 'special opportunities' or 'risks.' Initially, researchers and politicians had hoped that compensatory preschool intervention would inoculate socially disadvantaged children against early school failure. Although generally a relative success story, these very ambitious aims of early interventionists were not met.

At-risk versus established risk

Occasionally, special populations of children with well-diagnosed physical or mental disorders (e.g., Down's syndrome) have been called 'at-risk.' Strictly speaking, the at-risk concept can be only meaningfully applied to these sub-groups with established risks when referring to secondary handicaps (see Table 1). Secondary handicaps are, for instance, particularly poor learning strategies, poor social strategies, or an inadequate self-esteem, or other kinds of problem behaviors that are likely to result from inappropriate parenting. Intuitive parenting seems to be developed fairly well in parents with 'normal' children. With physically or behaviorally deviant children, it is often more difficult to establish the optimal fit between the child's developmental needs and parental behavior. Parents often tend to be either overprotective, or insensitive to the weak behavioral signs of their infant. An attitude of learned helplessness may ensue in the child that inhibits active learning and exploration, both of which are important prerequisites for healthy psychological development.

Risk factors and protective factors

Risk factors are influences on the young child and the developing person that are likely to alter that individual's personal resources. Specific kinds of risks and outcomes have proven to be only loosely related (Rutter, 2002). It is more likely that the accumulation of different kinds of risks increases the probability of some kind of negative outcome, generally speaking. Two classes of risk factors are roughly distinguished in developmental research: biological risk factors (e.g., preterm birth, perinatal complications) and social risk factors (e.g., low parental education, poverty, parental discord, parental mental illness, maternal depression). Scores constructed from cumulated biological risks are supposed to indicate an increased probability of psychobiological vulnerability, and scores from cumulated, chronic or acute, social risks a heightened probability of psychosocial stress.

Risk models differ as to whether they combine both risk sources additively or multiplicatively. An additive model implies that maladaptation or psychopathology increase linearly with the number of biological and social risk factors, and a multiplicative model that the effect of social risk factors is relatively higher for children with biological risks, and the effect of biological risks is greater for children living in adverse social circumstances. It appears that the additive models hold well for children born slightly preterm. For children of epileptic mothers, the multiplicative model seems to be more adequate. In the case of control children from similar social backgrounds, however, only the quality of the family environment (e.g., as measured by the HOME inventory) during early childhood seems to affect their cognitive abilities during adolescence. For children of epileptic mothers, especially those exposed in utero to antiepileptic drugs taken by their mothers, the quality of the family environment during the school years and in early adolescence adds to variations in outcome measures. It seems that children of epileptic mothers are both more sensitive, and sensitive over a longer period of development, to adverse social influences, but also to positive social influences (Titze et al.,2001).

As a complement to the study of risk factors, research into potential protective factors has come into focus. In many instances, they are simply the positive counter-parts of risk factors, as applies to poor or good parenting. Also, cultural factors can act as protective factors (and probably also as risk factors). Infants with a 'difficult temperament' seem to develop inconspicuously in a cultural environment that is accepting for those variations, as was observed in Latin-American families in New York. Variable-centered approaches concerned with what kinds of risk predict which outcomes tend now to yield to more person-centered approaches, with a focus on what kinds of risk affect which sub-group of children.

From risk factors to risk mechanisms

Recent research has focused on patterns of development, or trajectories, of children at high or low risk, and on potential mechanisms that, along the trajectories, translate biological and social risk factors into psycho-logical dysfunctioning (Rutter, 2002). Early biological risks (e.g., preterm birth) can change the infant's appearance or temperament in such a way that the caregivers respond less adequately (e.g., less sensitively, or with overprotection), thus creating a sub-optimal rearing climate. Biological risks can generally reduce a child's physical and psychological resources, constrain his or her information-processing capacities, or de-stabilize the child's self-regulation abilities (Lengua, 2002).

Supportive environments may partially compensate for the child's reduced resources, but quite often a less supportive, or a disadvantaged, environment provokes situational coping strategies (e.g., aggressive or shy behavior) that, in the long run, may lead to problem behavior. Children at biological risk or in threatening environments tend to show fewer developmentally beneficial cognitive and social behaviors, such as curiosity and exploration. Instead, they tend either to avoid challenging situations or to overreact with disruptive emotions, both kinds of coping that will restrain their developmental potential even further (Rauh, 1989).

Resilience

Children are considered at-risk when they encounter hazardous life circumstances or events that clearly exceed normal resources (e.g., warfare, natural or social disasters). Those who, against all predictions, do not succumb to these adversities are considered to have special resiliencies (i.e., a pre- or acquired disposition enabling them to withstand major hazards and to return to a normal life course). It is a kind of self-righting potential, and also refers to a child's ability to draw effectively on all available personal and social resources.

Successful coping with everyday challenges appears to be a kind of 'stress training' or 'steeling,' and may help to build up a repertoire of personal resources (Rutter, 2002). Coping with risky situations can, to some degree, be learned and can serve as preparations for future difficult situations. The term 'at-risk' could conse–quently also be applied to those children who, in spite of a sufficient health status, and in spite of general abilities and social conditions within the normal range, do not develop an adequate repertoire of personal or social resources to cope with stressful or risk-carrying situations. These would be the children who as adolescents, without any obvious risk factors, succumb to drug abuse or are seduced to partake in risky behaviors.

Risk-provoking behaviors

Particularly during adolescence, but also in childhood, some individuals engage in risky behaviors in that they actively provoke risky situations. Most of these youths seem to lack a proper sensitivity to dangers and threats. Their self-concept is disproportionately positive, their social perception appears to be inadequate, and their role-taking underdeveloped. While some of these characteristics are reminiscent of adolescent egocen-trism, others refer to inadequate emotion regulation (e.g., a reduced ability to attend, an inability to learn systematically, difficulties in controlling impulses), or to a need for sensation. These young people seem to literally select, and attract, or even produce, adverse events and hazardous experiences.

Debatable issues

There has been a debate about whether the same mechanisms account for behavioral variations within the normal range, as well as for psychopathology (Rutter, 2002). In a similar vein, there has also been debate about whether the same kinds of processes account for the development of competence or dysfunction, or whether different ones should be considered for children with either heightened or reduced susceptibility to specific risk influences. Moreover, the concepts of resiliency and vulnerability as general personality traits seem to yield to ideas of domain-specific, or even age-specific characteristics.

Conclusions

The at-risk concept combines research on biological and psychological development with that on socialization, as well as models of developmental psychology and differential psychology, with those of developmental

psychopathology. Research based on this concept provides ideas for the prevention of adverse develop-mental outcomes and for early intervention, with its focus not only on the individual, but also on the social and cultural context in which the child develops.

The different aspects of 'at-risk' that have been detailed here have given rise to quite diverse and sometimes divergent research traditions that, in the future, will need to communicate with each other. To date, most developmental risk research has been limited too narrowly to the nuclear family, and to the periods of early childhood and of adolescence. Future research needs to take a broader perspective in developmental time and in social space, and, at the same time, needs to study in more detail the transformations of risk experi-ences into concrete transactions and coping behaviors at the personal level. This implies a more dynamical view of the developing person in his or her immediate environment.

Furthermore, very little is known about the impact of cultural differences, and of social and cultural changes on kinds of risk and protective factors, and on related changes in risk outcomes. Epidemiological studies with longitudinal and time-sequential designs that would take these cultural factors into account are still extremely rare. Even if we might know what have been risk influences in the past with effects in the present time, we are still broadly ignorant of the future impact that contemporary risk factors may have on children when they become adolescents and adults.

Finally, there are studies suggesting that some risk effects (e.g., maltreatment, holocaust) may extend even into the next generation. This appears to be plausible for extreme personal experiences. Life circumstances have changed markedly in the past decades. Children survive who would never have done so before, such as extremely preterm children and those with chronic illnesses. Many children are protected today from adverse circumstances that were regular events in previous generations (e.g., certain types of illnesses, family member losses). New life patterns and new challenges in children's lives have appeared. We do not know, for example, whether growing up in single-parent households, although usually coped with well by most children, may affect these children's behavior as parents, or whether experiences with street violence will extend into the next generation.

See also:
Cross-cultural comparisons; Epidemiological designs; Cross-sectional and longitudinal designs; Indices of efficacy; Normal and abnormal prenatal development; Aggressive and prosocial behavior; Attention; Parenting and the family; Schooling and literacy; Siblings and peers; Socialization; Temperament; Behavioral and

learning disorders; Blindness; Down's syndrome; Hearing disorders; Prematurity and low birthweight; Pediatrics; Sociology

Further reading

Bailey, D. B., Bruer, J. T., Symons, F. J. and Lichtman, J. W. (eds.) (2001). *Critical Thinking about Critical Periods.* Baltimore, MD: Paul H. Brookes.

Bronfenbrenner, U. and Morris, P. A. (1998). The ecology of developmental processes. In W. Damon (editor-in-chief), *Handbook of Child Psychology*, Vol. I: *Theoretical Models of Human Development* (vol. ed., R. M. Lerner), 5th. edn. New York: Wiley, pp. 993–1028.

Leavitt, L. A. and Fox, N. A. (eds.) (1993). *The Psychological Effects of War and Violence on Children.* Hillsdale, NJ: Erlbaum.

Sameroff, A. J., Seifer, R., Baldwin, A. and Baldwin, C. (1993). Stability of intelligence from preschool to adolescence: the influence of social and family risk factors. *Child Development*, 64, 80–97.

Werner, E. E. and Smith, R. S. (1992). *Overcoming the Odds: High Risk Children from Birth to Adulthood.* Ithaca, NY: Cornell University Press.

Werner, E. E. and Smith, R. S. (2001). *Journey from Childhood to Midlife: Risk and Recovery.* Ithaca, NY: Cornell University Press.

Autism

SIMON BARON-COHEN

Introduction

Autism, a condition of neurodevelopment, is more common in males, with onset typically in infancy. It is diagnosed when a child or adult has abnormalities in a 'triad' of behavioral domains: social development, communication, and repetitive behavior / obsessive interests. People with autism typically may appear to be self-absorbed, or 'in a different world,' due to their lack of responsiveness to those around them. It can occur at any point on the IQ continuum, and IQ is a strong predictor of outcome. Autism is also invariably accompanied by language delay (e.g., no single words before 2 years old). Asperger's syndrome (AS) is a sub-group on the autistic spectrum. Those with AS share many of the same features as are seen in autism, but with no history of language delay and their IQ is in the average range or above. Typically, classic autism is identified before age 3, and can be diagnosed as early as 18 months. AS is typically identified later than this, usually around age 6 years old.

Frequency and clustering in the population

Early estimates of the prevalence of autism suggested it was quite rare (4 in 10,000 children), but over the 1990s a series of reports suggested that it was far more common than this. The highest estimate is that autism spectrum conditions (i.e., autism and AS) occur at a rate of 1 child in every 166. This massive change in reported figures has been interpreted by some to indicate that there is some new environmental cause (e.g., vaccine damage), but critics of this view argue that the increase can be explained more simply as the result of widening the diagnostic category (e.g., previously AS was not included). Other explanations have included improved awareness among clinicians and the general public (previously there was no special training or media coverage of autism), and the existence of many services for autism (which hitherto simply did not exist).

Psychological causes of autism

It is widely recognized that people with autism spectrum conditions process information differently to other people. Information as a psychological construct is referred to as cognition. The main cognitive theories of autism are summarized below.

Mindblindness theory

The mindblindness theory proposed that in autism spectrum conditions there are deficits in the normal process of empathizing, relative to mental age (Baron-Cohen, 1995). These deficits can occur by degrees. The term 'empathizing' encompasses a range of other terms: 'theory of mind,' 'mind-reading,' and 'empathy,' and involves two major elements – (a) the ability to attribute mental states to oneself and others, as a natural way to make sense of other people; and (b) having an emotional reaction that is appropriate to the other person's mental state. In this sense, it goes beyond what is normally meant by the term 'theory of mind' to include having some affective reaction (e.g., sympathy).

Since the first evaluation of mindblindness, there have been more than thirty experimental tests. The vast majority of these have revealed profound impairments in the development of empathizing ability in people with autism. This is manifested in the form of reduced shared attention, reduced use of mental state terms in language, reduced production and comprehension of pretense, difficulties in appreciating other people's different beliefs, and difficulties in understanding subtle emotions.

Empathizing-Systemizing (E-S) theory

Systemizing is the drive to analyze and build systems, in order to understand and predict the behavior of events that do not involve agents. Systems are all around us in our environment, and include technical systems (e.g., machines and tools), natural systems (e.g., biological

Empathizing and Systemizing

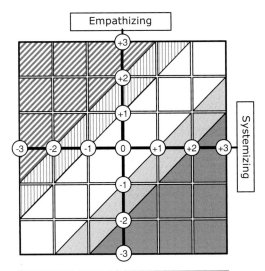

*Axes show standard deviations from the mean

Figure 1. Empathizing and Systemizing. These two psychological processes are plotted as independent dimensions (E and S). Research on sex differences in the general population shows that more females than males have stronger E relative to S (E > S), and that more males than females have stronger S relative to E (S > E). People on the autistic spectrum tend to show intact or even superior S, alongside impaired E (S≫E), relative to controls matched for mental age. Put succinctly, females are more likely to have a brain of Type E, males are more likely to have a brain of Type S, and people with autism are more likely to have a brain of Extreme Type S.

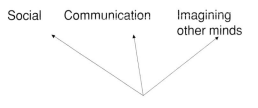

Figure 2. The triad of impairments. These are core areas of difficulty with people on the autistic spectrum. These behavioral 'symptoms' may reflect an underlying impairment in empathizing.

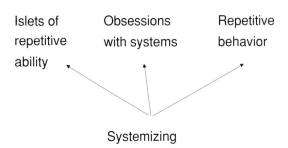

Figure 3. The triad of strengths. These are core qualities that are usually very strong in people with autism, and may not be unwanted. Islets of ability may be expressed as a talent in one skill, or at least an uneven cognitive profile relative to the person's other skills. Obsessions often focus on systems of one kind or another, and are an example of the person with autism going into a topic or activity in great depth, becoming a 'specialist.' Repetitive behavior was traditionally viewed as undesirable. These core qualities may, however, reflect an intact or even superior drive to systemize.

and geographical phenomena), abstract systems (e.g., mathematics or computer programs), and even social systems (e.g., profits and losses in a business, or a football league table). The way we make sense of any of these systems is in terms of underlying rules and regularities, or specifically an analysis of input-operation-output relationships.

E-S theory holds that alongside their deficits in the ability to empathize, the ability to systemize is either intact or superior in people with autism (Baron-Cohen, 2002). Initial studies of systemizing are consistent with these predictions. The systemizing talent found in a significant proportion of people with autism may help account for why 'islets of ability' in music, mathematics, drawing, and memorizing lists of information (e.g., train time-tables, calendrical calculation) may be found more often in autism than in other neurodevelopmental conditions. Because in the general population,

empathizing tends to be stronger in females and systemizing tends to be stronger in males, it has been proposed that autism may represent an 'extreme of the male brain' (Figs. 1, 2 and 3).

Executive dysfunction theory

People with autism spectrum conditions show 'repetitive behavior,' a strong desire for routines, and a 'need for sameness.' To date, the only cognitive account to attempt to explain this aspect of the syndrome is the executive dysfunction theory (Ozonoff *et al.*, 1994; Pennington *et al.*, 1997; Russell, 1997). This paints an essentially negative view of repetitive behavior, assuming that it is a form of frontal lobe perseveration (a tendency to repeat the response to a particular situation in other, inappropriate conditions), or an inability to shift attention. People with autism who have additional learning disabilities are more likely to show executive deficits. But the fact that it is possible for those with AS to exist who have no demonstrable executive dysfunction, while still having deficits in empathizing and talents in systemizing, suggests that executive dysfunction cannot be a core feature of autism spectrum conditions.

The executive account has also traditionally ignored the content of repetitive behavior. The E-S theory, in contrast, draws attention to the fact that much repetitive behavior involves the child's 'obsession' with, or strong interest in, mechanical systems (e.g., light switches, water faucets), or other systems that can be understood in terms of rules and regularities. Rather than these behaviors being a sign of executive dysfunction, they may reflect the child's intact or even superior interest in systems. A study of obsessions suggests that autistic obsessions are not random with respect to content, which would be predicted by the content-free executive dysfunction theory, but that these tend to cluster in the domain of systemizing.

Central coherence (CC) theory

'Weak' central coherence refers to the individual's preference for local detail over global processing (Frith, 1989). People with autism have been demonstrated to have a superior ability in the Embedded Figures Task – a test that involves locating a hidden part within a whole design as quickly and accurately as possible. This confirms that in autism there is superior attention to detail. Systemizing requires, as a first stage, excellent attention to detail, identifying parameters that may then be tested for their role in the behavior of the system under examination. So both the E-S theory and the CC theory predict excellent attention to detail. However, both theories also make opposite predictions when it comes to an individual with autism being able to understand a whole system.

The E-S theory predicts that a person with autism, faced with a new system to learn, will show a stronger drive to learn the system, compared to someone without autism, as long as there are underlying rules and regularities that can be discovered. Moreover, they will readily grasp that a change of one parameter in one part of the system may have distant effects on another part of the system. In contrast, the CC theory should predict that they will fail to understand whole (global) systems or the relationships between parts of a system. This prediction has not yet been tested.

Neurological causes of autism

A neural basis of empathy or social intelligence was first proposed by Brothers (1990). She suggested, from animal lesion studies, single cell recording studies, and neurological studies, that social intelligence was a function of three regions: the amygdala, the orbitofrontal cortex (OFC), and the superior temporal sulcus and gyrus (STG). Together, she called these the 'social brain.' There are several important lines of evidence implicating the amygdala in primate social behavior.

Amygdala-lesioned monkeys become socially isolated. They fail to initiate social interactions, and to respond appropriately to social gestures. When the amygdala-lesioned monkeys were released into the wild, they were unresponsive to group members, failed to display appropriate social signals (both affiliative and aggressive), and they withdrew from other animals.

Jocelyne Bachevalier lesioned either the medial temporal lobe (including the amygdala), or just the amygdala. The lesioned animal infants were raised and paired with an age-matched control animal. At 2 months, the infants with medial temporal lobe lesions were more passive, displayed increased temper tantrums, and initiated fewer social contacts. At 6 months, they interacted very little with the control animal, and actively withdrew from all approaches by the normal animals. Those with medial temporal lobe lesions also displayed emotionally expressionless faces, and showed more self-directed behavior and stereotypies (repetitive movements). Such abnormalities were still evident in adulthood. Amygdala lesions alone produced a similar pattern of social abnormalities, but to a lesser extent.

The human amygdala is activated when decoding signals of social importance, such as gaze, expression-recognition (especially of fearful faces), and body movements. There are several lines of evidence for an amygdala deficit in autism. A neuroanatomical study of autism at post-mortem found increased cell density in the amygdala, although its volume was normal. In addition, patients with amygdala lesions show impairments in social judgment that have been likened to 'acquired autism.' The age of onset of deficits in acquired autism compared to idiopathic cases is likely to mean that the two syndromes also differ in many ways. Likewise, patients with autism tend to show a similar pattern of deficits to those seen in patients with amygdala lesions. A recent structural magnetic resonance imaging (sMRI) study of autism reported reduced amygdala volume, while in a recent functional magnetic resonance imaging (fMRI) study, adults with autism but with normal intelligence, or with AS, showed significantly less amygdala activation during an empathizing task.

While these sorts of findings highlight the likely role an amygdala abnormality might play in autism, it is likely that it is not the only abnormal neural region. For example, the case has been made for anomalous functioning in the cerebellum, hippocampal formation, medial frontal cortex, and fronto-limbic connections in autism. Reduced neuron size and increased cell-packing density has also been found in the limbic system, specifically the hippocampus, subiculum, entorhinal cortex, amygdala, mammillary bodies, anterior cingulate, and septum in people with autism. Research is also focusing on the role of neurotransmitters, especially serotonin, in the autistic brain.

Genetic causes of autism

Ultimately, the behavioral, cognitive, affective, and neural abnormalities in autism spectrum conditions are likely to be due to genetic factors, as there is evidence for autism and AS being strongly heritable. Moreover, studies in molecular genetics are beginning to narrow down candidate regions on chromosomes (e.g., chromosome 7) that might be different in autism (International Molecular Genetics Study of Autism Consortium [IMGSAC], 2001).

Conclusions

Currently, there are no specific medications that are recommended for autism, but it is recognized that early identification of children with autism spectrum conditions is desirable, and special education in the form of highly structured, intensive programs is beneficial. Some of these programs are based on techniques from speech therapy (including the encouragement of social communication, such as joint attention behavior), whilst others are reward-based behavioral programs, where the children can use their natural systemizing skills to learn rules for social interaction. Some new tailor-made educational software is also being developed for people with autism, capitalizing on the fact that many of them enjoy using computers to learn about the world. The future of research in this field will be to understand the relationships between these different causal levels in autism, and to evaluate the most effective treatments.

See also:
Theories of the child's mind; Magnetic Resonance Imaging; Brain and behavioral development (I): sub-cortical; Brain and behavioral development (II): cortical; Executive functions; Face recognition; Intelligence; Selfhood; Socialization; Behavioral and learning disorders; Behavior genetics; Cognitive neuroscience; Ethology

Further reading

Baron-Cohen, S. (2003). *The Essential Difference: Men, Women and the Extreme Male Brain.* London: Allen Lane.

Baron-Cohen, S. and Bolton, P. (1993). *Autism: The Facts.* Oxford: Oxford University Press.

Wing, L. (2002). *The Autistic Spectrum.* London: Constable Robinson.

Acknowledgments

The author was supported by the MRC during the period of this work. Portions of this article also appeared in *Encarta* (2004).

Behavioral and learning disorders

CHRISTOPHER GILLBERG

Introduction

Non-autism behavior and learning disorders are common in the general population of children. Teachers often report that one in three of all primary school children have an academic, psychosocial, emotional, or behavioral problem (Kadesjö, 2000). However, the number of cases turns out to be much less, as revealed by epidemiological studies in child psychiatry and child development that report major behavior and learning disorders affect under 10 percent of all school-age children (Gillberg, 1995). Such disorders comprise major behavioral, emotional, and/or cognitive problems, usually with onset in the first five to eight years of life leading to functional impairment and handicap. Developmental disorders, such as specific reading/writing disorders and developmental coordination disorder (DCD) would not be included in this estimate. Conduct disorder, cases of child maltreatment, sexual or physical abuse are not included either, because they represent at once a huge and controversial area which there is not enough room to cover in this entry. The major diagnostic categories inferred – and which will be covered in this entry – are learning disability, behavioral phenotype syndromes, attention deficit hyperactivity disorder (ADHD), oppositional defiant disorder (ODD), Tourette's syndrome as well as other tic disorders, and obsessive compulsive disorder (OCD). Much less is known about depression, and anxiety disorders (including school refusal and selective mutism) in young children, and these conditions will only be briefly dealt with here.

Learning disability

A small percentage of the general population of children score under 70 on standardized IQ tests. When low scores in this range are combined with need for services or support specifically for the intellectual problems, a diagnosis of learning disability (or mental retardation) is made. The majority of children with learning disability have mild problems (IQ: 55–69), and only about 0.5 percent have moderate (IQ: 35/40–54), severe (IQ: 20–34/39), or profound learning disability (IQ<20). Boys are affected more often than girls, but the over-representation is not as marked as in other behavioral/cognitive disorders with symptom onset early in life (e.g., autism and ADHD). Brain damage and major genetic/chromosomal disorders (e.g., Down's syndrome, Rett's syndrome, tuberous sclerosis) are often identifiable causes in the latter group, whereas a likely specific cause cannot be identified in at least half of the cases with mild learning disability. Genetically determined low IQ, however, that is part of the normal distribution, and psychosocial factors, often interact in a complex fashion in such cases (Gillberg & Söderström, 2003).

Children with learning disability have a much increased rate of psychiatric disorder compared to the general population. If learning disability is associated with epilepsy, then the rate goes up even further. Among those with mild learning disability, the types of problems encountered are not widely discrepant from those seen in children of normal intellectual ability. Among those with more severe learning disability, the panorama shifts markedly. Thus, autistic disorder and atypical autism, ADHD, self-injurious behaviors, repetitive and stereotyped behaviors, and pica are much over-represented.

Children with learning disability are in need of appropriate assessment by a multidisciplinary team consisting of a neuropsychiatrist or developmental pediatrician / child neurologist, a neuropsychologist, and a special education expert. The level of learning disability and the type of co-morbid conditions (both psychiatric and physical), and possible etiologies, need to be determined at an early age so that appropriate interventions can be tailored individually to the specific needs of each child and family.

Behavioral phenotype syndromes

There are a number of conditions with a well-established etiology, or at least a very strong suspicion of a pathogenesis fairly unique to that condition, which present with a relatively typical behavioral phenotype. These are the behavioral phenotype syndromes. They include conditions such as the syndromes named after Williams, Rett, Prader-Willi, Angelman, and the 22q11-deletion (CATCH-22) syndromes. Individually, they are rare, occurring in 1 in 600 to about 1 in 10,000 children of school age. Male:female ratios are often consistent with those of the general population, except in the case of Rett's and Turner's syndromes, which are exclusively female conditions. Together, they are quite common, however, and as many as 0.5 percent of the general population of school-age children may be affected by one of these syndromes.

Most of the behavioral phenotype syndromes have a large sub-group with learning disability. However, some, such as the 22q11-deletion syndrome, have a large sub-population with only slightly sub-normal intelligence, or indeed normal or above normal levels of intelligence. Many of these conditions have typical physical stigmata, but they may be so slight, particularly when children are young, that they do not immediately alert the clinician to the possibility of an underlying specific (usually genetic) disorder.

The behavioral phenotype syndromes are particularly important because children often present with clinical indicators of an autism spectrum disorder, ADHD, Tourette's syndrome, or another major behavioral 'diagnosis.' The examining specialist needs to be well acquainted with the very real possibility of an underlying behavioral phenotype syndrome in such cases. Only a few brief examples of these syndromes will be given in the following.

Williams syndrome is usually associated with an abnormality of the elastin gene on the long arm of chromosome 7. It is hallmarked by overfriendliness, overtalkativeness, a drive for social interaction coupled with social anxiety and non-verbal neuropsychological problems, as well as a number of physical problems including cardiovascular disease.

Rett's syndrome is often associated with an abnormality of the MecP2-gene at the distal end of the long arm of the X chromosome. It is characterized by stagnating development (including stunted head growth) in the first few years of life, loss of communication skills, autistic-type behaviors, regression of purposeful hand movements, and a wide variety of other neurological and physical signs.

Prader-Willi syndrome is caused by a lack of a normal paternal gene at chromosome 15q11–13. It usually presents with hypotonia and feeding problems in the first days of life, but is substituted after a year or so by overeating, extreme overweight, skin-picking, and other ritualistic behaviors, as well as typical (but sometimes minor) physical stigmata and hypogonadism.

Angelman's syndrome is mostly caused by a lack of a normal maternal gene in the same broad region involved in the Prader-Willi syndrome. It often presents with severe learning disability, autistic (including ritualistic) behaviors, hyperactivity, ataxia, failure to walk unaided, and a peculiar tendency to unprovoked laughter.

The *22q11-deletion syndrome*, also called CATCH-22 for Cardiac abnormality, Anomalous face, Thymus hypoplasia, Cleft palate and Hypocalcemia associated with chromosome 22 abnormality, is of special interest because of its relatively high prevalence (about 0.03 percent of the general population of school-age children), the fact that learning disability is often minor or not present at all (in spite of the fact that the vast majority have problems coping with mainstream schooling), and that the clinical presentation often is that of ADHD, more rarely of an autistic-like condition. A typical nasal voice due to a sub-mucosal cleft soft palate, a history of a cardiac murmur, feeding problems, and preschool infections might guide the clinician toward the appropriate FISH analysis for a deletion at chromosome 22q11. Neuropsychologically, these children usually have considerably better verbal than non-verbal IQ at school age in spite of being very late in acquiring speech and language abilities.

Attention deficit hyperactivity disorder (ADHD)

The constellation of (1) inattention, (2) hyperactivity, and (3) impulsivity symptoms subsumed under the diagnostic label of 'ADHD' constitutes the single most common disorder in child and adolescent psychopathology (Kadesjö, 2000). It is believed to affect at least 3 percent of all school-age children in severe form, with mild and moderate cases affecting several more percent. Boys are affected on average three to four times as often as girls, but there is a suspicion that currently girls with the disorder may often go undiagnosed in spite of major academic and adjustment problems. ADHD is not synonymous with ICD-10 hyperkinetic disorder that requires the presence of symptoms from all three domains (viz., inattention, hyperactivity, and impulsivity). In contrast, ADHD has three sub-categories (viz., mainly inattentive sub-type, mainly hyperactive-impulsive sub-type, and combined sub-type) as reviewed in Table 1. In clinical settings, the combined sub-type is often seen already in very young

Table 1. Diagnostic criteria for Attention Deficit Hyperactivity Disorder[*].

A. Either (1) or (2)

  (1) six (or more) of the following symptoms of **inattention** have persisted for at least 6 months to a degree that is maladaptive and inconsistent with developmental level:

Inattention

    (a) often fails to give close attention to details or makes careless mistakes in schoolwork, work, or other activities

    (b) often has difficulty sustaining attention in tasks or play activities

    (c) often does not seem to listen when spoken to directly

    (d) often does not follow through on instructions and fails to finish schoolwork, chores, or duties in the workplace (not due to oppositional behavior or failure to understand instructions)

    (e) often has difficulty organizing tasks and activities

    (f) often avoids, dislikes, or is reluctant to engage in tasks that require sustained mental effort (such as schoolwork or homework)

    (g) often loses things necessary for tasks or activities (e.g., toys, school assignments, pencils, books, or tools)

    (h) is often easily distracted by extraneous stimuli

    (i) is often forgetful in daily activities

  (2) six (or more) of the following symptoms of **hyperactivity-impulsivity** have persisted for at least 6 months to a degree that is maladaptive and inconsistent with developmental level:

Hyperactivity

    (a) often fidgets with hands or feet or squirms in seat

    (b) often leaves seat in classroom or in other situations in which remaining seated is expected

    (c) often runs about or climbs excessively in situations in which it is inappropriate (in adolescents or adults may be limited to subjective feelings of restlessness)

    (d) often has difficulty playing or engaging in leisure activities quietly

    (e) is often 'on the go,' or often acts as if 'driven by a motor'

    (f) often talks excessively

Impulsivity

    (a) often blurts out answers before questions have been completed

    (b) often has difficulty awaiting turn

    (c) often interrupts or intrudes on others (e.g., butts into others' conversations or games)

B. Some hyperactive-impulsive or inattentive symptoms that caused impairment were present before age 7 years

C. Some impairment from the symptoms is present in two or more settings (e.g., at school [or work] and at home)

D. There must be clear evidence of clinically significant impairment in social, academic, or occupational functioning

E. The symptoms do not occur exclusively during the course of a Pervasive Developmental Disorder, Schizophrenia, or other Psychotic Disorder and are not better accounted for by another mental disorder (e.g., Mood Disorder, Anxiety Disorder, Dissociative Disorder, or a Personality Disorder).

Code based on type:

  314.01 Attention-Deficit/Hyperactivity Disorder, Combined Type: if both Criteria A1 and A2 are met for the past 6 months

  314.00 Attention-Deficit/Hyperactivity Disorder, Predominantly Inattentive Type: if Criterion A1 is met but Criterion A2 is not met for the past 6 months

  314.01 Attention-Deficit/Hyperactivity Disorder, Predominantly Hyperactive-Impulsive Type: if Criterion A2 is met but Criterion A1 is not met for the past 6 months

  Coding note: For individuals (especially adolescents and adults) who currently have symptoms that no longer meet full criteria, "In Partial Remission" should be specified.

[*]American Psychiatric Association, 1994. *DSM-IV: Diagnostic and Statistical Manual of Mental Disorders*, 4th. edn. Washington, DC: American Psychiatric Association.

children. The inattentive sub-type sometimes comes to the attention of clinicians only several years later, including in adolescence, and even adult life.

Co-morbidities are common. In a recent study, 87 percent of a general population sample with ADHD had at least one co-morbid diagnosis, which included DCD, reading/writing disorder, ODD, anxiety, depression, and social interaction difficulties sometimes amounting to autism spectrum disorder (Kadesjö & Gillberg, 2001).

ADHD is probably genetic in more than half of all cases, and oligo- or polygenic modes of inheritance are likely, given the available evidence from twin, adoption, and extended family studies. Risk factors also include potentially brain damaging events, such as preterm birth with complications and intrauterine alcohol exposure. Psychosocial factors probably play a role in determining the risk for some of the co-morbid problems (such as oppositional-defiant and conduct problems). On the other hand, the child-rearing situation and long-term outcome, but without direct consequences for brain development *per se*, do not appear to be involved in the basic pathophysiology. However, dopamine dysfunction has been suggested as an underlying common pathway on the basis, for example, of several molecular genetic studies implicating dopamine receptors and dopamine transporter gene variation/dysfunction in ADHD.

Neuropsychological findings associated with the syndrome include poor results on one or more of the arithmetic, coding, digit span, and information sub-tests of the Wechsler scales. They can also include a slight reduction in overall IQ, executive dysfunction, poor results on various tests of auditory and visual attention, and a limited capacity for impulse control. These findings, and those from neuroimaging (including functional neuroimaging), suggest variation/dysfunction in the prefrontal-frontal-striatal loops. Brain size appears to be significantly reduced in ADHD, but it is not clear yet whether this finding is associated with the overall lower IQ in ADHD, or is more specifically linked to the core behavioral and neuro-psychological problems inherent in the syndrome.

ADHD in the severe cases usually presents with major signs already during the preschool years. Parents are in need of an early diagnosis, and are often helped by good information and training in respect of how best to rear a child with a disruptive behavior disorder. The children themselves are often in need of an individually tailored educational program that can provide a lot of structure and short-term rewards. Stimulant and other medications affecting the catecholamine systems are often effective in controlling symptoms of ADHD (and ODD) in the short term, and appear to have some persistent positive effects also in the rather longer-term perspective. Drug treatment, when prescribed, should always be seen as an integral part of a more holistic approach to intervention in which educational and psychosocial aspects need to be fully integrated.

Untreated ADHD may carry a gloomy prognosis, with 40–70 percent of population-representative and clinic cases having a poor psychosocial outcome in early adult life. Substance-use disorders, including alcohol abuse, personality disorders, and antisocial development, are all quite common. Conversely, a large proportion of all adults with such problems have a childhood history of ADHD. The available evidence suggests that substance-use disorder is not predicted by prior stimulant treatment, but by ADHD *per se*. Stimulant-treated children may actually have a much reduced risk of later drug and alcohol abuse in adolescence.

Oppositional defiant disorder (ODD)

ODD is a very common co-morbid problem in ADHD, with 60 percent of children having the latter diagnosis meeting full criteria already in the early preschool years (Kadesjö, 2000). Some of the symptoms of ODD (Table 2) are so common in ADHD (e.g., loss of temper) that it is currently difficult to determine whether they should be considered intrinsic to ADHD rather than to ODD. Several percent of all preschool and school-age children meet diagnostic criteria for ODD, but it is unclear how large a proportion of all cases have ODD 'only' (without co-morbid ADHD, Tourette's syndrome, etc.). Boys are much over-represented. Children with ODD have a much increased risk of conduct disorder and antisocial development, particularly when the condition is co-morbid with ADHD, but it is not known what proportion of those meeting childhood criteria for ODD will go on to meet criteria for antisocial personality disorder in adult life (Kazdin & Wassell, 2000).

The roots of ODD have not been well elucidated. It is clear that psychosocial factors play a major role, but the exact mechanisms involved, and the validity of the disorder as a separate condition, are not as strong as in the case of ADHD. Genetic factors may also play a role in the pathogenetic chain of events – but conclusive evidence is lacking.

Guidelines for intervention are similar to those for ADHD. It goes without saying that this is the case particularly when ODD is co-morbid with ADHD.

Tourette's syndrome and other tic disorders

Tics are very common in the general population. At least 10 percent of school-age children are affected (or have been affected) by motor or vocal tics, or a combination

---

Table 2. Diagnostic criteria for Oppositional Defiant Disorder*.

A. A pattern of negativistic, hostile, and defiant behavior lasting at least 6 months, during which four (or more) of the following are present:

   (1) often loses temper

   (2) often argues with adults

   (3) often actively defies or refuses to comply with adults' requests or rules

   (4) often deliberately annoys people

   (5) often blames others for his or her mistakes or misbehavior

   (6) is often touchy or easily annoyed by others

   (7) is often angry and resentful

   (8) is often spiteful or vindictive

   Note: Consider a criterion met only if the behavior occurs more frequently than typically observed in individuals of comparable age and developmental level.

B. The disturbance in behavior causes clinically significant impairment in social, academic, or occupational functioning.

C. The behaviors do not occur exclusively during the course of a Psychotic or Mood Disorder.

D. Criteria are not met for Conduct Disorder, and, if the individual is age 18 years or older, criteria are not met for Antisocial Personality Disorder.

* American Psychiatric Association, 1994.

---

of both. If there are multiple motor tics, at least one vocal tic, and the child is functionally disabled because of them, then a diagnosis of Tourette's syndrome is often appropriate (Table 3). Recent population estimates suggest that at least 1 percent of the general population of school-age children are affected by a clinically handicapping Tourette's syndrome. Again, boys are much over-represented, and they are usually reported to be affected at three to five times the rate for girls.

Tourette's syndrome is usually genetic (Pauls, 2001). While long believed to be an autosomal dominant condition, it is now considered to be one of the many psychiatric disorders in which several susceptibility genes may act in concert to produce either sub-clinical variants or clinically handicapping conditions. Recently, interest has focused on the possibility that Tourette's syndrome can sometimes be caused or exacerbated by autoimmune processes (e.g., as occur after some coccal infections) affecting the basal ganglia or frontostriatal brain systems.

The majority of individuals with clinically important Tourette's syndrome are usually affected by one or more major co-morbidities. The most common of these are ADHD and OCD. Two-thirds of all those with Tourette's syndrome have one or both of these, and more often than not the co-morbidities are the major reason for psychosocial maladjustment and handicap, not the tics in themselves. Autism spectrum disorders also appear to be much overrepresented in Tourette's syndrome and other tic disorders. Moreover, tics are very common in some autism spectrum disorders, such as Asperger's syndrome. A very common developmental trajectory is one in which ADHD (often mainly hyperactive) is diagnosed in the preschool child (very often also with ODD). In such cases, tics emerge during the early school years, and OCD problems may then become the most handicapping symptoms a few years later.

Children with Tourette's syndrome are usually of normal (or high) intelligence, even though learning disability is certainly not excluded. Neuropsychological tests have revealed decreased impulse control, and some studies suggest an increased rate of blue-yellow color blindness (supporting basal ganglia dysfunction in the condition). By and large, however, the neuropsychological deficits documented in patients with Tourette's syndrome are often accounted for by their commonly co-morbid conditions, such as ADHD and OCD.

Tourette's syndrome should be diagnosed during the school years, parents and child informed about the implications, and possible interventions made available. Tics, although amenable to treatment with old and new neuroleptics, should not be considered target symptoms unless severely handicapping. There is usually a much stronger indication for medication treatment of one or more of the co-morbidities. Tics are not, as was once believed, a sign that stimulants should not be used in the treatment of ADHD, but rather that observation and caution should be increased. When gently titrated,

Table 3. Diagnostic criteria for Tourette's Disorder[*].

A. Both multiple motor and one or more vocal tics have been present at some time during the illness, although not necessarily concurrently. (A tic is a sudden, rapid recurrent, nonrhythmic, stereotyped motor movement or vocalization.)

B. The tics occur many times a day (usually in bouts), nearly every day or intermittently throughout a period of more than 1 year, and during this period there was never a tic-free period of more than 3 consecutive months.

C. The disturbance causes marked distress or significant impairment in social, occupational, or other important areas of functioning.

D. The onset is before age 18 years.

E. The disturbance is not due to the direct physiological effects of a substance (e.g., stimulants) or a general medical condition (e.g., Huntington's disease or postviral encephalitis).

[*]American Psychiatric Association, 1994.

stimulants usually do not cause major problems in the treatment of ADHD in Tourette's syndrome.

The outcome for Tourette's syndrome is not well known because of a dearth of population-representative studies. However, all the available evidence suggests that a large proportion of all individuals do well in adult life. Some have periods in which the symptoms wax and wane, sometimes with impairment, sometimes not. A small proportion have a continuation into adult life of severely handicapping tics. It seems likely that the ultimate prognosis in Tourette's syndrome is determined more by the presence of ADHD or OCD or both than by the tics themselves.

Obsessive compulsive disorder (OCD)

OCD is also quite a common condition, affecting about 1 percent of the general population of school-age children. It may be only marginally overrepresented in boys (the increased rate being contributed by the boys with the combination of Tourette's syndrome and OCD/Asperger's syndrome).

Obsessions and compulsions, just like tics, are very common in the general population of school-age children. However, it is only when they become severely handicapping in everyday life situations that there is a need to make a specific diagnosis of OCD (Table 4). It was once believed to be the classical example of a psychosocially determined 'neurosis,' but is now generally accepted to be the phenotypic expression of a neuropsychiatric disorder, in which basal ganglia dysfunction is a key player (Giedd *et al.*, 2000). The neuropsychological profile has not yet been shown to be specific to the disorder. Most children with this condition are of normal intelligence. Treatment with serotonin reuptake inhibitors and cognitive behavior therapy have both been shown to have independent positive effects on the manifestations of the disorder,

and should be attempted in most instances with clinically impairing symptomatology.

Emotional disorders

Although not a focus of this entry, the emotional disorders of childhood, depression, and anxiety disorders often show co-morbidity with the disruptive behavior disorders, such as ADHD and ODD. Whilst some authors would list OCD among the anxiety disorders, it now seems that it has more in common with the tic disorders as outlined in the foregoing. Separation anxiety disorder often manifests itself as school refusal in children. Selective mutism is a relatively rare condition affecting about 0.2 percent of all school-age children, and is believed by some authors to be a disorder of social anxiety. Be that as it may, children with selective mutism often have autism spectrum problems which, unfortunately, tend to go undiagnosed. Selective mutism is diagnosed in children who have normal or near-normal capacity for spoken language, but who, for whatever reason, refuse to speak in certain (usually most) settings.

Conclusions

Behavior and learning disorders requiring interventions affect about one in six boys and one in twelve girls. This epidemiological perspective needs to be taken on board by all teachers, school health officers, developmental pediatricians, and child psychiatrists so that better services can be provided in the future. There is a great need for further study both of the risk factors (including genetic, other biological, and psychosocial ones) leading to disorder, and of interventions that may help in halting the often negative psychosocial and academic development currently faced by many of those affected. There is also a need to focus more specifically on research in girls, who are currently underdiagnosed and

Table 4. Diagnostic criteria for Obsessive-Compulsive Disorder*.

A. Either obsessions or compulsions:

Obsessions as defined by (1), (2), (3), and (4):

(1) recurrent and persistent thoughts, impulses, or images that are experienced, at some time during the disturbance, as intrusive and inappropriate and that cause marked anxiety or distress

(2) the thoughts, impulses, or images are not simply excessive worries about real-life problems

(3) the person attempts to ignore or suppress such thoughts, impulses, or images, or to neutralize them with some other thought or action

(4) the person recognizes that the obsessional thoughts, impulses, or images are a product of his or her own mind (not imposed from without as in thought insertion)

Compulsions as defined by (1) and (2):

(1) repetitive behaviors (e.g., hand washing, ordering, checking) or mental acts (e.g., praying, counting, repeating words silently) that the person feels driven to perform in response to an obsession, or according to rules that must be applied rigidly

(2) the behaviors or mental acts are aimed at preventing or reducing distress or preventing some dreaded event or situation; however, these behaviors or mental acts either are not connected in a realistic way with what they are designed to neutralize or prevent or are clearly excessive

B. At some point during the course of the disorder, the person has recognized that the obsessions or compulsions are excessive or unreasonable. **Note:** This does not apply to children.

C. The obsessions or compulsions cause marked distress, are time consuming (take more than 1 hour a day), or significantly interfere with the person's normal routine, occupational (or academic) functioning, or usual social activities or relationships.

D. If another Axis I disorder is present, the content of the obsessions or compulsions is not restricted to it (e.g., preoccupation with food in the presence of an Eating Disorder; hair pulling in the presence of Trichotillomania; concern with appearance in the presence of Body Dysmorphic Disorder; preoccupation with drugs in the presence of Substance Use Disorder; preoccupation with having a serious illness in the presence of Hypochondriasis; preoccupation with sexual urges or fantasies in the presence of a Paraphilia; or guilty ruminations in the presence of Major Depressive Disorder).

E. The disturbance is not due to the direct physiological effects of a substance (e.g., a drug of abuse, a medication) or a general medical condition.

Specify if:

With Poor Insight: if, for most of the time during the current episode, the person does not recognize that the obsessions and compulsions are excessive or unreasonable

*American Psychiatric Association, 1994.

---

receive little in the way of intervention, even when they have major problems.

See also:
Theories of the child's mind; Magnetic Resonance Imaging; Epidemiological designs; Twin and adoption studies; Aggressive and prosocial behavior; Attention; Executive functions; Reading and writing; Sex differences; 'At-risk' factor; Autism; Child depression; Developmental coordination disorder; Prematurity and low birthweight; Williams syndrome; Behavior genetics; Pediatrics

Further reading

Gillberg, C., Harrington, R. and Steinhausen, H.-C. (2004). *Clinician's Deskbook of Child and Adolescent Psychiatry*. Cambridge: Cambridge University Press.

Harris, J. (1995). *Developmental Neuropsychiatry*. Oxford: Oxford University Press.

The Multimodal Cooperative Group (1999). A 14-month randomized clinical trial of treatment strategies for attention-deficit/hyperactivity disorder. The MTA Cooperative Group. Multimodal Treatment Study of Children with ADHD. *Archives of General Psychiatry*, 56, 1073–1086.

Blindness

ANN BIGELOW

Introduction

Blindness affects children's understanding of both the social and physical environment, yet it is the understanding of the latter that is more profoundly challenged. Language becomes blind children's most useful tool for deciphering the external world. Consequently, research on the effect of blindness on early development has focused primarily on spatial cognition and language, and to a lesser extent on social development.

Pervasive in the research is evidence of how blindness impacts on children's ability to sense the effect of their behavior on their physical and social surroundings. Blindness inhibits children's development of a sense of self-efficacy, an awareness that they are effective agents in the world and that their actions have consequences that can become predictable. Blind children's difficulty acquiring an early sense of self-efficacy affects their curiosity and exploration of the physical environment and their social exchanges with others.

Spatial cognition

Blind infants have difficulties in object and spatial understanding, particularly in determining objects' spatial locations and securing objects through their own actions. These difficulties result in delays in their ability to reach for objects and to locomote independently, but other motor milestones tend not to be affected.

Search for objects

Blind infants' understanding of space is initially body centered. They will reach for objects touching their bodies before they will reach to objects on sound cues alone. In her pioneering study of blind children's development, Fraiberg (1977) found the infants' early searches to sound were to objects directly in front of their bodies. Only later do sounding objects positioned

out of the midline elicit successful directional reaches (Bigelow, 1995). Even after sound begins to elicit and direct blind infants' reaches, if sound is in directional conflict with the location of immediate prior tactile contact with the object, the infants will reach to the area where they lost physical contact with the object rather than toward the sound (Fig. 1). With development, blind infants' search moves from the subjectively circumscribed space that is limited to the space directly in front of them, or to the space in which they last contacted the desired object, to allocentric search directed from external cues.

Electronic sensory aids have been developed to help blind children locate objects in space. The Sonicguide has received the most research. This is a sonar-based system that provides a complex auditory signal containing information about the distance, direction, and surface characteristics of objects within range. Research results on the effectiveness of the Sonicguide have been mixed, although clearly it has been shown to assist some infants. Nevertheless, its usefulness is questioned because of the possible negative impact on selective auditory perception and intermodal coordination (Warren, 1994).

Sensory aids which stimulate the development of natural experience and opportunity are more promising. For example, Nielsen (1992) has developed a miniature environment to teach reaching that utilizes blind children's initial subjective body-centered sense of space. The children lie on their backs in three-sided cubicles to which tactually interesting objects are attached to the walls and ceiling within reachable distance. Through random arm and hand movements, the children discover the objects that remain in constant positions. The experience of contacting particular objects in non-varying positions relative to their bodies allows the children to perceive their actions as having predictable consequences. This experience stimulates the children's interest in, and expectation of, using their bodies to locate and explore objects in the larger world.

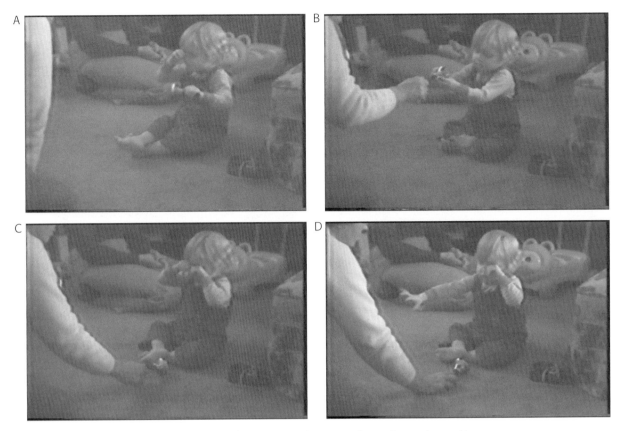

Figure 1. A blind child is playing with a bell (A), which is taken from him (B), and moved to another position where it is rung (C). The child reaches to where he lost contact with the bell rather than toward the sound of the object (D).

Locomotion

Fraiberg (1977) proposed that reaching is the key to locomotion because blind children begin to crawl shortly after they begin to reach to sound cues. She took such reaching as an indication of the emergence of Stage 4 of object permanence. Bigelow (1995) developed ten sound and touch tasks that assess the development of blind infants' object permanence from Stage 3, through Stage 4, into Stage 5. Table 1 shows the emergence of locomotor abilities and the development of object permanence, as indicated by the mastery of key tasks, in three blind infants. Although the infants mastered the tasks and locomotor abilities at different ages, the relation between their acquisition of object permanence and locomotion was similar. Crawling coincided with the emergence of Stage 4 behavior and walking coincided with or was subsequent to the transition to Stage 5. Blind children appear to have a protracted Stage 4, and a more extended period between learning to crawl and learning to walk than sighted children. They are as physically mature as their sighted peers, yet they know less about objects and space. To walk independently and release themselves from the four-point tactile contact with the environment that crawling provides, the children must advance in their object and spatial awareness.

Once mobile, blind children readily negotiate familiar environments, but they are at a disadvantage if they must coordinate information from different routes to produce novel routes or integrate spatial knowledge among objects that are not sequentially encountered. Spatial information that can be acquired by sighted children in a single glance must for blind children be explored, synthesized, and reconstructed. Knowing where one is in physical space, where objects are in relation to each other and to self, and how these relations change with self-movement, are life-long challenges for the blind.

Early social interaction

Blindness puts infants' social development at risk. There is no turning to face the parent in greeting or reaching out to be picked up. Although smiles are present, they are fleeting, not socially elicited, and not directionally oriented toward the cause of pleasure. Many important avenues for interaction, such as mutual gaze and pointing, are absent. Lack of vision makes it difficult for children to perceive what others are attending to and, therefore, to understand the emotional reactions and intentions of others. Blind infants are particularly

Table 1. Age in months for blind children's mastery of locomotive abilities and tasks indicative of stages of object permanence.

	Blind children			Age of sighted children's acquisition
	1	2	3	
Age in months when first seen	17	13	32	
Stage 3 (task 1)	20	*	*	4[a]
Stage 4 (task 2)	23	*	*	8[a]
Crawling	23	*	*	7[b]
Transition between Stages 4 and 5 (task 8)	28	17	35	
Stage 5 (task 9)	30	21	34	12[a]
Walking unsupported	32	17	36	12[b]

[a] Age taken from J. H. Flavell (1963). *The Developmental Psychology of Jean Piaget.* New York: Van Nostrand.
[b] Age taken from N. Bayley (1969). *Bayley Scales of Infant Development.* New York: Psychological Corporation.
Note. An asterisk indicates the child showed mastery on the first session.
Adapted from A. E. Bigelow (1992). Locomotion and search behavior in blind infants. *Infant Behavior and Development,* 15, 184. Copyright 1992, with permission from Elsevier Science.

dependent on others to present the physical and social affordances available because they cannot easily predict these affordances themselves. Joint attention is delayed because of the difficulties in detecting the spatial relations among self, other, and object as well as the focus of others' attention. Once blind children begin to use language effectively to engage others and to acquire and discuss objects, they can more easily initiate social interactions.

Parents of blind children must learn to be sensitive to alternative means of interaction. Fraiberg (1977) suggested that infants' hand movements may be more indicative of their emotional responses than their facial expressions. The blind baby, who does not turn to greet the parent, may move the hands excitedly upon hearing the parent's voice and become immobile upon hearing a stranger's voice. Parents must become attuned to such cues in order to establish interactive social patterns with their children. By providing sensitive tactile and vocal responses to their infants' behavior, parents facilitate the infants' learning that they can influence the actions and eventually the feelings and thoughts of others. In so doing, blind infants become active social partners.

Language development

Similarities between blind and sighted children's language development suggest that common processes are at work in the early language acquisition of children with quite diverse perceptual awareness. Blindness does not delay the age of first words or growth of early vocabulary. Words for objects and people dominate the early vocabulary of both blind and sighted children. Commonalities also exist in the underlying characteristics of what blind and sighted children choose to label with their early words. Piaget proposed that young children label things or events that acquire their meaning in the sensorimotor period. The early words of sighted children label objects that children act upon (e.g., *ball, cookie*), or objects that produce perceptual change such as *dog, car*. The early words of blind children also support Piaget's prediction, despite the children's restricted self-actions and ability to perceive external action. Table 2 shows the general nominals of three blind children's initial fifty-word vocabularies. In addition to labels for objects acted upon, the blind children's early words labeled objects that produce auditory change (e.g., *music*), changes in tactile sensation such as *dirt*, and even olfactory change (e.g., *furnace*, used to refer to the object and any heating vent).

The differences between the early language of blind and sighted children are influenced by experiential factors. In comparing the findings of several researchers, Mulford (1988) noted that young blind children have more specific nominals and fewer general nominals than sighted children. Blind children's difficulty with extending their labels to classes of objects may be because they are less likely to encounter multiple instances of the objects; they cannot readily perceive objects from a distance and do not have access to pictures. Alternatively, blind children may have difficulty with category formation. Their inability to perceive the visual attributes of objects reduces their ability to perceive similarities among objects, making it difficult for them to abstract the critical features of objects necessary to extend the application of their early words. Their action words label self-actions. Relational terms (e.g., *no, more*) are used to satisfy their own needs, but do not encode information about the dynamical state of external events. Like sighted children, blind children's language initially is aligned closely with their perceptual experience, but this experience is reduced essentially to what they are currently doing or interacting with. It is primarily the close perceptual experiences of touch, taste, and smell that are commented upon. References to the experiences of others or events they have not participated in, both of which might be perceived with interest by sighted children, are rare in blind children.

Other differences between the early language of blind and sighted children may stem from the way blind children are spoken to (Mulford, 1988). Parents of blind children provide many labels but fewer descriptions of objects or events, resulting in the children having few modifiers (adjectives and adverbs). Parental speech to blind children tends to be more directive and less elaborate than to sighted children. The differences in the speech directed to blind children and their reduced perceptual experience may affect social-cognitive factors upon which language is based.

Other behaviors associated with blindness

Some behaviors of blind children resemble characteristics that are associated with pathology in sighted children. Yet these behaviors may be a natural result of lack of vision and serve a useful function for blind children. Echolalia, which rarely occurs in the absence of other more appropriate uses of language, may be a means of maintaining contact with others or engaging them when it is not clear what others are focused on or talking about. The reversal of first and second person pronouns may indicate that blindness inhibits the encoding of the reciprocal nature of speaker and addressee inherent in these pronouns.

The inability to readily engage in pretend play may be due to the reduced perceptual access to behaviors that could be imitated in play. Also many toys and props for play are miniatures of larger items whose overall shape is unknown to blind children (e.g., toy cars or animals), and thus the miniatures are not recognizable as representations of the larger objects.

Blind children are prone to self stimulating, autistic-like behaviors, such as rocking, headshaking, and limb flapping. These behaviors may be comforting in their predictability compared to the relative unpredictability of external acts and sensory input. Such behaviors tend to reduce as the children gain mastery over their environment.

Although the lack of visual experience can account for many of the behaviors of concern, the constellation of autistic-like behaviors, echolalia, difficulties in symbolic play and in linguistic reference to self and other suggest that blind children are at risk for problems in the development of self-understanding. Key to this understanding is blind children's ability to perceive the effect of their behavior on the external world, be it social or physical.

Conclusions

The study of blind children both informs our understanding of the development of these children and reveals the importance of vision to developmental processes. In the past, comparisons often have been made between blind and sighted children's performance

Table 2. Blind children's general nominals in first fifty-word vocabulary by semantic category.

Food	Household items	Clothes	Toys
Cookie[a] (2)	High chair (2)	Hat[a] (2)	Rockinghorse (2)
Juice[a] (2)	Blanket[a] (1)	Shoes[a] (1)	Truck (2)
Toast[a] (1)	Telephone[a] (1)	Diaper (1)	Ball[a] (1)
Gum[a] (1)	Rocking chair (1)	Sweater (1)	Bike[a] (1)
Candy[a] (1)	Radio (1)	Snowsuit (1)	Top (1)
Cracker[a] (1)	Furnace (1)		Wagon (1)
Water[a] (1)	Piano (1)		Drum (1)
Drink[a] (1)	Newspaper (1)		Guitar (1)
Pickle[a] (1)			
Dinner (1)			
Treat (1)			
French fries (1)			
Tea (1)			
Sandwich (1)			
Yogurt (1)			
Cone (1)			
Fruit loops (1)			
Vehicles	Animals	People	Place
Car[a] (3)	Puppy[a] (2)	Baby (2)	Basement (1)
	Bird[a] (1)	Boy (1)	Kitchen (1)
Body part	Personal items	Miscellaneous	
Bum (1)	Key[a] (1)	Music (2)	
Eye (1)	Money[a] (1)	Bath (2)	
	Powder (1)	Dirt (1)	
	Bell (1)	Car seat (1)	

[a]General nominals also in sighted children's first fifty words, as indicated in K. Nelson (1973). Structure and strategy in learning to talk. *Monographs of the Society for Research in Child Development*, 38, No. 149.
[b]Numbers in parentheses are number of blind children in the sample of three who have word among first fifty words.
From A. E. Bigelow [1987]. Early words of blind children *Journal of Child Language*, 14, 51. Copyright 1987, with permission from Cambridge University Press.

on tasks that are facilitated by vision or visual imagery. Such comparisons have led to conclusions of delays or deficits in blind children. Research on individual differences within blind children's development is a promising alternative (Warren, 1994). This approach examines the nature of variation within the population and searches for causal factors of the variation. The search for causality is facilitated by adopting a dynamical systems framework, which necessitates the asking of complex questions, such as how the changing relations among the children's capabilities, their environment, and as how others respond to their disability impact on their development. By addressing such questions, a more productive understanding of blind children's development will emerge.

The study of blind children also provides a unique context in which to examine the role of vision in early development. Important headways have been made in understanding the importance of vision to object awareness, locomotion, spatial knowledge, and language and communication skills. Knowledge of blind children's ability to acquire a sense of self, despite initial difficulties, has also been useful in understanding the unique impediments of autistic children in understanding self and others. Future research with blind children promises to expand and deepen knowledge of the ways vision facilitates development and to illustrate that, although important, vision is not essential to normal development.

See also:
Dynamical systems approaches; Cognitive development in infancy; Perceptual development; Motor development; Social development; Language development; Locomotion; Play; Prehension; Selfhood; 'At-risk' concept; Autism; Jean Piaget

Further reading

Dunlea, A. (1989). *Vision and the Emergence of Meaning: Blind and Sighted Children's Early Language.* Cambridge: Cambridge University Press.

Landau, B. and Gleitman, L. R. (1985). *Language and Experience: Evidence from the Blind Child.* Cambridge, MA: Harvard University Press.

Lewis, V. and Collis, G. (eds.) (1997). *Blindness and Psychological Development in Young Children.* Leicester, UK: The British Psychological Society.

Millar, S. (1994). *Understanding and Representing Space: Theory and Evidence from Studies with Blind and Sighted Children.* Oxford: Oxford University Press.

Pérez-Pereira, M. and Conti-Ramsden, G. (1999). *Language Development and Social Interaction in Blind Children.* Hove, UK: Psychology Press.

Cerebral palsies

FIONA STANLEY

Introduction

This overview of the cerebral palsies is given from the perspective of an epidemiologist describing the patterns of occurrence and possible causal pathways to these motor disorders from population data. It does not go into details about clinical, therapeutic, or management issues, which are complex and currently being challenged. Hard evidence of effectiveness of early interventions to reduce the disability and enhance capacity is still needed, but well worth pursuing. Current therapies include drugs, Botulinus toxin injections, surgery (including neuro/spinal-cord surgery), and a variety of physiotherapeutic activities. None of these will be reviewed here as the focus is on the epidemiology. There are several other entries in this volume that contribute to our understanding of the cerebral palsies. Hence, an appreciation of normal and abnormal prenatal development, behavioral and learning disorders, of developmental coordination disorder, the birth process, the status of the newborn, and motor development all help in better understanding the complex pathways to the cerebral palsies, and the large number of possible pathologies that can interfere with motor development in utero and in early childhood. The advent and increasing use of brain imaging techniques has opened a whole new world of diagnosis of brain structure and function, which promises to contribute enormously to knowledge about the timing and etiologies of the cerebral palsies (and other brain disorders). In addition, epidemiology needs to become more sophisticated in both measuring and analyzing, as well as collaborating with other disciplines, to enable better elucidation of causal pathways (Stanley, Blair, & Alberman, 2000; Blair & Stanley, 2002).

Definition and descriptions of the cerebral palsies

The cerebral palsies are a heterogeneous collection of motor disorders, best defined as a group of non-progressive, but often changing, motor impairment syndromes secondary to lesions or anomalies of the brain arising in the early stages of its development (Mutch et al., 1992). They are heterogeneous as regards cause, severity, outcome, and clinical features. The term refers to clinical descriptions of motor disorders of cerebral origin, but there is no definitive test nor an underlying classical etiology, brain pathology, or genetic defect that is 'cerebral palsy.' In spite of the recent increased use of brain imaging in children with neurological problems, in the majority of children labeled as having cerebral palsy no definitive cerebral diagnosis is obvious. Thus, it is a clinical description with fairly poorly defined parameters ('non-progressive,' 'early stages of brain development,' 'brain anomaly'). Why still use the term 'cerebral palsy'? Reasons mostly relate to management, services, and funding for children with motor disorders, rather than to it being an acceptable or useful definition that helps with etiological investigations. Moreover, no other term has come into common usage to replace it.

Since the early 1980s, epidemiologists have become increasingly interested in neurological problems such as the cerebral palsies, and total population collections of cases (or registers) have been crucial in describing patterns and occurrence. For the purposes of epidemiological registers, both the minimum age at which ascertainment of a birth-year cohort will be considered complete and accurate and the maximum age at which post-neonatally acquired cases will be included, needs to be decided. The challenge is that it takes time for many children with cerebral palsy to demonstrate their impairments and, this awaits the development of challenging motor activity, even in the most severe cases. Thus, it can vary from months (when severe) to years (when mild) of age, and the impairment can change as the child develops, in spite of the brain lesion not being progressive. Since most of the known causes of motor impairment can also result in death, either before birth (early or late fetal death) or after (neonatal, infant, or child death), the diagnosis of cerebral palsy is therefore a

Table 1. Distribution of types of cerebral palsy in six registers, excluding post-neonatally acquired cases.

CP type	W. Australia[1] 1975–1990 (N – 756) Predominant %	Pure %	W. Sweden[2] 1983–1990 (N – 383) Predominant %	Mersey, UK[3] 1966–1977 (N – 695) Predominant %	Avon, UK[4] 1969–1988 (N – 489) Predominant %	E. Denmark[5] 1965–1974 (N – 788) Predominant %	N. Ireland[6] 1978–1992 (N – 662) Predominant %
Hemiplegia	36.2	33.1	33.7	27.0	36.2	26.8	37.0
Diplegia	31.6	18.0	44.9*	21.0	28.4	32.2	17.8
Quadriplegia	15.9	9.1	8.4	27.7	14.3	21.1	31.6
Non-classical spastic		16.0					
All spastic	83.7	76.2	87.0	75.7	78.9	80.1	86.4
Ataxia	7.0*	5.0	5.5	4.5		5.6	5.0
Dyskinesia	8.6	5.8	7.6	4.1		10.0	6.0
Hypotonia	0.6	0.5		2.0			0.2
Mixed							
– Mainly spastic		7.5		10.8**			
– Mainly non-spastic		4.9					
Other					21.1	4.3	
Unclassified				2.8			2.4

* Includes ataxic diplegia
** Mixed CP associated with spasticity, not necessarily predominantly spastic
1 Unpublished data from the Western Australian Cerebral Palsy Register
2 Hagberg *et al.* (1993, 1996)
3 Pharoah *et al.* (1987)
4 MacGillivray & Campbell (1995)
5 Topp *et al.* (1997)
6 Parkes *et al.* (1998)

function of the survival of a cerebrally damaged child at any age before development is considered to be complete. If death occurs before ascertainment, then differing survival rates in different study populations can influence cerebral palsy rates, providing further challenges to those of us interested in how often the various cerebral palsies occur and what causes them.

Table 1 shows the distribution of types of cerebral palsies from six population registers. The majority are spastic, with proportions of sub-types (diplegia, hemiplegia, and quadriplegia) varying markedly between countries due mostly to differences in how their pediatric neurologists classify them more than to etiological differences. Table 2 shows the Western Australian (WA) Cerebral Palsy Register form that is a modification of the one used by the Oxford Register of Early Childhood Impairments. This limb-by-limb coding system allows different types of cerebral palsy to be inferred by a central coder, hence reducing the inter-observer variation seen in Table 1.

Many cases of cerebral palsy also have associated sensory defects, cognitive disability, behavioral disorders, and epilepsy. These correlate with severity: the more severe the motor disorder, the more likely the child will also have additional impairments. In the WA Cerebral Palsy Register, of those with severe motor problems 52% also had severe intellectual impairment (IQ < 35) compared with only 4.4% of those with mild motor disorder; 60% had seizures compared with 20% of the mild group; and 24% were blind compared with only 3% of the mild group. These problems present enormous challenges to the assessment of children in the severe groups.

Occurrence of cerebral palsy

Table 3 compares prevalence and incidence of the cerebral palsies. In a condition in which there is lifelong handicap, these two are markedly different. Prevalence not only depends on how many children are born with cerebral palsy, but how many survive to be counted. Prevalence is essential for studies to plan the needs for care and support for this population of disabled children and adults. We can never measure true incidence as we have inadequate information on how many brain-damaged children died as fetuses, neonates, or at older ages before they were diagnosed. Incidence, or some

Table 2. Western Australian Cerebral Palsy Register form.

WESTERN AUSTRALIAN CEREBRAL PALSY REGISTER
Description of motor and other disabilities

Name _____   Date of birth _____

Address _____

_____

Centre _____   Record No. _____

Examiner _____   Date _____

MOTOR DISABILITY

SEVERITY CODES	
Signs	Function
Minimal = 1 =	Motor signs present but no functional impairment.
Mild = 2 =	Symptoms result in some functional impairment.
Moderate = 3 =	Between mild and severe; e.g. ambulant with walking frame.
Severe = 4 =	Little purposeful voluntary action, though function may be acquired, IQ permitting

Use severity codes 1–4 in appropriate boxes to refer to function in (1) and to indicate severity of motor signs in (2) and (3).

	RUL	LUL	RLL	LLL	Head	Trunk

(1) **Function:** ☐ ☐ ☐ ☐ ☐ ☐

(2) **Signs Felt (tone):**

Predominantly hypertonic
With clasp-knife effect (yes/no)
Predominantly hypotonic
Variable tone

(3) **Signs Observed (abnormal movements):**

	At rest	With excitement or intention
Short and jerky	☐	☐
Slow and writhing	☐	☐
Tremor	☐	☐
Inco-ordination *(code only if this is the predominant motor dysfunction)*	☐	☐
Movements resulting in abnormal postures and grimacing	☐	☐

(4) Verbal description of motor disability including severity (as you would record in medical notes):

_____

_____

_____

_____

Table 3. Cerebral palsy: measures of occurrence.		
	Prevalence	*Incidence*
Definition	Existing/current cases in a population	New cases arising in a population
Used for	Planning of services	Etiological studies
Relationship	Prevalence is incidence minus mortality and migration	
How measured	Surveys to identify cases as a proportion of specific populations	• Follow up a birth cohort • Register cases of cerebral palsy and relate these to their birth cohorts
Problems with measure	Very large surveys required to establish precise estimates	• True incidence of brain defect/damage causing (likely to cause) cerebral palsy is not measurable • Delay in ascertainment (months or years from cerebral defect) • Cases lost due to deaths, out migration, and other losses from birth cohorts

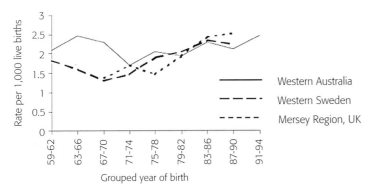

Figure 1. Cerebral palsy rates per 1,000 live births in three populations, 1959–1994. Cerebral palsy due to postneonatal causes excluded. Mersey Region data: 1967–1989 only. Swedish data: to 1990.

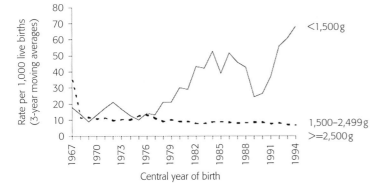

Figure 2. Birthweight-specific cerebral palsy rates per 1,000 live births (3-year moving averages), Western Australia, 1967–1994. Cerebral palsy due to postneonatal causes excluded. Two-year average used for 1967 and 1994. >=: greater than or equal to.

measure of it, is essential for studies of etiology, as we are interested in new cases arising in a population.

The proxy incidence measure we use is the number of children in the population described as having cerebral palsy by age 5 years, including all those who have died, per 1,000 children born alive or per 1,000 neonatal survivors. Figure 1 shows the best estimates of occurrence from three of the longest standing registers, all of which use multiple sources of ascertainment. Data are available in these registers for birth cohorts from 1959 to 1962 to those born in 1991–1994; 2–2.5 children per 1,000 born were classified with a cerebral palsy syndrome by the age of 5 years, which probably is the best measure of incidence we have for developed countries with modern perinatal care. Data from developing countries are far less reliable as survival rates of those with impairments are low, and there are more preventable causes of brain damage (e.g., iodine deficiency, malnutrition, and infections).

Trends have been remarkably stable since the early 1970s. However, overall trends have masked increases in cerebral palsy in preterm and low birthweight infants that have occurred as a result of the dramatic increase in the survival of very preterm infants due to the introduction of neonatal intensive care. Figure 2 illustrates clearly the increase in <1,500g cerebral palsy rates as mortality in those low-birthweight groups fell (gestational age data were not available before 1980 in Western Australia; thus, birth weight was used to obtain these long-term trends). The increase in very preterm cerebral palsy rates is likely to have occurred from increased survival of neonates who were already damaged, as well as from the increased risks of neonatal complications in the surviving very preterm infants (Fig. 3).

Table 4. Periconceptional and early antenatal causes of the cerebral palsies.

Type of factor	Description	Timing
Maternal	Genetic, family history (e.g., epilepsy)	Periconceptional
	Infertility, related problems	Periconceptional
Fetal malformation syndromes	Known and unknown genetic or teratogenic influences	Periconceptional and early gestation
Infections	TORCH, other organisms	Early gestation
Deficiencies	Iodine	Early-mid gestation
	Thyroid hormone	?Throughout gestation
Toxic	Methylmercury	Throughout gestation
	Alcohol	Early-mid gestation
	Carbon monoxide poisoning	Throughout gestation
Vascular	Hypoxia, ischemia, thrombotic disorders (e.g., maternal)	Mid-late gestation

The implications of these data for neonatal care are enormously important. If most cerebral palsy in very preterm infants is coming from antenatal damage and increased survival, then neonatal care will be keeping alive severely impaired children, but if the damage occurs after birth, then neonatal interventions may well prevent cerebral palsy. A significant research effort is employed in tackling these issues, as well as attempting to elucidate the causes and prevention of preterm births.

The extraordinary observation that the huge effort to reduce so-called birth asphyxia has not influenced cerebral palsy rates, particularly in term births, has been instrumental in shifting the interest (in terms of etiological and prevention research) from the period around birth to antenatal factors.

Causal pathways to the cerebral palsies

There has been a considerable change in our thinking about cause in the cerebral palsies, away from the single episode of preventable birth asphyxia that dominated research, influenced litigation against obstetricians, and resulted in obstetrical practices to avoid birth asphyxia – none of which has eventuated in a reduction in the cerebral palsies. The focus is now on earlier factors and complexity of causal pathways. There is an increasing understanding of the multiplicity of causes, how their interactions cause brain damage, and that many factors thought to be causes are actually associations or early signs of the brain pathology (such as low Apgar scores or newborn encephalopathy).

Table 4 lists the many causes of cerebral palsy that commence antenatally. Although individually rare in developed countries, they may actually account for the majority of cases. The large number of different neuronal migration disorders now being described with neuroimaging have obviously been missed in the past. The most important preventable cause of cerebral palsy

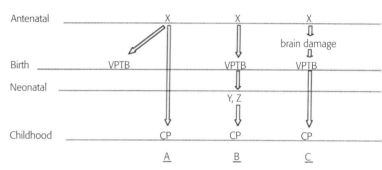

Figure 3. How could very preterm birth be associated with cerebral palsy? Shown are three possible pathways (A, B, C) between very preterm birth (VPTB) and cerebral palsy (CP). Pathway A involves one or more antenatal events (X) that independently cause preterm delivery, and lead to CP. Together, these events and VPTB cause CP. Pathway B represents the claim that VPT infants may be more susceptible to neonatal (Y) or perinatal (Z) complications than fullterm infants, which in turn give rise to CP. Pathway C holds that antenatal events X cause brain damage associated with CP, and that the damage itself is also responsible for VPTB. What is common to all three pathways is that antenatal events X cause VPTB.

worldwide is endemic cretinism, diplegia, and deaf mutism due to severe maternal iodine deficiency in early pregnancy. Since many of these early factors result in preterm birth, low birthweight or neonatal encephalopathy, as well as cerebral palsy, one can understand how clinicians and others presumed that these other outcomes on the causal pathway were responsible for the brain damage.

The risks of cerebral palsy in infants born very preterm (i.e., before 28 weeks) is nearly 100 times higher than in those born at term. These risks vary depending upon the causal pathway to the preterm birth (Fig. 3). Some causes, such as ascending genital tract infection/inflammation may be direct, and the preterm delivery is not on the causal pathway. Other causes, such as postnatal cerebral haemorrhage, may be a direct result of the very preterm delivery, as well as of other factors, on a causal pathway to cerebral palsy. Interest in the patterns of inflammatory cytokines among children with cerebral palsy (measured from neonatal Guthrie spots), that appear to differ from control children, may develop into useful research about these pathways to brain damage. Other new and promising hypotheses being investigated include pathways involving complex genetic risks and thrombophilic disorders in the mother (associated with hemiplegias).

The dramatic increase in twins and higher-order multiple births due to more older mothers and the use of infertility treatments has resulted in increased rates of cerebral palsy in populations. Rates of cerebral palsy are higher in multiples due to the much higher proportions of very preterm multiples than of singletons, and to an increased risk of cerebral palsy in term multiples as well, suggesting that the increased risks are not just due to their skewed gestational age and birthweight distributions, but also something connected to being multiple as well.

The most preventable of the cerebral palsies are the group caused by identifiable post-neonatal causes such as head injury, meningitis/encephalitis, cerebro-vascular accidents, status epilepticus, and other rarer causes. While reductions have occurred following widespread Haemophilus influenzae type B vaccination campaigns, in Western Australia we have observed an increase in non-accidental injury resulting in brain damage. Social factors thus dominate this group of disorders (accidents, child abuse, infections), and the rates are much higher in Aboriginal children than Caucasian children in Australia.

Conclusions

While 'cerebral palsy' is not a single entity, it provides a useful umbrella term to describe the group of cerebral motor disorders that are most severe and common in children. There is no evidence that the occurrence of these problems is falling and in fact some evidence that it is rising, possibly due to increasing perinatal survival and to social factors in post-neonatal cases. The challenge is to better identify their antenatal and perinatal causal pathways that are likely to be many and complex, much like the group of syndromes and causes that result in the intellectual disabilities.

There are many exciting possible new areas of research as well as scope for using existing research disciplines in more collaborative ways. The increase in knowledge about how the brain develops, with complex interactions between multiple genes and between genetic and environmental influences, will enhance our capacity to identify why this development can go wrong. Better ways of measuring exposures, influences, and their biological effects in utero will help tease out the pathways that remain hidden in so many cases of even severe cerebral palsy. Linking in the contributions of careful clinical, neurological descriptions (phenotype) and their measurement in population data by epidemiologists to this new research will be exciting and helpful. Pathways in very preterm and low birthweight infants are likely to differ substantially from those in fullterm infants, and the better we become at measuring growth patterns in utero and their causes, the more likely we will be able to understand their pathological consequences. Considerable research needs to be done to ensure that as new treatments emerge in perinatal care, we continue to ensure that if they increase survival they do not contribute to increases in cerebral palsy.

We need to ensure that we continue to collect complete and accurate data on total populations of children that describe their neurological disabilities. This not only is valuable for planning of services for children with motor disorders like the cerebral palsies, but can provide helpful monitoring of influences that either increase or decrease their occurrence.

See also:

Magnetic Resonance Imaging; Epidemiological designs; Indices of efficacy; Normal and abnormal prenatal development; The birth process; The status of the human newborn; Motor development; Intelligence; 'At-risk' concept; Behavioral and learning disorders; Developmental coordination disorder; Prematurity and low birthweight; Developmental genetics; Pediatrics

Further reading

Gibson, C. S., MacLennan, A. H., Goldwater, P. N. and Dekker, G. A. (2003). Antenatal causes of cerebral palsy: associations between inherited thrombophilias, viral and bacterial infection, and inherited susceptibility to infection. *Obstetrical and Gynecological Survey*, 58, 209–220.

Nelson, K. B. and Grether, J. K. (1999). Causes of cerebral palsy [review]. *Current Opinion in Pediatrics*, 11, 487–491.

Yeargin-Allsopp, M. and Boyle, C. (eds.) (2002). The epidemiology of neurodevelopmental disorders. *Mental Retardation and Developmental Disabilities Research Reviews*, 8, 113–211.

Child depression

IAN M. GOODYER & CARLA SHARP

Introduction

'Depression' refers to an alteration in mood state that consists one of or more of three components: a feeling of sadness, an accompanying sense of unease (dysphoria), and a loss of the positive sense of pleasure (anhedonia). In children and adolescents, irritability may dominate the mood state perhaps as a consequence of dysphoric elements. Clinical consequences of lowered mood occur when there are accompanying adverse alterations in thinking about the self, the world, and others, and reductions in normal physiological and metabolic processes resulting in undesirable changes to the vital functions that involve sleep patterns, eating, energy levels, and general activity.

Need for a developmental approach

The clinical syndromes of depressive illnesses lack a developmentally sensitive framework for detecting depressive states in childhood. Even amongst adolescents, there are age-sensitive variations in clinical presentations. High levels of negative cognitive symptoms are more apparent in those over 14 years of age, while self-reports of current symptoms are less likely to indicate clinically valid disorders in younger adolescents. In adolescent girls, for example, the same score on a depression self-report measure obtained from different age groups has a substantially different probability of indicating clinical depression (Fig. 1). This indicates developmental effects on the liability for depressive disorders.

Children as young as 6 years of age can describe their mental state in a valid way. For the preschool and infancy period, we lack sensitive, valid, and reliable indices of mood dysregulation and their cognitive and physiological correlates. Thus, current nosological classification systems (DSM-IV; ICD-10) do not take into account differential changes in the levels and types of moods, thoughts, and behaviors that occur through periods of rapid biological maturation in the first two decades of life.

The present focus: major depression

Most of our knowledge regarding depressive disorders comes from investigations of unipolar Major Depressive Disorder (using the DSM-IV criteria). The remainder of this entry focuses on this clinical syndrome. Major depression is diagnosed when at least five of the following symptoms are present during the same two-week period. To begin with, there must be a mood symptom of depressed or irritable mood or anhedonia. Then, there must be four other symptoms from the following list: a significant decrease or increase in weight or appetite or failure to make expected weight gain, insomnia or hypersomnia, psychomotor agitation or retardation, fatigue or loss of energy, feelings of worthlessness or inappropriate guilt, concentration difficulties or indecisiveness, and thoughts of death and/or suicide attempts or ideation. The child or adolescent should also be clearly impaired in their personal and/or social functioning.

Other shortcomings of present classifications

It is important to note that clinical classifications have considerable limitations. The disorders they characterize, including depression, are invariably heterogeneous at the levels of both presentation and etiology. Meeting syndrome criteria generally applies to only a small number of individuals. Community-based studies have indicated a large number of individuals who may fail to reach clinical criterion by only one or two features, and yet report significant distress and impairment (Pickles, Rowe, *et al.*, 2001). It is, therefore, not surprising that revisions of diagnostic criteria occur quite frequently in an effort to capture the full range of depressive

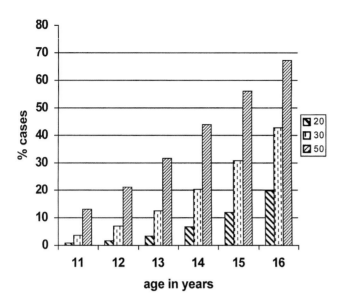

Figure 1. Estimated proportion of adolescent girls with major depression at each age year according to level of self-report depression scores.

conditions. Some authorities advocate a dimensional approach to mood states in general, suggesting that there is one underlying construct or quantitative trait indexed by the number and severity of symptoms. However, the extent to which variation in self-report scores represents a latent etiological construct at the psychological, physiological, or genetic level that predicts subsequent abnormal developmental trajectory and/or affective disorder is unclear.

Epidemiology and course

The twelve-month-period prevalence estimates for major depression is approximately 1 percent for pre-pubertal children and between 3 and 4 percent for post-pubertal children. This substantive and non-linear increase occurs primarily in adolescents between 14 and 16 years of age, particularly in those who have reached an observable level of physical change (Tanner's stage three). In pre-pubertal children, there is no sex difference in prevalence, whereas in post-pubertal adolescents there is a marked increase in females compared to males (whose prevalence continues to rise but at a much slower rate). The increases in incidence and prevalence through this post-pubertal period are somewhat more correlated with rises in sex steroid levels rather than with age or particular stage of physical sexual development (Angold, Costello, & Worthman, 1998).

The course of major depression shows remarkable variation in the short and long term. In clinical studies of adolescents with their first episode of depression, 50 percent continue to meet diagnostic criteria at twelve months, even with treatment. Recurrence risk is high for

both child, and adolescent onset cases and continuity into adult life occurs in about 30 percent of cases.

Etiology

Genetic factors

Unipolar major depression is highly familial, but the mode of transmission is complex and developmentally sensitive. Childhood forms appear to be lower in genetic risk than adolescent and adult forms (Rice, Harold, & Thapar, 2002). Exactly what it is that is familial is not clear. One possible genetically mediated psychosocial process is that parents with a lifetime history of affective disorder may fail to protect their offspring at a time of social adversity, rendering the child more prone to adverse life events. This may occur because such parents can put their offspring at risk through an increased exposure to personally disappointing life events. For example, a depressed mother may put her child at increased risk for depression by being unable to terminate a violent relationship with a partner due to her own symptoms of anhedonia, negative thoughts of herself, and low energy.

Neurobiological factors

At present, there is good evidence that biological dysregulation in the hypothalamic-pituitary-adrenal-axis (HPA) occurs once a depressive episode is triggered. In young people who are currently depressed, evening cortisol hypersecretion occurs in about 30 percent of cases. This steroid abnormality is associated with a worse short-term outcome, and may indicate a compromised neurocognitive system that may in turn increase the liability for further undesirable life events. This patho-physiological process is significantly more likely in the post-pubertal adolescent than the pre-pubertal child. Morning cortisol and DHEA hypersecretion predict the onset of major depression in adolescents at high risk for major depression, indicating a potential causal role for steroid abnormalities in the onset of affective disorders (Goodyer, Herbert *et al.* 2000). Morning cortisol may be an index of genetic risk for psychopathology, whereas evening cortisol may reflect increases of daily environmental influences on physiological function.

With regard to the role of neurotransmitters in the etiology of childhood depression, blunted growth hormone responses in children following a pharmacological challenge test that activates central serotonergic systems have suggested impairments in serotonin function in children at high risk and suffering from major depression. There is increasing evidence that a sub-group of children and adolescents are at risk for major depression because of abnormalities in monoamine system functions. That there may be such putative physiological vulnerabilities preceding the onset of clinically recognizable major depressive disorder remains to be confirmed in prospective studies of children at high risk for psychopathology.

Cognitive factors

Good or successful competence in interpersonal development during adolescence, both with peers and in more personal confiding relationships, is a potentially important protective factor in diminishing the risk for depressive disorder. High levels of negative self-perception of competence (e.g., "I am not socially attractive, I am a poor scholar, I am not good at sport") is a critical moderator of subsequent increases in depressive thinking styles for both sexes during adolescence. Errors in estimating self-competence are predictive of increases in depressive symptoms.

Several aspects of social cognition that may be related to negative self-perception and low social competence have been found to be associated with childhood depression. For instance, dysfunctional attitudes and negative attributional styles are weakly associated with the subsequent onset of clinical depression with effects most apparent for individuals exposed to severe personally undesirable events. Overall, social-cognitive factors appear to be best understood as having reciprocal relationships, with depressive symptoms over the adolescent period increasing the liability additively for clinical disorder. Whether sub-populations of young people possess mood and/or cognitive vulnerability processes that increase the risk for the subsequent onset of major depression remains unclear (Alloy, Abramson *et al.* 1999).

Biases in information processing about the self have been demonstrated in children and adolescents. For example, compared with controls, depressed children and adolescents recall more negative words describing the self from an adjective checklist, but there are no differences in recognizing such words. This bias may reflect a deficit or distortion of episodic event memory processes in depressed young people. In normal subjects, such processes can be unavailable to consciousness (i.e., latent), becoming apparent only following activation by mood change. Thus, adolescents at high risk for depression are more likely to show increases in negative self-description during dysphoric, compared to neutral, moods. This putative cognitive vulnerability for depression is associated with the temperamental trait of high emotionality. It is these adolescents, who, in the presence of social adversities, may become dysphoric and most at risk for clinical affective disorders.

Recent advances in cognitive neuroscience examining the roles of executive functions in affective psychopathologies have yet to be systematically investigated in young people at risk for depression. Impairments in episodic event memory are closely associated with deficits in attention, behavioral inhibition, and decision-making processes. These may arise in childhood, thereby increasing the liability for subsequent emotional and behavioral disorders. The empirical support for such an 'executive vulnerability' arising in early development is emerging, but has yet to be specifically tied to the onset of subsequent depressive disorders.

Life events and difficulties

The cognitive models of affective disorder across the lifespan indicate a strong relationship between social adversity and depressive thoughts, feelings, and behaviors. The relationship between depression and life events is most likely reciprocal, because over the adolescent period there appears to be an evolving pattern of interpersonal difficulties within the family that can lead to the gradual evolution of clinically observable emotional disorders. These 'slow growing' depressive conditions that evolve over a period of months or years may be distinct from relatively fast onset disorders provoked by highly psychologically 'toxic' life events (e.g., the break-up of a close friendship or romantic relationship). These very adverse experiences serve to bring forward the onset of depression in already at-risk adolescents. In slowly evolving conditions, onset occurs after adolescents appear to be exposed to continuing low-level difficulties (e.g., chronic family arguments, but not family breakdown) over time.

How such social adversities exert their effects is not clear. Additive statistical models, demonstrating correlates over time between experience and perceptions of self and others, are only the first step to delineating the intermediate psychological and physiological processes that determine depressive states. Thus, life events and difficulties are likely to exert effects on self-perception, social competence, and related behavioral styles. These may lead to persistent biases in how the self and social systems are perceived and interpreted over time. It is also increasingly likely that some young people may themselves increase the liability for negative experiences through genetically mediated styles of risk behavior. Depressions may therefore be brought about in part through interplays between risk environments, their cognitive appraisal, and how coping processes are activated and utilized to maintain well-being. This rather unspecified theoretical position requires much greater understanding than has occurred hitherto. The psychological processes required for effective appraisal of, and efficient problem solving in, negative social experiences remain unclear in children and adolescents at high risk for affective disorders.

Treatment

Therapeutic interventions for childhood and adolescent depression include psychosocial and psychopharmacological interventions, both of which have proven, but limited, efficacy (Michael & Crowley, 2002). Cognitive behavior therapy is the treatment of choice for mild to moderate depression in clinical settings, but there is no treatment trial that has compared different psychological treatments to each other. For more severe disorders, anti-depressants are invariably required. In our view, no treatment should be given to children or adolescents without a clear diagnosis and a multidisciplinary approach to treatment. This is likely to happen best in specialist services with psychiatry, psychology, and nursing staff educated and trained in child cognitive abilities. Combinations of psychological and pharmacological treatments may prove to be effective in reducing relapse and promoting continuous well-being in young people with high levels of impairment and severe disorders. However, the long-term effects of treatments on adult adjustment are not yet clear.

Conclusions

There is clear-cut evidence that depressive conditions can occur in children as young as 6 and probably younger. Techniques for detecting depression in the preschool child are not currently available. Their absence does not allow us to assert that such individuals are too immature to suffer from depressive conditions. There is increasing evidence for important developmental influences on the nature and characteristics of depressions. The internal milieu of the brain requires much greater understanding than hitherto if we are to delineate the maturational processes that increase the liability for major depressions in particular.

More emphasis is required on longitudinal studies that can track concurrently individual differences in the trajectory of physiological, psychological, and social processes through a developmentally sensitive period of time, such as puberty. Such designs would be further informed by considering the potential early risks formed by genetic indices and preschool environmental markers that may form the general vulnerability constructs for later psychopathology. Since depression appears to be preceded by the mood change of dysphoria, further experimental studies should consider evaluating psychological characteristics of vulnerable and recovered individuals under emotional demand as well as neutral conditions. A major challenge for clinical services is the development and provision of safe, effective, and deliverable treatments. There is a high non-compliance rate for medication, low availability of time-intensive psychological treatments (e.g., cognitive-behavioral therapy), and a shortage of specialist skills to deliver either in most countries worldwide. The 21st century is a good time for health-care systems to begin taking child and adolescent mental health disorders, and depression in particular, as seriously as it does cancer and heart disease.

See also:

Psychoanalytical theories; Theories of the child's mind; Developmental testing; Self and peer assessment of competence and well-being; Cross-sectional and longitudinal designs; Emotional development; Executive functions; Parenting and the family; Selfhood; Sex differences; Siblings and peers; 'At-risk' concept; Autism; Behavioral and learning disorders; Behavior genetics; Milestones of motor development and indicators of biological maturity

Further reading

Goodyer, I. M. (ed.) (2001). *The Depressed Child and Adolescent*, 2nd edn. Cambridge: Cambridge University Press.
Hammen, C. (2001). *Depression Runs in Families: The Social Context of Risk and Resilience in Children of Depressed Mothers.* Berlin: Springer.
Ingram, R. E., Miranda, J. and Segal, Z. (eds.) (1998). *Cognitive Vulnerability to Depression.* London: Guilford Press.

Acknowledgment

Ian Goodyer is supported by program and project grants from the Wellcome Trust. Carla Sharp is supported by an NHS Research Fellowship.

Developmental coordination disorder

MARY M. SMYTH & MARGARET COUSINS

Introduction

Unusual motor clumsiness, not attributable to a syndrome such as cerebral palsy, has been observed in around 4 to 7 percent of children. Functional difficulties manifested by such children may include poor fine motor skills (motor-graphic proficiency, manual dexterity, tool use) and/or gross motor abilities (walking, running, jumping). Posture and balance may be impaired. There may be difficulties with learning motor skills, and delays in attaining motor milestones. Component aspects of coordinated movement, such as the regulation of timing and force, have also been found to be impaired. Studies of preterm and low birthweight infants show that such children are at greater risk for poor motor function in later life, but this is not the inevitable outcome of non-optimal perinatal factors, and neither do all clumsy children have a history of such difficulties. As with other developmental disorders, poor coordination is more prevalent in boys than girls, with the estimated ratio varying from around 2:1 to as high as 4:1, depending on the method of recruitment.

Problems of terminology

The terminology used to describe the difficulties of such children has been broad ranging: from the essentially descriptive 'physically awkward' and 'clumsy child syndrome' to terms implying causality, such as 'minimal brain dysfunction' and 'minor neurological dysfunction.' Additionally, terms such as 'developmental dyspraxia,' or 'sensory-integrative dysfunction,' reflect attempts to place the problem in a specific sphere of cognitive operations, though there is little evidence to support their widespread use.

The World Health Organization classification (ICD-10) lists the disorder as a Specific Developmental Disorder of Motor Function (SDD-MF), but this term is not in widespread use. Developmental coordination disorder (DCD) is the term adopted by the American Psychiatric Association (DSM-IV), and is the one of preference in the research literature. While these medical classifications lend weight to the notion of the specificity of a developmental motor disorder, the prevalent model in some countries (e.g., the Netherlands and Sweden) is one of co-morbidity, particularly one of overlapping motor and attentional disorders, forming a syndrome sometimes referred to as Deficits in Attention, Motor Control, and Perception (DAMP). Incidence of language and reading disorders has also been found to be higher in the motor-disordered than non-motor-disordered population.

The problem of diagnosis

Diagnosis of DCD is based on behavioral definition. Both DSM-IV and ICD-10 maintain that no diagnosable neurological condition may be present. DSM-IV states that "motor coordination is substantially below that expected given the person's chronological age and measured intelligence," whereas ICD-10 specifies that the disparity between expected-for-age and observed performance should be at least two standard deviations below the population mean on a standardized test. Both definitions state that the disorder should significantly interfere with academic achievement or activities of daily living in order for a diagnosis to be given. The two definitions differ with regard to clumsiness in conjunction with learning difficulties: ICD-10 excludes a diagnosis if IQ is less than 70, whereas DSM-IV states that it may be given if the motor impairment is in excess of that normally associated with the level of retardation. The degree of impairment that would constitute an 'excess' is left unspecified.

These diagnostic criteria have been criticized on a number of grounds. Serious concerns have been raised about all the criteria adopted by DSM-IV and ICD-10 (Henderson & Barnett, 1998). Definition in terms of discrepancy between observed and expected performance is problematic on the grounds that different test batteries identify slightly different groups of children, and there is no real consensus as to what level of performance should constitute a problem. There is no evidence that the motor difficulties experienced by children with low IQ differ in any respect from those with high global or verbal IQ, provided they are able to understand task instructions. Regarding exclusion on the basis of neurological disorder, modern brain imaging techniques are now able to identify minor brain lesions that would previously have gone unnoticed. Indeed, in countries where the disorder is conceptualized as part of a wider spectrum of disorders (e.g., DAMP), a neural sub-strate has usually been assumed.

The use of screening tests

Screening procedures for motor disorders vary according to purpose. For experimental work, children may be screened from the general population or be clinically referred, the latter usually being the case when testing the efficacy of proposed remedial therapies. Some researchers, if concerned with a single causal hypothesis such as a specific sensory deficit, have screened on the basis of that deficit. For this reason, it is not always sensible to assume that children described in one study are directly comparable to those in another. In addition, the issue of heterogeneity is frequently raised. For this reason, the use of wide-ranging test batteries is recommended for the purposes of identifying children with DCD.

Several test batteries are available for screening motor disorders in children. Most are wide-ranging, testing both gross and fine motor skills. In the UK, the Movement Assessment Battery for Children (Movement ABC; Henderson & Sugden, 1992) is frequently the instrument of choice. It comprises a motor competence checklist to be completed by teachers, and a motor battery that includes tests of balance, ball skills, and manual dexterity, with norms provided for different age groups. Some differences have been found when the battery has been tested in countries other than the UK, indicating that some motor skills are culturally specific in, for example, the age at which they are expected to be acquired. Broader-based neurodevelopmental tests can also be employed. These are used to assess reflexes, balance, posture, and musculature, and to look for the presence of neurological 'soft signs,' such as choreiform and athetotiform movements and tremor. Such devices have been used as screening instruments in major epidemiological studies conducted in Groningen and Gothenburg, where a substantial number of children have been studied from birth, and developmental abnormalities recorded.

Observational and empirical studies

The abundance of test batteries and the consequent variety in inclusion criteria present difficulties for the interpretation of investigative research of children with DCD (Geuze *et al.*, 2001). Such studies have taken the form either of observational work, which essentially details the functional deficits noted above, or of investigations aimed at establishing an association between clumsiness and some hypothesized underlying processing deficit. The evidence to date suggests that there may be a mild generalized processing deficit with regard to any task involving motor control, as well as areas of more specific impairment. This may manifest as slowness or variability of movement time. In addition, there may be specific areas that are problematic for individuals with DCD, such as visuo-spatial processing.

Many studies have focused on single sensory modalities, such as impaired visual or proprioceptive processing. While studies of visual perceptual processing show that children with DCD, as a group, are impaired, there is little evidence that the visual system itself is compromised. For example, strabismus (squint) has been reported in only a small percentage of clumsy children. Children with DCD have been found to be poorer at tasks measuring visual discrimination, and those requiring visual attention and memory.

Impairment of the sense of movement (kinesthesis) has also been explored as a potential causal factor in DCD and strong claims have been made for kinesthetic difficulties as a major contributory factor, as well as an area for remediation. Studies have used a specific set of discrimination and recognition tests, but results have not always been replicated. A number of them have failed to find a relationship between performance on these tests, and motor performance more generally.

In addition to single modality explanations, researchers have investigated the extent to which the integration of sensory information, or the pathways linking perceptual input to motor output, may be disturbed in children with DCD. Converging evidence from studies of repeated movements, cross-modal matching, and balance indicates that children with DCD may be more reliant on visual information related to action than age-matched controls. This may indicate difficulties with processing of proprioceptive information, particularly in relation to posture and balance. Increased use of vision may also arise from difficulties in prospective control, and in controlling motor noise. A striking characteristic of children with

DCD is that their performance on a range of tasks is more variable than children without coordination problems, an example of which is provided in Figure 1. In addition, they have greater difficulty when performance is stressed (e.g., when placed under time constraints), indicating that feedback is more necessary for competent performance than it is in other children.

Sub-types of DCD

While group studies of children with DCD have been useful in identifying potential areas where deficits may be found, they are far from providing a causal explanation of impoverished motor ability. There are difficulties in ensuring that studies are comparable in the way they select children. Additionally, there is very little evidence of homogeneity among children designated DCD. All studies that use a large enough sample may therefore find group differences between the DCD population and controls. Very few studies have published individual data, or given an indication of the proportion of index children who have difficulty with any given task. From an analysis of those that did, it was concluded that, on average, half the DCD group are likely to have difficulty with any given experimental task (Geuze *et al.*, 2001).

Cluster studies that have looked specifically at the issue of sub-typing have produced varying accounts. This probably reflects both variations in inclusion criteria, and different underlying assumptions about the nature of the disorder, resulting in differences in the ways in which multivariate analyses are conducted. Most cluster studies have identified one sub-group of children with DCD that is impaired across all tasks. In addition, these analyses have tended to show that balance performance does not correlate well with locomotor abilities, in that some children with DCD have normal balance despite their poor gross motor abilities (Henderson & Barnett, 1998).

Remediation

Available remedial treatments for DCD form two categories: those aimed at remediating poor function, or those at remediating a proposed underlying process deficit. For example, treatments have been proposed on the assumption of a kinesthetic deficit, or of difficulties with 'sensory integration.' While the remediation of some hypothesized deficit underlying DCD remains a laudable goal, the degree of heterogeneity among these children suggests that a process-oriented approach will be limited in its efficacy if applied over the whole range of motor-disordered children. A meta-analysis of intervention studies demonstrated that functional

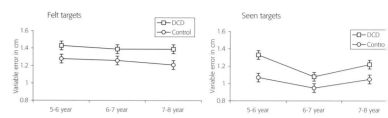

Figure 1. Mean variable error in non-visual aiming by children in DCD and control groups. Children aimed under a board at targets that they could either see on top of the board, or feel on top of the board, but with their eyes closed. Variable error reflects the spread of error round the mid-point of the aiming responses. Children in the DCD group produced larger variable error. Data taken from M. M. Smyth & U. C. Mason, 1997. Planning and execution of action in children with and without Developmental Coordination Disorder. *Journal of Child Psychology and Psychiatry*, 38, 1023–1037.

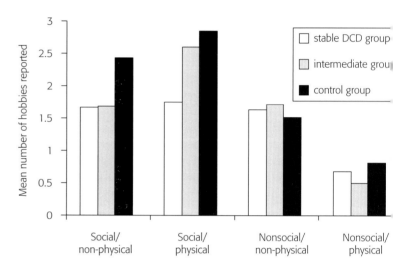

Figure 2. Mean numbers and types of pastimes reported by 15-year-olds (a) with DCD, (b) an intermediate group diagnosed with DCD as children but showing improvement in the teen years, and (c) without DCD. Data taken from M. H. Cantell, M. M. Smyth, & T. P. Ahonen, 1994. Clumsiness in adolescence: educational, motor, and social outcomes of motor delay detected at 5 years. *Adapted Physical Activity Quarterly*, 11, 115–129.

approaches – repeated and supervised practice of the specific skills that the child lacks – are the most likely to be effective (Pless & Carlsson, 2000). Thus, each child should be assessed and treated on the basis of individual need.

Follow-up studies

Outcome studies relating to DCD have been emerging since the 1980s. While early accounts suggested a good prognosis, testing was often done using the same test batteries as at the earlier age. Studies that have used more age-appropriate tasks with older children have been less optimistic. Not only do a substantial number

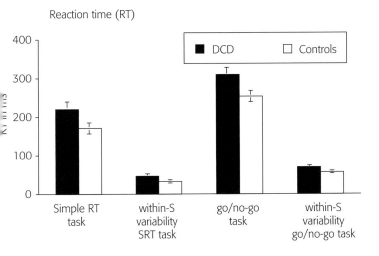

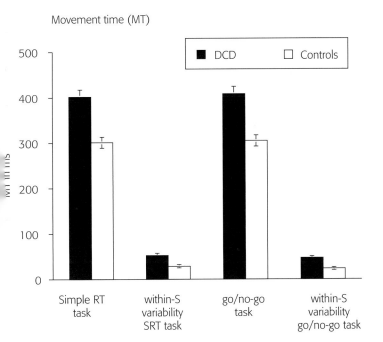

Figure 3. Adults with DCD and control participants: mean time taken to react to an auditory stimulus, and movement time to a target, in simple reaction time (SRT) and go/no-go tasks, together with mean within-subject variability. Adults with DCD were slower and more variable in reaction time and movement time in both tasks.

of children continue to perform poorly on motor tasks, but they may be more at risk of educational under-achievement in their teens than children without DCD (Cantell, Smyth, & Ahonen, 1994). Teenagers with DCD are aware of their motor problems, and rate themselves as poor on tasks involving motor skills. They may be at risk of feeling socially excluded, a pattern that begins in early school years, and may choose more solitary pursuits than other children (Fig. 2).

As yet, no lifespan developmental course for the disorder has been established. The longest reported follow-up study consists of a sub-set of the children in the Gothenburg cohort, who were last reported on at the age of 22. However, only five of this group had motor impairments in the absence of an attentional disorder, and the motor outcome for the group was not fully recorded. Despite the lack of research into the persistence of DCD into later teens and adulthood, it is now not unusual for medical and educational professionals to make a retrospective diagnosis of DCD or developmental dyspraxia in adults presenting with a history consistent with a developmental motor impairment.

We have recently demonstrated that DCD can persist into adulthood, and may have significant effects on an individual's quality of life. Figure 3 shows reaction time and movement time data from a recent study of adults with continuing coordination impairments. Like children with DCD, adults may show unusual slowness and variability of movement. Affected adults also have difficulties acquiring complex motor skills such as driving, and may be unable to gain employment commensurate with qualifications because of the inability to learn occupation-specific skills.

Conclusions

'DCD' refers to a heterogeneous group of disabilities affecting significant numbers of children and adults. Its etiology is not known, though adverse environmental factors at birth are implicated in some cases. A significant number of children with DCD do not outgrow their motor problems, and some are at risk for social, emotional, and educational difficulties in later life. DCD can co-occur with a range of other developmental disorders such as dyslexia and ADHD. At present, remediation attempts for the motor difficulties are most likely to be successful if they target specific areas of poor function.

See also:
Neuromaturational theories; Magnetic Resonance Imaging; Developmental testing; Parental and teacher rating scales; Epidemiological designs; Cross-sectional and longitudinal designs; Motor development; Attention; Sex differences; 'At-risk' concept; Behavioral and learning disorders; Cerebral palsies; Dyslexia; Prematurity and low birthweight; Cognitive neuroscience; Pediatrics; Milestones of motor development and indicators of biological maturity

Further reading

Henderson, S. E. and Henderson, L. (2002). Toward an understanding of Developmental Coordination

Disorder. *Adapted Physical Activity Quarterly*, 19, 12–31.

Polatajko, H. J. (1999). Developmental Coordination Disorder (DCD): alias the Clumsy Child Syndrome. In K. Whitmore, H. Hart, and G. Willems (eds.), *A Neurodevelopmental Approach to Specific*

Learning Disorders. London: MacKeith Press, pp. 119–133.

Wann, J. P., Mon-Williams, M. and Carson, R. G. (1998). Assessing manual control in children with coordination difficulties. In K. Connolly (ed.), *The Psychobiology of the Hand.* London: MacKeith Press, pp. 213–229.

Down's syndrome

DIGBY ELLIOTT

Introduction

Down's syndrome (DS) is named after the physician John Langdon Down (1832–1896) who, in 1866, published a description of a number of physical characteristics shared by people belonging to this group. Although there is some cultural variation, DS is associated with approximately 1 in every 700 live births in North America and Europe. There are slightly more males born with DS than females (1.3:1).

Almost all persons with DS exhibit some degree of intellectual impairment. There is, however, a great deal of variability in intellectual ability within this group, with the degree of mental retardation ranging from mild (IQs in the 55 to 70 range) to severe (IQs in the 25 to 40 range). In spite of this variation, DS persons exhibit a unique pattern of ability-disability. For example, when compared to other intellectually challenged persons, children with DS often have greater difficulty with cognitive activities involving speech and language, but display superior visual-motor skill. Thus, when one considers perceptual-motor and cognitive development in DS individuals, it is important to distinguish between performance and learning patterns that can be attributed to the general level of intellectual functioning, and the patterns associated with the syndrome.

Diagnosis and classification

DS is classified as a chromosomal disorder. Although there are three types of the syndrome, trisomy 21 is the most prevalent (i.e., 94 percent of all cases). Trisomy 21 occurs following faulty chromosomal distribution in the formation of the sperm or egg prior to fertilization. Specifically, non-dysjunction during meiosis results in either the sperm or the egg having an extra 21st chromosome. As a consequence, the fertilized egg contains a complement of 47, as opposed to 46, chromosomes (Fig. 1). In a less frequent number of cases (about 2 percent), non-dysjunction occurs after fertilization during one of the initial cell divisions. When this takes place the individual has a mixture of cells containing 46 and 47 chromosomes. People with this 'mosaic' form of DS may be less intellectually disadvantaged than persons with trisomy 21. Although it is unknown why non-dysjunction of the 21st chromosome occurs, the risk of trisomy 21 and mosaicism increases exponentially with maternal age (Fig. 2).

The third type of DS is termed translocation (about 4 percent of all cases). Translocation is not associated with parental age. It occurs when part of the 21st chromosome becomes detached from the rest of the chromosome during cell division and attaches to another chromosome. Although the total number of chromosomes is 46, the presence of the extra genetic material associated with the 21st chromosome results in the individual developing features similar to persons with non-dysjunction. In approximately a third of the cases of translocation, one of the parents is a carrier of a translocated chromosome. Thus, the risk of reoccurrence of translocation is greater.

Prenatal diagnosis of DS can be made at between 12 and 20 weeks of gestation by extracting tissue from the placenta in order to examine the chromosomes of the fetus. Because procedures such as chorionic villus sampling and amniocentesis entail a small risk of miscarriage, they are typically conducted only when the mother is at risk for carrying a fetus with a trisomy (e.g., maternal age over 35 years). Less invasive screening procedures, involving the measurement of various substances in the blood (e.g., the triple screen) and a detailed sonogram, are often used with younger women. These screening procedures can detect about 60 percent of the fetuses with DS, but also result in many false-positive readings.

At birth, a preliminary diagnosis of DS is usually made based on a number of physical characteristics common to the syndrome. These include a flat facial profile with small skin folds on the inner corner of the eyes, and a single deep crease across the center of the palm. A karyotype is then performed to confirm the diagnosis.

Risks associated with Down's syndrome

Persons with DS are at increased risk for a number of health problems. For example, the syndrome is associated with a greater frequency of congenital heart defects and an increased likelihood of childhood leukemia. Children and adults with DS are also more susceptible to respiratory and digestive problems, and various types of infection. As well, adults with DS are four times more likely to develop Alzheimer's disease than other individuals. Because of these various health problems, the average life expectancy of DS persons is shorter than that of the general population. However, with the many recent improvements in medical practices, about 50 percent of people affected now live past the age of 55 years.

DS is associated with atypical fetal development of the central nervous system. As a result, DS persons display a number of brain abnormalities. These include a reduced neuronal density in a number of cortical areas, poor myelination of nerve fibers, and abnormalities in the formation of dendritic spines. At a macroscopic level, those with DS typically have smaller frontal lobes, brain stem, and cerebellum. There also appears to be incomplete development of the corpus callosum at the fifth rostrum. The challenge these brain abnormalities present to perceptual-motor and cognitive development are often compounded by a number of hearing and ophthalmic disorders associated with the syndrome.

As well as the unique structural features associated with the brain of persons with DS, there are both behavioral and neuroimaging evidence to suggest that many persons with the syndrome develop atypical right cerebral hemisphere specialization for the perception of speech sounds. This apparent reversal in brain organization for speech perception, in conjunction with left hemisphere specialization for speech production and the organization of movement, may present some unique obstacles for language development, as well as verbal-motor abilities. These obstacles may in turn have an impact on overall intellectual development (Fig. 3).

Perceptual-motor development

Much of the work on early perceptual-motor development has focused on when infants and young children with DS achieve various developmental milestones such as sitting, grasping objects, and walking. Although such children are generally delayed in achieving these milestones, the development of sensorimotor functioning is still very rapid over the first three years, and mastery in this area is usually found to outstrip development in the communication and cognitive domains. Delays in some motor behaviors have been attributed to hypotonia,

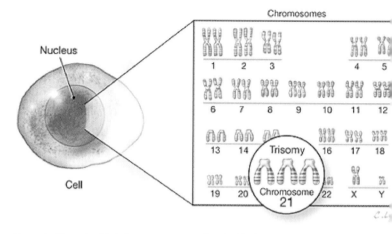

Figure 1. The extra 21st chromosome associated with trisomy 21.

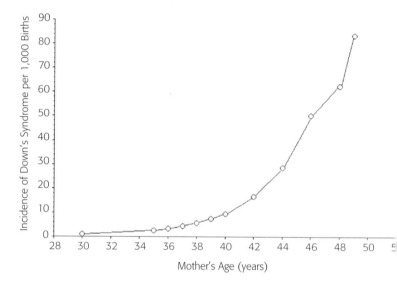

Figure 2. The incidence of Down's syndrome as a function of maternal age.

which is a condition associated with reduced levels of electrical activity in the skeletal muscles. While hypotonia may play a role in the delayed development of early motor behaviors, studies on joint stiffness and stretch reflex activity with older children indicate that poor muscle tone does not present a disadvantage to perceptual-motor development in later childhood.

Although most developmental milestones are achieved later, children with DS usually exhibit the same sequence of development as other children. This occurs because simple motor behaviors provide the basis for more complex motor abilities. For example, it has been suggested that DS children are late in developing the alternating leg movement patterns needed for crawling and walking, because they exhibit diminished spontaneous kicking behaviors in their first four to seven months of life. Given that locomotor behaviors are delayed, DS children may not have the same early opportunities to interact with their environment. These

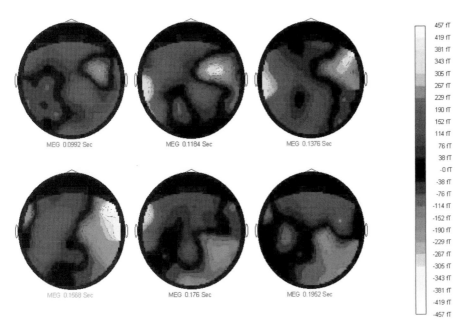

Figure 3. These images are isocontour maps of magnetoencephalographic activity in an adolescent with Down's syndrome after listening to the auditory presentation of a single word. Of interest is the unusual amount of right hemisphere activity approximately .16 sec after word onset.

additive consequences of delayed motor development appear to be responsible for the widening developmental gap between DS children and others with increasing age. In the same way, the late development of basic motor behaviors can impinge on various aspects of intellectual development. This, of course, highlights the importance of early intervention programs in reducing the developmental gap.

One area in which perceptual-motor development appears to be qualitatively different in DS children is in the control of reaching and grasping movements. Specifically, although reaching movements to objects occur at the appropriate time relative to other motor behaviors, infants with DS are less likely to manipulate an object once it has been grasped. They are also less adept at changing their grip to conform to the size and the shape of the object. The reaching trajectories of DS children also appear to be less influenced by the specific task requirements, and numerous discontinuities in the trajectories indicate that children with DS may have difficulty planning the appropriate movements. These motor control differences could reflect a problem in programming the timing and intensity of muscular force, or they could simply represent a strategic approach to goal-directed behavior that is designed to reduce the impact of possible movement error.

Although there is evidence to indicate that children and adults with DS have difficulty preparing goal-directed upper limb movements, they generally perform as well as or better than other intellectually challenged individuals if they are able to regulate their movements on the basis of visual and kinesthetic feedback. However, DS children and adults exhibit difficulty relative to other people of a similar mental age when they are required to organize a sequence of movements on the basis of verbal information. These sorts of verbal-motor problems may be related to an atypical pattern of brain organization, unique to DS. Specifically, right hemisphere specialization of receptive language function along with left hemisphere specialization for praxis may present a communication challenge to the neural systems responsible for speech perception and movement organization (Weeks, Chua, & Elliott, 2000).

Language and cognitive development

During infancy and early childhood, DS children generally perform better on sensorimotor, symbolic play, social, and adaptive aspects of various developmental inventories than they do in the communication and cognitive domains. Language production appears to lag behind language comprehension. In particular, children with DS have difficulty with the grammatical/syntactical components of language (Rondal & Buckley, 2003). As a consequence of these difficulties, some children with DS attempt to communicate with gestures rather than verbal utterances. This situation has led a number of investigators to explore the effectiveness of visual language systems. The use of sign language has been shown to facilitate the early stages of language acquisition, and is now routinely recommended by intervention specialists working with the families of young children with DS.

Over the course of childhood development, it becomes clear that the language problems associated with DS spill over into other cognitive areas. For example, DS children exhibit specific difficulties on tasks involving verbal short-term memory and sequential language processing. There also appears to be a strong link between auditory memory and language ability. Based on the finding that DS children often perform better than their mental-age counterparts on tasks that involve visual discrimination and other types of spatial processing, a number of researchers have suggested that some of the cognitive and language-based problems associated with the syndrome may reflect a more general sequential processing deficit. This idea has been linked by some investigators to work on atypical cerebral specialization in this group of people (e.g., Pipe, 1988).

Although people with DS do exhibit a unique pattern of ability-disability for language and cognitive function, it is also the case that many of the information-processing difficulties exhibited by this group reflect their more general intellectual deficits. Consequently, some of the memory and other cognitive problems experienced by children and adults with DS appear to be due to the absence of appropriate control strategies. Because control strategies such as rehearsal and elaboration can be taught, this presents a degree of optimism to educators. However, it is also the case that control procedures taught in one information-processing context do not generalize well to other situations.

Conclusions

Over the last several years, the most exciting research associated with the DS has been the multinational effort to map the 21st chromosome. A recent landmark paper detailed the gene structure of 99.7 percent of the chromosome (Hattori *et al.*, 2000). Researchers interested in DS will now be able to assess how specific genes contribute to the many physical and mental characteristics exhibited by children and adults with the syndrome. This research may in turn lead to the development of environmental interventions designed to reduce deleterious effects associated with having an extra 21st chromosome.

Another exciting research direction is associated with the development of non-invasive neuroimaging techniques, such as head-only functional magnetic resonance imaging devices and magnetoencephalography, which can be used with young children. These technologies, along with appropriate behavioral testing, will provide researchers with a much richer window into the development of brain-behavior relationships in this population. A better understanding of these relationships, and how they change with age and experience, might once again help us identify the educational interventions that will be effective for individual children with DS.

See also:
Magnetic Resonance Imaging; Developmental testing; Normal and abnormal prenatal development; Cognitive development beyond infancy; Perceptual development; Motor development; Speech development; Language development; Intelligence; Locomotion; Play; Prehension; 'At-risk' concept; Pediatrics

Further reading

Cuskelly, M., Jobling, A. and Buckley, S. (2002). *Down Syndrome Across the Lifespan*. London: Whurr.

Hassold, T. J. and Patterson, D. (eds.) (1999). *Down Syndrome: A Promising Future, Together*. New York: Wiley-Liss.

Nadel, L. and Rosenthal, D. M. (eds.) (1994). *Down Syndrome: Living and Learning in the Community*. New York: Wiley.

Dyslexia

MARGARET J. SNOWLING

Introduction

Although the majority of children learn to read without difficulty, a substantial minority (between 4 and 10 percent) have significant problems. These children are usually described as dyslexic; their literacy problems, encompassing those with word recognition, decoding, and spelling, are unexpected in that their skills are poorer than predicted given their general cognitive ability and educational opportunity. Dyslexia can occur in pure form, but is frequently observed in combination with attention deficit hyperactivity disorder or developmental coordination disorder. The co-occurrence of two developmental disorders is referred to as co-morbidity. Dyslexia has been reported in readers of a large number of the world's languages, although its manifestations differ according to the nature of the writing system, and it is generally believed that it is rarer in logographic writing systems, such as Chinese, than in alphabetic systems, such as English.

Early reports of dyslexia came primarily from medical specialists. These were gradually replaced from the 1960s onward by a more scientific approach involving epidemiological studies of whole child populations. Such studies have provided data about what differentiates children with specific reading problems like dyslexia from those who are delayed in reading development, but for whom reading is in line with generally low cognitive ability, and who are referred to as 'garden-variety' poor readers in the USA. The group differences reported include a higher preponderance of males among children with specific reading difficulties, and more specific delays and difficulties with speech and language development, whilst there are more 'hard' neurological signs (e.g., seizures) amongst those with generally poor attainments. However, there is still no agreement about whether it is useful to differentiate these two types of reading problem, particularly since recent studies have suggested that rate of progress in reading does not differ between the two groups (Shaywitz et al., 1992).

Characteristics of dyslexia

Although the role of sensorimotor factors in dyslexia continues to be debated, a widely accepted view is that it can be considered part of the continuum of language disorders. Since the 1980s, there has been a gradual shift from theories that implicate verbal deficits in dyslexia to a more specific theory that it is characterized by speech processing or phonological difficulties.

The most consistently reported phonological difficulties found in dyslexia are limitations of verbal short-term memory and problems with phonological awareness. Phonological awareness refers to the ability to reflect consciously on the sound structure of words in order to make judgments about their rhyming relationships (e.g., the odd one out of *sun*, *gun*, *rub*, *fun*), or about the phonemes they contain (e.g., 'bice' without the /b/ is ice). Dyslexic children also have difficulties with the retrieval of phonological information from long-term memory. Word finding difficulties are seen clinically and investigations of rapid naming of alphanumeric symbols report deficiencies. It is possible that these problems stem from more basic deficits in speech perception or production although current research has failed to find consistent deficits in these processes. The strength of the evidence pointing to the phonological deficits associated with dyslexia has led to the proposal that it should be defined as a core phonological deficit. Importantly, within the phonological deficit model of dyslexia, poor phonology is related to poor reading performance, irrespective of IQ (Snowling, 2000).

Phonological deficits and learning to read

Studies of normal reading development offer a framework for considering the impact of phonological deficits on learning to read. At a basic level, learning to read requires the child to establish a set of mappings between the letters (graphemes) of printed words and the sounds

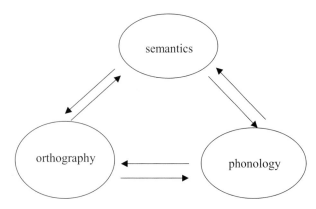

Figure 1. Interactive framework of reading development. After M. S. Seidenberg, & J. McClelland, 1989. A distributed developmental model of word recognition. *Psychological Review*, 96, 523–568.

(phonemes) of spoken words. In connectionist models of reading, such a phonological pathway interacts with a semantic pathway that makes contact with word meaning. It is argued that the mappings between orthography and phonology in the phonological pathway (Fig. 1) allow novel words to be decoded. In English, they can be considered to provide a scaffold for learning multi-letter (e.g., -ough, -igh), morphemic (-tion, -cian), and inconsistent (-ea) spelling-sound correspondences. In the early stages of reading, it is assumed that resources are directed toward establishing letter-sound connections. Later in development, the semantic pathway begins to be more involved in the development of reading fluency, and, in English, this pathway becomes specialized for reading irregular or exception words.

Within this model of reading development, deficits at the level of phonological representation constrain the reading development of dyslexic children (Harm & Seidenberg, 1999). A consequence is that, although dyslexic children can learn to read words (possibly relying on context), they have difficulty generalizing this knowledge. For dyslexic readers of English, a notable consequence is that decoding ability is not well developed, as evidenced by poor performance on non-word reading tasks.

Individual differences in dyslexia

An important issue for the phonological deficit theory of dyslexia is that of individual differences in reading profile. The theory provides a good explanation for the problems of a child with poor word-attack skills (ineffective grapheme-phoneme mappings), who cannot read non-words and whose spelling is non-phonetic. Such children are sometimes referred to as showing developmental phonological dyslexia. However, there are also dyslexic children who appear to have mastered phonic skills for reading and writing. Such children have

been referred to as showing developmental 'surface' dyslexia. The classic characteristic of these children is that, in single-word reading, they rely heavily upon a phonological strategy. Thus, they tend to pronounce irregular English words as though they were regular (e.g. glove → "gloave"; island → "izland"), they have particular difficulty distinguishing between homophones like pear-pair and leek-leak, and their spelling is usually phonetic (e.g. biscuit → BISKT; pharmacist → FARMASIST).

While evidence in favor of distinct sub-types that are stable across time is lacking, most systematic studies of individual differences among dyslexics have revealed variations in their reading and spelling skills. Dyslexic children who have relatively more difficulty in reading non-words than exception words perform significantly less well than controls of similar reading level on tests of phonological awareness, whereas those who have more difficulty with exception words than non-words show milder phonological deficits. Arguably, therefore, a dimensional view of individual differences is preferable to a taxonomy. In essence, the more severe a child's phonological deficit, the greater their impairment in non-word reading. In contrast, variation in exception word reading appears to be more closely tied to reading experience, reflecting the fact that print exposure is required to learn about the inconsistencies of the English orthographic system.

The behavioral characteristics of dyslexia change across the lifespan. While reading problems are the key symptoms of dyslexia in the early school years, adults with a childhood history of dyslexia often become proficient readers though most lack reading fluency and have difficulty decoding novel words, and few overcome their spelling problems. Moreover, adult dyslexic readers have persisting problems with phonological awareness, speeded naming, and verbal short-term memory tasks. At the other end of the age spectrum, preschool children at genetic risk of dyslexia show phonological difficulties in the context of slower than expected vocabulary development. Indeed, problems of phonological awareness, together with limitations of letter knowledge, presage reading difficulties in high-risk children (Snowling, Gallagher, & Frith, 2003).

Cross-linguistic manifestations of dyslexia

Until recently, most research on dyslexia has been conducted in the English language. English, however, is not typical even of European writing systems in that it contains a large number of spellings with inconsistent mappings between sounds and letters, as well as exception words. In this respect, it is interesting to note that the ubiquitous difficulties with phonological

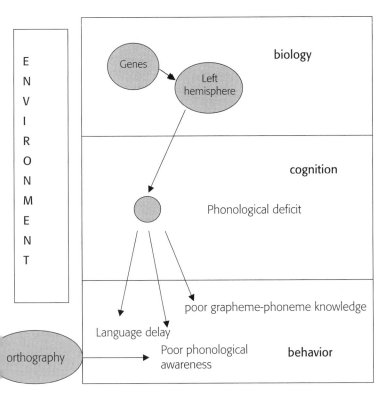

Figure 2. Biological and environmental influences on dyslexia. After J. Morton, & U. Frith, 1995. Causal modelling: a structural approach to developmental psychopathology. In D. Cicchetti and D. J. Cohen (eds.), *Manual of Developmental Psychopathology*. New York: Wiley, pp. 357–390.

awareness associated with dyslexia are not a universal phenomenon. Rather, they appear to be specific to children who learn to read in irregular or opaque orthographies, such as English. In more regular or transparent orthographies, where the relationships between spellings and their sounds are consistent (e.g., German, Italian, Spanish, and Greek), children learn to decode quickly, and at the same time they rapidly acquire awareness of the phonemic structure of spoken words. It follows that, in these languages, deficits in phonological awareness are not a good marker of dyslexia. Indeed, it is impairments of automatic phonological processing, such as performance on rapid naming tasks, that are the hallmark of dyslexia in these writing systems. Moreover, in regular orthographies, dyslexia is primarily a disorder of reading fluency rather than of reading accuracy, as in English.

Biological bases of dyslexia

It has been known for many years that poor reading tends to run in families, and there is now conclusive evidence that dyslexia is heritable. Population genetics suggest that there is as much as a 50 percent probability of a boy becoming dyslexic if his father is dyslexic and

about 40 percent if his mother is affected, with a somewhat lower probability of a girl developing dyslexia. Results of large-scale twin studies suggest that both phonological and orthographic reading skills are significantly heritable, and at the molecular level gene markers for dyslexia have been identified on chromosomes 6, 15, and 18, though the precise genetic mechanisms involved are not understood (Grigorenko, 2001).

Studies of dyslexic readers using functional brain imaging techniques have also burgeoned in recent years. Taken together, these studies suggest that regions of the temporal cortex in the left hemisphere function differently in dyslexic and normal readers, with dyslexic readers showing underactivation of these areas during reading and phonological processing tasks (Grigorenko, 2001). Interestingly, minor structural abnormalities have also been documented in these brain regions, although the causal significance of these findings remains uncertain.

Interventions for dyslexia

There is considerable evidence that phonological awareness training brings benefits for subsequent literacy development, and is a particularly effective intervention when combined with highly structured reading tuition. However, initial phonological skill is one of the best predictors of responsiveness to intervention in such training regimes. It follows that dyslexic children and those at risk of dyslexia may respond relatively less well to these techniques than normally developing readers. For dyslexic children who do not respond to such treatments, more intensive therapies need to be designed and special school placement considered.

Conclusions

The phonological deficit theory of dyslexia provides a parsimonious explanation of the disparate symptoms of dyslexia that persist through preschool to adulthood. It also makes contact with theories of normal reading development and reading intervention, and is consistent with the available biological evidence. The behavioral manifestations of dyslexia, however, differ between individuals, with such differences depending upon the severity of the phonological deficit, the integrity of other language skills, the teaching the child receives, and the language in which they learn. Putative interactions between biology and environment, mediated by cognition, are summarized, in Figure 2.

Future research on dyslexia is likely to be directed toward increasing knowledge of its neurobiological foundations, and ultimately to the development of more effective prevention and/or interventions. To this end, researchers could fruitfully compare the development of children with dyslexia and those with other language learning disorders, such as specific language impairment, at both cognitive and biological levels of description. A further item for the agenda is the evaluation of interventions that address the learning needs of so-called treatment resisters.

See also:
Magnetic Resonance Imaging; Epidemiological designs; Twin and adoption studies; Speech development; Language development; Connectionist modeling; Reading and writing; Sex differences; Developmental coordination disorder; Behavior genetics

Further reading

Blachman, B. A. (ed.) (1997). *Foundations of Reading Acquisition and Dyslexia.* Hillsdale, NJ: Erlbaum.

Cestnick, L. and Coltheart, M. (1999). The relationship between language-processing and visual-processing deficits in developmental dyslexia. *Cognition,* 71, 231–255.

Klein, R. M. and McCullen, P. A. (eds.) (1999). *Converging Methods for Understanding Reading and Dyslexia.* Cambridge, MA: MIT Press.

Hearing disorders

ROGER D. FREEMAN, MARYKE GROENVELD, &
FREDERICK K. KOZAK

Introduction

Hearing is the basis of human communication. The effects of hearing loss on a child's speech and language development are dependent on age of onset, age of diagnosis and intervention, individual differences in the child, and environmental influences. It is not solely the inability to hear that is involved. The purpose of this entry is to introduce the reader to some of the more important factors in this area as it relates to child development, and to stimulate further reading. The main focus pertains to sensorineural hearing loss. Conductive hearing loss, albeit important, is addressed in the sub-section on 'Otitis media with effusion.'

Definitions

Sensorineural hearing loss (SNHL) results from an abnormality in the sensory organ or cochlea, or an abnormality of the cochlear or hearing nerve. Alternatively, conductive hearing loss (CHL) refers to hearing loss that results from an abnormality of the ear canal, tympanic membrane (ear drum), or ear bones (ossicles). Mixed hearing loss (MHL) includes both sensorineural and conductive hearing loss affecting the patient's auditory system. Hearing loss may not affect all frequencies equally, nor does it necessarily affect both ears equally. The decibel (dB) is a unit that describes hearing loss. The severity of hearing loss may range from slight (16–25 dB), mild (26–40 dB), moderate (41–55 dB), moderately-severe (56–70 dB), severe (71–90 dB), to profound (91 or > dB).

If the hearing loss is present at birth it is considered congenital. Hearing loss after birth is categorized as acquired. If the onset is prior to the development of speech it is prelingual; during speech acquisition, peri-lingual; and if it is after the acquisition of speech, postlingual. The hearing loss may be unilateral (present in one ear only) or bilateral (present in both ears). Individuals with a severe to profound loss are usually considered to be deaf or hard of hearing depending on the benefit of their hearing aids. The community of deaf people who identify and foster a distinct deaf culture is referred to as the Deaf.

The cochlea is the snail shaped end-organ of hearing containing special sensory cells that convert mechanical forces of sound into electrical impulses to the brain via the auditory nerve. A cochlear implant is an electronic device that converts sound into electrical impulses that can stimulate the auditory nerve. Meningitis is a serious inflammation of the coverings of the brain (meninges), and is usually due to bacterial or viral infection. Acute Otitis Media (AOM) is inflammation of the middle ear lining. In Otitis Media with Effusion (OME), non-purulent fluid (fluid without pus) is present in the middle ear, OME being synonymous with the term 'serous otitis media.' The tympanic membrane separates the external ear canal from the middle ear. It transmits sound waves to the cochlea through the small bones of the middle ear (ossicles). The external ear canal is the opening of the ear that brings sound to the ear drum.

Factors to consider

The major factors to take into account when considering hearing loss and the effect on the child's speech and language development include:

– age at onset (congenital versus acquired; pre-, peri-, or postlingual)
– age at diagnosis and age when intervention begins (e.g., utilization of hearing aids)
– degree of hearing loss (mild, moderate, severe, profound)
– course (stable, progressive)
– unilateral or bilateral
– frequencies affected (i.e., high, low, or mid-frequency loss)
– other coincidental impairments or disabilities, whether or not part of a syndrome

- associated conductive hearing loss
- speech understanding
- cultural environment (hearing parents versus Deaf parents)

Prevalence and etiology

Epidemiological investigations have shown that a bilateral, sensorineural hearing loss of 40 dB HL (decibel hearing loss) or greater occurs in approximately 1–2 per 1,000 children generally, and in 6 per 1,000 children by age 18. Children treated in neonatal intensive care units (NICU) have a risk of a similar hearing loss of about 1 in 200. If the criterion for hearing loss is defined as greater than 26 dB for the better hearing ear, the incidence increases significantly. Unilateral sensorineural hearing loss affects about 3 in 1,000 children. Conductive hearing loss in the pediatric population is best broken down into permanent and transient. Transient conductive hearing loss is primarily a result of build-up of fluid in the middle ear space (OME). Permanent conductive hearing loss frequently affects patients with syndromic head and neck abnormalities, or can occur as an isolated abnormality of the external or middle ear in patients without any type of syndrome. Approximately 33–40 percent of children with hearing loss have at least one other associated disability or developmental problem, such as language or learning disorders not directly caused by the hearing loss.

Genetic defects are believed to be responsible for approximately half of childhood sensorineural hearing loss, with the remaining 50 percent due to environmental or acquired factors such as those due to prematurity, meningitis, and viral infection. Many genes responsible for genetic hearing loss have been identified. A large proportion of cases attributed to genetic and acquired causes remain at this time in the category of unknown etiology (about 35 percent). Hearing loss and damage to the central nervous system, such as that following meningitis, may be associated with general or specific cognitive impairment, and to effects such as increased irritability, decrease in impulse control, or decreased attention.

Types of hearing loss

Partial/minimal/moderate hearing loss

Minimal/moderate or partial hearing loss may affect the ability of a child to hear, especially in noisy environments, with multiple persons speaking, with persons having certain voice characteristics (frequency range, accents), or when feeling anxious or vulnerable. A child with even a mild severity of hearing loss may perform more poorly in school. Intercurrent illnesses, such as middle ear infections or a simple cold, may cause a temporary threshold shift in hearing loss, and therefore exacerbate the pre-existing loss. The quality of supportive services, such as hearing aids, FM systems in classrooms, general health care, education of family members and teachers, are all important factors in childhood education (Bess, Dodd-Murphy, & Parker, 1998).

Unilateral hearing loss

Unilateral sensorineural hearing loss (45 dB or greater) in school-age children occurs in approximately 3 per 1,000 children. If a loss of 26 dB or greater is considered, this number triples. Loss is frequently found through school screening and detection, often at age 5 or 6 years. Children with unilateral hearing loss vary in their academic success. Impairment of localization of sound and of filtering out sounds in noisy environments may explain the sometimes poor performance of these children in school. With the implementation of universal newborn screening programs, it is projected that many of these children will be picked up earlier.

Otitis Media with Effusion (OME) and developmental outcome

Since the 1970s, there has been a concern among professionals caring for young children that a decrease in hearing from OME will lead to a delay in speech, language, and psychosocial development. Fluid in the middle ear will cause on average a 28.5 dB hearing loss. Methodological problems with these studies may explain why results have been conflicting. Clarification of this question is an important area of ongoing research. Although a number of studies with improved methodology and outcome measures have found very little correlation between OME and associated hearing loss with effects on language and behavior, longer term follow-up studies into late childhood and the early teens may help to clarify the effect of OME on children's educational success (Paradise et al., 2001).

Cognitive, social, and educational considerations

The majority of cognitive testing materials have been developed and standardized for hearing children; therefore it is unclear which test materials are appropriate for children with hearing loss. If tests are used that are standardized on children without a hearing loss, a delay in verbal skills is likely to be found in hearing-impaired children. Is this delay an effect of hearing loss, or is it due to unrelated problems with language acquisition? Hearing-impaired or deaf children are as likely as children without hearing loss to have other learning disabilities.

If a hearing-impaired child is fully integrated in a regular classroom, a case can be made to assess this child with material that has been standardized on children without hearing loss; this information might help determine whether the child is able to keep up with the level of language required. However, this measure will not be a reflection of the general intelligence of the child. Fortunately, some language-free tests have evolved into instruments that access a much larger array of cognitive functions, such as the revised Leiter International Performance Scale (an individually administered test of intelligence originally designed for deaf children that does not require verbal communication).

In order to reach their potential, hearing-impaired children will need a curriculum that draws much more heavily on visual and tactile information than is customary. So as to receive all the necessary non-verbal information, they need to be able to see their teacher and other children when they speak, and may need to have a sign language interpreter and/or learning assistance. The academic development of a child with hearing impairment is likely to follow a somewhat different course from that of a typical child.

There are few psychologists who are familiar with deaf or hearing-impaired children, and even fewer who are able to sign fluently. In the case of deaf children who depend on sign language, an interpreter may be necessary, but it should be noted that most test material has not been standardized for such a procedure. Test results may be useful in monitoring the progress of an individual child, and to help define needed adaptations in the academic environment and teaching style. It should be remembered that cognitive assessments only address a very narrow area of functioning, and are generally not predictive of life success (Freeman & Groenveld, 2000).

Isolation of the hard-of-hearing

Children with hearing difficulty often learn to guess in social situations and are frequently very isolated. Amplification, and other systems within the classroom, cannot fully compensate for hearing loss. Hearing aids are often akin to turning up the volume of an unclear radio transmission – louder but not clearer. As an invisible handicap, often little or no information is given to the patient or family about social isolation, the fact that hearing people will forget that there is a hearing loss, and that hearing aids do not completely correct the

problem. For the Deaf who do not acquire speech through hearing, it is typically a different story because their impairment is usually obvious, and there is a community to join, if desired, in which communication is easy (even if that community is somewhat isolated from larger communities).

The 'methods controversy'

For prelingually deaf children, more than 100 years of controversy over methods of education have cast a shadow over their lives. It may be hard for parents of newly diagnosed hearing-impaired children to obtain timely, balanced, and individualized information with which to make their choice of methods of education. Space limitations allow only a brief exposition of the complexities involved.

Those believing deafness is a deficiency to be corrected insisted upon a pure auditory/oral approach that forbade signing. Sign language was disparaged as a non-language. It was confidently stated that signing would inhibit auditory/aural success by 'taking the easy way out.' Those who saw deafness as a difference to be respected advocated signing as natural and possible, along with any other means of communication available. Sign language was seen as part of Deaf culture. Linguists who have studied sign languages have validated the concept that they are languages in their own right. However, the expectation that, by providing a first language early, signing would lead to adequate reading and writing (English as a second language approach) has not been realized.

Children who are deaf or hard of hearing commonly achieve a poor level of proficiency in English. This may be explained by the observation that a natural sign language such as American or British Sign Language does not follow the patterns of English. The child trying to learn English will still need to learn the rules of English syntax. Since about 90 percent of deaf children have hearing parents, immersion in sign language would require rapid learning by the parents and immediate family, and use of a 'foreign' language in the extended family. This would be a high expectation and realistically not achievable for the majority of hearing parents. Many parents are now opting for cochlear implantation as noted above, with concomitant use of sign language.

Signing

Signed English, sign language, and fingerspelling are not equivalent methods of non-speech communication. Signed English attempts to convey all the inflections of English in a gestural system. This can be tedious, appear

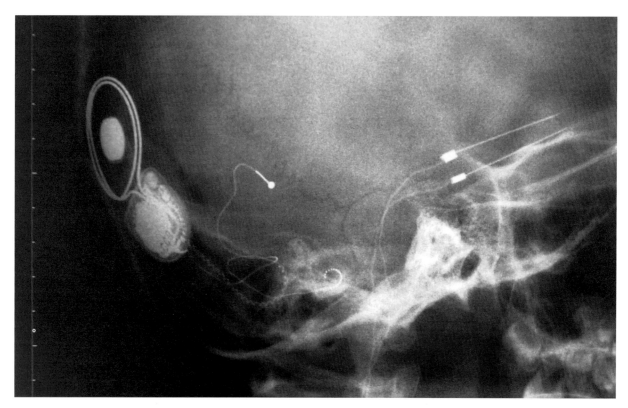

Figure 1. Multichannel cochlear implant (internal device), demonstrating insertion of the electrode into the cochlea. Also seen is the attached ball electrode that is placed under the temporalis muscle, and two sharp electrodes from the facial nerve monitor that it used during surgery.

unnatural and may not be truly equivalent to English. Fingerspelling, which spells words in the air, is inefficient for communication and also requires sound English literacy. Sign language is a defined language unto itself. The signs are linguistic approximations of words or phrases. Although once an area of controversy, the use of sign language by children who are deaf or hard of hearing neither suppresses the development of speech in those capable of it, nor does its use completely compensate for difficulties in acquiring written/read English.

Early identification and intervention

Neuronal growth is explosive during very early infancy. The deprivation of sound has been shown to have lasting effects. The earlier the age of identification and subsequent intervention for the hearing loss, the less the impact on the developing child (Yoshinaga-Itano, Coulter, & Thomson, 2000). For this reason, many developed countries have mandated universal newborn screening to ensure early intervention. Without newborn hearing screening, the average age at detection of bilateral sensorineural hearing loss is between 3 and 4 years of age in the Western world, and even higher in developing countries. This can occur despite concerns being raised by parents that their children may have a hearing loss. However, universal newborn screening will not detect the child who has normal hearing at birth and subsequently develops a progressive loss.

Parental concerns that their child does not hear properly should never be taken lightly; that child requires testing by a qualified audiologist. School children with even minimal sensorineural hearing loss can do poorly in the areas of academic performance, behavior, and self-esteem. Due to methodological limitations inherent in comparative studies, it is difficult to be sure that lags in development are not a marker for psychosocial adversity, rather than a direct effect of hearing loss.

Access to language either through sign language, cochlear implantation, or both provides a very strong argument for universal screening programs to detect hearing loss so intervention can be instituted as early as possible. Hearing resource teachers are invaluable in carrying out their role for such children (Calderon & Greenberg, 1997).

Hearing aids

Hearing aids are battery-operated devices that amplify sound. Each has a microphone, amplifier, and a receiver that sends the amplified sound out of the hearing aid and into the ear. In recent years, hearing aids have advanced from analog to digital technology. Digital aids can be adjusted to improve speech intelligibility, and also protect the ears from loud sounds. Some patients still prefer analog devices over digital technology. Many of the early digital hearing aids were designed for adult use. Today, more advanced digital aids can be modified for very young or special-needs children. Recent improvements include circuitry to make automatic adjustments to different environmental settings (e.g., background noise) and built-in FM receivers.

Cochlear implants

Children with sensorineural hearing loss usually experience hearing loss secondary to loss of sensory receptors (hair cells) in the inner ear. The hearing nerve endings beyond the receptors within the cochlea are generally still intact. A cochlear implant is an electronic device inserted surgically into the cochlea that converts acoustical information into electrical impulses. The impulses stimulate the nerve endings electrically, bypassing the sensory receptors (see Fig. 1). This device has achieved acceptance over the last several years as a treatment for severe to profound hearing loss not amenable to amplification with hearing aids. Factors such as age of onset, age of detection and intervention for hearing loss, age of implantation, and communication method post-implantation, all play a role in the success of hearing habilitation of the implanted child.

In general, the earlier a child is implanted following loss of hearing (or in the case of congenital hearing loss, the earlier the child is implanted after birth), the more successful the child will be in developing speech and verbal language communication skills (Niparko & Blankenhorn, 2003). Implants have been successful with many children. Morbidity related to the surgical procedure is minimal. The success of cochlear implantation provides a strong argument for universal neonatal screening programs to detect hearing loss so intervention can be instituted as early as possible.

Conclusions

Children with hearing loss constitute a heterogeneous group, subject to many differing risks and barriers, though some do very well. Even minimal permanent hearing loss appears to place children at higher risk for later language, learning, and behavioral problems. Early detection and intervention are believed essential, but there remain many unsolved problems in their implementation. Emphasis upon hearing may obscure other less obvious impairments, such as learning disability and central language impairment. Because of interacting factors, the care of children with hearing loss and the study of their development needs to be approached from a multidisciplinary perspective.

See also:
Epidemiological designs; Perceptual development; Speech development; Language development; Prematurity and low birthweight; Pediatrics

Further reading

Fortnum, H. M., Marshall, D. H. and Summerfield, A. Q. (2002). Epidemiology of the UK population of hearing-impaired children, including characteristics of those with and without cochlear implants – audiology, aetiology, comorbidity and affluence. *International Journal of Audiology*, 41, 170–179.

Gravel, J. S. and O'Gara, J. (2003). Communication options for children with hearing loss. *Mental Retardation and Developmental Disabilities Research Reviews*, 9, 243–251.

Mayberry, R. I., Locke, E. and Kazmi, H. (2002). Linguistic ability and early language exposure. *Nature*, 417, 38.

Meadow-Orlans, K. P., Sass-Lehrer, M., Scott-Olson, K. and Mertens, D. M. (1998). Children who are hard of hearing: are they forgotten? *Perspectives in Education and Deafness*, 16, 6–8, 24.

Roberts, J. E., Burchinal, M. R. and Zeisel, S. A. (2002). Otitis media in early childhood in relation to children's school-age language and academic skills. *Pediatrics*, 110, 696–706.

Prematurity and low birthweight

MIJNA HADDERS-ALGRA

Introduction

A low weight at birth can be caused by birth at preterm age (which is defined as a birth prior to 37 completed weeks of gestation), or by intrauterine growth retardation or restriction. These two causal pathways for low birthweight may have different effects on brain development. Nevertheless, a major part of research about low-birthweight infants deals with groups defined simply in terms of weight. More specifically, infants are considered to be either low birthweight (LBW, < 2,500 gr), very low birthweight (VLBW, < 1,500 gr), or extremely low birthweight (ELBW, < 1,000 gr) at birth. It should be realized, however, that LBW groups consist of a mixture of growth-retarded infants born at term and infants born preterm, whereas VLBW and ELBW populations mainly consist of preterm infants, with or without fetal growth retardation. In what follows, the differential effects of intrauterine growth retardation and preterm birth on child development will be discussed.

Fetal growth retardation

Clinically, the infant with intrauterine growth retardation or restriction (IUGR) presents as a baby with a birthweight that is less than expected for its age, and therefore as small-for-gestational-age (SGA). However, not all SGA infants have suffered from IUGR, because other factors, such as the infant's genetic growth potential, may result in a birthweight that is relatively low for the duration of gestation.

IUGR is mostly related to placental dysfunction involving a reduction in the delivery of nutrients and oxygen to the fetus. The fetus responds to this situation with a hemodynamic adaptation consisting of preferential perfusion of the brain. As a result, the effect of growth restriction is less for the brain than for the rest of the body, a phenomenon called brain sparing. Hemodynamic protection is not perfect, however. Animal studies indicate that IUGR is associated with a reduced number of neurons, and a significant reduction of neuropil in central structures, such as the hippocampus and cerebellum. In addition, the situation of chronic stress induced by IUGR may lead to subtle changes in the setting of the monoaminergic systems, such as the serotonergic circuitries. Studies in human infants evaluating latencies to auditory- and visual-evoked responses indicate that the hemodynamic changes related to brain sparing are associated with an accelerated maturation of the (central) nervous system. It is not clear whether this acceleration is mediated by stress-related substances, such as glucocorticoids or monoamines.

Studies addressing the long-term consequences of IUGR have generally assessed the development of groups of SGA and appropriate-for-gestational-age infants. On the basis of these studies, it can be concluded that minor degrees of IUGR, specified as a birthweight between one and two standard deviations below the mean, or a birthweight between the third and tenth percentiles of the growth curve, do not affect the child's motor, cognitive, or behavioral development. However, severe IUGR, defined as a birthweight two standard deviations below the norm or below the third percentile, does result in a significant increase of minor neurological dysfunctions, learning disorders, and behavioral problems, such as attention deficit disorder with or without hyperactivity at school age (Hadders-Algra, 2002). There is some evidence that the harmful effects of IUGR on cognitive abilities at school age are related to the phenomenon of brain sparing, and the occurrence of accelerated cerebral maturation during infancy (Scherjon et al., 2000). This suggests that such maturation during infancy may be a negative rather than a positive sign. Other studies have suggested that the effects of severe IUGR on cognitive achievement may persist beyond adolescence (Larroque et al., 2001).

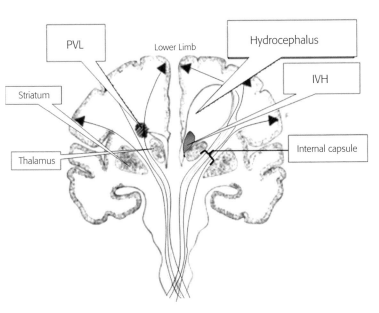

PVL

Lower Limb

Hydrocephalus

IVH

Striatum

Internal capsule

Thalamus

Figure 1. Schematic diagram of the two major types of brain lesion occurring in preterm infants (coronal section through the brain). On the left-hand side, the black spot at the corner of the lateral ventricle (the boomerang shaped open structure) represents a lesion of the periventricular white matter (PVL = periventricular leukomalacia). On the right-hand side, a hemorrhage in the germinal layer surrounding the ventricle has occurred. The hemorrhage extends into the ventricle (the gray spot in the ventricle, IVH = intraventricular hemorrhage), and results in an expansion of the ventricle (hydrocephalus). Note that the lesions in the periventricular region easily affect the fibers of the corticospinal tract running through the internal capsule between the striatum and thalamus. The fact that the corticospinal fibers involved in the control of lower limb activity lie most closely to the ventricles explains why cerebral palsy in preterm children often affects the control of the legs (spastic diplegia).

Prematurity

Epidemiological aspects

In Western countries, 6–10 percent of pregnancies end with preterm delivery. Recently, the prevalence of preterm birth has been increasing, especially births before 28 weeks of gestation. The increase in preterm birth is related to the increase of assisted reproductive therapy and ovulation induction, which increase the risk of multiple birth, and the increasing proportion of births among women over 34 years (Lumley, 2003). In addition, improvements in neonatal care have resulted in an increased survival of preterm infants, in particular those with a gestational age of less than 28 weeks. Thus, the absolute number of preterm survivors steadily increases, and amongst them the proportion of vulnerable infants born at very young gestational age.

Problems encountered in the newborn preterm infant

The basic problem of the preterm infant is that the organ systems are not appropriately adapted to the

requirements of extrauterine life. The problems that probably have the most impact on the development of the preterm infant's brain are those related to the cardio-vascular and respiratory systems. In the respiratory domain, two major problems can be distinguished. Firstly, the immaturity of the lungs in terms of the units of gas-exchange (viz., the alveoli) makes them prone to collapse easily due to a deficiency in the lipoprotein surfactant. This immaturity of the lungs may lead to a respiratory distress syndrome, which can be treated by oxygen therapy or by means of assisted ventilation. In some preterm infants with respiratory distress, the use of assisted ventilation in conjunction with high concentrations of oxygen results in a chronic respiratory disease called bronchopulmonary dysplasia. The second frequently encountered respiratory problem in preterm infants is the occurrence of apnea, meaning a cessation of spontaneous respiration due to immaturity of respiratory control.

In the cardiovascular domain, the following problems occur frequently. Firstly, the ductus Botalli (or ductus arteriosus) of the fetal circulation may persist as a consequence of low oxygen levels due to inadequate respiration. A patent ductus arteriosus results in hypoxemia, or reduced oxygenation of the blood cells. Secondly, cerebral autoregulation is immature, which means that the preterm infant cannot adapt cerebral blood flow appropriately in response to changes in blood pressure. Despite this, the preterm infant easily exhibits substantial variability and swings in blood pressure due to an immaturity of blood pressure control. This immaturity and that of cerebral autoregulation appear to be important factors in the causal pathways for the majority of intracranial lesions in preterm infants.

Intracranial lesions in preterm infants typically are located in the periventricular areas. Basically, two types of lesions can be distinguished: hemorrhagic and ischemic ones (Fig. 1). Hemorrhagic lesions most frequently occur in the sub-ependymal periventricular germinal matrix, which at this time of life is richly vascularized in order to fulfill the energy requirements of active glial cell proliferation. As the vessels in the germinal matrix are thin-walled, they are pre-disposed to be a ready source of bleeding. More often than not, the hemorrhage extends into the ventricles, thereby creating an intraventricular hemorrhage. Occasionally intraventricular hemorrhages are complicated by a periventricular hemorrhagic infarction. The ischemic lesions mainly occur in the periventricular white matter, which at preterm age is the watershed zone of centri-fugal and centripetal arterial systems. The condition resulting from ischemic lesions is called periventricular leukomalacia.

For the majority of preterm infants, neonatal life is a period of chronic stress due to the presence of minor or major illnesses. The combination of immaturity, stress, and physical disorders affects the infant's ability to regulate behavioral states and motor behavior. Moreover, the hospital stay is stressful not only for the tiny preterm infant, but also for the parents who worry about the disorders and the unfamiliar behavior of the baby, as well as the infant's developmental outcome. In addition, they suffer from a lack of comforting bodily contact with the infant.

At present, preterm infants are offered various types of intervention aimed at improving behavioral state and self-regulation by the infant, and at facilitating parent-infant interaction and understanding. Some intervention programs increase the infant's sensory input in order to compensate for the deficit of specific intrauterine experiences, whereas others aim at reducing the sensory stimulation produced by the artificial world of neonatal intensive care. Remarkably, positive effects on neonatal behavior and morbidity have been reported for both types of intervention. Possibly, the so-called kangaroo-care is the most promising method of intervention in preterm infants as it integrates parent–infant interaction with a natural mix of sensory enrichment and protection.

Motor development in preterm infants without cerebral palsy

Posture in awake preterm infants younger than 32 weeks postmenstrual age (PMA) is characterized by a predominant extension of arms and legs and an absence of head control. From 32 weeks PMA onward, the extension of the limbs changes into a preference for flexion, at first in the legs and then, from about 36 weeks onward, in the arms. Head control in healthy preterm infants at term age is identical to that of infants born at term. This means that the infant can keep the head upright for a few seconds when supported in a sitting position.

The most frequently occurring movement pattern of the preterm infant is referred to as general movements (GMs). This pattern consists of movements in which all parts of the body participate. Normal GMs prior to term age are very variable, and complex. At 36–38 weeks PMA, 'preterm' GMs change into the more slow, forceful, variable, and complex 'writhing' GMs, which are the GMs observed in fullterm neonates. Most likely, the age of 36–38 weeks PMA can be regarded as a period of real transition in the (central) nervous system. This transition is associated with an increase in motoneuronal excitability, a significant reduction of apneas, the emergence of the efficient and well-coordinated sucking behavior of the fullterm infant, and the development of full-blown newborn behavioral states.

In principle, motor development of preterm infants after term age follows the same route as that in fullterm infants. In fullterm infants, the emergence of motor

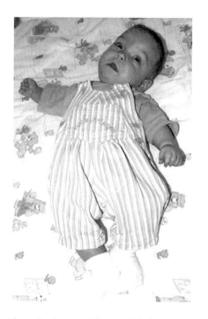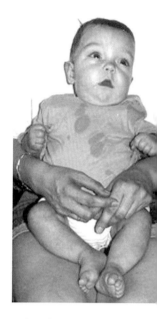

Figure 2. Preterm infant at birth (27 weeks and 1,100 gr) and at 4 months postterm. His spontaneous motor behavior in supine and sitting position was characterized by hyperextension of neck and trunk, and shoulder retraction.

milestones is characterized by considerable between-subject variability. For the assessment of motor milestones in preterm infants, the infant's age should be corrected for prematurity (i.e., functional age should be calculated from term age onward). This rule is especially useful during the first half-year postterm, when the normal variability in the emergence of motor abilities is in the order of about 2–3 months, which is more or less equivalent to the degree of prematurity in many infants. At later ages, the variability in attainment of motor abilities (e.g., standing and walking without help) exceeds the degree of prematurity, thereby reducing the significance of age correction in older preterm infants. It is still a matter of debate as to whether preterm infants develop motor milestones at an earlier or a later age than their fullterm peers. Probably, the controversy is due in part to the fact that preterm infants may show either type of development (Fallang et al., 2003). An accelerated motor development during early infancy may occur in healthy preterm infants who can benefit from the extrauterine experience during preterm life, as well as in those who suffered from chronic stress. A delayed motor development can be the result of physical illness, such as respiratory morbidity or neurological disorders.

Preterm infants without cerebral palsy frequently exhibit minor dysfunctions in motor behavior. During the first few months after birth, they often present with mildly abnormal GMs, which in particular are characterized by a limited amount of variation and complexity (Hadders-Algra et al., 2004). Another frequently observed motor phenomenon in preterm infants is hyperextension of the neck and trunk or

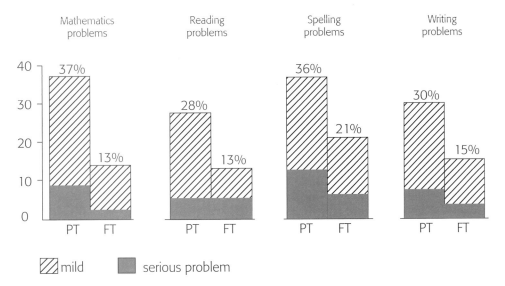

Figure 3. Prevalence of learning problems in VLBW infants without serious neurological handicap at 12 years of age. PT = VLBW group (n = 132), FT = fullterm, normal birthweight control group (n = 155). Data based on N. Botting, A. Powls, R. W. I. Cooke, & N. Marlow, 1998. Cognitive and educational outcome of very-low-birthweight children in early adolescence. *Developmental Medicine and Child Neurology*, 40, 652–660.

'transient dystonia' (Fig. 2). It mainly occurs during the first postnatal year, and is associated with a lack of trunk rotations and minor deviations in the development of reaching and grasping behavior (de Groot, 2000).

EMG studies on postural development in preterm infants demonstrated that these infants often exhibit an excess of activity in the postural muscles during reaching. In addition, it has been shown that preterm children frequently have a deficiency in postural control mechanisms that are guided by feedforward processes (i.e., processes involving anticipation and preparatory planning) based on prior experience. Preterm children with and without lesions on a neonatal ultrasound brain scan more strongly rely on postural strategies that are dominated by feedback mechanisms. Those with lesions of the periventricular white matter have not only a reduced capacity for feedforward postural control, but also a reduced number of postural strategies (Hadders-Algra *et al.*, 1999). Some evidence indicates that early motor signs such as mildly abnormal GMs and hyperextension of the neck and trunk point to an increased vulnerability for the development of clumsiness, as well as behavioral and learning problems at school age.

Long-term outcome in preterm infants

VLBW and preterm birth are associated with an increased risk for the development of major handicaps. The prevalences of major handicaps amongst survivors with a VLBW vary from 2.4% to 9% for cerebral palsy, 2% to 38% for visual impairment, 2% to 44% for hearing loss, and 7% to 27% for mental retardation (Ornstein *et al.*, 1991). The development of major handicaps is related primarily to periventricular leukomalacia and

periventricular haemorrhagic infarction. Visual impairment in preterm children has two major sources of origin. Visual problems may be due to the retinopathy of prematurity, which is caused by retinal vulnerability to oxygen toxicity prior to 36 weeks PMA. They may also be caused by deficits in the processing of visual information in the central nervous system, generally in association with periventricular leukomalacia.

Preterm birth is also associated with an increased risk for minor neurological dysfunctions and behavior and learning disorders at school age and in adolescence (Hadders-Algra, 2002). Typical forms of neurological dysfunction are a mild disturbance of the regulation of muscle tone, and problems in coordination and balance control, and fine manipulative disability. In addition, preterm children often suffer from minor dysfunctions in the visual system, such as refractive errors, a reduced stereoacuity, and problems in the analysis of complex visual patterns.

A substantial portion of children born preterm suffer from learning problems (Fig. 3). The less favorable educational outcome occurs despite the fact that the majority of preterm children without a serious neurological disorder have an IQ within the normal range. Still, the distribution of IQ scores at early adolescence in children with a VLBW is shifted toward the lower end of the distribution in comparison to those with a normal birthweight (Fig. 4). The shift is larger for performance IQ than for verbal IQ.

Attention deficit and hyperactivity disorder (ADHD) is the most frequently reported behavioral problem in preterm infants. Yet, Botting and colleagues (1997), who carried out an extensive psychiatric assessment at the age of 12 years in VLBW children and normal birthweight

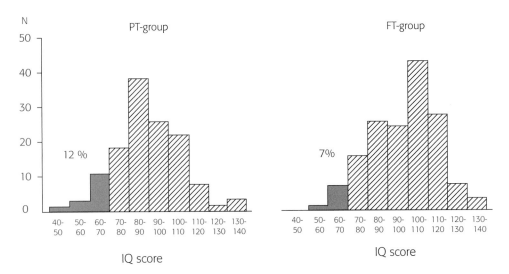

Figure 4. Distribution of IQ scores in VLBW infants (PT-group) without serious neurological handicap (n = 132) and normal birthweight controls (FT-group, n = 155) at 12 years. Data based on Botting et al., 1998.

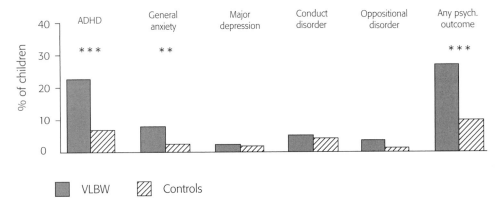

Figure 5. Psychiatric morbidity at 12 years of age in VLBW infants (n = 137) and normal birthweight controls (n = 148). Statistically significant differences between the two groups: ∗∗ p < 0.01, ∗∗∗ p < 0.001. Data based on N. Botting, A. Powls, R. W. I. Cooke, & N. Marlow, 1997. Attention Deficit Hyperactivity Disorders and other psychiatric outcomes in very low birthweight children at 12 years. *Journal of Child Psychology and Psychiatry*, 38, 931–941.

controls, concluded that VLBW children showed an excess not only of ADHD, but also of anxiety and major depression (Fig. 5). The two groups did not differ in the prevalence of conduct disorders. Remarkably, ADHD occurred in the VLBW group equally often in boys as in girls. This finding contrasts with the gender-specific prevalence of ADHD in the general population, where it occurs three times as often in males as in females. This could imply that the etiology of ADHD in VLBW children differs from that in the general population. It is conceivable that ADHD in the general population is mainly rooted in the genetic constitution of the child, whereas ADHD in VLBW children could be due to adversities during early life leading to micro- or macrostructural changes in the brain.

The relationships between minor neurological dysfunction, cognitive and behavioral disorders, and risk factors during early life are far from clear. The occurrence of minor developmental disorders in groups of VLBW infants is not directly related to gestational age at birth, birthweight, or mild degrees of intraventricular hemorrhage, and to a limited extent only to the neonatal need for artificial ventilation and mild degrees of periventricular leukomalacia detected from ultrasound brain scans. The obscurity of the relationships between brain and behavior in preterm children is illustrated by the study of Stewart et al. (1999). They performed structural magnetic resonance imaging (sMRI) scans of the brains of preterm children at the age of 14–15 years. Forty of the seventy-two children had abnormal findings on the MRI, in particular, abnormalities of the white matter. The prevalence of MRI abnormalities in the preterm group was significantly higher than that in the fullterm control group (one out of twenty-one). However, the abnormalities on the MRI were not related to minor neurological dysfunction, school achievement, or reading abilities, but they were associated with a general score on problem behavior.

Conclusions

Infants born growth-retarded or preterm are at risk for major and minor developmental disorders. Major developmental handicaps are, in general, related to overt lesions of the brain such as periventricular leukomalacia. But the etiology and pathogenesis of so-called minor developmental disorders, such as clumsy motor behavior, learning disorders, and behavioral problems is less clear. Possibly two major pathogenetic pathways can be distinguished (Hadders-Algra, 2002). Firstly, a pathway related to chronic stress in early life, which may induce alterations in the setting of certain neurotransmitter systems like that involving monoaminergic neurons. Such a 'differently set' brain would be more pre-disposed to the generation of simple forms of minor neurological dysfunction or behavioral problems. The second pathway could be related to macrostructural damage of the brain, such as small lesions of the white matter that possibly arise when physical disorders surpass the stress-related compensatory mechanisms of the fetus or infant. Minor lesions of the brain may result in the development of complex forms of minor neurological dysfunction, and a high vulnerability for the development of attention disorder and learning problems.

In order to elucidate the problem of developmental outcome in low-birthweight infants, future research could aim at trying to understand the following issues. (1) Which phenomena are perceived as stressful events by the fetus during the third trimester of pregnancy and by the newborn preterm infant? (2) What are the consequences of stress during early life for infant development and in particular for the development of the infant's brain? (3) When do the stress-related compensatory mechanisms of the fetus or preterm infant fail and what are the consequences of this failure in terms of lesions of the brain and developmental outcome? (4) By which means can adversities in early life be prevented or the negative sequelae be reduced?

These questions can be answered by carefully designed longitudinal studies. Examples are in-depth studies in which relatively small groups of infants are studied with the combination of sensitive brain imaging techniques, neuroendocrine and neurophysiogical assessments, and daily life developmental outcome parameters, and studies in which the long-term outcome of well-defined, larger populations of preterm or growth-retarded infants is evaluated by means of standardized neurological, cognitive, psychiatric, and neuroimaging assessment techniques.

See also:

Neuromaturational theories; Magnetic Resonance Imaging; Developmental testing; Epidemiological designs; Cross-sectional and longitudinal designs; Normal and abnormal prenatal development; The birth process; The status of the human newborn; Motor development; Attention; Brain and behavioral development (I): sub-cortical; Brain and behavioral development (II): cortical; Intelligence; Locomotion; Parenting and the family; Prehension; Sex differences; Sleep and wakefulness; 'At-risk' concept; Behavioral and learning disorders; Cerebral palsies; Child depression; Developmental coordination disorder; Hearing disorders; Sudden Infant Death Syndrome; Pediatrics; Milestones of motor development and indicators of biological maturity

Further reading

Hadders-Algra, M. (2003). Developmental Coordination Disorder: is clumsy motor behavior caused by a lesion of the brain at early age? *Neural Plasticity*, 10, 39–50.

Hadders-Algra, M. and Forssberg, H. (2002). Development of motor functions in health and disease. In H. Lagercrantz, M. Hanson, P. Evrard, and C. Rodeck (eds.), *The Newborn Brain. Neuroscience and Clinical Applications*. Cambridge: Cambridge University Press, pp. 479–507.

Volpe, J. J. (2001). *Neurology of the Newborn*, 4th. edn. Philadelphia: Saunders.

Prolonged infant crying and colic

IAN ST. JAMES-ROBERTS

Introduction

In keeping with western traditions, the little girl's birth in Figure 1 is being celebrated with a lusty cry. This recognition of a baby's cry as evidence of health and vigor stands in marked contrast to another widely held western belief, that prolonged unexplained crying in a young infant – often referred to as 'colic' – is a sign that something is wrong with the baby. This issue, of whether crying in a young baby signifies well-being, or ill health, underlies much of the recent research, so that it is helpful to start by considering how and why this has come about. The focus will be on crying in 1- to 3-month-old infants and its outcomes since infant crying and clinical concern about it peak during this period. The lack of an agreed definition of colic is a source of much confusion. Here, the term 'colic' will be used broadly to refer to prolonged bouts of crying that occur without apparent reason in 1- to 3-month-old infants, together with parental concern about the crying. The aim is to clarify this phenomenon.

Infant crying as a developing behavior and a clinical problem

For many parents and clinicians, the word 'colic' suggests periods of 'paroxysmal' crying, marked by intense, painful-sounding vocalization and stiffening and writhing of the trunk and limbs, which occur for no apparent reason. This view can be traced back to three lines of research in the 1950s and 1960s: (1) Ole Wasz-Höckert and colleagues' work that introduced the idea of cry 'types,' such as hunger, anger, and pain cries, which were presumed to allow a listener to use the cry's sound to identify the cause of the crying; (2) Morris Wessel and colleagues' study of "paroxysmal fussing . . . sometimes called colic"; (3) Ronald Illingworth's review, which attributed the crying to gastrointestinal pain. The word 'colic' – from the Greek word for the intestine –

implies that the cause of the crying lies in the gastrointestinal system. Thus, Illingworth and others inferred that it involved gastrointestinal pain.

Much ensuing research has sought to describe more precisely what Wessel, Illingworth, and others were writing about, with regard to both phenomenology and causation. The results depart from the predominant 1950/1960 perspective in important ways. The first is an acknowledgment that, although infant crying is an important part of the picture, the clinical starting point is parental complaint to a professional about 'problem' crying. This has three consequences. Firstly, it has become clear that parents' personal, and possibly cultural, characteristics influence the likelihood that they will be disturbed by their baby's crying and seek professional help. Secondly, direct measurement of infant crying is needed to distinguish the behavior that underlies parental complaint. Thirdly, infant samples selected by parental referral give a biased view of infant crying. General community samples are needed to understand how crying affects all caregivers, whether or not they seek help.

The second departure from the 1950/1960 viewpoint is that objective measures of infant crying, although confirming that parents are often correct in reporting that their baby cries a lot, have not confirmed the crying to be a discrete, clinical condition restricted to a small minority of babies. Rather, prolonged crying bouts have been found in 1- to 3-month-old western babies in general. Their crying peaks at around 5–6 weeks of age, and includes an evening crying peak as well as other features reported in clinical samples. Together with cross-cultural and other findings, this has been taken as evidence that a peak in infant crying is normative in the first 12 weeks. Most babies who cry a lot at this age are at the extremes of the normal distribution, rather than suffering from a clinical condition. Surveys of western parents' concerns and complaints about problem crying have found that it follows the developmental curve for infant crying, peaking at around the same age that

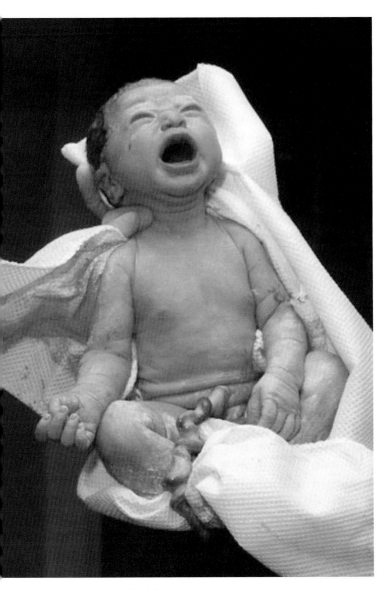

Figure 1. A birth cry.

infants cry the most. The implication is that the factors underlying the crying in most clinical cases are shared, to a greater or lesser degree, by western infants in general, and are probably linked to normal development.

The third departure from the earlier perspective concerns the quality of the babies' cries. Audiorecordings have confirmed that babies who cry a lot in the first three months tend to cry relatively intensely, but have not provided much evidence that the crying sounds themselves are abnormal, or that they clearly identify pain. This remains controversial. However, a careful review of the evidence by Gustafson, Wood, & Green (2000) has questioned the underlying assumption that crying behavior maps directly onto, and so identifies, its cause. Instead of discrete cry types, such as hunger, anger, and pain cries, they conclude that crying in young

babies is a 'graded signal,' which conveys information about the degree of an infant's distress, but not what is causing it. If so, attempts to distinguish between cries believed to signify colic and other cries in terms of their acoustic and behavioral features may prove fruitless.

The fourth departure is that the unsoothability of 1- to 3-month-old babies' crying, rather than its sound, has emerged as a central feature. Babies selected for high amounts of crying have proved to be objectively difficult or impossible to soothe, even for trained researchers using standardized consoling procedures. Other studies have confirmed that infants who cry a lot at home are highly reactive and hard to soothe when given standard clinical examinations involving undressing and handling. These findings point to individual differences in young infants' reactivity and ability to regulate their crying in response to challenging stimulation as the basis for variations in how much they cry at home. They also give some indication of the kinds of stimulation that provoke crying in such babies, since undressing, being put down, and being handled seem to be important triggers. We do not yet know the precise nature of the stimuli that give rise to crying in these babies, but understanding this will be important, in order to provide information that helps parents to manage the crying.

In summary, recent studies have increased our knowledge of infant crying and its impact on parents. While the amount of crying and length of cry bouts remain central issues, the emphasis has shifted from a focus solely on the sound of young babies' cries to more interactive aspects of their behavior and, particularly, to soothability. Since hard-to-soothe crying is aversive and uncontrollable for parents, it is easy to understand why many western parents find it upsetting. The puzzle is why many, apparently healthy, 1- to 3-month-old western infants should have these prolonged bouts of hard-to-soothe crying.

Causes of the infant crying bouts

Crying is metabolically costly, raising metabolism by 10–15 percent according to one study. This might seem to justify the belief that prolonged crying means something is wrong, since why otherwise would a baby maintain a behavioral state that is hazardous to growth? However, a view drawn from evolutionary theory is that infants who cry a lot are demonstrating their biological 'fitness': they can afford to cry in spite of its metabolic costs. By doing so, they increase parental involvement and promote their own survival. Here, too, the approaches can be sub-divided into those that view crying mainly as a sign of abnormality or those that see it as a function of normal development.

Explanations that attribute the infant crying to organic disturbance

The view that prolonged crying means that there is something wrong with a baby has led to studies of possible antecedent risk factors, such as maternal stress, cigarette smoking, and alcohol consumption during pregnancy, and medical complications and drugs used during labor and childbirth. While significant correlations between these variables and infant crying have sometimes been reported, they are weak, often fail to replicate, and are always difficult to interpret since they are interlaced with other biological and social factors. Furthermore, although controlled animal studies have shown that antenatal maternal stress and alcohol consumption predict deficits in offspring, the deficits have been predominantly in attentional and cognitive abilities, rather than increases in distressed vocalizations.

Evidence for causal links between concurrent organic disturbances and infant crying is, however, stronger. Gormally's (2001) review concluded that a variety of rare conditions, ranging from maternal drug ingestion to infant migraine, can give rise to prolonged crying in 1- to 5-month-old babies. She also found evidence that intolerance for cow's milk protein and fructose can lead to increased crying, as posited in the traditional, gastro-intestinal view of infant colic noted above.

This evidence is important for theories of causation and clinical practice, but there are two major qualifications. Firstly, organic disturbance is often obvious from symptoms of illness such as fever. Indeed, where crying is secondary to an illness, the origins of the crying are usually not at issue and the infants would be excluded from most colic studies. Secondly, in the absence of fever, crying due to organic disturbances is rare. Gormally (2001) concluded that 5–10 percent of cases presenting for prolonged unexplained crying in the first few months of infancy may have an associated organic disturbance. Treem (2001) estimated that around 10 percent of infants presenting for colic cannot tolerate cow's milk protein, pointing out that they can often be identified from symptoms such as vomiting, diarrhoea, and eczema. The implication is that about 90 percent of infants who cry for prolonged periods in early infancy do not have an organic disturbance.

Explanations attributing crying to inadequate parenting

Clinical studies have reported that interventions that change parental behavior can reduce young babies' crying. The studies were inconsistent in the kinds of parenting strategies that proved effective, but the implication seems to be that shortcomings in parental behavior caused the crying in the first place.

It is plausible that inexperienced or neglectful parents occasionally contribute to infant crying. Since babies often stop crying when parents intervene, it is also unsurprising that changes such as increasing parents' speed of response should lead to reduced crying. However, as noted above, the phenomenon at issue is not crying in general but bouts of hard-to-soothe crying. Furthermore, parents often know of strategies, such as car rides, which stop the crying bouts, but these too are not a solution, since the crying recurs. There is little evidence that changes in parenting practices can prevent the unsoothable crying bouts that are of most concern. Increased carrying, which proved promising in an early study, has not proved effective in others.

For practical reasons, it is difficult to study parental behavior before such crying occurs, but several studies have observed the home behavior of parents whose babies cry a lot, compared to other infants' parents. These studies found the parents to be highly responsive and sensitive, so that the few distinguishing features, such as high amounts of time spent carrying their babies, seemed to be responses to the crying. The conclusion was that these infants continued to fret and cry in spite of care that would usually work with most babies. Cross-cultural studies provide another source of evidence about parenting and crying. Anecdotal accounts and one systematic study of 1- to 3-month-old infants suggest that 'proximal care,' in which babies are held continuously and fed often, are associated with very little crying. More evidence is needed since, if confirmed, the differences could be related to variations in climate, diet, and gene pool between the families in such studies and western samples. Consequently, the findings may not implicate parental care.

Causal explanations that attribute the infant crying to individual differences in developmental processes

Human infants undergo a major 'neurodevelopmental transition' in the first three months after birth, evidence of which can be seen in the disappearance of the 'primitive reflexes' and the emergence of attentional and learning abilities and social behaviors such as smiles. Infant crying itself is considered to change from a reflex to a voluntary, social-communicative, behavior during this period. These changes are attributed to growth of the cerebral cortex and its increasing influence on behavior regulation.

Several authors have argued that prolonged crying in 1- to 3-month-old infants is linked to this developmental transition. This argument fits the normative evidence about crying, and moves the focus from the gut to the central nervous system. Individual differences in growth rate and maturation of central processes may partly explain variations between infants in the age at which crying peaks, and in how much they cry. However, this leaves unclear why a developmental transition shared by infants should lead some, but not others, to cry unsoothably for prolonged periods of time.

Based on the finding that infants who cry a lot are objectively hard-to-soothe following challenging stimulation, recent theorizing about this has centered on the concepts of 'reactivity' and 'regulation' of response. Adopted from temperament research, these terms refer to individual differences in how rapidly and intensely infants respond to a given stimulus (reactivity), and in how quickly and effectively they inhibit their responses and return to baseline (regulation of response). They refer to dispositions within infants, but do not necessarily carry the implication of a long-lived temperamental characteristic. The concept of 'regulation' of a response maps closely onto the finding that infants who cry a lot at this age are hard-to-soothe, implying that their main difficulty may be with inhibiting, or stopping, crying.

It is not yet clear whether low inhibitory ability, high reactivity, or both, are most responsible for the 'hard-to-soothe' character of the infants' prolonged crying bouts, and the term 'high responsivity' has been used to include both these characteristics. This focus on how the nervous system modulates crying is a promising avenue for future research. Figure 2 illustrates how infant responsivity may combine with infant neuro-developmental change and environmental triggers to produce the prolonged, unsoothable crying bouts often referred to as 'colicky crying.'

The management and outcomes of prolonged infant crying and colic

The evidence that organic disturbances can give rise to prolonged crying in young babies highlights the need for clinical protocols that allow these rare, but important, cases to be distinguished. Equally, the recognition that colic as a complaint to clinicians is about parents, as well as infants, implies the need to assess the factors that influence parental perceptions of, and responses to, their babies' crying. Attention is being paid to the links between infant crying and the 'shaken baby syndrome,' while parental vulnerabilities, such as maternal depression, need to be taken into account. The evidence that most infants who cry a lot at this early age are in good health requires a change in how many parents and professionals think about prolonged crying in early infancy. Based on the views of an expert panel, Barr, St. James-Roberts, & Keefe (2001) have put forward guidelines for assessment and management which recognize these goals.

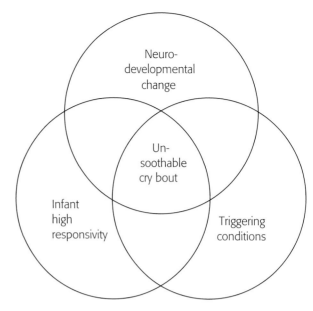

Figure 2. Three-component causal model for the onset of an unsoothable ('Colic') crying bout. A normal neurodevelopmental change is assumed to provide the necessary, underlying circumstances. Individual differences in reactivity or regulation of response ('responsivity') account for why some infants cry more often, intensely, and persistently, than others during this transition. Since even babies judged to have colic crying bouts cry normally most of the time (only about one in seven of their crying bouts is judged to be colic crying), a third factor, stimulation from the environment or internal milieu of the infant, is needed to trigger a crying bout that resists an infant's and parents' soothing attempts.

In the absence of parental and family risk factors, the long-term prognosis for babies who cry a lot in the early months is good. They have usually proved indistinguishable from their peers in follow-up studies (Lehtonen, 2001). This optimistic prognosis may not apply where prolonged crying has its onset at a later age or continues after 3 months of age, and poor outcomes for such cases have been reported (Papoušek, Wurmser, & von Hofacker, 2001). It is not yet clear what distinguishes these cases, but they imply the need for particular concern when infants over 3 months of age are brought to attention for persistent crying.

Conclusions

Recent research has produced substantial changes in our conceptualization of prolonged, unexplained crying during early infancy. Instead of viewing this as a symptom of an infant medical condition, the main focus has shifted to the impact of the crying on parents and consequent parent-infant interactions and relationships. Research into the neurodevelopmental processes that occur during early infancy should advance our understanding of the crying. In most cases, the clinical goal is to support parents in how to manage the crying, rather than to try to cure it, and guidelines for this purpose have been put forward. Practice-oriented trials are needed to establish the effectiveness of diagnostic schemes designed to distinguish between cases where infants are healthy, the rare cases where infants have organic disturbances, and cases where parents are vulnerable to the effects of the crying. Prolonged crying beyond 3 months of age appears to be associated with poor outcomes, so that research into the distinguishing etiological features of these cases, and which identifies effective treatments, needs to be a priority.

See also:

Magnetic Resonance Imaging; Cross-cultural comparisons; The status of the human newborn; Speech development; Sleep and wakefulness; Temperament; 'At-risk' concept

Further reading

Barr, R. G., Hopkins, B. and Green, J. A. (eds.) (2000). *Crying as a Sign, a Symptom, and a Signal.* London: MacKeith Press.

Lutz, T. (1999). *Crying: The Natural History and Cultural History of Tears.* New York: Norton.

Sudden Infant Death Syndrome

JAMES J. MCKENNA

Introduction

Since its formal recognition as a medical entity in 1969, well over 290,000 babies in the western world alone have died from the Sudden Infant Death Syndrome (SIDS). Also known as cot or crib death, it is presumed to be a sleep-related infant disorder primarily, but not exclusively, affecting infants in the first year of life, and especially between eight and sixteen weeks after birth. Still aptly described as a 'diagnosis by exclusion,' the pathophysiology of SIDS remains elusive. Yet, after more than forty years of research in which no public health policy or medical intervention reduced SIDS appreciably if at all, SIDS rates per 1,000 live births since 1990 continue to decline to unprecedented levels worldwide (Byard & Krous, 2001).

Sleeping position and related factors implicated in the decline of SIDS

The breakthrough in reducing SIDS risks came from an unexpected source, namely, child-care practices, or, more specifically, the position in which infants are placed for sleep. In the middle to late 1980s and early 1990s, observations by a number of researchers in different countries pointed to the prone infant sleeping position as being potentially dangerous, and associated with high rates of SIDS. Their observations, preceded by similar observations made in the 1940s, were followed by national, state-of-the-art epidemiological studies in Australia, New Zealand, the United Kingdom, and the Netherlands, all of which confirmed that the prone sleeping position was a significant risk factor for SIDS (Fleming et al., 1996). Between 1990 and 1992, when well-organized national campaigns recommended a change away from the prone position to the supine or side position, dramatic declines in SIDS were experienced in at least eight countries: Tasmania, New Zealand, the United Kingdom, Australia, Denmark, Norway, Sweden, and the Netherlands. In the United

States, the National Institutes of Health and the American Academy of Pediatrics initiated the 'Back to Sleep' campaign in 1992. Since then, SIDS rates have fallen no less than 40 percent nationally.

That a behavioral child-care practice over which parents assert control could make such a difference in reducing SIDS rates worldwide continues to astonish researchers. Its discovery marked the beginning of an important paradigm shift. It is now thought that, regardless of whatever the internal biological defects or causes of SIDS prove to be, they cannot fully be understood without reference to the overall social and physical environment within which they find expression.

The physical environment refers to the qualities of furnishings on which the infant sleeps. Characteristics of the bedding, especially the quality and firmness of the infant's mattress, including the total weight and insularity of the infant's blankets, are thought relevant. Researchers are also interested in whether or not the infant sleeps alone in a separate room, or with another person, whether sleeping partners are sober, and whether the infant sleeps with others on the same sleeping surface, as well as the ages and levels of responsibility of the sleeping partners. Whether or not the parents smoke, as well as the nature and quality of the caregiver-infant interactions and mother's choice of feeding method (breast, bottle, mixed), all constitute additional factors potentially able to increase or decrease the chances of an infant dying from SIDS.

The special characteristics of the human infant, including a relatively slow rate of biological and social development and extreme neurological immaturity at birth, suggest that social care of infants is practically synonymous with physiological regulation. In fact, compared with other mammals, young human infants are subject to the most extensive external physiological regulation and support by the mother for the longest period of time. For example, mothers' touches and whispers and odors cause changes in the infant's heart rates, breast feeding, and breathing patterns, to name but a few physiological responses (McKenna & Mosko,

2001). With this in mind, it is not surprising that at least for some types of SIDS, the quality of the social and physical setting within which the infant's development (including sleep) occurs might prove important.

Potential causes and risk factors associated with SIDS

Although the primary causes of SIDS are still unknown, the most salient SIDS risk factors include the following: infants sleeping prone, maternal smoking during and after pregnancy, prematurity and/or low birthweight, use of soft sleeping surfaces, covering of an infant's head, placing infants on soft pillows to sleep, over heating, lack of breast feeding, and bedsharing with a mother who smokes, takes drugs or who otherwise is unfamiliar with safety factors associated with bedsharing. Infants are also more likely to die from SIDS if their mothers are single, unsupported, less than 20 years of age, exhibit socially chaotic lifestyles, are poor, and lack consistent pre- and/or postnatal care (Byard & Krous, 2001).

It is generally thought that there may well be more than one cause of SIDS, but the most compelling general hypothesis is that the fatal event is related to the control of breathing and/or arousal during sleep. Perhaps an infant has a normal breathing pause during some phase of sleep, but the arousal mechanisms in the brain are unable to awaken the baby thus permitting the use of voluntary brain structures to breathe, or to reinitiate breathing. We know that deeper stages of sleep (Stage 3 or 4) as measured by EEG, which are prolonged by solitary infant sleep environments, are more difficult stages of sleep from which to awaken during a respiratory crisis than are lighter stages of sleep (viz., Stage 1 or 2, the latter complying with REM sleep). Or, it could be that some kind of fast-acting bacteria place a strain on the entire cardiorespiratory apparatus of an infant and, in combination with an arousal deficit, or some other as yet unidentified factor, the bacteria prove fatal.

One current theory is that, for one sub-class of infants, a fast-acting bacteria strain, which in one study was found in all SIDS victims, might paralyze the respiratory muscles leading to death. It has also been proposed that SIDS generally tends to occur after the regulatory mechanisms of the cardiorespiratory system have failed to monitor some combination of oxygen levels, breathing, heart-rate rhythm, and body temperature, which altogether fails to promote the minimal number of breaths or heart rates per minute required for life.

The unfolding pattern and characteristics of infant sleep architecture, including how many minutes infants spend in the various stages or types of sleep (light, deep, or REM sleep) and how infants arouse, are believed to be controlled by the brain stem. This area is composed of clusters of differentiated cells that receive and send messages from and to the heart, hormonal centers, lungs, muscles surrounding the ribs, diaphragm, and airway passages, as well as structures that specifically help to balance the proper amounts of oxygen and carbon dioxide in the blood and regulate body temperature.

One series of SIDS studies focused on the arcuate nucleus located on the ventral surface of the brain stem that monitors the proper balance of carbon dioxide and oxygen. When carbon dioxide builds up in the blood, the respiratory neurons are activated to expel it, thereby causing fresh oxygen to be inhaled and reducing the acidity of the blood. A significant number of SIDS victims compared with control infants had fewer 'acethylcholine binding sites' in this area of the brain (Kinney et al., 1995). This suggests that in a variety of circumstances, including prone sleeping, infants may not have optimal or even minimal ability to reinitiate breathing following some types of apnoea or exposure to their own exhaled carbon dioxide. This could occur, for example, if the carbon dioxide is trapped in a mattress as the baby lies face down, or if the infant is under thick blankets. Alternatively, it might mean that some infants simply cannot arouse to breathe after particularly long breathing pauses or apnoeas.

Diversity among SIDS victims

The fact remains that there is no single, consistent criterion or pathological marker that can be used either to predict potential SIDS victims or identify them post-mortem on autopsy. Nor is there an animal model of SIDS since there is no condition like it that is known to occur in any species other than humans (Rognum, 1995; Byard & Krous, 2001).

The SIDS population remains exceedingly heterogeneous. However, SIDS rates remain highest amongst minorities who are economically disadvantaged. The rate of SIDS for African-Americans, for example, is at least twice as high as it is for Caucasians, being about 1.4 per 1,000 live births and 0.6, respectively. Politically, socially, economically marginalized and often indigenous groups (e.g., Maori, Cree, Australian Aboriginal, Native Americans, Alaskan Inuits) around the world likewise experience significantly higher rates of SIDS than do members of the majority, usually white, cultures (Byard & Krous, 2001). Some SIDS victims may appear to suffer from subtle deficits that develop during intrauterine life, but are not apparent in the neonate. In addition, preterm and low-birthweight infants are at increased risk.

One group of researchers suggests that especially SIDS victims found 'faces straight down' could actually have suffocated. These deaths are labeled 'other infant deaths.' The thinking here is that some infants sleeping prone may not yet be strong enough to turn or lift their heads well enough to get fresh air, especially when sleeping face down on soft mattresses. Unfortunately, on postmortem examination death by asphyxiation is practically indistinguishable from SIDS. With this in mind, dead infants found sleeping on beanbag cushions, with an obese adult on a couch, or found sleeping in a bed with a mother who smokes or is intoxicated, or found with the head covered by blankets, increasingly are thought to have been asphyxiated rather than as having died from SIDS. In some of these cases, infants may have been forced to re-breathe lethal doses of their own expelled carbon dioxide, and been unable to get enough oxygen.

Epidemiological findings

Although the situation may change with recommendations to position infants on their backs for sleep, in many countries SIDS occurs most frequently in winter, and usually in the early morning or evening hours, when the infant is out of sight of the caregiver and presumably asleep. However, SIDS is also known to occur while babies are riding around in strollers, sitting in car seats, dozing in baby carriers, and even sleeping on their mother's chests, following a breastfeeding episode.

In the United States, the highest SIDS rates occur amongst mothers less than 20 years of age, who smoked during their pregnancies, are unmarried, and lack access to prenatal care. From an international perspective, and where comparative protocols for identifying SIDS victims are used, SIDS rates appear lowest within Japanese, Dutch, Swedish, Finnish, Norwegian, English, and Israeli populations. In these low SIDS countries, infants are positioned to sleep in the supine position and most mothers breastfeed.

Some countries claim that SIDS is virtually unknown (e.g., China, former Czechoslovakia). While this might be true, it is difficult to know until more careful and standardized autopsy procedures are employed in these countries. The most recent international study of child-care practices in relationship to SIDS rates was conducted by the SIDS Global Task Force (Nelson *et al.*, 2001). It revealed an unexpected finding. The study shows dramatically that low SIDS 'awareness' and low SIDS rates per 1,000 live births are also associated with cultures within which parents and infant sleep within proximity to each other, such that they co-sleep often in the form of some sort of bedsharing (Fig. 1).

Bedsharing is, however, controversial in many western industrialized cultures. Particularly in the context of SIDS research, this is because amongst at-risk urban, impoverished populations, most notably African-Americans in the United States and the Maori in New Zealand, bedsharing is associated with relatively high SIDS. This leads some SIDS researchers to argue that mother-infant bedsharing is inherently dangerous (Kemp *et al.*, 2000). Other researchers point out that the positive relationship between high SIDS and high bedsharing rates in these sub-groups can be explained by the convergence of multiple SIDS risk factors in conjunction with bedsharing (McKenna & Mosko, 2001; Fleming *et al.*, 1996), and is not due to bedsharing *per se*. For example, higher rates of infants sleeping prone, maternal smoking or drug use, lack of breastfeeding, and an array of other unsafe sleep practices including use of unsafe sleep furnishings for infants are found in those populations where infant death rates are high. The growing consensus is that bedsharing behavior is diverse, and can be practiced safely or unsafely. One way to conceptualize this issue is to think in terms of a 'risks-benefits continuum' wherein, depending on the presence or absence in the bedsharing environment of known risk factors, bedsharing can be protective in some situations and risky in others (McKenna & Mosko, 2001; Fig. 2).

Bedsharing is not the only issue around which SIDS researchers disagree. Only a relatively small number of SIDS victims show any signs that something might be wrong with them before they die. As a result, the medical community is engaged in another volatile debate, and is continuing research, on whether or not infants with a history of repeated apnoeas should be sent home from the hospital with breathing monitors. At any given time, between 40,000 and 45,000 monitors are put to use in the United States. As yet, however, no evidence indicates that monitors prevent SIDS deaths, and there are no data to suggest how or under what circumstances infants die from SIDS when monitors are available. At present, the effectiveness of home monitors in preventing SIDS deaths is highly questionable (Byard & Krous, 2001).

New perspectives on SIDS: the importance of parental night-time contact, breastfeeding, and how the brain uses serotonin

Regardless of routine sleep practices, most infants in western countries die outside the supervision of a responsible adult caregiver, either from SIDS or from various kinds of asphyxial deaths. Indeed, an infant who sleeps within proximity of an adult caregiver in the same room is only half as likely to die from SIDS than is an infant sleeping in a crib in a room by itself (Blair *et al.*, 1999).

Historically, infants sleeping alone is a relatively new cultural custom no more than 100 years old, and limited

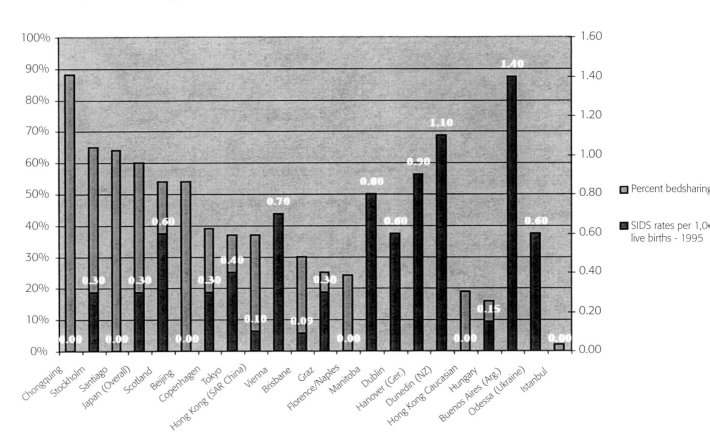

Figure 1. SIDS rates (1995) per 1,000 live births in relationship to percent bedsharing across various cities and countries throughout the world. From E. A. S. Nelson, B. J. Taylor, A. Jenite *et al.* 2001. International Child Care Practice Study: infant sleeping environment. *Early Human Development*, 62, 43–55.

to the industrialized western world. There is no scientific doubt that mother-infant co-sleeping in conjunction with baby-controlled night-time breastfeeding is the usual human pattern practiced by almost all contemporary people. Given this fact, it seems appropriate to ask whether the biological mechanisms evolved to control human infant sleep and breathing, and which function alongside and in relationship to night-time breastfeeding, are subject to physiological regulation through maternal contact. The more specific question is whether or not breathing and arousal mechanisms thought to be involved in some SIDS are able to change as quickly in any particular infant as do culturally based social ideas about where infants should sleep. In other words, where and when infants sleep alone, their sleep, breathing, thermoregulation, and arousal mechanisms could be functioning in environments for which they were not selected for during evolution. As a consequence of this, perhaps some human infants, especially those born with deficits, have an increased risk of dying from SIDS, when the mother's body is not present during sleep to provide what some call 'physiological (sensory) regulatory stimuli.'

In our behavioral and physiological studies of mother-infant co-sleeping and breastfeeding in a sleep

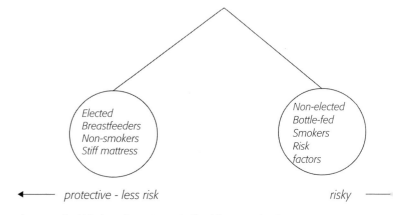

Figure 2. The 'risks-benefit continuum' of bedsharing with infants.

laboratory, we find that, compared with when they slept by themselves, bedsharing mothers and infants aroused more frequently, usually as a result of the other's movement or sound. Bedsharing mother-baby pairs spent more time in the same state of sleep and wakefulness simultaneously, and significantly more sleep time in lighter stages of sleep (Stages 1 and 2). We also found that, compared with infants who regularly slept in a different room from their mothers, bedsharing infants spent less time in deeper stages of sleep (Stage 3 or 4), the stages of an infant's sleep from which awakening to arouse the re-initiation of breathing is more difficult. We postulate that more infant arousals, and increased sleep time in light rather than deep sleep, may be advantageous for young infants. Our thinking is that some infants might also need more 'practice' in learning how to awaken quickly and effectively than do other infants, and that mother-infant co-sleeping with breastfeeding provides the appropriate biological context for such practice (Byard & Krous, 2001).

While not all epidemiological studies suggest that breastfeeding reduces the chances of SID, at least half of them do. Research from several laboratories shows that, in contrast to breastfeeding mothers and infants who sleep apart, bedsharing mother-infant pairs breastfeed twice as much per night and for three times the total night-time duration than do solitary-sleeping, breastfeeding infants. This finding raises the possibility that with more of mother's milk, and thus more of her antibodies consumed, the intensely breastfed infant might better fight off any threatening fast-action bacteria potentially involved in SIDS.

Most recently Deborah Weese-Mayer and her colleagues at Rush-Presbyterian St. Lukes Medical Center in Chicago found that SIDS victims tended to have a different version of one key gene called 5-HTT, which effects how the brain uses serotonin, an important brain neurotransmitter involved in maintaining (among other functions) rhythmical breathing. In her control group, 71 percent of African-Americans (who have high SIDS rates) had the suspect variant, while only 47 percent of the white population did. This same gene appears to be relatively rare among the Japanese whose babies die much less frequently from SIDS than all other groups. Gene-environment interactions are still thought to be very important in determining whether or not the gene finds expression in the form of SIDS, but this is the first time an underlying genetic component has potentially been identified.

Conclusions

Much research is needed in these and other areas. No answer will come easily, and no one solution to the SIDS tragedy will be applicable to all infants. The fact remains that an understanding of what causes SIDS and what can prevent it has not been achieved. However, since the early 1990s, an appreciation has been acquired of the importance of the infant's caregiving environment in moderating whatever the primary causes prove to be. This acceptance of the fact that the human infant's biology is best understood in terms of the context of the mother-infant dyad promises to yield a better understanding of this syndrome, and makes it more likely that this tragic syndrome will be eliminated sooner rather than later.

See also:
Cross-cultural comparisons; Epidemiological designs; The status of the human newborn; Brain and behavioral development (I): sub-cortical; Sleep and wakefulness; 'At-risk' concept; Prematurity and low birthweight; Anthropology

Further reading

McKenna, J. J. (1986). An anthropological perspective on the sudden infant death syndrome (SIDS): the role of parental breathing cues and speech breathing adaptations. *Medical Anthropology*, 10, 9–53.

McKenna, J. J., Mosko, S. and Richard, C. (1997). Bedsharing promotes breast feeding. *Pediatrics*, 100, 214–219.

McKenna J. J., Mosko, S. and Richard, C. (1999). Breast feeding and mother-infant cosleeping in relation to SIDS prevention. In W. Trevathan, N. Smith and J. J. McKenna (eds.), *Evolutionary Medicine*. New York: Oxford University Press, pp. 53–74.

Williams syndrome

MICHELLE DE HAAN

Introduction

Williams syndrome (WS) is a rare neurogenetic disorder that affects boys and girls equally and is estimated to occur in 1 in 20,000 live births. Individuals with this syndrome are missing a number of genes on a specific region of the seventh chromosome (7q11.23). The deletion of these genes is associated with physical abnormalities, mild to moderate intellectual impairment, and an outgoing, overly friendly personality. WS has attracted interest from researchers in a number of fields because it involves a unique pattern of strengths and weaknesses in specific cognitive abilities. Verbal abilities, face recognition, and social competence are relative strengths, while visuo-spatial abilities and mathematics are relative weaknesses (Bellugi & Wang, 1996). This uneven cognitive profile has provided fuel for debates about the links between genes and cognition (Bellugi & St. George, 2000; Donnai & Karmiloff-Smith, 2000). In this entry, the genetic and behavioral profile of WS will be described, and its relevance to these debates discussed.

Description of Williams syndrome genotype and phenotype

Genotype

Most individuals with WS have a sub-microscopic deletion of about twenty genes on one of the usual two copies of chromosome 7, meaning that every cell in the body is missing one copy of the affected genes. Genes provide the 'recipes' for making proteins used in the body. With only one intact copy of the genes, there will be only half the usual amount of proteins. This is known as haploinsufficiency, and means that the abilities affected in WS must depend on the amount of one or more of these proteins, and not merely their presence or absence.

Most cases of WS are caused by copying errors: when the chromosomes are being duplicated for reproduction, a section is accidentally left out. The size of the deletion is similar in most individuals, although not identical. One gene that is deleted in over 90 percent of cases, and the first of the genes to be identified is the elastin gene. A blood test using a molecular genetic technique called Fluorescent In Situ Hybridization (FISH) can be used to detect whether one or two copies of this gene are present, with a finding of only one copy confirming a diagnosis of WS.

Phenotype: physical, neurological, and behavioral characteristics

Infants with WS are often colicky in the first months of life, have severe difficulties with feeding, and failure to thrive. In some cases, these features lead to an early diagnosis, but in other cases individuals remain undiagnosed until a later age. Other characteristics include transiently elevated calcium levels in infancy, short height, early puberty, heart and blood vessel abnormalities, and hypersensitivity to certain sounds. Individuals with WS, like some other genetic disorders such as Down's syndrome, have a characteristic facial appearance as shown in Figure 1.

The link between the deleted genes and the behavioral profile of WS must occur via the brain, thus there has been interest in identifying brain abnormalities in the syndrome. There is no evidence for clear damage to specific areas, but the relative sizes of different brain regions are atypical. Generally the brains are smaller than normal. However, within this overall reduction, anterior areas of the brain are proportionately intact, while posterior areas, especially the right occipital region, are proportionately small. Certain regions of the cerebellum are larger than normal, and, interestingly, these are the same regions that are affected (but are smaller) in autism.

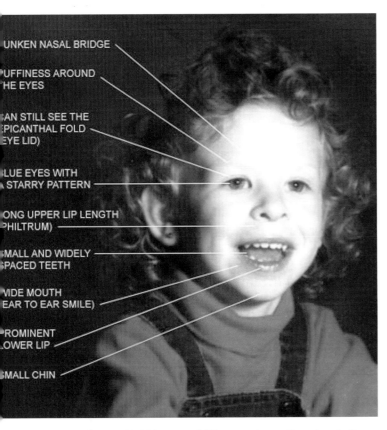

SUNKEN NASAL BRIDGE

PUFFINESS AROUND
THE EYES

CAN STILL SEE THE
EPICANTHAL FOLD
(EYE LID)

BLUE EYES WITH
A STARRY PATTERN

LONG UPPER LIP LENGTH
(PHILTRUM)

SMALL AND WIDELY
SPACED TEETH

WIDE MOUTH
(EAR TO EAR SMILE)

PROMINENT
LOWER LIP

SMALL CHIN

Figure 1. Facial features of Williams syndrome. Reproduced with permission from childrenheartinstitute.org – Hasan Abdallah, MD.

Behavioral characteristics

Intellectual abilities

Individuals with WS typically have mildly to moderately impaired intellect. However, the range of abilities across individuals is quite large, with some obtaining the lowest possible scores and others with values close to normal (Mervis *et al.*, 2000). Despite this broad range in overall level of intellectual abilities, people with WS tend to show a similar cognitive profile of strengths and weaknesses in particular abilities.

Cognitive profile

Much effort has been put into describing the cognitive profile of WS and its distinctive features (Bellugi & Wang, 1996; Mervis *et al.*, 2000). The reason is that a precise description of the cognitive phenotype is necessary for understanding the link between cognition and its underlying genetic and neural substrates. The general cognitive profile of WS is relative strengths in verbal, face processing, and social abilities, and relative weaknesses in visuo-spatial and number abilities. Figure 2 gives an example of a drawing and a verbal description of an elephant by a 15-year-old with WS. It

is important to note that the strengths are *relative* strengths, meaning that performance is better than might be expected given overall intellectual abilities or weaknesses in other areas, but not necessarily meaning performance in the normal range.

WS individuals tend to be quite talkative and articulate. Indeed, their verbal abilities are strikingly good in comparison to individuals with other genetic syndromes and of a similar intellectual level. Many people have noted their use of rather sophisticated words (e.g., *alleviate*, *evacuate*) that are surprising given their overall cognitive abilities. Results of standardized testing confirm these observations. For example, WS adolescents score higher than their mental age would predict on vocabulary tests involving matching a word to a picture. While their vocabularies are certainly impressive, their proclivity for unusual words and other evidence suggest that they may have atypical organization of semantic knowledge. It is possible that the very good auditory rote memory of individuals with WS helps them to acquire their impressive vocabulary, but with atypical semantic organization. They also perform well on tests of other aspects of language. In particular, they show strengths on the structural aspects of language, such as knowledge of syntax (e.g., understanding passive sentences and processing conditional questions).

Their good verbal abilities contrast with their impaired visuo-spatial abilities. Their difficulty is often described as being 'unable to see the forest for the trees' – they appear to have a bias to attend to information about the parts of a pattern and fail to see the whole. This causes severe difficulty with tasks involving drawing or copying. For example, if asked to draw a bicycle, they may draw recognizable components but with an unusual arrangement (Figure 3). This difficulty is not limited to situations in which they must construct a pattern, as they also have difficulty in tasks involving matching spatial relations (e.g., matching line orientation). In everyday life, this can give rise to difficulties in tasks such as learning left from right, telling time from a circular clock, or tying shoelaces. It is important to note that these difficulties with spatial processing do not reflect a general impairment in visual perception *per se*, because they have normal visual priming and are unexpectedly good at recognition of faces. Some have interpreted the difficulty with spatial information as reflecting atypical development of the dorsal (spatial) visual pathway relative to the ventral (object recognition) pathway.

Social behavior

WS individuals are often described as 'hypersociable' or over-friendly. They tend to score higher than typical

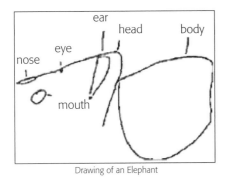

And what an elephant is, it is one of the animals. And what the elephant does, it lives in the jungle. It can also live in the zoo. And what it has, it has long gray ears, fan ears, ears that can blow in the wind. It has a long trunk that can pick up grass, or pick up hay . . . If they're in a bad mood it can be terrible . . . If the elephant gets mad it could stomp; It could charge, like a bull can charge. They have long big tusks. They can damage a car . . . It could be dangerous. When they're in a pinch, when they're in a bad mood it can be terrible. You don't want an elephant as a pet. You want a cat or a dog or a bird . . .

Drawing of an Elephant   Verbal Description of an Elephant

Figure 2. Contrast between visual-spatial and language abilities in Williams syndrome.

individuals, or those with other developmental disorders, on tests measuring behavior in social situations, including their ability to remember names and faces, their tendency to initiate social interactions with strangers, and their empathy with others' emotions.

What is the relationship between the genotype and phenotype?

One reason for the scientific interest in WS is that it provides an opportunity of linking genes with behavior. The deleted genes must in some way be responsible for the impaired abilities, but how? One approach to this question is to compare those with WS to patients with smaller gene deletions in the same region of chromosome 7 (e.g., Tassabehji *et al.*, 1999). By comparing these groups, it can be possible to determine which genes are related to which characteristics of WS.

This approach has been successful in identifying the gene involved in one of the physical characteristics of WS, supravalvular aortic stenosis (SVAS). SVAS is an obstructive vascular lesion that can take the form of a discrete hourglass deformity or diffuse aortic hypoplasia. It has been linked to the deletion of the elastin gene. Elastin belongs to the class of connective tissue proteins found in tissues that can readily be stretched (e.g., tendons, ligaments, bladder wall, and large blood vessels). The observation that individuals with a point deletion of only that gene show SVAS, but not the WS cognitive profile, demonstrates that deletion of that gene underlies this physical characteristic of the syndrome.

A similar approach has been adopted to try to identify which genes underlie the cognitive characteristics of WS, but the results of these studies are in disagreement. One study of patients with small deletions involving the elastin and limkinase 1 genes found evidence connecting deletion of limkinase 1 with the impaired visuo-spatial construction abilities in WS. However, another study did not support this result: patients with similar

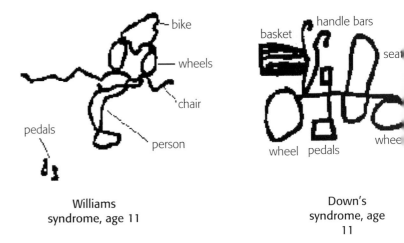

Williams syndrome, age 11   Down's syndrome, age 11

Figure 3. Drawing of a bicycle by Williams and Down's syndrome children matched on age and IQ.

deletions showed no impairments in visuo-spatial abilities. Thus, the question concerning the link between the deleted genes and the cognitive characteristics of WS remains controversial.

How do cognitive modules develop?

Another reason for researchers' interest in WS is because of the clues it might provide into the developing brain and mind. Studies of adults suggest that the mature brain is organized into modules – that specific brain regions carry out specific cognitive functions. There are two rival explanations as to how this organization develops: (a) the innate modularity hypothesis, and (b) the interactive specialization hypothesis.

Innate modularity hypothesis

According to the innate modularity view, the cognitive modules observed in adults are genetically specified and already present from birth. This view predicts that, even early in development, one or more modules can be impaired without affecting other modules. WS, together with another developmental disorder called Specific Language Impairment (SLI), provides support for this view. In WS, language is a strength in spite of lowered intellect, while in SLI, language is impaired in spite of normal intellect. The double dissociation of language and general intellect across the two developmental disorders supports the view that there is a language module that can be selectively spared or impaired.

Interactive specialization hypothesis

According to this view, the brain is not initially organized into distinct modules, and only becomes so during development as an emergent property of both biological maturation and experience. One piece of evidence in support of this view is that the cognitive profile of WS is not constant over development. For example, while adults and older children with WS show a strength in verbal abilities and weakness in number abilities, WS infants show the opposite pattern. This finding is incompatible with the innate modularity hypothesis that certain modules are impaired or intact from the start, since it shows that early abilities do not necessarily predict later ones. It also illustrates the important point that the process of development is critical for understanding developmental disorders.

Advocates of innate modularity might argue that there could still be innate modules because face processing has been noted as a strength, even from early in life in WS. Moreover, WS adults can achieve near normal performance on standardized tests of this ability. Could this be an intact innate module? Proponents of the interactive specialization hypothesis point out that, if so, face recognition should be accomplished by the same cognitive mechanisms as in typically developing individuals. However, several studies show this is not the case. For example, WS individuals appear to rely less than normal on cues from the configuration of features in the face to recognize identity. In addition, their event-related brain potentials show atypical patterns within the first several hundred milliseconds of processing. Together, these results argue against the view that the cognitive strengths in WS reflect the operation of intact modules. The challenge that remains for the interactive specialization view is to delineate more precisely the roles of biological maturation and experience in the process, and in failures of the process in forming mature cognitive modules.

Conclusions

Investigations of WS are providing an increasingly detailed picture of its cognitive and genetic profile. Several studies cast doubt on the view that the uneven cognitive profile reflects spared and impaired modules specifically linked to the genetic deletion. Instead, it is possible that the genetic deletions affect more basic, lower-level abilities that ultimately affect development of higher-level ones. These sorts of findings have implications for the types and timings of interventions that might be most effective.

There are several important directions for future research in WS. Firstly, functional neuroimaging techniques can provide a window into the brain organization that underlies cognitive abilities in WS, and allow further testing of the innate modularity and interactive specialization hypotheses. Secondly, more longitudinal studies focused on brain and cognitive development during infancy and early childhood in WS will allow a better understanding of how the mature profile is established. Thirdly, genetic studies have provided important first clues about the identity of the deleted genes and their protein products. Ultimately, it is possible that they may also lead to development of gene or pharmacological treatments. These types of research are all critical to understanding the links from genes to brain to behavior.

See also:
Understanding ontogenetic development: debates about the nature of the epigenetic process; Theories of the child's mind; Magnetic Resonance Imaging; Cognitive development beyond infancy; Language development; Brain and behavioral development (I): sub-cortical; Brain and behavioral development (II): cortical; Face recognition; Autism; Behavioral and learning disorders; Down's syndrome; Prolonged infant crying and colic; Cognitive neuroscience; Developmental genetics

Further reading

Atkinson, J., Braddick, O. J., Anker, S., Curran, W., Andrew, R., Wattam-Bell, J. and Braddick, F. (2003). Neurobiological models of visuo-spatial cognition in young Williams syndrome children: measures of dorsal-stream and frontal function. *Developmental Neuropsychology*, 23, 139–172.

Levitin, D. J., Menon, V., Schmitt, J. E., Eliez, S., White, C. D., Glover, G. H., Kadis, J., Korenberg, J. R., Bellugi, U. and Riess, A. L. (2003). Neural correlates of auditory perception in Williams syndrome: an fMRI study. *Neuroimage*, 18, 74–82.

Paterson, S. J., Brown, J. H., Gsodl, M. K., Johnson, M. H. and Karmiloff-Smith, A. (1999). Cognitive modularity and genetic disorders. *Science*, 286, 2355–2358.

Tager-Flusberg, H., Boshart, J. and Baron-Cohen, S. (1998). Reading the windows to the soul: evidence of domain-specific sparing in Williams syndrome. *Journal of Cognitive Neuroscience*, 10, 631–639.

PART VII
Crossing the borders

This final part aims to indicate how developmental psychology can benefit from cooperation with other disciplines in the study of child development. The benefits are in terms of potential gains of knowledge concerning both fundamental and applied issues about the development of children. Where possible, examples are based on programs of research rather than single studies. Each section is written by an expert in a discipline other than developmental psychology. Thus, for example, a linguist writes about what has been done and what can be achieved in forging links with developmental psychology to study language development.

Anthropology **Michael Cole & Jennifer Cole**
Behavioral embryology **Scott R. Robinson**
Behavior genetics **Thalia C. Eley**
Cognitive neuroscience **Mark H. Johnson**
Developmental genetics **William A. Harris**
Education **Leslie Smith**
Ethology **John C. Fentress**
Linguistics **Melissa Bowerman**
Pediatrics **Martin C. O. Bax**
Sociology **Elizabeth G. Menaghan**

Anthropology

MICHAEL COLE & JENNIFER COLE

Introduction

The anthropological study of human development has been intertwined with the work of psychologists since at least the latter half of the 19th century. This common interest had several sources. These included the nature of human evolution, the new roles that children were playing in social life as a consequence of the spread of the industrial revolution, and the effects of these large social and economic changes on the nature of individual human development.

Influence of Darwinism

After the publication of Charles Darwin's *On The Origin of Species* in 1859, children came to be viewed as scientifically interesting, instead of imperfect adults to be seen and not heard, because their behavior provided clues to human evolution. It became fashionable, for example, to compare the behavior of human children with other primates to see if individual children went through, for example, a 'chimpanzee stage' similar to the one through which the human species was thought to have evolved. This was a time when many adhered to Ernst Haeckel's aphorism that "ontogeny recapitulates phylogeny", or that the development of the individual repeats the same stages as that of the human species. This belief later led to the claim that societies could be ranked with respect to their level of development, a view that made it almost irresistible to conclude that 'primitives' think like children.

Darwin's follower, Herbert Spencer (1886), justified the view that social and mental development go hand in hand by arguing that, in the early stages of history, societies were so simple and their experience so limited that humans could not even hold as many as two ideas in mind, so weak were their powers of generalization. But with repeated experience and growth in the variety of experience, humans could begin to ". . . move toward the concept of a truth higher in generality than these different experiences themselves" (p. 221).

The analogy to children seemed obvious, so it is no surprise to find that James Mark Baldwin, who had a strong influence on Piaget and many other 20th-century psychologists, should write a book entitled *Mental Development in the Child and the Race, Methods and Processes* (1895), or that a student of G. Stanley Hall, another central figure in the history of developmental psychology, should write a monograph entitled *The Child: Study in the Evolution of Man* (Chamberlain, 1900). In a similar vein, the German anthropologist, Carl Vogt (1864) claimed that the brains of African adults resembled those of 7-year-old European children.

A focus on children and subsequent neglect

Once anthropologists actually began to observe children, they found that the story of parallel primitivisms and developmental progress was not altogether convincing. Young children from non-technological societies sometimes exhibited impressive, even precocious, abilities. But this counter-evidence met with a ready explanation: although they may develop quickly, primitive people's development ceases early. For example, in his largely anthropological approach to the study of South African children, Dudley Kidd (1906) claimed that, with puberty, degenerative processes set in, so that early growth soon tapered off.

Given this intense interest in similarities between the development of children and societies, it is a curious fact that when anthropology began to mature as a profession, children found little place in anthropological writings. One explanation for this sudden loss of interest is probably the trenchant criticisms of social evolutionary theories mounted by Franz Boas (1858–1942), a German-born anthropologist who started his professional career as a student of the psychologist Wilhelm Wundt (1832–1920). Boas, unlike many of his predecessors, spent a good deal of time in the field, learning the language and customs of the people among whom he lived.

On the basis of his own experience, Boas argued that when Europeans with superficial knowledge of another society sought to judge the intellectual merits of its members, they generally mistook their own lack of understanding for lack of understanding on the part of the people with whom they had come into superficial contact. Boas (1911) proposed instead the idea that all humans everywhere share the same psychological capabilities that find their unique expression in the culture formed by the social group in response to ecological conditions. When the first joint Cambridge Torres Straits expedition of anthropologists and psychologists was organized, there was a good deal of ethnographic and experimental-psychological research carried out among adults, but children did not figure in the research at all.

The influence of Freudianism

While the emphasis on a universal sequence of social and psychological progress and the psychic unity of mankind waned within anthropology in the early decades of the 20th century, anthropologists found themselves faced with a new kind of universalism in the form of Freudian theories of the relationship between culture and human development. Freud put forward a wide-ranging set of hypotheses about how features of cultures represent universal manifestations of basic human psychodynamic processes that begin at birth. In response, anthropologists sought to put Freud's claims to the test of anthropological fieldwork.

Several anthropologists, most notably Bronislaw Malinowski (1884–1942) and Margaret Mead (1901–1978), used data gathered during long-term participant observation in other cultures to challenge Freudian orthodoxies. On the basis of his research in the Trobriand Islands, Malinowski questioned the universality of the Oedipal complex in childhood, as well as sexual repression in adolescence. Mead (1928) also contested Freud's notion that adolescence is universally associated with intergenerational conflict and sexual inhibitions, as well as Stanley Hall's claim that adolescence was always a time of inner turmoil, in her famous study of Samoan adolescents. Drawing on her Samoan ethnography, she developed the idea that ethnographic fieldwork could disprove universal theories of human nature by finding one negative case, which she dubbed the 'anthropological veto.'

In a more cognitive vein, Mead explicitly sought to test Piaget's theory of universal sequences of cognitive development using a variety of methods borrowed from his work in conjunction with ethnographic observation

on the Pacific island of Manus. Based on her findings, and contrary to Piaget's observations that western children initially think animistically, and are therefore comparable to primitive adults, Mead found that children on Manus thought in distinct cause and effect terms. Indeed, it was the adults who thought animistically! Rejecting psychological explanations, Mead suggested that culturally accepted adult theories and local socialization practices explained the shift from childhood to adult forms of thinking.

Other anthropologists, however, derived inspiration from Freudian ideas. In the 1930s, the psychoanalyst, Abram Kardiner (1891–1981), in conjunction with anthropologists Ralph Linton (1893–1953) and Cora Du Bois (1903–1991), sought to illuminate the causal mechanisms through which culture shaped personality development. They proposed a scheme in which 'primary institutions' of subsistence and child-rearing practices create a 'basic personality' comprised of shared anxieties and neuroses, which in turn give rise to 'secondary institutions' of religion and folklore that mediate and ameliorate psychodynamic tensions.

The influence of the Whitings and the Six Cultures study

Anthropologists also followed prominent psychologists in seeking to understand processes of socialization, but they did so by providing scientific accounts of the socialization of children in so-called primitive societies. In their massive Six Cultures study, John and Beatrice Whiting (1975) sought to trace causal relationships beginning with a group's environment and history. Then, they considered maintenance systems (e.g., subsistence patterns, social structure, division of labor), which in turn shape child-rearing practices and the 'projective expressive systems' (e.g., religion, magic beliefs) that formed the child's proximal environment, and consequently the overall process of socialization in development. This work successfully demonstrated, for example, that gender-related personality traits taken as universal by Euro-American psychologists (e.g., the presumed innately greater nurturance of females) could be traced to child-rearing patterns shaped by maintenance systems. Thus, for instance, boys assigned child-care duties in agricultural societies developed more nurturant personalities than boys in a New England town.

Psychologists on culture and development

With the exception of the Whitings and their students, the 1970s and 1980s were a period when research on culture and development was dominated by

Figure 1. Young men in Tanzania borrow images and styles taken from American rap music. Photograph courtesy of Brad Weiss.

psychologists interested in testing the extent to which presumably universal laws of cognitive development were in fact subject to conditions of culture that had been insufficiently investigated (Berry *et al.*, 2002). This work generally met with a chilly reception from anthropologists who were skeptical about the application of psychological tests as culture-free instruments for the measurement of development.

More recently, one witnesses a growing appreciation on the part of psychologists for the need to make their methods more culture-sensitive, to acknowledge the centrality of cultural context to both their theories and methods, and to allow the use of qualitative methods such as discourse analysis and participant observation into their pantheon of methods for studying human development.

Contemporary anthropology

Within cultural anthropology, most work during the 1980s and early 1990s ignored issues of individual human development, focusing instead on broad issues of power and representation, political economy and history. At present, anthropological interest in development is often macro in scale, focused largely on processes of cultural and economic globalization, which many argue undermine older forms of social reproduction. However, the resurgence of concern in issues of social reproduction brought about by globalization, which draws together political, economic,

cultural, and biological factors, creates new possibilities for a fruitful interaction among different disciplines around issues of human development.

One important line of contemporary anthropological writing focuses on youth, the period roughly between 15 and 25 years of age. Taking place within the context of a growing interest in processes of globalization, which involves both novel interconnections among different parts of the world and new forms of exclusion, several anthropologists have examined how youths are implicated in newly emergent patterns of production and consumption, politics and power. In many societies around the world, youth are the first to seize on, and modify their behavior and expectations in response to globally circulated forms of media. As a result, they provide a particularly sharp lens through which to explore issues of social reproduction and transformation, and the role of the media in these processes (Fig. 1).

In middle childhood (6–12 years), a major focus has been placed upon education and enculturation, with special attention to apprenticeship and schooling. For example, Robert LeVine and his colleagues (1994) have shown that schooling exerts a kind of 'sleeper effect' on females. When educated females marry and have families, they have fewer children than uneducated peers and interact with their children more verbally. Their children in turn have higher cognitive test scores, higher levels of achievement in schooling, and smaller families, while gaining preparation to engage in the globalized practices of modern economic formations.

In infancy, great interest has been shown in the reciprocal effects of culture and biology, such as in James Chisholm's (1983) work with the Navajo. He showed that the temperamental characteristics of the children of urbanized Navajo women are more volatile than those of their rural counterparts. This effect was mediated by the stress of involvement in modern life and the differential amounts of cortisol induced in the expectant urbanized mothers, which in turn influenced their children-to-be.

Conclusions

Psychologists have recognized the simplicity of early approaches to identifying stages of development with chronological age, and they, too, are questioning the nature, and causes, of different patterns of development to adulthood. For their part, anthropologists are cooperating with psychologists to clarify the ways in which universal processes of development place constraints on cultural variation.

It currently appears that several fruitful lines of collaboration between psychologists and anthropologists show promise for future understanding of human development. For example, psychologists are becoming aware that cultural variations in young children's play have brought into question classical psychological accounts of the role of play in children's cognitive and social development. Collaborative studies of the development of category systems have given both anthropologists and psychologists a deeper appreciation of the roles of maturation and local cultural practices in the formation of basic category systems. The impact of schooling on development has brought anthropologists and psychologists together in efforts to understand the mechanisms at work, and to help design more effective educational environments that are sensitive to local cultural conditions. And, as a last example, the ways in which cultural and economic globalization are transforming adolescence and early adulthood is an area of rapidly growing concern and collaboration among practitioners of the two disciplines.

See also:

What is ontogenetic development?; Constructivist theories; Psychoanalytical theories; Cross-cultural comparisons; Cognitive development beyond infancy; Play; Schooling and literacy; Sex differences; Socialization; Temperament; Sociology; James Mark Baldwin; Jerome S. Bruner; Erik Erikson; Jean Piaget; Lev S. Vygotsky

Further reading

Cole, M. (1996). *Cultural Psychology: A Once and Future Discipline.* Cambridge, MA: Harvard University Press.

D'Andrade, R. and Strauss, C. (1992). *Human Motives and Cultural Models.* Cambridge: Cambridge University Press.

Shweder, R. A., Goodnow, J., Hatano, G., LeVine, R. A., Markus, H. and Miller, P. (1998). The cultural psychology of development: one mind, many mentalities. In W. Damon and R. M. Lerner (eds.), *Handbook of Child Psychology*, Vol. I: *Theoretical Models of Human Development*, 5th edn. New York: Wiley, pp. 865–938.

Behavioral embryology

SCOTT R. ROBINSON

Introduction

William James speculated that infants are born into a "blooming, buzzing confusion," which stemmed from the long, dark sleep within the womb devoid of experience. Although this passive view of the neonate has remained influential for nearly a century, a conceptual revolution has occurred more recently in developmental psychology. This new view sees the newborn as an active participant in its own behavioral development. One reason for the dramatic change in perspective is that investigators have become more proficient at asking questions. Rather than evaluating infants in terms of adult perceptual or behavioral abilities, research programs have addressed neonatal behavior and cognition by adapting experimental procedures to abilities that are relevant to the infant. This research strategy has yielded important demonstrations of behavioral competence in infants within days after birth.

Appreciation of neonatal behavioral competence raises a fundamental question: what is the source of these behavioral abilities? It is possible that the competencies of the newborn arise abruptly, preformed in the maturation of the nervous system in utero. Alternatively, the abilities of the newborn may be foreshadowed by an extended period of *behavioral* development, which includes the expression of organized movement and sensory experience before birth (Smotherman & Robinson, 1996). It is to the prenatal period that researchers have turned to seek answers to this dilemma, which has brought developmental psychology into contact with the field of embryology.

The embryo as foundation

Embryology literally is the study of embryos. An embryo is an immature animal that develops within the egg or womb, comprising the span from fertilization to hatching or birth. A prevalent view of the relationship between embryonic development and life after birth is expressed by the analogy of a house. A completed house comprises many rooms with different purposes, just as a mature body comprises many functional systems. But the different rooms cannot be used, the house cannot even be built, without first laying down a solid foundation to support later construction. Embryonic development is also a period of foundation building, in which neural substrates are constructed that later will permit the elaboration of more complex networks for governing behavior.

A presumption of the foundation analogy is that prenatal development is biology, and psychology begins after birth. This depiction may be accurate only during early embryogenesis, in which the basic structural organization of the organism is created. Interactions between cells and tissues, governed by a complex network of membrane-bound proteins, growth factors, extracellular chemical signals, and many other products of gene activity, are responsible for creating the raw materials from which the nervous system will be constructed. For the developmental psychologist interested in the prenatal roots of behavior, a more relevant beginning may be the inception of motility, when activity within the central nervous system results in active movement by the embryo. All vertebrate species show spontaneous movement before birth. But the relationship between embryonic activity and later behavior has been the subject of considerable debate.

Behavior as a factor in prenatal development

Teratology provides perhaps the most dramatic evidence that prenatal events can have an impact on postnatal behavior. A teratogen is any substance that can be transmitted to the fetus in utero to alter prenatal development. Alcohol is probably the best-known example of a teratogen. Chronic abuse of alcohol can lead to Fetal Alcohol Syndrome (FAS), which involves a collection of dysmorphologies including facial abnormalities and lung hypoplasia. Lesser exposure can produce more subtle behavioral effects such as irritability, hyperactivity, poor attention, decreased motor coordination, and cognitive deficits in language acquisition, problem solving, and learning. Many other substances, including pesticides, heavy metals, and drugs of abuse, have joined the list of recognized teratogenic agents.

Less widely appreciated are the teratogen-like effects that result from a simple absence of embryonic motor activity (Moessinger, 1983). Fetuses that experience a period of akinesia (loss of movement through drug exposure or myopathy) exhibit a suite of morphological effects, including microstomia (small mouth), retarded lung development, skin and facial abnormalities, immobilized joints and altered bone growth, short umbilical cord, and long-term movement disabilities (Fig. 1). Fetal Akinesia Deformation Sequence is a stark demonstration that fetal movement is an important contributor to prenatal morphological and behavioral development.

Early behavioral embryologists disagreed over whether embryonic movements were the result of endogenous neural activity, or reflexive responses to indeterminate environmental stimuli. This controversy was resolved through the work of Viktor Hamburger and colleagues, who demonstrated that chick embryos continued to produce spontaneous activity in the central nervous system after the ventral spinal cord was surgically isolated from the brain and from incoming sensory information. Spontaneous neural activity now is recognized to play a crucial role in guiding neuromotor development. Activity in motoneurons and their associated muscle fibers is necessary for normal processes of cell death, synapse elimination, and re-structuring of neuronal connectivity within the motor system. Moreover, the amount of activity appears to be less important than the pattern; bursts of electrical stimulation are more effective in promoting selective elimination of synapses than a steady rate of stimulation.

Although activity-dependent processes such as selective pruning in the nervous system mark the embryo as an active participant in its own development, embryonic movements seem far removed from behavioral abilities traditionally studied by developmental psychologists. Indeed, classic studies of fetal motility stressed how embryonic movements appeared random, purposeless, and lacking in coordination. However, more careful analyses of chick embryos observed in ovo and rodent fetuses in utero have demonstrated a remarkable degree of organization underlying embryonic movement. Chick embryos show patterns of muscle activity and leg movement that are highly similar during spontaneous motor activity, hatching behavior, and post-hatching locomotion

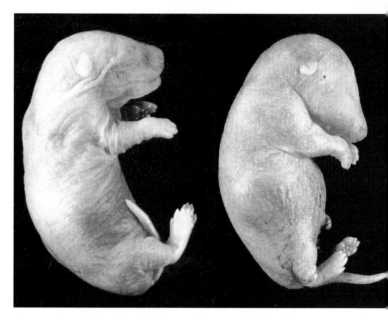

Figure 1. Photographs of term rat fetuses after normal gestation (left) and akinesia induced by curare during the last three days of gestation (right). The curarized fetus exhibits thin, tight skin, immobilized joints, and underdeveloped hindlimbs, and retains the flexed head position characteristic of a younger fetus. From A. C. Moessinger, 1983. Fetal akinesia deformation sequence: an animal model. *Pediatrics*, 72, 857–863.

(Bekoff, 1992; see Fig. 2). The spontaneous movements of mammalian fetuses express organization in multiple dimensions, including temporal rhythmicity, movement synchrony, organization of active and quiet sleep, and motor coordination during species-typical action patterns that are related to postnatal grooming, suckling, and locomotor behavior (Robinson & Smotherman, 1992). Given the wealth of recent discoveries about fetal behavioral organization, the historical depiction of the fetus as a passive object during prenatal development is no longer defensible.

The principle of induction

Late in the 19th century, Hans Spemann (1869–1941) was among a handful of experimental embryologists who formulated the principle of induction as a mechanism of embryological change. Induction is a form of interaction in which the presence of one cell type causes a second cell type to undergo change. The concept is well illustrated by interactions that occur during the process of gastrulation (Fig. 3). As cells of the blastula invaginate, an intermediate layer of cells (mesoderm) migrates beneath the outermost layer of cells (ectoderm). The migration of the underlying mesoderm layer provides an inductive trigger to the overlying ectoderm, causing it to thicken, lengthen and

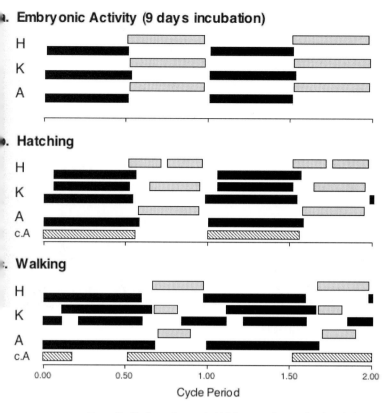

a. Embryonic Activity (9 days incubation)

b. Hatching

c. Walking

Cycle Period

Figure 2. Similar patterns of chick leg muscle coordination during spontaneous embryonic movement, hatching behavior, and postnatal walking. Bar graphs depict normalized bursts of EMG activity for muscles of the right hip (H), knee (K), and ankle (A); extensor muscles are indicated by black bars and flexors by gray. Hatched bars show activity of the contralateral ankle extensor (c. A) as a measure of interlimb coordination during hatching and walking. Redrawn from A. C. Bekoff, 1992. Neuroethological approaches to the study of motor development in chicks: achievements and challenges. *Journal of Neurobiology*, 23, 1486–1505.

roll up into the neural tube, which is the earliest rudiment of the brain and spinal cord. In embryological terms, the neural tube forms as a consequence of the inductive influence of mesoderm on ectoderm.

The most relevant aspect of the concept of induction for developmental psychology is the flexible definition of what constitutes environment. Psychologists may be inclined to see a clear delineation between the organism and its environment: everything under the skin is organism; everything else is environment. But to embryologists, environment denotes a relationship. The extracellular matrix can be environment to individual cells, one tissue can be environment to another, and the dispersed products of cellular biosynthesis can be environment to other tissues. The concept of induction necessitates that environment be defined relative to the thing that changes.

A flexible definition of environment helps to clarify the multilevel, interactive process of development. This is especially important in studies of prenatal

development, where the contribution of environment often is assumed to be minimal. For example, considerable attention has been devoted to determining what environmental stimuli may be available to the fetus in utero. Stimuli in some modalities, such as light, are effectively excluded by the barriers that surround the fetus: the mother's abdomen, the uterus, the chorion and amnion that envelop the fetus, and the amniotic fluid filling the space within these membranes (Fig. 4, left). But sound and mechanical vibration can be transmitted through these barriers, and chemical stimuli, including constituents of maternal diet, can cross the placenta to enter amniotic fluid. Human and animal experiments have confirmed that fetuses can detect and respond to environmental stimulation in these modalities.

The world outside the mother's skin is not the only relevant source of environmental influence for the fetus (Fig. 4, left). In mammals, the mother also serves as a critical component of the fetal environment. The fetus' needs for nutrition, oxygen, and waste removal are met by the mother through the placenta. Chemical signals, including hormones, can be transmitted across the placenta to provide communication between mother and fetus. Although the fetus possesses an independent neural substrate for generating 24-hour rhythms in its activity (in the suprachiasmatic nucleus of the hypothalamus), the rhythm is synchronized to the circadian pattern of the mother by chemicals that cross the placenta. Sounds produced by the mother, such as voice, or physical forces that result from changes in posture or maternal exercise also can be detected by the fetus. These are but a few examples that illustrate the complexity of environmental influences that derive from the maternal-fetal relationship.

Self-stimulation by the embryo

The embryo also can influence its own environment. Avian embryos typically begin to vocalize several days before hatching. In some species, the rate of vocalization is a reliable indicator of egg temperature, which provides feedback for the mother to regulate incubation. Embryonic vocalizations also can influence auditory development. Newly hatched ducklings exhibit a bias to approach the source of maternal calls, whether it is produced by the mother duck or a mechanical speaker. Experimental dissection of this bias has revealed that prenatal auditory experience is both sufficient and necessary for the auditory preference to develop. The embryo's *own* vocalizations provide the necessary auditory experience to create a post-hatching bias; ducklings that are experimentally de-vocalized and isolated from acoustic stimuli fail to express a preference for the maternal call.

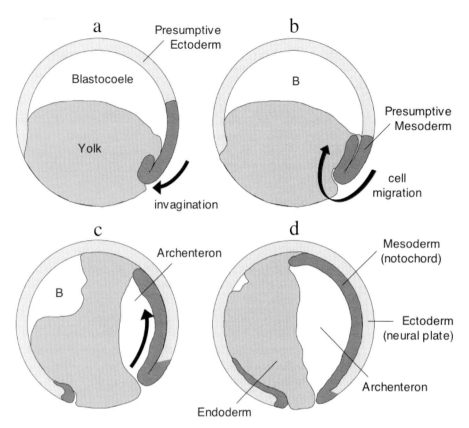

Figure 3. Diagram of midsagittal sections of frog embryos during gastrulation. The developmental sequence depicts: (a) early invagination of presumptive mesoderm cells in the late blastula stage, (b) migration of cells into the hollow blastocoele (B), (c) formation of the primitive gut or archenteron, and (d) disappearance of the blastocoele and formation of the three primary germ layers (ectoderm, mesoderm, endoderm) of the gastrula.

Mammalian fetuses may benefit from self-stimulation in a chemical modality. The fetus is surrounded by amniotic fluid (AF), which is derived partly from chemical constituents of maternal blood, and partly from chemicals produced in the placenta, umbilical cord, embryonic membranes, or the skin, lungs, and kidneys of the fetus. AF provides a fluid space in which fetal movements can occur. The presence of membranes and fluid around the fetus can serve as a kind of scaffolding, facilitating some aspects of early motor coordination. Too little fluid (oligohydramnios), however, results in movement restriction and its deleterious consequences. AF is swallowed and breathed by the fetus, and thereby contributes to the development of the mouth, gastrointestinal tract, and lungs. In addition to its physical properties, AF contains a complex assortment of phospholipids, carbohydrates, and proteins, including hormones that can influence the sexual development of neighboring fetuses in the womb.

Fetuses show distinctive behavioral responses upon oral exposure to AF (Korthank & Robinson, 1998), which triggers changes in fetal motor activity and responsiveness to sensory stimuli (Fig. 4, right). During parturition, the pregnant rat distributes AF on her own ventrum, and the odor of AF helps newborn rats to locate the nipple for the first time. Pups prefer the odor of AF and odor cues introduced into AF before birth. Such exposure learning can produce olfactory memories that are retained after birth to influence orientation and ingestive behavior of newborn, juvenile, and adult rats. Thus, it is evident that AF, which is produced largely by the fetus, can contribute in important ways to perinatal behavioral development. In these ways, the fetus helps to construct its own environment within the womb.

Conclusions

Prenatal self-stimulation, whether through movement, sound, or the chemical milieu, is instructive as a model for the bidirectional and interactive processes that characterize embryonic development. A relational definition of environment, including self-stimulation, can help to clarify the multiple determinants of behavior and neural development before birth. Indeed, understanding the complex ways that experience can contribute to early development represents one of the major challenges facing developmental neuroscience.

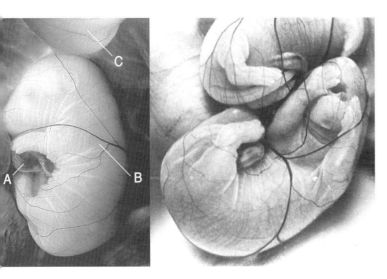

Figure 4. Rat fetuses photographed in vivo two days before birth (day 20). At left, key features of the fetal environment are indicated: (A) umbilical cord, which restricts the range of fetal movement but grows in response to tension produced by motility; (B) chorion and amnion, membranes that contain amniotic fluid and constrain fetal movements; (C) an adjacent sibling, which is a source of physical stimulation and may produce hormones that can affect development of other fetuses. Fetal movements are further constrained by the uterus; non-labor contractions of the uterine myometrium compress the fetus, which stimulates endocrine activity and promotes certain aspects of brain development. At right, a fetus responds to amniotic fluid with mouthing, swallowing, and forelimb treadling. Oral exposure to amniotic fluid alters sensory responsiveness and the organization of fetal movements, and can influence postnatal olfactory behavior.

Little of the motor activity of embryos can be characterized as explicit practice, nor can most of the sensory features of the intrauterine environment be thought of as providing specific experience with contingencies relevant for postnatal behavior. Rather, the challenge for developmental researchers is to explain how general motor or sensory experience in utero may help to build neural systems that govern coordinated action and sensorimotor integration after birth. Similarly, the advent of molecular technology in modern embryology has fostered the search for genetic causes of developmental change. But much remains to be discovered about how embryonic activity and sensory experience serve to regulate gene expression or the modification of gene products in the developing embryo. In these ways, concepts and research methods that originally were developed within the respective disciplines of developmental psychology and embryology will continue to be useful in deciphering the tangle of cause and effect in prenatal behavioral ontogeny.

See also:
The concept of development: historical perspectives; Understanding ontogenetic development: debates about the nature of the epigenetic process; Neuromaturational theories; Ethological theories; Learning theories; Cross-species comparisons; Conceptions and misconceptions about embryonic development; Normal and abnormal prenatal development; The status of the human newborn; Perceptual development; Motor development; Development of learning and memory; Brain and behavioral development (I): sub-cortical; Locomotion; Sleep and wakefulness; Developmental genetics; Ethology; George E. Coghill; Viktor Hamburger; Wilhelm T. Preyer

Further reading

Gottlieb, G. (1997). *Synthesizing Nature-Nurture*. Mahwah, NJ: Erlbaum.
Lecanuet, J.-P., Krasnegor, N. A., Fifer, W. P. and Smotherman, W. P. (eds.) (1995). *Fetal Development: A Psychobiological Perspective*. New York: Erlbaum.
Nathanielsz, P. W. (1999). *Life in the Womb: The Origin of Health and Disease*. Ithaca, NY: Promethean Press.

Behavior genetics

THALIA C. ELEY

Introduction

Since the 1980s, there has been a proliferation of behavior genetic studies exploring psychological development. These studies have assessed phenotypes reflecting both normal and abnormal development. For example, some studies use measures of variation in normal traits such as personality, where others explore variation in more unusual emotions and behaviors using symptom scales. There is also some data available on child psychiatric disorders.

There have been two major results from this work. To begin with, individual differences in virtually every developmental psychological trait are heritable to some extent (see Appendix 3 for the statistics of behavior genetics). That is, there is genetic influence on almost all aspects of psychological development. Exceptions to this may include religious affiliation, early studies of which suggested no heritable influence, although recent data suggest that every aspect of religiosity is genetically influenced. One other exception is the quality and character of romantic relationships, which have no detectable genetic influence (Plomin *et al.*, 2001).

The highest heritability estimates ($h^2 \approx 60–70\%$) are seen for hyperactivity, both as a disorder and as a trait (Thapar, 2003). Slightly lower heritability ($h^2 \approx 40–60\%$) is seen for language disorders, antisocial behavior, and general cognitive ability (Plomin *et al.*, 2001; Eley, Moffitt, & Lichtenstein, 2003). The lowest heritability estimates ($h^2 \approx 20–40\%$) tend to be for emotional symptoms such as anxiety and depression, and language development (Eley, 1999; Plomin *et al.*, 2001).

The second major advance in this field relates to the environment. Behavior genetic studies tell us as much about the influence of environmental factors as they do about genetics. The environmental influences are divided into those that result in within-family similarity (shared environment) and those that result in differences between family members (non-shared environment). Studies exploring psychological traits during childhood have found, as in the adult literature, that environmental influences are almost exclusively of the non-shared kind. As such, aspects of the environment within the family are likely to be operating in a child-specific manner that had not been previously recognized.

Contemporary behavior genetics

The field of behavior genetics is now moving beyond simple examination of heritability, and level of environmental influence, to examine more specific theoretically relevant questions. Firstly, studies have begun to explore the role of genes and environment on the origins of the high levels of trait covariation seen with findings from developmental psychology. Secondly, the relative influence of genes and environment on continuity and change over time has begun to be considered. Thirdly, there are studies exploring the validity of discrete diagnostic categories (e.g., language delay) versus considering such individuals as extreme groups on related continua (measures of language development). Fourthly, although rare, there are phenotypes for which shared environment is substantial and significant, and this may give us specific insight into those phenotypes. The final two groups of studies are those exploring aspects of gene-environment interplay: gene-environment correlations and gene-environment interactions.

Co-morbidity and trait covariation

Several competing theories have been put forward to explain the high levels of co-morbidity and trait covariation seen in developmental psychology. These models can be summarized as follows: (1) that the two phenotypes share etiological factors; (2) that the co-morbid disorder has a specific risk factor; (3) that the two disorders are temporally associated with one another (i.e., the two are developmental stages of one

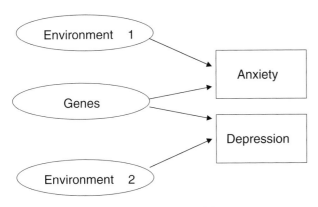

Figure 1. Shared genetic risks for anxiety and depression contrast with symptom-specific environmental risk.

underlying syndrome); and (4) that the two disorders are distinct entities, with one creating increased risk for the other (i.e., there is a causal association).

The first of these hypotheses has received the greatest attention in the behavior genetic literature, with the exploration of shared and specific familial, or genetic and environmental influences on different traits (see Appendix 3). For example, the covariation between anxiety and depression in children and adolescents appears to be largely due to shared genetic influences that are associated with both traits (Fig. 1). This shared genetic vulnerability also influences individual differences in neuroticism, which may act as a mediator of genetic influence on emotional symptoms. In contrast, environmental influences are more trait-specific (Eley, 1999). This suggests a diathesis-stress model in which there is a shared genetic diathesis to emotional symptoms, with the type of environmental stress resulting in the specific symptom type. Similar results have been obtained for the covariation between conduct and hyperactivity symptoms, with genetic influences largely shared between these two (Thapar, 2003). Similarly, aspects of cognitive development appear to be highly genetically linked, supporting the notion of a heritable higher-order factor (Plomin *et al.*, 2001).

Developmental studies

A further important area linking behavior genetic studies to issues in developmental psychology has been the exploration of sources of continuity and discontinuity in symptoms and traits, and the examination of specific developmental theories. Several studies have explored the etiology of continuity across time, and in general these have shown that genetic influences are more important for continuity of traits, whereas environmental influences tend to be time-specific. For example, continuity in both emotional and behavioral

symptoms across middle childhood to early adolescence is largely due to continuity of genetic influences (Reiss, Neiderhiser, Hetherington, & Plomin, 2000).

Furthermore, behavior genetic studies have clarified issues regarding heterogeneity within the domain of antisocial behavior. As predicted by a recent developmental taxonomy of antisocial behavior, aggressive antisocial behavior is highly heritable, more so than non-aggressive antisocial behavior that is also significantly influenced by the shared environment. Genetic influences are also central to the continuity of aggressive antisocial behavior, whereas continuity in non-aggressive antisocial behavior is mediated by environmental influences (Eley *et al.*, 2003). Interestingly, a further area in which behavior genetic studies have shed light on developmental issues has been within the field of cognition, where studies have demonstrated a steady increase in genetic influence throughout the lifespan, accompanied by a parallel decrease in shared environment influence (Plomin *et al.*, 2001).

Categories versus continua

One of the most intriguing questions in developmental psychology is whether those with high levels of symptoms are a qualitatively distinct category from individuals in the normal range on related traits, or whether they are merely the quantitative extreme of such continua. Several behavior genetic studies have explored this issue, and overall they have indicated that the influence of genetic and environmental factors is similar for those in the extremes, as compared to those in the normal range for most psychological traits (Eley, 1999; Thapar, 2003). The exception to this is language delay (Plomin *et al.*, 2001). Studies of language delay generally find high heritability, in the 40–60% range, whereas individual differences in language development are only modestly heritable ($h^2 \approx 20\%$).

Shared environment influences

The phenotypes that have replicated evidence for shared environment influence are aspects of anxiety, antisocial behavior, and cognitive development in infancy and childhood (less so in adolescence). Within studies of anxiety, it appears to be separation anxiety and social anxiety/fear that demonstrate high shared environmental influences (Eley, 1999). This is particularly interesting given the likely role of features of the family environment, such as learning effects and parent-child interaction in the etiology of these types of anxiety. Within studies of antisocial behavior, it appears to be non-aggressive aspects or covert antisocial behaviors that are influenced by the shared environment. This may be due to the tendency for 'birds of a feather to flock together' (i.e., for siblings with a tendency toward antisocial behavior to hang out together with antisocial peers). Finally, the influence of shared environment on early cognitive development is likely to reflect features of the environment, such as the number of books and puzzles in the home, the manner in which the parents speak to the children, the educational level of the parents, and other socio-demographic characteristics of the home environment.

Gene-environment correlations

In addition to identifying the substantial role the environment plays in developmental outcomes, behavior genetics has also taught us that environmental influences do not operate in a purely environmental manner. Genes and the environment are often correlated with one another, such that exposure to certain environmental influences is related in some way to genetic factors. There are three types of gene-environment (g-e) correlation: passive, evocative, and active.

Parents with an outgoing personality may pass onto their child genes for traits such as extraversion or sociability, and in addition provide an environment where the child is also encouraged to be outgoing (passive g-e correlation). An outgoing and fun-loving child is also likely to evoke positive reactions from others (evocative g-e correlations). Finally, an outgoing child may seek out social situations more often than a child who is less outgoing (active g-e correlation). These correlations can result in apparently environmental variables being genetically influenced (Plomin *et al.*, 2001). For example, there is evidence that life events and aspects of parenting (e.g., negativity) are heritable (Fig. 2). Furthermore, the relationship between these environmental variables and outcomes such as depression scores are mediated by shared genetic influences. As such, the same genes influence depression symptoms that in turn influence aspects of the child's environment, such as life events or parenting (Reiss *et al.*, 2000). Gene-environment correlations are also likely to be of importance with regard to the relationship between maternal depression symptoms and emotional symptoms in children.

Gene-environment interactions

A further mechanism by which genes and environment may influence outcome is via gene-environment interactions. This refers to individuals being at increased vulnerability to environmental influences depending on their genotype (Plomin *et al.*, 2001; Reiss *et al.*, 2000). For example, genetic risks for depression may be found

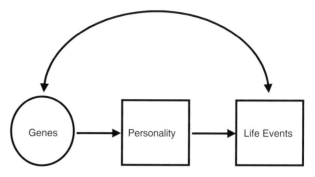

Figure 2. Gene-environment correlation: there is a genetic influence on life events that appears to be mediated by personality.

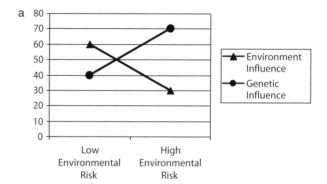

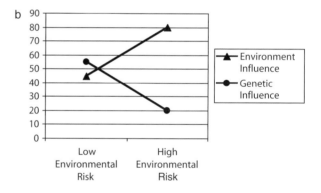

Figure 3. Gene-environment interaction effects: the moderation of level of genetic (and environmental) influence by a specific measured environmental variable. (a) Increasing genetic influence. (b) Decreasing genetic influence with increasing environmental risk.

to act by making children particularly susceptible to life events, such as the loss of a family member. To date, there have been very few studies examining gene-environment interactions, but there have been some positive findings. Indirect studies examine the extent to which heritability varies in sub-sets of the population, and results from these include both those in which heritability is *greater* for those situations with environmental risk, and those where genetic influences are *minimized* by environmental risk (Fig. 3). More recently, studies have begun to explore direct evidence for interactions between specific genotypes and specific environmental influences. For example, recent work suggests that the association between the dopamine receptor D4 and hyperactivity may be stronger in those subjects who are stimulant medication responders (Thapar, 2003).

Conclusions

The future of behavior genetics is likely to lie in studies exploring specific mechanisms by which genetic influences affect psychological development. This has already begun in the field of developmental genetics, in which specific genes are being identified that play a role in the etiology of psychological traits. Much of this work has focused on adult traits and disorders, but molecular genetic studies exploring the associations between specific genes and child development are already underway. Other studies aim to explore the mechanisms between the gene and the outcome, utilizing approaches ranging from genetic functional studies, to brain imaging and neuropsychiatric and cognitive testing. The most exciting aspect of behavior genetic work in the 21st century will depend on the extent of the collaboration between behavior geneticists, developmental psychologists, cognitive neuroscientists, and those in other related areas. Approaching questions from multiple levels (e.g., genetic risk, neurocognitive processes, environmental stress) within single studies will enable the greatest advances in terms of understanding the processes involved in psychological development.

See also:
Understanding ontogenetic development: debates about the nature of the epigenetic process; Twin and adoption studies; Cognitive development in infancy; Cognitive development beyond infancy; Language development; Aggressive and prosocial behavior; Brain and behavioral development (II): cortical; Parenting and the family; Siblings and peers; 'At-risk' concept; Behavioral and learning disorders; Child depression; Developmental genetics; The statistics of quantitative genetic theory

Further reading

Benjamin, J., Ebstein, R. and Belmaker, R. H. (2002). *Molecular Genetics of Human Personality*. Washington, DC: American Psychiatric Press.

Plomin, R., DeFries, J. C., Craig, I. W. and McGuffin, P. (2003). *Behavior Genetics in the Postgenomic Era*. Washington, DC: American Psychological Association.

Rutter, M. and Silberg, J. (2002). Gene-environment interplay in relation to emotional and behavioral disturbance. *Annual Review of Psychology*, 53, 463–490.

Acknowledgments

The author is supported by a Career Development Award from the Medical Research Council.

Cognitive neuroscience

MARK H. JOHNSON

Introduction

There is a dramatic increase in the volume of the human brain between conception and adulthood. Over the postnatal years, there are equally dramatic improvements in motor, cognitive, and perceptual abilities. While aspects of human behavioral development have been studied in their own right for decades, only recently has interest turned to the issue of how the growth of the brain relates to the emergence of novel behavioral abilities, a new field that has become known as Developmental Cognitive Neuroscience (Johnson, 2005). This entry briefly reviews the merits of three general approaches to developmental cognitive neuroscience: the maturational perspective, the interactive specialization approach, and the skill learning hypothesis. It is suggested that while the former approach has been useful, the future lies in further investigation of the latter two approaches.

The maturational perspective

Since the early 1990s, the cognitive neuroscience approach to developmental psychology has been heavily dominated by a maturational viewpoint in which the goal is to relate the maturation of particular regions of the brain, usually regions of the cerebral cortex, to newly emerging sensory, motor, and cognitive functions (Fig. 1A). Evidence concerning the differential neuroanatomical development of cortical regions was used to determine an age when a particular region is likely to become functional. Success in a new behavioral task at this same age is attributed to the maturation of a new brain region, with maturation assumed to be an 'all or none' phenomenon, or at least to have a sudden onset. Comparisons are then made between the behavioral performance of adults with acquired lesions and behaviors during infancy.

One example of this approach comes from the neurodevelopment of visual orienting and attention. In this respect, several researchers have argued that control over visually guided behavior is exerted initially by sub-cortical structures, but with age and development posterior cortical regions, and finally anterior regions, come to influence behavior. In another example, maturation within the frontal lobes has been related to advances in the ability to reach for hidden objects toward the end of the first year.

Infants younger than 9 months often fail to retrieve a hidden object accurately after a short delay period if its location is changed from one where it was previously successfully retrieved. Instead, they perseverate by reaching to the hiding location where the object was found on the immediately preceding trial. This error is similar to those made by human adults with frontal lesions and monkeys with lesions to the dorsolateral prefrontal cortex, leading to the proposal that the maturation of this region in human infants allows them to retain information over space and time, and to inhibit pre-potent responses (Diamond, 2001). In turn, these developments allow successful performance in object retrieval paradigms. Converging evidence for this claim comes from associations with resting frontal EEG responses and deficits in children with a neurochemical deficit in the prefrontal cortex resulting from phenylketonuria (PKU). However, obtaining functional imaging data on human infants during such object retrieval tasks to date has been difficult.

Despite these successes of the maturational approach, and its support from some animal studies, there are reasons to believe that it may not successfully explain all aspects of human functional brain development. For example, such development, in which regions mature sequentially, cannot easily account for the dynamical changes in patterns of cortical activation observed during postnatal development, or for activity in frontal cortical regions during the first months (see later). Furthermore, comparison of the performance of preterm with fullterm infants on the object retrieval task discussed above indicates that length of experience in the postnatal environment is critical. Evidence reviewed

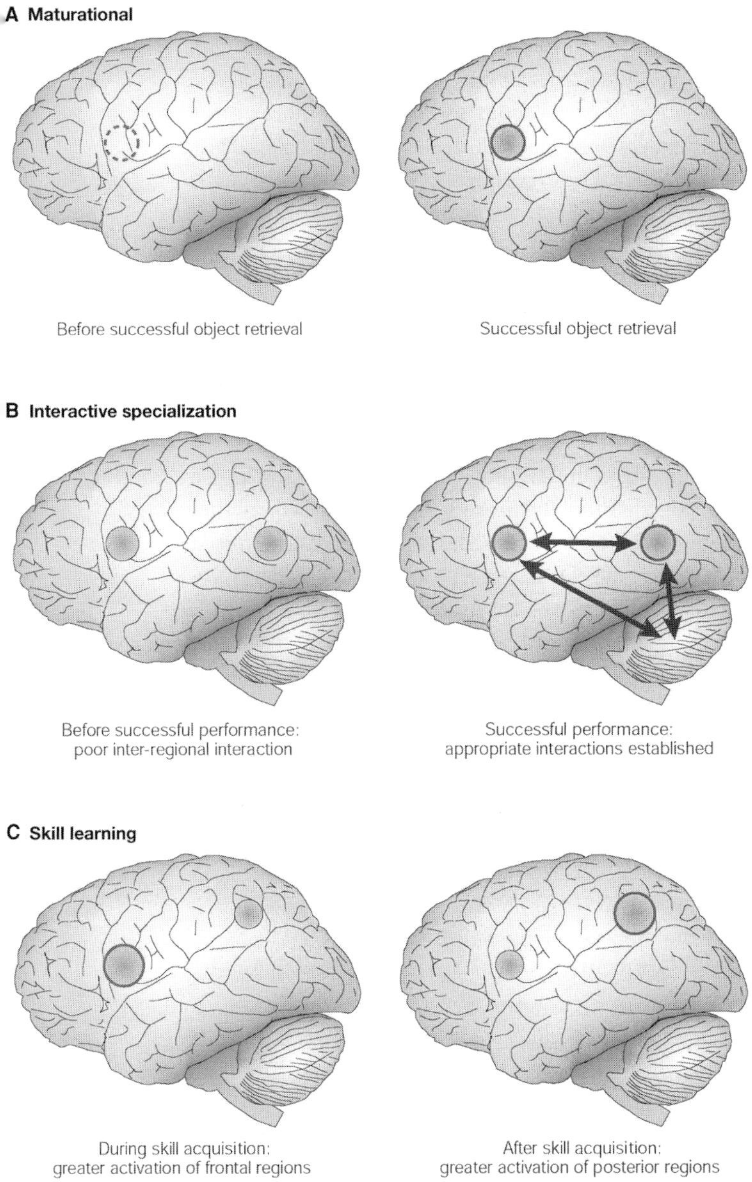

A Maturational

Before successful object retrieval

Successful object retrieval

B Interactive specialization

Before successful performance:
poor inter-regional interaction

Successful performance:
appropriate interactions established

C Skill learning

During skill acquisition:
greater activation of frontal regions

After skill acquisition:
greater activation of posterior regions

Figure 1. Three accounts of the neural basis of an advance in behavioral abilities in infants. Panel A represents a maturational view in which maturation of one region (in this case the dorsolateral prefrontal cortex, DLPC) enables new behavioral abilities to appear. Panel B illustrates an interactive specialization view in which the onset of a new behavioral ability is due to changes in the interactions between several regions that were already partially active. In this purely hypothetical illustration, it is suggested that changes in the interactions between DLPC, parietal cortex and cerebellum may give rise to successful performance in the object retrieval paradigm. Panel C shows a third perspective, skill learning, in which the pattern of activation of cortical regions changes during the acquisition of new skills throughout the lifespan. In the example illustrated, there is decreasing activation of DLPC and medial frontal cortex, accompanied by increasing activation of more posterior regions as human adults perform a visuo-motor sequence learning task. It is suggested that similar changes may occur during the acquisition of new abilities by infants. These three accounts are not necessarily mutually exclusive. Figure reprinted from M. H. Johnson, 2001. Functional brain development in humans. *Nature Reviews Neuroscience*, 2, 475–483.

in the next section suggests that consideration of the emerging interactions between regions of the brain is at least as important as the development of connectivity within a region.

The interactive specialization approach

In contrast to the maturational approach in which behavioral developments are attributed to the onset of functioning in one region or system, an alternative viewpoint assumes that postnatal functional brain development, at least within the cerebral cortex, involves a process of organizing inter-regional interactions (Fig. 1B). Referring to adult brain imaging data, Friston & Price (2001) point out that it may be an error to assume that particular cognitive functions can be localized within a certain cortical region. Rather, they suggest that the response properties of a specific region may be determined by its patterns of connectivity to other regions and their current activity states. According to this view ". . . the cortical infrastructure supporting a single function may involve many specialized areas whose union is mediated by the functional integration among them" (p. 276).

Extending this notion to development means we should observe changes in the response properties of cortical regions during ontogeny as regions interact and compete with each other to acquire their role in new computational abilities. The onset of new behavioral competencies during infancy will be associated with changes in activity over several regions, and not just by the onset of activity in one or more additional region(s). In further contrast to the maturational approach, this view predicts that during infancy patterns of cortical activation during behavioral tasks may be more extensive than those observed in adults, and involve different patterns of activation. Within broad constraints, even apparently the same behavior in infants and adults could involve different patterns of cortical activation.

Recent evidence indicates that the same behavior in infants and adults can be mediated by different structures and pathways, and that there are dynamical changes in the cortical processing of stimuli during infancy. Experiments with scalp-recorded electrical potentials have suggested that both for word learning and face processing, there is increasing spatial localization of selective processing with age or experience of a stimulus class (M. H. Johnson, 2000). For example, word recognition differences between known words and control stimuli are initially found over large areas, but this difference narrows to the leads over the left temporal lobe only when vocabulary reaches around 200 words, irrespective of maturational age.

In parallel with changes in the patterns of regional activation are those in the 'tuning' or specialization of individual regions. For example, when event-related potentials (ERPs) are recorded during passive exposure to faces, the resulting component that is sensitive to upright human faces in adults (the N170) is much more broadly tuned in its response in infants. Specifically, in adults, the N170 shows a different amplitude and latency to human upright faces than to animal or inverted faces. In infants, the equivalent ERP component responds similarly to upright and inverted human faces. This evidence for dynamical changes in cortical processing during infancy is consistent with a process in which inter-regional interactions help to shape intra-regional connectivity, such that several regions together come to support particular perceptual and cognitive functions.

Further evidence for this viewpoint comes from studies of developmental disorders of genetic origin in which functional brain development goes awry. Neuroimaging studies of groups with disorders such as autism and Williams syndrome have yet to produce a clear consensus on their neural basis. However, it is agreed from structural imaging studies that abnormalities in white matter are at least as extensive as those in grey matter, and from functional imaging that multiple cortical and sub-cortical regions are involved in these disorders. These general conclusions suggest that initial brain abnormalities are subsequently compounded by deviant patterns of interaction and connectivity between regions. This idea is supported by the observation that cortical activation patterns are different in these disorders, even in areas of behavior in which they perform as successfully as controls. This view stands in contrast to the maturational account in which developmental disorders could result in a deficit localizable to a particular cortical area, with an associated specific cognitive deficit.

The skill learning hypothesis

Recent neuroimaging evidence from adults has highlighted changes in the neural basis of behavior that result as a consequence of acquiring perceptual or motor expertise. One hypothesis is that the regions active in infants during the onset of new perceptual or behavioral abilities are the same as those involved in skill acquisition in adults. This hypothesis predicts that some of the changes in the neural basis of behavior during infancy will mirror those observed during more complex skill acquisition in adults (Fig. 1C).

In contrast to more precocial mammals, one of the most striking features of human infants is their initial inability to perform simple motor tasks, such as reaching for an object. Work on complex motor skill learning tasks in adult primates shows that prefrontal cortex is often activated during the early stages of acquisition, but this activation recedes to more posterior regions as expertise is acquired (M. H. Johnson, 2001). In addition to the examples of prefrontal involvement described earlier, activity in this region, or at least within the frontal lobe, has been reported in a number of infancy studies where action is elicited, and early damage to these structures has more severe long-term effects than damage to other cortical regions. For example, Csibra, Tucker, & Johnson (2001) examined the cortical activity associated with the planning of eye movements in 6-month-old infants. They observed eye-movement-related potentials over frontal sites, but not over the more posterior (parietal) sites where they are normally observed in adults. Converging results are obtained when eye movement tasks are studied in infants with perinatal focal damage to the cortex. Infants with damage to the frontal quadrants of the brain show long-lasting deficits in visual orienting tasks, but those with the more posterior damage that causes deficits in adults do not.

With regard to perceptual expertise, Isabel Gauthier and colleagues have shown that extensive training of adults with artificial objects, 'greebles,' eventually results in activation of a cortical region previously associated with face processing, the 'fusiform face area.' This suggests that the region is normally activated by faces in adults, not because it is pre-specified for faces, but due to our extensive expertise with that class of stimulus, and this encourages parallels with the development of face processing abilities in infants. The extent of the parallels between adult perceptual expertise and infant perceptual development remains unclear. However, in both cases, ERP studies have revealed effects of stimulus inversion only after substantial expertise has been acquired with faces or greebles. Future experiments need to trace in more detail changes in the patterns of cortical activation during training in adults and development in infants.

From the view of functional brain development outlined in this section, it is interesting to study cases in which there has been a period of visual deprivation early in postnatal life. As predicted by this account, after the surgical restoration of vision following a period of deprivation, there is often rapid improvement in abilities to close to normal levels. However, in some important domains, such as the configural processing of faces, recovery is never complete, with deficits still remaining after many years of visual experience. These findings suggest that the order in which motor and perceptual abilities are acquired during development may be important, and that there are periods of development during which the brain is particularly sensitive to certain types of experience.

Conclusions

While progress has been made by considering functional brain development in terms of the sequential maturation of different cortical regions and their associated functions, it is becoming increasingly evident that new cognitive functions during infancy and childhood may coincide with emerging patterns of interactions between different regions. Some of these changing patterns of interactions between regions may also be characteristic of perceptual and motor learning in adults. By directing the infant to orient and attend to certain types of external stimuli, some brain systems effectively 'tutor' others with appropriate input for subsequent specialization. In this sense, the human child plays an active role in the later stages of his own functional brain specialization.

Further assessment of the three different cognitive neuroscience perspectives on developmental psychology outlined in this entry will require more improved methods for non-invasive functional imaging, such as Near Infra-Red Spectroscopy / optical imaging, and more detailed computational models that generate predictions about both neuroanatomy and behavior. Whatever the outcome of these investigations, a better understanding of functional brain development in human infants and children will have profound consequences for educational and social policies. Four specific areas that merit further research are: (1) determining the role of the prefrontal cortex in development, (2) developing functional imaging methods suitable for very young infants including newborns, (3) studying the early precursors of developmental disorders such as autism, and (4) understanding individual variability in development from genetics to brain to cognition.

See also:
Understanding ontogenetic development: debates about the nature of the epigenetic process; Neuromaturational theories; Ethological theories; Magnetic Resonance Imaging; Cognitive development in infancy; Perceptual development; Attention; Brain and behavioral development (II): cortical; Connectionist modeling; Executive functions; Face recognition; Prehension; Autism; Prematurity and low birthweight; Williams syndrome; Developmental genetics; Ethology

Further reading

Fuster, J. M. (1997). *The Prefrontal Cortex.* 3rd. edn. New York: Raven Press.

Johnson, M. H., Munakata, Y. and Gilmore, R. O. (2002). *Brain Development and Cognition: A Reader*, 2nd. edn. Oxford: Blackwell.

Nelson, C. A. and Luciana, M. (2001). *Handbook of Developmental Cognitive Neuroscience.* Cambridge, MA: MIT Press.

Acknowledgments

The UK Medical Research Council supports the author's research. This chapter is based on sections from M. H. Johnson (2001).

Developmental genetics

WILLIAM A. HARRIS

Introduction

The evolution of nervous systems has led to animals that respond to their particular environmental niches in ways that are species-specific. Species-specific neural circuits are built during development so that as newly emerging postembryonic creatures venture out into their worlds, their behaviors are immediately adaptive. Consider the larva of a fly, but in this case a mutant in which all sensory neurons fail to develop. Yet, this animal crawls across the surface of a dish in perfectly coordinated peristaltic waves. Similarly, amphibian embryos raised in the presence of blocking doses of anesthetics are able to swim in a coordinated fashion immediately upon recovery. This evidence implies that the motor circuits underlying these types of locomotion are constructed independently of sensory input and strongly suggests that other developmental factors, such as genetic programs, are involved in building behaviors into the nervous system. This is not to discount the role of genes in building sensory systems as well as motor ones, as we recognize that the young of different species are born with sensory cells that are tuned in to their specific ecological niches. Thus, there are sensory systems in hatchling sea turtles that detect the magnetic field so that the young can orient at sea and later return to the beach where they were born. Animals also process information using species-specific circuitry. Thus, some cortical neurons in the auditory cortex of bats respond best to particular Doppler shifts in the echo of a screech, informing the bat how fast it is closing in on a moth. Many of us wonder how these neural systems are built in these precise and ethologically adaptive ways.

This developmental question has attracted interest from developmental biologists, developmental psychologists, and developmental psychobiologists. At present, we may be able to eliminate an influence (e.g., certain spinal motor circuits develop in the absence of sensory input), or implicate others (e.g., certain motoneurons do not develop properly in the absence of a particular target muscle), but we do not yet know how the various genetic and epigenetic influences are co-ordinated to build neural systems that have these very specific and interesting capacities. We know that genes are involved in the evolution of species-specific behaviors through their roles in neural development, but we are still working toward a better understanding of how specific genes are mechanistically involved in the development of specific behaviors. In this entry, I hope to provide a brief account of the genetic approach to understanding neural and behavioral development.

The roles of genes in building nervous systems

The task of understanding how nervous systems are built to produce adaptive behaviors is daunting as they are probably the most structurally and cellularly diverse organs in animal biology (Sanes, Reh, & Harris, 2000). They are also the most molecularly complex. The small roundworm *C. elegans* only has 959 somatic cells, but 302 of these are neurons. Of the organism's 20,000 genes, approximately 3,000 are expressed preferentially or solely in the nervous system (Kim *et al.*, 2001). What fraction of these are involved in building the nervous system is difficult to guess. A similar number of genes are selectively expressed in the *Drosophila* nervous system, and two-thirds of these are expressed in embryonic or larval stages.

Studies of the patterns of expression of thousands of different mRNAs randomly selected from whole organism cDNA libraries in *Xenopus* and zebrafish also suggest that in the brain and spinal cord more genes are turned on than in any other tissue, and many of these genes are turned on during development. Around 50 percent of human hereditary illnesses are neurological, and many of these are likely to have developmental etiologies. Some problems of neural development are caused by single genes. One striking example is the insensitivity to pain caused by the absence of a receptor to a growth factor necessary for the development of pain neurons. Others, like Down's syndrome, reflect multigene problems. By studying mutants and deletions in many organisms, we have improved our understanding of the genes that are necessary for building behaviors.

Genes, it must be emphasized, do not contain sufficient information to write an individual's behavioral biography. They operate in a developing organism within a huge context of epigenetic influences that also contribute to development of the nervous system, and the behaviors themselves operate and adapt when this organism is exposed to the external influences of the world around it. It must also be emphasized, however, that investigations into the growing arrays of mutants in genes that affect behavior is leading to a better understanding of the basic circuitry underlying these behaviors, especially with respect to how these circuits are originally built.

What kinds of genes are used to build a nervous system? To approach this question, laboratories have screened for mutants that affect neural development or function (Yoshihara, Ensminger, & Littleton, 2001). Many mutations in flies that were initially identified because they affected specific adult behaviors, like jumping in response to a passing shadow, turned out to be genes that code for proteins involved in development. The synapse between the visual interneurons and the leg extensor motoneurons are necessary for jumping in response to a shadow. In one fly mutant called *bendless*, a specific set of synapses between higher-level visual neurons and jump motoneurons are not made. Sets of synapses in other, but certainly not most, neural circuits are also affected in the mutant. The normal gene *bendless* codes for a factor that is involved in the rapid degradation of targeted proteins that are likely to participate in synapse formation. The identification of these proteins may well be important for understanding this process.

There are a host of uncoordinated mutant varieties of nematodes with a medley of underlying neural defects caused by the malfunction of genes encoding a variety of interesting proteins involved in different aspects of neural development. One way to explore this problem in detail is the massive genetic screen approach. In *Drosophila*, such large-scale screens have been done to find mutations in every single gene that was involved in embryonic morphogenesis and pattern formation. Many of the genes discovered by such screens were critical for very early neural development. Many of these were later shown to be homologous to genes that affected the development of the vertebrate nervous system in similar ways. Those such as the *notch* gene, the segment polarity genes, and the *Hox* genes are obvious examples. These genetic entries into early neural development were also accompanied by large-scale screens for mutants

Table 1. Some general categories of gene function during neural development based on mutant phenotypes.

1. Genes that are involved in specifying neural versus epidermal fate.
2. Genes that are involved in sub-dividing or regionalizing the nervous system along the body axes.
3. Genes that are involved in giving local fate or character to specific neural structures.
4. Genes that are involved in cell proliferation, survival, and death in the nervous system.
5. Genes that are involved in giving polarity and topography to individual neural areas.
6. Genes that are involved in cellular specification and determination.
7. Genes that are involved in providing generic molecular and anatomical character to neurons and glia.
8. Genes that are involved with neuronal migration.
9. Genes that are involved in axon pathfinding.
10. Genes that are involved in synapse formation.
11. Genes that are involved with synaptic modification.

directly involved in particular aspects of later neuronal development or behavior, such as mutants that affect the way the retina is formed or mutants that lead to blindness. The kinds of phenotypes that showed up using these various screens have helped us build a framework for thinking about the developmental genetic steps involved in building a nervous system. Table 1 lists some of these.

Examples of the developmental genetic approach

One example comes from a screen in flies for mutants with impaired phototaxis. Among many that were isolated is a mutant called *sevenless*, in which the ultraviolet photoreceptor, R7, in each facet of the eye fails to develop. Instead, the cells that would have given rise to these receptors turn into lens-secreting non-neuronal cells. The *sevenless* gene was found to be transmembrane tyrosine kinase receptor, a finding that raised obvious questions. If *sevenless* codes for a receptor, what is the signal? How does activation of the receptor cause the cell to choose one fate over another? To answer these questions, further screens were done to find new mutants with similar phenotypes, or mutants that enhanced or suppressed a partial phenotype in a hypomorphic *sevenless* allele. A complex transduction pathway that included activation of the fly homologue of the *ras* oncogene and downstream transcription factors were identified.

Another rewarding finding was the identification of the signal that binds to the *sevenless* receptor. A screen for UV-insensitive flies yielded a membrane-bound signaling molecule, called *bride-of-sevenless* (boss), that is expressed specifically in the R8 cells, the normal neighbors of the R7 cells. Thus, cells that touch R8 cells get a signal that activates a tyrosine kinase pathway, which drives the responding cell to a photoreceptor R7 fate. Because of this extensive analysis, the *sevenless* pathway is one of the best-understood pathways from ligand through receptor activation to transcriptional control in all of biology (Fig. 1). About twenty proteins have now been identified as involved in the R7 pathway.

Is this all of them? It is unlikely. It seems that the researchers may simply have run out of steam in screening for new pathway components. There may be as many as hundreds of genes involved in this pathway, although most of these would have a very peripheral role or minor influence. Though perhaps perpetually incomplete for this reason, this analysis is nevertheless a paradigm for investigating a developmental pathway.

If there are so many genes involved in the pathway for developing this one neuronal type, what might this mean for complicated circuits involving many neurons? Genetic work on two types of behavior in nematodes may be relevant here. Large-scale screens have been done for mutants that fail to respond appropriately to touch and for mutants that fail to lay eggs. Each screen defined dozens of genes involved in the development of the specific neurons that underlie these circuits. Surprisingly, many of these are involved in the development of either the touch circuit neurons or the egg laying circuit neurons, and are not shared between the two developmental pathways, indicating an astonishing amount of specificity in the genetic programs that govern the development of different specific neural pathways.

Focusing on particular aspects of neural development has led to the discovery of molecules that control specific developmental processes. An example of this is the genetic investigation into the proteins involved in axon navigation during the wiring-up of the nervous system. It took dedicated screens for mutants in which the axonal navigation was disrupted to shed real light on molecules involved in axonal guidance. Such screens done in *Drosophila*, nematodes, and more recently zebrafish, have yielded many of the key players now known to participate in the guidance of axons in all species studied, including mammals. For example, the *unc-6* mutant in nematodes was found to code for both an attractive and a repellent midline signal for axon migration. In *unc-5* mutants, axons show attraction but not repulsion to the *unc-6* guidance cue.

The vertebrate homologue of *unc-6* is called netrin. Netrin is expressed in the ventral midline of the spinal

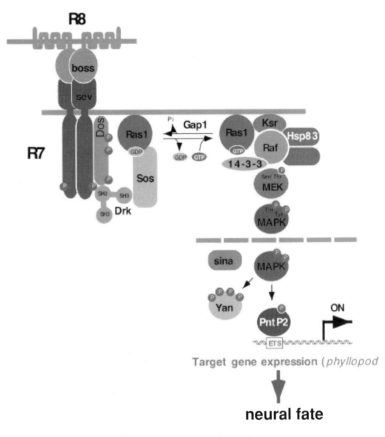

Figure 1. Components of the *sevenless* transduction pathway as elucidated by genetic screens for modifiers of *sevenless* function. From Professor Ernst Hafen.

cord where it attracts the axons of dorsal commissural interneurons and repels the axons of motoneurons. The commissural interneurons express the 'attractive' netrin receptor DCC ('deleted in colon cancer'), the homologue of *C. elegans unc-40*. Motoneurons that express a different 'repulsive' netrin receptor, the vertebrate homologue of *C. elegans unc-5*, grow away from the ventral midline. This is a dramatic example of the conservation of genetic pathways involved in neural development throughout animal kingdom.

Forward and reverse genetics

Developmental genetics as discussed above is a 'forward genetics' approach, where the genes are discovered by mutations that disrupt neural development. There is a great advantage to this approach because it makes no assumptions about the kinds of genes involved. Furthermore, by saturation screening, followed by enhancer-suppressor screening, one can potentially find most or even all of the important genetic components in the processes under investigation. But forward genetics

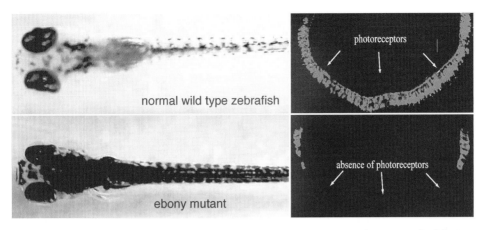

Figure 2. Ebony mutants are darker than wild types because their photoreceptors degenerate. The fish tries to adapt its body color to the background, and so visually impaired mutants like ebony ones that 'think' they are in the dark are easy to recognize and screen.

demands a species with a short generation time and the possibility of screening thousands of mutagenized animals. This is why most of this work is done with nematodes and flies. Recently, however, zebrafish have come onto the scene as a 'forward genetic' animal.

Zebrafish have two additional striking advantages. The first is that the embryos are transparent, and so it is possible to screen for neural defects morphologically and without any dissection. In this way, for example, a large class of mutants have been found that disrupt the development of the midbrain-hindbrain boundary, and these mutants have helped elucidate development pathways involving signaling pathways and transcription factors that are used to organize the brain around this region. The other distinct advantage is that zebrafish are vertebrates like humans, and their nervous systems are organized like ours. A microscopic section through the zebrafish retina looks very much like a section through the human retina. It has the same cell types in the same laminae. The many mutations that cause blindness in zebrafish by affecting the development or the survival of cells in the retina (Fig. 2) are therefore likely models at both morphological and molecular levels for understanding some hereditary retinal malformations and degenerations in humans (Goldsmith, 2001). In general, zebrafish may be relevant for understanding the genetic basis of the neural development that underlies emergent human behavior. While the beginning of this entry focused on species-specific circuits, it is obvious that the developmental genetic approach often leads to the discovery of molecules and mechanisms that are of a more general significance.

Mice are not such a good 'forward genetic' system for investigating neural development. Yet, some spontaneous mouse mutants have been the starting point for detailed investigations of neural development. For example, the spontaneous reeler mutant, discovered because of its unstable gait, was found to code for a protein, called 'reelin.' Reelin defines a molecular pathway that is critical for the proper migration of cortical cells and cerebellar cells during embryogenesis. Mutations in components of this pathway lead to the mouse equivalent of human lissencephaly, mild forms of which have been linked to mood disorders and schizophrenia.

Mice are a better 'reverse genetic' system, in which specific genes are deliberately knocked out or introduced to test their roles in development. Often the results are surprising and the phenotypes seen are not what are predicted. It was dumbfounding to find surprisingly normal-looking brains in mice where the gene that coded for all forms of the neural cell adhesion molecule, N-CAM, had been knocked out, as previous work suggested that N-CAM was involved in several different key aspects of neural development.

As is the case with N-CAM, a high fraction of mouse knockouts yield subtle phenotypes given the precedent work in vitro. It sometimes takes the targeted knockout of two or more genes simultaneously to achieve an obvious or striking phenotype, implying the overlapping or intersecting functions of different genes involved in particular processes. *Noggin*, for example, has clearly been implicated as a neural inducer in lower vertebrates, yet *noggin* knockout mice have fully formed nervous systems. It is not until one combines this mutant with the knockout of another inducer, *chordin*, that hypomorphic nervous systems are seen in the doubly mutant mice.

Many other strategies have been introduced to developmental genetics in response to particular issues and challenges in the field. Gene traps are used to find genes, knock them out, and label the cells that normally express them – all in one go. A recent study in mice identified hundreds of new genes that appear to be involved in neural development using this technique (Leighton *et al.*, 2001). There is also a great deal to be learned from conditional knockouts in which a specific gene function can be impaired in specific cell types at specific times in development.

Developmental genetics and psychological development: future perspectives?

It is clear that the biological basis of psychology is centered in the brain, and that psychological development is linked with brain development. The field of developmental genetics as it applies to brain development has shown that we are still in the infancy of understanding this process. Many thousands of genes are necessary for the proper building of particular neural circuits, and we have identified only a small fraction of these. And, although we may be able to explain the aberrant behavior of a mutant fly through a gene's effect on a specific developmental process, we are a long way from understanding the developmental processes that underlie different personality traits, or how these processes are influenced by particular genes that affect these traits. Syndromes, such as some types of autism and dyslexia and psychological attributes like sexual orientation, may be influenced by the activity of specific genes, but we do not yet know what these genes do in development that is the basis of such conditions or attributes.

If a measure of a person's behavioral psychology is found to have a more complex hereditary component than the function of a single gene, as must be the case for most such measures, then it will be an even longer time, although hopefully not impossibly long, before developmental geneticists can describe the causal connections between the genes involved and their combined developmental effects on the brain. To understand how genes work in this regard, the developmental consequences of genetic influences must be unpacked to reveal the intrinsic genetic effects (interactions among genes), the epigenetic effects (interactions with the cellular and organismal environment), maternal effects (including in mammals uterine and postnatal nursing/caregiving activities), and non-maternal environmental factors. To sort out how genes involved in neural development work in all these situations is an enormous challenge for the future.

Conclusions: nature and nurture

From the perspective of developmental genetics, nature versus nurture is not much of an issue. The issue is simply how genes are involved in brain development. The structure of the nervous system is largely the product of thousands of genes involved in every aspect of its development from its earliest to its most mature stages. Genes are involved in building the brain and helping the brain build itself, as in the ability of neurons and synapses to respond to the environment and learn new things. For example, there are *Drosophila* mutants that are unable to form memories because of defects in single genes whose products are involved in synapse plasticity. Males of these strains do not recall being rejected by females during courtship, and thus have unusual sexual behavior when paired with new females. The concepts of nature and nurture thus translate into questions about how genes are involved in making the neural substrate of developing behavior, and questions about how the effects of experience are translated through gene products to changes in the brain.

See also:
Understanding ontogenetic development: debates about the nature of the epigenetic process; Ethological theories; Cross-species comparisons; Twin and adoption studies; Conceptions and misconceptions about embryonic development; Brain and behavioral development (II): cortical; Autism; Down's syndrome; Dyslexia; Williams syndrome; Behavioral embryology; Behavior genetics

Further reading

Dickson, B. J. (2002). Molecular mechanisms of axon guidance. *Science*, 298, 1959–1964.

Jessell, T. M. and Sanes, J. R. (2000). Development. The decade of the developing brain. *Current Opinions in Neurobiology*, 10, 599–611.

Kyriacou, C. P. and Hall, J. C. (1994). Genetic and molecular analysis of Drosophila behavior. *Advances in Genetics*, 31, 139–186.

Education

LESLIE SMITH

Introduction

Developmental psychology (DP) is an empirical science whose standard question is how children in fact develop as individuals in sociocultural worlds. Developmental models set out answers to this question with the intention of serving the same function as Albert Einstein's model in physics. In this sense, DP is a theoretical science. Education is different in three ways.

Firstly, education is similar to DP since it does include empirical investigation guided by developmental models, notably as to the psychology of teaching and learning in schools, classrooms, and other contexts. Even so, education differs from DP in combining multiple disciplines cutting across all of the social sciences, as well as history and philosophy. Secondly, education is an applied science whose standard question is how teaching and learning could or should – not merely do – occur in practice. Just as one model in physics may be applied to the design of both nuclear power stations and nuclear weapons, the same developmental model may be put to divergent, even incompatible, uses. This leads to the third difference. Education is a normative discipline due to its central concern with values in the improvement of individuals or society. It is well known that individuals and societies differ with regard to what counts as worthwhile, or important, or good. It is worth noticing here that value diversity rules out monism, but this admission leaves open the pluralism versus relativism debate about values. These three differences between DP and education lead to a problem amounting to a border dispute.

Border dispute problem

DP and education are not the same thing. Although a co-extensive position about development and education has been set out – according to the claim by John Dewey (1859–1952) in 1916 that ". . . education is development" – this is not the only position. To see why, an instructive example is provided by John Ruskin (1819–1900), whose view of education (Palmer, 2001) invoked in the 1992 British Command Paper *Choice and Diversity* was that ". . . the duty on government and parents is identical. For without good schools there can be little development."

This view is arresting. Psychologists are likely to interpret this as a commitment to the importance of human development in schooling. The interpretation of educational politicians was different, and their sub-text made clear that economic development at the national level was at issue. The same dual focus on 'learning unlocking the treasures within us all [and on] economic prosperity' was evident in the 1997 Command Paper *Excellence in Schools*. The bitter irony is that this is to miss Ruskin's main point: ". . . there is no wealth but life." This point is unlikely to be lost in DP. Unfortunately, it is not the sole point in education. A rationale runs like this.

Egan (1997) has argued that any adequate account of education includes three elements, which taken together are jointly inconsistent. These three elements are identifiable by reference to paradigm examples: (1) Plato (L. Smith, 2002) on intellectual search for truth about reality; (2) Emile Durkheim (1859–1918) on enculturation by society; and (3) Jean Jacques Rousseau (1712–1778) on human development (Palmer, 2001). According to Egan, this trinity has to be combined, though in different proportions in different accounts. However, none eliminates incompatibilities due to their joint presence.

Adapting Egan's argument to DP with reference to George Orwell's hero in *1984* who did know that $2 + 2 = 4$, it is paradoxical to claim that: (1) developmental differences are real (cf., Dewey: a child may develop into a sturdy oak, a bending willow, a thorny cactus, or a poisonous weed); (2) developmental differences reflect the contingencies of local contexts in variable cultures (cf., Vygotsky: sociocultural interactions are intrinsically different); and (3) developmental sequences have misperceptions, 'false memories,' pseudo-concepts as intermediaries to true knowledge of reality. The problems here are two-fold. One is that it is a valid task in DP to investigate developmental processes – individual differences, contextual variations, and deviant rationality in developmental sequences – without also investigating their successful outcomes (i.e., their contribution to the formation of true knowledge such as $2 + 2 = 4$). Yet in education, this formation problem has to be addressed. The other is that in view of the conceptual difference between norms and facts, there is no consensus – neither in DP nor in education – about how to combine the causality of development with the normativity of knowledge in a unitary account (Smith in Goswami, 2002).

The question follows on. What difference would the removal of DP make to education? As a heuristic, consider a thought-experiment about two teachers who are identical (training, expertise, experience) in every respect except one: DP makes a contribution to the educational beliefs and practices of one of these teachers, but not the other. Well then: what difference does this make? Or is this a distinction without a difference? Five ways to answer this question follow, five views of education from a vantage point in DP (Table 1).

Independence

This is comparable to ships passing in the night without meeting. From a unilaterally defined research perspective on each of the good ships DP and education, the research programs can be defined, and refined, internally by contributors to the discipline. Research in DP can deal with psychological processes and techniques devoid of educational relevance. Educational research can deal with non-developmental aspects of schooling. Either way, this amounts to internalism (i.e., ideas and evidence are unique to one particular discipline, and to no other). This makes sense as one way to augment any academic discipline. Indeed, psychological accounts in education over the last century have become regarded as unnecessary, either because their potential has been overestimated, or else psychology has underperformed. In DP, educational accounts are typically by-passed altogether due to judgments about their non-relevance.

To repeat, internalism as a research strategy makes sense. It also has an opportunity-cost in that a comprehensively internal position breaks down. Guided exclusively by internalism, the cross-over points with other disciplines are non-detectable from within that discipline. Yet common ground is plain to see, for example, in the UK National Curriculum whose principal aim is to promote development in all main areas of learning and experience. This is missed by internalism in DP, as this aim too is not thereby an

Table 1. Five ways to fit developmental psychology to education.		
View	Function	Principle
1 Independence	Truth. Utility	This is the case. That is the case or is useful
2 Relevance	Speculation	If this is the case, that appears to be the case or appears to be useful.
3 Implication	Validity	If this is the case, that is the case.
4 Application	Utility	If this is the case, that is useful.
5 Inter-dependence	Truth and Utility	If and only if this is the case, that is the case or is useful.

educational aim of all children, all parents, all teachers, the general public, and all governments. Conversely, the differences detected in DP between children's development from baseline to Ph.D. will not be detected by internalists in education.

Relevance

This is a way-station promising much and providing little. An elegant and powerful account of human development is combined with global conclusions about education. Such conclusions are comparable to arresting messages in bottles floating on vast oceans. Their clarity is problematic. Conclusions about global relevance from this way-station often lag behind commonsense, leading to charges of psychobabble. Relevance is a two-termed relationship and both terms should be specified. This is carried through for DP, but not for education. Nativist and evolutionary accounts of development in general, along with accounts of number development during infancy in particular, are especially problematic, educationally speaking. Relevance alone is not enough, any more than the sign 'Good Food Tonight' with neither menu nor recipe available.

Implication

An implication is comparable to a directive with a unidirectional flow from source to target. Informative, explicit, elucidatory, or distinctive, an implication goes beyond relevance, and so can be checked in three ways. One check is whether an asserted implication really is an implication. Jean Piaget disowned many implications about curriculum design attributed to him by commentators (such as implications for the mathematics curriculum that Piaget regarded as "modern mathematics taught by an archaic method"), about individualized learning (his long-stated view was that "group work in the classroom is more active than individual work"), and about teaching requiring readiness (his view was "a teacher creates a learning context"). Piaget's (1995) remark that ". . . each individual is led to think and re-think the system of collective notions" is an affirmation of a major problem, namely, how any individual develops autonomous and novel knowledge in spite of sociocultural assistance that is as pervasive as it is predominating (L. Smith, 2002). This problem has largely gone without remark in most psychological and educational commentary, and is re-visited in the Conclusions.

A second check is whether an implication is distinctive at the level of educational beliefs in consequence of which it changes the way in which education can be interpreted. Her Majesty's Inspectorate's proposal for schooling to promote "lively enquiring minds" can be distinctively interpreted through Margaret Donaldson's model of four modes of mental functioning that develop by their use in *here/now* contexts through to transcendent contexts not directly or imaginatively derived from personal experience (Palmer, 2001). A non-developmental account leaves development out of account. This is a tautology, but not all tautologies are banal. Cyril Burt's psychometric account of the development of intelligence had exclusive implications for secondary education based on school-specific selection regimented by the bell-curve (Palmer, 2001). By contrast, Donaldson's account had inclusive implications for the schooling of all children. A third check is whether an implication, which has led to an improved understanding in education, has also led to improvement in educational practices.

Application

An educational application is the testing of a corresponding implication. Does the implication work in practice? Even if it does, is it practicable? Can it become common practice? Does it amount to good practice? Two pedagogical functions are relevant to all applications. One is assessment, whose two main forms are diagnostic and formative. The other is treatment or instructional intervention. The intervention projects such as Cognitive Acceleration in Science Education (CASE) in the UK, exploited both pedagogical functions in four steps (Shayer & Adey, 2002): (1) Piaget's model of the development of children's reasoning through serial levels; (2) diagnostic assessment survey of below-level functioning by two-thirds of youngsters during schooling; (3) intervention model based on mastery, formative assessment, group learning, and reflection over Years 7–8 science classrooms, leading to 'good' A-C passes in three core GCSE subjects (Science, Maths, English) at Year 11 in experimental over control classes (25 percent gain in CASE I; 20 percent gain in CASE II); and (4) on-going extensions across all years and the whole curriculum. Effective interventions with these properties are as rare as they are welcome.

Inter-dependence

An application is typically driven by an external resource imported into educational practices. The flow is uni-directional. Inter-dependence is bi-directional, requiring a unitary account that is designed and tested at the intersection of both disciplines. Intersection does not mean the reduction of one discipline to the other, but rather the staking out of common ground between them. This can be done at five levels:

(1) common phenomena such as intellectual, moral, or emotional development;
(2) overarching model combining developmental and educational principles;
(3) convergent methods for triangulation covering the whole model;
(4) complementary evidence for quantitative and qualitative analysis;
(5) interdisciplinary interpretation in a single account.

We are not yet at (5), but have at least left (1), notably in work due to Ann Brown and her colleagues (Bransford, Brown, & Cocking, 2001) in which the 'basic-applied' distinction was recast, such that classrooms are as basic as laboratories for generalization by colleagues. This required in (2) dual principles in the study of school-based learning communities, such as reciprocal teaching based on Vygotskian developmental zones, and Robert Slavin's social process models of instruction. A commitment to (3) was assured through design experiments to engineer educational innovation, leading to rich data sets in (4). There are three blockages prior to arrival at (5). One is the Tower of Babel: contributions are typically several and proliferating, reflecting current practices in independent disciplines. Multidisciplinarity is not the same as (5). A second is the mismatch between methodological sophistication at (4), and theoretical over-simplification at (2). A model is neither a method nor a data set, and unitary models are rare. A third blockage is the value-difference, both within and between each discipline. Fundamental questions about "what should be" and "what should be done" are central to education, and are normative. These questions could not be resolved in the absence of developmental models; yet their origin is in DP that is a non-normative discipline. This theoretical issue is taken up in the Conclusions.

Conclusions

DP and education are not the same thing. But they are related in that the former makes a necessary, though not sufficient, contribution to the latter. In contrast to the theoretical science which is DP, education is an applied science that tests the means to normatively defined ends or values. Egan has provided a timely reminder of the fundamental difference between DP and education.

Changing educational beliefs through DP. Education can be viewed in five ways from DP with the 'two teachers' thought-experiment as a heuristic. Both independence and relevance currently predominate, though neither is likely to change educational beliefs. Implication continues to be the standard way to do this.

Changing educational practices through DP. Application has been demonstrated to be effective notably in terms of a stringent criterion for improving current practice in educationally significant ways. This position is set to be generalized. Inter-dependence is a promissory note for research programs in the 21st century. It will not advance under a division of labor that makes losers in research communities whose members work in a context marked by the politicization of education.

DP and developmental epistemology. DP is not the only empirical study of development. Developmental epistemology (DE) is also an empirical study. DP and DE are both empirical disciplines, but their focus is different. DP's focus is on causal facts related to children and their development. DE's focus is on normative facts related to knowledge or values and their development. All facts can be empirically investigated, but these two types of facts are irreducible. Interestingly, there is co-instantiation, co-development both of children and of knowledge (L. Smith, 2002). The elaboration and use of a joint model covering both DP and DE is set to be productive in both developmental and educational research. A notable question is the individualization of knowledge and values (i.e., how the advance is made from normative pressure to valid normativity).

See also:
Constructivist theories; Developmental testing; Cognitive development in infancy; Cognitive development beyond infancy; Intelligence; Schooling and literacy; Sociology; Jerome S. Bruner; Jean Piaget; Lev S. Vygotsky

Further reading

Bereiter, C. (2002). *Education and Mind in the Knowledge Age*. Mahwah, NJ: Erlbaum.

De Corte, E. (2000). Marrying theory building and the improvement of school practice. *Learning and Instruction*, 10, 249–266.

Dewey, J. (1966). *Democracy and Education*. New York: The Free Press.

Ethology

JOHN C. FENTRESS

Introduction

Ethology can be defined broadly as the naturalistic study of behavior in diverse animal species. A primary goal of ethological research is to dissect streams of animal action into their component parts or properties, and also to determine how these dissected components fit together at the level of the intact organism. Careful observation and description of intact organism behavior under specified contexts of expression are thus the starting-points for most ethological research. The comparative method is used to document both the similarities and differences in action sequences across different species. In recent years, developmental studies have added importantly to earlier ethological emphases upon 'instinct' and 'innate' action patterns, for it has become clear that both nature and nurture operate together in a subtle mix throughout ontogeny (Edelman, 1987; Ridley, 2003).

Today, many ethologists are reaching out into other fields, including child psychology (Posner, Rothbart, Farah, & Bruer, 2001). For example, in areas such as social relationships and attachment, research has shown that the precise timing, quality, and quantity of specific as well as more broadly defined sources of information offer insights into ontogeny that are applicable across many species (including humans) and levels of inquiry. It is important to remember that nature, at its mechanistic level, is basically conservative – with a wide variety of animal and human phenotypes being constructed from the same principal ingredients. Thus, both similarities and differences are critical to the comparative approach, whether across species, individuals, or developmental time frames.

For developmental analyses, both ethologists and psychologists have become increasingly aware that genetic foundations are involved in all behavior, but that these biological building blocks are always utilized in the context of ontogenetic experiences. Thus, while early ethological studies provided useful service to developmental studies with their emphases upon 'instinctive' actions, the lines between 'innate,' 'learned,' and 'experience dependent' have begun to blur. Developmental systems are importantly both interactive with their broader surround and self-organizing. Precisely how this dance between interactive and self-organizing processes operates in specific systems is the subject of much active investigation.

Pattern formation and movement as unifying themes

One useful framework for seeking links between developmental psychology and ethology – as well as each of these fields with disciplines such as neuroscience, developmental biology, and endocrinology – is that of pattern formation in behavior. In basic terms, a pattern in behavior must be evaluated in terms both of component parts or processes and of the organization of these abstracted units with regard to their higher-order arrangements and broader contexts of expression.

Through their studies of pattern formation in behavior, ethologists have highlighted three fundamental ways to think about the operation of components and contexts (Fentress & Gadbois, 2001). In each case, it is the dynamical balance among intrinsically and extrinsically defined factors that is critical. Thus, the task is to evaluate: (1) intrinsic gene actions, in the context of environmental factors; (2) action performances, in terms of events within the organism as they relate to the impingement of sensory and other externally defined events; and (3) each action itself, in terms of other actions that precede, follow, or which might have (co-)occurred.

Animal movement patterns have played an important part in ethological research, and the development of movement has recently become important to a wide range of issues in child development (Thelen & Smith, 1994). Movement is observed behavior, and as such reminds us that our models of behavior must be dynamically ordered, as well as relational and multilayered, for a more complete understanding. Development is similar to movement in that it too is dynamical, relational, and multilayered.

Example one: rodent grooming

The richness of animal actions, even apparently 'simple' actions, offers perspectives that can be applied to many areas in child development. An illustration is self-grooming, which is a common behavioral pattern in rodents (Fentress & Gadbois, 2001). Abstracted principles of expressive and developmental organization seen in rodent grooming may also apply to human movement in that: (1) grooming does not occur randomly in time, but most often in particular transitions between other behavioral states; (2) the interactions between grooming expression and alternative forms of action can be either positive or negative, depending upon both relative strengths and timing; (3) grooming actions are not unitary, but can be broken into a variety of sub-components, or 'sub-units'; (4) the actions occur within a hierarchically ordered 'action syntax,' where individual acts (think 'letters') are formed into various combinations (as in 'words'), which are in turn combined into still higher-order patterns ('phrases,' etc.); and (5) each abstracted action 'type' can be further dissected into individual movement properties, such as kinematic variables that may be differentially shared across higher-order action categories.

In development, these action properties and their combinations also follow distinct rules of assembly, disassembly, and re-assembly, much as in the progression of motor abilities and language in children. From a neurological perspective, the separation and combination of action components and their underlying processes is important, as different regions of the brain are differentially associated with particular levels of organization. In behavioral terms, actions such as self-grooming in rodents can often be elicited early in ontogeny through appropriate postural support, even though these same actions normally do not appear until much later (Fig. 1). Similar results have been confirmed in humans (Thelen & Smith, 1994). The study of animal actions can thus provide model systems to clarify similar profiles in child development.

Differentially maturing parts of the brain interconnect in complex ways, and in doing so can alter one another's properties. This can be seen dramatically both in animal actions and in human actions, such as language development in deaf children, where cortical areas that normally sub-serve linguistic aspects of auditory processing can be re-structured within limits to handle analogous

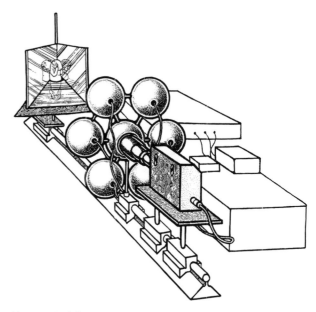

Figure 1. An infant mouse given postural support in special chair used for analysis of early self-grooming behavior. With postural support, young animals and humans will often exhibit movement capacities that are normally not seen until later in ontogeny.

functions via vision. The observed plasticity is in itself constrained, and much current research is being devoted to defining both plasticity and its limits for specific functions and brain regions ontogenetically (Posner *et al.*, 2001).

Many early mammalian movements occur prior to birth, aided by gravitational support via the prenatal environment. In both animals and humans, a cascade of functions can emerge, with aspects of expression that only much later in life serve communicative functions. Often the early movements exhibit a high level of spontaneity, and they are not simple reflexes that need to be triggered by environmental stimuli.

An important contribution of ethology is the realization that young organisms can often express complex and well-formed actions the first time they have the opportunity (e.g., breathing, crying, and nursing in human neonates). The young organism is thus not just an incomplete older organism; at each stage of development well-formed actions may play a critical role in survival, by means of what have been termed ontogenetic adaptations. Often these early actions cease to be expressed later, due to either the elimination of circuits, or the blocking from later-developing forms of expression. Furthermore, the circuitry for many actions develops 'pre-functionally,' thus indicating a limited role for learning or related practice effects. There are many cases in the clinical literature where neurological insult later in life, through either disease or physical trauma, will cause the individual to behave in ways reminiscent of earlier life stages. Importantly, however, neurological damage in adults often leads toward actions

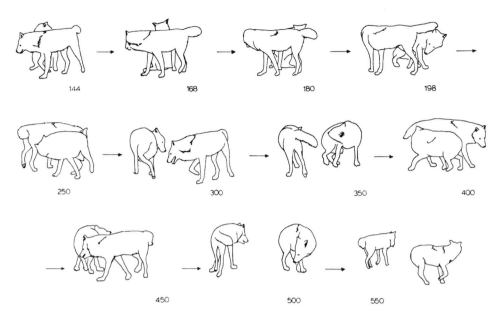

144   168   180   198

250   300   350   400

450   500   550

Figure 2. A pair of wolves moving around one another in a rule-governed partner-wise 'dance.' Such rules of inter-animal coordination emphasize the importance of relational measures in social behavior. Similar relational measures can be applied to coordinated limb movements within individuals.

that are 'stereotyped' and lack the 'fluency' with which movements are performed by young infants (Brian Hopkins, personal communication).

Example two: social communication in wolves

Many actions serve communicative functions. Thus, early ethological work on animal displays served to broaden the contexts within which particular action properties are evaluated. In studies of communication, actions are in some sense shared, where both actor and receiver play essential roles. In young animals, such as wolves, subsequent communicative actions are often first emitted in what seem like inappropriate contexts. In addition, these actions may be elicited prior to the time that the young animals exhibit sensitivity to those of others. Moreover, actions that are most effective in communication with young individuals may be replaced by others in the future.

To illustrate further from animal social behavior, young wolves often emit fragmented actions that are later combined into complex communicative sequences. In addition, they may emit these actions in initially unexpected, even apparently inappropriate, contexts, with few signs of sophisticated processing of signals generated by other animals. The developmental sequence of many forms of both animal and human behavior follows the trajectory of refinement of aspects of expression prior to any obvious adjustment to similar or alternative signals from their social neighbors. Individual components of action may occur more or less

in isolation, giving the entire sequence of expression a fragmented appearance (Fentress & Gadbois, 2001; Thelen & Smith, 1994). The ontogenetic assembly, and also disassembly, as well as reassembly, of parts and their connections, are equally important foci for developmental inquiry, whatever the action or species.

An important lesson from studies of wolf and other forms of animal social behavior is that relational perspectives are often essential to capture the essence of dyadic and higher interactions. Thus, two or more animals may show clear rules of order when the movements of each are described explicitly with reference to the movements of others, rather than through descriptions based upon other external referents, such as a camera or the eyes of the observer (Fig. 2). Note that in studies, coordinated actions *within* an individual are also often most usefully described in terms of relational coordinates defined for individual limbs and limb segments. These facts highlight that behavioral order can cohere at a number of complementary levels, and that similar descriptive perspectives can be applied across these levels.

Young wolves show often striking individual differences in both their actions and the contexts within which these actions are employed. In analogy to rodent grooming, the connections between two animals may at first appear very loosely structured, then simplified and rigid, and subsequently re-elaborated as social roles and individual temperaments emerge. A difficult, but important, goal is to see how such layers of organization in development fit together.

There are numerous developmental events that are involved in effective communication, including the

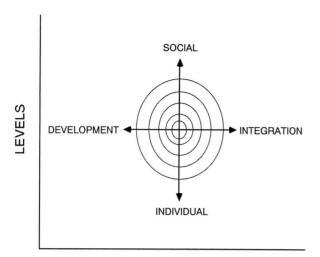

TIME FRAMES

Figure 3. Both developmental psychology and ethology conduct studies on topics that range from actions of the individual through complex forms of social behavior. The developmental foundations of behavior and processes of integrated performance can be viewed together in terms of pattern formation and its phenotypic expression.

Table 1. Terms such as 'innate' and 'instinctive' have been used diversely in the literature to emphasize the importance of evolutionary and genetic foundations of behavior. Several common uses are listed. In each case, there are limitations and potential confusions. In addition, the individual characterizations cited do not logically entail the others.

Term	Limitation
PRESENT AT BIRTH	Many characteristic actions occur only late in ontogeny
INEVITABLE	Total non-modifiability can rarely if ever be established
UNLEARNED	Many definitions and presumed consequences of learning
INDEPENDENT OF EXPERIENCE	At many levels, 'experience' contributes to all phenotypes
UNIVERSAL	Ignores individual variations within species
AUTOMATIC	Often vague and can apply to learned skills, as in sports
CENTRALLY PROGRAMMED	Can ignore diverse roles of sensory experience
RIGID	Often a relative term, in both performance and ontogeny

establishment of basic perceptual abilities, processes of cognitive evaluation, motivation, and so forth. The analysis of action is critical to studies of behavioral development, but must always be connected to the operation of other processes that may have distinct time courses and causes. A major contribution of ethology has been to emphasize this fact (Fig. 3).

On genes and experience

Determining the role of intrinsic or spontaneous factors in behavioral ontogeny has been an important contribution of ethology to all branches of developmental psychology. Blank-slate models are impossible to maintain. Ethologists have performed a valuable task in pointing out how early actions in development must often occur for the first time in a well-coordinated fashion, even when not taught. These ontogenetic adaptations are supported by many observations at the neuroembryological level, as well as in terms of whole organism behavior (Ridley, 2003). What role does experience play?

Later research has made it clear that, even in cases of apparently innate and spontaneous behavior, the foundations for adaptive expression must always involve subtle and changing interplays between intrinsic and extrinsic variables (Table 1). The sensitivity to particular sources of input can change radically during development, as clarified by such notions as sensitive periods. Many examples can be cited, ranging from learning of song in birds, to language in children, to the

establishment of attachments in both animals and humans. Furthermore, in addition to often highly specific factors underlying particular features of behavior, ethological research has led to investigations of processes that are often far-reaching, spreading across both actions and their substrates.

As the psychologist Donald O. Hebb (1904–1985) pointed out, one cannot construct a rectangle without having two dimensions, length and width. Analogously, an organism, whatever its final shape, also always has two interlocked dimensions-genes plus experience. How these two fundamental processes work together is the subject of much current research, ranging from child development to developmental neurobiology. The effects of an experience always depend upon genes and earlier gene products, and in turn affect the actions of these genes and their products (Ridley, 2003).

Clinical issues

While ethologists have emphasized adaptive patterns of action, which are often remarkably robust under diverse developmental conditions, they have also evaluated behavioral disorders at a variety of levels of inquiry. Perhaps the most striking example is in the area of social attachment where, as in the case of humans, many animal species deprived of normal social experience may suffer from a number of other disorders (e.g., deviant maternal behavior, temperament modifications, cognitive deficits).

Serious mental disorders such as schizophrenia are now known to reflect genetic distinctions between individuals, such as events that modify the production and utilization of dopamine in particular areas of the brain. Various forms of mental retardation are also known to have genetic precursors. But in each of these cases, environmental events during ontogeny can exert important influences upon which genes are expressed during any given developmental period.

Ethologists have also been attentive to such issues as flexibility and rigidity in behavior. For example, under conditions of stress, animals as well as humans often fall back onto routines that are relatively simple and well established, thus losing the flexibility to deal effectively with changing environmental events. Ethologists have traditionally looked at conditions under which actions appear to be irrelevant to the primary tasks of the animal, such as displacement activities, where, for example, a rodent suddenly and vigorously grooms its face when confronted with various approach-avoidance conflicts (Fentress & Gadbois, 2001). Actions may also be 're-directed' to non-primary targets, such as when a child kicks a dog after being angered by a more powerful playmate.

Many of these actions may become selectively persistent and rigid, as in the case of pacing often observed in environmentally deprived (e.g., zoo) animals, or certain obsessive-compulsive movements in humans (Fentress & Gadbois, 2001). Animal analogies to schizophrenia can often be seen both in animals that are environmentally deprived and in those with genetically connected disorders of neural function (e.g., genes that result in excessive dopamine production).

Potential genetically based compromises in behavior and neural circuitry can often be ameliorated by special training. An illustration of the latter case concerns mice who normally have genetic cerebellar and behavioral abnormalities that can to varying degrees be 'rescued' through specialized training methods. In terms of physically produced trauma, it is now clear that the prognosis for recovery is also highly dependent upon the age at which the trauma occurs. The connection between reactions to physically induced trauma and genetic/phenotypic factors remains an area of active investigation (Posner *et al.*, 2001).

One important perspective that can be linked to ethological research, and that is directly relevant to child development, is that experiences in ontogeny can be 'permissive' and 'selective' as well as 'instructional' (Edelman, 1987). Experiences can thus trigger genetic events that in turn 'self-organize' subsequent stages of phenotypic development, rather like opening up a file drawer to read the messages that are otherwise hidden from view. Selection is also used in a different and important sense. Promotion of certain developmental pathways can either facilitate or inhibit the development of alternative pathways in analogy to Darwinian selection. While the details will obviously differ for different systems, such results challenge the developmental psychologist (and ethologist) to ask when and to what extent particular developmental events operate independently, synergistically, or antagonistically to one another.

Conclusions

What is clear in both ethology and developmental psychology is that blank-slate 'mirror' models of ontogeny are not sufficient. Organisms do not in a simple way mirror the details of the experiences to which they have been exposed, but utilize these inputs in ways that depend upon both genes and previously established phenotypic states. Evolutionary and genetic factors interplay with both species-characteristic and individual forms of experience within dynamical constraints throughout life. Certainly, the marriage of ethology and developmental psychology as each is pursued today, along with sister disciplines that range from cellular biology through the study of social/ecological contexts of intact organism expressions, holds great promise for the establishment of such organizational principles in the future.

There are deeper conceptual issues that have not been touched upon thus far in this entry. One example is the theme of interdependencies in development. Systems may at times appear to operate more or less independently, and at other times interact, thus producing higher-order products (Fentress & Gadbois, 2001). But in development, simple interactions only scratch the surface. Thus, when systems A and B interact, in part because of their own intrinsic properties, they may change the 'rules' of subsequent interactions by altering the properties of their partners, and so on. Indeed, the distinction between acts and their connections is often moot.

Systems during development may not only interact and isolate, but also become interdependent upon one another (i.e., 'mutual molding' among individual properties) in ways that remain poorly understood. The future marriage of ethology and developmental psychology may do much to clarify such issues.

See also:

The concept of development: historical perspectives; Understanding ontogenetic development: debates about the nature of the epigenetic process; Ethological theories; Learning theories; Dynamical systems approaches; Cross-species comparisons; Observational methods; Conceptions and misconceptions about embryonic development; Motor development; Social development; Language development; Brain and behavioral development (I): sub-cortical; Brain and behavioral development (II): cortical; Play; Sleep and wakefulness; Temperament; Behavior and learning disorders; Behavioral embryology; Developmental genetics

Further reading

Fentress, J. C. (1999). The organization of behavior revisited. *Canadian Journal of Experimental Psychology*, 53, 8–19.

Karmiloff-Smith, A. (1997). *Beyond Modularity*. Cambridge, MA: MIT Press.
Tinbergen, N. (1972). *The Animal in its World*, Vol. I: *Field Studies*. London: Allen and Unwin.

Acknowledgments

The preparation of this entry has been aided by grants from the Canadian Institute of Health Sciences (CIHS) and the Natural Sciences and Engineering Research Council of Canada (NSERC). I am indebted to each for many years of support. I thank Brian Hopkins for his invitation to contribute to this volume, for his patience, and for his editorial expertise.

Linguistics

MELISSA BOWERMAN

Introduction

The study of language development and the study of linguistics have long been intertwined. Ties between the two disciplines were given a deeper theoretical grounding in the 1950s–1960s through Noam Chomsky's paradigm-changing challenge to behaviorist accounts of language acquisition. Chomsky argued that the structure of language is far more complex than behaviorists had envisioned, and that the child's task is not simply to build up a stock of sentence patterns or responses, but to formulate a highly abstract underlying rule system. Learning mechanisms commonly invoked at the time, such as modeling, imitation, and reinforcement, were, Chomsky urged, inadequate to this task. He proposed that certain aspects of grammatical structure (viz., language universals, or constraints honored by all languages) are not in fact learned at all, but are known innately, as part of the child's inborn capacity for language acquisition.

Interest in the relationship between language universals and children's capacity for language acquisition remains strong, although linguistic frameworks have diverged and there is now a range of approaches to characterizing the linguistic structures a child must master. In the generative grammar tradition of Chomsky and his followers, grammatical structure is held to be autonomous (i.e., independent of meaning or other external factors and shaped by the domain-specific architecture of the mind). This architecture is seen as guiding the process of language acquisition: children rely on innately known abstract categories and principles in analyzing the structure of the language they are exposed to. This approach may be contrasted with that of cognitive-functionalist ('usage-based') approaches to linguistics, which view language structure as intimately related to the semantic and pragmatic properties of the messages being communicated, as well as to mechanisms of perception and production (Tomasello, 1998, 2000). Researchers working within this framework assume that most aspects of language are learned, not innate, although children are credited with a species-specific capacity for this kind of learning. The cognitive-functionalist perspective offers many points of contact with traditional concerns of developmentalists, and it will be the main focus of this entry. An introduction to the generative grammar approach to language acquisition can be found in Crain & Lillo-Martin (1999).

Discovering the mapping between form and function

According to the cognitive-functionalist perspective, the structure of human languages can be seen as a set of strategies that have evolved over time to solve communicative problems. Examples include how to direct someone's attention to a particular entity, how to express basic relations among entities (who did what to whom), how to elicit specific kinds of information (what, where, when, etc.), how to indicate what information is new and what is assumed to be shared by the listener, and how to describe an event from the perspective of one participant rather than another. Strategies differ across languages, and the 'choices' a language makes for how to solve one kind of problem often have repercussions for how it may solve another. For instance, English uses word order to distinguish agent and patient (cf. 'Bill kissed Ellen' versus 'Ellen kissed Bill'). Turkish, in contrast, marks the direct object with a suffix (accusative case ending): *Bill Ellen-i öptü* 'Bill Ellen-accusative kissed' ('Bill kissed Ellen'). The use of explicit markers to indicate basic relationships among sentence elements leaves word order free to express other meanings, such as emphasis or speaker perspective. For example, simply by switching the positions of agent and patient – *Ellen-i Bill öptü* 'Ellen-accusative Bill kissed' – a speaker of Turkish can convey that 'It was *Bill* who kissed Ellen.' To express this meaning in English requires the use of emphatic stress or a special construction, or both (as shown here).

Form

Within this perspective on language structure, children's task is to work out the mapping between form and function (e.g., to discover the devices their language uses for communicating information of various kinds). Research since the 1970s has yielded substantial insights into how children approach the 'form' side of the mapping problem. For example, drawing on acquisition data from many different languages, Slobin (1985–1997, Vol. II) has explored which kinds of form-meaning mappings are easy for children and which are more difficult (i.e., learned later with more errors). Such data provide clues to learners' procedures for discovering and representing linguistic structure. For example, children do better with mappings that are 'iconic,' in the sense that the meaning to be communicated is in some way diagrammed or mirrored by the arrangement of the linguistic elements (e.g., when each element of meaning is expressed by one element of form, or the order in which two events take place is reflected in the order of clauses within a sentence). In further studies of the learning of forms, Tomasello (2003) and his colleagues have explored how children build up knowledge of grammatical structure over time, arguing that – contrary to generativist claims – learners' early grammars lack system-wide syntactic categories or parameters, and are instead item-based, reflecting, for example, knowledge of how to combine particular verbs with other elements.

Meaning

In much functionally oriented work on language acquisition, it has been assumed that while forms vary, the meanings to be expressed are more or less universal. Several factors have contributed to this view. Firstly, cross-linguistic work of the 1970s showed that, all over the world, children's first word combinations revolve around a restricted set of meanings to do with agency, action, location, possession, and the existence, recurrence, non-existence, and disappearance of objects. These were exactly the kinds of meanings that Piaget had stressed in his work on sensorimotor development, which suggested that children's early meanings originate through universal cognitive processes, and are later mapped onto language (Brown, 1973). Further inspiration came from early cross-linguistic studies of semantic categorization in adult languages (e.g., the domain of color terms), which suggested that semantic variation is more strongly constrained than had been supposed. Children's early meanings often show striking correspondences to candidate semantic universals, which has suggested that the organization of meaning both in languages and in language learners is molded by fundamental propensities of human perception and cognition (E. V. Clark in Bowerman & Levinson, 2001).

Meanings of grammatical elements

A domain for which semantic correspondences between child and adult speech have been explored in particular detail is that of grammatical elements or 'closed class' forms (e.g., tense and agreement markers on verbs, plural markers and case endings on nouns, prepositions, conjunctions). In adult languages, these elements (as opposed to 'open class' items like nouns and verbs) convey restricted and schematic kinds of information (e.g., whether an entity is one or more than one – book versus books – but not that there are exactly five of them, or that their color is red). One explanation attributes these special meanings to biases inherent in the language learner. For instance, Slobin (1985–1997, Vol. II) proposed that children come to the language acquisition task with a pre-structured semantic space in which there is a "privileged set of grammaticizable notions" to which grammatical elements are initially mapped. Although the forms that get mapped vary across languages, of course, the meanings themselves are constant, and the result is a "universally specifiable 'Basic Child Grammar' that reflects an underlying ideal form of human language." A related hypothesis is Bickerton's (1981) proposal for an innate 'language bioprogram' – a universal cognitive/semantic sub-stratum for language that privileges certain meaning distinctions over others.

In a recent reconceptualization of the problem, Slobin has concluded that it is not, after all, necessary to explain the special meanings of grammatical elements by building them directly into the child (D. I. Slobin in Bowerman & Levinson, 2001). He argues that the schematic nature of these meanings can be adequately accounted for by reference to discourse factors that guide 'grammaticization', the diachronic process through which forms such as nouns or verbs may, over time, become restricted in their positioning, phonologically reduced, and semantically 'bleached,' until eventually they end up as new grammatical elements. This example shows that semantic universals can in principle be accounted for in different ways (e.g., by reference either to semantic predispositions inherent in the child, or to discourse processes at play in rapid speech among fluent speakers).

Semantic and syntactic bootstrapping

A second area in which a close relationship has been posited between language acquisition and semantic universals is that of 'argument linking' – the mapping between the semantic roles associated with a verb, such as agent and patient, and the syntactic treatment of the noun phrases that play these roles. Both within and across languages, there are strong regularities in this mapping (e.g., in most languages an agent argument appears as the subject of a sentence, and a patient argument as the direct object of the verb).

According to generative linguistic approaches to language acquisition, these regularities suggest that linking rules are innate, which means that children can draw on them to solve important acquisition problems. According to the hypothesis of 'semantic bootstrapping' put forward by Pinker (1984), children use meaning to predict syntax. For example, they assume that if a word names the agent of an action (like "Daddy," in "Daddy threw the ball"), it is the subject of its sentence. From this starting point, they can work out further properties of the target language, such as the basic ordering of subject, verb, and object. A second proposal, 'syntactic bootstrapping' (Gleitman, 1990), runs the process the other way, from syntax to meaning: when faced with a new verb, the child uses the number and syntactic arrangement of its arguments to make a first-pass prediction about its meaning (e.g., in "Mary *blicks* the ball to John," *blick* is likely to be a verb of object transfer, such as 'give,' while in "Mary *blicks* that the ball is red," it is probably a verb of perception or cognition, such as 'see' or 'think').

Like the question of whether children are really pre-disposed to assign certain kinds of meanings to grammatical elements, semantic and syntactic bootstrapping have been hotly debated. Some critics focus on whether linking regularities are indeed universal enough to plausibly be considered innate, while others argue that children's knowledge of semantic-syntactic correspondences is built up over time in a process of schema abstraction (Goldberg, 1995; Tomasello, 2003).

Cross-linguistic variation in the structure of meaning

Since the early 1990s there has been a trend away from emphasis on universals of meaning and their role in language acquisition, and toward exploration of cross-linguistic differences in semantic structure. Languages may be constrained, but they are by no means identical: in every conceptual domain, there is significant variation in the categories of meanings to which the forms of language are linked. Wherever there is variation, children's non-linguistic conceptualizations of the world cannot be counted on to supply directly the meanings to be encoded. Between non-linguistic cognition and the forms of language lies another level of linguistic

organization that has often been neglected in research on language development, namely, the semantic system of the target language. Current studies often stress that, just as learners must discover the syntax, morphology, and phonology of their language, so too must they work out its semantic system (Bowerman & Levinson, 2001, Part 4).

One kind of semantic difference among languages lies in what *must* be said – obligatory categories of meaning. For example, speakers of English must indicate in every sentence the time of the situation being talked about (a tensed verb is obligatory). Speakers of Turkish must also specify time, but, in addition, they must indicate (for past events) how they know about the situation (through direct perception versus hearsay or inference). Speakers of Mandarin, in contrast, need specify neither of these meanings. Children must, then, determine which meanings must be marked in their language, and which are optional, or left to inference.

A second and more fundamental kind of semantic difference across languages lies in the partitioning of basic conceptual domains such as space, time, and causality (e.g., how many categories are distinguished, and what these categories encompass). For example, the English prepositions *in* and *on* pick out concepts of 'containment' and 'support' that seem fundamental to native speakers of this language. But many languages lack close translation equivalents for these words, and classify spatial situations according to different criteria. Compare, for example, the classification of four spatial manipulations in English (Fig. 1A) and Korean (Fig. 1B): the English distinction between containment and support is crosscut in Korean by the category picked out by the verb *kkita*, which is used for fitting objects with complementary shapes snugly together regardless of whether the moved object goes 'into' or 'onto' the stationary object (M. Bowerman & S. Choi in Bowerman & Levinson, 2001).

Acquiring a language-specific semantic system

Recent research has shown that children tune in to language-specific classification principles remarkably early (Bowerman & Levinson, 2001.) For example, learners of English and Korean reveal sensitivity to the language-specific spatial categories shown in Figure 1 by as early as 18 to 24 months, both in their early production of spatial forms and in their comprehension, even before production begins. By the one- and two-word stage, very young children learning Tzeltal, a Mayan language of Mexico, sub-divide 'eating' events more finely than children learning English, using different verbs, as is appropriate, for eating meat versus soft things versus crunchy things. These studies suggest that in addition to mapping already-available concepts

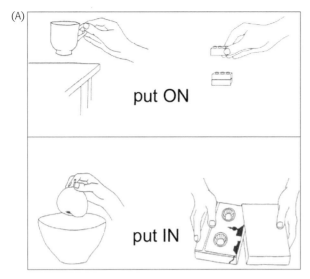

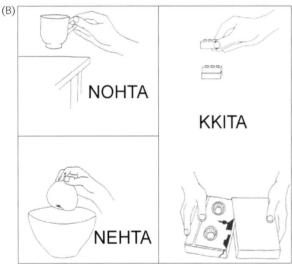

Figure 1. A – Semantic classification of four actions in English; B – Semantic classification of four actions in Korean.

directly to the forms of language, children may be capable, even from a very young age, of *constructing* categories of meaning through observing the distribution of forms across contexts in the speech of fluent speakers.

One factor that may contribute to rapid, language-specific acquisition is that cross-linguistic semantic variation is not unrestrained, but tends to pattern along a limited number of dimensions. As noted earlier, limitations on semantic variation might reflect either inborn cognitive-perceptual constraints or the shaping of meaning by the demands of fluent discourse; either way, the fewer the possibilities the child has to consider, the more tractable the learning task. Another factor that may facilitate early language-specific semantic development is that although there is diversity in the organization of meaning *across* languages, systems tend to be coherent *within* languages. For example, English characteristically encodes the path of motion with *particles* (e.g., 'go *in, out, down*'), while Spanish provides

verbs for this purpose (*entrar* 'go in'; *salir* 'go out' *bajar* 'go down'). These languages exemplify two of the major typological patterns according to which languages express motion (Talmy, 1985), where 'typology' refers to how languages cohere into distinct 'types' in their characteristic solutions to given communicative problems. The existence of intra-language systematicity means that whatever children have already learned about one part of their language can help them to make accurate predictions about other parts. This process has been termed 'typological bootstrapping' (D. I. Slobin in Bowerman & Levinson, 2001).

Influence of language on thought?

In the last few years, renewed attention to language-specificity in the organization of meaning has led to a resurgence of interest in an old question: does the language we learn affect the way we think about the world (the Whorfian hypothesis)? The possibility of linguistic influences on thought (perception, memory, similarity judgments, problem-solving, etc.) was for many years summarily rejected, but recently there have been several tantalizing lines of evidence. For example: (1) the presence of a distinction between two copulas in Spanish (*ser* 'to be' for inherent properties and *estar* 'to be' for transient properties) is associated with an earlier appreciation of the 'appearance-reality' distinction in learners of Spanish than in learners of English (Sera, 1997); (2) in early childhood, learners of both English and Yucatec Mayan strongly tend to classify objects by shape. This preference continues into adulthood for English speakers, but for Yucatec speakers it declines by 7–9 years of age and is replaced by a preference for material. These differences were predicted on the basis of systematic differences in the semantics of nouns in the two languages (J. Lucy & S. Gaskins in Bowerman & Levinson, 2001); and (3) adults who have learned a language that habitually presents spatial situations from the speaker's perspective (e.g., 'the cup is *to the left of / behind the bowl*') solve spatial problems differently from adults who have learned languages that habitually use a geocentric perspective ('the cup is *to the west of / uphill of the bowl*') (Levinson in Bowerman & Levinson, 2001). Of course, the proper interpretation of such findings is controversial, but the recent stress on language specificity has brought the relationship between language and thought back into the mainstream, and we can expect much future work on this issue.

Conclusions

Over the last several decades, there has been a close relationship between the study of linguistics and the study of child language development. Following Chomsky, linguists have often explained hypothesized language universals by attributing them to properties of the child's inborn capacity for language acquisition. In their turn, acquisitionists have tried to explain how children draw on this innate knowledge to work out the structure of the language being acquired. The ensuing debates have typically revolved around what kind of innate knowledge of language structure, if any, it is plausible to attribute to the child.

Recent years have seen the rise of alternative 'usage-based' linguistic frameworks that emphasize cognitive and functional motivations for syntax and morphology, and describe the structure of any particular language as a complex set of interacting strategies, constantly in flux, for solving communicative problems. These approaches are attractive to child language researchers who favor 'learning' over 'innate knowledge,' because the child's task can be seen as one of discovering the mapping between forms (words, grammatical morphemes, construction patterns) and their meanings. Early attempts to understand the acquisition of form-meaning mapping concentrated primarily on the forms, with the assumption that the meanings are supplied by non-linguistic cognition and so are more or less universal. But researchers now emphasize that there are in fact striking differences in the way languages partition conceptual domains. To the extent that semantic categories differ across languages, the traditional assumption that children map the forms of language directly onto non-linguistic concepts becomes less plausible. Rather, the acquisition of semantic categories begins to look like an integral part of linguistic development, albeit a process that must interact with children's non-linguistic conceptual understanding of the world.

In the coming years, cognitive-functional approaches to linguistics are likely to take on increasing importance for the study of language acquisition. On the one hand, scholars are attempting to characterize the mechanisms for pattern finding and schema abstraction that children use to discover patterns of form-meaning mapping in their language. On the other hand, they are trying to determine how the construction of language-specific semantic categories draws upon, interacts with, and possibly even influences children's general conceptual understanding of the world. Both developments will tend to pull the study of language acquisition back closer to traditional concerns of developmental psychologists than has been the case for child language research carried out within the framework of generative grammar.

See also:
Constructivist theories; Theories of the child's mind; Cross-cultural comparisons; Cognitive development beyond infancy; Language development; Williams syndrome; Ethology; Jean Piaget

Further reading

Berman, R. and Slobin, D. I. (eds.) (1994). *Relating Events in Narrative: A Crosslinguistic Developmental Study.* Hillsdale, NJ: Erlbaum.

Gentner, D. and Goldin-Meadow, S. (eds.) (2003). *Language in Mind: Advances in the Study of Language and Thought.* Cambridge, MA: MIT Press.

Pinker, S. (1989). *Learnability and Cognition: The Acquisition of Argument Structure.* Cambridge, MA: MIT Press.

Pediatrics

MARTIN C. O. BAX

Introduction

Although Hippocrates (460–377 BP) wrote about specific diseases in children and the Elizabethan physician Thomas Phaire (1510–date of death unknown) wrote his book on children in 1545, the notion of doctors specializing in child health as opposed to all health did not really develop until the 1930s. It was during the early years of the 20th century that European and American pediatricians began to be appointed or set up in practice and soon after that associations of pediatricians were formed. It is of interest that children's hospitals had been built in the 19th century to deal with the very large numbers of sick children there were, but doctors saw no reason to specialize in caring for children. The reason for this was partly that acute infectious diseases and mortality in children had such high incidences, and at that time doctors did not perceive any particular difference between illness in adults as opposed to children, although children were clearly more vulnerable and had high mortality rates from these illnesses.

In one year in the early 1800s, infant mortality rates in the City of London were actually recorded as being over 100%, infant mortality being the percentage of deaths to the number of births. In that year not only every infant born in the city died, but also those who had been brought into the city from outside. It was only as public health measures and hygiene began to evolve and started to bring this terrible mortality under control that the specific diseases of children, or those starting in childhood, began to be recognized.

The contributions of Down, Freud, and others to the emergence of pediatrics

Another development in the 18th century was the recognition that lunatics and criminals should be separated. Chronic conditions that originated in childhood were recognized, and doctors began to look beyond the acute illnesses to pathologies that affected the child's growth and development. Famously in 1887, John Langdon Down (Fig. 1) gave his Lettsomian lectures on the mental affections of childhood and youth (reprinted in 1990 under the title *Mental Affection of Childhood and Youth*). He should be recognized as probably one of the first pediatricians as he opened his lecture by saying:

> I bethought myself that mental devotions in childhood and youth have never been the subject of a disquisition from this chair and that probably a period of nearly 30 years spent among children with various phases of mental affection might entitle me to bring before the members of the Society material, which from the nature of the subject can only be accumulated by a few.
>
> (p. 1)

Children with what he termed idiocy had particular characteristics. Again, he recognized developmental problems: "Their language is one of gesture only. Living in a world of their own they are regardless of the ordinary circumstances around them and yield only to the counter fascination of music." Down's description of those 'idiots' whom he called 'mongols' is discussed elsewhere in this volume.

It is interesting to note another famous Victorian physician who was interested in diseases of children initially: Sigmund Freud (1856–1939). His book on the cerebral palsies, published in the 1890s, was preceded by work on aphasias. In a brief section on 'idiocy,' he noted the fact that many children with cerebral palsy were retarded in their mental development. The writings of Langdon Down and Freud signaled the beginning of a move in medicine from mere anecdote to some systematic account of the problems of childhood. Another person who should be mentioned here is Hector Charles Cameron (1878–1958) who wrote a book entitled *The Nervous Child*, initially published in 1919. He eventually became the first physician to be put in charge of the Children's Department at Guy's Hospital in London. In his book, he presented a systematic account of the child's development from the nursery through to maturity. He

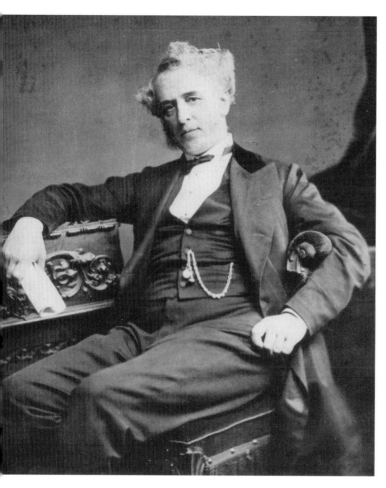

Figure 1. John Langdon Down (1832–1896), by kind permission of the John Langdon Down Centre.

Figure 2. Albrecht Peiper (1889–1968).

wrote sensibly about feeding and sleeping disorders in the young child. In the older child, he recognized the importance of positive reinforcement of appropriate behavior, as opposed to the opposite course of rebuking inappropriate behavior.

It should be noted that pediatrics, unlike other specialities (except for geriatrics), is a specialization in a group of people rather than a part of the body (as, for example, cardiology, surgery, and neurology, all of which are specializations in adults). This has many advantages as the health professional is involved in the needs of the whole child, and attempts to take a comprehensive approach to the child and the problems of the family. Inevitably, however, sub-speciality has crept in so that there are now neurologists, cardiologists, orthopedic surgeons, and the like who specialize in these particular areas in pediatrics. Some countries have resisted this specialization, so, for example, in Denmark there are no pediatric neurologists. There could be a similar discussion about the different sub-groups of psychologists who are involved in the care of children.

During the early part of the 20th century, physicians were beginning to be appointed who specialized in pediatrics. Initially, they were more interested in the acute illnesses that resulted in children being taken to hospital, but over time they began to be increasingly attracted to understanding aspects of childhood disease that had a bearing on the child's psychological development. The first major publication that retains considerable interest today was that of Albrecht Peiper whose *Cerebral Function in Infancy and Childhood* (1962) initially appeared in the 1920s (Fig. 2).

Peiper had major interests in all aspects of development and carried out many studies on topics such as, for example, the development of respiration. His studies of locomotion showed that neonatal stepping (or what others have called primary walking) was not subjected to labyrinthine influences. This is demonstrated very clearly in Figure 3, which shows a newborn held upside down by Peiper ascending a staircase fastened to the ceiling and stepping across a horizontal surface. In his chapter on the environment, he talks about attachment and behavior under the heading 'Home Sickness.' He was one of the first people to recognize fully the dangers of separating mother and child, and was familiar with the early work of John Bowlby (1907–1990) and Konrad Lorenz (1903–1986).

Pediatricians and developmental psychologists: differences in approach to child assessment

An advantage pediatricans often have over psychologists is that they see a large number of children. For example, when I worked in a Child Health Clinic at Guy's Hospital in London, on average, in three and a half hours, between twelve and eighteen children and their parents would be seen. In the short time available, an assessment of the child's development would be routinely made. I stress assessment and not a screening examination. Later in research, when we compared our assessments of language against those made by developmental psychologists, we found that there was a very high correlation in those children whom we thought had potential developmental language delay at the age of 3. The difference is that we had done the assessment in our overall twenty-minute paediatric evaluation (Bax, Hart, & Jenkins, 1990), in contrast to psychologists who took at least thirty minutes using the Reynell language test. Furthermore, we categorized the outcome as normal, possibly abnormal, definitely abnormal, whereas the psychologists came up with a quantitative score.

The advantages of both approaches seemed to me obvious, and the importance of collaboration emphasized. The children whom we classified as having a definite delay were all scored by the psychologists as being below 1.5 standard deviation on the Reynell Test, except in one case that we had scored as having normal, possibly delayed, language. However, on inspecting the Reynell form, we found that the psychologists had been unable in many instances to get a response from this child for particular items. We had scored the child's language based on a rich vocabulary of obscenities that we had heard. Thus, we considered the child to have a very significant behavioral problem, and identified that as the principal issue to be confronted with this child.

Three ways in which pediatricians collaborate with developmental psychologists

Developmental psychology now informs many of the activities and approaches used by pediatricians toward children with acute and chronic illness. Some of developmental psychology's findings, such as the benefit of encouraging parents to stay with their sick child, are now readily put into practice in most hospital pediatric wards and clinics. However, actual collaboration between pediatricians and developmental psychologists can be highlighted by discussing their rather specific

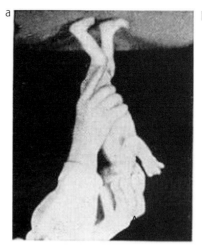

Figure 3. Newborn stepping upside down on a horizontal surface (a) and ascending a small staircase affixed to the ceiling (b). For Peiper, stepping under these conditions was evidence that the labyrinthines did not play a role in this neonatal response.

roles with three groups of children: (1) assessment of neonates; (2) dealing with children who are routinely subjected to developmental (functional) assessment; and (3) diagnosing or treating children with disabilities and behavioral problems.

Neonatal assessment

From the 1960s onward, pediatricians began to care for preterm infants. Now, all over the developed world, most maternity hospitals have Special Care or Premature Baby Units (Neonatal Intensive Care Units, NICUs) into which something like 6–7 percent of infants will be admitted. About half that number will spend a substantial amount of time (several weeks) in the Unit. Since the 1990s, very small infants born after only 24–26 weeks' gestation have been cared for in these Units. Apart from taking physiological measures, the neonatologist needs to understand at what level the newborn is developmentally. This is to gain some understanding of the child's functional ability (e.g., sucking and swallowing are not integrated until 34 weeks, thus allowing one to estimate the child's actual age and which, of course, reflects back to function). Moreover, the neonatologist has to make some clinical assessments of the child's condition.

Prechtl's (1977) manual on the neurological examination of the healthy fullterm normal newborn includes the description of classic, age-specific neurological signs, but also begins to look at developmental patterns. His more recent work on spontaneous movements, which has involved some collaboration with developmental psychologists, traces the pattern of developmental changes in the output of the motor system from prenatal life to the early postnatal weeks and months. Other aspects of the developing neuro-motor function have been studied by looking at sucking and swallowing abilities in newborns (Gewold *et al.*, 2003).

As an adjunct to the mother's estimate of the date of the onset of the gestation, the Dubowitz scale (Dubowitz & Mercuri, 1999) has been developed to estimate gestational age from the time of conception. In contrast, the Brazelton Newborn Neonatal Behavioral Assessment Scale (Brazelton & Nugent, 1995), devised in collaboration with developmental psychologists, attempts to capture many aspects of the fullterm newborn's behavioral repertoire. The scale has been used, for example, to evaluate potential insults to the brain in babies born to women who used drugs such as cocaine during pregnancy.

A proportion of all babies from NICUs go on to have significant neurodevelopmental problems. These include cerebral palsy, since half of children with this disorder are born prematurely. In addition to abnormal neurological findings, most who eventually manifest cerebral palsy will have a developmental delay. Children who have been in NICUs may have other difficulties later on including behavioral and learning problems. The neonatologist has urgent need of the assistance of developmental psychologists to study the later development of preterm infants, and to ensure that babies from NICU have their outcomes monitored. The developmental psychologist's training in behavioral assessment allows him or her to advise parents about care. The information obtained needs to be used to ensure that neonatal care can be further developed.

Developmental assessments

In all parts of the developed world, children are seen by pediatricians on a regular basis and, depending on the circumstances, by other health personnel such as physiotherapists. The aim is to monitor not only physical health and growth, but also development across a number of domains. Building on the work of Arnold Gesell, developmental scales have been devised by pediatricians such as William Frankenberg in the USA, with his Denver Developmental Scale, and by the likes of Ronald S. Illingworth (1909–1990) and Mary D. Sheridan in the UK. In such instances, the scales have been developed in collaboration with developmental psychologists. Other scales are the products of psychologists such as Nancy Bayley (1899–1994) in the USA and Ruth F. Griffiths (1895–1973) in the UK working closely with pediatricians.

In most parts of the developed world, some sort of assessment takes place when the child enters school, and to a varying degree the child is followed up in a Child Development Center. The pediatrician who carries out these assessments may choose to include a neurologically based developmental examination. If any evidence is found of developmental delay, help is often sought from a developmental psychologist and others, such as speech and language therapists, physiotherapists, and occupational therapists. Developing assessment instruments for children is a fruitful area for multi-disciplinary cooperation. It is also an area of great contention as there are differing views in different countries as to what is an appropriate way to try to monitor the developmental status of a population. Nevertheless, the concept of neurodevelopmental disorders is broadly recognized.

Children with disabilities

As infectious diseases began to be overcome and chronic illnesses such as tuberculosis were beginning to disappear from the developed world, pediatricians found they had time to look at the 'idiots and imbeciles' who had attracted the attention of Langdon Down. Many of these children at the time (1950s, 1960s) were in long-stay hospitals with minimal medical staffing and minimal treatment or management. In many developed countries, these institutions have now been largely closed down and the care of such children is carried out at home. There remain, however, many parts of the world where quite large numbers of children are still in institutions (e.g., the former Soviet Union). Children with disabilities, and they are usually neurodisabilities, are now seen, assessed, and diagnosed at some sort of Child Development or Disability Center in the UK, and there are now some 300 or more of these centers spread round the country. In these centers, pediatricians and psychologists, together with therapists, will jointly assess children and, together with the family, develop a management plan.

Many children with disabilities have some developmental delay, but also often some abnormalities of development (e.g., those with the Prader Willi syndrome have feeding difficulties). With the recent emergence of the field of behavioral phenotypes (O'Brien, 2002), the investigations routinely carried out by the pediatrician have become of more value to the developmental psychologist, and help in better understanding the child's problems. Thus, in the Prader Willi syndrome, the lack of any sense of satiety leads to gross overfeeding and, unless controlled, excessive weight gain will ensue. Genetic investigations, while in early stages at present, will eventually clearly provide much more information not only about the child's likely prognosis or outcome, but also about behavior and developmental profiles.

Conclusions

In addition to genetic investigations, some sort of imaging such as Magnetic Resonance Imaging (MRI) may be carried out on the child's brain. Currently, this is usually done in a static situation and, while abnormal findings will indicate that there has been damage to the brain, scans are not always predictive of a one-to-one basis of outcome. Thus, as an example, in terms of movement, the child with the form of cerebral palsy known as spastic diplegia will usually have damage to the periventricular white matter in posterior areas, but the extent of the damage and the clinical features in the child are often not very highly correlated. With more complex disabilities such as reading problems, evidence from MRI scanning of some damage in an area of brain associated with language development may be of doubtful significance. However, various forms of functional imaging are becoming available. For example, it is possible to demonstrate, with functional scanning, activity in different parts of the brain in a child with attention deficit hyperactivity disorder (ADHD), compared to the brain of one without these difficulties.

We used single photon emission computed tomography to compare regional blood flow in a normal child and a child with ADHD. The child with ADHD had lower flow in the striatal regions and high flow in occipital regions. Many similar studies have been performed showing, for example, different cortical blood flows when a person is reading as opposed to listening (Born & Lou, 1999).

While there are 2 percent of children who have a moderate to severe disability, there are a further 10 percent who have some specific learning disorder such as ADHD, dyslexia, or dysgraphia (Whitmore, Hart, & Willems, 1999). The application of this new technology mentioned above will require in future close cooperation between psychology and medicine. The work of the pediatric neurologist and the neuro-imager in identifying areas of the brain that show abnormalities will need to be interpreted in terms of the functional outcome. Bearing in mind that while there is now a good general correlation often displayed between findings on neuroimaging and function, this is not always the case. The assessment of behavior and the cognitive functions of the child by the psychologist will need to be intimately linked to the work of the pediatrician in describing and understanding the basic impairments within the central nervous system. It is in these sorts of disorders where the use of functional imaging, and the collaboration between pediatric neurologists and developmental psychologists, have much to offer in the future.

See also:

Neuromaturational theories; Magnetic Resonance Imaging; Developmental testing; Normal and abnormal prenatal development; The status of the human newborn; Motor development; Language development; Attention; Brain and behavioral development (I): sub-cortical; Brain and behavioral development (II): cortical; 'At-risk' concept; Behavioral and learning disorders; Cerebral palsies; Developmental coordination disorder; Down's syndrome; Hearing disorders; Prematurity and low birthweight; Behavior genetics; Cognitive neuroscience; Sociology; John Bowlby; Milestones of motor development and indicators of biological maturity

Further reading

Aicardi, J. (1998). *Diseases of the Nervous System in Children*. London: Mac Keith Press.
Behrman, R. E., Kliegman, R. M. and Jensen, H. B. (2003). *Nelson Textbook of Pediatrics*, 17th. edn. Amsterdam: Elsevier.
Rutter, M., Graham, P., Yule, W. and Birch, H. (1970). *A Neuropsychiatric Study in Childhood*. London: Heinemann.

Sociology

ELIZABETH G. MENAGHAN

Introduction

How can the work of sociologists and of developmental psychologists enrich each other? Although divergent starting points and emphases make this difficult, researchers in both fields have begun to bridge disciplinary boundaries to provide new knowledge. Each field brings different emphases to these collaborations: sociologists highlight social arrangements, organizations, and patterns, as well as social interaction between and among individuals and groups, whereas developmental psychologists focus on internal processes within individuals. Both are concerned with the scope and generalizability of their theories and findings, but sociologists are more likely to consider whether these are maintained across major social categories defined by education, income, socio-economic status, region, race-ethnicity, and sex, while developmentalists ask how they vary by age or developmental stage. When sociologists *do* consider age, they often conceptualize it in terms of age-linked social expectations or social constraints, rather than as capturing something about the human organism or psyche that changes predictably over time.

Despite these disciplinary biases and blinders, there are encouraging indications that these barriers are not impassable. We can identify collaborations in data collection and data analysis that draw on the strengths of both fields, as well as studies that challenge and enrich both areas.

National longitudinal studies as arenas for collaboration

Regarding data, one major example in the United States is the development of longitudinal studies of infants, children, and adolescents that are linked to extensive interviews with one or both of their parents. The National Longitudinal Survey of Youth – 1979 (NLSY79), begun in 1979 to follow a nationally representative cohort of young men and women born between 1958 and 1965 as they moved into work and family roles, was dramatically expanded in 1986 to begin following all of the children who had been born to all of the women in this study. Interviews and direct assessments of these children have been conducted every other year. By 2002, these children numbered more than 9,000, and for the oldest children these data included information at nine time points spanning eighteen years of their lives.

This effort combined traditional sociological survey research methods with expertise from the child development research community to identify age-appropriate assessment domains and measures. Sociologists also developed workshops and user guides that helped to acquaint developmental psychologists with this new data resource and with large-scale surveys more generally. A special section of the November 1991 issue of the journal *Developmental Psychology* highlighted the possibilities that such large data sources contained (Chase-Lansdale, Mott, Brooks-Gunn, & Phillips, 1991).

Other large US national longitudinal data sets include the National Educational Longitudinal Surveys (NELS), which follow adolescents who were 8th graders in 1988; the National Longitudinal Study of Adolescent Health (Add Health), which has been following adolescents in grades 7–12 since 1994; the National Institute for Child Health and Human Development (NICHD) Study of Early Child Care, which follows over 1,300 children from ten sites from birth through grade 5; and the Early Childhood Longitudinal Studies (ECLS), one of which (ECLS-B) follows 13,500 children born in 2001 from 9 months of age through first grade, and the other of which (ECLS-K) follows about 22,000 children who entered kindergarten in fall 1998 from their first year of kindergarten through fifth grade. Cross-national analyses are possible using similar surveys conducted in other countries, such as Canada's National Longitudinal Survey of Children and Youth (NLSCY) and the United

Kingdom's National Child Development Study of children born in 1958 (Table 1).

These large data collection efforts highlight the combination of traditional sociological methodologies regarding systematic and representative sampling and closed-ended interviewing with concerns regarding developmental processes and trajectories, and bring together social demographers, economists, sociological social psychologists, and life-course analysts with developmental psychologists. The prospective longitudinal approach taken, rather than cross-sectional snapshots at single points in time, is a major strength of these efforts. As these studies continue over time, they permit analyses of how aspects of early development may be linked to later opportunities and difficulties, and to adult social and economic status and family formation. Their size and representativeness also permit analyses of how these links may vary for children in differing birth cohorts and in differing social and economic circumstances.

Other collaborations intentionally depart from representative sampling to focus on a high-risk segment of the population. For example, Furstenberg *et al.*'s(1999) book, *Managing to Make it: Urban Families and Adolescent Success*, focuses on 500 families living in impoverished Philadelphia neighborhoods. Examining neighborhood conditions, parental strategies, and adolescent development, this multidisciplinary team documents the wide range in parenting competence among low-income parents, and the importance of that competence for adolescent outcomes.

The life-course perspective

Perhaps the strongest theoretical and substantive links from sociology to child development have been made by sociologists who embrace life-course principles. As articulated most clearly by sociologist Glen H. Elder, the life-course perspective emphasizes that: (1) individuals are agents who make choices within social constraints; (2) these choices have emerging consequences for themselves and for those whose lives are linked with theirs; and (3) both historical context and developmental age must be taken into account in understanding individual and family trajectories. Elder's landmark study, *Children of the Great Depression*, first published in 1974, demonstrated that small differences in children's age at the time their families experienced severe economic losses altered the meaning and consequences of that experience. Those old enough to 'pitch in' and contribute labor to the household were less negatively affected, while younger children were less able to understand the difficulties their families faced, less able to feel themselves part of any adaptations made,

and more vulnerable to parental anger or depression. Following up these children years later, Elder also explored how the timing of their military experiences in the Second World War further qualified and sometimes re-shaped their life chances and later adult outcomes.

Sara McLanahan's work on family composition and child and adolescent outcomes similarly suggests that the timing of parents' marital disruption matters in part because the behaviors associated with greater distress around the time of the breakup have differing social consequences at different ages. For example, younger children might act out in school and play groups with relatively few long-term consequences, while the same upheaval and misbehavior in the high school years may be associated with poorer school records and higher drop out, as well as early sexual debut and its associated risks. Finally, consistent with a life-course orientation, family sociologists increasingly focus not only on socialization efforts by parents and other adults, but on children as agents of their own socialization.

The social stress perspective

Sociologists working within social stress frameworks, such as those developed by Pearlin *et al.*(1981), also have clear theoretical and substantive links to developmental psychology. Key to the idea of social stress is its attention both to objective social demands and circumstances, and to the social and psychological resources that children and adults can mobilize. Stress occurs when there is a discrepancy between these resources and demands. Thus, the same event or condition may have much larger effects depending on factors such as age, family supports, and individual attitudes, particularly self-esteem and mastery.

Recent work in this tradition has re-awakened a greater appreciation for the long-term importance of childhood experience. Sociologists studying social stress and mental health have long emphasized the impact of *current* circumstances on mental health and illness, and have typically focused on adult rather than child samples. But Kessler and Shanyang (1999) showed that current social circumstances are not as tightly linked to current mental health outcomes as theorized. By collecting information about both social circumstances and mental health as well as illness and organizing it by age, they found that most episodes of diagnosable mental illness in adulthood are *not* first episodes, but recurrences that occur to the sub-set of people who have already had a prior episode. This finding pushes the search for factors shaping adult mental health back earlier into the life course, and calls for increased attention to childhood and adolescent experiences that may create long-term reductions in individual

Table 1. Longditudinal surveys of child development.

Title and acronym	Nation	Starting date	Age range at initial round	Sample size initial round	Substantive focus	Web site
Early Childhood Longitudinal Studies-Birth (ECLS-B)	United States	2001	9 months	13,500	child development; child care; early school years	www.nichd.nih.gov/about/cpr/dbs/res_early.htm http://nces.ed.gov/ecls/
Early Childhood Longitudinal Studies-Kindergarten (ECLS-K)	United States	1998	Students entering kindergarten	22,000	transition to school grades K-5	www.nichd.nih.gov/about/cpr/dbsr/res_early.htm http://nces.ed.gov/ecls/
National Child Development Study (NCDS)	United Kingdom	1958	Birth	17,000	child development	www.cls.ioe.ac.uk/Ncds/nhome.htm
Linked: Children of the National Child Development Study (C-NCDS)	United Kingdom	1991	Birth	4,229	family processes; cognitive skills; social behavior	www.nichd.nih.gov/about/cpr/dbs/res_child.htm
National Educational Longitudinal Surveys (NELS)	United States	1988	Students in 8th grade	24,599	education	http://nces.ed.gov/surveys/nels88/
National Longitudinal Survey of Youth (NLSY79) Child-Mother Data Set	United States	1986	Birth to age 14	5,255	family processes; cognitive skills; social behavior	www.bls.gov/nls/nlsy79ch.htm www.chrr.ohio-state.edu/nls-info/
National Longitudinal Survey of Children and Youth (NLSCY)	Canada	1994	Birth to age 11	22,000	child development	www.hrdc-drhc.gc.ca/sp-ps/arb-dgra/nlscy-elnej/home.shtml
National Longitudinal Study of Adolescent Health (AddHealth)	United States	1994–1995	Students in grades 7–12	21,000	health behaviors; health outcomes	www.nichd.nih.gov/about/cpr/dbs/res_add.htm www.cpc.unc.edu/addhealth/
Study of Early Child Care (NICHD SECC)	United States	1991	Birth	over 1,300	child care; parental care	http://secc.rti.org/summary.cfm

emotional and psychological resources, and thus increase vulnerability to later difficult circumstances.

New questions about development

Sociological work can also raise new questions about accepted ideas regarding developmental readiness and vulnerability. An intriguing example is the work of Arline Geronimus, Sanders Korenman, and Marianne Hillemeier, who have challenged assumptions that it is the psychological immaturity of adolescent mothers that adversely affects their children's social and cognitive development. Drawing on data from the NLSY79 study of mothers and children, they were able to identify sisters who shared the same social and economic circumstances in their families, but differed in whether they had become adolescent mothers, and to compare outcomes for their children. Despite postponing their first births at least five years later than their sisters, the older mothers did not have children with better outcomes. These investigators concluded that the poorer social and economic resources these sisters could command, not age at first birth in itself, are the culprits in producing worse outcomes.

A second example is the findings of recent welfare-to-work studies that have examined the effects of new policies requiring US mothers with very low incomes to increase their labor force participation in order to receive cash benefits. These studies typically posited high vulnerability of infants and toddlers to greater maternal absence from the home, but are instead reporting worse outcomes for adolescents. These findings suggest how ideas about children's developmental needs may affect the implementation of social policies and thus their consequences. At many of the sites studied, concern about very young children's vulnerability led to active efforts to mitigate harm by providing additional funds for infant and toddler child-care and after-school programs, but there were no parallel efforts for adolescents. Thus, these studies may be interpreted as supporting age-appropriate protective efforts for all children, rather than casting doubt on the idea of developmental vulnerabilities.

Conclusions

As these examples illustrate, the differing perspectives of sociologists and developmental psychologists can be usefully combined to improve research designs, and to suggest new and more complex arguments about both social circumstances and human development. Perhaps the most promising strategies for future data collection efforts and analyses are those that: (1) conceptualize both adults and children as active agents who make choices and attempt to shape their own lives, consider the role of both children and parents in forging the linkages between them, and collect data from both generations; (2) view individual lives within social contexts, develop more nuanced arguments regarding the theoretically important dimensions of those contexts, and improve the measurement of those dimensions; and (3) utilize longitudinal designs that study children and their families, as well as their social contexts, over considerable time periods. Ideally, these studies will embrace sufficient diversity in sex, social class, region, and ethnicity, as well as age, for researchers to be able to examine the generalizability of their explanations across social contexts.

Some of the most promising topics for further collaboration between sociologists and developmental psychologists are those that focus on work, family, and their inter-connections. Today, both occupational/economic circumstances and romantic/marital and parent-child relationships are characterized by increased uncertainties and discontinuities. Jobs disappear, family ties unravel, and community resources erode; over time, new occupational conditions may emerge, new partners may be found, and new communities joined. Children and adolescents observe the diversity of their parents' experiences, and also seek to understand and to shape their own emerging work identities and family commitments. These experiences are not likely to affect individuals uniformly, but will vary in their impacts depending on the resources that family and individuals bring to these experiences.

Multidisciplinary research should study how and under what conditions these experiences impact both parents and children. Examined conditions should include both resources and vulnerabilities that have their origins earlier in the life course, and those that are linked to current developmental stages. This simultaneous attention to both past and present, and to both social factors and psychological and developmental processes, promises to yield new insights for the future.

See also:
Clinical and non-clinical interview methods; Developmental testing; Parental and teacher rating scales; Epidemiological designs; Cross-sectional and longitudinal designs; Parenting and the family; Socialization; 'At-risk' concept; Education

Further reading

Elder, G. H., Jr., Modell, J. and Parke, R. D. (eds.) (1993). *Children in Time and Place: Developmental and Historical Insights.* New York: Cambridge University Press.

Mortimer, J. T. and Shanahan, M. J. (eds.) (2003). *Handbook of the Life Course.* New York: Kluwer Academic / Plenum.

Phelps, E., Furstenberg, F. F., Jr. and Colby, A. (eds.) (2002). *Looking at Lives: American Longitudinal Studies in the Twentieth Century.* New York: Russell Sage Foundation.

Appendices

1. Biographical sketches of key figures

Concise overviews are given of twelve historically important individuals whose work has had a major influence in formulating current theories of ontogenetic development. Reference is made in the companion website to others from a variety of disciplines who have also contributed in their disparate ways to theory and method as they relate to the study of individual development.

James Mark Baldwin: **Robert H. Wozniak**
Alfred Binet: **Peter Bryant**
John Bowlby: **Peter Fonagy**
Jerome S. Bruner: **David Olson**
George E. Coghill: **Ronald W. Oppenheim**
Erik Erikson: **Peter Fonagy**
Viktor Hamburger: **Ronald W. Oppenheim**
Jean Piaget: **Pierre Mounoud**
Wilhelm T. Preyer: **Kurt Kreppner**
Lev S. Vygotsky: **Eugene Subbotsky**
Heinz Werner: **Willis F. Overton & Ulrich Müller**
Donald Winnicott: **Peter Fonagy**

2. Milestones of motor development and indicators of biological maturity

Up-to-date norms for both the achievement of motor milestones and what constitute markers of biological maturity are presented in a readily accessible style. This important contribution complements those entries on 'Neuromaturational theories' (Part I), 'Developmental testing' (Part II), 'Motor development' (Part IV), and 'Pediatrics' (Part VII).

3. The statistics of quantitative genetic theory

A reader-friendly overview is presented of the main statistical techniques currently used in behavior genetics to separate the variance that can be attributed to genetic and environmental factors, as well as to their co-contributions in human development. In these respects, it serves as a very helpful addendum to the important entries concerned with 'Twin and adoption studies' (Part II) and 'Behavior genetics' (Part VII).

4. Glossary of terms

A limited glossary of some of the main terms used in each of the entries is provided. A more extensive version will be available on the companion web-site.

Biographical sketches of key figures

James Mark Baldwin (1861–1934)

ROBERT H. WOZNIAK

James Mark Baldwin published psychology's first well-controlled experimental studies of infant behavior, and elaborated a biosocial theory of development that introduced a new level of complexity into conceptualization of the mind, its evolutionary origins, ontogenetic growth, and sociocultural formation. Baldwin addressed topics as varied as the nature of developmental and evolutionary mechanisms, the relationship between reason and reality, the genesis of logic, and the nature and development in children of habit, imitation, creative invention, altruism, egoism, morality, social suggestibility, self-awareness, theory of mind, and enculturation. His use, and in some cases introduction of concepts such as multiplicity of self, ideal self, self-esteem, assimilation, accommodation, primary circular reaction, genetic logic, and genetic epistemology, exerted a formative influence on later scholars such as George Herbert Mead, Jean Piaget, and Lev Vygotsky.

Born in Columbia, South Carolina, on January 12, 1861, Baldwin attended Princeton (AB, 1884; MA, 1887; Ph.D. 1888), where he studied the Scottish mental philosophy of James McCosh (1811–1894), the experimental psychology of Wilhelm Wundt (1832–1920), and the mental evolutionism of Herbert Spencer (1820–1903). Much of Baldwin's later work can be seen as an attempt to transcend the limitations and contradictions inherent in these views (Wozniak, 1982).

Following a semester in Wundt's Leipzig laboratory, two years at Princeton as an instructor, and two years at Lake Forest University, Baldwin moved in 1889 to the University of Toronto. There, he carried out psychology's first systematic studies of infant reaching (*Science*, 1890–1893), and developed a passionate interest in the genesis of mind. Returning to Princeton in 1893, he soon published his two most important theoretical contributions, *Mental Development in the Child and the Race* (1895) and *Social and Ethical Interpretations in Mental Development* (1897).

Assuming that organisms naturally relate to objects by acting on them, Baldwin conceived of intellectual growth as a process of adaptation. All action, he argued, is characterized by 'habit' – a system of mental tendencies to action – and 'accommodation' – ability to vary activity in relationship to circumstance and to select progressively more useful actions. 'Circular reaction' – repetition of action with variation and selection – constitutes an invariant, functional mechanism through which the mind develops toward greater understanding of reality. This theory of sensorimotor adaptation was later incorporated into that of Piaget.

Baldwin, however, went beyond individual adaptation, extending his model to the genesis of the social self. Consciousness of self, he suggested, develops through social interaction in which social habit is accommodated to a changing social environment through circular social action. In social action, the child both imitates and elaborates on the behavior of social others. The consciousness of self thereby comes to reflect the consciousness of the other just as consciousness of the other reflects consciousness of self (a view adopted by G. H. Mead).

Finally, Baldwin recognized that the behavior of the social other exists in a broader social context from which it receives cultural meaning. He described this context as a "mass of organized tradition, custom, usage, social habit . . . already embodied in the institutions and ways of acting, thinking . . . of a given social group . . ."

(Baldwin, 1897, p. 301). This idea, among others, significantly influenced Vygotsky.

In 1903, Baldwin moved to Johns Hopkins University to work on a three-volume genetic epistemology, *Thought and Things* (1906–1911), tracing cognitive development from pre-logical through discursive to 'hyper-logical' thought. Dense and conceptually difficult, *Thought and Things* was little read and less appreciated.

In 1908, at the pinnacle of his career, Baldwin was arrested in a raid on a Baltimore bordello and forced to resign from Hopkins. The ensuing scandal led to his being ostracized from American psychology; and he spent most of the rest of his life in Europe. There he wrote an autobiography, *Between Two Wars* (1926). He died in Paris on November 9, 1934, and was buried in Princeton.

Alfred Binet (1857–1911)

PETER BRYANT

Alfred Binet, a gifted French experimental psychologist, was one of the first researchers to do systematic experimental work on children's perception and cognition. He also devised the first successful intelligence test. These two massive achievements qualify him well for the title of the father of the study of cognitive development.

Binet originally studied Law but, finding this subject uncongenial, taught himself Psychology. His first research, starting in 1882, was in the area of psychopathology. In this enterprise, he reached the conclusion, which influenced much of his later work on intelligence, that in the study of abnormal behavior one "must start with the normal state" before concluding anything about what constituted the abnormalities.

Binet did his initial developmental research with his own two daughters. His reports of this work in 1890 showed that he was already interested in developmental changes (Pollack and Brenner, 1969). For instance, he studied the bilaterality of his two children's hand movements, and reported a striking development in unilaterality between 2 and 3 years. Binet also looked at his daughters' ability to distinguish differences in the length of two straight lines. Having established virtually no difference between their length judgments and those of adults, he looked for quantitative judgments that might show developmental differences. This led him to study number judgments, and, in a highly original study that anticipated and almost certainly influenced many of Piaget's ideas half a century later, he showed that children often confuse number with physical extent. When his 4-year-old daughter compared the number of counters in a row of large and a row of small counters, she said that there were more in the row with larger counters even when there were fewer in that row than in the other one. Binet's conclusion, that the child confused the number in a row with the amount of space that the row occupied, is still as significant and provocative in the 21st century as it was when he reached it in the 19th.

Binet's work with his daughters covered many aspects of development, including perception and memory, and, in 1892, in cooperation with Victor Henri (1872–1940), he began a series of studies of perception and of visual and verbal memory in large numbers of school children. This work showed large and consistent developmental differences, as well as an appreciable superiority in children's memory for meaningful sentences over their memory for lists of words.

In 1904, Binet was made a member of a government commission on the treatment of mentally handicapped children, and quickly realized that there was an urgent need for an objective way of detecting such children. Together with his new colleague Theodore Simon (1873–1961), he used his considerable experience with cognitive tasks that he knew to be appropriate for children to construct a scale consisting of thirty items varying in difficulty. This scale, which was first published in 1905 and revised and extended in 1908 and 1911, was a breakthrough. Having administered the scale to a large number of children, Binet and Simon were able to give it to individual children to establish their 'niveau mental' (mental level).

Binet always avoided using the scale to give precise measurements. The terms 'Mental Age' or 'IQ' were actually introduced and applied to the Binet/Simon scale by Wilhem Stern (1871–1938). These terms were the last step in the creation of the first systematic and effective intelligence test, which transformed Psychology and its relations to the community.

Binet's test also set the scene for the study of cognitive development because it demonstrated, again for the first time, systematic developmental changes in fundamental cognitive abilities, such as the ability to make inferences and to draw analogies. Binet was, as his biographer Theta Wolf (1973) first said, "an individual who made a difference."

John Bowlby (1907–1990)

PETER FONAGY

The son of a London surgeon, the British psychiatrist John Bowlby studied Medicine and Psychology at Cambridge University. After service as an army psychiatrist, he took up an appointment at the Tavistock Clinic in 1946, where he remained for the rest of his working life. From that time onward, he became increasingly dissatisfied with prevailing views in the first half of the 20th century concerning the origin of affectional bonds.

Photograph © Lucinda Douglas-Menzies.

Both psychoanalytic and Hullian learning theory stressed that the emotional bond to the primary caregiver was a secondary drive, based on feeding. Yet, evidence was already available that in the animal kingdom at least, the young of the species could become attached to conspecific adults (as well as non-conspecifics and even man-made artifacts) who did not feed them. Bowlby was among the first to recognize that the human infant enters the world pre-disposed to participate in social interaction. His critical contribution was his unwavering focus on the infant's need for an unbroken (secure) early attachment to the mother. He thought that the child who does not have this was likely to show signs of partial deprivation (i.e., an excessive need for love or for revenge, gross guilt and depression), or complete deprivation (i.e., listlessness, quiet unresponsiveness, and retardation of development) and, later in development, signs of superficiality (i.e., want of real feeling, lack of concentration, deceit, and compulsive thieving).

Bowlby's attachment theory has a biological focus (Bowlby, 1969). He emphasized the survival value of attachment in enhancing safety through proximity to the caregiver, in addition to promoting feeding, learning about the environment, and social interaction, as well as providing protection from predators. It was the latter that Bowlby considered the biological function of attachment behaviors, which were seen as part of a behavioral system (a term he borrowed from ethology). This is key to understanding the heated nature of the controversy between psychoanalysis and attachment theory. A behavioral system involves inherent motivation. It is not reducible to another drive. It explains why feeding is not causally linked to attachment and why attachment can occur to abusive caretakers.

Bowlby identified three behavioral systems (viz., attachment, exploration, and fear), which regulate the child's developmental adaptation. In combination, they provide a means for the child to learn and develop without straying too far or remaining away too long. The fear system inhibits exploration and activates the attachment system, the urgent call for reassurance. The caregiving system is the complementary biological system in the adult to meet attachment needs. It is important to note that in Bowlby's theory the goal of the system is initially a physical state, the reduction of fear through the maintenance of a desired degree of proximity to the mother. The extent to which the attachment figure's proximity can ensure that a sense of safety or security has been achieved will determine the strength of the infant's bond with the caregiver. In general, the caregiver's sensitivity to the infant's mind state is regarded as critical in this context.

In the second volume of his trilogy, Bowlby established the set goal of the attachment system as maintaining the caregiver's accessibility and responsiveness that he covered with a single term: 'availability' (Bowlby, 1973, p. 202). In fact, it was not until the third section of the book that he addressed the critical role of appraisal in the operation of the attachment system. Here, he asserted that availability means confident expectation – gained from "tolerably accurately" (p. 202) represented experience over a significant time period – that the attachment figure will be available. The attachment behavioral system thus came to be underpinned by a set of cognitive mechanisms, discussed by Bowlby as representational models or, following Craik (1943), as internal working models. It is this model, originating in infancy, that is thought to continue to organize the individual's behavior in later childhood and adult attachment relationships. Attachment needs being adequately met creates a long-term sense of expectation that relationships are safe and one is worthy of love. In insecure attachment, the long-term expectation may be an emphasis on managing alone without support or feeling insecure in being constantly and unduly concerned that one's attachment needs may not be met.

In his later work, Bowlby (1980) was increasingly influenced by cognitive psychology and particularly by the information-processing model of neural and cognitive functioning. Just as cognitive psychologists defined representational models in terms of access to particular kinds of information and data, Bowlby suggested that different patterns of attachment reflect differences in the individual's degree of access to certain kinds of thoughts, feelings, and memories. For example, avoidant insecure models of attachment permit only limited access to attachment-related thoughts, feelings, and memories whereas others provide exaggerated or distorted access to attachment-relevant information. Thus, for Bowlby, cognitive as well as emotional access to such information emerges as a function of the nature of the past relationship between infant and caregiver. Evidence consistent with Bowlby's ideas has been accumulating over past decades (Cassidy & Shaver, 1999), and links to the psychoanalytic origins of his ideas have been clarified (Fonagy, 2001).

Jerome S. Bruner (b. 1915)

DAVID OLSON

For some sixty years, Jerome Bruner has more or less presided over the coming-of-age of developmental psychology as a mature social-cognitive science. His influence is seen in every aspect of the development of mind and from infant inter-subjectivity to adult rationality, and from language acquisition to reflective thought. His writings inspired dramatically new research initiatives while remaining accessible to the general, informed reader. He is adored by more than two generations of younger scholars and widely regarded as the world's greatest living psychologist.

Jerome Bruner was born on October 15, 1915, in New York, the youngest of four children in a "nominally observant" Jewish family. He played a formative role in the cognitive revolution that swept through psychology in the 1960s, ending a half-century of domination by behaviorism. As a Professor of Psychology at Harvard University and as Co-Director with George A. Miller of the Harvard Center for Cognitive Studies, he led a large group of researchers in the study of cognitive and linguistic processes and their development. As Watts Professor of Psychology at Oxford University, he came to treat his study of language and cognitive development as an aspect of social development, with an increased emphasis on the role of education in that development. As Research Professor of Psychology at New York University Law School, he continues to examine the role of narrative structures in the organization of autobiography, literature, and law.

His association as an undergraduate at Duke University with the contrarian views of William McDougall (1871–1938) shaped Bruner's understanding

of the mind. Whereas American psychologists were primarily empiricists and materialists, McDougall emphasized nativism and mentalism. Bruner's contrarian views were sharpened at Harvard as a graduate student where he encountered the conflicts between the whole-person theorists Gordon W. Allport (1897–1967) and Henry A. Murray (1893–1988), and the experimentalists Edwin G. Boring (1886–1968) and Karl S. Lashley (1890–1958). The eventual product was an experimental approach to the higher mental processes involved in the talk and thought of whole persons that is best represented in the landmark volume he authored with Jacqueline Goodnow and George Austin, *A Study of Thinking* (1956).

Bruner's contributions to developmental psychology are equally distinctive. He introduced the work of Jean Piaget and Lev Vygotsky to the attention of North Americans, extending and adding a cognitive process perspective to intellectual development, work that is amply exemplified in the volume he produced with his students and edited with Patricia Greenfield and Rose Olver, *Studies in Cognitive Growth* (1966). Along with his collaborators, Colwyn Trevarthen and T. Berry Brazelton, Bruner pioneered the study of infant perception, intersubjectivity, and their predispositions to language, work well represented by his important book *Child's Talk* (1983a).

Bruner has been a strong proponent of the importance of culture in human development, emphasizing education as a fundamental aspect of culture. Minds, he argues, have the properties they do, not just because they are human, but because of their predispositions to culture, the language, rules, rituals, and stories much amplified by formal schooling. These themes are advanced in *The Culture of Education* (1996).

An informative account of his development as a psychologist through his first sixty years is provided by his intellectual autobiography, *In Search of Mind: Essays in Autobiography* (1983b). His recent work on the cultural and personal uses of narrative and interpretation is exemplified by his book with Anthony Amsterdam, *Minding the Law* (2000), and, most recently, *Making Stories: Law, Literature, Life* (2003).

Bruner's impact on psychology, philosophy, and scholarship generally has been acknowledged through two *Festschrifts* dedicated to him: *The Social Foundations of Language and Thought: Essays in Honor of Jerome S. Bruner* (Olson, 1980) and *Language, Culture, Self: The Philosophy of Jerome Bruner* (Bakhurst & Shanker, 2001). Acknowledgment has also come through the award of the International Balzan prize (1987); and by being in receipt of twenty-four honorary degrees from around the world, including the University of Geneva, Harvard University, Yale University, and the University of California, Berkeley.

George E. Coghill (1872–1941)

RONALD W. OPPENHEIM

Historically, the contributions of pioneers and great innovators, and even the pioneers themselves, are often forgotten as their ideas become incorporated into the prevailing conceptual and intellectual framework. This appears to have happened to George E. Coghill whose role as one of the founders of the fields of neuroembryology (developmental neuroscience), developmental psychobiology, and modern neuroscience has not been fully appreciated (Cowan, 1998).

Beginning in the early years of the 20th century, Coghill, together with the Herrick brothers (C. Judson and Clarence L.), helped to lay the foundation for the field of modern neuroscience (Herrick, 1949; Windle, 1979). They envisioned an interdisciplinary field called 'psychobiology' that transcended the traditional boundaries of biology, neurology, psychiatry, psychology, neuroanatomy, embryology, and animal behavior, and that even included an analysis of higher cognitive processes in humans. In 1891, the *Journal of Comparative Neurology*, the first journal of neuroscience, was founded by C. L. Herrick (1858–1904) as the official voice of this new discipline (Palay, 1991). It is quite clear that what we now consider as modern neuroscience had its origins with these pioneers more than a century ago.

Although Coghill made many fundamental empirical contributions to neuroembryology, he is best known for his detailed studies of neuroanatomical and behavioral development in amphibians (Coghill, 1929). This work, begun in 1906, represented the first scientific demonstration that behavioral ontogeny was an orderly, non-random, process related to equally orderly changes in the development of the nervous system. As an embryologist and anatomist with an abiding interest in behavior and evolution, Coghill was in a unique position to synthesize the findings from these various disciplines into a biologically valid theory of neurobehavioral development.

The approach Coghill championed was comparative, and thus evolutionary, in the sense that it supported attempts to establish major phylogenetic trends in the development of behavior. His approach was also based upon the assumption that ontogenetic changes in behavior were mediated by orderly, predictable epigenetic changes in the anatomy and physiology of the nervous system and related organ system. However, because of his embryological background, Coghill's use of the concept of epigenesis included early embryonic inductions and cellular interactions, as well as function, use, experience, and learning. He believed that the environment made important contributions to both neural and behavioral development and that adaptive modifications in the nervous system and behavior during development were often mediated by neural function and experience.

The developing animal was viewed from an organismic perspective in which behavior was thought to be partly regulated by intrinsic constraints that served to organize and guide development along specific pathways. Coghill rejected the prevailing trends in physiology and psychology (i.e., reflexology and behaviorism), which argued that complex, integrated behavior patterns developed out of earlier reflexes or from simple stimulus-response relations. He argued, instead, that from the earliest stages behavior was integrated or patterned, that this integration was guided by intrinsic (self-regulatory) mechanisms, and that at each stage environmental influences had to be accommodated to these mechanisms to be adaptively useful. One of the central tenets of Coghill's theory was that behavior develops from a relatively undifferentiated state to a state of increasing differentiation (i.e., from a state of generalized, global activity to one of increasing refinement and detail).

Although Coghill's views were derived in a large measure from his own observations on the behavior and anatomy of the salamander embryo, these ideas were almost immediately recognized as having potential value as a basis for the formulation of a more general theory of vertebrate behavioral development. Beginning in the 1920s and 1930s, Coghill's work and ideas served as a source of inspiration for child psychologists such as Arnold Gesell, Orvis C. Irwin, Karl C. Pratt, Heinz Werner, and Myrtle McGraw. His work on the salamander embryo also stimulated a great deal of research during the 1920s and 1930s into the prenatal development of behavior. Historically, the period between 1925 and 1940 can now be seen to have been, in many respects, a halcyon era for the neuroembryological study of behavior. Motivated by the theoretical challenge of Coghill, investigators throughout the world studied the embryos and fetuses of a wide variety of vertebrate species, ranging from the primitive dogfish to humans.

Shortly after Coghill's death, the prominent British biologist Julian Huxley remarked that ". . . his death is a devastating loss to science. In my opinion, Coghill stood among the twenty outstanding biological scientists of our time, although so few people were cognizant of his work that perhaps not many others would agree with me" (Oppenheim, 1978). Coghill and his work remained relatively unknown until after the publication of his book *Anatomy and the Problem of Behavior* (1929), which represented a series of lectures he gave at University College London in 1928. It was only in the last decade of his life that Coghill's work finally began to be recognized. During this period, he was elected to the National Academy of Sciences, received several honorary degrees, and served as President of the American Association of Anatomists. Although his work lives on today in some contemporary textbooks (e.g., Sanes, Reh, & Harris, 2000), his conceptual contributions to the establishment of the closely aligned fields of developmental neuroscience and developmental psychobiology are still not fully appreciated.

Erik Erikson (1902–1994)

PETER FONAGY

Born in Germany, Erik Erikson had no university education there and went to art school in Italy. During the 1920s, he got to know the Freud family and was accepted as a co-worker at the Vienna Psychoanalytical Institute. In 1934, he moved to Boston and became the first child analyst in New England. During his long career, which included appointments at the universities of Yale and Harvard, his primary concern was the interaction of social norms and biological drives in generating self and identity (Erikson, 1950a).

His original training as a teacher freed him from the 19th-century heritage of neurological psychiatry that bedeviled the psychoanalysts of the first post-Freudian generation. His well-known description of eight developmental stages covering the lifespan (Erikson, 1950b) was based on biological events that disturb the equilibrium between drives and social adjustment. Personality would be arrested if the developmental challenge was not mastered through the evolution of new skills and attitudes. This would compromise later developmental stages. Erikson was remarkable amongst psychoanalysts for his attention to cultural and family factors, and his extension of the developmental model to the entire life cycle. His theory introduced plasticity to the psychoanalytical developmental model, as well as stressing the need for a coherent self-concept fulfilled in a supportive social milieu.

Erikson was the first to expand Freud's problematic erotogenic zone model in his subtle concept of 'organ modes.' Prior to Erikson, it was assumed that activity associated with the pleasure inherent in each zone provided the basis for psychological modalities such as dependency and oral aggression, and for specific mechanisms such as incorporation and projection. Erikson's concept of organ modes extended the psychic function aspect of bodily fixation. In 1950, he wrote: ". . . in addition to the overwhelming need for food, a baby is, or soon becomes receptive in many other respects. As he is willing and able to suck on appropriate objects and to swallow whatever appropriate fluids they emit, he is soon also willing and able to 'take in' with his eyes whatever enters his visual field. His tactile senses, too, seem to 'take in' what feels good" (p. 57). In this way, he made a critical distinction between drive expression and mode of functioning, which opened up new vistas for the psychoanalytic understanding of human behavior.

The drive expression model binds understanding of social interaction to the gratification of biological needs. The notion of 'mode of functioning,' on the other hand, frees us to think about characteristic manners of obtaining gratification or relating to objects at particular developmental stages. Erikson showed us how a person may find that a means of gratification, originally associated with a particular phase or erogenous zone, offers a useful way of expressing later wishes and conflicts. This enabled him to introduce a whole series of constructs, including identity, generativity, and basic trust. He expanded the drive model while remaining in a biological framework. His description of libido theory as tragedies and comedies taking place around the orifices of the body aptly summarizes Erikson's widening perspective enriched by anthropology and developmental study.

For Erikson, basic trust was the mode of functioning of the oral stage. The mouth was seen as the focus of a general approach to life – the 'incorporative' approach. He stressed that these processes established interpersonal patterns that were centered on the social modality of taking, and holding onto, objects, physical and psychic. Erikson (1950a) defined basic trust as a capacity ". . . to receive and accept what is given" (p. 58).

By emphasizing the interactional psychosocial aspects of development, Erikson quietly altered the central position assigned to excitement in Freud's theory of psychosexual development. Although he accepted the libidinal phase model and its timings as givens, his formulation was one of the first to shift the emphasis from a mechanistic drive theory view to the inherently interpersonal and transactional nature of the child-caregiver dyad as these are currently understood, related to the child's development of a sense of self.

Erikson's (1950a) brilliant insight, far ahead of his time, was that seemingly insignificant experiences would eventually become aggregated, leading to ". . . the firm establishment of enduring patterns for the balance of basic trust over basic mistrust . . . [the] amount of trust derived from earliest infantile experience does not seem to depend on absolute quantities of food or demonstrations of love, but rather on the quality of the maternal relationship" (Erikson, 1959, p. 63). While many of his ideas have been so generally adopted that they are rarely nowadays linked with his name (e.g., the crisis of identity in adolescence), his imperative to make psychodynamic theory socially relevant is as pertinent now as it was at the time of its publication.

Viktor Hamburger (1900–2001)

RONALD W. OPPENHEIM

Born on July 9, 1900, in Silesia (then part of Germany), Viktor Hamburger was conceived in the 19th century, lived during the entire 20th century – an era prophetically declared to be the "century of the child" (Key, 1909) – and died on June 12, 2001, in the 21st century. Educated in Germany, he received his Ph.D. in 1925 in the laboratory of the embryologist Hans Spemann (1869–1941) who later won the Nobel Prize for his discovery of embryonic induction. Because of his Jewish background, following the rise of the Nazis Hamburger was forced to give up his first academic position at the University of Freiburg and immigrate with his family to the United States in the early 1930s (Oppenheim, 2001). In 1935, he accepted a faculty position in the Department of Zoology at Washington University in St. Louis where he remained for the rest of his life.

Hamburger's major contributions were made in the two disciplines he helped to found, experimental neuroembryology and developmental neurobiology. In a research career spanning more than sixty-five years, he carried out seminal studies on the formation of nerve pathways, synaptogenesis, neuronal cell death, neurotrophic factors, and the ontogeny of behavior (Hamburger, 1996). Outside of his studies on the emergence of behavior in the embryo, described below,

his most important contributions were the discovery with Rita Levi-Montalcini and Stanley Cohen of the prototypical neurotrophic factor, nerve growth factor (NGF), and the recognition of the role of programmed cell death in neuronal development (Hamburger, 1996). More than half a century after these discoveries, both areas continue to be at the cutting edge of biomedical research (Oppenheim & Johnson, 2003).

After more than forty years of studying aspects of neuronal development, beginning in the 1960s, at an age when many of us are anticipating retirement, Hamburger began an entirely new line of investigation on the embryology of behavior (Hamburger, 1977). Building upon the pioneering work of Wilhelm Preyer in the late 19th century and inspired by the studies of George Coghill on neurobehavioral development (Oppenheim, 1992), Hamburger and his colleagues used the chick embryo as a model for re-examining the early ontogeny of vertebrate behavior. Although the period spanning the 1920s, 1930s, and 1940s is unprecedented for the many studies of behavioral development during embryonic and prenatal stages (Carmichael, 1954), virtually all of the studies were descriptive in nature. By contrast, Hamburger set out to merge descriptive studies with a variety of classical as well as modern experimental techniques. Beginning with a detailed description and quantification of emerging motor patterns, followed by surgical manipulations, pharmacological perturbations, electrophysiology, and modern neuroanatomical techniques, a comprehensive picture of neurobehavioral development gradually emerged, from the onset of the first simple movements and reflexes to the complex, coordinated motor patterns involved in hatching (Hamburger, 1977; Bekoff, 2001).

In the chick embryo, Hamburger and his colleagues were able to show that behavioral development was mediated by endogenously generated neuronal activity involving stereotyped central and peripheral nervous system circuits that are established prior to and in the absence of sensory input. Although previous studies of adult vertebrates and invertebrates had revealed similar central pattern generators that are the basis of locomotor patterns, such as walking, swimming, and flying (Oppenheim, 1992), the work of Hamburger provided the first unambiguous evidence for the developmental origins of these mechanisms. Furthermore, these studies provided a compelling experimental refutation of the then popular view that early neurobehavioral development was largely a matter of early experience shaping neuronal connectivity and the resulting behavior patterns.

When his experimental work came to an end in the mid-1980s, Hamburger began a series of important historical studies of embryology and neuroembryology that continued until the end of his life (Oppenheim,

2001). Few of us will have the opportunity, and fewer still will have the inclination, to remain active and productive in science for over eight decades. By virtue of his longevity, creativity, and hard work, Viktor Hamburger managed this, and by doing so he will be remembered as one of the most influential scientists in neurobiology in the 20th century, and one of the few who made significant contributions to our understanding of both neuronal and behavioral development.

Jean Piaget (1896–1980)

PIERRE MOUNOUD

Given the abundant literature on Jean Piaget's life and work (Montangero, 2001), we concentrate here on crucial aspects of his theory on cognitive development that too often have been misinterpreted. To begin with:

Photograph by Alain Perruchoud.

- Piaget introduced a structuralist and constructivist approach to developmental psychology. His major contribution was to interpret children's behavior in terms of structures and transformations. Transformations are conceived as actions (physically or mentally produced) modifying the object's positions or its dimensions. Structures are the coordination of a set of objects' positions or dimensions and actions.
- Coordination may, for example, entail a relationship between a set of displacements of an object (e.g., placing an object inside, under, or behind another one) and its various localizations (to be contained, recovered, hidden); or the coordination of a set of transformations of a collection of objects (e.g., spacing and re-grouping) and its numerical invariance.
- At the core of Piaget's theory, there is the idea of the construction of new structures as ". . . a passing from a simpler to a more complex structure, this process . . . being endless" (Piaget, 1968/1971, pp. 54/62). These changes (i.e., "passing") are realized by means of adaptive processes such as abstractions and reconstructions.

These ideas remain relevant today. For example, Ungerleider & Mishkin (1982) have introduced a distinction between two broad streams of projections of visual pathways: a ventral stream playing a critical role in the identification and recognition of objects and a dorsal stream mediating the localization of those same objects. A successful integration of these two streams is actually considered as the origin of adaptive goal-directed behavior. This perspective sounds very close to Piaget's ideas.

We shall now illustrate the constructivist aspect of Piaget's theory, taking as an example the development of object permanence, inseparable from the structuration of space in terms of displacements, in order to specify how such construction is only possible if starting from previous structures related to the same type of problems (Piaget, 1968/1971). This construction takes place during the first eighteen months of life.

In the standard tasks, the infant has to look for an object hidden under or behind another one. Infants' difficulties are related to the organization of the successive displacements and locations taken by the object. They are misled by the tasks. They try, for example, to reach for the object in the direction of its initial location when in fact it has been displaced to a different location, or they search for it at the location where previously found.

According to Piaget, the progressive changes in behavior are made possible by the previously constituted structures enabling the infant to solve similar problems of object permanence at other levels of organization. Looking at the reflex behavior of the neonate for evidence of these primitive structures, Piaget considered that various reflex schemes could realize simple forms of permanence, which he qualified as "practical" (Piaget, 1937/1955, pp. 182/210). For instance, the rooting reflex is a behavior that allows the newborn to capture the mother's breast in order to maintain its practical permanence. In a similar way, oculomotor reflexes can be defined as the capacity to keep the permanence of visual contact with a moving object by means of visual tracking and capture. It is a form of coordination between object displacements and eye-head rotations.

We have considered two levels of object permanence dealing with the organization of space in terms of displacements, one at the level of the reflex schemes and the other one at the level of the sensorimotor schemes, as referred to by Piaget. Changes from one level to another are realized by abstractive and reconstructive processes. The new structures do not result from a simple re-description or generalization of the previous one, but instead from "convergent reconstructions with overtaking (dépassement)" or "reflective abstraction" (see Piaget, 1967/1971, pp. 366, 376 / 320, 329, for a definition). Thus, we can understand that recent discoveries related to the complexity of primary structures (e.g., numerical knowledge in infants) do not necessarily contradict Piaget's constructivist theory.

In conclusion, Piaget's view on cognitive development is characterized by the construction of new structures that are based on previous ones. However, recent progress in infancy research shows that these primary structures are more sophisticated than initially thought by Piaget. These sophisticated primary structures foreshadow future structures without entirely predetermining them.

Wilhelm T. Preyer (1841–1897)

KURT KREPPNER

Wilhelm Thierry Preyer was the son of a German industrialist who had moved to England. He was born in Manchester and, after finishing school in Germany, began to study Natural Sciences and Medicine at the University of Bonn. Preyer completed his doctoral dissertation at the University of Heidelberg in 1861, where he applied for the first time in Germany Charles Darwin's theory for explaining the disappearence of *plautus impennis*, a large Nordic penguin from Iceland. From Heidelberg, Preyer went to Vienna (1862–1863) and from here again to Berlin (1863–1864) where he was a student of Hermann von Helmholtz (1821–1894), and then to Paris (1865) where he attended lectures of the French physiologist Claude Bernard (1813–1878).

He became a university lecturer at the University of Bonn in late 1865 and, in 1866, a medical doctor. In 1869, he was offered a professorship in physiology at the University of Jena. There, he was a colleague of the zoologist Ernst Haeckel (1839–1919), the inventor of the Theory of Recapitulation, which claimed that the evolution of species is repeated during the development of both the embryo and the infant. As an advocate of Darwin's theory of evolution, Preyer was in continuous discussion with Haeckel, and his studies on chick embryos (1883) as well as his famous observational studies centering on the mental development of his son Axel (1882) were attempts to follow Haeckel's new bio-genetic approach. Preyer's observation of his son can be taken as one part of his general attempt to link embryology and early childhood on the one hand, and animal and human development on the other. For his work on prenatal development with both the chick embryo and the human fetus, Preyer is sometimes regarded as the founding father of behavioral embryology in general, and of scientific child psychology in particular.

In his observations of his son, he followed a strict schedule and claimed that only direct observations had to be recorded, and that each day observations had to be made three times. With these criteria, Preyer set new standards for scientific observations that are still valuable. Another innovation for looking at a child's development was the distinction of three areas (perception, will, and mind), which he tried to describe separately. Here, he applied the recommendations of Johannes Nicolaus Tetens (1736–1805), a German philosopher who had sub-divided human consciousness into these areas.

Intense observation of the infant's perceptual and mental activities clearly played a central role in Preyer's work. He hoped that, with his sometimes extremely fine-grained descriptions of changes over time, it would become possible to reconcile two controversial positions of his time, nativism and empiricism. Moreover, with his recordings of infant development, Preyer opened a new view that opposed Haeckel's theory. Within the framework of Haeckel's recapitulation theory, the process of human development during infancy was thought to be largely predefined by evolution. Preyer, however, after reviewing his own observations, concluded that developmental processes in the human species seemed to be slower than in other animals and therefore more open to environmental influences. This might, according to Preyer, result in a high degree of adaptability and flexibility during individual development, even during infancy. His two-volume book *Die Seele des Kindes* was first published in 1882, and soon translated into English and published by G. Stanley Hall (1844–1924) in 1888.

In 1888, Preyer made an extraordinary decision: he gave up his professorship in Jena and went to Berlin without being offered a proper position there. Perhaps he was bored with living in Jena and intended to participate in the more stimulating atmosphere of Berlin, or he speculated on getting a more attractive professorship in experimental psychology there. A third possible reason for his decision is based on the fact that Preyer had bad working conditions in Jena that had already ruined his health. Although sick during his time in Berlin, he continued to work on topics that were closer to psychology. He published on hypnotism and translated the work of James Braid (1795–1860) on this topic into German (1890), and turned to writing and graphology (1895). At Berlin University, he gave lectures – without payment – on physiology as well as on Darwin's theory, and also engaged in school reform. To earn some money, Preyer directed a department at the Berlin Urania, an institution of adult education for the dissemination of knowledge about the natural sciences. For health reasons, Preyer finally moved to Wiesbaden and lived there as a private scholar. He died on July 15, 1897.

Lev S. Vygotsky (1896–1934)

EUGENE SUBBOTSKY

Vygotsky was born in 1896 in Orsha (Belarus) to a middle-class Jewish family, the second of eight children. He grew up in Gomel (Belarus). As a child, he studied with private tutors, then entered the Jewish gymnasium, graduating with honors in 1913. He was a passionate reader, attracted to classical literature and philosophy, particularly the writings of Georg Wilhelm Friedrich Hegel (1770–1831) and Baruch Spinoza (1632–1677).

Vygotsky's early interests were in the humanities and social sciences. While he received a degree in law from Moscow University in 1917, he also studied in the Department of History and Philology at Shanyavsky Public University. Returning to Gomel, he worked at the Teachers College there. In January 1924, Vygotsky delivered a talk about the methodology of reflexological and psychological research at the Second Psycho-neurological Congress in Leningrad, and as a result he was invited to join the Psychological Institute in Moscow. From 1924 until his death from tuberculosis in 1934, he lived mainly in Moscow, working in close collaboration with Alexander Luria (1902–1977), Alexej N. Leontiev (1903–1979), and others, with whom he created his cultural historical approach toward psychological development. In 1925, he was awarded a Ph.D. in psychology for his thesis entitled *The Psychology of Art*. In the same year, he traveled to Berlin, Amsterdam, Paris, and London. In London he delivered a lecture at the International Congress on the Education of the Deaf.

Vygotsky participated in the founding of the Moscow Institute of Defectology, and lectured extensively in various institutions in Moscow, Leningrad, and other major cities of the Soviet Union while holding various posts in the Academy of Communist Education, Higher Women's Courses, 1st and 2nd Moscow Universities, Institute for Protection of Children's and Adolescents' Health, Moscow Conservatory, 2nd Medical Institute, and Hertzen's Pedagogical Institute (Leningrad). In his works and lectures, he maintained a broad interdisciplinary approach toward education and development, creating a dialogue between psychological theories and those coming from linguistics, psycholinguistics, history, biology, philosophy, and other areas of the arts and sciences. Because of the novelty and originality of Vygotsky's thinking, many of his major works (see Bibliography) were not published until long after his death. Six works by Vygotsky were published in international journals and special issues abroad before and soon after his death. However, it was only after the English translation of *Thought and Language* in 1962, with the introduction by Jerome Bruner and the subsequent response by Jean Piaget (1995), that Vygotsky's ideas started to influence developmental scientists in the West.

Vygotsky's cultural-historical theory emphasizes the role of social context in psychological development. Cognitive development is viewed as a qualitative transformation of the innate 'lower mental functions' (LMFs) of a newborn into 'higher mental functions' (HMFs) of older children and adults. Unlike LMFs that are unmediated and isolated abilities, HMFs are mediated and linked to each other. The most powerful mediator is language. With language, children acquire the ability to reflect on their thoughts and actions and to exercise control over their actions. Agency and executive function are, therefore, key features of higher mental functioning. According to his 'main law of the development of HMFs,' any HMF (i.e., logical thinking) appears first within the shared interaction between a child and his or her instructors (the 'inter-psychological plane'), and is then appropriated by the child and transferred into the mental ('intra-psychological') plane. A crucial factor in this transformation belongs to the instructors who actively help the child to construct his or her HMFs and acquire new abilities and knowledge. The scope of cognitive tasks and skills that the child can only manage with the help of instructors is viewed as the child's Zone of Proximal Development (ZPD). The effect in cognitive development is achieved when the child becomes able to manage independently those tasks and skills that earlier were a part of ZPD. Thus, instruction (i.e., teaching) is considered as an 'engine' in children's cognitive development.

This 'bird's eye' view of Vygotsky's work does not do justice to the richness and persisting relevance of his theory. Comprehensive and acccessible coverages can be found, for example, in Kozulin (1990), van der Veer & Valsiner (1991), and Vygotskaya and Lifanova (1996).

Heinz Werner (1890–1964)

WILLIS F. OVERTON & ULRICH MÜLLER

Heinz Werner grew up and received his entire education in Vienna. In 1914, he completed his dissertation, entitled *About the Psychology of Esthetic Joy*, at the University of Vienna. Three lines of interest can be identified in Werner's early publications (1913 to 1915): conceptual development, perceptual phenomena, and esthetic-expressive phenomena. These topics would occupy Werner throughout his lifetime.

In 1917, after postdoctoral work in the Physiological Institute in Vienna directed by Sigmund Exner (1846–1926), and experimental work at the Psychological Laboratory under Oswald Külpe (1862–1915) and Karl Bühler (1879–1963) in Munich, Werner became a research assistant at the Psychological Institute at Hamburg, which was directed by Wilhelm Stern (1871–1938). In 1921, he became a *privatdozent* at the Psychological Institute, which was part of the newly founded University of Hamburg. In 1926, Werner was appointed Professor and Vice-Director of this institute.

During his tenure at Hamburg (1917 to 1933), Werner was extremely productive and engaged in interdisciplinary exchanges with prominent colleagues, such as the philosopher Ernst Cassirer (1874–1945) and the comparative psychologist Jakob von Uexküll (1864–1944). Influenced by the genetic psychology of Felix Krueger (1874–1948), Werner applied the concept of development to esthetic-expressive phenomena, as reflected in his work on the origins of metaphor and lyric.

During this time, Werner also began to approach perceptual phenomena from a developmental perspective, and became interested in the primordial, expressive aspect of perception. He coined the term "physiognomic" perception to refer to this way of being-in-the-world. In this mode, objects are experienced in a pre-objective, intersensorial, and expressive way. To study how percepts develop across a short time span, Werner created and applied the microgenetic method. He also applied this method to the study of the expressive, physiognomic aspect of language. Physiognomic perception is contrasted with logical-analytical forms of cognition in which objects are unambiguous and precisely determined. Werner held that psychologists wrongly ignore physiognomic perception at the expense of logical-analytical cognition.

To quote him: "The living world of things, in which the human being participates with his feelings, strivings and reflections, does virtually not exist for this psychology (i.e., the psychology that studies logical-analytical thought) but only the cold, thing-like, and distanced world of relative closure, which in truth is hardly ever realized" (Werner, 1932, p. 2, our translation).

In 1926, Werner published *The Comparative Psychology of Mental Development*, which was eventually translated in 1948. In this book, he articulates the organismic-holistic framework for developmental psychology (see also Werner & Kaplan, 1963). This framework is characterized by two basic assumptions: (1) activity is dependent on the context or whole of which it is a part, and (2) activity is directed toward an end. The field of developmental psychology is defined as transcending the boundaries of child psychology and is applied to all life sciences (biological development, anthropology, psychopathology, and comparative psychology). Werner (1957) proposed the orthogenetic principle as the key theoretical principle that unifies the study of development across different disciplines. This principle states that wherever development occurs it proceeds from a state of relative globality and lack of differentiation to a state of increasing differentiation, articulation, and hierarchical integration.

When the National Socialists seized power in Germany, Werner emigrated to the United States. In the 1930s and 1940s, while affiliated with the University of Michigan, the Wayne County Training School, and Brooklyn College, Werner worked on perception and cognition in children with mental retardation. In 1947, he was appointed Professor and Chair of the Department of Psychology and Education at Clark University in Worcester, Massachusetts. At Clark University, Werner continued and expanded his work on perception (Werner & Wapner, 1952), and on the development of esthetic-expressive, symbolic phenomena (Werner and Kaplan, 1963), using the organismic-holistic framework. The work on perception led to the formulation of the sensory-tonic field theory, according to which perception is a process that depends on the dynamical interplay between the properties of the stimuli and the existing affective-motor states of the organism.

Werner & Kaplan (1963) described symbol formation as a socially motivated, directive form-building process that starts from non-linguistic, affective-motor forms of functioning, and results, in the course of successive differentiations and integrations, in a rule-governed, autonomous linguistic system. In particular, they show how crucial conceptual pre-requisites for language acquisition such as reference and depiction are rooted in non-linguistic forms of functioning.

Werner's early work is not well known today, and his theoretical works in developmental psychology as well as that on perception are less influential than they were in the 1960s and 1970s. However, the book on symbol formation continues to influence current research on social development in infancy (e.g., the development of pointing) and language acquisition.

Donald Winnicott (1896–1971)

PETER FONAGY

The developmental model of Donald Winnicott, a British pediatrician and psychoanalyst who worked for over forty years at Paddington Green Hospital in London and who was influenced by the writings of Melanie Klein (1882–1960), described the child's development from the early unity of infant and mother (Winnicott, 1965). Central to his ideas is the radical claim that the strength or weakness of the child's ego is a function of his caregiver's capacity to respond appropriately to his initially absolute dependence. The baby's ego can only master and integrate the drives in so far as his mother can perceive and act on his rudimentary needs and intentions. Winnicott thus saw the stability and power of the infant's ego, before the separation of the mother from the *self*, as directly determined by the mother's ability to think about her infant's mind.

Self-development depends on the emergence of differentiation of 'me' from 'not me,' and the experience of the infant's own feelings and perceptions as distinct from those of others. The infant-mother relationship has three functions that facilitate this: holding-integration, handling-personalization, and object-relating (Winnicott, 1965). Maternal holding is based on comprehension, holding in mind, of the infant's mental state. Winnicott (1967) suggested that optimal development of self-esteem depends on the mother's capacity for affective 'mirroring' of the infant. Her primary maternal pre-occupation (a partial withdrawal from activities other than the baby and a state of heightened sensitivity to her own self, her body, and the baby) helps the mother give the baby the 'illusion' that she responds accurately to his gestures because his wish creates her (and she is part of him).

Winnicott, however, does not assume that even early infancy is an idyllic era. The mother has to be 'good-enough,' but her failure is inevitable and is the motivator of growth. He stresses that the baby must not be

challenged too soon about the mother's 'realness' (her independent existence), and asked to negotiate the 'me and the not-me' (Winnicott, 1956a; 1956b). The baby's sense of omnipotence gives rise to the ego nuclei, which will in time become integrated in the real experience of the I (the true self).

An 'active and adaptive' handling environment contributes to the integration of bodily and mental states, thereby establishing personalization. The handling of the baby is adaptive when he neither feels overwhelmed, nor experiences himself as a mere collection of organs and limbs surmounted by a wobbling head. The mother's sensitivity to the baby's moods is critical, as is the coherence lent to him by the goal-orientedness of his physical being (activity as opposed to passivity). If handled satisfactorily, the baby looks at the mother's face rather than breast, such that his concerns with mind and meaning come to override his preoccupation with his physical needs.

Winnicott (1971) described how object-relating arises from the experience of magical omnipotence. The mother's survival of her infant's physical 'attacks' facilitate the development of the self and the mother's release from omnipotent control. The infant begins to be able to perceive her as a real or separate other. Failure and frustration are essential for ultimate adaptation in that they facilitate the break away from infantile omnipotence.

Winnicott (1953) also introduced the idea of transitional phenomena in his study of the infant's use of the mother to facilitate independent functioning. A favorite blanket may help to soothe the infant because it is grasped in the moment when the infant fantasizes about breast feeding, and is associated with conjuring up the mother (and the breast) in her absence. The physical object is both the infant (the 'me' aspect) and the mother (the 'not-me' aspect); it is transitional in facilitating the move from the omnipotence of relating to a subjectively created object, to relating to the 'real' mother who is part of external reality. Because the transitional object helps to bridge the gap between 'me and not-me' as the baby becomes aware of separation, the baby and his comforter may become inseparable, with the object crucially under the omnipotent control of the baby. Transitional objects are in the space between the self and external reality, a space in which symbolization occurs, meaningful, affectionate, sharing-yet-separate companionship and love grow, as well as where play and illusion are maintained in the spontaneous, creative activities of healthy people (Winnicott, 1971).

The self can develop when the person looking after the child does not unnecessarily impinge on him, by substituting her own impulses while curtailing or re-directing the infant's creative gestures. Lack of good-enough mothering distorts the ego's development, forestalling the establishment of an internal environment that could become the essence of the self. If the mother cannot 'comprehend' the infant through her gestures, he will be forced into a compliance that is alien to his true self. As the mother's gestures do not 'give meaning' to the infant's reactions, symbolic communication cannot be said to develop between them. The infant, and then the child, will have the capacity to 'go through the motions' of interpersonal relationships, but these encounters will be with the false self, which will serve to hide the true self (Winnicott, 1965).

The false self is marked by lack of spontaneity or originality. Such individuals later tend to seek further impingements to recreate the experience of compliant relating and, with it, a sense of realness about their own existence. A self whose own creative gestures have not been recognized is an empty self that will often look for powerful others to merge with, to fill itself with borrowed strength or ideals. Only when challenged by the need to act spontaneously as a whole person, particularly in intense relationships, will the limitations become evident. Change in these cases comes about when interactions (e.g., with a therapist) convince the hidden true self that its creative gestures will be permitted, and its sense of existence affirmed within that relationship.

APPENDIX 2

Milestones of motor development and indicators of biological maturity

ROBERT M. MALINA

Introduction

Three interacting processes, physical growth, biological maturation, and behavioral development, are major demands in the daily lives of children and adolescents for approximately the first two decades of life. The processes occur simultaneously and interact to influence self-concept, self-esteem, body image, and perceived competence. The interactions emphasize the biocultural context of childhood and adolescence.

Defining terms

Growth refers to the increase in the size of the body as a whole and of its parts. As children grow, they increase in height and weight and in lean and fat tissues, their organs increase in size, and so on. Different parts of the body grow at different rates and different times, resulting in altered body proportions.

Maturation refers to progress toward the biologically mature state, maturity. Maturation is a process, while maturity is a state. Maturation occurs in all organs and organ systems – enzymes, chemical composition, functions, shapes, and so on. Maturity varies with the biological system considered. Sexual maturity is fully functional reproductive capability. Skeletal maturity is a fully ossified adult skeleton. Maturation of the nervous and endocrine systems is a major factor underlying sexual, skeletal, and somatic growth and maturation.

Timing and tempo of growth and maturation vary considerably among individuals. Timing refers to when specific events in growth and maturation occur, while tempo addresses the rate at which the processes progress.

The processes underlying biological growth and maturation, and aspects of behavioral development, are cellular. The cellular processes cannot be observed or measured directly. The study of growth and maturation is based on standardized measurements and observations of outcomes of cellular activities (e.g., height attained reflects the proliferation of cartilage cells at growth plates of individual bones, stage of sexual maturity reflects neuroendocrine influences on gonadal cells, activities in the motor cortex regulate voluntary movements).

The term 'development' is often used regarding growth and maturation. It is used most commonly in the context of behavioral development during infancy, childhood, and adolescence. Some aspects of behavioral development refer to the timing of specific events during infancy and early childhood (i.e., ages at which specific landmarks are attained, such as age at walking alone and use of language). These are referred to as developmental milestones. Milestones related to the development of motor control, such as age at independent walking or overhand throwing with opposition of movement can be viewed to some extent as indicators of neuromuscular maturation.

The term 'development' is also used to describe the biological processes of differentiation of pluripotent embryonic stem cells into specific cell types, tissues, organs, and functional units. Accordingly, development depends upon the activation and repression of genes or sets of genes interacting with hormones, nutrients, and the prenatal environment. The development of biological functions continues postnatally as different systems of the body become functionally refined.

Milestones in motor development

Motor development is the process through which a child acquires movement patterns (i.e., basic movements comprising a task and skills involving accuracy,

Table 1. Percentiles for ages (months) at which healthy, fullterm infants attain developmental milestones leading to independent walking. Adapted from R. H. Largo, L. Molinari, M. Weber, L. Comenale Pinto, G. Duc, 1985. Early development of locomotion: significance of prematurity, cerebral palsy and sex. *Developmental Medicine and Child Neurology*, **27, 183–191.**[1]

Developmental milestone	Boys Percentiles			Girls Percentiles		
	10	50	90	10	50	90
Roll to supine	3.7	5.0	6.2	3.8	5.2	6.7
Roll to prone	4.8	6.0	8.8	4.6	6.0	8.7
Pivot[2]	5.0	6.4	8.6	4.7	6.8	8.8
Crawl on stomach[3]	6.1	7.0	8.7	5.8	6.9	8.9
Creep on hands/knees	6.8	8.3	10.4	6.5	8.8	11.8
Creep on hands/feet	8.1	9.0	11.8	7.7	9.6	11.9
Sit up	7.3	9.1	11.8	6.8	8.9	11.5
Stand at rail	7.4	8.4	9.8	7.1	8.7	10.5
Pull to stand	7.5	8.5	11.3	7.3	8.9	11.5
Cruise at rail[4]	8.0	9.5	11.7	8.0	9.8	11.8
Stand momentarily	9.9	12.4	15.6	9.8	12.5	14.9
Walk, one hand held	9.2	11.5	13.0	9.5	11.8	13.5
Walk alone	10.8	13.0	15.9	11.0	13.1	15.7
Walk up and down stairs	16.2	18.9	23.7	16.0	19.7	23.8

[1] Data are based on 56 boys and 55 girls from the second Zurich Longitudinal Study.
[2] Pivoting – child on stomach moves in circular manner by actions of arms and legs.
[3] Crawling on stomach – child pulls forward by coordinated action of arms and legs.
[4] Cruise at rail – sideways walking while holding on to a table or similar stable object.

precision, and economy in performance of a task). It is a seemingly continuous process of modification that involves the interactions of several factors: (1) neuromuscular maturation, that has a significant genotypic component; (2) the growth characteristics of the child (e.g., size, proportions, and body composition); (3) the tempo of growth, maturation, and development; (4) the residual effects of prior motor experiences; and (5) new motor experiences. All of these occur in the context of the physical and sociocultural environments within which the young child is reared. Environmental experiences interact with the biological substrate of growth and maturation to determine the motor proficiency of the individual.

The acquisition of motor abilities and skills is a common focus in the child development and exercise science literature. All children, except some with severe disabilities, have the potential to develop and learn a variety of fundamental movement patterns and more specialized skills. Although movements are behaviors, they have a major biological substrate related to morphology and physiology.

The term 'developmental milestone' is used to denote the acquisition of control and coordination of specific voluntary movements during infancy and childhood. Motor achievements involving postural, locomotor, and prehensile control are accounted for in developmental scales (e.g., Bayley Scales of Infant Development). While such scales are used to evaluate the integrity of the developing central nervous system in infants and young children, one of their main applications is as a screening device to identify children with developmental problems, or who might be at risk for developing such problems (e.g., Denver Developmental Screening Test). Emphasis is on early detection and diagnosis so that physical therapy or other forms of intervention can be initiated as necessary.

Ages and associated variation for the attainment of specific motor milestones during infancy and early childhood indicate levels of overall motor development that infants and young children are expected to demonstrate by particular ages. The range of interindividual variation in early motor development is substantial (Table 1). It also includes sequence variations and occasional omissions. Such variation is often overlooked in research on motor development. The sequential age-related appearance of motor milestones that is apparent in developmental scales was considered to be the product of a genotypically controlled neuromuscular maturation. In contrast, current views stemming from dynamical systems approaches to development emphasize the ongoing interactions between the development of specific movements, the growth characteristics of the child, and environmental circumstances.

Independent walking is the major motor development task during the first two years of life. The developmental changes leading to walking are essentially a series of postural changes through which the child gains the motor control necessary, first to assume upright posture, then to maintain upright posture, and finally to walk independently. With the refinement of the walking pattern, control of locomotor and manipulative abilities improves so that more independent action is possible. Thus, early childhood is a time of increasing experimentation with a variety of motor tasks, and the acquisition of competence in fundamental movement patterns is one of the more important developmental tasks of early childhood.

A good deal of early and current motor development research has described the temporal, spatial, and sequential elements of specific movement patterns as they develop. Specific elements are often summarized in a sequence of stages reflecting progress from the immature to the mature pattern for specific movement tasks. The definition and delineation of stages are to some extent arbitrary, but are a convenience to facilitate understanding the acquisition of achievements in motor development. Developmental sequences have been described for locomotor (running, jumping, hopping,

Table 2. Estimated ages (months) at which 60% of children performed at specific developmental levels for several fundamental motor patterns: B = boys, G = girls. Adapted from V. Seefeldt & J. Haubenstricker, 1982. Patterns, phases, or stages: an analytical model for the study of developmental movement. In J. A. S. Kelso & J. E. Clark (eds.), *The Development of Movement Control and Co-ordination.* New York: Wiley, pp. 309–319.[1]

Fundamental pattern	Stages									
	1		2		3		4		5	
	B	G	B	G	B	G	B	G	B	G
Run	23	20	27	25	40	40	51	62	–	–
Standing long jump	23	24	47	48	76	76	117	120	–	–
Overhand throw	10	10	40	44	45	56	50	73	63	102
Hop	34	28	46	41	64	58	90	86	–	–
Skip	59	56	65	63	78	70	–	–	–	–
Catch	24	23	41	40	51	50	73	61	80	77
Strike	24	23	32	34	44	46	88	101	–	–
Kick	22	20	40	47	56	73	90	99	–	–

[1] Number of stages from immature (Stage 1) to mature varies for each basic skill. The last stage indicated is the mature stage; other stages indicate intermediate levels in the development of each movement. The data were provided by courtesy of Dr. Vern Seefeldt, Michigan State University.

skipping), projection (throwing, kicking, striking), and interceptive (catching) abilities and skills.

The mixed-longitudinal Motor Performance Study at Michigan State University provides insights into the development of eight fundamental motor patterns (Table 2). Development of most patterns progresses rapidly during early childhood, but continues into middle childhood for others. Boys tend to attain each stage of overhand throwing and kicking earlier than girls, whereas girls tend to attain each stage of hopping and skipping earlier than boys. The sex differences may be related to cultural influences on practice and appropriateness of activities that involve these movement patterns. The attainment of specific stages, especially intermediate ones, of other movement patterns (running, jumping, catching, and striking) shows similarity between boys and girls, but there is variation between the sexes in the ages at which mature stages are attained.

Assuming the stages are correctly described, several aspects of these developmental milestones of motor development need further study: (1) variability in duration of stages within each movement pattern; (2) the relationship between age at entry into a stage and subsequent progress through the stage; (3) characteristics of children (e.g., size, physique, body composition, behavior, prior movement experiences, environmental circumstances) who progress through stages of a specific pattern quickly, compared to those who do so more slowly; and (4) relationships between ages at attaining specific stages, or duration of progress through them, and subsequent motor performance.

Maturity indicators

Maturity indicators refer to specific landmarks of skeletal, sexual, and somatic maturation that document progress to the mature state. As noted, the processes underlying maturation of these systems cannot be observed or measured directly. Rather, outcomes of these processes are used to define indicators of maturity that are used in growth studies. Eruption and calcification of the dentition are also maturity indicators, but the teeth tend to proceed independently of other indicators.

Skeletal maturity

All children start with a skeleton of cartilage prenatally and have a fully developed skeleton of bone in early adulthood. Progression from the cartilage model, to initial bone formation, in the shape of the bone, and to adult morphology provides the basis for assessing skeletal maturity. The changes are monitored in standardized radiographs of the hand and wrist. Three types of information provide the basis for estimating skeletal maturity: (1) initial appearance of bone centers on an X-ray, which indicates the replacement of cartilage by bone tissue; (2) definition and characterization of each bone through gradual shape differentiation; and (3) union or fusion of epiphyses with their respective diaphyses in long bones (metacarpals, phalanges, radius, ulna), and attainment of adult contours and shapes by carpal ebones.

There are three commonly used methods for the assessment of skeletal maturity: the Greulich-Pyle,

Tanner-Whitehouse, and Fels methods (Malina, Bouchard, & Bar-Or, 2004). All are similar in principle in that they entail matching a hand-wrist radiograph to a set of criteria specific to each method. Each method provides a skeletal age (SA), which corresponds to the level of skeletal maturity attained by a child relative to the reference sample for each method. Skeletal age is expressed relative to a child's chronological age (CA) to provide an indication of maturity status. The methods for assessing skeletal maturity differ in criteria, scoring, and reference samples, and have strengths and limitations. SAs derived with each method are not equivalent.

Secondary sex characteristics

Puberty is a transitional period between childhood and adulthood, which includes the appearance of secondary sex characteristics, maturation of the reproductive system, and the adolescent growth spurt, in addition to psychological and behavioral changes. Pubertal status is based on the assessment of secondary sex characteristics – the breasts and menarche in girls, the penis and testes in boys, and pubic hair in both sexes. Development of the breasts (B), penis and testes (genitals, G), and pubic hair (PH) is summarized in five or six stages specific for each characteristic. The criteria described by Tanner (1962) are used most often. Stage 1 represents the prepubertal state (B 1, G 1, PH 1). It is often assumed that prepubertal children are homogeneous in maturation, but they do vary in skeletal maturity and hormonal status.

Stage 2 indicates the initial, overt development of each characteristic, namely, the elevation of the breasts in girls (B 2), the enlargement of the genitals in boys (G 2), and the appearance of pubic hair in both sexes (PH 2). Stages 3 and 4 represent continued maturation of each characteristic and are more difficult to evaluate. Stages 2 through 4 indicate the pubertal state, and Stage 5 the mature or adult state. Some scales for pubic hair include a Stage 6, which marks the expansion of pubic hair upwardly in the midline of the abdomen in many males, and laterally and, but to a lesser extent, upwardly in some females.

Ratings of stages of sexual maturation are ordinarily made by direct observation at clinical examination. Such assessments may have limited application outside of the clinical setting because the method requires invasion of individual privacy. Given this limitation, self-assessments are increasingly used. Youngsters are asked to rate their stage of sexual maturity by comparison with photographs of the characteristics, or with schematic drawings of the respective stages prepared from the criterion photographs. Good-quality photographs of the stages, with simplified descriptions, should be used (excellent colored photographs of the stages are available in the national survey of youth in the Netherlands as reported by van Wieringen *et al.*, 1971). Self-assessment should be done privately in a quiet room after careful explanation of the procedures and purpose of the assessment. A private cubicle with a full-length mirror is preferred. The mirror assists the adolescent in self-examination and assignment of stages. There are limited data on the concordance of self-ratings by youth and those by experienced assessors. The reproducibility of clinical assessments by physicians or other experienced raters and by youth is not generally reported.

It is common in the pediatric and adolescent literature to refer to the assessment of secondary sex characteristics as Tanner staging, often without indicating which characteristics were assessed. This is not correct. Secondary sex characteristics are assessed using the criteria of Tanner (1962). Stages are specific to the breasts, genitals, and pubic hair, respectively, and are not equivalent or interchangeable (e.g., G 2 is not equivalent to PH 2 in boys, and G 3 in boys is not equivalent to B 3 in girls). The average of breast and pubic hair ratings in girls and of genital and pubic hair ratings in boys are occasionally used as a composite indicator, but this has limitations. What does a composite rating of 1.5 refer to? Is it B 1 and PH 2, or B 2 and PH 1? Half-stages do not exist, and two individuals can have the same composite rating and be assessed quite differently. One boy can be rated in G 3 and PH 3 with an average rating of 3, whereas another boy can be rated as G 2 and PH 4 with an average rating of 3. Ratings of specific characteristics should be reported.

At assessment, the individual is in a specific stage of sexual maturation. The initial appearance of a stage usually cannot be observed. Age at onset of a specific stage is estimated as the midpoint of the interval between examinations when the stage was not observed and when it was first observed so that estimated ages at onset are generally later than the actual time of onset. Ranges of median or mean ages at onset of stages of secondary sex characteristics in longitudinal and cross-sectional samples of European and North American girls and boys are summarized in Table 3.

Age at menarche

Menarche refers to the first menstrual period, and the age at which it occurs is the most commonly reported maturity indicator of female adolescence. It is a late event in puberty that occurs after peak height velocity (see below). There is no corresponding physiological event in male adolescence. Menarche also has significant value judgments associated with its attainment in many cultures, and the psychological importance of menarche in the development of girls has no counterpart in the sexual maturation of boys.

Age at menarche can be estimated in three ways. In longitudinal studies, the girl or her mother is interviewed on each occasion as to whether menarche has or has not occurred, and if it has occurred, when it did so. Girls are ordinarily examined at three- or six-month intervals so that a reasonably accurate estimate of the age at menarche can be determined. Sample sizes in prospective studies are generally small, and thus the range of variation may be reduced.

The status quo method provides a sample or population estimate of the age at menarche. As the name implies, the menarcheal status (i.e., pre- or post-menarcheal) of each girl in the sample is assessed. Two pieces of information are needed for a large cross-sectional sample that spans 9 through 17 years of age: the exact CA of each girl and whether or not she has attained menarche. The percentages of post-menarcheal girls in each CA group are fitted with probits or logits. The point at which the fitted line intersects 50% is the estimated median age at menarche for the sample. Each method provides a standard deviation and confidence intervals (5th and 95th). Status quo estimates apply only to the population and not to individuals. Ranges of median ages at menarche from status quo surveys of European and North American populations in the mid-1970s through the mid-1990s are summarized in Table 4.

The retrospective method is limited to those who are post-menarcheal. Girls are asked to recall as accurately as possible when menarche had occurred. If the interview is done at close intervals as in longitudinal studies, the method is quite accurate. However, if it is done with older girls or with adult women, it has an error component. The method relies on the individual's memory and includes potential error associated with accuracy of recall. Most teenagers and women can recall this landmark within a range of about three months. The use of prompts (e.g., season of the year, holidays, special activities, examinations) during an interview can assist in recall. The retrospective method should not be used in a sample of adolescents that includes girls who have not yet attained menarche. The mean will be biased toward a younger age by the inclusion of girls who have attained menarche and by the exclusion of those who have not yet attained menarche.

Other secondary sex characteristics

Appearance of axillary hair in both sexes, and facial hair and voice change in boys, are additional maturity indicators. They are often rated on three stage scales (i.e., absent/unbroken, present/breaking, adult/mature). These characteristics are rather late events in the

Table 3. Range of median/mean ages (years) at the onset of stages of secondary sex characteristics (B = breasts, PH = pubic hair, G = genitals) in European and North American girls and boys. Adapted from R. M. Malina, C. Bouchard, & O. Bar-Or, 2004. *Growth, Maturation and Physical Activity*, **2nd. edn. Champaign, IL: Human Kinetics.**

Girls					
Europe					
	B 2	10.0–11.6	PH 2	10.4–12.	
	B 3	11.0–12.5	PH 3	11.4–13.	
	B 4	12.8–14.6	PH 4	12.3–14.	
	B 5	14.0–15.7	PH 5	13.6–15.	
North America					
	B 2	8.9–11.2	PH 2	8.8–11.	
	B 3	10.2–12.2	PH 3	10.3–12.	
	B 4	12.2–13.9	PH 4	11.9–14.	
	B 5	13.7–15.5	PH 5	13.1–16.	
Boys					
Europe					
	G 2	10.8–12.2	PH 2	11.5–13.	
	G 3	12.9–13.7	PH 3	13.4–13.	
	G 4	13.8–14.7	PH 4	14.1–15.0	
	G 5	14.7–16.1	PH 5	14.9–16.	
North America					
	G 2	9.2–12.4	PH 2	11.2–12.8	
	G 3	11.8–13.5	PH 3	12.1–13.	
	G 4	13.4–14.6	PH 4	13.4–14.	
	G 5	14.3–17.3	PH 5	14.3–16.	

Table 4. Range of median ages at menarche (years) in samples of European and North American girls in the mid-1970s through the mid-1990s. Adapted from Malina, Bouchard, & Bar-Or (2004).[1]

Europe	12.3–13.5
North America	12.1–12.9

[1] Ages are based on probit analysis.

sequence of pubertal events, and are not very often compared to other indicators of sexual maturity.

Somatic maturity

It is not possible to assess maturity from body measurements as body size by itself is not an indicator of maturity. However, if longitudinal data for height that span adolescence are available, the inflection in the growth curve that marks the adolescent growth spurt can be used to derive a valuable indicator of maturity. The two primary parameters of the growth curve are

Table 5. Ranges of mean ages at peak height velocity (PHV) in samples of European and North American adolescents.[1]		
	Ages at Peak Height Velocity (years)	
	Girls	*Boys*
Europe	11.4–12.2	13.8–14.2
North America	10.8–12.0	13.3–14.1

[1] Adapted from Malina, Bouchard, & Bar-Or (2004). At times, several estimates of the parameters of the adolescent growth spurt are reported for the same sample; the parameters are derived from different curve-fitting models.

take-off (TO) or initiation of the spurt, and peak height velocity (PHV) or maximum rate of growth during the spurt. The age, size, and rate of growth at TO, and at PHV, can be derived. Age at PHV is a commonly used indicator of somatic maturity in longitudinal studies.

Note that some children show a small growth spurt in height (an increase in velocity of growth) several years prior to the onset of the adolescent growth spurt. The spurt usually occurs between 6.5 and 8.5 years of age, and is called the mid-growth spurt. Corresponding spurts have been identified for body weight and other body dimensions. There does not appear to be a sex difference in the timing of maximum velocity of the mid-growth spurt in height, but the spurt occurs more frequently in boys than in girls. Not all children show a mid-growth spurt. This reflects biological variation among individuals, and also variation in the frequency of measurements in childhood. Children are usually measured annually during childhood, and such an interval may not be sufficiently sensitive to detect the change in velocity of growth that defines the spurt. The mid-growth spurt has not been established as an indicator of somatic maturity.

Earliest efforts at identifying the age at PHV and PHV (cm/yr) were graphic. Presently, curves are mathematically fitted to longitudinal records of heights of individual children to estimate velocity and acceleration of growth, and in turn to derive the timing and magnitude of PHV. In mathematically fitting longitudinal growth records, a distinction is made between structural and non-structural models. The former have a pre-selected form for the growth curve and the parameters or constants of the model have a pre-determined biological meaning. The latter do not have a pre-selected form and their parameters may not be easy to interpret biologically. If longitudinal data are available for other body dimensions (e.g., weight, sitting height, leg length) or performance variables (e.g., muscular strength, vertical jump), estimates of the timing and magnitude of the growth spurts in each can be derived.

Ages at PHV for samples of North American and European youth are summarized in Table 5. Sample sizes in longitudinal studies are not usually large enough to derive population estimates. Moreover, they may not reflect the normal range of variation in a large sample of adolescent boys and girls.

Age at PHV also serves as a landmark against which attained sizes and velocities of other body dimensions or physical performances, as well as stages of sexual maturity, can be expressed. Menarche, for example, occurs after PHV. Peak gains in weight and muscle strength occur after PHV in both sexes, while peak gains in maximal aerobic power occur close to the time of PHV.

Interrelationships among maturity indicators

A question of relevance is the interrelationship among indicators of skeletal, sexual, and somatic maturation. Do they measure the same kind of biological maturity? The issue of interrelationships is complex because only skeletal maturity spans the prepubertal and pubertal years, whereas indicators of sexual maturity and age at PHV are limited to puberty and adolescence.

Evidence suggests that the tempo of prepubertal growth and maturation is independent of the timing and tempo of pubertal growth and maturation. Prepubertal growth and skeletal maturation depend principally upon the stimulation of growth hormones and related growth factors. Sexual maturation, the adolescent growth spurt, and the final stages of skeletal maturation (i.e., epiphyseal union) are primarily under the influence of growth hormones, related growth factors, and steroid hormones, among others. There appears to be a general maturity factor that underlies the timing of growth and maturation during adolescence, and discriminates among individuals who are early, average (i.e., 'on time'), or late in the timing of adolescent events. There is, however, variation among maturity indicators so that no one system provides a complete description of adolescent events in individuals. Variation in tempo of maturation is an additional factor. There is no consistent relationship between the age at which a stage of a secondary sex characteristic develops (timing), and the rate of progress to the next stage (tempo). Limitations of the methods for assessing maturity and associated intra- and inter-individual technical errors also contribute to the variability.

Conclusions

Milestones in motor development and indicators of biological maturation provide important tools for understanding the individuality of growth, maturation, and development of infants, children, and adolescents.

There is a need to validate stages of fundamental movement patterns and perhaps to expand the concept to other movements, and for analysis of interrelationships among milestones of motor development, including fundamental patterns. Studies of motor development have not systematically included indicators of growth and biological maturity status.

The independence of pre-pubertal growth and maturation from the events of adolescence raises the question of a maturity indicator during childhood. The timing of the mid-growth spurt has not been included in studies of interrelationships among maturity indicators. Skeletal maturity was the primary indicator. SA can vary by three to four years among prepubertal children of the same CA, and this is reflected in growth status. Newer technologies that are currently used for the assessment of body composition and which require lower-level radiation exposure (e.g., dual X-ray absorptiometry [DEXA]) or no exposure (Magnetic Resonance Imaging [MRI]), may potentially be modified for the assessment of skeletal maturity.

See also:

The concept of development: historical perspectives; Neuromaturational theories; Dynamical systems approaches; Cross-cultural comparisons; Developmental testing; Epidemiological designs; Cross-sectional and longitudinal designs; Motor development; Brain and behavioral development (I): sub-cortical; Locomotion; Prehension; Sex differences; Ethology; Pediatrics

Further reading

Beunen, G. and Malina, R. M. (1988). Growth and physical performance relative to the timing of the adolescent spurt. *Exercise and Sports Sciences Reviews*, 16, 503–540.

Eveleth, P. H. and Tanner, J. M. (1990). *Worldwide Variation in Human Growth*, 2nd edn. Cambridge: Cambridge University Press.

Hauspie, R. and Chrastek-Spruch, H. (1999). Growth models: possibilities and limitations. In F. E. Johnston, B. Zemel and P. B. Eveleth (eds.), *Human Growth in Context*. London: Smith-Gordon, pp. 15–24.

Marubini, E. and Milani, S. (1986). Approaches to the analysis of longitudinal data. In F. Falkner and J. M. Tanner (eds.), *Human Growth*, Vol. III, 2nd edn. New York; Plenum, pp. 79–94.

The statistics of quantitative genetic theory

THALIA C. ELEY

Introduction

The majority of behavior genetic studies quantifying genetic and environmental influences on psychological phenotypes in children have used the twin design, and as such the analysis of this type of data will be the focus. Most studies to date have been primarily interested in exploring the sources of variance, or individual differences within a population. The concept of heritability in the broadest sense refers to the proportion of variance due to genetic influence. It is sometimes referred to as h^2, but more commonly in the behavior genetic literature it is described in terms of additive genetic influence (a^2 also referred to as A) and/or non-additive genetic influence or dominance (d^2 or D).

Environmental influences are also divided into two sources of variance: common or shared environmental influences (c^2 or C) are defined as those that make members of a family similar to one another (i.e., result in familial resemblance), whereas non-shared environmental factors (e^2 or E) are those which make members of a family different from one another (i.e., result in differences between family members). It is important to note that it is not that the experience of the environment itself is shared or not shared, but that the effect of that influence results in resemblance between family members or in differences between them. The non-shared environment term also includes error as this also lowers familial resemblance in a random way.

The ACE model

In this simplest mode, variance in the phenotype is divided into three latent factors: additive genetic (A), common or shared environment (C), and non-shared environment (E), as illustrated by the following equation:

1. $\quad V_p = a^2 + c^2 + e^2$

Monozygotic or MZ (identical) twins both share their entire genome and also, by definition, share their shared environment. As such, their similarity (or correlation) is described as the sum of these two types of influence:

2. $\quad r_{MZ} = a^2 + c^2$

In contrast, dizygotic or DZ (fraternal) twins only share half their additive genetic material on average – the same as any other sibling pair. In addition, as with MZ twin pairs, they entirely share the shared environment. As such, within-pair resemblance for DZ twin pairs can be described as the sum of half the genetic influence and the shared environment influence:

3. $\quad r_{DZ} = \frac{1}{2}a^2 + c^2$

When data are available on MZ and DZ twin pairs, the correlations within each of these two groups can be incorporated into these equations, from which heritability can then be estimated as in the following equation:

4. $\quad a^2 = 2\,(r_{MZ} - r_{DZ})$

From these equations, the contributions of shared and non-shared environmental influences can also be calculated. Three examples of how different pairs of correlations result in very different parameter estimates are given in Table 1.

In all of the pairs of data in Table 1, the DZ correlation was never less than half of the MZ correlation, and as such these were all examples where any genetic influence was additive. As there are two copies of each chromosome (except the X and Y chromosomes in males), a complete human genome includes two copies of most segments of DNA. However, some sections of DNA occur in variant forms called alleles. Additive genetic influences are those in which having two copies of the risk allele confers twice as much risk as having only one copy, and in which the effects of genes at different loci are additive (rather than the effects of genes at different loci interacting, a process know as epistasis). In some genes, the action of one allele is dominant over

Table 1. Some examples of different pairs of monozygotic and dizygotic twin correlations and the different parameter estimates calculated from them.

r_{MZ}	r_{DZ}	a^2	c^2	e^2
.6	.3	.6	.0	.4
.6	.4	.4	.2	.4
.6	.6	.0	.6	.4

Note: r_{MZ} = monozygotic twin correlation, r_{DZ} = dizygotic twin correlation, a^2 = additive genetic influence, c^2 = shared environment influence, e^2 = non-shared environment influence.

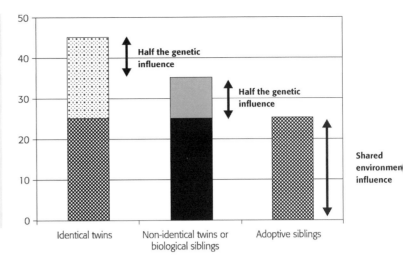

Figure 1. Similarity for twins, and biological and adoptive siblings.

the others, and in this case having either one or two copies of this allele will result in the same outcome. This is called genetic dominance. MZ twins share their whole genome, and therefore share all their dominance genetic influence, whereas DZ twins only share one quarter. This results in much lower resemblance in DZ pairs relative to MZ pairs for phenotypes influenced by genetic dominance. Such a pattern of correlations (with DZ correlations being less than half those for the MZ) indicates the presence of genetic dominance.

As twin data lead to just three observed statistics (variance in the phenotype, and to the correlations for MZ and DZ twins), only three parameters can be estimated at any one time. Dominance genetic effects are therefore only explored when there is no evidence for shared environment (c^2), and this parameter can be dropped from the analyses and replaced by d^2. Rough estimates of additive and dominance genetic influences can be calculated as follows:

5. $\quad V_p = a^2 + d^2 + e^2$
6. $\quad r_{MZ} = a^2 + d^2$
7. $\quad r_{DZ} = \frac{1}{2}a^2 + \frac{1}{4}d^2$
8. $\quad a^2 = 4r_{DZ} - r_{MZ}$

Consider an example where the MZ correlation is .6, and the DZ correlation is .2. If the heritability estimate was calculated using equation 4, this would result in a value of .8, which is greater than the MZ correlation, and therefore not possible. In this case, equations 5 to 8 are used, which result in estimates of .2 for a^2 ($4 \times .2 = .8$ and $.8 - .6 = .2$), .4 for d^2, and .4 for e^2. In this instance, the total heritability (sometimes referred to as broad sense heritability or h^2) is the sum of a^2 and d^2.

Adoption studies

The adoption design is based on the same principles. Members of an adoptive family share their shared

environment, but not their genes. In contrast, members of non-adoptive biological families share their shared environment and 50% of their genes. The correlations between dyads within such families are calculated from these principles. For example, the correlation for a trait within a biological sibling pair, or biological parent-child pair is $a^2 + c^2$, the same as for a pair of DZ twins. In contrast, the correlation between adoptive siblings or an adoptive parent-child dyad will be just c^2 as they share no genes.

The contrasting correlations between these two are used comparatively in just the same way as correlations between MZ and DZ twins. Figure 1 illustrates the division of within-pair resemblance for MZ twin pairs, DZ twin pairs and biological sibling pairs, and adoptive siblings into additive genetic and shared environment estimates. One of the advantages of the adoption study is the direct estimate of c^2 obtained from adopted family members, as this parameter has to be indirectly inferred from twin data, and a direct estimate is thus less likely to be contaminated with error.

Testing significance

Correlations can provide a rough estimate of heritability, but cannot test whether each of the terms is significantly different from zero. Furthermore, they do not take into account the variance in the measures, as they simply use the correlations alone. In order to take into account the variance within the measures, variance-covariance matrices are parameterized using model-fitting analysis (e.g., using Mx; Neale & Cardon, 1992). In such analyses, the covariation within a twin pair is parameterized rather than just the correlation (which has been standardized, thereby removing all influence of variance).

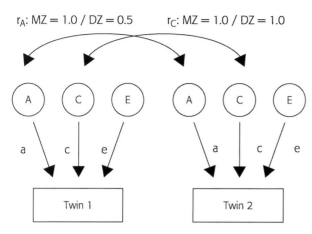

Figure 2. A univariate model of twin data.

Figure 2 is a diagramatic representation of equations 1 to 3. The variance in the phenotype for each twin is accounted for by the paths from the three latent factors A, C, and E. The correlation between the twins is accounted for by two sets of paths: genetic ($a \times 1.0 \times a = a^2$ for MZ pairs and $a \times 0.5 \times a = \frac{1}{2}a^2$ for DZ pairs) and shared environment ($c \times 1.0 \times c = c^2$ for all twins). It can be seen from this figure that the correlation between MZ twins, for example, is therefore $a^2 + c^2$ as given in equation 2.

Models are fitted to the variance-covariance matrices for the MZ and DZ pairs. The fit of the model is tested using chi-square, which should be small and non-significant indicating that the data do not differ significantly from the model. The significance of any path can be tested by comparing the chi-square of a model with that path included to a model that does not include the path. For example, in order to establish whether the shared environment parameter is significant in the model, the full model is first run, which includes the parameter C (ACE), followed by a reduced model without the C term (AE). In univariate analyses, an ACE model and an AE model differ in their degrees of freedom by one, as one path has been dropped. The chi-square for the difference in fit between the two models is the difference between the ACE model chi-square and that for the AE model. If the difference in chi-square values between the two models is significant for one degree of freedom, then the path is significantly different from zero and cannot be dropped from the model. In this way, it is possible to ascertain which factors are significant in the etiology of the phenotype being studied.

Two other fit indices commonly used are the comparative fit index (CFI) that should be between 0.9 and 1.0, and Akaike's Information Criterion (AIC), which should be large and negative. The model of best fit is said to be that which has the fewest paths in it, without significant deterioration in the fit of the model.

All these fit indices are negatively influenced by sample size, so larger twin studies tend also to use a fit index that takes sample size into account such as the Root Mean Squared Error Approximation (RMSEA), in which values below 0.1 indicate good fit, values below 0.05 an excellent fit. More detailed discussions of model-fitting approaches with twin data are given elsewhere (technical notes on running models can be found in the appendix in Plomin *et al.*, 2001, and in Neale *et al.*, 1999).

Multivariate genetic analyses

Multivariate genetic analyses explore the role of genetic and environmental influences on the covariation between traits or co-morbidity of disorders. There are many different multivariate models, which can be used to ask different theoretical questions. Figure 3 presents partial diagrams of four widely used multivariate models. It should be noted that in these figures just one member of the twin pair is presented (hence they are partial diagrams) in contrast to the univariate model (Figure 2) in which both members of the pair are illustrated. All models are bivariate, but each can easily be extended to three or more variables.

The first model is probably the most common bivariate model in the child psychology literature, and has tended to dominate bivariate analyses in particular (Simonoff, 2000). In this model, one set of influences account for variance in both variable 1 and variable 2. A second set of influences are specific to variable 2. This model is particularly appropriate for longitudinal data in which one set of factors influences both time points, with an additional set of new influences coming in at time 2. This model can also be converted into model 2, the correlated factors model (Loehlin, 1996), which allows the estimation of the correlation between genetic, shared environmental, and non-shared environmental influences on the two variables. The genetic correlation can range from 1.0, indicating that all the genes on variable 1 also influence variable 2, to 0 indicating no sharing of genes, to −1.0 indicating that all the genes on variable 1 influence variable 2 in the reverse direction. The same applies to the shared environmental and non-shared environmental correlations. These two models have been widely used in the behavior genetic literature on developmental phenotypes, and have tended to show that genetic influences account for covariance across traits and across time, whereas environmental variance is more commonly measure- or time-specific.

The third model has a structure imposed on the shared and specific aspects of the influences on the two variables. It should be noted that in the bivariate case only nine paths can be estimated, and as such this model

1: Cholesky Decomposition

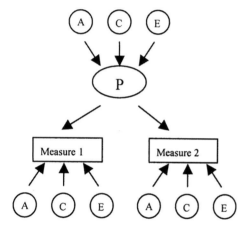

2: Correlated Factors Model

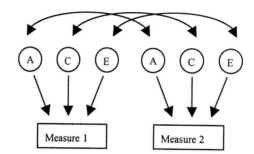

3: Common Pathway Model

4: Independent Pathway Model

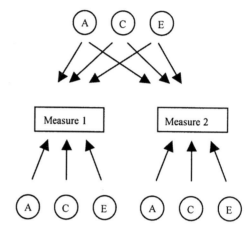

Figure 3. Four multivariate models.

is generally only used for analyses of three variables or more, or in the bivariate instance it can be used where there is no evidence for one set of parameters. For example, this model might be run with only A and E terms. It can be used to test the hypothesis that there is one underlying phenotype (or endophenotype) that mediates the effects of all shared genetic and environmental factors on the measured phenotypes.

The final (independent pathway) model also allows one set of genetic, shared, and non-shared environment influences on the two variables, but this time the magnitude of their influence on the two measured variables is independent. This model also has to be limited in the bivariate case, with the size of the paths from the shared A, C, and E terms to the measured variables being equal for both. In both models 3 and 4, there are variable-specific proportions of variance (those represented below the measured variable boxes) in addition to shared variables (those represented above the measured variable boxes). Both these models test specific hypotheses regarding the structure of the shared

genetic and environmental variance on the measured phenotypes, such as whether there is a mediating endophenotype. Although these models have not been widely used to date in the behavior genetic literature on child psychological phenotypes, they are likely to be more popular as interest grows in identifying mechanisms of genetic and environmental risks on outcome.

Conclusions

Model-fitting techniques using behavior genetic data allow the testing of specific hypotheses regarding the etiology of the development of psychological phenotypes. These techniques are constantly refined and updated to meet the changing demands of behavior geneticists (Neale *et al.*, 1999). It is clear that there is still much that this discipline can tell us about the development of psychological abilities.

See also:
Cross-sectional and longitudinal designs; Twin and adoption studies; Structural equation modeling; 'At-risk' concept; Behavior genetics

Further reading

Neale, M. C. and Kendler, K. S. (1995). Models of comorbidity for multifactorial disorders. *American Journal of Human Genetics*, 57, 935–953.

Purcell, S. (2002). Variance components models for gene-environment interaction in twin analysis. *Twin Research*, 5, 554–571.

Sham, P. C. (1998). *Statistics in Human Genetics*. London: Arnold.

Acknowledgments

The author is supported by a Career Development Award from the Medical Research Council.

Glossary of terms

22q11 deletion (CATCH 22) syndrome: genetic disorder consisting of cardiac abnormality, anomalous face, thymus hypoplasia, cleft palate, and hypocalcemia, associated with specific abnormality on chromosome 22.

α-bungarotoxin (α-BTX): a substance that presynaptically blocks neuromuscular transmission.

A-not-B task/error: devised by Jean Piaget (1896–1980) to investigate the development of object permanence in infancy, the task involves hiding a desirable object at location A for several trials and then hiding it at a new location B. The error is that infants below about 12 months perseverate in searching at A from where they have successfully retrieved the object several times, sometimes even when the object is visible at the new location B. Introducing a delay imposed between the moment the toy is hidden and the reaching action is initiated before allowing the infant to search increases the difficulty of this task, resulting in perseveration, and suggesting that memory constraints have to be overcome in order to perform the task correctly. Thus, the task requires infants both to hold a retrieval plan in mind, and to suppress a previously reinforced response.

abruptio placentae: premature separation of the placenta from the site of implantation on the uterus before the delivery of the fetus. It is a life-threatening condition for the fetus and occurs about 1 in 500 to 750 deliveries.

absolute distance: the precise metric distance of an object or surface relative to the self.

abstractions: in Fischer's neo-Piagetian skill theory, the fourth and final tier of skill development. Abstractions represent generalized or intangible content and stand in contrast to concrete representations, which refer to things that are tangible, concrete, and able to be imaged or imitated.

acceleration: linear acceleration is the rate of change of velocity measured in meters per second per second (ms^{-2}). Angular acceleration is the rate of change of angular velocity measured in radians per second per second (ws^{-2}).

accommodation: the process of modifying or adjusting an existing scheme or psychological structure in order to act upon or know an object, event, or person. For example, a child accommodates his grasping scheme when he adjusts his hand movements to fit the contours of a particular object. In Piaget's theory, accommodation must occur in tandem with assimilation.

acethycholine: hormone-like, neurotransmitter protein, produced by cells to create or stimulate central nervous system reactions necessary for life.

action sequences: organization of behavior in time, where specific actions follow one another in various temporal patterns.

action theory: a theoretical approach that views individuals as both products and producers of their developmental histories.

action unit: a term to describe the different facial muscles involved in an expression.

activation: a concept from neuroscience and connectionism in which the state of a neuron codes information according to a coding principle such as space code in higher parts of the nervous system or rate code in more peripheral parts.

active intermodal matching: this concept pertains to Meltzoff and Moore's proposed mechanism for facial imitation. Facial imitation involves intermodal matching because the infant sees the adult's gesture, but does not see his own response (the infant does not see his own response as his own face remains unseen by him). Facial imitation thus requires matching across different sensory modalities (hence 'intermodal'). It is 'active' because infants correct and improve their responses over successive attempts; the responses do not simply pop out fully formed.

active sleep (also referred to as Irregular or REM sleep and State II): that condition of the infant when the eyes are closed, intermittent rapid eye movements can be observed through the eyelids, respirations are irregular and variable in frequency and amplitude, and motor activity varies from apparently random small limb movements to occasionally trunk movements and periods of inactivity. Vocalizations are not present.

activity-dependent organization: the property of the nervous system to use the pattern of its own activity to wire itself. The central concept is "fire together, wire together," a shorthand term for the Hebbian synapse.

adaptation: in evolutionary biology, the process by which those behavioral or other characteristics of individuals that promote survival in their particular environment evolve through the action of natural selection. Also refers to the outcome of the process.

additive model: a statistical model in which the effects explain variance of the dependent variable such that the total portion of explained variance is the sum of the portions explained by each individual effect.

adrenal cortex: the outermost layer of the adrenal gland derived from mesoderm situated on top of the kidneys that releases corticosteroid hormones into the blood stream in response to stress.

adrenal medulla: the innermost part of the adrenal gland derived from neural crest cells of the ectoderm that releases adrenalin (epinephrine) and noradrenalin (norepinephrine) into the blood stream in response to stress and fear.

Adult Attachment Interview: an instrument developed by Mary Main and co-workers designed to measure individual differences in representations of attachment figures in adults.

affordance: a neologism devised by James J. Gibson (1904–1979). Defined as functional possibilities of an object or environmental layout relative to what an individual can do with respect to them. It involves two sorts of properties: objective properties (what something affords depends on its physical characteristics) and subjective properties (what something affords depends in addition on relevant characteristics of the perceiver, such as body size and action abilities). For example, whether a chair affords sitting for an infant will, in part, depend on the size and action capabilities of the infant relative to the height of the chair. The affordance concept derives directly from the concept of organism-mutualism.

agentic processes: in neo-Piagetian skill theory, the capacity to exert control over action, thought, or feeling.

Infants act as agents soon after birth as they begin to exert control over simple reflexes and action elements. Although individuals exert control over their actions, controlled action always occurs under coactive control of the social context and the biological medium within which agentic behavior emerges and is used. This is the process of epigenesis.

agnosia: complete or partial loss of the ability to recognize familiar objects or stimuli (including faces), usually as a result of brain damage.

akinesia: absence of movement, used in reference to conditions or drugs that result in immobilization of the fetus and cessation of spontaneous motor activity.

allele: a specific gene sequence that is one of a number of different mutated or natural forms of a particular gene or DNA sequence.

allocentric search: search for objects based on external cues from the objects independently of one's body position or locations of previous successful searches for the objects.

allometry: in biology, the study of relationships between size and shape. During mammalian growth, different parts of the body grow at different rates, but in a proportional manner so that body shape is noticeably altered during this period without distorting a recognizable species-characteristic form.

altricial: species that are born immature at birth, requiring parental care to survive.

alveoli: the vesicles in the lungs in which the exchange of oxygen and carbon dioxide takes place.

Alzheimer's disease: a progressive, incurable, neurological disease characterized by premature senile dementia that affects brain functions, including short-term memory loss, inability to reason, and the deterioration of language and the ability to care for oneself.

ambidexterity: literally means a condition of 'equal hand' (ambi) dexterity or skill across a range of tasks. For tasks requiring little skill, virtually all adults are ambidextrous. For skilled tasks, even writing, many adults, with sufficient practice, might be able to achieve ambidexterity or near ambidexterity. However, by 'ambidexterity,' they may mean that they preferentially use one hand on some tasks, their other hand on other tasks. The latter condition is more accurately described as 'mixed,' 'inconsistent,' or 'weak left- or right-handedness.' By any of these loose usages, ambidexterity would be fairly common in the population. In its strict and literal sense, however, it is extremely rare.

amino acid: an organic acid that forms the fundamental components of proteins, peptides, and polypetides that go to make up all living cells.

amniocentesis: a technique that involves extracting and analyzing fetal cells from the amniotic fluid.

amnion (or amniotic sac): the innermost of two membranous sacs that completely surround the developing embryo and fetus.

amniotic fluid: the watery fluid that fills the cavity created by the embryonic membranes (amnion and chorion). It is produced by several sources, including a filtrate from maternal plasma, secretion by the amnion, and urination by the fetus.

amodal: intermodal information that is not unique to one sensory channel, as when a single event is specified by more than one modality.

amygdala: a key structure in the limbic system of the forebrain involved in emotion recognition and other social emotional functions such as fear, aggression, and defensive behaviors, as well as learning and memory.

analysis of variance (ANOVA): the statistical analysis of mean differences that are traced back to the effects of one or more factors. The simplest ANOVA is a one-way design in which N subjects are (randomly) allocated to a number of different levels of a single factor. The total variation in observations is then partitioned into the between-groups sum of squares (between level means), and the within-groups (or residual) sum of squares (differences between subjects in the same group). The desired outcome in most cases is that the between-groups sum of squares is greater than that for the within-groups.

anemia: a condition in which there is a low red blood cell count in the blood, usually marked by a decrease in hemoglobin, the pigment in red blood cells that transports oxygen.

anencephaly: a congenital malformation due to failure of the neural tube to close at the rostral end and which consists of the absence of the cerebral hemispheres in all cases and of the diencephalon and midbrain in most.

Angelman syndrome: a genetic disorder dominated by learning disability, ataxia, jerky puppet-like movements, epilepsy, and various behavioral problems, including autistic features; associated with loss of maternal alleles on chromosome 15q11–13 and other genetic abnormalities. First reported by Harry Angelman (1915–1996) in 1965.

anhedonia: a loss of interest in and withdrawal from all regular and pleasurable activities, often associated with depression.

anlage: a primordium or developmental precursor.

antecedent-consequent relationships: in its weakest form, it is assumed that a precursor or antecedent is simply a forerunner to some later-occurring event in development, without the implication that there is a functional connection between them. In the stronger form, a precursor is a necessary condition for that later event, which would not occur without it.

anterior cingulate gyrus: a structure in the prefrontal cortex that is closely associated with executive attention and executive function.

anthropology: the study of human beings worldwide in relation to distribution, origin, classification, and the relationships between variations in environmental and social influences as well as physical characteristics and dietary intake relative to culture. The concept of culture is central to the work of anthropologists, along with the variations it creates (e.g., in beliefs and many other psychological functions such as social learning, child-rearing practices, development, and growth).

aortic hypoplasia: decreased growth of the aorta, the blood vessel that delivers oxygen-rich blood from the left ventricle to the body.

Apgar score: an evaluation of a newborn's physical status by assigning numerical values (0–2) to each of five criteria: (1) heart rate, (2) respiratory effort, (3) muscle tone, (4) response stimulation, and (5) skin color; a score of 8–10 indicates the best possible condition. Devised by Virginia Apgar (1909–1974).

apical ectodermal ridge: the layer of surface ectodermal cells at the apex of the embryonic limb bud. Considered to exert an inductive influence on the condensation of underlying mesenchyme.

apnea: a pause between breaths in a respiratory cycle, usually lasting between three and forty seconds, and due to obstructions to nasal, oral, or tracheal passageways, or by malfunctioning of the brain stem itself.

apoptosis: programmed cell death and replacement. It is a normal biological process that allows the elimination of unwanted cells through activation of the cell death program. The products of apoptosis are absorbed by neighboring cells. Abnormal control of apoptosis can have serious consequences and can lead to a wide range of diseases.

application: empirical testing of implications with regard both to whether any implication actually does work in educational practice and to the extent to which it amounts to an improvement.

apraxia: a neurological syndrome involving the loss of the ability to perform complex movements, despite no obvious impairments in the muscles or sensory organs themselves.

arcuate nucleus: an area of the brain stem thought to be responsible, among other things, for stimulating reactions necessary for waking and arousing from sleep.

articulation: the process of producing and modifying airflow above the larynx and voice tone into distinctive connected speech through coordinating movements of the jaw, mouth, tongue, and vocal cords.

artificial intelligence (AI): problem-solving, recognition, and other intelligent-like behavior exhibited by an inanimate device. Computers led to an explosion of interest in AI.

ascending genital tract infection: lower genital tract microorganisms from the vagina or cervix ascending to infect or cause inflammation of the amniotic fluid, placenta, choriodecidua, chorioamnion, or uterus that is associated with an increased risk of preterm labor/ delivery.

Asperger's syndrome: a sub-group on the autistic spectrum. This syndrome and classical autism share the same features, but in Asperger language development is normal, and cognitive development proceeds on time.

asphyxial death: a suffocation wherein the organism is mechanically prevented from breathing, sometimes due to being wedged between furniture or being pushed against soft materials or objects blocking the air passages.

assimilation: the process of incorporating an object into a scheme or psychological structure. In Piaget's theory, assimilation must occur in tandem with accommodation.

astrocyte: one type of a number of different glial cells found in the white and gray matter of the central nervous system (CNS). They are star-shaped, with many processes, and provide mechanical support for neurons by wrapping around them and attaching them to their blood vessels.

asymmetrical tonic neck posture or response (ATNR): from the flexed and symmetrical posture of the supine fullterm newborn, an asymmetry develops in which the upper extremity on the side to which the head is rotated extends, while that on the side of the occiput is flexed (thus being described as a 'fencing position'). Also, the leg on the side of the face tends to be extended, while the other leg is flexed.

asymptote: a line on a growth curve that gets increasingly near the ceiling, but does not reach it.

'at-risk' concept: one implying the probability of an adverse outcome.

athetoid (or athetotiform) movements: those resembling the slow, involuntary writhing movements characteristic of athetosis, and especially evident in the hands and fingers and sometimes in the feet.

attachment theory: usually refers to the theory proposed by John Bowlby (1907–1990) and developed further by Mary D. Salter Ainsworth (1913–1999) that is meant to explain how an infant develops emotional relationships with the mother or another caregiver and how they relate to subsequent development. Attachment behaviors, forming a system, are assumed to be biological predispositions that have evolved to maintain the survival of the species by ensuring the proximity of caregivers committed to providing care and protection during early childhood. The crux of the theory in its present form is the notion of an 'internal working model': ways of coping with the world that are developed in response to the responsivity of the caregiver. Such styles carry through from infancy into the adult's style as a caregiver.

attention deficit hyperactivity disorder (ADHD): a relatively common and diffuse childhood disorder, it is a constellation of problems that become manifest in children entering school, characterized by inattentiveness, hyperactivity, poor impulse control, behavior management problems, and a high risk of other co-morbid behaviors and academic problems.

attentional flexibility: the capacity to shift the focus of attention from one task to another. This capacity is typically measured by performance on card sorting tasks, in which the sorting rule is periodically changed; impaired performance on such tasks can involve difficulties in disengaging from the previously correct rule or in establishing and attending to the new rule.

attractor: a particular solution of a dynamical system to which other solutions converge in time. Attractors can be constant in time, periodic, or have more complex time dependencies (e.g., chaos). They are (asymptotically) stable in the sense that the dynamical system evolves such as to approach the attractor in whose vicinity the system starts out. If the state of a dynamical system is exposed to perturbations, then this attractive property reduces deviations from stable states.

attributable fraction: the proportion of cases of some negative outcome that may be attributable to a particular risk.

attributional style: a cognitive style that may be depressive or not and which refers to the interpretation of events (i.e., in a task testing for attributional style, subjects are asked to give reasons why a hypothetical event might have occurred).

attrition: drop-out or loss to follow-up of participants in a study because of refusal to continue, failure to locate, or other problems. The concern is that non-random drop-out may make the sample no longer representative of the original population.

auditory nerve: the set of neural pathways that communicates between the cochlea and the cochlear nucleus in the medulla.

autism: a neurodevelopmental condition nowadays conceptualized as a spectrum, involving difficulties in social development, verbal and non-verbal communication, absence of imaginative play, and a focus on unusually strong and narrow interests.

auto-encoder networks: connectionist models in which the input is the same as the target. These models have to learn to reproduce the input on the output layer. Often an intermediate layer has fewer processing units than either input and output layers and so forms a bottleneck. In order to learn the task, the model therefore needs to extract statistical information from the input and form compact internal representations.

autonomic nervous system (ANS): a self-regulating division of the nervous system that controls involuntary functions having to do with the cardiovascular, digestive, reproductive, and respiratory systems of the body. It is sub-divided into the parasympathetic and sympathetic nervous systems.

autoregressive series/model: a specific form of time-series analysis where a score at some occasion on a variable ($X[t]$) is predictive of a score at some later occasion on the same variable ($X[t + 1]$). These models are typically used in time-series analysis, but they can be useful in longitudinal panel analyses as well.

autosomal dominant condition/disease: genetic condition caused by one mutated gene located on one of the autosomal ('non-sex') chromosomes. One of the parents will usually have the disease as it is dominant in this mode of inheritance.

avoidance learning: learning to make a response to a warning signal in order to avoid an aversive event.

axon: nerve cell process transporting outgoing or efferent information.

axon retraction: a phenomenon often seen in early development, where axons extend farther, or to more places or terminal zones, than they will at maturity, and then refine their connections by retracting.

Babinski response: extension of the big toe upward and the spreading out of the other toes when the external portion of the newborn's foot is stroked from the back of the heel to base of the toes. Absent when there is damage to the lower spinal cord. First reported by François F. Babinski (1857–1932).

backpropagation: the best-known algorithm for training neural network models with more than two layers of units. The principle of the backpropagation algorithm is to change the weights in the neural network so that the discrepancy between the network's output and the desired output (supplied by a 'teacher') is minimized.

balance scale task: a task in which children have to predict the movement of a balance scale that has weights attached on either side of the fulcrum, and where the weights and their distance to the fulcrum vary.

balanced (or orthogonal) design: ANOVA design in which the cells contain equal numbers of cases.

basal ganglia: the complex of striatum (caudate nucleus and putamen), sub-thalamic nucleus, globus pallidus, and substantia nigra, which is involved in motor control and cognitive functions.

behavior genetics: the study of behavioral variation among individuals, which is separated into genetic versus environmental components. The most common research methodologies employed are family, twin, and adoption studies. Environmental influences are divided into two classes, shared and non-shared (or unique) environment.

behavior mechanism: a hypothetical structure in the central nervous system that, when activated, produces an event of behavioral interest such as a particular perception, a specific motor pattern, or an identifiable internal state. Similar to cognitive structure.

behavioral embryology: reputedly founded by Wilhelm T. Preyer (1841–1897), it is a branch of developmental biology that studies the prenatal development of the nervous system and behavior. Its main animal models are the chick and rat embryo. Among its successes are the Preyer-Tracy hypothesis of autogeneous motility and more recent studies showing the anticipatory nature of prenatal development and thus the continuities between it and postnatal development.

behavioral phenotype syndromes: describe behaviors associated with specific genetic conditions and where these behaviors are related to that particular condition. These syndromes have fairly predictable behavioral presentations and may also be induced by environmental conditions.

behavioral state concept: this concept can be defined in at least two distinct ways. The taxonomic definition assumes that the classification of states is an arbitrary but convenient heuristic device. It specifies a small number of exclusive combinations among four directly observable state criteria. The dynamical definition assumes that behavioral states are the a posteriori consequences of spontaneous interactions among many fluctuating systems; that they are 'real' attributes of the organism, and that only some combinations of sub-systems are dynamically stable.

behavior system: any organization of perceptual, central, and motor units that acts as a larger unit in some situations.

behaviorism: a school of psychology that studied only unambiguous behavior, which had to be measurable in order to derive scientific laws of human behavior needing only to refer to events that could be objectively defined in physical terms. It left out consciousness and introspection and avoided subjective notions such as imagining.

beneficence: the obligation upon researchers to maximize possible benefits, and minimize possible harms, for research participants.

bias (cultural): cross-cultural differences in data that are not related to the trait or concept presumably assessed by an instrument (or some other method), and that tend to distort the interpretation of these data.

bifurcation: a mathematical term for instability or a transition in a dynamical system.

bilabial: speech sounds formed using both lips.

bimanual task: many tasks must be performed with two hands (e.g., lifting a large two-handled platter of food or a bulky package). Such tasks do not require hand differentiation; each hand (and arm) does essentially the same thing.

binocular disparity: the difference in inputs to the two eyes that can contribute to perception of relative depth of nearby objects.

binocular rivalry: the phenomenon where, if different images are presented to each eye, the perception is not fusion of the two, but alternation between them.

binocular vision: a combination and comparison of the information received from the eyes, used in the stereoscopic aspect of depth perception, but also in a number of other ways.

biogenetic processes: in neo-Piagetian skill theory, all life processes that function below the level of psychological experience and action. In a hierarchical view of development, organism-environment systems function as multileveled processes. Higher levels emerge from integrations of lower-level systems, but have properties that are absent from and not reducible to lower-level systems. As such, while psychological processes (e.g.,

meaning making, experience, mediated action) are biological processes that occur within a biogenetic medium, a distinction is made between lower-level biogenetic processes (gene action, cell metabolism, brain functioning) and higher-order individual-agentic and sociocultural processes and systems.

biological motion: perception of the motion of independent stimulus elements as part of a moving human or animal figure, as when luminous dots are placed on a walking person and recorded in isolation.

biological risk factor: biological conditions of the child (e.g., appearance), and influences on the child's health status, particularly the nervous system (e.g., prenatal teratogens, preterm birth, illnesses) that increase the probability of the child's physical and/or psychological vulnerability.

birth asphyxia: a vague term referring to the process whereby hypoxia occurring during the intrapartum period causes some chronic ill effect, the duration or severity of which is not specified but understood to be more than the expected compensatory responses. Some factors, such as acidosis or fetal distress, are followed by abnormal neurological signs and hypoxic damage to other organs may be consistent with birth asphyxia, but they are not specific to it and can be indicators of damage occurring before labor.

birth prevalence: cases of a specified condition that can be identified by a given age. Excludes cases that cannot be ascertained because they die before the condition is recognized, as well as those that outgrow the condition by the given age and those who migrate in. Includes cases who die after being diagnosed and those who migrate out. Rates are calculated using live births or neonatal deaths as the denominator.

blastula: the first stage in the development of an embryo formed by cleavage of the zygote. It consists of a hollow sphere containing undifferentiated dividing cells (blastomeres), which form a layer (blastoderm) around a central cavity (blastocoele). In mammals, the embryo at this stage is referred to as the blastocyst.

Bock's profile analysis: a variant of multivariate repeated measures analysis of variance, in which time-adjacent means are compared.

BOLD signal: the *b*lood *o*xygen *l*evel *d*ependent signal that serves as the basis for current methods in fMRI.

botulinus: toxin injections made from a chemical produced by bacteria that temporarily paralyze muscle by acting on nerve impulse transmission. They produce reduction of hypertonicity by reversible denervation.

brachial plexus: a group of nerves formed from vertebral levels C5-T1 that are responsible for innervating most of the structures in the upper limb.

brain derived neurotrophic factor (BDNF): in contrast to nerve growth factor (NGF), BDNF is mainly, though not exclusively, localized in the central nervous system. It supports the survival of primary sensory neurons originating from the neural crest and ectodermal placodes that are not responsive to NGF.

brain (neuro-)imaging: identified by two broad categories – structural and functional imaging. Structural imaging evolved from radiographic techniques for imaging the brain through non-invasive techniques such as computerized axial tomography (CAT) to two-dimensional structural Magnetic Resonance Imaging (sMRI). Functional imaging, which began with xenon gas inhalation, really started to develop with the discovery of radioligands that remained in the blood stream or entered the brain to bind to certain receptors, which gave rise to single photon emission computerized tomography (SPECT) and positron emission tomography (PET). A subsequent breakthrough came with the development of oxygen-15 labeled water ($H_2^{15}O$ or H20-15) imaging. H20-15 emits positrons and creates images based on regional blood flow within the brain. Since active neurons recruit a robust blood supply, H20-15 PET allowed regional maps of brain activity to be made during a variety of cognitive tasks. When it was discovered that blood flow changes could be measured by H20-15, functional magnetic resonance imaging (fMRI) appeared on the scene. Instead of radiation or X-rays, MRI uses variation in the signal produced by the body's protons when it is placed in a strong magnetic field. Other imaging or brain mapping techniques include electroencephalography (EEG), magnetoencephalography (MEG), and optical imaging.

brain sparing: a notion derived from animal studies, which holds that when the developing organism is subjected to perinatal insults such as hypoxia, then the supply of oxygen and nutrients is preferentially directed to the brain at the expense of other vital organs like the kidneys and liver. Recent research, including that with preterm infants suffering from intrauterine growth retardation, has questioned the validity of this claim.

brain stem: an older, more 'primitive' part of the lower central mammalian brain responsible for organizing fundamental emotions related to fear, hunger, sex, protective drives, and temperature control, emotionality, arousal, sleep, heart and breathing rates, water retention, blood pressure and volume, as well as possibly the ratio of carbon dioxide to oxygen.

bridge law (or principle): also known as reduction function, it is a law (or set of laws) connecting the predicates of the reduced theory (the theory to be reduced) with the predicates of the reducing theory (the theory to which the first is reduced). First introduced by Ernest Nagel (1901–1985) as a means of integrating different levels of organization in a supratheoretic system and thus a step toward achieving the unity of science, he held that one theory could be reduced to another if it was possible to logically derive the first from the second, together with bridge laws. One claim for a bridge law that has been made is self-organization, something that is evident at all levels of organization.

bridging: in neo-Piagetian skill theory, a change process in which persons use a target skill (called a shell) to guide their construction of a new skill. People use the higher-level target like an algebraic equation in action, a target with unspecified components that are used to shape and direct the development of lower-level skills. In this way, the higher-level target serves as a bridge in the construction of the lower-level components to form a new skill.

broncopulmonary dysplasia: a respiratory disorder in preterm infants due to the treatment of severe respiratory distress and which can result in considerable damage of the lung tissue.

Caenorhabditis (c.) elegans (or nematode): a species of microscopic roundworm found in the soil and used for genetic studies as it has a small genome of only six chromosomes.

calcarine sulcus: sulcus that begins under the posterior end of the corpus callosum and arches to the occipital pole. The visual cortex is arranged around this sulcus.

canalization: according to Conrad H. Waddington (1905–1975), this concept represents a general summary of a number of facts in genetics and embryology. Broadly speaking, it can be defined as the capacity of the epigenetic system to attain developmental end-states despite minor variations in initial conditions and conditions met during subsequent development (viz., genetic and environmental perturbations). The depth to which a developmental pathway is canalized or buffered is taken to represent the strength of its homeorhetic properties.

case-comparison design: a research design in which cases of a given disease or other condition are sampled for study. A comparison sample of persons not having the condition is also recruited, as far as possible from the same basic population. These samples are then compared on exposure to hypothesized risks for the condition.

catastrophe theory: devised originally by René F. Thom (1923–2002) to mathematically model Waddington's epigenetic landscape. It is a theory of dynamical systems based on analogy with topographical form and dealing with instabilities in a limited sub-class of such systems that can be described by potential functions.

category learning: the ability to group objects together that are perceptually dissimilar (e.g., different cats) and treat them as members of a single category. The ability to form categories has been shown to exist even in 3-month-old infants. However, the category structures of infants differ from those of adults.

causal determinism (or causalism): the doctrinal assertion of the causality principle. In general terms, it advocates the idea that every event is necessitated by antecedent events and conditions, together with the laws of nature. Pursued thoroughly enough it will explain all phenomena and thus give rise to a theory of everything.

cell adhesion molecules (CAMs): receptors on the neuronal membrane with a configuration having a specific attraction to outgrowing axons and thus leading to specific connectivity.

cell assemblies: a group of neurons that act together in processing a certain task. One neuron can be part of several cell assemblies.

cell recognition molecules: particular proteins or other complex molecules generated by one cell type that another cell type has receptors for and can 'recognize' (i.e., receptor uptake of these molecules causes some change in the cell's physiology, usually by genetic instruction).

cell theory: in its modern form, the theory that all cells come from previously existing cells and that they are the fundamental functional units of all living organisms. Considered to be one of the most important theories in biology, it was originally proposed by Matthias Schleiden (1804–1881) in 1838 and again the following year by Theodor Schwann (1810–1882), it became known as the Schleiden-Schwann cell theory.

central nervous system (CNS): that part of the nervous system in vertebrates consisting of the brain and cerebral ganglia together with retina and the spinal cord. Anything else is considered to be the peripheral nervous system.

central pattern generator (CPG): a network of spontaneously active interneurons that emit modulated rhythmical activity. Those situated in the spinal cord are implicated in the coordination of rhythmical activities such as locomotion.

cerebellar cortex: the outer layer of the cerebellum (also known as the molecular layer), mainly consisting of parallel fibers and cerebellar interneurons.

cerebellum: the 'small brain,' a major structure of the metencephalon (hindbrain), lying above the medulla and pons, that occupies most of the posteriocranial fossa. It is generally considered to be involved in a feedback circuit governing the activity of the extrapyramidal motor system. As an important part of the motor system, it controls muscle tone and involuntary movements and provides coordination and integration of movements as well as other timing functions in behavior. Damage to the cerebellum impairs motor learning.

cerebral cortex: the six-layered, convoluted sheet of neural tissue (gray matter) that dominates the outside view of the human brain, forming the cerebrum. A more literary term than isocortex or neocortex, which refer to the same structure.

cerebral palsy: the cerebral palsies are a heterogenous collection of motor disorders, best defined as a group of non-progressive, but often changing, motor impairment syndromes secondary to lesions or abnormalities of the brain arising in the early stages of its development.

character: in evolutionary biology, characters, in contrast to traits, are shared similarities, which are regarded as properties (structures or behaviors) in different organisms. They are treated as being heritable and homologous.

child development: a vast multidisciplinary area of study that includes, for example, child psychology, child psychiatry, developmental psychology, and pediatrics as well as various sub-fields of biological and cultural anthropology, linguistics, neuroscience, and sociology. It is distinguished by methodological pluralism (e.g., experimental and correlational) and a range of theoretical and applied concerns. There tends to be a divide between research carried out during and beyond infancy, especially with regard to cognitive development, and some (e.g., Society for Research in Child Development) contend that child development does not include the period of adolescence. In recent years, there has been a noticeable tendency for the study of child development to incorporate theory and findings from developmental and evolutionary biology as well as concerned efforts to relate prenatal and postnatal development in terms of identifying the continuities and discontinuities between them.

child psychology: a branch of psychology supposedly founded by Wilhelm T. Preyer (1841–1897) that typically studies the behavior of children at key ages or makes comparisons between adjacent ages using experimental methods in order to tease out age-specific functions, processes, and mechanisms that may be deemed to be cognitive, emotional, social, etc., in nature. Often it is used interchangeably with developmental psychology, but strictly speaking there are differences between them, the main one being that the chief concern of developmental psychology should be the study of both intra- and inter-individual differences as a function of age. Child psychology as generally practiced does not deal with change in this way, nor with the identification of developmental transitions between states or stages, but at most with age differences in a variable-oriented approach.

childhood amnesia: the inability of adults to recall early autobiographical memories.

cholinergic neurotransmitter system: a system in the brain using the neurotransmitter acetylcholine that is based in the mesencephalic reticular activating system and which distributes acetylcholine throughout the brain. This system has a widespread energizing influence on brain activity and is closely tied to sustained attention and alerting.

chorionic villus sampling: the removal and genetic analysis of tissue that will eventually form the placenta.

chromosome: a threadlike, deeply stained, structure contained in the nucleus of a cell of eukaryotic organisms and composed mainly of DNA and protein in the form of chromatin. Each chromosome consists of two chromatids bound together at the centromere. According to classical genetics, it is the bearer of the genes in a linear order and thus like 'beads on a string,' which molecular genetics now compares to 'a string on the beads.' As for all diploid organisms, human cells normally have 46 chromosomes or 23 pairs (22 matched pairs and one pair of sex chromosomes), with one of each pair being contributed by the mother and the other by the father at conception. The number of chromosomes is constant for the somatic cells into which chromatin resolves itself during mitosis and meiosis.

classical conditioning: a form of learning where an initially neutral stimulus is paired with a response-eliciting stimulus.

cleavage: the series of mitotic cell divisions during which a single fertilized egg, the zygote, is transformed into a multicelluar body, the blastula.

closed-class: a grammatical class of words with limited membership and which have primarily grammatical meaning (e.g., conjunctions, demonstratives, determiners, pronouns, auxiliary verbs).

closed-ended interviewing: interaction between a researcher/interviewer and a respondent in which the interviewer presents a prepared set of questions to each respondent in the same words and in the same order, and asks each respondent to select from a prepared set of possible responses. It can be contrasted with open-ended interviewing in which respondents are free to respond in their own words, and interviewers may re-phrase questions, probe for additional information, and construct new questions, so that the content of the interview varies across respondents.

closed-loop and open-loop control: terms originating in engineering and transferred to the study of motor control. Closed-loop control refers to control achieved by feedback such that the actual response conforms to the desired response (or set point) by means of correcting any difference between them. The feedback path, input to output and back to input, forms what is called a closed loop (e.g., monosynaptic reflex arc, cortico-cerebellar loops). In contrast, open-loop or predictive control involves control only by an input signal, without the benefit of feedback. In this form of control, the input signal is amplified so as to drive the motor to perform the desired outcome. Aiming movements of the hand toward a target that are performed too quickly for proprioceptive feedback to have occurred are typically given as an example of open-loop control.

cluster reduction: a phonological pattern of deletion of one or more elements in a consonant cluster as in 'tick' for 'stick.'

co-factor: an accompanying condition, circumstance, or characteristic necessary or sufficient to produce a particular outcome, result, or event.

co-occurrence learning: learning what words can occur before or after a given word.

co-regulation: the idea that in face-to-face social interaction, social partners simultaneously and continuously adjust their thoughts, feelings, and actions to those of their interlocutor. The concept of co-regulation implies that individuals are not autonomous in their social behavior.

co-sleeping: refers to a diverse, generic class of human-wide sleeping arrangements (mother-infant, husband-wife-children, brother-sister, etc.) wherein at least two or more persons sleep within proximity or close enough to permit each (or all) to detect, monitor, and exchange sensory stimuli (e.g., odors, sound, movement, touch, gaze, etc.).

co-twin method: a method for comparing the development of monozygotic twins in which one is given regular practice or training on a specific ability or a range of them, while such experiences are withheld from the other twin. If practice does not make a difference, then it is taken as evidence that the environment plays little role in development and thus it is genetically determined.

coccal infections: infections with certain bacteria, including streptococci, and staphylococci.

cochlea: the organ of the inner ear that detects frequency variations in incoming sound waves.

cochlear nucleus: the portion of the medulla in the lower brain to which the auditory nerve connects. This area is organized by frequency response characteristics.

coding scheme: a set or sets of mutually exclusive and exhaustive categories used when coding behavior, either live or video-recorded or from transcripts.

cognition: a generic term involving high-level functions such as recognizing, concept formation, imagining, judging, problem-solving, reasoning, remembering, and thinking. Applied to the social domain (i.e., social cognition) it refers to how people select, interpret, remember, and use social information to make judgments and decisions. It is intimately related to perception and difficult to distinguish from it as, for example, when studying attentional processes.

cognitive behavior therapy (CBT): developed from Ellis and Beck's cognitive theories of depression. It aims to challenge and eliminate negative distortions and replace negative automatic thoughts with alternative adaptive thoughts by using logical analysis and behavioral experiments. Behavioral techniques include increasing rewarding activities (activity scheduling), decreasing behavior that is followed by unpleasant consequences, training of family/friends to praise/encourage constructive behaviors and not to reinforce depressive behaviors, and assertiveness and social skills training.

cognitive development: in very general terms, the development of abilities necessary for understanding and organizing the world and including, for example, the acquisition of those required for discrimination, memory, and problem-solving. Piaget's genetic epistemology had a major impact on conceptualizing and studying cognitive development, with his functional universals of assimilation and accommodation interacting in the process of equilibration. In more recent times, the theory of embodiment is beginning to have an impact on theorizing about the nature of cognitive development: the acquisition of knowledge is attained through exploratory cycles of perception and action that result from a brain interacting with a body and the body interacting with the external world.

cognitive-functionalist approach: in linguistics, the view that language structure is shaped by the semantic and pragmatic properties of the messages being communicated and by the mechanisms of language perception and production. Stands in contrast with the 'generative approach.'

cognitive psychology: the branch of psychology that studies the processes and mechanisms underlying all forms of cognition, mainly by experimental methods. To begin with, it was based on testing information-processing models of cognitive functioning, but in recent years these models have been challenged by dynamical systems approaches and the theory of embodiment.

Cohen's kappa coefficient: an index of the extent to which two observers agree when applying a nominal scale (i.e., a set of mutually exclusive and exhaustive categories), that corrects for chance agreement, and which provides a measure of inter-rater reliability.

cohort: a number of people who share a common characteristic linked to a specified place and time (e.g., born in a particular geographical location over a specified time period, or the year of marriage). The birth cohort of 1958 is comprised of all individuals born in that calendar year, while the marriage cohort of 1982 consists of all individuals married in 1982.

cohort effect: a characterization of a group such as a variable mean or an association between variables that changes for persons born at different times or places.

colic: refers to prolonged, unexplained crying in 1- to 3-month-old infants. It may be used to refer to amounts of crying, to the inference that the crying is caused by gastrointestinal pain, or to the reports of parents that the crying is a problem.

common coding: a recent hypothesis in cognitive psychology stating that perception and action are not independent systems, but rather share resources and mutually influence each other. Thus, action perception and action planning draw on the same psychological codes and representations.

community survey: a research design in which conclusions are intended to be drawn about the whole of the people in the community (usually defined geographically) or a particular sub-group within it. Attention is therefore given to the representativeness of the sample from which data are recorded.

co-morbidity: the co-occurrence of two or more disorders in the same individual and usually used in relation to psychiatric disorders.

comparative method: the combined evaluation of both similarities and differences in behavior and its roots across species, developmental periods, individuals, and cultures.

competence (embryology): a reactive state permitting directional development and differentiation in response to a stimulus or organizer. Closely associated with the concept of sensitive period.

competence (psychology): the display of adequate abilities or qualities for a particular task or situation.

competitive exclusion model: a model of imprinting proposed by Patrick Bateson that posits experience with the imprinting stimulus as the causal factor for the end of the sensitive period.

composite scale: a score created by aggregating several of the items in a questionnaire or set of tests.

compound symmetry: constant variances and constant covariances of the dependent measure across the levels of a factor in analysis of variance. This property of the variance-covariance matrix is present when the main diagonal elements of a set of multivariate data are equal to one another, and which must also be the case for the off-diagonal elements. It is a condition that is important in the analysis of longitudinal data.

computational models: computer programs that are used to explain different aspects of cognitive and behavioral development and processing. A computational model implements a theory of development and can be used to test this theory and to generate predictions that can be tested empirically.

conditional knockouts: usually transgenic animals in which specific genes can be knocked out only in certain cells or at certain times under experimental control.

conduct disorder: a psychiatric diagnosis, created by the American Psychiatric Association, for children who violate age-appropriate social norms and rules, especially by physically aggressing persons, damaging property, stealing, running away from home, and not going to school. Thus, it is a consistent pattern of socially non-acceptable, norm-breaking behavior leading to functional disability.

configural processing: assignment of the spatial relationship between facial features during face processing.

confirmatory factor analysis (CFA): a type of factor analysis where the specific number of factors and the pattern of the zero and non-zero loadings are hypothesized a priori and in advance of the estimation. CFA is often used to compare one specific alternative factor model hypothesis to another.

confound: means literally to throw something into disorder. In the research context, this term is used when there are two or more explanations for a significant result, usually because a study cannot control extraneous variables.

confounding variable: a factor that generates an apparent association between two variables because it has a prior association with both. For example, height and school achievement may both be associated with socioeconomic status. Thus, an apparent link between size and success could be said to be subject to confounding by social class.

congenital malformations: deformities acquired early in development and, prior to detection by ultrasound, noted only at birth.

CONLERN: a term coined by John Morton and Mark Johnson to reflect the infant's acquisition of face knowledge by virtue of experience viewing faces. Presumed to be mediated cortically.

connectionism: a theoretical framework in which networks of interconnected nodes (analogous to neural networks) process information through an activation dynamics while their connectivity evolves according to learning dynamics. Connectionist networks receive inputs that ultimately arise from sensor systems. Particular output layers are assumed to ultimately determine behavior. By generating activation at the output nodes in response to sensory inputs, connectionist networks process information. Through the learning dynamics, the connectivity of the network over the long run comes to reflect the sensory environment of the system.

connectionist models: a class of computational models that consist of a number of interconnected simple processing units. Often the units are arranged in several layers. Connectionist models learn from experience and have been used to explain several aspects of infant cognitive and behavioral development.

conscience: internalization of the rules and restrictions of society; it determines which behaviors are permissible and punishes wrongdoing with feelings of guilt.

consciousness: a phenomenon that the philosopher William James (1842–1910) likened to a 'stream' or process by which a sense of self is attained through a succession of experiences. The pragmatist John Dewey (1859–1952) added that consciousness is an emergent property of sentient creatures, which develops and enables discrimination and choice based on the satisfaction of needs and desires. He also argued that, while consciousness involves privately experienced states, categorical thinking must be communicable or based on shared meanings to sustain self-consciousness. Other pertinent features of consciousness have to do with the limited capacity of the brain to sustain perception and memory. Attention controls access to consciousness and memory establishes the extent to which on-going events can be re-categorized to include novel and unexpected situations. Some developmental psychologists (e.g., Myrtle McGraw, Jerome Kagan) have contended that infant sensitivity to balance, novelty, and discrepancy paves the way for the emergence of consciousness by stimulating the neural mechanisms of arousal and attention. Neuroscientists, however, remain divided about the neural correlates of conscious states. Some contend (Michael Posner) that consciousness is strongly correlated with the firing patterns of neurons in specific brain regions, while others believe (Gerald Edelman) that consciousness involves the synchrony and coherence of widely distributed neuron groups.

conservation: in general, the concept that some quantitative aspect of an entity remains unchanged despite a transformation in its appearance. Piaget devised a series of tasks to test children's understanding of conservation in a variety of entity domains (e.g., mass, number, volume, weight). For example, in conservation-of-mass tasks, children are tested on whether or not they understand that two identical balls of clay will have the same amount (mass) even if one of them is rolled out into a sausage. In terms of number, if two rows containing equal numbers of counters are presented in one-to-one alignment, and then the counters in one row are moved closer together, the number of counters in the two rows remains the same.

CONSPEC: a term coined by Morton and Johnson to reflect an innate bias to orient to face-like stimuli in the first two months of life. Presumed to be mediated by the superior colliculus.

constraint: a condition that preserves the symmetry of a system and restricts its degrees of freedom. When the system is perturbed, it may lead to symmetry breaking. Applied to behavior, a constraint is a boundary condition that eliminates or restrains certain configurations of action while permitting or enabling others. There are two classes of constraints: holonomic or law-governed constraints that restrict without having any material embodiment in the system (e.g., Newton's laws of motion) and non-holonomic or rule-governed constraints that are physically embodied in the system (e.g., a schema) and which serve as prescriptions for action. Computational models incorporate the latter constraints (e.g., model architecture, training algorithm, training regime). In terms of cognition, a constraint is anything that makes representational development selective in what becomes represented or how the representation occurs. Typically, a constraint has the function of guiding the child's learning within biological boundaries to the extent to which the child can process

information and prepare action. In developmental biology, four classes of holonomic constraints are recognized: developmental constraints, physical constraints, morphological constraints, and phyletic constraints.

construct equivalence: the measurement principle asserting that a construct or factor can be measured under different circumstances or at different occasions yet still retain its basic property. In practice, several levels of equivalence may be investigated, including factor loading equivalence (or factorial invariance) and factor score equivalence.

construct validity: the process of assessing the significance and utility of a measure by examining whether it predicts associations (and lack of associations) with other variables in the way predicted by the theoretical concept being studied.

constructivism: the philosophical idea that knowledge and meaning are constructed by action on objects and are neither innate nor simply transmitted through experience. Constructivists believe that events have no meaning by themselves, but instead that individuals must create meaning through the application of existing actions or ways of knowing. It is the epistemological theory that underlies Piaget's approach to cognitive development.

contamination: the influence of one measure of behavior upon the measurement of another (e.g., if parents know how a teacher has rated their child and modify their own rating accordingly).

content analysis: the systematic coding of the contents of a text or narrative.

context (cultural): the ecological and social environment in which individuals function and that they share with members of a larger group (e.g., ethnic group or national group).

context (interview): that which surrounds or accompanies a behavior or event. For example, the verbal or linguistic context of a question in an interview may include the other questions and answers that preceded it. The non-verbal or non-linguistic context may include the interviewer's non-verbal behaviors (e.g., gestures and facial expressions), salient props (e.g., pictures, toys, or other objects), and actions carried out by the interviewer and/or child (e.g., picking up a toy). Broader aspects of the context would include where and when the interview took place, the degree of familiarity between the interviewer and child, and the formality/informality of the interviewer's style.

contexts (of expression): variations in behavior and its control that occur as a function of internal and external events.

continuous performance task: a type of task that demands active cognitive performance over an extended period. Good performance in such a task requires extended periods of sustained attention, and extended activation of brain areas involved in sustained attention. Children with attention deficit hyperactivity disorder (ADHD) show deficits on continuous performance tasks, which are taken to imply deficits in the brain regions controlling sustained attention.

contour: the pattern of upward and downward pitch change.

contrast sensitivity: visual sensitivity to varying levels of brightness.

control group: a group of individuals who do not receive the experimental treatment being studied. This group serves as a comparison for the experimental group who do receive the treatment of interest.

control parameter: in dynamical systems terminology, it is not an ordering principle, but guides a system through its respective collective states (as defined by order parameters) in non-specific ways. Looked at another way, it is a boundary condition that acts as a constraint on the dynamics of the order parameter. When increased or scaled up beyond some critical value, it can transiently lose its constraining influence on the order parameter, which may then manifest stochastic or even chaotic behavior before making a sudden jump to another state. The important point about control parameters is they do not prescribe variations in the patterning of the order parameter in a strictly deterministic fashion. Instead, they control in only leading the order parameter unspecifically through regions of instabilities or keeping the system within a stable operating range.

convergent evolution: when unrelated species evolve comparable characteristics that are derived from different features. This is in contrast to parallel evolution, where related species independently evolve characteristics that are derived from the same features.

convergent validity: the converse of discriminant validity. An aspect of construct validity, in which measures of constructs that theoretically should be related to each other are shown, in fact, to be related to each other (i.e., you should be able to show a correspondence or convergence between similar constructs).

coordination: the maintenance of a particular relationship between components of an action system. Coordination most typically refers to the timing of movement, although some authors have applied the term to describe spatial relationships as well. Interlimb coordination refers to the maintenance of a particular pattern of timing between the movements of different limbs. Intralimb coordination refers to the maintenance of a particular pattern of timing between different joints within a limb. Maintaining a relationship between the timing of a movement and the time of occurrence of a particular event in the outside environment is also a form of coordination (e.g., when catching a ball).

coordinative structure: a term introduced by Nikolai A. Bernstein (1896–1966) to indicate a functional grouping of muscles spanning a number of joints that is flexibly assembled to achieve a specific goal. Also referred to as a synergy or functional generator. It is seen as a solution to the degrees-of-freedom problem in that muscles are not controlled as separate units, but as task-specific, functional groupings.

copying errors: refers to mistakes made when chromosomes are being replicated (e.g., deletion of certain genes or making too many copies of certain genes).

corpus callosum: the large midline band or collection of commissural fibers connecting the right and left hemispheres of the cerebral cortex.

corrected age: postnatal age minus the number of weeks born before the gestational age of 40 weeks. For example, an infant born at 30 weeks gestation and tested at 20 weeks after birth has a corrected age of $20 - (40 - 30) = 10$ weeks. This preterm infant can then be compared to fullterm infants with a postnatal age of 10 weeks. The rationale for using corrected age is that development is a function of time since conception and not time from birth. Thus, corrected age matches preterm and fullterm infants in terms of 'level of maturity.'

correspondence problem: the problem of how the imitator knows what acts of their own 'match' those they see in others. What is the metric of equivalence? Traditional theories assume that visual and motor systems are separate; this poses the correspondence problem.

cortical area: a fundamental division of the cerebral cortex, containing many columns. Each cortical area is usually recognized by a topographic representation of some feature, like the visual field, characteristic structure of its layers, and particular inputs and outputs.

cortical column: a cyclinder of cells extending the depth of the cerebral cortex, and which is the fundamental repeating unit of the cortex. Each column does a stereotyped intake, transformation, and distribution of a particular class of information.

cortical inhibition hypothesis: associated with reflexology, it seemingly originated with the founding father of British neurology John Hughlings Jackson (1835–1911) and his idea of physiological inhibition or encephalization based on the brain possessing a hierarchical organization such that 'higher' centers (i.e., the cortex) suppressed the expression of behaviors assumed to be controlled by 'lower' centers (i.e., sub-cortical structures like the brain stem and spinal cord). Applied to development, it holds that earlier appearing behaviors (e.g., reflexes) are tonically inhibited by the emerging influences descending from the newly developing cortex, and in this way voluntarily controlled actions emerge. In adult neurology, it was used by Jackson to account for the disappearance of reflexes under pathological conditions and is a reason why the hypothesis is inappropriate for the study of normal development.

cortical plate: the term for the developing cortex in embryogenesis, before it contains all its cellular components and has differentiated into its mature structure.

covariance: the expectancy of the cross-product of the differences of two strings of random scores from their respective means. Weighting by the strings' respective standard deviations yields the correlation of the two strings. Thus, it is the summary statistic of association among a pair of variables calculated as the average of the products of the deviations of each variable.

covert attention: selection of targets in the absence of actual eye movements (e.g., when 'looking out of the corner of one's eye').

cranial nerve: motor and sensory nerves that carry the special senses, and control certain movements, the nuclei of which reside in the brainstem.

critical literacy: a way of teaching literacy that emphasizes looking at the meanings embedded within texts and making explicit the author's purpose in writing the text in a particular way. Teaching entails questioning the construction of texts and analyzing the power of language to convey different things to different people. Students are encouraged to reflect on their own and others' attitudes and values.

critical period: a concept originating in embryology that referred to a time in development or growth that was most susceptible to the induction of new structures by neurochemical agents and whose effects were considered to be irreversible. Today, the term 'sensitive period' is generally used and applied to the development of both structure and function (e.g., learning).

cross-cultural psychology: a methodological approach to the study of the relationships between (human) behavior and cultural context.

cross-lagged correlation/regression model: a statistical technique used in longitudinal research in which the relative influences of two variables upon one another are examined, while the correlations between each within time and within each across time are taken into account. More technically, it is a linear regression model where scores on at least two variables (X and Y) are measured on at least two occasions (t = 1 and 2) and the scores at the later occasion (X[t + 1]) are predicted by the same variable 'lagged' in time (X[t]) and the other variable 'crossed' in time (Y[t + 1]).

cross-modal coordination: coordination of information that is picked up by different sensory modalities. For example, cross-modal coordination allows humans to recognize that a person's face (visual modality) and voice (auditory modality) go together. There are cross-modal connections among all five sensory modalities (sight, sound, smell, taste, and touch).

cross-modal matching: the integration of information from different perceptual systems (e.g., the mapping of visuo-spatial coordinates onto proprioceptive information about the position of the body in space).

cross-sectional design: a study that cuts across a population to compare different groups. It may compare the sexes or different social groups, but usually is used to compare different age groups.

crying peak: epidemiological studies, carried out mainly in western societies, have found a peak in minutes of infant crying per twenty-four hours at around 5–6 weeks of age. However, the same phenomenon has also been found in non-western cultures and in preterm infants of the same corrected age, which suggest it is a universal feature of early infancy.

cumulative incidence (CI): the proportion of people who become diseased during a specified period of time and calculated as:

$$CI = \frac{\text{number of new cases of a disease during a given period of time}}{\text{total population at risk}}$$

An even more precise estimate of incidence that utilizes all available information is called the incidence rate (IR), force of morbidity or mortality, or incidence density (ID). This is considered to be a measure of the instantaneous rate of development of disease in a population and is defined as:

$$CI = \frac{\text{number of new cases of a disease during a given time period}}{\text{total person-time of observation}}$$

cytokines: any of numerous hormone-like, low-molecular-weight proteins, secreted by various cell types that regulate the intensity and duration of immune response and mediate cell-cell communication, as well as acting as signals in cell survival, growth, differentiation, and apoptosis. Examples include interferon, interleukin, lymphokine, chemokines, and various growth factors.

cytoplasm: the jelly-like material surrounding the nucleus of a cell. It is differentiated into ectoplasm (concerned mainly with cell movement) and less dense endoplasm containing most of the cell's structures.

Darwinism: Darwin's theory of natural selection of small, inherited variations that increase an individual's ability to compete for resources, survive, and reproduce. The problems for Darwin were how such genetic variations arose and how they were transmitted from one generation to the next. The answer to the first problem was random mutation, with chromosomal rearrangement and genetic recombination being added at a later date.

data-driven processes: processes that operate in response to information coming into the system. A young child might try to keep her balance on a roundabout by feeling her way to where it seems safest; an older child might have reasoned out that the rim of the roundabout is the most challenging. Where the younger child's decision is driven by sensory data on the platform motion, the older child may take a theory-driven decision on the layout of the platform.

décalage: Piagetian idea that cognitive abilities develop at different rates in the same individual. For example, children solve conservation of number tasks before they solve conservation of mass tasks.

declarative (or explicit) and procedural memory: both are classes of long-term memory. Declarative memory is the portion of long-term memory where information about facts and specific events is stored, involves structures in the temporal lobe (especially the hippocampus), and is distinguished in terms of episodic and semantic memory. Procedural memory, which is governed by different brain systems, is a storage system for information concerning complex activities that have become highly automatized and are performed without much conscious effort, but which are acquired by a relatively slow process of learning (e.g., driving a car, riding a bicycle).

decoding ability: a reading sub-skill involving the ability to translate letters into sounds to derive the pro-nunciation of a printed word.

dehydroepiandrosterone (DHEA): an endogenous hormone secreted by the adrenal cortex. Levels are virtually non-existent in the pre-school child, increase markedly between 6 and 20 years of age and then decline. The developmental functions of DHEA remain unclear.

delay(ed) conditioning: a classical conditioning procedure in which the conditional stimulus begins before and overlaps with the onset of the unconditional stimulus. The two stimuli then terminate together.

demand characteristics: the degree to which participants in an experiment experience an expectation that they should behave in a particular way.

dendrite: branch-like nerve cell process collecting incoming or afferent information.

denervation: injury to a peripheral nerve, resulting in disconnection from its target (synapse).

deoxyribose: the sugar in DNA, which is similar to ribose, but lacks one oxygen atom.

dependent differentiation: the idea that activity and interaction among structures and functions is necessary to embryonic development.

dermomyotome: tissue derived from somites that goes on to form muscle and dermis.

design matrix: contains vectors that specify the effects under study in linear models.

determination: the developmental process in which cells and tissues of the embryo become progressively restricted in what they may become. Cells of the early embryo may be totipotent, capable of producing cells of any organ system of the adult. But as development proceeds, cells become increasingly limited in their potential and directed toward a definite structure and function.

determinism: the doctrine of linear causality, which holds that the state of a system at one moment determines its states at all subsequent times. Its roots lie in the idea that everything can be explained, at least in principle (termed 'universal determinism'). While they are in some sense deterministic, non-linear dynamical systems do not show such long-range predictability. This is because their initial conditions do not dictate their subsequent behavior in the same way. Chaos is a form of non-linear determination without predictability.

developmental acceleration: units of change in developmental velocity during a specified time interval. After having subtracted the mean velocity value at a previous age from that at a subsequent adjacent age to give one for speed of development, then the resulting adjacent scores are again subtracted from each other (double differentiation) to give a measure of accele-ration (the unit of change) between the two ages.

Developmental acceleration obtained in this way can be used to indicate sudden changes in a process of continuous development.

developmental biology: the study of mechanisms and processes of ontogenetic development, differentiation, growth, and morphogenesis in animals and plants at the genetic, molecular, cellular, and functional levels. Its model organisms include, for example, the roundworm (*Caenorhabditis elegans*), the fruit fly (*Drosophila melanogaster*), the zebrafish (*Brachydanio rerio*), and the African clawed toed frog (*Xenopus laevis*). Starting in the 1990s, there have been further attempts to unite developmental and evolutionary biology in what is called a 'new synthesis.'

developmental bootstrapping: a term used in developmental psychology to indicate that one ability provides leverage for acquiring a second, different ability. The prior ability sets conditions under which the latter can be more easily acquired.

developmental cognitive neuroscience: the study of how the development and growth of the brain relates to the emergence of new behavioral abilities.

developmental coordination disorder (DCD): as defined by the American Psychiatric Association in DSM-IV (1994), it is a generic term encompassing a range of developmental motor impairments of less severity than recognized syndromes such as cerebral palsy. Some researchers now consider DCD to share some of the same dysfunctional mechanisms as cerebral palsy, although much less severely.

developmental delay: describes the development in a child who is slower than the accepted norms. For example, walking is usually achieved by 18 months of age and walking after that time would be described as delayed, although it might not necessarily be an indication of something wrong with the child.

developmental disorders: disorders, often caused by genetic or chromosomal defects, that lead to abnormal development. The resulting disorder can be general or affect different aspects of behavior to different degrees. Well-known developmental disorders are Asperger's syndrome, autism, Down's syndrome, the fragile-X syndrome, and Williams syndrome.

developmental dyspraxia: difficulties with movement planning resulting in impairments of gesture and sequencing. Often used synonymously with Developmental Coordination Disorder (DCD) by groups interested in raising public awareness of coordination disorders.

developmental emergence: the appearance of new abilities and structures in the child as a result of

dynamical interactions involving the brain, body, and society. For example, the emergence of babbling can occur as the coupling of the oscillatory movements of the jaw with those of the vocal cords.

developmental epistemology: epistemology is the branch of philosophy that deals with the theory of knowledge. Its standard questions – What is knowledge? How does knowledge differ from true belief? – are normative and non-empirical. Developmental epistemology (i.e., Piaget's genetic epistemology) deals with the genesis or development of knowledge in two respects: (1) its initial formation, and (2) its valid constitution.

developmental evolutionary biology: see *evolutionary developmental biology*.

developmental function: a term applied, originally by Joachim Wohlwill (1928–1987), to the form or mode of the relationship between the chronological age of an individual and the changes occurring in that person on some specified dimension of behavior. By 'form or mode' is meant either qualitative change (e.g., in terms of a sequence of stages) or quantitative change (e.g., in terms of an exponential function). Sometimes referred to as a developmental trajectory.

developmental genetics: an important and burgeoning part of developmental biology that can be broadly defined as the study of how the genotype is transformed into the phenotype during development. Thus, it concerns identifying the mechanisms of differential gene expression from the same nuclear material during development. It arose from a division between embryologists and geneticists as to the role of genes in development during the first half of the 20th century. Today, its two main methods are forward and reverse genetics, the former for identifying genes responsible for particular genotypes and the latter for discovering phenotypes through changing the functions of specific genes.

developmental gradients: see *maturational gradients*.

developmental neuropsychology: the study of the appearance and development of language, perception, memory, and other cognitive processes as they relate to brain functions and structures across the lifespan.

developmental plasticity: in the context of the nervous system, this refers to the role of neuronal activity and sensory experience in the normal development and maintenance of neuronal anatomy and function. It can also apply to compensatory changes in the nervous system following perturbations at any stage in the lifespan.

developmental psychobiology: a field of study that endeavors to integrate developmental psychology and developmental biology, largely by means of experimental methods. Mainly this is done by combining topics in psychology (e.g., attachment, emotion) with techniques from biology (e.g., heart rate), neurophysiology (e.g., single cell recordings), and genetics (e.g., gene mapping). A large part of the research is animal-based, with the rat being a prominent model, but attempts are made to forge theoretical links between this research and that on developing humans.

developmental psychology: a branch of psychology devoted to the study of age-related change in psychological functions in both humans and animals, using a variety of both experimental and observational methods. It has theoretical implications for other branches of psychology and practical applications (e.g., in providing more effective techniques for teaching children who are developmentally delayed). More recently, lifespan psychology has extended the focus of study to adult development in considering systematic change from conception to death as its subject matter. The areas covered include cognitive, emotional, perceptual, moral, motor, language, memory, and social development, with increasing attempts to forge theoretical links between them (e.g., between developmental cognitive and developmental social psychology). Overall, the main defining feature of developmental psychology (or at least it should be), and one that distinguishes it from child psychology, is a concern to account for inter-individual differences in intra-individual change.

developmental readiness: the age-related capacity of the individual to function effectively in specific situations.

developmental research: systematic study of constancy and change across the lifespan.

developmental risks: risks that are associated with some probability of a deviant developmental course, or trajectory; risks with outcomes later in a child's development.

developmental screening: refers to some form of assessment carried out to see that the child's development is proceeding as expected. The word 'screening' suggests a limited number of tests that allow an initial prognosis to be made.

developmental trajectories: patterns of developmental change that are either hypothesized or actual and in the latter case that may be used to identify sub-groups of individuals.

developmental velocity: units of change in a developmental variable during a specified time interval.

It is obtained by subtracting two age-related values from each other. For example, if a group of infants had a mean score of say 10 seconds for looking at a display followed by 15 seconds at the next age, then the measure of mean velocity between these two ages (or the unit of change) would be +5 seconds. It can also be the case that the velocity value obtained is negative. Such a measure of developmental velocity can sometimes be more informative than just the group mean in certain studies (e.g., in those comparing the development of fullterm and preterm infants), showing that the speed or tempo of development is faster for one group compared to another.

deviance statistic: used to compare the fit of two models after one or more parameters have been added or deleted.

diachronic biology: the label used by Conrad H. Waddington (1903–1975) to indicate his attempt at integrating genetics, embryology, and evolutionary biology into a unified developmental science based on dynamical principles. It can be considered as the forerunner of current attempts at creating an evolutionary developmental biology.

diachronic emergence: the emergence of new structures in the language through pressures from social group differentiation and stylistic variation.

diagnosis (or diacrisis): determining the cause or causes of a congenital defect, injury, or illness and account for its symptoms and signs. Diagnosis implies that a causative mechanism for the condition is known.

diaphysis: the shaft of a long bone lying between the epiphyses (plural: diaphyses).

diarthrodial joints: synovial joints having a joint capsule filled with fluid.

diencephalon: the basal cell mass of the forebrain that contains the thalamus and hypothalamus.

differentiation (general): according to Waddington, this term was borrowed by embryology from psychology. In developmental biology, it refers to the fact that cells not only increase in number during development, but also change in structure and function and become different in their specializations from their earlier forms and from one another.

differentiation (specific): in developmental biology, the commitment or specialization of embryonic stem cells to becoming a specific cell type or tissue.

diffusion anisotropy: an important consideration in brain imaging, it refers to the ability of water to move more in certain directions than in others. In the brain, this tendency is most often dependent on the orientation of white matter fiber tracts surrounding water.

diffusion tensor imaging: a technique used to visualize elements with directional structure, such as bundles of myelinated axons, in the brain.

diffusion tensor magnetic resonance imaging: as applied to neuroimaging, this Magnetic Resonance Imaging technique uses information about the direction of water movement in white matter to determine the size and orientation of its constituent fiber tracts.

digitigrade locomotion: locomotion with the toes at the end of the stance phase being in contact with the floor; typical pattern of adult human locomotion.

digraphs: combinations of letters that represent a single phoneme (e.g., 'gh' in 'laugh'). For the most part, these combinations are of consecutive letters, but sometimes they are split (e.g., the 'o-e' combination signifies a long 'o' sound, as in 'hope').

diploid organisms: a cell having two sets of chromosomes and thus twice the haploid number. Nearly all animal cells are diploid, except for the gametes.

direct corticomotoneuronal connections or tracts: the pyramidal fibers originating in the motor cortex and extending down the spinal cord. They connect to the muscles of the hand with just one synapse.

direct (monogenesis) and indirect (metagenesis and metamorphosis) development: monogenesis is the direct development of an embryo, without metamorphosis, into an organism similar to the parent. Metagenesis, like the other form of indirect development, metamorphosis, consists of marked changes undergone in a series of successively produced individuals, extending from the one developed from the ovum to the final mature individual. Unlike metamorphosis, metagenesis involves the production of sexual individuals by non-sexual means, either directly or through intervening sexless generations.

direct realist account: J. J. Gibson's theory of perception according to which the structure of the world is directly available to perception. According to this account, there is no need to postulate cognitive processes to interpret sensory input (i.e., converting sensations to perceptions) because the structure of the surroundings is objectively present in the available perceptual information.

disability: according to the International Classification of Impairments, Disabilities, and Handicaps (World Health Organization, 2001), any restriction or lack of ability to perform an activity in a manner or within the range considered normal for a human being. The term reflects the consequences of impairment with regard to

functional performance and activity by the individual; disabilities thus represent disturbances at the level of the whole person. Some would include developmental problems associated with social deprivation in the definition.

discourse analysis: an analysis of spoken language that moves beyond the study of grammar to try and understand how language is used, and what its effects are, in particular social and cultural contexts.

discriminant validity: an aspect of construct validity, in which measures of constructs that theoretically should not be related to each other are shown, in fact, not to be related to each other (i.e., you should be able to discriminate between dissimilar constructs).

displacement activities: actions studied by ethologists that appear out of context or irrelevant to the situation, such as scratching movements during conflict or anxiety.

display rules: the understanding of when, where, and how to control emotional expressions according to cultural expectations.

distributed representation: the concept that single perceptual, cognitive, or motor functions may be found over physically separate regions of the central nervous system, and that single regions of the nervous system may participate in multiple functions.

dizygotic twins: a pair of twins created from two separately fertilized eggs.

DNA (deoxyribonucleic acid): the self-replicating molecule forming the hereditary material as chromosomes in the nuclei of eukaryotes and as strands in prokaryotes. It is a nucleic acid made up of two chains of nucleotides composed of deoxyribose sugar and the bases adenine, cytosine, guanine, and thymine. The two chains wind round each other and are linked by hydrogen bonds between specific complementary bases to form a spiral ladder-shaped molecule called the double helix.

DNA double helix: the helical structure assumed by two strands of deoxyribonucleic acid (nucleotides), which are held together throughout their length by hydrogen bonds between bases on opposite strands like rungs on a ladder, referred to as Watson-Crick base pairing.

domain (interactive): the theoretical view that although systems of knowledge may be characterized by distinct properties, domains can interact with each other and are connected through a common underlying process.

domain (theory of mind): area of knowledge structured by a set of principles that have application to a set of distinctive phenomena. The child's theory of mind comes to apply to the domain of psychology by organizing phenomena of what people say and do according to the idea that there are relationships between people's intentions, beliefs, and desires. The child's theory of language comes to apply to the domain of speech by organizing the sounds according to the idea that there are chunks of meaning that sound distinct in regular ways.

domain specificity: an aspect of knowledge or its acquisition that is peculiar to the development of representations within a particular domain. The domain of number needs specific attention being paid to how numerous items happen to be, and specific counting skills have to be acquired. The domain of language needs attention to speech-sounds, and words have to be acquired.

dopamine: neurotransmitter that can initiate and modulate a wide range of actions and brain functions; often depleted or unbalanced in various disorders (e.g., Parkinson's disease, hyperactivity, and schizophrenia).

dorsal horn: column at dorsal side of the spinal cord (i.e., situated toward spine) and one of two major routes by which afferent information (i.e., somaesthesis) is carried to the thalamus (the other being the spinothalamic tract that transmits information about pain and temperature).

dorsal root ganglia (DRG): location of cell bodies of sensory neurons, lying lateral and dorsal to the spinal cord.

dorsal visual pathway (or stream): a cortical visual processing pathway that runs from the occipital lobes to parietal lobes and processes information relative to spatial locations or actions related to objects. Together with the ventral stream forms part of the influential two-visual systems hypothesis.

dorsolateral prefrontal cortex: one of the three main sub-divisions of the frontal cortex encompassing Broadman's areas 9–12, 47, and 48.

double dissociation: when an impairment in one ability can occur independently of another ability and vice versa, the two abilities are said to show a double dissociation.

Down's syndrome: a chromosomal abnormality characterized by the presence of extra genes associated with the 21st chromosome. Its incidence is about 1 per 700 live births.

downward causation (or macrocausation): a concept introduced by Donald T. Campbell in 1974 in order to combat radical reductionism and the excesses of bottom-up explanations as provided by genetic determinism. It is evident when a higher level of a system determines the behavior of lower levels of organization. Under this influence, all processes at lower levels are constrained to act according to the laws of the higher level. However, determination is not complete as the whole is to some degree constrained by the lower levels (upward or bottom-up causation), but at the same time the parts are to some degree constrained by the whole (downward or top-down causation). Such 'two-way causation' is said to typify the behavior of complex systems.

dual x-ray energy absorptiometry (DEXA): a method for estimating body composition, specifically bone mineral, fat-free soft tissues, and fat. The method requires a low radiation exposure in the form of two photon beams, one of low energy and the other of high energy.

dualism: a theory of ontology that there are only two real substances in the universe, one being material and the other being mental. Thus, the mind and body (or brain) exist independently of each other and have entirely different essences or natures.

Dubowitz scale: a method for the neurological assessment of the preterm and fullterm infant, which makes possible an adequate prediction of the child's gestational age (i.e., the age from conception).

ductus Botalli (or ductus arteriosus): part of the fetal circulation. It directly connects the left pulmonary artery to the aorta, thereby bypassing circulation of the non-ventilated lungs.

dynamic field theory: a theoretical framework in which ideas from the dynamical systems approach are extended to address how information is processed. The concept of activation is used similarly as in connectionism, but strong interactions within an activation dynamics lead to attractors and instabilities.

dynamic systems theory (development and evolution): a theory of biological form, intended to integrate biological evolution and ontogenetic development, that considers the whole organism rather than just genes as in the Modern synthesis. Its main thrust is that gene action takes place within self-organizing morphogenetic fields, which impose constraints on what forms can be generated, both in development and during evolution. While genes are acknowledged as being involved at every stage in the generation of form, the unity of developing and evolving organisms derives from the relational processes embodied in morphogenetic fields. One of a number of recent attempts to derive a new synthesis of development and evolution, the theory's main author is Brian Goodwin.

dynamical balance: flexible rules that alter the relative salience of defined factors such as those which control behavior.

dynamical coupling: the parameters describing how the process of changes within a variable emerge from one variable to another.

dynamical parameters: the parameters describing the process of changes within a variable.

dynamical system: any system that changes over time. Change can be continuous or discontinuous, and there are mathematical tools available (e.g., catastrophe theory) for distinguishing between these two types of change (and whether discontinuous changes are quantitative or qualitative in nature). The dynamics involved do not necessarily refer only to mechanical forces and masses as in Newtonian mechanics, but also to the most simple and abstract description of how the global behavior of a system evolves over time. Based on this distinction, there are two general classes of dynamical systems: linear and non-linear. More mathematically, when the temporal evolution of a system can be predicted based on its current state, then the system is a dynamical system. It can be characterized by a differential equation (or an iterative map if time is measured in discrete units). The mathematical theory of dynamical systems emphasizes qualitative properties of the solutions of such equations (e.g., their convergence in time to attractor states and their sensitivity to small changes of the equation).

dynamical systems approaches: in the wide sense, the use of concepts from the mathematical theory of dynamical systems to describe how the behavior of complex systems is generated over time. In the narrow sense, a specific theoretical framework, in which behavior is assumed to arise as stable states or attractors of dynamical systems, which depend on sensory information, task, intention, and interaction. Instabilities lead to change of behavior and thus demarcate qualitatively different behaviors or states.

dyslexia: a disorder of reading in which oral language skill and non-verbal cognitive ability are normal. May be acquired or developmental in origin. In developmental dyslexia, reading and spelling are both impaired.

dysmorphology: abnormal physical or morphological development, especially of a particular anatomical feature.

dysphoria: feelings of low or unpleasant mood often associated with depression.

Early Childhood Environment Rating Scale (ECERS): an instrument for measuring aspects of the environment of pre-school children, which can be considered to be measures of the quality of the preschool environment.

Early Childhood Longitudinal Studies (ECLS): sponsored by the US National Institute for Child Health and Human Development (NICHD), these studies focus on child development, child care, and the early school years and include two separate longitudinal panels: ECLS-B, that follows children from 9 months of age through first grade, and ECLS-K, which follows through from kindergarten entry to fifth grade.

echolalia: repetitive parroting of the words of others.

ecological fallacy: a bias derived for the inference of individual characteristics from aggregate data or an error of inference due to a failure to distinguish between different levels of organization. The bias or error may occur because an association that is observed among variables at an aggregate level does not necessarily exist at an individual level.

ecological systems theory: Uri Bronfenbrenner's theory, which states that family relationships must be understood as a network of interacting parts in a whole that is itself influenced by wider social processes.

ecological validity: how well a study generalizes to or represents everyday, real life. Studies with high ecological validity can be generalized beyond the setting in which they were carried out.

ecology: a term invented by Ernst H. Haeckel (1834–1919) in 1866 and which now denotes the interdisciplinary study of the relationships among organisms and their environments, including both living and non-living components. It addresses three levels of organization: the individual, the population, and community levels.

ectoderm: the outermost primary germ layer that originates during gastrulation, which gives rise to the nervous system and outer integument (i.e., outer protective covering such as skin and cuticle).

EEG stage 1 sleep: considered to be NREM (non-Rem, or quiet sleep), a transitional stage from wake to sleep wherein a person is close to being awake, but whose eyes exhibit slow, rolling movements, while the recorded brain waves are about 8 to 13 cycles per second.

EEG stage 2 sleep: considered to be NREM light sleep, follows stage 1 in both children and adults with brain wave forms occurring about 12–14 cycles per second of low voltage but mixed frequencies, and marked by K-complexes and sleep spindles; arousal threshold is a bit higher than what is needed to awaken a person from stage 1 sleep.

EEG stage 3 sleep: a phase of NREM sleep, often considered along with stage 4 sleep as 'slow wave sleep,' with about 2 brain wave cycles per second or slower.

EEG stage 4 sleep: a phase of NREM sleep in humans that has a higher voltage associated with the wave than stage 3 and is the most resistant to arousals; a person requires the most amount of stimuli (noise) to awaken from this stage of sleep.

effect size: a statistical measure of the extent to which variation in one variable predicts variation in an outcome variable.

efference copy (or corollary discharge): a concept introduced into the study of motor control by Erich von Holst (1908–1962) to indicate the sending of a copy of the efferent signal ahead of a movement so that it prepares the system for incoming sensory feedback or for a future motor command. 'Efferent' means the conduction of nerve impulses 'away from the central nervous system' to muscles and glands.

efficacy: the degree to which a clinical intervention has a desired effect.

elastin (gene): the main protein in elastic tissues of the body such as tendons, ligaments, and large blood vessels.

electroencephalogram (EEG): an instrument with a variable number of channels designed to record electrical activity (in microvolts) generated in the upper layer of the cortex from electrodes attached to the scalp. First demonstrated by Hans Berger (1873–1941) in 1924.

electromyography (EMG): electrical activity recorded from muscles by means of skin electrodes affixed to the belly of muscles or needle electrodes inserted into the muscles.

embodied cognition: stands for the research program attempting to understand cognition in close association with the sensory and motor processes through which cognition manifests itself and the neural structures on which cognition is based. Embodied cognition also includes the notion of 'situatedness,' which postulates that cognition takes place in contexts provided by highly structured and specific environments, and by an individual's behavioral history.

embodiment: the theory that cognitive and behavioral development can only be understood as occurring in a body. As such, it grounds much of cognition on an internal model of the human body and its actions. While frequently theories of development focus on abstract algorithms describing information processing, the embodiment view maintains that processing in a body is different because in effect the body itself participates in the information processing. Moreover, the developing body allows the infant or child to explore her environment in different ways at different ages. The theory, allied to dynamical systems approaches, is beginning to have a theoretical impact on the study of development, especially infant development as it relates to object permanence.

embryo: an organism between the time of conception and hatching or birth. In mammalian development, the period of the embryo comprises the span from the first cell divisions until the organism begins to take the form of the adult, when it is referred to as a fetus. Mammalian embryos are all but indistinguishable from each other with the naked eye.

embryogenesis: the formation, growth, and development of the embryo during approximately the first two months of human life after conception.

embryology: see *developmental biology*.

emergence: an abstract concept, considered to be a property of non-linear systems, that is meant to express the state of affairs in which multiple combinations of factors can lead to a particular behavioral outcome. The behavior is emergent if no single factor by itself determines whether the behavior may arise. Put another way, it is the appearance in either evolution or development of a structure or function from lower-level processes that were not pre-specified to determine that structure or function. The distinction between emergent and non-emergent properties is credited to John Stuart Mill (1806–1873) in his book *System of Logic* (1843).

emotional competence: term applied to the emotional processes (emotion expression, emotion regulation, and emotion understanding) responsible for effective social interaction.

emotional development: the study of the emergence of specific emotions and emotional states such as disgust, fear, and sadness, as well as the development of the ability to recognize or appraise emotions in both self and others and to communicate them appropriately. A striking feature of this area of study in developmental psychology is the ongoing attempt to integrate emotional and cognitive development as a means of understanding the development of emotional processes such as awareness and regulation or the cognitive mediation of emotional states. More recently, emotional development has been studied in the context of the growing area of affective neuroscience, which endeavors to gain insights into brain-behavior relationships involved, for example, in emotional awareness and the regulation of emotional states, mainly by means of EEG recordings.

emotional regulation: the ability to modulate, maintain, or enhance emotion.

empathy: a sharing of the negative or painful feelings of another. It involves being sensitive to another's emotions or emotional state, even though one's own situation is different. For example, I may be empathetic when I see a friend in pain, even though I recognize that I am not actually in pain myself. Thus, it is the ability to place oneself in the role of another that provides information on how the other may feel or think without directly being informed.

empowerment: to invest with power. In the context of education, this entails the equipping of individuals and groups with abilities and skills that enable them to take control of their own educational futures.

emulation: duplicating the outcomes produced by another, but using different actions to reach this same end.

encoding: the input of events into memory.

encoding specificity: Endel Tulving's hypothesis that memory retrieval is improved when information present at encoding, including contextual details, is also available at the time of retrieval.

enculturation: the process of socialization by which children come to internalize the values, practices, and knowledge judged to be central by their own culture or group.

endemic cretinism: a clinical syndrome of intellectual disability, spastic-rigid motor disorder, and deaf-mutism strongly associated with low maternal thyroid hormone levels during pregnancy and with severe periconceptional iodine deficiency.

entoderm (or endoderm): the innermost primary germ layer that originates during gastrulation, which gives rise to the alimentary tract and other internal organs of the body.

environment: in ecology, it is the sum total of biological, chemical, and physical factors in some circumscribed area. It really only exists because it is inhabited by an organism. For example, a field is an environment for a horse, its dropping the environment for beetles, and their exoskeletons the environment for parasitic mites. Thus, the field comprises a series of overlapping environments. Ecologists use the term interchangeably with habitat or niche. In psychology, following Kurt Lewin (1890–1947), there is also a psychological environment: a selective representation of the physical environment and the way in which the holder of that representation thinks it determines his or her behavior.

enzyme: a biological catalyst produced in cells and capable of speeding up and specifying chemical reactions essential for life. A globular protein, it is specific to a particular reaction or group of similar reactions and therefore there are a great number of them. The exact mechanism by which enzymes act is not fully understood, but it seems that certain parts of the enzyme molecule (the 'active centers') combine with a substrate molecule so that the substrate undergoes chemical changes much more rapidly than in the absence of the enzyme, but the enzyme itself remains unchanged. Most enzymes have the suffix-ase, which is added to the names of the substrate they act on. Thus, lactase is the enzyme that acts to break down lactose.

epidemiology: the study of the incidence, prevalence, and distribution of diseases, disorders, and infections in specified populations (e.g., as defined by age, sex, occupation), with the aim of providing information about their causes and how they might be controlled. Other important features of epidemiology are the identification of risk factors for particular diseases (e.g., child abuse) and disorders (e.g., cerebral palsy), and its crucial role in evidence-based medicine. It can be thought of as the who, where, when, what, and why of diseases, etc.: who has it, where they are located geographically and in relation to each other, when it is occurring, what the cause is, and why it occurred.

epigenesis: 'epi' means something upon or in addition to. Thus, development of structures and functions is not determined solely by the 'unfolding' of instructions in the genes nor only by environmental instruction. It involves complicated ongoing interactions between different levels of organization from genes to cells to brain parts to body parts, and all in interaction (or coaction) with specific tasks and with functional activity itself. The meaning of epigenesis has undergone a number of changes since William Harvey (1578–1657) first defined it in the 17th century.

epigenetic emergence: the emergence of a structure during the development of the embryo through interactions between tissues and ongoing gene expression. For example, the heart can induce the development of the retina at an early point in development because of their proximity in the embryo.

epigenetic landscape: a visual aid, representing a multidimensional space that includes the dimension of time, devised by Conrad H. Waddington (1905–1975) to capture some of the main features of genotype-phenotype interaction during development (i.e., those of epigenetics) such as canalization, equifinality, and homeorhesis. The landscape varies between individuals, but nevertheless maintains its basic shape of a sloping surface ending in the same valley. No matter how the phenotype (depicted by a rolling ball) traverses the landscape, it will always end up in that valley. It is interesting to note that Waddington originally trained as a geologist and thus drew on this experience to devise this visual analogy between a geographical structure, consisting of hills and intersecting valleys, and ontogenetic development.

epigenetics: a term first used by Waddington in 1942, although it seems to go back to Oscar Hertwig (1849–1892) who referred to it in his book *Biological Problem of Today: Preformation or Epigenesis?* (1896). For Waddington, it denoted a branch of biology concerned with studying how the phenotype develops as a consequence of interactions between structural genes and their products (i.e., the phenotype), but without change in the sequence of nuclear DNA. What developed according to Waddington was the epigenetic system, which he defined as one in which there was an ongoing balance achieved between genetic instructions, phenotypical changes, and environmental influences that brings about development of the zygote into a reproductive adult. In recent years, there has been considerable progress made in understanding epigenetic mechanisms, which include DNA methylation, histone acetylation, and RNA interference, with their effects activating and suppressing gene action. As a consequence, epigenetics is given a central role in evolutionary developmental biology.

epiglottis: cartilaginous, flap-like structure that prevents the entry of food into the larynx. In the human newborn, the entrance to the larynx is above the level of the tongue, which means it is possible to drink and breathe at the same time. Within the next six months, the epiglottis descends in the pharynx in order to close off the trachea and with this it is no longer possible to breathe while drinking.

epilepsy: a chronic disorder, found in cerebral palsy, that is characterized by paroxysmal brain dysfunction due to excessive neuronal discharge, and usually associated with some alteration of consciousness. The clinical manifestations of the attack may vary from complex abnormalities of behavior including generalized or focal convulsions to momentary spells of impaired consciousness.

epiphyses: the portion of a long bone formed during secondary ossification, and initially separated from the diaphyses by cartilage. They ossify separately and eventually fuse with the diaphysis.

episodic event and semantic memory: a distinction introduced by Endel Tulving, both are classes of declarative memory. Episodic memory refers to a type of long-term memory for personal events or experiences that is stored as information to provide a sense of personal continuity and familiarity with the past. It can be distinguished from semantic memory (a type of long-term memory for factual information about the world, excluding personal episodes in one's life, such as the dates of the Second World War), and from procedural memory (a storage system for information about how to carry out sequences of operations – knowing how to do things in contrast to knowing that, which refers to semantic memory).

epistatic/epistasis: the interaction of two or more genes or gene-gene influences, such that one gene is suppressed by an unrelated gene.

equilibrium: in Piagetian theory, the state that exists when assimilation and accommodation are in balance, or when cognitive structures and processes are successful in assimilating objects of action.

equivalence (of data across cultures): invariance of measurement scale properties across cultures, which is a necessary condition for meaningful cross-cultural comparison (also called comparability of scores).

escape learning: learning to make a response in order to escape from an aversive event.

essentialism: a philosophical belief that it is possible to identify the essence of a property or, in the context of a study, a variable.

established risk: manifest adverse conditions (e.g., blindness, chromosomal aberrations, autism) that pose a special challenge for amelioration.

ethology: the scientific study of the natural patterns of behavior of animals in relation to their natural environment or contexts of expression. Alternatively, it is referred to as behavioral biology.

etiology: the science and study of the causes of disease and their mode of operation (cf. *pathogenesis*). Within behavior genetics, etiology is used to describe the combined influence of genetic, shared environmental, and non-shared environmental influences on outcome.

eugenics: the doctrine put forward by Francis Galton (1822–1911) that encouraged breeding among persons of presumed higher moral and intellectual standing and discouraged breeding of lower classes or those considered to be 'inferior.' Eugenics was still practiced in parts of Europe until the middle of the 1970s.

eukaryote cell (or organism): a term used to cover all living organisms except bacteria and blue-green algae (i.e., cyanobacteria) that belong to the prokaryote grouping. The cells of eukaryotes have a clearly defined nucleus bounded by a membrane, within which DNA is formed into distinct chromosomes. In addition to a well-defined nucleus, they also contain mitochondria, choloroplasts (structures within the cells of plants containing the green pigment chlorophyll), and organelles that are lacking in the cells of prokaryotes.

event-related (brain) potentials (ERPs): these reflect brain activity generated by large populations of neurons acting synchronously and then volume conducting to the scalp surface, where the activity can be recorded non-invasively with small sensors or electrodes placed on the surface of the scalp. Following, for example, the presentation of a visual stimulus on a computer monitor, positive- or negative-going deflections in the on-going EEG are referred to as ERP components and are thought to reflect distinct neural and mental operations in the processing of that stimulus or event. There are, for example, not only visually evoked potentials (VEP), but also auditory-evoked potentials (AEP).

evolutionary biology: one of the two major branches of biology (the other being functional biology). Covers two main topics: (1) phylogeny, determining ancestor-descendant relationships among all species, their times of origin and extinction, and the rate (gradual or abrupt) and course of change in their characters; (2) biological evolution: aims to understand the origins of hereditary variations, what the levels and units of natural selection are, how and under what conditions the purported mechanisms of evolutionary change operate and give rise to adaptations, the relative importance of these co-acting mechanisms, how populations become different species, the interrelationships between biological and cultural evolution, and between ontogenetic development and biological evolution. Sub-fields include, for example: palaeontology, systematics, population genetics, molecular evolution, and more recently evolutionary developmental biology.

evolutionary developmental biology: a renewed attempt to bring about a synthesis of developmental and evolutionary biology in order to understand: (1) the evolution of ontogenetic development, and (2) how developmental processes or rather epigenetics (as well as morphological processes) constrain or facilitate phenotypical evolution.

evolutionary emergence: the appearance of a new structure in a species as a result of exaptation or adaptation of other structures that were initially serving somewhat different purposes.

executive attention: an executive function ability to allocate attention in a way that is consistent with self-established goals and plans. Executive attention shows the most extended developmental changes, beginning in the late phases of infancy (18 months) and showing changes throughout adolescence.

executive function (EF): an umbrella term for the set of (neuro-)cognitive processes underlying flexible goal-directed responses to novel or complex situations. Such situations may involve: (1) planning and decision making; (2) error correction or troubleshooting; (3) initiation of novel sequences of actions; (4) danger or technical difficulty; or (5) the need to overcome a strong habitual response. For some, the term has no precise definition, but broadly it refers to processes through which perceptual information or information in memory is used in the guidance of action (i.e., the maintenance of an appropriate problem-solving set for the attainment of a future goal). EF is closely related to the concept of working memory, and the neural substrate supporting the function is generally recognized as the dorsolateral prefrontal cortex.

experience-dependent processes: the idea that the development and functioning of a system are shaped by its experience with the environment. It has been shown that many cortical areas develop in an experience-dependent way, and this idea has been taken up in different connectionist models of cognitive development.

experience-expectant processes: examples include overproduction of nerve cells, dendrites, and synapses prenatally that await fine-tuning and adjustment with first experiences postnatally involving, for instance, vision and hearing.

experimental embryology: came to replace descriptive embryology in the middle of the 19th century as a means of trying to identify experimentally the 'mechanics' of growth and development (the causal-analytic approach). Experimental manipulations included the selective destruction of tissues (Wilhelm Roux, 1850–1924; Hans Driesch, 1867–1941) or the transplantation of one body part to another part of the body (Hans Spemann, 1869–1941). The latter manipulation was aimed at finding the organizer or organizing center that induced the formation of the neural tube. In general terms, an organizer is a part of the embryo that provides a stimulus for the direction of morphogenesis and the differentiation of other parts.

experimental method: the control and manipulation of variables in order to test scientific theories.

explicit (or declarative) and implicit (or non-declarative) memory: both are classes of long-term memory. Explicit memory, also referred to as episodic memory, is conscious memory (i.e., the conscious recollection and recall of information previously learnt). Implicit memory is unconscious memory (i.e., memory that does not require the conscious or intentional recognition of information previously learnt). Amnesic patients typically perform normally on tasks involving implicit memory, but poorly on those requiring explicit memory.

exploratory factor analysis (EFA): a type of factor analysis where neither the specific number of factors nor the pattern of the zero and non-zero loads are hypothesized in advance of the estimation. EFA is often used to estimate a reasonable description of data in terms of a multiple factor model in situations where no other description is available.

exponential: a function that varies as the power or exponent of another quantity. If $y = a^x$, then y varies exponentially with x. Exponential functions or series involve the constant $e = 2.71828 . . .$ (the base of natural or Napierian logarithms).

exponential change: continuous change that either accelerates or decelerates so that the pattern of change is curvilinear (J-shaped or S-shaped [sigmoid]). A snowball rolling downhill changes exponentially with time since when it is twice as big, it gathers snow twice as fast.

exposure: in epidemiological studies, the duration or intensity of the presence of a risk for a negative outcome.

exposure learning: a simple form of learning expressed by young animals in which mere exposure to a stimulus leads to establishment of a preference for that stimulus later in life. Postnatal examples of exposure learning include imprinting and the development of bird song; during prenatal development, exposure learning can lead to preferences for sounds or odor cues that are important in mother-infant interaction, choice of diet, or social interactions after birth.

external validity: the degree to which the results of an experiment or study on particular groups of participants generalize to the population at large.

externalism: the view that an educational account should focus on the beliefs and practices of teachers and learners with reference to the interpretations available in other disciplines in the social sciences, including psychology.

externalizing disorders: responses to stress that are directed toward others, such as aggression, anti-social behavior, conduct disorder, delinquency, and rule-breaking behaviors.

exteroceptive pain reflexes: a class of reflexes mediated by receptors located at or close to the body surface. They include, for example, the contraction of the muscles of the abdominal wall when the overlying skin is stroked briskly.

extracellular matrix: a complex network of macromolecules made up of water, ions, proteins and long-chain sugars (polysaccharides) that is dispersed in the spaces between cells and tissues of the body, and in which cells are embedded. Thus, it is often referred to as a 'biological glue.' It provides a regulated environment that is crucial to the functioning of cells, such as neurons, and plays an important role in embryonic development. It also forms part of connective tissues such as bone and skin.

extrafusal fibers: the vast majority of skeletal muscle fibers that are not found within muscle spindles at their polar ends and are innervated by alpha motoneurons. When stimulated by a motoneuron, actin filaments slide to overlap with myosin filaments, resulting in the muscle contracting.

extraversion: a broad factor of temperament, including characteristics of gregariousness, assertiveness, activity, excitement-seeking, and positive emotions.

eyeblink conditioning: a classical conditioning procedure in which an association is formed between a neutral stimulus such as a tone and a response-eliciting stimulus such as a puff of air directed toward the eye.

factor analysis: a set of mathematical and statistical techniques for the analysis of a set of observed or manifest variables (M) in terms of a smaller set of unobserved or latent variables (K<M).

factor loadings: a set of coefficients indicating the linear regression of a set of observed or manifest variables (M) on to a smaller set of underlying latent variables (K<M).

fallopian tubes: the bilaterally paired tubes that allow for the egg to travel from the ovary to the uterus during the menstrual cycle by means of muscular and ciliary action.

false belief test: a standard test of being able to take into account that other people can have different beliefs to one's own. Typically, a child of 4 years old can pass a false belief test. There are beliefs that do not correspond to the actual state of affairs in the real world. For example, if John puts a bar of chocolate into a drawer and then his mother moves it to a cupboard in his absence, he is likely to hold the false belief that the chocolate is in the drawer, whereas in reality it is in the cupboard. The ability to reason about false beliefs (e.g., to predict that John will look in the drawer for the chocolate) is generally regarded as a key component of a theory of mind.

fasciculation: a small, localized, involuntary muscle contraction involving groups of muscle fibers visible beneath the skin.

feedback: information about the results of a process that is used to change the process itself. There are two types of feedback. Negative feedback, invented by Henry S. Black (1898–1983) in 1927 to stabilize vacuum tube amplifiers, is a circular or closed-loop causal process in which the system's output is returned to its input, which is then compared to desired outcome in a comparator. If the desired outcome and the input deviate (i.e., if there is an error signal), then the discrepancy is corrected so that the two are equal and homeostasis is maintained. Hence, it is also referred to as deviation-reducing, error-reducing, or stabilizing feedback. It is a self-regulating mechanism involved in many biological processes such as EEG waves, postural control, and the control of slow goal-directed movements, with Piaget even claiming that his concept of equilibration is an example of negative feedback. Positive feedback, in contrast, is when the correction is made in the same direction as the original displacement and thus serves to amplify it. Hence, it is referred to as deviation-amplifying feedback.

feedforward: an anticipatory process in which trends in the input signal lead to modulations of the output signal that prevent or suppress subsequent errors. An example is the provision of an efference copy of the extra-ocular muscles during a saccade that suppresses the sensation of movement, which would otherwise be generated by the motion of images across the retina during such an eye movement.

fetal akinesia deformation sequence (FADS): a specific pattern of abnormal fetal growth and physical defects that result from a period of reduced motor activity or akinesia during fetal development.

fetal alcohol syndrome (FAS): a fetal condition characterized by a specific pattern of growth, mental development, and physical birth defects, caused by excessive exposure to alcohol in utero. The distinctive and often severe effects associated with FAS are more commonly expressed in milder or incomplete form, referred to as fetal alcohol effects or fetal alcohol spectrum disorder.

fetal breathing movements: first identified in 1888, they are rhythmical, but paradoxical, chest wall and abdominal movements, which are the precursors of postnatal respiration.

fetal programming: the process whereby interactions between the genome and the environment, in utero and during infancy, produce structural and functional adaptations that alter susceptibility to common diseases in adult life.

fetus: a mammalian embryo from the time it begins to assume the form of the adult until birth.

fibrillation: a small, localized, involuntary muscle contraction involving single muscle fibers.

filial imprinting: the process through which early social preferences become restricted to a particular stimulus, or class of stimuli, as a result of exposure to that stimulus.

final common pathway: introduced into neurophysiology by Charles S. Sherrington (1857–1952), it forms part of the principle of convergence of connections. Take, for example, the case of one neuron that has many synaptic connections with other nerve cells. The sum of the excitatory and inhibitory synaptic effects at any one moment determines the activity of the neuron. This neuron is then said to represent the final common pathway for the neurons connecting with it, as it integrates the information from various sources into a unified response. Examples of a final common pathway are peripheral motoneurons that send axons and signals from the central nervous system to skeletal muscle fibers. In developmental psychology, it has been borrowed as a metaphor to carry the idea that certain functions (e.g., motor ones) may serve as a sort of conduit for the development of other functions (e.g., those labeled 'cognitive' or 'social').

finger-tapping task: in such tasks, the participant must tap the forefinger of each hand at a specified rate, either at a 'comfortable' rate or "as fast as you can." Some investigators complicate the task by requiring both hands to tap a regular rhythm, but with one hand tapping twice for each single tap of the other.

FISH analysis: see *fluorescent in situ hybridization*

Five Factor model: a theory developed using factor analyses of ratings of the words people use to describe personality characteristics, stating that personality is composed of five primary dimensions – neuroticism, extraversion, openness, agreeableness, and conscientiousness.

fixed, free, and equal parameters: in the estimation of any structural model, parameters can be (1) fixed at a known value (e.g., 0, $\frac{1}{2}$ or 0.5), (2) free to take on a value based on the available data, or (c) required to be equal (or invariant) to any other parameter in the model.

fixed action pattern (FAP): in ethology, a stereotyped behavior pattern, the form of which is determined by a specific pattern of impulses generated in the central nervous system and which is relatively uninfluenced by learning.

fluorescent in situ hybridization (FISH): a laboratory technique that helps diagnose Williams syndrome among other disorders. A DNA probe for the elastin gene is made with a fluorescent label, and mixed with a sample of the patient's DNA. If the elastin DNA is present, the probe will be attached (hybridize). This allows a determination of whether there are one or two copies of the elastin gene present.

FM system: a wireless system in the classroom or other area with teacher and student supplied with microphone and receiver, respectively, so that the deaf person can hear the teacher's voice better than with a hearing aid alone.

follow-back design: for a given sample on whom past data are available, data at a later age are obtained such as medical or criminal justice records. Also known as retrospective design.

form-meaning mapping: patterns of correspondence between elements of language (forms) and elements of meaning (e.g., agent, patient, number, gender, definiteness, time, location, or trajectory). Such patterns are typically many-to-one or one-to-many: a given form, such as the English 'my,' can express more than one meaning (here, possession by 1st person, definiteness), and a given meaning, such as number (one, more than one), can be marked by more than one form (e.g., "a duck is eating my sandwich"). Form-meaning correspondences differ systematically across languages. Compare, for example, the characteristic 'packaging' of the notions of trajectory and manner of motion in English and Spanish: "run out / dance down / swim across" versus "salir corriendo" (exit running) / "bajar bailando" (descend dancing) / "cruzar nadando" (cross swimming).

form perception: sometimes referred to as shape perception, this term is generally applied to the ability to extract form or shape information from a two-dimensional stimulus.

formal operations: the last of Piaget's four broad stages of cognitive development. In formal operations, adolescents become capable of thinking in terms of abstract forms. Because they involve manipulation of formal rules and abstract expression, algebra and symbolic logic provide examples of formal operational thinking.

forward genetics: the process of discovering, through random mutation, genes that lead to particular phenotypes.

frequency: the rate of oscillation in a sound wave. High-pitched sounds have a high fundamental frequency (F_0).

fricative: speech sounds (i.e., consonants) characterized by a long interval of turbulence noise due to forcing air through a constricted passage.

frontal cortex: the front third of the cortex, which has as its posterior boundary the motor cortex. Involved in aspects of motor planning, working memory, organization of behavior with respect to future goals (i.e., executive functions).

frontal lobes: refer to the rostral cerebral region superior to the Sylvian fissure and anterior to the Rolandic fissure, and encompass approximately 24–33 percent of the adult human brain.

frontal quadrants: the anterior portions of the brain.

functional experience: experience that appears to the observer to be functionally relevant to the behavior in question. For example, the experience of ingesting food appears to be functionally relevant to the behavior of pecking in birds.

functional imaging: a procedure that measures the quick, tiny metabolic and/or electrical changes taking place in an active part of the brain (e.g., by means of positron emission tomography [PET], functional magnetic resonance imaging [fMRI], electrical measurements of evoked responses [ERP], and magnetoencephalography [MEG]).

functional magnetic resonance imaging (fMRI): an imaging technique utilizing the small differences in regional blood flow that accompany the neural activity in the brain associated with performance of a cognitive or motor task as compared to that found during a period of rest (the baseline).

fundamental frequency (F_0): the lowest frequency (first harmonic) of a periodic signal, such as the tone of the human voice.

fusiform gyrus: a specific gyrus or 'outfolding' in the inferior temporal lobe that appears to be involved in recognizing faces and objects with which we have become familiar.

fussing: this term refers to distressed vocal and other behavior that is less intense than crying and often considered to be either an intermediate state or a transition between crying and settled behavior.

'g': a general ability factor that contributes to the observed correlation between many measures of cognitive ability and thereby constitutes one way of conceptualizing general intelligence.

gametes: mature haploid cells that fuse to form a zygote in sexual reproduction. In many organisms, the male gamete is called a spermatozoon, spermatozoid, or antherozoid. The female gamete is referred to as an ovum. As haploid cells, they contain half the normal complement of chromosomes and thus when they fuse the diploid number is restored. Gametes are formed by meiosis.

ganglia: group of nerve cells (outside or inside the central nervous system) conveying information from the environment (touch, temperature), or from the body (muscle length), to a group of nerve cells in the spinal cord (autonomic ganglion) connecting preganglionic and postganglionic nerve fibers of the autonomic nervous system.

gastrulation: the developmental process in which the cells of the blastula are reorganized by folding and migration into the blastocoele, resulting in an embryo with three distinct layers of cells. These primary germ layers consist of the ectoderm (outer), mesoderm (middle), and entoderm (inner).

gender: has become a term to denote the social meanings of masculine and feminine. Thus, while sex is biological, gender is socially constructed or determined, and its meaning can change from place to place and over time. It has become an analytical tool for understanding social processes.

gender identity disorder (GID): a strong and persistent lack of comfort with one's sex (e.g., an individual with male reproductive structures who feels psychologically like a female). In childhood, it is evident in a child's insistence that he or she is the wrong sex; persistent preferences for clothing, games, and pastimes of the other sex; and taking on cross-sex roles in fantasy play.

gene: the functional unit of inheritance based upon the coding of DNA molecules, which directs the synthesis of a particular protein.

gene traps: a strategy using a genetic construct that is a kind of mutagen that acts as a cellular marker. If the construct integrates into a gene that is transcribed in a specific cell type at a specific time, the marker will be expressed in those cells at that time.

General system theory (GST): a courageous attempt by Ludwig von Bertalanffy (1901–1972) to provide a systems framework for promoting interdisciplinary research. Drawing largely on irreversible thermodynamics and exploring its application to living systems, he devised not so much a theory, as a general model of organization applicable to open systems at different levels of analysis.

generalized linear model (GLM): group of statistical models that models some function of the expected value of the dependent variable as a linear combination of the independent variables.

generalized sequential querier (GSEQ): a general-purpose computer program for analyzing sequential observational data that has been expressed using SDIS conventions.

generative grammar approach: a theoretical linguistic framework based on ideas promoted by Noam Chomsky in the 1950s. A generative grammar attempts to describe a native speaker's tacit grammatical knowledge by a system of rules or constraints that specify all of the well-formed, or grammatical, sentences of the language while excluding all ungrammatical, or impossible, sentences. Grammatical structure is assumed to be autonomous (i.e., determined by domain-specific principles and independent of meaning or more general cognitive or communicative pressures). Universal rules or constraints ('Universal Grammar') are hypothesized to be innate, and to guide children in acquiring the grammar of any particular language. Stands in contrast to the cognitive-functionalist approach to language.

genetic determinism: the doctrine that our genes determine who we are at every level of organization or that both structure and function are inherited rather than acquired through learning.

genetic epistemology: see *developmental epistemology*

genome: the total genetic material of any organism (i.e., in humans, the 23 pairs of chromosomes that make up the genome).

genotype and phenotype: a distinction first made by Wilhelm Johannsen (1857–1927) in 1909. Genotype is the genetic constitution of a cell or individual. When it refers to the whole organism, the term is sometimes exchanged with genome. Phenotype is the organism's characters (structural and functional) determined by the combined influences of its genetic constitution and environment. Phenome is sometimes used when reference is made to the whole organism.

geocentric perspective: also called the 'absolute' frame of reference, this is one of three frames of reference languages provide to specify how something (the 'figure') is located with respect to something else (the 'ground') on the horizontal plane. In the geocentric frame of reference, the speaker uses fixed external bearings, as in "the fork is to the north/south/east/west of the spoon" – or "uphill of," "inland of," etc. In the relative frame of reference, the speaker specifies the position of the objects from his own point of view ("the fork is to the left/right of the spoon / . . . is in front of / behind the spoon"). In the intrinsic frame of reference, the speaker relies on features or axes of the ground object ("the fork is beside the spoon . . . is at the tip of the spoon").

germ plasm: a term devised by Augustus Weismann (1834–1914) for a kind of protoplasm in the nuclei of the reproductive or germ cells and tissues of the body, which constituted the hereditary material. It is thus analogous to DNA.

germinal (or germ) layers: the three primary germinal cell layers formed during gastrulation that line the central cavity of the gastrula, and which are partially determined in their developmental potential. Ectoderm, the outermost layer, gives rise to the nervous system and outer integument. Mesoderm, the middle layer, produces muscles, connective tissues, and the urogenital system. Entoderm, the innermost layer, differentiates into the alimentary tract and other internal organs (e.g., the liver).

Gesell's developmental schedules (or scales): a standardized procedure for observing and evaluating a child's developmental status at ten ages from 1 month to 5 years. Evaluations are carried out in five, rather arbitrarily designated, domains or sub-tests labeled: gross motor, fine-motor, language, personal-social and adaptive. Gesell cautioned against deriving a composite score or developmental quotient (DQ) and argued instead that DQs for each domain together with clinical judgments should be used to arrive at decisions about each child's developmental status. While Gesell never published information on the reliability or validity of the schedules, they have spawned many other infant tests.

glial cells: cell types in the central nervous system (astroglial cells and oligoglial cells) connected to neural cells and, in contrast to these cells, having no role in information transport over long distances. However, they support non-neuronal cells of the nervous system. In development, they perform the special function of supplying guides to migration of neurons on their extended processes; other glial cells form the myelin sheaths of axons.

glottal: speech sounds formed at the glottis (the space between the vocal folds).

glycogen: a polysaccharide that is the chief carbohydrate store in animal cells and produced from glucose. It is broken down into lactic acid when it is used as an energy source in the liver or muscles.

go/no-go test: originally devised by Alexander R. Luria (1902–1977), this simple task involves forming a habitual response to a stimulus (e.g., pressing a button in response to a light) and then suppressing that prepotent response on selected trials. Performance is rated by error frequency and type (e.g., errors of commission or omission) as well as reaction times.

Golgi apparatus (or complex or organ): a cell organelle consisting of a system of smooth-surfaced, double-membraned vesicles in the cytoplasm. It stores and transports lipids and proteins and has a role in the formation of the cell wall.

Golgi tendon organ: a proprioceptive receptor found embedded in muscle tendons. It is compressed and activated by any increase of the tendon's tension, due either to active contraction or to passive stretch of the corresponding muscle.

graded signal: this theory proposes that an infant's cry conveys the degree of the infant's distress or state of arousal, but not its specific cause. It contrasts with the idea of 'cry types,' where the audible, acoustic features of a cry are assumed to vary so as to signal its particular cause (e.g., 'hunger' versus 'anger' versus 'pain' cries). According to graded signal theory, parents and others use contextual information to work out the cause.

grammaticization (or grammaticalization): a central phenomenon of language change in which a contentful word such as a noun or a verb develops over time. It does so through a process of becoming more fixed in position, phonologically reduced, and semantically bleached into a grammatical element like an inflection, preposition, or conjunction.

granular cells: neurons giving rise to parallel fibers in the cerebellum and the most numerous cell type in the brain.

gray matter: grayish nervous tissue in regions of the brain in which are found aggregations of unmyelinated neurons as well as fibers. This portion of the brain is divided into: (1) the cortical gray matter, consisting of unmyelinated neurons, found at the surface of the brain, and (2) the sub-cortical gray matter situated in the deep central regions of the brain (caudate, putamen, globus pallidus, and thalamus).

Greenhouse-Geisser epsilon: a correction factor that is smaller than 1 if the sphericity assumption in an ANOVA is violated. The factor is multiplied with F, making the test more conservative. It is a method of correcting the degrees of freedom of the within-subject F-tests in the analysis of variance of repeated measures or longitudinal data so as to allow for departures of the variance-covariance matrix from the assumption of sphericity.

growth cone: the actively growing, most distal, expanded part of a neurite or outgrowing axon extended from a neuron, instrumental in target location.

growth factors: regulatory chemicals produced by specific cells or tissues (e.g., cells in the developing nervous system) that stimulate cellular growth, differentiation, or tissue development. One example is nerve growth factor (NGF), which stimulates the outgrowth of nerve fibers during the differentiation of neurons.

growth hormone (or somatotropin): a hormone produced by the anterior pituitary gland. It decreases the rate of carbohydrate uptake, enhances the mobilization of lipids from adipose tissue, and stimulates the production of insulin-like growth factors by the liver to enhance growth of muscle and bone.

growth-mixture model: a theoretical model where a growth process supposedly exists for two or more groups, but the identification of the persons in the groups is unknown or unmeasured (i.e., latent). The mixture analysis attempts to determine the optimal number of groups (G>1), isolate the growth parameters of the separate groups, and assign a probability of group membership to each person.

Guthrie test: a universal screening test in which a spot of blood is extracted by means of a heelprick and which is carried out in the newborn period to detect treatable conditions such as phenylketonuria (PKU) or congenital hypothyroidism, conditions which can lead to irreversible brain damage, if not treated early.

gyrus: an outfolding or convolution of the cerebral cortex of brain that lies between sulci (fissures).

habituation: a decrease in responding to the repeated presentation of a particular stimulus. Habituation to a specific stimulus is generally believed to reflect the progressive encoding of that stimulus in memory and a simple form of learning.

haemophilus influenza type B (Hib): a species of gram-negative bacteria that is the major cause of bacterial meningitis and acute epiglottitis in children. Invasive Hib rates have fallen dramatically since the introduction of infant vaccines.

handedness (bimanual versus unimanual): this distinction refers to: (1) the hand that performs faster or more precisely on manual tasks; and (2) the hand preferred for use, regardless of performance. In addition, there is another ongoing debate about how many types of handedness there are: right versus left, right versus non-right, and whether or not ambidexterity should be included. Handedness should be distinguished from manual specialization: a division of labor between the two hands in performing a bimanual task (e.g., one hand writes, other hand and arm used to support body while writing).

handicap: a physical, mental, or emotional condition that interferes with an individual's normal functioning. Reduction in a person's capacity to fulfill a social role as a consequence of an impairment, inadequate training for the role, or other circumstances.

haploid: a nucleus, cell, or organism having a single set of unpaired chromosomes. Gametes, formed as a result of meiosis, are haploid. Fusion of two reproductive cells during fertilization restores the normal diploid number.

haploinsufficiency: genetic mutations that result in half the normal level of the gene product leading to phenotypic effects. In other words, such effects are sensitive to gene dosage.

Hawthorne effect: the effect of simply being studied, usually improving performance no matter what changes are made to the circumstances.

hazard ratio: a unit-free ratio of the odds of onset of a given outcome in any given unit of time for individuals with a given risk, divided by the odds of onset over the same period for individuals without such a risk.

Hebbian learning: a method of weight adaptation in connectionist models that is biologically plausible. Weights between two units get strengthened if both units are active at the same time ('what fires together wires together'). Several variations of Hebbian learning exist (e.g., involving weight decay and temporal aspects of unit activation).

Hebbian synapse: a basic mechanism for synaptic plasticity, posited to underlie learning and memory, through which an increase in synaptic efficacy arises from the persistent stimulation of the postsynaptic cell by the presynaptic cell. Thus, when as axon of cell A is close enough to excite cell B and is repeatedly involved in firing it, some growth process or metabolic change ensues in one or both cells such that efficiency of A, as one of the cells firing B, is increased. However, if A fires and B does not, then the connection between them is weakened. In connectionist modeling, it has become a technique for selectively weighting the strength of connections between neurons.

hedonism: the doctrine that the pursuit of pleasure is the chief good.

hemoglobin: a pigmented protein that contains iron located in red blood cells of vertebrates and responsible for the delivery of oxygen to tissues.

hereditary: genetic material and information passed on from individuals of one generation to the next. Genetic material and hereditary are not synonymous, as, for example, a fertilized egg contains much cytoplasm that is non-genetic. Also, material passed from the mother to the embryo via the placenta is in a sense hereditary, but again not genetic.

heritability: a statistic that estimates what proportion of the total population variation in a character or phenotype is due to genetic differences between individuals.

heterochrony: originally introduced into evolutionary biology by Gavin de Beer (1899–1972) to account for evolutionary change in the onset or timing of development. Applied to development, the term portrays it as a mixture of different timings in the appearance of structures and functions, with some being accelerated and others relatively retarded. Slower-developing structures and functions act as constraints on the process of developmental change that are 'lifted' once they mature, resulting in the emergence of new abilities.

heterogeneity: the presence of two or more sub-groups within a population or group of behaviors.

heteronomy: acceptance of externally defined rules, laws, and norms; originating outside the self.

heuristic: a rule-of-thumb procedure or trial-and-error problem-solving process for making a decision or forming a judgment, without resorting to an algorithm or formal reasoning. The use of analogies or metaphors can be part of such a process.

hierarchical models of motor control: models involving a distinction between higher (e.g., cortical) and lower (e.g., sub-cortical) levels of control.

hierarchy: the arrangement of items and/or sub-items by size or other criteria such as relative control; can be applied to actions, underlying operations, and social relationships.

hippocampus: a forebrain structure of the temporal lobe, shaped like a seahorse, and part of the limbic system, it is thought to be important in emotion, motivation, spatial abilities (e.g., 'navigation by cognitive maps'), and the consolidation of declarative (but not procedural) memory. Damage to the hippocampus is consistently associated with significant loss of this sort of memory.

histology: the branch of anatomy that studies the structure and function of cells and tissue at the microscopical level. The four major tissues that make up the bodies of animals are epithelial, nervous, muscle, and connective tissue.

holism: a term accredited to Jan C. Smuts (1870–1950) who first used it in the 1920s as the antithesis of radical reductionism, and which is understood to mean that the properties of a system cannot be determined or explained by the sum of its constituent parts alone. Accordingly, systems are hierarchically organized, with the emergence of new properties between its levels of organization. Adopted in the developmental sciences by the likes of Paul Weiss (1898–1989), an embryologist, and other so-called organismic biologists.

homeodomain proteins: proteins encoded by homeobox genes that are involved in the control of gene expression during morphogenesis and development.

homeorhesis: a term derived by Waddington from the Greek word *rhesis* meaning 'to flow' and intended to convey the self-righting properties inherent to developing organisms. In contrast to homeostasis, which is concerned with the maintenance of an initial state (e.g., as with a thermostat), homeorhesis is depicted as a mechanism for maintaining an orderly sequence of developmental change in the face of both internal and external perturbations.

homology: objects or events that have common origins and similar structures, even though their surface properties or functions may differ. In biology, where it is a controversial concept, it refers to similarities among species that are derived from a common ancestor, and which can apply to a morphological structure, a chromosome, or an individual gene or DNA segment. The forelimbs of chickens, dogs, humans, and whales are examples of homologies in that the skeletons of these appendages are constructed of bones arranged in the same pattern due to the fact they were inherited from a common ancestor with a similar arrangement. As in the case of the wings of bats and birds, structures can be partially homologous and partially analogous (i.e., the wings are homologous because of common descent from the forelimb of a reptilian ancestor, but the modifications for flying are different and have evolved independently and are thus analogous).

homoscedasticity: the condition of equal residual variances in analysis of variance.

Hox genes: a family of homeobox transcription factors that specify position information along the body axis. They are defined by a specific sequence of amino acids and nucleotides (the homeobox) that allows the *Hox* genes to bind to specific regions of DNA and thereby control transcription of these target genes. In this way, vertebrate *Hox* genes help control the craniocaudal (i.e., head-to-tail axis) segmentation of neural and non-neural structures (i.e., they specify position information). *Hox* genes are part of the Antennapedia gene sub-family originally identified in the fruit fly.

Human Genome Project (HGP): officially started in 1990, it is an international research effort to map the estimated 30,000 genes in human DNA and to completely sequence the 3 billion chemical bases that make up these genes. Findings, collected in shared databases, are expected to provide better diagnoses and treatments for a range of human disorders, some of which, like muscular dystrophy and Alzheimer's disease, can be found in genetic variations in DNA called single nucleotide polymorphisms or SNP (pronounced 'snips'). Another feature of the program is to analyze the DNA of a set of non-human model organisms such as the fruit fly and laboratory mouse to provide comparative information that is essential for understanding how the human genome works. The plan was for all databases to be publicly available by the end of 2005, but that was brought forward to 2003. The organization of the databases (some of which are already available) and the algorithm for making use of the data have led to a new area of study labeled bioinformatics.

Huntington's disease (or chorea): an inherited adult-onset disorder of the nervous system due to a dominant gene mutation on chromosome 4 causing neurological degeneration. Signs include uncoordinated movements, irritability, and attention span deficits.

Hunyh-Feldt epsilon: a correction factor that is smaller than 1 if the sphericity assumption in a repeated measures ANOVA is violated. The factor is multiplied with F, making the test more conservative. This factor is comparable to the Greenhouse-Geisser epsilon, but it tends to be less conservative.

hyoid bone: a fine bone lying inferior to the mandible (jawbone) and from which the larynx is suspended.

hyperextension: a posture in which the neck and trunk are overextended (i.e., curved too much backwards).

hypomorphic nervous system: a smaller than normal nervous system usually due to fewer cells.

hypoplasia: reduced size owing to the underdevelopment of all or part of an organ.

hypothalamic-pituitary-adrenal axis: a complex and important physiological pathway between brain and peripheral structures whereby the amount of steroids released from the adrenal glands is controlled by a negative feedback mechanism involving release of peptides from the pituitary (ACTH) and the hypothalamus (CRH). Peptide release is itself under control of the glucocorticoid receptors in the hippocampus. Receptor saturation diminishes peptide release and therefore adrenal activity. The reverse occurs when receptors are unsaturated.

hypothalamus: a small region of the brain located just beneath the thalamus that is responsible for regulating many physiological systems of the body, including hormones produced by the pituitary gland, body temperature, thirst, hunger, water balance, and sexual function. It is also closely connected with emotional activity and sleep, and functions as a center for the integration of hormonal and autonomic nervous system activity through its control of pituitary secretions.

hypothesis: a conjecture or tentative explanation of certain facts that is testable empirically and then supported or rejected by the findings (i.e., on the basis of one or other inferential statistic). It is also a term applied in cognitive psychology to strategies for solving problems or making decisions such as participants in

experiments inferring what sort of responses are required under different conditions from one trial to the next.

hypotonia: lower than normal muscle tone as assessed by the manipulation or palpation of body parts.

hypoxia: deficiency or decrease below normal levels of oxygen in inspired gases, arterial blood, or tissue, and just short of anoxia. Ischemic tissue hypoxia is characterized by tissue oligemia (deficient amount of blood) and caused by arterial or arteriolar obstruction or vasoconstriction. It is not possible to measure hypoxia directly in the brain of a fetus or neonate during labor.

hysteresis: also termed jump resonance by electrical engineers, it involves scaling up the value of some parameter in a non-linear system to a critical value at which point there can be a sudden jump to a new and qualitatively different state, without any intermediary states. Scaling down or decreasing the value of the parameter may result in an abrupt change back to the original state, but at a different critical value. Repeatedly scaling up and down can result in a hysteresis cycle (i.e., 'progression' followed by 'regression' and so on). Subsequently, the cycle is broken and the system settles into a stable regime as defined by the new state.

iconic mapping: a mapping between form and meaning in which the form in some way reflects or diagrams the conceptual structure it expresses (e.g., forms for meanings that 'belong together' conceptually are positioned close together in a sentence). There is debate over the extent to which grammar is iconic: for those within the generativist framework, iconicity is marginal (sound symbolism as in "cuckoo" would be an example) and most form-meaning mappings are considered arbitrary, whereas for those who take a cognitive-functional approach, iconicity is pervasive.

illusory contours: boundaries of objects that are not visible, but are implied by the arrangement of line segments and other visual stimuli.

imitation: involves observing and duplicating a model performing a behavior. More formally, imitation is said to occur when three conditions are met: (1) the observer produces similar behavior to the model; (2) the perception of an act causes the observer's response; and (3) the equivalence between the acts of self and other plays a role in generating the response.

immediate-early genes: genes that are expressed rapidly (within minutes) and transiently following a variety of cellular signals, and which apparently do not require protein synthesis.

impairment: a physical or mental defect at the level of a body system or organ. The official World Health

Organization (2001) definition is: any loss or abnormality of psychological, physiological, or anatomical structure or function.

imprinting: rapid early learning of identifying features of parents (filial imprinting) and/or of mating partners (sexual imprinting). Also considered to be the process by which early experience promotes the development of perceptual mechanisms.

impulsivity: pathological decrease of impulse control, often encountered in ADHD and Tourette's syndromes.

incidence: in contrast to prevalence, it quantifies the number of new events or cases of disease that develop in a population of individuals at risk during a specified time interval, including those who die later or migrate out. Rates are calculated using live births or total births as the denominator.

individuation: according to Waddington, he introduced this term from psychology into embryology as a means of denoting the way in which separate elements become organized into a single functioning unit. For others (e.g., George E. Coghill, 1872–1941), it referred to behaviors emerging from a total integrated pattern and progressing to increasing individuation as a consequence of inhibitory influences acting on the integrated pattern.

induction (embryology): a process of interaction during development by which one part of the embryo (such as a specific tissue or cell type) causes another part to differentiate. It can be positive or instructive (specification of a developmental fate) or negative (restriction of developmental potential). Primary and secondary inductions take place early and later in development, respectively.

infancy/infant: from the Latin *infans* meaning incapable of speech; the developmental period extending from birth to about 2 years of age and which is thus demarcated by the acquisition of articulated speech.

infantile amnesia: the more rapid forgetting of memories during infancy than later in development. There is much speculation about its particular function.

infantile grandiosity: a number of psychoanalysts writing about infant development assume that infants imagine themselves to be all-powerful as they are responsible for creating the caretaking that they experience. Other analysts believe that their picture of themselves as powerful is created to protect them against their sense of helplessness and vulnerability. In either case, caregiving that does not allow them the illusion of being in control is considered to make them vulnerable to a persistence of this unrealistically grand image.

infantile responses: organized behaviors that can be elicited from the newborn under specific environmental conditions.

infantile sexuality: early in his work, Sigmund Freud (1856–1939) recognized that young children had an intense orientation toward pleasure and considered these aspects of sexuality in a broad sense that encompassed oral pleasure related to eating and stimulation of the mouth, anal pleasures focused on sensations around the anal sphincter and the sense of control, as well as sexual feelings focused on the genitals.

inferior parietal lobe: part of the brain on the top side of the head, just above the ear, which is involved in understanding where things are in space and also in comparing equivalences in actions performed by ourselves and other people during imitation tasks. It also plays a role in keeping track of who produces an action (self versus other), and thus is believed to be implicated in determining 'agency.'

influence efficacy: a measure of effect size including indices with a fixed potential range of -1.0 to $+1.0$, such as a correlation coefficient, measures expressed in the units of the variables, such as regression coefficients, and measures with a theoretically infinite range, such as odds ratios.

information: a technical term, measured in 'bits' (log base 2), that is often used informally to account for a range of events and the sources of constraints on expression.

information-processing theories: in cognitive psychology, a set of theories derived from formal automata theory originally put forward by John von Neumann (1903–1957) at the Hixon symposium (1948). Such theories make the distinction between that which controls (a controlling device) and that which is controlled (a controlled system). Broadly speaking, they contain one of three types of models: cybernetic (closed-loop) models, algorithmic (open-loop) models, or some combination of the two. Furthermore, processing is depicted as taking place via series of step- or stage-like cognitive and perceptual operations. In recent years these models have been challenged by those derived from connectionist theories and dynamical systems approaches.

inhibitory control: a psychological process in which routine, habitual, or over-practiced responses to a stimulus may be suppressed when such responses are at odds with a higher-order goal. Different types of inhibitory control may be distinguished according to either the inhibited response (e.g., simple act or more complex responses such as speech) or the nature of inhibition (e.g., delay versus production of a conflicting sub-dominant response).

innate: having arisen within the species through evolution rather than through learning by that individual. Innate propensities are typically expressed at or by birth. Some innate behaviors may be 'blocked' or 'masked' due to poor motor abilities and not manifest at the moment of birth. If an ability emerges after birth and is not attributable to postnatal learning, it may still be deemed innate; however, such cases are rare and require extraordinary evidence that they are not attributable to learning.

innate modularity hypothesis: the hypothesis that the brain is organized into distinct modules or regions that are specifically devoted to particular cognitive abilities, and that this neurocognitive organization is present from birth.

innate releasing mechanism (IRM): a term introduced by Konrad Z. Lorenz (1903–1989) into ethology to describe a hard-wired device somewhere in the central nervous system that causes a species-specific sign stimulus or releaser to evoke a fixed action pattern.

innate versus acquired dichotomy: similar to the nature-nurture debate in that heredity and learning are viewed as independent determinants of development.

insecure attachment: a pattern of attachment of an individual (usually a child) toward another individual (usually a caregiver) where anxiety or avoidance behavior is observed, as opposed to secure attachment where affection and proximity-seeking predominate.

instability: the loss of stability of attractors of dynamical systems induced by gradual change of parameter values of the associated differential equation (or iterative map). Such instabilities, also called bifurcations, are accompanied by increased variability and reduced resistance against perturbations of the state of the system. They can lead to large changes in state (e.g., switching to a new attractor).

integration: according to Coghill, the coordination of related but separate functions by the brain during development.

intentional stance: see *mind reading*.

inter-rater reliability: a measure of agreement between raters such as the intraclass correlation or kappa, the latter accounting for chance agreements.

interactive specialization approach (or hypothesis): one of three general approaches to developmental cognitive neuroscience that assumes postnatal functional brain development involves a process of organizing inter-regional interactions so that the response

properties of a specific region may be determined by its patterns of connectivity to other regions and their current activity states. It means that the brain is not initially organized into distinct modules and only becomes so during development as an emergent property of both biological maturation and experience.

interdigital necrotic zone (INZ): the regions lying between the newly forming digits, where programmed cell death (apoptosis) occurs.

intermodal coordination: the ability to associate sensory input from one modality to that of another.

intermodal perception: perceiving relationships among different types of sensory input.

internal capsule: white matter located between the basal ganglia and the thalamus, and through which the lateral and medial bundles of the corticospinal tracts (CST) descend.

internal validity: the degree to which differences between experimental and control groups can be attributed to the variables manipulated in an experiment, as opposed to extraneous factors.

internalism: the view that an educational account should focus on the beliefs and practices of teachers and learners without reference to the interpretations available in allied disciplines in the social sciences, including psychology.

internalizing disorders/problems: responses to stress that are directed toward the self, such as anxiety, depression, fearfulness, self-destructive behaviors, withdrawal, and worrying.

International Phonetic Alphabet (IPA): an alphabet designed to provide universal symbols to represent all the known speech sounds used in human languages.

interneurons: classically, neurons between sensory neuron and motoneuron; more commonly, neurons with short axons and part of local neural circuits. They often contain neuromodulators that alter the direct excitatory or inhibitory connections of other cells.

interval recording: an observational data recording strategy for which successive short (e.g., 10 or 15 seconds) intervals are assigned behavioral codes.

intra-individual differences: differences in the expression of a behavior by an individual over time.

intrapsychic conflicts: classical Freudian psychoanalysis assumes that mental disorder is due to contradictory and irreconcilable wishes and beliefs on the part of the sufferer. Freud and some of his followers conceived of these conflicts as generally occurring between instinctual (sexual and aggressive) desires, an awareness of the constraints of reality, and moral imperatives.

intrauterine growth retardation or restriction (IUGR): an insufficient growth of the fetus, due, for example, to placental dysfunction. It may result in a weight at birth that is inappropriate for the duration of gestation, such as one below the 10th percentile of the growth curve.

intrinsic dynamics: the set of factors that determine the changing properties of body parts during movements. These factors include the elasticity of tendons, the resistance of joints, size and weight of the body part, the forces generated by muscles, etc.

introspective method: traced back to Aristotle (384–322 BP), this is a method of data collection in which observers record their own mental processes and experiences. Refined by Wilhelm Wundt (1832–1920) from uncontrolled to controlled introspection (or rather immediate retrospection), it was finally banished from psychology by the behaviorists and John B. Watson (1878–1958) in particular.

intuitive parenting: an unlearned inclination of adults (and even children as young as 2 years of age) to react adequately to an infant's physical, social, and emotional needs, and learning abilities.

intuitive theory of something: a child's set of ideas on a domain. Intuitive physics may include the notion that one moving object has just one speed, a notion that applies well to the front mudguard of a bicycle, but not to the front wheel whose spin is very rapid at the tire surface and much slower next to the hub. Intuitive biology may include the notion that all living things are capable of self-propelled movement, a notion that applies better to animals than to plants, with odd exceptions in both the sub-domains of zoology and botany.

invagination: the inward folding of an unbroken layer of cells into the central cavity of the blastula during the early stages of gastrulation.

iodine deficiency: an insufficient quantity of iodine and its essential constituents of thyroxine (T4) and triiodothyronine (T3), which are essential for normal growth and development. The sensitivity of different organs to iodine deficiency varies, with the brain being particularly susceptible during the fetal and early postnatal period. If severe enough, this leads to endemic cretinism, or mental deficiency, deaf-mutism, and spastic diplegia. Later effects are growth failure and retardation of bone growth.

ischemia: local anemia due to mechanical obstruction (mainly arterial narrowing or disruption) of the blood supply.

isocortex: same as cerebral cortex, but the preferred technical term; 'iso' refers to the similar six-layered structure the cortex has throughout its extent.

joint capsule: connective tissue surrounding a synovial joint and containing synovial fluid.

kangaroo-care: also known as the kangaroo mother method, it originated in Bogotá, Colombia, as a cost-effective means of caring for the very preterm or low-birthweight infant during the period of neonatal intensive care. The method, which has spread to neonatal intensive care units in Europe and North America, involves periods of skin-to-skin contact between infant and parent achieved by means of carrying the infant in a sling. The few evaluation studies carried out on the method have reported that infants in the treatment group had lower rates of serious illness and fewer readmissions, but did not differ from controls with regard to mortality and growth.

karyotype: the specific characteristics of chromosomes in the nucleus of a somatic cell or organism in terms of their number, sizes, and shapes. In humans, the karyotype consists of 46 chromosomes, while for crayfish, fruit flies, and mice the numbers are 200, 8, and 40, respectively.

kinematics: studies of object motions and their relations to reference frames that may involve the relative motions of other objects.

kinesiology: the interdisciplinary study of physical activity. Originally employed as a term describing the study of movement using the principles of mechanics and anatomy. The term derives from 'kines' meaning movement and '-ology' the study of something. Today, the term is used to define an academic area of study of human movement broadly defined (i.e., physical activity).

kinesthesis: a general term used to describe sensations associated with movement arising from receptors in the muscles, tendons, joints, and skin. While it is more or less synonymous with proprioception, J. J. Gibson included the visual modality (i.e., the act of seeing) under proprioception.

kinetic depth information: information from object or surface movement that specifies its relative distance from the observer.

kinetic occlusion: movement of an object against a background.

language development: the acquisition of the ability to understand the meaning of words (semantics) and to use them in ways that are grammatically correct (syntactics) relative to a child's linguistic environment. In general, there are two features of this process: the production and reception of language, with the latter developing in advance of the former, and perhaps even starting in utero. Once the first words become evident, subsequent development consists of word perfection involving relating predicates to arguments. Theories of language development tend to be divided between treating language as a 'special gift' (i.e., innate) or as something that has emergent properties.

larynx: situated at the bottom of the vocal tract between the vocal cords and the oral cavity, it is part of the cartilaginous air passage structure, located above the trachea and below the pharynx, that houses the vocal folds and the various muscles serving laryngeal vocal mechanisms.

latent factor/score/variable: a hypothetical variable that is not directly measured, but is presumed to have some influence on the scores of the observed or manifest variables. Put another way, it is a hidden commonality that has to be derived from the data generated by a group of measured variables.

latent growth model: the representation of a longitudinal process for many individuals where the components of growth are hypothesized to be unobserved or latent scores and the errors of measurement at each occasion are independent. It is also possible to add a latent shape to this model so the changes represented by the latent slopes are not equal over equal intervals of time.

latent trait: a mathematical abstraction, combining several different measures in order to achieve a more precise measure of the underlying construct.

lateral bias: a generic term referring to any kind of bias favoring one side of the body over the other. It includes biases in head-turning and hand and arm use as well as biases of the feet, legs, eyes, ears, and even side-of-mouth for chewing.

laterality: a structural (i.e., neural) asymmetry or a functional one expressed in behavior. In the latter case, it is performed in a consistent manner. The ongoing question is how structural asymmetries relate to functional asymmetries.

learned helplessness: a learned attitude of passivity in the face of a problem situation and of awaiting help from someone or somewhere indiscriminately.

learning disability: also known as mental retardation and defined as an intellectual impairment (IQ<70) leading to functional disability.

Leiter International Performance Scale: an individually administered test of intelligence originally designed for deaf children that does not require verbal communication.

levels of analysis: the analysis and interpretation of behavioral and social phenomena at various levels (individual, organizational, cultural, ecological), without reduction to explanation at a less inclusive level.

levels of development: in Kurt Fischer's neo-Piagetian skill theory, an indication of the degree of hierarchical integration of a cognitive skill. According to the theory, there are four levels of hierarchical integration within each of four broad tiers of development. The levels correspond to single sets, mappings, systems, and systems of systems. Each higher level emerges as an integration of lower-level skill components. Individual skills develop through four tiers that embody a total of thirteen levels of hierarchical integration throughout development.

life course analysis: analysis using as its framework key tenets of a life course perspective including: (1) individuals are agents who make choices within social constraints; (2) these choices have emerging consequences for themselves and for those whose lives are linked with theirs; and (3) both historical context and developmental age must be taken into account in understanding individual and family trajectories.

ligands: molecules that bind to receptors or proteins and thereby induce a signal in a cell.

likelihood ratio (LR): in statistics the ratio of two likelihoods, particularly that of a likelihood function to the maximum likelihood. Widely used as a test statistic, especially for examining relationships among categorical variables arranged in a contingency table. In goodness-of-fit modeling, the smaller the LR, the stronger the relationship because in using it in this way we attempt to accept a particular model rather than reject a null hypothesis.

limb bud: the initial outgrowth of tissue from the embryo, which will go on to form fore- and hindlimbs.

limbic cortices: a collective term for a number of different cortices on the edge of the cortical sheet.

limbic system: the brain region consisting of highly interconnected cortical and sub-cortical areas folded into the inner surface of the temporal lobe surrounding the brain stem and bordering on the corpus callosum that are centrally involved in the generation and expression of arousal, emotion, and hunger, as well as memory. The areas included are, typically, the amygdala, cingulate gyrus, fornix, hippocampus, parahippocampal gyrus, and the septum pellucidum.

limkinase 1 gene: a gene located on the 7th chromosome that is typically deleted in Williams syndrome and that some studies have linked to visuo-spatial abilities.

linear dynamical systems: systems in which their behavior is fully prescribed by their initial conditions. In such systems, there is a one-to-one relationship between input and output (or a proportionality between the intensity of input and the intensity of output). Such systems demonstrate only quantitative change.

linear growth model: the representation of a longitudinal process for many individuals where there are equal changes over equal intervals of time. The resultant group and individual trajectories (or integral) can be plotted (in Cartesian coordinates) as a set of straight lines over time.

lissencephaly: a condition of cortical dysgenesis in which cellular layers are improperly formed and thus the cerebral cortex lacks the typical convolutional pattern.

locomotion: to move from place to place by changing the jumping body's base of support. There are many forms of locomotion in humans. Locomotion that involves moving from one foot to the other is referred to as bipedal locomotion and includes movement patterns such as walking, running, galloping, jumping, and skipping. Quadrupedal locomotion involves moving on four limbs (the hands and either the knees or feet). Crawling is an example of quadrupedal locomotion in humans.

logistical growth function: a growth curve in which the rate of growth is proportional to the product of the size at the time and the amount of growth remaining. It has an S-shaped or sigmoid curve, indicating little growth, followed by a sudden spurt to an asymptote, and has been used to identify continuous accelerations in the development of particular behaviors.

logographic writing systems: a system of writing in which the printed symbols represent entire words without relating to pronunciation.

longitudinal design: a study that takes place over time, preferably with at least three time points so that change both between and within individuals can be charted.

longitudinal-experimental studies: studies of large samples followed over long periods of time, in which a preventive intervention is targeted to a randomly selected part of an at-risk group.

longitudinal studies: ones that follow people over an extended period of time, usually several or more years, to examine patterns involving earlier and later experiences and development.

lumboscaral plexus: a group of nerves formed from vertebral levels L4-S3, which are responsible for innervating most of the structures in the lower limb.

Magnetic Resonance Imaging (MRI): based on magnetic fields and pulsed radio frequencies without ionizing radiation, this is a class of techniques that use the static or changing properties of polar molecules in the brain, such as hemoglobin, to visualize its structures, or activity in structures. Also used to estimate body composition, specifically images of fat, muscle, and bone tissues.

magnetoencephalography (MEG): a technique of brain imaging that measures the magnetic fields created by the induction of electrical activity of nerve cells.

major depressive disorder: at least five of the following symptoms must be present during the same two-week period (according to ICD-10, the International Classification of Disorders, less than a two-week period if symptoms are severe and of rapid onset) –
(1) depressed or irritable mood; (2) anhedonia; (3) significant decrease or increase in weight or appetite or failure to make expected weight gain; (4) insomnia or hypersomnia; (5) psychomotor agitation or retardation; (6) fatigue or loss of energy; (7) feelings of worthlessness or inappropriate guilt; (8) concentration difficulties or indecisiveness; and (9) thoughts of death and/or suicide attempts or ideation.

mappings: in Fischer's neo-Piagetian skill theory, a concept borrowed from mathematics to describe a level of functioning in which an individual is able to control the relationship between two units of behavior. For example, using representational mappings, a 4-year-old child can hold in mind the relationship between two representations. In so doing, she maps one representation onto a second representation (also used to refer to reflex mappings, sensorimotor mappings, abstract mappings).

Marfan syndrome: a disorder inherited as an autosomal dominant trait and marked by defective formation of elastic fibers that affects the skeleton, large arteries, suspensory ligaments of the lens of the eye, tendons, and joint capsules. Sufferers have abnormally long slender extremities, spidery fingers, high palate, displacement of the lens, lax joints, and aneurysm of the aorta.

masked threshold: the ability of a listener to detect an auditory signal (e.g., a pure tone) amongst noise.

maturation: like 'growth,' a term that has assumed a variety of inconsistent meanings. A definition apparently in contemporary usage is that particular functions develop without any specific environmental influences as long as non-specific influences (e.g., temperature, oxygen levels, nutrition) remain constant or within certain ranges.

maturation versus learning debate: a controversy replacing that on the dichotomy between heredity and environment in the 1930s and 1940s. Essentially, it boiled down to whether ontogenetic development was genetically controlled or determined purely by learning effects. In fact, none of the protagonists in this sterile controversy, generated largely by the media of the time, actually subscribed to such extreme views, except perhaps as debating points.

maturational gradients: gradation of onset or rate of events in early development over the area for a physical substrate (e.g., initiating the making of connections starting in the front and finishing in the back of a structure).

maturational perspective/approach: one of three general approaches to developmental cognitive neuroscience in which the goal is to relate the maturation of particular regions of the brain to newly emerging sensory, motor, and cognitive functions.

maximal aerobic power: the highest amount of chemical energy that can be transformed in the aerobic machinery of muscle mitochondria per unit time (generally per minute). It is measured as maximal O_2 uptake during an exercise test on a motorized treadmill or cycle ergometer.

measurement efficacy: any of several indices of agreement between ordinal measures.

measurement error: a hypothetical variable defined as the part of an observed item indicating the lack of measurement of an attribute of interest. The error score is traditionally assumed to be uncorrelated with the true score and is the reason several different observed items are uncorrelated.

measurement theory: the set of principles used to determine how attributes of an individual can be quantified from measured behaviors. One of the simplest versions of this theory is that any observed item is considered to be the sum of the true score and an independent error score.

MecP2 gene: a gene often mutated in Rett's syndrome.

medial (pre-)frontal cortex: part of the brain situated at the front, right in the center of the head, which is involved in high-level processes such as thinking about oneself and other people, and especially taking the perspective of others and determining their goals (i.e., 'mind reading'). It becomes more activated while the person is solving theory of mind tasks and performing imitation tasks that involve inferring others' goals and intentions.

meiosis (or reduction division): a stage in the development of egg and sperm cells in which the cell divides and the number of chromosomes is halved. Put another way, it is the cellular process that results in chromosomal division where one of each pair of homologous chromosomes passes to each daughter cell.

memory: the encoding of information, its storage and retention, and subsequent retrieval. The information can range from stimuli, events, and images through to ideas. Many different memory systems have been identified such as perceptual memory, working memory, and the distinctions between long-term memory (of which perceptual memory is a part), sensory and short-term memory (of which working memory is a part), declarative and procedural memory, episodic and semantic memory, as well as explicit and implicit memory. There are some overlaps in meaning between these different systems.

menarche: the first menstrual period.

meningitis: inflammation of the membranes (the meninges) covering the brain and spinal cord. It can be caused by bacterial infection, viral infection, and infection due to the micro-organism meningococcus.

mental image: in Piagetian theory, the reconstruction of action on concrete objects in the absence of those objects. Mental images are formed as a result of the abbreviation and internalization of action on objects. To construct a mental image is to engage in abbreviated actions that are similar to the actions that one would perform if one were actually operating on the object. Mental images are active constructions rather than static mental pictures.

mental modules: relatively fixed mental systems that have unique inputs and processes that operate on those inputs.

mental retardation: a condition of significantly below-average intellectual development (IQ<70) and adaptive functioning in, for example, self-care, that is manifested before 18 years of age. An IQ between 50 and 70 is taken to signify mild mental retardation, 35 to 50 the moderate form, 20 to 35 the severe manifestation, and below 20 profound mental retardation.

mesencephalic reticular activating system: a system in the brain stem that controls arousal of other parts of the brain and is closely tied to sustained attention.

mesoderm: the middle primary germ layer that originates during gastrulation, and which gives rise to the muscles, elements of the skeleton, connective tissues, and the urogenital system.

meta-analysis: systematic and quantitative examination of the results from different studies, pooling them so that robust conclusions can be reached and the nature of agreements or disagreements can be clarified and understood. It is not the same as metanalysis (i.e., forming a new word due to mistaking the boundary between existing words).

metamorphosis (or indirect development): the hormonally driven transition from a larval stage to an adult in which a significant proportion of the organism's structure changes such that the larval and adult stages are often not recognizable as the same individual. Thus, it is a process of qualitative and radical change in both structure and function from the embryo to the adult in two or more stages.

metazoan: refers to all vertebrates and invertebrates, but excludes the Protozoa (i.e., unicellular or acellular micro-organisms) and Porifora (i.e., sponges). More generally, it refers to the sub-kingdom of animals having a body made of cells organized into tissues and coordinated by a nervous system.

method bias: differences in score distributions between (cultural) samples that are similar for all items/stimuli of an instrument, but that are not related to the trait or concept presumably measured by that instrument.

methylphenidate: a drug that is often prescribed to control ADHD. Paradoxically, methylphenidate is a stimulant that arouses the brain. It has its effect on ADHD by increasing the arousal of the part of the brain that controls inhibition, allowing ADHD children to exhibit inhibitory control over behavior.

microgenetic method: an intensive investigation of a group at a time when it is known that change is likely to occur. The aim is to chart the complexity of this change, sometimes by speeding up the process through training.

mind reading: the ability to infer what someone else is thinking or feeling. Also known as adopting the 'international stance.'

mind-body problem: the philosophical issue of how the mind is related to the body, which brings with it what properties, functions, and occurrences should be ascribed to each. The problem impinges not only on the philosophy of the mind, but also on the philosophy of psychology. The modern version of the problem is usually depicted as starting with René Descartes (1596–1650).

mindblindness theory: a theory claiming that in people with autism, there are degrees of mindblindness, or difficulties in imagining other people's mental states. This is often the result of a specific developmental delay.

minor neurological dysfunction (MND): the presence of mild impairments observed during a neurological examination such as mild problems in muscle tone regulation and with co-ordination or fine manipulation.

mirror neurons: these neurons were discovered in a particular region (called F5) of the monkey brain in the mid-1990s. The special property of mirror neurons is that they are activated by both the observation and the execution of a specific action. For example, mirror neurons fire both when the monkey grasps a piece of food and when it sees someone else grasp the food. These neurons do not fire when the monkey uses the hand to perform a different action (e.g., pushing away the food). They seem to code 'grasping the food' whether done by self or other.

missing at random (MAR): the assumption that, for the sub-set of persons for whom data are not measured (i.e., incomplete or missing), data can be indicated by scores on variables that are measured (i.e., complete). The MAR assumption is different than the traditional assumption of 'missing completely at random' (MCAR), and it permits a correction for the bias due to selection using maximum-likelihood estimation (MLE).

mitochondria: minute, rod-shaped or granular bodies, about $\frac{1}{4}$ to 3μm in length or diameter that occur in the cytoplasm of most cells responsible for aerobic respiration. They contain many of the enzymes of the cell, particularly those required for the citric acid or Krebs cycle. They are the site for not only the Krebs cycle, but also the electron transport chain and thus, the cell's energy production. Consequently, they are most numerous in cells with a high level of metabolic activity.

mitosis: the generation of new cells by cell division.

mixed-effects models: a set of statistical techniques used to estimate parameters about (1) fixed effects based on groups (i.e., mean differences and regressions), as well as (2) random effects based on individual differences (i.e., variance and covariances).

mobile conjugate reinforcement: an operant conditioning procedure in which infants aged between 2 and 6 months learn to kick a foot in order to produce movement in an overhead mobile.

model: a formalized representation of a class of phenomena (e.g., complex systems) that is simplified by ignoring certain details. It derives from a theory and can become a kind of mini-theory when it characterizes a process and serves to guide and develop the theory further. In science, a model can be either descriptive or predictive.

model representation: a representation of something using principles that allow you to map properties of the model onto theoretically selected properties of something else. By their very nature, all models are selective, and the selection is determined by the purpose of the modeler and the materials available.

model systems: simplified representations of more complex systems, often used to isolate and highlight specific properties of organization.

moderate-discrepancy hypothesis: the view that infants prefer stimuli that are moderately discrepant, or different, from what they already know.

Modern synthesis: the idea that biological evolution is a consequence of natural selection acting on variability in phenotypes created by changes in gene frequencies in populations brought about by mutations, genetic recombination, or drift.

modularity: sometimes imputed to cortical areas, this is a conception of the mind as composed of an innately provided set of independently operating mental computers, each tuned to accept different input and to subject it to different processing. A number module would be tuned to detect how numerous items were, and the occurrence of addition or subtraction could be observed. A language module would be tuned to accept speech-sounds and assign them meaning. No cross-talk would occur between modules. The same line of thinking applies to specific perceptual and cognitive abilities as being physically and computationally isolated from each other.

monosynaptic reflex arc: single-synapse reflex arc connecting sensory input with motor output.

monosynaptic reflexes: motor responses to discrete stimuli that require only one synapse to complete the circuit. They include, for example, the biceps and triceps reflexes, and the patellar stretch reflex or knee jerk.

monozygotic twins: a pair of twins created from a single fertilized egg.

moral development: broadly considered, this is the development of an increasing ability to understand social reality and to integrate social experience so that distinctions can be made between what is right and what is wrong in order to make responsible decisions and to act on them. It also involves a concern for others, the desire to do right, and the ability to reflect on the consequences of one's actions. A matter of some controversy is whether the ability to reason logically is a necessary, but not sufficient, condition for morality to develop fully.

Moro response: the spreading (abduction) of a newborn's arms and fingers, followed by strong flexion (adduction) at the shoulder, after a sudden change in head or whole body position. It is assumed to be a labyrinthine reaction, but there is some debate about this, as there is about whether the response is symmetrical or asymmetrical in healthy fullterm newborns. Named after the pediatrican Ernst Moro (1874–1951).

morphogenesis: a dynamical process involving growth and differentiation through which form and pattern are generated in biological systems. More specifically, it describes the process of cellular differentiation, distribution, and growth that takes place during the embryonic development of an organism, which gives rise to tissues, organs, and anatomy. The term 'morphogenesis' is also used to describe the development of unicellular life forms that do not have an embryonic stage in their life cycle, or to refer to the evolution of a body structure within a taxonomic group.

morphological marking: the inflection of words to mark changes in meaning or grammatical function, such as the addition of 's' to nouns to mark their plurality.

morula: a stage in the development of the embryo in which a cluster of complex cells form after the zygote splits.

mosaicism: a type of Down's syndrome in which there is a mixture of cells containing 46 and 47 chromosomes.

motility: the ability to move spontaneously, used particularly with reference to independent cell locomotion (e.g., by spermatozoa) and the first movements of the embryo. The latter are generated by spontaneous activity in the central nervous system and are not related to a specific task or goal.

motion parallax: the relative motions of individual objects viewed as an observer moves, as in looking at trees in a forest when driving past. It is one of the monocular cues for depth perception.

motion perception: the ability to discriminate between different directions of motion of visual stimuli.

motor ability: the qualities, power, competence, faculties, proficiencies, dexterities, talents, etc., that enable one to perform a particular motor feat at a specified time. It is a theoretical construct regarding factors that underlie proficiency in motor tasks (e.g., strength, speed, power, agility, balance, coordination, flexibility, accuracy, endurance). The factors are ordinarily measured with standardized tests (e.g., vertical power jump).

motor control: the control of the kinematics and dynamics (i.e., force) of movements by the brain that involves the regulation of the positions and motions of the various parts of the body in relation to each other and to one or more external reference frames in order to achieve a particular goal. More technically, it is the process by which values are assigned to the variables in a coordinative structure.

motor development: starting early in prenatal life, progressive, and sometimes regressive, changes in recognizable movement and postural patterns from simple to more complex forms of organization, associated with growth, maturation, and experience. Theoretically, the study of motor development, largely through the application of dynamical systems thinking, involves a number of issues such as how the couplings between movement, perception, and posture develop, the degrees of freedom problem, and the dual state problem (i.e., how the developing child discovers the dynamics of coordination while at the same time learning to control the system). The development of action is now integrated with, for example, the cognitive and social domains through the medium of theories of embodiment and in which movement is seen as 'final common pathway' for the attainment of achievements in such domains.

motor equivalence: based on the biological concept of equifinality (i.e., employing different means to achieve the same end state), this can be defined as performing an action or a task in a variety of different ways. To put it another way, it involves using movements in a flexible manner so as to achieve a particular outcome such that there is more than one solution to solve a particular problem. Accordingly, a variety of different muscle contractions and joint rotations can produce the same outcome.

motor inhibition: the ability to inhibit a behavioral response.

motor learning: a process associated with practice or experience leading to relatively permanent changes in motor skill capacities. While it is a very general term, it has been used in the past to contrast forms of learning in which perception or cognition are considered to be more critical, which in essence is a sort of dualism.

motor milestone: a key movement behavior or an identifiable state of organization of body parts or the whole body that appears during the first years of life and is used to signal that development is proceeding normally. Examples of motor milestones include sitting, crawling, standing, and walking.

motor noise: excessive background neural activity in the motor system, resulting in poor motor control and increased variation in movement response.

Motor Performance Study (Michigan State University): a mixed-longitudinal study begun in 1967, including observations on developmental stages for several fundamental movement patterns. The study also includes measures of growth status and several motor performance variables.

MRI morphometry: use of quantitative three-dimensional Magnetic Resonance Imaging techniques to determine the volume of the imaged brain and its sub-structures of interest.

multilevel modeling (MLM): a statistical technique developed by Harvey Goldstein and colleagues to analyze longitudinal data in which there are variables at several levels, with the lower levels being nested in the higher ones. While analogous to multivariate analysis of variance for repeated measures, MLM has the advantage of the inclusion of a powerful algorithm for dealing with missing data, an ever-present problem in longitudinal studies. It involves the estimation of parameters by means of an iterative model fitting to the data, which enables the inclusion of incomplete records. The statistics associated with main and interaction effects follow a chi-square distribution.

multivariate analysis of variance (MANOVA): a set of statistical techniques for the analysis of mean differences when there are multiple outcome (i.e., dependent) variables. It is comparable to the analysis of variance of univariate data, but in MANOVA groups are compared on n dependent variables simultaneously. The most commonly used test is Wilk's lambda that is based on three matrices (viz., the within-, the between-, and the total matrix of sums of squares and cross products).

muscle spindle: a specialized sensory receptor with wrapped neurites, embedded in muscle, and relaying information regarding muscle length and change of length (i.e., stretch).

musculoskeletal system: in the human, the complex of about 800 muscles, 200 bones, more than 100 joints, and a host of ligaments and tendons. The ligaments connect and constrain two or more bones or cartilages at a moveable joint. The inelastic tendons connect muscles with moveable structures such as a bone and ensure that the force exerted by a muscle is transmitted to that part of the body to be moved. Also includes the innervation of muscles (i.e., motor end plates).

mutation (biology): a term originally devised by Hugo M. de Vries (1848–1935) in 1901, it refers to a random alteration in the arrangement or amount of genetic material in a cell that may cause it and all cells derived from it to differ in structure and function. An organism affected by a mutation is called a mutant. There are two types of mutations: point mutations consisting of minor changes in the genetic material such as single-base pair substitutions in structural genes, and macromutations involving larger sections of chromosomes. Mutations most often occur during DNA replication when so-called 'copying errors' can arise. More often than not, mutations are lethal, but sometimes they can be advantageous, given particular environmental circumstances, in the sense of increasing the chances of survival and reproductive success.

myelination: the process of myelin elaboration that covers, insulates, and promotes rapid signal conduction in axons and which is principally a postnatal event in humans.

myofibril: the structural unit of striated muscle, with several found in each fiber. They are, in fact, long, contractile cells with many nuclei, of which striated muscle is formed.

myotube: the basic multinucleate muscle cell formed from the fusion of multiple myoblasts.

N170: a specific component of the event-related potential (ERP) elicited by upright faces, and observed in adults but not infants.

narcissism: in psychoanalytic theory, this is concerned with the emotional investment in the self (self-esteem). It is generally held that individuals whose self-esteem is chronically low have not experienced sufficient love and appreciation in their early development, and are therefore unable to experience genuine deep feelings toward others and constantly struggle with doubts about their own value, often swinging between extremes of grandiosity and self-deprecation.

National Child Development Study (NCDS): a longitudinal study of all infants born in the United Kingdom during a single week in 1958, which has collected data on these children at various time points and was expanded in 1991 to study children born to these respondents. This expansion was intended to produce UK data that would parallel the US study of children of the NLSY-79 female respondents.

National Educational Longitudinal Surveys (NELS): sponsored by the US Department of Education, this study began by studying eighth-graders in public and private schools and has conducted biennial interviews and assessments since 1988 focused on educational attainment and occupational and family outcomes.

National Institute for Child Health and Human Development Study of Early Child Care (NICHD-SECC): a study of infants living in ten US communities in 1991, it follows these children from birth through fifth grade focusing on parental and non-parental care and social and cognitive development.

National Longitudinal Study of Adolescent Health (Add-Health): sponsored by the US National Institute for Child Health and Human Development, this study of children and adolescents enrolled in seventh through twelfth grade in 1994 has focused on social networks, health behaviors, and health outcomes, including sexual and reproductive health.

National Longitudinal Survey of Children and Youth (NLSCY): sponsored by Statistics Canada, this study, focused on child development broadly conceived, began in 1994 with the intention of studying children from birth to age 11, and is expected to follow them to age 25.

National Longitudinal Survey of Youth (NLSY): sponsored by the US National Institute for Child Health and Human Development, the NLSY refers to a series of longitudinal studies of various birth cohorts, begun in the 1960s and 1970s. Of particular interest is the NLSY-79, which began in 1979 to study adolescents and young adults born between 1958 and 1965, and its related Child-Mother data set begun in 1986, which conducts biennial interviews and assessments of all children born to female NLSY-79 respondents. Children born after 1986 were added as new child respondents in subsequent waves, so that eventually the sample will include all the children born to this cohort.

nativism: a general school of thought according to which abilities are claimed to be inborn and not developed through experience. Recent nativist accounts of infant ability treat core knowledge as innate along with ways of interpreting events on the basis of that knowledge. However, they are not so extreme as to rule out a major contribution of experience in refining and modifying the core knowledge that infants enter the world possessing.

natural selection: a major force in evolution co-discovered by Charles Darwin (1809–1882) and Alfred Russel Wallace (1823–1913), natural selection serves as a filter in preserving reproductively successful developmental outcomes and acting against outcomes that impede successful reproduction and the rearing of offspring.

nature-nurture debate: an almost outmoded controversy over the relative importance of heredity or genes (nature) and environment or experience (nurture) as independent causal agents in the development of the individual.

negative predictive value: the proportion of the sample identified as negative (or normal) that subsequently had a negative (or normal) outcome.

neo-Darwinism: sometimes equated with the Modern synthesis, which is not strictly speaking correct as it was a fusion between the ideas contained in the *Origin of*

Species (1859) and the mechanisms of heredity discovered by Gregor Mendel (1822–1894). However, by the turn of the 20th century, neo-Darwinism has become a three-way split between Mendelians, mutationists, and selectionists. It was the Modern synthesis that brought together these different strands into one overarching theory.

neo-Piagetian theories of cognitive development: theories of cognitive development that preserve important tenets of Piaget's theory of cognitive development while addressing important criticisms of the theory. Neo-Piagetian theorists generally reject a strong doctrine of developmental stages (*structures d'ensemble*) while retaining the notion of domain-specific transformations of cognitive structures in terms of a series of levels. Theorists include Robbie Case, Theo Dawson, Andreas Demetriou, Kurt Fischer, Graem Halford, Juan Pascual-Leone, and others.

nerve growth factor (NGF): a neurotrophic substance emitted from smooth muscle and tissues innervated by neurons. Its role is thought to be the guidance of neuronal growth during embryonic development, especially in the peripheral nervous system, and in the maintenance of sympathetic and sensory neurons.

neural cell adhesion molecule (N-CAM): a cell adhesion molecule expressed on the surfaces of most neurons.

neural determinism: the doctrine that development arises from genetically determined changes in neural structures.

neural net: computer simulation of biological inter-activation of neurons. A common simple structure involves an input layer of nodes, a middle or 'hidden' layer, and an output layer. Cognitive tasks are solved by progressive change in the pattern of activation over the network of interconnections. The methodology and related theory is referred to as connectionism.

neural networks: see *connectionist models*.

neural plate: the embryonic precursor of the neural tube, this is a region of embryonic ectodermal cells called neuroectoderm that lie directly about the notochord.

neural tube: containing neural cells in early stages of differentiation, this is the earliest rudiment of the central nervous system, which forms from a thickened plate of ectoderm that rolls up around its long axis to form a hollow tubular structure (i.e., the neural tube) extending from the rostral to caudal end of the embryo, and which ultimately will differentiate into the brain and spinal cord.

neurodevelopmental disorder: a disorder of development associated with dysfunctioning of the central nervous system.

neurogenesis: proliferation of neurons in early development by division of precursor cells.

neuroimaging studies: studies of the brain that allow scientists to see the structure and workings of the brain during mental or motor tasks, which helps to understand their localization, sequencing, and network interactions. Includes PET (positron emission tomography), fMRI (functional magnetic resonance imaging), ERPs (event-related potentials), and magnetoencephalography (MEG).

neurological 'soft' signs: minor versions of signs seen in some acquired motor disorders or severe neurodevelopmental syndromes.

neuromaturation: the genetically determined process by which the nervous system becomes mature, and a relatively vacuous concept.

neuromaturational theories: theories supposedly holding the view that development is determined solely by the genetic regulation of maturational processes. On closer inspection, no such monocausal theories have existed since at least the end of the 19th century.

neuron: nerve cell, consisting of cell body or soma and processes, that collects incoming or afferent information (via the dendrites) and transports outgoing or efferent information (via the axon). Typical neurons have 1,000 to 10,000 synapses and axons that can vary in length from 3 micrometers to more than 1 meter. Often neuron is confused with nerve, the latter having no cell body and being made up of bundles of axons.

neuronal migration disorders: a group of disorders resulting from genetic, chromosomal, or environmental causes that disturb the process by which newly generated neural cells migrate to their proper position in the brain, causing distinctive morphological patterns according to the causal agent, affected site, and gestational age at which the disturbance occurs.

neuroscience: a term that has been defined in various ways. It is best considered to be an umbrella term for all those sciences that try to understand how the brain and nervous system mediate behavior, in terms of the mechanisms and processes involved in this mediation. At one level, it combines with cognitive psychology and cognitive science to create cognitive neuroscience and at the other extreme with molecular biology giving rise to molecular neuroscience.

neuroticism: a broad factor of temperament, including characteristics of fearfulness, sadness, shyness, irritability, and proneness to distress or discomfort.

neurotrophic factor: chemical substance in the nervous system attracting and maintaining specific outgrowing axons.

neurulation: formation of the neural tube from the ectoderm by a process of invagination and closure, including the caudal and rostral ends.

newborn encephalopathy: a clinically defined syndrome of disturbed neurological function occurring during the first week of life manifested by seizures, abnormal consciousness, difficulty maintaining respiration, difficulty feeding, and abnormal tone and reflexes. It is sometimes erroneously referred to as hypoxic-ischemic encephalopathy without evidence of causation by hypoxia-ischemia.

New York Longitudinal Study (NYLS): a pioneering retrospective and longitudinal study of temperament begun by Alexander Thomas (1914–2000) and Stella Chess in the late 1950s. Parent descriptors of their infants' behaviors in questionnaires and interviews resulted in the identification of nine dimensions of temperament, subsequently reduced to three broad categories ('easy babies,' 'difficult babies,' and 'slow-to-warm-up babies'). As the children became older, interviews with teachers and tests of the children were added. The subjects of the NYLS have been followed up to middle age.

niche: in ecology, the status of an organism in the ecosystem, including its habitat and its effect on other organisms and the environment.

non-dysjunction: failure of a pair of chromosomes to separate during cell division.

non-linear associator: a system that associates a number of inputs with a number of outputs in a non-linear way. This could mean that, for example, inputs that are only slightly different are associated with outputs that are very different, and vice versa. In neural network models, non-linearity is achieved by the non-linear activation function of the processing units, such as a threshold, sigmoid (S-shaped) or Gaussian (bell-shaped) function.

non-linear dynamical system: a system whose behavior is not predictable over long periods of time, either from its initial conditions or from its history of inputs. The equations of motion for such a system include threshold values that when breached result in sudden discontinuous changes to qualitatively different states.

non-structural growth model: a non-parametric model for mathematically fitting longitudinal growth data for individuals. Non-structural models (e.g., polynomial, kernel regression, cubic splines) do not assume an a priori functional form of the growth curve. The model has been applied to measures of growth and physical performance.

non-univocality principle: an unequivocal relationship between impulses and movements does not and cannot exist (i.e., the relationship between neural impulses and resulting movement is not one-to-one, but many-to-many).

noradrenergic neurotransmitter system: a system in the brain using the neurotransmitter noradrenaline (norepinephrine) that is based in the mesencephalic reticular activating system and which distributes noradrenaline throughout the brain. This system has a widespread energizing influence on brain activity and is closely tied to sustained attention and alerting.

normative: norms are directives or imperatives dealing with obligations and necessity in action and thought (i.e., 'what has to be done' and 'what has to be'). They are manifest as rules, commands/obligations, and technical directives. Their formation includes acquisition, constitution, and development.

nosology: the classification of disorders based on observable and detectable signs and symptoms on observation and interview, or more generally the study of disorders.

nuclear family: family comprising parents and children (i.e., not members of the extended family such as grandparents, aunts, and uncles). Taken to be the dominant family form in late industrial cultures in which the unit of analysis is the household consisting of mother, father, and children. In fact, since the 1970s, this type of family represents a minority of households.

nucleic acid: a complex organic acid in living cells made up of a long chain of nucleotides, of which there are two types: DNA and RNA.

nucleus (of a cell): a double-membrane-bounded body found within the cytoplasm of most cells of plants and animals, but not bacteria. It contains the chromosomes that can be seen with the aid of a microscope during meiosis and mitosis. It functions as the control center of the cell. The double membrane, or nuclear membrane, contains many pores through which there is an exchange of material between the nucleus and the cytoplasm.

numerical identity: this term is often used to describe the ability to identify the number of objects involved in an event on the basis of the structure of the event. For instance, a discontinuity in a moving object event, or moving object events, both sides of an impenetrable barrier signals that more than one object is involved.

object identity: the ability to perceive an object as the same object despite a gap in perceiving it, such as being able to identify an object as the same entity although it passes behind a screen on part of its trajectory. Movement on a constant trajectory is one cue that may be used to infer identity. Identity does not imply permanence, since attribution of identity does not include any assumptions regarding continuity of existence.

object permanence: the knowledge or awareness that objects continue to exist when they are out of sight, either through being in view but out of the visual field, or through being hidden by another object. According to Piaget, infants develop the beginnings of object permanence at 9 months, with further progress taking place up to 24 months. More recent accounts suggest object permanence is present by 3 or 4 months or that it is an innate ability.

object reversal test: an experimental paradigm that involves reversal of a previously learnt association. In a typical example, subjects are repeatedly presented with a pair of objects, one of which is associated with a reward (the sample) and one of which is not (the foil). After learning the association between the sample and reward, the association is unexpectedly reversed such that the sample now becomes the foil and vice versa. Dealing successfully with this reversal involves both learning a new association and inhibiting a previously learnt, but now outdated association.

object segregation: the ability to identify an object as a bounded whole separate from its background, supporting surfaces, and other objects.

object unity: the ability to perceive a unitary object despite the fact that parts of it are out of sight or partly occluded. In infancy, common motion of parts leading to constant deletion and accretion of background, and Gestalt good form, contribute to perception of object unity.

obsessive-compulsive disorder: a disorder dominated by obsessions and compulsions usually with child or adolescent onset, which often occur with a high probability and rigid manner, even at the expense of more adaptive patterns of action.

occipital-temporal pathway: connections between the occipital lobe (involved in vision) and temporal lobe (involved in visual cognition).

ocular dominance columns: segregation of the inputs from the right and left eyes into columns that form alternating bands in the primary visual cortex.

odds ratio: the odds of a given outcome ($= p/q$, where p is the proportion with the outcome and q is the proportion without the outcome) for participants with a particular characteristic, divided by the odds of that outcome for participants without the characteristic (or with one unit less of the characteristic).

Oedipal complex: the stage of development hypothesized by Freud in which a boy, at around 2–3 years of age, falls in love with his mother, but fears castration by his father. The successful resolution of this dilemma is supposed to lead to male gender identification.

ontogenetic adaptation: an anatomical, physiological, or behavioral characteristic that serves a transient, age-specific, biological function during development and which may occur relatively independent of experience.

ontogenetic development: concerns the processes and mechanisms of change during species-characteristic ontogeny.

ontogenetic skills: those abilities in infants designated by Myrtle McGraw (1899–1988) to have a recent evolutionary history and which are therefore more susceptible to the effects of experience than those she classified as phylogenetic skills.

ontogeny: a description of the life history of the *typical* individual of a particular species from a zygote to sexual maturity. Ontogenesis is sometimes used interchangeably, but at other times taken to refer to the life history of a *particular* individual.

open system: a system that exchanges energy, information, and matter with its environment and thus one that disobeys the second law of thermodynamics.

operant (or instrumental) conditioning: learning the relationship between one's own behavior and environmental consequences. A process of learning in which the relative frequency of a response increases as the result of a reward or reinforcement contingent on the response that is emitted. Also called respondent conditioning and Skinnerian conditioning.

operant train task: an operant conditioning procedure in which infants aged between 6 and 18 months learn to press a lever in order to produce movement of a train around a track.

oppositional defiant disorder: common childhood-onset symptom constellation dominated by negativism, temper tantrums, labile mood, aggression, and quarrelsome attitude.

optical imaging: a technique for studying brain activity that involves measuring tiny changes in the scattering or bending of infra-red light.

orbitofrontal cortex: a key region of the frontal cortex, located on the ventral surface, which appears to play a role in social judgment.

order: outside the context of mathematics where it is the number of times a given function has to be differentiated to obtain a given derivative, this is a qualitative statistical concept applicable to the law of entropy that refers to the regularity of arrangements or sequences of objects, numbers, or events. In this respect, it is different from organization. When entropy is evident, it is order rather than organization that tends to decrease in irreversible processes. Stating that a system is highly ordered conveys nothing about its level of organization. Thus, order and organization are not synonymous.

order parameter: a low-dimensional descriptor that expresses cooperative relationships between the many degrees of freedom found in complex systems, and which serves to simplify this description for an external observer. Order parameters are determined by and created from the cooperation of microscopical quantities, while at the same time they govern the qualitative behavior of the whole system in a form of circular causality. Behavioral states as described for the human newborn can be considered to be analogous to order parameters.

ordinal variables: variables in which higher numbers indicate higher levels of that which is measured, but the differences between adjacent numbers are not necessarily equal.

organelle: a generic term for minute structures in a cell that have a particular function. Examples include: the nucleus, mitochondria, and lysosomes (an enzyme in a membrane-bound sac in the cytoplasm required for the digestion of material in food, the destruction of foreign particles entering the cell, and the breakdown of all cell structures when it dies).

organization: a complex and non-random set of relationships among components of a system, which are functional, spatial, and temporal in nature. Unlike order, it is a physical attribute of a system and not subject to the law of entropy.

organism-environment mutualism: having assumed the status of a principle in J. J. Gibson's ecological psychology, this holds that animal and environment, as well as perception and action, are yoked by the two fundamental reciprocities that function in distinct, but complementary ways – a reciprocity between internal and external frames of references (i.e., between internal and external degrees of freedom) and a reciprocity between movement and the detection of the resultant information it generates (i.e., between the generation of force fields and the generation of flow fields).

organogenesis: formation of an organ through the assembly of tissues of different kinds once the three germ layers (viz., ectoderm, entoderm, mesoderm) have been established. Many organs consist of cells from more than one germ layer. During organogenesis, some cells undergo long migrations to their final location from their place of origin. They include precursors of the blood cells, lymph cells, pigment cells, and gametes. For example, cells migrating ventrally from the dorsal region of the head form the facial bones.

orthogonality: (1) characteristic of ANOVA designs – equal numbers of cases in each cell; and (2) independence of effects that are specified in a design matrix.

orthographic reading skills: a set of skills that include the ability to read words directly without translating them to sound, usually with automaticity.

other minds problem: a classical problem in philosophy pertaining to how we know that others have internal mental states such as beliefs, desires, emotions, and intentions. We cannot directly see these internal states in others. Why do we believe others have such invisible states, and are we justified in holding this belief (philosophical queries); where does such a view of others come from (developmental query)?

otitis media with effusion (OME): an inflammation of the middle ear with a collection of liquid in the middle-ear space. The signs and symptoms of acute infection are absent and there is no perforation of the tympanic membrane.

oversampling: increasing the proportionate representation of a given group in a study in order to increase the statistical power of tests comparing associations among variables in that group with associations in other study groups.

overt attention: eye movements to selected targets in the visual field.

own-sex schema: organized sets of beliefs about the characteristics associated with one's own sex.

oxyhemoglobin: oxygenated hemoglobin (a protein present in red blood cells or erythrocytes).

P400: a specific component of the event-related potential, thought to be elicited by faces, and observed in infants but not adults.

palmar grasp: clutching objects with the whole hand.

panel design: a research design in which a group of participants is selected without regard to risks and is followed repeatedly to determine factors related to developmental outcomes or later onset of diseases or other conditions.

panel studies: the longitudinal collection of information on a set of individuals (N) at multiple occasions (T) where the number of persons far exceeds the number of occasions (N>T; e.g., N>1,000 and T = 3).

parameter (statistics): a characteristic of the distribution of a population or a distribution of scores such as the mean or standard deviation as distinct from the property of a sample drawn from a population. Often used interchangeably with variable, but this is incorrect as it differs in meaning.

parasympathetic nervous system: one of the two major sub-divisions of the autonomic nervous system that conserves and restores energy in opposition to physical responses from the sympathetic nervous system. Typically causes, for example, lower heart rate, blood vessel dilation, and increased digestive secretions.

parietal cortex: the region of cortex lying between primary visual and primary/somatosensory cortex, and involved in complex aspects of navigation and visual recognition.

parietal lobe: this area comprising about a fifth of the cerebral cortex, can be divided into three segments: the postcentral gyrus, the inferior parietal lobule, and the superior parietal lobule.

participant observation: a technique of contemporary anthropological fieldwork in which the fieldworkers live with the group they have chosen to study and participate in their daily activities as much as possible.

path analysis: a set of mathematical and statistical models based on an organized set of multiple linear regression equations with multiple outcome variables. These techniques can be used in an exploratory or confirmatory fashion.

path diagram: a technique for path analysis developed by Sewall Wright (1889–1988), and first published in 1921, for the display of a set of linear relationships among measured (manifest) and unmeasured (latent) variables. If the diagrams are drawn in complete form, all structural expectations of the model can be generated using a set of 'path tracings' rules.

pathogenesis (or pathogeny): the origin and development of a disease. Also referred to as nosogenesis and nosogeny.

pathophysiology: the scientific study of the unfolding, sometimes complex, process by which an otherwise healthy biological system, partially or wholly, either slowly or instantaneously, breaks down or somehow fails to serve its intended function, potentially harming or killing the organism.

pattern of variances and covariances: pattern of variability of variances and covariances in a variance-covariance matrix. An example is compound symmetry.

pedagogy: the art, science, or profession of teaching. More specifically, consciously planned teaching, philosophy, and practices underpinned by beliefs about, and/or theories of, teaching and learning.

pediatrics: the practice of medicine devoted to the care and treatment of children as well as the diagnosis and prevention of certain developmental disorders.

peer group: any group in which most members have roughly equal status within the confines and functions of the group.

peg-moving task: one of a number of tasks used to measure speed and accuracy of hand movement. The individual must move dowelling pegs either from one pegboard to another or from the back to the front of the same board. On the premise that such tasks are less practiced than those normally listed in handedness questionnaires, or inventories, it is widely supposed that they provide a 'purer' measure of handedness (i.e., one that is less contaminated by prior experience).

perception: generally speaking, the active process of recognizing and identifying something. As such, it is distinguished from sensation: the sensitivity of neural receptors to internal and external stimuli. Putting the two terms together, perception is then a process of converting 'meaningless' sensations into 'meaningful' percepts. This interpretation represents the concept of indirect perception that can be traced back to the work of Hermann L. F. Helmholtz (1821–1894). This concept is opposed by that of direct perception as espoused by J. J. Gibson and his followers in ecological psychology: all the information necessary for accurate perception is contained in the environment, perception is immediate and spontaneous, and perception and action cannot be separated as perception guides action and action generates more new perceptual information. An attempt to integrate these two concepts and also cognition with perception was made by Ulrich Neisser (1976) in his book *Cognition and Reality* based on his three-part perception-action cycle: schemata (past knowledge directs perception to task-relevant stimuli), perceptual exploration (sampling and selection of available information relevant to completion of the task), and schemata modification (arising from discrepancies between information obtained and information in the schemata).

perception-action coupling: circular causality between perception and movement in order to achieve a particular action relative to a particular task. This type of causality is exemplified by J. J. Gibson as follows: "We perceive in order to act and we act in order to perceive."

perceptual development: the development of perceptual modalities, either individually or in some combination (i.e., cross-modal matching or intermodal perception), from before birth to weeks, months, and sometimes years postnatally. Most research concerned with perceptual development has focused on the visual system during the period of infancy, particularly the first six months after birth, as visual functions undergo rapid and relatively clear-cut changes during this period. This is particularly the case for so-called low-level abilities such as depth perception, visual accommodation, and visual acuity. The study of higher-level abilities involved in various attentional processes such as search strategies overlaps considerably with research on cognitive development. Overall, there has been a relative neglect of auditory development and, more especially, with regard to gustatory and olfactory modalities. In recent years, a growing trend is evident to study the developing inter-relationships between perception and action, mainly (but not exclusively) within the context of ecological psychology.

perceptual memory: a class of long-term memory for visual (e.g., faces, appearance of things), auditory (e.g., tunes, voices), and other perceptual information (e.g., odor, taste). It is sometimes included in the category of semantic memory.

perinatal: the period from onset of labor to the complete expulsion of the fetus, or to departure from the delivery suite. Sometimes, and especially in the USA, it covers a much larger time period (viz., from 28 weeks of pregnancy to 7 days and even 1 month after a fullterm delivery).

perinatal focal damage: localized damage to the brain of a fetus or infant, occurring during the period around birth (5 months before to 1 month after).

period effect: an effect on a mean value or association that changes over historical time.

peripheral nervous system (PNS): that part of the nervous system consisting of 12 pairs of cranial nerves, 31 pairs of spinal nerves, their peripheral combinations, and the peripheral portions of the autonomic nervous system (consisting in turn of the sympathetic and parasympathetic nervous systems). The cranial nerves are connected directly to the brain, the spinal nerves at regular intervals to the spinal cord, and the autonomic system originates from both the brain and the spinal cord. Together, these three components of the PNS inform the central nervous system about events in the environment and transmit output from it to the body.

permissive: used in embryology to denote developmental events with intrinsic origins that support ontogenetic change, but which would not otherwise be expressed.

perseverate: reaching to the hiding location where the object was found on the immediately preceding trial.

person-centered approaches: a research strategy organized around specific kinds of persons and addressing issues such as what kinds of problems handicapped children meet in comparison to non-handicapped ones.

person-specific variance: systematic variance that characterizes an individual or a group of individuals.

pharynx: the throat; a respiratory and digestive passageway from the larynx to the oral and nasal cavities.

phenylketonuria (PKU): a recessive genetic disorder that leads to functional deficits in children arising from a neurochemical deficit in the prefrontal cortex (i.e., the enzyme converting dietary phenylalanine to tyrosine is deficient, resulting in the excretion of phenylpyruvate, or phenylalanine, into the urine).

phonological deficit hypothesis/model/theory: terms used to refer to the theory that dyslexia is caused by a difficulty in the way in which the sounds of words are represented and processed.

phonological dyslexia: term used to refer to the reading profile in which real words can be read more accurately than non-words. Derived from studies of adult patients with acquired dyslexia, but also used to refer to a 'sub-type' of developmental dyslexia.

phonological loop: an element of Alan Baddeley's model of working memory. It acts as a relatively passive slave system for the temporary storage of verbal information, under the direction of the central executive.

phonological pathway: system of mappings within a connectionist model of reading connecting orthographic and phonological units of representation.

phonological process: a systematic sound pattern, typically one that can be demonstrated to occur across a number of words containing a particular sound or sound sequence.

phonological rule: a formal expression that expresses a systematic relationship in sound patterns.

phonology: a term that refers to the structure of speech sounds in a language, and also to the study of speech sounds. The importance of phonology for the development of reading is that children's awareness of the phonology of their own language (phonological awareness) has a considerable impact on the progress that they make in learning to read and write.

phototaxis: reflexive locomotion toward light.

phylogenetic abilities/behaviors (as opposed to ontogenetic abilities): those abilities and behaviors that are typical of the species. For example, walking is a phylogenetic ability of humans. Ontogenetic abilities are those supported by the culture. An example would be a specific dance step (e.g., a polka) that is unique to the individual or culture, but not seen in all humans.

phylogenetic (or geological) time: the time scale required for speciation to occur and thus consisting of time measured in units of a million years.

phylogenetic relationship: the pattern of relatedness among a group of species.

phylogenetic skills: those abilities in infants designated by McGraw to have a long evolutionary history (e.g., locomotion) and which are therefore much less susceptible to experience than ontogenetic skills. Attempting to distinguish between the two was rather unfortunate as it assumes that evolutionary influences have less of an effect on the development of ontogenetic skills, when in fact the latter would not be evident in the behavioral repertoire without such influences.

phylogeny: the historical paths taken by evolving groups of animals and plants over geological time. Often used interchangeably with biological evolution, the two terms need to be distinguished from each other. The distinction is between providing a descriptive evolutionary history of a species (phylogeny) and attempting to explain the processes (phyletic gradualism or punctuated equilibrium) and mechanisms behind this history such as gene recombination, genetic drift, mutation, and natural selection (biological evolution).

Piaget's stage theory: according to Piaget's theory, development occurs through a series of major periods or stages that contain their own sub-stages and in which psychological activity differs qualitatively from one period to the next. The main principle that makes the stage progression necessary and non-arbitrary is that the major achievement of one period sets the necessary starting condition for the next. Most secondary accounts name four major periods, although in his full elaboration of the account, Piaget identified only three periods with sub-divisions.

pictorial depth cues: information about relative distance that can be depicted in a picture or photograph.

placenta: in mammalian species, the organ in the uterus that unites the fetus and mother, providing the fetus with oxygen and nutrients while also removing waste products.

placenta previa: a condition in which the placenta is implanted into a lower than usual segment of the uterus, obstructing the cervical opening to the vagina.

planned comparison: a priori determined mean comparison, to be performed when a main effect or interaction in an ANOVA is significant; replaces across-the-board post-hoc tests.

plantigrade locomotion: locomotion with the plantar side of the foot in contact with the floor during the whole stance phase; typical pattern of early walking in humans, which gradually becomes digitigrade (heel-strike) locomotion.

plasticity (experiential): where organisms, objects, or events have the capacity to change through experience.

plasticity (neural): the property of the brain to reorganize itself after damage or in response to any developmental variation.

pleonastic extensions: an overgeneralization of a word that uses not only perceptual features, but also fortuitous event conjunctions, such as referring to a lake as a 'duck' because sometimes ducks are found there.

plexus: a network or interweaving of nerves and blood vessels (plural: plexuses).

Poisson distribution: named after Siméon-Denis Poisson (1781–1840), this is a skewed probability distribution with a long tail representing the number of randomly occurring events with a constant mean rate in a specified time interval. Its most frequent use is to model the random occurrence of infrequent events that have a fixed probability of occurrence. It has also been used to model developmental changes in the temporal organization of infant nutritive sucking and turn-taking during face-to-face interaction in older infants.

polarizer: signaling molecule that designates the front or back of a structure in early development.

polycyclic aromatic hydrocarbons: a group of over 100 different chemicals that form during the incomplete burning of coal, oil and gas, garbage, or other organic substances like tobacco.

polygenes: genes at more than one locus on a chromosome. Their variations in a particular population can have a combined effect on a discrete phenotypic character. The individual genes have a small quantitative effect, but together produce a wide range of phenotypical variation. Also called multiple factor quantitative genes.

polygenic mode of inheritance: inheritance pattern requiring the influence of several (four or more) genes.

The inheritance of characters such as height, weight, and behavior depends on the simultaneous action of a number of genes in interaction with the environment. It is a form of inheritance that increases the probability that a character or trait will show continuous variation in a population.

polygynous households: where one man is married to more than one woman.

polyneural to mononeural innervation: first observed in neonatal muscles in 1917. Starting early in prenatal life, one spinal motoneuron synaptically innervates more than one fiber in skeletal muscle (polyinnervation). Subsequently, supernumerary or collateral axons are retracted so that one motoneuron innervates one muscle fiber (monoinnervation), a process that takes place mainly prenatally, but also after birth depending on the muscle. The details of the mechanisms responsible for synapse elimination, axon retraction, and the loss of polyinnervation are still not completely understood, but are thought to involve competition for the uptake of neurotrophic substances in the target sites (i.e., muscle fibers).

polynomial: a mathematical expression containing three or more terms, denoted by letters. It has the general form: $a_0 x^{n-2} + a_1^{n-1} + a_2^{n-2} + \cdots + a_n$, where a_0, a_1, etc., are constants and n is the highest power of the variable, termed the degree or order of the polynomial. A polynomial of degree one (i.e., whose highest power of n is one) is called a linear polynomial.

polynomial analysis of variance: analysis of variance that describes the relationships between dependent and independent variables using polynomials of first and higher order.

polysynaptic reflexes: rapid automatic responses to stimulation that are mediated through at least two synapses and one interneuron. They include, for example, the automatic withdrawal of the leg when the foot steps on a sharp object.

population (biology and ecology): a group of inter-breeding organisms of one species living in a certain geographical range at a given time.

population thinking: the view that measures of central tendency such as the mean and median are abstractions from reality. What is real is variation both within and between individuals with regard to physical and behavioral traits, and there is no such thing as the 'average person.'

positive predictive value: the proportion of the sample identified as positive (or abnormal) that subsequently had a positive (or abnormal) outcome.

positive reinforcement: a reward that reliably follows a behavior and increases the likelihood that the behavior will be produced again.

posture: state of the body consisting of the maintenance of relationships between body parts (body-referenced definition) and relationships between body and ground and the gravitational vector (environmental-referenced definition). Posture has three functions: (1) to maintain stability in the face of gravity (i.e., an anti-gravity response); (2) stability in the face of self-induced change (e.g., when reaching for an object) and which requires anticipation or feedforward control; and (3) stability in the face of externally induced change (e.g., after a shoulder push when sitting or standing).

Prader-Willi syndrome: a genetic disorder, originally identified by John Langdon Down (1826–1896), with congenital symptoms of hypotonia and minor physical stigmata, later characterized by some cognitive impairment, gross overeating that can lead to obesity, adipositas, hypogenitalism, and various other symptoms not always present such as self-mutilation of the face; associated with loss of paternal alleles at chromosome 15q11–13.

praxis: skilled movement.

pre-functional: neural circuits that develop more or less completely prior to behavioral expression, thus limiting dependence upon prior learning or practice.

pre-reaching: organized but incomplete reaching movements before functional reaching has developed. First identified by Colwyn Trevarthen and subsequently subjected to motion analysis by Claes von Hofsten, they consist of arm movements toward an object with an open hand, which bring the hand in the vicinity of the object, but it does not contact it. Only seen in the newborn under appropriate conditions when in the right 'alert' state and seated in a semi-upright position.

precision: in statistics, the magnitude of the standard error or the associated confidence limits of a statistical estimate such as a mean or a correlation.

predetermined epigenesis: the almost outmoded idea that the sequential development of structures and functions proceeds from the genetic through the neural to the behavioral and environmental levels in a unidirectional (bottom-up) fashion.

preformationism: the age-old doctrine that the entire organism is preformed within the egg or sperm, but only begins to grow to a visible size after fertilization occurs.

prefrontal cortex (PFC): the most anterior part of the frontal cortex in front of the primary and secondary motor cortices (areas 4 and 6) and the frontal eye field of the frontal lobe.

prefrontal-frontal-striatal loops: neural circuits linking frontal areas of the brain with the sub-cortical area called the corpus striatum in the basal ganglia.

prehension: reaching for and grasping an object.

premotor cortex consisting of frontal lobe cortical regions located anterior to the primary motor cortex and about six times larger, it serves a number of functions such as the initiation of movements controlled by vision and touch, and is involved in postural control.

pretence: the use of objects in non-literal ways. It involves assertions that do not depend on being either true or false, and actions that do not depend upon being in factual accord with reality.

preterm birth: the live birth of an infant with a gestational age of 36 weeks or less.

preterm infant: one delivered or born before 37 completed weeks of pregnancy have elapsed since the last normal menstrual period.

prevalence: current cases of a specified condition or disease in a defined age group. Includes cases who have migrated in, but excludes those who have died or migrated out. It provides an estimate of the probability (P, risk) that an individual will be ill at that point in time, with the total relevant population as the denominator. Thus: P = number of existing cases at a given time point/total population.

preventive interventions: programs targeted toward at-risk individuals or populations to prevent the development of social adjustment problems, injuries, and illnesses.

Preyer-Tracy hypothesis of autogeneous motility: the idea that movements of the embryo begin before it is capable of responding to external stimulation as there are as yet no connections between motor and sensory neurons. Thus, the first movements of the embryo result solely from the autonomous discharge of motoneurons. The hypothesis gave rise to the notion of fixed action patterns in ethology and can be seen to be a forerunner of the central pattern generator in neurophysiology.

primacy effect: in contrast to the recency effect, the elevated recall for words at the beginning of a list; due presumably to items being stored in and retrieved from long-term memory.

primary motor cortex: precentral gyrus in the cortical area frontal to the central sulcus in each hemisphere with topographic representations of contralateral face, arm, trunk, and leg movement. Involved in the steering of movements.

primary sensory cortices: the parts of the cortex that get the most direct input from the retina (eye), cochlea (ear), or skin surface.

primary visual cortex: the part of the cortex that receives direct input from the lateral geniculate nucleus of the thalamus, which in turn gets direct retinal input. Also called the striate cortex or area VI in non-human primates and Brodmann area 17 in humans.

principle of the integration and individuation of behavior: Coghill's theory of development stems from this principle, which states that development begins as a coordinated pattern of behaviors from which individual behaviors emerge due to inhibitory influences imposing themselves on the original integrated pattern. Sometimes descriptively referred to as the mass-to-specific trend in development, which ignores Coghill's efforts to explain the mechanisms in his principle.

prion (proteinaceous infectious particle): abnormal or malformed version of normal cellular proteins that is believed to play a role in various neurological disorders (e.g., Creutzfeldt-Jakob disease). A hundred times smaller than a virus, it is neither a virus nor a bacterium and does not contain nucleic acid, yet nevertheless can self-replicate.

probabilistic epigenesis: the current idea that development is a consequence of bidirectional horizontal and vertical influences among genetic activity, neural activity, behavior, and the environment. Developmental outcomes are probable rather than predetermined because of the necessarily somewhat uncertain operation of a variety of endogenous and exogenous stimulative events.

processing units: the units in a connectionist model. A processing unit normally receives input from other units and/or from the environment. Depending on the magnitude of this input and on the activation function of the processing unit (e.g., a threshold function), it can itself become active. In this way, a processing unit shares basic properties with biological neurons.

prognosis: the prediction or forecast of the outcome of any condition, illness, or disease, thus whether the person involved will get better, worse, or stay the same.

proprioception: sensory information about position and movement of body parts relative to gravity available via sensory receptors (i.e., proprioceptors) in joints, muscle, and skin as well as the vestibular system.

prosocial behavior: an act that can be of help, aid, or assistance to another person. The behavior can take different forms, such as physical, verbal, intellectual, emotional, social, economic, and spiritual.

prosopagnosia: complete or partial loss of the ability to recognize familiar faces, usually the result of brain damage to the posterior right hemisphere.

prospective cohort: a cohort of living individuals followed over time to gather information on changes as they occur.

prospective control (neurophysiology): motor control relying on feedforward mechanisms.

protective factor: influences on a child's development that are likely to compensate for the effects of risk factors (e.g., sensitive parenting for a preterm child) or to protect a child from very likely risks (e.g., a reliable older sibling, positive teacher-student relationship).

protein-folding problem: the problem of determining the three-dimensional structure of a protein when the linear sequence of amino acids that identify the protein is known. Protein folding is the process, lasting a few tens of milliseconds, by which a protein evolves to this structure (termed its natural conformation) from an amino acid chain so that it can achieve its biological function (e.g., as an enzyme that repairs and replicates DNA, as a contractile element like myosin in muscle, or as a hormone such as insulin that regulates glucose metabolism). Errors in protein folding are thought to be the main causes of neurodegenerative diseases such as Alzheimer's and Huntington's, and possibly implicated in some developmental disorders.

protein tyrosine kinase: a protein kinase phosphorylating tyrosine participating in numerous processes in the regulation of cell growth and differentiation.

protoplasm: a term for the granular matter of which all living cells consist. It comprises a nucleus embedded in the cytoplasm.

proxemic cues: movements and positioning of the body during conversation.

proximal care: this term distinguishes parental care involving high amounts of holding and body contact from distal care, where infants are put down, which is more common in Western cultures. The term derives from anthropological research, where hunter-gatherer bands have been found to carry their babies more than 80 percent of daylight hours, to respond rapidly to infant frets, and to breastfeed frequently on demand.

proximal processes: those processes involving the individual directly and a term usually applied to immediate interpersonal interaction.

proximate mechanisms (or causes): determinants of behavior that are effective in moments of time or across the whole lifespan. They include social influences and internal regulating mechanisms such as behavioral state. These determinants are contrasted with ultimate causes.

psychoanalysis: a term that has three meanings – (1) a theory of mental function and human development originated by Sigmund Freud; (2) an intensive method of psychotherapy that involves free association and interpretation; and (3) an approach to a range of disciplines including literature, history, and art using the psychoanalytic model of the mind.

psychodynamic theory: theory influenced by psychoanalysis that stresses the importance of unconscious mental processing.

psycholinguistic guessing game: the hypothesis proposed by Kenneth Goodman that children learn to read by guessing the meaning of words with the help of their context. The hypothesis makes two claims, both of which are controversial: (1) that children depend heavily on the context to read new texts, and particularly texts that contain difficult or unfamiliar words; and (2) that children learn to recognize the written word on the basis of having guessed its meaning in the first place.

psychopathology: (1) the scientific study of aberrant behaviors and mental disorders; and (2) the collective signs and symptoms of a mental disorder (i.e., psychopathy).

psychosocial stress: adverse social circumstances, hardship, problematic social relationships, emotional distress, and misfortunes that bind, or even strain and overtax, the psychological and social resources of a person.

Pupil Evaluation Inventory: a form of peer assessment like the Revised Class Play.

Purkinje cells: cells in the middle layer of the cortex of the cerebellum that process the input from parallel and climbing fibers. Their axons provide the sole output from the cerebellum. Discovered by Johannes E. Purkinje (1787–1869) in 1837.

qualitative research: research with an emphasis on the understanding of processes and meanings; often these are considered not to be open to experimental and/or psychometric examination, and not to be measurable in terms of quantity, amount, etc.

quantifier: a predicate that expresses the amount of its argument, as in 'five dollars' where 'five' describes the quantity of dollars.

quantitative and qualitative change: change that is continuous, and which follows certain trends over time (e.g., asymptotic, exponential, logistic, monotonic), is considered to be quantitative. Appositional growth is a good example of this type of change. Allometric growth is an example of qualitative change, with metamorphosis being its most extreme expression. It not only signifies changes in form and function, but also the emergence of new properties via transitional periods of re-organization.

quantitative and qualitative regressions: during development, reductions in the numbers of axons, cells, neurons, and synapses (quantitative regression), and the loss of structures and their replacement by new ones, with possibly new functions (qualitative regression). Behavioral examples of both are less clear cut and in particular with regard to human development. A major problem, especially for the different forms of qualitative regression, is to know what happens to those structures that have been replaced by others.

quantitative research: research in which the measurement/assessment (in terms of quantity, amount, or frequency) of the phenomena that are being examined is emphasized.

race-ethnicity: a set of categories used to distinguish sub-groups of a larger society. The categories used have varied over time and in different societies. In the USA, categories used for the 2000 Census refer to both race (based on physical characteristics) and ethnicity (based on cultural characteristics such as common language or religious tradition). The Census Bureau distinguishes Hispanics (who can be of any race group) from non-Hispanics, and simultaneously distinguishes five race groups: White, Black or African-American, Asian, American Indian and Alaskan Native, Native Hawaiian and Pacific Islander. Much social research combines this information into a set of race-ethnic categories, typically distinguishing White non-Hispanics, Black non-Hispanics, and Hispanics.

radial glia: cells of a special class of astrocytes that extend from the ventricles to the cortex and along which migrating neurons travel to final destinations. With the completion of migration, the radial glia fibers break apart and the cells are transformed into fibrous astrocytes. Some neurons do not follow radial paths. The transformation of radial glia into astrocytes is an example of a qualitative regression.

radical behaviorism (or environmentalism): the most extreme form of behaviorism developed by John B. Watson (1878–1958) in which he claimed that classical conditioning contained both the necessary and sufficient conditions for development to occur. He became so extreme in his views on development partly as a consequence of his clashes with those he saw as maturationists.

ras: an intracellular tyrosine kinase (an enzyme) originally discovered through its role in oncogenesis, now found to be involved in a variety of developmental pathways.

rate ratio: the rate of a given outcome for participants with a particular characteristic divided by the rate of that outcome for participants without the characteristic.

rating scale: a questionnaire in which a person who knows a particular child is asked to make judgments, usually quantitative, about aspects of the child's behavior that are defined in the questionnaire.

reactivation: in contrast to reinstatement, a single passive re-exposure to an isolated component of the original training event that increases the accessibility of memory for the original training experience.

reading comprehension: the understanding of the meaning of any text.

recall: a form of information retrieval that occurs in the absence of any cues or prompts to aid the process.

recall memory: access to a memory trace in the absence of the stimulus that formed the memory (e.g., remembering the name of a friend without hearing the name repeated). Recall memory is typically 'cued' (e.g., a cue to recalling the name of a long-lost friend may be seeing a picture of him). Considered to require more cognitive effort than recognition memory.

recapitulation theory (or biogenetic law): the brainchild of Ernst Haeckel (1834–1919). The theory held that an ontogenetic sequence is a recapitulation in proper order of the corresponding sequence in phylogeny, with the absolute time from conception to maturation remaining the same from ancestors to descendants. In other words, organisms repeat the adult stages of their ancestors during their own ontogeny (metaphorically, they 'climb up their own family tree'). The theory has been summarized with the catch phrase 'ontogeny repeats phylogeny.' The theory eventually lost its credence when it was shown to be incompatible with Mendelian genetics.

recency effect: in contrast to the primacy effect, the elevated recall for words at the end of a list, due presumably to items being stored in and retrieved from short-term memory.

receptive field: the area of a sensory surface such as the retina or other receptor surfaces like the skin that will excite a neuron. For example, a neuron might have a receptive field in a small part of the skin surface, or the retina.

reciprocal assimilation: integration of one scheme into another. For Piaget, 'touch teaches vision' in the development of reaching so a visual scheme is assimilated to a scheme for touching. Results in a more complex scheme, which enables more proficient performance of an action.

reciprocity: the return of like behavior between individuals who are interacting with one another. For example, if one person is insulting, the other is insulting, and if one person is supportive, the other is supportive.

recognition memory: memory that occurs when a previously perceived stimulus is re-presented and registered as familiar. For example, a subject may recognize a voice, face, or visual pattern as being familiar, based on past exposure to it, even though there was no recollection of the stimulus before it was re-presented. People have excellent recognition memory for faces as they can recognize a person's face as familiar after lengthy delays. Considered to require less cognitive effort than recall memory.

reflex: a reflex should be distinguished from an action as it is a stereotyped response or movement (e.g., an eye blink to a specific external stimulus such as a puff of air) involving little or no cortical mediation. As such, it lacks the hallmark features of an action such as motor equivalence, which allow movements to be organized in a flexible and variable way to achieve a particular outcome in a particular task. Moreover, reflexes lack intentionality, whether it be an intentional act or an intentional sign. The above represents a reflex originally described by Sherrington. It is important to distinguish it from a reflex in Piagetian and neo-Piagetian theory. Here, they are more molar units of behavior, over which infants exert some cortical control, and constitute the first level of development. Examples include sucking, the palmar grasp, and looking at a seen object.

reflex arc: a simple model of the neural circuit that includes an afferent fiber conveying sensory information in the central nervous system and an efferent fiber to an end-organ (muscle, blood vessel, gland).

reflexology: the doctrine that behavioral mechanisms reside in the chaining of reflexes that is triggered by external stimulation. Closely allied to stimulus-response theory, it led to the human newborn being regarded as nothing more than a bundle of reflexes, and thus a passive rather than an active organism.

register: a list of individuals with a defined condition that enables the burden of disease to be measured in a given population over a given period of time.

regressive event: cell death, axon retraction, and synapse elimination in development.

regulator (or regulatory) gene: also known as a transacting element and a transcriptional regulatory element, this is a gene whose protein controls the activity and expression of one or more structural genes or metabolic pathways. In the Jacob-Monod operon model, these hypothetical genes acted only as repressors, but in later models they were assigned both repressor and activator roles. Thus, they became genes for turning on and off the transcription of structural genes and therefore for controlling the timing of development. It is thought that regulator genes account for differences in morphological development among primates, and thus indirectly have an influence on behavior.

reinforcement schedule: a well-defined procedure for reinforcing a given response only a certain proportion of the time it occurs.

reinforcer: a stimulus that has the power to alter the strength or probability of a behavior if it is made contingent on that behavior.

reinstatement: in contrast to reactivation, a periodic re-exposure to a small amount of partial practice or repetition of the original training experience that maintains the memory of that experience.

relativism (or cultural relativism): the anthropological doctrine originating with the Greek Sophists, and especially as espoused by J. Melville Herskovits (1895–1963), that the values and institutions of any culture are self-validating. Thus, there are no universals in human behavior or anything like a 'psychic unity of mankind', and no universal standards of good, bad, right, and wrong. The issue can be resolved if it is recognized that both the actual and expected consequences of behavior differ among cultures as a consequence of their differences in knowledge and experience.

REM sleep: abbreviation for 'rapid-eye movement sleep,' referred to also as paradoxical or active sleep, and one of the five EEG sleep stages identified by the eyes moving side-to-side underneath the lids and by electrophysiological wave signals emitted by the brain that are relatively fast, short in height, and somewhat erratic (as is heart rate and breathing during this stage). It is also a sleep stage in which an organism is likely to be dreaming.

repeated measures analysis of variance: analysis of variance of measures that are repeatedly observed on the same respondents.

representation (mental): (1) the capacity to make one thing stand for something else. Representations consist of a symbolic vehicle and a referent. The symbolic vehicle is that which does the representing (e.g., a word, an image, a picture). The referent consists of that which is represented (e.g., an event, a meaning, an object) in the real or imagined world. (2) In Fischer's skill theory, the third tier of skill development in which children gain the capacity to construct concrete meanings using signs and symbols.

representational re-description: a process whereby mental representations are iteratively re-represented to the mind in different formats, rendering what was originally encapsulated knowledge accessible to other parts of the cognitive system.

reproductive success: the number of offspring an individual produces, usually per unit time (reproductive rate) or over a given period of time.

residuals: differences between observed scores (the empirical observations) and the scores that a model predicts (the mathematical prediction of these observations).

respiratory distress syndrome (RDS): a respiratory disorder in preterm infants due to an immature surfactant system. The deficiency in surfactant results in a collapse of the gas-exchange units of the lungs and an increase of lung compliance. There are two sorts of RD: idiopathic respiratory distress (IRDS) or hyaline membrane disease when the lungs become lined with a glassy-like substance, and bronchial pulmonary dysplasia consisting of abnormal tissues in the bronchi of the lungs. In preterm infants, the former is one of the main causes of death during the first forty-eight hours after birth.

response inhibition tasks: tasks where the directed response to a number of cues is not to respond, and often used in tests of frontal lobe function.

resultant: a single force or velocity producing the same effect as the two or more forces or velocities acting in concert.

retina: the sensory membrane lining the eye that receives the image formed by the lens, and then transfers it to the primary visual cortex through the optic nerve and via the lateral geniculate bodies.

retinopathy of prematurity: previously termed retrolental fibroplasia, it consists of damage to the blood vessels of the retina, which may become detached if the resulting scar tissue contracts. Linked to hyperpoxia resulting from an overly high level of oxygen therapy, it can lead to blindness in very preterm and very low birthweight infants. Previously thought to have been eradicated, it has become prevalent again as more very preterm infants requiring lung ventilation are kept alive.

retrovirus: a class of enveloped viruses (e.g., HIV) that have their genetic material in the form of RNA. They infiltrate RNA and establish a template for foreign DNA to be established in the host, a process known as reverse transcription or transcriptase involving RNA → DNA information transfer. Can result in production of abnormal protein (e.g., prions).

Rett's syndrome: a progressive neurogenetic disorder with onset in the first few years of life and for which the first sign is usually hypotonia (a loss of muscle tone). Characterized by stunted development, a lag in brain and head growth, loss of purposeful hand use, and a number of major neurological problems, including epilepsy and decreased mobility involving gait abnormalities. Also presents as a diminished ability to express feelings and avoidance of eye contact. Unlike most genetically based disorders, it is almost exclusively restricted to females and associated with mutation of MecP2-gene on the X chromosome in the majority of cases. Both its incidence and prevalence are 1 in 10,000 to 15,000 live births.

reverse genetics: the process of searching for phenotypes through altering specific gene functions. The experimental procedure involved begins with a cloned segment of DNA, or a protein sequence, and uses this knowledge to introduce programmed mutations (through directed mutagenesis) back into the genome in order to investigate gene and protein function.

Revised Class Play: a peer assessment technique in children's reports on the behavior and reputations of others in their classroom. This assessment consistently yields three broad dimensions of social reputation amongst children: (1) Sociable-Leader; (2) Aggressive-Disruptive; and (3) Sensitive-Isolated.

rhythmical stereotypies: rapid, repetitive movements in infancy displayed, for example, in rocking, kicking, or banging. Rocking on all fours, for example, is shown just before the transition to crawling. Thus, repetition of rhythmical movement patterns may herald the onset of a developmental transition in healthy infants.

risk-benefit ratios: an analysis of the potential advantages and disadvantages of research participation for any particular individual.

risk factors: characteristics of individuals or influences that increase the probability or risk of some negative outcome (e.g., cerebral palsy or a learning disorder). Typically, they are distinguished in terms of biological risk factors (e.g., preterm birth) and environmental risk factors (e.g., poverty, which is a risk factor for poor educational achievement).

risk mechanisms: translation of risk factors into an individual's biological functioning (e.g., maternal alcohol intake that affects the fetal brain development) or behavior (inadequate information processing, emotion regulation, coping, inadequate attention deployment, inadequate emotional reaction as a consequence of insecurity, lack of interest in exploration as a consequence of adverse experiences).

Ritalin: a trade name for the drug methylphenidate.

RNA (ribonucleic acid): a complex nucleic acid in living cells that is concerned with protein synthesis. Most RNA is synthesized in the nucleus and then distributed to various parts of the cytoplasm. An RNA molecule consists of a long chain of nucleotides of alternating ribose sugar units and phosphate groups with bases adenine, guanine, and uracil attached to the sugar units.

rooting response: present in normal fullterm newborns (e.g., to locate the nipple) and characterized by head-turning, followed by sucking movements, toward the side of the mouth or cheek (i.e., perioral region) touched.

rostral: at the front of the longitudinal axis of the body.

sampling ratios: the number of sub-group persons to be included in a given study divided by the number of sub-group persons in the population from which the study sample is drawn. Also used to describe the proportions of the study population of various sub-groups in comparison to the proportions of the target population.

scaffolding: in sociocultural and neo-Piagetian skill theories of development, the ways in which adults assist and support children in their attempts to perform complex tasks. Scaffolding occurs when adults or more accomplished peers perform part of a task for a child, direct, or otherwise structure a child's actions in order to support task performance.

schema: a type of perceptual mechanism that can be said to recognize particular objects. Also refers to a mental representation of some feature of experience or the interpretation of new knowledge in terms of existing knowledge, following the meaning given by Frederic C. Bartlett (1886–1969) in his book *Remembering: A Study in Experimental and Social Psychology* (1932). Not the same as a scheme.

scheme: in Piaget's theory, a sensorimotor structure (e.g., a grasping scheme) that serves as an internal model for performing a particular movement such as looking, grasping, and touching in similar circumstances. Not the same as a schema.

Scholastic Aptitude Test (SAT): a commonly used set of verbal, mathematical, and analytical problems designed in the USA to compare performance of high school students to determine college entry.

'screw-you' effect: the term used by social psychologists when participants do not try to perform in a test because they are unhappy with the research process. This may apply in longitudinal research involving intensive interventions.

search errors in infancy: prior to 8 months, infants do not search for an object when someone hides it from them. After 8 months, they begin to search and do so accurately provided the object is hidden in the same place each time. If the object is hidden in a new location, infants of less than 12 months search in the original location. Following 12 months of age, the error recurs if the task is made more complex. For instance, if an object is hidden in a box, the box is moved under a cover where the object is tipped out, and the box is moved back to its original location, infants will search only in the box. Piaget takes the onset of search at 8 months as evidence for the beginnings of object permanence, and uses the errors that occur up to 24 months as evidence for the limitations in its early forms.

secondary visual cortex (V2): the area of visual cortex that immediately adjoins primary visual cortex (V1) and gets direct input from it. It is responsive to color information and the direction of motion.

segment polarity: the anterior-posterior polarity of each segment of an animal. As found for the *Drosophila* fly, there are segment polarity genes, mutations of which cause a disruption in pattern formation in each segment.

segmentation: a consistent feature of developing invertebrate and vertebrate embryos, composed of a number of repeating units with some common structure, with potential variation in each segment. Both the insect and vertebrate body are initially segmented, as is the spinal cord.

selective (or elective) mutism: a rare childhood-onset disorder dominated by refusal to speak in certain social settings (e.g., in school, with peers), in spite of being able to speak in other situations; often co-morbid with other neuropsychiatric disorders, including autism.

self: the definitions of self are perhaps as many as the theorists who have thought about it. Beside the bodily activities of the self of a person, including their brain and central nervous system, the self is made up of at least two major aspects. These can be referred to as the machinery of the self and the mental state or the idea of me. The machinery of the self involves all unconscious, unreferenced actions of the body, including its physiology and its processing of information that in turn includes cognitions and emotions, which are unavailable to consciousness. The mental state, or the idea of me, is that part of the self that can make reference to itself. It includes what is referred to as explicit consciousness. In the animal kingdom, the ability to reflect upon the person constitutes perhaps the most unique feature of the human self.

self-competence: refers to the perception that one has necessary and sufficient skills in various life domains, (academic, athletic, social, appearance, and behavior) to respond adaptively to demands within these environments.

self-concept: conscious attributes and characteristics of one's self.

self-differentiation: in embryology, the idea that heredity alone promotes early maturation of structure and function within a developing organism in a non-interactive fashion.

self-efficacy: the awareness that self actions can be effective in producing consequences that can become predictable.

self-esteem: a person's evaluation of his or her own worth; the extent to which one values oneself in terms of worth and competence. Higher self-esteem is considered a psychological resource (or protective factor) that may reduce social stress when the person faces undesirable events or conditions.

self-organization: a process by which new structures emerge without specification from outside. Thus, these new spatial and temporal patterns arise as a result of some internal regulation in response to changing external conditions that do not specify what should be changed, and not through the external imposition of a particular form of organization. The simplest form of self-organization is a phase transition between two stable states.

self-perception: the way in which one perceives oneself. This does not refer to a single, global entity but rather a multifaceted structure, which becomes more differentiated as a child becomes older. Several domains with different correlates have been suggested to include academic, athletic, social, and behavioral conduct, as well as appearance. Negative self-perception in certain domains, as well as global negative self-perception, is related in general to psychopathology in childhood and adolescence.

self-recognition: the ability of an organism to recognize itself, most often referenced by recognition of the physical self. It is measured by observing people's reaction to their mirror image. Prior to the middle of the second year of life, the human infant does not show self-recognition. Of the great apes only chimpanzees, but not gorillas and orangutans, appear to show self-recognition as defined by this test, as do porpoises with a different testing procedure. Thus, as yet, it would

not be appropriate to deny gorillas or orangutans are able to recognize their own reflections based on the one test, as there may be other tests that in fact show they do so. Self-recognition is one of the earliest markers of a human child's ability to make reference to itself, something referred to as the mental state of the idea of me.

self-regulation: the process of controlling one's own behavior or internal states.

self-report questionnaire for handedness: with such inventories, individuals indicate their preferred hand for a variety of common tasks, including writing, drawing, cutting with a knife, using a toothbrush, hammer, scissors, and other utensils and tools. Participants also may be asked to rate their consistency of use on a scale with anywhere from three to seven values (e.g., 'always left,' 'usually left,' 'either,' 'usually right,' 'always right'). There is usually a good association between measures of handedness obtained from these questionnaires and having individuals actually perform the tasks referred to in them.

self-stimulation: the stimulation of sensory systems that is the consequence of the embryo's own behavior or physiological activity (e.g., bird embryos hear their own vocalizations, mammalian fetuses produce amniotic fluid that they subsequently ingest).

semantic bootstrapping: a hypothesized learning procedure in which children use the meaning of linguistic elements to make inferences about their word class or syntactic role (e.g., a word for an object is likely to be a noun, a word naming an agent is probably the sentence-subject).

semantic pathway: a system of mappings within a connectionist model of reading connecting orthographic and phonological units of representation via meaning (semantics).

semi-circular canals: a sensory organ in the inner ear (labyrinth) that is associated with the maintenance of the body's balance and the detection of angular or rotational acceleration of the head. They are structurally developed by about 8 weeks after conception, but it is still a matter of debate as to whether they, and the vestibular system in general, are functional before birth.

sensitive period: a phase in development when the organism is sensitive or has a greater susceptibility to particular forms of experience and learning that may be essential to later behavior, and which is followed by a period of less sensitivity. It should be distinguished from 'critical period' that refers among other things to a period in life during which behavior must develop.

sensitivity (attachment theory): a sensitive mother is able to see things from the baby's point of view. She is alert to perceive her baby's signals, interprets them accurately, and responds appropriately and promptly, unless no response is most appropriate. She tends to give the baby what he seems to want, and when she does not she is tactful in acknowledging his communication. Furthermore, she makes her responses temporarily contingent upon the baby's signals.

sensitivity (epidemiology): the proportion of the sample with a positive (or abnormal) outcome that were previously identified as positive (or abnormal).

sensitivity threshold: the point at which a listener can detect a change in an auditory signal that is increased along some continuous dimension, such as loudness.

sensorimotor actions: the first of four stages of cognitive development identified by Piaget. Sensorimotor actions consist of integrations of the sensory and motor aspects of organized actions. In Piaget's theory, infants are capable of sensorimotor action, but not thought. Thought requires the ability to represent images of objects or events in the absence of direct action on those objects. In sensorimotor action, an infant is capable of representing an object only when receiving sensory input from that object.

sensory memory, short-term memory (STM), and long-term memory (LTM): sensory memory, which should not be confused with perceptual memory, is in effect a very short STM store that corresponds approximately to the moment when an item is perceived. STM is a memory system for holding a limited memory for periods up to about 20 to 30 seconds (but that can be renewed if information within it is rehearsed), and which is essential for language comprehension. LTM, sometimes referred to as secondary or permanent memory, is memory consisting of information that is stored for periods of about 30 seconds up to decades, and which is often broken down into episodic and semantic memory.

sequential data interchange standard (SDIS): a set of conventions for representing sequential observational data, developed by Bakeman & Quera (1995).

serial homology (or homonomy): originally termed a homotypy by Ernst H. Haeckel (1834–1919), that great coiner of neologisms, it refers to similarities in repetitive or serial structures within the same organism. Examples include the arms and legs of humans or among the branches and leaves of a tree. A more complex example is the jointed appendages of anthropods: in the crayfish, there are nineteen pairs of appendages that have the same pattern, but serve different functions (e.g., chewing, egg carrying, food handling, locomotion, mating, and

swimming). The concept has also been applied tentatively to the study of ontogenetic development within species in terms of whether structure-function relationships remain the same or change.

serial ordering: first raised by Karl S. Lashley (1890–1958), this is a major issue in the study of motor control, and also in the development of movement coordination. It can be defined as the sequencing or stringing together of a number of movements into an efficient pattern in order to achieve a particular outcome (e.g., reaching → grasping → prehension). The ordering of the movements is important as an incorrect order will give rise to an inefficient or energy-demanding action as occurs in motor disorders such as cerebral palsy.

serotonin: an indoleamine found in plants and animals, and that with dopamine, norepinephrine, epinephrine, acetylcholine, and histamine, is one of the biogenic amine neurotransmitters or neuromodulators. They are widely dispersed through the brain, but are particularly dense in the cortex. Serotonin has been implicated in feeding, emotions, mood and anxiety disorders, sexual activity, and sleep. Most anti-depressants like Prozac are thought to have their major effect on serotonergic systems in that they block serotonin uptake.

sex: in biology, it takes on two meanings. (1) Hetero-gametic sex: the gender that has two different sex chromosomes (e.g., in humans, the male is heterogametic because he has an X and a Y chromosome, while in avian species, the female is heterogametic because she has a W and a Z chromosome). (2) Homogametic sex: the gender that has two copies of the same sex chromosome (e.g., in humans, the female is homogametic because she is XX, while, in birds, the male is homogametic because he is ZZ).

sex category: dichotomous classification as either male or female.

sex chromosomes: the genetic material that determines whether one develops male or female reproductive structures. In humans, it is typically XX for female and XY for male.

sex role: behaviors that conform to an individual's sex category.

sex-typing: behaviors that are associated with either males or females.

sexual imprinting: the process by which early social experience determines the object to which later sexual behavior will be shown preferentially.

sexual orientation: the category of individuals with whom one has sex; generally heterosexual, homosexual, or bisexual.

sexually dimorphic: having behaviors and physical characteristics that differ for males and females, with, for most non-human species, males being bigger and more colorful.

shaken baby syndrome: often precipitated by crying, this refers to violent and excessive shaking of a baby by a caregiver. It may cause bleeding from the small vessels at the back of the eye, brain damage, or even infant death in severe cases.

shared neural representations: to a large extent the human brain codes visual analysis and motor control in distinct regions. However, there are also overlapping neural networks serving both, especially the perception and production of human movement patterns. These overlapping regions constitute shared neural representations, or shared neural circuitry, for perception and action.

shell: in neo-Piagetian skill theory (Granott, Fischer), a cognitive structure used in the process of bridging. A shell consists of a higher-order psychological structure whose specific content is only partially constructed. During the process of bridging, shells function as self-scaffolding structures that support an individual's attempt to order knowledge construction in the direction specified by the shell.

single unit recording studies: electrophysiological studies, generally performed on non-human animals, in which electrical activity is recorded from groups of neurons via electrodes placed directly in the brain.

Six Cultures study: a classic ethnographic study of enculturation in several parts of the world conducted by the anthropologists John W. M. Whiting (1908–1995) and Beatrice B. Whiting (1914–2003). It was initiated in 1954 as the Six Culture Study of Socialization of the Child and the main findings were published by the Whitings in 1975. The study had involved comparing everyday behaviors of children in the six different cultures and reported on cultural values and practice, adults' ideas and expectations about children, and how children play and work.

skill: in Fischer's (1980) dynamic skill theory, the capacity to control elements of acting, thinking, and feeling within particular conceptual domains and social contexts. Rather than being attributes of individual children, skills are properties of persons-in-contexts. Person and context collaborate in the production of any given level of controlled action.

skill learning hypothesis/approach: one of three general approaches to developmental cognitive neuroscience that assumes changes in the neural basis of behavior result as a consequence of acquiring perceptual or motor

expertise. Brain regions active in infants during the onset of new perceptual or behavioral abilities are hypothesized to be the same as those involved in skill acquisition in adults.

sleep architecture: refers to the time, duration, and order (structure and total sleep time involved) by which EEG sleep stages (stages 1, 2, 3, 4, and REM) or awakenings and arousals are expressed throughout an organism's sleep behavior, including the number of minutes spent in each stage and the order and/or re-occurrences of each stage at any given time of the day or night when sleep occurs.

sleeper effect: the claim that experiences during development may be latent and thus do not have an immediate effect. Rather, they become evident at a much later age, perhaps in some cases only in adulthood.

slot-filler relations: predicates open up slots for arguments, which then fill these slots.

social attachment: clearly oriented preferences for interactions involving particular individuals as a function of earlier experience.

social development: a vast area that covers many topics such as how the ability to communicate both verbally and non-verbally is acquired, the roles of family dynamics in child development and the establishment of attachments. At the risk of oversimplifying things, a major and persistent concern in studying social development concerns the formation of friendships and relationships and the effects they have on gaining independence from caregivers. Each of these topics can include taking account of cognitive and emotional development.

social ecology: the social aspects of the environment, both current and historical, which includes social relationships, social institutions, and political aspects.

social identities: identities specified by our membership of social categories, such as gender, ethnic, and religious categories.

social learning theory: following Albert Bandura, the theory that draws attention to learning through the observation and imitation of others' behavior in the acquisition of social skills.

social network: a complex constellation of interdependent social relationships, such as close friendships and family relationships, as well as the larger peer group and social community.

social psychology: the branch of psychology that focuses on studying individual attitudes, beliefs, and behaviors when other people (real, implied, or imagined) are present. Perhaps a similar definition proposed by

Gordon W. Allport (1897–1967) in 1954 words it somewhat better: an attempt to understand and explain how the thought, feeling, and behavior of individuals is influenced by the actual, imagined, or implied presence of others. Thus, social psychology is the study of social influences such as attitude change, coercion, conformity, persuasion, and prejudice. From this definition stems the central task of social psychology: to explain the ways in which interaction between people affects the way they think and behave.

social referencing: a form of appraisal in which an infant looks toward another person, often a parent, for information about how to react and feel about an ambiguous event or uncertain situations in the environment.

social relations model: a statistical model designed to determine the extent to which behavior is determined by the Actor (the person whose behavior is under consideration), the Partner (the target of the behavior), or the qualities of the Relationship between the Actor and Partner.

social reproduction: a term used by anthropologists and other social scientists to refer to the social processes through which families and groups reproduce themselves across generations.

social risk factor: adverse social conditions for a child's development, such as poverty, poor parenting, sick parents, poor education, violent environment, and lack of emotional support.

social stress: the discrepancy between objective social demands, circumstances, and opportunities and the social and psychological resources that a person can mobilize. Because social stress refers to the discrepancy between demands and resources, it permits the same objective event or condition to have varying effects on individuals with differing resources.

socialization: the process by which children gain the norms, values, practices, and knowledge of the culture or society into which they are born, and which are necessary for them to function as effective members of a group or organization. Usually, it is depicted as consisting of a two-step process in development: primary socialization (viz., the upbringing of a dependent infant) which is then followed by secondary socialization (viz., training for roles in society through education and social groups). Both involve learning your identity relative to others.

socioeconomic status (SES): a categorization of people's relative standing based on some combination of their educational attainment, the prestige of their occupation, and their income. Studies of children typically use their parents' socioeconomic status as an indicator of the status of the family.

sociological survey research methods: these methods are characterized by systematic sampling of members of a larger population to produce samples with a known relation to the distribution of characteristics in the population, and closed-ended interviewing aimed at obtaining the same information from each member of the sample.

sociology: the study of human social behavior, including patterns of interaction among individuals and in groups, forms of organization of social groups, and their influence on individual action. Its origins can be traced back to the Enlightenment in the 18th century and to Immanuel Kant (1724–1804), with the first person to use the term 'sociology' being Auguste Comte (1798–1857), who is considered to be the founding father of sociology.

soma (or somatic cells): a term used by Augustus Weismann (1834–1914) for the animal or plant body as a whole, with the exception of the germ cells. In contrast to the germ cells, they die with the individual (and thus are 'mortal').

somatic nervous system (SNS): that part of the nervous system concerned with sensory signals for external sense organs and with the control of skeletal muscles.

somatosensory cortex: the area of cortex that gets input from part of the thalamus (ventrobasal complex), which in turn receives the most direct input from the skin. It consists of three areas. The primary (or somesthetic) somatosensory area occupies the postcentral gyrus just behind the central sulcus of the temporal lobe and maps body parts, with disproportionate representations for the hands, lips, and tongue. The much smaller, secondary somatosensory area in the parietal lobes responds specifically to painful stimuli conveyed by the peripheral nervous system. Finally, the somatosensory (or somesthetic or supplementary) association area, just behind the primary somatosensory cortex, is the site for stereognosis (the tactile or haptic identification of solid or 3-D objects).

space code principle: neural coding according to this principle is based on the assumption that neural activation indicates the presence or absence of information, while the location of the neuron in the network determines what the information is about. Cortical neurons are assumed to implement the space code principle.

spastic diplegia: spasticity mainly affecting the lower limbs; typically there is involvement of the upper limbs, but to a milder degree.

spastic hemiplegia: spasticity involving one side of the body only; typically the upper limb is more affected than the lower limb.

spastic quadriplegia: spasticity of all four limbs, the upper limbs being affected equally to, or more than, the lower limbs.

spatial reasoning: cognition, reasoning, and problem-solving having to do with spatial matters. This is often contrasted to verbal skills. For example, spatial reasoning is needed to insert 3-D forms into openings of different shapes.

specific language impairment (SLI): also known as specific developmental disorder of language, it refers to disorders in language ability that appear in children who seem to be otherwise developing normally and who do not suffer from neurological or sensory impairments, mental retardation, or environmental deprivation.

specificity: the proportion of the sample with a negative (or normal) outcome that were previously identified as negative (or normal).

speech development: the process by which speech is acquired in children and that can be demarcated into age-related speech milestones. More often than not, speech development is described as consisting of two processes: the production and mastery of phonemes and the perception or recognition of the acoustic cues for phonemes, but there are also phonetic features, syllables, and words to take into consideration. The development of the production of speech sounds is a highly complex process, involving as it does the coordination of respiratory movements and articulatory movements of the larynx and vocal tract, the latter ones including as well the jaw, lips, tongue, pharynx, and velum. The role of preverbal speech sounds (crying, cooing, and babbling) in the development of speech continues to be a topic of much debate and divided opinions. Even if they are not necessary conditions for speech acquisition, then it is possible that they may facilitate the fine-tuning of sound production in that they constitute a form of 'vocal play' for exploring the limits of laryngeal and pharyngeal movements.

spermatozoa: mature male gametes produced by the testis and consisting of a head containing a haploid nucleus and a macrodome allowing sperm to penetrate the egg at fertilization, a middle part containing mito-chondria to generate the energy for movement, and a tail piece of locomotory flagella to drive the sperm forward.

sphericity: the condition under which the variance of the difference is constant between any two estimated factor level means in an analysis of variance, but one that is less restrictive than compound symmetry. As with compound sphericity, it is important in the analysis of variance of repeated measures or longitudinal data. Whether or not this condition has been met can be examined by means of the Mauchly test.

sphericity assumption: repeated measures analysis of variance must display the variance pattern of sphericity for proper application.

spinal reflex: movement or movement pattern resulting from stimulation of reflex arcs in the spinal cord.

spindle: a structure resembling a spinning-machine spindle that is formed from fine fibers of protein in the cytoplasm of cells at the beginning of metaphase of cell division. Chromosomes are attached to the spindle fibers by their centromeres at the equator. The equator is the widest part of the spindle.

spontaneous motor activity: movements expressed by the embryo or fetus that are not a response to explicit stimulation by an experimenter. At least some spontaneous movements are generated by activity in the central nervous system, although in intact embryos movements may be influenced by uncontrolled sources of environmental stimuli or self-stimulation.

stage: in Piagetian theory, a period of time in which a child's thinking or action assumes a stable or homogeneous form.

stage of cognitive development: a developmental period during which there is a level of thinking across many domains that is qualitatively different from the thinking undertaken before or afterwards.

statistical learning: the ability of humans, particularly children, to rapidly appreciate correlations and patterns in the information they perceive visually.

statistical power: in inferential statistics, the probability of detecting a population difference or association of a specified magnitude in a study of a representative sample from that population made up of a given number of participants. More specifically, it is the probability that a statistical test can reject the null hypothesis when it is false. It increases with increasing sample size and forms the basis for estimating the sample size needed to detect an effect of a particular magnitude.

steady state: the time-series hypothesis that a construct may deviate over time from some initial or average level, but as time goes by will eventually return to this initial state.

stem cells: undifferentiated embryonic or adult cells that have the potential to give rise to any type of differen-tiated cells. There are three basic sorts of stem cells: multipotent (give rise to only specific types of cells), pluripotent (can form most kinds of tissue, but not a whole organism), and totipotent (can form a whole organism as well as the placenta).

stepping response: movements of the legs that can be elicited in the human newborn. When held upright, supported under the armpits, and the soles of the feet are brought into contact with a surface, the infant displays an alternating stepping pattern. It is usually observed for two to three months postnatally and then can no longer be elicited.

stereoscopic depth perception: computation or detection of an aspect of object distance by comparison of the images of the same scene in the two eyes (i.e., by means of binocular disparity resulting from slightly different viewpoints of the eyes).

steroids: refers to a class of chemicals defined by their chemical structure, an important group of which is steroid hormones. Cortisol and DHEA are both members of the steroid family because of their chemical structure. They have critical and widespread functions in metabolism, including adjustment to physical and psychological stress.

stigmata: minor physical anomalies, such as low-seated or soft and pliable ears, epicanthus, and Greig hypertelorism (a congenital malformation of the skull characterized by an enlarged sphenoid bone, extremely wide bridge of the nose with great width between the eyes, exophtalnos or abnormal eyeball protusion, divergent strabismus, and optic atrophy).

still-face procedure: a procedure in which a person, usually the caregiver, after interacting in a normal manner and on instruction, becomes unresponsive (i.e., does not use facial or vocal cues). This usually results in changes in the infant's state (e.g., crying), attention, or affect. It is taken to indicate that the young infant (typically, 2–3 months of age) has some form of communicative awareness.

stimulus enhancement: an object may become the focus of attention by virtue of the fact that someone else uses it. Such attention may lead the observer to increased manipulation of it, which in turn leads to the chance production of behaviors. Studies of imitation often attempt to distinguish stimulus enhancement from imitation.

stimulus orienting: a form of attention in which sensory organs and perceptual systems are aligned to increase responsivity to environmental events. This type of attention is present at birth and is fully developed very early in infancy.

stimulus-response compatibility: a situation in which critical features of the stimulus and the response are the same. For example, this arises when subjects are asked to press the 'left' key (the response) when they see a dot appear on the left side of the visual field (the stimulus). Humans respond more quickly and with fewer errors in situations of stimulus-response compatibility than incompatibility (the latter occurs if they are asked to press the right key when they see a signal in the left of the visual field). Stimulus-response compatibility can be tested with spatial compatibilities, color ("Press the red key when you see the red signal"), and other dimensions.

stochasticity: refers to any process in which there is a random variable or element of probability in its structure and which as such depends on some parameter that may be discrete or continuous. In a stochastic process consisting of a sequence of discrete events, the outcome of one event has no bearing on the outcome of any other.

strange situation test: a test developed and standardized by Mary D. Salter Ainsworth in which a stranger approaches an infant with and without the caregiver being present, and various aspects of the infant's behavior are measured.

stress (or adrenal) hormones: the hormones, typically corticosteroids, which are involved during the stress response. The hormones of the adrenal cortex respond to internal physiological stress, while those of the adrenal medulla are released in response to stress situations outside the body.

striated (or striped or voluntary) muscle: a voluntary muscle that contracts faster than smooth muscle and is unlike it in having transverse alternating stripes of myosin and actin myofilaments. They are made up of myofibrils, which have many nuclei. Cardiac muscle is striped, but is exceptional in being involuntary.

Stroop test: in the classical Stroop test, subjects are asked to name the color of ink (red, green, blue, etc.) in which are written various color words. These either match the ink color (congruent condition) or contrast with it (incongruent condition). Performance is rated by differences in errors and reaction times across these two conditions. Other versions of the task involve congruent and incongruent non-verbal stimuli (e.g., matching one or two taps, or producing the opposite number of taps; copying a hand action, or producing a different hand action). The test is named after J. Ridley Stroop (1897–1973) who first reported the effect in 1935.

structural equation modeling (SEM): a general set of mathematical and statistical techniques for the estimation and evaluation of a variety of 'structural' hypotheses represented by a set of parameters compared to observed summary statistics. In effect, it combines features of multiple regression and factor analysis to identify relationships between latent variables.

structural gene: a gene that controls and specifies the production of a specific structural protein or peptide rather than transcription factors, its main product being messenger RNA.

structural growth model: a parametric model for mathematically fitting longitudinal growth data for individuals (e.g., double and triple logistic, Preece-Baines modified logistic). The form of the curve to be fitted is defined by a set of predetermined parameters of the growth process. The model is applied primarily to height and skeletal dimensions.

structural imaging: began with early radiographic techniques (e.g., angiogram), but the brain and any abnormalities remained unclear due to the fact it mainly consists of soft tissue. Images of the ventricles (fluid-filled spaces) within the brain were obtained by the painful procedure of air injection. With the advent of computerized axial tomography (CAT) using X-rays, detailed anatomical images of the brain became available for diagnostic and research purposes, and this was followed by structural magnetic resonance imaging.

structural magnetic resonance imaging (sMRI): an imaging technique that characterizes neuroanatomical structures of the brain and other body parts through the influence of a large magnet that polarizes hydrogen atoms in tissues, followed by monitoring the summation of the spinning energies to reconstruct an overall image with the aid of computer processing.

structural proteins: the basic components of cells that produce their physical form in combination with other molecules.

structure-function relationships: in the social sciences, the problem is to relate observable functions to unobservable and hypothetical structures. In the neurosciences, brain structures can be identified by various means and the problem is then to know what functions they serve. In the study of ontogenetic development, the ongoing issue is to account for the ways in which changes in neural structure relate to changes in function. Certainly, it is now generally accepted that structure-function relationships during development are not ones to be construed as those between an independent (i.e., structure) and a dependent (i.e., function) variable. Rather, there is an ongoing reciprocal relationship between structure and function throughout the whole of development as well as between function and changes in body dimensions and environmental circumstances.

structures d'ensemble: a Piagetian concept meaning 'structures of the whole.' Refers to the idea that within a given stage of cognitive development (e.g., concrete or formal operations), thinking is organized as a general structure that has wide applicability to many different tasks. This stands in contrast to the idea that thinking is modular or composed of multiple different abilities or types of intelligence.

stuttering: an articulatory or phonatory disorder that typically presents in childhood and is characterized by anxiety about spoken communication, along with a disfluent speech pattern that may involve repetitions of sounds or words, prolongations of pauses or sounds, or other breaks in the normal flow of speech.

stylopharyngeus: a muscle of the palate involved in swallowing.

sub-ependymal periventricular germinal matrix: tissue surrounding the ventricles, located just below their surface layer (the ependym), and in which neurons and glial cells are produced.

suckling: the behavioral interaction between infant mammals and their mothers associated with attachment to the nipple and ingestion of milk. In non-human animals, suckling conventionally refers to the behavior of the infant, whereas nursing refers to the behavior of the mother. With reference to humans, the terms often are reversed, with nursing referring to the infant's behavior and suckling to the mother.

sudden infant death syndrome (SIDS, cot or crib death): the sudden death of a young infant or child that is unexpected by history and in which a thorough post-mortem examination fails to demonstrate an adequate cause of death.

superior temporal polysensory (STS) area: a region of the inferior temporal lobe thought to be involved in processing faces.

superior temporal sulcus and gyrus: an area of the temporal lobes of the brain in which there are cells that respond to human faces and actions.

supernumerary connections: superfluous synaptic connections that disappear during development.

supervisory attentional system (SAS): a key element within a model of higher-order cognitive control originally devised by Donald Norman and Tim Shallice, the SAS is proposed to deal with the non-routine selection of actions, not by directly controlling behavior, but by modulating the activity of lower-level systems. A parallel may be drawn between the supervisory function of the SAS and the activity of the central executive in Alan Baddeley's model of working memory.

supplementary motor area (SMA): a large premotor area located in the medial prefrontal region of each hemisphere in primates that represents contralateral body movements and contralateral sensory receptors in a somatotopic pattern. Involved in the initiation of movements and in the temporal sequencing of multiple movements.

supravalvular aortic syndrome (SVAS): an obstruction of the largest blood vessel of the body, the aorta. It is associated with deletion of the elastin gene and found in individuals with Williams syndrome.

surface dyslexia: a term used to refer to the reading profile in which regular words and non-words can be read more accurately than exception words. Derived from studies of adult patients with acquired dyslexia, but also used to refer to a relatively rare sub-type of developmental dyslexia.

surfactant: a complex lipoprotein lining the air sacs in the lungs, which stabilizes the alveoli (i.e., the small gas-exchange units in the lungs) against collapse and enhances expansion of lungs during inhalation. Some preterm infants lack a sufficient amount of this substance, thus affecting respiratory function.

surgency: a positive affect and rapid approach of rewarding stimuli.

survival analysis: analysis of time to a given dichotomous outcome in one or more groups. It is a type of regression analysis using the 'time to first event' as the outcome for instances when not all the individuals will have experienced any events. The most frequently employed type of survival is Cox's regression analysis. It is used, for example, in medicine to study the duration of illnesses and in demography to analyze life expectancy.

symbols: a type of signifier or representational vehicle. In Piagetian theory, symbols include such representations as images, pictures, gestures, and the use of objects or movements to represent meanings. In contrast to signs (words), symbolic meanings are more personal, less generative, and are more likely to resemble their referents in some way.

sympathetic nervous system: the branch of the autonomic nervous system that plays the major role in an activated state or stress response, and associated with, for example, increased heart rate, dilated pupils, higher blood pressure, and inhibited digestive processes.

synapse: contact site between axon and nerve cell, with chemical transmission of information across the synaptic cleft from the axon of a presynaptic neuron to the axon, dendrite, or cell body of a postsynaptic neuron (or sometimes from one dendrite to another).

synapse elimination: the patterned reduction in the number of functional connections among nerve cells or between multiple neurons and muscles that occurs as a normal process of neural development. In early

development, there are many more synaptic connections than at maturity and the process of elimination, though not completely understood, involves functional activity and learning processes.

synaptic stabilization: the phenomenon of change in the lability of connections between neurons after learning, caused by loss of the receptors that promote synapse generation and removal.

synaptogenesis: making a synapse, the site of chemical-to-electrical transmission between neurons. Synapses are generated in both development and adulthood.

synergistic: two or more processes that facilitate the actions of one another, as when enzymes, hormones, or behavioral priming enhance the effectiveness of other factors.

synergy: the correlated activation of several muscles underlying functional movements.

syntactic bootstrapping: a hypothesized learning procedure involving the use by children of the syntactic frames in which a novel verb appears (i.e., the number of associated noun phrases and their syntactic arrangements) to narrow in on the kind of meaning it is likely to express. Thus, the child would infer that a novel verb, say, 'gorp,' has a different kind of meaning if it appears in "Mary gorped the book on the table" (= put? threw?) than if it appears in "Mary gorped that the book is on the table" (= thought? saw?).

systemic causality: a term coined by Jaan Valsiner in opposition to simple linear causality or what he referred to as elementaristic causality. It holds that the outcomes of a developing system are not due to one of its elements, but rest on functional relationships between them. As a consequence, if there is a change in one of them, then the whole system changes. Furthermore, these relationships are due to the actions of a catalyzing agent, which neither produces effects nor is an immediate party of the system. Nevertheless, its action is a necessary condition for the new outcome to emerge.

systemogenesis: as formulated by Piortr Kur'mich Anokhin (1899–1966), and based on the principle of heterochrony, it holds that development consists of the selective and accelerated maturation of particular structures and functions. Accordingly, prenatal development follows a heterochronous sequence of events to ensure optimal adaptation and survival, especially in the neonatal period. While not an explanatory concept, it does serve to stress that there are environmentally expectant and environmentally dependent processes in development, a distinction that continues to have heuristic value in the developmental sciences. Similar to the 'law of anticipatory maturation' proffered by the psychologist Leonard Carmichael (1898–1973), it represents a direct challenge to concepts such as morphogenesis and organogenesis in which growth and development constitute an orderly sequence of events.

systems approach: a theoretical approach that emphasizes reciprocal influences between the levels and components of a system, which give rise to emergence of new properties.

Tanner stages: assigning the level of current pubertal development to a male or female based on the observable characteristics of physical and sexual development. Pictures or line drawings are used for the individual and/or parent to denote which of five stages of physical maturity (pre-pubertal with no secondary sexual characteristics through to fully post-pubertal with a completed set of these features) the individual is currently at.

Tay-Sachs disease: an inherited genetic disorder involving an autosomal recessive condition that causes progressive destruction of the central nervous system through the accumulation of lipids due to the absence of a vital enzyme called hexosaminidase that is important in the metabolism of gangliosides (fatty substances necessary for brain development). It is acquired early in gestation, but does not manifest itself until the child is several months old. A fatal disease, with death usually occurring by 5 years of age, it is most frequent among individuals of Eastern European Jewish (Ashkenazi) descent, with 1 in 25 of them carrying the gene.

TE cortex: a region of the inferior temporal lobe that receives input from the occipital cortex, processes it, and then sends it on to other regions further upstream (e.g., hippocampus).

temporal contiguity window: the temporal span over which auditory-visual pairings are perceived as synchronous.

temporal resolution: either the smallest detectable gap that can be perceived in an ongoing auditory passage, or the smallest change in tempo that can be detected.

teratogen: any agent (e.g., alcohol, rubella) or environmental influence (e.g., exposure to X-rays, PCBs) that results in the abnormal development of the growing fetus, particularly non-heritable birth defects.

teratology: the field of study concerned with the causes, mechanisms, and manifestations of abnormal development, whether the result of genetic defect or environmental influence.

term birth: the live birth of an infant with a gestational age of 37 weeks or more.

testosterone: often defined as a 'male' sex (androgen) anabolic steroid hormone, because it is produced in large quantity by the Leydig cells of the testes. It is also produced by the ovaries as it is required for the production of oestrogen, and in smaller quantities by the cortex of the adrenal gland. Thus, testosterone is present in females and males soon after conception, but at higher levels in males during fetal life and from pre-adolescence onward.

thalamus: a collection of nuclei in the forebrain that receives input from all the senses (except olfaction), as well as from various parts of the motor and motivational systems, and relays it to the cerebral cortex. The thalamus also has reciprocal connections with the cortex.

The Observer: a sophisticated software system that allows for the recording and analysis of observational data either live or from video recordings.

Theory of Everything (TOE): sometimes referred to as the grand unified theory (GUT), and the holy grail of some physicists, it is the search for a theory that would bring together all known phenomena to explain the nature of all matter and energy in existence, as well as, for example, the underlying symmetries of nature. It is a descendant of the claim made by Pierre-Simon Laplace (1749–1827) around 1814 that if we knew the position and velocity of every single particle in the universe as well as the laws that governed them, then we could work out (with enough computing power) the state of the universe and everything in it.

theory of multiple intelligences: a view put forward by Howard Gardner that there are eight multiple intelligences: linguistic, logical-mathematical, spatial, musical, bodily kinesthetic, naturalist, interpersonal, and intrapersonal.

theory of neuronal group selection (TNGS): derived from Darwin's theory of natural selection and also referred to as 'Neural Darwinism,' this is process-oriented approach to brain functioning. In a nutshell, TNGS posits non-instructive sensorimotor systems that can adapt to their environment. Based on a multi-agent architecture rather than a connectionist network, the resulting autonomous agent imposes perceptual categorization on the environment, while learning arises from re-entrant links between agents of the control device. According to TNGS, the brain operates on the basis of two processes: a developmental process involving Darwinian competition between populations of neurons only constrained in part by the genes, and a learning process accomplished by a faster, less permanent, selective process that temporarily strengthens or weakens neuronal connections. Pruning of redundant connections is accomplished by re-entrant links between maps composed of neuronal groups organized by the first selectional process. The theory emphasizes the epigenetic nature of the entire developmental process that leads to enormous diversity at the microscopic level, and treats degenerative neuronal nets as the basis for selective processes occurring postnatally that result from experience. Due to both developmental and experiential selection as well as self-organizing processes at many levels of neuronal organization, behavior emerges in ways that cannot be predicted by environmental instructionism or by knowledge of brain evolution. TNGS is not entirely new as there have been previous attempts to devise theories of development based on Darwinian mechanisms in the brain (e.g., by means of genetic algorithms).

theory of sexual selection: a theory, originally put forward by Darwin but not accepted by Wallace, that one sex preferred certain traits in the other sex that allowed individuals with the valued traits to reproduce at higher than average levels.

theory of the child's mind (ToM): a set of interrelated principles and propositions that explains something of why children think and feel as they do, how they come to understand other people's minds or mental states, and why and how changes come about.

theory of the germ plasm: the theory of Augustus Weismann (1834–1914) that the cells destined to become reproductive cells are segregated very early in development and are thus untouched by influences from the environment or from anywhere else in the body. They are transmitted unchanged from generation to generation (and thus are 'immortal') and have no role in development, but do undergo differentiation themselves. The theory stood in marked opposition to the form of Lamarckism that existed in the 19th century (termed 'neo-Lamarckism') and in which heredity was considered to be like learning and memory (i.e., characteristics acquired in one generation are passed on to, and retained in the next one).

thrombophilic disorders: a disorder of the hemopoietic system responsible for the formation of blood cells in which there is a tendency to the occurrence of thrombosis (blood clots). When these occur in the brain, they can cause hemiplegia.

tiers: in Fischer's neo-Piagetian skill theory, the broadest set of distinctions in the degree of hierarchical integration of an action and thought. Accordingly, there are four tiers of development: reflexes, sensorimotor actions, representations, and abstractions. The concept of tier and the related concept of levels stands parallel but in contrast to the Piagetian notion of stage. Whereas stages imply general and integrated structures of action and thought (as in *structures d'ensemble*), the concept of tier implies no such holistic organization. Instead, different skills develop relatively independently of one another, some reaching higher-order levels and tiers whereas others do not.

timbre: tonal quality of sounds that distinguishes one vowel from another.

time-adjacent observations: repeated measures directly next to each other in the temporal sequence of observations.

time-lag design: the study of one age group across developmental or historical time.

time-series: a set of data where observations on a variable or set of variables are collected over a well-defined sequence of time intervals. In traditional time-series, a single entity might be observed (i.e., N = 1) over a long period of time (T > 100). It is typical to use the time-series label when the data collection includes more time points than individuals (i.e., T > N).

time-specific variance: systematic variance that characterizes the time interval under study.

topographical representation: a characteristic feature of the arrangement of sensory and motor processing regions in the central nervous system. Neighboring elements in the sensory surface or muscles are represented by physically neighboring elements in the processing region.

TORCH: an acronym for *Toxoplasmosis*, *Other* infections, *Rubella*, *Cytomegalovirus* infection, and *Herpes* simplex. The TORCH syndrome is a group of mostly viral infections seen in neonates that have crossed the placental barrier with similar clinical manifestations, although signs may vary in degree and time of appearance. They can cause abnormalities in the brains of children, with subsequent motor impairment.

Tourette's syndrome: a neurological disorder characterized by multiple involuntary motor tics and a least one vocal tic, commencing in childhood and leading to some functional disability. Most individuals with the syndrome are often impulsive and show other signs of ADHD. Its prevalence is conservatively estimated at 2 percent of the general population and is four times more likely to occur in boys. Named after the physician Georges Gilles de la Tourette (1859–1904), its onset is usually around the age of 6 years. Reputedly, Mozart had the syndrome.

trace conditioning: a classical conditioning procedure in which the conditional stimulus occurs and terminates before the onset of the unconditional stimulus.

trait: in biology, a particular character of a phenotype as opposed to a character mode. For example, in fruit flies, eye color is a character mode, while a red eye color is a trait. Traits can be autosomal or sex-linked, and determined by a single locus or by polygenes. In psychology, the term is a theoretical concept used to denote enduring characteristics or qualities of an individual (e.g., aggressive, friendly), and has a role in accounting for that person's observed regularities in behavior relative to others, but not for the regularities themselves. In 1936, Gordon W. Allport (1897–1967) and Henry S. Odbert (1909–1995) reported 4,505 trait names indicating psychological differences between individuals.

transcranial magnetic stimulation (TMS): a non-invasive method that uses an externally applied coil to generate magnetic field impulses that stimulate neurons in a focused region of underlying brain. By measuring responses to the stimulations and tracking the position of the coil relative to the topology of the brain, functional brain maps can be generated.

transforming growth factor (TGF): a member of a family of polypeptide growth factors, which together with their receptors are involved in the induction of neural tissue from ectoderm.

transient dystonia: a dysfunctional regulation of posture, where neck and trunk are over- or hyperextended (i.e., curved too much backward).

translocation: a form of chromosomal mutation, this is the process by which all or part of one chromosome becomes attached to another chromosome, and which can result in serious congenital disorders. Translocations can be balanced (no loss or gain of chromosomal material) or unbalanced (overall or partial loss of chromosomal material).

transparent orthographies: a system of writing in which the relationships between letters and sounds are largely consistent for reading (but usually less so for spelling), and the language contains exception words (e.g., in Finnish and Italian).

triarchic theory of intelligence: a view put forward by Robert J. Sternberg that there are three different aspects of intelligence: analytical intelligence, creative intelligence, and practical intelligence.

trisomy 21: the most prevalent form of Down's syndrome in which each cell contains an extra 21st chromosome, often by non-disjunction (a chromosomal mutation resulting in cells having too many or one too few chromosomes).

true score: a hypothetical variable defined as the part of an observed item indicating the measurement of an attribute of interest. The true score is traditionally assumed to be uncorrelated with the error score and is the reason why several different observed items are correlated.

Turner's syndrome: a chromosomal disorder with 45 chromosomes (often with non-disjunction), including only a single X chromosome in some or all cells of a female. Girls with the syndrome usually have short stature, webbing of the skin of the neck, absent or retarded development of secondary sexual characteristics at puberty, absence of menstruation, narrowing of the aorta, bicuspid aortic valve, and abnormalities of the eyes and bones. IQ is generally normal although some children have learning difficulties, especially involving spatial abilities.

typological thinking: having its roots in Plato's idealistic philosophy, this is a view that there are a limited number of fixed types in nature and thus that any variation is an illusion. A focus on central tendencies such as means to the neglect of standard deviations represents a modern form of typological thinking, as do racism and sexism. It was Darwin's theory of natural selection that replaced typological thinking with population thinking.

tyrosine kinase receptor/pathway: the proteins down-stream of the active receptor that are involved in transducing the signal into a biologically relevant response.

U-shaped learning: the learning curve that describes the unlearning of previously learned knowledge and its subsequent re-learning. For example, in the acquisition of the English past tense, children often produce incorrect inflections of irregular verbs (e.g., "comed") after previously having produced the correct "came." In the end, they learn to produce the correct form again.

ultimate mechanisms (or causes): determinants that have been incorporated into a system over many thousands of generations (i.e., over evolutionary time) by means of natural selection or other evolutionary mechanisms (e.g., genetic drift in isolated populations).

unit: in behavior, an action or process that is relatively indivisible and separate from other actions or processes.

uric acid: a crystalline solution in the urine of mammals and other urotelic animals (e.g., amphibians, fish). It is also a source of stimulation for fetal taste and olfactory receptors.

value difference: such a difference arises in two ways – (1) either the same value may be accepted by some and rejected by others; or (2) two values may be ranked in one order by some, but in the converse order by others.

value-monism: the view that one set of values is binding on all people in all societies in the way in which the question "What is 2 + 2?" has one true answer such that no other answer could be true. It is in this sense that values are objective.

value-pluralism: the view that different sets of values are binding on different individuals or societies, but with their objectivity preserved.

value-relativism: the view that different values are accepted by different individuals or societies in the way in which tastes and preferences differ. From this, it follows that values are subjective.

variable: an attribute or characteristic that can change or vary or be expressed as more than one value or in various values or categories. The opposite of a variable is a constant.

variable-centered approaches: a research strategy that analyzes the effect of specific variables (e.g., age, maternal alcohol intake) on children's current or later development.

variance-covariance matrix: a symmetric square matrix with variances of the variables in its main diagonal and covariances of pairs of variables in its off-diagonal cells.

variance within: the variance of the individuals' raw scores in an analysis of variance.

vasoconstriction: narrowing of the blood vessels. Nicotine, for example, elicits vasoconstriction in placental and fetal vascular beds, reducing oxygen and nutrients accessible to the fetus.

vector: in statistics, a set of ordered values in a column (or row) of a matrix, or a matrix with only one column or row. In mathematics and physics, it includes a quantity for which the magnitude and direction must be stated. Examples of vector quantities are force and velocity, the latter being different from speed in that it has a direction as well as a magnitude. In medicine, a vector is a disease-carrying agent such as an insect or tic that transmits parasites from one host to another.

vector field: a plot of the relationships among two or more variables in terms of the changes that are expected from any set of initial starting points. In physics, it stands, for example, for a gravitational or magnetic field in which the magnitude and direction of the vector quantity are one-valued functions of position.

velocity: linear or tangential velocity is the instantaneous or average rate of change of position or displacement of a rigid body. It is speed of a body in a specified direction measured in meters per second (ms^{-1}). Angular velocity is the rate at which a rigid body or point rotates around a fixed axis, which is measured in degrees, revolutions per unit time, or radians per second.

velum: the soft palate and adjacent nasopharynx that closes during normal swallowing and during the production of certain speech sounds.

ventral horn: column at the ventral side of the spinal cord (i.e., situated toward the same side of the body as the stomach), and that carries descending efferent information via the corticospinal tracts to striated muscles.

ventral plate in limb bud: a plate-like concentration of (ventrally located) mesenchymal cells in the extremities, giving rise to extensor and antigravity muscles.

ventral visual pathway (or stream): a cortical visual processing pathway that runs from the occipital to temporal lobes, and processes information about object form.

ventricle: one of the interconnected cavities in the vertebrate brain that is filled with cerebrospinal fluid, which it circulates through. There are a pair in the cerebral cortex (the lateral ventricles), one in the rest of the forebrain, and another in the medulla.

ventricular zone: the part of the embryonic brain where neurons are generated.

vernix caseosa: a fatty substance consisting of epithelial cells and sebaceous matter that covers the skin of the fetus during late gestation.

vestibular system: a sensory system that detects position and motion (specifically acceleration of the head), and which is a crucial organ of balance. It is comprised of bilateral semi-circular canals, the utricle and otoliths, all located in the inner ear, and includes the vestibular ganglion, and the vestibular nuclei in the brain stem as well as the medially descending vestibulospinal projections.

violation of expectation technique: this technique involves presenting two events to infants successively, one of which accords to a given physical principle, and the other of which violates the principle. It is assumed that if infants are aware of the principle, they will look longer at the violation event because it departs from their expectation. In many applications, this technique involves prior familiarization or habituation to a 'lawful' event, followed by test events that are variants of the original, one still lawful and the other unlawful.

visual accommodation: adjustments, voluntary or involuntary, of the crystalline lens of the eye to compensate for the distance of the object of focus from the retina and to keep the image focused on the fovea. The degree of curvature of the lens provides information about the distances of objects, and as such constitutes one of the monocular cues for visual depth perception (another one being motion parallax).

visual acuity: the ability to see fine details in a visual stimulus, typically measured by the number of degrees of visual arc subtended by object that can just be discriminated or by the width of the object itself.

visual cliff: an apparatus used to test an infant's visual depth perception and fear of heights. Typically made of Plexiglas with a shallow side and a deep side.

visual cortex: the part of the cortex that represents visual information. Can refer to either primary visual cortex, or all of the primary and secondary visual cortices.

visual-manual loop: the recurrent flow of information from vision to the motor system of the hand and back again.

visually reinforced preferential looking technique: a method for the study of early word comprehension that presents one auditory form (e.g., a word) from a speaker to the left of the child and one from a speaker to the right of the child. If the child turns toward the 'correct' direction, a rewarding stimulus such as a bunny playing a drum reinforces the correct looking.

voxel: elemental image unit that constitutes a 3-D magnetic resonance image.

wavelength sensitivity: visual sensitivity to varying colors.

Wechsler Intelligence Scales for Children and Adults (WISC-III): commonly used individually administered intelligence test consisting of a set of verbal and performance problems designed to determine whether a child or adult can solve the same problems as typical individuals of the same age. Originally developed in 1939 as the Wechsler-Bellevue scale by David Wechsler (1896–1981).

welfare-to-work studies: research studies that examine the effects of the changes in US federal policies regarding cash welfare receipt embodied in the Personal Responsibility and Work Opportunity Reconciliation Act (PROWRA) of 1996. These studies particularly focus on its repeal of the Aid for Families with Dependent Children (AFDC) program and its replacement with Temporary Aid to Needy Families (TANF) block grants,

which increased requirements for employment even for parents of very young children and set lifetime time-limits on the receipt of cash assistance. As a result, single mothers who had been receiving cash assistance while remaining out of the labor force were under considerable pressure to begin to engage in work-related activities and to find employment that would provide sufficient income to replace cash assistance. Welfare-to-work studies were aimed at following women as they attempted to make this transition.

white matter: whitish nervous tissue of the central nervous system consisting of neurons, connective fibers, and their myelin sheaths, together with associated glia cells and blood vessels.

Whorfian hypothesis (or linguistic relativity): the proposal that language, by providing habitual modes of expression, predisposes people to see the world in a certain way – different for different languages – and thus guides their thinking and behavior. Sometimes referred to as the Sapir-Whorf hypothesis after the anthropologist Edward Sapir (1884–1939) and his student the linguist Benjamin L. Whorf (1897–1943), who formulated it in the 1920s.

Williams syndrome: a rare disorder in which a small number of genes are deleted from a specific region of the 7th chromosome (7q11.23). It is characterized by physical abnormalities, mild to moderate intellectual impairment, and an outgoing, overly friendly personality.

working memory: a model of short-term memory, originally proposed by Alan D. Baddeley and Graham J. Hitch in 1974, conceived as a system for temporarily storing and manipulating information. It is composed of two temporary storage or buffer systems (the phonological loop and the visuo-spatial scratchpad), responsible for verbal and visual information respectively, and the central executive, which is responsible for the selection, initiation, and termination of processing routines involving these stores. This type of memory has been shown to be located in the prefrontal cortex.

zero-one time sampling: a historically important observational data-recording strategy for which successive brief intervals (e.g., 10 or 15 seconds) are checked as 'yes' (1) or 'no' (0) when a particular behavioral code predominates during the interval.

zone of proximal development (ZPD): in Vygotsky's sociohistorical theory of development, the distance between a child's actual developmental level as she performs a task independently and her potential level of development as she works with an adult or more accomplished peer. Vygotsky held that, because children's level of functioning is raised to new heights when working with others, their learning occurs in the 'zone of proximal development.'

zygosity: types of twins determined by the number of zygotes (fertilized eggs) giving rise to them. Twins are either genetically identical (monozygous, i.e., from just one zygote that later divides into two) or non-identical, sometimes called fraternal (dizygous, i.e., from two separate zygotes).

zygote: a fertilized female gamete, which is the product of the union of the nucleus of the ovum with the nucleus of the sperm.

BIBLIOGRAPHY

Achenbach, T. M., McConaughy, S. H. and Howell, C. T. (1987). Child/adolescent behavioral and emotional problems: implications of cross-informant correlations for situational specificity. *Psychological Bulletin*, 101, 213–232.

Adolph, K. E., Vereijken, B. and Denny, M. A. (1998). Learning to crawl. *Child Development*, 69, 1299–1312.

Adolph, K. E., Vereijken, B. and Shrout, P. E. (2003). What changes in infant walking and why. *Child Development*, 74, 475–497.

Adolphs, R., Tranel, D., Damasio, H. and Damasio, A. R. (1995). Fear and the human amygdala. *Journal of Neuroscience*, 15, 5879–5891.

Agresti, A. (2002). *Categorical Data Analysis*, 2nd. edn. Hoboken, NJ: Wiley.

Alderson, P. (1995). *Listening to Children: Children, Ethics and Social Research*. London: Barnardos.

Alderson, P. (2000). Children as researchers: the effects of participation rights on research methodology. In P. Christensen and A. James (eds.), *Research with Children: Perspectives and Practices*. London: Falmer Press, pp. 241–257.

Alloy, L. B., Abramson, L. Y., Whitehouse, W. G., Hogan, M. E., Tashman, N. A., Steinberg, D. L., Rose, D. T. and Donovan, P. (1999). Depressogenic cognitive styles: predictive validity, information processing and personality characteristics, and developmental origins. *Behaviour Research and Therapy*, 37, 503–531.

Altmann, J. (1974). Observational study of behaviour: sampling methods. *Behaviour*, 49, 227–267.

Aman, C. J., Roberts, R. J. and Pennington, B. F. (1998). A neuropsychological examination of the underlying deficit in Attention Deficit Hyperactivity Disorder: frontal lobe versus right parietal lobe theories. *Developmental Psychology*, 34, 956–969.

Anderson, K. E., Lytton, H. and Romney, D. M. (1986). Mothers' interactions with conduct disordered boys: who affects whom? *Developmental Psychology*, 22, 604–609.

Angold, A., Costello, E. J. and Worthman, C. M. (1998). Puberty and depression: the roles of age, pubertal status and pubertal timing. *Psychological Medicine*, 28, 51–61.

Annett, M. A. (1985). *Left, Right, Hand and Brain: The Right Shift Theory*. London: Erlbaum.

Arroliga, A. C., Newman, S., Longworth, D. L. and Stoller, J. K. (2002). Metaphorical medicine: using metaphors to enhance communication with patients who have pulmonary disease. *Annals of Internal Medicine*, 137, 376–379.

Aslin, R. N., Saffran, J. R. and Newport, E. L. (1998). Computation of conditional probability statistics by 8-month-old infants. *Psychological Science*, 9, 321–324.

Atkinson, J. (2000). *The Developing Visual Brain*. Oxford: Oxford University Press.

Baillargeon, R. (1987). Object permanence in 3.5 and 4.5-month-old infants. *Developmental Psychology*, 23, 655–664.

Bakeman, R. and Gottman, J. M. (1997). *Observing Interaction: an Introduction to Sequential Analysis*, 2nd. edn. Cambridge: Cambridge University Press.

Bakeman, R. and Quera, V. (1995). *Analyzing Interaction: Sequential Analysis with SDIS and GSEQ*. Cambridge: Cambridge University Press.

Bakhurst, D. and Shanker, S. (eds.) (2001). *Language, Culture, Self: the Philosophy of Jerome S. Bruner*. London: Sage.

Baldwin, J. M. (1895). *Mental Development in the Child and the Race*. New York: Macmillan.

Baldwin, J. M. (1897). *Social and Ethical Interpretations in Mental Development*. New York: Macmillan.

Baldwin, J. M. (1906–1911). *Thought and Things*. New York: Macmillan.

Baldwin, J. M. (1926). *Between Two Wars: 1861–1921*. Boston: Stratford.

Baltes, P. B. and Nesselroade, J. R. (1979). History and rationale of longitudinal research. In J. R. Nesselroade and P. B. Baltes (eds.), *Longitudinal Research in the Study of Behaviour and Development*. London: Academic Press, pp. 1–39.

Bandura, A., Ross, D. and Ross, S. A. (1963). Imitation of film-mediated aggressive models. *Journal of Abnormal and Social Psychology*, 66, 3–11.

Baron-Cohen, S. (1995). *Mindblindness: An Essay on Autism and Theory of Mind*. Boston: MIT Press / Bradford Books.

Baron-Cohen, S. (2002). The extreme male brain theory of autism. *Trends in Cognitive Sciences*, 6, 248–254.

Barr, R. and Hayne, H. (2000). Age-related changes in imitation: implications for memory development. In

C. Rovee-Collier, L. P. Lipsitt, and H. Hayne (eds.), *Progress in Infancy Research*. Hillsdale, NJ: Erlbaum, vol. I, pp. 21–67.

Barr, R. G., St. James-Roberts, I. and Keefe, M. R. (eds.) (2001). *New Evidence on Unexplained Early Infant Crying: Its Origins, Nature and Management*. Skillman, NJ: Johnson & Johnson Pediatric Institute.

Barr, R. G. and Young, S. N. (1999). A two-phase model of the soothing taste response: implications for a taste probe of temperament and emotion regulation. In M. Lewis and D. Ramsay (eds.), *Soothing and Stress*. Mahwah, NJ: Erlbaum, pp. 109–138.

Bates, E., Thal, D., Finlay, B. L. and Clancy, B. (2002). Early language development and its neural correlates. In F. Boller and J. Grafman (series eds.), *Handbook of Neuropsychology*, Vol. VIII: *Child Neurology* (vol. ed. S. J. Segalowitz and I. Rapin), 2nd. edn. Amsterdam: Elsevier, pp. 109–176.

Bax, M., Hart, H. and Jenkins, S. (1990). *Child Development and Child Health*. Oxford: Blackwell.

Behrman, R. E. (ed.) (1995). Long-term outcomes of early childhood programs. *The Future of Children*, 5, 3, whole issue.

Bekoff, A. (2001). Spontaneous embryonic motility: an enduring legacy. *International Journal of Developmental Neuroscience*, 19, 155–160.

Bell, A.-M. and Fox, N. A. (1994). Brain development over the first year of life: relations between EEG frequency and coherence and cognitive and affective behaviors. In G. Dawson and K. W. Fischer (eds.), *Human Behavior and the Developing Brain*. New York: Guilford, pp. 314–345.

Bell, R. Q. (1968). A reinterpretation of the direction of effects in studies of socialization. Psychological Review, 75, 81–95.

Bell, R. Q. and Harper, L. V. (1974). *Child Effects on Adults*. Lincoln, NE: University of Nebraska Press.

Bellugi, U. and St. George, M. (eds.) (2000). Linking cognitive neuroscience and molecular genetics: new perspectives from Williams syndrome. Special supplement of *Journal of Cognitive Neuroscience*, 12.

Bellugi, U. and Wang, P. (1996). Williams syndrome: from brain to cognition. In G. Adelman and B. H. Smith (eds.), *Encyclopedia of Neuroscience*. Amsterdam: Elsevier.

Belsky, J. (2001). Developmental risks (still) associated with early child care. *Journal of Child Psychology and Psychiatry*, 42, 845–859.

Bernstein, N. A. (1967). *The Co-ordination and Regulation of Movements*. Oxford: Pergamon Press.

Bernstein, N. A. (1996). On dexterity and its development. In M. L. Latash and M. T. Turvey (eds.), *Dexterity and its Development*. Hillsdale, NJ: Erlbaum, pp. 1–244.

Berry, J. W., Dasen, P. R. and Saraswathi, T. W. (eds.) (1997). *Handbook of Cross-Cultural Psychology*, Vol. II: *Basic Processes and Human Development*. Boston: Allyn and Bacon.

Berry, J. W., Poortinga, Y. H., Segall, M. H. and Dasen, P. R (2002). *Cross-Cultural Psychology Research and Application*, 2nd. edn. Cambridge: Cambridge University Press.

Bertenthal, B. I. and Fischer, K. W. (1978). Development of self-recognition in the infant. *Developmental Psychology*, 14, 44–50.

Bess, F. H., Dodd-Murphy, J. and Parker, R. A. (1998). Children with minimal sensorineural hearing loss: prevalence, educational performance, and functional status. *Ear & Hearing*, 19, 339–354.

Bickerton, D. (1981). *Roots of Language*. Ann Arbor, MI: Karoma Publishers.

Bigelow, A. E. (1995). The effects of blindness on the early development of the self. In P. Rochat (ed.), *The Self in Early Infancy: Theory and Research*. Amsterdam: North-Holland, pp. 327–347.

Bishop, D. V. M. (1983). How sinister is sinistrality? *Journal of the Royal College of Physicians of London*, 17, 161–172.

Blair, E. and Stanley, F. (2002). Causal pathways to cerebral palsy. *Current Paediatrics*, 12, 179–185.

Blair, P. S., Fleming, P. J., Smith, I. J., Platt, M. W., Young, J., Nadin, P., Berry, P. J. and Golding, J. (1999). Babies sleeping with parents: case-control study of the factors influencing the risk of sudden infant death syndrome. CESDI SUDI research group. *British Medical Journal*, 319, 1457–1461.

Blakemore, S.-J. and Decety, J. (2001). From the perception of action to the understanding of intention. *Nature Reviews Neuroscience*, 2, 561–567.

Blass, E. M. (1999). The ontogeny of human infant face recognition: orogustatory, visual, and social influences. In P. Rochat (ed.), *Early Social Cognition*. Mahwah, NJ: Erlbaum, pp. 35–65.

Bloom, P. (2001). *How Children Learn the Meanings of Words*. Cambridge, MA: MIT Press.

Boas, F. (1911). Introduction. In F. Boas (ed.), *Introduction to the Handbook of American Indian Languages*. Washington, DC: Government Printer, pp. 5–83.

Bock, R. D. (1975). *Multivariate Statistical Methods in Behavioral Research*. New York: McGraw-Hill.

Bogartz, R. (2000). Object permanence in infants. *Infancy*, 1, 4, whole issue.

Bolhuis, J. J. and Hogan, J. A. (eds.) (1999). *The Development of Animal Behavior: A Reader*. Oxford: Blackwell.

Bolhuis, J. J. and Macphail, E. M. (2001). A critique of the neuroecology of learning and memory. *Trends in Cognitive Sciences*, 5, 426–433.

Bonner, J. T. (ed.) (1982). *Evolution and Development: Report of the Dahlem Workshop on Evolution and Development*. Berlin: Springer.

Born, P. and Lou, H. C. (1999). Imaging in learning disorders. In K. Whitmore, H. Hart, and G. Willems (eds.), *A Neurodevelopmental Approach to Specific Learning Disorders*. London: MacKeith Press, pp. 247–258.

Bowerman, M. and Levinson, S. C. (eds.) (2001). *Language Acquisition and Conceptual Development*. Cambridge: Cambridge University Press.

Bowlby, J. (1958). The nature of the child's tie to its mother. *International Journal of Psychoanalysis*, 39, 350–373.

Bowlby, J. (1969). *Attachment and Loss*, Vol. I: *Attachment*. London: Hogarth Press.

Bowlby, J. (1972). *Attachment and Loss*, Vol. II: *Separation*. New York: Basic Books.

Bowlby, J. (1973). *Attachment and Loss*, Vol. II: *Separation: Anxiety and Anger*. London: Hogarth Press and Institute of Psycho-Analysis.

Bowlby, J. (1980). *Attachment and Loss*, Vol. III: *Loss: Sadness and Depression*. London: Hogarth Press and Institute of Psycho-Analysis.

Bransford, J., Brown, A. and Cocking, R. (2001). *How People Learn*. Washington, DC: National Academy Press.

Brazelton, T. B. and Nugent, K. (1995). *The Neonatal Behaviour Scale*, 3rd. edn. London: MacKeith Press.

Bremner, J. G. (2000). Developmental relationships between perception and action. *Infant Behavior & Development*, 23, 567–582.

Bremner, J. G. (2001). Cognitive development: knowledge of the physical world. In J. G. Bremner and A. Fogel (eds.), *Blackwell Handbook of Infant Development*. Oxford: Blackwell, pp. 99–138.

Brody, G. H. (1998). Sibling relationship quality: its causes and consequences. *Annual Review of Psychology*, 49, 1–24.

Broidy, L. M., Nagin, D. S., Tremblay, R. E., Brame, B., Dodge, K., Fergusson, D., Horwood, J., Loeber, R., Laird, R., Lynam, D., Moffitt, T., Bates, J. E., Pettit, G. S. and Vitaro, F. (2003). Developmental trajectories of childhood disruptive behaviors and adolescent delinquency: a six site, cross national study. *Developmental Psychology*, 39, 222–245.

Bronfenbrenner, U. (1979). *The Ecology of Human Development*. Cambridge, MA: Harvard University Press.

Bronfenbrenner, U. (1989). Ecological systems theory. In R. Vasta (ed.), *Annals of Child Development*. Greenwich, CT: JAI Press, Vol. VI, pp. 187–250.

Bronson, G. (1972). Infants' reactions to unfamiliar persons and novel objects. *Monographs of the Society for Research in Child Development*, 37, 46.

Brooks, W. K. (1902). The intellectual conditions for embryological science. II. *Science*, 15, 481–492.

Brothers, L. (1990). The social brain: a project for integrating primate behaviour and neurophysiology in a new domain. *Concepts in Neuroscience*, 1, 27–51.

Brown, R. (1973). *A First Language: The Early Stages*. Cambridge, MA: Harvard University Press.

Bruck, M., Ceci, S. J. and Hembrooke, H. (1998). Reliability and credibility of young children's reports. *American Psychologist*, 53, 136–151.

Bruml, H. (1972). Age changes in preference and skill measures of handedness. *Perceptual and Motor Skills*, 34, 3–14.

Bruner, J. S. (1983a). *Child's Talk: Learning to Use Language*. New York: Norton.

Bruner, J. S. (1983b). *In Search of Mind: Essays in Autobiography*. New York: Harper & Row.

Bruner, J. S. (1996). *The Culture of Education*. Cambridge, MA: Harvard University Press.

Bruner, J. S. (2003). *Making Stories: Law, Literature, Life*. New York: Farrar, Strauss, and Giroux.

Bruner, J. S. and Amsterdam, A. (2000). *Minding the Law*. Cambridge, MA: Harvard University Press.

Bruner, J. S., Goodnow, J. and Austin, G. (1956). *A Study of Thinking*. New York: Wiley.

Bruner, J. S., Greenfield, P. and Olver, R. (1966). *Studies in Cognitive Growth*. New York: Wiley.

Bukowski, W. M. and Cillessen, A. H. N. (1998). *Sociometry Then and Now: Six Decades of the Sociometric Study of Children in Peer Groups*. New Directions for Child Development, 80. San Francisco: Jossey Bass.

Bukowski, W. M., Sippola, L., Hoza, B. and Newcomb, A. F. (2000). Pages from a sociometric notebook: an analysis of nomination and rating scale measures of acceptance, rejection, and social preference. In A. H. N. Cillessen and W. M. Bukowski (eds.), *Recent Advances in the Measurement of Acceptance and Rejection in the Peer System*. New Direction for Child and Adolescent Development, 88. San Francisco, CA: Jossey-Bass/Pfeiffer, pp. 11–26.

Butterworth, G. and Hopkins, B. (1988). Hand-mouth coordination in the new-born baby. *British Journal of Developmental Psychology*, 8, 303–314.

Byard, R. and Krous, H. (eds.) (2001). *Sudden Infant Death Syndrome: Problems, Puzzles, Possibilities*. London: Arnold.

Calderon, R. and Greenberg, M. (1997). The effectiveness of early intervention for deaf children and children with hearing loss. In M. J. Guralnick (ed.), *The Effectiveness of Early Intervention. Directions for Second Generation Research*. Baltimore, MD: Paul H. Brookes, pp. 455–482.

Cameron, H. C. (1919). *The Nervous Child*. London: H. Frowde.

Campbell, A. (2002). *A Mind of her Own: The Evolutionary Psychology of Women*. New York: Oxford University Press.

Campbell, B. A. and Campbell, E. H. (1962). Retention and extinction of learned fear in infant and adult rats. *Journal of Comparative and Physiological Psychology*, 55, 1–8.

Campbell, D. T. and Stanley, J. C. (1966). *Experimental and Quasi-Experimental Designs for Research*. Chicago: Rand McNally.

Campos, J. J., Anderson, D. I., Barbu-Roth, M. A., Hubbard, E. M., Hertenstein, M. J. and Witherington, D. (2000). Travel broadens the mind. *Infancy*, 1, 149–219.

Carlson, S. M. and Moses, L. J. (2001). Individual differences in inhibitory control and children's theory of mind. *Child Development*, 72, 1032–1053.

Carmichael, L. (1954). The onset and early development of behavior. In L. Carmichael (ed.), *Manual of Child Psychology*. New York: Wiley, pp. 60–185.

Carroll, J. B. (1993). *Human Cognitive Abilities: A Survey of Factor-Analytic Studies*. New York: Cambridge University Press.

Cashon, C. H. and Cohen, L. B. (2000). Eight-month-old infants' perception of possible and impossible events. *Infancy*, 1, 429–446.

Cassidy, J. and Shaver, P. R. (eds.) (1999). *Handbook of Attachment: Theory, Research and Clinical Applications*. New York: Guilford.

Cernoch, J. M. and Porter, R. H. (1985). Recognition of maternal axillary odors by infants. *Child Development*, 56, 1593–1598.

Chamberlain, A. F. (1900). *The Child: A Study in the Evolution of Man*. London: W. Scott.

Chance, J. E., Turner, A. L. and Goldstein, A. G. (1982). Development of differential recognition for own- and other-race faces. *Journal of Psychology*, 112, 29–37.

Chase-Lansdale, P. L., Mott, F. L., Brooks-Gunn, J. and Phillips, D. A. (1991). Children of the National Longitudinal Survey of Youth: a unique research opportunity. *Developmental Psychology*, 27, 918–931.

Chen, H. H., Hippenmeyer, S., Arber, S. and Frank, E. (2003). Development of the monosynaptic stretch reflex circuit. *Current Opinion in Neurobiology*, 13, 96–102.

Chisholm, J. S. (1983). *Navajo Infancy: An Ethnological Study of Child Development*. Hawthorne, NY: Aldine.

Chomsky, N. (1982). *Some Concepts and Consequences of the Theory of Government and Binding*. Cambridge, MA: MIT Press.

Christensen, P. and James, A. (2000). *Research with Children: Perspectives and Practices*. London: Falmer Press.

Christie, F. and Misson, R. (eds.) (1998). *Literacy and Schooling*. London: Routledge.

Churchland, P. S. (1986). *Neurophilosophy: Toward a Unified Science of the Mind-Brain*. Cambridge, MA: MIT Press.

Cirelli, C., Pompeiano, M. and Tononi, G. 1996. Neuronal gene expression in the waking state: a role for locus coeruleus. *Science*, 274, 1211–1215.

Clark, J. E. and Whitall, J. (1989). Changing patterns of locomotion: from walking to skipping. In M. H. Woollacott and A. Shumway-Cook (eds.), *Development of Posture and Gait across the Life Span*. Columbia, SC: University of South Carolina Press, pp. 128–151.

Coghill, G. E. (1929). *Anatomy and the Problem of Behavior*. Cambridge: Cambridge University Press.

Cohen, J. (1968). Weighted kappa: nominal scale agreement provision for scaled disagreement or partial credit. *Psychological Bulletin*, 70, 213–220.

Collins, L. M. and A. G. Sayer (eds.) (2001). *New Methods for the Analysis of Change*. Washington, DC: American Psychological Association.

Cornwell, K. S., Harris, L. J. and Fitzgerald, H. E. (1991). Task effects in the development of hand preference in 9-, 13-, and 20-month-old girls. *Developmental Neuropsychology*, 7, 19–34.

Cosmides, L. and Tooby, J. (1997). *Evolutionary Psychology: A Primer* Online: www.psych.ucsb.edu/research/CEP/primer.html.

Côté, S., Tremblay, R. E., Nagin, D. S., Zoccolillo, M. and Vitaro, F. (2002). The development of impulsivity, fearfulness, and helpfulness during childhood: patterns of stability and change in the trajectories of boys and girls. *Journal of Child Psychology and Psychiatry*, 43, 609–618.

Cowan, W. M. (1998). The emergence of modern neuroanatomy and developmental neurobiology. *Neuron*, 20, 413–426.

Cowan, W. M., Jessell, T. M. and Zipursky, S. L. (eds.) (1997). *Molecular and Cellular Approaches to Neural Development*. Oxford: Oxford University Press.

Craik, K. (1943). *The Nature of Explanation*. Cambridge: Cambridge University Press.

Crain, S. and Lillo-Martin, D. (1999). *An Introduction to Linguistic Theory and Language Acquisition*. Oxford: Blackwell.

Crick, F. (1970). Central dogma of molecular biology, *Nature*, 227, 561–563.

Csibra, G., Tucker, L. A. and Johnson, M. H. (2001). Differential frontal cortex activation before anticipatory and reactive saccades in infancy. *Infancy*, 2, 159–174.

Dale, J. K., Maroto, M., Dequeant, M. L., Malapert, P., McGrew, M. and Pourquie, O. (2003). Periodic notch inhibition by lunatic fringe underlies the chick segmentation clock. *Nature*, 421, 275–278.

Dale, K. J. and Pourquie, O. (2000). A clock-work somite. *Bioessays*, 22, 72–83.

Dalton, T. C. and Bergenn, V. W. (eds.) (1995a). *Beyond Heredity and Environment: Myrtle McGraw and the Maturation Controversy*. Boulder, CO: Westview Press.

Dalton, T. C. and Bergenn, V. W. (1995b). Reconsidering Myrtle McGraw's contribution to developmental psychology. In T. C. Dalton and V. W. Bergenn (eds.), *Beyond Heredity and Environment: Myrtle McGraw and the Maturation Controversy*. Boulder, CO: Westview Press, pp. 1–36.

Damon, W. and Eisenberg, N. (eds.) (1998). *Handbook of Child Psychology*, Vol. III: *Social, Emotional, and Personality Development*. New York: Wiley.

Darwin, C. (1859). *On the Origin of Species by Means of Natural Selection*. London: Murray.

Darwin, C. (1872). *The Expression of the Emotions in Man and Animals*. London: John Murray.

Davidson, R. J. (1993). The neuropsychology of emotion and affective style. In M. Lewis and J. Haviland (eds.), *Handbook of Emotions*. New York: Guilford, pp. 143–154.

Davis, M. (1992). The role of the amygdala in fear-potentiated startle: implications for animal models of anxiety. *Pharmacological Science*, 13, 35–41.

DeCasper, A. J., Lecanuet, J. P., Maugais, R., Granier-Defeme, C. and Busnel, M. C. (1994). Fetal reactions to recurrent maternal speech. *Infant Behavior and Development*, 17, 159–164.

DeCasper, A. J. and Spence, M. J. (1986). Prenatal maternal speech influences newborns' perception of speech sounds. *Infant Behavior and Development*, 9, 133–150.

DeFries, J. C., Plomin, R. and Fulker, D. W. (1994). *Nature and Nurture during Middle Childhood*. Cambridge, MA: Blackwell.

de Groot, L. (2000). Posture and motility in preterm infants. *Developmental Medicine and Child Neurology*, 42, 65–68.

de Haan, M. (2001). The neuropsychology of face processing during infancy and childhood. In C. A. Nelson and M. Luciana (eds.), *Handbook of Developmental Cognitive Neuroscience*. Cambridge, MA: MIT Press, pp. 381–398.

Deater-Deckard, K. (2000). Parenting and child behavioral adjustment in early childhood: a quantitative genetic approach to studying family processes. *Child Development*, 71, 468–484.

Diamond, A. (2001). A model system for studying the role of dopamine in the prefrontal cortex during early development in humans. In C. A. Nelson and M. Luciana, *Handbook of Developmental Cognitive Neuroscience*. Cambridge, MA: MIT Press, pp. 433–472.

Dick, D. M. and Rose, R. J. (2002). Behavior genetics: what's new? What's next? *Current Directions in Psychological Science*, 11, 70–74.

Donaldson, M. (1978). *Children's Minds*. London: Fontana.

Donnai, D. and Karmiloff-Smith, A. (2000). Williams syndrome: from genotype through to cognitive phenotype. *American Journal of Medical Genetics*, 97, 164–171.

Dubowitz, V. and Mercuri, E. (1999). *The Neurological Assessment of the Preterm and Fullterm Newborn Infant*. London: MacKeith Press.

Dunn, J. and Plomin, R. (1990). *Separate Lives: Why Siblings are so Different*. New York: Basic Books.

Duval, S. and Wicklund, R. A. (1972). *A Theory of Self-Awareness*. New York: Academic Press.

Eckerman, C. O., Whatley, J. L. and Kutz, S. L. (1975). Growth of social play with peers during the second year of life. *Developmental Psychology*, 11, 42–49.

Edelman, G. M. (1987). *Neural Darwinism: The Theory of Group Selection*. New York: Basic Books.

Egan, K. (1997). *The Educated Mind: How Cognitive Tools Shape our Understanding*. Chicago: University of Chicago Press.

Eisenberg, A. R. (1992). Conflicts between mothers and their young children. *Merrill-Palmer Quarterly*, 38, 21–43.

Ekman, P., Friesen, W. and Ellsworth, P. (1972). *Emotion in the Human Face: Guidelines for Research and an Integration of Findings*. Oxford: Pergamon.

Elder, G. H., Jr. (1999). *Children of the Great Depression: Social Change in Life Experience*, 25th. anniversary edn. Boulder, CO: Westview Press.

Eley, T. C. (1999). Behavioral genetics as a tool for developmental psychology: anxiety and depression in children and adolescents. *Clinical Child and Family Psychology Review*, 2, 21–36.

Eley, T. C., Moffitt, T. E. and Lichtenstein, P. (2003). A longitudinal behavioral genetic analysis of the etiology of aggressive and non-aggressive antisocial behavior. *Development & Psychopathology*, 15, 383–402.

Elman, J. L. (1993). Learning and development in neural networks: the importance of starting small. *Cognition*, 48, 71–99.

Erikson, E. H. (1950a). *Childhood and Society*. New York: Norton.

Erikson, E. H. (1950b). Growth and crises of the "healthy personality." In M. J. E. Senn (ed.), *Symposium on the Healthy Personality*. New York, Josiah Macy Jr. Foundation, pp. 91–146.

Erikson, E. H. (1959). *Identity and the Life Cycle*. New York: International Universities Press.

Eyer, D. E. (1992). *Mother-Infant Bonding: A Scientific Fiction*. New Haven: Yale University Press.

Fagan, J. (1972). Infants' recognition memory for faces. *Journal of Experimental Child Psychology*, 14, 453–476.

Fagard, J. and Jacquet, A. Y. (1989). Onset of bimanual coordination and symmetry versus asymmetry of movement. *Infant Behavior and Development*, 12, 229–235.

Fairbairn, W. R. D. (1952). *An Object-Relations Theory of the Personality*. New York: Basic Books.

Fallang, B., Saugstad, O. D., Grøgaard, J. and Hadders-Algra, M. (2003). Kinematic quality of reaching movements in preterm infants. *Pediatric Research*, 53, 836–842.

Farah, M. J., Levinson, K. L. and Klein, K. L. (1995). Face perception and within-category discrimination in prosopagnosia. *Neuropsychologica*, 33, 661–674.

Feldman, H. M., Dollaghan, C. A., Campbell, T. F., Kurs-Lasky, M., Janosky, J. E. and Paradise, J. L. (2000). Measurement properties of the MacArthur communicative development inventories ages one and two years. *Child Development*, 71, 310–322.

Fennell, E., Satz, P. and Morris, P. (1983). The development of handedness and dichotic ear listening asymmetries in relation to school achievement: a longitudinal study. *Journal of Experimental Child Psychology*, 35, 248–262.

Fentress, J. C. and Gadbois, S. (2001). The development of action sequences. In E. M. Blass (ed.), *Handbook of Behavioral Neurobiology*, Vol. XIII: *Developmental Psychobiology*. New York: Kluwer Academic / Plenum Publishers, pp. 393–431.

Fergusson, D. M. (1997). Annotation: structural equation models in developmental research. *Journal of Child Psychology and Psychiatry*, 38, 877–887.

Ferreiro, E. and Teberosky, A. (1983). *Literacy before Schooling*. Exeter, NH: Heinemann.

Finkelstein, J. W., von Eye, A. and Preece, M. A. (1994). The relationship between aggressive behavior and puberty in normal adolescents: a longitudinal study. *Journal of Adolescent Health*, 15, 319–326.

Fischer, K. W. (1980). A theory of cognitive development: the control and construction of hierarchies of skills. *Psychological Review*, 87, 477–531.

Fivush, R. (1993). Emotional content of parent-child conversations about the past. In C. A. Nelson (ed.), *The Minnesota Symposium on Child Psychology: Memory and Affect in Development*. Hillsdale, NJ: Erlbaum, vol. XXVI, pp. 39–79.

Fleming, P. J., Blair, P. S., Bacon, C., Bensley, D., Smith, I., Taylor, E., Berry, J., Golding, J. and Tripp, J. (1996). Environments of infants during sleep and risk of the sudden infant death syndrome: results of 1993–1995 case-control study for confidential inquiry into stillbirths and deaths in infancy. *British Medical Journal*, 313, 191–195.

Fletcher, P. and MacWhinney, B. (eds.) (1995). *The Handbook of Child Language*. Oxford: Blackwell.

Fodor, J. A. (1975). *The Language of Thought*. New York: Crowell.

Fombonne, E. (1991). The use of questionnaires in child psychiatry research: measuring their performance and choosing an optimal cut-off. *Journal of Child Psychology and Psychiatry*, 32, 677–693.

Fonagy, P. (2001). *Attachment Theory and Psychoanalysis*. New York: Other Press.

Fonagy, P., Gergely, G., Jurist, E. and Target, M. (2002). *Affect Regulation, Mentalization and the Development of the Self*. New York: Other Press.

Fox, N. A. and Davidson, R. J. (1986). Taste elicited changes in facial signs of emotion and the asymmetry of brain electrical activity in human newborns. *Neuropsychologia*, 24, 417–422.

Fox, N. A. and Davidson, R. J. (1988). Patterns of brain electrical activity during facial signs of emotion in 10-month-old infants. *Development Psychology*, 24, 230–236.

Fraiberg, S. (1977). *Insights from the Blind: Comparative Studies of Blind and Sighted Infants*. New York: Basic Books.

Freeman, R. D. and Groenveld, M. G. (2000). The behaviour of children and youth with visual and hearing disability. In C. Gillberg and G. O Brien (eds.), *Developmental Disability and Behaviour*. London: MacKeith Press, pp. 27–42.

Freud, A. (1965). *Normality and Pathology in Childhood: Assessments of Development*. Madison, CT: International Universities Press.

Freud, S. (1905). Three essays on the theory of sexuality. In J. Strachey (ed.), *The Standard Edition of the Complete Psychological Works of Sigmund Freud*. London: Hogarth Press, vol. VII, pp. 123–230.

Friston, K. J. and Price, C. J. (2001). Dynamic representations and generative models of brain function. *Brain Research Bulletin*, 54, 275–285.

Frith, U. (1989). *Autism: Explaining the Enigma*. Oxford: Blackwell.

Furstenberg, F., Jr., Cook, T. D., Eccles, J., Elder, G. H., Jr. and Sameroff, A. (1999). *Managing to Make It: Urban Families and Adolescent Success*. Chicago: University of Chicago Press.

Galton, F. (1907). *Inquiries into Human Faculty and Its Development*. London: J. M. Dent, and New York: E. P. Dutton. (Originally published in 1883.)

Gardner, H. (1999). *Intelligence Reframed*. New York: Basic Books.

Gergely, G., Bekkering, H. and Kiraly, I. (2002). Rational imitation in preverbal infants. *Nature*, 415, 755.

Gesell, A. (1946). The ontogenesis of infant behavior. In L. Carmichael (ed.), *Manual of Child Psychology*. New York: Wiley, pp. 295–331.

Gesell, A. and Thompson, H. (1934). *Infant Behavior: Its Genesis and Growth*. New York: McGraw Hill.

Geuze, R. H., Jongmans, M. J., Schoemaker, M. M. and Smits-Engelsman, B. C. M. (2001). Clinical and research diagnostic criteria for developmental coordination disorder: a review and discussion. *Human Movement Science*, 20, 7–47.

Gewold, I., Bosma, J. F., Reynolds, E. W. and Vice, F. L. (2003). Integration of suck and swallow rhythms during feeding in preterm infants with and without bronchopulmonary dysplasia. *Developmental Medicine & Child Neurology*, 45, 344–348.

Gibson, E. J. (1988). Exploratory behavior in the development of perceiving, acting, and the acquiring of knowledge. *Annual Review of Psychology*, 39, 1–41.

Giedd, J. N., Blumenthal, J., Jeffries, N. O., Castellanos, F. X., Lin, H., Zijdenbos, A., Paus, T., Evans, A. C. and Rapoport, J. L. (1999). Brain development during childhood and adolescence: a longitudinal MRI study. *Nature Neuroscience*, 2, 861–863.

Giedd, J. N., Rapoport, J. L., Garvey, M. A., Perlmutter, S. and Swedo, S. E. (2000). MRI assessment of children with obsessive-compulsive disorder or tics associated with streptococcal infection. *American Journal of Psychiatry*, 157, 281–283.

Gilbert, S. F. (2003). *Developmental Biology*, 7th. edn. Sunderland, MA: Sinauer.

Gillberg, C. (1995). *Clinical Child Neuropsychiatry*. Cambridge: Cambridge University Press.

Gillberg, C. and Söderström, H. (2003). Learning disability. *Lancet*, 362, 9386, 811–821.

Gilliam, W. S. and Mayes, L. C. (2000). Developmental assessment of infants and toddlers. In C. H. Zeanah (ed.), *Handbook of Infant Mental Health*, 2nd. edn. London: Guilford Press, pp. 236–248.

Glaser, R., Kennedy, S., Lafuse, W. P., Bonneau, R. H., Speicher, C., Hillhouse, J. and Kiecolt-Glaser, J. K. (1990). Psychological-stress-induced modulation of interleukin 2 receptor gene expression and interleukin 2 production in peripheral blood leukocytes. *Archives of General Psychiatry*, 47, 707–712.

Gleitman, L. R. (1990). The structural sources of verb meanings. *Language Acquisition*, 1, 3–55.

Godfrey, K. M. and Barker, D. J. (2001). Fetal programming and adult health. *Public Health Nutrition*, 4, 611–624.

Goldberg, A. (1995). *Constructions: A Construction Grammar Approach to Argument Structure*. Chicago: University of Chicago Press.

Goldsmith, P. (2001). Modelling eye diseases in zebrafish. *Neuroreport*, 12, A73–77.

Goldstein, H. (2003). *Multilevel Statistical Models*, 3rd. edn. London: Arnold.

Goodyer, I. M., Herbert, J. *et al.* (2000). Recent life events, cortisol, dehydroepiandrosterone and the onset of major depression in high-risk adolescents. *British Journal of Psychiatry*, 177, 499–504.

Gormally, S. (2001). Clinical clues to organic etiologies in infants with colic. In R. G. Barr, I. St. James-Roberts, and M. R. Keefe (eds.), *New Evidence on Unexplained Early Infant Crying: Its Origins, Nature and Management*. Skillman, NJ: Johnson & Johnson Pediatric Institute, pp. 133–148.

Goswami, U. (ed.) (2002). *Blackwell Handbook of Childhood Cognitive Development*. Oxford: Blackwell.

Gottlieb, G. (1997). *Synthesizing Nature-Nurture: Prenatal Roots of Instinctive Behavior*. Mahwah, NJ: Erlbaum.

Gottman, J. and Mettetal, G. (1986). Speculations about social and affective development: friendship and acquaintanceship through adolescence. In J. M. Gottman and J. G. Parker (eds.), *Conversations of Friends: Speculations on Affective Development*. Cambridge: Cambridge University Press, pp. 192–237.

Gottman, J. M. (1995). *The Analysis of Change*. Mahwah, NJ: Erlbaum.

Gould, S. J. (1977). *Ontogeny and Phylogeny*. Cambridge, MA: Harvard University Press.

Granott, N., Fischer, K. W. and Parziale, J. (2002). Bridging to the unknown: a fundamental mechanism in learning and problem-solving. In N. Granott and J. Parziale (eds.), *Microdevelopment*. Cambridge: Cambridge University Press, pp. 131–156.

Granott, N. and Parziale, J. (eds.) (2002). *Microdevelopment: Transition Processes in Development and Learning*. Cambridge: Cambridge University Press.

Graue, M. E. and Walsh, D. J. (1998). *Studying Children in Context: Theories, Methods, and Ethics*. Thousand Oaks, CA: Sage.

Greenland, S. and Drescher, K. (1993). Maximum likelihood estimation of the attributable fraction from logistic models. *Biometrics*, 49, 865–872.

Grigorenko, E. L. (2001). Developmental dyslexia: an update on genes, brains and environments. *Journal of Child Psychology & Psychiatry*, 42, 91–126.

Grove, E. A. and Fukuchi-Shimogori, T. (2003). Generating the cerebral cortical area map. *Annual Review of Neuroscience*, 26, 355–380.

Gustafson, G. E., Wood, R. M. and Green, J. A. (2000). Can we hear the causes of infants' crying? In R. G. Barr, I. St. James-Roberts, and M. R. Keefe (eds.), *New Evidence on Unexplained Early Infant Crying: Its Origins, Nature and Management*. Skillman, NJ: Johnson & Johnson Pediatric, pp. 8–22.

Hadders-Algra, M. (2002). Two distinct forms of minor neurological dysfunction – perspectives emerging from a review of the data of the Groningen Perinatal Project. *Developmental Medicine and Child Neurology*, 44, 561–571.

Hadders-Algra, M., Brogren, E., Katz-Salamon, M. and Forssberg, H. (1999). Periventricular leukomalacia and preterm birth have a different detrimental effect on postural adjustments. *Brain*, 122, 727–740.

Hadders-Algra, M., Mavinkurve-Groothuis, A. M. C., Groen, S. E., Stremmelaar, E. F., Martijn, A. and Butcher, P. R. (2004). Quality of general movements and the development of minor neurological dysfunction at toddler and school age. *Clinical Rehabilitation*, 18, 287–299.

Hagberg, B., Hagberg, G. and Olow, I. (1993). The changing panorama of cerebral palsy in Sweden VI. Prevalence and origin during the birth year period 1983–1986. *Acta Pædiatrica*, 82, 387–393.

Hagberg, B., Hagberg, G., Olow, I. and von Wendt, L. (1996). The changing panorama of cerebral palsy in Sweden. VII. Prevalence and origin in the birth year period 1987–90. *Acta Pædiatrica*, 85, 954–960.

Hall, B. K. and Miyake, T. (2000). All for one and one for all: condensations and the initiation of skeletal development. *Bioessays*, 22, 38–147.

Hamburger, V. (1977). The developmental history of the motor neuron. *Neuroscience Research Program Bulletin*, 15, 1–37.

Hamburger, V. (1996). Viktor Hamburger. In L. R. Squire (ed.), *The History of Neuroscience in Autobiography*, Vol. I. Washington, DC: Society for Neuroscience, pp. 222–250.

Han, W., Waldfogel, J. and Brooks-Gunn, J. (2001). The effects of early maternal employment on later cognitive and behavioral outcomes. *Journal of Marriage and the Family*, 63, 336–354.

Harm, M. W. and Seidenberg, M. S. (1999). Phonology, reading acquisition, and dyslexia: insights from connectionist models. *Psychological Review*, 106, 491–528.

Harris, J. R. (1998). *The Nurture Assumption*. New York: Free Press.

Harris, L. J. and Carlson, D. F. (1993). Hand preference for visually-guided reaching in human infants and adults. In J. Ward (ed.), *Current Behavioral Evidence of Primate Asymmetries*. New York: Springer-Verlag, pp. 285–305.

Harter, S. (1998). The development of self-representations. In W. Damon (series ed.) and N. Eisenberg (vol. ed.), *The Handbook of Child Psychology* New York: Wiley, pp. 619–700.

Hartmann, H., Kris, H. and Loewenstein, R. (1949). Notes on the theory of aggression. *Psychoanalytic Study of the Child*, 3–4, 9–36.

Hartshorn, K. (2003). Reinstatement maintains a memory in human infants for $1\frac{1}{2}$ years. *Developmental Psychobiology*, 42, 269–282.

Hattori, M., Fujiyama, A., Taylor, T. D., Watanabe, H., Yada, T., Park, H. S., Toyoda, A., Ishii, K., Totoki, Y., Hhoi, D. K. and Soeda, E. (2000). The DNA sequence of human chromosome 21. *Nature*, 405, 311–319.

Hay, D. and Nash, A. (2002). Social development in different family arrangements. In P. K. Smith and C. Hart (eds.), *Blackwell Handbook of Childhood Social Development*. Oxford: Blackwell, pp. 238–261.

Hayne, H., Boniface, J. and Barr, R. (2000). The development of declarative memory in human infants. Age-related changes in deferred imitation. *Behavioral Neuroscience*, 114, 77–83.

Hearnshaw, L. S. (1979). *Cyril Burt: Psychologist*. London: Hodder and Staughton.

Heath, S. B. (1983). *Ways with Words*. Cambridge: Cambridge University Press.

Henderson, S. E. and Barnett, A. L. (1998). The classification of specific motor coordination disorders in children: some problems to be solved. *Human Movement Science*, 17, 449–469.

Henderson, S. E. and Sugden, D. (1992). *Movement Assessment Battery for Children*. London: The Psychological Corporation.

Hepper, P. G., McCartney, G. R. and Shannon, E. A. (1998). Lateralised behaviour in first trimester human foetuses. *Neuropsychologia*, 36, 531–534.

Herrick, C. J. (1949). *George Elliott Coghill, Naturalist and Philosopher*. Chicago: University of Chicago Press.

Heston, L. (1966). Psychiatric disorders in foster-reared children of schizophrenic mothers. *British Journal of Psychiatry*, 112, 819–825.

Hetherington, E. M., Henderson, S. H., O'Connor, T. G., Insabella, G. M., Taylor, L. C., Anderson, E. R., Skaggs, M. J., Jodl, K. M., Bridges, M., Kim, J. E., Mitchell, A. S. and Chan, R. W. (1999). Adolescent siblings in stepfamilies: family functioning and adolescent adjustment. *Monographs of the Society for Research in Child Development*, 64, 4, 1–208.

Hirschfeld, L. and Gelman, S. (1994). *Mapping the Mind: Domain Specificity in Cognition and Culture*. Cambridge: Cambridge University Press.

Hobel, C. and Culhane, J. (2003). Role of psychosocial and nutritional stress on poor pregnancy outcome. *Journal of Nutrition*, 133, 1709S–1717S.

Hobson, R. P. (1990). On the origins of self and the case of autism. *Development and Psychopathology*, 2, 163–181.

Hoeksma, J. B. and Knol, D. L. (2001). Testing predictive developmental hypotheses. *Multivariate Behavioral Research*, 36, 227–248.

Hogan, J. A. (2001). Development of behavior systems. In E. M. Blass (ed.), *Handbook of Behavioral Neurobiology*. New York: Kluwer Academic, Vol. XIII, pp. 229–279.

Holland, P. (2003). *We Don't Play with Guns Here: War, Weapon and Superhero Play in the Early Years*. Maidenhead and Philadelphia: Open University Press.

Hopkins, B. and Rönnqvist, L. (2002). Facilitating postural control: effects on the reaching behavior of 6 month-old infants. *Developmental Psychobiology*, 40, 1–15.

Hoppe-Graff, S. (1989). The study of transitions in development: potentialities of the longitudinal approach. In A. de Ribaupierre (ed.), *Transition Mechanisms in Child Development: the Longitudinal Perspective*. Cambridge: Cambridge University Press, pp. 1–32.

Howes, C. (1996). The earliest friendships. In W. M. Bukowski, A. F. Newcomb and W. W. Hartup (eds.), *The Company they Keep: Friendship in Childhood and Adolescence*. Cambridge: Cambridge University Press, pp. 66–86.

Hughes, C. (1998). Finding your marbles: does preschoolers' strategic behaviour predict later understanding of mind? *Developmental Psychology*, 34, 1326–1339.

Hughes, C., White, A., Sharper, J. and Dunn, J. (2000). Antisocial, angry and unsympathetic: "Hard to manage" preschoolers' peer problems, and possible social and cognitive influences. *Journal of Child Psychology and Psychiatry*, 41, 169–179.

Humphrey, D. E. and Humphrey, G. K. (1988). Sex differences in lateralized preference for grasping and reaching in infants. In M. A. Goodale (ed.), *Vision and Action: The Control of Grasping*. Norwood, NJ: Ablex, pp. 80–97.

Huppi, P. S., Warfield, S., Kikinis, R., Barnes, P., Zientara, G. P., Jolesz, F. A., Tsuji, M. K. and Volpe, J. J. (1998). Quantitative magnetic resonance imaging of brain development in premature and term newborns. *Annals of Neurology*, 43, 224–235.

IMGSAC (2001). A genomewide screen for autism: strong evidence for linkage to chromosomes 2q, 7q and 16p. *American Journal of Human Genetics*, 69, 570–581.

Izard, C. E. (1977). *Human Emotions*. New York: Plenum.

Jacobson, M. (1991). *Developmental Neurobiology*. New York: Plenum Press.

James, W. (1890). *The Principles of Psychology*. New York: Holt, Rinehart, and Winston.

Johnson, J. E., Christie, J. F. and Yawkey, T. D. (1999). *Play and Early Childhood Development*, 2nd. edn. New York: Longman.

Johnson, M. H. (2005). *Developmental Cognitive Neuroscience*. 2nd. edn. Oxford: Blackwell.

Johnson, M. H. (2000). Functional brain development in infants: elements of an interactive specialization framework. *Child Development*, 71, 75–81.

Johnson, M. H. (ed.) (2002). Imaging techniques and the application in developmental science. *Developmental Science*, 5, special issue.

Johnson, M. H. and Bolhuis, J. J. (2000). Predispositions in perceptual and cognitive development. In J. J. Bolhuis (ed.), *Brain, Perception, Memory. Advances in Cognitive Neuroscience*. Oxford: Oxford University Press, pp. 69–84.

Johnson, S. P. (2000). The development of visual surface perception: insights into the ontogeny of knowledge. In C. Rovee-Collier, L. Lipsitt, and H. Hayne (eds.), *Progress in Infancy Research*. Mahwah, NJ: Erlbaum, Vol. I, pp. 113–154.

Johnston, T. D. (1987). The persistence of dichotomies in the study of behavioral development. *Developmental Review*, 7, 149–182.

Jusczyk, P. W. (1997). *The Discovery of Spoken Language*. Cambridge, MA: MIT Press.

Kadesjö, B. (2000). *Neuropsychiatric and Neurodevelopmental Disorders in a Young School-Age Population: Epidemiology and Comorbidity in a School Health Perspective*. Gothenburg: Göteborg University.

Kadesjö, B. and Gillberg, C. (2001). The comorbidity of ADHD in the general population of Swedish school-age children. *Journal of Child Psychology and Psychiatry*, 42, 487–492.

Kalverboer, A. F. and Gramsbergen, A. (eds.) (2001). *Handbook of Brain and Behaviour in Human Development*. Dordrecht: Kluwer.

Karmiloff-Smith, A. (1992). *Beyond Modularity: A Developmental Perspective on Cognitive Science*. Cambridge, MA: MIT Press.

Karsenty, G. and Wagner, E. F. (2002). Reaching a genetic and molecular understanding of skeletal development. *Developmental Cell*, 2, 389–406.

Kauffman, S. A. (1993). *The Origins of Order: Self-Organization and Selection in Evolution*. New York: Oxford University Press.

Kazdin, A. E. and Wassell, G. (2000). Therapeutic changes in children, parents, and families resulting from treatment of children with conduct problems. *Journal of the American Academy of Child and Adolescent Psychiatry*, 39, 4, 414–420.

Keil, F. C. (1989). *Concepts, Kinds, and Cognitive Development*. Cambridge, MA: MIT Press.

Keller, E. F. (1995). *Refiguring Life: Metaphors of Twentieth-Century Biology*. New York: Columbia University Press.

Keller, H., Poortinga, Y. H. and Schöelmerich, A. (eds.) (2002). *Between Biology and Culture: Perspectives on Ontogenetic Development*. Cambridge: Cambridge University Press.

Kelley, M. F. and Surbeck, E. (1991). History of preschool assessment. In B. A. Bracken (ed.), *The Psychoeducational Assessment of Preschool Children*. Needham Heights, MA: Allyn & Bacon, pp. 1–17.

Kelsey, J. L., Whitemore, A. S., Evans, A. S. and Thompson, W. D. (1996). *Methods in Observational Epidemiology*, 2nd. edn. Oxford: Oxford University Press.

Kemp, J. S., Unger, B., Wilkins, D., Psara, R. M., Ledbetter, T. L., Graham, M. A., Case, M. and Thach, S. T. (2000). Unsafe sleep practices and an analysis of bedsharing among infants dying suddenly and unexpectedly: results of a four-year, population-based, death-scene investigation study of sudden infant death syndrome and related deaths. *Pediatrics*, 106, 41–59.

Kemp, N. and Bryant, P. (2003). Do beez buzz? Rule-based and frequency-based knowledge in learning to spell plural -s. *Child Development*, 74, 63–74.

Kenny, D. A. and La Voie, L. (1984). The social relations model. In L. Berkowitz (ed.), *Advances in Experimental Social Psychology*. New York: Academic Press, Vol. XIX, pp. 141–182.

Kernberg, O. F. (1987). Borderline personality disorder: a psychodynamic approach. *Journal of Personality Disorders*, 1, 344–346.

Kessen, W. (ed.) (1983). *Handbook of Child Psychology*, Vol. I: *History, Theory, and Methods*. New York: Wiley.

Kessler, R. C. and Shanyang, Z. (1999). Overview of descriptive epidemiology of mental disorders. In C. S. Aneshensel and J. C. Phelan (eds.), *Handbook of the Sociology of Mental Health*. New York: Kluwer, pp. 127–150.

Key, E. (1909). *The Century of the Child*. New York: Putnam.

Kidd, D. (1906). *Savage childhood: A Study of Kafir Children*, 1st. edn. London: Adam & Charles Black.

Kim, S. K., Lund, J., Kiraly, M., Duke, K., Jiang, M., Stuart, J. M., Eizinger, A., Wylie, B. N. and Davidson, G. S. (2001). A gene expression map for Caenorhabditis elegans. *Science*, 293, 2087–2092.

Kimura, D. (1999). *Sex and Cognition*. Cambridge, MA: MIT Press.

Kinney, H. C., Filana, J. J., Sleeper, L. A., Mandell, F., Valdes-Dapena, M. and White, W. F. (1995). Decreased musarinic receptor binding in sudden infant death syndrome. *Science*, 269, 1446–1447.

Klaus, M. H., Kennell, J., Berkowitz, G. and Klaus, P. (1992) Maternal assistance and support in labor: father, nurse, midwife, or doula? *Clinical Consultations in Obstetrics and Gynecology*, 4, 211–217.

Klaus, M. H. and Kennell, J. H. (1976). *Maternal-Infant Bonding*. St. Louis: Mosby.

Klebanov, P. K., Brooks-Gunn, J., McCarton, C. and McCormick, M. C. (1998). The contribution of neighborhood and family income to developmental test scores over the first three years of life. *Child Development*, 69, 1420–1436.

Kleitman, N. (1963). *Sleep and Wakefulness*, 2nd. edn. Chicago: University of Chicago Press.

Kochanska, G., Murray, K. and Harlan, E. (2000). Effortful control in early childhood: continuity and change, antecedents, and implications for social development. *Developmental Psychology*, 36, 220–232.

Konner, M. and Shostak, M. (1987). Timing and management of birth among the !Kung: biocultural interaction in reproductive adaptation. *Cultural Anthropology*, 2, 11–28.

Korthank, A. J. and Robinson, S. R. (1998). Effects of amniotic fluid on opioid activity and fetal sensory responsiveness. *Developmental Psychobiology*, 33, 235–248.

Kozulin, A. (1990). *Vygotsky's Psychology: A Biography of Ideas*. London: Harvester Wheatsheaf.

Laird, N. M. and Wair, J. H. (1982). Random Effects Models for longitudinal data. *Biometrics*, 38, 963–974.

Lamborn, S. D., Fischer, K. W. and Pipp, S. L. (1994). Constructive criticism and social lies: a developmental sequence for understanding honesty and kindness in social relationships. *Developmental Psychology*, 30, 495–508.

Lander, E. S. and Weinberg, R. A. (2000). Genomics: journey to the center of biology. *Science*, 287, 1777–1782.

Landmesser, L. T. (2001). The acquisition of motoneuron subtype identity and motor circuit formation. *International Journal of Developmental Neuroscience*, 19, 175–182.

Larroque, B., Bertrais, S., Czernichov, B. and Leger, J. (2001). School difficulties in 20-year-olds who were born small-for-gestational-age at term in a regional cohort study. *Pediatrics*, 108, 111–115.

Lawrence, D. G. and Hopkins, D. A. (1976). The development of motor control in the rhesus monkey: evidence concerning the role of corticomotoneuronal connections. *Brain*, 99, 235–254.

Lecanuet, J. P. and Schaal, B. (1996). Fetal sensory competencies. *European Journal of Obstetrics, Gynecology, Reproductive Biology*, 68, 1–23.

LeDoux, J. (1990). Cognitive and emotional interactions in the brain. *Cognition and Emotions*, 3, 265–289.

LeDoux, J. (1996). *The Emotional Brain: The Mysterious Underpinnings of Emotional Life*. New York: Touchstone.

Lee, C. and Smagorinsky, P. (2000). *Vygotskian Perspectives on Literacy Research*. Cambridge: Cambridge University Press.

Lehtonen, L. (2001). From colic to toddlerhood. In R. G. Barr, I. St. James-Roberts and M. R. Keefe (eds.), *New Evidence on Unexplained Early Infant Crying: Its Origins, Nature and Management*. Skillman, NJ: Johnson & Johnson Pediatric Institute, pp. 259–272.

Leighton, P. A., Mitchell, K. J., Goodrich, L. V., Lu, X., Pinson, K., Scherz, P., Skarnes, W. C. and Tessier-Lavigne, M. (2001). Defining brain wiring patterns and mechanisms through gene trapping in mice. *Nature*, 410, 174–179.

Lengua, L. J. (2002). The contribution of emotionality and self-regulation to the understanding of children's response to multiple risk. *Child Development*, 73, 144–161.

Leslie, A. M. (1987). Pretence and representation: the origins of "theory of mind." *Psychological Review*, 94, 412–426.

Leventhal, T. and Brooks-Gunn, J. (2000). The neighborhoods they live in: the effects of neighborhood residence in child and adolescent outcomes. *Psychological Bulletin*, 126, 309–337.

LeVine, R. A., Dixon, S. and Richman, A. (1994). *Child Care and Culture: Lessons from Africa*. Cambridge: Cambridge University Press.

Lewis, C., Newson, J. and Newson, E. (1982). Father participation and its relation to career aspirations and protodelinquency. In N. Beail and J. McGuire (eds.),

Fathers: Psychological Perspectives. London: Junction, pp. 174–193.

Lewis, M. (1992). *Shame, The Exposed Self.* New York: The Free Press.

Lewis, M. (1993). Self-conscious emotions: embarrassment, pride, shame, and guilt. In M. Lewis and J. Haviland (eds.), *Handbook of Emotions.* New York: Guilford Press, pp. 563–573.

Lewis, M. (1997). *Altering Fate: Why the Past does not Predict the Future.* New York: Guilford.

Lewis, M. and Brooks-Gunn, J. (1979). *Social Cognition and the Acquisition of Self.* New York: Plenum.

Lewis, M., Feiring, C. and Rosenthal, S. (2000). Attachment over time. *Child Development*, 71, 707–720.

Lewkowicz, D. J. (2000). The development of intersensory temporal perception: an epigenetic systems/limitations view. *Psychological Bulletin*, 126, 281–308.

Lieberman, P., Crelin, E. S. and Klatt, D. H. (1972). Phonetic ability and related anatomy of the newborn, adult human, Neanderthal man, and the chimpanzee. *American Anthropologist*, 74, 287–307.

Locke, J. L. (1993). *The Child's Path to Spoken Language.* Cambridge, MA: Harvard University Press.

Loehlin, J. C. (1996). The Cholesky approach: a cautionary note. *Behavior Genetics*, 26, 65–69.

Logothetis, N. K., Pauls, J., Augath, M., Trinath, T. and Oeltermann, A. (2001). Neurophysiological investigation of the basis of the fMRI signal. *Nature*, 31, 150–157.

Lozoff, B., Jimenez, E., Hagen, J., Mollen, E. and Wolf, A. W. (2000). Poorer behavioral and developmental outcome more than 10 years after treatment for iron deficiency in infancy. *Pediatrics*, 105, E51.

Lumley, J. (2003). Defining the problem: the epidemiology of preterm birth. *British Journal of Obstetrics and Gynaecology*, 110, suppl. 20, 3–7.

Luria, A. R. (1966). *Higher Cortical Functions in Man*, 1st. edn. New York: Basic Books.

Maccoby, E. E. (1998). *The Two Sexes: Growing Up Apart, Coming Together.* Cambridge, MA: Harvard University.

MacGillivray, I. and Campbell, D. M. (1995). The changing pattern of cerebral palsy in Avon. *Paediatric and Perinatal Epidemiology*, 9, 146–155.

MacWhinney, B. (1978). The acquisition of morphophonology. *Monographs of the Society for Research in Child Development*, 43, 1, 1–123, whole issue.

Maddison, W. P. and Maddison, D. R. (1992). *MacClade: Analysis of Phylogeny and Character Evolution*, Version 3.05. Sunderland, MA: Sinauer.

Mahler, M. (1968). *On Human Symbiosis and the Vicissitudes of Individuation.* New York: International Universities Press.

Mareschal (2001). Connectionist methods in infancy research. In J. Fagen and H. Hayne (eds.), *Progress in Infancy Research.* Mahwah, NJ: Erlbaum, Vol. II, pp. 71–119.

Martin, C. L. (2000). Cognitive theories of gender development. In T. Eckes and H. M. Trautner, *The Developmental Social Psychology of Gender.* Mahwah, NJ: Erlbaum, pp. 91–121.

Martin, N., Boomsma, D. and Machin, G. (1997). A twin-pronged attack on complex traits. *Nature Genetics*, 17, 387–392.

Masten, A. S., Morison, P. and Pellegrini, D. S. (1985). A Revised Class Play method of peer assessment. *Developmental Psychology*, 21, 523–533.

Matousek, M. and Petersen, I. (1973). Frequency analysis of the EEG in normal children and adolescents. In P. Kellaway and I. Petersen (eds.), *Automation of Clinical Electroencephalography.* New York: Raven Press, pp. 75–102.

Maurer, D. and Salapatek, P. (1976). Developmental changes in the scanning of faces by young infants. *Child Development*, 47, 523–527.

Mayr, E. (1982). *The Growth of Biological Thought.* Cambridge, MA: Harvard University Press.

McCall, R. B. (1977). Challenges to a science of developmental psychology. *Child Development*, 48, 333–344.

McCartney, G. and Hepper, P. (1999). Development of lateralised behaviour in the human fetus from 12 to 27 weeks' gestation. *Developmental Medicine and Child Neurology*, 41, 83–86.

McGraw, M. B. (1935). *Growth: A Study of Johnny and Jimmy.* New York: Appleton Century Crofts.

McGraw, M. B. (1940). Neuromuscular development of the human infant as exemplified in the achievement of erect locomotion. *Journal of Pediatrics*, 17, 747–771.

McGraw, M. B. (1946). Maturation of behavior. In L. Carmichael (ed.), *Manual of Child Psychology.* New York: Wiley, pp. 332–369.

McKenna, J. J. and Mosko, S. (2001). Mother-infant cosleeping with breast feeding as adaptation not pathology: toward a new scientific beginning point. In R. Byard and H. Krous (eds.), *Sudden Infant Death Syndrome: Problems, Puzzles and Paradoxes.* London: Arnold, pp. 258–272.

Mead, M. (1928). *Coming of Age in Samoa.* New York: William Morrow.

Mednick, S. A., Gabrielli, W. F. and Hutchings, B. (1984). Genetic influences in criminal behavior – evidence from an adoption cohort. *Science*, 224, 891–894.

Mehler, J., Jusczyk, P., Lambertz, G., Halsted, N., Bertoncini, J., and Amiel-Tison, C. (1988). A precursor of language acquisition in young infants. *Cognition*, 29, 143–178.

Melhuish, E. C. (2002). Prospects for research on the quality of the pre-school experience. In W. W. Hartup and R. K. Silbereisen (eds.), *Growing Points in Developmental Science.* Hove, UK: Psychology Press, 85–101.

Meltzoff, A. N. (2002). Imitation as a mechanism of social cognition: origins of empathy, theory of mind, and the representation of action. In U. Goswami (ed.), *Handbook of Childhood Cognitive Development.* Oxford: Blackwell, pp. 6–25.

Meltzoff, A. N. and Decety, J. (2003). What imitation tells us about social cognition: a rapprochement between developmental psychology and cognitive neuroscience. *Philosophical Transactions of the Royal Society B*, 358, 491–500.

Mervis, C. B., Robinson, B. F., Bertrand, J., Morris, C. A., Klein-Tasman, B. P. and Armstrong, S. C. (2000). The

Williams syndrome cognitive profile. *Brain and Cognition*, 44, 604–628.

Michael, K. D. and Crowley, S. L. (2002). How effective are treatments for child and adolescent depression? A meta-analytic review. *Clinical Psychology Review*, 22, 247–269.

Michel, G. F. and Harkins, D. A. (1986). Postural and lateral asymmetries in the ontogeny of handedness during infancy. *Developmental Psychobiology*, 19, 247–258.

Michel, G. F., Sheu, C.-F. and Brumley, M. R. (2002). Evidence of a right-shift factor affecting infant hand-use preferences from 7 to 11 months of age as revealed by latent class analysis. *Developmental Psychobiology*, 40, 1–13.

Mitchell, S. A. (1988). *Relational Concepts in Psychoanalysis: An Integration*. Cambridge, MA: Harvard University Press.

Montagu, A. (1989). *Growing Young*, 2nd. edn. Granby, MA: Bergin and Garvey.

Montangero, J. (2001). Piaget, J. (1896–1980). In N. J. Smelser and P. B. Baltes (eds.), *International Encyclopedia of the Social and Behavioral Sciences*. Amsterdam: Elsevier.

Mook, D. G. (1983). In defence of external invalidity. *American Psychologist*, 38, 379–387.

Morange-Majoux, F., Peze, A. and Bloch, H. (2000). Organisation of left and right hand movement in a prehension task: a longitudinal study from 20 to 32 weeks. *Laterality*, 5, 351–362.

Morris, J. S., Buchel, C. and Dolan, R. J. (2001). Parallel neural responses in amygdala sub-regions and sensory cortex during implicit fear conditioning. *NeuroImage*, 13, 1044–1052.

Morris, J. S., Frith, C. D., Perrett, D. I. and Rowland, D. (1996). A differential neural response in the human amygdala to fearful and happy facial expressions. *Nature*, 383, 812–815.

Morton, J. and Johnson, M. H. (1991). CONSPEC and CONLERN: a two-process theory of infant face recognition. *Psychological Review*, 2, 164–181.

Moses, L. J., Baldwin, D. A., Rosicky, J. G. and Tidball, G. (2001). Evidence for referential understanding in the emotions domain at twelve and eighteen months. *Child Development*, 72, 718–735.

MTA Cooperative Group. (1999). A 14-month randomized clinical trial of treatment strategies for attention deficit/hyperactivity disorder. *Archives of General Psychiatry*, 56, 1073–1086.

Mulder, E. J., Robles de Medina, P. G., Huizink, A. C., van den Bergh, B. R., Buitelaar, J. K. and Visser, G. H. (2002). Prenatal maternal stress: effects on pregnancy and the (unborn) child. *Early Human Development*, 73, 1–14.

Mulford, R. (1988). First words in the blind child. In M. D. Smith and J. L. Locke (eds.), *The Emergent Lexicon: The Child's Development of a Linguistic Vocabulary*. New York: Academic Press, pp. 293–338.

Munakata, Y. (1998). Infant perseveration and implications for object permanence theories: a PDP Model of the A-not-B task. *Developmental Science*, 1, 161–184.

Murray, L. and Trevarthen, C. (1986). The infant's role in mother-infant communications. *Journal of Child Language*, 13, 15–29.

Mutch, L. W., Alberman, E., Hagberg, B., Kodama, K. and Perat, M. V. (1992). Cerebral palsy epidemiology: where are we now and where are we going? *Developmental Medicine and Child Neurology*, 34, 547–555.

Nagel, E. (1957). Determinism and development. In D. B. Harris (ed.), *The Concept of Development: An Issue in the Study of Human Behavior*. Minneapolis: University of Minnesota Press, pp. 15–26.

National Commission for the Protection of Human Subjects of Biomedical and Behavioral Research (1979). *The Belmont Report*. Washington, DC: Department of Health, Education and Welfare.

Neale, M. C., Boker, S. M., Xie, G. and Maes, H. (1999). *Mx: Statistical Modeling*, 5th. edn. VCU Box 900126, Richmond, VA 23298: Department of Psychiatry.

Neale, M. C. and Cardon, L. R. (1992). *Methodology for Genetic Studies of Twins and Families*. Dordrecht: Kluwer.

Nelson, C. A. (2001). The development and neural bases of face recognition. *Infant and Child Development*, 10, 3–18.

Nelson, C. A. and Luciana, M. (eds.) (1999). *Handbook of Developmental Cognitive Neuroscience*. Cambridge, MA: MIT Press.

Neter, J., Kutner, M. H., Nachtsheim, C. J. and Wasserman, W. (1996). *Applied Linear Statistical Models*. Chicago: Irwin.

NICHD (2002). Early child care and children's development prior to school entry: results from the NICHD Study of Early Child Care. *American Educational Research Journal*, 39, 133–164.

Nielsen, L. (1992). *Space and Self*. Copenhagen: Sikon.

Niparko, J. K. and Blankenhorn, R. (2003). Cochlear implants in young children. *Mental Retardation and Developmental Disabilities Research Reviews*, 9, 267–275.

Noldus, L. P. J. J., Trienes, R. J. H., Henriksen, A. H. M., Jansen, H. and Jansen, R. G. (2000). The Observer Video-Pro: new software for the collection, management, and presentation of time-structured data from videotapes and digital media files. *Behavior Research Methods, Instruments, and Computers*, 32, 197–206.

Nussbaum, M. C. (1999). *Sex and Social Justice*. New York: Oxford University Press.

O'Brien, G. (ed.) (2002). *Behavioural Phenotypes in Clinical Practice*. London: MacKeith Press.

O'Connor, T. G. (2002). The effects of parenting reconsidered: findings, challenges and applications. *Journal of Child Psychology and Psychiatry*, 43, 555–572.

O'Connor, T. G., Deater-Deckard, K., Fulker, D., Rutter, M. and Plomin R. (1998). Genotype-environment correlations in late childhood and early adolescence: antisocial behavioral problems and coercive parenting. *Developmental Psychology*, 34, 970–981.

O'Connor, T. G. and Rutter, M. (1996). Risk mechanisms in development: some conceptual and methodological considerations. *Developmental Psychology*, 32, 787–795.

Oller, D. K. (2000). *The Emergence of the Speech Capacity*. Mahwah, NJ: Erlbaum.

Olson, D. (ed.) (1980). *The Social Foundations of Language and Thought: Essays in Honor of Jerome S. Bruner.* New York: Norton.

Oppenheim, R. W. (1978). G. E. Coghill (1872–1941): pioneer neuroembryologist and developmental psychobiologist. *Perspectives in Biology & Medicine,* 22, 44–64.

Oppenheim, R. W. (1981). Ontogenetic adaptations and retrogressive processes in the development of the nervous system and behavior: a neuroembryological perspective. In K. J. Connolly and H. F. R. Prechtl (eds.), *Maturation and Development, Biological and Psychological Perspectives.* Philadelphia: J. B. Lippincott, pp. 73–109.

Oppenheim, R. W. (1982a). The neuroembryological study of behavior: progress, problems, perspectives. *Current Topics in Developmental Biology,* 17, 257–309.

Oppenheim, R. W. (1982b). Preformation and epigenesis in the origins of the nervous system and behavior: issues, concepts and their history. In P. P. G. Bateson and P. H. Klopfer (eds.), *Perspectives in Ethology.* New York: Plenum Press, Vol. V, pp. 1–100.

Oppenheim, R. W. (1984). Ontogenetic adaptation in neural development: toward a more ecological developmental psychobiology. In H. F. R. Prechtl (ed.), *Continuity of Neural Functions from Prenatal to Postnatal Life.* Philadelphia: Lippincott, pp. 31–45.

Oppenheim, R. W. (1992). Pathways in the emergence of developmental neuroethology: antecedents to current views of neurobehavioral ontogeny. *Journal of Neurobiology,* 23, 1370–1403.

Oppenheim, R. W. (2001). Viktor Hamburger (1900–2001): journey of a neuroembryologist to the end of the millennium and beyond. *Neuron,* 31, 179–190.

Oppenheim, R. W. and Johnson J. E. (2003). Programmed cell death and neurotrophic factors. In M. J. Zigmond (ed.), *Fundamental Neuroscience,* 2nd. edn. New York: Elsevier, pp. 501–532.

Ornstein, M., Ohlsson A., Edmonds, J. and Asztalos, E. (1991). Neonatal follow-up of very low birthweight / extremely low birthweight infants to school age: a critical overview. *Acta Paediatrica,* 80, 741–748.

Overton, W. F. (1998). Developmental psychology: philosophy, concepts, and methodology. In W. Damon (editor-in-chief) and R. M. Lerner (vol. ed.), *Handbook of Child Psychology,* Vol. I, *Theoretical Models of Human Development,* 5th. edn. New York: Wiley, pp. 107–188.

Ozonoff, S., Rogers, S. J., Farnham, J. M. and Pennington, B. F. (1993). Can standard measures identify subclinical markers of autism? *Journal of Autism and Developmental Disorders,* 23, 429–441.

Pacton, S., Perruchet, P., Fayol, M. and Cleermans, A. (2001). Implicit learning out of the lab: the case of orthographic regularities. *Journal of Experimental Psychology: General,* 130, 401–426.

Palay, S. L. (1991). The founding of the *Journal of Comparative Neurology. Journal of Comparative Neurology,* 314, 1–8.

Pallas, S. L. (2001). Intrinsic and extrinsic factors shaping cortical activity. *Trends in Neurosciences,* 24, 417–423.

Palmer, J. (2001). *50 Classical and 50 Modern Thinkers on Education.* 2 vols. London: Routledge.

Papoušek, H. (1961). Conditioned head rotation reflexes in infants in the first months. *Acta Paediatrica,* 50, 565–576.

Papoušek, M., Wurmser, H. and von Hofacker, N. (2001). Clinical perspectives on unexplained early crying: challenges and risks for infant mental health and parent-infant relationships. In R. G. Barr, I. St. James-Roberts, and M. R. Keefe (eds.), *New Evidence on Unexplained Early Infant Crying: Its Origins, Nature and Management.* Skillman, NJ: Johnson & Johnson Pediatric Institute, pp. 289–316.

Paradise, J. L., Feldman, H. M., Campbell, T. F., *et al.* (2001). Effect of early or delayed insertion of tympanostomy tubes for persistent otitis media on developmental outcomes at the age of 3 years. *New England Journal of Medicine,* 344, 1179–1187.

Parke, R. D., Simkins, S., McDowell, D. J., Kim, M., Killian, C., Dennis, J., Flyr, M. L., Wild, M. and Rah, Y. (2002). Relative contributions of families and peers to children's social development. In P. K. Smith and C. Hart (eds.), *Blackwell Handbook of Childhood Social Development.* Oxford: Blackwell, pp. 156–178.

Parke, R. D., Ornstein, P. A., Reiser, J. J. and Zahn-Waxler, C. (1994). The past as prologue: an overview of a century of developmental psychology. In R. D. Parke, P. A. Ornstein, J. J. Reiser, and C. Zahn-Waxler (eds.), *A Century of Developmental Psychology.* Washington, DC: American Psychological Society, pp. 1–75.

Parker, S. T. and McKinney, M. L. (1999). *Origins of Intelligence: The Evolution of Cognitive Development in Monkeys, Apes, and Humans.* Baltimore, MA: Johns Hopkins University Press.

Parkes, J., Dolk, H. and Hill, N. (1998). *The Northern Ireland Cerebral Palsy Research Project 1997 Report: A Register of Children in Northern Ireland who Have Motor Deficit – Children born 1977–1992.* Belfast: Health and Health Care Research Unit, The Queen's University of Belfast, February 1998.

Parten, M. B. (1932). Social participation among preschool children. *Journal of Abnormal and Social Psychology,* 27, 243–369.

Pascalis, O., de Haan, M. and Nelson, C. A. (2002). Is face processing species specific during the first year of life? *Science,* 296, 1321–1323.

Pauls, D. L. (2001). Update on the genetics of Tourette syndrome. *Advances in Neurology,* 85, 281–293.

Pearlin, L. I., Lieberman, M. A., Menaghan, E. G. and Mullan, J. T. (1981). The stress process. *Journal of Health and Social Behavior,* 22, 337–356.

Peiper, A. (1962). *Cerebral Function in Infancy and Childhood.* London: Pitman. (Original German text, Leipzig: George Thine, 1961.)

Peisner-Feinberg, E. S., Burchinal, M. R., Clifford, R. M., Culkin, M. L., Howes, C., Kagan, S. L. and Yazejian, N. (2001). The relation of preschool child-care quality to children's cognitive and social developmental trajectories through second grade. *Child Development,* 72, 1534–1553.

Pellegrini, A. D. and Smith, P. K. (1998). Physical activity play: the nature and function of a neglected aspect of play. *Child Development,* 69, 577–598.

Pellis, S. M. and Pellis, V. C. (1998). The structure-function interface in the analysis of play fighting. In M. Bekoff and J. A. Byers (eds.), *Play Behavior: Comparative, Evolutionary, and Ecological Perspectives.* Cambridge: Cambridge University Press, pp. 115–140.

Pennington, B. F., Rogers, S., Bennetto, L., Griffith, E., Reed, D. and Shyu, V. (1997). Validity test of the Executive Dysfunction Hypothesis of autism. In J. Russell (ed.), *Executive Functioning in Autism.* Oxford: Oxford University Press, pp. 143–178.

Perlman, M. and Ross, H. S. (1997). Who's the boss? Parents' failed attempts to influence the outcomes of conflicts between their children. *Journal of Social and Personal Relationships*, 14, 463–480.

Perner, J., Leekam, S. R. and Wimmer, H. (1987). Three-year-olds' difficulty with false belief: the case for a conceptual deficit. *British Journal of Developmental Psychology*, 5, 125–137.

Peters, R. S. (1965). *Brett's History of Psychology.* Cambridge, MA: MIT Press.

Peterson, C., Maier, S. F. and Seligman, M. E. P. (1993). *Learned Helplessness: A Theory for the Age of Personal Control.* New York: Oxford University Press.

Pharoah, P. O. D., Cooke, T., Rosenbloom, L. and Cooke, R. W. I. (1987). Trends in birth prevalence of cerebral palsy. *Archives of Disease in Childhood*, 62, 379–384.

Piaget, J. (1932). *The Moral Judgment of the Child.* London: Routledge and Kegan Paul.

Piaget, J. (1937/1955). *La construction du réel chez l'enfant.* Neuchâtel: Delachaux & Nestlé. (English translation, 1955. *The Child's Construction of Reality.* London: Routledge.)

Piaget, J. (1951/1995). Egocentric thought and sociocentric thought. In J. Piaget, *Sociological Studies.* London: Routledge, pp. 276–286.

Piaget, J. (1954). *The Construction of Reality in the Child.* New York: Basic Books.

Piaget, J. (1962). *Play, Dreams and Imitation in Childhood* (trans. C. Gattegno and F. M. Hodgson). New York: Norton. (Original French edition, 1951.)

Piaget, J. (1967/1971). *Biologie et connaissance.* Paris: Gallimard. (English translation, 1971. *Biology and Knowledge.* Chicago: University of Chicago Press.)

Piaget, J. (1968/1971). Le structuralisme. Paris: PUF. (English translation, 1971. *Structuralism.* New York: Harper & Row.)

Piaget, J. (1972). *The Psychology of Intelligence.* Totowa, NJ: Littlefield Adams.

Piaget, J. (1995). *Sociological Studies.* London: Routledge.

Pickles, A., Rowe R., *et al.* (2001). Child psychiatric symptoms and psychosocial impairment: relationship and prognostic significance. *British Journal of Psychiatry*, 179, 230–235.

Pinker, S. (1984). *Language Learnability and Language Development.* Cambridge, MA: Harvard University Press.

Pinker, S. (1994). *The Language Instinct: How the Mind Creates Language.* New York: Morrow.

Pipe, M. E. (1988). Atypical laterality and retardation. *Psychological Bulletin*, 104, 343–349.

Pless, M. and Carlsson, M. (2000). Effects of motor skill intervention on developmental coordination disorder: a meta-analysis. *Adapted Physical Activity Quarterly*, 17, 381–401.

Plewis, I. (2001). Explanatory models for relating growth processes. *Multivariate Behavioral Research*, 36, 207–225.

Plomin, R., DeFries, J. C., McClearn, G. E. and McGuffin, P. (2001). *Behavioral Genetics*, 4th. edn. New York: Worth.

Pollack, R. H. and Brenner, M. J. (1969). *The Experimental Psychology of Alfred Binet.* New York: Springer.

Porter, R. H. and Winberg, J. (1999). Unique salience of maternal breast odors for newborn infants. *Neuroscience and Biobehavioral Reviews*, 23, 439–449.

Posner, M. I., Rothbart, M., Farah, M. and Bruer, J. (eds.) (2001). The developing human brain. *Developmental Science*, 4, 3, special issue.

Prechtl, H. F. R. (1977). *The Neurological Examination of the Healthy Full Term Newborn.* London: Heinemann.

Prechtl, H. F. R. (ed.) (1984). *Continuity of Neural Functions from Prenatal to Postnatal Life.* Blackwell: Oxford.

Prechtl, H. F. R. (1990). Qualitative changes of spontaneous movements in fetus and preterm infant are a marker of neurological dysfunction. *Early Human Development*, 23, 151–158.

Prechtl, H. F. R. and O'Brien, M. J. (1982). Behavioural states of the full term newborn: emergence of a new concept. In P. Stratton (ed.), *Psychobiology of the Newborn.* New York: Wiley, pp. 53–73.

Preyer, W. (1882). *Die Seele des Kindes. Beobachtungen über die geistige Entwicklung des Menschen in den ersten Lebensjahren* (The mind of the child. Observations on the mental development of man during the first years of life). 2 vols. Leipzig: Grieben.

Preyer, W. (1883). *Specielle Physiologie des Embryo. Untersuchungen über die Lebenserscheinungen vor der Geburt* (Specific physiology of the embryo. Studies on the phenomena of life before birth). Leipzig: Grieben. Also published partly in: Embryonic motility and sensitivity. *Monographs for the Society for Research in Child Development*, Volume II, No. 6, Serial No. 13, 114 pp.

Preyer, W. (1888/1889). *The Mind of the Child.* 2 vols. (trans. G. Stanley Hall). New York: Appleton Century Crofts.

Preyer, W. (1890). *Der Hypnotismus* (Hypnotism). Vienna: Urban & Schwarzenberg.

Preyer, W. (1895). *Zur Psychologie des Schreibens* (On the psychology of writing). Hamburg: Voss.

Prinz, W. and Hommel, B. (eds.) (2002). *Common Mechanisms in Perception and Action*, Attention and Performance 19. Oxford: Oxford University Press.

Pulkkinen, L., Virtanen, T, Klinteberg, B. A. and Magnusson, D. (2000). Child behavior and adult personality: comparisons between criminality groups in Finland and Sweden. *Criminal Behaviour and Mental Health*, 10, 155–169.

Quine, W. V. O. (1960). *Word and Object.* Cambridge, MA: MIT Press.

Rakic, P. (1990). Critical cellular events in cortical evolution: radial unit hypothesis. In B. L. Finlay, G. Innocenti and H. Scheich (eds.), *The Neocortex: Ontogeny and Phylogeny.* New York: Plenum, pp. 21–32.

Raudenbush, S. W. and Bryk, A. S. (2002). *Hierarchical Linear Models: Applications and Data Analysis Methods 2002*, 2nd. edn. Newbury Park, CA: Sage.

Rauh, H. (1989). The meaning of risk and protective factors in infancy. *European Journal of Psychology of Education*, 4, 161–173.

Ravid, D. and Tolchinsky, L. (2002). Developing linguistic literacy: a comprehensive model, with commentaries by M. Bamberg, R. Berman, D. Biber, R. Reppen and S. Conrad, M. Kail, N. Kemp, J. Miller, M. Nippold, C. Parisse, D. Sharpe and P. Zelazo, L. Verhoeven, *Journal of Child Language*, 29, 417–494.

Rawls, J. (1971). *A Theory of Justice*. Cambridge, MA: Harvard University Press.

Reese, H. W. (2001). Watson's social philosophy and activism. *Behavioral Development Bulletin*, 1, 17–22.

Reiss, A. and Roth, J. A. (eds.) (1993). *Understanding and Preventing Violence*. Washington, DC: National Academy Press.

Reiss, D., Neiderhiser, J. M., Hetherington, E. M. and Plomin, R. (2000). *The Relationship Code: Deciphering Genetic and Social Patterns in Adolescent Development*. Cambridge, MA: Harvard University Press.

Rice, F., Harold, G. and Thapar, A. (2002). The genetic aetiology of childhood depression: a review. *Journal of Child Psychology and Psychiatry*, 43, 65–79.

Richards, J. E. (1997). Effects of attention on infants' preference for briefly exposed visual stimuli in the paired-comparison recognition-memory paradigm. *Developmental Psychology*, 33, 22–31.

Richards, J. E. (2001). Attention in young infants: a developmental psychophysiological perspective. In C. A. Nelson and M. Luciana (eds.), *Developmental Cognitive Neuroscience*. Cambridge, MA: MIT Press, pp. 321–338.

Richards, M., Hardy, R., Kuh, D. and Wadsworth, M. (2001). Birth weight and cognitive function in the British 1946 birth cohort: longitudinal population based study. *British Medical Journal*, 322, 199–203.

Ridley, M. (2003). *Nature Via Nurture*. New York: Harper Collins.

Rivkin, M. J., Vajapeyam, S., Mulkern, R. V., Wolraich, D., Hall, E. K., Hutton, C., Yoo, S. S., Weiler, M. and Waber, D. (2003). A fMRI study of paced finger tapping in children. *Pediatric Neurology*, 28, 89–95.

Rizzolatti, G., Fadiga, L., Fogassi, L. and Gallese, V. (2002). From mirror neurons to imitation, facts, and speculations. In A. N. Meltzoff and W. Prinz (eds.), *The Imitative Mind: Development, Evolution, and Brain Bases*. Cambridge: Cambridge University Press, pp. 247–266.

Robbins, T. W. and Everitt, B. J. (1995). Arousal systems and attention. In M. S. Gazzaniga (ed.), *Cognitive Neurosciences*. Cambridge, MA: MIT Press, pp. 703–720.

Robins, L. N. (1966). *Deviant Children Grown Up*. Baltimore: Williams & Wilkins.

Robinson, S. R. and Smotherman, W. P. (1992). Fundamental motor patterns of the mammalian fetus. *Journal of Neurobiology*, 23, 1574–1600.

Rochat, P. (2001). *The Infant's World*. Cambridge, MA: Harvard University Press.

Rochat, P. and Senders, S. J. (1991). Active touch in infancy: action systems in development. In M. J. S. Weiss and P. R. Zelazo (eds.), *Newborn Attention: Biological Constraints and the Influence of Experience*. Norwood, NJ: Ablex, pp. 412–442.

Rognum, O. T. (1995). *Sudden Infant Death Syndrome: Trends in the 90s*. Oslo: Scandinavian University Press.

Rogoff, B. (1998). Cognition as a collaborative process. In W. Damon (series ed.) and D. Kuhn and R. S. Siegler (vol. eds.), *Handbook of Child Psychology*, Vol. II: *Cognition, Perception, and Language*, 5th. edn. New York: Wiley, pp. 679–744.

Rogoff, B. (2003). *The Cultural Nature of Human Development*. New York: Oxford University Press.

Rogosa, D. (1988). Myths about longitudinal research. In S. W. Schaie, R. T. Campbell, W. M. Meredith, and C. E. Rawlings (eds.), *Methodological Problems in Aging*. New York: Springer, pp. 171–209.

Rondal, J. A. and Buckley, S. (eds.) (2003). *Language Intervention in Down Syndrome*. London: Whurr.

Rose, S. A., Feldman, J. F., Futterweit, L. R. and Jankowski, J. J. (1997). Continuity in visual recognition memory: infancy to 11 years. *Intelligence*, 24, 381–392.

Rosenberg, K. and Trevathan, W. (1996). Bipedalism and human birth: the obstetric dilemma revisited. *Evolutionary Anthropology*, 4, 161–168.

Ross, H. S. and den Bak-Lammers, I. M. (1998). Consistency and change in children's tattling on their siblings: children's perspectives on the moral rules and procedures of family life. *Social Development*, 7, 275–300.

Rothbart, M. K., Ahadi, S. A. and Evans, D. E. (2000). Temperament and personality: origins and outcomes. *Journal of Personality and Social Psychology*, 78, 122–135.

Rothbart, M. K. and Bates, J. E. (1998). Temperament. In W. Damon (series ed.) and N. Eisenberg (vol. ed.), *Handbook of Child Psychology*, Vol. III: *Social, Emotional and Personality Development*, 5th. edn. New York: Wiley, pp. 105–176.

Rothbart, M. K. and Bates, J. E. (in press). Temperament in children's development: In W. Damon, R. Lerner (series eds.) and N. Eisenberg (vol. ed.), *Handbook of Child Psychology*, Vol. III: *Social, Emotional and Personality Development*, 6th edn. New York: Wiley.

Rothman, K. J. and Greenland, S. (1998). *Modern Epidemiology*, 2nd. edn. Philadelphia: Lippincott-Raven.

Rovee-Collier, C., Hayne, H. and Colombo, M. (2000). *The Development of Implicit and Explicit Memory*. Philadelphia, PA: John Benjamins.

Rowe, D. (1994). *The Limits of Family Influence: Genes, Experience, and Behavior*. New York: Guilford.

Rubin, K. H., Bukowski, W. M. and Parker, J. G. (1998). Peer interactions, relationships and groups. In W. Damon (series ed.) and N. Eisenberg (vol. ed.), *Handbook of Child Psychology*, Vol. III: *Social, Emotional, and Personality Development*, 5th edn. New York: Wiley, pp. 619–700.

Rumelhart. D. E., Hinton, G. E. and Williams, R. J. (1986). Learning internal representations by error propagation. In D. E. Rumelhart and J. L. McClelland (eds.), *Parallel Distributed Processing: Explorations in the Microstructure of Cognition*, Vol. I: *Foundations*. Cambridge, MA: MIT Press, pp. 318–364.

Russell, J. (1997). How executive disorders can bring about an inadequate theory of mind. In J. Russell (ed.), *Autism as an Executive Disorder*. Oxford: Oxford University Press, pp. 256–299.

Rutter, M. (2002). Nature, nurture, and development: from evangelism through science toward policy and practice. *Child Development*, 73, 1–21.

Sadato, N. A., Pascual-Leone, A., Grafman, J. *et al.* (1996). Activation of the primary visual cortex by Braille reading in blind subjects. *Nature*, 380, 526–528.

Sameroff, A. J. (1983). Developmental systems: context and evolution. In P. H. Mussen and W. Kessen (vol. eds.), *Handbook of Child Psychology*, Vol. I: *History, Theory and Methods*. New York: Wiley, pp. 237–294.

Sammons, P., Sylva, K., Melhuish, E. C., Siraj-Blatchford, I., Taggart, B. and Elliot, K. (2002). *The Effective Provision of Pre-school Education Project, Technical Paper 8a: Measuring the Impact on Children's Cognitive Development over the Pre-School Years*. London: Institute of Education / DfES.

Sandler, J. (1987). *From Safety to the Superego: Selected Papers of Joseph Sandler*. New York: Guilford Press.

Sanes, D., Reh, T. A. and Harris, W. A. (2000). *Development of the Nervous System*. New York: Academic Press.

Sarkar, S. and Robert, J. S. (eds.) (2003). Special section on evolutionary developmental biology. *Biology and Philosophy*, 18, 209–370.

Schaal, B., Orgeur, P. and Rognon, C. (1995). Odor sensing in the human fetus: anatomical, functional, and chemoecological bases. In J. P. Lecanuet, W. P. Fifer, N. A. Krasnegor, and W. P. Smotherman (eds.), *Fetal Development: A Psychobiological Perspective*. Hillsdale, NJ: Erlbaum, pp. 205–237.

Scherjon, S., Briët, J., Oosting, H. and Kok, J. (2000). The discrepancy between maturation of visual-evoked potentials and cognitive outcome at five years in very preterm infants with and without hemodynamic signs of fetal brain-sparing. *Pediatrics*, 105, 385–391.

Schneider, W. (1993). The longitudinal study of motor development: methodological issues. In A. F. Kalverboer, B. Hopkins, and R. Geuze (eds.), *Motor Development in Early Childhood*. Cambridge: Cambridge University Press, pp. 317–342.

Schöner, G. and Kelso, J. A. S. (1988). Dynamic pattern generation in behavioral and neural systems. *Science*, 239, 1513–1520.

Schöner, G., Zanone, P. G. and Kelso, J. A. S. (1992). Learning as change of coordination dynamics: theory and experiment. *Journal of Motor Behavior*, 24, 29–48.

Schuster, C. and von Eye, A. (2001). The relationship between mixed models and repeated measurement designs in ANOVA. *Journal of Adolescent Research*, 16, 205–220.

Scribner, S. and Cole, M. (1981). *The Psychology of Literacy*. Cambridge, MA: Harvard University Press.

Sera, M. D. (1997). *Ser* helps Spanish speakers identify "real" properties. *Child Development*, 68, 820–831.

Shayer, P. and Adey, P. (2002). *Learning Intelligence*. Buckingham: Open University Press.

Shaywitz, B. A., Fletcher, J. M., Holahan, J. M. and Shaywitz, S. E. (1992). Discrepancy compared to low achievement definitions of reading disability: results from the Connecticut longitudinal study. *Journal of Learning Disabilities*, 25, 10, 639–648.

Shekelle, P. G., Woolf, S. H., Eccles, M. and Grimshaw, J. (1999). Developing guidelines. *British Medical Journal*, 318, 593–596.

Shrout, P. and Fleiss, J. (1979). Intraclass correlations: uses in assessing rater reliability. *Psychological Bulletin*, 86, 420–428.

Shultz, T. R., Mareschal, D. and Schmidt, W. C. (1994). Modeling cognitive development on balance scale phenomena. *Machine Learning*, 16, 57–86.

Siegler, R. S. (1996). *Emerging Minds*. Oxford: Oxford University Press.

Simonoff, E. (2000). Extracting meaning from comorbidity: genetic analyses that make sense. *Journal of Child Psychology and Psychiatry*, 41, 667–674.

Slater, A. (ed.) (1998). *Perceptual Development: Visual, Auditory and Speech Perception in Infancy*. Hove, UK: Psychology Press.

Slater, A. (2001). Visual perception. In J. G. Bremner and A. Fogel (eds.), *Blackwell Handbook of Infant Development*. Oxford: Blackwell, pp. 5–34.

Slobin, D. I. (ed.) (1985–1997). *The Crosslinguistic Study of Language Acquisition*. Vols. I and II, 1985; Vol. III, 1992; Vols. IV and V, 1997. Hillsdale/Mahwah, NJ: Erlbaum.

Smilansky, S. (1968). *The Effects of Sociodramatic Play on Disadvantaged Preschool Children*. New York: Wiley.

Smith, L. (2002). *Reasoning by Mathematical Induction in Children's Arithmetic*. Oxford: Pergamon Press.

Smith, L. B. (1999). Children's noun learning: how general processes make specialized learning mechanisms. In B. MacWhinney (ed.), *The Emergence of Language*. Mahwah, NJ: Erlbaum, pp. 277–304.

Smith, L. B., Thelen, E., Titzer, R., and McLin, D. (1999). Knowing in the context of acting: the task dynamics of the A-not-B error. *Psychological Review*, 106, 235–260.

Smith, P. K. (1988). Children's play and its role in early development: a re-evaluation of the "play ethos." In A. D. Pellegrini (ed.), *Psychological Bases for Early Education*. Chichester: Wiley, pp. 207–226.

Smotherman, W. P. and Robinson, S. R. (1996). The development of behavior before birth. *Developmental Psychology*, 32, 425–434.

Snowling, M. J. (2000). *Dyslexia*. Oxford: Blackwell.

Snowling, M. J., Gallagher, A. and Frith, U. (2003). Family risk of dyslexia is continuous: individual differences in the precursors of reading skill. *Child Development*, 74, 358–373.

Spencer, H. (1886). *The Principles of Psychology*, Vol. V. New York: Appleton.

Spencer, J. P., Smith, L. B. and Thelen, E. (2001). Tests of a dynamic systems account of the A-not-B error: the influence of prior experience on the spatial memory abilities of 2-year-olds. *Child Development*, 72, 1327–1346.

Stanley, B. and Sieber, J. (eds.) (1992). *Social Research on Children and Adolescents: Ethical Issues*. Thousand Oaks, CA: Sage.

Stanley, F., Blair, E. and Alberman, E. (2000). *Cerebral Palsies: Epidemiology and Causal Pathways*. London: MacKeith Press.

Stanton, M. E. and Freeman, J. H., Jr. (2000). Developmental studies of eyeblink conditioning in the rat. In D. S. Woodruff-Pak and J. E. Steinmetz (eds.), *Eyeblink Classical Conditioning*, Vol. II: *Animal Models*. Boston: Kluwer, pp. 105–134.

Staudt, M., Schropp, C., Staudt, F., Obletter, N., Bise, K., Breit, A. and Weinmann, H. M. (1994). MRI assessment of myelination: an age standardization. *Pediatric Radiology*, 24, 122–127.

Stern, C. D. and Vasiliauskas, D. (1998). Clocked gene expression in somite formation. *Bioessays*, 20, 528–531.

Stern, D. N. (1985). *The Interpersonal World of the Infant: A View from Psychoanalysis and Developmental Psychology*. New York: Basic Books.

Sternberg, R. J. (1997). *Successful Intelligence*. New York: Plume.

Stewart, A. L., Rifkin, L., Amess, P. N., Kirkbride, V., Townsend, J. P., Miller, D. H., Lewis, S. W., Kingsley, D. P. E., Moseley, I. F., Foster, O. and Murray, R. M. (1999). Brain structure and neurocognitive and behavioural function in adolescents who were born very preterm. *Lancet*, 353, 1653–1657.

Swain, I. W., Zelazo, P. R. and Clifton, R. K. (1993). Newborn infants memory for speech sounds retained over 24 hours. *Developmental Psychology*, 29, 312–323.

Talmy, L. (1985). Lexicalization patterns: semantic structure in lexical form. In T. Shopen (ed.), *Language Typology and Semantic Description*, Vol. III: *Grammatical Categories and the Lexicon*. Cambridge: Cambridge University Press, pp. 57–149.

Tan, Ü., Örs, R., Kürçuoglu, M. and Kutlu, N. (1992). The lateralization of the grasp reflex in human newborns. *International Journal of Neuroscience*, 62, 1–8.

Tanner, J. M. (1962). *Growth at Adolescence*, 2nd. edn. Oxford: Blackwell.

Tassabehji, M., Metcalfe, K., Karmiloff-Smith, A., Carrette, M. J., Grant, J., Dennis, N., Reardon, W., Splitt, M., Read, A. P. and Donnai, D. (1999). Williams syndrome: use of microdeletions as a tool to dissect cognitive and physical phenotypes. *American Journal of Human Genetics*, 64, 118–125.

Teitel, D. (1998). Physiologic development of the cardiovascular system. In R. Polin and W. Fox (eds.), *Fetal and Neonatal Physiology*. Philadelphia: W. B. Saunders, pp. 827–836.

Thapar, A. (2003). Attention Deficit Hyperactivity Disorder: new genetic findings, new directions. In R. Plomin, J. C. DeFries, I. W. Craig and P. McGuffin (eds.), *Behavioral Genetics in the Postgenomic Era*. Washington, DC: American Psychological Association, pp. 445–462.

Thelen, E. (1995). Motor development: a new synthesis. *American Psychologist*, 50, 79–95.

Thelen, E. (2000). Grounded in the world: developmental origins of the embodied mind. *Infancy*, 1, 3–28.

Thelen, E., Corbetta, D., Kamm, K., Spencer, J. P., Schneider, K. and Zernicke, R. F. (1993). The transition to reaching: mapping intention and intrinsic dynamics. *Child Development*, 64, 1058–1099.

Thelen, E., Fisher, D. M. and Ridley-Johnson, R. (1984). The relationship between physical growth and a newborn reflex. *Infant Behavior and Development*, 7, 479–493.

Thelen, E., Schöner, G., Scheier, C. and Smith, L. B. (2001). The dynamics of embodiment: a field theory of infant perseverative reaching. *Behavioral and Brain Sciences*, 24, 1–33.

Thelen, E. and Smith, L. B. (1994). *A Dynamic Systems Approach to the Development of Cognition and Action*. Cambridge, MA: MIT Press.

Thomas, A. and Chess, S. (1977). *Temperament and Development*. New York: Brunner.

Thompson, P. M., Giedd, J. N., Woods, R. P., MacDonald, D., Evans, A. C. and Toga, A. W. (2000). Growth patterns in the developing brain detected by using continuum mechanical tensor maps. *Nature*, 40, 41, 90–193.

Thompson, R. (1992). Developmental changes in research risk and benefit: a changing calculus of concerns. In B. Stanley and J. Sieber (eds.), *Social Research on Children and Adolescents: Ethical Issues*. Thousand Oaks, CA: Sage, pp. 31–64.

Thompson, R. A. (1994). Emotion regulation: a theme in search of a definition. *Monographs of the Society for Research in Child Development*, Serial No. 240, 59, 25–52.

Titze, K., Koch, S., Lehmkuhl, U. and Rauh, H. (2001). Psychische und familiäre Belastungen bei Kindern von Müttern mit Epilepsie (Psychical and familial stress of children with epileptic mothers). *Kindheit und Entwicklung* (Childhood and Development), 10, 114–123.

Tomasello, M. (1998, 2000). *The New Psychology of Language: Cognitive and Functional Approaches to Language Structure*, Vols. I and II. Mahwah, NJ: Erlbaum.

Tomasello, M. (2003). *Constructing a Language: A Usage-based Theory of Language Acquisition*. Cambridge, MA: Harvard University Press.

Topp, M., Uldall, P. and Langhoff-Roos, J. (1997). Trend in cerebral palsy birth prevalence in eastern Denmark – birth-year period 1979–86. *Paediatric and Perinatal Epidemiology*, 11, 451–460.

Touwen, B. C. L. (1976). *Neurological Development in Infancy*. London: Heinemann.

Treem, W. R. (2001). Assessing crying complaints: the interaction with gastroesophageal reflux and cow's milk protein intolerance. In R. G. Barr, I. St. James-Roberts, and M. R. Keefe (eds.), *New Evidence on Unexplained Early Infant Crying: Its Origins, Nature and Management*. Skillman, NJ: Johnson & Johnson Pediatric Institute, pp. 165–176.

Treiman, R. (1993). *Beginning to Spell*. Oxford: Oxford University Press.

Tremblay, R. E. (2003). Why socialization fails? The case of chronic physical aggression. In B. B. Lahey, T. E. Moffitt and A. Caspi (eds.), *The Causes of Conduct Disorder and Serious Juvenile Delinquency*. New York: Guilford, pp. 182–224.

Tremblay, R. E. and Nagin, D. S. (in press). The developmental origins of physical aggression in humans. In R. E. Tremblay, W. W. Hartup, and J. Archer (eds.), *The Developmental Origins of Aggression*. New York: Guilford.

Trevathan, W. R. (1987). *Human Birth: An Evolutionary Perspective*. Hawthorne, NY: Aldine de Gruyter.

Tulving, E. (1985). How many emotions systems are there? *American Psychologist*, 40, 385–398.

Turiel, E. (2002). *The Culture of Morality: Social Development, Context, and Conflict*. Cambridge: Cambridge University Press.

Ungerleider, L. G. and Mishkin, M. (1982). Two cortical visual systems. In D. J. Ingle, M. A. Goodale, and R. J. W. Mansfield (eds.), *Analysis of Visual Behavior*. Cambridge MA: MIT Press, pp. 549–586.

Uvnäs-Moberg, K. (1999). Effects on mother and infant of oxytocin released in the postpartum period. In N. A. Fox, L. A. Leavitt, and J. G. Warhol (eds.), *The Role of Early Experience in Infant Development*. Skillman, NJ: Johnson & Johnson Pediatric Institute, pp. 283–288.

Vajapeyam, S., Rivkin, M. J., McAnulty, G., *et al.* (2002). DTI study of the premature infant brain shows that change in diffusion properties of white matter may precede myelination. *Proceedings of the 10th Scientific Meeting. ISMRM.*

Valentine, T. (1988). Upside-down faces: a review of the effects of inversion upon face recognition. *British Journal of Psychology*, 79, 471–491.

Valsiner, J. (2000). *Culture and Human Development*. London: Sage.

van der Knapp M. S., van der Wezel-Meijler, G., Barth, P. G., Barkhof, F., Ader, H. J. and Valk, J. (1996). Normal gyration and sulcation in preterm and term neonates: appearance on MR images. *Radiology*, 200, 389–396.

van de Vijver, F. J. R. and Leung, K. (1997). *Methods and Data Analysis for Cross-Cultural Research*. Newbury Park, CA: Sage.

van de Vijver, F. J. R. and Poortinga, Y. H. (2002). Structural equivalence in multicultural research. *Journal of Cross-Cultural Psychology*, 33, 141–156.

van der Meer, A. L. H. (1997). Keeping the arm in the limelight: advanced visual control of arm movements in neonates. *European Journal of Paediatric Neurology*, 4, 103–108.

van der Meer, A. L. H., van der Weel, F. R. and Lee, D. N. (1995). The functional significance of arm movements in neonates. *Science*, 267, 693–695.

van der Veer, R. and Valsiner, J. (1991). *Understanding Vygotsky: A Quest for Synthesis*. Oxford: Blackwell.

van Geert, P. (1998). A dynamic systems model of basic developmental mechanisms: Piaget, Vygotsky, and beyond. *Psychological Review*, 105, 634–677.

van Wieringen, J. C., Wafelbakker, F., Verbrugge, H. P. and de Haas, J. H. (1971*). Growth Diagrams 1965 Netherlands*. Groningen: Wolters–Noordhoff.

Vihman, M. M. (1996). *Phonological Development: The Origins of Language in the Child*. Cambridge, MA: Blackwell.

Vogt, K. C. (1864). *Lectures on Man, His Place in Creation, and in the History of the Earth*. London: Longman, Green, Longman & Roberts.

von Hofsten, C. (1982). Eye-hand coordination in newborns. *Developmental Psychology*, 18, 450–461.

von Hofsten, C. (1993). Prospective control: a basic aspect of action development. *Human Development*, 36, 253–270.

von Hofsten, C. (2003). On the development of perception and action. In J. Valsiner and K. J. Connolly (eds.), *Handbook of Developmental Psychology*. London: Sage, pp. 114–140.

Vygotskaya, G. L. and Lifanova, T. L. (1996). *L. S. Vygotsky: Life, Works and Psychological Portrait*. Moscow: Smysl-Academia.

Vygotsky, L. S. (1965). *The Psychology of Art*. Moscow: Iskusstvo. (Completed in 1925.)

Vygotsky, L. S. (1978). *Mind in Society: The Development of Higher Psychological Processes*. Cambridge, MA: Harvard University Press.

Vygotsky, L. S. (1982). The historic meaning of the crisis in psychology. In A. R. Luria and M. G. Yaroshevsky (eds.), *The Collected Works of L. S. Vygotsky*. Moscow: Pedagogica, Vol. I, pp. 291–436. (Written in 1925.)

Vygotsky, L. S. (1987). Thinking and speech. In R. W. Rieber and A. S. Carton (eds.), *The Collected Works of L. S. Vygotsky*. New York: Plenum, Vol. I, pp. 39–243. (Written in 1934.)

Vygotsky, L. S. (1999a). The teaching about emotions. In R. W. Rieber (ed.), *The Collected Works of L. S. Vygotsky*. New York: Kluwer, Vol. VI, pp. 71–235. (Written in 1931/1933.)

Vygotsky, L. S. (1999b). Tool and sign in the development of the child. In R. W. Rieber (ed.), *The Collected Works of L. S. Vygotsky*. New York: Kluwer, Vol. VI, pp. 3–65. (Written in 1930.)

Wallen, K. (1996). Nature needs nurture: the interaction of hormonal and social influences on the development of behavioral sex differences in rhesus monkeys. *Hormones and Behavior*, 30, 364–378.

Warren, D. H. (1994). *Blindness and Children: An Individual Differences Approach*. Cambridge: Cambridge University Press.

Waterman, A., Blades, M. and Spencer, C. (2001). Is a jumper angrier than a tree? *The Psychologist*, 14, 474–477.

Waters, E., Merrick, S., Treboux, D., Crowell, J. and Albersheim, L. (2000). Attachment security in infancy and early adulthood: a twenty-year longitudinal study. *Child Development*, 71, 684–689.

Watson, J. S. (2001). Contingency perception and misperception in infancy: some potential implications for attachment. *Bulletin of the Menninger Clinic*, 65, 296–320.

Weaver, A. and de Waal, F. B. M. (2002). An index of relationship quality based on attachment theory. *Journal of Comparative Psychology*, 116, 93–106.

Weeks, D. J., Chua, R. and Elliott, D. (eds.) (2000). *Perceptual-Motor Behavior in Down Syndrome*. Champaign, IL: Human Kinetics.

Weiskrantz, L. (1986). *Blindsight: A Case Study and Implications*. Oxford: Oxford University Press.

Werker, J. F. and Tees, R. C. (1999). Influences on infant speech processing: toward a new synthesis. *Annual Review of Psychology*, 50, 509–535.

Werner, H. (1932). *Grundfragen der Sprachphysiognomik* (Basic issues in the physiognomy of language). Leipzig: Barth.

Werner, H. (1948). *The Comparative Psychology of Mental Development*, 3rd edn. New York: International Universities Press. (Original work published in 1926.)

Werner, H. (1957). The concept of development from a comparative and organismic point of view. In D. B. Harris (ed.), *The Concept of Development: An Issue in the Study of Human Behavior*. Minneapolis: University of Minnesota Press, pp. 125–148.

Werner, H. and Kaplan, B. (1963). *Symbol Formation*. New York: Wiley.

Werner, H. and Wapner, S. (1952). Toward a general theory of perception. *Psychological Review*, 59, 324–338.

Werner, L. A. and Gray, L. (1998). Behavioral studies of hearing development. In E. W. Rubel, A. N. Popper, and R. R. Fay (eds.), *Springer Handbook of Auditory Research*, Vol. IX, *Development of the Auditory System*. New York: Springer, pp. 12–79.

Westermann, G. and Miranda, E. R. (2004). A new model of sensorimotor coupling in the development of speech. *Brain and Language*, 89, 393–400.

Whishaw, I. Q., Getz, G. A. S., Kolb, B. and Pellis, S. M. (2001). Accelerated nervous system development contributes to behavioral efficiency in the laboratory mouse: a behavioral review and theoretical proposal. *Developmental Psychobiology*, 39, 151–170.

Whiting, J. W. M. and Whiting, B. (1975). *Children of Six Cultures: A Psychocultural Analysis*. Cambridge, MA: Harvard University Press.

Whitmore, K., Hart, H. and Willems, G. (eds.) (1999). *A Neurodevelopmental Approach to Specific Learning Disorders*. London: MacKeith Press.

Wilkins, A. S. (2002). *The Evolution of Developmental Pathways*. Sunderland, MA: Sinauer.

Willet, J. B and Singer, J. D. (1995). It's déjà vu all over again: using multiple-spell discrete-time survival analysis. *Journal of Educational and Behavioral Statistics*, 20, 41–67.

Wilson, R. S. (1983). The Louisville Twin Study: developmental synchronies in behavior. *Child Development*, 54, 298–316.

Windle, W. F. (1979). *The Pioneering Role of Clarence Luther Herrick in American Neuroscience*. Hicksville, NY: Exposition Press.

Winnicott, D. W. (1953). Transitional objects and transitional phenomena. *International Journal of Psycho-Analysis*, 34, 1–9.

Winnicott, D. W. (1956a). Mirror role of mother and family in child development. In D. W. Winnicott (ed.), *Playing and Reality*. London: Tavistock, pp. 111–118.

Winnicott, D. W. (1956b). Primary maternal preoccupation. In D. W. Winnicott (ed.), *Collected Papers: Through Paediatrics to Psycho-analysis*. London: Tavistock, pp. 300–305.

Winnicott, D. W. (1965). *The Maturational Process and the Facilitating Environment*. London: Hogarth Press.

Winnicott, D. W. (1967). Mirror-role of the mother and family in child development. In P. Lomas (ed.), *The Predicament of the Family: A Psycho-Analytical Symposium*. London: Hogarth Press, pp. 26–33.

Winnicott, D. W. (1971). *Playing and Reality*. London: Tavistock.

Wohlwill, J. F. (1973). *The Study of Behavioral Development*. New York: Academic Press.

Wolf, T. H. (1973). *Alfred Binet*. Chicago: University of Chicago Press.

Wolff, P. H. (1987). *The Development of Behavioral States and the Expression of Emotions in Early Infancy*. Chicago: University of Chicago Press.

Wolff, P. H. (1993). Behavioral and emotional states in infancy. A dynamic perspective. In L. B. Smith and E. Thelen (eds.), *A Dynamic Systems Approach to Development: Applications*. Cambridge, MA: MIT Press, pp. 189–208.

Woodward, C. A., Thomas, H. B., Boyle, M. H., Links, P. S. and Offord, D. R. (1989). Methodologic note for child epidemiological surveys: the effects of instructions on estimates of behavior prevalence. *Journal of Child Psychology and Psychiatry*, 30, 919–924.

Wozniak, R. H. (1982). Metaphysics and science, reason and reality: the intellectual origins of genetic epistemology. In J. Broughton and D. J. Freeman-Moir (eds.), *The Cognitive Developmental Psychology of James Mark Baldwin: Current Theory and Research in Genetic Epistemology*. Norwood, NJ: Ablex, pp. 13–45.

Wrangham, R. W. (1999). Evolution of coalitionary killing. *Yearbook of Physical Anthropology*, 42, 1–30.

Yonas, A. and Granrud, C. E. (1984). The development of sensitivity to kinetic, binocular, and pictorial depth information in human infants. In D. Engle, D. Lee, and M. Jennerod (eds.), *Brain Mechanisms and Spatial Vision*. Dordrecht: Martinus Nijhoff, pp. 113–145.

Yoshihara, M., Ensminger, A. W. and Littleton, J. T. (2001). Neurobiology and the Drosophila genome. *Functional & Integrative Genomics*, 1, 235–240.

Yoshinaga-Itano, C., Coulter, D. and Thomson, V. (2000). The Colorado Newborn Hearing Screening Project: effects on speech and language development for children with hearing loss. *Journal of Perinatology*, 20, S132–137.

Zelazo, P. R., Zelazo, N. A. and Kolb, S. (1972). "Walking" in the newborn. *Science*, 176, 314–315.

Zeller, M., Vannatta, K., Schafer, J. and Noll, R. B. (2003). Behavioral reputation: a cross-age perspective. *Developmental Psychology*, 39, 1, 129–139.

AUTHOR INDEX

SUBJECT INDEX